The Oxford-Duden German Minidictionary

Second Edition
with new Phrasefinder

GERMAN–ENGLISH
ENGLISH–GERMAN

DEUTSCH–ENGLISCH
ENGLISCH–DEUTSCH

Gunhild Prowe
Jill Schneider

Phrasefinder prepared by
Neil and Roswitha Morris

OXFORD
UNIVERSITY PRESS

OXFORD
UNIVERSITY PRESS

Great Clarendon Street, Oxford OX2 6DP

Oxford University Press is a department of the University of Oxford.
It furthers the University's objective of excellence in research, scholarship,
and education by publishing worldwide in

Oxford New York

Athens Auckland Bangkok Bogotá Buenos Aires Calcutta
Cape Town Chennai Dar es Salaam Delhi Florence Hong Kong Istanbul
Karachi Kuala Lumpur Madrid Melbourne Mexico City Mumbai
Nairobi Paris São Paulo Singapore Taipei Tokyo Toronto Warsaw

with associated companies in Berlin Ibadan

Oxford is a registered trade mark of Oxford University Press
in the UK and in certain other countries

Published in the United States
by Oxford University Press Inc., New York

British Library Cataloguing in Publication Data
Data available

Library of Congress Cataloging in Publication Data
Data available

ISBN 0-19-860252-9

10 9 8 7 6 5 4 3

Typeset in Nimrod and Arial
by Latimer Trend & Company
Printed in Great Britain by
Charles Letts (Scotland) Ltd
Dalkeith, Scotland

....

Contents

....

Preface

This new edition of the Oxford-Duden German Minidictionary reflects the changes to the spelling of German ratified by the governments of Germany, Austria, and Switzerland in July 1996.

It provides a handy and comprehensive reference work for tourists and business people, and covers the needs of the student for GCSE.

The dictionary also includes a unique Phrasefinder, which groups together all the essential phrases you will need for everyday conversation. The section is thematically arranged and covers 8 key topics: going places, keeping in touch, food and drink, places to stay, shopping and money, sports and leisure, time and dates, and conversion charts.

Introduction

The text of this new edition reflects recent changes to the spelling of German ratified in July 1996. The symbol (NEW) has been introduced to refer from the old spelling to the new, preferred one:

Ass *nt* -ses, -se (NEW) **Ass**

Diät *f* -,-en (*Med*) diet; **D~ leben** be on a diet. **d~** *adv* **d~ leben** (NEW) **D~ leben**, *s.* **Diät**.

absein† *vi sep* (*sein*) (NEW) **ab sein**, *s.* **ab**

schneuzen (sich) *vr* (NEW) **schnäuzen** (sich)

Rolladen *m* (NEW) **Rollladen**

When the two forms follow each other alphabetically or are used in phrases, the old form is shown in brackets after the new, preferred one:

Abfluss (**Abfluß**) *m* drainage; (*Öffnung*) drain. **A~rohr** *nt* drain-pipe

arm *a* (ärmer, ärmst) poor; **Arm und Reich** (**arm und reich**) rich and poor

Where both the old and new forms are valid, an equals sign = is used to refer to the preferred form:

aufwändig *a* = **aufwendig**

Tunfisch *m* = **Thunfisch**

Rand *m* . . . **zu R~e kommen mit** = **zurande kommen mit**, *s.* **zurande**.

Stand *m* . . . **in S~ halten/setzen** = **instand halten/setzen**, *s.* **instand** . . .

When such forms follow each other alphabetically, they are given with commas, with the preferred form in first place:

Panther, Panter *m* -s, - panther

In phrases, *od* (oder) is used:

> . . . **deine(r,s)** *poss pron* yours;
> **die D~en** *od* **d~en** *pl* your family *sg*

> . . . **seine(r,s)** *poss pron* his; **das**
> **S~e** *od* **s~e tun** do one's share

On the English–German side, only the preferred German form is given.

- A swung dash ~ represents the headword or that part of the headword preceding a vertical bar |. The initial letter of a German headword is given to show whether or not it is a capital.

- The vertical bar | follows the part of the headword which is not repeated in compounds or derivatives.

- Square brackets [ ] are used for optional material.

- Angled brackets < > are used after a verb translation to indicate the object; before a verb translation to indicate the subject; before an adjective to indicate a typical noun which it qualifies.

- Round brackets ( ) are used for field or style labels (see list on page vii) and for explanatory matter.

- A box □ indicates a new part of speech within an entry.

- *od* (oder) and *or* denote that words or portions of a phrase are synonymous. An oblique stroke / is used where there is a difference in usage or meaning.

- ≈ is used where no exact equivalent exists in the other language.

- A dagger † indicates that a German verb is irregular and that the parts can be found in the verb table on page 705. Compound verbs are not listed there as they follow the pattern of the basic verb.

- The stressed vowel is marked in a German headword by ‿(long) or ‿(short). A phonetic transcription is only given for words which do not follow the normal rules of pronunciation. These rules can be found on page 703.

- Phonetics are given for all English headwords and for derivatives where there is a change of pronunciation or stress. In blocks of compounds, if no stress is shown, it falls on the first element.

- A change in pronunciation or stress shown within a block of compounds applies only to that particular word (subsequent entries revert to the pronunciation and stress of the headword).

- German headword nouns are followed by the gender and, with the exception of compound nouns, by the genitive and plural. These are only given at compound nouns if they present some difficulty. Otherwise the user should refer to the final element.

- Nouns that decline like adjectives are entered as follows: **-e(r)** *m/f*, **-e(s)** *nt*.

- Adjectives which have no undeclined form are entered in the feminine form with the masculine and neuter in brackets **-e(r,s)**.

- The reflexive pronoun **sich** is accusative unless marked (*dat*).

Proprietary terms

This dictionary includes some words which are, or are asserted to be, proprietary names or trademarks. Their inclusion does not imply that they have acquired for legal purposes a non-proprietary or general significance, nor is any other judgement implied concerning their legal status. In cases where the editor has some evidence that a word is used as a proprietary name or trademark this is indicated by the letter (P), but no judgement concerning the legal status of such words is made or implied thereby.

Abbreviations / Abkürzungen

adjective	a	Adjektiv
abbreviation	abbr	Abkürzung
accusative	acc	Akkusativ
Administration	Admin	Administration
adverb	adv	Adverb
American	Amer	amerikanisch
Anatomy	Anat	Anatomie
Archaeology	Archaeol	Archäologie
Architecture	Archit	Architektur
Astronomy	Astr	Astronomie
attributive	attrib	attributiv
Austrian	Aust	österreichisch
Motor vehicles	Auto	Automobil
Aviation	Aviat	Luftfahrt
Biology	Biol	Biologie
Botany	Bot	Botanik
Chemistry	Chem	Chemie
collective	coll	Kollektivum
Commerce	Comm	Handel
conjunction	conj	Konjunktion
Cookery	Culin	Kochkunst
dative	dat	Dativ
definite article	def art	bestimmter Artikel
demonstrative	dem	Demonstrativ-
dialect	dial	Dialekt
Electricity	Electr	Elektrizität
something	etw	etwas
feminine	f	Femininum
familiar	fam	familiär
figurative	fig	figurativ
genitive	gen	Genitiv
Geography	Geog	Geographie
Geology	Geol	Geologie
Geometry	Geom	Geometrie

Grammar	Gram	Grammatik
Horticulture	Hort	Gartenbau
impersonal	impers	unpersönlich
indefinite article	indef art	unbestimmter Artikel
indefinite pronoun	indef pron	unbestimmtes Pronomen
infinitive	inf	Infinitiv
inseparable	insep	untrennbar
interjection	int	Interjektion
invariable	inv	unveränderlich
irregular	irreg	unregelmäßig
someone	jd	jemand
someone	jdm	jemandem
someone	jdn	jemanden
someone's	jds	jemandes
Journalism	Journ	Journalismus
Law	Jur	Jura
Language	Lang	Sprache
literary	liter	dichterisch
masculine	m	Maskulinum
Mathematics	Math	Mathematik
Medicine	Med	Medizin
Meteorology	Meteorol	Meteorologie
Military	Mil	Militär
Mineralogy	Miner	Mineralogie
Music	Mus	Musik
noun	n	Substantiv
Nautical	Naut	nautisch
North German	N Ger	Norddeutsch
nominative	nom	Nominativ
neuter	nt	Neutrum
or	od	oder
Proprietary term	P	Warenzeichen
pejorative	pej	abwertend
Photography	Phot	Fotografie
Physics	Phys	Physik
plural	pl	Plural
Politics	Pol	Politik

possessive	poss	Possessiv-
past participle	pp	zweites Partizip
predicative	pred	prädikativ
prefix	pref	Präfix
preposition	prep	Präposition
present	pres	Präsens
present participle	pres p	erstes Partizip
pronoun	pron	Pronomen
Psychology	Psych	Psychologie
past tense	pt	Präteritum
Railway	Rail	Eisenbahn
reflexive	refl	reflexiv
regular	reg	regelmäßig
relative	rel	Relativ-
Religion	Relig	Religion
see	s.	siehe
School	Sch	Schule
separable	sep	trennbar
singular	sg	Singular
South German	S Ger	Süddeutsch
slang	sl	Slang
someone	s.o.	jemand
something	sth	etwas
Technical	Techn	Technik
Telephone	Teleph	Telefon
Textiles	Tex	Textilien
Theatre	Theat	Theater
Television	TV	Fernsehen
Typography	Typ	Typographie
University	Univ	Universität
auxiliary verb	v aux	Hilfsverb
intransitive verb	vi	intransitives Verb
reflexive verb	vr	reflexives Verb
transitive verb	vt	transitives Verb
vulgar	vulg	vulgär
Zoology	Zool	Zoologie

Pronunciation of the alphabet
Aussprache des Alphabets

English/Englisch		German/Deutsch
eɪ	a	a:
biː	b	be:
siː	c	tse:
diː	d	de:
iː	e	e:
ef	f	ɛf
dʒiː	g	ge:
eɪtʃ	h	ha:
aɪ	i	i:
dʒeɪ	j	jɔt
keɪ	k	ka:
el	l	ɛl
em	m	ɛm
en	n	ɛn
əʊ	o	o:
piː	p	pe:
kjuː	q	ku:
aː(r)	r	ɛr
es	s	ɛs
tiː	t	te:
juː	u	u:
viː	v	fau
'dʌbljuː	w	ve:
eks	x	ɪks
waɪ	y	'ʏpsilɔn
zed	z	tsɛt
eɪ umlaut	ä	ɛ:
əʊ umlaut	ö	ø:
juː umlaut	ü	y:
es'zed	ß	ɛs'tsɛt

A

Aal *m* -[e]s,-e eel. **a~en (sich)** *vr* laze; *(ausgestreckt)* stretch out

Aas *nt* -es carrion; *(sl)* swine

ab *prep* (+ *dat*) from; **ab Montag** from Monday □ *adv* off; *(weg)* away; *(auf Fahrplan)* departs; **ab sein** *(fam)* have come off; *(erschöpft)* be worn out; **von jetzt ab** from now on; **ab und zu** now and then; **auf und ab** up and down

abändern *vt sep* alter; *(abwandeln)* modify

abarbeiten *vt sep* work off; **sich a~** slave away

Abart *f* variety. **a~ig** *a* abnormal

Abbau *m* dismantling; *(Kohlen-)* mining; *(fig)* reduction. **a~en** *vt sep* dismantle; mine *(Kohle)*; *(fig)* reduce, cut

abbeißen† *vt sep* bite off

abbeizen *vt sep* strip

abberufen† *vt sep* recall

abbestellen *vt sep* cancel; **jdn a~** put s.o. off

abbiegen† *vi sep (sein)* turn off; **[nach] links a~** turn left

Abbild *nt* image. **a~en** *vt sep* depict, portray. **A~ung** *f* -,-en illustration

Abbitte *f* **A~ leisten** apologize

abblättern *vi sep (sein)* flake off

abblend|en *vt/i sep (haben)* **[die Scheinwerfer]** dip one's headlights. **A~licht** *nt* dipped headlights *pl*

abbrechen† *v sep* □ *vt* break off; *(abreißen)* demolish □ *vi (sein/haben)* break off

abbrennen† *v sep* □ *vt* burn off; *(niederbrennen)* burn down; let off *(Feuerwerkskörper)* □ *vi (sein)* burn down

abbringen† *vt sep* dissuade **(von from)**

Abbruch *m* demolition; *(Beenden)* breaking off; **etw** *(dat)* **keinen A~ tun** do no harm to sth

abbuchen *vt sep* debit

abbürsten *vt sep* brush down; *(entfernen)* brush off

abdank|en *vi sep (haben)* resign; *(Herrscher:)* abdicate. **A~ung** *f* -,-en resignation; abdication

abdecken *vt sep* uncover; *(abnehmen)* take off; *(zudecken)* cover; **den Tisch a~** clear the table

abdichten *vt sep* seal

abdrehen *vt sep* turn off

Abdruck *m* (*pl* -e) impression; *(Finger-)* print; *(Nachdruck)* reprint. **a~en** *vt sep* print

abdrücken *vt/i sep (haben)* fire; **sich a~** leave an impression

Abend *m* -s,-e evening; **am A~** in the evening; **heute A~** this evening, tonight; **gestern A~** yesterday evening, last night. **a~** *adv* **heute/gestern a~**, NEW **heute/gestern A~,** *s.* **Abend. A~brot** *nt* supper. **A~essen** *nt* dinner; *(einfacher)* supper. **A~kurs[us]** *m* evening class. **A~mahl** *nt (Relig)* [Holy] Communion. **a~s** *adv* in the evening

Abenteuer *nt* -s,-: adventure; *(Liebes-)* affair. **a~lich** *a* fantastic; *(gefährlich)* hazardous

Abenteurer *m* -s,- adventurer

aber *conj* but; **oder a~** or else □ *adv (wirklich)* really; **a~ ja!** but of course! **Tausende und a~ Tausende** thousands upon thousands

Aber|glaube *m* superstition. **a~gläubisch** *a* superstitious. **aber|mals** *adv* once again. **A~tausende**, **a~tausende** *pl* thousands upon thousands

abfahr|en† *v sep* □ *vi* (*sein*) leave; (*Auto:*) drive off □ *vt* take away; (*entlangfahren*) drive along; use (*Fahrkarte*). **a~t** *f* departure; (*Talfahrt*) descent; (*Piste*) run; (*Ausfahrt*) exit

Abfall *m* refuse, rubbish, (*Amer*) garbage; (*auf der Straße*) litter; (*Industrie-*) waste. **A~eimer** *m* rubbish-bin; litter-bin

abfallen† *vi sep* (*sein*) drop, fall; (*übrig bleiben*) be left (**für** for); (*sich neigen*) slope away; (*fig*) compare badly (**gegen** with); **vom Glauben a~** renounce one's faith. **a~d** *a* sloping

Abfallhaufen *m* rubbish-dump

abfällig *a* disparaging, *adv* -ly

abfangen† *vt sep* intercept; (*beherrschen*) bring under control

abfärben *vi sep* (*haben*) (*Farbe:*) run; (*Stoff:*) not be colour-fast; **a~auf** (+ *acc*) (*fig*) rub off on

abfassen *vt sep* draft

abfertigen *vt sep* attend to; (*zollamtlich*) clear; **jdn kurz a~** (*fam*) give s.o. short shrift

abfeuern *vt sep* fire

abfind|en† *vt sep* pay off; (*entschädigen*) compensate; **sich a~en mit** come to terms with. **A~ung** *f* -,-en compensation

abflauen *vi sep* (*sein*) decrease

abfliegen† *vi sep* (*sein*) fly off; (*Aviat*) take off

abfließen† *vi sep* (*sein*) drain or run away

Abflug *m* (*Aviat*) departure

Abfluss (**Abfluß**) *m* drainage; (*Öffnung*) drain. **A~rohr** *nt* drain-pipe

abfragen *vt sep* **jdn** *od* **jdm Vokabeln a~** test s.o. on vocabulary

Abfuhr *f* - removal; (*fig*) rebuff

abführ|en *vt sep* take or lead away. **a~end** *a* laxative. **A~mittel** *nt* laxative

abfüllen *vt sep* **auf** *od* **in Flaschen a~** bottle

Abgabe *f* handing in; (*Verkauf*) sale; (*Fußball*) pass; (*Steuer*) tax

Abgang *m* departure; (*Theat*) exit; (*Schul-*) leaving

Abgase *ntpl* exhaust fumes

abgeben† *vt sep* hand in; (*abliefern*) deliver; (*verkaufen*) sell; (*zur Aufbewahrung*) leave; (*Fußball*) pass; (*ausströmen*) give off; (*abfeuern*) fire; (*verlauten lassen*) give; cast (*Stimme*); **jdm etw a~** give s.o. a share of sth; **sich a~ mit** occupy oneself with

abgedroschen *a* hackneyed

abgehen† *v sep* □ *vi* (*sein*) leave; (*Theat*) exit; (*sich lösen*) come off; (*abgezogen werden*) be deducted; (*abbiegen*) turn off; (*verlaufen*) go off; **ihr geht jeglicher Humor ab** she totally lacks a sense of humour □ *vt* walk along

abgehetzt *a* harassed. **abgelegen** *a* remote. **abgeneigt** *a* **etw** (*dat*) **nicht abgeneigt sein** not be averse to sth. **abgenutzt** *a* worn.

Abgeordnete(r) *m/f* deputy; (*Pol*) Member of Parliament. **abgepackt** *a* pre-packed. **abgerissen** *a* ragged

abgeschieden *a* secluded. **A~heit** *f* - seclusion

abgeschlossen *a* (*fig*) complete; (*Wohnung*) self-contained. **abgeschmackt** *a* (*fig*) tasteless. **abgesehen** *prep* apart (**from von**). **abgespannt** *a* exhausted. **abgestanden** *a* stale. **abgestorben** *a* dead; (*Glied*) numb. **abgetragen** *a* worn. **abgewetzt** *a* threadbare

abgewinnen† *vt sep* win (**jdm** from s.o.); **etw** (*dat*) **Geschmack a~** get a taste for sth

abgewöhnen *vt sep* **jdm/sich das Rauchen a~** cure s.o. of/give up smoking

abgezehrt *a* emaciated

abgießen† vt sep pour off; drain (Gemüse)

ableiten† vi sep (sein) slip

Abgott m idol

abgöttisch adv a~ lieben idolize

abgrenz|en† vt sep divide off; (fig) define. **A~ung** f - demarcation

Abgrund m abyss; (fig) depths pl

abgucken vt sep (fam) copy

Abguss (**Abguß**) m cast

abhacken vt sep chop off

abhaken vt sep tick off

abhalten† vt sep keep off; (hindern) keep, prevent (von from); (veranstalten) hold

abhanden adv a~ kommen get lost

Abhandlung f treatise

Abhang m slope

abhängen¹ vt sep (reg) take down; (abkuppeln) uncouple

abhäng|en²† vi sep (haben) depend (von on). a~ig a dependent (von on). **A~igkeit** f - dependence

abhärten vt sep toughen up

abhauen† v sep □ vt chop off □ vi (sein) (fam) clear off

abheben† v sep □ vt take off; (vom Konto) withdraw; **sich a~** stand out (**gegen** against) □ vi (haben) (Cards) cut [the cards]; (Aviat) take off; (Rakete:) lift off

abheften vt sep file

abhelfen† vt sep (+ dat) remedy

Abhilfe f remedy; **A~ schaffen** take [remedial] action

abholen vt sep collect; call for (Person); **jdn am Bahnhof a~** meet s.o. at the station

abhorchen vt sep (Med) sound

abhör|en vt sep listen to; (überwachen) tap; **jdn od jdm Vokabeln a~en** test s.o. on vocabulary. **A~gerät** nt bugging device

Abitur nt -s ≈ A levels pl. **A~ient(in)** m -en,-en (f -,-nen) pupil taking the 'Abitur'

abkanzeln vt sep (fam) reprimand

abkaufen vt sep buy (dat from)

abkehren (sich) vr sep turn away

abkette[l]n vt/i sep (haben) cast off

abklingen† vi sep (sein) die away; (nachlassen) subside

abkochen vt sep boil

abkommen† vi sep (sein) a~ von stray from; (aufgeben) give up; **vom Thema a~** digress. **A~** nt -s,- agreement

abkömmlich a available

Abkömmling m -s,-e descendant

abkratzen v sep □ vt scrape off □ vi (sein) (sl) die

abkühlen vt/i sep (sein) cool; **sich a~** cool [down]; (Wetter:) turn cooler

Abkunft f - origin

abkuppeln vt sep uncouple

abkürz|en vt sep shorten; abbreviate (Wort). **A~ung** f short cut; (Wort) abbreviation

abladen† vt sep unload

Ablage f shelf; (für Akten) tray

ablager|n vt sep deposit; **sich a~n** be deposited. **A~ung** f -,-en deposit

ablassen† v sep □ vt drain [off]; let off (Dampf); (vom Preis) knock off □ vi (haben) **a~ von** give up; **von jdm a~** leave s.o. alone

Ablauf m drain; (Verlauf) course; (Ende) end; (einer Frist) expiry. **a~en**† v sep □ vi (sein) run or drain off; (verlaufen) go off; (enden) expire; (Zeit:) run out; (Uhrwerk:) run down □ vt walk along; (absuchen) scour (nach for); (abnutzen) wear down

ablegen v sep □ vt put down; discard (Karte); (abheften) file; (ausziehen) take off; (aufgeben) give up; sit, take (Prüfung); **abgelegte Kleidung** cast-offs pl □ vi (haben) take off one's coat; (Naut) cast off. **A~er** m -s,- (Bot) cutting; (Schössling) shoot

ablehn|en *vt sep* refuse; *(missbilligen)* reject. **A~ung** *f* -,-en refusal; rejection

ableit|en *vt sep* divert; **sich a~en** be derived (**von/aus** from). **A~ung** *f* derivation; *(Wort)* derivative

ablenk|en *vt sep* deflect; divert *(Aufmerksamkeit)*; *(zerstreuen)* distract. **A~ung** *f* -,-en distraction

ablesen† *vt sep* read; *(absuchen)* pick off

ableugnen *vt sep* deny

ablichten *vt sep* photocopy. **A~ung** *f* photocopy

abliefern *vt sep* deliver

ablös|en *vt sep* detach; *(abwechseln)* relieve; **sich a~en** come off; *(sich abwechseln)* take turns. **A~ung** *f* relief

abmach|en *vt sep* remove; *(ausmachen)* arrange; *(vereinbaren)* agree; **abgemacht!** agreed! **A~ung** *f* -,-en agreement

abmager|n *vi sep (sein)* lose weight. **A~ungskur** *f* slimming diet

abmarschieren *vi sep (sein)* march off

abmelden *vt sep* cancel *(Zeitung)*; **sich a~** report that one is leaving; *(im Hotel)* check out

abmess|en† *vt sep* measure. **A~ungen** *fpl* measurements

abmühen (sich) *vr sep* struggle

abnäh|en *vt sep* take in. **A~er** *m* -s,- dart

Abnahme *f* - removal; *(Kauf)* purchase; *(Verminderung)* decrease

abnehm|en† *v sep* □ *vt* take off, remove; pick up *(Hörer)*; **jdm etw a~en** take/*(kaufen)* buy sth from s.o. □ *vi (haben)* decrease; *(nachlassen)* decline; *(Person:)* lose weight; *(Mond:)* wane. **A~er** *m* -s,- buyer

Abneigung *f* dislike (**gegen** of)

abnorm *a* abnormal, *adv* -ly

abnutz|en *vt sep* wear out; **sich a~en** wear out. **A~ung** *f* - wear [and tear]

Abon|nement /abɔnə'mãː/ *nt* -s,-s subscription. **A~nent** *m* -en,-en subscriber. **a~nieren** *vt* take out a subscription to

Abordnung *f* -,-en deputation

abpassen *vt sep* wait for; **gut a~** time well

abprallen *vi sep (sein)* rebound; *(Geschoss:)* ricochet

abraten† *v sep (haben)* **jdm von etw a~** advise s.o. against sth

abräumen *vt/i (haben)* clear away; clear *(Tisch)*

abrechn|en *v sep* □ *vt* deduct □ *vi (haben)* settle up; *(fig)* get even. **A~ung** *f* settlement [of accounts]; *(Rechnung)* account

Abreise *f* departure. **a~n** *vi sep (sein)* leave

abreißen† *v sep* □ *vt* tear off; *(demolieren)* pull down □ *vi (sein)* come off; *(fig)* break off

abrichten *vt sep* train

abriegeln *vt sep* bolt; *(absperren)* seal off

Abriss (**Abriß**) *m* demolition; *(Übersicht)* summary

abrufen† *vt sep* call away; *(Computer)* retrieve

abrunden *vt sep* round off; **nach unten/oben a~** round down/up

abrupt *a* abrupt, *adv* -ly

abrüst|en *vt sep (haben)* disarm. **A~ung** *f* disarmament

abrutschen *vi sep (sein)* slip

Absage *f* -,-n cancellation; *(Ablehnung)* refusal. **a~n** *v sep* □ *vt* cancel □ *vi (haben)* **[jdm] a~n** cancel an appointment [with s.o.]; *(auf Einladung)* refuse [s.o.'s invitation]

absägen *vt sep* saw off; *(fam)* sack

Absatz *m* heel; *(Abschnitt)* paragraph; *(Verkauf)* sale

abschaffen *vt sep* abolish; get rid of *(Auto, Hund)*. **A~ung** *f* abolition

abschalten vt/i sep ⟨haben⟩ switch off

abschätzig a disparaging, adv -ly

Abschaum m ⟨fig⟩ scum

Abscheu m - revulsion

abscheulich a revolting; ⟨fam⟩ horrible, adv -lig

abschicken vt sep send off

Abschied m -[e]s,-e farewell; ⟨Trennung⟩ parting; A~ nehmen say goodbye (von to)

abschießen† vt sep shoot down; ⟨abtrennen⟩ shoot off; ⟨abfeuern⟩ fire; launch ⟨Rakete⟩

abschirmen vt sep shield

abschlagen† vt sep knock off; ⟨verweigern⟩ refuse; ⟨abwehren⟩ repel

abschlägig a negative; a~e Antwort refusal

Abschlepp|dienst m breakdown service. a~en vt sep tow away. A~seil nt tow-rope. A~wagen m breakdown vehicle

abschließen† v sep □vt lock; ⟨beenden, abmachen⟩ conclude; make ⟨Wette⟩; balance ⟨Bücher⟩; sich a~ ⟨fig⟩ cut oneself off □vi ⟨haben⟩ lock up; ⟨enden⟩ end. a~d adv in conclusion

Abschluss (Abschluß) m conclusion. A~prüfung f final examination. A~zeugnis nt diploma

abschmecken vt sep season

abschmieren vt sep lubricate

abschneiden† v sep □vt cut off; den Weg a~ take a short cut □vi ⟨haben⟩ gut/schlecht a~ do well/badly

Abschnitt m section; ⟨Stadium⟩ stage; ⟨Absatz⟩ paragraph; ⟨Kontroll-⟩ counterfoil

abschöpfen vt sep skim off

abschrauben vt sep unscrew

abschreck|en vt sep ⟨Culin⟩ put in cold water ⟨Ei⟩. a~end a repulsive, adv -ly; a~endes Beispiel warning. a~ungsmittel nt deterrent

abschreib|en† v sep □vt copy; ⟨Comm & fig⟩ write off □vi ⟨haben⟩ copy. A~ung f ⟨Comm⟩ depreciation

Abschrift f copy

Abschuss (Abschuß) m shooting down; ⟨Abfeuern⟩ firing; ⟨Raketen⟩ launch

abschüssig a sloping; ⟨steil⟩ steep

abschwächen vt sep lessen; sich a~ lessen; ⟨schwächer werden⟩ weaken

abschweifen vi sep ⟨sein⟩ digress

abschwellen† vi sep ⟨sein⟩ go down

abschwören† vi sep ⟨haben⟩ (+ dat) renounce

abseh|bar a in a~barer Zeit in the foreseeable future. a~en† vt/i sep ⟨haben⟩ copy; ⟨voraussehen⟩ foresee; a~en von disregard; ⟨aufgeben⟩ refrain from; es abgesehen haben auf (+ acc) have one's eye on; ⟨schikanieren⟩ have it in for

abseitn† vi sep ⟨sein⟩ NEW ab sein, s. ab

abseits adv apart; ⟨Sport⟩ offside □prep (+ gen) away from. A~ nt - ⟨Sport⟩ offside

absend|en† vt sep send off. A~er m sender

absetzen v sep □vt put or set down; ⟨ablagern⟩ deposit; ⟨abnehmen⟩ take off; ⟨absagen⟩ cancel; ⟨abbrechen⟩ stop; ⟨entlassen⟩ dismiss; ⟨verkaufen⟩ sell; ⟨abziehen⟩ deduct; sich a~ be deposited; ⟨fliehen⟩ flee □vi ⟨haben⟩ pause

Absicht f -,-en intention; mit A~ intentionally, on purpose

absichtlich a intentional, adv -ly, deliberate, adv -ly

absitzen† v sep □vi ⟨sein⟩ dismount □vt ⟨fam⟩ serve ⟨Strafe⟩

absolut a absolute, adv -ly

Absolution /-'tsio:n/ f - absolution

absolvieren vt complete; ⟨bestehen⟩ pass

absonderlich *a* odd

absonder|n *vt sep* separate; (*ausscheiden*) secrete; **sich a∼n** keep apart (**von** from). **A∼ung** *f* -,-en secretion

absor|bieren *vt* absorb. **A∼ption** /-'tsio:n/ *f* - absorption

abspeisen *vt sep* fob off (**mit** with)

abspenstig *a* **a∼ machen** take (**jdm** from s.o.)

absperr|en *vt sep* cordon off; (*abstellen*) turn off; (*SGer*) lock. **A∼ung** *f* -,-en barrier

abspielen *vt sep* play; (*Fußball*) pass; **sich a∼** take place

Absprache *f* agreement

absprech|en *vt sep* arrange; **sich a∼** agree; **jdm etw a∼** deny s.o. sth

abspringen† *vi sep* (*sein*) jump off; (*mit Fallschirm*) parachute; (*abgehen*) come off; (*fam: zurücktreten*) back out

Absprung *m* jump

abspülen *vt sep* rinse; (*entfernen*) rinse off

abstamm|en *vi sep* (*haben*) be descended (**von** from). **A∼ung** *f* - descent

Abstand *m* distance; (*zeitlich*) interval; **A∼ halten** keep one's distance; **A∼ nehmen von** (*fig*) refrain from

abstatten *vt sep* **jdm einen Besuch a∼** pay s.o. a visit

abstauben *vt sep* dust

abstech|en† *vi sep* stand out. **A∼er** *m* -s,- detour

abstehen† *vi sep* (*haben*) stick out; **a∼ von** be away from

absteigen† *vi sep* (*sein*) dismount; (*niedersteigen*) descend; (*Fußball*) be relegated

abstell|en *vt sep* put down; (*lagern*) store; (*parken*) park; (*abschalten*) turn off; (*fig: beheben*) remedy. **A∼gleis** *nt* siding. **A∼raum** *m* box-room

absterben† *vi sep* (*sein*) die; (*gefühllos werden*) go numb

Abstieg *m* -[e]s,-e descent; (*Fußball*) relegation

abstimm|en *v sep □vi* (*haben*) vote (**über** + *acc* on) □ *vt* coordinate (**auf** + *acc* with). **A∼ung** *f* vote

Abstinenz /-st-/ *f* - abstinence. **A∼ler** *m* -s,- teetotaller

abstoßen† *vt sep* knock off; (*schieben*) push off; (*verkaufen*) sell; (*fig: ekeln*) repel. **a∼d** *a* repulsive, *adv* -ly

abstrakt /-st-/ *a* abstract

abstreifen *vt sep* remove; slip off (*Kleidungsstück, Schuhe*)

abstreiten† *vt sep* deny

Abstrich *m* (*Med*) smear; (*Kürzung*) cut

abstufen *vt sep* grade

Absturz *m* -[e]s (*Aviat*) crash

abstürzen *vi sep* (*sein*) fall; (*Aviat*) crash

absuchen *vt sep* search; (*ablesen*) pick off

absurd *a* absurd

Abszess *m* -es,-e (*Abszeß m -sses,-sse*) abscess

Abt *m* -[e]s,-e abbot

abtasten *vt sep* feel; (*Techn*) scan

abtauen *vt/i sep* (*sein*) thaw; (*entfrosten*) defrost

Abtei *f* -,-en abbey

Abteil *nt* compartment

abteilen *vt sep* divide off

Abteilung *f* -,-en section; (*Admin, Comm*) department

abtragen† *vt sep* clear; (*einebnen*) level; (*abnutzen*) wear out; (*abzahlen*) pay off

abträglich *a* detrimental (*dat* to)

abtreib|en† *v sep □vt* (*Naut*) drive off course; **ein Kind a∼ lassen** have an abortion □ *vi* (*sein*) drift off course. **A∼ung** *f* -,-en abortion

abtrennen *vt sep* detach; (*abteilen*) divide off

abtret|en† *v sep □vt* cede (**an** + *acc* to); **sich** (*dat*) **die Füße a∼en** wipe one's feet □ *vi* (*sein*) (*Theat*) exit; (fig) resign. **A~er** m -s,- doormat

abtrocknen vt/i sep (haben) dry; **sich a~** dry oneself

abtropfen vi sep (sein) drain

abtrünnig a renegade; **a~ werden** (+ dat) desert

abtun† vt sep (fig) dismiss

abverlangen vt sep demand (dat from)

abwägen† vt sep (fig) weigh

abwandeln vt sep modify

abwandern vi sep (sein) move away

abwarten v sep ⃞ vt wait for ⃞ vi (haben) wait [and see]

abwärts adv down[wards]

Abwasch m -[e]s washing-up; (Geschirr) dirty dishes pl. **a~en†** v sep ⃞ vt wash; wash up (Geschirr); (entfernen) wash off ⃞ vi (haben) wash up. **A~lappen** m dishcloth

Abwasser nt -s,- sewage. **A~kanal** m sewer

abwechseln vi/r sep (haben) [sich] **a~** alternate; (Personen:) take turns. **a~d** a alternate, adv -ly

Abwechslung f -,-en change; **zur A~** for a change. **a~sreich** a varied

Abweg m **auf A~e geraten** (fig) go astray. **a~ig** a absurd

Abwehr f -defence; (Widerstand) resistance; (Pol) counter-espionage. **a~en** vt sep ward off; (abwehren) repel; (zurückweisen) dismiss. **A~system** nt immune system

abweich|en† vi sep (sein) deviate/(von Regel) depart (von from); (sich unterscheiden) differ (von from). **a~end** a divergent; (verschieden) different. **A~ung** f -,-en deviation; difference

abweis|en† vt sep turn down; turn away (Person); (abwehren) repel. **a~end** a unfriendly. **A~ung** f rejection; (Abfuhr) rebuff

abwenden† vt sep turn away; (verhindern) avert; **sich a~** turn away; (den Blick a~) look away

abwerfen† vt sep throw off; throw (Reiter); (Aviat) drop; (Kartenspiel) discard; shed (Haut, Blätter); yield (Gewinn)

abwert|en vt sep devalue. **a~end** a pejorative, adv -ly. **A~ung** f -,-en devaluation

abwesen|d a absent; (zerstreut) absent-minded. **A~heit** f - absence; absent-mindedness

abwickeln vt sep unwind; (erledigen) settle

abwischen vt sep wipe; (entfernen) wipe off

abwürgen vt sep stall (Motor)

abzahlen vt sep pay off

abzählen vt sep count

Abzahlung f instalment

abzapfen vt sep draw

Abzeichen nt badge

abzeichnen vt sep copy; (unterzeichnen) initial; **sich a~** stand out

Abzieh|bild nt transfer. **a~en†** v sep ⃞ vt pull off; take off (Laken); strip (Bett); (häuten) skin; (Phot) print; run off (Kopien); (zurückziehen) withdraw; (abrechnen) deduct ⃞ vi (sein) go away, (Rauch:) escape

abzielen vi sep (haben) **a~ auf** (+ acc) (fig) be aimed at

Abzug m withdrawal; (Abrechnung) deduction; (Phot) print; (Korrektur) proof; (am Gewehr) trigger; (A~söffnung) vent; **A~e** pl deductions

abzüglich prep (+ gen) less

Abzugshaube f [cooker] hood

abzweig|en v sep ⃞ vi (sein) branch off ⃞ vt divert. **A~ung** f -,-en junction; (Gabelung) fork

ach int oh; **a~ ja!** oh dear! **a~ so** I see; **mit A~ und Krach** (fam) by the skin of one's teeth

Achse f -,-n axis; (Rad-) axle

Achsel f -,-n shoulder; **die A∼n zucken** shrug one's shoulders. **A∼höhle** f armpit. **A∼zucken** nt -s shrug

acht[1] inv a A∼¹ f -,-en eight; **heute in a∼ Tagen** a week today

acht[2] außer a∼ lassen/sich in a∼ nehmen (NEW) außer Acht lassen/sich in Acht nehmen, s. Acht²

Acht² f A∼ geben a∼ auf (+ acc) look after; **außer A∼ lassen** disregard; **sich in A∼ nehmen** be careful

acht|e(r,s) a eighth. **A∼eckig** a octagonal. **a∼el** inv a eighth. **A∼el** nt -s,- eighth. **A∼elnote** f quaver, (Amer) eighth note

achten vt respect □ vi (haben) a∼ auf (+ acc) pay attention to; (aufpassen) look after; **darauf a∼, dass** take care that

ächten vt ban; ostracize (Person)

Achter|bahn f roller-coaster. **a∼n** adv (Naut) aft

achtgeben† vi sep (haben) (NEW) Acht geben, s. Acht²

achtlos a careless, adv -ly

achtsam a careful, adv -ly

Achtung f - respect (vor + dat for); **A∼!** look out! (Mil) attention! **'A∼ Stufe'** 'mind the step'

acht|zehn inv a eighteen. **a∼zehnte(r,s)** a eighteenth. **a∼zig** a inv eighty. **a∼zigste(r,s)** a eightieth

ächzen vi (haben) groan

Acker m -s,-: field. **A∼bau** m agriculture. **A∼land** nt arable land

addieren vt/i (haben) add; (zusammenzählen) add up

Addition /-'tsjo:n/ f -,-en addition

ade int goodbye

Adel m -s nobility

Ader f -,-n vein; **künstlerische A∼** artistic bent

Adjektiv nt -s,-e adjective

Adler m -s,- eagle

adlig a noble. **A∼e(r)** m nobleman

Administration /-'tsjo:n/ f - administration

Admiral m -s,-e admiral

adop|tieren vt adopt. **A∼tion** /-'tsjo:n/ f -,-en adoption. **A∼tiveltern** pl adoptive parents. **A∼tivkind** nt adopted child

Adrenalin nt -s adrenalin

Adres|se f -,-n address. **a∼sieren** vt address

adrett a neat, adv -ly

Adria f - Adriatic

Advent m -s Advent. **A∼skranz** m Advent wreath

Adverb nt -s,-ien /-jə:n/ adverb

Affäre f -,-n affair

Affe m -n,-n monkey; (Menschen-) ape

Affekt m -[e]s,-e im A∼ in the heat of the moment

affektiert a affected. **A∼heit** f - affectation

affig a affected; (eitel) vain

Afrika nt -s Africa

Afrikan|er(in) m -s,- (f -,-nen) African. **a∼isch** a African

After m -s,- anus

Agent|(in) m -en,-en (f -,-nen) agent. **A∼tur** f -,-en agency

Aggres|sion f -,-en aggression. **a∼siv** a aggressive, adv -ly. **A∼sivität** f - aggressiveness

Agitation /-'tsjo:n/ f - agitation

Agnostiker m -s,- agnostic

Ägypt|en /ɛ'gyptən/ nt -s Egypt. **Ä∼er(in)** m -s,- (f -,-nen) Egyptian. **ä∼isch** a Egyptian

ähneln vi (haben) (+ dat) resemble; **sich ä∼** be alike

ahnen vt have a presentiment of; (vermuten) suspect

Ahnen mpl ancestors. **A∼forschung** f genealogy. **A∼tafel** f family tree

ähnlich a similar, adv -ly; **jdm ä∼sehen** resemble s.o.; (typisch sein) be just like s.o. **A∼keit** f -,-en similarity; resemblance

Ahnung f -,-en premonition; (Vermutung) idea, hunch; **keine**

A~ (*fam*) no idea. **a~slos** *a* unsuspecting

Ahorn *m* -s,-e maple

Ähre *f* -,-n ear [of corn]

Aids /e:ts/ *nt* - Aids

Akademie *f* -,-n academy

Akadem|iker(in) *m* -s,- (*f* -,-nen)
university graduate. **a~isch** *a*
academic, *adv* -ally

akklimatisieren (sich) *vr* become acclimatized

Akkord *m* -[e]s,-e (*Mus*) chord;
im A~ arbeiten be on piece-
work. **A~arbeit** *f* piece-work

Akkordeon *nt* -s,-s accordion

Akkumulator *m* -s,-en /-'to:rən/
(*Electr*) accumulator

Akkusativ *m* -s,-e accusative.
A~objekt *nt* direct object

Akrobat|(in) *m* -en,-en (*f* -,-nen)
acrobat. **a~isch** *a* acrobatic

Akt *m* -[e]s,-e act; (*Kunst*) nude

Akte *f* -,-n file; **A~n** documents.
A~ndeckel *m* folder. **A~n-**
koffer *m* attaché case. **A~n-**
schrank *m* filing cabinet.
A~ntasche *f* briefcase

Aktie /'aktsjə/ *f* -,-n (*Comm*)
share. **A~ngesellschaft** *f* joint-
stock company

Aktion /ak'tsjo:n/ *f* -,-en action;
(*Kampagne*) campaign. **A~är** *m*
-s,-e shareholder

aktiv *a* active, *adv* -ly. **a~ieren** *vt*
activate. **A~ität** *f* -,-en activity

Aktualität *f* -,-en topicality;
A~en current events

aktuell *a* topical; (*gegenwärtig*)
current; **nicht mehr a~** no
longer relevant

Akupunktur *f* - acupuncture

Akustik *f* - acoustics *pl*. **a~isch**
a acoustic, *adv* -ally

akut *a* acute

Akzent *m* -[e]s,-e accent

akzept|abel *a* acceptable. **a~ie-**
ren *vt* accept

Alarm *m* -s alarm; (*Mil*) alert;
A~schlagen raise the alarm.

a~ieren *vt* alert; (*beunruhigen*)
alarm. **a~ierend** *a* alarming

Albdruck *m* = **Alpdruck**

albern *a* silly ● *adv* in a silly way
● *vi* (*haben*) play the fool

Albtraum *m* = **Alptraum**

Album *nt* -s,-ben album

Algebra *f* - algebra

Algen *fpl* algae

Algerien /-jən/ *nt* -s Algeria

Alibi *nt* -s,-s alibi

Alimente *pl* maintenance *sg*

Alkohol *m* -s alcohol. **a~frei** *a*
non-alcoholic

Alkohol|iker(in) *m* -s,- (*f* -,-nen)
alcoholic. **a~isch** *a* alcoholic.
A~ismus *m* - alcoholism

all *inv pron* **all das/mein Geld** all
the/my money; **all dies** all this;
all *nt* -s universe

alle *pred a* finished, (*fam*) all
gone; **a~ machen** finish up

alle(r,s) *pron a* all; (*jeder*) every;
a~es everything, all; (*alle Leute*)
everyone; **a~e** *pl* all; **a~es Geld**
all the money; **a~e meine**
Freunde all my friends; **a~e**
beide both [of them/us]; **wir a~e**
we all; **a~e Tage** every day; **a~e**
drei Jahre every three years; **in**
a~er Unschuld in all innocence;
ohne a~en Grund without any
reason; **vor a~em** above all;
a~es in a~em all in all; **a~es**
aussteigen! all change! **a~e** *pl*
pron **bei/trotz a~edem**
with/despite all that

Allee *f* -,-n avenue

Alleg|orie *f* -,-n allegory. **a~o-**
risch *a* allegorical

allein *adv* alone; (*nur*) only; **a~-**
stehend single; **a~ der Gedanke**
the mere thought; **a~e a~[e]** of
its/(*Person*) one's own accord;
(*automatisch*) automatically;
einzig und a~ solely ● *conj* but.
A~erziehende(r) *m/f* single
parent. **a~e a** sole. **a~stehend**
(a NEW) **a~ stehend**, *s*. **allein**.
A~stehende *pl* single people

allemal *adv* every time; *(gewiss)* certainly; **ein für a~** NEW **ein für alle Mal**, s. **Mal**

allenfalls *adv* at most; *(eventuell)* possibly

aller|beste(r,s) *a* very best; **am a~besten** best of all. **a~dings** *adv* indeed; *(zwar)* admittedly. **a~erste(r)** *a* very first

Allergie *f* -,-n allergy

allergisch *a* allergic (**gegen** to)

aller|hand *inv a* all sorts of □ *pron* all sorts of things; **das ist a~hand!** that's quite something! *(empört)* that's a bit much! **A~heiligen** *nt* -s All Saints Day. **a~höchstens** *adv* at the very most. **a~lei** *inv a* all sorts of □ *pron* all sorts of things. **a~letzte(r,s)** *a* very last. **a~liebst** *a* enchanting. **a~liebste(r,s)** *a* favourite □ *adv* **am a~liebsten** for preference; **am a~liebsten haben** like best of all. **a~meiste(r,s)** *a* most □ *adv* **am a~meisten** most of all. **A~seelen** *nt* -s All Souls Day. **a~seits** *adv* generally; **guten Morgen a~seits!** good morning everyone! **a~wenigste(r,s)** *a* very least □ *adv* **am a~wenigsten** least of all

alle|s, alle(r,s). a~samt *adv* all. **A~swisser** *m* -s,- *(fam)* know-all

allgemein *a* general, *adv* -ly; **im A~en** (**a~en**) in general. **A~heit** *f* - community; *(Öffentlichkeit)* general public

Allheilmittel *nt* panacea

Allianz *f* -,-en alliance

Alligator *m* -s,-en /-'to:rən/ alligator

alliiert *a* allied; **die A~en** *pl* the Allies

alljährlich *a* annual, *adv* -ly. **a~mächtig** *a* almighty; **der A~mächtige** the Almighty. **a~mählich** *a* gradual, *adv* -ly

Alltag *m* working day; **der A~** *(fig)* everyday life

alltäglich *a* daily; *(gewöhnlich)* everyday; *(Mensch)* ordinary □ *adv* daily

alltags *adv* on weekdays

allzu *adv* [far] too; **a~ bald/oft** all too soon/often; **a~ sehr/viel** far too much; **a~ vorsichtig** over-cautious. **a~bald** NEW **a~ bald**, s. allzu. **a~oft** *adv* NEW **a~ oft**, s. allzu. **a~sehr** *adv* NEW **a~ sehr**, s. allzu. **a~viel** *adv* NEW **a~ viel**, s. allzu

Alm *f* -,-en alpine pasture

Almosen *ntpl* alms

Alpdruck *m* nightmare

Alpen *pl* Alps. **A~veilchen** *nt* cyclamen

Alphabet *nt* -[e]s,-e alphabet. **a~isch** *a* alphabetical, *adv* -ly

Alptraum *m* nightmare

als *conj* as; *(zeitlich)* when; *(mit Komparativ)* than; **nichts a~** nothing but; **als ob** as if or though; **so tun als ob** *(fam)* pretend

also *adv & conj* so; **a~ gut** all right then; **na a~!** there you are!

alt *a* (**älter**, **ältest**) old; *(gebraucht)* second-hand; *(ehemalig)* former; **alt werden** grow old; **alles beim A~en (a~en) lassen** leave things as they are

Alt *m* -s *(Mus)* contralto

Altar *m* -s,-e altar

Alte(r) *m/f* old man/woman; **die A~en** old people. **A~eisen** *nt* scrap iron. **A~enheim** *nt* old people's home

Alter *nt* -s,- age; *(Bejahrtheit)* old age; **im A~ von** at the age of; **im A~** in old age

älter *a* older; **mein ä~er Bruder** my elder brother

altern *vi* (*sein*) age

Alternative *f* -,-n alternative

Alters|grenze *f* age limit. **A~heim** *nt* old people's home. **A~rente** *f* old-age pension. **a~schwach** *a* old and infirm; *(Ding)* decrepit

Alter|tum *nt* -s,-̈er antiquity. **a~-tümlich** *a* old; *(altmodisch)* old-fashioned

ältest|e(r,s) *a* oldest; **der ä~e Sohn** the eldest son

althergebracht *a* traditional

altklug *a* precocious, *adv* -ly

ältlich *a* elderly

alt|modisch old-fashioned □ *adv* in an old-fashioned way. **A~papier** *nt* waste paper. **A~stadt** *f* old [part of a] town. **A~warenhändler** *m* second-hand dealer. **A~weibermärchen** *nt* old wives' tale. **A~weibersommer** *m* Indian summer; *(Spinnfäden)* gossamer

Alufolie *f* [aluminium] foil

Aluminium *nt* -s aluminium; *(Amer)* aluminum

am *prep* = **an dem; am Montag** on Monday; **am Morgen** in the morning; **am besten/meisten** [the] best/most; **am teuersten sein** be the most expensive

Amateur /-'tø:ɐ/ *m* -s,-e amateur

Ambition /-'tsjo:n/ *f* -,-en ambition

Amboss *m* -es,-e (Amboß *m* -sses,-sse) anvil

ambulan|t *a* out-patient . . . □ *adv* **a~t behandeln** treat as an out-patient. **A~z** *f* -,-en out-patients' department; *(Krankenwagen)* ambulance

Ameise *f* -,-n ant

amen *int,* **A~** *nt* -s amen

Amerika *nt* -s America

Amerikan|er(in) *m* -s,- *(f* -,-nen) American. **a~isch** *a* American

Ami *m* -s,-s *(fam)* Yank

Ammoniak *nt* -s ammonia

Amnestie *f* -,-n amnesty

amoralisch *a* amoral

Ampel *f* -,-n traffic lights *pl;* *(Blumen-)* hanging basket

Amphib|ie /-jə/ *f* -,-n amphibian. **a~isch** *a* amphibious

Amphitheater *nt* amphitheatre

Amput|ation /-'tsjo:n/ *f* -,-en amputation. **a~ieren** *vt* amputate

Amsel *f* -,-n blackbird

Amt *nt* -[e]s,-̈er office; *(Aufgabe)* task; *(Teleph)* exchange. **a~ieren** *vi (haben)* hold office; be in office. **a~ierend** acting. **a~lich** *a* official, *adv* -ly. **A~szeichen** *nt* dialling tone

Amulett *nt* -[e]s,-e [lucky] charm

amüs|ant *a* amusing, *adv* -ly. **a~ieren** *vt* amuse; **sich a~ieren** be amused **(über** + *acc* at); *(sich vergnügen)* enjoy oneself

an *prep* (+ *dat/acc)* at; *(haftend, berührend)* on; *(gegen)* against; (+ *acc) (schicken)* to; **an der/die Universität** at/to university; **an dem Tag** on that day; **es ist an mir** it is up to me; **an [und für] sich** actually; **die Arbeit an sich** the work as such □ *adv (angeschaltet)* on; *(auf Fahrplan)* arriving; **an die zwanzig Mark/Leute** about twenty marks/people; **von heute an** from today

analog *a* analogous; *(Computer)* analog. **A~ie** *f* -,-n analogy

Analphabet *m* -en,-en illiterate person. **A~entum** *nt* -s illiteracy

Analy|se *f* -,-n analysis. **a~sieren** *vt* analyse. **A~tiker** *m* -s,- analyst. **a~tisch** *a* analytical

Anämie *f* - anaemia

Ananas *f* -,-[se] pineapple

Anarch|ie *f* - anarchy. **A~ist** *m* -en,-en anarchist

Anat|omie *f* - anatomy. **a~omisch** *a* anatomical, *adv* -ly

anbahnen (sich) *vr sep* develop

Anbau *m* cultivation; *(Gebäude)* extension. **a~en** *vt sep* build on; *(anpflanzen)* cultivate, grow

anbehalten† *vt sep* keep on

anbei *adv* enclosed

anbeißen† *vt sep* take a bite of □ *vi (haben) (Fisch:)* bite; *(fig)* take the bait

anbelangen *vt sep* = **anbetreffen**

anbellen vt sep bark at

anbeten vt sep worship

Anbetracht m in A~ (+ gen) in view of

anbetreffen† vt sep **was mich/das anbetrifft** as far as I am/that is concerned

Anbetung f - worship

anbiedern (sich) vr sep ingratiate oneself (**bei** with)

anbieten† vt sep offer; **sich a~** offer (**zu** to)

anbinden† vt sep tie up

Anblick m sight. **a~en** vt sep look at

anbrechen† v sep □ vt start on; break into (Vorräte) □ vi (sein) begin; (Tag:) break; (Nacht:) fall

anbrennen† v sep □ vi light □ vi (sein) burn; (Feuer fangen) catch fire

anbringen† vt sep bring [along]; (befestigen) fix

Anbruch m (fig) dawn; **bei A~ des Tages/der Nacht** at daybreak/nightfall

anbrüllen vt sep (fam) bellow at

Andacht f -,-en reverence; (Gottesdienst) prayers pl

andächtig a reverent, adv -ly; (fig) rapt, adv -ly

andauern vi sep (haben) last; (anhalten) continue. **a~d** a persistent, adv -ly; (ständig) constant, adv -ly

Andenken nt -s,- memory; (Souvenir) souvenir; **zum A~ an** (+ acc) in memory of

ander|e(r,s) a other; (verschieden) different; (nächste) next; **ein a~er, eine a~e** another □ pron **der a~e/die a~en** the other/others; **ein a~er** another [one]; (Person) someone else; **kein a~er** no one else; **einer nach dem a~en** one after the other; **alles a~e/nichts a~es** everything/nothing else; **etwas ganz a~es** something quite different; **alles a~e als** anything but; **unter a~em** among other things. **a~enfalls** adv otherwise. **a~erseits** adv on the other hand. **a~mal** adv **ein a~mal** another time

ändern vt alter; (wechseln) change; **sich ä~** change

andernfalls adv otherwise

anders pred a different; **a~ werden** change □ adv differently; (riechen, schmecken) different; (sonst) else; **jemand/niemand/irgendwo a~** someone/no one/somewhere else

anderseits adv on the other hand

anders|herum adv the other way round. **a~wo** adv (fam) somewhere else

anderthalb inv a one and a half; **a~ Stunden** an hour and a half

Änderung f -,-en alteration; (Wechsel) change

anderweitig a other □ adv otherwise; (anderswo) elsewhere

andeut|en vt sep indicate; (anspielen) hint at. **A~ung** f -,-en indication; hint

andicken vt sep (Culin) thicken

Andrang m rush (**nach** for); (Gedränge) crush

andre a & pron = andere

andrehen vt sep turn on; **jdm etw a~** (fam) palm sth off on s.o.

andrerseits adv = andererseits

androhen vt sep **jdm etw a~** threaten s.o. with sth

aneignen vt sep sich (dat) **a~** appropriate; (lernen) learn

aneinander adv & pref together; (denken) of one another; **a~ vorbei** past one another; **a~ geraten** quarrel. **a~geraten†** vi sep (sein) (NEW) **a~ geraten**, s. **aneinander**

Anekdote f -,-n anecdote

anekeln vt sep nauseate

anerkannt a acknowledged

anerkenn|en† vt sep acknowledge, recognize; (würdigen) appreciate. **a~end** a approving, adv -ly. **A~ung** f - acknowledgement, recognition; appreciation

anfahren† v sep □vt deliver; (streifen) hit; (schimpfen) snap at □vi (sein) start; **angefahren kommen** drive up

Anfall m fit, attack. **a~en†** v sep □vt attack □vi (sein) arise; (Zinsen:) accrue

anfällig a susceptible (**für** to); (zart) delicate. **A~keit** f - susceptibility (**für** to)

Anfang m -s,-e beginning, start; **zu** od **am A~** at the beginning; (anfangs) at first. **a~en†** vt/i sep (haben) begin, start; (tun) do

Anfänger|in m -s,- (-f-,-nen) beginner. **a~lich** a initial, adv -ly

anfangs adv at first. **A~buchstabe** m initial letter. **A~gehalt** nt starting salary. **A~gründe** mpl rudiments

anfassen v sep □vt touch; (behandeln) treat; tackle (Arbeit); jdn **a~** take s.o.'s hand; sich **a~** hold hands; sich weich **a~** feel soft □vi (haben) mit **a~** lend a hand

anfechten† vt sep contest; (fig: beunruhigen) trouble

anfertigen vt sep make

anfeuchten vt sep moisten

anfeuern vt sep spur on

anflehen vt sep implore, beg

Anflug m (Aviat) approach; (fig: Spur) trace

anforder|n vt sep demand; (Comm) order. **A~ung** f demand

Anfrage f enquiry. **a~n** vi sep (haben) enquire, ask

anfreunden (sich) vr sep make friends (**mit** with); (miteinander) become friends

anfügen vt sep add

anfühlen vt sep feel; sich weich **a~** feel soft

anführ|en vt sep lead; (zitieren) quote; (angeben) give; jdn **a~en** (fam) have s.o. on. **A~er** m

leader. **A~ungszeichen** ntpl quotation marks

Angabe f statement; (Anweisung) instruction; (Tennis) service; (fam: Angeberei) showing-off; **nähere A~n** particulars

angeb|en† v sep □vt state; give (Namen, Grund); (anzeigen) indicate; set (Tempo) □vi (haben) (Tennis) serve; (fam: protzen) show off. **A~er(in)** m -s,- (f -,-nen) (fam) show-off. **A~erei** f - (fam) showing-off

angeblich a alleged, adv -ly

angeboren a innate; (Med) congenital

Angebot nt offer; (Auswahl) range; **A~ und Nachfrage** supply and demand

angebracht a appropriate

angebunden a **kurz a~** curt

angegriffen a worn out; (Gesundheit) poor

angeheiratet a (Onkel, Tante) by marriage

angeheitert a (fam) tipsy

angehen† v sep □vi (sein) begin, start; (Licht, Radio:) come on; (anwachsen) take root; **a~ gegen** fight □vt attack; tackle (Arbeit); (bitten) ask (**um** for); (betreffen) concern; **das geht dich nichts an** it's none of your business. **a~d** a future; (Künstler) budding

angehör|en vi sep (haben) (+ dat) belong to. **A~ige(r)** m/f relative; (Mitglied) member

Angeklagte(r) m/f accused

Angel f -,-n fishing-rod; (Tür-) hinge

Angelegenheit f matter; auswärtige **A~en** foreign affairs

Angel|haken m fish-hook. **a~n** vi (haben) fish (**nach** for); **a~n gehen** go fishing □vt (fangen) catch. **A~rute** f fishing-rod

angelsächsisch a Anglo-Saxon

angemessen a commensurate (dat with); (passend) appropriate, adv -ly

angenehm a pleasant, adv -ly; (bei Vorstellung) **a~**! delighted to meet you!

angenommen a (Kind) adopted; (Name) assumed

angeregt a animated, adv -ly

angesehen a respected; (Firma) reputable

angesichts prep (+ gen) in view of

angespannt a intent, adv -ly; (Lage) tense

Angestellte(r) m/f employee

angetan a **a~ sein von** be taken with

angetrunken a slightly drunk

angewandt a applied

angewiesen a dependent (**auf** + acc on); **auf sich selbst a~** on one's own

angewöhnen vt sep **jdm etw a~** get s.o. used to sth; **sich** (dat) **etw a~** get into the habit of doing sth

Angewohnheit f habit

Angina f - tonsillitis

angleichen† vt sep adjust (dat to)

Angler m -s, - angler

anglikanisch a Anglican

Anglistik f - English [language and literature]

Angorakatze f Persian cat

angreifen† vt sep attack; tackle (Arbeit); (schädigen) damage; (anbrechen) break into; (anfassen) touch. **A~er** m -s, - attacker; (Pol) aggressor

angrenzen vi sep (haben) adjoin (**an etw** acc sth). **a~d** a adjoining

Angriff m attack; **in A~ nehmen** tackle. **a~slustig** a aggressive

Angst f -,¨e fear; (Psych) anxiety; (Sorge) worry (**um** about); **A~ haben** be afraid (**vor** + dat of); (sich sorgen) be worried (**um** about); **jdm A~ machen** frighten s.o. □ **mir ist a~** I am frightened; **I am worried** (**um** about); **jdm ... machen**
(NEW) **jdm A~ machen**

ängstigen vt frighten; (Sorge machen) worry; **sich ä~** be frightened; be worried (**um** about)

ängstlich a nervous, adv -ly; (scheu) timid, adv -ly; (verängstigt) frightened, scared; (besorgt) anxious, adv -ly; **Ä~keit** f - nervousness; timidity; anxiety

angstvoll a anxious, adv -ly; (verängstigt) frightened

angucken vt sep (fam) look at

angurten (sich) vr sep fasten one's seat-belt

anhaben† vt sep have on; **er/es kann mir nichts a~** (fig) he/it cannot hurt me

anhalten|en† vt sep stop; hold (Atem); **jdn zur Arbeit/Ordnung a~** urge s.o. to be tidy □ vi (haben) stop; (andauern) continue. **a~end** a persistent, adv -ly; (Beifall) prolonged. **A~er(in)** m -s,- (f -,-nen) hitchhiker; **per A~er fahren** hitchhike. **A~spunkt** m clue

anhand prep (+ gen) with the aid of

Anhang m appendix; (fam: Angehörige) family

anhängen vt sep (reg) hang up; (befestigen) attach; (hinzufügen) add

anhängen|en†2† vi (haben) be a follower of. **A~er** m -s,- follower; (Auto) trailer; (Schild) [tie-on] label; (Schmuck) pendant; (Aufhänger) loop. **A~erin** f -,-nen follower. **A~erschaft** f - following, followers pl. **a~lich** a affectionate. **A~sel** nt -s, - (Anhängsel) appendage

anhäufen vt sep pile up; **sich a~** pile up, accumulate

anheben† vt sep lift; (erhöhen) raise

Anhieb m **auf A~** straight away

Anhöhe f hill

anhören vt sep listen to; **mit a~** overhear; **sich gut a~** sound good

animieren *vt* encourage (**zu** to)

Anis *m* aniseed

Anker *m* **-s,-** anchor; **vor A~ gehen** drop anchor. **a~n** *vi* (*haben*) anchor; (*liegen*) be anchored

anketten *vt sep* chain up

Anklage *f* accusation; (*Jur*) charge; (*Anklagen*) prosecution. **A~bank** *f* dock. **a~n** *vt sep* accuse (*gen* of); (*Jur*) charge (*gen* with)

Ankläger *m* accuser; (*Jur*) prosecutor

anklammern *vt sep* clip on; peg on the line (*Wäsche*); **sich a~n** cling (**an** + *acc* to)

Anklang *m* **bei jdm A~ finden** meet with s.o.'s approval

ankleben *vt sep* stick on □ *vi* (*sein*) stick (**an** + *dat* to)

Ankleide|kabine *f* changing cubicle; (*zur Anprobe*) fitting-room. **a~n** *vt sep* **sich a~n** dress

anklopfen *vi sep* (*haben*) knock

anknipsen *vt sep* (*fam*) switch on

anknüpfen *vt sep* □ *vt* tie on; (*fig*) enter into (*Gespräch, Beziehung*) □ *vi* (*haben*) refer (**an** + *acc* to)

ankommen† *vi sep* (*sein*) arrive; (*sich nähern*) approach; **gut a~** arrive safely; (*fig*) go down well (**bei** with); **nicht a~ gegen** be no match for; **a~ auf** (+ *acc*) depend on; **es a~ lassen auf** (+ *acc*) risk; **das kommt darauf an** it [all] depends

ankreuzen *vt sep* mark with a cross

ankündigen *vt sep* announce. **A~ung** *f* announcement

Ankunft *f* - arrival

ankurbeln *vt sep* (*fig*) boost

anlächeln *vt sep* smile at

anlachen *vt sep* smile at

Anlage *f* **-,-n** installation; (*Industrie-*) plant; (*Komplex*) complex; (*Geld-*) investment; (*Plan*) layout; (*Beilage*) enclosure; (*Veranlagung*) aptitude; (*Neigung*)

predisposition; [öffentliche] **A~n** [public] gardens; **als A~** enclosed

Anlass *m* **-es,-̈e** (*Anlaß m* **-sses,** **-̈sse**) reason; (*Gelegenheit*) occasion; **A~ geben zu** give cause for

anlass|en† *vt sep* (*Auto*) start; (*fam*) leave on (*Licht*); keep on (*Mantel*); **sich gut/schlecht a~en** start off well/badly. **A~er** *m* **-s,-** starter

anlässlich (**anläßlich**) *prep* (+ *gen*) on the occasion of

Anlauf *m* (*Sport*) run-up; (*fig*) attempt. **a~en†** *vi sep* □ *vi* (*sein*) start; (*beschlagen*) mist up; (*Metall*) tarnish; **rot a~en** go red; (*erröten*) blush; **angelaufen kommen** come running up □ *vt* (*Naut*) call at

anlegen *v sep* □ *vt* put (**an** + *acc* against); put on (*Kleidung, Ohren*); lay back (*Ohren*); aim (*Gewehr*); (*investieren*) invest; (*ausgeben*) spend (*für* on); (*erstellen*) build; (*gestalten*) lay out; draw up (*Liste*); **[mit] Hand a~** lend a hand; **es darauf a~** (*fig*) aim (**zu** to); **sich a~ mit** quarrel with □ *vi* (*haben*) (*Schiff*) moor; **a~ auf** (+ *acc*) aim at

anlehnen *vt sep* lean (**an** + *acc* against); **sich a~** lean (**an** + *acc* on); **eine Tür angelehnt lassen** leave a door ajar

Anleihe *f* **-,-n** loan

anleinen *vt sep* put on a lead

anleit|en *vt sep* instruct. **A~ung** *f* instructions *pl*

anlernen *vt sep* train

Anliegen *nt* **-s,-** request; (*Wunsch*) desire

anliegen|en† *vi sep* (*haben*) [eng] **a~en** fit closely; [eng] **a~end** close-fitting. **A~er** *mpl* residents; **'A~er frei'** 'access for residents only'

anlocken *vt sep* attract

anlügen† *vt sep* lie to

anmachen vt sep (fam) fix; (anschalten) turn on; (anzünden) light; (Culin) dress ⟨Salat⟩

anmalen vt sep paint

Anmarsch m (Mil) approach

anmaßen vt sep sich (dat) a∼en presume (zu to); sich (dat) ein Recht a∼en claim a right. **a∼end** a presumptuous, (arrogant) arrogant, adv -ly. **A∼ung** f - presumption; arrogance

anmeld|en vt sep announce; (Admin) register; sich a∼en say that one is coming; (Admin) register; (Sch) enrol; (im Hotel) check in; (beim Arzt) make an appointment. **A∼ung** f announcement; (Admin) registration; (Sch) enrolment; (Termin) appointment

anmerk|en vt sep mark; sich (dat) etw a∼en lassen show sth. **A∼ung** f -,-en note

Anmut f - grace; (Charme) charm

anmuten vt sep es mutet mich seltsam/vertraut an it seems odd/familiar to me

anmutig a graceful, adv -ly; (lieblich) charming, adv -ly

annähen vt sep sew on

annäher|n a approximate, adv -ly. **A∼ungsversuche** mpl advances

Annahme f -,-n acceptance; (Adoption) adoption; (Vermutung) assumption

annehm|bar a acceptable. **a∼en†** vt sep accept; (adoptieren) adopt; acquire ⟨Gewohnheit⟩; (sich zulegen, vermuten) assume; sich a∼en (+ gen) take care of; angenommen, dass assuming that. **A∼lichkeiten** fpl comforts

annektieren vt annex

Anno adv A∼ 1920 in the year 1920

Annon|ce /a'nõːsə/ f -,-n advertisement. **a∼cieren** /-'siː-/ vt/i (haben) advertise

annullieren vt annul; cancel ⟨Flug⟩

anöden vt sep (fam) bore

Anomalie f -,-n anomaly

anonym a anonymous, adv -ly

Anorak m -s,-s anorak

anordn|en vt sep arrange; (befehlen) order. **A∼ung** f arrangement; order

anorganisch a inorganic

anormal a abnormal

anpacken v sep □ vt grasp; tackle ⟨Arbeit, Problem⟩ □ vi (haben) mit a∼ lend a hand

anpass|en vt sep try on; (angleichen) adapt (dat to); sich a∼ adapt (dat to). **A∼ung** f - adaptation. **a∼ungsfähig** a adaptable. **A∼ungsfähigkeit** f adaptability

Anpfiff m (Sport) kick-off; (fam: Rüge) reprimand

anpflanzen vt sep plant; (anbauen) grow

Anprall m -[e]s impact. **a∼en** vi sep (sein) strike (an etw acc sth)

anprangern vt sep denounce

anpreisen† vt sep commend

anprob|e f fitting. **a∼ieren** vt sep try on

anrechnen vt sep count (als as); (berechnen) charge for; (verrechnen) allow ⟨Summe⟩; ich rechne ihm seine Hilfe hoch an I very much appreciate his help

Anrecht nt right (auf + acc to)

Anrede f [form of] address. **a∼n** vt sep address; (ansprechen) speak to

anreg|en vt sep stimulate; (ermuntern) encourage (zu to); (vorschlagen) suggest. **a∼end** a stimulating. **A∼ung** f stimulation; (Vorschlag) suggestion

anreichern vt sep enrich

Anreise f journey; (Ankunft) arrival. **a∼n** vi sep (sein) arrive

Anreiz m incentive

anrempeln vt sep jostle

Anrichte f -,-n sideboard. **a∼n** vt sep (Culin) prepare; (garnieren) garnish (**mit** with); (*verursachen*) cause

anrüchig *a* disreputable

Anruf *m* call. **A~beantworter** *m* **-s,-** answering machine. **a~en†** *v sep* □ *vt* call to; (*bitten*) call on (**um** for); (*Teleph*) ring □ *vi* (*haben*) ring (**bei jdm** s.o.)

anrühren *vt sep* touch; (*ver-rühren*) mix

ans *prep* = **an das**

Ansage *f* announcement. **a~n** *vt sep* announce; **sich a~n** say that one is coming. **A~r(in)** *m* **-s,-** (*f -,-nen*) announcer

ansamm|eln *vt sep* collect; (*an-häufen*) accumulate; **sich a~eln** collect; (*sich häufen*) accumulate; (*Leute:*) gather. **A~lung** *f* collection; (*Menschen:*) crowd

ansässig *a* resident

Ansatz *m* beginning; (*Haar-*) hair-line; (*Versuch*) attempt; (*Techn*) extension

anschaff|en *vt sep* [**sich** *dat*] etw **a~en** acquire/(*kaufen*) buy sth. **A~ung** *f* **-,-en** acquisition; (*Kauf*) purchase

anschalten *vt sep* switch on

anschau|en *vt sep* look at. **a~lich** *a* vivid, *adv* -ly. **A~ung** *f* **-,-en** (*fig*) view

Anschein *m* appearance; **den A~ haben** seem. **a~end** *adv* apparently

anschicken (sich) *vr sep* be about (**zu** to)

anschirren *vt sep* harness

Anschlag *m* notice; (*Vor-*) estimate; (*Überfall*) attack (**auf** + *acc* on); (*Mus*) touch; (*Techn*) stop; **240 A~e in der Minute** ≈ 50 words per minute. **A~brett** *nt* notice board. **a~en†** *v sep* □ *vt* put up (*Aushang*); strike (*Note, Taste*); cast on (*Masche*); (*be-schädigen*) chip □ *vi* (*haben*) strike/(*stoßen*) knock (**an** + *acc* against); (*Hund:*) bark; (*wirken*) be effective □ *vi* (*sein*) knock (**an** + *acc* against); **mit dem Kopf**

a~en hit one's head. **A~zettel** *m* notice

anschließen† *v sep* □ *vt* connect (**an** + *acc* to); (*zufügen*) add; **sich a~** **an** (+ *acc*) (*anstoßen*) adjoin; (*folgen*) follow; (*sich anfreunden*) become friendly with; **sich jdm a~** join s.o. □ *vi* (*haben*) **a~an** (+ *acc*) (*folgen*) follow. **a~d** *a* adjoining; (*zeitlich*) following □ *adv* afterwards; **a~d an** (+ *acc*) after

Anschluss (**Anschluß**) *m* connection; (*Kontakt*) contact; **A~ finden** make friends; **im A~ an** (+ *acc*) after

anschmieg|en (sich) *vr sep* snug-gle up/(*Kleid:*) cling (**an** + *acc* to). **a~sam** *a* affectionate

anschmieren *vt sep* smear; (*fam: täuschen*) cheat

anschnallen *vt sep* strap on; **sich a~** fasten one's seat-belt

anschneiden† *vt sep* cut into; broach (*Thema*)

anschreiben† *vt sep* write (**an** + *acc* on); (*Comm*) put on s.o.'s account; (*sich wenden*) write to; **bei jdm gut/schlecht angeschrieben sein** be in s.o.'s good/bad books

anschreien† *vt sep* shout at

Anschrift *f* address

anschuldig|en *vt sep* accuse. **A~ung** *f* **-,-en** accusation

anschwellen† *vi sep* (*sein*) swell

anschwemmen *vt sep* wash up

anschwindeln *vt sep* (*fam*) lie to

ansehen† *vt sep* look at; (*ein-schätzen*) regard (**als** as); [**sich** *dat*] etw **a~** look at sth; (*TV*) watch sth. **A~** *nt* -s respect; (*Ruf*) reputation

ansehnlich *a* considerable

ansetzen† *v sep* □ *vt* put on (**an** + *acc* to); (*festsetzen*) fix; (*veran-schlagen*) estimate; **Rost a~** get rusty; **sich a~** form □ *vi* (*haben*) (*anbrennen*) burn; **zum Sprung a~** get ready to jump

Ansicht f view; **meiner A~ nach** in my view; **zur A~** (Comm) on approval. **A~s[post]karte** f picture postcard. **A~ssache** f matter of opinion

ansiedeln (sich) vr sep settle

ansonsten adv apart from that

anspannen vt sep hitch up; (anstrengen) strain; tense (Muskel)

anspiel|en vi sep (haben) **a~en auf** (+ acc) allude to; (versteckt) hint at. **A~ung** f -,-en allusion; hint

Anspitzer m -s,- pencil-sharpener

Ansporn m (fig) incentive. **a~en** vt sep spur on

Ansprache f address

ansprechen v sep □ vt speak to; (fig) appeal to □ vi (haben) respond (**auf** + acc to). **a~d** a attractive

anspringen† v sep □ vt jump at □ vi (sein) (Auto) start

Anspruch m claim/(Recht) right (**auf** + acc to); **A~ haben** be entitled (**auf** + acc to); **in A~ nehmen** make use of; (erfordern) demand; take up (Zeit); occupy (Person); **hohe A~e stellen** be very demanding. **a~slos** a undemanding; (bescheiden) unpretentious. **a~svoll** a demanding; (kritisch) discriminating; (vornehm) up-market

anspucken vt sep spit at

anstacheln vt sep (fig) spur on

Anstalt f -,-en institution; **A~en/keine A~en machen** prepare/make no move (**zu** to)

Anstand m decency; (Benehmen) [good] manners pl

anständig a decent, adv -ly; (ehrbar) respectable, adv -bly; (fam: beträchtlich) considerable, adv -bly; (richtig) proper, adv -ly

Anstands|dame f chaperon. **a~los** adv without any trouble; (bedenkenlos) without hesitation

anstarren vt sep stare at

anstatt conj & prep (+ gen) instead of; **a~ zu arbeiten** instead of working

anstecken vt sep tap (Fass)

ansteck|en v sep □ vt pin (**an** + acc to/on); put on (Ring); (anzünden) light; (in Brand stecken) set fire to; (Med) infect; **sich a~en** catch an infection (**bei** from) □ vi (haben) be infectious. **a~end** a infectious; (fam) catching. **A~ung** f -,-en infection

anstehen† vi sep (haben) queue, (Amer) stand in line

ansteigen† vi sep (sein) climb; (Gelände, Preise) rise

anstelle prep (+ gen) instead of

anstell|en vt sep put, stand (**an** + acc against); (einstellen) employ; (anschalten) turn on; (tun) do; **sich a~en** queue [up], (Amer) stand in line; (sich haben) make a fuss. **A~ung** f employment; (Stelle) job

Anstieg m -[e]s,-e climb; (fig) rise

anstiften vt sep cause; (anzetteln) instigate; **jdn a~n** put s.o. up (**zu** to). **A~er** m instigator

Anstoß m (Anregung) impetus; (Stoß) knock; (Fußball) kick-off; **A~ erregen/nehmen** give/take offence (**an** + dat at). **a~en**† v sep □ vt knock; (mit dem Ellbogen) nudge □ vi (sein) knock (**an** + acc against) □ vi (haben) adjoin (**an etw** acc sth); [**mit den Gläsern**] **a~en** clink glasses; **a~en auf** (+ acc) drink to; **mit der Zunge a~en** lisp

anstößig a offensive, adv -ly

anstrahlen vt sep floodlight; (anlachen) beam at

anstreichen† vt sep paint; (anmerken) mark. **A~er** m -s,- painter

anstreng|en vt sep strain; (ermüden) tire; **sich a~en** exert oneself; (sich bemühen) make an effort (**zu** to). **a~end** a strenuous; (ermüdend) tiring. **A~ung** f -,-en strain; (Mühe) effort

Anstrich *m* coat [of paint]

Ansturm *m* rush; (*Mil*) assault

Ansuchen *nt* -s,- request

Antagonismus *m* - antagonism

Antarktis *f* - Antarctic

Anteil *m* share; **A~ nehmen** take an interest (**an** + *dat* in); (*mitfühlen*) sympathize. **A~nahme** *f* - interest (**an** + *dat* in); (*Mitgefühl*) sympathy

Antenne *f* -,-n aerial

Anthologie *f* -,-n anthology

Anthropologie *f* - anthropology

Anti|alkoholiker *m* teetotaller.

A~biotikum *nt* -s,-ka antibiotic

antik *a* antique. **A~e** *f* - [classical] antiquity

Antikörper *m* antibody

Antilope *f* -,-n antelope

Antipathie *f* - antipathy

Anti|quariat *nt* -[e]s,-e antiquarian bookshop. **a~quarisch** *a* & *adv* second-hand

Antiquitäten *fpl* antiques. **A~händler** *m* antique dealer

Antisemitismus *m* - anti-Semitism

Antisept|ikum *nt* -s,-ka antiseptic. **a~isch** *a* antiseptic

Antrag *m* -[e]s,-e proposal; (*Pol*) motion; (*Gesuch*) application. **A~steller** *m* -s,- applicant

antreffen† *vt sep* find

antreiben† *vt sep* □ *vt* urge on; (*Techn*) drive; (*anschwemmen*) wash up □ *vi* (*sein*) be washed up

antreten† *v sep* □ *vt* start; take up (*Amt*) □ *vi* (*sein*) line up; (*Mil*) fall in

Antrieb *m* urge; (*Techn*) drive; **aus eigenem A~** of one's own accord

antrinken† *vt sep* **sich** (*dat*) **einen Rausch a~** get drunk; **sich** (*dat*) **Mut a~** give oneself Dutch courage

Antritt *m* start; **bei A~ eines Amtes** when taking office. **A~srede** *f* inaugural address

antun† *vt sep* **jdm etw a~** do sth to s.o.; **sich** (*dat*) **etwas a~** take one's own life; **es jdm angetan haben** appeal to s.o.

Antwort *f* -,-en answer, reply (**auf** + *acc* to). **a~en** *vt/i* (*haben*) answer (**jdm** s.o.)

anvertrauen *vt sep* entrust/(*mitteilen*) confide (**jdm** to s.o.); **sich jdm a~** confide in s.o.

anwachsen† *vi sep* (*sein*) take root; (*zunehmen*) grow

Anwalt *m* -[e]s,-e, **Anwältin** *f* -,-nen lawyer; (*vor Gericht*) counsel

Anwandlung *f* -,-en fit (**von** of)

Anwärter(in) *m*(*f*) candidate

anweis|en† *vt sep* assign (*dat* to); (*beauftragen*) instruct. **A~ung** *f* instruction; (*Geld-*) money order

anwend|en† *vt sep* apply (**auf** + *acc* to); (*gebrauchen*) use. **A~ung** *f* application; use

anwerben† *vt sep* recruit

Anwesen *nt* -s,- property

anwesen|d *a* present (**bei** at); **die A~den** those present. **A~heit** *f* - presence

anwidern *vt sep* disgust

Anwohner *mpl* residents

Anzahl *f* number

anzahl|en *vt sep* pay a deposit on; pay on account (*Summe*). **A~ung** *f* deposit

anzapfen *vt sep* tap

Anzeichen *nt* sign

Anzeige *f* -,-n announcement; (*Inserat*) advertisement; **A~ erstatten gegen jdn** report s.o. to the police. **a~n** *vt sep* announce; (*inserieren*) advertise; (*melden*) report [to the police]; (*angeben*) indicate, show. **A~r** *m* indicator

anzieh|en† *vt sep* □ *vt* attract; (*festziehen*) tighten; put on (*Kleider, Bremse*); draw up (*Beine*); (*ankleiden*) dress; **sich a~en** get dressed; **was soll ich a~en?** what shall I wear? **gut angezogen** well-dressed □ *vi* (*haben*) start pulling; (*Preise:*) go up.

a~end a attractive. A~ung f - attraction. A~ungskraft f attraction; (Phys) gravity

Anzug m suit; **im A~ sein** (fig) be imminent

anzüglich a suggestive; (Bemerkung) personal

anzünden vt sep light; (in Brand stecken) set fire to

anzweifeln vt sep question

apart a striking, adv -ly

Apathie f - apathy

apathisch a apathetic, adv -ally

Aperitif m -s,-s aperitif

Apfel m -s,: apple. **A~mus** nt apple purée

Apfelsine f -,-n orange

Apostel m -s apostle

Apostroph m -s,-e apostrophe

Apotheke|e f -,-n pharmacy. **A~er(in)** m -s,- (f -,-nen) pharmacist, [dispensing] chemist

Apparat m -[e]s,-e device; (Phot) camera; (Radio, TV) set; (Teleph) telephone; **am A~!** speaking! **A~ur** f -,-en apparatus

Appell m -s,-e appeal; (Mil) rollcall. **a~ieren** vi (haben) appeal (**an** + acc to)

Appetit m -s appetite; **guten A~!** enjoy your meal! **a~lich** a appetizing, adv -ly

applaudieren vi (haben) applaud

Applaus m -es applause

Aprikose f -,-n apricot

April m -[s] April; **in den A~schicken** (fam) make an April fool of

Aquarell nt -s,-e water-colour

Aquarium nt -s,-ien aquarium

Äquator m -s equator

Ära f - era

Araber(in) m -s,- (f -,-nen) Arab

arabisch a Arab; (Geog) Arabian; (Ziffer) Arabic

Arbeit f -,-en work; (Anstellung) employment, job; (Aufgabe) task; (Sch) [written] test; (Abhandlung) treatise; (Qualität) workmanship; **bei der A~** at work;

zur A~ gehen go to work; **an die A~ gehen, sich an die A~ machen** set to work; **sich** (dat) **viel A~ machen** go to a lot of trouble. **a~en** v sep ◻ vi (haben) work (**an** + dat on) ◻ vt make; **einen Anzug a~en lassen** have a suit made; **sich durch etw a~en** work one's way through sth. **A~er(in)** m -s,- (f -,-nen) worker; (Land-, Hilfs-) labourer. **A~erklasse** f working class

Arbeit|geber m -s,- employer. **A~nehmer** m -s,- employee. **a~sam** a industrious

Arbeits|amt nt employment exchange. **A~erlaubnis, A~genehmigung** f work permit. **A~kraft** f worker; **Mangel an A~kräften** shortage of labour. **A~los** a unemployed; **A~los sein** be out of work. **A~lose(r)** m/f unemployed person; **die A~losen** the unemployed pl. **A~losenunterstützung** f unemployment benefit. **A~losigkeit** f - unemployment

arbeitsparend a labour-saving

Arbeits|platz m job. **A~tag** m working day. **A~zimmer** nt study

Archäo|loge m -n,-n archaeologist. **A~logie** f - archaeology. **a~logisch** a archaeological

Arche f - **die A~** Noah Noah's Ark

Architek|t(in) m -en,-en (f -,-nen) architect. **a~tonisch** a architectural. **A~tur** f - architecture

Archiv nt -s,-e archives pl

Arena f -,-nen arena

arg a (ärger, ärgst) bad; (groß) terrible; **sein ärgster Feind** his worst enemy ◻ adv badly; (sehr) terribly

Argentin|ien /-jən/ nt - Argentina. **a~isch** a Argentinian

Ärger m -s annoyance; (Unannehmlichkeit) trouble. **ä~lich** a annoyed; (leidig) annoying;

ä~lich sein be annoyed. ä~n *vt* annoy; (*necken*) tease; sich a~n get annoyed (über jdn/etw with s.o./ about sth). Ä~nis *nt* -ses, -se annoyance; öffentliches Ä~nis public nuisance

Arglist *f* - malice. a~ig *a* malicious, *adv* -ly

arglos *a* unsuspecting; (*unschuldig*) innocent, *adv* -ly

Argument *nt* -[e]s,-e argument. a~ieren *vi* (*haben*) argue (dass that)

Argwohn *m* -s suspicion

argwöhn|en *vt* suspect. a~isch *a* suspicious, *adv* -ly

Arie /'a:rjə/ *f* -,-n aria

Aristo|krat *m* -en,-en aristocrat. A~kratie *f* - aristocracy. a~kratisch *a* aristocratic

Arithmetik *f* - arithmetic

Arkt|is *f* - Arctic. a~isch *a* Arctic

arm *a* (ärmer, ärmst) poor; **Arm und Reich** (arm und reich) rich and poor

Arm *m* -[e]s,-e arm; **jdn auf den Arm nehmen** (*fam*) pull s.o.'s leg

Armaturenbrett *nt* instrument panel; (*Auto*) dashboard

Armband *nt* (*pl* -bänder) bracelet; (*Uhr*-) watch-strap. A~uhr *f* wrist-watch

Arm|e(r) *m/f* poor man/woman; **die A~en** the poor *pl*; **du A~e** *od* **Ärmste!** you poor thing!

Armee *f* -,-n army

Ärmel *m* -s,- sleeve. Ä~kanal *m* [English] Channel. ä~los *a* sleeveless

Arm|lehne *f* arm. A~leuchter *m* candelabra

ärmlich *a* poor, *adv* -ly; (*elend*) miserable, *adv* -bly

armselig *a* miserable, *adv* -bly

Armut *f* - poverty

Arom|a *nt* -s,-men & -mas aroma; (*Culin*) essence. a~atisch *a* aromatic

Arran|gement /arãʒə'mã:/ *nt* -s,-s arrangement. a~gieren /-'ʒi:rən/ *vt* arrange; sich a~gieren come to an arrangement

Arrest *m* -[e]s (*Mil*) detention

arrogan|t *a* arrogant, *adv* -ly. A~z *f* - arrogance

Arsch *m* -[e]s,ˉe (*vulg*) arse

Arsen *nt* -s arsenic

Art *f* -,-en manner; (*Weise*) way; (*Natur*) nature; (*Sorte*) kind; (*Biol*) species; **auf diese Art** in this way. a~en *vi* (*sein*) a~en **nach** take after

Arterie /-jə/ *f* -,-n artery

Arthritis *f* - arthritis

artig *a* well-behaved; (*höflich*) polite, *adv* -ly; **sei a~!** be good!

Artikel *m* -s,- article

Artillerie *f* - artillery

Artischocke *f* -,-n artichoke

Artist(in) *m* -en,-en (*f* -,-nen) [circus] artiste

Arznei *f* -,-en medicine. A~mittel *nt* drug

Arzt *m* -[e]s,ˉe doctor

Ärztin *f* -,-nen [woman] doctor. ä~lich *a* medical

As *nt* -ses,-se (NEW) **Ass**

Asbest *m* -[e]s asbestos

Asche *f* - ash. A~nbecher *m* ashtray. A~rmittwoch *m* Ash Wednesday

Asiat(in) *m* -en,-en (*f* -,-nen) Asian. a~isch *a* Asian

Asien /'a:zjən/ *nt* -s Asia

asozial *a* antisocial

Aspekt *m* -[e]s,-e aspect

Asphalt *m* -[e]s asphalt. a~ieren *vt* asphalt

Ass *nt* -es,-e ace

Assistent(in) *m* -en,-en (*f* -,-nen) assistant

Ast *m* -[e]s,ˉe branch

ästhetisch *a* aesthetic

Asthm|a *nt* -s asthma. a~atisch *a* asthmatic

Astro|loge *m* -n,-n astrologer. A~logie *f* - astrology. A~naut *m* -en,-en astronaut. A~nom *m*

-en,-en astronomer. **A~nomie** *f*
- astronomy. **a~nomisch** *a* as-
tronomical

Asyl *nt* **-s,-e** home; (*Pol*) asylum.
A~ant *m* **-en,-en** asylum-seeker

Atelier /-'lje:/ *nt* **-s,-s** studio

Atem *m* **-s** breath; **tief A~ holen**
take a deep breath. **a~berau-
bend** *a* breath-taking. **a~los** *a*
breathless, *adv* -ly. **A~pause** *f*
breather. **A~zug** *m* breath

Atheist *m* **-en,-en** atheist

Äther *m* **-s** ether

Äthiopien /-jən/ *nt* **-s** Ethiopia

Athlet|(in) *m* **-en,-en** (*f* -,-nen)
athlete. **a~isch** *a* athletic

Atlant|ik *m* **-s** Atlantic. **a~isch**
a Atlantic; **der A~ische Ozean**
the Atlantic Ocean

Atlas *m* **-lasses,-lanten** atlas

atmen *vt/i* (*haben*) breathe

Atmosphär|e *f* **-,-n** atmosphere.
a~isch *a* atmospheric

Atmung *f* **-** breathing

Atom *nt* **-s,-e** atom. **a~ar** *a*
atomic. **A~bombe** *f* atom bomb.
A~krieg *m* nuclear war

Atten|tat *nt* **-[e]s,-e** assassination
attempt. **A~täter** *m* [would-be]
assassin

Attest *nt* **-[e]s,-e** certificate

Attrak|tion /-'tsjo:n/ *f* **-,-en** at-
traction. **a~tiv** *a* attractive, *adv*
-ly

Attrappe *f* **-,-n** dummy

Attribut *nt* **-[e]s,-e** attribute.
a~iv *a* attributive, *adv* -ly

ätzen *vt* corrode; (*Med*) cauterize;
(*Kunst*) etch. **ä~d** *a* corrosive;
(*Spott*) caustic

au *int* ouch; **au fein!** oh good!

Aubergine /ober'ʒi:nə/ *f* **-,-n** aubergine

auch *adv* & *conj* also, too; (*außerdem*) what's more; (*selbst*) even;
a~ wenn even if; **ich mag ihn—
ich a~** I like him—so do I; **ich
bin nicht müde—ich a~ nicht**
I'm not tired—nor or neither am
I; **sie weiß es a~ nicht** she

doesn't know either; **wer/
wie/was a~ immer** whoever/
however/whatever; **ist das a~
wahr?** is that really true?

Audienz *f* **-,-en** audience

audiovisuell *a* audio-visual

Auditorium *nt* **-s,-ien** (*Univ*) lecture hall

auf *prep* (+ *dat*) on; (+ *acc*) on
[to]; (*bis*) until, till; (*Proportion*)
to; **auf Deutsch/Englisch** in
German/English; **auf einer/
eine Party** at/to a party; **auf der
Straße** in the street; **auf seinem
Zimmer** in one's room; **auf einem Ohr taub** deaf in one ear;
auf einen Stuhl steigen climb
on [to] a chair; **auf die Toilette
gehen** go to the toilet; **auf ein
paar Tage verreisen** go away for
a few days; **auf 10 Kilometer zu
sehen** visible for 10 kilometres
□ *adv* open; (*in die Höhe*) up; **auf
sein** be open; (*Person:*) be up; **auf
und ab** up and down; **sich auf
und davon machen** make off;
Tür auf! open the door!

aufarbeiten *vt sep* do up; **Rückstände a~** clear arrears [of
work]

aufatmen *vi sep* (*haben*) heave a
sigh of relief

aufbahren *vt sep* lay out

Aufbau *m* construction;
(*Struktur*) structure. **a~en** *v sep*
□ *vt* construct, build; (*errichten*)
erect; (*schaffen*) build up; (*arrangieren*) arrange; **wieder
a~en** reconstruct; **sich a~en**
(*fig*) be based (**auf** + *dat* **on**) □ *vi*
(*haben*) be based (**auf** + *dat* **on**)

aufbäumen (sich) *vr sep* rear
[up]; (*fig*) rebel

aufbauschen *vt sep* puff out; (*fig*)
exaggerate

aufbehalten† *vt sep* keep on

aufbekommen† *vt sep* get open;
(*Sch*) be given [as homework]

aufbessern *vt sep* improve; (*erhöhen*) increase

aufbewahr|en *vt sep* keep; *(lagern)* store. **A~ung** *f* safe keeping; storage; *(Gepäck-)* left-luggage office

aufbieten† *vt sep* mobilize; *(fig)* summon up

aufblas|bar *a* inflatable. **a~en†** *vt sep* inflate; **sich a~en** *(fig)* give oneself airs

aufbleiben† *vi sep (sein)* stay open; *(Person:)* stay up

aufblenden *vt/i sep (haben)* *(Auto)* switch to full beam

aufblicken *vi sep (haben)* look up **(zu** at/*(fig)* to)

aufblühen *vi sep (sein)* flower; *(Knospe:)* open

aufbocken *vt sep* jack up

aufbraten† *vt sep* fry up

aufbrauchen† *vt sep* use up

aufbrausen *vi sep (sein)* *(fig)* flare up. **a~d** *a* quick-tempered

aufbrechen† *v sep* □ *vt* break open □ *vi (sein)* *(Knospe:)* open; *(sich aufmachen)* set out, start

aufbringen† *vt sep* raise *(Geld)*; find *(Kraft)*; *(wütend machen)* infuriate

Aufbruch *m* start, departure

aufbrühen *vt sep* make *(Tee)*

aufbürden *vt sep* **jdm etw a~** *(fig)* burden s.o. with sth

aufdecken *vt sep* *(auflegen)* put on; *(abdecken)* uncover; *(fig)* expose

aufdrängen *vt sep* force *(dat* on); **sich jdm a~** force one's company on s.o.

aufdrehen *vt sep* turn on

aufdringlich *a* persistent

aufeinander *adv* one on top of the other; *(schießen)* at each other; *(warten)* for each other; **a~folgen** follow one another; **a~folgend** successive; *(Tage)* consecutive. **a~folgen** *vi sep (sein)* NEW **a~ folgen**, *s.* **aufeinander**. **a~folgend** *a* NEW **a~ folgend**, *s.* aufeinander

Aufenthalt *m* stay; **10 Minuten A~ haben** *(Zug:)* stop for 10 minutes. **A~serlaubnis**, **A~sgenehmigung** *f* residence permit. **A~sraum** *m* recreation room; *(im Hotel)* lounge

auferlegen *vt sep* impose *(dat* on)

auferstehen|en† *vi sep (sein)* rise from the dead. **A~ung** *f -* resurrection

aufessen† *vt sep* eat up

auffahr|en† *vi sep (sein)* drive up; *(aufprallen)* crash, run **(auf +** *acc* into); *(aufschrecken)* start up; *(aufbrausen)* flare up. **A~t** *f* drive; *(Autobahn-)* access road, slip road; *(Bergfahrt)* ascent

auffallen† *vi sep (sein)* be conspicuous; **unangenehm a~** make a bad impression; **jdm a~** strike s.o. **a~d** *a* striking, *adv* **-ly**

auffällig *a* conspicuous, *adv* **-ly**; *(grell)* gaudy, *adv* **-ily**

auffangen† *vt sep* catch; pick up *(Funkspruch)*

auffassen *vt sep* understand; *(deuten)* take; **falsch a~en** misunderstand. **A~ung** *f* understanding; *(Ansicht)* view. **A~ungsgabe** *f* grasp

auffordern *vt sep* ask; *(einladen)* invite; **jdn zum Tanz a~** ask s.o. to dance. **A~ung** *f* request; invitation

auffrischen *v sep* □ *vt* freshen up; revive *(Erinnerung)*; **seine Englischkenntnisse a~** brush up one's English

aufführ|en† *vt sep* perform; *(angeben)* list; **sich a~en** behave. **A~ung** *f* performance

auffüllen *vt sep* fill up; **[wieder] a~** replenish

Aufgabe *f* task; *(Rechen-)* problem; *(Verzicht)* giving up; **A~n** *(Sch)* homework *sg*

Aufgang *m* way up; *(Treppe)* stairs *pl*; *(Astr)* rise

aufgeben† *v sep* □ *vt* give up; post *(Brief)*; send *(Telegramm)*; place *(Bestellung)*; register *(Gepäck)*;

put in the paper ⟨Annonce⟩; **jdm eine Aufgabe/ein Rätsel a~** set s.o. a task/a riddle; **jdm Suppe a~** serve s.o. with soup □ vi (haben) give up

aufgeblasen a (fig) conceited
Aufgebot nt contingent (**an** + dat of); (Relig) banns pl; **unter A~ aller Kräfte** with all one's strength

aufgebracht a (fam) angry
aufgedunsen a bloated
aufgehen† vi sep (sein) open; (sich lösen) come undone; ⟨Teig, Sonne:⟩ rise; ⟨Saat:⟩ come up; (Math) come out exactly; **in Flammen a~** go up in flames; **in etw** (dat) **a~** (fig) be wrapped up in sth; **ihm ging auf** (fam) he realized (**dass** that)
aufgelegt a sein zu be in the mood for; **gut/schlecht a~ sein** be in a good/bad mood
aufgelöst a (fig) distraught; **in Tränen a~** in floods of tears
aufgeregt a excited, adv -ly; (erregt) agitated, adv -ly
aufgeschlossen a (fig) open-minded
aufgesprungen a chapped
aufgeweckt a (fig) bright
aufgießen† vt sep pour on; (aufbrühen) make ⟨Tee⟩
aufgreifen† vt sep pick up; take up ⟨Vorschlag, Thema⟩
aufgrund prep (+ gen) on the strength of

Aufguss (**Aufguß**) m infusion
aufhaben† v sep □ vt have on; **den Mund a~** have one's mouth open; **viel a~** (Sch) have a lot of homework □ vi (haben) be open
aufhalsen vt sep (fam) saddle with
aufhalten† vt sep hold up; (anhalten) stop; (offenhalten) keep, detain; (offenhalten) hold open; hold out ⟨Hand⟩; **sich a~** stay; (sich befassen) spend some time (**mit** on)

aufhängen vt/i sep (haben) hang up; (henken) hang; **sich a~en** hang oneself. **A~er** m -s,- loop. **A~ung** f - (Auto) suspension
aufheben† vt sep pick up; (hochheben) raise; (aufbewahren) keep; (beenden) end; (rückgängig machen) lift; (abschaffen) abolish; (Jur) quash ⟨Urteil⟩; repeal ⟨Gesetz⟩; (ausgleichen) cancel out; **sich a~** cancel each other out; **gut aufgehoben sein** be well looked after. **A~** nt -s **viel A~s machen** make a great fuss (**von** about)
aufheitern vt sep cheer up; **sich a~** ⟨Wetter:⟩ brighten up
aufhellen vt sep lighten; **sich a~** ⟨Himmel:⟩ brighten
aufhetzen vt sep incite
aufholen v sep □ vt make up □ vi (haben) catch up; (zeitlich) make up time
aufhorchen vi sep (haben) prick up one's ears
aufhören vi sep (haben) stop; **mit der Arbeit a~, a~ zu arbeiten** stop working
aufklappen vt/i sep (sein) open
aufklär|en vt sep (haben) enlighten s.o.; (sexuell) tell s.o. the facts of life; **sich a~en** be solved; ⟨Wetter:⟩ clear up. **A~ung** f solution; enlightenment; (Mil) reconnaissance; **sexuelle A~ung** sex education
aufkleben vt sep stick on. **A~er** m -s,- sticker
aufknöpfen vt sep unbutton
aufkochen v sep □ vt bring to the boil □ vi (sein) come to the boil
aufkommen† vi sep (sein) start; ⟨Wind:⟩ spring up; ⟨Mode:⟩ come in; **a~ für** pay for
aufkrempeln vt sep roll up
aufladen† vt sep load; (Electr) charge
Auflage f impression; (Ausgabe) edition; (Zeitungs-) circulation; (Bedingung) condition; (Überzug) coating

auflassen† *vt sep* leave open; leave on ⟨Hut⟩

auflauern *vi sep (haben)* jdm a~ lie in wait for s.o.

Auflauf *m sep (haben); (Culin)* ≈ soufflé. **a~en**† *vi sep (sein) (Naut)* run aground

auflegen *v sep* □ *vt* apply ⟨auf + acc to⟩; put down ⟨Hörer⟩; **neu a~** reprint □ *vi (haben)* ring off

auflehn|en (sich) *vr sep (fig)* rebel. **A~ung** *f* - rebellion

auflesen† *vt sep* pick up

aufleuchten *vi sep (haben)* light up

aufliegen† *vi sep (haben)* rest ⟨auf + dat on⟩

auflisten *vt sep* list

auflockern *vt sep* break up; ⟨entspannen⟩ relax; *(fig)* liven up

auflös|en *vt sep* dissolve; close ⟨Konto⟩; **sich a~en** dissolve; ⟨Nebel:⟩ clear. **A~ung** *f* dissolution; ⟨Lösung⟩ solution

aufmach|en *v sep* □ *vt* open; ⟨lösen⟩ undo; **sich a~en** set out ⟨nach for⟩; ⟨sich schminken⟩ make oneself up □ *vi (haben)* open; **jdm a~en** open the door to s.o. **A~ung** *f* -,-en get-up; *(Comm)* presentation

aufmerksam *a* attentive, *adv* -ly; **a~ werden auf** (+ *acc*) notice; **jdn a~ machen auf** (+ *acc*) draw s.o.'s attention to. **A~keit** *f* -,-en attention; ⟨Höflichkeit⟩ courtesy

aufmucken *vi sep (fam)* rebel

aufmuntern *vt sep* cheer up

Aufnahme *f* -,-n acceptance; ⟨Empfang⟩ reception; (in Klub, Krankenhaus) admission; ⟨Einbeziehung⟩ inclusion; ⟨Beginn⟩ start; ⟨Foto⟩ photograph; ⟨Film-⟩ shot; *(Mus)* recording; ⟨Band-⟩ tape recording. **a~fähig** *a* receptive. **A~prüfung** *f* entrance examination

aufnehmen† *vt sep* pick up; ⟨absorbieren⟩ absorb; take ⟨Nahrung, Foto⟩; ⟨fassen⟩ hold;

⟨annehmen⟩ accept; ⟨leihen⟩ borrow; ⟨empfangen⟩ receive; (in Klub, Krankenhaus) admit; ⟨beherbergen, geistig erfassen⟩ take in; ⟨einbeziehen⟩ include; ⟨beginnen⟩ take up; ⟨niederschreiben⟩ take down; ⟨filmen⟩ film, shoot; *(Mus)* record; **auf Band a~** tape[-record]; **etw gelassen a~** take sth calmly; **es a~ können mit** *(fig)* be a match for

aufopfer|n *vt sep* sacrifice; **sich a~n** sacrifice oneself. **a~nd** *a* devoted, *adv* -ly. **A~ung** *f* self-sacrifice

aufpassen *vi sep* pay attention; ⟨sich vorsehen⟩ take care; **a~auf** (+ *acc*) look after

aufpflanzen (sich) *vr sep (fam)* plant oneself

aufplatzen *vi sep (sein)* split open

aufplustern *vt sep* ⟨Vogel:⟩ ruffle up its feathers

Aufprall *m* -[e]s impact. **a~en** *vi sep (sein)* **a~en auf** (+ *acc*) hit

aufpumpen *vt sep* pump up, inflate

aufputsch|en *vt sep* incite; **sich a~en** take stimulants. **A~mittel** *nt* stimulant

aufquellen *vi sep (sein)* swell

aufraffen *vt sep* pick up; **sich a~** pick oneself up; *(fig)* pull oneself together; ⟨sich aufschwingen⟩ find the energy ⟨zu for⟩

aufragen *vi sep (sein)* rise [up]

aufräumen *vt/i sep* tidy up; ⟨wegräumen⟩ put away; **a~mit** *(fig)* get rid of

aufrecht *a & adv* upright. **a~erhalten**† *vt sep (fig)* maintain

aufreg|en *vt* excite; ⟨beunruhigen⟩ upset; ⟨ärgern⟩ annoy; **sich a~en** get excited; ⟨sich erregen⟩ get worked up. **a~end** *a* exciting. **A~ung** *f* excitement

aufreiben† *vt sep* chafe; *(fig)* wear down; **sich a~en** wear oneself out. **a~d** *a* trying, wearing

aufreißen† *v sep* □ *vt* tear open; dig up ⟨Straße⟩; open wide

⟨Augen, Mund⟩ □ vi (sein) split open

aufreizend a provocative, adv -ly

aufrichten vt sep erect; (fig: trösten) comfort; **sich a~** straighten up; (sich setzen) sit up

aufrichtig a sincere, adv -ly. **A~keit** f - sincerity

aufriegeln vt sep unbolt

aufrollen vt sep roll up; (entrollen) unroll

aufrücken vi sep (sein) move up; (fig) be promoted

Aufruf m appeal (**an** + dat to); **a~en**† vt sep call out ⟨Namen⟩; **jdn a~en** call s.o.'s name; (fig) call on s.o. (**zu** to)

Aufruhr m -s,-e turmoil; (Empörung) revolt

aufrühr|en vt sep stir up. **A~er** m -s,- rebel. **a~erisch** a inflammatory; (rebellisch) rebellious

aufrunden vt sep round up

aufrüsten vi sep (haben) arm

aufs prep = **auf das**

aufsagen vt sep recite

aufsammeln vt sep gather up

aufsässig a rebellious

Aufsatz m top; (Sch) essay

aufsaugen† vt sep soak up

aufschauen vi sep (haben) look up (**zu** at/(fig) to)

aufschichten vt sep stack up

aufschieben† vt sep slide open; (verschieben) put off, postpone

Aufschlag m impact; (Tennis) service; (Hosen-) turn-up; (Ärmel-) upturned cuff; (Revers) lapel; (Comm) surcharge. **a~en**† v sep □ vt open; crack ⟨Ei⟩; (hochschlagen) turn up; (errichten) put up; (erhöhen) increase; cast on ⟨Masche⟩; sich (dat) das Knie **a~en** cut [open] one's knee □ vi (haben) hit (**auf** etw acc/dat sth); (Tennis) serve; (teurer werden) go up

aufschließen† v sep □ vt unlock □ vi (haben) unlock the door

aufschlitzen vt sep slit open

Aufschluss (**Aufschluß**) m A~ geben give information (**über** + acc on). **a~reich** a revealing; (lehrreich) informative

aufschneid|en† v sep □ vt cut open; (in Scheiben) slice; carve ⟨Braten⟩ □ vi (haben) (fam) exaggerate. **A~er** m -s,- (fam) showoff

Aufschnitt m sliced sausage, cold meat [and cheese]

aufschrauben vt sep screw on; (abschrauben) unscrew

aufschrecken v sep □ vt startle □ vi† (sein) start up; **aus dem Schlaf a~** wake up with a start

Aufschrei m [sudden] cry

aufschreiben† vt sep write down; (fam: verschreiben) prescribe; **jdn a~** ⟨Polizist:⟩ book s.o.

aufschreien† vi sep (haben) cry out

Aufschrift f inscription; (Etikett) label

Aufschub m delay; (Frist) grace

aufschürfen vt sep sich (dat) das Knie **a~** graze one's knee

aufschwatzen vt sep jdm etw **a~** talk s.o. into buying sth

aufschwingen† (sich) vr sep find the energy (**zu** for)

Aufschwung m (fig) upturn

aufsehen† vi sep (haben) look up (**zu** at/(fig) to). **A~** nt -s **A~ erregen** cause a sensation; **A~ erregend** sensational. **a~erregend** a NEW **A~ erregend**, s. **Aufsehen**

Aufseher(in) m -s,- (f -,-nen) supervisor; (Gefängnis-) warder

aufsein† vi sep (sein) NEW **auf sein**, s. **auf**

aufsetzen vt sep put on; (verfassen) draw up; (entwerfen) draft; **sich a~** sit up

Aufsicht f supervision; (Person) supervisor. **A~srat** m board of directors

aufsitzen† vi sep (sein) mount

aufspannen vt sep put up

aufsparen vt sep save, keep

aufsperren vt sep open wide

aufspielen v sep □ vi (haben) play □ vr **sich a~** show off; **sich als Held a~** play the hero

aufspießen vt sep spear

aufspringen† vi sep (sein) jump up; (aufprallen) bounce; (sich öffnen) burst open; (Haut:) become chapped; **a~ auf** (+ acc) jump on

aufspüren vt sep track down

aufstacheln vt sep incite

aufstampfen vi sep (haben) **mit dem Fuß a~** stamp one's foot

Aufstand m uprising, rebellion

aufständisch a rebellious. **A~e(r)** m rebel, insurgent

aufstapeln vt sep stack up

aufstauen vt sep dam [up]

aufstehen† vi sep (sein) get up; (offen sein) be open; (fig) rise up

aufsteigen† vi sep (sein) get on; (Reiter:) mount; (Bergsteiger:) climb up; (hochsteigen) rise [up]; (fig: befördert werden) rise (**zu** to); (Sport) be promoted

aufstell|en vt sep put up; (Culin) put on; (postieren) post; (in einer Reihe) line up; (nominieren) nominate; (Sport) select (Mannschaft); make out (Liste); set up (Behauptung); set up (Rekord); **sich a~en** line up; (in einer Reihe) line up. **A~ung** f nomination; (Liste) list

Aufstieg m -[e]s, -e ascent; (fig) rise; (Sport) promotion

aufstöbern vt sep flush out; (fig) track down

aufstoßen† v sep □ vt push open □ vi (haben) burp; **a~ auf** (+ acc) strike. **A~** nt -s burping

aufstrebend a (fig) ambitious

Aufstrich m [sandwich] spread

aufstützen vt sep rest (**auf** + acc on); **sich a~** lean (**auf** + acc on)

aufsuchen vt sep look for; (besuchen) go to see

Auftakt m (fig) start

auftauchen vi sep (sein) emerge; (U-Boot:) surface; (fig) turn up; (Frage:) crop up

auftauen vt/i sep (sein) thaw

aufteil|en vt sep divide [up]. **A~ung** f division

auftischen vt sep serve [up]

Auftrag m -[e]s, ¨-e task; (Kunst) commission; (Comm) order; **im A~** (+ gen) on behalf of. **a~en†** v sep □ vt apply; (servieren) serve; (abtragen) wear out; **jdm a~en** instruct s.o. (**zu** to) □ vi (haben) **dick a~en** (fam) exaggerate. **A~geber** m -s,- client

auftreiben† vt sep distend; (fam: beschaffen) get hold of

auftrennen vt sep unpick, undo

auftreten† v sep □ vi (sein) tread; (sich benehmen) behave, act; (Theat) appear; (die Bühne betreten) enter; (vorkommen) occur □ vt kick open. **A~** nt -s occurrence; (Benehmen) manner

Auftrieb m buoyancy; (fig) boost

Auftritt m (Theat) appearance; (auf die Bühne) entrance; (Szene) scene

auftun† vt sep **jdm Suppe a~** serve s.o. with soup; (dat) etw **a~** help oneself to sth; **sich a~** open

aufwachen vi sep (sein) wake up

aufwachsen† vi sep (sein) grow up

Aufwand m -[e]s expenditure; (Luxus) extravagance; (Mühe) trouble; **A~ treiben** be extravagant

aufwändig a = aufwendig

aufwärmen vt sep heat up; (fig) rake up; **sich a~** warm oneself; (Sport) warm up

Aufwartefrau f cleaner

aufwärts adv upwards; (bergauf) uphill; **es geht a~ mit jdm/etw** s.o./sth is improving. **a~gehen†** vi sep (sein) (NEW) **a~ gehen**, s. aufwärts

Aufwartung f - cleaner; **jdm seine A~ machen** call on s.o.

aufwaschen† *vt/i sep* (*haben*) wash up

aufwecken *vt sep* wake up

aufweichen *v sep* □ *vt* soften □ *vi* (*sein*) become soft

aufweisen† *vt sep* have, show

aufwend|en† *vt sep* spend; **Mühe a~en** take pains. **a~ig** *a* lavish, *adv* -ly; (*teuer*) expensive, *adv* -ly

aufwerfen† *vt sep* (*fig*) raise

aufwert|en *vt sep* revalue. **A~ung** *f* revaluation

aufwickeln *vt sep* roll up; (*auswickeln*) unwrap

aufwiegeln *vt sep* stir up

aufwiegen† *vt sep* compensate for

Aufwiegler *m* -s,- agitator

aufwirbeln *vt sep* **Staub a~** stir up dust; (*fig*) cause a stir

aufwischen *vt sep* wipe up; wash (*Fußboden*). **A~lappen** *m* floor-cloth

aufwühlen *vt sep* churn up; (*fig*) stir up

aufzähl|en *vt sep* enumerate, list. **A~ung** *f* list

aufzeichn|en *vt sep* record; (*zeichnen*) draw. **A~ung** *f* recording; **A~ungen** notes

aufziehen† *v sep* □ *vt* pull up; hoist (*Segel*); (*öffnen*) open; draw (*Vorhang*); (*auftrennen*) undo; (*großziehen*) bring up; rear (*Tier*); mount (*Bild*); thread (*Perlen*); wind up (*Uhr*); (*arrangieren*) organize; (*fam: necken*) tease □ *vi* (*sein*) approach

Aufzucht *f* rearing

Aufzug *m* hoist; (*Fahrstuhl*) lift, (*Amer*) elevator; (*Prozession*) procession; (*Theat*) act; (*fam: Aufmachung*) get-up

Augapfel *m* eyeball

Auge *nt* -s,-n eye; (*Punkt*) spot; **vier A~n werfen** throw a four; **gute A~n** good eyesight; **unter vier A~n** in private; **aus den A~n verlieren** lose sight of; **im A~ behalten** keep in sight; (*fig*) bear in mind

Augenblick *m* moment; **im/jeden A~** at the/at any moment; **A~!** just a moment! **a~lich** *a* immediate; (*derzeitig*) present □ *adv* immediately; (*derzeit*) at present

Augen|braue *f* eyebrow. **A~höhle** *f* eye socket. **A~licht** *nt* sight. **A~lid** *nt* eyelid. **A~schein** *m* in **A~schein nehmen** inspect. **A~zeuge** *m* eyewitness

August *m* -[s] August

Auktion *f* -,-en auction. **A~ator** *m* -s,-en /-'to:rən/ auctioneer

Aula *f* -,-len (*Sch*) [assembly] hall

Aupairmädchen, **Au-pair-Mädchen** /o'pɛ:r-/ *nt* au pair

aus *prep + dat* out of; (*von*) from; (*bestehend*) [made] of; **aus Angst** from or out of fear; **aus Spaß** for fun □ *adv* out; (*Licht, Radio*) off; **aus sein** be out; (*Licht, Radio:*) be off; (*zu Ende sein*) be over; **aus sein auf** (+ *acc*) be after; **mit ihm ist es aus** he's had it; **aus und ein** in and out; **nicht mehr aus noch ein wissen** be at one's wits' end; **von . . . aus** from . . .; **von sich aus** of one's own accord; **von mir aus** as far as I'm concerned

ausarbeiten *vt sep* work out

ausarten *vi sep* (*sein*) degenerate (**in** + *acc* into)

ausatmen *vt/i sep* (*haben*) breathe out

ausbaggern *vt sep* excavate; dredge (*Fluss*)

ausbauen *vt sep* remove; (*vergrößern*) extend; (*fig*) expand

ausbedingen† *vt sep* **sich** (*dat*) **a~** insist on; (*zur Bedingung machen*) stipulate

ausbessern *vt sep* mend, repair. **A~ung** *f* repair

ausbeulen *vt sep* remove the dents from; (*dehnen*) make baggy

Ausbeut|e *f* yield. **a~en** *vt sep* exploit. **A~ung** *f* exploitation

ausbild|en *vt sep* train; (*formen*) form; (*entwickeln*) develop; **sich**

a∼en train (als/zu as); (entstehen) develop. A∼er m -s,- instructor. A∼ung f training; (Sch) education

ausbitten† vt sep sich (dat) a∼ ask for; (verlangen) insist on

ausblasen† vt sep blow out

ausbleiben vi sep (sein) fail to appear; (Erfolg:) materialize; (nicht heimkehren) stay out; es konnte nicht a∼ it was inevitable. A∼ nt -s absence

Ausblick m view

ausbrech|en vi sep (sein) break out; (Vulkan:) erupt; (fliehen) escape; **in Tränen a∼en** burst into tears. A∼er m runaway

ausbreit|en vt sep spread [out]; sich a∼en spread. A∼ung f spread

ausbrennen† v sep □ vt cauterize □ vi (sein) burn out; (Haus:) be gutted [by fire]

Ausbruch m outbreak; (Vulkan-) eruption; (Wut-) outburst; (Flucht) escape, break-out

ausbrüten vt sep hatch

Ausbund m A∼der Tugend paragon of virtue

ausbürsten vt sep brush; (entfernen) brush out

Ausdauer f perseverance; (körperlich) stamina. a∼nd a persevering; (unermüdlich) untiring; (Bot) perennial □ adv with perseverance; untiringly

ausdehn|en vt sep stretch; (fig) extend; sich a∼en stretch; (Phys & fig) expand; (dauern) last. A∼ung f expansion; (Umfang) extent

ausdenken† vt sep sich (dat) a∼ think up; (sich vorstellen) imagine

ausdrehen vt sep turn off

Ausdruck m expression; (Fach-) term; (Computer) printout. a∼en vt sep print

ausdrück|en vt sep squeeze out; squeeze (Zitrone); stub out (Zigarette); (äußern) express; sich

a∼en express oneself. a∼lich a express, adv -ly

ausdrucks|los a expressionless. a∼voll a expressive

auseinander adv apart; (entzwei) in pieces; a∼ falten unfold; a∼ gehen part; (Menge:, Meinungen:) diverge; (Menge:) disperse; (Ehe:) break up; (entzweigehen) come apart; a∼ halten tell apart; a∼ nehmen take apart or to pieces; a∼ setzen place apart; (erklären) explain (jdm to s.o.); sich a∼ setzen set apart; (sich aussprechen) have it out (mit jdm with s.o.); come to grips (mit einem Problem with a problem).

a∼falten† vt sep NEW a∼ falten, s. auseinander. a∼gehen† vi sep (sein) NEW a∼ gehen, s. auseinander. a∼halten† vt sep NEW a∼ halten, s. auseinander. a∼nehmen† vt sep NEW a∼ nehmen, s. auseinander. a∼setzen vt sep NEW a∼ setzen, s. auseinander. A∼setzung f -,-en discussion; (Streit) argument

auserlesen a select, choice

ausfahr|en v sep □ vt take for a drive; take out (Baby) [in the pram] □ vi (sein) go for a drive. A∼t f drive; (Autobahn-, Garagen-) exit

Ausfall m failure; (Absage) cancellation; (Comm) loss. a∼en† vi sep (sein) fall out; (versagen) fail; (abgesagt werden) be cancelled; **gut/schlecht a∼en** turn out to be good/poor

ausfallend, ausfällig a abusive

ausfertig|en vt sep make out. A∼ung f -,-en in doppelter/dreifacher A∼ung in duplicate/triplicate

ausfindig a a∼ machen find

ausflippen vi (sein) freak out

Ausflucht f -,-e excuse

Ausflug m excursion, outing

Ausflügler m -s,- (fam) tripper

Ausfluss (**Ausfluß**) m outlet; (Abfluss) drain; (Med) discharge

ausfragen *vt sep* question

ausfransen *vi sep* (*sein*) fray

Ausfuhr *f* -,-en (*Comm*) export

ausführ|**en** *vt sep* take out; (*Comm*) export; (*durchführen*) carry out; (*erklären*) explain. **a~lich** *a* detailed □ *adv* in detail. **A~ung** *f* execution; (*Comm*) version; (*äußere*) finish; (*Qualität*) workmanship; (*Erklärung*) explanation

Ausgabe *f* issue; (*Buch-*) edition; (*Comm*) version

Ausgang *m* way out, exit; (*Flugsteig*) gate; (*Ende*) end; (*Ergebnis*) outcome, result; **A~** haben time off. **A~spunkt** *m* starting-point. **A~ssperre** *f* curfew

ausgeben† *vt sep* hand out; issue (*Fahrkarten*); spend (*Geld*); buy (*Runde Bier*); **sich a~ als** pretend to be

ausgebeult *a* baggy

ausgebildet *a* trained

ausgebucht *a* fully booked; (*Vorstellung*) sold out

ausgedehnt *a* extensive; (*lang*) long

ausgedient *a* worn out; (*Person*) retired

ausgefallen *a* unusual

ausgefranst *a* frayed

ausgeglichen *a* [well-]balanced; (*gelassen*) even-tempered

ausgeh|en† *vi sep* (*sein*) go out; (*Haare:*) fall out; (*Vorräte, Geld:*) run out; (*verblassen*) fade; (*herrühren*) come (*von* from); (*abzielen*) aim (**auf** + *acc* at); **gut/schlecht a~en** end well/badly; **leer a~en** come away empty-handed; **davon a~en, dass** assume that. **A~verbot** *nt* curfew

ausgelassen *a* high-spirited; **a~ sein** be in high spirits

ausgelernt *a* [fully] trained

ausgemacht *a* agreed; (*fam: vollkommen*) utter

ausgenommen *conj* except; **a~ wenn** unless

ausgeprägt *a* marked

ausgerechnet *adv* **a~ heute** today of all days; **a~er/Rom** he of all people/Rome of all places

ausgeschlossen *pred a* out of the question

ausgeschnitten *a* low-cut

ausgesprochen *a* marked □ *adv* decidedly

ausgestorben *a* extinct; **[wie] a~** ⟨*Straße:*⟩ deserted

Ausgestoßene(r) *m/f* outcast

ausgewachsen *a* fully-grown

ausgewogen *a* [well-]balanced

ausgezeichnet *a* excellent, *adv* -ly

ausgiebig *a* extensive, *adv* -ly; (*ausgedehnt*) long; **a~ Gebrauch machen von** make full use of; **a~ frühstücken** have a really good breakfast

ausgießen† *vt sep* pour out; (*leeren*) empty

Ausgleich *m* -[e]s balance; (*Entschädigung*) compensation. **a~en†** *v sep* □ *vt* balance; even out (*Höhe*); (*wettmachen*) compensate for; **sich a~en** balance out □ *vi* (*haben*) (*Sport*) equalize. **A~sgymnastik** *f* keep-fit exercises *pl*. **A~streffer** *m* equalizer

ausgleiten† *vi sep* (*sein*) slip

ausgrab|en† *vt sep* dig up; (*Archaeol*) excavate. **A~ung** *f* -,-en excavation

Ausguck *m* -[e]s,-e look-out post; (*Person*) look-out

Ausguss (**Ausguß**) *m* [kitchen] sink

aushaben† *vt sep* have finished (*Buch*); **wann habt ihr Schule aus?** when do you finish school?

aushalten† *v sep* □ *vt* bear, stand; hold (*Note*); (*Unterhalt zahlen für*) keep; **nicht auszuhalten, nicht zum A~** unbearable □ *vi* (*haben*) hold out

aushandeln *vt sep* negotiate

aushändigen vt sep hand over

Aushang m [public] notice

aushängen[1] vt sep (reg) display; take off its hinges ⟨Tür⟩

aushängen[2]† vi sep (haben) be displayed. **A~eschild** nt sign

ausharren vi sep (haben) hold out

ausheben† vt sep excavate; take off its hinges ⟨Tür⟩

aushecken vt sep (fig) hatch

aushelfen† vi sep (haben) help out (**jdm** s.o.)

Aushilfe f [temporary] assistant; **zur A~e** to help out. **A~s- kraft** f temporary worker. **a~sweise** adv temporarily

aushöhlen vt sep hollow out

ausholen vi sep (haben) [**zum Schlag**] **a~** raise one's arm [ready to strike]

aushorchen vt sep sound out

auskennen† (sich) vt sep know one's way around; **sich mit/in etw** (dat) **a~** know all about sth

auskleiden vt sep undress; ⟨Techn⟩ line; **sich a~** undress

ausknipsen vt sep switch off

auskommen† vi sep (sein) manage (**mit/ohne** with/without); ⟨sich vertragen⟩ get on (**gut** well). **A~** nt -s **sein A~/ein gutes A~ haben** get by/be well off

auskosten vt sep enjoy [to the full]

auskugeln vt sep **sich** (dat) **den Arm a~** dislocate one's shoulder

auskühlen vt/i sep (sein) cool

auskundschaften vt sep spy out; ⟨erfahren⟩ find out

Auskunft f -,-e information; ⟨A~sstelle⟩ information desk/ ⟨Büro⟩ bureau; ⟨Teleph⟩ enquiries pl; **eine A~** a piece of information. **A~sbüro** nt information bureau

auslachen vt sep laugh at

ausladen† vt sep unload; ⟨fam: absagen⟩ put off ⟨Gast⟩. **a~d** a projecting

Auslage f [window] display; **A~n** expenses

Ausland nt **im/ins A~** abroad

Ausländ|er(in) m -s,- (f -,-nen) foreigner. **a~isch** a foreign

Auslandsgespräch nt international call

auslass|en† vt sep let out; let down ⟨Saum⟩; ⟨weglassen⟩ leave out; ⟨versäumen⟩ miss; ⟨Culin⟩ melt; (fig) vent ⟨Ärger⟩ (**an** + dat on); **sich a~en über** (+ acc) go on about sth. **A~ungszeichen** nt apostrophe

Auslauf m run. **a~en**† vi sep (sein) run out; ⟨Farbe:⟩ run; ⟨Naut⟩ put to sea; ⟨leerlaufen⟩ run dry; ⟨enden⟩ end; ⟨Modell:⟩ be discontinued

Ausläufer m ⟨Geog⟩ spur; ⟨Bot⟩ runner, sucker

ausleeren vt sep empty [out]

ausleg|en vt sep lay out; display ⟨Waren⟩; ⟨bedecken⟩ cover/ ⟨auskleiden⟩ line (**mit** with); ⟨bezahlen⟩ pay; ⟨deuten⟩ interpret. **A~ung** f -,-en interpretation

ausleihen† vt sep lend; **sich** (dat) **a~** borrow

auslernen vi sep (haben) finish one's training

Auslese f - selection; (fig) pick; ⟨Elite⟩ élite. **a~n**† vt sep finish reading ⟨Buch⟩; ⟨auswählen⟩ pick out, select

ausliefer|n vt sep hand over; ⟨Jur⟩ extradite; **ausgeliefert sein** (+ dat) be at the mercy of. **A~ung** f handing over; ⟨Jur⟩ extradition; ⟨Comm⟩ distribution

ausliegen† vi sep (haben) be on display

auslöschen vt sep extinguish; ⟨abwischen⟩ wipe off; (fig) erase

auslosen vt sep draw lots for

auslös|en vt sep set off, trigger; (fig) cause; arouse ⟨Begeisterung⟩; ⟨einlösen⟩ redeem; pay a ransom for ⟨Gefangene⟩. **A~er** m -s,- trigger; ⟨Phot⟩ shutter release

Auslosung f draw

auslüften vt/i sep (haben) air

ausmachen *vt sep* put out; (*abschalten*) turn off; (*abmachen*) arrange; (*erkennen*) make out; (*betragen*) amount to; (*darstellen*) represent; (*wichtig sein*) matter; **das macht mir nichts aus** I don't mind

ausmalen *vt sep* paint; (*fig*) describe; **sich** (*dat*) **a∼** imagine

Ausmaß *nt* extent; **A∼e** dimensions

ausmerzen *vt sep* eliminate

ausmessen† *vt sep* measure

Ausnahme *f* -,-n exception. **A∼ezustand** *m* state of emergency. **a∼slos** *adv* without exception. **a∼sweise** *adv* as an exception

ausnehmen† *vt sep* take out; gut (*Fisch*) draw (*Huhn*); (*ausschließen*) exclude; (*fam: schröpfen*) fleece; **sich gut a∼** look good. **a∼d** *adv* exceptionally

ausnutz|en, ausnütz|en *vt sep* exploit; make the most of (*Gelegenheit*). **A∼ung** *f* exploitation

auspacken *v sep* □*vt* unpack; (*auswickeln*) unwrap □ *vi* (*haben*) (*fam*) talk

auspeitschen *vt sep* flog

auspfeifen† *vt sep* whistle and boo

ausplaudern *vt sep* let out, blab

ausplündern *vt sep* loot; rob (*Person*)

ausprobieren *vt sep* try out

Auspuff *m* -s exhaust [system]. **A∼gase** *ntpl* exhaust fumes. **A∼rohr** *nt* exhaust pipe

auspusten *vt sep* blow out

ausradieren *vt sep* rub out

ausrangieren *vt sep* (*fam*) discard

ausrauben *vt sep* rob

ausräuchern *vt sep* smoke out; fumigate (*Zimmer*)

ausräumen *vt sep* clear out

ausrechnen *vt sep* work out, calculate

Ausrede *f* excuse. **a∼n** *v sep* □*vi* (*haben*) finish speaking; **lass**

mich a∼n! let me finish! □ *vt* **jdm etw a∼n** talk s.o. out of sth

ausreichen *vi sep* (*haben*) be enough; **a∼ mit** have enough. **a∼d** *a* adequate, *adv* -ly; (*Sch*) ≈ pass

Ausreise *f* departure [from a country]. **a∼n** *vi sep* (*sein*) leave the country. **A∼visum** *nt* exit visa

ausreiß|en† *v sep* □*vt* pull or tear out □ *vi* (*sein*) (*fam*) run away. **A∼er** *m* (*fam*) runaway

ausrenken *vt sep* dislocate; **sich** (*dat*) **den Arm a∼** dislocate one's shoulder

ausrichten *vt sep* align; (*bestellen*) deliver; (*erreichen*) achieve; **jdm a∼** tell s.o. (*dass* that); **kann ich etwas a∼?** can I take a message? **ich soll Ihnen Grüße von X a∼** X sends [you] his regards

ausrotten *vt sep* exterminate; (*fig*) eradicate

ausrücken *vi sep* (*sein*) (*Mil*) march off; (*fam*) run away

Ausruf *m* exclamation. **a∼en†** *vt sep* exclaim; call out (*Namen*); (*verkünden*) proclaim; call (*Streik*); **jdn a∼en lassen** have s.o. paged. **A∼ezeichen** *nt* exclamation mark

ausruhen *vt/i sep* (*haben*) rest; **sich a∼** have a rest

ausrüst|en *vt sep* equip. **A∼ung** *f* equipment; (*Mil*) kit

ausrutschen *vi sep* (*sein*) slip

Aussage *f* -,-n statement; (*Jur*) testimony, evidence; (*Gram*) predicate. **a∼n** *vt/i sep* (*haben*) state; (*Jur*) give evidence, testify

Aussatz *m* leprosy

Aussätzige(r) *m/f* leper

ausschachten *vt sep* excavate

ausschalten *vt sep* switch or turn off; (*fig*) eliminate

Ausschank *m* sale of alcoholic drinks; (*Bar*) bar

Ausschau *f* - **A∼ halten nach** look out for. **a∼en** *vi sep* (*haben*)

(SGer) look; **a~en nach** look out for

ausscheiden† v sep □vi (sein) leave; (Sport) drop out; (nicht in Frage kommen) be excluded; **aus dem Dienst a~** retire □vt eliminate; (Med) excrete

ausschenken vt sep pour out; (verkaufen) sell

ausscheren vi sep (sein) (Auto) pull out

ausschildern vt sep signpost

ausschimpfen vt sep tell off

ausschlachten vt sep (fig) exploit

ausschlafen† v sep □vi/r (haben) [sich] a~ get enough sleep; (morgens) sleep late; **nicht ausgeschlafen haben** od **sein** be still tired □vt sleep off ⟨Rausch⟩

Ausschlag m (Med) rash; **den A~ geben** (fig) tip the balance. **a~en†** v sep □vi (haben) kick [out]; (Bot) sprout; ⟨Baum.⟩ come into leaf □vt knock out; (auskleiden) line; (ablehnen) refuse. **a~gebend** a decisive

ausschließen† vt sep lock out; (fig) exclude; (entfernen) expel. **a~lich** a exclusive, adv -ly

ausschlüpfen vi sep (sein) hatch

Ausschluss (**Ausschluß**) m exclusion; expulsion; **unter A~ der Öffentlichkeit** in camera

ausschmücken vt sep decorate; (fig) embellish

ausschneiden† vt sep cut out

Ausschnitt m excerpt, extract; (Zeitungs-) cutting; (Hals-) neckline

ausschöpfen vt sep ladle out; (Naut) bail out; exhaust ⟨Möglichkeiten⟩

ausschreiben† vt sep write out; (ausstellen) make out; (bekanntgeben) announce; put out to tender ⟨Auftrag⟩

Ausschreitungen fpl riots; (Exzesse) excesses

Ausschuss (**Ausschuß**) m committee; (Comm) rejects pl

ausschütten vt sep tip out; (verschütten) spill; (leeren) empty; **sich vor Lachen a~** (fam) be in stitches

ausschweif|end a dissolute. **A~ung** f -,-en debauchery; **A~ungen** excesses

ausschwenken vt sep rinse [out]

aussehen† vi sep (haben) look; **es sieht nach Regen aus** it looks like rain; **wie sieht er/es aus?** what does he/it look like? **ein gut a~der Mann** a good-looking man. **A~** nt -s appearance

aussein† vi sep (sein) (NEW) **aus sein**, s. aus

außen adv [on the] outside; **nach a~** outwards. **A~bordmotor** m outboard motor. **A~handel** m foreign trade. **A~minister** m Foreign Minister. **A~politik** f foreign policy. **A~seite** f outside. **A~seiter** m -s,- outsider; (fig) misfit. **A~stände** mpl outstanding debts. **A~stehende(r)** m/f outsider

außer prep (+ dat) except [for], apart from; (außerhalb) out of; **a~ Atem/Sicht** out of breath/sight; **a~ sich** (fig) beside oneself □ conj except; **a~ wenn** unless. **a~dem** adv in addition, as well □ conj moreover

äußer|e(r,s) a external; ⟨Teil, Schicht⟩ outer. **Ä~e(s)** nt exterior; (Aussehen) appearance

außer|ehelich a extramarital. **a~gewöhnlich** a exceptional, adv -ly. **a~halb** prep (+ gen) outside □ adv **a~halb wohnen** live outside town

äußer|lich a external, adv -ly; (fig) outward, adv -ly. **ä~n** vt express; **sich ä~n** comment; (sich zeigen) manifest itself

außerordentlich a extraordinary, adv -ily; (außergewöhnlich) exceptional, adv -ly

äußerst adv extremely

außerstande adv unable (**zu** to)

äußerste(r,s) a outermost; (*weiteste*) furthest; (*höchste*) utmost, extreme; (*letzte*) last; (*schlimmste*) worst; **am ä~n Ende** at the very end; **aufs ä~** = **aufs Ä~**, s. **Äußerste(s)**. **Ä~(s)** nt das Ä~ the limit; (*Schlimmste*) the worst; **sein Ä~s tun** do one's utmost; **aufs Ä~** extremely

Äußerung f -,-en comment; (*Bemerkung*) remark

aussetzen v sep □ vt expose (*dat* to); abandon (*Kind, Hund*); launch (*Boot*); offer (*Belohnung*); **etwas auszusetzen haben** an (+ *dat*) find fault with □ vi (*haben*) stop; (*Motor:*) cut out

Aussicht f -,-en prospect; (*auf* + *acc* of); **in A~ stellen** promise; **weitere A~en** (*Meteorol*) further outlook sg. **a~slos** a hopeless; **a~sreich** a promising, adv -ly.

aussöhnen vt sep reconcile; **sich a~** become reconciled

aussortieren vt sep pick out; (*ausscheiden*) eliminate

ausspannen v sep □ vt spread out; unhitch (*Pferd*); (*fam: wegnehmen*) take (*dat* from) □ vi (*haben*) rest. **A~ung** f rest

aussperr|en vt sep lock out. **A~ung** f -,-en lock-out

ausspielen v sep □ vt (*play* (*Karte*); (*fig*) play off (*gegen* against) □ vi (*haben*) (*Kartenspiel*) lead

Aussprache f pronunciation; (*Sprechweise*) diction; (*Gespräch*) talk

aussprechen† v sep □ vt pronounce; (*äußern*) express; **sich a~** talk; come out (*für/gegen* in favour of/against) □ vi (*haben*) finish [speaking]

Ausspruch m saying

ausspucken v sep □ vt spit out □ vi (*haben*) spit

ausspülen vt sep rinse out

ausstaffieren vt sep (*fam*) kit out

Ausstand m strike; **in den A~ treten** go on strike

ausstatt|en vt sep equip; **mit Möbeln a~en** furnish. **A~ung** f -,-en equipment; (*Innen-*) furnishings pl; (*Theat*) scenery and costumes pl; (*Aufmachung*) get-up

ausstehen† v sep □ vt suffer; **Angst a~** be frightened; **ich kann sie nicht a~** I can't stand her □ vi (*haben*) be outstanding

aussteig|en vi sep (*sein*) get out; (*aus Bus, Zug*) get off; (*fam: aussteigen*) opt out; (*aus einem Geschäft*) back out; **alles a~en!** all change! **A~er(in)** m -s,- (f -,-nen) (*fam*) drop-out

ausstell|en vt sep exhibit; (*Comm*) display; (*ausfertigen*) make out; issue (*Pass*). **A~er** m -s,- exhibitor. **A~ung** f exhibition; (*Comm*) display. **A~ungsstück** nt exhibit

aussterben† vi sep (*sein*) die out; (*Biol*) become extinct. **A~** nt -s extinction

Aussteuer f trousseau

Ausstieg m -[e]s, -e exit

ausstopfen vt sep stuff

ausstoßen† vt sep emit; utter (*Fluch*); heave (*Seufzer*); (*ausschließen*) expel

ausstrahl|en vt/i sep (*sein*) radiate, emit; (*Radio, TV*) broadcast. **A~ung** f radiation; (*fig*) charisma

ausstrecken vt sep stretch out; put out (*Hand*); **sich a~** stretch out

ausstreichen† vt sep cross out

ausstreuen vt sep scatter; spread (*Gerüchte*)

ausströmen v sep □ vi (*sein*) pour out; (*entweichen*) escape □ vt emit; (*ausstrahlen*) radiate

aussuchen vt sep pick, choose

Austausch m exchange. **a~bar** a interchangeable. **a~en** vt sep exchange; (*auswechseln*) replace

austeilen vt sep distribute; (*ausgeben*) hand out

Auster f -,-n oyster

austoben (sich) vr sep ⟨Sturm:⟩ rage; ⟨Person:⟩ let off steam; ⟨Kinder:⟩ romp about

austragen† vt sep deliver; hold ⟨Wettkampf:⟩; play ⟨Spiel⟩

Austral|ien /-jən/ nt -s Australia. **A~ier(in)** m -s, (f-,-nen) Australian. **a~isch** a Australian

austreiben v sep □ vt drive out; ⟨Relig⟩ exorcize □ vi (haben) ⟨Bot⟩ sprout

austreten† v sep □ vt stamp out; ⟨abnutzen⟩ wear down □ vi (sein) come out; ⟨ausscheiden⟩ leave **(aus etw** sth); **[mal]** a~ ⟨fam⟩ go to the loo; ⟨Sch⟩ be excused

austrinken† vt/i sep (haben) drink up; ⟨leeren⟩ drain

Austritt m resignation

austrocknen vt/i sep (sein) dry out

ausüben vt sep practise; carry on ⟨Handwerk:⟩; exercise ⟨Recht:⟩; exert ⟨Druck, Einfluss:⟩; have ⟨Wirkung⟩

Ausverkauf m [clearance] sale. **a~t** a sold out; **a~tes Haus** full house

auswachsen† vt sep outgrow

Auswahl f choice, selection; ⟨Comm⟩ range; ⟨Sport⟩ team

auswählen vt sep choose, select

Auswander|er m emigrant. **a~n** vi sep (sein) emigrate. **A~ung** f emigration

auswärt|ig a non-local; ⟨ausländisch⟩ foreign. **a~s** adv outwards; ⟨Sport⟩ away; **a~s essen** eat out; **a~s arbeiten** not work locally. **A~ sspiel** nt away game

auswaschen† vt sep wash out

auswechseln vt sep change; ⟨ersetzen⟩ replace; ⟨Sport⟩ substitute

Ausweg m ⟨fig⟩ way out. **a~los** a ⟨fig⟩ hopeless

ausweich|en vi sep (sein) get out of the way; **jdm/etw a~en** avoid; ⟨sich entziehen⟩ evade s.o./sth. **a~end** a evasive, adv -ly

ausweinen vt sep **sich** ⟨dat⟩ **die Augen a~** cry one's eyes out; **sich a~** have a good cry

Ausweis m -es,-e pass; ⟨Mitglieds-, Studenten:⟩ card. **a~en†** vt sep deport; **sich a~en** prove one's identity. **A~papiere** ntpl identification papers. **A~ung** f deportation

ausweiten vt sep stretch; ⟨fig⟩ expand

auswendig adv by heart

auswerten vt sep evaluate; ⟨nutzen⟩ utilize

auswickeln vt sep unwrap

auswirk|en (sich) vr sep have an effect **(auf + acc** on). **A~ung** f effect; ⟨Folge⟩ consequence

auswischen vt sep wipe out; **jdm eins a~** ⟨fam⟩ play a nasty trick on s.o.

auswringen vt sep wring out

Auswuchs m excrescence; **Auswüchse** ⟨fig⟩ excesses

auszahlen vt sep pay out; ⟨entlohnen⟩ pay off; ⟨abfinden⟩ buy out; **sich a~** ⟨fig⟩ pay off

auszählen vt sep count; ⟨Boxen⟩ count out

Auszahlung f payment

auszeichn|en vt sep ⟨Comm⟩ price; ⟨ehren⟩ honour; ⟨mit einem Preis⟩ award a prize to; ⟨Mil⟩ decorate; **sich a~en** distinguish oneself. **A~ung** f honour; ⟨Preis⟩ award; ⟨Mil⟩ decoration; ⟨Sch⟩ distinction

ausziehen v sep □ vt pull out; ⟨auskleiden⟩ undress; take off ⟨Mantel, Schuhe⟩; **sich a~** take off one's coat; ⟨sich entkleiden⟩ undress □ vi (sein) move out; ⟨sich aufmachen⟩ set out

Auszubildende(r) m/f trainee

Auszug m departure; ⟨Umzug⟩ move; ⟨Ausschnitt⟩ extract, excerpt; ⟨Bank-⟩ statement

authentisch a authentic

Auto nt -s,-s car; **A~ fahren** drive; ⟨mitfahren⟩ go in the car.

A~bahn f motorway, (*Amer*) freeway

Autobiographie f autobiography

Auto|bus m bus. **A~fähre** f car ferry. **A~fahrer(in)** m(f) driver, motorist. **A~fahrt** f drive

Autogramm nt -s,-e autograph

autokratisch a autocratic

Automat m -en,-en automatic device; (*Münz-*) slot-machine; (*Verkaufs-*) vending-machine; (*Fahrkarten-*) machine; (*Techn*) robot. **A~ik** f - automatic mechanism; (*Auto*) automatic transmission

Auto|mation /-'tsjo:n/ f - automation. **a~matisch** a automatic, adv -ally

autonom a autonomous. **A~ie** f - autonomy

Autonummer f registration number

Autopsie f -,-n autopsy

Autor m -s,-en /-'to:rən/ author

Auto|reisezug m Motorail. **A~rennen** nt motor race

Autorin f -,-nen author[ess]

Autori|sation /-'tsjo:n/ f - authorization. **a~sieren** vt authorize. **a~tär** a authoritarian. **A~tät** f -,-en authority

Auto|schlosser m motor mechanic. **A~skooter** /sku:tɐ/ m -s,-dodgem. **A~stopp** m -s per **A~stopp fahren** hitch-hike. **A~verleih** m car hire [firm]. **A~waschanlage** f car wash

autsch int ouch

Aversion f -,-en aversion (**gegen** to)

Axt f -,-e axe

B

B, b /be:/ nt - (*Mus*) B flat

Baby /'be:bi/ nt -s,-s baby. **B~ausstattung** f layette. **B~sitter** /-sɪtɐ/ m -s,- babysitter

Bach m -[e]s,-e stream

Backbord nt -[e]s port [side]

Backe f -,-n cheek

backen v □ vt/i† (haben) bake; (*braten*) fry □ vi (reg) (haben) (*kleben*) stick (**an** + dat to)

Backenzahn m molar

Bäcker m -s,- baker. **B~ei** f -,-en, **B~laden** m baker's shop

Back|form f baking tin. **B~obst** nt dried fruit. **B~ofen** m oven. **B~pfeife** f (fam) slap in the face. **B~pflaume** f prune. **B~pulver** nt baking-powder. **B~rohr** nt oven. **B~stein** m brick. **B~werk** nt cakes and pastries pl

Bad nt -[e]s,-er bath; (im Meer) bathe; (*Zimmer*) bathroom; (*Schwimm-*) pool; (*Ort*) spa

Bade|anstalt f swimming baths pl. **B~anzug** m swim-suit. **B~hose** f swimming trunks pl. **B~kappe** f bathing-cap. **B~mantel** m bathrobe. **B~matte** f bath-mat. **B~mütze** f bathing-cap. **b~n** vi (haben) have a bath; (im Meer) bathe □ vt bath; (*waschen*) bathe. **B~ort** m seaside resort; (*Kurort*) spa. **B~tuch** nt bath-towel. **B~wanne** f bath. **B~zimmer** nt bathroom

Bagatelle f -,-n trifle; (*Mus*) bagatelle

Bagger m -s,- excavator; (*Nass-*) dredger. **b~n** vt/i (haben) excavate; dredge. **B~see** m flooded gravel-pit

Bahn f -,-en path; (Astr) orbit; (*Sport*) track; (*einzelne*) lane; (*Rodel-*) run; (Stoff-, Papier-) width; (*Rock-*) panel; (*Eisen-*) railway; (*Zug*) train; (*Straßen-*) tram; **auf die schiefe B~ kommen** (fig) get into bad ways. **b~brechend** a (fig) pioneering. **b~en** vt sich (dat) einen Weg **b~en** clear a way (**durch** through). **B~hof** m [railway] station. **B~steig** m -[e]s,-e platform. **B~übergang** m level crossing, (*Amer*) grade crossing

Bahre f -,-n stretcher; (Toten-)bier

Baiser /bɛ'zeː/ nt -s,-s meringue

Bajonett nt -[e]s,-e bayonet

Bake f -,-n (Naut, Aviat) beacon

Bakterien /-jən/ fpl bacteria

Balance /ba'lãːs/ f - balance; **die B~ halten/verlieren** keep/lose one's balance. **b~ieren** vt/i (haben/sein) balance

bald adv soon; (fast) almost; **b~ ... b~...** now ... now ...

Baldachin /-xiːn/ m -s,-e canopy

bald|ig a early; (Besserung) speedy. **b~möglichst** adv as soon as possible

Balg m & nt -[e]s,̈er (fam) brat. **b~en** (sich) vr tussle. **B~erei** f -,-en tussle

Balkan m -s Balkans pl

Balken m -s,- beam

Balkon /bal'kõː/ m -s,-s balcony; (Theat) circle

Ball[1] m -[e]s,̈e ball

Ball[2] m -[e]s,̈e (Tanz) ball

Ballade f -,-n ballad

Ballast m -[e]s,-e ballast. **B~stoffe** mpl roughage sg

ballen vt **die [Hand zur] Faust b~** clench one's fist; **sich b~** gather, mass. **B~** m -s,- bale; (Anat) ball of the hand/(Fuß-)foot; (Med) bunion

Ballerina f -,-nen ballerina

Ballett nt -s,-e ballet

Balletttänzer(in) (**Ballettänzer(in)**) m(f) ballet dancer

ballistisch a ballistic

Ballon /ba'lõː/ m -s,-s balloon

Ball|saal m ballroom. **B~ungsgebiet** nt conurbation. **B~wechsel** m (Tennis) rally

Balsam m -s balm

Balt|ikum nt -s Baltic States pl. **b~isch** a Baltic

Balustrade f -,-n balustrade

Bambus m -ses,-se bamboo

banal a banal. **B~ität** f -,-en banality

Banane f -,-n banana

Banause m -n,-n philistine

Band[1] nt -[e]s,̈er ribbon; (Naht-, Ton-, Ziel-) tape; (Anat) ligament; **auf B~ aufnehmen** tape; **laufendes B~** conveyor belt; **am laufenden B~** (fam) non-stop

Band[2] m -[e]s,̈e volume

Band[3] m -[e]s,-e (fig) bond; **B~e der Freundschaft** bonds of friendship

Band[4] /bɛnt/ f -,-s [jazz] band

Bandage /ban'daːʒə/ f -,-n bandage. **b~ieren** vt bandage

Bande f -,-n gang

bändigen vt control, restrain; (zähmen) tame

Bandit m -en,-en bandit

Band|maß nt tape-measure. **B~nudeln** fpl noodles. **B~scheibe** f (Anat) disc. **B~scheibenvorfall** m slipped disc. **B~wurm** m tapeworm

bang[e] a (bänger, bängst) anxious; **jdm b~e machen** (NEW) **jdm B~e machen**, s. Bange. Für **e** f B~e haben be afraid; **jdm B~e machen** frighten s.o. **B~e** m vi (haben) fear (um for); **mir b~t davor** I dread it

Banjo nt -s,-s banjo

Bank[1] f -,̈e bench

Bank[2] f -,-en (Comm) bank. **B~einzug** m direct debit

Bankett nt -s,-e banquet

Bankier /baŋ'kjeː/ m -s,-s banker

Bank|konto nt bank account. **B~note** f banknote

Bankrott m -s bankruptcy; **B~ machen** od **gehen** go bankrupt. **b~** a bankrupt

Bankwesen nt banking

Bann m -[e]s,-e (fig) spell; **in jds B~** under s.o.'s spell. **b~en** vt exorcize; (abwenden) avert; **[wie] gebannt** spellbound

Banner nt -s,- banner

Baptist(in) m -en,-en (f -,-nen) Baptist

bar a (rein) sheer; (Gold) pure; **b~es Geld** cash; **[in] bar bezahlen** pay cash; **etw für b~e**

Münze nehmen (*fig*) take sth as gospel

Bar *f* -,-s bar

Bär *m* -en,-en bear; **jdm einen B~en aufbinden** (*fam*) pull s.o.'s leg

Baracke *f* -,-n hut

Barbar *m* -en,-en barbarian. **b~arisch** *a* barbaric

bar|fuß *adv* barefoot. **B~geld** *nt* cash

Bariton *m* -s,-e /-'to:nə/ baritone

Barkasse *f* -,-n launch

Barmann *m* (*pl* -männer) barman

barmherzig *a* merciful. **B~keit** *f* -mercy

barock *a* baroque. **B~** *nt* & *m* -[s] baroque

Barometer *nt* -s,- barometer

Baron *m* -s,-e baron. **B~in** *f* -,-nen baroness

Barren *m* -s,- (*Gold*-) bar, ingot; (*Sport*) parallel bars *pl*. **B~gold** *nt* gold bullion

Barriere *f* -,-n barrier

Barrikade *f* -,-n barricade

barsch *a* gruff, *adv* -ly; (*kurz*) curt, *adv* -ly

Barsch *m* -[e]s,-e (*Zool*) perch

Barschaft *f* - **meine ganze B~** all I have/had on me

Bart *m* -[e]s,⸗e beard; (*der Katze*) whiskers *pl*

bärtig *a* bearded

Barzahlung *f* cash payment

Basar *m* -s,-e bazaar

Base[1] *f* -,-n [female] cousin

Base[2] *f* -,-n (*Chem*) alkali, base

Basel *nt* -s Basle

basieren *vi* (*haben*) be based (**auf** + *dat* on)

Basilikum *nt* -s basil

Basis *f* -,**Basen** base; (*fig*) basis

basisch *a* (*Chem*) alkaline

Bask|enmütze *f* beret. **b~isch** *a* Basque

Bass *m* -es,⸗e (**Baß** *m* -sses,⸗sse) bass; (*Kontra*-) double-bass

Bassin /ba'sɛ̃:/ *nt* -s,-s pond; (*Brunnen*-) basin; (*Schwimm*-) pool

Bassist *m* -en,-en bass player; (*Sänger*) bass

Bassstimme (Baßstimme) *f* bass voice

Bast *m* -[e]s raffia

basta *int* [**und damit**] **b~!** and that's that!

bast|eln *vt* make □ *vi* (*haben*) do handicrafts; (*herum*-) tinker (**an** + *dat* with). **B~ler** *m* -s,- amateur craftsman; (*Heim*-) do-it-yourselfer

Bataillon /batal'jo:n/ *nt* -s,-e battalion

Batterie *f* -,-n battery

Bau[1] *m* -[e]s,-e burrow; (*Fuchs*-) earth

Bau[2] *m* -[e]s,-ten construction; (*Gebäude*) building; (*Auf*-) structure; (*Körper*-) build; (*B~stelle*) building site; **im Bau** under construction. **B~arbeiten** *fpl* building work *sg*; (*Straßen*-) roadworks. **B~art** *f* design; (*Stil*) style

Bauch *m* -[e]s, **Bäuche** abdomen, belly; (*Magen*) stomach; (*Schmer*-) paunch; (*Bauchung*) bulge. **b~ig** *a* bulbous. **B~nabel** *m* navel. **B~redner** *m* ventriloquist. **B~schmerzen** *mpl* stomach-ache *sg*. **B~speicheldrüse** *f* pancreas. **B~weh** *nt* stomach-ache

bauen *vt* build; (*konstruieren*) construct; (*an*-) grow; **einen Unfall b~** (*fam*) have an accident □ *vi* (*haben*) build (**an etw** *dat* sth); **b~ auf** (+ *acc*) (*fig*) rely on

Bauer[1] *m* -s,-n farmer; (*Schach*) pawn

Bauer[2] *nt* -s,- [bird]cage

Bäuer|in *f* -,-nen farmer's wife. **b~lich** *a* rustic

Bauern|haus *nt* farmhouse. **B~hof** *m* farm

bau|fällig *a* dilapidated. **B~genehmigung** *f* planning permission. B~gerüst nt scaffolding. B~jahr nt year of construction; B~jahr 1985 (Auto) 1985 model. B~kasten m box of building bricks; (Modell-) model kit. B~klotz m building brick. B~kunst f architecture. b~lich a structural, adv -ly. B~lichkeiten fpl buildings

Baum m -[e]s, Bäume tree

baumeln vi (haben) dangle; die Beine b~ lassen dangle one's legs

bäumen (sich) vr rear [up]

Baum|schule f [tree] nursery. B~stamm m tree-trunk. B~wolle f cotton. b~wollen a cotton

Bauplatz m building plot

bäurisch a rustic; (plump) uncouth

Bausch m -[e]s, Bäusche wad; in B~ und Bogen (fig) wholesale. b~en vt puff out; sich b~en billow [out]. b~ig a puffed [out]; (Ärmel) full

Bau|sparkasse f building society. B~stein m building brick; (fig) element. B~stelle f building site; (Straßen-) roadworks pl. B~unternehmer m building contractor. B~werk nt building. B~zaun m hoarding

Bayer|(in) m -s,-n (f -,-nen) Bavarian. B~n nt -s Bavaria

bay[e]risch a Bavarian

Bazillus m -,-len (fam: Keim) germ

beabsichtig|en vt intend. b~t a intended; (absichtlich) intentional

beacht|en vt take notice of; (einhalten) observe; (folgen) follow; nicht b~en ignore. b~lich a considerable. B~ung f -observance; etw (dat) keine B~ung schenken take no notice of sth

Beamte(r) m, Beamtin f -,-nen official; (Staats-) civil servant; (Schalter-) clerk

beängstigend a alarming

beanspruchen vt claim; (erfordern) demand; (brauchen) take up; (Techn) stress; die Arbeit beansprucht ihn sehr his work is very demanding

beanstand|en vt find fault with; (Comm) make a complaint about. B~ung f -,-en complaint

beantragen vt apply for

beantworten vt answer

bearbeiten vt work; (weiter-) process; (behandeln) treat (mit with); (Admin) deal with; (redigieren) edit; (Theat) adapt; (Mus) arrange; (fam: bedrängen) pester; (fam: schlagen) pummel

Beatmung f künstliche B~ artificial respiration. B~sgerät nt ventilator

beaufsichtig|en vt supervise. B~ung f - supervision

beauftrag|en vt instruct; (Künstler) commission. jdn mit einer Arbeit b~en assign a task to s.o. B~te(r) m/f representative

bebauen vt build on; (bestellen) cultivate

beben vi (haben) tremble

bebildert a illustrated

Becher m -s,- beaker; (Henkel-) mug; (Joghurt-, Sahne-) carton

Becken nt -s,- basin; (Schwimm-) pool; (Mus) cymbals pl; (Anat) pelvis

bedacht a careful; b~ auf (+ acc) concerned about; darauf b~ anxious (zu to)

bedächtig a careful, adv -ly; (langsam) slow, adv -ly

bedanken (sich) vr thank (bei jdm s.o.)

Bedarf m -s need/(Comm) demand (an + dat for); bei B~ if required. B~sartikel mpl requisites. B~shaltestelle f request stop

a regrettable. b~licherweise adv unfortunately. b~n vt regret; (bemitleiden) feel sorry for; bedaure!

sorry; **B~n** *nt* **-s** regret; *(Mitgefühl)* sympathy. **b~nswert** *a* pitiful; *(bedauerlich)* regrettable

bedeck|en *vt* cover; **sich b~en** *(Himmel:)* cloud over. **b~t** *a* covered; *(Himmel)* overcast

bedenken† *vt* consider; *(überlegen)* think over; **jdn b~** give s.o. a present; **sich b~** consider. **B~** *pl* misgivings; **ohne B~** without hesitation. **b~los** *a* unhesitating, *adv* -ly

bedenklich *a* doubtful; *(verdächtig)* dubious; *(bedrohlich)* worrying; *(ernst)* serious

bedeut|en *vi (haben)* mean; **jdm viel/nichts b~en** mean a lot/nothing to s.o.; **es hat nichts zu b~en** it is of no significance. **b~end** *a* important; *(beträchtlich)* considerable. **b~sam** *a* = **b~ungsvoll. B~ung** *f* -,-en meaning; *(Wichtigkeit)* importance. **b~unglos** *a* meaningless; *(unwichtig)* unimportant. **b~ungsvoll** *a* significant; *(vielsagend)* meaningful, *adv* -ly

bedien|en *vt* serve; *(betätigen)* operate; **sich [selbst] b~en** help oneself. **B~ung** *f* -,-en service; *(Betätigung)* operation; *(Kellner)* waiter; *(Kellnerin)* waitress. **B~ungsgeld** *nt*, **B~ungszuschlag** *m* service charge

bedingt *a* conditional; *(eingeschränkt)* qualified

Bedingung *f* -,-en condition; **B~en** conditions; *(Comm)* terms. **b~slos** *a* unconditional, *adv* -ly; *(unbedingt)* unquestioning, *adv* -ly

bedrängen *vt* press; *(belästigen)* pester

bedrohen *vt* threaten. **b~lich** *a* threatening. **B~ung** *f* threat

bedrück|en *vt* depress. **b~end** *a* depressing. **b~t** *a* depressed

bedruckt *a* printed

bedürf|en† *vi (haben)* (+ *gen*) need. **B~nis** *nt* -ses,-se need.

B~nisanstalt *f* public convenience. **b~tig** *a* needy

Beefsteak /ˈbiːfsteːk/ *nt* **-s,-s** steak; **deutsches B~** hamburger

beeil|en (sich) *vr* hurry; hasten (zu to); **beeil euch!** hurry up!

beeindrucken *vt* impress

beeinflussen *vt* influence

beeinträchtigen *vt* mar; *(schädigen)* impair

beend|igen *vt* end

beengen *vt* restrict; **beengt wohnen** live in cramped conditions

beerben *vt* jdn **b~** inherit s.o.'s property

beerdig|en *vt* bury. **B~ung** *f* -,-en funeral

Beere *f* -,-n berry

Beet *nt* **-[e]s,-e** *(Hort)* bed

Beete *f* -,-n **rote B~** beetroot

befähig|en *vt* enable; *(qualifizieren)* qualify. **B~ung** *f* - qualification; *(Fähigkeit)* ability

befahr|bar *a* passable. **b~en†** *vt* drive along; **stark b~ene Straße** busy road

befallen† *vt* attack; *(Angst:)* seize

befangen *a* shy; *(gehemmt)* self-conscious; *(Jur)* biased. **B~heit** *f* - shyness; self-consciousness; bias

befassen (sich) *vr* concern oneself/*(behandeln)* deal (mit with)

Befehl *m* **-[e]s,-e** order; *(Leitung)* command (über + *acc* of). **b~en†** *vt* jdm etw **b~en** order s.o. to do sth □ *vi (haben)* give an order. **b~igen** *vt* *(Mil)* command. **B~sform** *f (Gram)* imperative. **B~shaber** *m* **-s,-** commander

befestig|en *vt* fasten (**an** + *dat* to); *(stärken)* strengthen; *(Mil)* fortify. **B~ung** *f* -,-en fastening; *(Mil)* fortification

befeuchten *vt* moisten

befind|en (sich) *vr* be. **B~** *nt* **-s** [state of] health

beflecken *vt* stain

beflissen *a* assiduous, *adv* -ly

befolgen vt follow

beförder|n vt transport; (im Rang) promote. **B~ung** f -, -en transport; promotion

befragen vt question

befrei|en vt free; (räumen) clear (von of); (freistellen) exempt (von from); **sich b~en** free oneself. **B~er** m -s, - liberator. **b~t** a (erleichtert) relieved. **B~ung** f liberation; exemption

befremd|en vt disconcert. **B~en** nt -s surprise. **b~lich** a strange

befreunden (sich) vr make friends; **befreundet sein** be friends

befriedig|en vt satisfy. **b~end** a satisfying; (zufrieden stellend) satisfactory. **B~ung** f - satisfaction

befruchten vt fertilize. **B~ung** f - fertilization; **künstliche B~ung** artificial insemination

Befug|nis f -, -se authority. **b~t** a authorized

Befund m result

befürcht|en vt fear. **B~ung** f -, -en fear

befürworten vt support

begab|t a gifted. **B~ung** f -, -en gift, talent

begatten (sich) vr mate

begeben† (sich) vr go; (liter: geschehen) happen; **sich in Gefahr b~** expose oneself to danger. **B~heit** f -, -en incident

begegn|en vi (sein) jdm/etw b~en meet s.o./sth; **sich b~en** meet. **B~ung** f -, -en meeting; (Sport) encounter

begehen† vt walk along; (verüben) commit; (feiern) celebrate

begehr|en vt desire. **b~enswert** a desirable. **b~t** a sought-after

begeister|n vt jdn b~n arouse s.o.'s enthusiasm; **sich b~n** be enthusiastic (für about). **b~t** a enthusiastic, adv -ally; (eifrig) keen. **B~ung** f - enthusiasm

Begier|de f -, -n desire. **b~ig** a eager (auf + acc for)

begießen† vt water; (Culin) baste; (fam: feiern) celebrate

Beginn m -s beginning; **zu B~** at the beginning. **b~en†** vt/i (haben) start, begin; (anstellen) do

beglaubigen vt authenticate

begleichen† vt settle

begleit|en vt accompany. **B~er** m -s, -, **B~erin** f -, -nen companion; (Mus) accompanist. **B~ung** f -, -en company; (Gefolge) entourage; (Mus) accompaniment

beglück|en vt make happy. **b~t** a happy. **b~wünschen** vt congratulate (zu on)

begnadigen vt (Jur) pardon. **B~ung** f -, -en (Jur) pardon

begnügen (sich) vr content oneself (mit with)

Begonie f -/ə/ f -, -n begonia

begraben† vt bury

Begräbnis n -ses, -se burial; (Feier) funeral

begreif|en† vt understand; **nicht zu b~en** incomprehensible. **b~lich** a understandable; jdm etw b~lich machen make s.o. understand sth. **b~licherweise** adv understandably

begrenz|en vt form the boundary of; (beschränken) restrict. **b~t** a limited. **B~ung** f -, -en restriction; (Grenze) boundary

Begriff m -[e]s, -e concept; (Ausdruck) term; (Vorstellung) idea; **für meine B~e** to my mind; **im B~ sein od stehen** be about (zu to); **schwer von B~** (fam) slow on the uptake. **b~sstutzig** a obtuse

begründ|en vt give one's reason for; (gründen) establish. **b~et** a justified. **B~ung** f -, -en reason

begrüß|en† vt greet; (billigen) welcome. **b~enswert** a welcome. **B~ung** f - greeting; welcome

begünstigen vt favour; (fördern) encourage

begutachten *vt* give an opinion on; (*fam: ansehen*) look at

begütert *a* wealthy

begütigen *vt* placate

behaart *a* hairy

behäbig *a* portly; (*gemütlich*) comfortable, *adv* -bly

behagen *vi* (*haben*) please (**jdm** s.o.). **B~en** *nt* -s contentment; (*Genuss*) enjoyment. **b~lich** *a* comfortable, *adv* -bly. **B~lichkeit** *f* - comfort

behalten† *vt* keep; (*sich merken*) remember; **etw für sich b~** (*verschweigen*) keep sth to oneself

Behälter *m* -s,- container

behände *a* nimble, *adv* -bly

behandeln *vt* treat; (*sich befassen*) deal with. **B~lung** *f* treatment

beharr|en *vi* (*haben*) persist (**auf** + *dat* in). **b~lich** *a* persistent, *adv* -ly; (*hartnäckig*) dogged, *adv* -ly. **B~lichkeit** *f* - persistence

behaupt|en *vt* maintain; (*vorgeben*) claim; (*sagen*) say; (*bewahren*) retain; **sich b~en** hold one's own. **B~ung** *f* -,-en assertion; claim; (*Äußerung*) statement

beheben† *vt* remedy; (*beseitigen*) remove

behelf|en† (**sich**) *vr* make do (**mit** with). **b~smäßig** *a* make-shift □ *adv* provisionally

behelligen *vt* bother

behende *a* (NEW) **behände**

beherbergen *vt* put up

beherrsch|en *vt* rule over; (*dominieren*) dominate; (*meistern, zügeln*) control; (*können*) know; **sich b~en** control oneself. **b~t** *a* self-controlled. **B~ung** *f* - control; (*Selbst-*) self-control; (*Können*) mastery

beherzigen *vt* heed. **b~t** *a* courageous, *adv* -ly

behilflich *a* **jdm b~ sein** help s.o.

behinder|n *vt* hinder; (*blockieren*) obstruct. **b~t** *a* handicapped; (*schwer*) disabled.

B~te(r) *m/f* handicapped/disabled person. **B~ung** *f* -,-en obstruction; (*Med*) handicap; disability

Behörde *f* -,-n [public] authority

behüten *vt* protect; **Gott behüte!** heaven forbid! **b~t** *a* sheltered

behutsam *a* careful, *adv* -ly; (*zart*) gentle, *adv* -ly

bei *prep* (+ *dat*) near; (*dicht*) by; at (*Firma, Veranstaltung*); **bei der Hand nehmen** take by the hand; **bei sich haben** have with one; **bei mir** at my place; (*in meinem Fall*) in my case; **Herr X bei Meyer** Mr X c/o Meyer; **bei Regen** when/(*falls*) if it rains; **bei Feuer** in case of fire; **bei Tag/Nacht** by day/night; **bei der Ankunft** on arrival; **bei Tisch/der Arbeit** at table/work; **bei guter Gesundheit** in good health; **bei der hohen Miete** [what] with the high rent; **bei all seiner Klugheit** for all his cleverness

beibehalten† *vt sep* keep

beibringen† *vt sep* **jdm etw b~** teach s.o. sth; (*mitteilen*) break sth to s.o.; (*zufügen*) inflict sth on s.o.

Beicht|e *f* -,-n confession. **b~en** *vt/i* (*haben*) confess. **B~stuhl** *m* confessional

beide *a* & *pron* both; **die b~n Brüder** the two brothers; **b~s** both; **dreißig b~** (*Tennis*) thirty all. **b~rseitig** *a* mutual. **b~rseits** *adv* & *prep* (+ *gen*) on both sides (of)

beidrehen *vi sep* (*haben*) heave to

beieinander *adv* together

Beifahrer|(in) *m(f)* [front-seat] passenger; (*Lkw*) driver's mate; (*Motorrad*) pillion passenger. **B~sitz** *m* passenger seat

Beifall *m* -[e]s applause; (*Billigung*) approval; **B~ klatschen** applaud

beifällig *a* approving, *adv* -ly

beifügen *vt sep* add; (*beilegen*) enclose

beige /beːʒ/ *inv a* beige

beigeben† *v sep* □*vt* add □*vi* (haben) **klein b~** give in

Beigeschmack *m* [slight] taste

Beihilfe *f* financial aid; (Studien-) grant; (Jur) aiding and abetting

beikommen† *vi sep* (sein) **jdm b~** get the better of s.o.

Beil *nt* -[e]s,-e hatchet, axe

Beilage *f* supplement; (Gemüse) vegetable; **als B~ Reis** (Culin) served with rice

beiläufig *a* casual, *adv* -ly

beilegen *vt sep* enclose; (schlichten) settle

beileibe *adv* **b~ nicht** by no means

Beileid *nt* condolences *pl*. **B~sbrief** *m* letter of condolence

beiliegend *a* enclosed

beim *prep* = **bei dem; b~ Militär** in the army; **b~ Frühstück** at breakfast; **b~ Lesen** when reading; **b~ Lesen sein** be reading

beimessen† *vt sep* (fig) attach (dat to)

Bein *nt* -[e]s,-e leg; **jdm ein B~ stellen** trip s.o. up

beinah[e] *adv* nearly, almost

Beiname *m* epithet

beipflichten *vi sep* (haben) agree (dat with)

Beirat *m* advisory committee

beirren *vt* **sich nicht b~ lassen** not let oneself be put off

beisammen *adv* together; **b~ sein** be together. **B~sein†** *vi sep* (sein) ⟨NEW⟩ **b~ sein**, s. **beisammen**. **B~sein** *nt* -s get-together

Beisein *nt* presence

beiseite *adv* aside; (abseits) apart; **b~ legen** put aside; (sparen) put by; **Spaß od Scherz b~** joking apart

beisetzen *vt sep* bury. **B~ung** *f* -,-en funeral

Beispiel *nt* example; **zum B~** for example. **b~haft** *a* exemplary. **b~los** *a* unprecedented. **b~sweise** *adv* for example

beispringen† *vi sep* (sein) **jdm b~** come to s.o.'s aid

beiß|en† *vt/i* (haben) (bren-nen) sting; **sich b~en** (Farben:) clash. **b~end** *a* (fig) biting; (Bemerkung) caustic. **B~zange** *f* pliers *pl*

Bei|stand *m* -[e]s help; **jdm B~stand leisten** help s.o. **b~stehen†** *vi sep* (haben) **jdm b~stehen** help s.o.

beisteuern *vt* contribute

beistimmen *vi sep* (haben) agree

Beistrich *m* comma

Beitrag *m* -[e]s,ːe contribution; (Mitglieds-) subscription; (Ver-sicherungs-) premium; (Zei-tungs-) article. **b~en†** *vt/i sep* (haben) contribute

bei|treten† *vi sep* (sein) (+ dat) join. **B~tritt** *m* joining

beiwohnen *vi sep* (haben) (+ dat) be present at

Beize *f* -,-n (Holz-) stain; (Culin) marinade

beizeiten *adv* in good time

beizen *vt* stain (Holz)

bejahen *vt* answer in the affirma-tive; (billigen) approve of

bejahrt *a* aged, old

bejubeln *vt* cheer

bekämpf|en *vt* fight. **B~ung** *f* -fight (gen against)

bekannt *a* well-known; (vertraut) familiar; **jdm b~ sein** be known to s.o.; **jdn b~ machen** introduce s.o.; **etw b~ machen** od **geben** announce sth; **b~ werden** be-come known. **B~e(r)** *m/f* ac-quaintance; (Freund) friend. **B~gabe** *f* announcement. **b~geben†** *vt sep* ⟨NEW⟩ **b~ geben**, s. **bekannt**. **b~lich** *adv* as is well known. **b~machen** *vt sep* ⟨NEW⟩ **b~ machen**, s. **bekannt**. **B~machung** *f* -,-en an-nouncement; (Anschlag) notice. **B~schaft** *f* - acquaintance; (Leute) acquaintances *pl*; (Freunde) friends *pl*. **b~werden†**

vi sep (*sein*) (NEW) **b∼** werden, *s.* **bekannt**

bekehr|en *vt* convert; **sich b∼** become converted. **B∼ung** *f* -,-en conversion

bekenn|en† *vt* confess, profess 〈*Glauben*〉; **sich [für] schuldig b∼en** admit one's guilt; **sich b∼en zu** confess to 〈*Tat*〉; profess 〈*Glauben*〉; 〈*stehen zu*〉 stand by. **B∼tnis** *nt* -ses,-se confession; 〈*Konfession*〉 denomination

beklag|en *vt* lament; 〈*bedauern*〉 deplore; **sich b∼en** complain. **b∼enswert** *a* unfortunate. **B∼te(r)** *m(f)* (*Jur*) defendant

beklatschen *vt* applaud

bekleid|en *vt* hold 〈*Amt*〉. **b∼et** *a* dressed (**mit** in). **B∼ung** *f* clothing

Beklemmung *f* -,-en feeling of oppression

beklommen *a* uneasy; 〈*ängstlich*〉 anxious, *adv* -ly

bekommen† *vt* get; have 〈*Baby*〉; catch 〈*Erkältung*〉; **Angst/ Hunger b∼** get frightened/hungry; **etw geliehen b∼** be lent sth □ *vi* (*sein*) **jdm gut b∼** do s.o. good; 〈*Essen:*〉 agree with s.o.

bekömmlich *a* digestible

beköstig|en *vt* feed; **sich selbst b∼en** cater for oneself. **B∼ung** *f* -board; 〈*Essen*〉 food

bekräftigen *vt* reaffirm; 〈*bestätigen*〉 confirm

bekreuzigen (sich) *vr* cross oneself

bekümmert *a* troubled; 〈*besorgt*〉 worried

bekunden *vt* show; 〈*bezeugen*〉 testify

belächeln *vt* laugh at

beladen† *vt* load □ *a* laden

Belag *m* -[e]s,-e coating; 〈*Fußboden-*〉 covering; 〈*Brot-*〉 topping; 〈*Zahn-*〉 tartar; 〈*Brems-*〉 lining

belager|n *vt* besiege. **B∼ung** *f* -,-en siege

Belang *m* von/ohne **B∼** of/of no importance; **B∼e** *pl* interests. **b∼en** *vt* (*Jur*) sue. **b∼los** *a* irrelevant; 〈*unwichtig*〉 trivial. **B∼losigkeit** *f* -,-en triviality

belassen† *vt* leave; **es dabei b∼** leave it at that

belasten *vt* load; 〈*fig*〉 burden; 〈*beanspruchen*〉 put a strain on; 〈*Comm*〉 debit; 〈*Jur*〉 incriminate

belästigen *vt* bother; 〈*bedrängen*〉 pester; 〈*unsittlich*〉 molest

Belastung *f* -,-en load; 〈*fig*〉 strain; 〈*Last*〉 burden; 〈*Comm*〉 debit. **B∼smaterial** *nt* incriminating evidence. **B∼szeuge** *m* prosecution witness

belaufen† (sich) *vr* amount (**auf** + *acc* to)

belauschen *vt* eavesdrop on

beleb|en *vt* 〈*fig*〉 revive; 〈*lebhaft machen*〉 enliven; **wieder b∼en** 〈*Med*〉 revive, resuscitate; 〈*fig*〉 vive 〈*Handel*〉; **sich b∼en** revive; 〈*Stadt:*〉 come to life. **b∼t** *a* lively; 〈*Straße*〉 busy

Beleg *m* -[e]s,-e evidence; 〈*Beispiel*〉 instance (**für** of); 〈*Quittung*〉 receipt. **b∼en** *vt* cover/ 〈*garnieren*〉 garnish (**mit** with); 〈*besetzen*〉 reserve; 〈*Univ*〉 enrol for; 〈*nachweisen*〉 provide evidence for; **den ersten Platz b∼en** 〈*Sport*〉 take first place. **B∼schaft** *f* -,-en work-force. **b∼t** *a* occupied; 〈*Zunge*〉 coated; 〈*Stimme*〉 husky; **b∼te Brote** open sandwiches; **der Platz ist b∼t** this seat is taken

belehren *vt* instruct; 〈*aufklären*〉 inform

beleibt *a* corpulent

beleidig|en *vt* offend; 〈*absichtlich*〉 insult. **B∼ung** *f* -,-en insult

belesen *a* well-read

beleucht|en *vt* light; 〈*anleuchten*〉 illuminate. **B∼ung** *f* -,-en illumination; 〈*elektrisch*〉 lighting; 〈*Licht*〉 light

Belg|ien /-jən/ *nt* -s Belgium.
B~ier(in) *m* -s,- (*f* -,-nen)
Belgian. **b~isch** *a* Belgian.

belicht|en *vt* (*Phot*) expose.
B~ung *f* - exposure

Belieb|en *nt* -s nach **B~en** [just]
as one likes; (*Culin*) if liked. **b~ig**
a **eine b~ige Zahl/Farbe** any
number/colour you like □ *adv*
b~ig lange/oft as long/often as
one likes. **b~t** *a* popular.
B~theit *f* - popularity

beliefern *vt* supply (**mit** with)

bellen *vi* (*haben*) bark

belohn|en *vt* reward. **B~ung** *f*
-,-en reward

belüften *vt* ventilate

belügen† *vt* lie to; **sich** [**selbst**]
b~ deceive oneself

belustig|en *vt* amuse. **B~ung** *f*
-,-en amusement

bemächtigen (sich) *vr* (+ *gen*)
seize

bemalen *vt* paint

bemängeln *vt* criticize

bemannt *a* manned

**bemerk|bar a sich b~bar
machen** attract attention;
(*Ding*:) become noticeable. **b~en**
vt notice; (*äußern*) remark.
b~enswert *a* remarkable, *adv*
-bly. **B~ung** *f* -,-en remark

bemitleiden *vt* pity

bemittelt *a* well-to-do

bemüh|en *vt* trouble; **sich b~en**
try (**zu** to; **um etw** to get sth);
(*sich kümmern*) attend (**um** to);
b~t sein endeavour (**zu** to).
B~ung *f* -,-en effort; (*Mühe*)
trouble

bemuttern *vt* mother

benachbart *a* neighbouring

benachrichtig|en *vt* inform;
(*amtlich*) notify. **B~ung** *f* -,-en
notification

benachteilig|en *vt* discriminate
against; (*ungerecht sein*) treat un-
fairly. **B~ung** *f* -,-en discrimination (*gen* against)

benehmen† (sich) *vr* behave. **B~**
nt -s behaviour

beneiden *vt* envy (**um etw** sth).
b~swert *a* enviable

Bengel *m* -s,- boy; (*Rüpel*) lout

benommen *a* dazed

benötigen *vt* need

benutz|en, (SGer) benütz|en *vt*
use; take (*Bahn*). **B~er** *m* -s,-
user. **b~erfreundlich** *a* user-
friendly. **B~ung** *f* use

Benzin *nt* -s petrol, (*Amer*) gasoline. **B~tank** *m* petrol tank

beobacht|en *vt* observe. **B~er** *m*
-s,- observer. **B~ung** *f* -,-en ob-
servation

bepacken *vt* load (**mit** with)

bepflanzen *vt* plant (**mit** with)

bequem *a* comfortable, *adv* -bly;
(*mühelos*) easy, *adv* -ily; (*faul*)
lazy. **b~en (sich)** *vr* deign (**zu** to).
B~lichkeit *f* -,-en comfort;
(*Faulheit*) laziness

berat|en† *vt* advise; (*überlegen*)
discuss; **sich b~en** confer; **sich
b~en lassen** get advice □ *vi*
(*haben*) discuss (**über etw** *acc*
sth); (*beratschlagen*) confer.
B~er(in) *m* -s,- (*f* -,-nen) ad-
viser. **b~schlagen** *vi* (*haben*)
confer. **B~ung** *f* -,-en guidance;
(*Rat*) advice; (*Besprechung*) discussion; (*Med, Jur*) consultation.
B~ungsstelle *f* advice centre

berauben *vt* rob (*gen* of)

berauschen *vt* intoxicate. **b~d** *a*
intoxicating, heady

berechn|en *vt* calculate; (*an-
rechnen*) charge for; (*abfordern*)
charge. **b~end** *a* (*fig*) calculat-
ing. **B~ung** *f* calculation

berechtig|en *vt* entitle; (*befugen*)
authorize; (*fig*) justify. **b~t** *a*
justified, justifiable. **B~ung** *f*
-,-en authorization; (*Recht*) right;
(*Rechtmäßigkeit*) justification

bered|en *vt* talk about; (*klatschen*)
gossip about; (*überreden*) talk
round; **sich b~en** talk sth.
B~samkeit *f* - eloquence

beredt *a* eloquent, *adv* -ly

Bereich m -[e]s,-e area; (fig)
realm; (Fach-) field

bereichern vt enrich; **sich b∼**
grow rich (**an** + dat on)

Bereifung f - tyres pl

bereinigen vt (fig) settle

bereit a ready. **b∼en** vt prepare;
(verursachen) cause; give (Überraschung). **b∼halten†** vt sep
have/(ständig) keep ready.
b∼legen vt sep put out [ready].
b∼machen vt sep get ready; **sich
b∼machen** get ready. **b∼s** adv
already

Bereitschaft f -,-en readiness;
(Einheit) squad. **B∼sdienst** m
B∼sdienst haben (Mil) be on
stand-by; (Ärzt:) be on call; (Apotheke:) be open for out-of-hours
dispensing. **B∼spolizei** f riot
police

bereit|stehen† vi sep (haben) be
ready. **b∼stellen** vt sep put out
ready; (verfügbar machen) make
available. **B∼ung** f - preparation. **b∼willig** a willing, adv -ly.
B∼willigkeit f - willingness

bereuen vt regret

Berg m -[e]s,-e mountain; (Anhöhe) hill; **in den B∼en** in the
mountains. **b∼ab** adv downhill.
b∼an adv uphill. **B∼arbeiter** m
miner. **b∼auf** adv uphill; **es geht
b∼auf** (fig) things are looking
up. **B∼bau** m -[e]s mining

bergen† vt recover; (Naut) salvage; (retten) rescue

Berg|führer m mountain guide.
b∼ig a mountainous. **B∼kette** f
mountain range. **B∼mann** m (pl
-leute) miner. **B∼steigen** nt -s
mountaineering. **B∼steiger(in)**
m -s,- (f -,-nen) mountaineer,
climber. **B∼und-Talbahn** f
roller-coaster

Bergung f -recovery; (Naut) salvage; (Rettung) rescue

Berg|wacht f mountain rescue
service. **B∼werk** nt mine

Bericht m -[e]s,-e report; (Reise-)
account; **b∼ erstatten** report

(über + acc on). **b∼en** vt/i
(haben) report; (erzählen) tell
(von of). **B∼erstatter(in)** m -s,-
(f -,-nen) reporter; (Korrespon-
dent) correspondent

berichtig|en vt correct. **B∼ung** f
-,-en correction

berieseln vt irrigate. **B∼ungs-
anlage** f sprinkler system

beritten a (Polizei) mounted

Berlin nt -s Berlin. **B∼er** a -s,-
Berliner; (Culin) doughnut □ a
Berlin . . .

Bernhardiner m -s,- St Bernard

Bernstein m amber

bersten† vi (sein) burst

berüchtigt a notorious

berückend a entrancing

berücksichtig|en vt take into
consideration. **B∼ung** f - consideration

Beruf m profession; (Tätigkeit)
occupation; (Handwerk) trade.
b∼en† vt appoint; **sich b∼en** refer (**auf** + acc to); (vorgeben)
plead (**auf etw** acc sth) □ a competent; **b∼en sein** be destined
(**zu** to). **b∼lich** a professional;
(Ausbildung) vocational □ adv
professionally; **b∼lich tätig
sein** work, have a job. **B∼saus-
sichten** fpl career prospects.
B∼sberater(in) m(f) careers
officer. **B∼sberatung** f vocational guidance. **b∼smäßig**
adv professionally. **B∼sschule** f
vocational school. **B∼ssoldat** m
regular soldier. **b∼stätig** a working; **b∼stätig sein** work, have a
job. **B∼stätige(r)** m/f working
man/woman. **B∼sverkehr** m
rush-hour traffic. **B∼ung** f -,-en
appointment; (Bestimmung) vocation; (Jur) appeal; **B∼ung einlegen** appeal. **B∼ungsgericht** nt
appeal court

beruhen vi (haben) be based (**auf**
+ dat on); **eine Sache auf sich
b∼ lassen** let a matter rest

beruhigen vt calm [down];
(zuversichtlich machen) reassure;

sich b~en calm down. **b~end** *a* calming; *(tröstend)* reassuring; *(Med)* sedative. **B~ung** *f* - calming; reassurance; *(Med)* sedation. **B~ungsmittel** *nt* sedative; *(bei Psychosen)* tranquillizer

berühmt *a* famous. **B~heit** *f* -,-en fame; *(Person)* celebrity

berühr|en *vt* touch; *(erwähnen)* touch on; *(beeindrucken)* affect; **sich b~en** touch. **B~ung** *f* -,-en touch; *(Kontakt)* contact

besag|en *vt* say; *(bedeuten)* mean. **b~t** *a* [afore]said

besänftigen *vt* soothe; **sich b~** calm down

Besatz *m* -es,-e trimming

Besatzung *f* -,-en crew; *(Mil)* occupying force

besaufen† (sich) *vr* (*sl*) get drunk

beschädig|en *vt* damage. **B~ung** *f* -,-en damage

beschaffen *vt* obtain, get □ *a* so **b~ sein, dass** be such that; **wie ist es b~ mit?** what about? **B~heit** *f* - consistency; *(Art)* nature

beschäftig|en *vt* occupy; *(Arbeitgeber:)* employ; **sich b~en** occupy oneself. **b~t** *a* busy; *(angestellt)* employed (**bei** at). **B~te(r)** *m/f* employee. **B~ung** *f* -,-en occupation; *(Anstellung)* employment. **b~ungslos** *a* unemployed. **B~ungstherapie** *f* occupational therapy

beschäm|en *vt* make ashamed. **b~end** *a* shameful; *(demütigend)* humiliating. **b~t** *a* ashamed; *(verlegen)* embarrassed

beschatten *vt* shade; *(überwachen)* shadow

beschau|en *vt* (*SGer*) [sich *(dat)*] etw **b~en** look at sth. **b~lich** *a* tranquil; *(Relig)* contemplative

Bescheid *m* -[e]s information; **jdm B~ sagen** *od* **geben** let s.o. know; **B~ wissen** know

bescheiden *a* modest, *adv* -ly. **B~heit** *f* - modesty

bescheinen† *vt* shine on; **von der Sonne beschienen** sunlit

bescheinig|en *vt* certify. **B~ung** *f* -,-en [written] confirmation; *(Schein)* certificate

beschenken *vt* give a present/presents to

bescher|en *vt* **jdn b~en** give s.o. presents; **jdm etw b~en** give s.o. sth. **B~ung** *f* -,-en distribution of Christmas presents; *(fam: Schlamassel)* mess

beschießen† *vt* fire at; *(mit Artillerie)* shell, bombard

beschildern *vt* signpost

beschimpf|en *vt* abuse, swear at. **B~ung** *f* -,-en abuse

beschirmen *vt* protect

Beschlag *m* in **B~ nehmen, mit B~ belegen** monopolize. **b~en†** *vt* shoe □ *vi (sein)* steam or mist up □ *a* steamed or misted up; *(erfahren)* knowledgeable (**in** + *dat* about). **B~nahme** *f* -,-n confiscation; *(Jur)* seizure. **b~nahmen** *vt* confiscate; *(Jur)* seize; *(fam)* monopolize

beschleunig|en *vt* hasten; *(schneller machen)* speed up; quicken *(Schritt, Tempo)*; **sich b~en** speed up; quicken □ *vi (haben)* accelerate. **B~ung** *f* - acceleration

beschließen† *vt* decide; *(beenden)* end □ *vi (haben)* decide (**über** + *acc* about)

Beschluss (Beschluß) *m* decision

beschmieren *vt* smear;/*(bestreichen)* spread (**mit** with)

beschmutzen *vt* make dirty; **sich b~** get [oneself] dirty

beschneid|en† *vt* trim; *(Hort)* prune; *(fig: kürzen)* cut back; *(Relig)* circumcise. **B~ung** *f* - circumcision

beschneit *a* snow-covered

beschnüffeln, beschnuppern *vt* sniff at

beschönigen *vt* (*fig*) gloss over

beschränken vt limit, restrict; **sich b~auf** (+ acc) confine oneself to; ⟨Sache:⟩ be limited to

beschränkt a ⟨Bahnübergang⟩ with barrier[s]

beschränkt|t a limited; ⟨geistig⟩ dull-witted; ⟨borniert⟩ narrowminded. **B~ung** f -,-en limitation, restriction

beschreiben†t vt describe; ⟨schreiben⟩ write on. **B~ung** f -,-en description

beschuldig|en vt accuse. **B~ung** f -,-en accusation

beschummeln vt ⟨fam⟩ cheat

Beschuss (Beschuß) m ⟨Mil⟩ fire; ⟨Artillerie-⟩ shelling

beschütz|en vt protect. **B~er** m -s,- protector

Beschwer|de f -,-n complaint; **B~den** ⟨Med⟩ trouble sg. **b~en** vt weight down; **sich b~en** complain. **b~lich** a difficult

beschwichtigen vt placate

beschwindeln vt cheat ⟨um out of⟩; ⟨belügen⟩ lie to

beschwingt a elated; ⟨munter⟩ lively

beschwipst a ⟨fam⟩ tipsy

beschwören† vt swear to; ⟨anflehen⟩ implore; ⟨herauf-⟩ invoke

besehen† vt look at

beseitig|en vt remove. **B~ung** f - removal

Besen m -s,- broom. **B~ginster** m ⟨Bot⟩ broom. **B~stiel** m broomstick

besessen a obsessed ⟨von by⟩

besetz|en vt occupy; fill ⟨Posten⟩; ⟨Theat⟩ cast ⟨Rolle⟩; ⟨verzieren⟩ trim ⟨mit with⟩. **b~t** a occupied; ⟨Toilette, Leitung⟩ engaged; ⟨Zug, Bus⟩ full up; **der Platz ist b~t** this seat is taken; **mit Perlen b~t** set with pearls. **B~tzeichen** nt engaged tone. **B~ung** f -,-en occupation; ⟨Theat⟩ cast

besichtig|en†vt look round ⟨Stadt, Museum⟩; ⟨prüfen⟩ inspect; ⟨besuchen⟩ visit. **B~ung** f -,-en

visit; ⟨Prüfung⟩ inspection; ⟨Stadt-⟩ sightseeing

besiedelt a **dünn/dicht b~** sparsely/densely populated

besiegeln vt ⟨fig⟩ seal

besieg|en vt defeat; ⟨fig⟩ overcome. **B~te(r)** m/f loser

besinn|en† ⟨sich⟩ vr think, reflect; ⟨sich erinnern⟩ remember ⟨auf jdn/etw s.o./sth⟩; **sich anders b~en** change one's mind. **b~lich** a contemplative; ⟨nachdenklich⟩ thoughtful. **B~ung** f - reflection; ⟨Bewusstsein⟩ consciousness; **bei/ohne B~ung** conscious/unconscious; **zur B~ung kommen** regain consciousness; ⟨fig⟩ come to one's senses. **b~ungslos** a unconscious

Besitz m possession; ⟨Eigentum, Land-⟩ property; ⟨Gut⟩ estate. **b~anzeigend** a ⟨Gram⟩ possessive. **b~en**† vt own, possess; ⟨haben⟩ have. **B~er(in)** m -s,- ⟨f -,-nen⟩ owner; ⟨Comm⟩ proprietor. **B~ung** f -,-en ⟨landed⟩ property; ⟨Gut⟩ estate

besoffen a ⟨sl⟩ drunken; **b~ sein** be drunk

besohlen vt sole

besold|en vt pay. **B~ung** f - pay

besonder|e(r,s) a special; ⟨bestimmt⟩ particular; ⟨gesondert⟩ separate; **nichts B~es** nothing special. **B~heit** f -,-en peculiarity. **b~s** adv [e]specially, particularly; ⟨gesondert⟩ separately

besonnen a calm, adv -ly

besorg|en vt get; ⟨kaufen⟩ buy; ⟨erledigen⟩ attend to; ⟨versorgen⟩ look after. **B~nis** f -,-se anxiety; ⟨Sorge⟩ worry. **b~niserregend** a worrying. **b~t** a worried/⟨bedacht⟩ concerned ⟨um about⟩. **B~ung** f -,-en errand; **B~ungen machen** go shopping

bespielt a recorded

bespitzeln vt spy on

besprech|en† vt discuss; ⟨rezensieren⟩ review; **sich b~en** confer ein Tonband b~en make a tape recording. **B~ung** f -,-en discussion; review; (*Konferenz*) meeting

bespritzen vt splash

besser a & adv better. **b~n** vt improve; **sich b~n** get better, improve. **B~ung** f - improvement; **gute B~ung!** get well soon! **B~wisser** m -s,- know-all

Bestand m -[e]s,ˆe existence; (*Vorrat*) stock (**an** + dat of); **B~haben, von B~ sein** last

beständig a constant, adv. -ly; (*Wetter*) settled; **b~ gegen** resistant to

Bestand|saufnahme f stocktaking. **B~teil** m part

bestärken vt (fig) strengthen

bestätig|en vt confirm; acknowledge (*Empfang*); **sich b~en** prove to be true. **B~ung** f -,-en confirmation

bestatt|en vt bury. **B~ung** f -,-en funeral. **B~ungsinstitut** nt [firm of] undertakers pl, (Amer) funeral home

bestäuben vt pollinate

bestaubt a dusty

Bestäubung f - pollination

bestaunen vt gaze at in amazement; (*bewundern*) admire

best|e(r,s) a best; **b~en Dank!** many thanks! **am b~en** sein be best; **zum B~en geben/ halten** NEW **zum B~en geben/ halten**, s. **Beste(r,s)**. **B~e(r,s)** m/f/nt best; **sein B~es tun** do one's best; **zum B~en der Armen** for the benefit of the poor; **zum B~n geben** recite (*Gedicht*); tell (*Geschichte, Witz*); sing (*Lied*); **jdn zum B~n halten** (fam) pull s.o.'s leg

bestech|en† vt bribe; (*bezaubern*) captivate. **b~lich** a corruptible. **B~ung** f -,-en bribery. **B~ungsgeld** nt bribe

Besteck nt -[e]s,-e [set of] knife, fork and spoon; (coll) cutlery

bestehen† vi (haben) exist; (*fortdauern*) last; (*bei Prüfung*) pass; ~ **aus** consist/(gemacht sein) be made of; ~ **auf** (+ dat) insist on □ vt pass (*Prüfung*). **B~** nt -s existence

bestehlen† vt rob

besteig|en† vt climb; (*einsteigen*) board; (*aufsteigen*) mount; ascend (*Thron*). **B~ung** f ascent

bestell|en vt order; (vor-) book; (*ernennen*) appoint; (*bebauen*) cultivate; (*ausrichten*) tell; **zu sich b~en** send for; **b~t sein** have an appointment; **kann ich etwas b~en?** can I take a message? **B~en Sie Ihrer Frau Grüße von mir** give my regards to your wife. **B~schein** m order form. **B~ung** f order; (*Botschaft*) message; (*Bebauung*) cultivation

besten|falls adv at best. **b~s** adv very well

besteu|ern vt tax. **B~ung** f - taxation

bestialisch /-st-/ a bestial

Bestie /'bɛstjə/ f -,-n beast

bestimm|en vt fix; (*entscheiden*) decide; (*vorsehen*) intend; (*ernennen*) appoint; (*ermitteln*) determine; (*definieren*) define; (*Gram*) qualify □ vi (haben) be in charge (**über** + acc of). **~t** a definite, adv ly; (*gewiss*) certain, adv -ly; (*fest*) firm, adv -ly. **B~theit** f - firmness; **mit B~theit** for certain. **B~ung** f fixing; (*Vorschrift*) regulation; (*Ermittlung*) determination; (*Definition*) definition; (*Zweck*) purpose; (*Schicksal*) destiny. **B~ungsort** m destination

Bestleistung f (Sport) record

bestraf|en vt punish. **B~ung** f -,-en punishment

bestrahl|en vt shine on; (*Med*) treat with radiotherapy; irradiate (*Lebensmittel*). **B~ung** f radiotherapy

Bestreb|en nt -s endeavour; (Absicht) aim. **b~t a b~t sein** endeavour (**zu** to). **B~ung** f -,-en effort

bestreichen† vt spread (**mit** with)

bestreikt a strike-hit

bestreiten† vt dispute; (leugnen) deny; (bezahlen) pay for

bestreuen vt sprinkle (**mit** with)

bestürmen vt (fig) besiege

bestürz|t a dismayed; (erschüttert) stunned. **B~ung** f - dismay, consternation

Bestzeit f (Sport) record [time]

Besuch m -[e]s,-e visit; (kurz) call; (Schul-) attendance; (Gast) visitor; (Gäste) visitors pl; **b~ haben** have a visitor/visitors; **bei jdm zu od auf B~ sein** be staying with s.o. **~en** vt visit; (kurz) call on; (teilnehmen an) attend; go to (Schule, Ausstellung); **gut b~t** well attended. **B~er(in)** m -s,- (f -,-nen) visitor; caller; (Theat) patron. **B~szeit** f visiting hours pl

betagt a aged, old

betasten vt feel

betätig|en vt operate; **sich b~en** work (**als** as); **sich politisch b~en** engage in politics. **B~ung** f -,-en operation; (Tätigkeit) activity

betäub|en vt stun; (Lärm:) deafen; (Med) anaesthetize; (lindern) ease; deaden (Schmerz); **wie b~t** dazed. **B~ung** f - daze; (Med) anaesthesia; **unter örtlicher B~ung** under local anaesthetic. **B~ungsmittel** nt anaesthetic

Bete f -,-n **rote B~** beetroot

beteilig|en vt give a share to; **sich b~en** take part (**an** + dat in); (beitragen) contribute (**an** + dat to). **b~t a b~t sein** take part/(an Unfall) be involved/(Comm) have a share (**an** + dat in); **alle B~ten** all those involved. **B~ung** f -,-en participation; involvement; (Anteil) share

beten vi (haben) pray; (bei Tisch) say grace □ vt say

beteuer|n vt protest. **B~ung** f -,-en protestation

Beton /be'tɔŋ/ m -s concrete

betonen vt stressed, emphasize

betonieren vt concrete

beton|t a stressed; (fig) pointed, adv -ly. **B~ung** f -,-en stress, emphasis

betören vt bewitch

betr., Betr. abbr (betreffs) re

Betracht m **in B~ ziehen** consider; **außer B~ lassen** disregard; **nicht in B~ kommen** be out of the question. **b~en** vt look at; (fig) regard (als as)

beträchtlich a considerable, adv -bly

Betrachtung f -,-en contemplation; (Überlegung) reflection

Betrag m -[e]s,⸚e amount. **b~en†** vt amount to; **sich b~en** behave. **B~en** nt -s behaviour; (Sch) conduct

betrauen vt entrust (**mit** with)

betrauern vt mourn

betreff|en† vt affect; (angehen) concern; **was mich betrifft** as far as I am concerned. **b~end** a relevant; **der b~ende Brief** the letter in question. **b~s** prep (+ gen) concerning

betreib|en† vt (leiten) run; (ausüben) carry on; (vorantreiben) pursue; (antreiben) run (mit on)

betreten† vt step on; (eintreten) enter; 'B~ verboten' 'no entry'; (bei Rasen) 'keep off [the grass]' □ a embarrassed □ adv in embarrassment

betreu|en vt look after. **B~er(in)** m -s,- (f -,-nen) helper; (Kranken-) nurse. **B~ung** f - care

Betrieb m business; (Firma) firm; (Treiben) activity; (Verkehr) traffic; **in B~** working; (in Gebrauch) in use; **außer B~** not in use; (defekt) out of order

Betriebs|anleitung, B~anweisung f operating instructions pl. **B~ferien** pl firm's holiday; '**B~ferien**' 'closed for the holidays'. **B~leitung** f management. **B~rat** m works committee. **B~ruhe** f 'montags **B~ruhe**' 'closed on Mondays'. **B~störung** f breakdown

betrinken† (sich) vr get drunk

betroffen a disconcerted; **b~ sein** be affected (**von** by); **die B~en** those affected □ adv in consternation

betrüb|en vt sadden. **b~lich** a sad. **b~t** a sad, adv -ly

Betrug m -[e]s deception; (Jur) fraud

betrüg|en† vt cheat, swindle; (Jur) defraud; (in der Ehe) be unfaithful to; **sich selbst b~en** deceive oneself. **B~er(in)** m -s,- (f -,-nen) swindler. **B~erei** f -,-en fraud. **b~erisch** a fraudulent; (Person) deceitful

betrunken a drunken; **b~ sein** be drunk. **B~e(r)** m drunk

Bett nt -[e]s,-en bed; **im B~** in bed; **ins** od **zu B~ gehen** go to bed. **B~couch** f sofa-bed. **B~decke** f blanket; (Tages-) bedspread

bettel|arm a destitute. **B~ei** f - begging. **b~n** vi (haben) beg

bett|en vt lay, put; **sich b~en** lie down. **b~lägerig** a bedridden. **B~laken** nt sheet

Bettler(in) m -s,- (f -,-nen) beggar

Bettpfanne f bedpan

Bettuch (Betttuch) nt sheet

Bett|vorleger m bedside rug. **B~wäsche** f bed linen. **B~zeug** nt bedding

betupfen vt dab (**mit** with)

beug|en vt bend; (Gram) decline; conjugate (Verb); **sich b~en** bend; (lehnen) lean; (sich fügen) submit (**dat** to). **B~ung** f -,-en (Gram) declension; conjugation

Beule f -,-n bump; (Delle) dent

beunruhig|en vt worry; **sich b~en** worry. **B~ung** f - worry

beurlauben vt give leave to; (des Dienstes entheben) suspend

beurteil|en vt judge. **B~ung** f -,-en judgement; (Ansicht) opinion

Beute f - booty, haul; (Jagd-) bag; (B~tier) quarry; (eines Raubtiers) prey

Beutel m -s,- bag; (Geld-) purse; (Tabak- & Zool) pouch. **B~tier** nt marsupial

bevölker|n vt populate. **B~ung** f -,-en population

bevollmächtig|en vt authorize. **B~te(r)** m/f [authorized] agent

bevor conj before; **b~ nicht** not until

bevormunden vt treat like a child

bevorstehen† vi sep (haben) approach; (unmittelbar) be imminent; **jdm b~** be in store for s.o. **b~d** a approaching, forthcoming; **unmittelbar b~d** imminent

bevorzug|en vt prefer; (begünstigen) favour. **b~t** a privileged; (Behandlung) preferential; (beliebt) favoured

bewachen vt guard; **bewachter Parkplatz** car park with an attendant

bewachsen a covered (**mit** with)

Bewachung f - guard; **unter B~** under guard

bewaffn|en vt arm. **b~et** a armed. **B~ung** f - armament; (Waffen) arms pl

bewahren vt protect (**vor** + dat from); (behalten) keep; **die Ruhe b~** keep calm; **Gott bewahre!** heaven forbid!

bewähren (sich) vr prove one's/(Ding:) its worth; (erfolgreich sein) prove a success

bewahrheiten (sich) vr prove to be true

bewähr|t a reliable; (erprobt) proven. **B~ung** f - (Jur) probation. **B~ungsfrist** f [period of] probation. **B~ungsprobe** f (fig) test

bewaldet a wooded

bewältigen *vt* cope with; (*überwinden*) overcome; (*schaffen*) manage

bewandert *a* knowledgeable

bewässer|n *vt* irrigate. **B~ung** *f* - irrigation

bewegen¹ *vt* (*reg*) move; **sich b~** move; (*körperlich*) take exercise

bewegen¹² *vt* jdn dazu b~, etw zu tun induce s.o. to do sth

Beweg|grund *m* motive. **b~lich** amovable, mobile; (*wendig*) agile. **B~lichkeit** *f* - mobility; agility. **b~t** *a* moved; (*ereignisreich*) eventful; (*See*) rough. **B~ung** *f* -,-en movement; (*Phys*) motion; (*Rührung*) emotion; (*Gruppe*) movement; **körperliche B~ung** physical exercise; **sich in B~ung setzen** [start to] move. **B~ungsfreiheit** *f* freedom of movement/(*fig*) of action. **b~ungslos** *a* motionless

beweinen *vt* mourn

Beweis *m* -es,-e proof; (*Zeichen*) token; **B~e** evidence *sg*. **b~en†** *vt* prove; (*zeigen*) show; **sich b~en** prove oneself/(*Ding:*) itself. **B~material** *nt* evidence

bewenden *vi* es dabei b~lassen leave it at that

bewerb|en† (sich) *vr* apply (**um** for; **bei** to). **B~er(in)** *m* -s,- (*f* -,-nen) applicant. **B~ung** *f* -,-en application

bewerkstelligen *vt* manage

bewerten *vt* value; (*einschätzen*) rate; (*Sch*) mark, grade

bewilligen *vt* grant

bewirken *vt* cause; (*herbeiführen*) bring about; (*erreichen*) achieve

bewirt|en *vt* entertain. **B~ung** *f* - hospitality

bewohn|bar *a* habitable. **b~en** *vt* inhabit, live in. **B~er(in)** *m* -s,- (*f* -,-nen) resident, occupant; (*Einwohner*) inhabitant

bewölk|en (sich) *vr* cloud over; **b~t** cloudy. **B~ung** *f* - clouds *pl*

bewunder|n *vt* admire. **b~nswert** *a* admirable. **B~ung** *f* - admiration

bewusst (bewußt) *a* conscious (*gen* of); (*absichtlich*) deliberate, *adv* -ly; (*besagt*) said; **sich** (*dat*) **etw** (*gen*) **b~ sein/werden** be/become aware of sth. **b~los** *a* unconscious. **B~losigkeit** *f* - unconsciousness; **B~sein** *n* -s consciousness; (*Gewissheit*) awareness; **bei** [**vollem**] **B~sein** [fully] conscious; **mir kam zum B~sein** I realized (**dass** that)

bez. *abbr* (**bezahlt**) paid; (**bezüglich**) re

bezahl|en *vt/i* (**haben**) pay; pay for (*Ware, Essen*); **gut b~te Arbeit** well-paid work; **sich b~t machen** (*fig*) pay off. **B~ung** *f* - payment; (*Lohn*) pay

bezähmen *vt* control; (*zügeln*) restrain; **sich b~** restrain oneself

bezaubern *vt* enchant. **b~d** *a* enchanting

bezeichn|en *vt* mark; (*bedeuten*) denote; (*beschreiben, nennen*) describe (**als** as). **b~end** *a* typical. **B~ung** *f* marking; (*Beschreibung*) description (**als** as); (*Ausdruck*) term; (*Name*) name

bezeugen *vt* testify to

bezichtigen *vt* accuse (*gen* of)

bezieh|en† *vt* cover; (*einziehen*) move into; (*beschaffen*) obtain; (*erhalten*) get, receive; take (*Zeitung*); (*in Verbindung bringen*) relate (**auf** + *acc* to); **sich b~en** (*bewölken*) cloud over; **sich b~en auf** (+ *acc*) refer to; **das Bett frisch b~en** put clean sheets on the bed. **B~ung** *f* -,-en relation; (*Verhältnis*) relationship; (*Bezug*) respect; **in dieser B~ung** in this respect; [**gute**] **B~ungen haben** have [good] connections. **b~ungsweise** *adv* respectively; (*vielmehr*) or rather

beziffern (sich) *vr* amount (**auf** + *acc* to)

Bezirk *m* -[e]s,-e district

Bezug m cover; (Kissen-) case; (Beschaffung) obtaining; (Kauf) purchase; (Zusammenhang) reference; **B~e** pl earnings; **B~nehmen** refer (**auf** + acc to); in **B~** (**b~**) **auf** (+ acc) regarding, concerning

bezüglich prep (+ gen) regarding, concerning □ a relating (**auf** + acc to); (Gram) relative

bezwecken vt (fig) aim at

bezweifeln vt doubt

bezwingen† vt conquer

BH /be:'ha:/ m -**[s]**,-**[s]** bra

bibbern vi (haben) tremble; (vor Kälte) shiver

Bibel f -,-n Bible

Biber[1] m -s,- beaver

Biber[2] m & nt -s flannelette

Biblio|graphie, **B~grafie** f -,-n bibliography. **B~thek** f -,-en library. **B~thekar(in)** m -s,- (f -,-nen) librarian

biblisch a biblical

bieder a honest, upright; (ehrenwert) worthy; (einfach) simple

biegen† vt bend; **sich b~en** bend; **sich vor Lachen b~en** (fam) double up with laughter □ vi (sein) curve (**nach** to); **um die Ecke b~en** turn the corner. **b~sam** a flexible, supple. **B~ung** f -,-en curve

Biene f -,-n bee. **B~nhonig** m natural honey. **B~nstock** m beehive. **B~nwabe** f honey-comb

Bier nt -[e]s,-e beer. **B~deckel** m beer-mat. **B~krug** m beer-mug

Biest nt -[e]s,-er (fam) beast

bieten† vt offer; (bei Auktion) bid; (zeigen) present; **das lasse ich mir nicht b~** I won't stand for that

Bifokalbrille f bifocals pl

Biga|mie f - bigamy. **B~mist** m -en,-en bigamist

Bikini m -s,-s bikini

Bilanz f -,-en balance sheet; (fig) result; **die B~ ziehen** (fig) draw conclusions (**aus** from)

Bild nt -[e]s,-er picture; (Theat) scene; **jdn ins B~ setzen** put s.o. in the picture

bilden vt form; (sein) be; (erziehen) educate; **sich b~** form; (geistig) educate oneself

Bild|erbuch nt picture-book. **B~ergalerie** f picture gallery. **B~fläche** f screen; **von der B~fläche verschwinden** disappear from the scene. **B~hauer** m -s,- sculptor. **B~hauerei** f - sculpture. **b~hübsch** a very pretty. **b~lich** a pictorial; (figurativ) figurative, adv -ly. **B~nis** nt -ses,-se portrait. **B~schirm** m (TV) screen. **B~schirmgerät** nt visual display unit, VDU. **b~schön** a very beautiful

Bildung f - formation; (Erziehung) education; (Kultur) culture

Billard /'biljart/ nt -s billiards sg. **B~tisch** m billiard table

Billett /bil'jet/ nt -[e]s,-e & -s ticket

Billiarde f -,-n thousand million million

billig a cheap, adv -ly; (dürftig) poor; (gerecht) just; **recht und b~** right and proper. **b~en** vt approve. **B~ung** f - approval

Billion /bil|jo:n/ f -,-en million million

bimmeln vi (haben) tinkle

Bimsstein m pumice stone

bin s. sein; **ich bin** I am

Binde f -,-n band; (Verband) bandage; (Damen-) sanitary towel. **B~hautentzündung** f conjunctivitis. **b~n†** vt tie (**an** + acc to); make ⟨Strauß⟩; bind ⟨Buch⟩; (fesseln) tie up; (Culin) thicken; **sich b~n** commit oneself. **b~nd** a (fig) binding. **B~strich** m hyphen. **B~wort** nt (pl -wörter) (Gram) conjunction

Bind|faden *m* string; **ein B~faden** a piece of string. **B~ung** *f* -,-en *(fig)* tie, bond; *(Beziehung)* relationship; *(Verpflichtung)* commitment; *(Ski-)* binding; *(Tex)* weave

binnen *prep* (+ *dat)* within; **b~kurzem** shortly. **B~handel** *m* home trade

Binse *f* -,-n *(Bot)* rush. **B~nwahrheit, B~nweisheit** *f* truism

Bio- *pref* organic

Bio|chemie *f* biochemistry. **b~dynamisch** *m* organic. **B~graphie, B~grafie** *f* -,-n biography

Bio|hof *m* organic farm. **B~laden** *m* health-food store

Biolog|e *m* -n,-n biologist. **B~ie** *f* - biology. **b~isch** *a* biological, *adv* -ly; **b~ischer Anbau** organic farming; **b~isch angebaut** organically grown

Birke *f* -,-n birch [tree]

Birma *nt* -s Burma. **B~anisch** *a* Burmese

Birn|baum *m* pear-tree. **B~e** *f* -,-n pear; *(Electr)* bulb

bis *prep* (+ *acc)* as far as, [up] to; *(zeitlich)* until, till; *(spätestens)* by; **bis zu** up to; **bis jetzt** up to now, so far; **bis dahin** until *(spätestens)* by then; **bis auf** (+ *acc)* *(einschließlich)* [down] to; *(ausgenommen)* except [for]; **drei bis vier Mark** three to four marks; **bis morgen!** see you tomorrow! □ *conj* until

Bischof *m* -s,-̈e bishop

bisher *adv* so far, up to now. **b~ig** *attrib a (Präsident)* outgoing; **meine b~igen Erfahrungen** my experiences so far

Biskuit|rolle /bɪsˈkviːt-/ *f* Swiss roll. **B~teig** *m* sponge mixture

bislang *adv* so far, up to now

Biss *m* -es,-e *(Biß m -sses,-sse)* bite

bisschen *(bißchen)* *inv pron* **ein b~** a bit, a little; **ein b~ Brot** a bit of bread; **kein b~** not a bit

Biss|en *m* -s,- bite, mouthful. **b~ig** *a* vicious; *(fig)* caustic

bist *s.* **sein; du b~** you are

Bistum *nt* -s,-̈er diocese, see

bisweilen *adv* from time to time

bitte *adv* please; *(nach Klopfen)* come in; *(als Antwort auf 'danke')* don't mention it, you're welcome; **wie b~e?** pardon? *(empört)* I beg your pardon? **möchten Sie Kaffee?—ja b~e** would you like some coffee?—yes please. **B~e** *f* -,-n request/*(dringend)* plea *(um* for). **b~en†** *vt/i* *(haben)* ask/*(dringend)* beg *(um* for); *(einladen)* invite, ask; **ich b~e dich!** I beg [of] you! *(empört)* I ask you! **b~end** *a* pleading, *adv* -ly

bitter *a* bitter, *adv* -ly. **B~keit** *f* - bitterness. **b~lich** *adv* bitterly

Bittschrift *f* petition

bizarr *a* bizarre, *adv* -ly

blähen *vt* swell; puff out ⟨*Vorhang*⟩; **sich b~en** swell; *(Vorhang, Segel.)* billow □ *vi* *(haben)* cause flatulence. **B~ungen** *fpl* flatulence *sg*, *(fam)* wind *sg*

Blamage /blaˈmaːʒə/ *f* -,-n humiliation; *(Schande)* disgrace

blamieren *vt* disgrace; **sich b~** disgrace oneself; *(sich lächerlich machen)* make a fool of oneself

blanchieren /blãˈʃiːrən/ *vt (Culin)* blanch

blank *a* shiny; *(nackt)* bare; **b~sein** *(fam)* be broke. **B~oscheck** *m* blank cheque

Blase *f* -,-n bubble; *(Med)* blister; *(Anat)* bladder. **B~balg** *m* -[e]s, -̈e bellows *pl*. **b~n†** *vt/i* *(haben)* blow; play ⟨*Flöte*⟩. **B~nentzündung** *f* cystitis

Bläser *m* -s,- *(Mus)* wind player; **die B~** the wind section *sg*

blasiert *a* blasé

Blas|instrument *nt* wind instrument. **B~kapelle** *f* brass band

Blasphemie *f* - blasphemy

blass *a* *(blaß) a (blasser, blassest)* pale; *(schwach)* faint; **b~ werden** turn pale

Blässe f - pallor

Blatt nt -[e]s,⸚er (Bot) leaf; (Papier) sheet; (Zeitung) paper; **kein B~ vor den Mund nehmen** (fig) not mince one's words

blätter|n vi (haben) b~n **in** (+ dat) leaf through. **B~teig** m puff pastry

Blattlaus f greenly

blau a, **B~** nt -s,- blue; **b~er Fleck** bruise; **b~es Auge** black eye; **b~ sein** (fam) be tight; **Fahrt ins B~** mystery tour. **B~beere** f bilberry. **B~licht** nt blue flashing light. **b~machen** vi sep (haben) (fam) skive off work

Blech nt -[e]s,-e sheet metal; (Weiß-) tin; (Platte) metal sheet; (Back-) baking sheet; (Mus) brass; (fam: Unsinn) rubbish. **b~en** vt/i (haben) (fam) pay. **B~[blas]instrument** nt brass instrument. **B~schaden** m (Auto) damage to the bodywork

Blei nt -[e]s lead

Bleibe f - place to stay. **b~n†** vi (sein) remain, stay; (übrig-) be left; **ruhig b~n** keep calm; **bei etw b~n** (fig) stick to sth; **bei Sie am Apparat** hold the line; **etw b~n lassen** not do sth.; (aufhören) stop doing sth. **b~nd** a permanent; (anhaltend) lasting. **b~nlassen†** vt sep (NEW) **b~n lassen,** s. **bleiben**

bleich a pale. **b~en†** vi (sein) bleach; (ver-) fade ∘ vt (reg) bleach. **B~mittel** nt bleach

blei|ern a leaden. **b~frei** a unleaded. **B~stift** m pencil. **B~stiftabsatz** m stiletto heel. **B~stiftspitzer** m -s,- pencil-sharpener

Blende f -,-n shade, shield; (Sonnen-) [sun] visor; (Phot) diaphragm; (Öffnung) aperture; (an Kleid) facing. **b~n** vt dazzle, blind. **b~nd** a (fig) dazzling; (prima) marvellous, adv -ly

Blick m -[e]s,-e look; (kurz) glance; (Aussicht) view; **auf den ersten B~** at first sight; **einen B~ für etw haben** (fig) have an eye for sth. **b~en** vi (haben) look; (kurz) glance (**auf** + acc at). **B~punkt** m (fig) point of view

blind a blind; (trübe) dull; **b~er Alarm** false alarm; **b~er Passagier** stowaway. **B~darm** m appendix. **B~darmentzündung** f appendicitis. **B~e(r)** m/f blind man/woman; **die B~en** the blind pl. **B~enhund** m guidedog. **B~enschrift** f braille. **B~gänger** m -s,- (Mil) dud. **B~heit** f - blindness. **b~lings** adv (fig) blindly

blink|en vi (haben) flash; (funkeln) gleam; (Auto) indicate. **B~er** m -s,- (Auto) indicator. **B~licht** nt flashing light

blinzeln vi (haben) blink

Blitz m -es,-e [flash of] lightning; (Phot) flash; **ein B~ aus heiterem Himmel** (fig) a bolt from the blue. **B~ableiter** m lightning-conductor. **b~artig** a lightning …∘ adv like lightning. **B~birne** f flashbulb. **b~en** vi (haben) flash; (funkeln) sparkle; **es hat geblitzt** there was a flash of lightning. **B~gerät** nt flash [unit]. **B~licht** nt (Phot) flash. **b~sauber** a spick and span. **b~schnell** a lightning …∘ adv like lightning. **B~strahl** m flash of lightning

Block m -[e]s,⸚e block ∘ -[e]s,-s & -e (Schreib-) [note-]pad; (Häuser-) block; (Pol) bloc

Blockade f -,-n blockade

Blockflöte f recorder

blockieren vt block; (Mil) blockade

Blockschrift f block letters pl

blöd[e] a feeble-minded; (dumm) stupid, adv -ly

Blödsinn m -[e]s idiocy; (Unsinn) nonsense. **b~ig** a feeble-minded; (verrückt) idiotic

blöken vi (haben) bleat

blond *a* fair-haired; (*Haar*) fair.
B~ine *f* -,-n blonde

bloß *a* bare; (*alleinig*) mere; mit
b~em Auge with the naked eye
□ *adv* only, just; was mache ich
b~? whatever shall I do?

Blöße *f* -,-n nakedness; sich (*dat*)
eine B~ geben (*fig*) show a
weakness

bloß|legen *vt sep* uncover.
b~stellen *vt sep* compromise;
sich b~stellen show oneself up

Bluff *m* -s,-s bluff. b~en *vt/i*
(*haben*) bluff

blühen *vi* (*haben*) flower; (*fig*)
flourish. b~d *a* flowering; (*fig*)
flourishing, thriving; (*Phantasie*)
fertile

Blume *f* -,-n flower; (*vom Wein*)
bouquet. B~nbeet *n* flower-bed.
B~ngeschäft *n* flower-shop,
florist's [shop]. B~nkohl *m* cauliflower. B~nmuster *n* floral
design. B~nstrauß *m* bunch
of flowers. B~ntopf *m* flower-
pot; (*Pflanze*) [flowering] pot
plant. B~nzwiebel *f* bulb

blumig *a* (*fig*) flowery

Bluse *f* -,-n blouse

Blut *nt* -[e]s blood. b~arm *a* an-
aemic. B~bahn *f* blood-stream.
b~befleckt *a* blood-stained.
B~bild *nt* blood count. B~bu-
che *f* copper beech. B~druck *m*
blood pressure. b~dürstig *a*
bloodthirsty

Blüte *f* -,-n flower, bloom; (*vom
Baum*) blossom; (B~zeit) flowering period; (*Baum-*) blossom
time; (*fig*) flowering; (*Höhepunkt*) peak, prime; (*fam: Banknote*) forged note, (*fam*) dud

Blut|egel *m* -s,- leech. b~en *vi*
(*haben*) bleed

Blüten|blatt *nt* petal. B~staub
m pollen

Blut|er *m* -s,- haemophiliac.
B~erguss (B~erguß) *m* bruise.
B~gefäß *nt* blood-vessel.
B~gruppe *f* blood group.
B~hund *m* bloodhound. b~ig *a*

bloody. b~jung *a* very young.
B~körperchen *nt* -s,- [blood]
corpuscle. B~probe *f* blood test.
b~rünstig *a* (*fig*) bloody, gory;
(*Person*) blood-thirsty. B~
schande *f* incest. B~
spender *m* blood donor. B~
sturz *m* haemorrhage. B~
verwandte(r) *m/f* blood relation.
B~transfusion, B~über-
tragung *f* blood transfusion.
B~ung *f* -,-en bleeding; (*Med*)
haemorrhage; (*Regel-*) period.
b~unterlaufen *a* bruised;
(*Auge*) bloodshot. B~vergießen
nt -s bloodshed. B~vergiftung *f*
blood-poisoning. B~wurst *f*
black pudding

Bö *f* -,-en gust; (*Regen-*) squall
Bob *m* -s,-s bob[-sleigh]
Bock *m* -[e]s,=e buck; (*Ziege*) billy
goat; (*Schaf*) ram; (*Gestell*) support; einen B~ schießen (*fam*)
make a blunder. b~en *vi* (*haben*)
(*Pferd:*) buck; (*Kind:*) be stubborn. b~ig *a* (*fam*) stubborn.
B~springen *nt* leap-frog

Boden *m* -s,= ground; (*Erde*) soil;
(*Fuß-*) floor; (*Grundfläche*) bottom; (*Dach-*) loft, attic.
B~kammer *f* attic [room].
b~los *a* bottomless; (*fig*)
incredible. B~satz *m* sediment.
B~schätze *mpl* mineral de-
posits. B~see (der) Lake Con-
stance

Bogen *m* -s,- & = curve; (*Geom*)
arc; (*beim Skilauf*) turn; (*Archit*)
arch; (*Waffe, Geigen-*) bow; (*Papier*) sheet; einen großen B~
um jdn/etw machen (*fam*) give
s.o./sth a wide berth. B~gang *m*
arcade. B~schießen *nt* archery

Bohle *f* -,-n [thick] plank

Böhm|en *nt* -s Bohemia. b~isch
a Bohemian

Bohne *f* -,-n bean; grüne B~n
French beans. B~nkaffee *m* real
coffee

bohner|n *vt* polish. B~wachs *nt*
floor-polish

bohr|en vt/i (haben) drill (nach for); drive (Tunnel); sink (Brunnen); (Insekt:) bore; **in der Nase b~en** pick one's nose. **B~er** m -s,- drill. **B~insel** f [offshore] drilling rig. **B~maschine** f electric drill. **B~turm** m derrick

Boje f -,-n buoy

Böllerschuss m gun salute

Bolzen m -s,- bolt; (Stift) pin

bombardieren vt bomb; (fig) bombard (mit with)

bombastisch a bombastic

Bombe f -,-n bomb. **B~nangriff** m bombing raid. **B~nerfolg** m huge success. **B~r** m -s,- (Aviat) bomber

Bon /bɔŋ/ m -s,-s voucher; (Kassen-) receipt

Bonbon /bɔŋˈbɔŋ/ m & nt -s,-s sweet

Bonus m -[sses],-[sse] bonus

Boot nt -[e]s,-e boat. **B~ssteg** m landing-stage

Bord[^1] nt -[e]s,-e shelf

Bord[^2] m (Naut) **an B~** aboard, on board; **über B~** overboard. **B~buch** nt log[-book]

Bordell nt -s,-e brothel

Bord|karte f boarding-pass. **B~stein** m kerb

borgen vt borrow; **jdm etw b~** lend s.o. sth

Borke f -,-n bark

borniert a narrow-minded

Börse f -,-n purse; (Comm) stock exchange. **B~nmakler** m stockbroker

Borst|e f -,-n bristle. **b~ig** a bristly

Borte f -,-n braid

bösartig a vicious; (Med) malignant

Böschung f -,-en embankment; (Hang) slope

böse a wicked, evil; (unartig) naughty; (schlimm) bad, adv -ly; (zornig) cross; **jdm od auf jdn b~ sein** be cross with s.o. **B~wicht**

m -[e]s,-e villain; (Schlingel) rascal

bos|haft a malicious, adv -ly; (gehässig) spiteful, adv -ly. **B~heit** f -,-en malice; spite; (Handlung) spiteful act/(Bemerkung) remark

böswillig a malicious, adv -ly. **B~keit** f - malice

Botani|k f - botany. **B~ker(in)** m -s,- (f -,-nen) botanist. **b~sch** a botanical

Bot|e m -n,-n messenger. **B~engang** m errand. **B~schaft** f -,-en message; (Pol) embassy. **B~schafter** m -s,- ambassador

Bottich m -[e]s,-e vat; (Wasch-) tub

Bouillon /bʊlˈjɔŋ/ f -,-s clear soup. **B~würfel** m stock cube

Bowle /ˈbo:lə/ f -,-n punch

box|en vi (haben) box □ vt punch. **B~en** nt -s boxing. **B~er** m -s,- boxer. **B~kampf** m boxing match; (Boxen) boxing

Boykott m -[e]s,-s boycott. **b~ieren** vt boycott; (Comm) black

brachliegen† vi sep (haben) lie fallow

Branche /ˈbrɑ̃:ʃə/ f -,-n [line of] business. **B~nverzeichnis** nt (Teleph) classified directory

Brand m -[e]s,ˉe fire; (Med) gangrene; (Bot) blight; **in B~ geraten** catch fire; **in B~ setzen** od **stecken** set on fire. **B~bombe** f incendiary bomb

branden vi (haben) surge; (sich brechen) break

Brand|geruch m smell of burning. **b~marken** vt (fig) brand. **B~stifter** m arsonist. **B~stiftung** f arson

Brandung f - surf. **B~sreiten** nt surfing

Brand|wunde f burn. **B~zeichen** nt brand

Branntwein m spirit; (coll) spirits pl. **B~brennerei** f distillery

bras|**ilianisch** a Brazilian. B~**ilien** /-jən/ nt -s Brazil

Brat|**apfel** m baked apple. b~**en†** vt/i roast; (in der Pfanne) fry. B~**en** m -s, roast; (B~stück) joint. B~**ensoße** f gravy. b~**fertig** a oven-ready. B~**hähnchen**, B~**huhn** nt roast/(zum Braten) roasting chicken. B~**kartoffeln** fpl fried potatoes. B~**klops** m rissole. B~**pfanne** f frying-pan

Bratsche f -,-n (Mus) viola

Brat|**spieß** m spit. B~**wurst** f sausage for frying; (gebraten) fried sausage

Brauch m -[e]s,Bräuche custom. b~**bar** a usable; (nützlich) useful. b~**en** vt need; (ge-, verbrauchen) use; take (Zeit); er b~t es nur zu sagen one only has to say; du b~st nicht zu gehen you needn't go

Braue f -,-n eyebrow

brau|**en** vt brew. B~**er** m -s, brewer. B~**erei** f -,-en brewery

braun a, B~ nt -s; brown; b~ **werden** (Person:) get a tan; b~ **[gebrannt] sein** a [sun-]tanned

Bräune f - [sun-]tan. b~**n** vt/i (haben) brown; (in der Sonne) tan

braungebrannt a NEW **braun gebrannt**, s. braun

Braunschweig nt -s Brunswick

Brause f -,-n (Dusche) shower; (an Gießkanne) rose; (B~limonade) fizzy drink. b~**n** vi (haben) roar; (duschen) shower ◊ vi (sein) rush [along] ◊ vr **sich** b~**n** shower. b~**nd** a roaring; (sprudelnd) effervescent

Braut f -,-e bride; (Verlobte) fiancée

Bräutigam m -s,-e bridegroom; (Verlobter) fiancé

Brautkleid nt wedding dress

bräutlich a bridal

Brautpaar nt bridal couple; (Verlobte) engaged couple

brav a good, well-behaved; (redlich) honest □ adv dutifully; (redlich) honestly

bravo int bravo!

BRD abbr (Bundesrepublik Deutschland) FRG

Brech|**eisen** nt jemmy; (B~stange) crowbar. b~**en†** vt break; (Phys) refract (Licht); (erbrechen) vomit; **sich** b~**en** (Wellen:) break; (Licht:) be refracted; **sich** (dat) **den Arm** b~**en** break one's arm ◊ vi (sein) break ◊ vi (haben) vomit, be sick; **mit jdm** b~**en** (fig) break with s.o. B~**er** m breaker. B~**reiz** m nausea. B~**stange** f crowbar

Brei m -[e]s,-e paste; (Culin) purée; (Grieß) pudding; (Hafer-) porridge. b~**ig** a mushy

breit a wide; (Schultern, Grinsen) broad □ adv b~ **grinsen** grin broadly. B~**e** f -,-n width; breadth; (Geog) latitude. b~ **en** vt spread (über + acc over). B~**engrad** m [degree of] latitude. B~**enkreis** m parallel. B~**seite** f long side; (Naut) broadside

Bremse f -,-n horsefly

Bremse² f -,-n brake. b~**n** vt slow down; (fig) restrain ◊ vi (haben) brake

Bremslicht nt brake-light

brenn|**bar** a combustible; leicht b~**bar** highly [in]flammable. b~**en†** vi (haben) burn; (Licht:) be on; (Zigarette:) be alight; (weh tun) smart, sting; **es brennt in X** there's a fire in X; **darauf** b~**en,** **etw zu tun** be dying to do sth ◊ vt burn; (rösten) roast; (im Brennofen) fire; (destillieren) distil. b~**end** a burning; (angezündet) lighted; (fig) fervent □ adv **ich würde** b~**end gern ...** I'd love to ... B~**erei** f -,-en distillery

Brennessel f NEW **Brennnessel**

Brenn|**holz** nt firewood. B~**nessel** f stinging nettle. B~**ofen** m kiln. B~**punkt** m (Phys) focus;

im B~punkt des Interesses stehen be the focus of attention. B~spiritus m methylated spirits. B~stoff m fuel

brenzlig a (fam) risky; b~er Geruch smell of burning

Bresche f -,-n (fig) breach

Bretagne /bre'tanjə/ (die) - Brittany

Brett nt -[e]s,-er board; (im Regal) shelf; schwarzes B~ notice board. B~chen nt -s,- slat; (Frühstücks-) small board (used as plate). B~spiel nt board game

Brezel f -,-n pretzel

Bridge /britʃ/ nt - (Spiel) bridge

Brief m -[e]s,-e letter. B~beschwerer m -s,- paperweight. B~block m writing pad. B~freund(in) m(f) penfriend. B~kasten m letter-box, (Amer) mailbox. B~kopf m letter-head. b~lich a & adv by letter. B~marke f (postage) stamp. B~öffner m paper-knife. B~papier nt notepaper. B~porto nt letter rate. B~tasche f wallet. B~träger m postman, (Amer) mailman. B~umschlag m envelope. B~wahl f postal vote. B~wechsel m correspondence

Brigade f -,-n brigade

Brikett nt -s,-s briquette

brillant /bril'jant/ a brilliant, adv -ly. B~t m -en,-en [cut] diamond. B~z f - brilliance

Brille f -,-n glasses pl, spectacles pl; (Schutz-) goggles pl; (Klosett-) toilet seat

bringen† vt bring; (fort-) take; (ein-) yield; (veröffentlichen) publish; (im Radio) broadcast; show (Film); ins Bett b~ put to bed; jdn nach Hause b~ take/(begleiten) see s.o. home; an sich (acc) b~ get possession of; mit sich b~ entail; um etw b~ deprive of sth; etw hinter sich (acc) b~ get sth over [and done] with;

jdn dazu b~, etw zu tun get s.o. to do sth; es weit b~ (fig) go far

brisant a explosive

Brise f -,-n breeze

Brit|e m -n,-n, B~in f -,-nen Briton. b~isch a British

Bröck|chen nt -s,- (Culin) crouton. b~elig a crumbly; (Gestein) friable. b~eln vt/i (haben/sein) crumble

Brocken m -s,- chunk; (Erde, Kohle) lump; ein paar B~ Englisch (fam) a smattering of English

Brokat m -[e]s,-e brocade

Brokkoli pl broccoli sg

Brombeer|e f blackberry. B~strauch m bramble [bush]

Bronchitis f - bronchitis

Bronze /'brõ:sə/ f -,-n bronze

Brosch|e f -,-n brooch. b~iert a paperback. B~üre f -,-n brochure; (Heft) booklet

Brösel mpl (Culin) breadcrumbs

Brot nt -[e]s,-e bread; ein B~ a loaf [of bread]; (Scheibe) a slice of bread; sein B~ verdienen (fig) earn one's living (mit by)

Brötchen nt -s,- [bread] roll

Brot|krümel m breadcrumb. B~verdiener m breadwinner

Bruch m -[e]s,-̈e break; (Brechen) breaking; (Rohr-) burst; (Med) fracture; (Eingeweide-) rupture, hernia; (Math) fraction; (fig) breach; (in Beziehung) break-up

brüchig a brittle

Bruch|landung f crash-landing. B~rechnung f fractions pl. B~stück nt fragment. b~stückhaft a fragmentary. B~teil m fraction

Brücke f -,-n bridge; (Teppich) rug

Bruder m -s,-̈ brother

brüderlich a brotherly, fraternal

Brügge nt -s Bruges

Brühe f -,-n broth; (Knochen-) stock; klare B~e clear soup. b~en vt scald; (auf-) make

(*Kaffee*) **B~würfel** *m* stock cube
brüllen *vt/i* (*haben*) roar; ⟨*Kuh:*⟩ moo; (*fam: schreien*) bawl

brumm|eln *vt/i* (*haben*) mumble. **b~en** *vi* (*haben*) (*Insekt:*) buzz; (*Bär:*) growl; (*Motor:*) hum; (*murren*) grumble □ *vt* mutter. **B~er** *m* -s,- (*fam*) bluebottle. **b~ig** *a* (*fam*) grumpy, *adv* -ily

brünett *a* dark-haired. **B~e** *f* -,-n brunette

Brunnen *m* -s,- well; (*Spring-*) fountain; (*Heil-*) spa water. **B~kresse** *f* watercress

brüsk *a* brusque, *adv* -ly. **b~ieren** *vt* snub

Brüssel *nt* -s Brussels

Brust *f* -,¨e chest; (*weibliche, Culin:* B~*stück*) breast. **B~bein** *nt* breastbone. **B~beutel** *m* purse worn round the neck

brüsten (sich) *vr* boast

Brust|fellentzündung *f* pleurisy. **B~schwimmen** *nt* breaststroke

Brüstung *f* -,-en parapet

Brustwarze *f* nipple

Brut *f* -,-en incubation; (*Junge*) brood; (*Fisch-*) fry

brutal *a* brutal, *adv* -ly. **B~ität** *f* -,-en brutality

brüten *vi* (*haben*) sit (*on eggs*); (*fig*) ponder (**über** + *dat* over); **b~de Hitze** oppressive heat

Brutkasten *m* (*Med*) incubator

brutto *adv.* **B~** *pref* gross

brutzeln *vi* (*haben*) sizzle □ *vt* fry

Bub *m* -en,-en (*SGer*) boy. **B~e** *m* -n,-n (*Karte*) jack, knave

Bubikopf *m* bob

Buch *nt* -[e]s,¨er book; **B~führen** keep a record (**über** + *acc* of); **die B~er führen** keep the accounts. **B~drucker** *m* printer

Buche *f* -,-n beech

buchen *vt* book; (*Comm*) enter

Bücher|bord, B~brett *nt* bookshelf. **B~ei** *f* -,-en library. **B~regal** *nt* bookcase, bookshelves *pl.*

B~schrank *m* bookcase.

B~wurm *m* bookworm

Buchfink *m* chaffinch

Buch|führung *f* bookkeeping. **B~halter(in)** *m* -s,- (*f* -,-nen) bookkeeper, accountant. **B~haltung** *f* bookkeeping, accountancy; (*Abteilung*) accounts department. **B~händler(in)** *m(f)* bookseller. **B~handlung** *f* bookshop. **B~macher** *m* -s,- bookmaker. **B~prüfer** *m* auditor

Büchse *f* -,-n box; (*Konserven-*) tin, can; (*Gewehr*) [sporting] gun. **B~nmilch** *f* evaporated milk. **B~nöffner** *m* tin or can opener

Buch|stabe *m* -n,-n letter. **b~stabieren** *vt* spell [out]. **b~stäblich** *adv* literally

Buchstützen *fpl* book-ends

Bucht *f* -,-en (*Geog*) bay

Buchung *f* -,-en booking, reservation; (*Comm*) entry

Buckel *m* -s,- hump; (*Beule*) bump; (*Hügel*) hillock; **einen B~ machen** (*Katze:*) arch its back

bücken (sich) *vr* bend down

bucklig *a* hunchbacked. **B~e(r)** *m/f* hunchback

Bückling *m* -s,-e smoked herring; (*fam: Verbeugung*) bow

buddeln *vt/i* (*haben*) (*fam*) dig

Buddhis|mus *m* - Buddhism. **B~t(in)** *m* -en,-en (*f* -,-nen) Buddhist. **b~tisch** *a* Buddhist

Bude *f* -,-n hut; (*Kiosk*) kiosk; (*Markt-*) stall; (*fam: Zimmer*) room; (*Studenten-*) digs *pl*

Budget /by'dʒe:/ *nt* -s,-s budget

Büfett *nt* -[e]s,-e sideboard; (*Theke*) bar; **kaltes B~** cold buffet

Büffel *m* -s,- buffalo. **b~n** *vt/i* (*haben*) (*fam*) swot

Bug *m* -[e]s,-e (*Naut*) bow[s *pl*]

Bügel *m* -s,- frame; (*Kleider-*) coathanger; (*Steig-*) stirrup; (*Brillen-*) sidepiece. **B~brett** *nt*

ironing-board. **B~eisen** nt iron.
B~falte f crease. **b~frei** a non-
iron. **b~n** vt/i (haben) iron

bugsieren vt (fam) manœuvre

buhen vi (haben) (fam) boo

Bühne f -,-n breakwater

Bühne f -,-n stage. **B~nbild** nt
set. **B~neingang** m stage door

Buhrufe mpl boos

Bukett nt -[e]s,-e bouquet

Bulette f -,-n (meat) rissole

Bulgarien /-jən/ nt -s Bulgaria

Bull auge nt (Naut) porthole.
B~dogge f bulldog. **B~dozer**
/-doːzɐ/ m -s,- bulldozer. **B~e** m
-n,-n bull; (sl: Polizist) cop

Bummel m -s,- (fam) stroll.
B~lant m -en,-en (fam) dawdler;
(Faulenzer) loafer. **B~n** vi -t-
(fam) dawdling; (Nachlässigkeit)
carelessness

bummel ig a (fam) slow; (nachlässig) careless. **b~n** vi (sein)
(fam) stroll □ vi (haben) (fam)
dawdle. **B~streik** m go-slow.
B~zug m (fam) slow train

Bums m -es,-e (fam) bump,
thump

Bund[1] nt -[e]s,-e bunch; (Stroh-)
bundle

Bund[2] m -[e]s,-e association;
(Bündnis) alliance; (Pol) federation; (Rock-, Hosen-) waistband.
im B~e sein be in league (mit
with); **der B~** the Federal Government; (fam: Bundeswehr) the
[German] Army

Bündel nt -s,- bundle. **b~n** vt
bundle [up]

Bundes- pref Federal.
B~genosse m ally. **B~kanzler**
m Federal Chancellor. **B~land**
nt [federal] state; (Aust) province.
B~liga f German national
league. **B~rat** m Upper House of
Parliament. **B~regierung** f Federal Government. **B~republik** f
die B~republik Deutschland
the Federal Republic of Germany.
B~straße f ≈ A road. **B~tag** m
Lower House of Parliament.

B~wehr f [Federal German]
Army

bünd ig a & adv kurz und b~ig
short and to the point. **B~nis** nt
-sses,-sse alliance

Bunker m -s,- bunker;
(Luftschutz-) shelter

bunt a coloured; (farbenfroh) col-
ourful; (grell) gaudy; (gemischt)
varied; (wirr) confused; **b~er
Abend** social evening; **b~e
Platte** assorted cold meats □ adv
b~ durcheinander higgledy-
piggledy; **es zu b~ treiben** (fam)
go too far. **B~stift** m crayon

Bürde f -,-n (fig) burden

Burg f -,-en castle

Bürge m -n,-n guarantor. **b~n** vi
(haben) **b~n für** vouch for; (fig)
guarantee

Bürger(in) m -s,- (f -,-nen) citizen. **B~krieg** m civil war.
b~lich a civil; (Pflicht) civic;
(mittelständisch) middle-class;
b~liche Küche plain cooking.
B~liche(r) m/f commoner.
B~meister m mayor. **B~rechte**
npl civil rights. **B~steig** m -[e]s,
-e pavement, (Amer) sidewalk

Burggraben m moat

Bürgschaft f -,-en surety; **B~
leisten** stand surety

Burgunder m -s,- (Wein) Burgundy

Burleske f -,-n burlesque

Büro nt -s,-s office. **B~ange-
stellte(r)** m/f office-worker.
B~klammer f paper-clip.
B~krat m -en,-en bureaucrat.
B~kratie f -,-n bureaucracy.
b~kratisch a bureaucratic

Bursch e m -n,-n lad, youth;
(fam: Kerl) fellow. **b~ikos** a
hearty; (männlich) mannish

Bürste f -,-n brush. **b~n** vt brush.
B~nschnitt m crew cut

Bus m -ses,-se bus; (Reise-) coach.
B~bahnhof m bus and coach
station

Busch m -[e]s,-e bush

Büschel nt -s,- tuft

buschig *a* bushy

Busen *m* -s,- bosom

Bussard *m* -s,-e buzzard

Buße *f* -,-n penance; (*Jur*) fine

büßen *vt/i* (haben) [**für**] etw b~ atone for sth; (*fig: bezahlen*) pay for sth

bußfertig *a* penitent. **B~geld** *nt* (*Jur*) fine

Büste *f* -,-n bust; (*Schneider-*) dummy. **B~nhalter** *m* -s,- bra

Butter *f* - butter. **B~blume** *f* buttercup. **B~brot** *nt* slice of bread and butter. **B~brotpapier** *nt* grease-proof paper. **B~fass** (**B~faß**) *nt* churn. **B~milch** *f* buttermilk. **b~n** *vi* (haben) make butter □ *vt* butter

b.w. *abbr* (bitte wenden) P.T.O.

bzgl. *abbr* s. bezüglich

bzw. *abbr* s. beziehungsweise

C

ca. *abbr* (circa) about

Café /ka'fe:/ *nt* -s,-s café

Cafeteria /kafete'ri:a/ *f* -,-s cafeteria

campen /'kɛmpən/ *vi* (haben) go camping. **C~ing** *nt* -s camping. **C~ingplatz** *m* campsite

Cape /ke:p/ *nt* -s,-s cape

Caravan /'ka[:]ravan/ *m* -s,-s (*Auto*) caravan; (*Kombi*) estate car

Cassette /ka'sɛtə/ *f* -,-n cassette. **C~nrecorder** /-rɛkɔrdɐ/ *m* -s,- cassette recorder

CD /tseː'deː/ *f* -,-s compact disc, CD

Cellist(in) /tʃɛ'lɪst(ɪn)/ *m* -en, -en (*f* -,-nen) cellist. **C~o** /'tʃɛlo/ *nt* -s,-los & -li cello

Celsius /'tsɛlzjus/ *inv* Celsius, centigrade

Cembalo /'tʃɛmbalo/ *nt* -s,-los & -li harpsichord

Champagner /ʃam'panjɐ/ *m* -s champagne

Champignon /'ʃampɪnjɔŋ/ *m* -s,-s [field] mushroom

Chance /'ʃã:s(ə)/ *f* -,-n chance

Chaos /'ka:ɔs/ *nt* - chaos

chaotisch /ka'o:tɪʃ/ *a* chaotic

Charakter /ka'raktɐ/ *m* -s,-e /-'te:rə/ character. **c~isieren** *vt* characterize. **c~istisch** *a* characteristic (**für** of), *adv* -ally

Charisma /ka'rɪsma/ *nt* -s charisma. **c~atisch** *a* charismatic

charmant /ʃar'mant/ *a* charming, *adv* -ly. **C~e** /ʃarm/ *m* -s charm

Charter|flug /'tʃ-, 'ʃartv-/ *m* charter flight. **c~n** *vt* charter

Chassis /ʃa'si:/ *nt* -,- /-'si:[s], -'si:s/ chassis

Chauffeur /ʃo'fø:ɐ/ *m* -s,-e chauffeur; (*Taxi-*) driver

Chauvinis|mus /ʃovi'nɪsmus/ *m* - chauvinism. **C~t** *m* -en,-en chauvinist

Chef /ʃɛf/ *m* -s,-s head; (*fam*) boss

Chem|ie /çe'mi:/ *f* - chemistry. **C~ikalien** /-jən/ *fpl* chemicals

Chem|iker(in) /'çe:-/ *m* -s,- (*f* -,-nen) chemist. **c~isch** *a* chemical, *adv* -ly; **c~ische Reinigung** dry-cleaning; (*Geschäft*) dry-cleaner's

Chicorée /'ʃikore:/ *m* -s chicory

Chiffre /'ʃɪfrə, 'ʃɪfɐ/ *f* -,-n cipher; (*bei Annonce*) box number. **c~iert** *a* coded

Chile /'çile/ *nt* -s Chile

Chin|a /'çi:na/ *nt* -s China. **C~ese** *m* -n,-n, **C~esin** *f* -,-nen Chinese. **c~esisch** *a* Chinese. **C~esisch** *nt* -[s] (*Lang*) Chinese

Chip /tʃɪp/ *m* -s,-s [micro]chip. **C~s** *pl* crisps, (*Amer*) chips

Chirurg /çi'rʊrk/ *m* -en,-en surgeon. **C~ie** /-'gi:/ *f* - surgery. **c~isch** /-g-/ *a* surgical, *adv* -ly

Chlor /klo:g/ *nt* -s chlorine. **C~o-form** /kloro'fɔrm/ *nt* -s chloroform

Choke /tʃoːk/ m -s,-s (Auto) choke

Cholera /ˈkoːlera/ f - cholera

cholerisch /koˈleːrɪʃ/ a irascible

Cholesterin /ço-, koleste'ri:n/ nt -s cholesterol

Chor /koːɐ̯/ m -[e]s,-e choir; (Theat) chorus; im C∼ in chorus

Choral /koˈraːl/ m -[e]s,-e chorale

Choreographie, Choreografie /koreografiː/ f -,-n choreography

Chor|knabe /ˈkoːɐ̯-/ m choirboy. **C∼musik** f choral music

Christ /krɪst/ m -en,-en Christian. **C∼baum** m Christmas tree. **C∼entum** nt -s Christianity. **C∼in** f -,-nen Christian. **C∼kind** nt Christ-child; (als Geschenkbringer) ≈ Father Christmas. **c∼lich** a Christian

Christus /ˈkrɪstʊs/ m -ti Christ

Chrom /kroːm/ nt -s chromium

Chromosom /kromo'zoːm/ nt -s,-en chromosome

Chronik /ˈkroːnɪk/ f -,-en chronicle

chron|isch /ˈkroːnɪʃ/ a chronic, adv -ally. **c∼ologisch** a chronological, adv -ly

Chrysantheme /kryzan'teːmə/ f -,-n chrysanthemum

circa /ˈtsɪrka/ adv about

Clique /ˈklɪka/ f -,-n clique

Clou /kluː/ m -s,-s highlight, (fam) high spot

Clown /klaʊn/ m -s,-s clown. **c∼en** vi (haben) clown

Club /klʊp/ m -s,-s club

Cocktail /ˈkɔkteːl/ m -s,-s cocktail

Code /koːt/ m -s,-s code

Cola /ˈkoːla/ f -,- (fam) Coke (P)

Comic-Heft /ˈkɔmɪk-/ nt comic

Computer /kɔm'pjuːtɐ/ m -s,- computer. **c∼isieren** vt computerize

Conférencier /kõ'ferãsjeː/ m -s,- compère

Cord /kɔrt/ m -s, **C∼samt** m corduroy. **C∼[samt]hose** f cords pl

Couch /kaʊtʃ/ f -,-es settee. **C∼tisch** m coffee-table

Coupon /kuˈpõː/ m -s,-s = **Kupon**

Cousin /kuˈzɛ̃ː/ m -s,-s [male] cousin. **C∼e** /-ˈziːnə/ f -,-n [female] cousin

Creme /kreːm/ f -s,-s cream; (Speise) cream dessert. **c∼efarben** a cream. **c∼ig** a creamy

Curry /ˈkari, ˈkœri/ nt & m curry powder □ nt -s,-s (Gericht) curry

D

da adv there; (hier) here; (zeitlich) then; (in dem Fall) in that case; von da an from then on; **da sein** be there/(hier) here; (existieren) exist; **wieder da sein** be back; **noch nie da gewesen** unprecedented □ conj as, since

dabehalten† vt sep keep there

dabei (emphatic: **dabei**) adv nearby; (daran) with it; (eingeschlossen) included; (hinsichtlich) about it; (währenddem) during this; (gleichzeitig) at the same time; (doch) and yet; **dicht d∼** close by; **d∼ sein** be present; (mitmachen) be involved; **d∼ sein, etw zu tun** be just doing sth; **d∼ bleiben** (fig) remain adamant; **was ist denn d∼?** (fam) so what? **d∼seint** vi sep (sein) **d∼ sein**, s. **dabei**

dableiben† vi sep (sein) stay there

Dach nt -[e]s,¨er roof. **D∼boden** m loft. **D∼gepäckträger** m roofrack. **D∼kammer** f attic room. **D∼luke** f skylight. **D∼rinne** f gutter

Dachs m -es,-e badger

Dach|sparren *m* -s,- rafter. **D~ziegel** *m* [roofing] tile

Dackel *m* -s,- dachshund

dadurch (*emphatic:* **dadurch**) *adv* through it/them; (*Ursache*) by it; (*deshalb*) because of that; **d~, dass** because

dafür (*emphatic:* **dafür**) *adv* for it/them; (*anstatt*) instead; (*als Ausgleich*) but [on the other hand]; **d~, dass** considering that; **ich kann nichts dafür** it's not my fault. **d~können†** *vi sep* (*haben*) NEW **d~ können**, s. **dafür**

dagegen (*emphatic:* **dagegen**) *adv* against it/them; (*Mittel, Tausch*) for it; (*verglichen damit*) by comparison; (*jedoch*) however; **hast du was d~?** do you mind? **d~halten†** *vt sep* argue (*dass* that)

daheim *adv* at home

daher (*emphatic:* **daher**) *adv* from there; (*deshalb*) for that reason; **das kommt d~, weil** that's because; **d~ meine Eile** hence my hurry □ *conj* that is why

dahin (*emphatic:* **dahin**) *adv* there; **bis d~** up to there; (*bis dann*) until;(*Zukunft*) by then; **jdn d~bringen, dass er etw tut** get s.o. to do sth; **d~sein** (*fam*) be gone. **d~gestellt** *a* **d~gestellt lassen** (*fig*) leave open; **das bleibt d~gestellt** that remains to be seen

dahinten *adv* back there

dahinter (*emphatic:* **dahinter**) *adv* behind it/them; **d~ kommen** (*fig*) get to the bottom of it. **d~kommen†** *vi sep* (*sein*) NEW **d~ kommen**, s. **dahinter**

Dahlie /-jə/ *f* -,-n dahlia

dalassen† *vt sep* leave there

daliegen† *vi sep* (*haben*) lie there

damalig *a* at that time; **der d~e Minister** the then minister

damals *adv* at that time

Damast *m* -es,-e damask

Dame *f* -,-n lady; (*Karte, Schach*) queen; (*D~spiel*) draughts *sg*, (*Amer*) checkers *sg*; (*Doppelstein*) king. **D~n-** *pref* ladies'/lady's... **d~nhaft** *a* ladylike

damit (*emphatic:* **damit**) *adv* with it/them; (*dadurch*) by it; **hör auf d~!** stop it! □ *conj* so that

dämlich *a* (*fam*) stupid, *adv* -ly

Damm *m* -[e]s,-e dam; (*Insel-*) causeway; **nicht auf dem D~** (*fam*) under the weather

dämmer|ig *a* dim; **es wird d~ig** dusk is falling. **D~licht** *nt* twilight. **d~n** *vi* (*haben*) (*Morgen:*) dawn; **der Abend d~t** dusk is falling; **es d~t** it is getting light; (*abends*) dark. **D~ung** *f* dawn; (*Abend-*) dusk

Dämon *m* -s,-en /-'mo:nən/ demon

Dampf *m* -[e]s,-e steam; (*Chem*) vapour. **d~en** *vi* (*haben*) steam

dämpfen *vt* (*Culin*) steam; (*fig*) muffle (*Ton*); lower (*Stimme*); dampen (*Enthusiasmus*)

Dampf|er *m* -s,- steamer. **D~kochtopf** *m* pressure-cooker. **D~maschine** *f* steam engine. **D~walze** *f* steamroller

Damwild *nt* fallow deer *pl*

danach (*emphatic:* **danach**) *adv* after it/them; (*suchen*) for it/them; (*riechen*) of it; (*später*) afterwards; (*entsprechend*) accordingly; **es sieht d~ aus** it looks like it

Däne *m* -n,-n Dane

daneben (*emphatic:* **daneben**) *adv* beside it/them; (*außerdem*) in addition; (*verglichen damit*) by comparison. **d~gehen†** *vi sep* (*sein*) miss; (*scheitern*) fail

Dän|emark *nt* -s Denmark. **D~in** *f* -,-nen Dane. **d~isch** *a* Danish

Dank *m* -es thanks *pl*; **vielen D~!** thank you very much! **d~** *prep* (+ *dat or gen*) thanks to. **d~bar** *a* grateful, *adv* -ly; (*erleichtert*)

thankful, *adv* -ly; *(lohnend)* rewarding. **D~barkeit** *f* - gratitude. **d~e** *adv* **d~e** *[schön od sehr]!* thank you [very much]! *[nein]* **d~e!** no thank you! **d~en** *vi (haben)* thank (**jdm** s.o.); *(ablehnen)* decline; **ich d~e!** no thank you! **nichts zu d~en!** don't mention it!

dann *adv* then; **d~ und wann** now and then; **nur/selbst d~, wenn** only/even if

daran *(emphatic:* **daran**) *adv* on it/them; at it/them; *(denken)* of it; **nahe d~** on the point (**etw zu tun** of doing sth); **denkt d~!** remember! **d~gehen†** *vi sep (sein),* **d~machen (sich)** *vr sep* set about (**etw zu tun** doing sth). **d~setzen** *vt sep* **alles d~setzen** do one's utmost (**zu** to)

darauf *(emphatic:* **darauf**) *adv* on it/them; *(warten)* for it; *(antworten)* to it; *(danach)* after that; *(d~hin)* as a result; **am Tag d~** the day after; **am d~folgenden Tag** the following *or* next day. **d~folgend** *a* (NEW) **d~ folgend**, s. **darauf. d~hin** *adv* as a result

daraus *(emphatic:* **daraus**) *adv* out of *or* from it/them; **er macht sich nichts d~** he doesn't care for it; **was ist d~ geworden?** what has become of it?

Darbietung *f* -,**-en** performance; *(Nummer)* item

darin *(emphatic:* **darin**) *adv* in it/them

darlegen *vt sep* expound; *(erklären)* explain

Darlehen *nt* -s,- loan

Darm *m* -[e]s,**-e** intestine; *(Wurst-)* skin. **D~grippe** *f* gastric flu

darstell|en *vt sep* represent; *(bildlich)* portray; *(Theat)* interpret; *(spielen)* play; *(schildern)* describe. **D~er** *m* -s,- actor. **D~erin** *f* -,**-nen** actress. **D~ung**

f representation; interpretation; description; *(Bericht)* account

darüber *(emphatic:* **darüber**) *adv* over it/them; *(höher)* above it/them; *(sprechen, lachen, sich freuen)* about it; *(mehr)* more; *(inzwischen)* in the meantime; **d~hinaus** beyond [it]; *(dazu)* on top of that

darum *(emphatic:* **darum**) *adv* round it/them; *(bitten, kämpfen)* for it; *(deshalb)* that is why; **d~, weil** because

darunter *(emphatic:* **darunter**) *adv* under it/them; *(tiefer)* below it/them; *(weniger)* less; *(dazwischen)* among them

das *def art & pron s. der*

dasein† *vi sep (sein)* (NEW) **da sein**, s. **da. D~** *nt* -s existence

dasitzen† *vi sep (haben)* sit there

dasjenige *pron s. derjenige*

dass *(daß)* *conj* that; **d~ du nicht fällst!** mind you don't fall!

dasselbe *pron s. derselbe*

dastehen† *vi sep (haben)* stand there; **allein d~** *(fig)* be alone

Daten *pl* visual display unit, VDU. **D~verarbeitung** *f* data processing

datieren *vt/i (haben)* date

Dativ *m* -s,-**e** dative. **D~objekt** *nt* indirect object

Dattel *f* -,-**n** date

Datum *nt* s,-**ten** date; **Daten** dates; *(Angaben)* data

Dauer *f* - duration, length; *(Jur)* term; **von D~** lasting; **auf die D~** in the long run. **D~auftrag** *m* standing order. **d~haft** *a* lasting, enduring; *(fest)* durable. **D~karte** *f* season ticket. **D~lauf m im D~lauf** at a jog. **D~milch** *f* long-life milk. **d~n** *vi (haben)* last; **lange d~n** take a long time. **d~nd** *a* lasting; *(ständig)* constant, *adv* -ly; **d~nd fragen** keep asking. **D~stellung** *f* permanent position. **D~welle** *f* perm. **D~wurst** *f* salami-type sausage

Daumen *m* -s,- thumb; **jdm den D~drücken** *od* **halten** keep one's fingers crossed for s.o.

Daunen *fpl* down *sg*. **D~decke** *f* [down-filled] duvet

davon (*emphatic*: **dạvon**) *adv* from it/them; (*dadurch*) by it; (*damit*) with it/them; (*darüber*) about it; (*Menge*) of it; **die Hälfte d~** half of it/them; **das kommt d~!** it serves you right!

d~kommen *vi sep* (*sein*) escape (**mit dem Leben** with one's life). **d~laufen** *vi sep* (*sein*) run away.

d~machen (**sich**) *vr sep* (*fam*) make off. **d~tragen** *vt sep* carry off; (*erleiden*) suffer; (*gewinnen*) win

davor (*emphatic*: **dạvor**) *adv* in front of it/them; (*sich fürchten*) of it; (*zeitlich*) before it/them

dazu (*emphatic*: **dạzu**) *adv* to it; (*damit*) with it/them; (*dafür*) for it; **noch d~** in addition to that; **jdn d~bringen, etw zu tun** get s.o. to do sth; **ich kam nicht d~** I didn't get round to [doing] it. **d~gehören** *vi sep* (*haben*) belong to it/them; **alles, was d~gehört** everything that goes with it. **d~kommen** *vi sep* (*sein*) arrive [on the scene]; (*hinzukommen*) be added; (*hinzukommt, dass er krank ist* on top of that he is ill. **d~rechnen** *vt sep* add to it/them

dazwischen (*emphatic*: **dazwischen**) *adv* between them; in between; (*darunter*) among them. **d~fahren** *vi sep* (*sein*) (*fig*) intervene. **d~kommen** *vi sep* (*sein*) (*fig*) crop up; **wenn nichts d~kommt** if all goes well. **d~reden** *vi sep* (*haben*) interrupt. **d~treten** *vi sep* (*sein*) (*fig*) intervene

DDR *f* -abbr (**Deutsche Demokratische Republik**) GDR

Debatt|**e** *f* -,-n debate; **zur D~te stehen** be at issue. **d~tieren** *vt/i* (*haben*) debate

Debüt /de'by:/ *nt* -s,-s début

dechiffrieren /deʃɪ'fri:rən/ *vt* decipher

Deck *nt* -[e]s,-s (*Naut*) deck; **an D~** on deck. **D~bett** *nt* duvet

Decke *f* -,-n cover; (*Tisch-*) tablecloth; (*Bett-*) blanket; (*Reise-*) rug; (*Zimmer-*) ceiling; **unter einer D~stecken** (*fam*) be in league

Deckel *m* -s,- lid; (*Flaschen-*) top; (*Buch-*) cover

decken *vt* cover; tile (*Dach*); lay (*Tisch*); (*schützen*) shield; (*Sport*) mark; meet (*Bedarf*); **jdn d~** (*fig*) cover up for s.o.; **sich d~** (*fig*) cover oneself (**gegen** against); (*übereinstimmen*) coincide

Deck|**mantel** *m* (*fig*) pretence. **D~name** *m* pseudonym

Deckung *f* - (*Mil*) cover; (*Sport*) defence; (*Mann-*) marking; (*Boxen*) guard; (*Fin*) security; **in D~gehen** take cover

Defekt *m* -[e]s,-e defect. **d~** *a* defective

defensiv *a* defensive. **D~e** *f* -defensive

defilieren *vi* (*sein/haben*) file past

defin|**ieren** *vt* define. **D~ition** /-'tsjo:n/ *f* -,-en definition. **d~itiv** *a* definite, *adv* -ly

Defizit *nt* -s,-e deficit

Deflation /-'tsjo:n/ *f* - deflation

deformiert *a* deformed

deftig *a* (*fam*) (*Mahlzeit*) hearty; (*Witz*) coarse

Degen *m* -s,- sword; (*Fecht-*) épée

degenerier|**en** *vi* (*sein*) degenerate. **d~t** *a* (*fig*) degenerate

degradieren *vt* (*Mil*) demote; (*fig*) degrade

dehn|**bar** *a* elastic. **d~en** *vt* stretch; lengthen (*Vokal*); **sich d~en** stretch

Deich *m* -[e]s,-e dike

Deichsel *f* -,-n pole; (*Gabel-*) shafts *pl*

dein poss pron your. **d~e(r,s)** poss pron yours; **die D~en** *od* **d~en** *pl* your family *sg*. **d~erseits** *adv*

for your part. **d~etwegen** *adv*
for your sake; (*wegen dir*) because of you, on your account.
d~etwillen *adv* um **d~etwillen**
for your sake. **d~ige** *poss pron*
der/die/das d~ige yours. **d~s**
poss pron yours

Deka *nt* -[s],- (*Aust*) = **Dekagramm**

dekadent *a* decadent. **D~z** *f* -
decadence

Dekagramm *nt* (*Aust*) 10 grams;
10 **D~** 100 grams

Dekan *m* -s,-e dean

Deklin|ation /-'tsjo:n/ *f* -,-en de-
clension. **d~ieren** *vt* decline

Dekolleté, Dekolletee /dekɔl'te:/
nt -s,-s low neckline

Dekor *m* & *nt* -s decoration.
D~ateur /-'tø:ɐ/ *m* -s,-e interior
decorator; (*Schaufenster-*) win-
dow-dresser. **D~ation** /-'tsjo:n/
f -,-en decoration; (*Schau-
fenster-*) window-dressing; (*Auslage*) display; **D~ationen**
(*Theat*) scenery *sg*. **d~ativ** *a* decorative. **d~ieren** *vt* decorate;
dress (*Schaufenster*)

Deleg|ation /-'tsjo:n/ *f* -,-en dele-
gation. **d~ieren** *vt* delegate.
D~ierte(r) *m/f* delegate

Delfin *m* -s,-e = **Delphin**

delikat *a* delicate; (*lecker*) delicious; (*taktvoll*) tactful, *adv* -ly.
D~esse *f* -,-n delicacy. **D~es-
sengeschäft** *nt* delicatessen

Delikt *nt* -[e]s,-e offence

Delinquent *m* -en,-en offender

Delirium *nt* -s delirium

Delle *f* -,-n dent

Delphin *m* -s,-e dolphin

Delta *nt* -s,-s delta

dem *def art* & *pron s.* **der**

Dement|i *nt* -s,-s denial. **d~ieren**
vt deny

dem|entsprechend *a* corres-
ponding; (*passend*) appropriate
□ *adv* accordingly; (*passend*) appropriately. **d~gemäß** *adv* accordingly. **d~nach** *adv*

according to that; (*folglich*) consequently. **d~nächst** *adv* soon;
(*in Kürze*) shortly

Demokrat *m* -en,-en democrat.
D~ie *f* -,-n democracy. **d~isch**
a democratic, *adv* -ally

demolieren *vt* wreck

Demonstr|ant *m* -en,-en demon-
strator. **D~ation** /-'tsjo:n/ *f* -,-en
demonstration. **d~ativ** *a*
pointed, *adv* -ly; (*Gram*) demonstrative. **D~ativpronomen** *nt*
demonstrative pronoun.
d~ieren *vt/i* (*haben*) demonstrate

demontieren *vt* dismantle

demoralisieren *vt* demoralize

Demoskopie *f* -opinion research

Demut *f* - humility

demütig *a* humble, *adv* -bly.
d~en *vt* humiliate; **sich d~en**
humble oneself. **D~ung** *f* -,-en
humiliation

demzufolge *adv* = demnach

den *def art* & *pron s.* **der**. **d~en**
pron s. **der**

denk|bar *a* conceivable. **d~en†**
vt/i (*haben*) think (**an** + *acc* of);
(*sich erinnern*) remember (**an**
etw *acc* sth); **für jdn gedacht**
meant for s.o.; **das kann ich mir
d~en** I can imagine [that]; **ich
d~e nicht daran** I have no intention of doing it; **d~t daran!**
don't forget! **D~mal** *nt* memorial; (*Monument*) monument.
d~würdig *a* memorable.
D~zettel *m* jdm einen **D~zettel**
geben (*fam*) teach s.o. a lesson

denn *conj* for; besser/mehr **d~je**
better/more than ever □ *adv*
wie/wo **d~**? but how/where?
warum **d~** nicht? why ever not?
es sei **d~** [, **dass**] unless

dennoch *adv* nevertheless

Denunz|iant *m* -en,-en informer.
d~ieren *vt* denounce

Deodorant *nt* -s,-s deodorant

**deplaciert, deplatziert (depla-
ziert)** /-'tsi:ɐt/ *a* (*fig*) out of place

Deponie *f* -,-n dump. **d~ren** *vt* deposit

deportieren *vt* deport

Depot /de'po:/ *nt* -s,-s depot; (*Lager*) warehouse; (*Bank-*) safe deposit

Depression *f* -,-en depression

deprimieren *vt* depress. **d~d** *a* depressing

Deputation /-'tsjo:n/ *f* -,-en deputation

der, die, das, *pl* **die** *def art* (*acc* **den, die, das,** *pl* **die**; *gen* **des, der, des, der**; *dat* **dem, der, dem,** *pl* **den**) the; **der Mensch** man; **die Natur** nature; **das Leben** life; **das Lesen/Tanzen** reading/dancing; **sich** (*dat*) **das Gesicht/die Hände waschen** wash one's face/hands; **5 Mark das Pfund** 5 marks a pound □ *rel pron* (*acc* **den, die, das,** *pl* **die**; *gen* **dessen, deren, dessen,** *pl* **deren**; *dat* **dem, der, dem,** *pl* **denen**) □ *dem pron* that; (*pl*) those; (*substantivisch*) he, she, it; (*Ding*) it; (*betont*) that; (**d~jenige**) the one; (*pl*) they, those; (*Dinge*) those; (**diejenigen**) the ones; **der und der** such and such; **um die und die Zeit** at such and such a time; **das waren Zeiten!** those were the days! □ *rel pron* who; (*Ding*) which, that

derart *adv* so; (*so sehr*) so much. **d~ig** *a* such □ *adv* = **derart**

derb *a* tough; (*kräftig*) strong; (*grob*) coarse, *adv* -ly; (*unsanft*) rough, *adv* -ly

deren *pron s.* **der**

dergleichen *inv a* such □ *pron* such a thing/such things; **nichts d~** nothing of the kind; **und d~** and the like

der-/die-/dasjenige, *pl* **diejenigen** *pron* the one; (*Person*) he, she; (*Ding*) it; (*pl*) those, the ones

dermaßen *adv* = **derart**

der-/die-/dasselbe, *pl* **dieselben** *pron* the same; **ein- und**

dasselbe one and the same thing

derzeit *adv* at present

des *def art s.* **der**

Desert|eur /-'tø:ɐ̯/ *m* -s,-e deserter. **d~ieren** *vi* (*sein/haben*) desert

desgleichen *adv* likewise □ *pron* the like

deshalb *adv* for this reason; (*also*) therefore

Designer(in) /di'zaɪne, -nərɪn/ *m* -s,- (*f,* -,-nen) designer

Desin|fektion /dɛs'ʔɪnfɛk'tsjo:n/ *f* disinfecting. **D~fektionsmittel** *nt* disinfectant. **d~fizieren** *vt* disinfect

Desodorant *nt* -s,-s deodorant

Despot *m* -en,-en despot

dessen *pron s.* **der**

Dessert /dɛ'se:ɐ̯/ *nt* -s,-s dessert, sweet. **D~löffel** *m* dessertspoon

Destill|ation /-'tsjo:n/ *f* - distillation. **d~ieren** *vt* distil

desto *adv* je **mehr/eher,** **d~besser** the more/sooner the better

destruktiv *a* (*fig*) destructive

deswegen *adv* = **deshalb**

Detail /de'taɪ/ *nt* -s,-s detail

Detektiv *m* -s,-e detective. **D~roman** *m* detective story

Deton|ation /-'tsjo:n/ *f* -,-en explosion. **d~ieren** *vi* (*sein*) explode

deut|en *vt* interpret; predict (*Zukunft*) □ *vi* (*haben*) point (**auf** + *acc* at/*fig* to). **d~lich** *a* clear, *adv* -ly; (*eindeutig*) plain, *adv* -ly. **D~lichkeit** *f* - clarity

deutsch *a* German; **auf d~** NEW **auf D~,** *s.* **Deutsch. D~** *nt* -[s] (*Lang*) German; **auf D~** in German. **D~e(r)** *m/f* German. **D~land** *nt* -s Germany

Deutung *f* -,-en interpretation

Devise /-'vi:zə/ *f* -,-n motto. **D~n** *pl* foreign currency or exchange *sg*

Dezember *m* -s,- December

dezent *a* unobtrusive, *adv* -ly; (*diskret*) discreet, *adv* -ly

Dezernat nt -[e]s,-e department
Dezimal|system nt decimal system. D~zahl f decimal
dezimieren vt decimate
dgl. abbr s. dergleichen
d.h. abbr (das heißt) i.e.
Dia nt -s,-s (Phot) slide
Diabet|es m -, diabetes. D~iker m -s,- diabetic
Diadem nt -s,-e tiara
Diagnos|e f -,-n diagnosis. D~tizieren vt diagnose
diagonal a diagonal, adv -ly. D~e f -,-n diagonal
Diagramm nt -s,-e diagram; (Kurven-) graph
Diakon m -s,-e deacon
Dialekt m -[e]s,-e dialect
Dialog m -[e]s,-e dialogue
Diamant m -en,-en diamond
Diameter m -s,- diameter
Diapositiv nt -s,-e (Phot) slide
Diaprojektor m slide projector
Diät f -,-en (Med) diet; D~ leben be on a diet. d~ adv d~ leben (NEW) D~ leben, s. Diät. D~assistent(in) m(f) dietician
dich pron (acc of du) you; (refl) yourself
dicht a dense; (dick) thick; (undurchlässig) airtight; (wasser-) watertight □ adv densely; thickly; (nahe) close (bei zu). D~e f density. d~en¹ vt make watertight; (ab-) seal
dicht|en² vi (haben) write poetry. □ vt write, compose. D~er(in) m -s,- (f -,-nen) poet. d~erisch a poetic. D~ung¹ f -,-en poetry; (Gedicht) poem
Dichtung² f -,-en seal; (Ring) washer; (Auto) gasket
dick a thick, adv -ly; (beleibt) fat; (geschwollen) swollen; (fam; eng) close; d~ werden get fat; d~ machen be fattening; ein d~es Fell haben (fam) be thick-skinned. d~ n thickness; (D~leibigkeit) fatness. d~fellig a (fam) thick-skinned. d~flüssig

a thick; (Phys) viscous. D~kopf m (fam) stubborn person; einen D~kopf haben be stubborn. d~köpfig a (fam) stubborn
didaktisch a didactic
die def art & pron s. der
Dieb|(in) m -[e]s,-e (f -,-nen) thief. d~isch a thieving; (Freude) malicious. D~stahl m -[e]s,-e theft; (geistig) plagiarism
diejenige pron s. derjenige
Diele f -,-n floorboard; (Flur) hall
dien|en vi (haben) serve. D~er m -s,- servant; (Verbeugung) bow. D~erin f -,-nen maid, servant. d~lich a helpful
Dienst m -[e]s,-e service; (Arbeit) work; (Amtsausübung) duty; außer D~ off duty; (pensioniert) retired; D~ haben work; (Soldat, Arzt.) be on duty; der D~ habende Arzt the duty doctor; jdm einen schlechten D~ erweisen do s.o. a disservice
Dienstag m Tuesday. d~s adv on Tuesdays
Dienst|alter nt seniority. D~bereit a obliging; (Apotheke) open. D~bote m servant. d~eifrig a zealous, adv -ly. d~frei a d~freier Tag day off; d~frei haben have time off; (Soldat, Arzt.) be off duty. D~grad m rank. d~habend a (NEW) d~habend, s. Dienst. D~leistung f service. d~lich a official □ adv ness. D~mädchen nt maid. D~reise f business trip. D~stelle f office. D~stunden fpl office hours. D~weg m official channels pl
dies inv pron this. d~bezüglich a relevant □ adv regarding this matter. d~e(r,s) pron this; (pl) these; (substantivisch) this [one]; (pl) these; d~e Nacht tonight; (letzte) last night
Diesel m -[s],- (fam) diesel
dieselbe pron s. derselbe
Diesel|kraftstoff m diesel [oil]. D~motor m diesel engine

diesig a hazy, misty

dies|mal adv this time. **d~seits** adv & prep (+ gen) this side of (an)

Dietrich m -s,-e skeleton key

Diffam|ation /-'tsjo:n/ f -defamation. **d~ieren** vt/i (haben) differentiate (**zwischen** + dat between)

Digital- pref digital. **D~uhr** f digital clock/watch

Dikt|at nt -[e]s,-e dictation. **D~ator** m -s,-en /-'to:rən/ dictator. **d~atorisch** a dictatorial. **D~atur** f -,-en dictatorship. **d~ieren** vt/i (haben) dictate

Dilemma nt -s,-s dilemma

Dilettant|(in) m -en,-en (f -,-nen) dilettante. **d~isch** a amateurish

Dill m -s dill

Dimension f -,-en dimension

Ding nt -[e]s,-e & (fam) -er thing; **guter D~e sein** be cheerful; **vor allem D~en** above all

Dinghi /'dɪŋgi/ nt -s,-s dinghy

Dinosaurier /-je/ m -s,- dinosaur

Diözese f -,-n diocese

Diphtherie f -,-n diphtheria

Diplom nt -s,-e diploma; (Univ) degree

Diplomat m -en,-en diplomat. **D~ie** f -,-n diplomacy. **d~isch** a diplomatic, adv -ally

dir pron (dat of **du**) [to] you; (refl) yourself; **ein Freund von dir** a friend of yours

direkt a direct □ adv directly; (wirklich) really. **D~ion** /-'tsjo:n/ f - management; (Vorstand) board of directors. **D~or** m -s, -en /-'to:rən/, **D~orin** f -,-nen director; (Bank-, Theater-) manager; (Sch) head; (Gefängnis-) governor. **D~übertragung** f live transmission

Dirig|ent m -en,-en (Mus) conductor. **d~ieren** vt direct; (Mus) conduct

Dirndl nt -s,- dirndl [dress]

Dirne f -,-n prostitute

Diskant m -s,-e (Mus) treble

Diskette f -,-n floppy disc

Disko f -,-s (fam) disco. **D~thek** f -,-en discothèque

Diskrepanz f -,-en discrepancy

diskret a discreet, adv -ly. **D~ion** /-'tsjo:n/ f - discretion

diskriminier|en vt discriminate against. **D~ung** f - discrimination

Diskus m -,-se & **Disken** discus

Disku|ssion f -,-en discussion. **d~tieren** vt/i (haben) discuss

disponieren vt (haben) make arrangements; **d~ [können] über** (+ acc) have at one's disposal

Disput m -[e]s,-e dispute

Disqualifi|kation /-'tsjo:n/ f disqualification. **D~zieren** vt disqualify

Dissertation /-'tsjo:n/ f -,-en dissertation

Dissident m -en,-en dissident

Dissonanz f -,-en dissonance

Distanz f -,-en distance. **d~ieren (sich)** vr dissociate oneself (**von** from). **d~iert** a aloof

Distel f -,-n thistle

distinguiert /dɪstɪŋ'gi:ɐ̯t/ a distinguished

Disziplin f -,-en discipline. **d~arisch** a disciplinary. **d~iert** a disciplined

dito adv ditto

diverse attrib a pl various

Divid|ende f -,-en dividend. **d~ieren** vt divide (**durch** by)

Division f -,-en division

DJH abbr (**Deutsche Jugendherberge**) [German] youth hostel

DM abbr (**Deutsche Mark**) DM

doch conj & adv but; (dennoch) yet; (trotzdem) after all; **wenn d~ ...!** if only ...! **nicht d~!** don't [do that]! **er kommt d~?** he is coming, isn't he? **kommst du nicht?—d~!** aren't you coming? —yes, I am!

Docht m -[e]s,-e wick

Dock nt -s,-s dock. **d~en** vt/i (haben) dock

Dogge f -,-n Great Dane

Dogm|a nt -s,-men dogma. **d~atisch** a dogmatic, adv -ally

Dohle f -,-n jackdaw

Doktor m -s,-en /-'to:rən/ doctor. **D~arbeit** f [doctoral] thesis. **D~würde** f doctorate

Doktrin f -,-en doctrine

Dokument nt -[e]s,-e document. **D~arbericht** m documentary. **D~arfilm** m documentary film

Dolch m -[e]s,-e dagger

doll a (fam) fantastic; (schlimm) awful □ adv beautifully; (sehr) very; (schlimm) badly

Dollar m -s,- dollar

dolmetsch|en vt/i (haben) interpret. **D~er(in)** m -s,- (f -,-nen) interpreter

Dom m -[e]s,-e cathedral

domin|ant a dominant. **D~ieren** vi (haben) dominate; (vorherrschen) predominate

Domino nt -s,-s dominoes sg. **D~stein** m domino

Dompfaff m -en,-en bullfinch

Donau f - Danube

Donner m -s,- thunder. **d~n** vi (haben) thunder

Donnerstag m Thursday. **d~s** adv on Thursdays

Donnerwetter nt (fam) telling-off; (Krach) row □ int /'--'--/ wow! (Fluch) damn it!

doof a (fam) stupid, adv -ly

Doppel nt -s,- duplicate; (Tennis) doubles pl. **D~bett** nt double bed. **D~decker** m -s,- double-decker [bus]. **d~deutig** a ambiguous. **D~gänger** m -s,- double. **D~kinn** nt double chin. **D~name** m double-barrelled name. **D~punkt** m (Gram) colon. **D~schnitte** f sandwich. **d~sinnig** a ambiguous. **D~stecker** m two-way adaptor. **d~t** a double; (Boden) false; in **d~ter**

Ausfertigung in duplicate; die **d~te** Menge twice the amount □ adv doubly; (zweimal) twice; **d~t so viel** twice as much.

D~zimmer nt double room

Dorf nt -[e]s,-er village. **D~bewohner** m villager

dörflich a rural

Dorn m -[e]s,-en thorn. **d~ig** a thorny

Dörrobst nt dried fruit

Dorsch m -[e]s,-e cod

dort adv there; **d~ drüben** over there. **d~her** adv [von] **d~her** from there. **d~hin** adv there.

d~ig a local

Dose f -,-n tin, can; (Schmuck-) box

dösen vi (haben) doze

Dosen|milch f evaporated milk. **D~öffner** m tin or can opener

dosieren vt measure out

Dosis f -, **Dosen** dose

Dotter m & nt -s,- [egg] yolk

Dozent(in) m -en,-en (f -,-nen) (Univ) lecturer

Dr. abbr (Doktor) Dr

Drache m -n,-n dragon. **D~n** m -s,- kite; (fam: Frau) dragon. **D~nfliegen** nt hang-gliding. **D~nflieger** m hang-glider

Draht m -[e]s,-e wire; **auf D~** (fam) on the ball. **d~ig** a (fig) wiry. **D~seilbahn** f cable railway

drall a plump; (Frau) buxom

Dram|a nt -s,-men drama. **D~atik** f - drama. **D~atiker** m -s,- dramatist. **d~atisch** a dramatic, adv -ally. **d~atisieren** vt dramatize

dran adv (fam) = **daran**; **gut/schlecht d~ sein** be well off/in a bad way; **ich bin d~** it's my turn

Dränage /-'na:ʒə/ f - drainage

Drang m -[e]s urge; (Druck) pressure

drängeln vt/i (haben) push; (bedrängen) pester. **d~en** vt push;

(bedrängen) urge; **sich d~en** crowd (**um** round) □ *vi (haben)* push; *(eilen)* be urgent; *(Zeit:)* press; **d~en auf** (+ *acc*) press for

dran|halten† **(sich)** *vr sep* hurry. **d~kommen†** *vi sep (sein)* have one's turn; **wer kommt dran?** whose turn is it?

drapieren *vt* drape

drastisch *a* drastic, *adv* -ally

drauf *adv (fam)* = **darauf**; **d~und dran sein** be on the point (**etw zu tun** of doing sth). **D~gänger** *m* -s, -daredevil. **d~gängerisch** *a* reckless

draus *adv (fam)* = **daraus**

draußen *adv* outside; *(im Freien)* out of doors

drechseln *vt (Techn)* turn

Dreck *m* -s *(fam)* dirt; *(Morast)* mud; *(fam: Kleinigkeit)* trifle; **in den D~ziehen** *(fig)* denigrate. **d~ig** *a* dirty; *(fig)* dirty; muddy

Dreh *m* -s *(fam)* knack; **den D~ heraushaben** have got the hang of it. **D~bank** *f* lathe. **D~bleistift** *m* propelling pencil. **D~buch** *nt* screenplay, script. **d~en** *vt* turn; *(in Kreis)* rotate; *(verschlingen)* twist; roll *(Zigarette)*; shoot *(Film)*; **lauter/leiser d~en** turn up/down; **sich d~en** turn; *(im Kreis)* rotate; *(schnell)* spin; *(Wind:)* change; **sich um ... d~en** revolve around; *(sich handeln)* be about □ *vi (haben)* turn; *(Wind:)* change. **an etw** *(dat)* **d~en** turn sth. **D~orgel** *f* barrel organ. **D~stuhl** *m* swivel chair. **D~tür** *f* revolving door. **D~ung** *f* -,-en turn; *(im Kreis)* rotation.

D~zahl *f* number of revolutions

drei *inv a*, **D~** *f* -,-en three; *(Sch)* ≈ pass. **D~eck** *nt* -[e]s,-e triangle. **d~eckig** *a* triangular. **D~einigkeit** *f* - **die [Heilige] D~einigkeit** the [Holy] Trinity. **d~erlei** *inv* a three kinds of □ *pron* three things. **d~fach** *a* triple; **in d~facher Ausfertigung** in triplicate. **D~faltigkeit**

f - = **D~einigkeit**. **d~mal** *adv* three times. **D~rad** *nt* tricycle

dreißig *inv a* thirty. **d~ste(r,s)** *a* thirtieth

dreist *a* impudent, *adv* -ly; *(verwegen)* audacious, *adv* -ly. **D~igkeit** *f* - impudence; audacity

dreiviertel *inv a* <NEW> **drei viertel**, *s.* **viertel**. **D~stunde** *f* three-quarters of an hour

dreizehn *inv a* thirteen. **d~te(r,s)** *a* thirteenth

dreschen† *vt* thresh

dressieren *vt* train. **D~ur** *f* -training

dribbeln *vi (haben)* dribble

Drill *m* -[e]s *(Mil)* drill. **d~en** *vt* drill

Drillinge *mpl* triplets

drin *adv (fam)* = **darin**; *(drinnen)* inside

dringen† *vi (sein)* penetrate (**in** + *acc* into; **durch etw** sth); *(heraus:)* come (**aus** out of); **d~en auf** (+ *acc*) insist on. **d~end** *a* urgent, *adv* -ly. **d~lich** *a* urgent. **D~lichkeit** *f* - urgency

Drink *m* -[s],-s [alcoholic] drink

drinnen *adv* inside; *(im Haus)* indoors

dritt *adv* **zu d~** in threes; **wir waren zu d~** there were three of us. **d~e(r,s)** *a* third; **ein D~er** a third person. **d~el** *inv a* third; **ein d~el Apfel** a third of an apple. **D~el** *nt* -s,- third. **d~ens** *adv* thirdly. **d~rangig** *a* third-rate

Droge *f* -,-n drug. **D~enabhängige(r)** *m/f* drug addict. **D~erie** *f* -,-n chemist's shop, *(Amer)* drugstore. **D~ist** *m* -en,-en chemist

drohen *vi (haben)* threaten (**jdm** s.o.). **d~d** *a* threatening; *(Gefahr)* imminent

dröhnen *vi (haben)* resound; *(tönen)* boom

Drohung *f* -,-en threat

drollig a funny; (seltsam) odd

Drops m -, [fruit] drop

Droschke f -,-n cab

Drossel f -,-n thrush

drosseln vt (Techn) throttle; (fig) cut back

drüb|en adv over there. **d~er** adv (fam) = darüber

Druck¹ m -[e]s,-̈e pressure; **unter D~setzen** (fig) pressurize

Druck² m -[e]s,-e printing; (Schrift, Reproduktion) print. **D~buchstabe** m block letter

Drückeberger m -s,- shirker

drucken vt print

drücken vt/i (haben) press; (aus-) squeeze; (Schuh:) pinch; (umar-men) hug; (fig: belasten) weigh down; **Preise** ~ force down prices; (an Tür) **d~** push; **sich** ~ (fam) make oneself scarce; **sich d~ vor** (+ dat) (fam) shirk. **d~d** a heavy; (schwül) oppressive

Drucker m -s,- printer

Drücker m -s,- push-button; (Tür-) door knob

Druckerei f -,-en printing works

Druck|fehler m misprint. **D~knopf** m press-stud; (Drücker) push-button. **D~luft** f compressed air. **D~sache** f printed matter. **D~schrift** f type; (Veröffentlichung) publication; **in D~schrift** in block letters pl

drucksen vi (haben) hum and haw

Druck|stelle f bruise. **D~taste** f push-button. **D~topf** m pressure-cooker

drum adv (fam) = darum

drunter adv (fam) = darunter; **alles geht d~ und drüber** (fam) everything is topsy-turvy

Drüse f -,-n (Anat) gland

Dschungel m -s,- jungle

du pron (familiar address) you; **auf Du und Du (auf du und du)** on familiar terms

Dübel m -s,- plug

duck|en vt duck; (fig: demütigen) humiliate; **sich~en** duck; (fig) cringe. **D~mäuser** m -s,- moral coward

Dudelsack m bagpipes pl

Duell nt -s,-e duel

Duett nt -[e]s,-e [vocal] duet

Duft m -[e]s,-̈e fragrance, scent; (Aroma) aroma. **d~en** vi (haben) smell (nach of). **d~ig** a fine; (zart) delicate

duld|en vt tolerate; (erleiden) suffer □ vi (haben) suffer. **d~sam** a tolerant

dumm a (dümmer, dümmst) stupid, adv -ly; (unklug) foolish, adv -ly; (fam: lästig) awkward; **wie d~!** what a nuisance! **der D~e sein** (fig) be the loser. **d~erweise** adv stupidly; (leider) unfortunately. **D~heit** f -,-en stupidity; (Torheit) stupidity; (Handlung) folly. **D~kopf** m (fam) fool.

dumpf a dull, adv -y; (muffig) musty. **d~ig** a musty

Düne f -,-n dune

Dung m -s manure

Düng|emittel nt fertilizer. **d~en** vt fertilize. **D~er** m -s,- fertilizer

dunkel a dark; (vage) vague, adv -ly; (fragwürdig) shady; **d~les Bier** brown ale; **im D~eln** in the dark

Dünkel m -s conceit

dunkel|blau a dark blue. **d~braun** a dark brown

dünkelhaft a conceited

Dunkel|heit f - darkness. **D~kammer** f dark-room. **d~n** vi (haben) get dark. **d~rot** a dark red

dünn a thin, adv -ly; (Buch) slim; (spärlich) sparse; (schwach) weak

Dunst m -es,-̈e mist, haze; (Dampf) vapour

dünsten vt steam

dunstig a misty, hazy

Dünung f - swell

Duo nt -s,-s [instrumental] duet

Duplikat nt -[e]s,-e duplicate

Dur nt - (Mus) major [key]; **in A-Dur** in A major

durch prep (+ acc) through; (mittels) by; [geteilt] **durch** divided by □adv **die Nacht d~** throughout the night; **sechs Uhr d~** (fam) gone six o'clock; **d~und d~ nass** wet through

durcharbeiten vt sep work through; **sich d~** work one's way through

durchaus adv absolutely; **d~nicht** by no means

durchbeißen† vt sep bite through

durchblättern vt sep leaf through

durchblicken vi sep (haben) look through; **d~ lassen** (fig) hint at

Durchblutung f circulation

durchbohren vt insep pierce

durchbrechen†1 vt/i sep (haben) break [in two]

durchbrechen†2 vt insep break through; break (Schallmauer)

durchbrennen† vi sep(sein) burn through; (Sicherung:) blow; (fam: weglaufen) run away

durchbringen† vt sep get through; (verschwenden) squander; (versorgen) support; **sich d~ mit** make a living by

Durchbruch m breakthrough

durchdacht a **gut d~** well thought out

durchdrehen v sep □vt mince □vi (haben/sein) (fam) go crazy

durchdringen†1 vt insep penetrate

durchdringen†2 vi sep (sein) penetrate; (sich durchsetzen) get one's way. **d~d** a penetrating; (Schrei) piercing

durcheinander adv in a muddle; (Person) confused; **d~ bringen** muddle [up]; confuse (Person); **d~ geraten** get mixed up; **d~ reden** all talk at once. **D~** nt -s muddle

durcheinander† vt sep

NEW **d~ bringen**, s. durcheinander. **d~geraten†** vi sep (sein) NEW **d~ geraten**, s. durcheinander. **d~reden** vi sep (haben) NEW **d~ reden**, s. durcheinander

durchfahren†1 vi sep (sein) drive through; (Zug:) go through

durchfahren†2 vt insep drive through; jdn d~ (Gedanke:) flash through s.o.'s mind

Durchfahrt f journey/drive through; **auf der D~** passing through; **'D~ verboten'** 'no thoroughfare'

Durchfall m diarrhoea; (fam: Versagen) flop. **d~en†** vi sep (sein) fall through; (fam: versagen) flop; (bei Prüfung) fail

durchfliegen†1 vi sep (sein) fly through; (fam: durchfallen) fail

durchfliegen†2 vt insep fly through; (lesen) skim through

durchfroren a frozen

Durchfuhr f - (Comm) transit

durchführ|bar a feasible. **d~en** vt sep carry out

Durchgang m passage; (Sport) round; **'D~ verboten'** 'no entry'. **D~sverkehr** m through traffic

durchgeben† vt sep pass through; (übermitteln) transmit; (Radio, TV) broadcast

durchgebraten a **gut d~** well done

durchgehen† v sep □vi (sein) go through; (davonlaufen) run away; (Pferd:) bolt; **jdm etw d~ lassen** let s.o. get away with sth □vt go through. **d~d** a continuous, adv -ly; **d~ geöffnet** open all day; **d~der Wagen/Zug** through carriage/train

durchgreifen† vi sep (haben) reach through; (vorgehen) take drastic action. **d~d** a drastic

durchhalte|n† v sep (fig) □vi (haben) hold out □vt keep up. **D~vermögen** nt stamina

durchhängen† vi sep (haben) sag

durchkommen† *vi sep* (*sein*) come through; (*gelangen, am Telefon*) get through; (*bestehen*) pass; (*überleben*) pull through; (*finanziell*) get by (**mit** on)

durchkreuzen *vt insep* thwart

durchlassen† *vt sep* let through

durchlässig *a* permeable; (*undicht*) leaky

durchlaufen†¹ *v sep* □ *vi* (*sein*) run through □ *vt* wear out

durchlaufen†² *vt insep* pass through

Durchlauferhitzer *m* -s,- geyser

durchleben *vt insep* live through

durchlesen† *vt sep* read through

durchleuchten *vt insep* X-ray

durchlöchert *a* riddled with holes

durchmachen *vt sep* go through; (*erleiden*) undergo; have (*Krankheit*)

Durchmesser *m* -s,- diameter

durchnässt (durchnäßt) *a* wet through

durchnehmen† *vt sep* (*Sch*) do

durchnummerieren (durchnumerieren) *a* numbered consecutively

durchpausen *vt sep* trace

durchqueren *vt insep* cross

Durchreiche *f* -,-n [serving] hatch. **d∼n** *vt sep* pass through

Durchreise *f* journey through; **auf der D∼** passing through. **d∼n** *vi sep* (*sein*) pass through

durchreißen† *vt/i sep* (*sein*) tear

durchs = **durch das**

Durchsage *f* -,-n announcement. **d∼n** *vt sep* announce

durchschauen *vt insep* (*fig*) see through

durchscheinend *a* translucent

Durchschlag *m* carbon copy; (*Culin*) colander. **d∼en†** *v sep* □ *vt* (*Culin*) rub through a sieve; **sich d∼en** (*fig*) struggle through □ *vi* (*sein*) (*Sicherung:*) blow

durchschlagen†² *vt sep* smash

durchschlagend *a* (*fig*) effective; (*Erfolg*) resounding

durchschneiden† *vt sep* cut

Durchschnitt *m* average; **im D∼** on average. **d∼lich** *a* average □ *adv* on average. **D∼s-** *pref* average

Durchschrift *f* carbon copy

durchsehen† *v sep* □ *vi* (*haben*) see through □ *vt* look through

durchseihen *vt sep* strain

durchsetzen¹ *vt sep* force through; **sich d∼** assert oneself; (*Mode:*) catch on

durchsetzen² *vt insep* intersperse; (*infiltrieren*) infiltrate

Durchsicht *f* check

durchsichtig *a* transparent

durchsickern *vi sep* (*sein*) seep through; (*Neuigkeit:*) leak out

durchsprechen† *vt sep* discuss

durchstehen† *vt sep* (*fig*) come through

durchstreichen† *vt sep* cross out

durchsuch|en *vt insep* search. **D∼ung** *f* -,-en search

durchtrieben *a* cunning

durchwachsen *a* (*Speck*) streaky; (*fam: gemischt*) mixed

durchwacht *a* sleepless (*Nacht*)

durchwählen *vi sep* (*haben*) (*Teleph*) dial direct

durchweg *adv* without exception

durchweicht *a* soggy

durchwühlen *vt insep* rummage through; ransack (*Haus*)

durchziehen† *v sep* □ *vt* pull through □ *vi* (*sein*) pass through

durchzucken *vt insep* (*fig*) shoot through; **jdn d∼** (*Gedanke:*) flash through s.o.'s mind

Durchzug *m* through draught

dürfen† *vt & v aux* etw [tun] d∼ be allowed to do sth; **darf ich?** may I? **sie darf es nicht sehen** she must not see it; **ich hätte es nicht tun/sagen d∼** I ought not to have done/said it; **das dürfte nicht allzu schwer sein** that should not be too difficult

dürftig *a* poor; (*Mahlzeit*) scanty

dürr *a* dry; ⟨*Boden*⟩ arid; ⟨*mager*⟩ skinny. **D∼e** *f* -,-n drought

Durst *m* -[e]s thirst; **D∼haben** be thirsty. **d∼en** *vi* (*haben*) be thirsty. **d∼ig** *a* thirsty

Dusche *f* -,-n shower. **d∼n** *vi/r* (*haben*) **[sich] d∼n** have a shower

Düse *f* -,-n nozzle. **D∼nflugzeug** *nt* jet

düster *a* gloomy, ⟨*dunkel*⟩ dark

Dutzend *nt* -s,-e dozen. **d∼weise** *adv* by the dozen

duzen *vt* jdn **d∼** call s.o. 'du'

Dynam|ik *f* - dynamics *sg*; ⟨*fig*⟩ dynamism. **d∼isch** *a* dynamic; ⟨*Rente*⟩ index-linked

Dynamit *nt* -es dynamite

Dynamo *m* -s,-s dynamo

Dynastie *f* -,-n dynasty

D-Zug /'de:-/ *m* express [train]

E

Ebbe *f* -,-n low tide

eben *a* level; ⟨*glatt*⟩ smooth; **zu e∼er Erde** on the ground floor □ *adv* just; ⟨*genau*⟩ exactly; **e∼ noch** only just; ⟨*gerade vorhin*⟩ just now; **das ist es e∼!** that's just it! **[na] e∼** exactly! **E∼bild** *nt* image. **e∼bürtig** *a* equal; **jdm e∼bürtig sein** be s.o.'s equal

Ebene *f* -,-n ⟨*Geog*⟩ plain; ⟨*Geom*⟩ plane; ⟨*fig: Niveau*⟩ level

eben|falls *adv* also; **danke, e∼falls** thank you, [the] same to you. **E∼holz** *nt* ebony. **e∼mäßig** *a* regular, *adv* -ly. **e∼so** *adv* just the same; ⟨*ebenso sehr*⟩ just as much; **e∼so schön/teuer** just as beautiful/expensive; **e∼so gut** just as good; *adv* just as well; **e∼so sehr** just as much; **e∼so viel** just as much/many; **e∼so wenig** just as little/few; (*noch*) no more. **e∼sogut** *adv* NEW **e∼so**

gut, *s.* **ebenso**. **e∼sosehr** *adv* NEW **e∼so sehr**, *s.* **ebenso**. **e∼soviel** *adv* NEW **e∼so viel**, *s.* **ebenso**. **e∼so wenig**, *s.* **ebenso**

Eber *m* -s,- boar. **E∼esche** *f* rowan

ebnen *vt* level; ⟨*fig*⟩ smooth

Echo *nt* -s,-s echo. **e∼en** *vt/i* (*haben*) echo

echt *a* genuine, real; ⟨*authentisch*⟩ authentic; ⟨*Farbe*⟩ fast; ⟨*typisch*⟩ typical □ *adv* ⟨*fam*⟩ really; typically. **E∼heit** *f* - authenticity

Eck|ball *m* ⟨*Sport*⟩ corner. **E∼e** *f* -,-n corner; **um die E∼e bringen** ⟨*fam*⟩ bump off. **e∼ig** *a* angular; ⟨*Klammern*⟩ square; ⟨*unbeholfen*⟩ awkward. **E∼stein** *m* cornerstone. **E∼stoß** *m* = **E∼ball**. **E∼zahn** *m* canine tooth

Ecu, ECU /e'ky:/ *m* -[s],-[s] ecu

edel *a* noble, *adv* -bly; ⟨*wertvoll*⟩ precious; ⟨*fein*⟩ fine. **E∼mann** *m* (*pl* -leute) nobleman. **E∼mut** *m* magnanimity. **e∼mütig** *a* magnanimous, *adv* -ly. **E∼stahl** *m* stainless steel. **E∼stein** *m* precious stone

Efeu *m* -s ivy

Effekt *m* -[e]s,-e effect. **E∼en** *pl* securities. **e∼iv** *a* actual, *adv* -ly; ⟨*wirksam*⟩ effective, *adv* -ly. **e∼voll** *a* effective

EG *f* - *abbr* (Europäische Gemeinschaft) EC

egal *a* **das ist mir e∼** ⟨*fam*⟩ it's all the same to me □ *adv* **e∼ wie/wo** no matter how/where. **e∼itär** *a* egalitarian

Egge *f* -,-n harrow

Ego|ismus *m* - selfishness. **e∼ist(in)** *m* -en,-en (*f* -,-nen) egoist. **e∼istisch** *a* selfish, *adv* -ly. **e∼zentrisch** *a* egocentric

eh *adv* ⟨*Aust fam*⟩ anyway; **seit eh und je** from time immemorial

ehe *conj* before; **ehe nicht** until

Ehe *f* -,-n marriage. **E∼bett** *nt* double bed. **E∼bruch** *m* adultery. **E∼frau** *f* wife. **E∼leute** *pl* married couple sg. e∼lich a marital; (Recht) conjugal; (Kind) legitimate

ehemal|ig a former. **e∼s** adv formerly

Ehe|mann m (pl -männer) husband. **E∼paar** nt married couple

eher adv earlier, sooner; (lieber, vielmehr) rather; (mehr) more

Ehering m wedding ring

ehr|bar a respectable. **E∼e** f -,-n honour; **jdm E∼e machen** do credit to s.o. **e∼en** vt honour. **e∼enamtlich** a honorary □ adv in an honorary capacity. **E∼endoktorat** nt honorary doctorate **E∼engast** m guest of honour. **e∼enhaft** a honourable, adv -bly. **E∼enmann** m (pl -männer) man of honour. **E∼enmitglied** nt honorary member. **e∼enrührig** a defamatory. **E∼enrunde** f lap of honour. **E∼ensache** f point of honour. **e∼enwert** a honourable. **E∼enwort** nt word of honour. **e∼erbietig** a deferential, adv -ly. **E∼erbietung** f - deference. **E∼furcht** f reverence; (Scheu) awe. **e∼fürchtig** a reverent, adv -ly. **E∼gefühl** nt sense of honour. **E∼geiz** m ambition. **e∼geizig** a ambitious. **e∼lich** a honest, adv -ly; **e∼lich gesagt** to be honest. **E∼lichkeit** f - honesty. **e∼los** a dishonourable. **e∼sam** a respectable. **e∼würdig** a venerable; (als Anrede) Reverend

Ei nt -[e]s,-er egg

Eibe f -,-n yew

Eiche f -,-n oak. **E∼l** f -,-n acorn.

E∼lhäher m -s, jay

eichen vt standardize

Eichhörnchen nt -s, squirrel

Eid m -[e]s,-e oath

Eidechse f -,-n lizard

eidlich a sworn □ adv on oath

Eidotter m & nt egg yolk

Eier|becher m egg-cup. **E∼kuchen** m pancake; (Omelett) omelette. **E∼schale** f eggshell.

E∼schnee m beaten egg-white. **E∼stock** m ovary. **E∼uhr** f eggtimer

Eifer m -s eagerness; (Streben) zeal. **E∼sucht** f jealousy. **e∼süchtig** a jealous, adv -ly.

eifrig a eager, adv -ly; (begeistert) keen, adv -ly

Eigelb nt -[e]s,-e [egg] yolk

eigen a own; (typisch) characteristic (dat of); (seltsam) odd, adv -ly; (genau) particular. **E∼art** f peculiarity. **e∼artig** a peculiar, adv -ly; (seltsam) odd. **E∼brötler** m -s,- crank. **e∼händig** a personal, adv -ly; (Unterschrift) own. **E∼heit** f -,-en peculiarity. **e∼mächtig** a high-handed; (unbefugt) unauthorized □ adv highhandedly; without authority. **E∼name** m proper name. **E∼nutz** m self-interest. **e∼nützig** a selfish, adv -ly. **e∼s** adv specially. **E∼schaft** f -,-en quality; (Phys) property; (Merkmal) characteristic; (Funktion) capacity. **E∼schaftswort** nt (pl -wörter) adjective. **E∼sinn** m obstinacy. **e∼sinnig** a obstinate, adv -ly

eigentlich a actual, real; (wahr) true □ adv actually, really; (streng genommen) strictly speaking; **wie geht es ihm e∼?** by the way, how is he?

Eigen|tor nt own goal. **E∼tum** nt -s property. **E∼tümer(in)** m -s,- (f -,-nen) owner. **e∼tümlich** a odd, adv -ly; (typisch) characteristic. **E∼tumswohnung** f freehold flat. **e∼willig** a self-willed; (Stil) highly individual

eign|en (sich) vr be suitable. **E∼ung** f - suitability

Eil|brief m express letter. **E∼e** f - hurry; **E∼e haben** be in a hurry; (Sache:) be urgent. **e∼en** vi (sein) hurry □ (haben) (drängen) be urgent. **e∼ends** adv hurriedly. **e∼ig** a hurried, adv -ly; (dringend) urgent, adv -ly; **es e∼ig**

haben be in a hurry. **E~zug** *m* semi-fast train

Eimer |**n** *m* -s,- bucket; (*Abfall-*) bin

ein[1] *adj* one; **e~es Tages/ A- bends** one day/evening; **mit jdm in einem Zimmer schlafen** sleep in the same room as s.o. □ *indef art* a, (*vor Vokal*) an; **so ein** such a; **was für ein** (*Frage*) what kind of a? (*Ausruf*) what a!

ein[2] *adv* **ein und aus** in and out; **nicht mehr ein noch aus wissen** (*fam*) be at one's wits' end

einander *pron* one another

einarbeiten *vt sep* train

einäschern *vt sep* reduce to ashes; cremate (*Leiche*). **E~ung** *f* -,-en cremation

einatmen *vt/i sep* (*haben*) inhale, breathe in

einäugig *a* one-eyed. **E~bahn- straße** *f* one-way street

einbalsamieren *vt sep* embalm

Einband *m* binding

Einbau *m* installation; (*Montage*) fitting. **e~en** *vt sep* install; (*mon- tieren*) fit. **E~küche** *f* fitted kitchen

einbegriffen *pred* a included

einberuf|**en**† *vt sep* convene; (*Mil*) call up, (*Amer*) draft. **E~ung** *f* call-up, (*Amer*) draft

Einbettzimmer *nt* single room

einbeulen *vt sep* dent

einbeziehen† *vt sep* [**mit**] **e~** in- clude; (*berücksichtigen*) take into account

einbiegen† *vi sep* (*sein*) turn

einbild|**en** *vt sep* **sich** (*dat*) **etw e~en** imagine sth; **sich** (*dat*) **viel e~en** be conceited. **E~ung** *f* imagination; (*Dünkel*) conceit. **E~ungskraft** *f* imagination

einbläuen *vt sep* **jdm etw e~** (*fam*) drum sth into s.o.

einblenden *vt sep* fade in

einbleuen *vt sep* ⟨NEW⟩ **einbläuen**

Einblick *m* insight

einbrech|**en**† *vt sep* (*haben/sein*) break in; **bei uns ist einge- brochen worden** we have been

burgled □ (*sein*) set in; ⟨*Nacht:*⟩ fall. **E~er** *m* burglar

einbring|**en**† *vt sep* get in; bring in (*Geld*); **das bringt nichts ein** it's not worth while. **e~lich** *a* profitable

Einbruch *m* burglary; **bei E~ der Nacht** at nightfall

einbürger|**n** *vt sep* naturalize; **sich e~n** become established. **E~ung** *f* - naturalization

Ein|**buße** *f* loss **(an +** *dat* **of)**. **e~ büßen** *vt sep* lose

eincheck|**en** /-ʧɛkən/ *vt/i sep* (*haben*) check in

eindecken (sich) *vr sep* stock up

eindeutig *a* unambiguous; (*deut- lich*) clear, *adv* -ly

eindicken *vt sep* (*Culin*) thicken

eindring|**en**† *vi sep* (*sein*) **e~ in** (+ *acc*) penetrate into; (*mit Ge- walt*) force one's/(*Wasser:*) its way into; (*Mil*) invade; **auf jdn e~en** (*fig*) press s.o.; (*bittend*) plead with s.o. **e~lich** *a* urgent, *adv* -ly. **E~ling** *m* -s,-e intruder

Eindruck *m* impression; **E~ machen** impress (**auf jdn** s.o.)

eindrücken *vt sep* crush

eindrucksvoll *a* impressive

ein|**e(r,s)** *pron* one; (*jemand*) someone; (*man*) one, you; **e~er von uns** one of us; **es macht e~en müde** it makes you tired

einebnen *vt sep* level

eineiig *a* (*Zwillinge*) identical

eineinhalb *inv a* one and a half; **e~ Stunden** an hour and a half

Einelternfamilie *f* one-parent family

einengen *vt sep* restrict

Einer *m* -s,- (*Math*) unit. **e~** *pron s.* **eine(r,s)**. **e~lei** *inv a* □ *attrib* a one kind of; (*gleichgültig*) the same □ *pred a* (*fam*) immater- ial; **es ist mir e~lei** it's all the same to me. **E~lei** *nt* -s mono- tony. **e~seits** *adv* on the one hand

einfach *a* simple, *adv* -ly; ⟨*Essen*⟩ plain; ⟨*Faden, Fahrt, Fahrkarte*⟩ single; **e~er Soldat** private. **E~heit** *f* - simplicity

einfädeln *vt sep* thread; (*fig; arrangieren*) arrange; **sich e~** ⟨*Auto*⟩ filter in

einfahr|en *v sep* □*vi* (*sein*) arrive; ⟨*Zug:*⟩ pull in □*vt* ⟨*Auto*⟩ run in; **die Ernte e~en** get in the harvest. **E~t** *f* arrival; (*Eingang*) entrance, way in; (*Auffahrt*) drive; (*Autobahn-*) access road; **keine E~t** no entry

Einfall *m* idea; (*Mil*) invasion. **e~en†** *vi sep* (*sein*) collapse; (*eindringen*) invade; (*einstimmen*) join in; **jdm e~en** occur to s.o.; **sein Name fällt mir nicht ein** I can't think of his name; **was fällt ihm ein!** what does he think he is doing! **e~sreich** *a* imaginative

Einfalt *f* - naïvety

einfältig *a* simple; (*naiv*) naïve

Einfaltspinsel *m* simpleton

einfangen† *vt sep* catch

einfarbig *a* of one colour; ⟨*Stoff, Kleid*⟩ plain

einfass|en *vt sep* edge; set ⟨*Edelstein*⟩. **E~ung** *f* border, edging

einfetten *vt sep* grease

einfinden† (sich) *vr sep* turn up

einfließen† *vi sep* (*sein*) flow in

einflößen *vt sep* **jdm etw e~** give s.o. sips of sth; **jdm Angst e~** (*fig*) frighten s.o.

Einfluss (**Einfluß**) *m* influence. **e~reich** *a* influential

einförmig *a* monotonous, *adv* -ly. **E~keit** *f* - monotony

einfried(ig)|en *vt sep* enclose. **E~ung** *f* -,-en enclosure

einfrieren† *vt/i sep* (*sein*) freeze

einfügen *vt sep* insert; (*einschieben*) interpolate; **sich e~** fit in

einfühl|en (sich) *vr sep* empathize (**in** + *acc* with). **e~sam** *a* sensitive

Einfuhr *f* -,-en import

einführ|en *vt sep* introduce; (*einstecken*) insert; (*einweisen*) initiate; (*Comm*) import. **e~end** *a* introductory. **E~ung** *f* introduction; (*Einweisung*) initiation

Eingabe *f* petition; (*Computer*) input

Eingang *m* entrance, way in; (*Ankunft*) arrival

eingebaut *a* built-in; ⟨*Schrank*⟩ fitted

eingeben† *vt sep* hand in; (*einflößen*) give ⟨**jdm** s.o.⟩; (*Computer*) feed in

eingebildet *a* imaginary; (*überheblich*) conceited

Eingeborene(r) *m/f* native

Eingebung *f* -,-en inspiration

eingedenk *prep* (+ *gen*) mindful of

eingefleischt *a* **e~er Junggeselle** confirmed bachelor

eingehakt *adv* arm in arm

eingehen† *v sep* □*vi* (*sein*) come in; (*ankommen*) arrive; (*einlaufen*) shrink; ⟨*sterben*⟩ die; ⟨*Tuch, Firma:*⟩ fold; **auf etw** (*acc*) **e~** go into sth; (*annehmen*) agree to sth □*vt* enter into; contract ⟨*Ehe*⟩; make ⟨*Wette*⟩; take ⟨*Risiko*⟩. **e~d** *a* detailed; (*gründlich*) thorough, *adv* -ly

eingelegt *a* inlaid; (*Culin*) pickled; (*mariniert*) marinaded

eingemacht *a* (*Culin*) bottled

eingenommen *pred a* (*fig*) taken (**von** with); prejudiced (**gegen** against); **von sich e~** conceited

eingeschneit *a* snowbound

eingeschrieben *a* registered

Einge|ständnis *nt* admission. **e~stehen†** *vt sep* admit

eingetragen *a* registered

Eingeweide *pl* bowels, entrails

eingewöhnen (sich) *vr sep* settle in

eingießen† *vt sep* pour in; (*einschenken*) pour

eingleisig *a* single-track

einglieder|n vt sep integrate. **E~ung** f integration

eingraben† vt sep bury

eingravieren vt sep engrave

eingreifen† vi sep (haben) intervene. **E~** nt -s intervention; (Med) operation

Eingriff m intervention; (Med) operation

einhaken vt/r sep jdn e~ od sich bei jdm e~ take s.o.'s arm

einhalten† v sep □ vt keep; (befolgen) observe □ vi (haben) stop

einhändigen vt sep hand in

einhängen v sep □ vt hang; put down ⟨Hörer⟩; sich bei jdm e~ take s.o.'s arm □ vi (haben) hang up

einheimisch a local; (eines Landes) native; (Comm) homeproduced. **E~e(r)** m/f local native

Einheit f -,-en unity; (Maß, Mil) unit. **e~lich** a uniform, adv -ly; (vereinheitlicht) standard. **E~s-preis** m standard price; (Fahrpreis) flat fare

einhellig a unanimous, adv -ly

einholen vt sep catch up with; (aufholen) make up for; (erbitten) seek; (einkaufen) buy; e~ gehen go shopping

einhüllen vt sep wrap

einhundert inv a one hundred

einig a united; [sich (dat)] e~ werden/sein come to an/be in agreement

einig|e(r,s) pron some; (ziemlich viel) quite a lot of; (substantivisch)—e~e pl some; (mehrere) several; (ziemlich viele) quite a lot; e~es sg some things; vor e~er Zeit some time ago. e~emal adv (NEW) e~e Mal, s. Mal

einigen vt unite; unify ⟨Land⟩; sich e~ come to an agreement; (ausmachen) agree (auf + acc on)

einigermaßen adv to some extent; (ziemlich) fairly; (ziemlich gut) fairly well

Einig|keit f -unity; (Übereinstimmung) agreement. **E~ung** f -unification; (Übereinkunft) agreement

einjährig a one-year-old; (ein Jahr dauernd) one year's...; e~e Pflanze annual

einkalkulieren vt sep take into account

einkassieren vt sep collect

Einkauf m purchase; (Einkaufen) shopping; Einkäufe machen do some shopping. e~en vt sep buy; e~en gehen go shopping. **E~skorb** m shopping/(im Geschäft) wire basket. **E~stasche** f shopping bag. **E~swagen** m shopping trolley. **E~szentrum** nt shopping centre

einkehren vi sep (sein) [in einem Lokal] e~ stop for a meal/drink [at an inn]

einklammern vt sep bracket

Einklang m harmony; in **E~ stehen** be in accord (mit with)

einkleben vt sep stick in

einkleiden vt sep fit out

einklemmen vt sep clamp; sich (dat) den Finger in der Tür e~ catch one's finger in the door

einkochen v sep □ vi (sein) boil down □ vt preserve, bottle

Einkommen nt -s income. **E~[s]steuer** f income tax

einkreisen vt sep encircle; rot e~ ring in red

Einkünfte pl income sg; (Einnahmen) revenue sg

einlad|en† vt sep load; (auffordern) invite; (bezahlen für) treat. e~end a inviting. **E~ung** f invitation

Einlage f enclosure; (Schuh-) arch support; (Zahn-) temporary filling; (Programm-) interlude; (Comm) investment; (Bank-) deposit; Suppe mit **E~** soup with noodles/dumplings

Ein|lass m (Einlaß m -sses) admittance. e~lassen† vt sep let in; run ⟨Bad, Wasser⟩; sich auf etw (acc)/mit jdm e~lassen get involved in sth/with s.o.

einlaufen† vi sep (sein) come in; (ankommen) arrive; (Wasser:) run in; (schrumpfen) shrink; [in den Hafen] e~ enter port

einleben (sich) vr sep settle in

Einlege|arbeit f inlaid work. e~n vt sep put in; lay in (Vorrat); lodge (Protest, Berufung); (einfügen) insert; (Auto) engage (Gang); (servieren) inlay; (Culin) pickle; (marinieren) marinade; **eine Pause e~n** have a break. **E~sohle** f insole

einleiten vt sep initiate; (eröffnen) begin. e~end a introductory. **E~ung** f introduction

einlenken vi sep (haben) (fig) relent

einleuchten vi sep (haben) be clear (dat to). e~d a convincing

einliefer|n vt sep take (ins Krankenhaus to hospital). **E~ung** f admission

einlösen vt sep cash (Scheck); redeem (Pfand); (fig) keep

einmachen vt sep preserve

einmal adv once; (eines Tages) one or some day; **noch/schon e~** again/before; **noch so teuer** twice as expensive; **auf e~** at the same time; (plötzlich) suddenly; **nicht e~** not even; **es geht nun e~ nicht** it's just not possible. **E~eins** nt — [multiplication] tables pl. e~ig a single; (einzigartig) unique; (fam: großartig) fantastic, adv -ally

einmarschieren vi sep (sein) march in

einmisch|en vr sep in~terfere. **E~ung** f interference

einmütig a unanimous, adv -ly

Einnahme f -,-n taking; (Mil) capture. **E~n** pl income sg; (Einkünfte) revenue sg; (Comm) receipts; (eines Ladens) takings

einnehmen† vt sep take; have (Mahlzeit); (Mil) capture; take up (Platz); (fig) prejudice (gegen

against); **jdn für sich e~** win s.o. over. e~d a engaging

einnicken vi sep (sein) nod off

Einöde f wilderness

einordnen vt sep put in its proper place; (klassifizieren) classify; **sich e~** fit in; (Auto) get in lane

einpacken vt sep pack; (einhüllen) wrap

einparken vt sep park

einpauken vt sep jdm etw e~ (fam) drum sth into s.o.

einpflanzen vt sep plant; implant (Organ)

einplanen vt sep allow for

einpräg|en vt sep impress (jdm [up]on s.o.); **sich** (dat) **etw e~en** memorize sth. e~sam a easy to remember; (Melodie) catchy

einquartieren vt sep (Mil) billet (bei on); **sich in einem Hotel e~** put up at a hotel

einrahmen vt sep frame

einrasten vi sep (sein) engage

einräumen vt sep put away; (zugeben) admit; (zugestehen) grant

einrechnen vt sep include

einreden v sep ▢ vt jdm/sich (dat) etw e~ persuade s.o./one-self of sth ▢ vi (haben) **auf jdn e~** talk insistently to s.o.

einreib|en† vt sep rub (mit with). **E~mittel** nt liniment

einreichen vt sep submit; **die Scheidung e~** file for divorce

Einreiher m -s,- single-breasted suit. e~ig a single-breasted

Einreise f entry. e~n vi sep (sein) enter (nach Irland Ireland). **E~visum** nt entry visa

einreiß|en† v sep ▢ vt tear; (abreißen) pull down ▢ vi (sein) tear; (Sitte:) become a habit

einrenken vt sep (Med) set

einricht|en vt sep fit out; (möblieren) furnish; (anordnen) arrange; (Med) set (Bruch); (eröffnen) set up; **sich e~en** furnish one's home; (sich einschränken) economize; (sich

einrollen

vorbereiten) prepare (**auf** + *acc*
for). **E∼ung** *f* furnishing; (*Möbel*) furnishings *pl*; (*Techn*)
equipment; (*Vorrichtung*) device;
(*Eröffnung*) setting up; (*Institution*) institution; (*Gewohnheit*)
practice. **E∼ungsgegenstand** *m*
piece of equipment/(*Möbelstück*)
furniture

einrollen *vt sep* roll up; put in rollers (*Haare*)

einrosten *vi sep* (*sein*) rust; (*fig*)
get rusty

einrücken *v sep* □ *vi* (*sein*) (*Mil*)
be called up; (*einmarschieren*)
move in □ *vt* indent

eins *inv a & pron* one; **noch e∼**
one other thing; **mir ist alles e∼**
(*fam*) it's all the same to me. **E∼**
f -,-en one; (*Sch*) ≈ A

einsam *a* lonely; (*allein*) solitary;
(*abgelegen*) isolated. **E∼keit** *f* -
loneliness; solitude; isolation

einsammeln *vt sep* collect

Einsatz *m* use; (*Mil*) mission;
(*Wett-*) stake; (*E∼teil*) insert; **im**
E∼ in action. **e∼bereit** *a* ready
for action

einschalten *vt sep* switch on;
(*einschieben*) interpolate (*fig: beteiligen*) call in; **sich e∼en** (*fig*)
intervene. **E∼quote** *f* (*TV*) viewing figures *pl*; ≈ ratings *pl*

einschärfen *vt sep* **jdm etw e∼**
impress sth [up]on s.o.

einschätz|en *vt sep* assess; (*bewerten*) rate. **E∼ung** *f* assessment; estimation

einschenken *vt sep* pour

einscheren *vi sep* (*sein*) pull in

einschicken *vt sep* send in

einschieben *vt sep* push in; (*einfügen*) insert; (*fig*) interpolate

einschiff|en (sich) *vr sep* embark. **E∼ung** *f* - embarkation

einschlafen *vi sep* (*sein*) go to
sleep; (*aufhören*) peter out

einschläfern *vt sep* lull to sleep;
(*betäuben*) put out; (*töten*) put to
sleep. **e∼d** *a* soporific

Einschlag *m* impact; (*fig: Beimischung*) element. **e∼en†** *v sep* □ *vt*
knock in; (*zerschlagen*) smash;
(*einwickeln*) wrap; (*falten*) turn
up; (*drehen*) turn; take (*Weg*); take
up (*Laufbahn*) □ *vi* (*haben*) hit/
(*Blitz:*) strike (**in etw** *acc* sth);
(*zustimmen*) shake hands [on a
deal]; (*Erfolg haben*) be a hit; **auf**
jdn e∼en beat s.o.

einschlägig *a* relevant

einschleusen *vt sep* infiltrate

einschließ|en† *vt sep* lock in;
(*umgeben*) enclose; (*einkreisen*)
surround; (*einbeziehen*) include;
sich e∼en lock oneself in; **Bedienung eingeschlossen** service included. **e∼lich** *adv* inclusive □ *prep* (+ *gen*) including

einschmeicheln (sich) *vr sep* ingratiate oneself (**bei** with)

einschnappen *vi sep* (*sein*) click
shut; **eingeschnappt sein** (*fam*)
be in a huff

einschneiden† *vt/i sep* (*haben*)
[**in**] **etw** *acc* **e∼** cut into sth. **e∼d**
a (*fig*) drastic, *adv* -ally

Einschnitt *m* cut; (*Med*) incision;
(*Lücke*) gap; (*fig*) decisive event

einschränk|en *vt sep* restrict; (*reduzieren*) cut back; **sich e∼en**
economize. **E∼ung** *f* -,-en restriction; (*Reduzierung*) reduction; (*Vorbehalt*) reservation

Einschreib|e[e]brief *m* registered letter. **e∼en†** *vt sep* enter;
register (*Brief*); **sich e∼en** put
one's name down; (*sich anmelden*) enrol. **E∼en** *nt* registered letter/packet; **als** *od per*
E∼en by registered post

einschreiten† *vi sep* (*sein*) intervene

einschüchter|n *vt sep* intimidate. **E∼ung** *f* - intimidation

einsegn|en *vt sep* (*Relig*) confirm.
E∼ung *f* -,-en confirmation

einsehen† *vt sep* inspect; (*lesen*)
consult; (*begreifen*) see. **E∼** *nt* -s

ein E~ haben show some understanding; (vernünftig sein) see reason

einseitig a one-sided; (Pol) unilateral □ adv on one side; (fig) one-sidedly; (Pol) unilaterally

einsenden† vt sep send in

einsetzen v sep □ vt put in; (einfügen) insert; (verwenden) use; put on (Zug); call out (Truppen); (Mil) deploy; (ernennen) appoint; (wetten) stake; (riskieren) risk; **sich e~für** support □ vi (haben) start; (Winter, Regen.) set in

Einsicht f insight; (Verständnis) understanding; (Vernunft) reason; **zur E~ kommen** see reason. **e~ig** a understanding; (vernünftig) sensible

Einsiedler m hermit

einsilbig a monosyllabic; (Person) taciturn

einsinken† vi sep (sein) sink in

einspannen vt sep harness; **jdn e~** (fam) rope s.o. in; **sehr eingespannt** (fam) very busy

einsparen vt sep save

einsperren vt sep shut/(im Gefängnis) lock up

einspielen (sich) vr sep warm up; **gut aufeinander eingespielt sein** work well together

einsprachig a monolingual

einspringen† vi sep (sein) step in (für for)

einspritzen vt sep inject

Einspruch m objection; **E~ erheben** object; (Jur) appeal

einspurig a single-track; (Auto) single-lane

einst adv once; (Zukunft) one day

Einstand m (Tennis) deuce

einstecken vt sep put in; post ⟨Brief⟩; (Electr) plug in; (behalten) pocket; (fam: hinnehmen) take; suffer ⟨Niederlage⟩; **etw e~** put sth in one's pocket

einstehen† vi sep (haben) **e~ für** vouch for; answer for (Folgen)

einsteigen† vi sep (sein) get in; (in Bus/Zug) get on

einstell|en vt sep put in; (anstellen) employ; (aufhören) stop; (regulieren) adjust, set; (Optik) focus; tune (Motor, Zündung); tune to ⟨Sender⟩; **sich e~en** turn up; (ankommen) arrive; (eintreten) occur; (Schwierigkeiten.) arise; **sich e~en auf** (+ acc) adjust to; (sich vorbereiten) prepare for. **E~ung** f employment; (Aufhören) cessation; (Regulierung) adjustment; (Optik) focusing; (TV, Auto) tuning; (Haltung) attitude

Einstieg m -[e]s,-e entrance

einstig a former

einstimmen vi sep (haben) join in

einstimmig a unanimous, adv -ly. **E~keit** f - unanimity

einstöckig a single-storey

einstudieren vt sep rehearse

einstufen vt sep classify

Ein|sturz m collapse. **e~stürzen** vi sep (sein) collapse

einstweil|en adv for the time being; (inzwischen) meanwhile. **e~ig** a temporary

eintagen vt sep key in

eintauchen vt/i sep (sein) dip in; (heftiger) plunge in

eintauschen vt sep exchange

eintausend inv a one thousand

einteil|en vt sep divide (in + acc into); (Biol) classify; **sich** (dat) **seine Zeit gut e~en** organize one's time well. **e~ig** a one piece. **E~ung** f division; classification

eintönig a monotonous, adv -ly. **E~keit** f - monotony

Eintopf m, **E~gericht** nt stew

Ein|tracht f - harmony. **e~trächtig** a harmonious □ adv in harmony

Eintrag m -[e]s,-̈e entry. **e~en†** vt sep enter; (Admin) register; (einbringen) bring in; **sich e~en** put one's name down

einträglich a profitable

Eintragung f -, -en registration; (Eintrag) entry

eintreffen† vi sep (sein) arrive; (fig) come true; (geschehen) happen. **E~** nt -s arrival

eintreiben† vt sep drive in; (einziehen) collect

eintreten v sep □ vi (sein) enter; (geschehen) occur; **in einen Klub e~** join a club; **e~ für** (fig) stand up for □ vt kick in

Eintritt m entrance; (zu Veranstaltung) admission; (Beitritt) joining; (Beginn) beginning. **E~skarte** f [admission] ticket

eintrocknen vi sep (sein) dry up

einüben vt sep practise

einundachtzig inv a eighty-one

einverleiben vt sep incorporate (dat into); **sich** (dat) **etw e~** (fam) consume sth

Einvernehmen nt -s understanding; (Übereinstimmung) agreement; **in bestem E~** on the best of terms

einverstanden a **e~ sein** agree

Einverständnis nt agreement; (Zustimmung) consent

Einwand m -[e]s, ̈-e objection

Einwanderer er m immigrant. **e~n** vi sep (sein) immigrate. **E~ung** f immigration

einwandfrei a perfect, adv -ly; (untadelig) impeccable, adv -bly; (eindeutig) indisputable, adv -bly

einwärts adv inwards

einwechseln vt sep change

einwecken vt sep preserve, bottle

Einweg- pref non-returnable; (Feuerzeug) throw-away

einweichen vt sep soak

einweihen vt sep inaugurate; (Relig) consecrate; (einführen) initiate; (fam) use for the first time; **in ein Geheimnis e~en** let into a secret. **E~ung** f -, -en inauguration; consecration; initiation

einweisen† vt sep direct; (einführen) initiate; **ins Krankenhaus e~** send to hospital

einwenden† vt sep etwas e~ object (**gegen** to); **dagegen hätte ich nichts einzuwenden** (fam) I wouldn't say no

einwerfen† vt sep insert; post (Brief); (Sport) throw in; (vorbringen) interject; (zertrümmern) smash

einwickeln vt sep wrap [up]

einwilligen vi sep (haben) consent, agree (**in** + acc to). **E~ung** f - consent

einwirken vi sep (haben) **e~ auf** (+ acc) have an effect on; (beeinflussen) influence

Einwohner(in) m -s, - (f -, -nen) inhabitant. **E~zahl** f population

Einwurf m interjection; (Einwand) objection; (Sport) throwin; (Münz-) slot

Einzahl f (Gram) singular

einzahlen vt sep pay in. **E~ung** f payment; (Einlage) deposit

einzäunen vt sep fence in

Einzel nt -s, - (Tennis) singles pl. **E~bett** nt single bed. **E~fall** m individual/(Sonderfall) isolated case. **E~gänger** m -s, - loner. **E~haft** f solitary confinement. **E~handel** m retail trade. **E~händler** m retailer. **E~haus** nt detached house. **E~heit** f -, -en detail. **E~karte** f single ticket. **E~kind** nt only child

einzeln a single, adv -gly; (individuell) individual, adv -ly; (gesondert) separate, adv -ly; odd (Handschuh, Socken); **e~e Fälle** some cases. **E~e(r,s) (e~e(r,s))** pron **der/die E~e (e~e)** the individual; **ein E~er (e~er)** a single one; (Person) one individual; **jeder E~e (e~e)** every single one; (Person) each individual; **E~e (e~e)** pl some; **im E~en (e~en)** in detail; **ins E~e (e~e)** gehen go into detail

Einzel|person f single person. **E~teil** nt [component] part. **E~zimmer** nt single room

einziehen v sep □ vt pull in; draw in ⟨Atem, Krallen⟩; (Zool, Techn) retract; indent ⟨Zeile⟩; (aus dem Verkehr ziehen) withdraw; (beschlagnahmen) confiscate; (eintreiben) collect; make ⟨Erkundigungen⟩; (Mil) call up; (einfügen) insert; (einbauen) put in; den Kopf e~ duck [one's head] □ vi (sein) enter; (umziehen) move in; (eindringen) penetrate

einzig a only; (einmalig) unique; **eine/keine e~e Frage** a/not a single question; **ein e~es Mal** only once □ adv only; **e~ und allein** solely. **e~artig** a unique; (unvergleichlich) unparalleled. **E~e(r,s)** (e~e(r,s)) pron der/die/das **E~e** (e~e) the only one; **ein/kein E~er** (e~er) a/not a single one; **das E~e** (e~e), was mich stört the only thing that bothers me

Einzug m entry; (Umzug) move (in + acc into). **E~sgebiet** nt catchment area

Eis nt -es ice; (Speise) ice-cream; **Eis am Stiel** ice lolly; **Eis laufen** skate. **E~bahn** f ice rink. **e~bär** m polar bear. **E~becher** m ice-cream sundae. **E~bein** nt (Culin) knuckle of pork. **E~berg** m iceberg. **E~diele** f ice-cream parlour

Eisen nt -s,- iron. **E~bahn** f railway. **E~bahn** m -s,- railwayman

eisern a iron; (fest) resolute, adv -ly; **e~er Vorhang** (Theat) safety curtain; (Pol) Iron Curtain

Eis|fach nt freezer compartment. **e~gekühlt** a chilled. **e~ig** a icy. **E~kaffee** m iced coffee. **e~kalt** a ice cold; (fig) icy, adv -ily. **E~kunstlauf** m figure skating. **E~lauf** m skating. **e~laufen†** vi sep (sein) **Eis laufen**, s. Eis. **E~läufer(in)** m(f) skater. **E~pickel** m ice-axe. **E~scholle** f ice-floe. **E~schrank** m refrigerator

E~vogel m kingfisher. **E~würfel** m icecube. **E~zapfen** m icicle. **E~zeit** f ice age

eitel a vain; (rein) pure. **E~keit** f - vanity

Eiter m -s pus. **e~n** vi (haben) discharge pus

Eiweiß nt -es,- e egg-white; (Chem) protein

Ekel m -s disgust; (Widerwille) revulsion

Ekel nt -s,- (fam) beast

ekel|erregend a nauseating. **e~haft** a nauseating; (widerlich) repulsive. **e~n** vt/i (haben) **mich** od **mir e~t [es]** davor it makes me feel sick □ vr **sich e~n vor** (+ dat) find repulsive

eklig a disgusting, repulsive

Ekstase f ecstasy. **e~tisch** a ecstatic, adv -ally

Ekzem nt -s,-e eczema

elasti|sch a elastic; (federnd) springy; (fig) flexible. **E~zität** f - elasticity; flexibility

Elch m -[e]s,-e elk

Elefant m -en,-en elephant

elegan|t a elegant, adv -ly. **E~z** f - elegance

elektrifizieren vt electrify

Elektr|iker m -s,- electrician. **e~isch** a electric, adv -ally

elektrisieren vt electrify; **sich e~** get an electric shock

Elektrizität f - electricity. **E~swerk** nt power station

Elektr|oartikel mpl electrical appliances. **E~ode** f -,-n electrode. **E~oherd** m electric cooker. **E~on** nt -s,-en /-'tro:nən/ electron. **E~onik** f - electronics sg. **e~onisch** a electronic

Element nt -[e]s,-e element; (Anbau-) unit. **e~ar** a elementary

Elend nt -s misery; (Armut) poverty. **e~** a miserable, adv -bly, wretched, adv -ly; (krank) poorly; (gemein) contemptible; (fam:

schrecklich) dreadful, *adv* -ly. **E~sviertel** *nt* slum

elf *inv a,* **E~** *f* -,-**en** eleven

Elfe *f* -,-**n** fairy

Elfenbein *nt* ivory

Elfmeter *m* (*Fußball*) penalty

elfte(r,s) *a* eleventh

eliminieren *vt* eliminate

Elite *f* -,-**n** élite

Elixier *nt* -s,-e elixir

Ell[en]bogen *m* elbow

Ellip|se *f* -,-**n** ellipse. **e~tisch** *a* elliptical

Elsass (Elsaß) *nt* - Alsace

elsässisch *a* Alsatian

Elster *f* -,-**n** magpie

elter|lich *a* parental. **E~n** *pl* parents. **E~nhaus** *nt* (*parental*) home. **e~nlos** *a* orphaned. **E~nteil** *m* parent

Email /e'maj/ *nt* -s,-s, **E~le** /e'maljə/ *f* -,-**n** enamel. **e~lieren** /ema[l]'ji:rən/ *vt* enamel

Emanzi|pation /-'tsjo:n/ *f* - emancipation. **e~piert** *a* emancipated

Embargo *nt* -s,-s embargo

Emblem *nt* -s,-e emblem

Embryo *m* -s,-s embryo

Emigr|ant(in) *m* -en,-en (*f* -,-nen) emigrant. **E~ation** /-'tsjo:n/ *f* - emigration. **e~leren** *vi* (*sein*) emigrate

eminent *a* eminent, *adv* -ly

Emission *f* -,-**en** emission; (*Comm*) issue

Emotion /-'tsjo:n/ *f* -,-**en** emotion. **e~al** *a* emotional

Empfang *m* -[e]s,-̈e reception; (*Erhalt*) receipt; **in E~ nehmen** receive; (*annehmen*) accept. **e~en** *vt* receive; (*Biol*) conceive

Empfäng|er *m* -s,- recipient; (*Post-*) addressee; (*Zahlungs-*) payee; (*Radio, TV*) receiver. **e~lich** *a* receptive·/(*Med*) susceptible (**für** to). **E~nis** *f* - (*Biol*) conception

Empfängnisverhütung *f* contraception. **E~smittel** *nt* contraceptive

Empfangs|bestätigung *f* receipt. **E~chef** *m* reception manager. **E~dame** *f* receptionist. **E~halle** *f* [hotel] foyer

empfehl|en† *vt* recommend; **sich e~en** be advisable; (*verabschieden*) take one's leave. **e~enswert** *a* to be recommended; (*ratsam*) advisable. **E~ung** *f* -,-**en** recommendation; (*Gruß*) regards *pl*

empfind|en† *vt* feel. **e~lich** *a* sensitive (**gegen** to); (*zart*) delicate; (*wund*) tender; (*reizbar*) touchy; (*hart*) severe, *adv* -ly. **E~lichkeit** *f* - sensitivity; delicacy; tenderness; touchiness. **e~sam** *a* sensitive; (*sentimental*) sentimental. **E~ung** *f* -,-**en** sensation; (*Regung*) feeling

emphatisch *a* emphatic, *adv* -ally

empor *adv* (*liter*) up[wards]

empören *vt* incense; **sich e~** be indignant; (*sich auflehnen*) rebel. **e~d** *a* outrageous

Empor|kömmling *m* -s,-e upstart. **e~ragen** *vi sep* (*haben*) rise [up]

empör|t *a* indignant, *adv* -ly. **E~ung** *f* - indignation; (*Auflehnung*) rebellion

emsig *a* busy, *adv* -ily

Ende *nt* -s,-n end; (*eines Films, Romans*) ending; (*fam: Stück*) bit; **E~ Mai** at the end of May; **zu E~sein/gehen** be finished/come to an end; **etw zu E~ schreiben** finish writing sth; **am E~** at the end; (*schließlich*) in the end; (*fam: vielleicht*) perhaps; (*fam: erschöpft*) at the end of one's tether. **end|en** *vi* (*haben*) end. **e~gültig** *a* final, *adv* -ly; (*bestimmt*) definite, *adv* -ly

Endivie /-jə/ *f* -,-**n** endive

end|lich *adv* at last, finally; (*schließlich*) in the end. **e~los** *a* endless, *adv* -ly. **E~resultat** *nt* final result. **E~spiel** *nt* final. **E~spurt** *m* -[e]s final spurt. **E~station** *f* terminus. **E~ung** *f* -,-en (*Gram*) ending

Energie *f* - energy

energisch *a* resolute, *adv* -ly; (*nachdrücklich*) vigorous, *adv* -ly; **e~werden** put one's foot down

eng *a* narrow; (*beengt*) cramped; (*anliegend*) tight; (*nah*) close, *adv* -ly; **e~anliegend** tight-fitting

Enga|gement /ãgaʒə'mã:/ *nt* -s,-s (*Theat*) engagement; (*fig*) commitment. **e~gieren** /-'ʒi:-rən/ *vt* (*Theat*) engage; **sich e~gieren** become involved; **e~giert** committed

eng|anliegend *a* (NEW) **e~ anliegend**, *s*. **eng**. **E~e** *f* -,-n narrowness; **in die E~e treiben** (*fig*) drive into a corner

Engel *m* -s,- angel. **e~haft** *a* angelic

engherzig *a* petty

England *nt* -s England

Engländer *m* -s,- Englishman; (*Techn*) monkey-wrench; **die E~** the English *pl.* **E~in** *f* -,-nen Englishwoman

englisch *a* English; **auf e~** (NEW) **auf E~**, *s*. **Englisch**. **E~** *nt* -[s] (*Lang*) English; **auf E~** in English

Engpass (Engpaß) *m* (*fig*) bottleneck

en gros /ã'gro:/ *adv* wholesale

engstirnig *a* (*fig*) narrowminded

Enkel *m* -s,- grandson; **E~** *pl* grandchildren. **E~in** *f* -,-nen granddaughter. **E~kind** *nt* grandchild. **E~sohn** *m* grandson. **E~tochter** *f* granddaughter

enorm *a* enormous, *adv* -ly; (*fam*: *großartig*) fantastic

Ensemble /ã'sã:bəl/ *nt* -s,-s ensemble; (*Theat*) company

entart|en *vi* (*sein*) degenerate. **e~et** *a* degenerate

entbehr|en *vt* do without; (*vermissen*) miss. **e~lich** *a* dispensable; (*überflüssig*) superfluous. **E~ung** *f* -,-en privation

entbind|en† *vt* release (**von** from); (*Med*) deliver (**von** of) □ *vi* (*haben*) give birth. **E~ung** *f* delivery. **E~ungsstation** *f* maternity ward

entblöß|en *vt* bare. **e~t** *a* bare

entdeck|en *vt* discover. **E~er** *m* -s,- discoverer; (*Forscher*) explorer. **E~ung** *f* -,-en discovery

Ente *f* -,-n duck

entehren *vt* dishonour

enteignen *vt* dispossess; expropriate (*Eigentum*)

enterben *vt* disinherit

Enterich *m* -s,-e drake

entfachen *vt* kindle

entfallen† *vi* (*sein*) not apply; **jdm e~** slip from s.o.'s hand; (*aus dem Gedächtnis*) slip s.o.'s mind; **auf jdn e~** be s.o.'s share

entfalt|en *vt* unfold; (*entwickeln*) develop; (*zeigen*) display; **sich e~en** unfold; develop. **E~ung** *f* - development

entfern|en *vt* remove; **sich e~en** leave. **e~t** *a* distant; (*schwach*) vague, *adv* -ly; **2 Kilometer e~t** 2 kilometres away; **e~t verwandt** distantly related; **nicht im E~testen** (**e~testen**) not in the least. **E~ung** *f* -,-en removal; (*Abstand*) distance; (*Reichweite*) range. **E~ungsmesser** *m* rangefinder

entfesseln *vt* (*fig*) unleash

entfliehen† *vi* (*sein*) escape

entfremd|en *vt* alienate. **E~ung** *f* - alienation

entfrosten *vt* defrost

entführ|en *vt* abduct, kidnap; hijack (*Flugzeug*). **E~er** *m* abductor, kidnapper; hijacker. **E~ung** *f* abduction, kidnapping; hijacking

entgegen *adv* towards □ *prep* (+ *dat*) contrary to. **e~gehen†** *vi sep* (*sein*) (+ *dat*) go to meet; (*fig*) be heading for. **e~gesetzt** *a* opposite; (*gegensätzlich*) opposing. **e~halten†** *vt sep* (*fig*) object. **e~kommen†** *vi sep* (*sein*) (+ *dat*) come to meet; (*zukommen auf*) come towards; (*fig*) oblige. **E∼kommen** *nt* -s helpfulness; (*Zugeständnis*) concession. **e∼kommend** *a* approaching; (*Verkehr*) oncoming; (*fig*) obliging. **e∼nehmen†** *vt sep* accept. **e∼sehen†** *vi sep* (*haben*) (+ *dat*) (*fig*) await; (*freudig*) look forward to. **e∼setzen** *vt sep* Widerstand **e∼setzen** (+ *dat*) resist. **e∼treten†** *vi sep* (*sein*) (+ *dat*) (*fig*) confront; (*bekämpfen*) fight. **e∼wirken†** *vi sep* (*haben*) (+ *dat*) counteract; (*fig*) oppose

entgegn|en *vt* reply (**auf** + *acc* to). **E∼ung** *f* -,-en reply

entgehen† *vi sep* (*sein*) (+ *dat*) escape; **jdm e∼** (*unbemerkt bleiben*) escape s.o.'s notice; **sich** (*dat*) **etw e∼ lassen** miss sth

entgeistert *a* flabbergasted

Entgelt *nt* -[e]s payment; **gegen E∼** for money. **e∼en** *vt* **jdm etw e∼en lassen** (*fig*) make s.o. pay for sth

entgleis|en *vi* (*sein*) be derailed; (*fig*) make a gaffe. **E∼ung** *f* -,-en derailment; (*fig*) gaffe

entgleiten† *vi* (*sein*) **jdm e∼** slip from s.o.'s grasp

entgräten *vt* fillet, bone

Enthaarungsmittel *nt* depilatory

enthalt|en *vt* contain; **in etw** (*dat*) **e∼en sein** be contained/ (*eingeschlossen*) included in sth; **sich der Stimme e∼en** (*Pol*) abstain. **e∼sam** *a* abstemious. **E∼samkeit** *f* - abstinence. **E∼ung** *f* (*Pol*) abstention

enthaupten *vt* behead

entheben† *vt* **jdn seines Amtes e∼** relieve s.o. of his post

enthüll|en *vt* unveil; (*fig*) reveal. **E∼ung** *f* -,-en revelation

Enthusias|mus *m* - enthusiasm. **E∼t** *m* -en,-en enthusiast. **e∼tisch** *a* enthusiastic, *adv* -ally

entkernen *vt* stone; core (*Apfel*)

entkleid|en *vt* undress; **sich e∼en** undress. **E∼ungsnummer** *f* strip-tease [act]

entkorken *vt* uncork

entkommen† *vi* (*sein*) escape

entkorken *vt* uncork

entkräft|en *vt* weaken; (*fig*) invalidate. **E∼ung** *f* - debility

entkrampfen *vt* relax; **sich e∼** relax

entladen† *vt* unload; (*Electr*) discharge; **sich e∼** discharge; (*Gewitter:*) break; (*Zorn:*) explode

entlang *adv & prep* (+ *preceding acc or following dat*) along; **die Straße e∼**, **e∼ der Straße** along the road; **an etw** (*dat*) **e∼** along sth. **e∼fahren†** *vi sep* (*sein*) drive along. **e∼gehen†** *vi sep* (*sein*) walk along

entlarven *vt* unmask

entlass|en† *vt* dismiss; (*aus Krankenhaus*) discharge; (*aus der Haft*) release; **aus der Schule e∼ werden** leave school. **E∼ung** *f* -,-en dismissal; discharge; release

entlast|en *vt* relieve the strain on; ease (*Gewissen, Verkehr*); relieve (*von of*); (*Jur*) exonerate. **E∼ung** *f* - relief; exoneration. **E∼ungszug** *m* relief train

entlaufen† *vi* (*sein*) run away

entledigen (**sich**) *vr* (+ *gen*) rid oneself of; (*ausziehen*) take off; (*erfüllen*) discharge

entleeren *vt* empty

entlegen *a* remote

entleihen† *vt* borrow (**von** from)

entlocken *vt* coax (*dat* from)

entlohnen *vt* pay

entlüft|en *vt* ventilate. **E∼er** *m* -s,- extractor fan. **E∼ung** *f* ventilation

entmündigen *vt* declare incapable of managing his own affairs

entmutigen *vt* discourage

entnehmen† *vt* take (*dat* from); (*schließen*) gather (*dat* from)

Entomologie *f* - entomology

entpuppen (sich) *vr* (*fig*) turn out (**als etw** to be sth)

entrahmt *a* skimmed

entreißen† *vt* snatch (*dat* from)

entrichten *vt* pay

entrinnen† *vi* (*sein*) escape

entrollen *vt* unroll; unfurl (*Fahne*); **sich e~** unroll; unfurl

entrüsten† *vt* fill with indignation; **sich e~en** be indignant (**über** + *acc* at). **e~et** *a* indignant, *adv* -ly. **E~ung** *f* - indignation

entsaften *vt* extract the juice from. **E~er** *m* -s, - juice extractor

entsagen *vi* (*haben*) (+ *dat*) renounce. **E~ung** *f* - renunciation

entschädigen *vt* compensate. **E~ung** *f* -,-en compensation

entschärfen *vt* defuse

entscheiden† *vt/i* (*haben*) decide; **sich e~en** decide; (*Sache*:) be decided. **e~end** *a* decisive, *adv* -ly; (*kritisch*) crucial. **E~ung** *f* decision

entschieden *a* decided, *adv* -ly; (*fest*) firm, *adv* -ly

entschlafen† *vi* (*sein*) (*liter*) pass away

entschließen† (sich) *vr* decide, make up one's mind; **sich anders e~** change one's mind

entschlossen *a* determined; (*energisch*) resolute, *adv* -ly, **kurz e~** without hesitation; (*spontan*) on the spur of the moment. **E~heit** *f* - determination

Entschluss (Entschluß) *m* decision; **einen E~ fassen** make a decision

entschlüsseln *vt* decode

entschuldbar *a* excusable. **e~igen** *vt* excuse; (*jdn*) apologize (**bei** to); **e~igen Sie [bitte]!** excuse me! **e~igen** Sie mich. **E~igung** *f* -,-en apology; (*Ausrede*) excuse; **[jdn] um E~igung bitten** apologize [to s.o.]. **E~igung!** sorry! (*bei Frage*) excuse me

entsetzen *vt* horrify. **E~en** *nt* -s horror. **e~lich** *a* horrible, *adv* -bly, (*schrecklich*) terrible, *adv* -bly. **e~t** *a* horrified

entsinnen† (sich) *vr* (+ *gen*) remember

Entsorgung *f* - waste disposal

entspannen *vt* relax; **sich e~en** relax; (*Lage*:) ease. **E~ung** *f* - relaxation; easing; (*Pol*) détente

entsprechen† *vi* (*haben*) (+ *dat*) correspond to; (*übereinstimmen*) agree with; (*nachkommen*) comply with. **e~end** *a* corresponding; (*angemessen*) appropriate; (*zuständig*) relevant □ *adv* correspondingly; appropriately; (*demgemäß*) accordingly □ *prep* (+ *dat*) in accordance with.
E~ung *f* -,-en equivalent

entspringen† *vi* (*sein*) (*Fluss*:) rise; (*fig*) arise, spring (*dat* from); (*entfliehen*) escape

entstammen *vi* (*sein*) come/(*abstammen*) be descended (*dat* from)

entstehen† *vi* (*sein*) come into being; (*sich bilden*) form; (*sich entwickeln*) develop; (*Brand*:) start; (*stammen*) originate/(*sich ergeben*) result (**aus** from). **E~ung** *f* - origin; formation; development; (*fig*) birth

entsteinen *vt* stone

entstellen *vt* disfigure; (*verzerren*) distort. **E~ung** *f* disfigurement; distortion

entstört *a* (*Electr*) suppressed

enttäuschen *vt* disappoint. **E~ung** *f* disappointment

entvölkern *vt* depopulate

entwaffnen *vt* disarm. **e~d** *a* (*fig*) disarming

Entwarnung *f* all-clear [signal]

entwässern *vt* drain. **E~ung** *f* - drainage

entweder *conj* & *adv* either

entweichen† *vi* (*sein*) escape

entweihen *vt* desecrate. **E~ung** *f* - desecration

entwenden vt steal (dat from)

entwerfen† vt design; (aufsetzen) draft; (skizzieren) sketch

entwert|en vt devalue; (ungültig machen) cancel. **E~er** m -s,- ticket-cancelling machine. **E~ung** f devaluation; cancelling

entwick|eln vt develop; **sich e~eln** develop. **E~lung** f -,-en development; (Biol) evolution. **E~lungsland** nt developing country

entwinden† vt wrench (dat from)

entwirren vt disentangle; (fig) unravel

entwischen vi (sein) jdm e~ (fam) give s.o. the slip

entwöhnen vt wean (gen from); cure (Süchtige)

entwürdigend a degrading

Entwurf m design; (Konzept) draft; (Skizze) sketch

entwurzeln vt uproot

entzieh|en† vt take away (dat from); jdm den Führerschein e~hen withdraw s.o. from driving; **sich e~hen** (+ dat) withdraw from; (entgehen) evade. **E~hungskur** f treatment for drug/alcohol addiction

entziffern vt decipher

entzücken vt delight. **E~** nt -s delight. **e~d** a delightful

Entzug m withdrawal; (Vorenthaltung) deprivation. **E~serscheinungen** fpl withdrawal symptoms

entzünd|en vt ignite; (anstecken) light; (fig: erregen) inflame; **sich e~en** ignite; (Med) become inflamed. **e~et** a (Med) inflamed. **e~lich** a inflammable. **E~ung** f (Med) inflammation

entzwei a broken. **e~en (sich)** vr quarrel. **e~gehen†** vi sep (sein) break

Enzian m -s,-e gentian

Enzyklo|pädie f -,-en encyclopaedia. **e~pädisch** a encyclopaedic

Enzym nt -s,-e enzyme

Epidemie f -,-n epidemic

Epi|lepsie f - epilepsy. **E~leptiker(in)** m -s,- (f -,-nen) epileptic. **e~leptisch** a epileptic

Epilog m -s,-e epilogue

episch a epic

Episode f -,-n episode

Epitaph nt -s,-e epitaph

Epoche f -,-n epoch. **e~machend** a epoch-making

Epos nt -/Epen epic

er pron he; (Ding, Tier) it

erachten vt consider (für nötig necessary). **E~** nt -s meines E~s in my opinion

erbarmen (sich) vr have pity/ (Gott:) mercy (gen on). **E~** nt -s pity; mercy

erbärmlich a wretched, adv -ly (stark) terrible, adv -bly

erbarmungslos a merciless, adv -ly

erbau|en vt build; (fig) edify; **sich e~en** be edified (an + dat); **nicht e~t von** (fam) not pleased about. **e~lich** a edifying

Erbe¹ m -n,-n heir

Erbe² nt -s inheritance; (fig) heritage. **e~n** vt inherit

erbeuten vt get; (Mil) capture

Erbfolge f (Jur) succession

erbiet|en (sich) vr offer (zu to)

Erbin f -,-nen heiress

erbitten† vt ask for

erbittert a bitter; (heftig) fierce, adv -ly

erblassen vi (sein) turn pale

erblich a hereditary

erblicken vt catch sight of

erblinden vi (sein) go blind

erbost a angry, adv -ily

erbrechen† vt vomit □ vi/r [sich] e~ vomit. **E~** nt -s vomiting

Erbschaft f -,-en inheritance

Erbse f -,-n pea

Erb|stück nt heirloom. **E~teil** nt inheritance

Erd|apfel m (Aust) potato. **E~beben** nt -s,- earthquake. **E~beere** f strawberry. **E~boden** m ground

Erde f -,-n earth; (Erdboden) ground; (Fußboden) floor; **auf der E~** on earth; (auf dem Boden) on the ground/floor. **e~n** vt (Electr) earth

erdenklich a imaginable

Erd|gas nt natural gas. **E~geschoss** (E~geschoß) nt ground floor, (Amer) first floor. **e~ig** a earthy. **E~kugel** f globe. **E~kunde** f geography. **E~nuss** (E~nuß) f peanut. **E~öl** nt [mineral] oil. **E~reich** nt soil

erdreisten (sich) vr have the audacity (**zu** to)

erdrosseln vt strangle

erdrücken vt crush to death. **e~d** a (fig) overwhelming

Erd|rutsch m landslide. **E~teil** m continent

erdulden vt endure

erejfern (sich) vr get worked up

ereignen (sich) vr happen

Ereignis nt -ses,-se event. **e~los** a uneventful. **e~reich** a eventful

Eremit m -en,-en hermit

ererbt a inherited

erfahr|en† vt learn, hear; (erleben) experience □ a experienced. **E~ung** f -,-en experience; **in E~ung bringen** find out

erfassen vt seize; (begreifen) grasp; (einbeziehen) include; (aufzeichnen) record; **von einem Auto erfasst werden** be struck by a car

erfind|en† vt invent. **E~er** m -s,- inventor. **e~erisch** a inventive. **E~ung** f -,-en invention

Erfolg m -[e]s,-e success; (Folge) result; **E~ haben** be successful; **E~ versprechend** promising. **e~en** vi (sein) take place; (geschehen) happen. **e~los** a unsuccessful, adv -ly. **e~reich** a successful, adv -ly. **e~versprechend** a (NEW) **E~ versprechend**, s. Erfolg

erforder|lich a required, necessary. **e~n** vt require, demand. **E~nis** nt -ses,-se requirement

erforschen vt explore; (untersuchen) investigate. **E~ung** f exploration; investigation

erfreuen vt please; **sich guter Gesundheit e~en** enjoy good health. **e~lich** a pleasing, gratifying; (willkommen) welcome. **e~licherweise** adv happily. **e~t** a pleased

erfrier|en† vi (sein) freeze to death; (Glied:) become frostbitten; (Pflanze:) be killed by the frost. **E~ung** f -,-en frostbite

erfrischen vt refresh; **sich e~en** refresh onself. **e~end** a refreshing. **E~ung** f -,-en refreshment

erfüll|en vt fill; (nachkommen) fulfil; serve (Zweck); discharge (Pflicht:) **sich e~en** come true. **E~ung** f fulfilment; **in E~ung gehen** come true

erfunden invented; (fiktiv) fictitious

ergänz|en vt complement; (nachtragen) supplement; (auffüllen) replenish; (vervollständigen) complete; (hinzufügen) add; **sich e~en** complement each other. **E~ung** f complement; supplement; (Zusatz) addition

ergeb|en† vt produce; (zeigen) show, establish; **sich e~en** result; (Schwierigkeit:) arise; (kapitulieren) surrender; (sich fügen) submit; **es ergab sich** it turned out (**dass** that) □ a devoted, adv -ly; (resigniert) resigned, adv -ly. **E~enheit** f - devotion

Ergebnis nt -ses,-se result. **e~los** a fruitless, adv -ly

ergehen† vi (sein) be issued; **etw über sich** (acc) **e~ lassen** submit to sth; **wie ist es dir ergangen?**

how did you get on? □ *vr* sich
e~**in** (+ *dat*) indulge in

ergiebig *a* productive; (*fig*) rich

ergötzen *vt* amuse

ergreifen† *vt* seize; take ⟨*Maß-
nahme, Gelegenheit*⟩; take up
⟨*Beruf*⟩; (*rühren*) move; **die
Flucht e~** flee. **e~d** *a* moving

ergriffen *a* deeply moved. **E~-
heit** *f* - emotion

ergründen *vt* get to the bottom of

erhaben *a* raised; (*fig*) sublime;
über etw (*acc*) **e~ sein** (*fig*) be
above sth

Erhalt *m* -[e]s receipt. **e~en†** *vt*
receive, get; (*gewinnen*) obtain;
(*bewahren*) preserve, keep; (*instand halten*) maintain; (*unterhalten*) support; **am Leben e~en**
keep alive □*a* **gut/schlecht
e~en** in good/bad condition;
e~en bleiben survive

erhältlich *a* obtainable

Erhaltung *f* - (*s.* **erhalten**) preservation; maintenance

erhängen (sich) *vr* hang oneself

erhärten *vt* (*fig*) substantiate

erheb|en† *vt* raise; levy ⟨*Steuer*⟩;
charge ⟨*Gebühr*⟩; **Anspruch
e~en** lay claim (**auf** + *acc* to);
Protest e~en protest; **sich
e~en** rise; ⟨*Frage:*⟩ arise; (*sich
empören*) rise up. **e~lich** *a* considerable, *adv* -bly. **E~ung** *f*
-,-en elevation; (*Anhöhe*) rise;
(*Aufstand*) uprising; (*Ermitt-
lung*) survey

erheitern *vt* amuse. **E~ung** *f* -
amusement

erhitzen *vt* heat; **sich e~** get hot;
(*fig*) get heated

erhoffen *vr* sich (*dat*) etw e~
hope for sth

erhöh|en *vt* raise; (*fig*) increase;
sich e~en rise, increase. **E~ung**
f -,-en increase. **E~ungszeichen**
nt (*Mus*) sharp

erhol|en (sich) *vr* recover (**von**
from); (*nach Krankheit*) convalesce, recuperate; (*sich ausru-*

hen) have a rest. **e~sam** *a* restful. **E~ung** *f* - recovery; convalescence; (*Ruhe*) rest. **E~ungs-
heim** *nt* convalescent home

erhören *vt* answer

erinner|n *vt* remind (**an** + *acc* of);
sich e~n remember (**an
jdn/etw** s.o./sth). **E~ung** *f* -,-en
memory; (*Andenken*) souvenir

erkält|en (sich) *vr* catch a cold;
sich e~en have a cold. **E~ung** *f*
-,-en cold

erkenn|bar *a* recognizable;
(*sichtbar*) visible. **e~en†** *vt* recognize; (*wahrnehmen*) distinguish; (*einsehen*) realize. **e~tlich**
a sich **e~tlich zeigen** show one's
appreciation. **E~tnis** *f* -,-se recognition; realization; (*Wissen*) knowledge; **die neuesten
E~tnisse** the latest findings

Erker *m* -s,- bay

erklär|en *vt* declare; (*erläutern*)
explain; **sich bereit e~en** agree
(**zu** to); **ich kann es mir nicht
e~en** I can't explain it. **e~end** *a*
explanatory. **e~lich** *a* explic-
able; (*verständlich*) understandable. **e~licherweise** *adv*
understandably. **e~t** *attrib a* de-
clared. **E~ung** *f* -,-en declaration; explanation; **öffentliche
E~ung** public statement

erkling|en† *vi* (*sein*) ring out

erkrank|en *vi* (*sein*) fall ill; be
taken ill (**an** + *dat* with). **E~ung**
f -,-en illness

erkunden *vt* explore; (*Mil*) reconnoitre

erkundig|en (sich) *vr* enquire
(**nach jdm/etw** after s.o./about
sth). **E~ung** *f* -,-en enquiry

erlahmen *vi* (*sein*) tire; ⟨*Kraft,
Eifer:*⟩ flag

erlangen *vt* attain, get

Erlass *m* -es,-̈e (**Erlaß** *m* -sses,
-̈sse) (*Admin*) decree; (*Befreiung*)
exemption; (*Straf-*) remission

erlassen† *vt* (*Admin*) issue; **jdm
etw e~** exempt s.o. from sth; let
s.o. off ⟨*Strafe*⟩

erlauben vt allow, permit; **sich e~, etw zu tun** take the liberty of doing sth; **ich kann es mir nicht e~** I can't afford it

Erlaubnis f - permission. **E~schein** m permit

erläuter|n vt explain. **E~ung** f -,-en explanation

Erle f -,-n alder

erleb|en vt experience; (mit-) see; have (Überraschung, Enttäuschung); **etw nicht mehr e~en** not live to see sth. **E~nis** nt -ses,-se experience

erledig|en vt do; (sich befassen mit) deal with; (beenden) finish; (entscheiden) settle; (töten) kill; **e~t sein** be done/settled/(fam: müde) worn out/(fam: ruiniert) finished

erleichter|n vt lighten; (vereinfachen) make easier; (befreien) relieve; (lindern) ease; **sich e~n** (fig) unburden oneself. **e~t** a relieved. **E~ung** f -relief

erleiden† vt suffer

erlernen vt learn

erlesen a exquisite; (auserlesen) choice, select

erleucht|en vt illuminate; **hell e~et** brightly lit. **E~ung** f -,-en (fig) inspiration

erliegen† vi (sein) succumb (dat to); **seinen Verletzungen e~** die of one's injuries

erlogen a untrue, false

Erlös m -es proceeds pl

erlöschen† vi (sein) go out; (vergehen) die; (aussterben) die out; (ungültig werden) expire; **erloschener Vulkan** extinct volcano

erlös|en vt save; (befreien) release (von from); (Relig) redeem. **e~t** a relieved. **E~ung** f release; (Erleichterung) relief; (Relig) redemption

ermächtig|en vt authorize. **E~ung** f -,-en authorization

ermahn|en vt exhort; (zurechtweisen) admonish.

E~ung f exhortation; admonition

ermäßig|en vt reduce. **E~ung** f -,-en reduction

ermatt|en vi (sein) grow weary □ vt weary. **E~ung** f -weariness

ermessen† vt appreciate. **E~** nt -s discretion; (Urteil) judgement; **nach eigenem E~** at one's own discretion

ermitt|eln vt establish; (herausfinden) find out □ vi (haben) investigate (**gegen jdn** s.o.). **E~lungen** fpl investigations. **E~lungsverfahren** nt (Jur) preliminary inquiry

ermöglichen vt make possible

ermord|en vt murder. **E~ung** f -,-en murder

ermüd|en vt tire □ vi (sein) get tired. **E~ung** f -tiredness

ermunter|n vt encourage; **sich e~n** rouse oneself. **E~ung** f -encouragement

ermutigen vt encourage. **e~d** a encouraging

ernähr|en vt feed; (unterhalten) support, keep; **sich e~en von** live/(Tier:) feed on. **E~er** m -s,- breadwinner. **E~ung** f -nourishment; nutrition; (Kost) diet

ernenn|en† vt appoint. **E~ung** f -,-en appointment

erneuer|n vt renew; (auswechseln) replace; change (Verband); (renovieren) renovate. **E~erung** f renewal; replacement; renovation. **e~t** a renewed; (neu) new □ adv again

erniedrig|en vt degrade; **sich e~en** lower oneself **e~end** a degrading. **E~ungszeichen** nt (Mus) flat

ernst a serious, adv -ly; **e~ nehmen** take seriously. **E~** m -es seriousness; **im E~** seriously; **mit einer Drohung E~ machen** carry out a threat; **ist das dein E~?** are you serious? **E~fall** m **im E~fall** when the real thing

happens. e~haft a serious, adv
-ly. e~lich a serious, adv -ly

Ernte f -,-n harvest; (Ertrag)
crop. E~dankfest nt harvest
festival. e~n vt harvest; (fig)
reap, win

ernüchter|n vt sober up; (fig)
bring down to earth;
(enttäuschen) disillusion. e~nd a
(fig) sobering. E~ung f - disillu-
sionment

Erober|er m -s,- conqueror. e~n
vt conquer. E~ung f -,-en conquest

eröffn|en vt open; jdm etw e~en
announce sth to s.o.; sich jdm
e~en (Aussicht) present itself to
s.o. E~ung f opening; (Mitteilung) announcement. E~ungs-
ansprache f opening address

erörter|n vt discuss. E~ung f
-,-en discussion

Erosion f -,-en erosion

Erot|ik f -eroticism. e~isch a er-
otic

Erpel m -s,- drake

erpicht a e~auf (+ acc) keen on

erpress|en vt extort; blackmail
(Person). E~er m -s,- black-
mailer. E~ung f - extortion;
blackmail

erprob|en vt test. e~t a proven

erquicken vt refresh

erraten† vt guess

erreg|bar a excitable. e~en vt ex-
cite; (hervorrufen) arouse; sich
e~en get worked up. e~end a
exciting. E~er m -s,- (Med) germ.
e~t a agitated; (hitzig) heated.
E~ung f - excitement; (Erregt-
heit) agitation

erreich|bar a within reach; (Ziel)
attainable; (Person) available.
e~en vt reach; catch (Zug); live
to (Alter); (durchsetzen) achieve

erretten vt save

errichten vt erect

erringen† vt gain, win

erröten vi (sein) blush

Errungenschaft f -,-en achievement; (fam: Anschaffung) acquisition; E~en der Technik
technical advances

Ersatz m -es replacement, substitute; (Entschädigung) compensation. E~dienst m = Zivildienst.
E~reifen m spare tyre. E~spie-
ler(in) m(f) substitute. E~teil nt
spare part

ersäufen† vt drown

erschaffen† vt create

erschallen† vi (sein) ring out

erschein|en vi (sein) appear;
(Buch:) be published; jdm merkwürdig e~en seem odd to s.o.
E~en nt -s appearance; (Buch)
publication. E~ung f -,-en appearance; (Person) figure;
(Phänomen) phenomenon;
(Symptom) symptom; (Geist) apparition

erschieß|en† vt shoot [dead].
E~ungskommando nt firing
squad

erschlaffen vi (sein) go limp;
(Haut, Muskeln:) become flabby

erschlagen† vt beat to death; (tödlich treffen) strike dead; vom
Blitz e~ werden be killed by
lightning □ a (fam) (erschöpft)
worn out; (fassungslos) stunned

erschließen† vt develop; (zugänglich machen) open up; (nutzbar machen) tap

erschöpf|en vt exhaust. e~end a
exhausting; (fig: vollständig) ex-
haustive. e~t a exhausted.
E~ung f - exhaustion

erschreck|en† vi (sein) get a
fright □ vt (reg) startle; (beunruhigen) alarm; du hast mich
e~t you gave me a fright □ vr (reg
& irreg) sich e~en get a fright.
e~end a alarming, adv -ly

erschrocken a frightened;
(erschreckt) startled; (bestürzt)
dismayed

erschütter|n vt shake; (ergreifen)
upset deeply. E~ung f -,-en
shock

erschweren vt make more difficult

erschwinglich a affordable

ersehen† vt (fig) see (aus from)

ersetzen vt replace; make good (Schaden); refund (Kosten); **jdm etw e~** compensate s.o. for sth

ersichtlich a obvious, apparent

erspar|en vt save; **jdm etw e~** save/(ersparren) spare s.o. sth. **E~nis** f -,-se saving; **E~nisse** savings

erst adv (zuerst) first; (noch nicht mehr als) only; (nicht vor) not until; **e~ dann** only then; **eben od gerade e~** [only] just; **das machte ihn e~ recht wütend** it made him all the more angry

erstarren vi (sein) solidify; (gefrieren) freeze; (steif werden) go stiff; (vor Schreck) be paralysed

erstatten vt (zurück-) refund; Bericht e~ report (jdm to s.o.)

Erstaufführung f first performance, première

erstaun|en vt amaze, astonish. **E~en** nt amazement, astonishment. **e~lich** a amazing, adv -ly. **e~licherweise** adv amazingly

Erst|ausgabe f first edition. **e~e(r,s)** a first; (beste) best; **(E~e)** Hilfe first aid; **der e~e Beste** (beste) the first to come along; (fam) any Tom, Dick or Harry; **e~e** NEW **als E~es/fürs E~e** e~e als E~es/fürs E~e; **Erste(r,s)** m/f first; (Beste) best; **fürs E~e** for the time being; **als E~es** first of all; **er kam als E~er** he arrived first; **er ist der/sie ist die E~e in Latein** he/she is top in Latin

erstechen† vt stab to death

erstehen† vt buy

ersteigern vt buy at an auction

erst|emal adv **das e~emal/zum e~enmal** NEW **das erste Mal/zum ersten Mal,** s. Mal. **e~ens** adv firstly, in the first place. **e~e~r(r,s)** a the former; **der/die/das E~ere** (e~ere) the former

ersticken vt suffocate; smother (Flammen); (unterdrücken) suppress □ vi (sein) suffocate. **E~** nt -s suffocation; **zum E~** stifling

erst|klassig a first-class. **e~mals** adv for the first time

erstreben vt strive for. **e~swert** a desirable

erstrecken (sich) vr stretch; **sich e~auf** (+ acc) (fig) apply to

ersuchen vt ask, request. **E~** nt -s request

ertappen vt (fam) catch

erteilen vt give (jdm s.o.)

ertönen vi (sein) sound; (erschallen) ring out

Ertrag m -[e]s,-e yield. **e~en†** vt bear

erträglich a bearable; (leidlich) tolerable

ertränken vt drown

ertrinken† vi (sein) drown

erübrigen (sich) vr be unnecessary

erwachen vi (sein) awake

erwachsen a grown-up. **E~e(r)** m/f adult, grown-up

erwäg|en† vt consider. **E~ung** f -,-en consideration; **in E~ung ziehen** consider

erwähn|en vt mention. **E~ung** f -,-en mention

erwärmen vt warm; **sich e~** warm up; (fig) warm (**für** to)

erwart|en vt expect; (warten auf) wait for. **E~ung** f -,-en expectation. **e~ungsvoll** a expectant, adv -ly

erwecken vt (fig) arouse; give (Anschein)

erweichen vt soften; (fig) move; **sich e~ lassen** (fig) relent

erweisen† vt prove; (bezeigen) do (Gefallen, Dienst, Ehre); **sich e~ als** prove to be

erweitern vt widen; dilate (Pupille); (fig) extend, expand

Erwerb m -[e]s acquisition; (Kauf) purchase; (Brot-) livelihood; (Verdienst) earnings pl.

e~en† vt acquire; (kaufen) purchase; (fig: erlangen) gain.

e~slos a unemployed. e~stätig a [gainfully] employed. E~ung f -,-en acquisition

erwider|n vt reply; return ⟨Besuch, Gruß⟩. E~ung f -,-en reply

erwirken vt obtain

erwischen vt (fam) catch

erwünscht a desired

erwürgen vt strangle

Erz nt -es,-e ore

erzähl|en vt tell ⟨jdm s.o.⟩ □ vi (haben) talk ⟨von about⟩. E~er m -s,-, narrator. E~ung f -,-en story, tale

Erzbischof m archbishop

erzeug|en vt produce; (Electr) generate; (fig) create. E~er m -s,-, producer; (Vater) father. E~nis nt -ses,-se product; landwirtschaftliche E~nisse farm produce sg. E~ung f - production; generation

Erz|feind m arch-enemy. E~herzog m archduke

erzieh|en† vt bring up; (Sch) educate. E~er m -s,-, [private] tutor. E~erin f -,-nen governess. E~ung f - upbringing; education

erzielen vt achieve; score ⟨Tor⟩

erzogen a gut/schlecht e~ well/badly brought up

erzürnt a angry

erzwingen† vt force

es pron it; (Mädchen) she; (acc) her; impers es regnet it is raining; es gibt there is/(pl) are; ich hoffe es I hope so

Esche f -,-n ash

Esel m -s,-, donkey; (fam: Person) ass. E~sohr nt E~sohren haben ⟨Buch:⟩ be dog-eared

Eskalation f -,-en escalation. e~ieren vt/i (haben) escalate

Eskimo m -[s],-[s] Eskimo

Eskort|e f -,-n (Mil) escort. e~ieren vt escort

essbar (eßbar) a edible. Essecke (Eßecke) f dining area

essen† vt/i (haben) eat; zu Mittag Abend e~ have lunch/supper; (auswärts) e~ gehen eat out; chinesisch e~ have a Chinese meal. E~ nt -s,- food; (Mahl) meal; (festlich) dinner

Essenz f -,-en essence

Esser(in) m -s,- (f -,-nen) eater

Essig m -s vinegar. E~gurke f [pickled] gherkin

Esskastanie (Eßkastanie) f sweet chestnut. Esslöffel (Eßlöffel) m ≈ dessertspoon. Essstäbchen (Eßstäbchen) ntpl chopsticks. Esstisch (Eßtisch) m dining-table. Esswaren (Eßwaren) fpl food sg; (Vorräte) provisions. Esszimmer (Eßzimmer) nt dining-room

Estland nt -s Estonia

Estragon m -s tarragon

etablieren (sich) vr establish oneself/⟨Geschäft:⟩ itself

Etage f -'ta:ʒə/ f -,-n storey. E~nbett nt bunk-beds pl. E~nwohnung f flat, (Amer) apartment

Etappe f -,-n stage

Etat /e'ta:/ m -s,-s budget

etepetete a (fam) fussy

Eth|ik f - ethic; (Sittenlehre) ethics sg. e~isch a ethical

Etikett nt -[e]s,-e[n] label; (Preis-) tag. E~e f -,-n etiquette; (Aust) = Etikett. e~ieren vt label

etliche|(r,s) pron some; (mehrere) several; e~e Mal several times; e~es a number of things; (ziemlich viel) quite a lot. e~emal adv NEW e~e Mal, s. etliche(r,s)

Etui /e'tvi:/ nt -s,-s case

etwa adv (ungefähr) about; (zum Beispiel) for instance; (womöglich) perhaps; nicht e~, dass ... not that ...; denkt nicht e~ ... don't imagine ...; du hast doch nicht e~ Angst? you're not afraid, are you? e~ig a possible

etwas *pron* something; (*fragend/verneint*) anything; (*ein bisschen*) some, a little; **ohne e~ zu sagen** without saying anything; **sonst noch e~?** anything else? **noch e~ Tee?** some more tea? **so e~ Ärgerliches!** what a nuisance! □ *adv* a bit

Etymologie *f* - etymology

euch *pron* (*acc of* **ihr** *pl*) you; (*dat*) [to] you; (*refl*) yourselves; (*einander*) each other; **ein Freund von e~** a friend of yours

euer *poss pron pl* your. **e~e, e~s. eure, euret-**

Eule *f* -,-n owl

Euphorie *f* - euphoria

eur|e *poss pron pl* your. **e~e(r,s)** *poss pron* yours. **e~erseits** *adv* for your part. **e~etwegen** *adv* for your sake; (*wegen euch*) because of you, on your account. **e~etwillen** *adv* **um e~etwillen** for your sake. **e~ige** *poss pron* **der/die/das e~ige** yours

Euro *m* -[s]/-[s] Euro. **E~** *pref* Euro-

Europa *nt* -s Europe. **E~** *pref* European

Europä|er(in) *m* -s,- (*f* -,-nen) European. **e~isch** *a* European; **E~ische Gemeinschaft** European Community

Euro|paß *m* Europassport. **E~scheck** *m* Eurocheque

Euter *nt* -s,- udder

evakuier|en *vt* evacuate. **E~ung** *f* - evacuation

evangelisch *a* Protestant. **E~gelist** *m* -en,-en evangelist. **E~gelium** *nt* -s,-ien gospel

evaporieren *vt/i* (*sein*) evaporate

Eventual|ität *f* -,-en eventuality. **e~ell** *a* possible □ *adv* possibly; (*vielleicht*) perhaps

Evolution /-'tsjo:n/ *f* - evolution

evtl. *abbr s.* **eventuell**

ewig *a* eternal, *adv* -ly; (*fam:* ständig) constant, *adv* -ly; (*endlos*) never-ending; **e~ dauern** (*fam*) take ages. **E~keit** *f* - eternity; **eine E~keit** (*fam*) ages

exakt *a* exact, *adv* -ly. **E~heit** *f* - exactitude

Examen *nt* -s,- & **-mina** (*Sch*) examination

Exekutive *f* - (*Pol*) executive

Exempel *nt* -s,- example; **ein E~ an jdm statuieren** make an example of s.o.

Exemplar *nt* -s,-e specimen; (*Buch*) copy. **e~isch** *a* exemplary

exerzieren *vt/i* (*haben*) (*Mil*) drill; (*üben*) practise

exhumieren *vt* exhume

Exil *nt* -s exile

Existenz *f* -,-en existence; (*Lebensgrundlage*) livelihood; (*pej: Person*) individual

existieren *vi* (*haben*) exist

exklusiv *a* exclusive. **e~e** *prep* (+ *gen*) excluding

exkommunizieren *vt* excommunicate

Exkremente *npl* excrement *sg*

exotisch *a* exotic

expandieren *vt/i* (*haben*) expand. **E~sion** *f* - expansion

Expedition /-'tsjo:n/ *f* -,-en expedition

Experiment *nt* -[e]s,-e experiment. **e~ell** *a* experimental. **e~ieren** *vi* (*haben*) experiment

Experte *m* -n,-n expert

explo|dieren *vi* (*sein*) explode. **E~sion** *f* -,-en explosion. **e~siv** *a* explosive

Export *m* -[e]s,-e export. **E~teur** /-'tø:ɐ/ *m* -s,-e exporter. **e~tieren** *vt* export

Express *m* -es,-e (**Expreß** *m* -sses,-sse) express

extra *adv* separately; (*zusätzlich*) extra; (*eigens*) specially; (*fam: absichtlich*) on purpose

Extrakt *m* -[e]s,-e extract

Extras *npl* (*Auto*) extras

extravagant *a* flamboyant, *adv* -ly; (*übertrieben*) extravagant. **E~z** *f* -,-en flamboyance; extravagance; (*Überspanntheit*) folly

extravertiert *a* extrovert

extrem a extreme, adv -ly. E~ nt -s,-e extreme. E~ist m -en,-en extremist. E~itäten fpl extremities

Exzellenz f - (title) Excellency

Exzentr|iker m -s,- eccentric. e~isch a eccentric

Exzess m -es,-e (Exzeß m -sses, -sse) excess

F

Fabel f -,-n fable. f~haft a (fam) fantastic, adv -ally

Fabrik f -,-en factory. F~ant m -en,-en manufacturer. F~at nt -[e]s,-e product; (Marke) make. F~ation /-'tsio:n/ f - manufacture

Facette /fa'sɛtə/ f -,-n facet

Fach nt -[e]s,¨er compartment; (Schub-) drawer; (Gebiet) field; (Sch) subject. F~arbeiter m skilled worker. F~arzt m, F~ärztin f specialist. F~ausdruck m technical term

fäch|eln (sich) vr fan oneself. F~er m -s,- fan

Fach|gebiet nt field. f~gemäß, f~gerecht a expert, adv -ly. F~hochschule f ≈ technical university. f~kundig a expert, adv -ly. f~lich a technical, adv -ly; (beruflich) professional. F~mann m (pl -leute) expert. f~männisch a expert, adv -ly. F~schule f technical college. f~simpeln vi (haben) (fam) talk shop. F~werkhaus nt half-timbered house. F~wort nt (pl -wörter) technical term

Fackel f -,-n torch. F~zug m torchlight procession

fade a insipid; (langweilig) dull

Faden m -s,¨ thread; (Bohnen-) string; (Naut) fathom. f~scheinig a threadbare; (Grund) flimsy

Fagott nt -[e]s,-e bassoon

fähig a capable (zu/gen of); (tüchtig) able, competent. F~keit f -,-en ability; competence

fahl a pale

fahnd|en vi (haben) search (nach for). F~ung f -,-en search

Fahne f -,-n flag; (Druck-) galley [proof]; eine F~ haben (fam) reek of alcohol. F~nflucht f desertion. f~nflüchtig a f~nflüchtig werden desert

Fahr|ausweis m ticket. F~bahn f carriageway; (Straße) road. f~bar a mobile

Fähre f -,-n ferry

fahren† vi (sein) go; travel; (Fahrer:) drive; (Radfahrer:) ride; (verkehren) run; (ab-) leave; (Schiff:) sail; mit dem Auto/Zug f~en go by car/train; in die Höhe f~en start up; in die Kleider f~en throw on one's clothes; mit der Hand über etw (acc) f~en run one's hand over sth; was ist in ihn gefahren? (fam) what has got into him? □ vt drive; ride (Fahrrad); take (Kurve). f~end a moving; (f~bar) mobile; (nicht sesshaft) travelling, itinerant. F~er m -s,- driver. F~erflucht f failure to stop after an accident. F~erhaus nt driver's cab. F~erin f -,-nen woman driver. F~gast m passenger; (im Taxi) fare. F~geld nt fare. F~gestell nt chassis; (Aviat) undercarriage. f~ig a nervy; (zerstreut) distracted. F~karte f ticket. F~kartenausgabe f, F~kartenschalter m ticket office. f~lässig a negligent, adv -ly. F~lässigkeit f - negligence. F~lehrer m driving instructor. F~plan m timetable. f~planmäßig a scheduled □ adv according to/(pünktlich) on schedule. F~preis m fare. F~prüfung f driving test. F~rad nt bicycle. F~schein m ticket

Fährschiff nt ferry

Fahr|schule f driving school.
F~schüler(in) m(f) learner
driver. **F~spur** f [traffic] lane.
F~stuhl m lift; (Amer) elevator.
F~stunde f driving lesson

Fahrt f -,-en journey; (Auto)
drive; (Ausflug) trip; (Tempo)
speed; **in voller F~** at full speed.
F~ausweis m ticket

Fährte f -,-n track; (Witterung)
scent; **auf der falschen F~** (fig)
on the wrong track

Fahr|kosten pl travelling expenses. **F~werk** nt undercarriage.
F~zeug nt -[e]s,-e vehicle;
(Wasser-) craft, vessel

fair /fɛːɐ̯/ a fair, adv -ly. **F~ness**
(**F~neß**) f -fairness

Fakten pl facts

Faktor m -s,-en /-'toːrən/ factor

Fakul|tät f -,-en faculty. **f~tativ**
a optional

Falke m -n,-n falcon

Fall m -[e]s,¨e fall; (Jur, Med,
Gram) case; **im F~[e]** in case
(gen of); **auf jeden F~,** **auf alle
F~e** in any case; (bestimmt) definitely; **für alle F~e** just in case;
auf keinen F~ on no account

Falle f -,-n trap; **eine F~ stellen**
set a trap (dat for)

fallen† vi (sein) fall; (sinken) go
down; **[im Krieg] f~** be killed in
the war; **f~ lassen** drop (etw, Bg-
Plan, jdn); make (Bemerkung)

fällen vt fell; (fig) pass (Urteil);
make (Entscheidung)

fallen|lassen† vt sep (NEW) **fallen
lassen,** s. **fallen**

fällig a due; (Wechsel) mature;
längst f~ long overdue. **F~keit**
f -(Comm) maturity

Fallobst nt windfalls pl

falls conj in case; (wenn) if

Fallschirm m parachute.
F~jäger m paratrooper.
F~springer m parachutist

Falltür f trapdoor

falsch a wrong; (nicht echt, unaufrichtig) false; (gefälscht) forged;

(Geld) counterfeit; (Schmuck)
fake □ adv wrongly; falsely;
(singen) out of tune; **f~ gehen**
(Uhr:) be wrong

fälsch|en vt forge, fake. **F~er** m
-s,- forger

Falsch|geld nt counterfeit
money. **F~heit** f - falseness

fälschlich a wrong, adv -ly; (irrtümlich) mistaken, adv -ly.
f~erweise adv by mistake

Falsch|meldung f false report;
(absichtlich) hoax report.
F~münzer m -s,- counterfeiter

Fälschung f -,-en forgery, fake;
(Fälschen) forging

Falte f -,-n fold; (Rock-) pleat;
(Knitter-) crease; (im Gesicht)
line; (Runzel) wrinkle

falten vt fold; **sich f~** (Haut:)
wrinkle. **F~rock** m pleated skirt

Falter m -s,- butterfly; (Nacht-)
moth

faltig a creased; (Gesicht) lined;
(runzlig) wrinkled

familiär a family ...; (vertraut,
zudringlich) familiar; (zwanglos)
informal

Familie /-jə/ f -,-n family.
F~nanschluss (**F~nanschluß**)
m **F~nanschluss haben** live as
one of the family. **F~nforschung** f genealogy. **F~nleben**
nt family life. **F~nname** m surname. **F~nplanung** f family
planning. **F~nstand** m marital
status

Fan /fɛn/ m -s,-s fan

Fana|tiker m -s,- fanatic. **f~tisch**
a fanatical, adv -ly. **F~tismus** m
- fanaticism

Fanfare f -,-n trumpet; (Signal)
fanfare

Fang m -[e]s,¨e capture; (Beute)
catch; **F~e** (Krallen) talons;
(Zähne) fangs. **F~arm** m tentacle. **f~en†** vt catch; (ein-) capture; **sich f~en** get caught (in +
dat in); (fig) regain one's balance/
(seelisch) composure; **gefangen**

nehmen take prisoner; **gefangen halten** hold prisoner; keep in captivity 〈*Tier*〉. **F~en nt -s F~en spielen** play day tag. **F~frage** *f* catch question. **F~zahn** *m* fang

Fantasie *f* -,-n = **Phantasie**

fantastisch *a* = **phantastisch**

Farb|aufnahme *f* colour photograph. **F~band** *nt* (*pl* -bänder) typewriter ribbon. **F~e** *f* -,-n colour; 〈*Maler*〉 paint; 〈*zum Färben*〉 dye; 〈*Karten*〉 suit. **f~echt** a colour-fast

färben *vt* colour; dye 〈*Textilien, Haare*〉; 〈*fig*〉 slant 〈*Bericht*〉; **sich [rot] f~** turn [red] □ *vi* 〈*haben*〉 not be colour-fast

farb|enblind *a* colour-blind. **f~enfroh** *a* colourful. **F~fernsehen** *nt* colour television. **F~film** *m* colour film. **F~foto** *nt* colour photo. **f~ig** *a* coloured □ *adv* in colour. **F~ige(r)** *m/f* coloured man/woman. **F~kasten** *m* box of paints. **f~los** *a* colourless. **F~stift** *m* crayon. **F~stoff** *m* dye; 〈*Lebensmittel-*〉 colouring. **F~ton** *m* shade

Färbung *f* -,-en colouring; 〈*fig: Anstrich*〉 bias

Farce /'farsə/ *f* -,-n farce; 〈*Culin*〉 stuffing

Farn *m* -[e]s,-e, **F~kraut** *nt* fern

Färse *f* -,-n heifer

Fasan *m* -[e]s,-e[n] pheasant

Fasch|ierte(s) *nt* 〈*Aust*〉 mince **F~ing** *m* -s 〈*SGer*〉 carnival

Faschis|mus *m* - fascism. **F~t** *m* -en,-en fascist. **f~tisch** *a* fascist

faseln *vt/i* 〈*haben*〉 〈*fam*〉 [Unsinn] **f~** talk nonsense

Faser *f* -,-n fibre. **f~n** *vi* 〈*haben*〉 fray

Fass *nt* -es,-er 〈*Faß nt* -sses,-sser〉 barrel, cask; **Bier vom F~** draught beer; **F~ ohne Boden** 〈*fig*〉 bottomless pit

Fassade *f* -,-n façade

fassbar (**faßbar**) *a* comprehensible; 〈*greifbar*〉 tangible

fassen *vt* take [hold of], grasp; 〈*ergreifen*〉 seize; 〈*fangen*〉 catch; 〈*ein-*〉 set; 〈*enthalten*〉 hold; 〈*fig: begreifen*〉 take in, grasp; conceive 〈*Plan*〉; make 〈*Entschluss*〉; **sich f~** compose oneself; **sich kurz/in Geduld f~** be brief/patient; **in Worte f~** put into words; **nicht zu f~** 〈*fig*〉 unbelievable □ *vi* 〈*haben*〉 **f~ an** (+ *acc*) touch; **f~ nach** reach for

fasslich (**faßlich**) *a* comprehensible

Fasson /fa'sõ:/ *f* - style; 〈*Form*〉 shape; 〈*Weise*〉 way

Fassung *f* -,-en mount; 〈*Edelstein-*〉 setting; 〈*Electr*〉 socket; 〈*Version*〉 version; 〈*Beherrschung*〉 composure; **aus der F~ bringen** disconcert. **f~slos** *a* shaken; 〈*erstaunt*〉 flabbergasted. **F~svermögen** *nt* capacity

fast *adv* almost, nearly; **f~ nie** hardly ever

fasten *vi* 〈*haben*〉 fast. **F~enzeit** *f* Lent. **F~nacht** *f* Shrovetide; 〈*Karneval*〉 carnival. **F~nachtsdienstag** *m* Shrove Tuesday. **F~tag** *m* fast-day

Faszin|ation /-'tsio:n/ *f* - fascination. **f~ieren** *vt* fascinate; **f~ierend** fascinating

fatal *a* fatal; 〈*peinlich*〉 embarrassing. **F~ismus** *m* - fatalism. **F~ist** *m* -en,-en fatalist

Fata Morgana *f* -,-nen mirage

fauchen *vi* 〈*haben*〉 spit, hiss □ *vt* snarl

faul *a* lazy; 〈*verdorben*〉 rotten, bad; 〈*Ausrede*〉 lame; 〈*zweifelhaft*〉 bad; 〈*verdächtig*〉 fishy

Fäule *f* - decay

faul|en *vi* 〈*sein*〉 rot; 〈*Zahn:*〉 decay; 〈*verwesen*〉 putrefy. **f~enzen** *vi* 〈*haben*〉 be lazy. **F~enzer** *m* -s,-lazy-bones *sg*. **F~heit** *f* - laziness. **f~ig** *a* rotting; 〈*Geruch*〉 putrid

Fäulnis *f* - decay

Faulpelz m (fam) lazy-bones sg
Fauna f - fauna
Faust f -,*Fäuste* fist; **auf eigene F~** (fig) off one's own bat.
F~handschuh m mitten.
F~schlag m punch
Fauxpas /foʹpa/ m -,- /-[s],-s/ gaffe
Favorit(in) /favoʹriːt(ɪn)/ m -en, -en (f -,-nen) (Sport) favourite
Fax nt -,-[e] fax. **f~en** vt fax
Faxen fpl (fam) antics; **F~ machen** fool about; **F~ schneiden** pull faces
Faxgerät nt fax machine
Feber m -s,- (Aust) February
Februar m -s,-e February
fecht|en vi (haben) fence. **F~er** m -s,- fencer
Feder f -,-n feather; (Schreib-) pen; (Spitze) nib; (Techn) spring. **F~ball** m shuttlecock; (Spiel) badminton. **F~busch** m plume. **f~leicht** a as light as a feather. **F~messer** nt penknife. **f~nd** vi (haben) be springy; (nachgeben) give; (hoch-) bounce. **f~nd** a springy; (elastisch) elastic. **F~ung** f - (Techn) springs pl; (Auto) suspension
Fee f -,-n fairy
Fegefeuer nt purgatory
fegen vt sweep □ vi (sein) (rasen) tear
Fehde f -,-n feud
fehl a **f~ am Platze** out of place. **F~betrag** m deficit. **f~en** vi (haben) be missing/(Sch) absent; (mangeln) be lacking; **es f~t an** (+ dat) there is a shortage of; **mir f~t die Zeit** I haven't got the time; **sie/es f~t mir sehr** I miss her/it very much; **was f~t ihm?** what's the matter with him? **es f~te nicht viel und er ... he** very nearly ...; **das hat uns noch gefehlt!** that's all we need!
f~end a missing; (Sch) absent
Fehler m -s,- mistake, error; (Sport & fig) fault; (Makel) flaw. **f~frei** a faultless, adv -ly. **f~haft** a

faulty. **f~los** a flawless, adv -ly
Fehl|geburt f miscarriage.
f~gehen† vi sep (sein) go wrong; (Schuss:) miss; (fig) be mistaken. **F~griff** m mistake. **F~kalkulation** f miscalculation. **F~schlag** m failure. **f~schlagen†** vi sep (sein) fail. **F~start** m (Sport) false start. **F~tritt** m false step; (fig) [moral] lapse. **F~zündung** f (Auto) misfire
Feier f -,-n celebration; (Zeremonie) ceremony; (Party) party. **F~abend** m end of the working day; **F~abend machen** stop work, (fam) knock off; **nach F~abend** after work. **f~lich** a solemn, adv -ly; (förmlich) formal, adv -ly. **F~lichkeit** f -,-en solemnity; (Party) festivity. **F~lichkeiten** festivities. **f~n** vt celebrate; hold (Fest); (ehren) fête □ vi (haben) celebrate; (lustig sein) make merry. **F~tag** m [public] holiday; (kirchlicher) feast-day; **erster/zweiter F~tag** Christmas Day / Boxing Day. **f~tags** adv on public holidays
feige a cowardly; **f~ sein** be a coward □ adv in a cowardly way
Feige f -,-n fig. **F~nbaum** m fig tree
Feigheit f - cowardice. **F~ling** m -s,-e coward
Feile f -,-n file. **f~n** vt/i (haben) file
feilschen vi (haben) haggle
Feilspäne mpl filings
fein a fine, adv -ly; (zart) delicate, adv -ly; (Strümpfe) sheer; (Unterschied) subtle; (scharf) keen; (vornehm) refined; (elegant) elegant; (prima) great; **sich f~ machen** dress up. **F~arbeit** f precision work
feind a jdm **f~ sein** (NEW) jdm **F~ sein**, s Feind. **F~(in)** m -es,-e (f -,-nen) enemy; **jdm F~ sein** be hostile towards s.o. **f~lich** a enemy; (f~selig) hostile.

F~schaft f -,-en enmity. f~selig a hostile. F~seligkeit f -,-en hostility

fein|fühlig a sensitive. F~gefühl nt sensitivity; (Takt) delicacy. F~heit f -,-en (s. fein) fineness; delicacy; subtlety; keenness; refinement. f~heiten subtleties. F~kostgeschäft nt delicatessen [shop]. F~schmecker m -s,- gourmet

feist a fat

feixen vi (haben) smirk

Feld nt -[e]s,-er field; (Fläche) ground; (Sport) pitch; (Schach-) square; (auf Formular) box. F~bau m agriculture. F~bett nt camp-bed, (Amer) cot. F~forschung f fieldwork. F~herr m commander. F~marschall m Field Marshal. F~stecher m -s,-, field-glasses pl. F~webel m -s,- (Mil) sergeant. F~zug m campaign

Felge f -,-n [wheel] rim

Fell nt -[e]s,-e rock. F~block m boulder. F~en m -s,- rock. f~enfest a (fig) firm, adv -ly. f~ig a rocky

feminin a feminine; (weiblich) effeminate

Femininum nt -s,-na (Gram) feminine

Feminist|(in) m -en,-en (f -,-nen) feminist. f~isch a feminist

Fenchel m -s fennel

Fenster nt -s,- window. F~brett nt window-sill. F~laden m [window] shutter. F~leder nt chamois-[leather]. F~putzer m -s,- window-cleaner. F~scheibe f [window-]pane

Ferien /'fe:rjən/ pl holidays; (Univ) vacation sg; F~ haben be on holiday. F~ort m holiday resort

Ferkel nt -s,- piglet

fern a distant; der F~e Osten the Far East; f~ halten keep away; sich f~ halten keep away □ adv far away; von f~ from a distance □ prep (+ dat) far [away] from. F~bedienung f remote control. f~bleiben† vi sep (sein) stay away (dat from). F~e f - distance; in/aus der F~e in/from a distance; in weiter F~e far away; (zeitlich) in the distant future. f~er a further □ adv (außerdem) furthermore; (in Zukunft) in future. f~gelenkt a remote-controlled, (Rakete) guided. F~gespräch nt long-distance call. f~gesteuert a = f~gelenkt. F~glas nt binoculars pl. f~halten† vt sep NEW = f~ halten, s. fern. F~kopierer m -s,- fax machine. F~kurs[us] m correspondence course. F~lenkung f remote control. F~licht nt (Auto) full beam. F~meldewesen nt telecommunications pl. F~rohr nt telescope. F~schreiben nt telex. F~schreiber m -s,- telex [machine]

Fernseh|apparat m television set. f~en† vi sep (haben) watch television. F~en nt -s television. F~er m -s,- [television] viewer; (Gerät) television set. F~gerät nt television set

Fernsprech|amt nt telephone exchange, (Amer) central. F~er m telephone. F~nummer f telephone number. F~zelle f telephone box

Fernsteuerung f remote control

Ferse f -,-n heel. F~ngeld nt F~ngeld geben (fam) take to one's heels

fertig a finished; (bereit) ready; (Comm) ready-made; (Gericht) ready-to-serve; f~ werden mit finish; (bewältigen) cope with; f~ sein have finished; (fig) be through (mit jdm with s.o.); (fam: erschöpft) be all in/(see-lisch) shattered; etw f~ bringen od (fam) **kriegen** manage to do sth; (beenden) finish sth; **ich bringe od** (fam) **kriege es nicht f~** I can't bring myself to do it; **etw/jdn f~ machen** finish sth; (bereitmachen) get sth/s.o. ready; (fam: erschöpfen) wear s.o. out; (seelisch) shatter s.o.; (fam: abkanzeln) carpet s.o.; **sich f~ machen** get ready; **etw f~ stellen** complete sth □ adv f~ **essen/lesen** finish eating/reading. **F~bau** m (pl -bauten) prefabricated building. **f~bringen†** vt sep NEW← **bringen**, s. **fertig**. **f~en** vt make. **f~gericht** nt ready-to-serve meal. **F~haus** nt prefabricated house. **F~keit** f -,-en skill. **f~kriegen** vt sep (fam) NEW← **kriegen**, s. **fertig**. **f~machen** vt sep NEW← f~ **machen**, s. **fertig**. **f~stellen** vt sep NEW← f~ **stellen**, s. **fertig**. **F~stellung** f completion. **F~ung** f - manufacture

fesch a (fam) attractive; (flott) smart; (Aust: nett) kind

Fessel f -,-n ankle

fesseln vt tie up; tie (an + acc to); (fig) fascinate; **ans Bett gefesselt** confined to bed. **F~** fpl bonds. **f~d** a (fig) fascinating; (packend) absorbing

fest a firm; (nicht flüssig) solid; (erstarrt) set; (haltbar) strong; (nicht locker) tight; (feststehend) fixed; (ständig) steady; (Anstellung) permanent; (Schlaf) sound; (Blick, Stimme) steady; **f~ werden** harden; (Gelee:) set; **f~e Nahrung** solids pl □ adv firmly; tightly; steadily; soundly; (kräftig, tüchtig) hard; **f~ schlafen** be fast asleep; **f~ angestellt** permanent

Fest nt -[e]s,-e celebration; (Party) party; (Relig) festival; **frohes F~!** happy Christmas!

fest|angestellt a NEW← f~ **angestellt**, s. **fest**. **f~binden†** vt sep tie (an + dat to). **f~bleiben†** vi

sep (sein) (fig) remain firm. **f~e** adv (fam) hard. **F~essen** nt = **F~mahl**. **f~fahren†** vi/r sep (sein) [sich] **f~fahren** get stuck; (Verhandlungen:) reach deadlock. **f~halten†** v sep vt hold on to; (aufzeichnen) record; **sich f~halten** hold on □ vi (haben) **f~halten** an (+ dat) (fig) stick to; cling to (Tradition). **f~igen** vt strengthen; (fig) grow stronger. **F~iger** m -s,- styling lotion/(Schaum-) mousse. **F~igkeit** f -(s. **fest**) firmness; solidity; strength; steadiness. **f~klammern** vt sep clip (an + dat to); **sich f~klammern** cling (an + dat to). **F~land** nt mainland; (Kontinent) continent. **f~legen** vt sep (fig) fix, settle; lay down (Regeln); tie up (Geld); **sich f~legen** commit oneself

festlich a festive, adv -ly. **F~keiten** fpl festivities

fest|liegen† vi sep (haben) be fixed, settled. **f~machen** v sep □ vt fasten/(binden) tie (an + dat to); (f~legen) fix, settle □ vi (haben) (Naut) moor. **f~mahl** nt feast; (Bankett) banquet. **F~nahme** f -,-n arrest. **f~nehmen†** vt sep arrest. **F~ordner** m steward. **f~setzen** vt sep fix, settle; (inhaftieren) gaol; **sich f~setzen** collect. **f~sitzen†** vi sep (haben) be firm/(Schraube:) tight; (haften) stick; (nicht weiterkommen) be stuck. **f~spiele** npl festival sg. **f~stehen†** vi sep (haben) be certain. **f~stellen** vt sep (ermitteln) establish; (bemerken) notice; (sagen) state. **F~stellung** f establishment; (Aussage) statement; (Erkenntnis) realization. **F~tag** m special day

Festung f -,-en fortress

Fest|zelt nt marquee. **F~ziehen†** vt sep pull tight. **F~zug** m [grand] procession

Fete /'fe:tə, 'fɛ:tə/ f -,-n party

fett a fat; ⟨f~reich⟩ fatty; ⟨fettig⟩ greasy; ⟨üppig⟩ rich; ⟨Druck⟩ bold; **f~ gedruckt** bold. **F~** nt -[e]s,-e fat; ⟨flüssig⟩ grease. **f~arm** a low-fat. **f~en** vt grease □ vi (haben) be greasy. **F~fleck** m grease mark. **f~ig** a greasy. **f~leibig** a obese. **F~näpfchen** nt **ins F~näpfchen treten** (fam) put one's foot in it

Fetzen m -s,- scrap; ⟨Stoff⟩ rag; **in F~** in shreds

feucht a damp, moist; ⟨Luft⟩ humid. **f~heiß** a humid. **F~igkeit** f -dampness; ⟨Nässe⟩ moisture; ⟨Luft-⟩ humidity. **F~igkeitscreme** f moisturizer

feudal a ⟨fam: vornehm⟩ sumptuous, adv -ly. **F~ismus** m -feudalism

Feuer nt -s,-fire; ⟨für Zigarette⟩ light; ⟨Begeisterung⟩ passion; **F~ machen** light a fire; **F~ fangen** catch fire; ⟨fam: sich verlieben⟩ be smitten; **jdm F~ geben** give s.o. a light; **F~ speiender Berg** volcano. **F~alarm** m fire alarm. **F~bestattung** f cremation. **f~gefährlich** a [in]flammable. **F~leiter** f fire-escape. **F~löscher** m -s,- fire extinguisher. **F~melder** m -s,- fire alarm. **f~n** vi (haben) fire (**auf** + acc on) □ vt (fam) ⟨schleudern⟩ fling; ⟨entlassen⟩ fire. **F~probe** f (fig) test. **F~rot** a crimson. **f~speiend** a ⟨NEW⟩ **F~ speiend,** s. **Feuer. F~stein** m flint. **F~stelle** f hearth. **F~treppe** f fire-escape. **F~wache** f fire station. **F~waffe** f firearm. **F~wehr** f -,-en fire brigade. **F~wehrauto** nt fire-engine. **F~wehrmann** m (pl -männer & -leute) fireman. **F~werk** nt firework display, fireworks pl. **F~werkskörper** m firework. **F~zeug** nt lighter

feurig a fiery; (fig) passionate

Fiaker m -s,- ⟨Aust⟩ horse-drawn cab

Fichte f -,-n spruce

fidel a cheerful

Fieber nt -[raised] temperature; **F~ haben** have a temperature. **f~haft** a (fig) feverish, adv -ly. **f~n** vi (haben) be feverish. **F~thermometer** nt thermometer

fiebrig a feverish

fies a (fam) nasty, adv -ily

Figur f -,-en figure; ⟨Roman-, Film-⟩ character; ⟨Schach-⟩ piece

Fiktion /-'tsio:n/ f -,-en fiction. **f~tiv** a fictitious

Filet /fi'le:/ nt -s,-s fillet

Filia|le f -,-n, **F~geschäft** nt ⟨Comm⟩ branch

Filigran nt -s filigree

Film m -[e]s,-e film; ⟨Kino-⟩ film, ⟨Amer⟩ movie; ⟨Schicht⟩ coating. **f~en** vt/i (haben) film. **F~kamera** f cine/⟨für Kinofilm⟩ film camera

Filt|er m & ⟨Techn⟩ nt -s,- filter; ⟨Zigaretten-⟩ filter-tip. **f~ern** vt filter. **F~erzigarette** f filter-tipped cigarette. **f~rieren** vt filter

Filz m -es felt. **f~en** vi (haben) become matted □ vt (fam) ⟨durchsuchen⟩ frisk; ⟨stehlen⟩ steal. **F~schreiber** m -s,-, **F~stift** m felt-tipped pen

Fimmel m -s,- (fam) obsession

Fina|le nt -s,- ⟨Mus⟩ finale; ⟨Sport⟩ final. **F~list(in)** m -en,-en (f -,-nen) finalist

Finanz f -,-en finance. **F~amt** nt tax office. **F~iell** a financial, adv -ly. **f~ieren** vt finance. **F~minister** m minister of finance

finden† vt find; ⟨meinen⟩ think; **den Tod f~en** meet one's death; **wie f~est du das?** what do you think of that? **f~est du?** do you think so? **es wird sich f~en** it'll turn up; (fig) it'll be all right □ vi (haben) find one's way. **F~er** m -s,- finder. **F~erlohn** m reward.

f~ig *a* resourceful. F~ling *m*
-s,-e boulder

Finesse *f* -,-n *(Kniff)* trick; F~n
(Techn) refinements

Finger *m* -s,-: finger; die F~
lassen von *(fam)* leave alone;
etw im kleinen F~ haben *(fam)*
have sth at one's fingertips.
F~abdruck *m* finger-mark; *(admin)* fingerprint. F~hut *m* thimble. F~nagel *m* finger-nail.
F~ring *m* ring. F~spitze *f* finger-tip. F~zeig *m* -[e]s,-e hint

fingieren *vt* fake. f~t *a* fictitious

Fink *m* -en,-en finch

Finn|e *m* -n,-n, F~in *f* -,-nen
Finn. f~isch *a* Finnish. F~land
nt -s Finland

finster *a* dark; *(düster)* gloomy;
(unheildrohend) sinister; im
F~n in the dark. F~nis *f* - darkness; *(Astr)* eclipse

Finte *f* -,-n trick; *(Boxen)* feint

Firma *f* -,-men firm, company

firmen *vt (Relig)* confirm

Firmen|wagen *m* company car.
F~zeichen *nt* trade mark, logo

Firmung *f* -,-en *(Relig)* confirmation

Firnis *m* -ses,-se varnish. f~sen
vt varnish

First *m* -[e]s,-e *[roof]* ridge

Fisch *m* -[e]s,-e fish; F~e *(Astr)*
Pisces. F~dampfer *m* trawler.
f~en *vt/i (haben)* fish; aus dem
Wasser f~en *(fam)* fish out of
the water. F~er *m* -s,- fisherman.
F~erei *f* -, F~fang *m* fishing.
F~gräte *f* fishbone. F~händler
m fishmonger. F~otter *m* otter.
F~reiher *m* heron. F~stäbchen
nt -s,- fish finger. F~teich *m* fishpond

Fiskus *m* - der F~ the Treasury

Fisole *f* -,-n *(Aust)* French bean

fit *a* fit. Fitness (Fitneß) *f* -fitness

fix *a (fam)* quick, adv -ly; *(geistig)*
bright; f~e Idee obsession; fix
und fertig all finished; *(bereit)* all
ready; *(fam: erschöpft)* shattered.
F~er *m* -s,- *(sl)* junkie

fixieren *vt* stare at; *(Phot)* fix

Fjord *m* -[e]s,-e fiord

FKK *abbr* (Freikörperkultur)
naturism

flach *a* flat; *(eben)* level; *(niedrig)*
low; *(nicht tief)* shallow; f~er
Teller dinner plate; die f~e
Hand the flat of the hand

Fläche *f* -,-n area; *(Ober-)* surface;
(Seite) face. F~nmaß *nt* square
measure

Flachs *m* -es flax. f~blond *a*
flaxen-haired; *(Haar)* flaxen

flackern *vi (haben)* flicker

Flagge *f* -,-n flag

flagrant *a* flagrant

Flair /flɛːɐ̯/ *nt* -s air, aura

Flak *f* -,-[s] anti-aircraft artillery/*(Geschütz)* gun

flämisch *a* Flemish

Flamme *f* -,-n flame; *(Koch-)*
burner; in F~n in flames

Flanell *m* -s *(Tex)* flannel

Flank|e *f* -,-n flank. f~ieren *vt*
flank

Flasche *f* -,-n bottle. F~nbier *nt*
bottled beer. F~nöffner *m*
bottle-opener

flatter|haft *a* fickle. f~n *vi (sein/
haben)* flutter; *(Segel-)* flap

flau *a (schwach)* faint; *(Comm)*
slack; mir ist f~ I feel faint

Flaum *m* -s down. f~ig *a*
downy; f~ig rühren *(Aust Culin)*
cream

flauschig *a* fleecy; *(Spielzeug)*
fluffy

Flausen *fpl (fam)* silly ideas;
(Ausflüchte) silly excuses

Flaute *f* -,-n *(Naut)* calm; *(Comm)*
slack period; *(Schwäche)* low

fläzen (sich) *vr (fam)* sprawl

Flechte *f* -,-n *(Med)* eczema; *(Bot)*
lichen; *(Zopf)* plait. f~n† *vt* plait;
weave *(Korb)*

Fleck *m* -[e]s,-e[n] spot; *(größer)*
patch; *(Schmutz-)* stain, mark;
blauer F~ bruise; nicht vom
F~kommen *(fam)* make no progress. f~en *vi (haben)* stain.

F~en m -s,- = Fleck; (Ortschaft) small town. f~enlos a spotless. F~entferner m -s,- stain remover. f~ig a stained; (Haut) blotchy

Fledermaus f bat

Flegel m -s,- lout. f~haft a loutish. F~jahre npl (fam) awkward age sg. f~n (sich) vr loll

flehen vi (haben) beg (um for). f~tlich a pleading, adv -ly

Fleisch nt -[es] flesh; (Culin) meat; (Frucht-) pulp; F~ fressend carnivorous. F~er m -s,- butcher. F~erei f -,-en, F~erladen m butcher's shop. f~fressend a (NEW) F~ fressend, s. Fleisch. F~fresser m -s,- carnivore. F~hauer m -s,- (Aust) butcher. f~ig a fleshy. f~lich a carnal. F~wolf m mincer. F~wunde f flesh-wound

Fleiß m -es diligence; mit F~ diligently; (absichtlich) on purpose. f~ig a diligent, adv -ly; (arbeitsam) industrious, adv -ly

flektieren vt (Gram) inflect

fletschen vt die Zähne f~ ⟨Tier⟩ bare its teeth

flexibel a flexible; (Einband) limp. F~ibilität f - flexibility. F~ion f -,-en (Gram) inflexion

flicken vt mend; (mit Flicken) patch. F~ m -s,- patch

Flieder m -s lilac. f~farben a lilac

Fliege f -,-n fly; (Schleife) bow-tie; zwei F~n mit einer Klappe schlagen kill two birds with one stone. f~n† vi (sein) fly; (geworfen werden) be thrown; (zu Fallen) fall; (fam: entlassen werden) be fired/(von der Schule) expelled; in die Luft f~n blow up □ vt fly. f~nd a flying; ⟨Händler⟩ itinerant; in f~nder Eile in great haste. F~r m -s,- airman; (Pilot) pilot; (fam: Flugzeug) plane. F~rangriff m air raid

fliehen† vi (sein) flee (vor + dat from); (entweichen) escape □ vt

shun. f~end a fleeing; ⟨Kinn, Stirn⟩ receding. F~kraft f centrifugal force

Fliese f -,-n tile

Fließband nt assembly line. f~en† vi (sein) flow; (aus Wasserhahn) run. f~end a flowing; ⟨Wasser⟩ running; (Verkehr) moving; (geläufig) fluent, adv -ly. F~heck nt fastback. F~wasser nt running water

flimmern vi (haben) shimmer; (TV) flicker; es flimmert mir vor den Augen everything is dancing in front of my eyes

flink a nimble, adv -bly; (schnell) quick, adv -ly

Flinte f -,-n shotgun

Flirt /flœrt/ m -s,-s flirtation. f~en vi (haben) flirt

Flitter m -s sequins pl; (F~schmuck) tinsel. F~wochen fpl honeymoon sg

flitzen vi (sein) (fam) dash; ⟨Auto:⟩ whizz

Flock|e f -,-n flake; (Wolle) tuft. f~ig a fluffy

Floh m -[e]s,ˈe flea. F~markt m flea market. F~spiel nt tiddlywinks sg

Flor m -s gauze; (Trauer-) crape; (Samt-, Teppich-) pile

Flora f - flora

Florett nt -[e]s,-e foil

florieren vi (haben) flourish

Floskel f -,-n (empty) phrase

Floß nt -es,ˈe raft

Flosse f -,-n fin; (Seehund-, Gummi-) flipper; (sl: Hand) paw

Flöt|e f -,-n flute; (Block-) recorder. f~en vi (haben) play the flute/recorder; (fam: pfeifen) whistle □ vt play on the flute/recorder. F~ist(in) m -en,-en (f -,-nen) flautist

flott a quick, adv -ly; (lebhaft) lively; (schick) smart, adv -ly. f~leben live it up

Flotte f -,-n fleet

flottmachen vt sep wieder f∼ (Naut) refloat; get going again (Auto); put back on its feet (Unternehmen)

Flöz nt -es,-e (coal) seam

Fluch m -[e]s,-e curse. **F∼en** vi (haben) curse, swear

Flucht¹ f -,-en (Reihe) line; (Zimmer-) suite

Flucht² f - flight; (Entweichen) escape; **die F∼ ergreifen** take flight. **f∼artig** a hasty, adv -ily

flücht|en vi (sein) flee (vor + dat from); (entweichen) escape ⊳ vr **sich f∼en** take refuge. f∼ig a fugitive; (kurz) brief, adv -ly; (Blick, Gedanke) fleeting; (Bekanntschaft) passing; (oberflächlich) cursory, adv -ily; (nicht sorgfältig) careless, adv -ly; (Chem) volatile; f∼ig sein be on the run; f∼ig kennen know slightly. F∼igkeitsfehler m slip. F∼ling m -s,-e fugitive; (Pol) refugee

Fluchwort nt (pl -wörter) swearword

Flug m -[e]s,-e flight. **F∼abwehr** f anti-aircraft defence. **F∼ball** m (Tennis) volley. **F∼blatt** nt pamphlet

Flügel m -s,- wing; (Fenster-) casement; (Mus) grand piano

Fluggast m [air] passenger

flügge a fully-fledged

Flug|gesellschaft f airline. **F∼hafen** m airport. **F∼lotse** m air-traffic controller. **F∼platz** m airport; (klein) airfield. **F∼preis** m air fare. **F∼schein** m air ticket. **F∼schneise** f flight path. **F∼schreiber** m -s,- flight recorder. **F∼schrift** f pamphlet. **F∼steig** m -[e]s,-e gate. **F∼wesen** nt aviation. **F∼zeug** nt -[e]s,-e aircraft, plane

Fluidum nt -s aura

Flunder f -,-n flounder

flunkern vi (haben) (fam) tell fibs; (aufschneiden) tell tall stories

Flunsch m -[e]s,-e pout

fluoreszierend a fluorescent

Flur m -[e]s,-e (entrance) hall; (Gang) corridor

Flusen fpl fluff sg

Fluss m -es,-e (Fluß m -sses,-sse) river; (Fließen) flow; **im F∼** (fig) in a state of flux. f∼abwärts adv down-stream. f∼aufwärts adv up-stream. **F∼bett** nt river-bed

flüssig a liquid; (Lava) molten; (fließend) fluent, adv -ly; (Verkehr) freely moving. **F∼keit** f -,-en liquid; (Anat) fluid

Flusspferd (Flußpferd) nt hippopotamus

Flut f -,-en high tide; (fig) flood; **F∼en** waters. **F∼licht** nt floodlight. **F∼welle** f tidal wave

Föderation /-'tsio:n/ f -,-en federation

Fohlen nt -s,- foal

Föhn m -s föhn [wind]; (Haartrockner) hair-drier. f∼en vt [blow-]dry

Folge f -,-n consequence; (Reihe) succession; (Fortsetzung) instalment; (Teil) part; **F∼ leisten** (+ dat) accept (Einladung); obey (Befehl). f∼en vi (sein) follow (jdm/etw s.o./sth); (zuhören) listen (dat to); **daraus f∼t, dass** it follows that; **wie f∼t** as follows ⊳ (haben) (gehorchen) obey (jdm s.o.). f∼end a following; **F∼endes** (f∼endes) the following. **f∼endermaßen** adv as follows

folger|n vt conclude (aus from). **F∼ung** f -,-en conclusion

folg|lich adv consequently. f∼sam a obedient, adv -ly

Folie /'fo:liə/ f -,-n foil; (Plastik-) film

Folklore f - folklore

Folter f -,-n torture; **auf die F∼ spannen** (fig) keep on tenterhooks. f∼n vt torture

Fön (P) m -s,-e hair-drier

fönen vt (NEW) **föhnen**

Fontäne f -,-n jet; (Brunnen) fountain

Förder|band nt (pl -bänder) conveyor belt. **f~lich** a beneficial

fördern vt demand; (beanspruchen) claim; (zum Kampf) challenge; **gefordert werden** (fig) be stretched

fördern vt promote; (unterstützen) encourage; (finanziell) sponsor; (gewinnen) extract

Forderung f -,-en demand; (Anspruch) claim

Förderung f - (s. fördern) promotion; encouragement; (Techn) production

Forelle f -,-n trout

Form f -,-en form; (Gestalt) shape; (Culin, Techn) mould; (Back-) tin; **[gut] in F~** in good form

Formalität f -,-en formality

Format nt -[e]s,-e format; (Größe) size; (fig: Bedeutung) stature

Formation /-'tsjo:n/ f -,-en formation

Formel f -,-n formula

formell a formal, adv -ly

formen vt shape, mould; (bilden) form; **sich f~** take shape

förmlich a formal, adv -ly; (regelrecht) virtual, adv -ly. **F~keit** f -,-en formality

form|los a shapeless; (zwanglos) informal, adv -ly. **F~sache** f formality

Formular nt -s,-e [printed] form

formulier|en vt formulate, word. **F~ung** f -,-en wording

forsch a brisk, adv -ly; (schneidig) dashing, adv -ly

forsch|en vi (haben) search (nach for). **f~end** a searching. **F~er** m -s,- research scientist; (Reisender) explorer. **F~ung** f -,-en research. **f~ungsreisende(r)** m explorer

Forst m -[e]s,-e forest

Förster m -s,- forester

Forstwirtschaft f forestry

Forsythie /-tsjə/ f -,-n forsythia

Fort nt -s,-s (Mil) fort

fort adv away; **f~ sein** be away; (gegangen/verschwunden) have gone; **und so f~** and so on; **in einem f~** continuously. **f~bewegen** vt sep move; **sich f~bewegen** move. **f~bewegung** f locomotion. **f~bildung** f further education/training. **f~bleiben†** vi sep (sein) stay away. **f~bringen†** vt sep take away. **f~fahren†** vi sep (sein) go away □ (haben/sein) continue (zu to). **f~fallen†** vi sep (sein) be dropped/(ausgelassen) omitted; (entfallen) no longer apply; (aufhören) cease. **f~führen** vt sep continue. **F~gang** m departure; (Verlauf) progress. **f~gehen†** vi sep (sein) leave, go away; (ausgehen) go out; (andauern) go on. **f~geschritten** a advanced; (spät) late. **F~geschrittene(r)** m/f advanced student. **f~gesetzt** a constant, adv -ly. **f~jagen** vt sep chase away. **f~lassen†** vt sep let go; (auslassen) omit. **f~laufen†** vi sep (sein) run away; (sich f~setzen) continue. **f~laufend** a consecutive, adv -ly. **f~nehmen†** vt sep take away. **f~pflanzen (sich)** vr sep reproduce; (Ton, Licht.) travel. **f~pflanzung** f reproduction. **F~pflanzungsorgan** nt reproductive organ. **f~reißen†** vt sep carry away; (entreißen) tear away. **f~schaffen†** vt sep take away. **f~schicken** vt sep send away; (abschicken) send off. **f~schreiten†** vi sep (sein) continue; (Fortschritte machen) progress, advance. **f~schreitend** a progressive; (Alter) advancing. **F~schritt** m progress; **F~schritte machen** make progress. **f~schrittlich** a progressive. **f~setzen** vt sep continue; **sich f~setzen** continue. **F~setzung** f -,-en continuation; (Folge) instalment; **F~setzung folgt** to be continued. F~setzungsroman *m* serialized novel, serial.

f~während *a* constant, *adv* -ly.

f~werfen† *vt sep* throw away.

f~ziehen† *v sep* □ *vt* pull away □ *vi (sein)* move away

Fossil *nt* -s,-ien /-jən/ fossil

Foto *nt* -s,-s photo. **F~apparat** *m* camera. **F~gen** *a* photogenic

Fotograf(in) *m* -en,-en (*f* -,-nen) photographer. **F~ie** *f* -,-n photography; (*Bild*) photograph. f~ieren *vt* take a photo[graph] of; sich f~ieren lassen have one's photo[graph] taken □ *vi (haben)* take photographs.

f~isch *a* photographic

Fotokopie *f* photocopy. f~ren *vt* photocopy. **F~rgerät** *nt* photocopier

Fötus *m* -,-ten foetus

Foul /faul/ *nt* -s,-s (*Sport*) foul. f~en *vt* foul

Foyer /foa'je:/ *nt* -s,-s foyer

Fracht *f* -,-en freight. **F~er** *m* -s,- freighter. **F~gut** *nt* freight. **F~schiff** *nt* cargo boat

Frack *m* -[e]s,-e & tailcoat; im **F~** in tails *pl*

Frage *f* -,-n question; ohne **F~** undoubtedly; eine **F~** stellen ask a question; etw in **F~** stellen = etw infrage stellen, *s.* infrage; nicht in **F~** kommen = nicht infrage kommen, *s.* infrage. **F~bogen** *m* questionnaire. f~n *vt* (*haben*) ask; sich f~n wonder (ob whether). f~nd *a* questioning, *adv* -ly; (*Gram*) interrogative. **F~zeichen** *nt* question mark

frag|lich *a* doubtful; (*Person, Sache*) in question. f~los *adv* undoubtedly

Fragment *nt* -[e]s,-e fragment. f~arisch *a* fragmentary

fragwürdig *a* questionable; (*verdächtig*) dubious

fraisefarben /'frɛ:s-/ *a* strawberry-pink

Fraktion /-'tsjo:n/ *f* -,-en parliamentary party

Franken *m* -s,- (*Swiss*) franc

Franken[2] *nt* -s Franconia

Frankfurter *f* -,- frankfurter

frankieren *vt* stamp, frank

Frankreich *nt* -s France

Fransen *fpl* fringe *sg*

Franz|ose *m* -n,-n Frenchman; die **F~osen** the French *pl*. **F~ösin** *f* -,-nen Frenchwoman. f~ösisch *a* French. **F~ösisch** *nt* -[s] (*Lang*) French

frapp|ant *a* striking. f~ieren *vt* (*fig*) strike; f~ierend striking

fräsen *vt* (*Techn*) mill

Fraß *m* -es feed; (*pej: Essen*) muck

Fratze *f* -,-n grotesque face; (*Grimasse*) grimace; (*pej: Gesicht*) face; **F~n schneiden** pull faces

Frau *f* -,-en woman; (*Ehe-*) wife; **F~ Thomas** Mrs/(*unverheiratet*) Miss/(*Admin*) Ms Thomas; **Unsere Liebe F~** (*Relig*) Our Lady. **F~chen** *nt* -s,- mistress

Frauen|arzt *m*, **F~ärztin** *f* gynaecologist. **F~rechtlerin** *f* -,-nen feminist. **F~zimmer** *nt* woman

Fräulein *nt* -s,- single woman; (*jung*) young lady; (*Anrede*) Miss

fraulich *a* womanly

frech *a* cheeky, *adv* -ily; (*unverschämt*) impudent, *adv* -ly. **F~dachs** *m* (*fam*) cheeky monkey. **F~heit** *f* -,-en cheekiness; impudence; (*Äußerung, Handlung*) impertinence

frei *a* free; (*freischaffend*) freelance; (*Künstler*) independent; (*nicht besetzt*) vacant; (*offen*) open; (*bloß*) bare; **f~er Tag** day off; sich (*dat*) **f~ nehmen** take time off; **f~ machen** (*räumen*) clear; vacate (*Platz*); (*befreien*) liberate; **f~ lassen** leave free; **jdm f~e Hand lassen** give s.o. a free hand; **ist dieser Platz f~?** is this seat taken? **'Zimmer f~'** 'vacancies' □ *adv* freely; (*ohne*

Notizen) without notes; (*umsonst*) free

Frei|bad *nt* open-air swimming pool. **f~bekommen†** *vt sep* get released; **einen Tag f~bekommen** get a day off. **f~beruflich** *a & adv* freelance. **F~e** *nt* im **F~en** in the open air, out of doors. **F~frau** *f* baroness. **F~gabe** *f* release. **f~geben** *v sep* □ *vt* release; (*eröffnen*) open; **jdm einen Tag f~geben** give s.o. a day off □ *vi* (*haben*) **jdm f~geben** give s.o. time off. **F~gebig** *a* generous, *adv* -ly. **F~gebigkeit** *f* - generosity. **f~haben†** *v sep* □ *vt* **eine Stunde f~haben** have an hour off; (*Sch*) have a free period □ *vi* (*haben*) be off work/(*Sch*) school; (*beurlaubt sein*) have time off. **f~halten†** *vt sep* keep clear; (*belegen*) keep; **einen Tag f~halten** keep a day/oneself free; **jdn f~halten** treat s.o. [to a meal/drink]. **F~handelszone** *f* free-trade area. **f~händig** *adv* without holding on

Freiheit *f* -,-en freedom, liberty; **sich** (*dat*) **F~en erlauben** take liberties. **F~sstrafe** *f* prison sentence

freiheraus *adv* frankly

Frei|herr *m* baron. **F~karte** *f* free ticket. **F~körperkultur** *f* naturism. **f~lassen†** *vt sep* release, set free. **F~lassung** *f* - release. **F~lauf** *m* free-wheel. **f~legen** *vt sep* expose. **f~lich** *adv* admittedly; (*natürlich*) of course. **F~lichttheater** *nt* open-air theatre. **f~machen** *v sep* □ *vt* (*frankieren*) frank; (*entkleiden*) bare; **einen Tag f~machen** take a day off □ *vi/r* (*haben*) [sich] **f~machen** take time off. **F~marke** *f* [postage] stamp. **F~maurer** *m* Freemason. **f~mütig** *a* candid, *adv* -ly. **F~platz** *m* free seat; (*Sch*) free place. **f~schaffend** *a* freelance.

f~schwimmen† (**sich**) *v sep* pass one's swimming test. **f~setzen** *vt sep* release; (*entlassen*) make redundant. **f~sprechen†** *vt sep* acquit. **F~spruch** *m* acquittal. **f~stehen†** *vi sep* (*haben*) stand empty; **es steht ihm f~** (*fig*) he is free (zu) to. **f~stellen** *vt sep* exempt (**von** from); **jdm etw f~stellen** leave sth up to s.o. **f~stempeln** *vt sep* frank. **F~stil** *m* freestyle. **F~stoß** *m* free kick. **F~stunde** *f* (*Sch*) free period

Freitag *m* Friday. **f~s** *adv* on Fridays

Frei|tod *m* suicide. **F~übungen** *fpl* (physical) exercises. **F~umschlag** *m* stamped envelope. **f~weg** *adv* freely; (*offen*) openly. **f~willig** *a* voluntary, *adv* -ily. **F~willige(r)** *m/f* volunteer. **F~zeichen** *nt* ringing tone; (*Rufzeichen*) dialling tone. **F~zeit** *f* free or spare time; (*Muße*) leisure; (*Tagung*) [weekend/holiday] course. **F~zeit-pref** leisure ... **F~zeitbekleidung** *f* casual wear. **f~zügig** *a* unrestricted; (*großzügig*) liberal; (*moralisch*) permissive

fremd *a* foreign; (*unbekannt, ungewohnt*) strange; (*nicht das eigene*) other people's; **ein f~er Mann** a stranger; **f~e Leute** strangers; **unter f~em Namen** under an assumed name; **jdm f~sein** be unknown/(*wesens-*) alien to s.o.; **ich bin hier f~** I'm a stranger here. **f~artig** *a* strange, *adv* -ly; (*exotisch*) exotic. **F~e** *f* in der **F~e** away from home; (*im Ausland*) in a foreign country. **F~e(r)** *m/f* stranger; (*Ausländer*) foreigner; (*Tourist*) tourist. **F~enführer** *m* [tourist] guide. **F~enverkehr** *m* tourism. **F~enzimmer** *nt* room [to let]; (*Gäste-*) guest room. **f~gehen†** *vi sep* (*sein*) (*fam*) be unfaithful. **F~körper** *m* foreign body.

f~**ländisch** *a* foreign; (*exotisch*) exotic. **F~ling** *m* -s,-e stranger. **F~sprache** *f* foreign language. **F~wort** *nt* (*pl* -wörter) foreign word

frenetisch *a* frenzied

frequen|tieren *vt* frequent. **F~enz** *f* -,-en frequency

Freske *f* -,-n, **Fresko** *nt* -s,-ken fresco

Fresse *f* -,-n (*sl*) (*Mund*) gob; (*Gesicht*) mug; **halt die F~!** shut your trap! **f~n†** *vt/i* (*haben*) eat. **F~n** *nt* -s feed; (*sl: Essen*) grub

Freßnapf (**Freßnapf**) *m* feeding bowl

Freud|e *f* -,-n pleasure; (*innere*) joy; **mit F~en** with pleasure; **jdm eine F~e machen** please s.o. **f~ig** *a* joyful, *adv* -ly; **f~iges Ereignis** *(fig)* happy event. **f~los** *a* cheerless; (*traurig*) sad

freuen *vt* please; **sich f~** be pleased (**über** + *acc* about); **sich f~ auf** (+ *acc*) look forward to; **es freut mich, ich freue mich** I'm glad *or* pleased (**daß** that)

Freund *m* -es,-e friend; (*Verehrer*) boyfriend; (*Anhänger*) lover (*gen* of). **F~in** *f* -,-nen friend; (*Liebste*) girlfriend; (*Anhängerin*) lover (*gen* of). **f~lich** *a* kind, *adv* -ly; (*umgänglich*) friendly; (*angenehm*) pleasant; **wären Sie so f~lich?** would you be so kind? **f~licherweise** *adv* kindly. **F~lichkeit** *f* -,-en kindness; friendliness; pleasantness

Freundschaft *f* -,-en friendship; **F~ schließen** become friends. **f~lich** *a* friendly

Frevel /ˈfreːfəl/ *m* -s,- (*liter*) outrage. **f~haft** *a* (*liter*) wicked

Frieden *m* -s peace; **F~ schließen** make peace; **im F~** in peace-time; **laß mich in F~!** leave me alone! **F~srichter** *m* ≈ magistrate. **F~svertrag** *m* peace treaty

fried|fertig *a* peaceable. **F~hof** *m* cemetery. **f~lich** *a* peaceful;

adv -ly; (*verträglich*) peaceable. **f~liebend** *a* peace-loving

frieren† *vi* (*haben*) (*Person:*) be cold; *impers* **es friert/hat gefroren** it is freezing/there has been a frost; **frierst du? friert [es] dich?** are you cold? □ *vt* (*sein*) (*gefrieren*) freeze

Fries *m* -es,-e frieze

Frikadelle *f* -,-n [meat] rissole

frisch *a* fresh; (*sauber*) clean; (*leuchtend*) bright; (*munter*) lively; (*rüstig*) fit; **sich f~ machen** freshen up □ *adv* freshly, newly; **f~ gelegte Eier** new-laid eggs; **im Bett f~ beziehen** put clean sheets on a bed; **f~ gestrichen!** wet paint! **F~e** *f* - freshness; brightness; liveliness; fitness. **F~haltepackung** *f* vacuum pack. **F~käse** *m* ≈ cottage cheese. **f~weg** *adv* freely

Fris|eur /friˈzøːɐ̯/ *m* -s,-e hairdresser; (*Herren-*) barber. **F~seursalon** *m* hairdressing salon. **F~seuse** /-ˈzøːzə/ *f* -,-n hairdresser

frisieren *vt* **jdn/sich f~en** do s.o.'s/one's hair; **die Bilanz/einen Motor f~en** (*fam*) fiddle the accounts/soup up an engine. **F~kommode** *f* dressing-table. **f~salon** *m* = **Friseursalon**. **F~tisch** *m* dressing-table

Frisör *m* -s,-e = **Friseur**

Frist *f* -,-en period; (*Termin*) deadline; (*Aufschub*) time; **drei Tage F~** three days' grace. **f~en** *vt* **sein Leben f~en** eke out an existence. **f~los** *a* instant, *adv* -ly

Frisur *f* -,-en hairstyle

frittieren (**fritieren**) *vt* deep-fry

frivol /friˈvoːl/ *a* frivolous, *adv* -ly; (*schlüpfrig*) smutty

froh *a* happy; (*freudig*) joyful; (*erleichtert*) glad; **f~e Ostern!** happy Easter!

fröhlich *a* cheerful, *adv* -ly; (*vergnügt*) merry, *adv* -ily; **f~e Weihnachten!** merry Christmas!

F~keit f - cheerfulness; merriment

frohlocken vi (haben) rejoice; (schadenfroh) gloat

Frohsinn m - cheerfulness

fromm a (frömmer, frömmst) devout, adv -ly; (gutartig) docile, adv -ly; f~er **Wunsch** idle wish

Frömm|igkeit f - devoutness, piety. **f~lerisch** a sanctimonious, adv -ly

frönen vi (haben) indulge (dat in)

Fronleichnam m Corpus Christi

Front f -,-en front. **f~al** a frontal; (Zusammenstoß) head-on □ adv from the front; (zusammenstoßen) head-on. **F~alzusammenstoß** m head-on collision

Frosch m -[e]s,-e frog. **F~laich** m frog-spawn. **F~mann** m (pl -männer) frogman

Frost m -[e]s,-e frost. **F~beule** f chilblain

frösteln vi (haben) shiver; mich fröstelte [es] I shivered/(fror) felt chilly

frost|ig a frosty, adv -ily. **F~schutzmittel** nt antifreeze

Frottee nt & m -s towelling

frottier|en vt rub down. **F~[hand]tuch** nt terry towel

frotzeln vt/i (haben) [über] jdn f~ make fun of s.o.

Frucht f -,-e fruit; **F~tragen** bear fruit. **f~bar** a fertile; (fig) fruitful. **F~barkeit** f - fertility. **f~en** vi (haben) wenig/nichts **f~en** have little/no effect. **f~los** a fruitless, adv -ly. **F~saft** m fruit juice

frugal a frugal, adv -ly

früh a early □ adv early; (morgens) in the morning; heute/gestern/morgen f~ this/yesterday/tomorrow morning; von f~an od auf from an early age. **f~auf** adv von f~auf <u>NEW</u> von f~ auf, s. früh. **F~aufsteher** m -s,- early riser. **F~e** f - in aller f~e bright and early; in der **F~e** (SGer) in the morning.

f~er adv earlier; (eher) sooner; (ehemals) formerly; (vor langer Zeit) in the old days; **f~er oder später** sooner or later; ich wohnte **f~er** in X I used to live in X. **f~ere(r,s)** a earlier; (ehemalig) former; (vorige) previous; in **f~eren Zeiten** in former times. **f~estens** adv at the earliest.

F~geburt f premature birth/(Kind) baby. **F~jahr** nt spring. **F~jahrsputz** m spring-cleaning. **F~kartoffeln** fpl new potatoes. **f~ling** m -s,-e spring. **f~morgens** adv early in the morning. **f~reif** a precocious

Frühstück nt breakfast. **f~en** vi (haben) have breakfast

frühzeitig a & adv early; (vorzeitig) premature, adv -ly

Frustration /-'tsjo:n/ f -,-en frustration. **f~ieren** vt frustrate; **f~ierend** frustrating

Fuchs m -es,-e fox; (Pferd) chestnut. **f~en** vt (fam) annoy

Füchsin f -,-nen vixen

fuchteln vi (haben) mit etw f~ (fam) wave with sth

Fuder nt -s,- cart-load

Fuge[1] f -,-n joint; aus den **F~n** gehen fall apart

Fuge[2] f -,-n (Mus) fugue

füg|en vt fit (in + acc into); (an-) join (an + acc on to); (dazu-) add (zu to); (fig: bewirken) ordain; sich **f~en** fit (in + acc into); adjoin/(folgen) follow (an etw acc sth); (fig: gehorchen) submit (dat to); sich in sein Schicksal **f~en** resign oneself to one's fate; es **f~te** sich it so happened (dass that). **f~sam** a obedient, adv -ly. **F~ung** f -,-en eine **F~ung des Schicksals** a stroke of fate

fühlbar a noticeable. **f~en** vt/i (haben) feel; sich **f~en** feel (krank/einsam ill/lonely); (fam: stolz sein) fancy oneself; sich [nicht] wohl **f~en** [not] feel well. **F~er** m -s,- feeler. **F~ung**

f - contact; **F~ung aufnehmen** get in touch

Fuhre *f* -,**-n** load

führ|en *vt* lead; guide ⟨*Tourist*⟩; (*geleiten*) take; (*leiten*) run; (*befehligen*) command; (*verkaufen*) stock; bear ⟨*Namen, Titel*⟩; keep ⟨*Liste, Bücher, Tagebuch*⟩; **bei** *od* **mit sich f~en** carry; **sich gut/schlecht f~en** conduct oneself well/badly □ *vi* (*haben*) lead; (*verlaufen*) go, run; **zu etw f~en** lead to sth. **f~end** *a* leading. **F~er** *m* -s,- leader; (*Fremden-*) guide; (*Buch*) guide[book]. **F~erhaus** *nt* driver's cab. **F~erschein** *m* driving licence; **den F~erschein machen** take one's driving test. **F~erscheinentzug** *m* disqualification from driving. **F~ung** *f* -,**-en** leadership; (*Leitung*) management; (*Mil*) command; (*Betragen*) conduct; (*Besichtigung*) guided tour; (*Vorsprung*) lead; **in F~ung gehen** go into the lead

Fuhr|unternehmer *m* haulage contractor. **F~werk** *nt* cart

Fülle *f* -,**-n** abundance, wealth (**an** + *dat* of); (*Körper-*) plumpness. **f~n** *vt* fill; (*Culin*) stuff; **sich f~n** fill [up]

Füllen *nt* -s,- foal

Füll|er *m* -s,- (*fam*), **F~federhalter** *m* fountain pen. **f~ig** *a* plump; (*Busen*) ample. **F~ung** *f* -,**-en** filling; (*Kissen-, Braten-*) stuffing; (*Pralinen-*) centre

fummeln *vi* (*haben*) fumble (**an** + *dat* with)

Fund *m* -[e]s,-e find

Fundament *nt* -[e]s,-e foundations *pl.* **f~al** *a* fundamental

Fund|büro *nt* lost-property office. **F~grube** *f* (*fig*) treasure trove. **F~sachen** *fpl* lost property

fünf *inv a* **f~,** -**en** five; (*Sch*) ≈ fail mark. **F~linge** *mpl* quintuplets. **f~te(r,s)** a fifth. **f~zehn** *inv a* fifteen. **f~zehnte(r,s)** a fifteenth. **f~zig** *inv a* fifty. **F~ziger**

m -s,- man in his fifties; (*Münze*) 50-pfennig piece. **f~zigste(r,s)** a fiftieth

fungieren *vi* (*haben*) act (**als** as)

Funk *m* -s radio; **über F~** over the radio. **F~e** *m* -n,-n spark. **f~eln** *vi* (*haben*) sparkle; (*Stern:*) twinkle. **f~elnagelneu** *a* (*fam*) brand-new. **f~en** *vt* radio. **F~er** *m* -s,- radio operator. **F~sprechgerät** *nt* walkie-talkie. **F~spruch** *m* radio message. **F~streife** *f* [police] radio patrol

Funktion /-'tsjo:n/ *f* -,**-en** function; (*Stellung*) position; (*Funktionieren*) working; **außer F~** out of action. **F~är** *m* -s,-e official. **f~ieren** *vi* (*haben*) work

für *prep* (+ *acc*) for; **Schritt für Schritt** step by step; **was für [ein]** what [a]! (*fragend*) what sort of [a]? **für sich** by oneself; (*Ding:*) itself. **Für** *nt* **das Für und Wider** the pros and cons *pl.*

F~bitte *f* intercession

Furche *f* -,**-n** furrow

Furcht *f* - fear (**vor** + *dat* of); **f~erregend** terrifying. **f~bar** *a* terrible, *adv* -ly

fürchten *vt/i* (*haben*) fear; **sich f~en** be afraid (**vor** + *dat* of); **ich f~e, das geht nicht** I'm afraid that's impossible. **f~erlich** *a* dreadful, *adv* -ly

furcht|erregend *a* (NEW) **F~ erregend.** s. **Furcht. f~los** *a* fearless, *adv* -ly. **f~sam** *a* timid, *adv* -ly

füreinander *adv* for each other

Furnier *nt* -s,-e veneer. **f~t** *a* veneered

fürs *prep* = **für das**

Fürsorge *f* care; (*Admin*) welfare; (*fam: Geld*) ≈ social security. **F~r(in)** *m* -s,- (*f* -,**-nen**) social worker. **f~lich** *a* solicitous

Fürsprache *f* intercession; **F~ einlegen** intercede

Fürsprecher *m* (*fig*) advocate

Fürst m -en,-en prince. F~entum nt -s,-er principality. F~in f -,-nen princess. f~lich a princely; (üppig) lavish, adv -ly

Furt f -,-en ford

Furunkel m -s,- (Med) boil

Fürwort nt (pl -wörter) pronoun

Furz m -es,-e (vulg) fart. f~en vi (haben) (vulg) fart

Fusion f -,-en fusion; (Comm) merger. f~ieren vi (haben) (Comm) merge

Fuß m -es,-e foot; (Aust: Bein) leg; (Lampen-) base; (von Weinglas) stem; zu Fuß on foot; zu Fuß gehen walk; auf freiem Fuß free; auf freundschaftlichem/großem Fuß on friendly terms/in grand style. F~abdruck m footprint. F~abtreter m -s,- doormat. F~bad nt footbath. F~ball m football. F~ballspieler m footballer. F~balltoto nt football pools pl. F~bank f footstool. F~boden m floor. F~bremse f footbrake

Fussel f -,-n & m -s,-[n] piece of fluff; F~n fluff sg. f~n vi (haben) shed fluff

fuß|en vi (haben) be based (auf + dat on). F~ende nt foot

Fußgänger|(in) m -s,- (f -,-nen) pedestrian. F~brücke f footbridge. F~überweg m pedestrian crossing. F~zone f pedestrian precinct

Fuß|geher m -s,- (Aust) = F~gänger. F~gelenk nt ankle. F~hebel m pedal. F~nagel m toenail. F~note f footnote. F~pflege f chiropody. F~pfleger(in) m(f) chiropodist. F~rücken m instep. F~sohle f sole of the foot. F~stapfen pl in jds F~stapfen treten (fig) follow in s.o.'s footsteps. F~tritt m kick. F~weg m footpath; eine Stunde F~weg an hour's walk

futsch pred a (fam) gone

Futter[1] nt -s,- feed; (Trocken-) fodder

Futter[2] nt -s,- (Kleider-) lining

Futteral nt -s,-e case

füttern[1] vt feed

füttern[2] vt line

Futur nt -s (Gram) future; zweites F~ future perfect. f~istisch a futuristic

G

Gabe f -,-n gift; (Dosis) dose

Gabel f -,-n fork. g~n (sich) vr fork. G~stapler m -s,- fork-lift truck. G~ung f -,-en fork

gackern vi (haben) cackle

gaffen vi (haben) gape, stare

Gag /gɛk/ m -s,-s (Theat) gag

Gage /'ga:ʒə/ f -,-n (Theat) fee

gähnen vi (haben) yawn. G~ nt -s yawn; (wiederholt) yawning

Gala f - ceremonial dress

galant a gallant, adv -ly

Galavorstellung f gala performance

Galerie f -,-n gallery

Galgen m -s,- gallows sg. G~frist f (fam) reprieve

Galionsfigur f figurehead

Galle f - bile; (G~nblase) gallbladder. G~nblase f gall-bladder. G~nstein m gallstone

Gallert nt -[e]s,-e, Gallerte f -,-n [meat] jelly

Galopp m -s gallop; im G~ at a gallop. g~ieren vi (sein) gallop

galvanisieren vt galvanize

gamm|eln vi (haben) (fam) loaf around. G~ler(in) m -s,- (f -,-nen) drop-out

Gams f -,-en (Aust) chamois

Gämse f -,-n chamois

gang pred a g~ und gäbe quite usual

Gang m -[e]s,-e walk; (G~art) gait; (Boten-) errand; (Funktionieren) running; (Verlauf, Culin) course; (Durch-) passage; (Korridor) corridor; (zwischen

Sitzreihen) aisle, gangway; *(Anat)* duct; *(Auto)* gear; **in G~ bringen/halten** get/keep going; **in G~ kommen** get going/*(fig)* under way; **im G~e/in vollem swing; Essen mit vier G~en** four-course meal. **G~art** f gait

gängig a common; *(Comm)* popular

Gangschaltung f gear change

Gangster /'gɛŋstɐ/ m -s,- gangster

Gangway /'gɛŋweː/ f -,-s gangway

Ganove m -n,-n *(fam)* crook

Gans f -,-̈e goose

Gänse|blümchen nt -s,- daisy. **G~füßchen** ntpl inverted commas. **G~haut** f goose-pimples pl. **G~marsch** m **im G~marsch** in single file. **G~rich** m -s,-e gander

ganz a whole, entire; *(vollständig)* complete; *(fam: heil)* undamaged, intact; **die g~e Zeit** all the time, the whole time; **eine g~e Weile/ Menge** quite a while/lot; **g~e zehn Mark** all of ten marks; **meine g~en Bücher** all my books; *inv* **g~ Deutschland** the whole of Germany; **g~ bleiben** *(fam)* remain intact; **wieder g~ machen** *(fam)* mend; **im G~en (g~en)** in all, altogether; **im Großen und G~en (im großen und g~en)** on the whole □ *adv* quite; *(völlig)* completely, entirely; *(sehr)* very; **nicht g~** not quite; **g~ allein** all on one's own; **ein g~ alter Mann** a very old man; **g~ wie du willst** just as you like; **es war g~ nett** it was quite nice; **g~ und gar** completely, totally; **g~ und gar nicht** not at all. **G~e(s)** nt whole; **es geht ums G~e** it's all or nothing.

g~jährig adv all the year round

gänzlich adv completely, entirely

ganz|tägig a & adv full-time; *(geöffnet)* all day. **g~tags** adv all day; *(arbeiten)* full-time

gar[1] a done, cooked

gar[2] adv **gar nicht/nichts/niemand** not/nothing/no one at all; **oder gar** or even

Garage /ga'ra:ʒə/ f -,-n garage

Garantie f -,-n guarantee. **g~ren** vt/i *(haben)* **[für]** etw **g~ren** guarantee sth; **er kommt g~rt zu spät** *(fam)* he's sure to be late.

Garbe f -,-n sheaf

Garderobe f -,-n *(Kleider)* wardrobe; *(Ablage)* cloakroom, *(Amer)* checkroom; *(Flur-)* coat-rack; *(Künstler-)* dressing-room. **G~nfrau** f cloakroom attendant

Gardine f -,-n curtain. **G~nstange** f curtain rail

garen vt/i *(haben)* cook

gären† vi *(haben)* ferment; *(fig)* seethe

Garn nt -[e]s,-e yarn; *(Näh-)* cotton

Garnele f -,-n shrimp; *(rote)* prawn

garnieren vt decorate; *(Culin)* garnish

Garnison f -,-en garrison

Garnitur f -,-en set; *(Wäsche)* set of matching underwear; *(Möbel-)* suite; **erste/zweite G~ sein** *(fam)* be first-rate/second best

garstig a nasty

Garten m -s,-̈ garden; **botanischer G~** botanical gardens pl. **G~arbeit** f gardening. **G~bau** m horticulture. **G~haus** nt, **G~laube** f summerhouse. **G~lokal** nt open-air café. **G~schere** f secateurs pl

Gärtner|(in) m -s,- (f -,-nen) gardener. **G~ei** f -,-en nursery; *(fam: Gartenarbeit)* gardening

Gärung f -fermentation

Gas nt -es,-e gas; **Gas geben** *(fam)* accelerate. **G~herd** m gas cooker. **G~maske** f gas mask. **G~pedal** nt *(Auto)* accelerator

Gasse f -,-n alley; (Aust) street

Gast m -[e]s,-e guest; (Hotel-, Urlaubs-) visitor; (im Lokal) patron; **zum Mittag G∼e haben** have people to lunch; **bei jdm zu G∼ sein** be staying with s.o. **G∼arbeiter** m foreign worker. **G∼bett** nt spare bed

Gäste|bett nt spare bed. **G∼buch** nt visitors' book. **G∼zimmer** nt [hotel] room; (privat) spare room; (Aufenthaltsraum) residents' lounge

gast|frei, a **∼freundlich** a hospitable, adv -bly. **G∼freundschaft** f hospitality. **G∼geber** m -s,- host. **G∼geberin** f -,-nen hostess. **G∼haus** nt, **G∼hof** m inn, hotel. **gastieren** vi (haben) make a guest appearance; (Truppe, Zirkus:) perform (in + dat in)

gastlich a hospitable, adv -bly. **G∼keit** f - hospitality

Gastro|nomie f - gastronomy. **g∼nomisch** a gastronomic

Gast|spiel nt guest performance. **G∼spielreise** f (Theat) tour. **G∼stätte** f restaurant. **G∼stube** f bar; (Restaurant) restaurant. **G∼wirt** m landlord. **G∼wirtin** f landlady. **G∼wirtschaft** f restaurant

Gas|werk nt gasworks sg. **G∼zähler** m gas-meter

Gatte m -n,-n husband

Gatter nt -s,- gate; (Gehege) enclosure

Gattin f -,-nen wife

Gattung f -,-en kind; (Biol) genus; (Kunst) genre. **G∼sbegriff** m generic term

Gaudi f - (Aust, fam) fun

Gaul m -[e]s, Gäule [old] nag

Gaumen m -s,- palate

Gauner m -s,- crook, swindler. **G∼ei** f -,-en swindle

Gaze /'ga:zə/ f - gauze

Gazelle f -,-n gazelle

geachtet a respected

geädert a veined

geartet a **gut g∼** good-natured; **anders g∼** different

Gebäck nt -s [cakes and] pastries pl; (Kekse) biscuits pl

Gebälk nt -s timbers pl

geballt a (Faust) clenched

Gebärde f -,-n gesture. **g∼n (sich)** vr behave (wie like)

Gebaren nt -s behaviour

gebär|en† vt give birth to, bear; **geboren werden** be born. **G∼mutter** f womb, uterus

Gebäude nt -s,- building

Gebeine ntpl (mortal) remains

Gebell nt -s barking

geben† vt give; (tun, bringen) put; (Karten) deal; (aufführen) perform; (unterrichten) teach; **etw verloren g∼** give sth up as lost; **von sich g∼** utter; (fam: erbrechen) bring up; **viel/wenig g∼ auf** (+ acc) set great/little store by; **sich g∼** (nachlassen) wear off; (besser werden) get better; (sich verhalten) behave; **sich geschlagen g∼** admit defeat □ impers **es gibt** there is/are; **was gibt es Neues/zum Mittag/im Kino?** what's the news/ for lunch/on at the cinema? **wird Regen g∼** it's going to rain; **das gibt es nicht** there's no such thing □ vi (haben) (Karten) deal

Gebet nt -[e]s,-e prayer

Gebiet nt -[e]s,-e area; (Hoheits-) territory; (Sach-) field

gebiet|en† vt command; (erfordern) demand □ vi (haben) rule. **G∼er** m -s,- master; (Herrscher) ruler. **g∼erisch** a imperious, adv -ly; (Ton) peremptory

Gebilde nt -s,- structure

gebildet a educated; (kultiviert) cultured

Gebirge nt -s,- mountains pl. **G∼ig** a mountainous

Gebiss nt -es,-e (Gebiß nt -sses, -sse) teeth pl; (künstliches) false teeth pl, dentures pl; (des Zaumes) bit

geblümt *a* floral, flowered

gebogen *a* curved

geboren *a* born; **g~er Deutscher** German by birth; **Frau X, g~e Y** Mrs X, née Y

geborgen *a* safe, secure. **G~heit** *f* - security

Gebot *nt* -[e]s,-e rule; (*Relig*) commandment; (*bei Auktion*) bid

gebraten *a* fried

Gebrauch *m* -[e]s (*Sprach-*) usage; **Gebräuche** customs; **in G~** in use; **G~ machen von** make use of. **g~en** *vt* use; **ich kann es nicht/gut g~en** I have no use for/can make good use of it; **zu nichts zu g~en** useless

gebräuchlich *a* common; (*Wort*) in common use

Gebrauch|sanleitung, G~s-anweisung *f* directions *pl* for use. **g~t** *a* used; (*Comm*) secondhand. **G~twagen** *m* used car

gebrechlich *a* frail, infirm

gebrochen *a* broken □ *adv* **g~Englisch sprechen** speak broken English

Gebrüll *nt* -s roaring; (*fam: Schreien*) bawling

Gebrumm *nt* -s buzzing; (*Motoren-*) humming

Gebühr *f* -,-en charge, fee; **über G~** excessively; **g~en** *vi* (*haben*) **ihm g~t Respekt** he deserves respect; **wie es sich g~t** as is right and proper. **g~end** *a* due, *adv* duly; (*geziemend*) proper, *adv* -ly. **g~enfrei** *a* free □ *adv* free of charge. **g~enpflichtig** *a* & *adv* subject to a charge; **g~enpflichtige Straße** toll road

gebunden *a* bound; (*Suppe*) thickened

Geburt *f* -,-en birth; **von G~** by birth. **G~enkontrolle, G~enregelung** *f* birth-control. **G~enziffer** *f* birth-rate

gebürtig *a* a native (*aus* of); **g~er Deutscher** German by birth

Geburts|datum *nt* date of birth. **G~helfer** *m* obstetrician. **G~hilfe** *f* obstetrics *sg*. **G~ort** *m* place of birth. **G~tag** *m* birthday. **G~urkunde** *f* birth certificate

Gebüsch *nt* -[e]s,-e bushes *pl*

Gedächtnis *nt* -ses memory; **aus dem G~** from memory

gedämpft *a* (*Ton*) muffled; (*Stimme*) hushed; (*Musik*) soft; (*Licht, Stimmung*) subdued

Gedanke *m* -ns,n- thought (**an** + *acc* of); (*Idee*) idea; **sich** (*dat*) **G~n machen** worry (**über** + *acc* about). **G~nblitz** *m* brainwave. **g~nlos** *a* thoughtless, *adv* -ly; (*zerstreut*) absent-minded, *adv* -ly. **G~nstrich** *m* dash. **G~nübertragung** *f* telepathy. **g~nvoll** *a* pensive, *adv* -ly

Gedärme *ntpl* intestines; (*Tier-*) entrails

Gedeck *nt* -[e]s,-e place setting; (*auf Speisekarte*) set meal; **ein G~auflegen** set a place. **g~t** *a* covered; (*Farbe*) muted

gedeihen† *vi* (*sein*) thrive, flourish

gedenken† *vi* (*haben*) propose (*etw zu tun* to do sth); **jds/etw g~** remember s.o./sth. **G~** *nt* -s memory; **zum G~ an** (+ *acc*) in memory of

Gedenk|feier *f* commemoration. **G~gottesdienst** *m* memorial service. **G~stätte** *f* memorial. **G~tafel** *f* commemorative plaque. **G~tag** *m* day of remembrance; (*Jahrestag*) anniversary

Gedicht *nt* -[e]s,-e poem

gediegen *a* quality ...; (*solide*) well-made; (*Charakter*) upright; (*Gold*) pure □ *adv* **g~gebaut** well built

Gedränge *nt* -s crush, crowd. **g~t** *a* (*knapp*) concise □ *adv* **g~t voll** packed

gedrückt *a* depressed

gedrungen *a* stocky

Geduld f - patience; **G~ haben** be patient. **g~en (sich)** vr be patient. **g~ig** a patient, adv -ly. **G~[s]spiel** nt puzzle

gedunsen a bloated

geehrt a honoured; **Sehr g~er Herr X** Dear Mr X

geeignet a suitable; **im g~en Moment** at the right moment

Gefahr f -,-en danger; **in/außer G~** in/out of danger; **auf eigene G~** at one's own risk; **G~ laufen** run the risk (**etw zu tun** of doing sth)

gefähr|den vt endanger; (fig) jeopardize. **g~lich** a dangerous, adv -ly; (riskant) risky

gefahrlos a safe

Gefährt nt -[e]s,-e vehicle

Gefährte m -n,-n, **Gefährtin** f -,-nen companion

gefahrvoll a dangerous, perilous

Gefälle nt -s,- slope; (Straßen-) gradient

gefallen† vi (haben) **jdm g~** please s.o.; **er/es gefällt mir** I like him/it; **sich** (dat) **etw g~ lassen** put up with sth

Gefallen¹ m -s,- favour

Gefallen² nt -s pleasure (**an** + dat in); **G~ finden an** (+ dat) like; **dir zu G~** to please you

Gefallene(r) m soldier killed in the war

gefällig a pleasing; (hübsch) attractive, adv -ly; (hilfsbereit) obliging; **jdm g~ sein** do s.o. a good turn; **[sonst] noch etwas g~?** will there be anything else? **G~keit** f -,-en favour; (Freundlichkeit) kindness. **g~st** adv (fam) kindly

Gefangen|e(r) m/f prisoner. **g~halten†** vt sep NEW **g~ halten**, s. **fangen**. **G~nahme** f - capture. **g~nehmen†** vt sep NEW **g~ nehmen**, s. **fangen**. **G~schaft** f - captivity; **in G~schaft geraten** be taken prisoner

Gefängnis nt -ses,-se prison; (Strafe) imprisonment. **G~strafe** f imprisonment; (Urteil) prison sentence. **G~wärter** m [prison] warder, (Amer) guard

Gefäß nt -es,-e container, receptacle; (Blut-) vessel

gefasst (**gefaßt**) a composed; (ruhig) calm, adv -ly; **g~ sein auf** (+ acc) be prepared for

Gefecht nt -[e]s,-e fight; (Mil) engagement; **außer G~ setzen** put out of action

gefedert a sprung

gefeiert a celebrated

Gefieder nt -s plumage. **g~t** a feathered

Geflecht nt -[e]s,-e network; (Gewirr) tangle; (Korb-) wicker-work

gefleckt a spotted

geflissentlich adv studiously

Geflügel nt -s poultry. **G~klein** nt -s giblets pl. **g~t** a winged; **g~tes Wort** familiar quotation

Geflüster nt -s whispering

Gefolge nt -s retinue, entourage. **G~schaft** f - followers pl, following; (Treue) allegiance

gefragt a popular; **g~ sein** be in demand

gefräßig a voracious; (Mensch) greedy

Gefreite(r) m lance-corporal

gefrier|en† vi (sein) freeze. **G~fach** nt freezer compartment. **G~punkt** m freezing point. **G~schrank** m upright freezer. **G~truhe** f chest freezer

gefroren a frozen. **G~e(s)** nt (Aust) ice-cream

Gefüge nt -s,- structure; (fig) fabric

gefügig a compliant; (gehorsam) obedient

Gefühl nt -[e]s,-e feeling; (Empfindung) sensation; (G~sregung) emotion; **im G~ haben** know instinctively. **g~los** a insensitive; (herzlos) unfeeling;

(taub) numb. **g~sbetont** *a* emotional. **g~skalt** *a (fig)* cold. **g~smäßig** *a* emotional, *adv* -ly; *(instinktiv)* instinctive, *adv* -ly. **G~sregung** *f* emotion. **g~voll** *a* sensitive, *adv* -ly; *(sentimental)* sentimental, *adv* -ly

gefüllt *a* filled; *(voll)* full; *(Bot)* double; *(Culin)* stuffed; *(Schokolade)* with a filling

gefürchtet *a* feared, dreaded

gefüttert *a* lined

gegeben *a* given; *(bestehend)* present; *(passend)* appropriate; **zu g~er Zeit** at the proper time. **g~enfalls** *adv* if need be. **G~heiten** *fpl* realities, facts

gegen *prep (+ acc)* against; *(Sport)* versus; *(g~über)* towards; *(Vergleich)* compared with; *(Richtung, Zeit)* towards; *(ungefähr)* around; **ein Mittel g~** a remedy for □ *adv* **g~ 100 Leute** about 100 people. **G~angriff** *m* counter-attack

Gegend *f* -,-en area, region; *(Umgebung)* neighbourhood

gegeneinander *adv* against/*(gegenüber)* towards one another

Gegen|fahrbahn *f* opposite carriageway. **G~gift** *nt* antidote. **G~leistung** *f* als **G~leistung** in return. **G~maßnahme** *f* countermeasure. **G~satz** *m* contrast; *(Widerspruch)* contradiction; *(G~teil)* opposite; **im G~satz zu** unlike. **g~sätzlich** *a* contrasting; *(widersprüchlich)* opposing; **g~seitig** *a* mutual, *adv* -ly; **sich g~seitig hassen** hate one another. **G~spieler** *m* opponent. **G~sprechanlage** *f* intercom. **G~stand** *m* object; *(Gram, Gesprächs-)* subject. **g~standslos** *a* unfounded; *(überflüssig)* irrelevant; *(abstrakt)* abstract. **G~stück** *nt* counterpart; *(G~teil)* opposite. **G~teil** *nt* opposite, contrary; **im G~teil** on the contrary. **g~teilig** *a* opposite

gegenüber *prep (+ dat)* opposite; *(Vergleich)* compared with; **jdm g~ höflich sein** be polite to s.o. □ *adv* opposite. **G~** *nt* -s person opposite. **g~liegen†** *vi sep (haben)* be opposite *(etw dat* sth). **g~liegend** *a* opposite. **g~stehen†** *vi sep (haben) (+ dat)* face; **feindlich g~stehen** *(+ dat)* be hostile to. **g~stellen** *vt sep* confront; *(vergleichen)* compare. **g~treten†** *vi sep (sein) (+ dat)* face

Gegen|verkehr *m* oncoming traffic. **G~vorschlag** *m* counterproposal. **G~wart** *f* - present; *(Anwesenheit)* presence. **g~wärtig** *a* present □ *adv* at present. **G~wehr** *f* - resistance. **G~wert** *m* equivalent. **G~wind** *m* head wind. **g~zeichnen** *vt sep* countersign

geglückt *a* successful

Gegner(in) *m* -s,- *(f* -,-nen) opponent. **g~isch** *a* opposing

Gehabe *nt* -s affected behaviour

Gehackte(s) *nt* minc., *(Amer)* ground meat

Gehalt¹ *m* -[e]s content

Gehalt² *nt* -[e]s,:er salary. **G~serhöhung** *f* rise, *(Amer)* raise

gehaltvoll *a* nourishing

gehässig *a* spiteful, *adv* -ly

gehäuft *a* heaped

Gehäuse *nt* -s, case; *(TV, Radio)* cabinet; *(Schnecken-)* shell; *(Kern-)* core

Gehege *nt* -s enclosure

geheim *a* secret; **g~ halten** keep secret; **im g~en** secretly. **G~dienst** *m* Secret Service. **g~halten†** *vt sep* NEW **g~ halten**, **s. geheim. G~nis** *nt* -ses,-se secret. **g~nisvoll** *a* mysterious, *adv* -ly. **G~polizei** *f* secret police

gehemmt *a (fig)* inhibited

gehen† *vi (sein)* go; *(zu Fuß)* walk; *(fort-)* leave; *(funktioniere* work; ⟨Teig:⟩ rise; **tanzen/ein-kaufen g~** go dancing/shopping; **an die Arbeit g~** set to work; **in Schwarz [gekleidet] g~** dress in black; **nach Norden g~** ⟨Fenster:⟩ face north; **wenn es nach mir ginge** if I had my way; **über die Straße g~** cross the road; **was geht hier vor sich?** what is going on here? **das geht zu weit** ⟨fam⟩ that's going too far; *impers* **wie geht es [Ihnen]?** how are you? **es geht ihm gut/besser/schlecht** he is well/better/not well; ⟨geschäftlich⟩ he is doing well/better/badly; **ein gut g~des Geschäft** a flourishing or thriving business; **es geht nicht/nicht anders** it's impossible/there is no other way; **es ging ganz schnell** it was very quick; **es geht um** it concerns; **es geht ihr nur ums Geld** she is only interested in the money; **es geht [so]** ⟨fam⟩ not too bad; **sich g~ lassen** lose one's self-control; ⟨sich vernachlässigen⟩ let oneself go □ *vt* walk. **g~lassen†** ⟨lassen⟩ *vr sep* NEW **g~ lassen (sich),** s. **gehen**

geheuer *a* **nicht g~** eerie; ⟨verdächtig⟩ suspicious; **mir ist nicht g~** I feel uneasy

Geheul *nt* -s howling

Gehilfe *m* -n,-n, **Gehilfin** *f* -,-nen trainee; ⟨Helfer⟩ assistant

Gehirn *nt* -s brain; ⟨Verstand⟩ brains *pl* **G~erschütterung** *f* concussion; **G~hautentzündung** *f* meningitis. **G~wäsche** *f* brainwashing

gehoben *a* ⟨fig⟩ superior; ⟨Sprache⟩ elevated

Gehöft *nt* -[e]s,-e farm

Gehölz *nt* -es,-e coppice, copse

Gehör *nt* -s hearing; **G~ schenken** (+ *dat*) listen to

gehorchen *vi* (haben) (+ *dat*) obey

gehören *vi* (haben) belong ⟨dat to⟩; **zu den Besten g~** be one of

the best; **dazu gehört Mut** that takes courage; **sich g~** be [right and] proper; **es gehört sich nicht** it isn't done

gehörig *a* proper, *adv* -ly; **jdn g~ verprügeln** give s.o. a good hiding

gehörlos *a* deaf

Gehörn *nt* -s,-e horns *pl*; ⟨Geweih⟩ antlers *pl*

gehorsam *a* obedient, *adv* -ly. **G~** *m* -s obedience

Geh|steig *m* -[e]s,-e pavement, ⟨Amer⟩ sidewalk. **G~weg** *m* = **Gehsteig**; ⟨Fußweg⟩ footpath

Geier *m* -s,- vulture

Geig|e *f* -,-n violin. **g~en** *vi* (haben) play the violin □ *vt* play on the violin. **G~er(in)** *m* -s,- (*f* -,-nen) violinist

geil *a* lecherous; ⟨fam⟩ randy; ⟨fam: toll⟩ great

Geisel *f* -,-n hostage

Geiß *f* -,-en ⟨SGer⟩ [nanny-]goat. **G~blatt** *nt* honeysuckle

Geißel *f* -,-n scourge

Geist *m* -[e]s,-er mind; ⟨Witz⟩ wit; ⟨Gesinnung⟩ spirit; ⟨Gespenst⟩ ghost; **der Heilige G~** the Holy Ghost or Spirit; **im G~** in one's mind. **g~erhaft** *a* ghostly

geistes|abwesend *a* absentminded, *adv* -ly. **G~blitz** *m* brainwave. **G~gegenwart** *f* presence of mind. **G~gegenwärtig** *adv* with great presence of mind. **g~gestört** *a* [mentally] deranged. **g~krank** *a* mentally ill. **G~krankheit** *f* mental illness. **G~wissenschaften** *fpl* arts. **G~zustand** *m* mental state

geist|ig *a* mental, *adv* -ly; ⟨intellektuell⟩ intellectual, *adv* -ly; **g~ige Getränke** spirits. **g~lich** *a* spiritual, *adv* -ly; ⟨religiös⟩ religious; ⟨Musik⟩ sacred; ⟨Tracht⟩ clerical. **G~liche(r)** *m* clergyman. **G~lichkeit** *f* - clergy. **g~los** *a* uninspired. **g~reich** *a* clever; ⟨witzig⟩ witty

Geiz m -es meanness. **g~en** vi (haben) be mean (**mit** with). **G~hals** m (fam) miser. **g~ig** a mean, miserly. **G~kragen** m (fam) miser

Gekicher nt -s giggling

geknickt a (fam) dejected, adv -ly

gekonnt a accomplished □ adv expertly

Gekrakel nt -s scrawl

gekränkt a offended, hurt

Gekritzel nt -s scribble

gekünstelt a affected, adv -ly

Gelächter nt -s laughter

geladen a loaded; (fam: wütend) furious

Gelage nt -s,- feast

gelähmt a paralysed

Gelände nt -s,- terrain; (Grundstück) site. **G~lauf** m cross-country run

Geländer nt -s,- railings pl; (Treppen-) banisters pl; (Brücken-) parapet

gelangen vi (sein) reach/(fig) attain (**zu etw/an etw** acc sth); **in jds Besitz g~** come into s.o.'s possession

gelassen a composed; (ruhig) calm, adv -ly. **G~heit** f - equanimity; (Fassung) composure

Gelatine /ʒela-/ f - gelatine

geläufig a common, current; (fließend) fluent, adv -ly; **jdm g~ sein** be familiar to s.o.

gelaunt a **gut/schlecht g~e Leute** good-humoured/bad-tempered people; **gut/schlecht g~ sein** be in a good/bad mood

gelb a yellow; (bei Ampel) amber; **g~e Rübe** (SGer) carrot; **das G~e vom Ei** the yolk of the egg. **G~** nt -s,- yellow; **bei G~** (Auto) on [the] amber. **g~lich** a yellowish. **G~sucht** f jaundice

Geld nt -[e]s money; **öffentliche G~er** public funds. **G~beutel** m, **G~börse** f purse. **G~geber** m -s,- backer. **g~lich** a financial, adv -ly. **G~mittel** ntpl

funds. **G~schein** m banknote. **G~schrank** m safe. **G~strafe** f fine. **G~stück** nt coin

Gelee /ʒe'le:/ nt -s,s jelly

gelegen a situated; (passend) convenient; **jdm sehr g~ sein** od **kommen** suit s.o. well; **mir ist viel/wenig daran g~** I'm very/not keen on it; (es ist wichtig) it matters a lot/little to me

Gelegenheit f -,-en opportunity; chance; (Anlass) occasion; (Comm) bargain; **bei g~** some time. **G~sarbeit** f casual work. **G~sarbeiter** m casual worker. **G~skauf** m bargain

gelegentlich a occasional □ adv occasionally; (bei Gelegenheit) some time □ prep (+ gen) on the occasion of

gelehrt a learned. **G~e(r)** m/f scholar

Geleise nt -s,- = **Gleis**

Geleit nt -[e]s escort; **freies G~** safe conduct. **g~en** vt escort. **G~zug** m (Naut) convoy

Gelenk nt -[e]s,-e joint. **g~ig** a supple; (Techn) flexible

gelernt a skilled

Geliebte(r) m/f lover; (liter) beloved

gelieren /ʒe-/ vi (haben) set

gelinde a mild, adv -ly; **g~ gesagt** to put it mildly

gelingen† vi (sein) succeed, be successful; **es gelang ihm, zu entkommen** he succeeded in escaping. **G~** nt -s success

gell int (SGer) = **gelt**

gellend a shrill, adv -y

geloben vt promise [solemnly]; **sich** (dat) **g~ vow** (**zu** to); **das Gelobte Land** the Promised Land

Gelöbnis nt -ses,-se vow

gelöst a (fig) relaxed

Gelse f -,-n (Aust) mosquito

gelt nt (SGer) **das ist schön, g~?** it's nice, isn't it? **ihr kommt**

doch, g~? you are coming, aren't you?

gelten† *vi* (*haben*) be valid; ⟨*Regel:*⟩ apply; **g~ als** be regarded as; **etw nicht g~ lassen** not accept sth; **wenig/viel g~** be worth/(*fig*) count for little/a lot; **jdm g~** be meant for s.o.; **das gilt nicht** that doesn't count. **g~d** *a* valid; ⟨*Preise*⟩ current; ⟨*Meinung*⟩ prevailing; **g~d machen** assert ⟨*Recht, Forderung*⟩; bring to bear ⟨*Einfluss*⟩

Geltung *f* - validity; ⟨*Ansehen*⟩ prestige; **G~ haben** be valid; **zur G~ bringen/kommen** set off/show to advantage

Gelübde *nt* -s,- vow

gelungen *a* successful

Gelüst *nt* -[e]s,-e desire/(*stark*) craving (**nach** for)

gemächlich *a* leisurely □ *adv* in a leisurely manner

Gemahl *m* -s,-e husband. **G~in** *f* -,-nen wife

Gemälde *nt* -s,- painting. **G~galerie** *f* picture gallery

gemäß *prep* (+ *dat*) in accordance with □ *a* **etw** (*dat*) **g~ sein** in keeping with sth

gemäßigt *a* moderate; ⟨*Klima*⟩ temperate

gemein *a* common; (*unanständig*) vulgar; (*niederträchtig*) mean; **g~er Soldat** private; **etw g~ haben** have sth in common □ *adv* shabbily; (*fam*: *schrecklich*) terribly

Gemeinde *f* -,-n [local] community; (*Admin*) borough; (*Pfarr-*) parish; (*bei Gottesdienst*) congregation. **G~rat** *m* local council/(*Person*) councillor. **G~wahlen** *fpl* local elections

gemein|**gefährlich** *a* dangerous. **G~heit** *f* -,-en (*s. gemein*) commonness; vulgarity; meanness; (*Bemerkung, Handlung*) mean thing [to say/do]; **so eine G~heit!** how mean! (*wie ärgerlich*) what a nuisance! **G~kosten**

pl overheads. **g~nützig** *a* charitable. **G~platz** *m* platitude. **G~sam** *a* common; **etw g~sam haben** have sth in common □ *adv* together

Gemeinschaft *f* -,-en community. **G~lich** *a* joint; (*Besitz*) communal □ *adv* jointly; (*zusammen*) together. **G~sarbeit** *f* team-work

Gemenge *nt* -s,- mixture

gemessen *a* measured; (*würdevoll*) dignified

Gemetzel *nt* -s,- carnage

Gemisch *nt* -[e]s,-e mixture. **g~t** *a* mixed

Gemme *f* -,-n engraved gem

Gemse *f* -,-n NEW **Gämse**

Gemurmel *nt* -s murmuring

Gemüse *nt* -s,- vegetable; (*coll*) vegetables *pl*. **G~händler** *m* greengrocer

gemustert *a* patterned

Gemüt *nt* -[e]s,-er nature, disposition; (*Gefühl*) feelings *pl*; (*Person*) soul

gemütlich *a* a cosy; (*gemächlich*) leisurely; (*zwanglos*) informal; (*Person*) genial; **es sich** (*dat*) **g~ machen** make oneself comfortable □ *adv* cosily; in a leisurely manner; informally. **G~keit** *f* - cosiness; leisureliness

Gemüts|**art** *f* nature, disposition. **G~mensch** *m* (*fam*) placid person. **G~ruhe** *f* **in aller G~ruhe** (*fam*) calmly. **G~verfassung** *f* frame of mind

Gen *nt* -s,-e gene

genau *a* exact, *adv* -ly, precise, *adv* -ly; ⟨*Waage, Messung*⟩ accurate, *adv* -ly; ⟨*sorgfältig*⟩ meticulous, *adv* -ly; (*ausführlich*) detailed; **nichts G~es wissen** not know any details; **es nicht so g~ nehmen** not be too particular; **g~ genommen** strictly speaking; **g~!** exactly! **g~ge-nommen** *adv* NEW **g~ genommen**, *s.* **genau**. **G~igkeit** *f* -

exactitude; precision; accuracy; meticulousness

genauso adv just the same; (g~sehr) just as much; g~ schön/teuer just as beautiful/ expensive; g~ gut just as good; adv just as well; g~ sehr just as much; g~ viel just as much/ many; g~ wenig just as little/ few; (noch) no more. g~gut adv (NEW) g~ gut, s. genauso. g~sehr adv (NEW) g~ sehr, s. genauso. g~viel adv (NEW) g~ viel, s. genauso. g~wenig adv (NEW) g~ wenig, s. genauso

Gendarm /ʒã'darm/ m -en,-en (Aust) policeman

Genealogie f - genealogy

genehmig|en vt grant; approve (Plan). G~ung f -,-en permission; (Schein) permit

geneigt a sloping, inclined; (fig) well-disposed (dat towards); [nicht] g~ sein (fig) [not] feel inclined (zu to)

General m -s,-e general. G~direktor m managing director. g~isieren vi (haben) generalize. G~probe f dress rehearsal. G~streik m general strike. g~überholen vt insep (inf & pp only) completely overhaul

Generation /-'tsio:n/ f -,-en generation

Generator m -s,-en /-'to:rən/ generator

generell a general, adv -ly

genes|en† vi (sein) recover. G~ung f recovery; (Erholung) convalescence

Genet|ik f - genetics sg. g~isch a genetic, adv -ally

Genf nt -s Geneva. G~er a Geneva ...; G~er See Lake Geneva

genial a brilliant, adv -ly; ein g~er Mann a man of genius. G~ität f - genius

Genick nt -s,-e [back of the] neck; sich (dat) das G~ brechen break one's neck

Genie /ʒe'ni:/ nt -s,-s genius

genier|en /ʒe'ni:rən/ vt embarrass; sich g~ feel or be embarrassed

genieß|bar a fit to eat/drink. g~en† vt enjoy; (verzehren) eat/ drink. G~er m -s,- gourmet. g~erisch a appreciative □ adv with relish

Genitiv m -s,-e genitive

Genosse m -n,-n (Pol) comrade. G~nschaft f -,-en cooperative

Genre /'ʒã:rə/ nt -s,-s genre

Gentechnologie f genetic engineering

genug inv a & adv enough

Genüge f zur G~ sufficiently. g~n vi (haben) be enough; jds Anforderungen g~n meet s.o.'s requirements. g~nd inv a sufficient, enough; (Sch) fair □ adv sufficiently, enough

genügsam a frugal, adv -ly; (bescheiden) modest, adv -ly

Genugtuung f - satisfaction

Genuss m -es,-e (Genuß m -sses, -sse) enjoyment; (Vergnügen) pleasure; (Verzehr) consumption

genüsslich (genüßlich) a pleasurable □ adv with relish

geöffnet a open

Geo|graphie f -, -grafie f - geography. g~graphisch a gra-fisch a geographical, adv -ly. G~loge m -n,-n geologist. G~logie f - geology. g~logisch a geological, adv -ly. G~meter m -s,- surveyor. G~metrie f - geometry. g~metrisch a geometric[al]

geordnet a well-ordered; (stabil) stable; alphabetisch g~ in alphabetical order

Gepäck nt -s luggage, baggage. G~ablage f luggage-rack. G~aufbewahrung f left-luggage office. G~schalter m luggage office. G~schein m left-luggage ticket; (Aviat) baggage check. G~stück nt piece of luggage. G~träger m porter;

(Fahrrad-) luggage carrier; *(Dach-)* roof-rack. **G~wagen** *m* luggage-van

Gepard *m* -s,-e cheetah

gepflegt *a* well-kept; *(Person)* well-groomed; *(Hotel)* first-class

Gepflogenheit *f* -,-en practice; *(Brauch)* custom

Gepolter *nt* -s [loud] noise

gepunktet *a* spotted

gerade *a* straight; *(direkt)* direct; *(aufrecht)* upright; *(aufrichtig)* straightforward; *(Zahl)* even; **etw g~ biegen** straighten sth; **sich g~ halten** hold oneself straight □ *adv* straight; directly; *(eben)* just; *(genau)* exactly; *(besonders)* especially; **g~ sitzen/stehen** sit/stand [up] straight; **nicht g~ billig** not exactly cheap; **g~ erst** only just; **g~ an dem Tag** on that very day. **G~ f** -,-n straight line. **G~aus** *adv* straight ahead/on

gerade|biegen† *vt sep* NEW g~ biegen, s. gerade. **g~halten**† *(sich) vr sep* NEW sich g~ halten, s. gerade. **g~heraus** *adv* *(fig)* straight out. **g~sitzen**† *vi sep (haben)* NEW g~ sitzen, s. gerade. **g~so** *adv* just the same; **g~so gut** just as good; *adv* just as well. **g~sogut** NEW g~so gut, s. geradeso. **g~stehen**† *vi sep (haben)* *(fig)* accept responsibility **(für)** for; *(aufrecht stehen)* NEW g~ stehen, s. gerade. **g~wegs** *adv* directly, straight. **g~zu** *adv* virtually; *(wirklich)* absolutely

Geranie /-jə/ *f* -,-n geranium

Gerät *nt* -[e]s,-e tool; *(Acker-)* implement; *(Küchen-)* utensil; *(Elektro-)* appliance; *(Radio-, Fernseh-)* set; *(Turn-)* piece of apparatus; *(coll)* equipment

geraten† *vi (sein)* get; **in Brand g~** catch fire; **in Wut g~** get angry; **in Streit g~** start quarrelling; **gut/schlecht g~** turn out

well/badly; **nach jdm g~** take after s.o.

Geratewohl *nt* **aufs G~** at random

geräuchert *a* smoked

geräumig *a* spacious, roomy

Geräusch *nt* -[e]s,-e noise. **G~los** *a* noiseless, *adv* -ly. **G~voll** *a* noisy, *adv* -ily

gerben *vt* tan

gerecht *a* just, *adv* -ly; *(fair)* fair, *adv* -ly; **g~ werden** (+ *dat*) do justice to. **g~fertigt** *a* justified. **G~igkeit** *f* - justice; fairness

Gerede *nt* -s talk; *(Klatsch)* gossip

geregelt *a* regular

gereift *a* mature

gereizt *a* irritable, *adv* -bly. **G~heit** *f* - irritability

gereuen *vt* **es gereut mich nicht** I don't regret it

Geriatrie *f* - geriatrics

Gericht[1] *nt* -[e]s,-e *(Culin)* dish

Gericht[2] *nt* -[e]s,-e court [of law]; **vor G~** in court; **das Jüngste G~** the Last Judgement; **mit jdm ins G~ gehen** take s.o. to task. **g~lich** *a* judicial; *(Verfahren)* legal □ *adv* legally; **g~lich vorgehen** take legal action. **G~sbarkeit** *f* - jurisdiction. **G~shof** *m* court of justice. **G~smedizin** *f* forensic medicine. **G~ssaal** *m* courtroom. **G~svollzieher** *m* -s,-bailiff

gerieben *a* grated; *(fam: schlau)* crafty

gering *a* small; *(niedrig)* low; *(g~fügig)* slight; **jdn/etw g~achten** have little regard for s.o./sth; *(verachten)* despise s.o./sth. **g~achten** *vt sep* NEW g~ achten, s. gering. **g~fügig** *a* slight, *adv* -ly. **g~schätzig** *a* contemptuous, *adv* -ly; *(Bemerkung)* disparaging. **g~ste(r,s)** *a* least; **nicht im G~sten** (g~sten) not in the least

gerinnen† *vi (sein)* curdle; *(Blut:)* clot

Gerippe nt -s,- skeleton; (fig) framework

gerissen a (fam) crafty

Germ m -[e]s & (Aust) f - yeast

German m -n,-n [ancient] German. **g~isch** a Germanic. **G~ist(in)** m -en,-en (f -,-nen) Germanist. **G~istik** f - German [language and literature]

gern[e] adv gladly; **g~ haben** like; (lieben) be fond of; **ich tanze/schwimme g~** I like dancing-/swimming; **das kannst du g~ tun** you're welcome to it; **willst du mit?—g~!** do you want to come?—I'd love to!

gerötet a red

Gerste f - barley. **G~nkorn** nt (Med) stye

Geruch m -[e]s,-e smell (von/nach of). **g~los** a odourless. **G~ssinn** m sense of smell

Gerücht nt -[e]s,-e rumour

geruhen vi (haben) deign (zu to)

gerührt a (fig) moved, touched

Gerümpel nt -s lumber, junk

Gerüst nt -[e]s,-e scaffolding; (fig) framework

gesalzen a salted; (fam: hoch) steep

gesammelt a collected; (gefasst) composed

gesamt a entire, whole. **G~ausgabe** f complete edition. **G~betrag** m total amount. **G~eindruck** m overall impression. **G~heit** f - whole. **G~schule** f comprehensive school. **G~summe** f total

Gesandte(r) m/f envoy

Gesang m -[e]s,-e singing; (Lied) song; (Kirchen-) hymn. **G~buch** nt hymn-book. **G~verein** m choral society

Gesäß nt -es buttocks pl. **G~tasche** f hip pocket

Geschäft nt -[e]s,-e business; (Laden) shop, (Amer) store; (Transaktion) deal; (fam: Büro) office; **schmutzige G~e** shady

dealings; **ein gutes G~ machen** do very well (mit out of); **sein G~ verstehen** know one's job. **g~ehalber** adv on business. **g~ig** a busy, adv -ily; (Treiben) bustling. **G~igkeit** f - activity. **g~lich** a business ... □ adv on business

Geschäfts|brief m business letter. **G~führer** m manager; (Vereins-) secretary. **G~mann** m (pl -leute) businessman. **G~reise** f business trip. **G~stelle** f office; (Zweigstelle) branch. **g~tüchtig** a **g~tüchtig sein** be a good businessman/-woman. **G~viertel** nt shopping area. **G~zeiten** fpl hours of business

geschehen† vi (sein) happen (dat to); **es ist ein Unglück g~** there has been an accident; **es ist um uns g~** we are done for; **das geschieht dir recht!** it serves you right! **gern g~!** you're welcome! **G~** nt -s events pl

gescheit a clever; **daraus werde ich nicht g~** I can't make head or tail of it

Geschenk nt -[e]s,-e present, gift. **G~korb** m hamper

Geschichte f -,-n history; (Erzählung) story; (fam: Sache) business. **g~lich** a historical, adv -ly

Geschick nt -[e]s fate; (Talent) skill; **G~ haben** be good (zu at). **G~lichkeit** f - skilfulness, skill. **g~t** a skilful, adv -ly; (klug) clever, adv -ly

geschieden a divorced. **G~e(r)** m/f divorcee

Geschirr nt -s,-e (coll) crockery; (Porzellan) china; (Service) service; (Pferde-) harness; **schmutziges G~** dirty dishes pl. **G~spülmaschine** f dishwasher. **G~tuch** nt tea-towel

Geschlecht nt -[e]s,-er sex; (Gram) gender; (Familie) family; (Generation) generation. **g~lich** a sexual, adv -ly. **G~skrankheit** f venereal disease. **G~steile** ntpl genitals. G~sverkehr *m* sexual intercourse. G~swort *nt* (*pl* -wörter) article

geschliffen *a* (*fig*) polished

geschlossen *a* closed □ *adv* unanimously; (*vereint*) in a body

Geschmack *m* -[e]s,⸚e taste; (*Aroma*) flavour; (*G~ssinn*) sense of taste; **einen guten G~ haben** (*fig*) have good taste; **finden an** (+ *dat*) acquire a taste for. **g~los** *a* tasteless, *adv* -ly; **g~los sein** (*fig*) be in bad taste. **G~ssache** *f* matter of taste. **g~voll** *a* tasteful, *adv* -ly

geschmeidig *a* supple; (*weich*) soft

Geschöpf *nt* -[e]s,-e creature

Geschoss *nt* -es,-e (**Geschoß** *nt* -sses,-sse) missile; (*Stockwerk*) storey, floor

geschraubt *a* (*fig*) stilted

Geschrei *nt* -s screaming; (*fig*) fuss

Geschütz *nt* -es,-e gun, cannon

geschützt *a* protected; (*Stelle*) sheltered

Geschwader *nt* -s,- squadron

Geschwätz *nt* -es talk. **g~ig** *a* garrulous

geschweift *a* curved

geschweige *conj* **g~ denn** let alone

geschwind *a* quick, *adv* -ly

Geschwindigkeit *f* -,-en speed; (*Phys*) velocity. **G~sbegrenzung, G~sbeschränkung** *f* speed limit

Geschwister *pl* brother[s] and sister[s]; siblings

geschwollen *a* swollen; (*fig*) pompous, *adv* -ly

Geschworene(r) *m/f* juror; **die G~n** the jury *sg*

Geschwulst *f* -,⸚e swelling; (*Tumor*) tumour

geschwungen *a* curved

Geschwür *nt* -s,-e ulcer

Geselle *m* -n,-n fellow; (*Handwerks-*) journeyman

gesellig *a* sociable; (*Zool*) gregarious; (*unterhaltsam*) convivial; **g~er Abend** social evening. **G~keit** *f* -,-en entertaining; **die G~keit lieben** love company

Gesellschaft *f* -,-en company; (*Veranstaltung*) party; **die G~** society; **jdm G~ leisten** keep s.o. company. **g~lich** *a* social, *adv* -ly. **G~sreise** *f* group tour. **G~sspiel** *nt* party game

Gesetz *nt* -es,-e law. **G~entwurf** *m* bill. **g~gebend** *a* legislative. **G~gebung** *f* legislation. **g~lich** *a* legal, *adv* -ly. **g~los** *a* lawless. **g~mäßig** *a* lawful, *adv* -ly; (*gesetzlich*) legal, *adv* -ly

gesetzt *a* staid; (*Sport*) seeded □ *conj* **g~ den Fall** supposing

gesetzwidrig *a* illegal, *adv* -ly

gesichert *a* secure

Gesicht *nt* -[e]s,-er face; (*Aussehen*) appearance; **zu G~ bekommen** set eyes on. **G~sausdruck** *m* [facial] expression. **G~sfarbe** *f* complexion. **G~spunkt** *m* point of view. **G~szüge** *mpl* features

Gesindel *nt* -s riff-raff

gesinnt *a* **gut/übel g~** well/ill disposed (*dat* towards)

Gesinnung *f* -,-en mind; (*Einstellung*) attitude; **politische G~** political convictions *pl*

gesittet *a* well-mannered; (*zivilisiert*) civilized

gesondert *a* separate, *adv* -ly

Gespann *nt* -[e]s,-e team; (*Wagen*) horse and cart/carriage

gespannt *a* taut; (*fig*) tense, *adv* -ly; (*Beziehungen*) strained; (*neugierig*) eager, *adv* -ly; (*erwartungsvoll*) expectant, *adv* -ly; **g~ sein, ob** wonder whether; **auf etw/jdn g~ sein** look forward eagerly to sth/to seeing s.o.

Gespenst *nt* -[e]s,-er ghost. **g~isch** *a* ghostly; (*unheimlich*) eerie

Gespött *nt* -[e]s mockery; **zum G~ werden** become a laughing-stock

Gespräch *nt* -[e]s-e conversation; *(Telefon-)* call; **ins G~ kommen** get talking; **im G~ sein** be under discussion. **g~ig** *a* talkative. **G~sgegenstand** *m*, **G~sthema** *nt* topic of conversation

gesprenkelt *a* speckled

Gespür *nt* -s feeling; *(Instinkt)* instinct

Gestalt *f* -,-en figure; *(Form)* shape, form; **G~ annehmen** *(fig)* take shape. **g~en** *vt* shape; *(organisieren)* arrange; *(schaffen)* create; *(entwerfen)* design; **sich g~en** turn out

geständig *a* confessed; **g~ig sein** have confessed. **G~nis** *nt* -ses,-se confession

Gestank *m* -s stench, [bad] smell

gestatten *vt* allow, permit; **nicht gestattet** prohibited; **g~ Sie?** may I?

Geste /'gɛ-, 'ge:stə/ *f* -,-n gesture

Gesteck *nt* -[e]s,-e flower arrangement

gestehen *vt/i (haben)* confess; confess to *(Verbrechen)*; **offen gestanden** to tell the truth

Gestein *nt* -[e]s,-e rock

Gestell *nt* -[e]s,-e stand; *(Flaschen-)* rack; *(Rahmen-)* frame

gestellt *a* **gut/schlecht g~** well/badly off; **auf sich** *(acc)* **selbst g~ sein** be thrown on one's own resources

gestelzt *a (fig)* stilted

gesteppt *a* quilted

gestern *adv* yesterday; **g~ Nacht (nacht)** last night

Gestik /'gɛstɪk/ *f* - gestures *pl*. **g~ulieren** *vi (haben)* gesticulate

gestrandet *a* stranded

gestreift *a* striped

gestrichelt *a (Linie)* dotted

gestrichen *a* **g~er Teelöffel** level teaspoon[ful]

gestrig /'gɛstrɪç/ *a* yesterday's; **am g~en Tag** yesterday

Gestrüpp *nt* -s,-e undergrowth

Gestüt *nt* -[e]s,-e stud [farm]

Gesuch *nt* -[e]s,-e request; *(Admin)* application. **g~t** *a* sought-after; *(gekünstelt)* contrived

gesund *a* healthy, *adv* -ily; **g~ sein** be in good health; *(Sport, Getränk:)* be good for one; **wieder g~ werden** get well again

Gesundheit *f* - health; **G~!** *(bei Niesen)* bless you! **g~lich** *a* health ...; *adv* for health reasons; **g~licher Zustand** state of health □ *adv* **es geht ihm g~lich gut/schlecht** he is in good/poor health. **g~shalber** *adv* for health reasons. **g~sschädlich** *a* harmful. **g~szustand** *m* state of health

getäfelt *a* panelled

getigert *a* tabby

Getöse *nt* -s racket, din, *adv* -ly

getragen *a* solemn, *adv* -ly

Getränk *nt* -[e]s,-e drink. **G~ekarte** *f* wine-list

getrauen *vt* **sich** *(dat)* **etw g~** dare [to] do sth; **sich g~** dare

Getreide *nt* -s *(coll)* grain

getrennt *a* separate, *adv* -ly; **g~ leben** live apart; **g~ schreiben** write as two words. **g~schreiben**† *vt sep* ⟨NEW⟩ **g~ schreiben,** *s.* **getrennt**

getreu *a* faithful, *adv* -ly □ *prep* (+ *dat)* true to; **der Wahrheit g~** *(+ dat)* true to; **der Wahrheit g~** truthfully. **g~lich** *adv* faithfully

Getriebe *nt* -s,-e bustle; *(Techn)* gear; *(Auto)* transmission; *(Gehäuse)* gearbox

getrost *adv* with confidence

Getto *nt* -s,-s ghetto

Getue *nt* -s *(fam)* fuss

Getümmel *nt* -s tumult

getüpfelt *a* spotted

geübt *a* skilled; *(Auge, Hand)* practised

Gewächs *nt* -es,-e plant; *(Med)* growth

gewachsen a jdm/etw g~ sein be a match for s.o./be equal to sth

Gewächshaus nt greenhouse; (Treibhaus) hothouse

gewagt a daring

gewählt a refined

gewahr a g~ werden become aware (acc/gen of)

Gewähr f -, guarantee

gewahren vt notice

gewähr|en vt grant; (geben) offer; jdn g~en lassen let s.o. have his way. **g~leisten** vt guarantee

Gewahrsam m -s safekeeping; (Haft) custody

Gewährsmann m (pl -männer & -leute) informant, source

Gewalt f -, -en power; (Kraft) force; (Brutalität) violence; **mit G~** by force; **g~ anwenden** use force; **sich in der G~ haben** be in control of oneself. **G~herrschaft** f tyranny. **g~ig** a powerful; (enorm) enormous, adv -ly; (stark) tremendous, adv -ly. **g~sam** a forcible, adv -bly; (Tod) violent. **g~tätig** a violent. **G~tätigkeit** f -,-en violence; (Handlung) act of violence

Gewand nt -[e]s,-er robe

gewandt a skilful, adv -ly; (flink) nimble, adv -bly. **G~heit** f -skill; nimbleness

Gewässer nt -s,- body of water; **G~** pl waters

Gewebe nt -s,- fabric; (Anat) tissue

Gewehr nt -s,-e rifle, gun

Geweih nt -[e]s,-e antlers pl

Gewerb|e nt -s,- trade. **g~lich** a commercial, adv -ly. **g~smäßig** a professional, adv -ly

Gewerkschaft f -,-en trade union. **G~ler(in)** m -s,- (f -,-nen) trade unionist

Gewicht nt -[e]s,-e weight; (Bedeutung) importance. **G~heben** nt -s weight-lifting. **g~ig** a important

gewieft a (fam) crafty

gewillt a g~ sein be willing

Gewinde nt -s,- [screw] thread

Gewinn m -[e]s,-e profit; (fig) gain, benefit; (beim Spiel) winnings pl; (Preis) prize; (Los) winning ticket; **G~ bringend** profitable, adv -bly. **G~beteiligung** f profit-sharing. **g~bringend** a (NEW) G~ bringend, s. Gewinn. **g~en†** vt win; (erlangen) gain; (fördern) extract; jdn für sich g~en win s.o. over □ vi (haben) win; **g~en an** (+ dat) gain in. **g~end** a engaging. **G~er(in)** m -s,- (f -,-nen) winner

Gewirr nt -s,-e tangle; (Straßen-) maze; **G~ von Stimmen** hubbub of voices

gewiss (gewiß) a (gewisser, gewissest) certain, adv -ly

Gewissen nt -s,- conscience. **g~haft** a conscientious, adv -ly. **g~los** a unscrupulous. **G~sbisse** mpl pangs of conscience

gewissermaßen adv to a certain extent; (sozusagen) as it were

Gewissheit (Gewißheit) f - certainty

Gewitter nt -s,- thunderstorm. **g~n** vi (haben) es g~ert it is thundering. **g~ig** a thundery

gewogen a (fig) well-disposed (dat towards)

gewöhnen vt jdn/sich g~an (+ acc) get s.o. used to/get used to; **[an] jdn/etw gewöhnt sein** be used to s.o./sth

Gewohnheit f -,-en habit. **g~smäßig** a habitual, adv -ly. **G~srecht** nt common law

gewöhnlich a ordinary, adv -ily; (üblich) usual, adv -ly; (ordinär) common

gewohnt a customary; (vertraut) familiar; (üblich) usual; **etw** (acc) **g~ sein** be used to sth

Gewöhnung f - getting used (an + acc to); (Süchtigkeit) addiction

Gewölb|e nt -s,- vault. **g~t** a curved; (Archit) vaulted

gewollt a forced
Gewühl nt -[e]s crush
gewunden a winding
gewürfelt a check[ed]
Gewürz nt -es,-e spice. **G~nelke** f clove
gezackt a serrated
gezähnt a serrated; ⟨Säge⟩ toothed
Gezeiten fpl tides
gezielt a specific; ⟨Frage⟩ pointed
geziemend a proper, adv -ly
geziert a affected, adv -ly
gezwungen a forced □ adv **g~ lachen** give a forced laugh. **g~ermaßen** adv of necessity; **etw g~ermaßen tun** be forced to do sth
Gicht f - gout
Giebel m -s,- gable
Gier f - greed (**nach** for). **g~ig** a greedy, adv -ily
gießen| vt pour; water ⟨Blumen, Garten⟩; ⟨Techn⟩ cast □ v impers **es g~t** it is pouring [with rain]. **G~erei** f -,-en foundry. **G~kanne** f watering-can
Gift nt -[e]s,-e poison; ⟨Schlangen⟩ venom; ⟨Biol, Med⟩ toxin. **g~ig** a poisonous; ⟨Schlange⟩ venomous; ⟨Med, Chem⟩ toxic; ⟨fig⟩ spiteful, adv -ly. **G~müll** m toxic waste. **G~pilz** m poisonous fungus, toadstool. **G~zahn** m [poison] fang
gigantisch a gigantic
Gilde f -,-n guild
Gimpel m -s,- bullfinch; ⟨fam: Tölpel⟩ simpleton
Gin /dʒɪn/ m -s gin
Ginster m -s ⟨Bot⟩ broom
Gipfel m -s,- summit, top; ⟨fig⟩ peak. **G~konferenz** f summit conference. **g~n** vi ⟨haben⟩ culminate (**in** + dat in)
Gips m -es plaster. **G~abguss** (**G~abguß**) m plaster cast. **G~er** m -s,- plasterer. **G~verband** m ⟨Med⟩ plaster cast
Giraffe f -,-n giraffe

Girlande f -,-n garland
Girokonto /ˈʒiːro-/ nt current account
Gischt m -[e]s & f - spray
Gitar|re f -,-n guitar. **G~rist(in)** m -en,-en ⟨f -,-nen⟩ guitarist
Gitter nt -s,- bars pl; ⟨Rost⟩ grating, grid; ⟨Geländer, Zaun⟩ railings pl; ⟨Fenster⟩ grille; ⟨Draht-⟩ wire screen; **hinter G~n** ⟨fam⟩ behind bars. **G~netz** nt grid
Glanz m -es shine; ⟨von Farbe, Papier⟩ gloss; ⟨Seiden-⟩ sheen; ⟨Politur⟩ polish; ⟨fig⟩ brilliance; ⟨Pracht⟩ splendour
glänzen vi ⟨haben⟩ shine. **g~d** a shining, bright; ⟨Papier, Haar⟩ glossy; ⟨fig⟩ brilliant, adv -ly
glanz|los a dull. **G~stück** nt masterpiece; ⟨einer Sammlung⟩ showpiece. **g~voll** a ⟨fig⟩ brilliant, adv -ly; ⟨prachtvoll⟩ splendid, adv -ly. **G~zeit** f heyday
Glas nt -es,-er glass; ⟨Brillen-⟩ lens; ⟨Fern-⟩ binoculars pl; ⟨Marmelade-⟩ [glass] jar. **G~er** m -s,- glazier
gläsern a glass ...
Glashaus nt greenhouse
glasieren vt glaze; ice ⟨Kuchen⟩
glas|ig a glassy; ⟨durchsichtig⟩ transparent. **G~scheibe** f pane
Glasur f -,-en glaze; ⟨Culin⟩ icing
glatt a smooth; ⟨eben⟩ even; ⟨Haar⟩ straight; ⟨rutschig⟩ slippery; ⟨einfach⟩ straightforward; ⟨eindeutig⟩ downright; ⟨Absage⟩ flat; **g~ streichen** smooth out □ adv smoothly; evenly; ⟨fam: völlig⟩ completely; ⟨gerade⟩ straight; ⟨leicht⟩ easily; ⟨ablehnen⟩ flatly; **g~ rasiert** clean-shaven; **g~ gehen** od **verlaufen** go off smoothly; **das ist g~ gelogen** it's a downright lie
Glätte f - smoothness; ⟨Rutschigkeit⟩ slipperiness
Glatteis nt [black] ice; **aufs G~ führen** ⟨fam⟩ take for a ride
glätten vt smooth; **sich g~** become smooth; ⟨Wellen⟩ subside

glatt|gehen† *vi sep (sein)* NEW **g~gehen**, *s.* **glatt**. **g~rasiert** *a* NEW **g~ rasiert**, *s.* **glatt**. **g~streichen**† *vt sep* NEW **g~streichen**, *s.* **glatt**. **g~weg** *adv (fam)* outright

Glatze|*e f -,-n* bald patch; *(Voll-)* bald head; **eine G~e bekommen** go bald. **g~köpfig** *a* bald

Glaube *m -ns* belief **(an** + *acc* in); *(Relig)* faith; **in gutem G~n** in good faith; **G~n schenken** (+ *dat)* believe. **g~n** *vt/i (fam)* believe **(an** + *acc* in); *(vermuten)* think; **jdm g~n** believe s.o.; **nicht zu g~n** unbelievable, incredible. **G~nsbekenntnis** *nt* creed

glaubhaft *a* credible; *(überzeugend)* convincing, *adv* -ly

gläubig *a* religious; *(vertrauend)* trusting, *adv* -ly. **G~e(r)** *m/f(Relig)* believer; **die G~en** the faithful. **G~er** *m -s,- (Comm)* creditor

glaub|lich *a* **kaum g~lich** scarcely believable. **g~würdig** *a* credible; *(Person)* reliable. **G~würdigkeit** *f* - credibility; reliability

gleich *a* same; *(identisch)* identical; *(g~wertig)* equal; **g~ bleibend** constant; **2 mal 5 [ist] g~ 10** two times 5 equals 10; **das ist mir g~** it's all the same to me; **ganz g~, wo/wer** no matter where/who □ *adv* equally; *(übereinstimmend)* identically, the same; *(sofort)* immediately; *(in Kürze)* in a minute; *(fast)* nearly; *(direkt)* right; **g~ gesinnt** like-minded; **g~ alt/schwer sein** be the same age/weight. **g~altrig** *a* [of] the same age. **g~artig** *a* similar. **g~bedeutend** *a* synonymous. **g~berechtigt** *a* equal. **G~berechtigung** *f* equality. **g~bleibend** *a* NEW **g~ bleibend**, *s.* **gleich**. **gleichen**† *vi (haben)* **jdm/etw g~** be like *or* resemble s.o./sth; **sich g~** be alike

gleich|ermaßen *adv* equally. **g~falls** *adv* also, likewise; **danke g~falls** thank you, the same to you. **g~förmig** *a* uniform, *adv* -ly; *(eintönig)* monotonous, *adv* -ly. **G~förmigkeit** *f* uniformity; monotony. **g~gesinnt** *a* NEW **g~ gesinnt**, *s.* **gleich**. **G~gewicht** *nt* balance; *(Phys & fig)* equilibrium. **g~gültig** *a* indifferent, *adv* -ly; *(unwichtig)* unimportant. **G~gültigkeit** *f* indifference. **g~heit** *f* - equality; *(Ähnlichkeit)* similarity. **g~machen** *vt sep* make equal; **dem Erdboden g~machen** raze to the ground. **g~mäßig** *a* even, *adv* -ly, regular, *adv* -ly; *(beständig)* constant, *adv* -ly; **G~mäßigkeit** *f* - regularity. **G~mut** *m* equanimity. **g~mütig** *a* calm, *adv* -ly

Gleichnis *nt -ses,-se* parable

gleich|sam *adv* as it were. **G~schritt** *m* **im G~schritt** in step. **g~sehen**† *vi sep (haben)* **jdm g~sehen** look like s.o.; *(fam: typisch sein)* be just like s.o. **g~setzen** *vt sep* equate/*(g~stellen)* place on a par *(dat/*mit with). **g~stellen** *vt sep* place on a par *(dat* with). **G~strom** *m* direct current. **g~tun**† *vi sep (haben)* **es jdm g~tun** emulate s.o.

Gleichung *f -,-en* equation

gleich|viel *adv* no matter *(ob/*wer whether/who). **g~wertig** *a* of equal value. **g~zeitig** *a* simultaneous, *adv* -ly

Gleis *nt -es,-e* track; *(Bahnsteig)* platform; **G~ 5** platform 5

gleiten† *vi (sein)* glide; *(rutschen)* slide. **g~d** *a* sliding; **g~de Arbeitszeit** flexitime

Gleitzeit *f* flexitime

Gletscher *m -s,-* glacier. **G~spalte** *f* crevasse

Glied *nt -[e]s,-er* limb; *(Teil)* part; *(Ketten-)* link; *(Mitglied)* member; *(Mil)* rank. **g~ern** *vt* arrange;

(*einteilen*) divide; **sich g~ern** be divided (*in* + *acc* into).
G~maßen *fpl* limbs

glimmen† *vi* (*haben*) glimmer

glimpflich *a* lenient, *adv* -ly; **g~ davonkommen** get off lightly

glitschig *a* slippery

glitzern *vi* (*haben*) glitter

global *a* global, *adv* -ly

Globus *m* - & -**busses,-ben** & -**busse** globe

Glocke *f* -,-n bell. **G~nturm** *m* bell-tower, belfry

glorifizieren *vt* glorify

glorreich *a* glorious

Glossar *nt* -s,-e glossary

Glosse *f* -,-n comment

glotzen *vi* (*haben*) stare

Glück *nt* -[e]s [good] luck; (*Zufriedenheit*) happiness; **G~ bringend** lucky; **G~/kein G~ haben** be lucky/unlucky; **zum G~** luckily, fortunately; **auf gut G~** on the off chance (*wahllos*) at random. **g~bringend** *a* NEW **G~ bringend,** s. **Glück. g~en** *vi* (*sein*) succeed; **es ist mir geglückt** I succeeded

gluckern *vi* (*haben*) gurgle

glücklich *a* lucky, fortunate; (*zufrieden*) happy; (*sicher*) safe □ *adv* happily; safely; (*fam: endlich*) finally. **g~erweise** *adv* luckily, fortunately

glückselig *a* blissfully happy. **G~keit** *f* bliss

glucksen *vi* (*haben*) gurgle

Glücksspiel *nt* game of chance; (*Spielen*) gambling

Glückwunsch *m* good wishes *pl*; (*Gratulation*) congratulations *pl*; **herzlichen G~!** congratulations! (*zum Geburtstag*) happy birthday! **G~karte** *f* greetings card

Glüh|birne *f* light-bulb. **g~en** *vi* (*haben*) glow. **g~end** *a* glowing; (*rot-*) red-hot; (*Hitze*) scorching; (*leidenschaftlich*) fervent, *adv* -ly. **G~faden** *m* filament. **G~wein**

m mulled wine. **G~würmchen** *nt* -s,- glow-worm

Glukose *f* - glucose

Glut *f* - embers *pl*; (*Röte*) glow; (*Hitze*) heat; (*fig*) ardour

Glyzinie /-jə/ *f* -,-n wisteria

GmbH *abbr* (**Gesellschaft mit beschränkter Haftung**) ≈ plc

Gnade *f* - mercy; (*Gunst*) favour; (*Relig*) grace. **G~nfrist** *f* reprieve. **g~nlos** *a* merciless, *adv* -ly

gnädig *a* gracious, *adv* -ly; (*mild*) lenient, *adv* -ly; **g~e Frau** Madam

Gnom *m* -en,-en gnome

Gobelin /gobaˈlɛ̃/ *m* -s,-s tapestry

Gold *nt* -[e]s gold. **g~en** *a* gold ...; (*g~farben*) golden; **g~ene Hochzeit** golden wedding. **G~fisch** *m* goldfish. **G~grube** *f* gold-mine. **g~ig** *a* sweet, lovely. **G~lack** *m* wallflower. **G~regen** *m* laburnum. **G~schmied** *m* goldsmith

Golf¹ *m* -[e]s,-e (*Geog*) gulf

Golf² *nt* -s golf. **G~platz** *m* golf-course. **G~schläger** *m* golf-club. **G~spieler(in)** *m(f)* golfer

Gondel *f* -,-n gondola; (*Kabine*) cabin

Gong *m* -s,-s gong

gönnen *vt* **jdm etw g~** not begrudge s.o. sth; **jdm etw nicht g~** begrudge s.o. sth; **sie gönnte sich** (*dat*) **keine Ruhe** she allowed herself no rest

Gönner *m* -s,- patron. **g~haft** *a* patronizing, *adv* -ly

Gör *nt* -s,-en, **Göre** *f* -,-n (*fam*) kid

Gorilla *m* -s,-s gorilla

Gosse *f* -,-n gutter

Gotlik *f* - Gothic. **g~isch** *a* Gothic

Gott *m* -[e]s, ¨er God; (*Myth*) god

Götterspeise *f* jelly

Gottes|dienst *m* service. **g~lästerlich** *a* blasphemous, *adv* -ly. **G~lästerung** *f* blasphemy

Gottheit f -,-en deity

Göttin f -,-nen goddess

göttlich a divine, adv -ly

gott|los a ungodly; (atheistisch) godless. **g~verlassen** a God-forsaken

Götze m -n,-n, **G~nbild** nt idol

Gouver|nante /guvər'nantə/ f -,-n governess. **G~neur** /-'nøːɐ/ m -s,-e governor

Grab nt -[e]s,-̈er grave

graben† vi (haben) dig

Graben m -s,-̈ ditch; (Mil) trench

Grab|mal nt tomb. **G~stein** m gravestone, tombstone

Grad m -[e]s,-e degree

Graf m -en,-en count

Grafik f -,-en graphics sg; (Kunst) graphic arts pl; (Druck) print

Gräfin f -,-nen countess

grafisch a graphic; **g~e Darstellung** diagram

Grafschaft f -,-en county

Gram m -s grief

grämen (sich) vr grieve

grämlich a morose, adv -ly

Gramm nt -s,-e gram

Gram|matik f -,-en grammar. **g~matikalisch**, **g~matisch** a grammatical, adv -ly

Granat m -[e]s,-e (Miner) garnet. **G~apfel** m pomegranate. **G~e** f -,-n shell; (Hand-) grenade

Granit m -s,-e granite

Graph|ik f, **g~isch** a = Grafik, grafisch

Gras nt -es,-̈er grass. **g~en** vi (haben) graze. **G~hüpfer** m -s,- grasshopper

grassieren vi (haben) be rife

grässlich (gräßlich) a dreadful, adv -ly

Grat m -[e]s,-e [mountain] ridge

Gräte f -,-n fishbone

Gratifikation /-'tsjoːn/ f -,-en bonus

gratis adv free [of charge]. **G~probe** f free sample

Gratu|lant(in) m -en,-en (f -,-nen) well-wisher. **G~lation** /-'tsjoːn/ f -,-en congratulations

pl; (Glückwünsche) best wishes pl. **g~lieren** vi (haben) jdm **g~lieren** congratulate s.o. (zu on); (zum Geburtstag) wish s.o. happy birthday; [ich] **g~liere!** congratulations!

grau a, **G~** nt -s,- grey. **G~brot** nt mixed rye and wheat bread

Gräuel m -s,- horror. **G~tat** f atrocity

grauen[1] vi (haben) der Morgen od es graut dawn is breaking

grauen[2] v impers mir graut [es] davor I dread it. **G~** nt -s dread. **g~haft**, **g~voll** a gruesome; (grässlich) horrible, adv -bly

gräulich[1] a greyish

gräulich[2] a horrible, adv -bly

Graupeln fpl soft hail sg

grausam a cruel, adv -ly. **G~keit** f -,-en cruelty

graus|en v impers mir graust davor I dread it. **G~en** nt -s horror, dread. **g~ig** a gruesome

gravieren vt engrave. **g~d** a (fig) serious

Grazie /'graːtsjə/ f - grace

graziös a graceful, adv -ly

greifbar a tangible; **in g~er Nähe** within reach

greifen† vt take hold of; (fangen) catch □ vi (haben) reach (nach for); **g~ zu** (fig) turn to; **um sich g~** (fig) spread. **G~** nt **G~spielen** play tag

Greis m -es,-e old man. **G~enalter** nt extreme old age. **g~enhaft** a old. **G~in** f -,-nen old woman

grell a glaring; (Farbe) garish; (schrill) shrill, adv -ly

Gremium nt -s,-ien committee

Grenz|e f -,-n border; (Staats-) frontier; (Grundstücks-) boundary; (fig) limit. **g~en** vi (haben) border (an + acc on). **g~enlos** a boundless; (maßlos) infinite, adv -ly. **G~fall** m borderline case

Greu|el m -s,- (NEW) Gräuel. **g~lich** a (NEW) gräulich[2]

Griech|e *m* -n,-n Greek. **G~en-land** *nt* -s Greece. **G~in** *f* -,-nen Greek woman. **g~isch** *a* Greek. **G~isch** *nt* -[s] (*Lang*) Greek

griesgrämig *a* (*fam*) grumpy

Grieß *m* -es semolina

Griff *m* -[e]s,-e grasp, hold; (*Hand*-) movement of the hand; (*Tür-, Messer-*) handle; (*Schwert*-) hilt. **g~bereit** *a* handy

Grill *m* -s,-s grill; (*Garten*-) barbecue

Grille *f* -,-n (*Zool*) cricket; (*fig: Laune*) whim

grill|en *vt/i*; (*im Freien*) barbecue □ *vi* (*haben*) have a barbecue. **G~fest** *nt* barbecue. **G~gericht** *nt* grill

Grimasse *f* -,-n grimace; **G~n schneiden** pull faces

grimmig *a* furious; (*Kälte*) bitter

grinsen *vi* (*haben*) grin. **G~** *nt* -s grin

Grippe *f* -,-n influenza, (*fam*) flu

grob *a* (*gröber, gröbst*) coarse, *adv* -ly; (*unsanft, ungefähr*) rough, *adv* -ly; (*unhöflich*) rude, *adv* -ly; (*schwer*) gross, *adv* -ly; (*Fehler*) bad; **g~e Arbeit** rough work; **g~ geschätzt** roughly. **G~ian** *m* -s,-e brute

gröblich *a* gross, *adv* -ly

grölen *vt/i* (*haben*) bawl

Groll *m* -[e]s resentment; **einen G~ gegen jdn hegen** bear s.o. a grudge. **g~en** *vi* (*haben*) be angry (*dat* with); (*Donner:*) rumble

Grönland *nt* -s Greenland

Gros[1] *nt* -ses,- (*Maß*) gross

Gros[2] /gro:/ *nt* - majority, bulk

Groschen *m* -s, (*Aust*) groschen, (*fam*) ten-pfennig piece; **der G~ ist gefallen** (*fam*) the penny's dropped

groß *a* (*größer, größt*) big; (*Anzahl, Summe*) large; (*bedeutend, stark*) great; (*g~artig*) grand; (*Buchstabe*) capital; **g~e Ferien** summer holidays; **g~e Angst haben** be very frightened; **der**

größte Teil the majority *or* bulk; **g~ werden** (*Person:*) grow up; **g~ in etw** (*dat*) **sein** be good at sth; **g~ geschrieben werden** (*fig*) be very important (**bei jdm** to s.o.); **G~ und Klein** (*und klein*) young and old; **in g~en und Ganzen** (**im g~en und ganzen**) on the whole □ *adv* (*feiern*) in style; (*fam: viel*) much; **jdn g~ ansehen** look at s.o. in amazement

großartig *a* magnificent, *adv* -ly. **G~aufnahme** *f* close-up. **G~britannien** *nt* -s Great Britain. **G~buchstabe** *m* capital letter. **G~e(r)** *m/f* **unser G~er** our eldest; **die G~en** the grown-ups; (*fig*) the great *pl*

Größe *f* -,-n size; (*Ausmaß*) extent; (*Körper*) height; (*Bedeutsamkeit*) greatness; (*Math*) quantity; (*Person*) great figure

Groß|eltern *pl* grandparents. **g~enteils** *adv* largely

Größenwahnsinn *m* megalomania

Groß|handel *m* wholesale trade. **G~händler** *m* wholesaler. **g~herzig** *a* magnanimous, *adv* -ly. **G~macht** *f* superpower. **G~mut** *f* -magnanimity. **g~mütig** *a* magnanimous, *adv* -ly. **G~mutter** *f* grandmother. **G~onkel** *m* great-uncle. **G~reinemachen** *nt* -s spring-clean. **g~schreiben**[*vt sep*] write with a capital [initial] letter; **g~geschrieben werden** (*fig*) NEW **g~ geschrieben werden**, *s*. **groß. G~schreibung** *f* capitalization. **g~sprecherisch** *a* boastful. **g~spurig** *a* pompous, *adv* -ly; (*überheblich*) arrogant, *adv* -ly. **G~stadt** *f* [large] city. **g~städtisch** *a* city ... **G~tante** *f* great-aunt. **G~teil** *m* large proportion; (*Hauptteil*) bulk

größtenteils *adv* for the most part

groß|tun† (sich) *vr sep* brag.
G~vater *m* grandfather.
g~ziehen† *vt sep* bring up; rear
⟨*Tier*⟩. **g~zügig** *a* generous, *adv*
-ly; (*weiträumig*) spacious.
G~zügigkeit *f* - generosity

grotesk *a* grotesque, *adv* -ly
Grotte *f* -,-n grotto
Grübchen *nt* -s,- dimple
Grube *f* -,-n pit
grübeln *vi* (haben) brood
Gruft *f* -,-e [burial] vault
grün *a* green; **im G~en** out in the
country; **die G~en** the Greens.
G~ nt -s,- green; (*Laub, Zweige*)
greenery
Grund *m* -[e]s,-e ground; (*Boden*)
bottom; (*Hinter-*) background;
(*Ursache*) reason; **aus diesem**
G~e for this reason; **von G~ auf**
(*fig*) radically; **im G~e** [*genom-*
men] basically; **auf G~ laufen**
(*Naut*) run aground; **auf G~** (+
gen) = **aufgrund**; **zu G~e rich-**
ten/gehen/liegen = **zugrunde**
richten/gehen/liegen, s. **zu-**
grunde. **G~begriffe** *mpl* basics.
G~besitz *m* landed property.
G~besitzer *m* landowner
gründ|en *vt* found; set up; start
⟨*Familie*⟩; (*fig*) base (**auf** + *acc*
on); **sich g~en** be based (**auf**
acc on). **G~er(in)** *m* -s,- (*f* -,-nen)
founder
Grund|farbe *f* primary colour.
G~form *f* (*Gram*) infinitive.
G~gesetz *nt* (*Pol*) constitution.
G~lage *f* basis, foundation.
g~legend *a* fundamental, *adv* -ly.
gründlich *a* thorough, *adv* -ly.
G~keit *f* - thoroughness
grund|los *a* bottomless; (*fig*)
groundless □ *adv* without reason.
G~mauern *fpl* foundations
Gründonnerstag *m* Maundy
Thursday
Grund|regel *f* basic rule. **G~riss**
(**G~riß**) *m* ground-plan; (*fig*) out-
line. **G~satz** *m* principle.
g~sätzlich *a* fundamental, *adv*
-ly; (*im Allgemeinen*) in principle;

(*prinzipiell*) on principle.
G~schule *f* primary school.
G~stein *m* foundation-stone.
G~stück *nt* plot [of land]
Gründung *f* -,-en foundation
grün|en *vi* (haben) become green.
G~gürtel *m* green belt. **G~span**
m verdigris. **G~streifen** *m* grass
verge; (*Mittel-*) central reservation, (*Amer*) median strip
grunzen *vi* (haben) grunt
Gruppe *f* -,-n group; (*Reise-*) party
gruppieren *vt* group; **sich g~**
form a group/groups
Grusel|geschichte *f* horror
story. **g~ig** *a* creepy
Gruß *m* -es,-e greeting; (*Mil*) salute; **einen schönen G~ an X**
give my regards to X; **vie-**
le/herzliche G~e regards; **Mit**
freundlichen G~en Yours sin-
cerely/(*Comm*) faithfully
grüßen *vt/i* (haben) say hallo (**jdn**
to s.o.); (*Mil*) salute; **g~ Sie X von**
mir give my regards to X; **jdn g~**
lassen send one's regards to s.o.;
grüß Gott! (*SGer, Aust*) good
morning/afternoon/evening!
guck|en *vi* (haben) (*fam*) look.
G~loch *nt* peep-hole
Guerilla /ge'rɪlja/ *f* - guerrilla
warfare. **G~kämpfer** *m* guerrilla
Gulasch *nt & m* -[e]s goulash
gültig *a* valid, *adv* -ly. **G~keit** *f* -
validity
Gummi *m & nt* -s,-[s] rubber;
(*Harz*) gum. **G~band** *nt* (*pl*
-bänder) elastic *or* rubber band;
(*G~zug*) elastic
gummiert *a* gummed
Gummi|knüppel *m* truncheon.
G~stiefel *m* gumboot, welling-
ton. **G~zug** *m* elastic
Gunst *f* - favour; **zu jds G~en** in
s.o.'s favour; **zu G~** (+ *gen*) =
zugunsten
günstig *a* favourable, *adv* -bly;
(*passend*) convenient, *adv* -ly
Günstling *m* -s,-e favourite

Gurgel f -,-n throat. **g~n** vi (haben) gargle. **G~wasser** nt gargle

Gurke f -,-n cucumber; (Essig-) gherkin

gurren vi (haben) coo

Gurt m -[e]s,-e strap; (Gürtel) belt; (Auto) safety-belt. **G~band** nt (pl -bänder) waistband

Gürtel m -s,- belt. **G~linie** f waistline. **G~rose** f shingles sg

GUS abbr (Gemeinschaft Unabhängiger Staaten) CIS

Guss m -es,-̈e (Guß m -sses,-̈sse) (Techn) casting; (Strom) stream; (Regen-) down-pour; (Torten-) icing. **G~eisen** nt cast iron. **g~eisern** a cast-iron

gut a (besser, best) good; (Gewissen) clear; (gütig) kind (zu to); **jdm gut sein** be fond of s.o.; **im G~en (g~en)** amicably; **zu g~er Letzt** in the end; **schon gut** that's all right □ adv well; (schmecken, riechen) good; (leicht) easily; **es gut haben** be well off; (Glück haben) be lucky; **gut zu sehen** clearly visible; **gut drei Stunden** a good three hours; **du hast gut reden** it's easy for you to talk

Gut nt -[e]s,-̈er possession, property; (Land-) estate; **Gut und Böse** good and evil; **Güter** (Comm) goods

Gutacht|en nt -s,- expert's report. **G~er** m -s,- expert

gut|artig a good-natured; (Med) benign. **g~aussehend** a (NEW) **gut aussehend,** s. aussehen. **g~bezahlt** a (NEW) **gut bezahlt,** s. bezahlen. **G~dünken** nt -s nach eigenem G~dünken at one's own discretion

Gute(s) nt etwas/nichts **G~s** something/nothing good; **G~s tun** do good; **das G~ daran** the good thing about it all; **alles G~!** all the best!

Güte f -,-n goodness, kindness; (Qualität) quality; **du meine G~!** my goodness!

Güterzug m goods-/(Amer) freight train

gut|gehen† vi sep (sein) (NEW) **gut gehen,** s. gehen. **g~gehend** a (NEW) **gut gehend,** s. gehen. **g~gemeint** a (NEW) **gut gemeint,** s. meinen. **g~gläubig** a trusting. **g~haben†** vt sep **fünfzig Mark g~haben** have fifty marks credit (bei with). **G~haben** nt -s,- [credit] balance; (Kredit) credit. **g~heißen†** vt sep approve of

gütig a kind, adv -ly

gütlich a amicable, adv -ly

gut|machen vt sep make up for; make good (Schaden). **g~mütig** a good-natured, adv -ly. **G~mütigkeit** f - good nature. **G~schein** m credit note; (Bon) voucher; (Geschenk-) gift token. **g~schreiben†** vt sep credit. **G~schrift** f credit

Guts|haus nt manor house. **G~hof** m manor

gut|situiert a (NEW) **gut situiert,** s. situiert. **g~tun†** vi sep (haben) (NEW) **gut tun,** s. tun. **g~willig** a willing, adv -ly

Gymnasium nt -s,-ien ≈ grammar school

Gymnast|ik f - [keep-fit] exercises pl; (Turnen) gymnastics sg. **g~isch** a **g~ische Übung** exercise

Gynäko|loge m -n,-n gynaecologist. **G~logie** f - gynaecology. **g~logisch** a gynaecological

H

H, h /haː/ nt, -,- (Mus) B, b

Haar nt -[e]s,-e hair; sich (dat) **die Haare** od **das H~ waschen** wash one's hair; **um ein H~** (fam) very nearly. **H~bürste** f hairbrush. **h~en** vi (haben) shed hairs; (Tier:) moult □ vr **sich**

h~en moult. h~ig *a* hairy;
(*fam*) tricky. **H~klammer,**
H~klemme *f* hair-grip. **H~na-**
del *f* hairpin. **H~nadelkurve** *f*
hairpin bend. **H~schleife** *f* bow.
H~schnitt *m* haircut.
H~spange *f* slide. **h~sträu-**
bend a hair-raising; (*empörend*)
shocking. **H~trockner** *m* -s,-
hair-drier. **H~waschmittel** *nt*
shampoo

Habe *f* - possessions *pl*

haben† *vt* have; Angst/Hunger/
Durst h~ be frightened/hungry/
thirsty; **ich kätte gern** I'd like;
sich h~ (*fam*) make a fuss; **es**
gut/schlecht h~ be well/badly
off; **etw gegen jdn h~** have sth
against s.o.; **was hat er?** what's
the matter with him? □ *v aux*
have; **ich habe/hatte geschrie-**
ben I have/had written; **er hätte**
ihr geholfen he would have
helped her

Habgier *f* greed. **h~ig** *a* greedy
Habicht *m* -[e]s,-e hawk
Hab|seligkeiten *fpl* belongings.
H~sucht *f* = Habgier
Hachse *f* -,-n (*Culin*) knuckle
Hack|beil *nt* chopper. **H~braten**
m meat loaf
Hacke¹ *f* -,-n hoe; (*Spitz-*) pick
Hacke² *f* -,-n, **Hacken** *m* -s,- heel
hack|en *vt* hoe; (*schlagen, zerklei-*
nern) chop; ⟨*Vogel:*⟩ peck; **ge-**
hacktes Rindfleisch minced/
(*Amer*) ground beef. **H~fleisch**
nt mince, (*Amer*) ground meat
Hafen *m* -s,¨ harbour; (*See-*) port.
H~arbeiter *m* docker.
H~damm *m* mole. **H~stadt** *f*
port
Hafer *m* -s oats *pl*. **H~flocken** *fpl*
[rolled] oats. **H~mehl** *nt* oatmeal
Haft *f* - (*Jur*) custody; (*H~strafe*)
imprisonment. **h~bar** *a* (*Jur*)
liable. **H~befehl** *m* warrant [of
arrest]
haften *vi* (*haben*) cling; (*kleben*)
stick; (*bürgen*) vouch/(*Jur*) be
liable (**für** for)

Häftling *m* -s,-e detainee
Haftpflicht *f* (*Jur*) liability.
H~versicherung *f* (*Auto*) third-
party insurance
Haftstrafe *f* imprisonment
Haftung *f* - (*Jur*) liability
Hagebutte *f* -,-n rose-hip
Hagel *m* -s hail. **H~korn** *nt* hail-
stone. **h~n** *vi* (*haben*) hail
hager *a* gaunt
Hahn *m* -[e]s,¨e cock; (*Techn*) tap,
(*Amer*) faucet
Hähnchen *nt* -,s- (*Culin*) chicken
Hai[fisch] *m* -[e]s,-e shark
Häkchen *nt* -s,- tick
häkel|n *vt/i* (*haben*) crochet.
H~nadel *f* crochet-hook
Haken *m* -s,- hook; (*Häkchen*)
tick; (*fam: Schwierigkeit*) snag.
h~ *vt* hook (**an** + *acc* to). **H~-**
kreuz *nt* swastika. **H~nase** *f*
hooked nose

halb *a* half; **eine h~e Stunde** half
an hour; **zum h~en Preis** at half
price; **auf h~em Weg** half-way
□ *adv* half; **h~drei** half past two;
fünf [Minuten] vor/nach
h~vier twenty-five [minutes]
past three/to four; **h~ und h~**
half and half; (*fast ganz*) more or
less. **H~blut** *nt* half-breed.
H~dunkel *nt* semi-darkness.
H~e(r,s) *f/m/nt* half [a litre]
halber *prep* (+ *gen*) for the sake of;
Geschäfte h~ on business
halbieren *vt* halve, divide in half;
(*Geom*) bisect
Halb|insel *f* peninsula. **H~kreis**
m semicircle. **H~kugel** *f* hemisphere. **h~laut** *a* low □ *adv* in an
undertone. **h~mast** *adv* at half-
mast. **H~messer** *m* -s,- radius.
H~mond *m* half moon. **H~pen-**
sion *f* half-board. **h~rund** *a* se-
micircular. **H~schuh** *m* [flat]
shoe. **h~stündlich** *a & adv* half-
hourly. **h~tags** *adv* [for] half a
day; **h~tags arbeiten** ≈ work
part-time. **H~ton** *m* semitone.

h~wegs *adv* half-way; (*ziemlich*) more or less. h~wüchsig *a* adolescent. H~zeit *f* (*Sport*) half-time; (*Spielzeit*) half

Halde *f* -,-n dump, tip

Hälfte *f* -,-n half; zur H~ half

Halfter[1] *m & nt* -s,- halter

Halfter[2] *f* -,-n & *nt* -s,- holster

Hall *m* -[e]s,-e sound

Halle *f* -,-n hall; (*Hotel-*) lobby; (*Bahnhofs-*) station concourse

hallen *vi* (*haben*) resound; (*wider-*) echo

Hallen- *pref* indoor

hallo *int* hallo

Halluzination /-'tsio:n/ *f* -,-en hallucination

Halm *m* -[e]s,-e stalk; (*Gras-*) blade

Hals *m* -es,-e neck; (*Kehle*) throat; aus vollem H~e at the top of one's voice; (*lachen*) out loud. H~ausschnitt *m* neckline. H~band *nt* (*pl* -bänder) collar. H~kette *f* necklace. H~schmerzen *mpl* sore throat *sg*. h~starrig *a* stubborn. H~tuch *nt* scarf

halt[1] *adv* (*SGer*) just; es geht h~ nicht it's just not possible

halt[2] *int* stop! (*Mil*) halt! (*fam*) wait a minute!

Halt *m* -[e]s,-e hold; (*Stütze*) support; (*innerer*) stability; (*Anhalten*) stop. h~ machen stop. h~bar *a* durable; (*Tex*) hardwearing; (*fig*) tenable; h~bar bis ... (*Comm*) use by ...

halten† *vt* hold; make (*Rede*); give (*Vortrag*); (*einhalten, bewahren*) keep; [sich (*dat*)] etw h~ keep (*Hund*); take (*Zeitung*); run (*Auto*); warm h~ keep warm; h~ für regard as; viel/nicht viel h~ von think highly/little of; sich h~ hold on (an + *dat* to); (*fig*) hold out; (*Geschäft:*) keep going; (*haltbar sein*) hold; (*Wetter:*) hold; (*Blumen:*) last; sich links h~ keep left; sich gerade h~ keep upright;

sich h~ an (+ *acc*) (*fig*) keep to □ *vi* (*haben*) hold; (*haltbar sein, bestehen bleiben*) last; (*Freundschaft, Blumen:*) last; (*Halt machen*) stop; (*fig*) set great store by; auf sich (*acc*) h~ take pride in oneself; an sich (*acc*) h~ contain oneself; zu jdm h~ be loyal to s.o.

Halter *m* -s,- holder

Halte|stelle *f* stop. H~verbot *nt* waiting restriction; 'H~verbot' 'no waiting'

halt|los *a* (*fig*) unstable; (*unbegründet*) unfounded. h~machen *vi sep* (*haben*) (NEW) H~ machen, s. Halt

Haltung *f* -,-en (*Körper-*) posture; (*Verhalten*) manner; (*Einstellung*) attitude; (*Fassung*) composure; (*Halten*) keeping; h~ annehmen (*Mil*) stand to attention

Halunke *m* -n,-n scoundrel

Hamburger *m* -s,- hamburger

hämisch *a* malicious, *adv* -ly

Hammel *m* -s,- ram; (*Culin*) mutton. H~fleisch *nt* mutton

Hammer *m* -s,- hammer

hämmern *vt/i* (*haben*) hammer; (*Herz:*) pound

Hämorrhoiden /hɛmɔro'i:dən/ Hämorriden /hɛmɔ'ri:dən/ *fpl* haemorrhoids

Hamster *m* -s,- hamster. h~n *vt/i* (*fam*) hoard

Hand *f* -,-e hand; eine H~ voll Kirschen a handful of cherries; jdm die H~ geben shake hands with s.o.; rechter/linker H~ on the right/left; [aus] zweiter H~ second-hand; unter der H~ unofficially; (*geheim*) secretly; H~ (+ *gen*) = anhand; H~ und Fuß haben (*fig*) be sound. H~arbeit *f* manual work; (*handwerklich*) handicraft; (*Nadelarbeit*) needlework; (*Gegenstand*) handmade article. H~ball *m* [German] handball. H~besen *m* brush. H~bewegung *f* gesture.

H~bremse f handbrake.
H~buch nt handbook, manual
Händedruck m handshake
Handel m -s trade, commerce;
(*Unternehmen*) business; (*Geschäft*) deal; **H~ treiben** trade.
h~n vi (haben) act; (*Handel treiben*) trade (**mit** in); **von etw** od
über etw (acc) **h~n** deal with
sth; **sich h~n um** be about, concern. **H~smarine** f merchant
navy. **H~sschiff** nt merchant
vessel. **H~sschule** f commercial
college. **h~süblich** a customary.
H~sware f merchandise
Hand|feger m -s, brush. **H~fertigkeit** f dexterity. **h~fest** a
sturdy; (fig) solid. **H~fläche** f
palm. **h~gearbeitet** a handmade. **H~gelenk** nt wrist.
h~gemacht a handmade.
H~gemenge nt -s, scuffle.
H~gepäck nt hand-luggage.
h~geschrieben a hand-written.
H~granate f hand-grenade.
h~greiflich a tangible; **h~greiflich werden** become violent.
H~griff m handle; **mit einem
H~griff** with a flick of the wrist
handhaben vt insep (reg) handle
Handikap /'hɛndikɛp/ nt -s, -s
handicap
Hand|kuss (Handkuß) m kiss on
the hand. **H~lauf** m handrail
Händler m -s, dealer, trader
handlich a handy
Handlung f -, -en act; (*Handeln*)
action; (*Roman-*) plot; (*Geschäft*)
shop. **H~sweise** f conduct
Hand|schellen fpl handcuffs.
H~schlag m handshake.
H~schrift f handwriting; (*Text*)
manuscript. **H~schuh** m glove.
H~schuhfach nt glove compartment. **H~stand** m handstand.
H~tasche f handbag. **H~tuch**
nt towel. **h~voll** a -, eine
H~voll (NEW) **eine H~ voll**, s.
Hand
Handwerk nt craft, trade; **sein
H~ verstehen** know one's job.

H~er m -s, -craftsman; (*Arbeiter*)
workman
Handy /'hɛndi/ nt -s, -s mobile
phone
Hanf m -[e]s hemp
Hang m -[e]s, ⸚e slope; (fig) inclination, tendency
Hänge|brücke f suspension
bridge. **H~lampe** f [light] pendant. **H~matte** f hammock
hängen[1] vt (reg) hang
hängen[2] vi (haben) hang; **h~ an**
(+ dat) (fig) be attached to; **h~
bleiben** stick (**an** + dat to);
(*Kleid.:*) catch (**an** + dat on); **h~
lassen** leave; **den Kopf h~
lassen** be downcast. **h~bleiben†**
vi sep (sein) (NEW) **h~ bleiben**, s.
hängen. h~lassen† vt sep
(NEW) **h~ lassen**, s. **hängen**
Hannover nt -s Hanover
hänseln vt tease
hantieren vi (haben) busy oneself
hapern vi (haben) **es hapert**
there's a lack (**an** + dat of)
Happen m -s, mouthful; **einen
H~ essen** have a bite to eat
Harfe f -, -n harp
Harke f -, -n rake. **h~n** vt/i
(haben) rake
harmlos a harmless; (*arglos*) innocent, adv -ly. **H~igkeit** f -
harmlessness; innocence
Harmonie f -, -n harmony. **h~
ren** vi (haben) harmonize; (*gut
auskommen*) get on well
Harmonika f -, -s accordion;
(*Mund-*) mouth-organ
harmonisch a harmonious, adv
-ly
Harn m -[e]s urine. **H~blase** f
bladder
Harpune f -, -n harpoon
hart (härter, härtest) a hard;
(*heftig*) violent; (*streng*) harsh
☐ adv hard; (*streng*) harshly
Härte f -, -n hardness; (*Strenge*)
harshness; (*Not*) hardship. **h~n**
vt harden

Hart|faserplatte f hardboard.
h∼gekocht a (NEW) **h∼ gekocht**, s. **kochen**. **h∼herzig** a hardhearted. **h∼näckig** a stubborn, adv ·ly; (ausdauernd) persistent, adv ·ly. **H∼näckigkeit** f - stubbornness; persistence

Harz nt -es, -e resin

Hasche nt -s,-s (Culin) hash

haschen vi (haben) **h∼ nach** try to catch

Haschisch nt & m -[s] hashish

Hase m -n,-n hare; **falscher H∼** meat loaf

Hasel f -,-n hazel. **H∼maus** f dormouse. **H∼nuss** (**H∼nuß**) f hazel-nut

Hasenfuß m (fam) coward

Hass m -es (**Haß** m -sses) hatred

hassen vt hate

hässlich (**häßlich**) a ugly; (unfreundlich) nasty, adv ·ily. **H∼keit** f - ugliness; nastiness

Hast f - haste. **h∼en** vi (sein) hasten, hurry. **h∼ig** a hasty, adv ·ily, hurried, adv ·ly

hast, hat, hatte, hätte s. **haben**

Haube f -,-n cap; (Trocken-) drier; (Kühler-) bonnet, (Amer) hood

Hauch m -[e]s breath; (Luft-) breeze; (Duft) whiff; (Spur) tinge. **h∼dünn** a very thin; (Strümpfe) sheer. **h∼en** vt/i (haben) breathe

Haue f - pick; (Prügel) beating. **h∼n†** vt beat; (hämmern) knock; (meißeln) hew; sich **h∼n** fight; **übers Ohr h∼n** (fam) cheat □ vi (haben) bang (**auf** + acc on); **jdm ins Gesicht h∼n** hit s.o. in the face

Haufen m -s,- heap, pile; (Leute) crowd

häufen vt heap or pile [up]; sich **h∼** pile up; (zunehmen) increase

haufenweise adv in large numbers; **h∼ Geld** pots of money

häufig a frequent, adv ·ly. **H∼keit** f - frequency

Haupt nt -[e]s, **Häupter** head. **H∼bahnhof** m main station.

H∼darsteller m, **H∼darstellerin** f male/female lead. **H∼fach** nt main subject. **H∼gericht** nt main course. **H∼hahn** m mains tap; (Wasser-) stopcock

Häuptling m -s,-e chief

Haupt|mahlzeit f main meal. **H∼mann** m (pl -leute) captain. **H∼person** f most important person; (Theat) principal character. **H∼post** f main post office. **H∼quartier** nt headquarters pl. **H∼rolle** f lead; (fig) leading role. **H∼sache** f main thing; **in der H∼sache** in the main. **h∼sächlich** a main, adv ·ly. **H∼satz** m main clause. **H∼schlüssel** m master key. **H∼stadt** f capital. **H∼straße** f main street. **H∼verkehrsstraße** f main road. **H∼verkehrszeit** f rush-hour. **H∼wort** nt (pl -wörter) noun

Haus nt -es, **Häuser** house; (Gebäude) building; (Schnecken-) shell; **zu H∼e** at home; **nach H∼e** home; **H∼ halten** s. **haushalten**. **H∼angestellte(r)** m/f domestic servant. **H∼arbeit** f housework; (Sch) homework. **H∼arzt** m family doctor. **H∼aufgaben** fpl homework sg. **H∼besetzer** m -s,- squatter. **H∼besuch** m house-call

hausen vi (haben) live; (wüten) wreak havoc

Haus|frau f housewife. **H∼gehilfin** f domestic help. **h∼gemacht** a home-made. **H∼halt** m -[e]s,-e household; (Pol) budget. **h∼halten†** vi sep (haben) **h∼halten mit** manage carefully, conserve (Kraft). **H∼hälterin** f -,-nen housekeeper. **H∼haltsgeld** nt housekeeping [money]. **H∼haltsplan** m budget. **H∼herr** m head of the household; (Gastgeber) host. **h∼hoch** a huge; (fam) big □ adv (fam) vastly; (verlieren) by a wide margin

hausier|en vi (haben) ~en mit
hawk. **H~er** m -s,- hawker

Hauslehrer m [private] tutor.
H~in f governess

häuslich a domestic, ⟨Person⟩
domesticated

Haus|meister m caretaker.
H~nummer f house number.
H~ordnung f house rules pl.
H~putz m cleaning. **H~rat** m
-[e]s household effects pl.
H~schlüssel m front-door key.
H~schuh m slipper. **H~stand** m
household. **H~suchung** f
[police] search. **H~suchungs-
befehl** m search-warrant.
H~tier nt domestic animal;
⟨Hund, Katze⟩ pet. **H~tür** f front
door. **H~wart** m -[e]s,-e care-
taker. **H~wirt** m landlord.
H~wirtin f landlady

Haut f -,Häute skin; ⟨Tier-⟩ hide;
aus der H~fahren ⟨fam⟩ fly off
the handle. **H~arzt** m dermatologist

häuten vt skin; sich **h~** moult

haut|eng a skin-tight. **H~farbe** f
colour; ⟨Teint⟩ complexion

Haxe f -,-n = Hachse

Hbf. abbr s. Hauptbahnhof

Hebamme f -,-n midwife

Hebel m -s,- lever. **H~kraft** f,
H~wirkung f leverage

heben† vt lift; ⟨hoch-, steigern⟩ raise; **sich h~** rise; ⟨Nebel:⟩ lift;
⟨sich verbessern⟩ improve

hebräisch a Hebrew

hecheln vi (haben) pant

Hecht m -[e]s,-e pike

Heck nt -s,-s ⟨Naut⟩ stern; ⟨Aviat⟩
tail; ⟨Auto⟩ rear

Hecke f -,-n hedge. **H~nschütze**
m sniper

Heck|fenster nt rear window.
H~motor m rear engine. **H~tür**
f hatchback

Heer nt -[e]s,-e army

Hefe f - yeast. **H~teig** m yeast
dough. **H~teilchen** nt Danish
pastry

Heft¹ nt -[e]s,-e haft, handle

Heft² nt -[e]s,-e booklet; ⟨Sch⟩ exercise book; ⟨Zeitschrift⟩ issue.
h~en vt ⟨nähen⟩ tack; ⟨stecken⟩
pin/⟨klammern⟩ clip/⟨mit Heft-
maschine⟩ staple (**an** + acc to).
H~er m -s,- file

heftig a fierce, adv -ly, violent, adv
-ly; ⟨Schlag, Regen⟩ heavy, adv
-ily; ⟨Schmerz, Gefühl⟩ intense,
adv -ly; ⟨Person⟩ quick-tempered.
H~keit f - fierceness, violence;
intensity

Heft|klammer f staple; ⟨Büro-⟩
paper-clip. **H~maschine** f
stapler. **H~pflaster** nt sticking
plaster. **H~zwecke** f -,-n draw-
ing-pin

hegen vt care for; ⟨fig⟩ cherish
⟨Hoffnung⟩; harbour ⟨Verdacht⟩

Hehl nt & m kein[en] **H~**
machen aus make no secret of.
H~er m -s,- receiver, fence

Heide¹ m -n,-n heathen

Heide² f -,-n heath; ⟨Bot⟩ heather.
H~kraut nt heather

Heidelbeere f -, ⟨Amer⟩
blueberry

Heid|in f -,-nen heathen.
h~nisch a heathen

heikel a difficult, tricky; ⟨delikat⟩
delicate; ⟨dial⟩ ⟨Person⟩ fussy

heil a undamaged, intact; ⟨Person⟩
unhurt; ⟨gesund⟩ well; **mit h~er
Haut** ⟨fam⟩ unscathed

Heil nt -s salvation; **sein H~ versuchen** try one's luck

Heiland m -s ⟨Relig⟩ Saviour

Heil|anstalt f sanatorium;
⟨Nerven-⟩ mental hospital.
H~bad nt spa. **H~bar** a curable

Heilbutt m -[e]s,-e halibut

heil|en vt cure; heal ⟨Wunde⟩ □ vi
⟨sein⟩ heal

heilfroh a ⟨fam⟩ very relieved

Heilgymnastik f physiotherapy

heilig a holy; ⟨geweiht⟩ sacred;
der H~e Abend Christmas Eve;
die h~e Anna Saint Anne; **h~-**

halten hold sacred; keep (*Feiertag*); h~ **sprechen** canonize. **H~abend** *m* Christmas Eve. **H~e(r)** *m/f* saint. h~en *vt* keep, observe. **H~enschein** *m* halo. h~halten† *vt sep* ⟨NEW⟩ h~ **halten**, *s.* halten. **H~keit** *f* - sanctity, holiness. h~sprechen† *vt sep* ⟨NEW⟩ h~ **sprechen**, *s.* heilig. **H~tum** *nt* -s,¨er shrine

heilkräftig *a* medicinal. **H~kräuter** *ntpl* medicinal herbs. h~los *a* unholy. **H~mittel** *nt* remedy. **H~praktiker** *m* -s,- practitioner of alternative medicine. h~sam *a* (*fig*) salutary. **H~sarmee** *f* Salvation Army. **H~ung** *f* - cure

Heim *nt* -[e]s,-e home; (*Studenten-*) hostel. h~ *adv* home. **Heimat** *f* -,-en home; (*Land*) native land. **H~abend** *m* folk evening. h~los *a* homeless. **H~stadt** *f* home town

heim|begleiten *vt sep* see home. h~bringen† *vt sep* bring home; (*begleiten*) see home. **H~computer** *m* home computer. h~fahren† *v sep* □*vi* (*sein*) go/drive home □*vt* take/drive home. **H~fahrt** *f* way home. h~gehen† *vi sep* (*sein*) go home; (*sterben*) die

heimisch *a* native, indigenous; (*Pol*) domestic; h~ **sein/sich** h~**fühlen** be/feel at home

Heim|kehr *f* - return [home]. h~kehren *vi sep* (*sein*) return home. h~kommen† *vi sep* (*sein*) come home

heimlich *a* secret, *adv* -ly; h~ **tun** be secretive; **etw** h~ **tun** do sth secretly *or* in secret. **H~keit** *f* -,-en secrecy; **H~keiten** secrets. **H~tuerei** *f* - secretiveness

Heim|reise *f* journey home. h~reisen *vi sep* (*sein*) go home. **H~spiel** *nt* home game. h~suchen *vt sep* afflict. h~tückisch *a* treacherous; (*Krankheit*) insidious. h~wärts *adv*

home. **H~weg** *m* way home. **H~weh** *nt* -s homesickness; **H~weh haben** be homesick. **H~werker** *m* -s,- [home] handyman. h~zahlen† *vt sep* jdm etw h~zahlen (*fig*) pay s.o. back for sth

Heirat *f* -,-en marriage. h~en *vt/i* (*haben*) marry. **H~santrag** *m* proposal; **jdm einen H~santrag machen** propose to s.o. **h~sfähig** *a* marriageable

heiser *a* hoarse, *adv* -ly. **H~keit** *f* - hoarseness

heiß *a* hot, *adv* -ly; (*hitzig*) heated; (*leidenschaftlich*) fervent, *adv* -ly; **mein H~ geliebter Sohn** my beloved son; **mir ist** h~ I am hot

heißen† *vi* (*haben*) be called; (*bedeuten*) mean; **ich heiße** ... my name is ...; **wie** h~ **Sie?** what is your name? **wie heißt** ... **auf Englisch?** what's the English for ...? **es heißt** it says; (*man sagt*) it is said; **das heißt** that is [to say]; **was soll das h~?** what does it mean? (*empört*) what is the meaning of this? □*vt* call; **jdn etw tun** h~ tell s.o. to do sth

heiß|geliebt *a* ⟨NEW⟩ h~ **geliebt**, *s.* heiß. h~**hungrig** *a* ravenous. **H~wasserbereiter** *m* -s,- water heater

heiter *a* cheerful, *adv* -ly; (*Wetter*) bright; (*amüsant*) amusing; **aus** h~**em Himmel** (*fig*) out of the blue. **H~keit** *f* - cheerfulness; (*Gelächter*) mirth

Heiz|anlage *f* heating; (*Auto*) heater. **H~decke** *f* electric blanket. h~en *vt* heat; light (*Ofen*) □*vi* (*haben*) put the heating on; (*Ofen:*) give out heat. **H~gerät** *nt* heater. **H~kessel** *m* boiler. **H~körper** *m* radiator. **H~lüfter** *m* -s,- fan heater. **H~material** *nt* fuel. **H~ofen** *m* heater. **H~ung** *f* -,-en heating; (*Heizkörper*) radiator

Hektar *nt & m* -s,- hectare

hektisch *a* hectic

Held *m* -en,-en hero. **h~enhaft**
a heroic, *adv* -ally. **H~enmut** *m*
heroism. **h~enmütig** *a* heroic,
adv -ally. **H~entum** *nt* -s heroism. **H~in** *f* -,-nen heroine

helfen† *vi* (*haben*) help (**jdm** s.o.);
(*nützen*) be effective; **sich** (*dat*)
nicht zu h~en wissen not know
what to do; **es hilft nichts** it's
no use. **H~er(in)** *m* -s,- (*f* -,-nen)
helper, assistant. **H~ershelfer**
m accomplice.

hell *a* light; (*Licht ausstrahlend,
klug*) bright; (*Stimme*) clear;
(*fam: völlig*) utter; **h~es Bier** ≈
lager ; *adv* brightly; **h~ begeistert** absolutely delighted. **h~hö-
rig** *a* poorly soundproofed;
h~hörig werden (*fig*) sit up and
take notice

hellicht *a* (NEW) **helllicht**

Hell|igkeit *f* - brightness.
H~seher(in) *m* -s,- (*f* -,-nen)
clairvoyant. **h~wach** *a* wide
awake

helllicht *a* **h~er Tag** broad daylight

Helm *m* -[e]s,-e helmet

Hemd *nt* -[e]s,-en vest, (*Amer*) un-
dershirt; (*Ober-*) shirt. **H~bluse**
f shirt

Hemisphäre *f* -,-n hemisphere

hemmen *vt* check; (*verzögern*)
impede; (*fig*) inhibit. **H~ung** *f*
-,-en (*fig*) inhibition; (*Skrupel*)
scruple; **H~ungen haben** be inhibited. **h~ungslos** *a* unre-
strained, *adv* -ly

Hendl *nt* -s,-[n] (*Aust*) chicken

Hengst *m* -[e]s,-e stallion.
H~fohlen *nt* colt

Henkel *m* -s,- handle

henken *vt* hang

Henne *f* -,-n hen

her *adv* here; (*zeitlich*) ago; **her
mit ...!** give me ...! **von oben
unten/Norden/weit her** from
above/below/the/north/far away;
von der Farbe/vom Thema her
as far as the colour/subject is
concerned; **vor/hinter jdm/etw**

her in front of/behind s.o./sth;
hinter jdm/etw her sein be
after s.o./sth; **her sein** come (**von**
from); **es ist schon lange/drei
Tage her** it was a long time/three
days ago

herab *adv* down [here]; **von oben
h~** from above; (*fig*) condescending, *adv* -ly. **h~blicken** *vi
sep* (*haben*) = **h~sehen**

herablass|en† *vt sep* let down;
sich~en condescend (**zu** to).
h~end *a* condescending, *adv* -ly.
H~ung *f* - condescension

herab|sehen† *vi sep* (*haben*) look
down (**auf** + *acc* on). **h~setzen**
vt sep reduce, cut; (*fig*) belittle.
h~setzend *a* disparaging, *adv*
-ly. **h~würdigen** *vt sep* belittle,
disparage

Heraldik *f* - heraldry

heran *adv* near; [**bis**] **h~ an** (+
acc) up to. **h~bilden** *vt sep* train.
h~gehen† *vi sep* (*sein*) **h~gehen
an** (+ *acc*) go up to; get down to
⟨*Arbeit*⟩. **h~kommen†** *vi sep*
(*sein*) approach; **h~kommen an**
(+ *acc*) come up to; (*erreichen*) get
at; (*fig*) measure up to.
h~machen (sich) *vr sep* **sich
h~machen an** (+ *acc*) approach;
get down to ⟨*Arbeit*⟩. **h~reichen**
vi sep (*haben*) **h~reichen an** (+
acc) reach; (*fig*) measure up to.
h~wachsen† *vi sep* (*sein*) grow
up. **h~ziehen†** *v sep* □ *vt* pull up
(**an** + *acc* to); (*züchten*) raise;
(*h~bilden*) train; (*hinzuziehen*)
call in □ *vi* (*sein*) approach

herauf *adv* up [here]; **die Treppe
h~** up the stairs. **h~beschwö-
ren** *vt sep* evoke; (*verursachen*)
cause. **h~kommen†** *vi sep* (*sein*)
come up. **h~setzen** *vt sep* raise,
increase

heraus *adv* out (**aus** of); **h~da-
mit** *od* **mit der Sprache!** out with
it! **h~ sein** be out; **aus dem
Gröbsten h~ sein** be over the
worst; **fein h~ sein** be sitting
pretty. **h~bekommen†** *vt sep* get
out; (*ausfindig machen*) find out;

(*lösen*) solve; **Geld h~bekommen** get change. **h~bringen†** *vt sep* bring out; (*fam*) get out. **h~finden†** *v sep* □ *vt* find out □ *vi* (*haben*) find one's way out. **H~forderer** *m* -s,-: challenger. **h~fordern** *vt sep* provoke; challenge (*Person*). **H~forderung** *f* provocation; challenge. **H~gabe** *f* handing over; (*Admin*) issue; (*Veröffentlichung*) publication. **h~geben†** *vt sep* hand over; (*Admin*) issue; (*veröffentlichen*) publish; edit (*Zeitschrift*); **jdm Geld h~geben** give s.o. change □ *vi* (*haben*) give change (**auf** + *acc* for). **H~geber** *m* -s,-: publisher; editor. **h~gehen†** *vi sep* (*sein*) (*Fleck:*) come out; **aus sich h~gehen** (*fig*) come out of one's shell. **h~halten†** (**sich**) *vr sep* (*fig*) keep out (**aus** *of*). **h~holen** *vt sep* get out. **h~kommen†** *vi sep* (*sein*) come out; (*aus Schwierigkeit, Takt*) get out; **auf eins od dasselbe h~kommen** (*fam*) come to the same thing. **h~lassen†** *vt sep* let out. **h~machen** *vt sep* get out; **sich gut h~machen** (*fig*) do well. **h~nehmen†** *vt sep* take out; **sich zu viel h~nehmen** (*fig*) take liberties. **h~platzen** *vi sep* (*haben*) (*fam*) burst out laughing. **h~putzen** (**sich**) *vr sep* doll oneself up. **h~ragen** *vi sep* jut out; (*fig*) stand out. **h~reden** (**sich**) *vr sep* make excuses. **h~rücken** *v sep* □ *vt* move out; (*hergeben*) hand over □ *vi* (*sein*) **h~rücken mit** hand over; (*fig: sagen*) come out with. **h~rutschen** *vi sep* (*sein*) slip out. **h~schlagen†** *vt sep* knock out; (*fig*) gain. **h~stellen** *vt sep* put out; **sich h~stellen** turn out (**als** to be; **daß** that). **h~suchen** *vt sep* pick out. **h~wollen†** *vi sep* (*haben*) **nicht mit der Sprache h~wollen** hum and haw. **h~ziehen†** *vt sep* pull out

herb *a* sharp; (*Wein*) dry; (*Landschaft*) austere; (*fig*) harsh

herbei *adv* here. **h~führen** *vt sep* (*fig*) bring about. **h~lassen** (**sich**) *vr sep* condescend (**zu** to).
h~schaffen *vt sep* get.
h~sehnen *vr sep* long for

Herberge *f* -,-n (*youth*) hostel; (*Unterkunft*) lodging. **H~svater** *m* warden

herbestellen *vt sep* summon
herbitten† *vt sep* ask to come
herbringen† *vt sep* bring [here]
Herbst *m* -[e]s,-e autumn. **h~lich** *a* autumnal
Herd *m* -[e]s,-e stove, cooker; (*fig*) focus
Herde *f* -,-n herd; (*Schaf-*) flock
herein *adv* in [here]; **h~!** come in! **h~bitten†** *vt sep* ask in. **h~brechen** *vi sep* (*sein*) burst in; (*Tag:*) set in; (*Nacht:*) fall; **h~brechen über** (+ *acc*) (*fig*) overtake. **h~fallen†** *vi sep* (*sein*) (*fam*) be taken in (**auf** + *acc* by). **h~kommen†** *vi sep* (*sein*) come in. **h~lassen†** *vt sep* let in. **h~legen** *vt sep* (*fam*) take for a ride. **h~rufen†** *vt sep* call in

Herfahrt *f* journey/drive here
herfallen† *vi sep* (*sein*) **h~ über** (+ *acc*) attack; fall upon (*Essen*)
hergeben† *vt sep* hand over; (*fig*) give up; **sich h~ zu** (*fig*) be a party to
hergebracht *a* traditional
hergehen† *vi sep* (*sein*) **h~ vor/neben/hinter** (+ *dat*) walk along in front of/beside/behind; **es ging lustig her** (*fam*) there was a lot of merriment
herhalten† *vt sep* (*haben*) hold out; **h~ müssen** be the one to suffer
herholen *vt sep* fetch; **weit hergeholt** (*fig*) far-fetched
Hering *m* -s,-e herring; (*Zeltpflock*) tent-peg
her|kommen† *vi sep* (*sein*) come here; **wo kommt das her?** where

does it come from? **h~kömmlich** *a* traditional. **H~kunft** *f* - origin

herlaufen† *vi sep* (sein) **h~ vor/ neben/hinter** (+ *dat*) run/ (*gehen*) walk along in front of/ beside/behind

herleiten *vt sep* derive

hermachen *vt sep* **viel/wenig h~** be impressive/unimpressive; (*wichtig nehmen*) make a lot of/little fuss (**von** of); **sich h~ über** (+ *acc*) fall upon; tackle (*Arbeit*)

Hermelin¹ *nt* -s,-e (*Zool*) stoat

Hermelin² *m* -s,-e (*Pelz*) ermine

hermetisch *a* hermetic, *adv* -ally

Hernie /'hɛrnjə/ *f* -,-n hernia

Heroin *nt* -s heroin

heroisch *a* heroic, *adv* -ally

Herr *m* -n,-en gentleman; (*Gebieter*) master (**über** + *acc* of); [**Gott,**] **der H~** the Lord [God]; **H~ Meier** Mr Meier; **Sehr geehrte H~en** Dear Sirs. **H~chen** *nt* -s,- master. **H~enhaus** *nt* manor [house]. **h~enlos** *a* ownerless; (*Tier*) stray. **H~ensitz** *m* manor

Herrgott *m* **der H~** the Lord; **H~ [noch mal]!** damn it!

herrichten *vt sep* prepare; **wieder h~** renovate

Herrin *f* -,-nen mistress

herrisch *a* imperious, *adv* -ly; (*Ton*) peremptory; (*herrschsüchtig*) overbearing

herrlich *a* marvellous, *adv* -ly; (*großartig*) magnificent, *adv* -ly. **H~keit** *f* -,-en splendour

Herrschaft *f* -,-en rule; (*Macht*) power; (*Kontrolle*) control; **meine H~en!** ladies and gentlemen!

herrsch|en *vi* (haben) rule; (*verbreitet sein*) prevail; **es h~te Stille/große Aufregung** there was silence/great excitement. **H~er(in)** *m* -s,- (*f* -,-nen) ruler. **h~süchtig** *a* domineering

herrühren *vi sep* (haben) stem (**von** from)

hersein† *vi sep* (sein) (NEW) **her sein**, *s.* **her**

herstammen *vi sep* (haben) come (**aus/von** from)

herstell|en *vt sep* establish; (*Comm*) manufacture, make. **H~er** *m* -s,- manufacturer, maker. **H~ung** *f* -establishment; manufacture

herüber *adv* over [here]. **h~kommen†** *vi sep* (sein) come over [here]

herum *adv* **im Kreis h~** [round] in a circle; **falsch h~** the wrong way round; **um . . . h~** round . . .; (*ungefähr*) [round] about . . .; **h~ sein** be over. **h~albern** *vi sep* (haben) fool around. **h~drehen** *vt sep* turn round/(*wenden*) over; turn (*Schlüssel*); **sich h~drehen** turn round/over. **h~gehen†** *vi sep* (sein) walk around; (*Zeit:*) pass; **h~gehen um** go round. **h~kommen†** *vi sep* (sein) get about; **h~kommen um** get round; come round (*Ecke*); **um etw [nicht] h~kommen** (*fig*) [not] get out of sth. **h~kriegen** *vt sep* **jdn h~kriegen** (*fam*) talk s.o. round. **h~liegen†** *vi sep* (sein) lie around. **h~lungern** *vi sep* (haben) loiter. **h~schnüffeln** *vi sep* (haben) (*fam*) nose about. **h~sitzen†** *vi sep* (haben) sit around; **h~sitzen um** sit round. **h~sprechen (sich)** *vr sep* (*Gerücht:*) get about. **h~stehen†** *vi sep* (haben) stand around; **h~stehen um** stand round. **h~treiben (sich)** *vr sep* hang around. **h~ziehen†** *vi sep* (sein) move around; (*ziellos*) wander about

herunter *adv* down [here]; **die Treppe h~** down the stairs; **h~ sein** be down; (*körperlich*) be run down. **h~fallen†** *vi* fall off. **h~gehen†** *vi sep* (sein) come down; (*sinken*) go/come down.

h~**gekommen** a (fig) run-down;
⟨Gebäude⟩ dilapidated; ⟨Person⟩
down-at-heel. h~**kommen†** vi
sep (sein) come down; (fig) go to
rack and ruin; ⟨Firma, Person:⟩
go downhill; ⟨gesundheitlich⟩ get
run down. h~**lassen†** vt sep let
down, lower. h~**machen** vt sep
(fam) reprimand; ⟨herabsetzen⟩
run down. h~**spielen** vt sep (fig)
play down. h~**ziehen†** vt sep pull
out

hervor adv out (**aus** of).
h~**bringen†** vt sep produce;
utter ⟨Wort⟩. h~**gehen†** vi sep
(sein) come/⟨sich ergeben⟩
emerge/⟨folgen⟩ follow (**aus**
from). h~**heben†** vt sep (fig)
stress, emphasize. h~**quellen†**
vi sep (sein) stream out;
⟨h~treten⟩ bulge. h~**ragen** vi sep
(haben) jut out; (fig) stand out.
h~**ragend** a (fig) outstanding.
h~**rufen†** vt sep (fig) cause.
h~**stehen†** vi sep (haben) protrude. h~**treten†** vi sep (sein)
protrude, bulge; (fig) stand out.
h~**tun†** (sich) vr sep (fig) distinguish oneself; ⟨angeben⟩ show off

Herweg m way here

Herz nt -ens,-en heart; ⟨Karten-
spiel⟩ hearts pl; **sich** (dat) **ein H~
fassen** pluck up courage. **H~an-
fall** m heart attack

herzeigen vt sep show

herz|en vt hug. **H~enslust** f
nach H~enslust to one's heart's
content. **h~haft** a hearty, (fig)
·ly; ⟨würzig⟩ savoury

herziehen† v sep vt **hinter sich**
(dat) **h~** pull along [behind one]
□ vi (sein) **hinter jdm h~** follow
along behind s.o.; **über jdn h~**
(fam) run s.o. down

herz|ig a sweet, adorable. **H~in-
farkt** m heart attack. **H~-
klopfen** nt -s palpitations pl;
ich hatte H~klopfen my heart
was pounding

herzlich a cordial, adv ·ly; ⟨warm⟩
warm, adv ·ly; ⟨aufrichtig⟩ sincere, adv ·ly; **h~en Dank!** many
thanks! **h~e Grüße** kind regards; **h~ wenig** precious little.
H~keit f - cordiality; warmth;
sincerity

herzlos a heartless

Herzog m -s,-̈e duke. **H~in** f
-,-nen duchess. **H~tum** nt
-s,-̈er duchy

Herz|schlag m heartbeat; ⟨Med⟩
heart failure. **h~zerreißend** a
heart-breaking

Hessen nt -s Hesse

heterosexuell a heterosexual

Hetze f - rush; ⟨Kampagne⟩ virulent campaign (**gegen** against).
h~n vt chase; **sich h~n** hurry
□ vi (haben) agitate; ⟨sich beeilen⟩
hurry □ vi (sein) rush

Heu nt -s hay; **Geld wie Heu
haben** (fam) have pots of money

Heuchelei f - hypocrisy

heuch|eln vt feign □ vi (haben)
pretend. **H~ler(in)** m -s,- (f
-,-nen) hypocrite. **h~lerisch** a
hypocritical, adv ·ly

heuer adv (Aust) this year

Heuer f -,-n ⟨Naut⟩ pay. **h~n** vt
hire; sign on ⟨Matrosen⟩

heulen vi (haben) howl; ⟨fam:
weinen⟩ cry; ⟨Sirene:⟩ wail

Heurige(r) m (Aust) new wine

Heu|schnupfen m hay fever.
H~schober m -s,- haystack.
H~schrecke f -,-n grasshopper;
⟨Wander-⟩ locust

heute adv today; ⟨heutzutage⟩
nowadays; **h~e früh** od **Morgen**
(**morgen**) this morning; **von
h~e auf morgen** from one day
to the next. **h~ig** a today's . . .;
⟨gegenwärtig⟩ present; **der
h~ige Tag** today. **h~zutage** adv
nowadays

Hexe f -,-n witch. **h~n** vi (haben)
work magic; **ich kann nicht
h~n** (fam) I can't perform miracles. **H~njagd** f witch-hunt.

H~**nschuss** (H~**nschuß**) *m* lumbago. H~**rei** *f* - witchcraft

Hieb *m* -[e]s,-e blow; (*Peitschen-*) lash. h~ **hiding** *sg*

hier adv here; h~ **sein/bleiben/ lassen/behalten** be/stay/leave/ keep here; h~ **und da** here and there; (*zeitlich*) now and again

Hierarchie /hjerar'çi:/ *f*-,-n hierarchy

hier|auf adv on this/these; (*antworten*) to this; (*zeitlich*) after this. h~**aus** adv out of or from this/these. h~**behalten**† *vt sep* ⟨NEW⟩ h~ **behalten**, *s*. **hier**. h~**bleiben**† *vi sep* ⟨NEW⟩ h~ **bleiben**, *s*. **hier**. h~**durch** adv through this/these; (*Ursache*) as a result of this. h~**für** adv for this/these. h~**her** adv here. h~**hin** adv here. h~**in** adv in this/these. h~**lassen**† *vt sep* ⟨NEW⟩ h~ **lassen**, *s*. **hier**. h~**mit** adv with this/these; (*Comm*) herewith; (*Admin*) hereby. h~**nach** adv after this/these; (*demgemäß*) according to this/ these. h~**sein**† *vi sep* (*sein*) ⟨NEW⟩ h~ **sein**, *s*. **hier**. h~**über** adv over/(*höher*) above this/these; (*sprechen, streiten*) about this/ these. h~**unter** adv under/ (*tiefer*) below this/these; (*dazwischen*) among these. h~**von** adv from this/these; (*h~über*) about this/these; (*Menge*) of this/these. h~**zu** adv to this/ these; (*h~für*) for this/these. h~**zulande** adv here

hiesig *a* local. H~**e(r)** *m/f* local

Hilf|e *f* -,-n help, aid; **um H~e rufen** call for help; **jdm zu H~e kommen** come to s.o.'s aid; **H~e** (+ *gen*) ⟨NEW⟩ **mithilfe**. h~**los** *a* helpless, adv -ly. H~**losigkeit** *f* -helplessness. h~**reich** *a* helpful

Hilfs|arbeiter *m* unskilled labourer. h~**bedürftig** *a* needy; h~**bedürftig sein** be in need of help. h~**bereit** *a* helpful, adv -ly. H~**kraft** *f* helper. H~**mittel** *nt* aid. H~**verb,** H~**zeitwort** *nt* auxiliary verb

Himbeere *f* raspberry

Himmel *m* -s,- sky; (*Relig* & *fig*) heaven; (*Bett-*) canopy; **am H~** in the sky; **unter freiem H~** in the open air. H~**bett** *nt* four-poster [bed]. H~**fahrt** *f* Ascension; **Mariä H~fahrt** Assumption. h~**schreiend** *a* scandalous. H~**srichtung** *f* compass point; **in alle H~srichtungen** in all directions. h~**weit** *a* (*fam*) vast

himmlisch *a* heavenly

hin adv there; **hin und her** to and fro; **hin und zurück** there and back; (*Rail*) return; **hin und wieder** now and again; **an** (+ *acc*) ... **hin** along; **auf** (+ *acc*) ... **hin** in reply to (*Brief, Anzeige*); on (*jds Rat*); **zu od nach** ... **hin** towards; **vor sich hin reden** talk to oneself; **hin sein** (*fam*) be gone; (*kaputt, tot*) have had it; **[ganz] hin sein von** be overwhelmed by; **es ist noch/nicht mehr lange hin** it's a long time yet/not long to go

hinab adv down [there]

hinauf adv up [there]; **die Treppe Straße h~** up the stairs/road. h~**gehen**† *vi sep* (*sein*) go up. h~**setzen** *vt sep* raise

hinaus adv out [there]; (*nach draußen*) outside; **zur Tür h~** out of the door; **auf Jahre h~** for years to come; **über etw** (*acc*) **h~** beyond sth; (*Menge*) [over and] above sth; **über etw** (*acc*) **h~ sein** (*fig*) be past sth. h~**fliegen** *v sep* □ *vi* (*sein*) fly out; (*fam*) get the sack □ *vt* fly out. h~**gehen**† *vi sep* (*sein*) go out; (*Zimmer:*) face (**nach Norden** north); h~**gehen über** (+ *acc*) go beyond, exceed. h~**kommen**† *vi sep* (*sein*) get out; h~**kommen über** (+ *acc*) get beyond. h~**laufen**† *vi sep* (*sein*) run out; h~**laufen auf** (+ *acc*) (*fig*) amount to. h~lehnen (sich) vr sep lean out. h~ragen vi sep (haben) h~ragen über (+ acc) project beyond; (in der Höhe) rise above; (fig) stand out above. h~schicken vt sep send out. h~schieben† vt sep push out; (fig) put off. h~sehen† vi sep (haben) look out. h~sein† vir sep (sein) ⟨NEW⟩ h~ sein, s. hinaus. h~werfen† vt sep throw out; (fam: entlassen) fire. h~wollen† vi sep (haben) want to go out; h~wollen auf (+ acc) (fig) be ambitious. h~ziehen† v ⊙ vt pull out; (in die Länge ziehen) drag out; (verzögern) delay; sich h~ziehen drag on; be delayed ⊙ vi (sein) move out. h~zögern vt delay; sich h~zögern be delayed

Hinblick m im H~ auf (+ acc) in view of, (hinsichtlich) regarding

hinbringen† vt sep take there; (verbringen) spend

hinder|lich a awkward; jdm h~lich sein hamper s.o. h~n vt hamper; (verhindern) prevent. H~nis nt -ses,-se obstacle. H~nisrennen nt steeplechase

hindeuten vi sep (haben) point (auf + acc to)

Hindu m -s,-s Hindu. H~ismus m -Hinduism

hindurch adv through it/them; den Sommer h~ throughout the summer

hinein adv in [there]; (nach drinnen) inside; h~ in (+ acc) into. h~fallen† vi sep (sein) fall in. h~gehen† vi sep (sein) go in; h~gehen in (+ acc) go into. h~laufen† vi sep (sein) run in; h~laufen in (+ acc) run into. h~reden vi sep (haben) jdm h~reden interrupt s.o.; (sich einmischen) interfere in s.o.'s affairs. h~versetzen (sich) vr sep sich in jds Lage h~versetzen put oneself in s.o.'s position. h~ziehen† vt sep pull in;

h~ziehen in (+ acc) pull into; in etw (acc) h~gezogen werden (fig) become involved in sth

hin|fahren† v sep ⊙ vi (sein) go/drive there ⊙ vt take/drive there. H~fahrt f journey/drive there; (Rail) outward journey. h~fallen† vi sep (sein) fall. h~fällig a (gebrechlich) frail; (ungültig) invalid. h~fliegen† v sep ⊙ vi (sein) fly there; (fam) fall ⊙ vt fly there. H~flug m flight there; (Admin) outward flight. H~gabe f - devotion; (Eifer) dedication

hingeb|en† vt sep give up; sich h~en (fig) devote oneself (einer Aufgabe to a task); abandon oneself (dem Vergnügen to pleasure). H~ung f - devotion. h~ungsvoll a devoted, adv -ly

hingegen adv on the other hand

hingehen† vi sep (sein) go/(zu Fuß) walk there; (vergehen) pass; h~ zu go up to; wo gehst du hin? where are you going? etw h~lassen (fig) let sth pass

hingerissen a rapt, adv -ly; h~ sein be carried away (von by)

hin|halten† vt sep hold out; (warten lassen) keep waiting. h~hocken (sich) vr sep squat down. h~kauern (sich) vr sep crouch down

hinken vi (haben/sein) limp

hin|knien (sich) vr sep kneel down. h~kommen† vi sep (sein) get there; (hingehören) belong, go; (fam: auskommen) manage (mit with); (fam: stimmen) be right. h~länglich a adequate, adv -ly. h~laufen† vi sep (sein) run/(gehen) walk there. h~legen vt sep lay or put down; sich h~legen lie down. h~nehmen† vt sep (fig) accept

hinreichen v sep ⊙ vt hand (dat to) ⊙ vi (haben) extend (bis to); (ausreichen) be adequate. h~d a adequate, adv -ly

Hinreise f journey there; (Rail) outward journey

hinreißen† vt sep (fig) carry away; **sich h~ lassen** get carried away. **h~d** a ravishing, adv -ly

hinricht|en vt sep execute. **H~ung** f execution

hinschicken vt sep send there

hinschleppen vt sep drag there; (fig) drag out; **sich h~** drag oneself along; (fig) drag on

hinschreiben† vt sep write there; (aufschreiben) write down

hinsehen† vi sep (haben) look [NEW] **hin sein**, s. hin

hinsetzen vt sep put down; **sich h~** sit down

Hinsicht f - **in dieser/gewisser H~** in this respect/in a certain sense; **in finanzieller H~** financially. **h~lich** prep (+ gen) regarding

hinstellen vt sep put or set down; park (Auto); (fig) make out (**als** to be); **sich h~** stand

hinstrecken vt sep hold out; **sich h~** extend

hintan|setzen, h~stellen vt sep ignore; (vernachlässigen) neglect

hinten adv at the back; **dort h~** back there; **nach/von h~** to the back/from behind. **h~herum** adv round the back; (fam) by devious means; (erfahren) in a roundabout way

hinter prep (+ dat/acc) behind; (nach) after; **h~ jdm/etw herlaufen** run after s.o./sth; **h~ etw** (dat) **stecken** be behind sth; **h~ etw** (acc) **kommen** (fig) get to the bottom of sth; **etw h~ sich** (acc) **bringen** get sth over [and done] with. **H~bein** nt hind leg

Hinterbliebene pl (Admin) surviving dependants; **die H~n** the bereaved family sg

hinterbringen† vt tell (jdm s.o.)

hintere(r,s) a back, rear; **h~s Ende** far end

hintereinander adv one behind/(zeitlich) after the other; **dreimal h~** three times in succession or (fam) in a row

Hintergedanke m ulterior motive

hintergehen† vt deceive

Hinter|grund m background. **H~halt** m -[e]s,-e ambush; **aus dem H~halt überfallen** ambush. **h~hältig** a underhand

hinterher adv behind, after; (zeitlich) afterwards. **h~gehen†** vi sep (sein) follow (jdm s.o.). **h~kommen†** vi sep (sein) follow [behind]. **h~laufen†** vi sep (sein) run after (jdm s.o.)

Hinter|hof m back yard. **H~kopf** m back of the head

hinterlassen† vt leave [behind]; (Jur) leave, bequeath (dat to). **H~schaft** f -,-en (Jur) estate

hinterlegen vt deposit

Hinter|leib m (Zool) abdomen. **H~list** f deceit. **h~listig** a deceitful, adv -ly. **h~m** prep = **hinter dem**. **H~mann** m (pl -männer) person behind. **h~n** prep = **hinter den**. **H~n** m -s,- (fam) bottom, backside. **H~rad** nt rear or back wheel. **H~rücks** adv from behind. **h~s** prep = **hinter das**. **h~ste(r,s)** a last; **h~ste Reihe** back row. **H~teil** nt (fam) behind

hintertreiben† vt (fig) block

Hinter|treppe f back stairs pl. **H~tür** f back door; (fig) loophole

hinterziehen† vt (Admin) evade

Hinterzimmer nt back room

hinüber adv over or across [there]; **h~ sein** (fam: unbrauchbar, tot) have had it; (betrunken) be gone. **h~gehen†** vi sep (sein) go over or across; **h~gehen** (+ acc) or cross

hinunter adv down [there]; **die Treppe/Straße h~** down the stairs/road. **h~gehen†** vi sep *(sein)* go down. **h~schlucken** *vt sep* swallow

Hinweg *m* way there

hinweg *adv* away, off; **h~ über** *(+ acc)* over; **über eine Zeit h~** over a period. **h~gehen†** *vi sep (sein)* **über** *(+ acc) (fig)* pass over. **h~kommen†** *vt sep (sein)* **h~kommen über** *(+ acc) (fig)* get over. **h~sehen†** *vi sep (haben)* **h~sehen über** *(+ acc)* see over; *(fig)* overlook. **h~setzen** *(sich)* **über sich h~setzen über** *(+ acc)* ignore

Hinweis *m* **-es,-e** reference; *(Andeutung)* hint; *(Anzeichen)* indication; **unter H~ auf** *(+ acc)* with reference to. **h~en†** *vt sep* ▢ *vi (haben)* point *(auf + acc* to) ▢ *vt* **jdn auf etw** *(acc)* **h~en** point sth out to s.o. **h~end** *a (Gram)* demonstrative

hin|wenden† *vt sep* turn; **sich h~wenden** turn *(zu* to). **h~werfen†** *vt sep* throw down; drop *(Bemerkung)*; *(schreiben)* jot down; *(zeichnen)* sketch; *(fam: aufgeben)* pack in

hinwieder *adv* on the other hand

hin|zeigen *vi sep (haben)* point *(auf + acc* to). **h~ziehen†** *vt sep* pull; *(fig: in die Länge ziehen)* drag out; *(verzögern)* delay; **sich h~ziehen** drag on; be delayed; **sich h~gezogen fühlen zu** *(fig)* feel drawn to

hinzu *adv* in addition. **h~fügen** *vt sep* add. **h~kommen†** *vi sep (sein)* be added; *(ankommen)* arrive [on the scene]; join *(zu* join s.o.). **h~rechnen** *vt sep* add. **h~ziehen†** *vt sep* call in

Hjobsbotschaft *f* bad news *sg*

Hirn *nt* **-s** brain; *(Culin)* brains *pl.* **H~gespinst** *nt* **-[e]s,-e** figment of the imagination. **h~hautentzündung** *f* meningitis. **h~verbrannt** *a (fam)* crazy

Hirsch *m* **-[e]s,-e** deer; *(männlich)* stag; *(Culin)* venison

Hirse *f* **-** millet

Hirt *m* **-en,-en**, **Hirte** *m* **-n,-n** shepherd

hissen *vt* hoist

Histor|iker *m* **-s,-** historian. **h~isch** *a* historical; *(bedeutend)* historic

Hit *m* **-s,-s** *(Mus)* hit

Hitze *f* **-** heat. **H~welle** *f* heatwave. **h~ig** *a (fig)* heated, *(abl-)ly*; *(Person)* hot-headed; *(jähzornig)* hot-tempered. **H~kopf** *m* hothead. **H~schlag** *m* heat-stroke

H-Milch */ˈhaː-/ f* long-life milk

Hobby *nt* **-s,-s** hobby

Hobel *m* **-s,-** *(Techn)* plane; *(Culin)* slicer. **h~n** *vt/i (haben)* plane. **H~späne** *mpl* shavings

hoch *a (höher, höchst; attrib* **hohe**(*r,s*)) high; *(Baum, Mast)* tall; *(Offizier)* high-ranking; *(Alter)* great; *(Summe)* large; *(Strafe)* heavy; **hohe Schuhe** ankle boots ▢ *adv* high; *(sehr)* highly; **h~wachsen** tall; **h~ begabt** highly gifted; **h~ gestellte Persönlichkeit** important person; **die Treppe/den Berg h~** up the stairs/hill; **sechs Mann h~** six of us/them. **H~** *nt* **-s,-s** cheer; *(Meteorol)* high

Hoch|achtung *f* high esteem. **H~achtungsvoll** *adv* Yours faithfully. **H~amt** *nt* High Mass. **h~arbeiten** (**sich**) *vr sep* work one's way up. **h~begabt** *attrib a* (NEW) **begabt, s. hoch.** **H~betrieb** *m* great activity; **in den Geschäften herrscht H~betrieb** the shops are terribly busy. **H~burg** *f (fig)* stronghold. **H~deutsch** *nt* High German. **H~druck** *m* High pressure. **H~ebene** *f* plateau. **h~fahren** *vi sep (sein)* go up; *(auffahren)* start up; *(aufbrausen)* flare up. **h~fliegend** *a (fig)* ambitious. **h~gehen** *vi sep (sein)* go up; *(explodieren)* blow up; *(aufbrausen)* flare up. **h~gestellt** *attrib a (Zahl)* superior;

(fig) NEW h~ gestellt, *s.* hoch.
h~gewachsen *a* NEW h~ gewachsen, *s.* hoch. **H~glanz** *m*
high gloss. **h~gradig** *a* extreme,
adv -ly. **h~hackig** *a* high-heeled.
h~halten† *vt sep* hold up; *(fig)*
uphold. **H~haus** *nt* high-rise
building. **h~heben**† *vt sep* lift up;
raise *(Kopf, Hand)*. **h~herzig** *a*
magnanimous, *adv* -ly. **h~kant**
adv on end. **h~kommen**† *vi sep*
(sein) come up; *(aufstehen)* get up;
(fig) get on [in the world].
H~konjunktur *f* boom.
h~krempeln *vt sep* roll up.
h~leben *vi sep (haben)* **h~leben**
lassen give three cheers for; ...
lebe hoch! three cheers for ...!
H~mut *m* pride, arrogance.
h~mütig *a* arrogant, *adv* -ly.
h~näsig *a (fam)* snooty.
h~nehmen† *vt sep* pick up;
(fam) tease. **H~ofen** *m* blast-fur-
nace. **h~ragen** *vi sep* rise [up];
(Turm:) soar. **H~ruf** *m* cheer.
H~saison *f* high season.
h~schätzung *f* high esteem.
h~schlagen† *vt sep* turn up
(Kragen). **h~schrecken**† *vi sep*
(sein) start up. **H~schule** *f* university; *(Musik-, Kunst-)* academy. **h~sehen**† *vi sep (haben)*
look up. **H~sommer** *m* midsum-
mer. **H~spannung** *f* high/*(fig)*
great tension. **h~spielen** *vt sep*
(fig) magnify. **H~sprache** *f*
standard language. **H~sprung**
m high jump

höchst *adv* extremely, most
Hochstapler *m* -s, confidence
trickster

höchst|e(r,s) *a* highest; *(Baum,
Turm)* tallest; *(oberste, größte)*
top; **es ist h~e Zeit** it is high
time. **h~ens** *adv* at most; *(es sei
denn)* except perhaps. **H~fall** *m*
im **H~fall** at most. **H~ge-
schwindigkeit** *f* top or maximum speed. **H~maß** *nt*
maximum. **h~persönlich** *adv* in
person. **H~preis** *m* top price.

H~temperatur *f* maximum
temperature. **h~wahrschein-
lich** *adv* most probably

hoch|trabend *a* pompous, *adv* -ly.
h~treiben† *vt sep* push up
(Preis). **H~verrat** *m* high treason. **H~wasser** *nt* high tide;
(Überschwemmung) floods *pl*.
h~würden *m* -s Reverend; *(Anrede)* Father

Hochzeit *f* -,-en wedding; **H~fei-
ern** get married. **H~skleid** *nt*
wedding dress. **H~sreise** *f*
honeymoon [trip]. **H~stag** *m*
wedding day/*(Jahrestag)* anniversary

hochziehen† *vt sep* pull up;
(hissen) hoist; raise *(Augenbrau-
en)*

Hocke *f* - in der **H~sitzen** squat;
in die H~ gehen squat down.
h~n *vi (haben)* squat □ *vr* sich
h~n squat down

Hocker *m* -s, stool

Höcker *m* -s, bump; *(Kamel-)*
hump

Hockey /hɔki/ *nt* -s hockey

Hode *f* -,-n, **Hoden** *m* -s, testicle

Hof *m* -[e]s, e [court]yard;
(Bauern-) farm; *(Königs-)* court;
(Schul-) playground; *(Astr)* halo;
Hof halten hold court

hoffen *vt/i (haben)* hope **(auf +**
acc for). **h~tlich** *adv* I hope, let
us hope; *(als Antwort)*
h~tlich/h~tlich nicht let's
hope so/not

Hoffnung *f* -,-en hope. **h~slos** *a*
hopeless, *adv* -ly. **h~svoll** *a* hope-
ful, *adv* -ly

höflich *a* polite, *adv* -ly, courteous, *adv* -ly. **H~keit** *f* -,-en po-
liteness, courtesy; *(Äußerung)*
civility

hohe(r,s) *a s.* hoch

Höhe *f* -,-n height; *(Aviat, Geog)*
altitude; *(Niveau)* level; *(einer
Summe)* size; *(An-)* hill; **in die
H~ gehen** rise, go up; **nicht auf
der H~** *(fam)* under the weather;

das ist die H∼! (fam) that's the limit!

Hoheit f -,-en (Staats-) sovereignty; (Titel) Highness. **H∼sgebiet** nt [sovereign] territory. **H∼szeichen** nt national emblem

Höhe|nlinie f contour line. **H∼nsonne** f sun-lamp. **H∼nzug** m mountain range. **H∼punkt** m (fig) climax, peak; (einer Vorstellung) highlight. **h∼r** a & adv higher; **h∼re Schule** secondary school

hohl a hollow; (leer) empty

Höhle f -,-n cave; (Tier-) den; (Hohlraum) cavity; (Augen-) socket

Hohl|maß nt measure of capacity. **H∼raum** m cavity

Hohn m -s scorn, derision

höhnen vt deride □ vi (haben) jeer. **h∼isch** a scornful, adv -ly

holen vt fetch, get; (kaufen) buy; (nehmen) take (aus from); **h∼ lassen** send for; **[tief] Atem od Luft h∼** take a [deep] breath; **sich** (dat) **etw h∼** get sth; catch (Erkältung)

Holland nt -s Holland

Holländ|er|m -s,- Dutchman; **die H∼er** the Dutch pl. **H∼erin** f -,-nen Dutchwoman. **h∼isch** a Dutch

Höll|e f - hell. **h∼isch** a infernal; (schrecklich) terrible, adv -bly

holpern vi (sein) jolt or bump along □ vi (haben) be bumpy

holp[e]rig a bumpy

Holunder m -s (Bot) elder

Holz nt -es,⸚er wood; (Nutz-) timber. **H∼blasinstrument** nt woodwind instrument

hölzern a wooden

Holz|hammer m mallet. **∼ig** a woody. **H∼kohle** f charcoal. **H∼schnitt** m woodcut. **H∼schuh** m [wooden] clog. **H∼wolle** f wood shavings pl. **H∼wurm** m woodworm

homogen a homogeneous

Homöopathie f - homoeopathy

homosexuell a homosexual. **H∼e(r)** m/f homosexual

Honig m -s honey. **H∼wabe** f honeycomb

Hono|rar nt -s,-e fee. **h∼rieren** vt remunerate; (fig) reward

Hopfen m -s hops pl; (Bot) hop

hopsen vi (sein) jump

Hör|apparat m hearing-aid. **h∼bar** a audible, adv -bly

horchen vi (haben) listen (auf + acc to); (heimlich) eavesdrop

Horde f -,-n horde; (Gestell) rack

hören vt hear; (an-) listen to □ vi (haben) hear; (horchen) listen; (gehorchen) obey; **h∼ auf** (+ acc) listen to. **H∼sagen** nt vom **H∼sagen** from hearsay

Hör|er m -s,- listener; (Teleph) receiver. **H∼funk** m radio. **H∼gerät** nt hearing-aid

Horizon|t m -[e]s horizon. **h∼tal** a horizontal, adv -ly

Hormon nt -s,-e hormone

Horn nt -s,⸚er horn. **H∼haut** f hard skin; (Augen-) cornea

Hornisse f -,-n hornet

Horoskop nt -[e]s,-e horoscope

Hörrohr nt stethoscope

Horrorfilm m horror film

Hörsaal m (Univ) lecture hall. **H∼spiel** nt radio play

Hort m -[e]s,-e (Schatz) hoard; (fig) refuge. **h∼en** vt hoard

Hortensie /-jə/ f -,-n hydrangea

Hörweite f in/außer H∼ within/out of earshot

Hose f -,-n, **Hosen** pl trousers pl. **H∼nrock** m culottes pl. **H∼nschlitz** m fly, flies pl. **H∼nträger** mpl braces, (Amer) suspenders

Hostess (Hosteß) f -,-tessen hostess; (Aviat) air hostess

Hostie /'hɔstjə/ f -,-n (Relig) host

Hotel nt -s,-s hotel; **H∼ garni** /gar'ni:/ bed-and-breakfast hotel. **H∼ier** /-'lje:/ m -s,-s hotelier

hübsch *a* pretty, *adv* ·ily; ⟨*nett*⟩ nice, *adv* ·ly; ⟨*Summe*⟩ tidy

Hubschrauber *m* -s,- helicopter

huckepack *adv* jdn h⟨~⟩ tragen give s.o. a piggyback

Huf *m* -[e]s,-e hoof. H⟨~⟩eisen *nt* horseshoe

Hüft|e *f* -,-n hip. H⟨~⟩gürtel, H⟨~⟩halter *m* -s,- girdle

Hügel *m* -s,-. hill. h⟨~⟩ig *a* hilly

Huhn *nt* -s,¨er chicken; ⟨*Henne*⟩ hen

Hühn|chen *nt* -s,- chicken. H⟨~⟩erauge *nt* corn. H⟨~⟩erbrühe *f* chicken broth. H⟨~⟩erstall *m* henhouse, chicken-coop

huldig|en *vi* (haben) pay homage (dat to). H⟨~⟩ung *f* - homage

Hülle *f* -,-n cover; ⟨*Verpackung*⟩ wrapping; ⟨*Platten-*⟩ sleeve; in H⟨~⟩ und Fülle in abundance. h⟨~⟩n *vt* wrap

Hülse *f* -,-n ⟨*Bot*⟩ pod; ⟨*Etui*⟩ case. H⟨~⟩nfrüchte *fpl* pulses

human *a* humane, *adv* ·ly. h⟨~⟩itär *a* humanitarian. H⟨~⟩ität *f* - humanity

Hummel *f* -,-n bumble-bee

Hummer *m* -s,- lobster

Hum|or *m* -s humour; H⟨~⟩or haben have a sense of humour. h⟨~⟩oristisch *a* humorous. h⟨~⟩orvoll *a* humorous, *adv* ·ly

humpeln *vi* (sein/haben) hobble

Humpen *m* -s,- tankard

Hund *m* -[e]s,-e dog; ⟨*Jagd-*⟩ hound. H⟨~⟩ehalsband *nt* dog-collar. H⟨~⟩ehütte *f* kennel. H⟨~⟩eleine *f* dog lead

hundert *inv a* one/a hundred. H⟨~⟩ *nt* -s,-e hundred; H⟨~⟩e od h⟨~⟩e von hundreds of. H⟨~⟩jahrfeier *f* centenary, (Amer) centennial. h⟨~⟩prozentig *a & adv* one hundred per cent. h⟨~⟩ste(r,s) *a* hundredth. H⟨~⟩stel *nt* -s,- hundredth

Hündin *f* -,-nen bitch

Hüne *m* -n,-n giant

Hunger *m* -s hunger; H⟨~⟩ haben be hungry. h⟨~⟩n *vi* (haben) starve; h⟨~⟩n nach (fig) hunger for. H⟨~⟩snot *f* famine

hungrig *a* hungry, *adv* ·ily

Hupe *f* -,-n ⟨*Auto*⟩ horn. h⟨~⟩n *vi* (haben) sound one's horn

hüpf|en *vi* (sein) skip; ⟨*Vogel, Frosch:*⟩ hop; ⟨*Grashüpfer:*⟩ jump. H⟨~⟩er *m* -s,- skip, hop

Hürde *f* -,-n ⟨*Sport & fig*⟩ hurdle; ⟨*Schaf-*⟩ pen, fold

Hure *f* -,-n whore

hurra *int* hurray. H⟨~⟩ *nt* -s,-s hurray; ⟨*Beifallsruf*⟩ cheer

Husche *f* -,-n [short] shower. h⟨~⟩n *vi* (sein) slip; ⟨*Eidechse:*⟩ dart; ⟨*Maus:*⟩ scurry; ⟨*Lächeln:*⟩ flit

hüsteln *vi* (haben) give a slight cough

husten *vi* (haben) cough. H⟨~⟩ *m* -s cough. H⟨~⟩saft *m* cough mixture

Hut¹ *m* -[e]s,¨e hat; ⟨*Pilz-*⟩ cap

Hut² *f* - auf der H⟨~⟩ sein be on one's guard (vor + dat against)

hüten *vt* watch over; tend ⟨*Tiere*⟩; ⟨*aufpassen*⟩ look after; das Bett h⟨~⟩ müssen be confined to bed; sich h⟨~⟩ be on one's guard (vor + dat against); sich h⟨~⟩, etw zu tun take care not to do sth

Hütte *f* -,-n hut; ⟨*Hunde-*⟩ kennel; ⟨*Techn*⟩ iron and steel works. H⟨~⟩nkäse *m* cottage cheese. H⟨~⟩nkunde *f* metallurgy

Hyäne *f* -,-n hyena

Hybride *f* -,-n hybrid

Hydrant *m* -en,-en hydrant

hydraulisch *a* hydraulic, *adv* ·ally

hydroelektrisch /hydroˀeˈlɛk-trɪʃ/ *a* hydroelectric

Hygiene /hyˈgjeːnə/ *f* - hygiene. h⟨~⟩isch *a* hygienic, *adv* ·ally

hypermodern *a* ultra-modern

Hypno|se *f* - hypnosis. h⟨~⟩tisch *a* hypnotic. H⟨~⟩tiseur /-ˈzøːɐ̯/ *m* -s,-e hypnotist. h⟨~⟩tisieren *vt* hypnotize

Hypochonder /hypo'xɔndɐ/ *m* -s,- hypochondriac

Hypothek *f* -,-en mortgage

Hypothe|se *f* -,-n hypothesis. **h~tisch** *a* hypothetical, *adv* -ly

Hys|terie *f* -, hysteria. **h~terisch** *a* hysterical, *adv* -ly

I

ich *pron* I; **ich bin's** it's me. **Ich** *nt* -[s],-[s] self; (*Psych*) ego

IC-Zug /i'tse:-/ *m* inter-city train

ideal *a* ideal. **I~** *nt* -s,-e ideal. **i~isieren** *vt* idealize. **I~ismus** *m* - idealism. **I~ist(in)** *m* -en, -en (*f* -,-nen) idealist. **i~istisch** *a* idealistic

Idee *f* -,-n idea; **fixe I~** obsession; **eine I~** (*fam: wenig*) a tiny bit

identifizieren *vt* identify

identi|sch *a* identical. **I~tät** *f* -,-en identity

Ideo|logie *f* -,-n ideology. **i~logisch** *a* ideological

idiomatisch *a* idiomatic

Idiot *m* -en,-en idiot. **i~isch** *a* idiotic, *adv* -ally

Idol *nt* -s,-e idol

idyllisch /i'dʏlɪʃ/ *a* idyllic

Igel *m* -s,- hedgehog

ignorieren *vt* ignore

ihm *pron* (*dat of* er, es) [to] him; (*Ding, Tier*) [to] it; **Freunde von ihm** friends of his

ihn *pron* (*acc of* er) him; (*Ding, Tier*) it. **i~en** *pron* (*dat of* sie *pl*) [to] them; **Freunde von i~en** friends of theirs. **I~en** *pron* (*dat of* Sie) [to] you; **Freunde von I~en** friends of yours

ihr *pron* (*2nd pers pl*) you □ (*dat of* sie *sg*) [to] her; (*Ding, Tier*) [to] it; **Freunde von ihr** friends of hers □ *poss pron* her; (*Ding, Tier*) its; (*pl*) their. **Ihr** *poss pron* your. **i~e(r,s)** *poss pron* hers; (*pl*) theirs. **I~e(r,s)** *poss pron* yours.

i~erseits *adv* for her/(*pl*) their part. **I~erseits** *adv* on your part. **i~etwegen** *adv* for her/(*Ding, Tier*) its/(*pl*) their sake; (*wegen*) because of her/it/them, on her/ its/their account. **I~etwegen** *adv* for your sake; (*wegen*) because of you, on your account. **i~etwillen** *adv* **um i~etwillen** for her/(*Ding, Tier*) its/(*pl*) their sake. **I~etwillen** *adv* **um I~etwillen** for your sake. **i~ige** *poss pron* **der/die/das i~ige** hers; (*pl*) theirs. **I~ige** *poss pron* **der/die/das I~ige** yours. **I~s** *poss pron* hers; (*pl*) theirs. **I~s** *poss pron* yours

Ikone *f* -,-n icon

illegal *a* illegal, *adv* -ly

Illusion *f* -,-en illusion; **sich** (*dat*) **I~ionen machen** delude oneself. **i~orisch** *a* illusory

Illustr|ation /-'tsio:n/ *f* -,-en illustration. **i~ieren** *vt* illustrate. **I~ierte** *f* -n,-[n] [illustrated] magazine

Iltis *m* -ses,-se polecat

im *prep* = **in dem**; **im Mai** in May; **im Kino** at the cinema

Image /'ɪmɪdʒ/ *nt* -[s],-s /-ɪs/ [public] image

Imbiss (**Imbiß**) *m* snack. **I~halle**, **I~stube** *f* snack-bar

Imit|ation /-'tsio:n/ *f* -,-en imitation. **i~ieren** *vt* imitate

Imker *m* -s,- bee-keeper

Immatrikul|ation /-'tsio:n/ *f* -, (*Univ*) enrolment. **i~ieren** *vt* (*Univ*) enrol; **sich i~ieren** enrol

immer *adv* always; **für i~** for ever; (*endgültig*) for good; **i~ noch** still; **i~ mehr/weniger/ wieder** more and more/less and less/again and again; **wer/was [auch] i~** whoever/whatever. **i~fort** *adv* = **i~zu**. **i~grün** *a* evergreen. **i~hin** *adv* (*wenigstens*) at least; (*trotzdem*) all the same; (*schließlich*) after all. **i~zu** *adv* all the time

Immobilien /-jən/ pl real estate sg. I~händler, I~makler m estate agent, (Amer) realtor

immun a immune (gegen to). i~isieren vt immunize. I~ität f - immunity

Imperativ m -s,-e imperative

Imperfekt nt -s,-e imperfect

Imperialismus m - imperialism

impf|en vt vaccinate, inoculate. I~stoff m vaccine. I~ung f -,-en vaccination, inoculation

Implantat nt -[e]s,-e implant

imponieren vi (haben) impress (jdm s.o.)

Impor|t m -[e]s,-e import. I~teur /-'tø:ɐ/ m -s,-e importer. i~tieren vt import

imposant a imposing

impoten|t a (Med) impotent. I~z f - (Med) impotence

imprägnieren vt waterproof

Impressionismus m - impressionism

improvisieren vt/i (haben) improvise

Impuls m -es,-e impulse. i~iv a impulsive, adv -ly

imstande pred a able (zu to); capable (etw zu tun of doing sth)

in prep (+ dat) in, (+ acc) into, in; (bei Bus, Zug) on; in der Schule/ Oper at school/the opera; in die Schule to school □ a in sein be in

Inbegriff m embodiment. i~en pred a included

Inbrunst f - fervour

inbrünstig a fervent, adv -ly

indem conj (während) while; (dadurch) by (+ -ing)

Inder(in) m -s,- (f -,-nen) Indian

indessen conj while (+ dat); (unterdessen) meanwhile; (jedoch) however

Indian m -s,-e (Aust) turkey

Indian|er(in) m -s,- (f -,-nen) (American) Indian. i~isch a Indian

Indien /'ɪndjən/ nt -s India

indigniert a indignant, adv -ly

Indikativ m -s,-e indicative

indirekt a indirect, adv -ly

indisch a Indian

indiskre|t a indiscreet. I~tion /-'tsjo:n/ f -,-en indiscretion

indiskutabel a out of the question

indisponiert a indisposed

Individu|alist m -en,-en individualist. I~alität f - individuality. i~ell a individual, adv -ly. I~um /-'vi:duom/ nt -s,-duen individual

Indizienbeweis /ɪn'di:tsjən-/ m circumstantial evidence

indoktrinieren vt indoctrinate

industr|ialisiert a industrialized. I~ie /-,-n industry. i~iell a industrial. I~ielle(r) m industrialist

ineinander adv in/into one another

Infanterie f - infantry

Infektion /-'tsjo:n/ f -,-en infection. I~skrankheit f infectious disease

Infinitiv m -s,-e infinitive

infizieren vt infect; sich i~ become/ (Person:) be infected

Inflation /-'tsjo:n/ f - inflation. i~är a inflationary

infolge prep (+ gen) as a result of. i~dessen adv consequently

Inform|atik f - information science. I~ation /-'tsjo:n/ f -,-en information; I~ationen pl information sg. i~ieren vt inform; sich i~ieren find out (über + acc about)

infrage adv etw i~ stellen question sth; (ungewiss machen) make sth doubtful; nicht i~ kommen be out of the question

infrarot a infra-red

Ingenieur /ɪnʒe'njø:ɐ/ m -s,-e engineer

Ingwer m -s ginger

Inhaber(in) m -s,- (f -,-nen) holder; (Besitzer) proprietor; (Scheck-) bearer

inhaftieren vt take into custody

inhalieren vt/i (haben) inhale

Inhalt m -[e]s,-e contents pl; (Bedeutung, Gehalt) content; (Geschichte) story. **I~sangabe** f summary. **I~sverzeichnis** nt list;/(in Buch) table of contents

Initiale /-'tsia:lə/ f -,-n initial

Initiative /initsia'ti:və/ f -,-n initiative

Injektion /-'tsio:n/ f -,-en injection. **injizieren** vt inject

inklusive prep (+ gen) including
☐ adv inclusive

inkognito adv incognito

inkonsequen|t a inconsistent,
adv -ly. **I~z** f -,-en inconsistency

inkorrekt a incorrect, adv -ly

Inkubationszeit /-'tsio:ns-/ f
(Med) incubation period

Inland nt -[e]s home country;
(Binnenland) interior. **I~sgespräch** nt inland call

inmitten prep (+ gen) in the
middle of; (unter) amongst ☐ adv
i~ von amongst, amidst

innehaben† vt sep hold, have.
i~halten† vi sep (haben) pause

innen adv inside; **nach i~** inwards. **I~architekt/in** m(f) interior designer. **I~minister** m
Minister of the Interior; (in UK)
Home Secretary. **I~politik** f
domestic policy. **I~stadt** f town
centre

inner|e(r,s) a inner; (Med, Pol) internal. **I~e(s)** nt interior; (Mitte)
centre; (fig: Seele) inner being.
I~eien fpl (Culin) offal sg. **i~halb** prep (+ gen) (zeitlich
& fig) within; (während) during
☐ adv **i~halb von** within. **i~lich** a internal; (seelisch) inner; (besinnlich) introspective ☐ adv
internally; (im Innern) inwardly.
i~ste(r,s) a innermost; **im I~sten** (fig) deep down

innig a sincere, adv -ly; (tief) deep,
adv -ly; (eng) intimate, adv -ly

Innung f -,-en guild

inoffiziell a unofficial, adv -ly

ins prep = **in das**; **ins Kino/Büro**
to the cinema/office

Insasse m -n,-n inmate; (im Auto)
occupant; (Passagier) passenger

insbesondere adv especially

Inschrift f inscription

Insekt nt -[e]s,-en insect. **I~envertilgungsmittel** nt insecticide

Insel f -,-n island

Inser|at nt -[e]s,-e [newspaper]
advertisement. **I~ent** m -en,-en
advertiser. **I~ieren** vt/i (haben)
advertise

insgeheim adv secretly. **i~samt**
adv [all] in all

Insignien /-jən/ pl insignia

insofern, insoweit adv /-'zo:-/
in this respect; **i~ als** in as much
as ☐ conj /-zo'fɛrn, -'vait/ **i~ als**
in so far as

Inspektion /ɪnspɛk'tsio:n/ f
-,-en inspection. **I~ektor** m
-en,-en /-'to:rən/ inspector

Inspiration /ɪnspira'tsio:n/ f
-,-en inspiration. **i~ieren** vt
inspire

inspizieren /-sp-/ vt inspect

Install|ateur /ɪnstala'tø:ɐ̯/ m
-s,-e fitter; (Klempner) plumber.
i~ieren vt install

instand adv **i~ halten** maintain;
(pflegen) look after; **i~ setzen** restore; (reparieren) repair. **I~haltung** f - maintenance, upkeep

inständig a urgent, adv -ly

Instandsetzung f - repair

Instant- /'ɪnstant-/ pref instant

Instanz /-st-/ f -,-en authority

Instinkt /-st-/ m -[e]s,-e instinct.
i~iv a instinctive, adv -ly

Institut /-st-/ nt -[e]s,-e institute. **I~tion** /-'tsio:n/ f -,-en institution

Instrument /-st-/ nt -[e]s,-e instrument. **I~almusik** f instrumental music

Insulin nt -s insulin

inszenier|en vt (Theat) produce.
I~ung f -,-en production

Integration /-'tsjo:n/ f - integration. i~**ieren** vt integrate; sich i~**ieren** integrate. I~**ität** f - integrity

Intellekt m -[e]s intellect. i~**uell** a intellectual

intelligen|t a intelligent, adv -ly. I~z f - intelligence; (Leute) intelligentsia

Intendant m -en,-en director

Intens|ität f - intensity. i~**iv** a intensive, adv -ly. i~**ivieren** vt intensify. I~**ivstation** f intensive-care unit

inter|essant a interesting. I~**esse** nt -s,-n interest; I~**esse haben** be interested (an + dat in). I~**essengruppe** f pressure group. I~**essent** m -en,-en interested party; (Käufer) prospective buyer. i~**essieren** vt interest; sich i~**essieren** be interested (für in)

intern a (fig) internal, adv -ly. **Inter|nat** nt -[e]s,-e boarding school. i~**national** a international, adv -ly. i~**nieren** vt intern. I~**nierung** f - internment. I~**nist** m -en,-en specialist in internal diseases. I~**pretation** /-'tsjo:n/ f -,-en interpretation. i~**pretieren** vt interpret. I~**punktion** /-'tsjo:n/ f - punctuation. I~**rogativpronomen** nt interrogative pronoun. I~**vall** nt -s,-e interval. I~**vention** /-'tsjo:n/ f -,-en intervention

Interview /'ıntvju:/ nt -s,-s interview. i~**en** /-'vju:ən/ vt interview

intim a intimate, adv -ly. I~**ität** f -,-en intimacy

intolerant a intolerant. I~z f - intolerance

intransitiv a intransitive, adv -ly

intravenös a intravenous, adv -ly

Intrig|e f -,-n intrigue. i~**ieren** vi (haben) plot

introvertiert a introverted

Intui|tion /-'tsjo:n/ f -,-en intuition. i~**tiv** a intuitive, adv -ly

Invalidenrente f disability pension

Invasion f -,-en invasion

Inven|tar nt -s,-e furnishings and fittings pl; (Techn) equipment; (Bestand) stock; (Liste) inventory. I~**tur** f -,-en stock-taking

investieren vt invest

inwendig a & adv inside

inwie|fern adv in what way. i~**weit** adv how far, to what extent

Inzest m -[e]s incest

inzwischen adv in the meantime

Irak (der) -[s] Iraq. i~**isch** a Iraqi

Iran (der) -[s] Iran. i~**isch** a Iranian

irdisch a earthly

Ire m -n,-n Irishman; **die I~n** the Irish pl

irgend adv **wer/was/wann** i~ whoever/whatever/whenever; **wenn** i~ **möglich** if at all possible; i~ **etwas** (NEW) i~**etwas**; i~ **jemand** (NEW) i~**jemand**. i~**ein** indef art some/any; i~**ein anderer** someone/anyone else. i~**eine(r,s)** pron any one; (jemand) someone/anyone. i~**etwas** pron something; (fragend, verneint) anything. i~**jemand** pron someone; (fragend, verneint) anyone. i~**wann** pron at some time [or other]/at any time. i~**was** pron (fam) something [or other]/anything. i~**welche(r,s)** pron any. i~**wer** pron someone/anyone. i~**wie** adv somehow [or other]. i~**wo** adv somewhere/anywhere; i~**wo anders** somewhere else

Irin f -,-nen Irishwoman

Iris f -,- (Anat, Bot) iris

irisch a Irish

Irland nt -s Ireland

Ironie f - irony

ironisch a ironic, adv -ally

irr a = **irre**

irrational a irrational

irre a mad, crazy; (*fam: gewaltig*) incredible, adv -bly; **i~ werden** (NEW) i~**werden**. I~**(r)** m/f lunatic. **i~führen** vt sep (*fig*) mislead. **i~gehen†** vi sep (*sich täuschen*) be wrong

irrelevant a irrelevant

irre|machen vt sep confuse. **i~n** vi/r (haben) [**sich**] **i~n** be mistaken; **wenn ich mich nicht i~** if I am not mistaken □ vi (*sein*) wander. **I~nanstalt** f, **I~nhaus** nt lunatic asylum. **i~reden** vi sep (haben) ramble. **i~werden†** vi sep (sein) be confused

Irr|garten m maze. **i~ig** a erroneous

irritieren vt irritate

Irr|sinn m madness, lunacy. **i~sinnig** a mad; (*fam: gewaltig*) incredible, adv -bly. **I~tum** m -s,-̈er mistake. **i~tümlich** a mistaken, adv -ly

Ischias m & nt - sciatica

Islam (der) -[s] Islam. **islamisch** a Islamic

Island nt -s Iceland

Isolier|band nt insulating tape. **i~en** vt isolate; (*Phys, Electr*) insulate; (*gegen Schall*) soundproof. **I~ung** f - isolation; insulation; soundproofing

Israel -['israe:l/] nt -s Israel. **I~eli** m -[s],-s & f -,-[s] Israeli. **i~elisch** a Israeli

ist s. **sein**; **er ist he** is

Ital|ien /-jən/ nt -s Italy. **I~iener(in)** m -s,- (f -,-nen) Italian. **i~ienisch** a Italian. **I~ienisch** nt -[s] (*Lang*) Italian

J

ja adv, **Ja** nt -[s] yes; **ich glaube ja** I think so; **ja nicht!** not on any account! **seid ja vorsichtig!** whatever you do, be careful! **da seid ihr ja!** there you are! **das ist es ja** that's just it; **das mag ja** wahr sein that may well be true

Jacht f -,-en yacht

Jacke f -,-n jacket; (*Strick-*) cardigan

Jackett /ʒa'kɛt/ nt -s,-s jacket

Jade m -[s] & f - jade

Jagd f -,-en hunt; (*Schießen*) shoot; (*Jagen*) hunting; shooting; (*fig*) pursuit (nach of); **auf die J~ gehen** go hunting/shooting. **J~flugzeug** nt fighter aircraft. **J~gewehr** nt sporting gun. **J~hund** m gun-dog: (*Hetzhund*) hound

jagen vt hunt; (*schießen*) shoot; (*verfolgen, wegjagen*) chase; (*treiben*) drive; **sich j~** chase each other; **in die Luft j~** blow up □ vi (haben) hunt, go hunting/shooting; (*fig*) chase (nach after) □ vi (*sein*) race, dash

Jäger m -s,- hunter

jäh a sudden, adv -ly; (*steil*) steep, adv -ly

Jahr nt -[e]s,-e year. **J~buch** nt year-book. **j~elang** adv for years. **J~estag** m anniversary. **J~eszahl** f year; (*Wein*) season. **J~gang** m year; (*Wein*) vintage. **J~hundert** nt century. **J~hundertfeier** f centenary. (*Amer*) centennial

jährlich a annual, yearly □ adv annually, yearly

Jahr|markt m fair. **J~tausend** nt millenium. **J~zehnt** nt -[e]s,-e decade

Jähzorn m violent temper. **j~ig** a hot-tempered

Jalousie /ʒalu'zi:/ f -,-n venetian blind

Jammer m -s misery, (*Klagen*) lamenting; **es ist ein J~** it is a shame

jämmerlich a miserable, adv -bly; (*Mitleid erregend*) pitiful, adv -ly

jammern vi (haben) lament □ vt **jdn j~n** arouse s.o.'s pity. **j~schade** a **j~schade sein** (*fam*) be a terrible shame

Jänner *m* -s,- *(Aust)* January

Januar *m* -s,-e January

Jap|an *nt* -s Japan. **J~aner(in)** *m* -s,- (*f* -,-nen) Japanese. **J~anisch** *a* Japanese. **J~anisch** *nt* -[s] *(Lang)* Japanese

Jargon /ʒarˈgõː/ *m* -s jargon

jäten *vt/i (haben)* weed

jauchzen *vi (haben) (liter)* exult

jaulen *vi (haben)* yelp

Jause *f* -,-n *(Aust)* snack

jawohl *adv* yes

Jawort *nt* jdm sein J~ geben accept s.o.'s proposal (of marriage)

Jazz /jats, dʒɛs/ *m* - jazz

je *adv (jemals)* ever; *(jeweils)* each; *(pro)* per; **je nach** according to; **seit eh und je** always; **besser denn je** better than ever □ *conj* je mehr, desto od umso besser the more the better □ *prep (+ acc)* per

Jeans /dʒiːns/ *pl* jeans

jed|e(r,s) *pron* every; *(j~er Einzelne)* each; *(j~er Beliebige)* any; *(substantivisch)* everyone; each one; anyone; **ohne j~en Grund** without any reason. **j~enfalls** *adv* in any case; *(wenigstens)* at least. **j~ermann** *pron* everyone. **j~erzeit** *adv* at any time. **j~esmal** *adv* [NEW] *jedes Mal, s. Mal*[^1]

jedoch *adv & conj* however

jeher *adv* von od seit j~ always

jemals *adv* ever

jemand *pron* someone, somebody; *(fragend, verneint)* anyone, anybody

jen|e(r,s) *pron* that; *(pl)* those; *(substantivisch)* that one; *(pl)* those. **j~seits** *prep (+ gen)* [on] the other side of

jetzig *a* present; *(Preis)* current

jetzt *adv* now. **J~zeit** *f* present

jeweil|ig *a* respective. **j~s** *adv* at a time

jiddisch *a*, **J~** *nt* -[s] Yiddish

Job /dʒɔp/ *m* -s,-s job. **j~ben** *vi (haben) (fam)* work

Joch *nt* -[e]s,-e yoke

Jockei, Jockey /ˈdʒɔki/ *m* -s,-s jockey

Jod *nt* -[e]s iodine

jodeln *vi (haben)* yodel

Joga *m & nt* -[s] yoga

joggen /ˈdʒɔgən/ *vi (haben/sein)* jog. **J~ing** *nt* -[s] jogging

Joghurt, Jogurt *m & nt* -[s] yoghurt

Johannisbeere *f* redcurrant; **schwarze J~** blackcurrant

johlen *vi (haben)* yell; *(empört)* jeer

Jolle *f* -,-n dinghy

Jong|leur /ʒõˈgløːɐ/ *m* -s,-e juggler. **j~lieren** *vi (haben)* juggle

Joppe *f* -,-n [thick] jacket

Jordanien /-jən/ *nt* -s Jordan

Journal|ismus /ʒʊrnaˈlɪsmʊs/ *m* - journalism. **J~ist(in)** *m* -en,-en *(f* -,-nen) journalist

Jubel *m* -s rejoicing, jubilation. **j~n** *vi (haben)* rejoice

Jubil|ar(in) *m* -s,-e *(f* -,-nen) person celebrating an anniversary. **J~äum** *nt* -s,-äen jubilee, *(Jahrestag)* anniversary

juck|en *vi (haben)* itch; **sich j~en** scratch; **es j~t mich** I have an itch; *(fam: möchte)* I'm itching (zu) to. **J~reiz** *m* itch[ing]

Jude *m* -n,-n Jew. **J~ntum** *nt* -s Judaism; *(Juden)* Jewry

Jüd|in *f* -,-nen Jewess. **j~isch** *a* Jewish

Judo *nt* -[s] judo

Jugend *f* - youth; *(junge Leute)* young people *pl.* **J~herberge** *f* youth hostel. **J~klub** *m* youth club. **J~kriminalität** *f* juvenile delinquency. **j~lich** *a* youthful. **J~liche(r)** *m/f* young man/woman; *(Admin)* juvenile; **J~liche** *pl* young people. **J~stil** *m* art nouveau. **J~zeit** *f* youth

Jugoslaw|ien /-jən/ *nt* -s Yugoslavia. **j~isch** *a* Yugoslav

Juli *m* -[s],-s July

[^1]: New spelling reference

jung a (jünger, jüngst) young;
⟨Wein⟩ new ~ pron J~ und Alt
(J~ und alt) young and old. J~e
m -n,-n boy. J~e(s) nt young
animal/bird; ⟨Katzen-⟩ kitten;
(Bären-, Löwen-) cub; (Hunde-,
Seehund-) pup; die J~en the
young pl. j~enhaft a boyish
Jünger m -s,- disciple
Jungfer f -,-n alte J~ old maid.
J~nfahrt f maiden voyage
Jung|frau f virgin; (Astr) Virgo.
j~fräulich a virginal. J~ge-
selle m bachelor
Jüngling m -s,-e youth
jüngst|e(r,s) a youngest; (neueste)
latest; in j~er Zeit recently
Juni m -[s],-s June
Junior m -s,-en /-'o:rən/ junior
Jura pl law sg
Jurist|(in) m -en,-en (f -,-nen)
lawyer. j~isch a legal, adv -ly
Jury /ʒy'ri:/ f -,-s jury; (Sport)
judges pl
justieren vt adjust
Justiz f - die J~ justice.
J~irrtum m miscarriage of jus-
tice. J~minister m Minister of
Justice
Juwel nt -s,-en & (fig) m -e jewel.
J~ier m -s,-e jeweller
Jux m -es,-e (fam) joke; aus Jux
for fun

K

Kabarett nt -s,-s & -e cabaret
kabbelig a choppy
Kabel nt -s,- cable. K~fernsehen
nt cable television
Kabeljau m -s,-e & -s cod
Kabine f -,-n cabin; (Umkleide-)
cubicle; (Telefon-) booth; (einer
K~nbahn) car. K~nbahn f
cable-car
Kabinett nt -s,-e (Pol) Cabinet
Kabriolett nt -s,-s convertible
Kachel f -,-n tile. k~n vt tile

Kadaver m -s,- carcass
Kadenz f -,-en (Mus) cadence;
(für Solisten) cadenza
Kadett m -en,-en cadet
Käfer m -s,- beetle
Kaff nt -s,-s (fam) dump
Kaffee /'kafe:, ka'fe:/ m -s,-s cof-
fee; (Mahlzeit) afternoon coffee.
K~grund m = satz.
K~kanne f coffee-pot. K~ma-
schine f coffee-maker. K~
mühle f coffee-grinder. K~satz
m coffee-grounds pl
Käfig m -s,-e cage
kahl a bare; (haarlos) bald; k~
geschoren shaven. k~gescho-
ren a ⟨NEW⟩ k~ geschoren, s.
kahl. k~köpfig a bald-headed
Kahn m -s,-e boat; (Last-) barge
Kai m -s,-e quay
Kaiser m -s,- emperor. K~in f
-,-nen empress. k~lich a im-
perial. K~reich nt empire.
K~schnitt m Caesarean [sec-
tion]
Kajüte f -,-n (Naut) cabin
Kakao /ka'kaʊ/ m -s cocoa
Kakerlak m -s & -en,-en cockroach
Kaktee /kak'te:ə/ f -,-n, **Kaktus**
m -,-teen /-'te:ən/ cactus
Kalb nt -[e]s,-er calf. K~fleisch
nt veal
Kalender m -s,- calendar; (Ta-
schen-, Termin-) diary
Kaliber nt -s,- calibre; (Gewehr-)
bore
Kalium nt -s potassium
Kalk m -[e]s,-e lime; (Kalzium)
calcium. k~en vt whitewash.
K~stein m limestone
Kalkul|ation f -/-'tsjo:n/ f -,-en cal-
culation. k~ieren vt/i (haben)
calculate
Kalorie f -,-n calorie
kalt a (kälter, kältest) cold; es ist
k~ it is cold; mir ist k~ I am
cold. k~blütig a cold-blooded,
adv -ly; (ruhig) cool, adv -ly
Kälte f -,(Gefühls-) coldness;
10 Grad K~ 10 degrees below
zero. K~welle f cold spell

kalt|herzig *a* cold-hearted.
k~schnäuzig *a (fam)* cold, *adv*
-ly

Kalzium *nt* -s calcium

Kamel *nt* -s *e* camel; *(fam: Idiot)*
fool

Kamera *f* -,-s camera

Kamerad|(in) *m* -en,-en *(f*
-,-nen) companion; *(Freund)*
mate; *(Mil, Pol)* comrade.
K~schaft *f* - comradeship

Kameramann *m (pl* -männer *&*
-leute) cameraman

Kamille *f* - camomile

Kamin *m* -s,-e fireplace; *(SGer:
Schornstein)* chimney. **K~feger**
m -s,- *(SGer)* chimney-sweep

Kamm *m* -[e]s,*e* comb; *(Berg-)*
ridge; *(Zool, Wellen-)* crest

kämmen *vt* comb; **jdn/sich k~**
comb s.o.'s/one's hair

Kammer *f* -,-n small room;
(Techn, Biol, Pol) chamber.
K~diener *m* valet. **K~musik** *f*
chamber music

Kammgarn *nt (Tex)* worsted

Kampagne /kam'panjə/ *f* -,-n
(Pol, Comm) campaign

Kampf *m* -es,*e* fight; *(Schlacht)*
battle; *(Wett-)* contest; *(fig)*
struggle; **schwere K~e** heavy
fighting *sg*; **den K~ ansagen** (+
dat) (fig) declare war on

kämpf|en *vi (haben)* fight; **sich
k~en** durch fight one's way
through. **K~er(in)** *m* -s,- *(f*
-,-nen) fighter

kampf|los *adv* without a fight.
K~richter *m (Sport)* judge

kampieren *vi (haben)* camp

Kanada *nt* -s Canada

Kanad|ier(in) /-/-jɐ, -jərɪn/ *m* -s,-
(f -,-nen) Canadian. **k~isch** *a*
Canadian

Kanal *m* -s,*e* canal; *(Abfluss-)*
drain, sewer; *(Radio, TV)* channel; **der K~** the [English] Channel

Kanalis|ation /-'tsjo:n/ *f* - sewer-
age system, drains *pl*. **k~ieren**

vt canalize; *(fig: lenken)* channel

Kanarienvogel /-jən-/ *m* canary

Kanarisch *a* **K~e Inseln** Canaries

Kandi|dat(in) *m* -en,-en *(f*
-,-nen)* candidate. **k~dieren** *vi
(haben)* stand *(für* for)

kandiert *a* candied

Känguru (Känguruh) *nt* -s,-s
kangaroo

Kaninchen *nt* -s,- rabbit

Kanister *m* -s,- canister; *(Benzin-)*
can

Kännchen *nt* -s,- [small] jug;
(Kaffee-) pot

Kanne *f* -,-n jug; *(Kaffee-, Tee-)*
pot; *(Öl-)* can; *(große Milch-)*
churn; *(Gieß-)* watering-can

Kannibal|e *m* -n,-n cannibal.
K~ismus *m* - cannibalism

Kanon *m* -s,-s canon; *(Lied)* round

Kanone *f* -,-n cannon, gun; *(fig:
Könner)* ace

kanonisieren *vt* canonize

Kantate *f* -,-n cantata

Kante *f* -,-n edge; **auf die hohe
K~ legen** *(fam)* put by

Kanten *m* -s,- crust [of bread]

Kanter *m* -s,- canter

kantig *a* angular

Kantine *f* -,-n canteen

Kanton *m* -s,-e *(Swiss)* canton

Kantor *m* -s,-en /-'to:rən/ choir-
master and organist

Kanu *nt* -s,-s canoe

Kanzel *f* -,-n pulpit; *(Aviat)* cockpit

Kanzleistil *m* officialese

Kanzler *m* -s,- chancellor

Kap *nt* -s,-s *(Geog)* cape

Kapazität *f* -,-en capacity; *(Experte)* authority

Kapelle *f* -,-n chapel; *(Mus)* band

Kaper *f* -,-n *(Culin)* caper

kapern *vt (Naut)* seize

kapieren *vt (fam)* understand,
(fam) get

Kapital *nt* -s capital; **K~
schlagen aus** *(fig)* capitalize on.
K~ismus *m* - capitalism. **K~ist**

m -en,-en capitalist. **k~istisch** *a* capitalist

Kapitän *m* -s,-e captain

Kapitel *nt* -s,- chapter

Kapitul|ation /-'tsjo:n/ *f* - capitulation. **k~ieren** *vi* (*haben*) capitulate

Kaplan *m* -s,-e curate

Kappe *f* -,-n cap. **k~n** *vt* cut

Kapsel *f* -,-n capsule; (*Flaschen-*) top

kaputt *a* (*fam*) broken; (*zerrissen*) torn; (*defekt*) out of order; (*ruiniert*) ruined; (*erschöpft*) worn out. **k~gehen†** *vi sep* (*sein*) (*fam*) break; (*zerreißen*) tear; (*defekt werden*) pack up; (*Ehe, Freundschaft:*) break up. **k~lachen** (**sich**) *vr sep* (*fam*) be in stitches. **k~machen** *vt sep* (*fam*) break; (*zerreißen*) tear; (*defekt machen*) put out of order; (*erschöpfen*) wear out; **sich k~machen** wear oneself out

Kapuze *f* -,-n hood

Kapuzinerkresse *f* nasturtium

Karaffe *f* -,-n carafe; (*mit Stöpsel*) decanter

Karambolage /karambo'la:ʒə/ *f* -,-n collision

Karamell (Karamel) *m* -s caramel. **K~bonbon** *m* & *nt* ≈ toffee

Karat *nt* -[e]s,-e carat

Karawane *f* -,-n caravan

Kardinal *m* -s,-e cardinal. **K~zahl** *f* cardinal number

Karfiol *m* -s (*Aust*) cauliflower

Karfreitag *m* Good Friday

karg *a* (**kärger, kärgst**) meagre; (*frugal*) frugal; (*spärlich*) sparse; (*unfruchtbar*) barren; (*gering*) scant. **k~en** *vi* (*haben*) be sparing (**mit** with)

kärglich *a* poor, meagre; (*gering*) scant

Karibik *f* - Caribbean

kar|iert *a* check[ed]; (*Papier*) squared; **schottisch k~** tartan

Karik|atur *f* -,-en caricature; (*Journ*) cartoon. **k~ieren** *vt* caricature

karitativ *a* charitable

Karneval *m* -s,-e & -s carnival

Karnickel *nt* -s,- (*dial*) rabbit

Kärnten *nt* -s Carinthia

Karo *nt* -s,-s (*Raute*) diamond; (*Viereck*) square; (*Muster*) check; (*Kartenspiel*) diamonds *pl*. **K~muster** *nt* check

Karosserie *f* -,-n bodywork

Karotte *f* -,-n carrot

Karpfen *m* -s,- carp

Karre *f* -,-n = **Karren**

Karree *nt* -s,-s square; **ums K~** round the block

Karren *m* -s,- cart; (*Hand-*) barrow. **k~** *vt* cart

Karriere /ka'rjɛːrə/ *f* -,-n career; **K~ machen** get to the top

Karte *f* -,-n card; (*Eintritts-, Fahr-*) ticket; (*Speise-*) menu; (*Land-*) map

Kartei *f* -,-en card index. **K~karte** *f* index card

Karten|spiel *nt* card-game; (*Spielkarten*) pack/(*Amer*) deck of cards. **K~vorverkauf** *m* advance booking

Kartoffel *f* -,-n potato. **K~brei** *m*, **K~püree** *nt* mashed potatoes *pl*. **K~salat** *m* potato salad

Karton /kar'tɔŋ/ *m* -s,-s cardboard; (*Schachtel*) carton, cardboard box

Karussell *nt* -s,-s & -e roundabout

Karwoche *f* Holy Week

Käse *m* -s,- cheese. **K~kuchen** *m* cheesecake

Kaserne *f* -,-n barracks *pl*

Kasino *nt* -s,-s casino

Kasperle *nt* & *m* -s,- Punch. **K~theater** *nt* Punch and Judy show

Kasse *f* -,-n till; (*Registrier-*) cash register; (*Zahlstelle*) cash desk; (*im Supermarkt*) check-out; (*Theater-*) box-office; (*Geld*) pool [of money], (*fam*) kitty; (*Kranken-*) health insurance scheme; (*Spar-*) savings bank;

knapp/gut bei K~ sein (fam) be short of cash/be flush. **K~npatient** m ≈ NHS patient.

K~nschlager m box-office hit. **K~nwart** m -[e]s,-e treasurer. **K~nzettel** m receipt

Kasserolle f -,-n saucepan [with one handle]

Kassette f -,-n cassette; (Film-, Farbband-) cartridge; (Geld-) money-box; (Schmuck-) case. **K~nrecorder** /-rɛkɔːdɐ/ m -s,- cassette recorder

kassier|en vt/i (haben) collect the money; (im Bus) take the fares □ vt collect. **K~er(in)** m -s,- (f -,-nen) cashier

Kastagnetten /kastan'jɛtən/ pl castanets

Kastanie /kas'taːnjə/ f -,-n [horse] chestnut, (fam) conker. **k~nbraun** a chestnut

Kaste f -,-n caste

Kasten m -s,- box; (Brot-) bin; (Flaschen-) crate; (Brief-) letterbox; (Aust: Schrank) cupboard; (Kleider-) wardrobe

kastrieren vt castrate; neuter (Tier)

Kasus m -,- /-uːs/ (Gram) case

Katalog m -[e]s,-e catalogue. **k~isieren** vt catalogue

Katalysator m -s,-en /-'toːrən/ catalyst; (Auto) catalytic converter

Katapult nt -[e]s,-e catapult. **k~ieren** vt catapult

Katarrh, Katarr m -s,-e catarrh

katastr|ophal a catastrophic. **K~ophe** f -,-n catastrophe

Katechismus m - catechism

Kateg|orie f -,-n category. **k~orisch** a categorical, adv -ly

Kater m -s,- tom-cat; (fam: Katzenjammer) hangover

Katheder nt -s,- [teacher's] desk

Kathedrale f -,-n cathedral

Kath|olik(in) m -en,-en (f -,-nen) Catholic. **k~olisch** a Catholic. **K~olizismus** m - Catholicism

Kätzchen nt -s,- kitten; (Bot) catkin

Katze f -,-n cat. **K~njammer** m (fam) hangover. **K~nsprung** m ein K~nsprung (fam) a stone's throw

Kauderwelsch nt -[s] gibberish

kauen vt/i (haben) chew; bite (Nägel)

kauern vi (haben) crouch; **sich k~** crouch down

Kauf m -[e]s, Käufe purchase; guter K~ bargain; in K~ nehmen (fig) put up with. **k~en** vt/i (haben) buy; **k~en bei** shop at

Käufer(in) m -s,- (f -,-nen) buyer; (im Geschäft) shopper

Kauf|haus nt department store. **K~kraft** f purchasing power. **K~laden** m shop

käuflich a saleable; (bestechlich) corruptible; **k~ sein** be for sale; **k~erwerben** buy

Kauf|mann m (pl -leute) businessman; (Händler) dealer; (dial) grocer. **k~männisch** a commercial. **K~preis** m purchase price

Kaugummi m chewing-gum

Kaulquappe f -,-n tadpole

kaum adv hardly; **k~ glaublich** od **zu glauben** hard to believe

kauterisieren vt cauterize

Kaution /-'tsjoːn/ f -,-en surety; (Jur) bail; (Miet-) deposit

Kautschuk m -s rubber

Kauz m -es, Käuze owl; **komischer K~** (fam) odd fellow

Kavalier m -s,-e gentleman

Kavallerie f -,- cavalry

Kaviar m -s caviare

keck a bold; (frech) cheeky

Kegel m -s,- skittle; (Geom) cone; **mit Kind und K~** (fam) with all the family. **K~bahn** f skittle-alley. **k~förmig** a conical. **k~n** vi (haben) play skittles

Kehle f -,-n throat; **aus voller K~** at the top of one's voice; **etw in die falsche K~ bekommen** (fam) take sth the wrong way.

K~kopf m larynx. K~kopf-
entzündung f laryngitis
Kehr|e f -,-n [hairpin] bend.
k~en vi (haben) (fegen) sweep
□ vt sweep; (wenden) turn; den
Rücken k~en turn one's back
(dat on); sich k~en turn; sich
nicht k~en an (+ acc) not care
about. K~icht m -[e]s sweepings
pl. K~reim m refrain. K~seite f
(fig) drawback; die K~seite der
Medaille the other side of the
coin. k~tmachen (sich) sep (haben)
turn back; (sich umdrehen) turn
round. K~twendung f about-
turn; (fig) U-turn.
keifen vi (haben) scold
Keil m -[e]s,-e wedge
Keile f -(fam) hiding. k~n (sich)
vr (fam) fight. K~rei f -,-en
(fam) punch-up
Keilkissen nt [wedge-shaped]
bolster. K~riemen m fan belt
Keim m -[e]s,-e (Bot) sprout;
(Med) germ; im K~ ersticken
(fig) nip in the bud. k~en vi
(haben) germinate; (austreiben)
sprout. K~frei a sterile
kein pron no; not a; auf k~en
Fall on no account; k~e fünf
Minuten less than five minutes.
k~e(r,s) pron no one, nobody;
(Ding) none, not one. k~esfalls
adv on no account. k~eswegs
adv by no means. k~mal adv not
once. k~s pron none, not one
Keks m -[es],-[e] biscuit, (Amer)
cookie
Kelch m -[e]s,-e goblet, cup; (Relig) chalice; (Bot) calyx
Kelle f -,-n ladle; (Maurer-,
Pflanz-) trowel
Keller m -s,- cellar. K~ei f -,-en
winery. K~geschoss (K~ge-
schoß) nt cellar; (bewohnbar)
basement. K~wohnung f basement flat
Kellner m -s,- waiter. K~in f
-,-nen waitress
keltern vt press
keltisch a Celtic

Kenia nt -s Kenya
kenn|en† vt know; k~en lernen
get to know; (treffen) meet; sich
k~en lernen meet; (näher) get
to know one another. k~en-
lernen vt sep (NEW) k~en lernen,
s. kennen. K~er m -s,-, K~erin
f -,-nen connoisseur; (Experte)
expert. K~melodie f signature
tune. k~tlich a recognizable;
k~tlich machen mark. K~tnis
f -,-se knowledge; zur K~tnis
nehmen take note of; in K~tnis
setzen inform (von of). K~wort
nt (pl -wörter) reference;
(geheimes) password.
K~zeichen nt distinguishing
mark or feature; (Merkmal)
characteristic, (Markierung)
mark, marking; (Abzeichen)
badge; (Auto) registration.
k~zeichnen vt distinguish;
(markieren) mark. k~zeich-
nend a typical (für of). K~ziffer
f reference number
kentern vi (sein) capsize
Keramik f -,-en pottery, ceramics
sg; (Gegenstand) piece of pottery
Kerbe f -,-n notch
Kerbholz nt etwas auf dem
K~haben (fam) have a record
Kerker m -s,- dungeon; (Gefängnis) prison
Kerl m -s,-e & -s (fam) fellow,
bloke
Kern m -s,-e pip; (Kirsch-) stone;
(Nuss-) kernel; (Techn) core;
(Atom-, Zell- & fig) nucleus;
(Stadt-) centre; (einer Sache)
heart. K~energie f nuclear energy. K~gehäuse nt core. k~ge-
sund a perfectly healthy. k~ig a
robust; (Ausspruch) pithy. K~los
a seedless. K~physik f nuclear
physics sg
Kerze f -,-n candle. k~ngerade
a & adv straight. K~nhalter m
-s,- candlestick
kess (keß) a (kesser, kessest)
pert

Kessel *m* -s, kettle; (*Heiz-*) boiler. **K~stein** *m* fur

Ketchup (**Ketchup**) /'kɛtʃap/ *m* -[s],-s ketchup

Kette *f* -,-n chain; (*Hals-*) necklace. **k~n** *vt* chain (**an** + *acc* to). **K~nladen** *m* chain store. **K~nraucher** *m* chain-smoker. **K~nreaktion** *f* chain reaction

Ketze|r(in) *m* -s,- (*f* -,-nen) heretic. **K~rei** *f* - heresy

keuch|en *vi* (*haben*) pant. **K~husten** *m* whooping cough

Keule *f* -,-n club; (*Culin*) leg; (*Hühner-*) drumstick

keusch *a* chaste. **K~heit** *f* - chastity

Kfz *abbr s.* Kraftfahrzeug

Khaki *nt* - khaki. **k~farben** *a* khaki

kichern *vi* (*haben*) giggle

Kiefer[1] *f* -,-n pine[-tree]

Kiefer[2] *m* -s,- jaw

Kiel *m* -s,-e (*Naut*) keel. **K~wasser** *nt* wake

Kiemen *fpl* gills

Kies *m* -es gravel. **K~el** *m* -s,-, **K~elstein** *m* pebble. **K~grube** *f* gravel pit

Kilo *nt* -s,-[s] kilo. **K~gramm** *nt* kilogram. **K~hertz** *nt* kilohertz. **K~meter** *m* kilometre. **K~meterstand** *m* ≈ mileage. **K~watt** *nt* kilowatt

Kind *nt* -es,-er child; **von K~ auf** from childhood

Kinder|arzt *m,* **K~ärztin** *f* paediatrician. **K~bett** *nt* child's cot. **K~ei** *f* -,-en childish prank. **K~garten** *m* nursery school. **K~gärtnerin** *f* nursery-school teacher. **K~geld** *nt* child benefit. **K~gottesdienst** *m* Sunday school. **K~lähmung** *f* polio. **k~leicht** *a* very easy. **k~los** *a* childless. **K~mädchen** *nt* nanny. **k~reich** **k~reiche Familie** large family. **K~spiel** *nt* children's game; **das ist ein/kein K~spiel** that is dead easy/not

easy. **K~tagesstätte** *f* day nursery. **K~teller** *m* children's menu. **K~wagen** *m* pram, (*Amer*) baby carriage. **K~zimmer** *nt* child's/children's room; (*für Baby*) nursery

Kind|heit *f* childhood. **k~isch** *a* childish, puerile. **k~lich** *a* childlike

kinetisch *a* kinetic

Kinn *nt* -[e]s,-e chin. **K~lade** *f* jaw

Kino *nt* -s,-s cinema

Kiosk *m* -[e]s,-e kiosk

Kippe *f* -,-n (*Müll-*) dump; (*fam: Zigaretten-*) fag-end; **auf der K~ stehen** (*fam*) be in a precarious position; (*unsicher sein*) hang in the balance. **k~lig** *a* wobbly. **k~ln** *vi* (*haben*) wobble. **k~n** *vt* tilt; (*schütten*) tip (**in** + *acc* into) □ *vi* (*sein*) topple

Kirch|e *f* -,-n church. **K~enbank** *f* pew. **K~endiener** *m* verger. **K~enlied** *nt* hymn. **K~enschiff** *nt* nave. **K~hof** *m* churchyard. **k~lich** *a* church … □ *adv* **k~lich getraut werden** be married in church. **K~turm** *m* church tower, steeple. **K~weih** *f* -,-en [village] fair

Kirmes *f* -,-sen = Kirchweih

Kirsch|e *f* -,-n cherry. **K~wasser** *nt* kirsch

Kissen *nt* -s,- cushion; (*Kopf-*) pillow

Kiste *f* -,-n crate; (*Zigarren-*) box

Kitsch *m* -es sentimental rubbish; (*Kunst*) kitsch. **k~ig** *a* slushy; (*Kunst*) kitschy

Kitt *m* -s [adhesive] cement; (*Fenster-*) putty

Kittel *m* -s,- overall, smock; (*Arzt-, Labor-*) white coat

kitten *vt* stick; (*fig*) cement

Kitz *nt* -es,-e (*Zool*) kid

Kitzel *m* -s,- tickle; (*Nerven-*) thrill. **k~eln** *vt/i* (*haben*) tickle. **k~lig** *a* ticklish

Kladde *f* -,-n notebook

klaffen vi (haben) gape

kläffen vi (haben) yap

Klage f -,-n lament; (Beschwerde) complaint; (Jur) action. **k~n** vi (haben) lament; (sich beklagen) complaint; (Jur) sue

Kläger(in) m -s,- (f -,-nen) (Jur) plaintiff

kläglich a pitiful, adv -ly; (erbärmlich) miserable, adv -bly

klamm a cold and damp; (steif) stiff. **K~** f -,-en (Geog) gorge

Klammer f -,-n (Wäsche-) peg; (Büro-) paper-clip; (Heft-) staple; (Haar-) grip; (für Zähne) brace; (Techn) clamp; (Typ) bracket. **k~n (sich)** vr cling (an + acc to)

Klang m -[e]s,-e sound; (K~farbe) tone. **k~voll** a resonant; ⟨Stimme⟩ sonorous

Klapp|bett nt folding bed. **K~e** f -,-n flap; (fam: Mund) trap. **k~en** vt fold; (hoch-) tip up □ vi (haben) (fam) work out. **K~entext** m blurb

Klapper f -,-n rattle. **k~n** vi (haben) rattle. **K~schlange** f rattlesnake

klapp|rig a rickety; (schwach) decrepit. **K~stuhl** m folding chair. **K~tisch** m folding table

Klaps m -es,-e pat; (strafend) smack. **k~en** vt smack

klar a clear; **k~ werden** clear; (fig) become clear (dat to); sich (dat) **k~ werden** make up one's mind; (erkennen) realize (dass that); sich (dat) **k~ od im K~en (k~en)** sein realize (dass that)

klären vt clarify; sich **k~** clear; (fig: sich klären) resolve itself

Klarheit f -,- clarity

Klarinette f -,-n clarinet

klar|machen vt sep make clear (dat to); sich (dat) etw **k~machen** understand sth.

K~sichtfolie f transparent/(haftend) cling film.

Klärung f - clarification

klarwerden† vi sep (sein) (NEW) **klar werden**, s. **klar**

Klasse f -,-n class; (Sch) class, form, grade; (Amer) (Zimmer) classroom; **erster/zweiter K~ reisen** travel first/second class. **k~** inv a (fam) super. **K~narbeit** f [written] test. **K~nbuch** nt register. **K~nkamerad(in)** m(f) class-mate. **K~nkampf** m class struggle. **K~nzimmer** nt classroom

klassifizier|en vt classify. **K~ung** f -,-en classification

Klass|ik f - classicism; (Epoche) classical period. **K~iker** m -s,- classical author/(Mus) composer. **k~isch** a classical; (mustergültig, typisch) classic

Klatsch m -[e]s gossip. **K~base** f (fam) gossip. **k~en** vt slap; Beifall **k~en** applaud □ vi (haben) make a slapping sound; (im Wasser) splash; (tratschen) gossip; (applaudieren) clap; [in die Hände] **k~en** clap one's hands □ vi (haben/sein) slap (gegen against). **K~maul** nt gossip. **k~nass (k~naß)** a (fam) soaking wet

klauben vt pick

Klaue f -,-n claw; (fam: Schrift) scrawl. **k~n** vt/i (haben) (fam) steal

Klausel f -,-n clause

Klaustrophobie f - claustrophobia

Klausur f -,-en (Univ) [examination] paper; (Sch) written test

Klaviatur f -,-en keyboard

Klavier nt -s,-e piano. **K~spieler(in)** m(f) pianist

kleb|en vt stick (mit Klebstoff glue (an + acc to) □ vi (haben) stick (an + dat. to). **k~rig** a sticky. **K~stoff** m adhesive, glue. **K~streifen** m adhesive tape

kleckern vi (haben) (fam) = **klecksen**

Klecks m -es,-e stain; (Tinten-) blot; (kleine Menge) dab. **k~en** vi (haben) make a mess

Klee m -s clover. **K~blatt** nt clover leaf

Kleid nt -[e]s,-er dress; **K~er** dresses; (Kleidung) clothes. **k~en** vt dress; (gut stehen) suit; **sich k~en** dress. **K~erbügel** m coat-hanger. **K~erbürste** f clothes-brush. **K~erhaken** m coat-hook. **K~errock** m pinafore dress. **K~erschrank** m wardrobe, (Amer) clothes closet. **k~sam** a becoming. **K~ung** f - clothes pl, clothing. **K~ungsstück** nt garment

Kleie f - bran

klein a small, little; (von kleinem Wuchs) short; **k~ hacken/schneiden** chop/cut up small or into small pieces; **k~ geschrieben werden** (fig) count for very little (bei jdm with s.o.); von **k~ auf** from childhood. **K~arbeit** f painstaking work. **K~bus** m minibus. **K~e(r,s)** m/f/nt little one. **K~geld** nt [small] change. **k~hacken** vt sep (NEW) = **k~ hacken, s. klein. K~handel** m retail trade. **K~heit** f - smallness; (Wuchs) short stature. **K~holz** nt firewood. **K~igkeit** f -,-en trifle; (Mahl) snack. **K~kind** nt infant. **K~kram** m (fam) odds and ends pl; (Angelegenheiten) trivia pl. **k~laut** a subdued. **k~lich** a petty. **K~lichkeit** f - pettiness. **k~mütig** a faint-hearted

Kleinod nt -[e]s,-e jewel

klein|schneiden vt sep (NEW) **k~schneiden, s. klein. k~schreiben** vt sep write with a small [initial] letter; **k~geschrieben werden** (fig) (NEW) = **k~ geschrieben werden, s. klein. K~stadt** f small town. **k~städtisch** a

provincial. **K~wagen** m small car

Kleister m -s paste. **k~n** vt paste

Klemme f -,-n [hair-]grip; **in der K~ sitzen** (fam) be in a fix. **k~n** vt jam; **sich** (dat) **den Finger k~n** get one's finger caught □ vi (haben) jam, stick

Klempner m -s,- plumber

Klerus (der) - the clergy

Klette f -,-n burr; **wie eine K~** (fig) like a limpet

kletter|n vi (sein) climb. **K~pflanze** f climber. **K~rose** f climbing rose

Klettverschluss (**Klettverschluß**) m Velcro (P) fastening

klicken vi (haben) click

Klient(in) /kli'ɛnt(ɪn)/ m -en,-en (f -,-nen) (Jur) client

Kliff nt -[e]s,-e cliff

Klima nt -s climate. **K~anlage** f air-conditioning

klimat|isch a climatic. **k~isiert** a air-conditioned

klimpern vi (haben) jingle; **k~ auf** (+ dat) tinkle on (Klavier); strum (Gitarre)

Klinge f -,-n blade

Klingel f -,-n bell. **k~n** vi (haben) ring; **es k~t** there's a ring at the door

klingen† vi (haben) sound

Klinik f -,-en clinic. **k~sch** a clinical, adv -ly

Klinke f -,-n [door] handle

klipp pred a **k~ und klar** quite plain, adv -ly

Klipp m -s,-s = **Klips**

Klippe f -,-n [submerged] rock

Klips m -es,-e clip; (Ohr-) clip-on ear-ring

klirren vi (haben) rattle; (Geschirr, Glas:) chink

Klischee nt -s,-s cliché

Klo nt -s,-s (fam) loo, (Amer) john

klobig a clumsy

klönen vi (haben) (NGer fam) chat

klopf|en vi (haben) knock; (leicht) tap; ⟨Herz:⟩ pound; **es k~te** there was a knock at the door □ vt beat; (ein-) knock

Klops m -es,-e meatball; (Brat-) rissole

Klosett nt -s,-s lavatory

Kloß m -es,-e dumpling; **ein K~ im Hals** (fam) a lump in one's throat

Kloster nt -s,- monastery; ⟨Nonnen-⟩ convent

klösterlich a monastic

Klotz m -es,-e block

Klub m -s,-s club

Kluft[1] f -,-e cleft; (fig: Gegensatz) gulf

Kluft[2] f -,-en outfit; (Uniform) uniform

klug a (klüger, klügst) intelligent, adv -ly; (schlau) clever, adv -ly, **nicht k~ werden aus** not understand. **K~heit** f - cleverness

Klump|en m -s,- lump. **k~en** vi (haben) go lumpy

knabbern vt/i (haben) nibble

Knabe m -n,-n boy. **k~nhaft** a boyish

Knäckebrot nt crispbread

knack|en vt/i (haben) crack. **K~s** m -es,-e crack; **einen K~s haben** be cracked/(fam: verrückt sein) crackers

Knall m -es,-e bang. **K~bonbon** m cracker. **k~en** vi (haben) go bang; ⟨Peitsche:⟩ crack □ vt ⟨jdn werfen⟩ chuck; **jdm eine k~en** (fam) clout s.o. **k~ig** a (fam) gaudy. **K~rot** a bright red

knapp a (gering) scant; (kurz) short; (mangelhaft) scarce; (gerade ausreichend) bare; (eng) tight; **ein k~es Pfund** just under a pound; **jdn k~ halten** (fam) keep s.o. short (**mit** of). **k~halten**[†] vt sep (NEW) **k~ halten**, s. **knapp**. **K~heit** f - scarcity

Knarre f -,-n rattle. **k~n** vi (haben) creak

Knast m -[e]s (fam) prison

knattern vi (haben) crackle; ⟨Gewehr:⟩ stutter

Knäuel m & nt -s,- ball

Knauf m -[e]s,-e Knäufe knob

knauser|ig a (fam) stingy. **k~n** vi (haben) (fam) be stingy

knautschen vt (fam) crumple □ vi (haben) crease

Knebel m -s,- gag. **k~n** vt gag

Knecht m -[e]s,-e farm-hand; (fig) slave. **k~en** vt (fig) enslave. **K~schaft** f - (fig) slavery

kneif|en[†] vt pinch □ vi (haben) pinch; (fam: sich drücken) chicken out. **K~zange** f pincers pl

Kneipe f -,-n (fam) pub, (Amer) bar

knet|en vt knead; (formen) mould. **K~masse** f Plasticine(P)

Knick m -[e]s,-e bend; (im Draht) kink; (Kniff) crease. **k~en** vt bend; (kniffen) fold; **geknickt sein** (fam) be dejected. **k~[e]rig** a (fam) stingy

Knicks m -es,-e curtsy. **k~en** vi (haben) curtsy

Knie nt -s,- /ˈkniːə/ knee. **K~bundhose** f knee-breeches pl. **K~kehle** f hollow of the knee

knien /ˈkniːən/ vi (haben) kneel □ vr **sich k~** kneel [down]

Knie|scheibe f kneecap. **K~strumpf** m knee-length sock

Kniff m -[e]s,-e pinch; (Falte) crease; (fam: Trick) trick. **k~en** vt fold. **k~[e]lig** a (fam) tricky

knipsen vt (lochen) punch; (Phot) photograph □ vi (haben) take a photograph/photographs

Knirps m -es,-e (fam) little chap; (P) ⟨Schirm⟩ telescopic umbrella

knirschen vi (haben) grate; ⟨Schnee, Kies:⟩ crunch; **mit den Zähnen k~** grind one's teeth

knistern vi (haben) crackle; ⟨Papier:⟩ rustle

Knitter|falte f crease. **k~frei** a crease-resistant. **k~n** vi (haben) crease

knobeln vi (haben) toss (**um** for); (fam: überlegen) puzzle

Knoblauch m -s garlic

Knöchel m -s,- ankle; (Finger-) knuckle

Knochen m -s,- bone. **K~mark** nt bone marrow. **k~trocken** a bone-dry

knochig a bony

Knödel m -s,- (SGer) dumpling

Knoll|e f -,-n tuber. **k~ig** a bulbous

Knopf m -[e]s,ᴗe button; (Kragen-) stud; (Griff) knob

knöpfen vt button

Knopfloch nt buttonhole

Knorpel m -s gristle; (Anat) cartilage

knorrig a gnarled

Knospe f bud

Knötchen nt -s,- nodule

Knoten m -s,- knot; (Med) lump; (Haar-) bun, chignon. **k~** vt knot. **K~punkt** m junction

knotig a knotty; (Hände) gnarled

knuffen vt poke

knüll|en vt crumple ▯ vi (haben) crease. **K~er** m -s,- (fam) sensation

knüpfen vt knot; (verbinden) attach (an + acc to)

Knüppel m -s,- club; (Gummi-) truncheon

knurr|en vi (haben) growl; (Magen:) rumble; (fam: schimpfen) grumble. **k~ig** a grumpy

knusprig a crunchy, crisp

knutschen vi (haben) (fam) smooch

k.o. /kaˈʔoː/ a **k.o. schlagen** knock out; **k.o. sein** (fam) be worn out. **K.o.** m -s,-s knock-out

Koalition /koaliˈtsi̯oːn/ f -,-en coalition

Kobold m -[e]s,-e goblin, imp

Koch m -[e]s,ᴗe cook; (im Restaurant) chef. **K~buch** nt cookery book, (Amer) cookbook. **k~en** vt cook; (sieden) boil; make ⟨Kaffee,

Tee⟩; hart gekochtes Ei hardboiled egg ▯ vi (haben) cook; (sieden) boil; (fam) seethe (**vor** + dat with). **K~en** nt -s cooking; (Sieden) boiling; **zum K~n bringen/kommen** bring/come to the boil. **k~end** a boiling ▯ adv **k~end heiß** boiling hot. **K~er** m -s,- cooker. **K~gelegenheit** f cooking facilities pl. **K~herd** m cooker, stove

Köchin f -,-nen [woman] cook

Koch|kunst f cookery. **K~löffel** m wooden spoon. **K~nische** f kitchenette. **K~platte** f hotplate. **K~topf** m saucepan

Kode /koːt/ m -s,-s code

Köder m -s,- bait

Koexist|enz /ˈkoːʔɛksɪstɛnts/ f coexistence. **k~ieren** vi (haben) coexist

Koffein /kɔfeˈiːn/ nt -s caffeine. **K~frei** a decaffeinated

Koffer m -s,- suitcase. **K~kuli** m luggage trolley. **K~radio** nt portable radio. **K~raum** m (Auto) boot, (Amer) trunk

Kognak /ˈkɔnjak/ m -s,-s brandy

Kohl m -[e]s cabbage

Kohle f -,-n coal. **K~[n]hydrat** nt -[e]s,-e carbohydrate. **K~nbergwerk** nt coal-mine, colliery. **K~ndioxid** nt carbon dioxide. **K~ngrube** f = **K~nbergwerk. K~nherd** m (kitchen) range. **K~nsäure** f carbon dioxide. **K~nstoff** m carbon. **K~papier** nt carbon paper **Kohl|kopf** m cabbage. **K~rabi** m -[s],-[s] kohlrabi. **K~rübe** f swede

Koje f -,-n (Naut) bunk

Kokain /kokaˈiːn/ nt -s cocaine

kokett a flirtatious. **k~ieren** vi (haben) flirt

Kokon /koˈkõ/ m -s,-s cocoon

Kokosnuss (**Kokosnuß**)/coconut

Koks m -es coke

Kolben m -s,- (Gewehr-) butt; (Mais-) cob; (Techn) piston; (Chem) flask

Kolibri *m* -s,-s humming-bird

Kolik *f* -,-en colic

Kollabora|teur /-'tø:ɐ̯/ *m* -s,-e collaborator. **K~tion** /-'tsjo:n/ *f* - collaboration

Kolleg *nt* -s,-s & -ien /-jən/ (*Univ*) course of lectures

Kollegle *m* -n,-n, **K~in** *f* -,-nen colleague. **K~ium** *nt* -s,-ien staff

Kollekt|e *f* -,-n (*Relig*) collection. **K~tion** /-'tsjo:n/ *f* -,-en collection. **K~tiv** *a* collective. **K~tivum** *nt* -s,-va collective noun

kolli|dieren *vi* (*sein*) collide. **K~sion** *f* -,-en collision

Köln *nt* -s Cologne. **K~isch-wasser, K~isch Wasser** *nt* eau-de-Cologne

Kolonialwaren *fpl* groceries

Koloni|e *f* -,-n colony. **k~isieren** *vt* colonize

Kolonne *f* -,-n column; (*Mil*) convoy

Koloss *m* -es,-e (Koloß *m* -sses,-sse) giant

kolossal *a* enormous, *adv* -ly

Kolumne *f* -,-n (*Journ*) column

Koma *nt* -s,-s coma

Kombi *m* -s,-s = **K~wagen**. **K~nation** /-'tsjo:n/ *f* -,-en combination; (*Folgerung*) deduction; (*Kleidung*) co-ordinating outfit. **k~nieren** *vt* combine; (*fig*) reason; (*folgern*) deduce. **K~wagen** *m* estate car, (*Amer*) station-wagon

Kombüse *f* -,-n (*Naut*) galley

Komet *m* -en,-en comet. **k~enhaft** *a* (*fig*) meteoric

Komfort /kɔm'foːɐ̯/ *m* -s comfort; (*Luxus*) luxury. **k~abel** /-'taː-bəl/ *a* comfortable, *adv* -bly; (*luxuriös*) luxurious, *adv* -ly

Komik *f* - humour. **K~er** *m* -s,-, comic, comedian

komisch *a* funny; (*Oper*) comic; (*sonderbar*) odd, funny □ *adv* funnily; oddly. **k~erweise** *adv* funnily enough

Komitee *nt* -s,-s committee

Komma *nt* -s,-s & -ta comma; (*Dezimal-*) decimal point; **drei K~ fünf** three point five

Komman|dant *m* -en,-en commanding officer. **K~deur** /-'dø:ɐ̯/ *m* -s,-e commander. **k~dieren** *vt* command; (*befehlen*) order; (*fam: herum-*) order about □ *vi* (*haben*) give the orders

Kommando *nt* -s,-s order; (*Befehlsgewalt*) command; (*Einheit*) detachment. **K~brücke** *f* bridge

kommen† *vi* (*sein*) come; (*eintreffen*) arrive; (*gelangen*) get (**nach** to); **k~ lassen** send for; **auf/hinter etw** (*acc*) **k~** think of/find out about sth; **um/zu etw k~** lose/acquire sth; **wieder zu sich k~** come round; **wie kommt das?** why is that? **K~** *nt* -s coming; **K~und Gehen** coming and going. **k~d** *a* coming; **k~den Montag** next Monday

Kommen|tar *m* -s,-e commentary; (*Bemerkung*) comment. **K~tator** *m* -s,-en /-'to:rən/ commentator. **k~tieren** *vt* comment on

kommer|zialisieren *vt* commercialize. **k~ziell** *a* commercial, *adv* -ly

Kommili|tone *m* -n,-n, **K~tonin** *f* -,-nen fellow student

Kommiss *m* -es (Kommiß *m* -sses) (*fam*) army

Kommissar *m* -s,-e commissioner; (*Polizei-*) superintendent

Kommission *f* -,-en commission; (*Gremium*) committee

Kommode *f* -,-n chest of drawers

Kommunalwahlen *fpl* local elections

Kommunikation /-'tsjo:n/ *f* -,-en communication

Kommunikee /kɔmyni'ke:/ *nt* -s,-s = **Kommuniqué**

Kommunion *f* -,-en [Holy] Communion

Kommuniqué /kɔmyni'ke:/ *nt* -s,-s communiqué

Kommun|ismus m - Communism. **K~ist(in)** m -en,-en (f -,-nen) Communist. **k~istisch** a Communist

kommunizieren vi (haben) receive [Holy] Communion

Komödie /ko'mø:djə/ f -,-n comedy

Kompagnon /'kɔmpanjõ:/ m -s,-s (Comm) partner

kompakt a compact. **K~schallplatte** f compact disc

Kompanie f -,-n (Mil) company

Komparativ m -s,-e comparative

Komparse m -n,-n (Theat) extra

Kompass m -es,-e (Kompaß m -sses,-sse) compass

kompati|bel a compatible

kompetent a competent. **K~z** f -,-en competence

komplett a complete, adv -ly

Komplex m -es,-e complex. **k~a** a complex

Komplikation /-'tsjo:n/ f -,-en complication

Kompliment nt -[e]s,-e compliment

Komplize m -n,-n accomplice

komplizier|en vt complicate. **k~t** a complicated

Komplott nt -[e]s,-e plot

kompo|nieren vt/i (haben) compose. **K~nist** m -en,-en composer. **K~sition** /-'tsjo:n/ f -,-en composition

Kompositum nt -s,-ta compound

Kompost m -[e]s compost

Kompott nt -[e]s,-e stewed fruit

Kompresse f -,-n compress

komprimieren vt compress

Kompromiss m -es,-e (Kompromiß m -sses,-sse) compromise; **einen K~ schließen** compromise. **k~los** a uncompromising

kompromittieren vt compromise

Konden|sation /-'tsjo:n/ f - condensation. **k~sieren** vt condense

Kondensmilch f evaporated/(gesüßt) condensed milk

Kondition /-'tsjo:n/ f - (Sport) fitness; **in K~** in form. **K~al** m -s,-e (Gram) conditional

Konditor m -s,-en /-'to:rən/ confectioner. **K~ei** f -,-en patisserie

Kondo|lenzbrief m letter of condolence. **k~lieren** vi (haben) express one's condolences

Kondom nt & m -s,-e condom

Konfekt nt -[e]s confectionery; (Pralinen) chocolates pl

Konfektion /-'tsjo:n/ f - ready-to-wear clothes pl

Konferenz f -,-en conference; (Besprechung) meeting

Konfession f -,-en [religious] denomination. **k~ell** a denominational. **k~slos** a nondenominational

Konfetti nt -s confetti

Konfirm|and(in) m -en,-en (f -,-nen) candidate for confirmation. **K~ation** /-'tsjo:n/ f -,-en (Relig) confirmation. **k~ieren** vt (Relig) confirm

Konfitüre f -,-n jam

Konflikt m -[e]s,-e conflict

Konföderation /-'tsjo:n/ f confederation

Konfront|ation /-'tsjo:n/ f -,-en confrontation. **k~ieren** vt confront

konfus a confused

Kongress m -es,-e (Kongreß m -sses,-sse) congress

König m -s,-e king. **K~in** f -,-nen queen. **k~lich** a royal, adv -ly; (hoheitsvoll) regal, adv -ly; (großzügig) handsome, adv -ly; (fam: groß) tremendous, adv -ly. **K~reich** nt kingdom

konisch a conical

Konjug|ation /-'tsjo:n/ f -,-en conjugation. **k~ieren** vt conjugate

Konjunktion /-'tsjo:n/ f -,-en (Gram) conjunction

Konjunktiv m -s,-e subjunctive

Konjunktur f - economic situation; (Hoch-) boom

konkav a concave

konkret a concrete

Konkurren|t(in) m -en,-en (f -,-nen) competitor, rival. **K~z** f - competition; **jdm K~z machen** compete with s.o. **k~zfähig** a (Comm) competitive. **K~zkampf** m competition, rivalry

konkurrieren vi (haben) compete

Konkurs m -es,-e bankruptcy; **K~ machen** go bankrupt

können† vt/i (haben) etw k~ be able to do sth; (beherrschen) know sth; **k~ Sie Deutsch?** do you know any German? **das kann ich nicht** I can't do that; **er kann nicht mehr** he can't go on; **für etw nichts k~** not be to blame for sth □v aux **lesen/schwimmen k~** be able to read/swim; **er kann/konnte es tun** he can/could do it; **das kann od könnte [gut] sein** that may [well] be. **K~** nt -s ability, (Wissen) knowledge.

Könner(in) m -s,- (f -,-nen) expert

konsequen|t a consistent, adv -ly; (logisch) logical, adv -ly. **K~z** f -,-en consequence

konservativ a conservative

Konserven fpl tinned or canned food sg. **K~nbüchse, K~ndose** f tin, can. **k~ieren** vt preserve; (in Dosen) tin, can **K~ierungsmittel** nt preservative

Konsistenz f - consistency

konsolidieren vt consolidate

Konsonant m -en,-en consonant

konsterniert a dismayed

Konstitution /-'tsio:n/ f -,-en constitution. **k~ell** a constitutional

konstruieren vt construct; (entwerfen) design

Konstruk|tion /-'tsio:n/ f -,-en construction; (Entwurf) design. **k~tiv** a constructive

Konsul m -s,-n consul. **K~at** nt -[e]s,-e consulate

Konsult|ation /-'tsio:n/ f -,-en consultation. **k~ieren** vt consult

Konsum m -s consumption. **K~ent** m -en,-en consumer. **K~güter** npl consumer goods

Kontakt m -[e]s,-e contact. **K~linsen** fpl contact lenses. **K~person** f contact

kontern vt/i (haben) counter

Kontinent /'kɔn-, kɔnti'nɛnt/ m -[e]s,-e continent

Kontingent nt -[e]s,-e (Comm) quota; (Mil) contingent

Kontinuität f - continuity

Konto nt -s,-s account. **K~auszug** m (bank) statement. **K~nummer** f account number. **K~stand** m [bank] balance

Kontrabass (Kontrabaß) m double-bass

Kontrast m -[e]s,-e contrast

Kontroll|abschnitt m counterfoil. **K~e** f -,-n control; (Prüfung) check. **K~eur** /-'løːɐ/ m -s,-e [ticket] inspector. **k~ieren** vt check; inspect (Fahrkarten); (beherrschen) control

Kontroverse f -,-n controversy

Kontur f -,-en contour

Konvention /-'tsio:n/ f -,-en convention. **k~ell** a conventional, adv -ly

Konversation /-'tsio:n/ f -,-en conversation. **K~slexikon** nt encyclopaedia

konvertieren vi (haben) (Relig) convert. **K~it** m -en,-en convert

konvex a convex

Konvoi /kɔn'vɔy/ m -s,-s convoy

Konzentration /-'tsio:n/ f -,-en concentration. **K~slager** nt concentration camp

konzentrieren vt concentrate; **sich k~** concentrate (auf + acc on)

Konzept nt -[e]s,-e [rough] draft; **jdn aus dem K~bringen** put s.o.

off his stroke. K~papier nt rough paper

Konzern m -s,-e (Comm) group [of companies]

Konzert nt -[e]s,-e concert; (Klavier-, Geigen-) concerto. K~meister m leader, (Amer) concertmaster

Konzession f -,-en licence; (Zugeständnis) concession

Konzil nt -s,-e (Relig) council

Kooperation /ko'ʔopera'tsjo:n/ f co-operation

Koordin|ation /ko'ʔɔrdina'tsjo:n/ f - co-ordination. k~ieren vt co-ordinate

Kopf m -[e]s,ˈe head; ein K~ Kohl/Salat a cabbage/lettuce; aus dem K~ from memory; (auswendig) by heart; auf dem K~ (verkehrt) upside down; K~ an K~ neck and neck; ⟨stehen⟩ shoulder to shoulder; K~ stehen stand on one's head; sich ⟨dat⟩ den K~ waschen wash one's hair; sich ⟨dat⟩ den K~ zerbrechen rack one's brains. K~ball m header. K~bedeckung f head-covering

Köpf|chen nt -s,- little head; K~chen haben (fam) to be clever. k~en vt behead; (Fußball) head

Kopf|ende nt head. K~haut f scalp. K~hörer m headphones pl. K~kissen nt pillow. K~kissenbezug m pillow-case. K~los a panic-stricken. K~nicken nt nod. K~rechnen nt mental arithmetic. K~salat m lettuce. K~schmerzen mpl headache sg. K~schütteln nt -s shake of the head. K~sprung m header, dive. K~stand m headstand. K~steinpflaster nt nt cobble-stones pl. K~stütze f head-rest. K~tuch nt headscarf. k~über adv head first; (fig) headlong. K~wäsche f shampoo. K~weh nt headache. K~zerbrechen nt -s sich ⟨dat⟩ K~zerbrechen machen

rack one's brains; (sich sorgen) worry

Kopie f -,-n copy. k~ren vt copy

Koppel[1] f -,-n enclosure; (Pferde-) paddock

Koppel[2] nt -s,- (Mil) belt. k~n vt couple

Koralle f -,-n coral

Korb m -[e]s,ˈe basket; jdm einen K~ geben (fig) turn s.o. down. K~ball m [kind of] netball. K~stuhl m wicker chair

Kord m -s (Tex) corduroy

Kordel f -,-n cord

Korinthe f -,-n currant

Kork m -s,- cork. K~en m -s,- cork. K~enzieher m -s,- corkscrew

Korn[1] nt -[e]s,ˈer grain, (Samen-) seed; (coll: Getreide) grain, corn; (am Visier) front sight

Korn[2] m -[e]s,- (fam) grain schnapps

Körn|chen nt -s,- granule. k~ig a granular

Körper m -s,- body; (Geom) solid. K~bau m build, physique. k~behindert a physically disabled. k~lich a physical, adv -ly; (Strafe) corporal. K~pflege f personal hygiene. K~puder m talcum powder. K~schaft f -,-en corporation, body. K~strafe f corporal punishment. K~teil m part of the body

Korps /ko:ɐ̯/ nt -,- /-[s],-s/ corps

korpulent a corpulent

korrekt a correct, adv -ly. K~or m -s,-en /-'to:rən/ proof-reader. K~ur f -,-en correction. K~urabzug, K~urbogen m proof

Korrespon|dent(in) m -en,-en (f -,-nen) correspondent. K~denz f -,-en correspondence. k~dieren vi (haben) correspond

Korridor m -s,-e corridor

korrigieren vt correct

Korrosion f - corrosion

korrumpieren vt corrupt

korrup|t a corrupt. **K~tion** /-'tsjo:n/ f - corruption

Korsett nt -[e]s,-e corset

koscher a kosher

Kose|name m pet name. **K~wort** nt (pl -wörter) term of endearment

Kosmet|ik f - beauty culture. **K~ika** ntpl cosmetics. **K~ikerin** f -,-nen beautician. **k~isch** a cosmetic; ⟨Chirurgie⟩ plastic

kosm|isch a cosmic. **K~onaut(in)** m -en,-en (f -,-nen) cosmonaut. **k~opolitisch** a cosmopolitan

Kosmos m - cosmos

Kost f - food; (Ernährung) diet; (Verpflegung) board

kostbar a precious. **K~keit** f -,-en treasure

kosten[1] vt/i (haben) [von] etw k~ taste sth

kosten[2] vt cost; (brauchen) take; **wie viel kostet es?** how much is it? **K~** pl expense sg, cost sg; (Jur) costs; **auf meine K~** at my expense. **K~[vor]anschlag** m estimate. **k~los** a free ⬡ adv free [of charge]

Kosthappen m taste

köstlich a delicious; (entzückend) delightful. **K~keit** f -,-en (fig) gem; (Culin) delicacy

Kost|probe f taste; (fig) sample. **k~spielig** a expensive, costly

Kostüm nt -s,-e (Theat) costume; (Verkleidung) fancy dress; (Schneider-) suit. **K~fest** nt fancy-dress party. **k~iert** a **k~iert sein** be in fancy dress

Kot m -[e]s excrement; (Schmutz) dirt

Kotelett /kɔt'lɛt/ nt -s,-s chop, cutlet. **K~en** pl sideburns

Köter m -s,- (pej) dog

Kotflügel m (Auto) wing, (Amer) fender

kotzen vi (haben) (sl) throw up; **es ist zum K~** it makes you sick

Krabbe f -,-n crab; (Garnele) shrimp; (rote) prawn

krabbeln vi (sein) crawl

Krach m -[e]s,-e din, racket; (Knall) crash; (fam: Streit) row; (fam: Ruin) crash. **k~en** vi (haben) crash; **es hat gekracht** there was a bang/(fam: Unfall) a crash ⬡ (sein) break, crack; (auftreffen) crash (gegen into)

krächzen vi (haben) croak

Kraft f -,-e strength; (Gewalt) force; (Arbeits-) worker; **in/außer K~** in/no longer in force; **in K~ treten** come into force. **k~** prep (+ gen) by virtue of. **K~ausdruck** m swear-word. **K~fahrer** m driver. **K~fahrzeug** nt motor vehicle. **K~fahrzeugbrief** m [vehicle] registration document

kräftig a strong; (gut entwickelt) sturdy; (nahrhaft) nutritious; (heftig) hard ⬡ adv strongly; (heftig) hard. **k~en** vt strengthen

kraft|los a weak. **K~post** f post bus service. **K~probe** f trial of strength. **K~rad** nt motorcycle. **K~stoff** m (Auto) fuel. **k~voll** a strong, powerful. **K~wagen** m motor car. **K~werk** nt power station

Kragen m -s,- collar

Krähe f -,-n crow

krähen vi (haben) crow

krakeln vt/i (haben) scrawl

Kralle f -,-n claw. **k~n (sich)** vr clutch (**an jdn/etw** s.o./sth); (Katze:) dig its claws (**in** + acc into)

Kram m -s (fam) things pl, (fam) stuff; (Angelegenheiten) business; **wertloser K~** junk. **k~en** vi (haben) rummage about (**in** + dat in; **nach** for). **K~laden** m [small] general store

Krampf m -[e]s,-e cramp. **K~adern** fpl varicose veins. **k~haft** a convulsive, adv -ly; (verbissen) desperate, adv -ly

Kran m -[e]s,-e (Techn) crane

Kranich m -s,-e (*Zool*) crane

krank a (**kränker**, **kränkst**) sick; ⟨*Knie*, *Herz*⟩ bad; **k~ sein/werden/machen** be/fall/make ill; **jdn k~ melden/schreiben** (NEW) **jdn k~melden/k~schreiben**, s. **krankmelden**, **krankschreiben**. **K~e(r)** m/f sick man/woman, invalid; **die K~en** the sick pl

kränkeln vi (*haben*) be in poor health. **k~d** a ailing

kränken vi (*haben*) (*fig*) suffer (**an** + *dat* from)

kränken vt offend, hurt

Kranken|bett nt sick-bed. **K~geld** nt sickness benefit. **K~gymnast(in)** m -en,-en (f -,-nen) physiotherapist. **K~gymnastik** f physiotherapy. **K~haus** nt hospital. **K~kasse** f health insurance scheme/(*Amt*) office. **K~pflege** f nursing. **K~pfleger(in)** m(f) nurse. **K~saal** m [hospital] ward. **K~schein** m certificate of entitlement to medical treatment. **K~schwester** f nurse. **K~urlaub** m sick-leave. **K~versicherung** f health insurance. **K~wagen** m ambulance. **K~zimmer** nt sick-room

krank|haft a morbid; (*pathologisch*) pathological. **K~heit** f -,-en illness, disease

kränklich a sickly

krank|melden vt sep jdn **k~melden** report s.o. sick; **sich k~melden** report sick. **k~schreiben†** vt sep jdn **k~schreiben** give s.o. a medical certificate; **sich k~schreiben lassen** get a medical certificate

Kränkung f -,-en slight

Kranz m -es,-e wreath; (*Ring*) ring

Krapfen m -s,- doughnut

krass (**kraß**) a (**krasser**, **krassest**) glaring; (*offensichtlich*) blatant; (*stark*) gross; rank (*Außenseiter*)

Krater m -s,- crater

kratz|bürstig a (*fam*) prickly. **k~en** vt/i (*haben*) scratch; **sich k~en** scratch oneself/(*Tier:*) itself. **K~er** m -s,- scratch; (*Werkzeug*) scraper

Kraul nt -s (*Sport*) crawl. **k~en¹** vi (*haben/sein*) (*Sport*) do the crawl

kraulen² vt tickle; **sich am Kopf k~** scratch one's head

kraus a wrinkled; (*Haar*) frizzy; (*verworren*) muddled; **k~ ziehen** wrinkle. **K~e** f -,-n frill, ruffle; (*Haar*) frizziness

kräuseln vt wrinkle; frizz (*Haar*); gather (*Stoff*); ripple (*Wasser*); **sich k~** wrinkle; (*Haar:*) go frizzy; (*Wasser:*) ripple

krausen vt wrinkle; frizz (*Haar*); gather (*Stoff*); **sich k~** wrinkle. (*Haar:*) go frizzy

Kraut nt -[e]s, Kräuter herb; (*SGer*) cabbage; (*Sauer-*) sauerkraut; **wie K~ und Rüben** (*fam*) higgledy-piggledy

Krawall m -s,-e riot; (*Lärm*) row

Krawatte f -,-n [neck]tie

kraxeln vi (*sein*) (*fam*) clamber

krea|tiv /krea'ti:f/ a creative. **K~tur** f -,-en creature

Krebs m -es,-e crayfish; (*Med*) cancer; (*Astr*) Cancer. **k~ig** a cancerous

Kredit m -s,-e credit; (*Darlehen*) loan; **auf K~** on credit. **K~karte** f credit card

Kreide f -,-n chalk. **k~bleich** a deathly pale. **k~ig** a chalky

kreieren /kre'i:rən/ vt create

Kreis m -es,-e circle; (*Admin*) district

kreischen vt/i (*haben*) screech; (*schreien*) shriek

Kreisel m -s,- [spinning] top; (fam: Kreisverkehr) roundabout

kreis|en vi (haben) circle; (um around). **k~förmig** a circular. **K~lauf** m cycle; (Med) circulation. **k~rund** a circular. **K~säge** f circular saw. **K~verkehr** m [traffic] roundabout, (Amer) traffic circle

Krem f -,-s & m -s,-e cream

Krematorium nt -s,-ien crematorium

Krempe f -,-n [hat] brim

Krempel m -s (fam) junk

krempeln vt turn, nach oben up)

Kren m -[e]s (Aust) horseradish

krepieren vi (sein) explode; (sl: sterben) die

Krepp m -s,-s & -e crêpe

Krepppapier (Kreppapier) nt crêpe paper

Kresse f -,-n cress; (Kapuziner-) nasturtium

Kreta nt -s Crete

Kreuz nt -es,-e cross; (Kreuzung) intersection; (Mus) sharp; (Kartenspiel) clubs pl; (Anat) small of the back; **über K~** crosswise; **das K~ schlagen** cross oneself. **k~** adv **k~ und quer** in all directions. **k~en** vt cross; **sich k~en** cross; (Straßen:) intersect; (Meinungen:) clash □ vi (haben/sein) cruise; (Segelschiff:) tack. **K~er** m -s,- cruiser. **K~fahrt** f (Naut) cruise; (K~zug) crusade. **K~feuer** nt crossfire. **K~gang** m cloister

kreuzig|en vt crucify. **K~ung** f -,-en crucifixion

Kreuz|otter f adder, common viper. **K~ung** f -,-en intersection; (Straßen:) crossroads sg; (Hybride) cross. **K~verhör** nt crossexamination; **ins K~verhör nehmen** cross-examine. **K~weg** m crossroads sg; (Relig) Way of the Cross. **K~weise** adv crosswise. **K~worträtsel** nt crossword [puzzle]. **K~zug** m crusade

kribbel|ig a (fam) edgy. **k~n** vi (haben) tingle; (kitzeln) tickle

kriech|en vi (sein) crawl; (fig) grovel (vor + dat to). **k~erisch** a grovelling. **K~spur** f (Auto) crawler lane. **K~tier** nt reptile

Krieg m -[e]s,-e war; **K~ führen** wage war (gegen on)

kriegen vt (fam) get; **ein Kind k~** have a baby

Krieger|denkmal nt war memorial. **k~isch** a warlike; (militärisch) military

kriegs|beschädigt a war-disabled. **K~dienstverweigerer** m -s,- conscientious objector. **K~gefangene(r)** m prisoner of war. **K~gefangenschaft** f captivity. **K~gericht** nt court martial. **K~list** f stratagem. **K~rat** m council of war. **K~recht** nt martial law. **K~schiff** nt warship. **K~verbrechen** nt war crime

Krimi m -s,-s (fam) crime story/film. **K~nalität** f -crime; (Vorkommen) crime rate. **K~nalpolizei** f criminal investigation department. **K~nalroman** m crime novel. **K~nell** a criminal. **K~nelle(r)** m criminal

kringeln (sich) vr curl [up]; (vor Lachen) fall about

Kripo f - = **Kriminalpolizei**

Krippe f -,-n manger; (Weihnachts-) crib; (Kinder-) crèche. **K~nspiel** nt Nativity play

Krise f -,-n crisis

Kristall[1] nt -s (Glas) crystal; (geschliffen) cut glass

Kristall[2] m -s,-e crystal. **k~isieren** vi/r (haben) [sich] k~isieren crystallize

Kriterium nt -s,-ien criterion

Kritik f -,-en criticism; (Rezension) review; **unter aller K~** (fam) abysmal

Kriti|ker m -s,- critic; (Rezensent) reviewer. **k~sch** a critical, adv -ly. **k~sieren** vt criticize; review

kritteln vi (haben) find fault (**an** + acc with)

kritzeln vt/i (haben) scribble

Krokette f -,-n (Culin) croquette

Krokodil nt -s,-e crocodile

Krokus m -,-[se] crocus

Krone f -,-n crown; (Baum-) top

krönen vt crown

Kron|leuchter m chandelier. **K~prinz** m crown prince

Krönung f -,-en coronation; (fig: Höhepunkt) crowning event/(Leistung) achievement

Kropf m -[e]s,ͤe (Zool) crop; (Med) goitre

Kröte f -,-n toad

Krücke f -,-n crutch; (Stock-) handle; **an K~n** on crutches

Krug m -[e]s,ͤe jug; (Bier-) tankard

Krume f -,-n soft part [of loaf]; (Krümel) crumb; (Acker-) topsoil

Krümel m -s,- crumb. **k~ig** a crumbly. **k~n** vt crumble □ vi (haben) be crumbly; (Person:) drop crumbs

krumm a crooked; (gebogen) curved; (verbogen) bent; **etw k~ nehmen** (fam) take sth amiss. **k~beinig** a bow-legged

krümmen vt bend; crook (Finger); **sich k~** bend; (sich winden) writhe; (vor Schmerzen/Lachen) double up

krummnehmen† vt sep (NEW) **krumm nehmen**, s. **krumm**

Krümmung f -,-en bend; (Kurve) curve

Krüppel m -s,- cripple

Kruste f -,-n crust; (Schorf) scab

Kruzifix nt -es,-e crucifix

Krypta /ˈkrypta/ f -,-ten crypt

Kuba nt -s Cuba. **k~nisch** a Cuban

Kübel m -s,- tub; (Eimer) bucket; (Techn) skip

Kubik- pref cubic. **K~meter** m & nt cubic metre

Küche f -,-n kitchen; (Kochkunst) cooking; **kalte/warme K~** cold/hot food; **französische K~** French cuisine

Kuchen m -s,- cake

Küchen|herd m cooker, stove. **K~maschine** f food processor, mixer. **K~schabe** f -,-n cockroach. **K~zettel** m menu

Kuckuck m -s,-e cuckoo; **zum K~!** (fam) hang it! **K~suhr** f cuckoo clock

Kufe f -,-n [sledge] runner

Kugel f -,-n ball; (Geom) sphere; (Gewehr-) bullet; (Sport) shot. **k~förmig** a spherical. **K~lager** nt ball-bearing. **k~n** vt/i (haben) roll; **sich k~n** roll/(vor Lachen) fall about. **k~rund** a spherical; (fam: dick) tubby. **K~schreiber** m -s,- ballpoint [pen]. **k~sicher** a bullet-proof. **k~stoßen** nt shot-putting

Kuh f -,ͤe cow

kühl a cool, adv -ly; (kalt) chilly. **K~box** f -,-en cool-box. **K~e** f - coolness; chilliness. **k~en** vt cool; refrigerate (Lebensmittel); chill (Wein). **K~er** m -s,- icebucket; (Auto) radiator. **K~erhaube** f bonnet, (Amer) hood. **K~fach** nt frozen-food compartment. **K~raum** m cold store. **K~schrank** m refrigerator. **K~truhe** f freezer. **K~ung** f - cooling; (Frische) coolness. **K~wasser** nt [radiator] water

Kuhmilch f cow's milk

kühn a bold, adv -ly; (wagemutig) daring. **K~heit** f - boldness

Kuhstall m cowshed

Küken nt -s,- chick; (Enten-) duckling

Kukuruz m -[es] (Aust) maize

kulant a obliging

Kuli m -s,- (fam: Kugelschreiber) ballpoint [pen], Biro (P)

kulinarisch a culinary

Kulissen fpl (Theat) scenery sg; (seitlich) wings; **hinter den K~** (fig) behind the scenes

kullern vt/i (sein) (fam) roll
Kult m -[e]s,-e cult
kultivier|en vt cultivate. **k~t** a
cultured
Kultur f -,-en culture; K~en
plantations. K~beutel m
toiletbag. k~ell a cultural.
K~film m documentary film
Kultusminister m Minister of
Education and Arts
Kümmel m -s caraway; (Getränk)
kümmel
Kummer m -s sorrow, grief;
(Sorge) worry; (Ärger) trouble
kümmer|lich a puny; (dürftig)
meagre; (armselig) wretched.
k~n vt concern; sich k~n um
look after; (sich befassen) concern
oneself with; (beachten) take notice of; ich werde mich darum
k~n I shall see to it; k~e dich
um deine eigenen Angele-
genheiten! mind your own business!
kummervoll a sorrowful
Kumpel m -s,- (fam) mate
Kunde m -n,-n customer. K~n-
dienst m [after-sales] service
Kund|gebung f -,-en (Pol) rally.
k~ig a knowledgeable; (sach-)
expert
kündig|en vt cancel (Vertrag);
give notice of withdrawal for
(Geld); give notice to quit
(Wohnung); seine Stellung
k~en give [in one's] notice □ vi
(haben) give [in one's] notice;
jdm k~en give s.o. notice of [his
dismissal/(Vermieter:) to quit].
K~ung f -,-en cancellation; notice [of withdrawal/dismissal/to
quit]; (Entlassung) dismissal.
K~ungsfrist f period of notice
Kund|in f -,-nen [woman] cus-
tomer. K~machung f -,-en
(Aust) [public] notice. K~schaft
f - clientele, customers pl
künftig a future □ adv in future
Kunst f -,e art; (Können) skill.
K~dünger m artificial fertilizer.
K~faser f synthetic fibre.

k~fertig a skilful. K~fertig-
keit f skill. K~galerie f art gallery. k~gerecht a expert, adv -ly.
K~geschichte f history of art.
K~gewerbe nt arts and crafts pl.
K~griff m trick. K~händler m
art dealer
Künstler m -s,- artist; (Könner)
master. K~in f -,-nen [woman]
artist. k~isch a artistic, adv
-ally. K~name m pseudonym;
(Theat) stage name
künstlich a artificial, adv -ly
kunst|los a simple. K~maler m
painter. K~stoff m plastic.
K~stopfen nt invisible mending. K~stück nt trick; (große
Leistung) feat. k~voll a artistic;
(geschickt) skilful, adv -ly; (kompliziert) elaborate, adv -ly.
K~werk nt work of art
kunterbunt a multicoloured; (gemischt) mixed □ adv k~ durcheinander higgledy-piggledy
Kupfer nt -s copper. k~n a cop-
per
kupieren vt crop
Kupon /ku'põ:/ m -s,-s voucher;
(Zins-) coupon; (Stoff-) length
Kuppe f -,-n [rounded] top;
(Finger-) end, tip
Kuppel f -,-n dome
kupp|eln vt couple (an + acc) □
□ vi (haben) (Auto) operate the
clutch. K~lung f -,-en coupling;
(Auto) clutch
Kur f -,-en course of treatment;
(im Kurort) cure
Kür f -,-en (Sport) free exercise;
(Eislauf) free programme
Kurbel f -,-n crank. k~n vt wind
(nach oben/unten up/down).
K~welle f crankshaft
Kürbis m -ses,-se pumpkin;
(Flaschen-) marrow
Kurgast m health-resort visitor
Kurier m -s,-e courier
kurieren vt cure
kurios a curious, odd. K~ität f
-,-en oddness; (Objekt) curiosity;
(Kunst) curio

Kur|ort m health resort; (*Bade-ort*) spa. **K∼pfuscher** m quack

Kurs m -es,-e course; (*Aktien-*) price. **K∼buch** nt timetable

kursieren vi (haben) circulate

K∼schrift f italics pl

Kursus m -,**Kurse** course

Kurswagen m through carriage

Kurtaxe f visitors' tax

Kurve f -,-n curve; (*Straßen-*) bend

kurz a (*kürzer, kürzest*) short; (*knapp*) brief; (*rasch*) quick; (*schroff*) curt; **k∼e Hosen** shorts; **vor k∼em** a short time ago; **seit k∼em** lately; **binnen k∼em** shortly; **den Kürzeren** (**kürzeren**) **ziehen** get the worst of it □ adv briefly; quickly; curtly; **k∼ vor/nach** a little way/(*zeitlich*) shortly before/after; **sich k∼ fassen** be brief; **k∼ und gut** in short; **über k∼ oder lang** sooner or later; **zu k∼ kommen** get less than one's fair share. **k∼arbeit** f short-time working. **k∼ärmelig** a short-sleeved. **k∼atmig** a **k∼atmig sein** be short of breath

Kürze f - shortness; (*Knappheit*) brevity; **in K∼** shortly. **k∼n** vt shorten; (*verringern*) cut

kurz|erhand adv without further ado. **k∼fristig** a short-term □ adv at short notice. **K∼geschichte** f short story. **k∼lebig** a short-lived

kürzlich adv recently

Kurz|meldung f newsflash. **K∼nachrichten** fpl news headlines. **K∼schluss** (**K∼schluß**) m short circuit; (*fig*) brainstorm. **K∼schrift** f shorthand. **k∼sichtig** a short-sighted. **K∼sichtigkeit** f - short-sightedness. **K∼streckenrakete** f short-range missile. **k∼um** adv in short

Kürzung f -,-en shortening; (*Verringerung*) cut (*gen*)

Kurz|waren fpl haberdashery sg, (*Amer*) notions. **k∼weilig** a amusing. **K∼welle** f short wave

kuscheln (**sich**) vr snuggle (**an** + acc up to)

Kusine f -,-n [female] cousin

Kuss m -es,ⁿe (**Kuß** m -sses,-sse) kiss

küssen vt/i (haben) kiss; **sich k∼** kiss

Küste f -,-n coast. **K∼nwache** f **K∼nwacht** f coastguard

Küster m -s,- verger

Kustos m -,-oden /-'to:/ curator

Kutsche f -,-n [horse-drawn] carriage/(*geschlossen*) coach. **K∼er** m -s,- coachman, driver. **k∼ieren** vt/i (haben) drive

Kutte f -,-n (*Relig*) habit

Kutter m -s,- (*Naut*) cutter

Kuvert /ku've:ɐ/ nt -s,-s envelope

KZ /ka:'tset/ nt -[s],-[s] concentration camp

L

labil a unstable

Labor nt -s,-s & -e laboratory. **L∼ant(in)** m -en,-en (f -,-nen) laboratory assistant. **L∼atorium** nt -s,-ien laboratory

Labyrinth nt -[e]s,-e maze, labyrinth

Lache f -,-n puddle; (*Blut-*) pool

lächeln vi (haben) smile. **L∼** nt -s smile. **l∼d** a smiling

lachen vi (haben) laugh. **L∼** nt -s laugh; (*Gelächter*) laughter

lächerlich a ridiculous, adv -ly; **sich l∼ machen** make a fool of oneself. **L∼keit** f -,-en ridiculousness; (*Kleinigkeit*) triviality

lachhaft a laughable

Lachs m -es,-e salmon. **l∼farben**, **l∼rosa** a salmon-pink

Lack m -[e]s,-e varnish; (*Japan-*) lacquer; (*Auto*) paint. **l∼en** vt varnish. **l∼ieren** vt varnish.

(spritzen) spray. **L~schuhe** mpl patent-leather shoes

Lade f -,-n drawer

laden† vt load; *(Electr)* charge; *(Jur: vor-)* summons

Laden m -s,: shop, *(Amer)* store; *(Fenster-)* shutter. **L~dieb** m shop-lifter. **L~diebstahl** m shoplifting. **L~schluss** (**L~schluß**) m [shop] closing-time. **L~tisch** m counter

Laderaum m *(Naut)* hold

lädieren vt damage

Ladung f -,-en load; *(Naut, Aviat)* cargo; *(elektrische, Spreng-)* charge; *(Jur: Vor-)* summons

Lage f -,-n position; *(Situation)* situation; *(Schicht)* layer; *(fam: Runde)* round; **nicht in der L~ sein** to be in a position *(zu* to)

Lager nt -s,- camp; *(L~haus)* warehouse; *(Vorrat)* stock; *(Techn)* bearing; *(Erz-, Ruhe-)* bed; *(eines Tieres)* lair; **[nicht] auf L~** [not] in stock. **L~haus** nt warehouse. **l~n** vt store; *(legen)* lay; **sich l~n** settle; *(sich legen)* lie down □ vi *(haben)* camp; *(liegen)* ·lie; *(Waren-)* be stored. **L~raum** m store-room. **L~stätte** f *(Geol)* deposit. **L~ung** f - storage

Lagune f -,-n lagoon

lahm a lame; **l~ legen** *(fig)* paralyse. **l~en** vi *(haben)* be lame

lähmen vt paralyse

lahmlegen vt sep (NEW) **lahm legen,** s. **lahm**

Lähmung f -,-en paralysis

Laib m -[e]s,-e loaf

Laich m -[e]s *(Zool)* spawn. **l~en** vi *(haben)* spawn

Laie m -n,-n layman; *(Theat)* amateur. **l~nhaft** a amateurish. **L~nprediger** m lay preacher

Lake f - brine

Laken nt -s,- sheet

lakonisch a laconic, adv -ally

Lakritze f - liquorice

lallen vt/i *(haben)* mumble; *(Baby:)* babble

Lametta nt -s tinsel

Lamm nt -[e]s,:er lamb

Lampe f -,-n lamp; *(Decken-, Wand-)* light; *(Glüh-)* bulb. **L~nfieber** nt stage fright. **L~nschirm** m lampshade

Lampion /lamˈpjoːn/ m -s,-s Chinese lantern

lancieren /lãˈsiːrən/ vt *(Comm)* launch

Land nt -[e]s,:er country; *(Fest-)* land; *(Bundes-)* state, Land; *(Aust)* province; **Stück L~** piece of land; **auf dem L~e** in the country; **an L~ gehen** *(Naut)* go ashore; **hier zu L~e** = **hierzulande. L~arbeiter** m agricultural worker. **L~ebahn** f runway. **l~einwärts** adv inland. **l~en** vt/i *(sein)* land; *(fam: gelangen)* end up

Ländereien pl estates

Länderspiel nt international

Landesteg m landing-stage

Landesverrat m treason

Land|karte f map. **l~läufig** a popular

ländlich a rural

Land|maschinen fpl agricultural machinery sg. **L~schaft** f -,-en scenery; *(Geog, Kunst)* landscape; *(Gegend)* country[side]. **l~schaftlich** a scenic; *(regional)* regional. **L~smann** m *(pl* -leute) fellow countryman, compatriot. **L~männin** f -,-nen fellow countrywoman. **L~straße** f country road; *(Admin)* ≈ B road. **L~streicher** m -s,- tramp. **L~tag** m state/*(Aust)* provincial parliament

Landung f -,-en landing. **L~sbrücke** f landing-stage

Land|vermesser m -s,- surveyor. **L~weg** m country lane; **auf dem L~weg** overland. **L~wirt** m farmer. **L~wirtschaft** f agriculture; *(Hof)* farm. **l~wirtschaftlich** a agricultural

lang[1] *adv & prep* (+ *preceding acc or preceding* an + *dat*) along; **den od am Fluss l~** along the river

lang[2] *a* (**länger, längst**) long; (*groß*) tall; **seit l~em** for a long time □ *adv* **eine Stunde/Woche l~** for an hour/a week; **mein Leben l~** all my life. **l~ärmelig** *a* long-sleeved. **l~atmig** *a* long-winded. **l~e** *adv* a long time; (*schlafen*) late; **wie/zu l~e** how/too long; **schon l~e** [for] a long time; (*zurückliegend*) a long time ago; **so l~e wie möglich** as possible; **l~e nicht** not for a long time; (*bei weitem nicht*) nowhere near

Länge *f* -,-n length; (*Geog*) longitude; **der L~nach** lengthways; (*liegen, fallen*) full length

langen *vt* hand (*dat* to) □ *vi* (*haben*) reach (**an etw** *acc* sth; **nach** for); (*genügen*) be enough

Längengrad *m* degree of longitude. **L~enmaß** *nt* linear measure. **l~ere** *a* & *adv* longer; (*längere Zeit*) [for] some time

Langeweile *f* - boredom; **l~ haben** be bored

lang|fristig *a* long-term; (*Vorhersage*) long-range. **l~jäh-rig** *a* long-standing; (*Erfahrung*) long. **l~lebig** *a* long-lived

länglich *a* oblong; **l~ rund** oval

langmütig *a* long-suffering

längs *adv & prep* (+ *gen/dat*) along; (*der Länge nach*) lengthways

lang|sam *a* slow, *adv* -ly. **L~samkeit** *f* - slowness. **L~schläfer(in)** *m(f)* (*fam*) late riser. **L~schrift** *f* longhand

längst *adv* [**schon**] l~ for a long time; (*zurückliegend*) a long time ago; **l~ nicht** nowhere near

Lang|strecken- *pref* long-distance; (*Mil, Aviat*) long-range. **l~weilen** *vt* bore; **sich l~weilen** be bored. **l~weilig** *a* boring, *adv* -ly. **L~welle** *f* long wave. **l~wierig** *a* lengthy

Lanze *f* -,-n lance

Lappalie /la'pa:liə/ *f* -,-n trifle

Lappen *m* -s,- cloth; (*Anat*) lobe

läppisch *a* silly

Lapsus *m* -,- slip

Lärche *f* -,-n larch

Lärm *m* -s noise. **l~en** *vi* (*haben*) make a noise. **l~end** *a* noisy

Larve /'larfə/ *f* -,-n larva; (*Maske*) mask

lasch *a* listless; (*schlaff*) limp; (*fade*) insipid

Lasche *f* -,-n tab; (*Verschluss-lappen*) flap; (*Zunge*) tongue

Laser /'le:-, 'la:zɐ/ *m* -s,- laser

lassen† *vt* leave; (*zulassen*) let; **jdn etw l~** let s.o. keep sth; **sein Leben l~** lose one's life; **etw [sein od bleiben] l~** not do sth; (*aufhören*) stop [doing] sth; **lass das!** stop it! **jdn schlafen/gewinnen l~** let s.o. sleep/win; **jdn warten l~** keep s.o. waiting; **etw machen/reparieren l~** have sth done/repaired; **etw verschwinden l~** make sth disappear; **sich [leicht] biegen/öffnen l~** bend/open [easily]; **sich gut waschen l~** wash well; **es lässt sich nicht leugnen** it is undeniable; **lass uns gehen!** let's go!

lässig *a* casual, *adv* -ly. **L~keit** *f* - casualness

Lasso *nt* -s,-s lasso

Last *f* -,-en load; (*Gewicht*) weight; (*fig*) burden; **L~en** charges; (*Steuern*) taxes; **jdm zur L~ fallen** be a burden on s.o. **L~auto** *nt* lorry. **l~en** *vi* (*haben*) weigh heavily; (*liegen*) rest (**auf** + *dat* on). **L~enaufzug** *m* goods lift

Laster[1] *m* -s,- (*fam*) lorry, (*Amer*) truck

Laster[2] *nt* -s,- vice. **l~haft** *a* depraved; (*zügellos*) dissolute

läster|lich *a* blasphemous. **l~n** *vt* blaspheme □ *vi* (*haben*) make disparaging remarks (**über** + *acc* about). **L~ung** *f* -,-en blasphemy

lästig *a* troublesome; **l~ sein/ werden** be/become a nuisance

Last|kahn *m* barge. **L~[kraft]wagen** *m* lorry, (*Amer*) truck. **L~zug** *m* lorry with trailer[s].

Latein *nt* -[s] Latin. **L~amerika** *nt* Latin America. **l~isch** *a* Latin

latent *a* latent

Laterne *f* -,-n lantern; (*Straßen-*) street lamp. **L~npfahl** *m* lamp-post

latschen *vi* (*sein*) (*fam*) traipse; (*schlurfen*) shuffle

Latte *f* -,-n slat; (*Tor-, Hoch-sprung-*) bar

Latz *m* -es,⁻e bib

Lätzchen *nt* -s,- [baby's] bib

Latzhose *f* dungarees *pl*

lau *a* lukewarm; (*mild*) mild

Laub *nt* -[e]s leaves *pl*; (*L~werk*) foliage. **L~baum** *m* deciduous tree

Laube *f* -,-n summer-house; (*gewachsen*) arbour. **L~ngang** *m* pergola; (*Archit*) arcades *pl*

Laub|säge *f* fretsaw. **L~wald** *m* deciduous forest

Lauch *m* -[e]s leeks *pl*

Lauer *f* **auf der L~ liegen** lie in wait. **l~n** *vi* (*haben*) lurk; **l~n auf** (+ *acc*) lie in wait for

Lauf *m* -[e]s, Läufe *m,pl* (*Laufen*) running; (*Verlauf*) course; (*Wett-*) race; (*Sport: Durchgang*) heat; (*Gewehr-*) barrel; **im L~[e]** (+ *gen*) in the course of. **L~bahn** *f* career. **l~en†** *vi* (*sein*) run; (*zu Fuß gehen*) walk; (*gelten*) be valid; **Ski/Schlittschuh l~en** ski/ skate; **jdn l~en lassen** (*fam*) let s.o. go. **l~end** *a* running; (*gegenwärtig*) current; (*regelmäßig*) regular; **l~ende Nummer** serial number; **auf dem L~enden (l~enden) sein/jdn auf dem L~enden (l~enden) halten** be/keep s.o. up to date □ *adv* continually. **l~enlassen†** *vt* sep (NEW) **l~en lassen**, *s.* laufen

Läufer *m* -s,- (*Person, Teppich*) runner; (*Schach*) bishop

Lauf|gitter *nt* play-pen. **L~masche** *f* ladder. **L~rolle** *f* castor. **L~schritt** *m* **im L~schritt** at a run; (*Mil*) at the double. **L~stall** *m* play-pen. **L~zettel** *m* circular

Lauge *f* -,-n soapy water

Laun|e *f* -,-n mood; (*Einfall*) whim; **guter L~e sein**, **gute L~e haben** be in a good mood. **l~enhaft** *a* capricious. **l~isch** *a* moody

Laus *f* -,Läuse louse; (*Blatt-*) greenfly. **L~bub** *m* (*fam*) rascal

lauschen *vi* (*haben*) listen; (*heimlich*) eavesdrop

lausig *a* (*fam*) lousy □ *adv* terribly

laut *a* loud, *adv* -ly; (*geräuschvoll*) noisy, *adv* -ily; **l~ lesen** read aloud; **l~er stellen** turn up □ *prep* (+ *gen/dat*) according to. **L~** *m* -es,-e sound

Laute *f* -,-n (*Mus*) lute

lauten *vi* (*haben*) (*Text:*) run, read; **auf jds Namen l~** be in s.o.'s name

läuten *vt/i* (*haben*) ring

lauter *a* pure; (*ehrlich*) honest; (*Wahrheit*) plain □ *a inv* sheer; (*nichts als*) nothing but. **L~keit** *f* - integrity

läutern *vt* purify

laut|hals *adv* at the top of one's voice, (*lachen*) out loud. **l~los** *a* silent, *adv* -ly; (*Stille*) hushed. **L~schrift** *f* phonetics *pl*. **L~sprecher** *m* loudspeaker. **l~stark** *a* vociferous, *adv* -ly. **L~stärke** *f* volume

lauwarm *a* lukewarm

Lava *f* -,-ven lava

Lavendel *m* -s lavender

lavieren *vi* (*haben*) manœuvre

Lawine *f* -,-n avalanche

lax *a* lax. **L~heit** *f* - laxity

Lazarett *nt* -[e]s,-e military hospital

leasen /ˈliːsən/ *vt* rent

Lebehoch nt cheer

leben vt/i (haben) live (von on); **leb wohl!** farewell! **L~** nt -s, - life, (Treiben) bustle; **am L~** alive. **l~d** a living

lebendig a live; (lebhaft) lively; (anschaulich) vivid, adv -ly; **l~ sein** be alive. **L~keit** f - liveliness; vividness

Lebens|abend m old age. **L~alter** nt age. **L~art** f manners pl. **l~fähig** a viable. **L~gefahr** f mortal danger; **in L~gefahr** in mortal danger; (Patient) critically ill. **l~gefährlich** a extremely dangerous; (Verletzung) critical □ adv critically. **L~größe** f in L~größe life-sized. **L~haltungskosten** pl cost of living sg. **l~lang** a lifelong. **l~länglich** a life □ adv for life. **L~lauf** m curriculum vitae. **L~mittel** ntpl food sg. **L~mittelgeschäft** nt food shop. **L~mittelhändler** m grocer. **l~notwendig** a vital. **L~retter** m rescuer; (beim Schwimmen) life-guard. **L~standard** m standard of living. **L~unterhalt** m livelihood; **seinen L~unterhalt verdienen** earn one's living. **L~versicherung** f life assurance. **L~wandel** m conduct. **l~wichtig** a vital. **L~zeichen** nt sign of life. **L~zeit** f **auf L~zeit** for life

Leber f -,-n liver. **L~fleck** m mole. **L~wurst** f liver sausage

Lebe|wesen nt living being. **L~wohl** nt -s,-s & -e farewell

leb|haft a lively; (Farbe) vivid. **L~haftigkeit** f - liveliness. **L~kuchen** m gingerbread. **l~los** a lifeless. **L~tag** m **mein/dein L~tag** all my/your life. **L~zeiten** fpl **zu jds L~zeiten** in s.o.'s lifetime

leck a leaking. **L~** nt -s,-s leak. **l~en¹** vi (haben) leak

lecken² vi (haben) lick

lecker a tasty. **L~bissen** m delicacy. **L~ei** f -,-en sweet

Leder nt -s,- leather. **l~n** a leathery; (wie Leder) leathery

ledig a single. **l~lich** adv merely

Lee f & nt - **nach Lee** (Naut) to leeward

leer a empty; (unbesetzt) vacant; **l~ laufen** (Auto) idle. **L~e** f - emptiness; (leerer Raum) void. **l~en** vt empty; **sich l~en** empty. **L~lauf** m (Auto) neutral. **L~ung** f -,-en (Post) collection

legal a legal, adv -ly. **l~isieren** vt legalize. **L~ität** f - legality

Legas|thenie f - dyslexia **L~theniker** m -s,- dyslexic

legen vt put; (hin-, ver-) lay; (Haare) set; **Eier l~** lay eggs; **sich l~** lie down; (Staub:) settle; (nachlassen) subside

legendär a legendary

Legende f -,-n legend

leger /leˈʒɛːɐ̯/ a casual, adv -ly

legieren vt alloy; (Culin) thicken. **L~ung** f -,-en alloy

Legion f -,-en legion

Legislative f - legislature

legitim a legitimate, adv -ly. **l~ieren (sich)** vr prove one's identity. **L~ität** f - legitimacy

Lehm m -s clay. **l~ig** a clayey

Lehne f -,-n (Rücken-) back; (Arm-) arm. **l~en** vt lean (an + acc against); **sich l~en** lean (an + acc against) □ vi (haben) be leaning (an + acc against). **L~sessel**, **L~stuhl** m armchair

Lehr|buch nt textbook. **L~e** f -,-n apprenticeship; (Anschauung) doctrine; (Theorie) theory; (Wissenschaft) science; (Ratschlag) advice; (Erfahrung) lesson; **jdm eine L~e erteilen** (fig) teach s.o. a lesson. **l~en** vt/i (haben) teach. **L~er** m -s,- teacher; (Fahr-, Ski-) instructor. **L~erin** f -,-nen teacher. **L~erzimmer** nt staff-room. **L~fach** nt (Sch) subject. **L~gang** m course.

L~kraft f teacher. L~ling m -s,-e apprentice; (Auszubildender) trainee. L~plan m syllabus. l~reich a instructive. L~stelle f apprenticeship. L~stuhl m (Univ) chair. L~zeit f apprenticeship

Leib m -es,-er body; (Bauch) belly. L~eserziehung f (Sch) physical education. L~eskraft f aus L~eskräften as hard/(schreien) loud as one can. L~gericht nt favourite dish. L~haftig a der l~haftige Satan the devil incarnate □ adv in the flesh. l~lich a physical; (blutsverwandt) real, natural. L~speise f = L~gericht. L~wache f (coll) bodyguard. L~wächter m bodyguard. L~wäsche f underwear

Leiche f -,-n [dead] body; corpse. L~nbegängnis nt -ses,-se funeral. L~nbestatter m -s,- undertaker. l~nblass (l~nblaß) a deathly pale. L~nhalle f mortuary. L~nwagen m hearse. L~nzug m funeral procession, cortège

Leichnam m -s,-e [dead] body

leicht a light, adv -ly; (Stoff, Anzug) lightweight; (gering) slight, adv -ly; (mühelos) easy, adv -ily; jdm l~ fallen be easy for s.o.; etw l~ machen make sth easy (dat for); es sich (dat) l~ machen take the easy way out; etw l~ nehmen (fig) take sth lightly. L~athletik f [track and field] athletics sg. l~fallen† vi sep (sein) (NEW) = l~ fallen, s. leicht. l~fertig a thoughtless, adv -ly; (vorschnell) rash, adv -ly; (frivol) frivolous, adv -ly. L~gewicht nt (Boxen) lightweight. l~gläubig a credulous. l~hin adv casually. L~igkeit f - lightness; (Mühelosigkeit) ease; (L~sein) easiness; mit L~igkeit with ease. l~lebig a happy-go-lucky. l~machen vt sep (NEW) = l~ machen, s. leicht. l~nehmen†

vt sep (NEW) l~ nehmen, s. leicht. L~sinn m carelessness; recklessness; (Frivolität) frivolity. l~sinnig a careless, adv -ly; (unvorsichtig) reckless, adv -ly; (frivol) frivolous, adv -ly

Leid nt -[e]s sorrow, grief; (Böses) harm; es tut mir L~ I am sorry; er tut mir L~ I feel sorry for him; jdm etw zu L~e tun = jdm etw zuleide tun, s. zuleide. l~ a jdn/etw l~ sein/werden be/get tired of s.o./sth; jdm l~ tun (NEW) jdm L~ tun, s. Leid

Leide|form f passive. l~n† vt/i (haben) suffer (an + dat from); jdn [gut] l~n können like s.o.; jdn/etw nicht l~n können dislike s.o./sth. L~n nt -s,- suffering; (Med) complaint; (Krankheit) disease. l~nd a suffering; l~nd sein be in poor health. L~nschaft f -,-en passion. l~nschaftlich a passionate, adv -ly

leid|er adv unfortunately; l~er ja/nicht I'm afraid so/not. l~ig a wretched. l~lich a tolerable, adv -bly. L~tragende(r) m/f person who suffers; (Trauernde) mourner. L~wesen nt zu meinem L~wesen to my regret

Leier f -,-n die alte L~ (fam) the same old story. L~kasten m barrel-organ. l~n vt/i (haben) wind; (herunter-) drone out

Leih|bibliothek, L~bücherei f lending library. l~en† vt (lent) lend; sich (dat) etw l~en borrow sth. L~gabe f loan. L~gebühr f rental; (für Bücher) lending charge. L~haus nt pawnshop. L~wagen m hire-car. l~weise adv on loan

Leim m -s glue. l~en vt glue

Leine f -,-n rope; (Wäsche-) line; (Hunde-) lead, leash

Leinen nt -s linen. l~en a linen. L~tuch nt sheet. L~wand f linen; (Kunst) canvas; (Film-) screen

leise *a* quiet, *adv* -ly; ⟨*Stimme, Musik, Berührung*⟩ soft, *adv* -ly; ⟨*schwach*⟩ faint, *adv* -ly; ⟨*leicht*⟩ light, *adv* -ly; **l~r stellen** turn down

Leiste *f* -,-n strip; ⟨*Holz-*⟩ batten; ⟨*Zier-*⟩ moulding; ⟨*Anat*⟩ groin

Leisten *m* -s,- [shoemaker's] last

leist|en *vt* achieve, accomplish; **sich** (*dat*) **etw l~en** treat oneself to sth; ⟨*fam: anstellen*⟩ get up to sth; **ich kann es mir nicht l~en** I can't afford it. **L~ung** *f* -,-en achievement; ⟨*Sport, Techn*⟩ performance; ⟨*Produktion*⟩ output; ⟨*Zahlung*⟩ payment. **l~ungs-fähig** *a* efficient. **L~ungsfähig-keit** *f* efficiency

Leit|artikel *m* leader, editorial. **L~bild** *nt* (*fig*) model. **l~en** *vt* run, manage; ⟨*an-/hinführen*⟩ lead; ⟨*Mus, Techn, Phys*⟩ conduct; ⟨*lenken, schicken*⟩ direct. **l~end** *a* leading; ⟨*Posten*⟩ executive

Leiter[1] *f* -,-n ladder

Leit|er[2] *m* -s,- director; ⟨*Comm*⟩ manager; ⟨*Führer*⟩ leader; ⟨*Sch*⟩ head; ⟨*Mus, Phys*⟩ conductor. **L~erin** *f* -,-nen director; manageress; leader; head. **L~faden** *m* manual. **L~kegel** *m* [traffic] cone. **L~planke** *f* crash barrier. **L~spruch** *m* motto. **L~ung** *f* -,-en ⟨*Führung*⟩ direction; ⟨*Comm*⟩ management; ⟨*Aufsicht*⟩ control; ⟨*Electr: Schnur*⟩ lead, flex; ⟨*Kabel*⟩ cable; ⟨*Telefon-*⟩ line; ⟨*Rohr-*⟩ pipe; ⟨*Haupt-*⟩ main. **L~ungswasser** *nt* tap water

Lektion /-'tsĭo:n/ *f* -,-en lesson

Lekt|or *m* -s,-en /-'to:rən/, **L~o-rin** *f* -,-nen ⟨*Univ*⟩ assistant lecturer; ⟨*Verlags-*⟩ editor. **L~üre** *f* -,-n reading matter; ⟨*Lesen*⟩ reading

Lende *f* -,-n loin

lenk|bar *a* steerable; ⟨*fügsam*⟩ tractable. **l~en** *vt* guide; ⟨*steuern*⟩ steer; ⟨*Aust*⟩ drive; ⟨*regeln*⟩ control; **jds Aufmerksamkeit auf sich** (*acc*) **l~en** attract s.o.'s

attention. **L~er** *m* -s,- driver; ⟨*L~stange*⟩ handlebars *pl*. **L~rad** *nt* steering-wheel. **L~stange** *f* handlebars *pl*. **L~ung** *f* - steering

Leopard *m* -en,-en leopard

Lepra *f* - leprosy

Lerche *f* -,-n lark

lernen *vt/i* ⟨*haben*⟩ learn; ⟨*für die Schule*⟩ study; **schwimmen l~** learn to swim

lesbar *a* readable; ⟨*leserlich*⟩ legible

Lesb|ierin /'lɛsbĭərɪn/ *f* -,-nen lesbian. **l~isch** *a* lesbian

Lese *f* - harvest. **L~buch** *nt* reader. **l~n†** *vt/i* ⟨*haben*⟩ read; ⟨*Univ*⟩ lecture □ *vt* pick, gather. **L~n** *nt* -s reading. **L~r(in)** *m* -s,- (*f* -,-nen) reader. **L~ratte** *f* (*fam*) bookworm. **l~rlich** *a* legible, *adv* -bly. **L~zeichen** *nt* bookmark

Lesung *f* -,-en reading

lethargisch *a* lethargic, *adv* -ally

Lettland *nt* -s Latvia

letzt|e(r,s) *a* last; ⟨*neueste*⟩ latest; **in l~er Zeit** recently; **l~en En-des** in the end; **er kam als L~er (l~er)** he arrived last. **l~emal** *adv* **das l~emal/zum l~en-mal** (*NEW*) **das l~e Mal/zum l~en Mal,** *s.* **Mal**[1]. **l~ens** *adv* recently; ⟨*zuletzt*⟩ lastly. **l~ere(r,s)** *a* the latter; **der/die/das L~ere (l~ere)** the latter

Leucht|e *f* -,-n light. **l~en** *vi* ⟨*haben*⟩ shine. **l~end** *a* shining. **L~er** *m* -s,- candlestick. **L~feuer** *nt* beacon. **L~kugel** *f* flare. **L~rakete** *f* flare. **L~reklame** *f* neon sign. **L~[stoff]röhre** *f* fluorescent tube. **L~turm** *m* lighthouse. **L~zifferblatt** *nt* luminous dial

leugnen *vt* deny

Leukämie *f* - leukaemia

Leumund *m* -s reputation

Leute *pl* people; ⟨*Mil*⟩ men; ⟨*Arbeiter*⟩ workers

Leutnant m -s,-s second lieutenant

leutselig a affable, adv -bly

Levkoje /'lef'ko:jə/ f -,-n stock

Lexikon nt -s,-ka encyclopaedia; (Wörterbuch) dictionary

Libanon (der) -s Lebanon

Libelle f -,-n dragonfly; (Techn) spirit-level; (Haarspange) slide

liberal a (Pol) Liberal

Libyen nt -s Libya

Licht nt -[e]s,-er light; (Kerze) candle; L~ machen turn on the light; hinter L~ führen (fam) dupe. L~ a bright; (Med) lucid; (spärlich) sparse. L~bild nt [passport] photograph; (Dia) slide. L~bildervortrag m lide lecture. L~blick m (fig) ray of hope. l~en vt line out; den Anker l~en (Naut) weigh anchor; sich l~en become less dense; (Haare:) thin. L~hupe f headlight flasher; die L~hupe betätigen flash one's headlights. L~maschine f dynamo. L~schalter m light-switch. L~ung f -,-en clearing

Lid nt -[e]s,-er [eye]lid. L~schatten m eye-shadow

lieb a dear; (nett) nice; (artig) good; jdn l~ haben be fond of s.o.; (lieben) love s.o.; jdn l~gewinnen grow fond of s.o.; es ist mir l~ I'm glad (dass that); es wäre mir l~er I should prefer it (wenn if). l~äugeln vi (haben) l~äugeln mit fancy; toy with (Gedanken)

Liebe f -,-n love. L~lei f -,-en flirtation. l~n vt love; (mögen) like; sich l~n love each other; (körperlich) make love. l~nd a loving □ adv etw l~nd gern tun love to do sth. l~nswert a lovable. l~nswürdig a kind. l~nswürdigerweise adv very kindly. L~nswürdigkeit f -,-en kindness

lieber adv rather; (besser) better; l~ mögen like better; ich trinke l~ Tee I prefer tea

Liebes|brief m love letter. L~dienst m favour. L~geschichte f love story. L~kummer m heartache; L~kummer haben be depressed over an unhappy love-affair. L~paar nt [pair of] lovers pl

lieb|evoll a loving, adv -ly; (zärtlich) affectionate, adv -ly. l~gewinnen† vt sep NEW l~ gewinnen, s. lieb; l~haben† vt sep NEW l~ haben, s. lieb. L~haber m -s,- lover; (Sammler) collector. L~haberei f -,-en hobby. l~kosen vt caress. L~kosung f -,-en caress. l~lich a lovely; (sanft) gentle; (süß) sweet. L~ling m -s,-e darling; (Bevorzugte) favourite. L~lings- pref favourite. l~los a loveless; (Eltern) uncaring; (unfreundlich) unkind □ adv unkindly; (ohne Sorgfalt) without care. L~schaft f -,-en [love] affair. l~ste(r,s) a dearest; (bevorzugt) favourite □ adv am l~sten best [of all]; jdn/etw am l~sten mögen like s.o./sth best [of all]; ich hätte am l~sten geweint I felt like crying. L~ste(r) m/f beloved; (Schatz) sweetheart

Lied nt -[e]s,-er song

liederlich a slovenly; (unordentlich) untidy; (ausschweifend) dissolute. L~keit f -,- slovenliness; untidiness; dissoluteness

Lieferant m -en,-en supplier

liefer|bar a (Comm) available. l~n vt supply; (zustellen) deliver; (hervorbringen) yield. L~ung f -,-en delivery; (Sendung) consignment; (per Schiff) shipment. L~wagen m delivery van

Liege f -,-n couch. L~nt vi (haben) lie; (gelegen sein) be situated; l~n bleiben remain lying [there]; (im Bett) stay in bed; (Ding:) be left; (Schnee:) settle; (Arbeit:) remain undone; (zurückgelassen werden) be left behind; (Panne haben) break down; l∼n lassen leave [lying there]; (zurücklassen) leave behind; (nicht fortführen) leave undone; l∼n an (+ dat) (fig) be due to; (abhängen) depend on; jdm [nicht] l∼n [not] suit s.o.; (ansprechen) [not] appeal to s.o.; mir liegt viel/nicht daran it is very/ not important to me. l∼nbleiben† vi sep (sein) NEW>l∼n bleiben, s. liegen. l∼nlassen† vt sep NEW> lassen, s. liegen. L∼sitz m reclining seat. L∼stuhl m deckchair. L∼stütz m -es,-e press-up, (Amer) push-up. L∼wagen m couchette car. L∼wiese f lawn for sunbathing

Lift m -[e]s,-e & -s lift, (Amer) elevator

Liga f -,-gen league

Likör m -s,-e liqueur

lila inv a mauve; (dunkel) purple

Lilie /'li:liə/ f -,-n lily

Liliputaner(in) m -s,- (f -,-nen) dwarf

Limo f -,-[s] (fam), L∼nade f -,-n fizzy drink, (Amer) soda; (Zitronen-) lemonade

Limousine /limu'zi:nə/ f -,-n saloon, (Amer) sedan; (mit Trennscheibe) limousine

lind a mild; (sanft) gentle

Linde f -,-n lime tree

linder|n vt relieve, ease. L∼ung f - relief

Line|al nt -s,-e ruler. l∼ar a linear

Linguistik f - linguistics sg

Linie /-jə/ f -,-n line; (Zweig) branch; (Bus-) route; L∼ 4 number 4 [bus/tram]; in erster L∼ primarily. L∼nflug m scheduled flight. L∼nrichter m linesman

lin|ijiert a lined, ruled

Link|e f -n,-n left side; (Hand) left hand; (Boxen) left; die L∼e (Pol) the left; zu meiner L∼en on my left. l∼e(r,s) a left; (Pol) leftwing;

l∼e Seite left[-hand] side; (von Stoff) wrong side; l∼e Masche purl. l∼isch a awkward, adv -ly

links adv on the left; (bei Stoff) on the wrong side; (verkehrt) inside out; von/nach l∼ from/to the left; l∼ stricken purl. L∼händer(in) m -s,- (f -,-nen) left-hander. l∼händig a & adv lefthanded. L∼verkehr m driving on the left

Linoleum /-leum/ nt -s lino, linoleum

Linse f -,-n lens; (Bot) lentil

Lippe f -,-n lip. L∼nstift m lipstick

Liquid|ation /-'tsjo:n/ f -,-en liquidation. l∼ieren vt liquidate

lispeln vt/i (haben) lisp

List f -,-en trick, ruse; (Listigkeit) cunning

Liste f -,-n list

listig a cunning, crafty

Litanei f -,-en litany

Litauen nt -s Lithuania

Liter m & nt -s,- litre

liter|arisch a literary. L∼atur f - literature

Litfaßsäule f advertising pillar

Liturgie f -,-n liturgy

Litze f -,-n braid; (Electr) flex

live /laif/ adv (Radio, TV) live

Lizenz f -,-en licence

Lkw /ɛlka've'/ m -[s],-s = Lastkraftwagen

Lob nt -[e]s praise

Lobby /'lɔbi/ f - (Pol) lobby

loben vt praise. l∼swert a praiseworthy, laudable

löblich a praiseworthy

Lobrede f eulogy

Loch nt -[e]s,-er hole. l∼en vt punch a hole/holes in; punch (Fahrkarte). L∼er m -s,- punch

löcher|ig a full of holes. l∼n vt (fam) pester

Locke f -,-n curl. l∼n¹ vt curl; sich l∼n vi curl

locken² vt lure, entice; (reizen) tempt. l∼d a tempting

Lockenwickler m -s, curler; ⟨Rolle⟩ roller

locker a loose, adv -ly; ⟨Seil⟩ slack; ⟨Erde, Kuchen⟩ light; ⟨zwanglos⟩ casual; ⟨zu frei⟩ lax; ⟨unmoralisch⟩ loose. **l~n** vt loosen; slacken ⟨Seil, Zügel⟩; break up ⟨Boden⟩; relax ⟨Griff⟩; **sich l~n** become loose; ⟨Seil:⟩ slacken; ⟨sich entspannen⟩ relax. **L~ungsübungen** fpl limbering-up exercises

lockig a curly

Lock|mittel nt bait. **L~ung** f -,-en lure; ⟨Versuchung⟩ temptation. **L~vogel** m decoy

loden m -s ⟨Tex⟩ loden

lodern vi ⟨haben⟩ blaze

Löffel m -s, spoon; ⟨L~ voll⟩ spoonful. **l~n** vt spoon up

Logarithmus m -,-men logarithm

Logbuch nt ⟨Naut⟩ log-book

Loge /ˈloːʒə/ f -,-n lodge; ⟨Theat⟩ box

Logierbesuch /loˈʒiːɐ̯-/ m house guest|guests pl

Log|ik f - logic. **l~isch** a logical, adv -ly

Logo nt -s,-s logo

Lohn m -[e]s,-e wages pl, pay; ⟨fig⟩ reward. **L~empfänger** m wage-earner. **l~en** vi|r ⟨haben⟩ [sich] **l~en** be worth it or worth while □ vt be worth; **jdm etw l~en** reward s.o. for sth. **l~end** a worthwhile; ⟨befriedigend⟩ rewarding. **L~erhöhung** f [pay] rise; ⟨Amer⟩ raise. **L~steuer** f income tax

Lok f -,-s ⟨fam⟩ = **Lokomotive**

Lokal nt -s,-e restaurant; ⟨Trink-⟩ bar. **l~** a local. **l~isieren** vt locate; ⟨begrenzen⟩ localize

Lokomotiv|e f -,-n engine, locomotive. **L~führer** m engine driver

London nt -s London. **L~er** a London … □ m -s,- Londoner

Lorbeer m -s,-en laurel; **echter L~** bay. **L~blatt** nt ⟨Culin⟩ bay-leaf

Lore f -,-n ⟨Rail⟩ truck

Los nt -es,-e lot; ⟨Lotterie-⟩ ticket; ⟨Schicksal⟩ fate; **das große Los ziehen** hit the jackpot

los pred a **los sein** be loose; **jdn/etw los sein** be rid of s.o./sth; **was ist [mit ihm] los?** what's the matter [with him]? □ adv los! go on! **Achtung, fertig, los!** ready, steady, go!

lösbar a soluble

losbinden f vt sep untie

Lösch|blatt nt sheet of blotting-paper. **l~¹** vt put out, extinguish; quench ⟨Durst⟩; blot ⟨Tinte⟩; ⟨tilgen⟩ cancel; ⟨streichen⟩ delete; erase ⟨Aufnahme⟩

löschen² vt ⟨Naut⟩ unload

Lösch|fahrzeug nt fire-engine. **L~gerät** nt fire extinguisher. **L~papier** nt blotting-paper

lose a loose, adv -ly

Lösegeld nt ransom

losen vt ⟨haben⟩ draw lots (**um** for)

lösen vt undo; ⟨lockern⟩ loosen; ⟨entfernen⟩ detach; ⟨klären⟩ solve; ⟨auflösen⟩ dissolve; cancel ⟨Vertrag⟩; break off ⟨Beziehung, Verlobung⟩; ⟨kaufen⟩ buy; **sich l~** come off; ⟨sich trennen⟩ detach oneself/itself; ⟨lose werden⟩ come undone; ⟨sich entspannen⟩ relax; ⟨sich klären⟩ resolve itself; ⟨sich auflösen⟩ dissolve

los|fahren vi sep ⟨sein⟩ start; ⟨Auto:⟩ drive off; **l~fahren auf** (+ acc) head for; ⟨fig: angreifen⟩ go for. **l~gehen** f vi sep ⟨sein⟩ set off; ⟨fam: anfangen⟩ start; ⟨fam: abgehen⟩ come off; ⟨Bombe, Gewehr:⟩ go off; **l~gehen auf** (+ acc) head for; ⟨fig angreifen⟩ go for. **l~kommen** f vi sep ⟨sein⟩ get away ⟨von from⟩; **l~kommen auf** (+ acc) come towards. **l~lachen** vi sep ⟨haben⟩ burst out laughing. l~lassen† vt sep let go of; (freilassen) release

löslich a soluble

los|lösen vt sep detach; **sich l~lösen** become detached; (fig) break away **(von** from). **l~machen** vt sep detach; (los-binden) untie; **sich l~machen** free oneself/itself. **l~platzen** vi sep (sein) (fam) burst out laughing. **l~reißen†** vt sep tear off; **sich l~reißen** break free; (fig) tear oneself away. **l~sagen (sich)** vr sep renounce **(von etw** sth). **l~schicken** vt sep send off. **l~sprechen†** vt sep absolve **(von** from). **l~steuern** vi sep (sein) head **(auf** + acc **for)**

Losung f -,-en (Pol) slogan; (Mil) password

Lösung f -,-en solution. **L~smittel** nt solvent

los|werden† vt sep get rid of. **l~ziehen†** vi sep (sein) set off; **l~ziehen gegen** od **über** (+ acc) (beschimpfen) run down

Lot nt -[e]s, -e perpendicular; (Blei-) plumb[-bob]; **im Lot sein** (fig) be all right. **l~en** vt plumb

löt|en vt solder. **L~lampe** f blow-lamp, (Amer) blowtorch. **L~metall** nt solder

lotrecht a perpendicular, adv -ly

Lotse m -n,-n (Naut) pilot. **l~n** vt (Naut) pilot; (fig) guide

Lotterie f -,-n lottery

Lotto nt -s,-s lotto; (Lotterie) lottery

Löw|e m -n,-n lion; (Astr) Leo. **L~enanteil** m (fig) lion's share. **L~enzahn** m (Bot) dandelion. **L~in** f -,-nen lioness

loyal /lǫa'jaːl/ a loyal. **L~ität** f - loyalty

Luchs m -es,-e lynx

Lücke f -,-n gap. **L~nbüßer** m -s,- stopgap. **l~nhaft** a incomplete; (Wissen) patchy. **l~nlos** a complete; (Folge) unbroken

Luder nt -s,- (sl) (Frau) bitch; **armes L~** poor wretch

Luft f -,-̈e air; **tief L~ holen** take a deep breath; **in die L~ gehen** explode. **L~angriff** m air raid. **L~aufnahme** f aerial photograph. **L~ballon** m balloon. **L~bild** nt aerial photograph. **L~blase** f air bubble

Lüftchen nt -s,- breeze

luft|dicht a airtight. **L~druck** m atmospheric pressure

lüften vt air; raise (Hut); reveal (Geheimnis)

Luft|fahrt f aviation. **L~fahrt-gesellschaft** f airline. **L~gewehr** nt airgun. **L~hauch** m breath of air. **l~ig** a airy; (Kleid) light. **L~kissenfahrzeug** nt hovercraft. **L~krieg** m aerial warfare. **L~kurort** m climatic health resort. **l~leer** a **l~leerer Raum** vacuum. **L~linie** f 100 km **L~linie** 100 km as the crow flies. **L~loch** nt air-hole; (Aviat) air pocket. **L~matratze** f air-bed, inflatable mattress. **L~pirat** m [aircraft] hijacker. **L~post** f airmail. **L~pumpe** f air pump; (Fahrrad-) bicycle-pump. **L~röhre** f windpipe. **L~schiff** nt airship. **L~schlange** f [paper] streamer. **L~schlösser** ntpl castles in the air. **L~schutz-bunker** m air-raid shelter

Lüftung f - ventilation

Luft|veränderung f change of air. **L~waffe** f air force. **L~weg** m **auf dem L~weg** by air. **L~zug** m draught

Lüg|e f -,-n lie. **l~en†** vt/i (haben) lie. **L~ner(in)** m -s,- (f -,-nen) liar. **l~nerisch** a untrue; (Person) untruthful

Luke f -,-n hatch; (Dach-) skylight

Lümmel m -s,- lout; (fam: Schelm) rascal. **l~n (sich)** vr loll

Lump m -en,-en scoundrel. **L~en** m -s,- rag; **in L~en** in rags, in rags; **sich nicht l~en lassen** be generous. **L~engesindel, L~enpack** nt

riff-raff. L~ensammler *m* rag-and-bone man. l~ig *a* mean, shabby; (*gering*) measley
Lunchpacket /'lan[t]ʃ-/ *nt* packed lunch
Lunge *f* -,-n lungs *pl*; (L~nflügel) lung. L~nentzündung *f* pneumonia
lungern *vi* (*haben*) loiter
Lunte *f* ~,-n riechen (*fam*) smell a rat
Lupe *f* -,-n magnifying glass
Lurch *m* -[e]s,-e amphibian
Lust *f* -,ˮe pleasure; (*Verlangen*) desire; (*sinnliche Begierde*) lust; L~ haben feel like (auf etw *acc* sth); ich habe keine L~ I don't feel like it; (*will nicht*) I don't want to
Lüster *m* -s,- lustre; (*Kronleuchter*) chandelier
lüstern *a* greedy (auf + *acc* for); (*sinnlich*) lascivious; (*geil*) lecherous
lustig *a* jolly; (*komisch*) funny; sich l~ machen über (+ *acc*) make fun of
Lüstling *m* -s,-e lecher
lust|los *a* listless, *adv* -ly. L~mörder *m* sex killer. L~spiel *nt* comedy
lutherisch *a* Lutheran
lutsch|en *vt*/*i* (*haben*) suck. L~er *m* -s,- (*fam*) lollipop; (*Schnuller*) dummy, (*Amer*) pacifier
lütt *a* (*NGer*) little
Lüttich *nt* -s Liège
Luv *f* & *nt* - nach Luv (*Naut*) to windward
luxuriös *a* luxurious, *adv* -ly
Luxus *m* - luxury. L~artikel *m* luxury article. L~ausgabe *f* de luxe edition. L~hotel *nt* luxury hotel
Lymph|drüse /'lymf-/ *f*, L~knoten *m* lymph gland
lynchen /'lynçən/ *vt* lynch

Lyr|ik *f* - lyric poetry. L~iker *m* -s,- lyric poet. l~isch *a* lyrical; (*Dichtung*) lyric

M

Mach|art *f* style. m~bar *a* feasible. m~en *vt* make; get (*Mahlzeit*); take (*Foto*); (*ausführen, tun, in Ordnung bringen*) do; (*Math: ergeben*) be; (*kosten*) come to, sich (*dat*) etw m~en lassen have sth made; was m~st du da? what are you doing? was m~t die Arbeit? how is work? das m~t 6 Mark [zusammen] that's 6 marks [altogether]; das m~t nichts it doesn't matter; sich (*dat*) wenig/nichts m~en aus care little/ nothing for □ *vr* sich m~en do well; sich an die Arbeit m~en get down to work □ *vi* (*haben*) ins Bett m~en (*fam*) wet the bed; schnell m~en hurry. M~enschaften *fpl* machinations
Macht *f* -,ˮe power; mit aller M~ with all one's might. M~haber *m* -s,- ruler
mächtig *a* powerful; (*groß*) enormous □ *adv* (*fam*) terribly
macht|los *a* powerless. M~wort *nt* ein M~wort sprechen put one's foot down
Mädchen *nt* -s,- girl; (*Dienst-*) maid. m~haft *a* girlish. M~name *m* girl's name; (*vor der Ehe*) maiden name
Made *f* -,-n maggot
Mädel *nt* -s,- girl
madig *a* maggoty; jdn m~ machen (*fam*) run s.o. down
Madonna *f* -,-nnen madonna
Magazin *nt* -s,-e magazine; (*Lager*) warehouse; (*Raum*) store-room
Magd *f* -,ˮe maid

Magen m -s,- stomach.
M~schmerzen mpl stomach-
ache sg. M~verstimmung f
stomach upset

mager a thin; (Fleisch) lean;
(Boden) poor; (dürftig) meagre.
M~keit f · thinness; leanness.
M~sucht f anorexia

Magie f · magic

Magier /'ma:giɐ/ m -s,- magician. m~isch a magic; (geheimnisvoll) magical

Magistrat m -[e]s,-e city council

Magnesia f · magnesia

Magnet m -en & -[e]s,-e magnet.
m~isch a magnetic. m~isieren
vt magnetize. M~ismus m · mag-
netism

Mahagoni nt -s mahogany

Mäh|drescher m · combine
harvester. m~en vt/i (haben)
mow

Mahl nt -[e]s,-er & -e meal

mahlen† vt grind

Mahlzeit f · meal; M~! enjoy your
meal!

Mähne f -,-n mane

mahn|en vt/i (haben) remind
(wegen about); (ermahnen) ad-
monish; (auffordern) urge (zu to);
zur Vorsicht/Eile m~en urge
caution/haste. M~ung f -,-en re-
minder; admonition; (Auffor-
derung) exhortation

Mai m -[e]s,-e May; der Erste
Mai May Day. M~glöckchen nt
-s,- lily of the valley. M~käfer m
cockchafer

Mailand nt -s Milan

Mais m -es maize, (Amer) corn;
(Culin) sweet corn. M~kolben m
corn-cob

Majestät f -,-en majesty. m~isch
a majestic, adv -ally

Major m -s,-e major

Majoran m -s,-e marjoram

Majorität f -,-en majority

makaber a macabre

Makel m -s,- blemish; (Defekt)
flaw; (fig) stain. m~los a flawless; (fig) unblemished

mäkeln vi (haben) grumble

Makkaroni pl macaroni sg

Makler m -s,- (Comm) broker

Makrele f -,-n mackerel

Makrone f -,-n macaroon

mal adv (Math) times; (bei Maßen)
by; (fam: einmal) once; (eines
Tages) one day; schon mal once
before; (jemals) ever; nicht mal
not even; hört/seht mal! listen!/look!

Mal[1] nt -[e]s,-e time; das ers-
te/zweite/letzte/nächste Mal
the first/second/last/next time;
zum ersten/letzten Mal for the
first/last time; mit einem Mal
all at once; ein für alle Mal once
and for all; jedes Mal every time;
jedes Mal, wenn whenever; ei-
nige/mehrere Mal a few/sev-
eral times

Mal[2] nt -[e]s,-e mark; (auf der
Haut) mole; (Mutter-) birthmark

Mal|buch nt colouring book.
m~en vt/i (haben) paint. M~er
m -s,- painter. M~erei f -,-en
painting. M~erin f -,-nen
painter. m~erisch a picturesque

Malheur /ma'lø:ɐ/ nt -s,-e & -s
(fam) mishap; (Ärger) trouble

Mallorca /ma'lɔrka, -'jɔrka/ nt -s
Majorca

malnehmen† vt sep multiply (mit
by)

Malz nt -es malt. M~bier nt malt
beer

Mama /'mama, ma'ma:/ f -,-s
mummy

Mammut nt -s,-e & -s mammoth

mampfen vt (fam) munch

man pron one, you; (die Leute)
people, they; man sagt they say,
it is said

Manager /'mɛnɪdʒɐ/ m -s,- manager

manch inv pron m~ ein(e) many
a; m~ einer/eine many a man/
woman. m~e(r,s) pron many a;
[so] m~es Mal many a time;

m~e Leute some people
□ (*substantivisch*) **m~er/m~e**
many a man/woman; **m~e** *pl*
some; (*Leute*) some people; (*viele*)
many [people]; **m~es** some
things; (*vieles*) many things.
m~erlei *inv a* various □ *pron*
various things

manchmal *adv* sometimes

Mandant(in) *m* -en,-en (*f* -,-nen)
(*Jur*) client

Mandarine *f* -,-n mandarin

Mandat *nt* -[e]s,-e mandate; (*Jur*)
brief; (*Pol*) seat

Mandel *f* -,-n almond; (*Anat*) tonsil. **M~entzündung** *f* tonsillitis

Manege /ma'ne:ʒə/ *f* -,-n ring;
(*Reit-*) arena

Mangel¹ *m* -s,⸗ lack; (*Knappheit*)
shortage; (*Med*) deficiency;
(*Fehler*) defect; **M~ leiden** go
short

Mangel² *f* -,-n mangle

mangel|haft *a* faulty, defective;
(*Sch*) unsatisfactory. **m~n¹** *vi*
(*haben*) **es m~t an** (+ *dat*) there
is a lack/(*Knappheit*) shortage of.
mangeln² *vt* put through the
mangle

mangels *prep* (+ *gen*) for lack of

Mango *f* -,-s mango

Manie *f* -,-n mania; (*Sucht*) obsession

Manier *f* -,-en manner; **M~en**
manners. **m~lich** *a* well-mannered □ *adv* properly

Manifest *nt* -[e]s,-e manifesto.
m~ieren (sich) *vr* manifest itself

Maniküre *f* -,-n manicure; (*Person*) manicurist. **m~n** *vt* manicure

Manipul|ation /-'tsjo:n/ *f* -,-en
manipulation. **m~ieren** *vt* ma-
nipulate

Manko *nt* -s,-s disadvantage;
(*Fehlbetrag*) deficit

Mann *m* -[e]s,⸗er man; (*Ehe-*) husband

Männchen *nt* -s,- little man;
(*Zool*) male; **M~ machen**
(*Hund:*) sit up

Mannequin /'manəkɛ̃/ *nt* -s,-s
model

Männerchor *m* male voice choir

Mannes|alter *nt* manhood.
M~kraft *f* virility

mannhaft *a* manful, *adv* -ly

mannigfaltig *a* manifold; (*verschieden*) diverse

männlich *a* male; (*Gram & fig*)
masculine; (*mannhaft*) manly;
(*Frau*) mannish. **M~keit** *f* - mas-
culinity; (*fig*) manhood

Mannschaft *f* -,-en team; (*Naut*)
crew. **M~sgeist** *m* team spirit

Manöver *nt* -s,- manoeuvre;
(*Winkelzug*) trick. **m~rieren**
vt/i (*haben*) manoeuvre

Mansarde *f* -,-n attic room;
(*Wohnung*) attic flat

Manschette *f* -,-n cuff; (*Blumen-
topf-*) paper frill. **M~nknopf** *m*
cuff-link

Mantel *m* -s,⸗ coat; (*dick*) overcoat; (*Reifen-*) outer tyre

Manuskript *nt* -[e]s,-e manuscript

Mappe *f* -,-n folder; (*Akten-*)
briefcase; (*Schul-*) bag

Marathon *m* -s,-s marathon

Märchen *nt* -s,- fairy-tale.
m~haft *a* fairy-tale...; (*phantastisch*) fabulous

Margarine *f* - margarine

Marienkäfer /ma'ri:ən-/ *m* lady-
bird, (*Amer*) ladybug

Marihuana *nt* -s marijuana

Marille *f* -,-n (*Aust*) apricot

Marinade *f* -,-n marinade

Marine *f* marine; (*Kriegs-*) navy.
m~blau *a* navy [blue]. **M~in-
fanterist** *m* marine

marinieren *vt* marinade

Marionette *f* -,-n puppet, marionette

Mark¹ *f* -,- mark; **drei M~** three
marks

Mark² nt -[e]s (Knochen-) marrow (Bot)pith; (Frucht-) pulp; **bis ins M~ getroffen** (fig) cut to the quick

markant a striking

Marke f -,-n token; (rund) disc; (Erkennungs-) tag; (Brief-) stamp; (Lebensmittel-) coupon; (Spiel-) counter; (Markierung) mark; (Fabrikat) make; (Tabak-) brand. **M~nartikel** m branded article

markier|en vt mark; (fam: vortäuschen) fake. **M~ung** f -,-en marking

Markise f -,-n awning

Markstück nt one-mark piece

Markt m -[e]s,ˆe market; (M~platz) market-place. **M~forschung** f market research. **M~platz** m market-place

Marmelade f -,-n jam; (Orangen-) marmalade

Marmor m -s marble

Marokko nt -s Morocco

Marone f -,-n [sweet] chestnut

Marotte f -,-n whim

Marsch¹ f -,-en marsh

Marsch² m -[e]s,ˆe march. **m~ int** (Mil) march! **m~ ins Bett!** off to bed!

Marschall m -s,ˆe marshal

marschieren vi (sein) march

Marter f -,-n torture. **m~n** vt torture

Martinshorn nt [police] siren

Märtyrer(in) m -s,- (f -,-nen) martyr

Martyrium nt -s martyrdom

Mar|xismus m - Marxism. **m~xistisch** a Marxist

März m -s,-e March

Marzipan nt -s marzipan

Masche f -,-n stitch; (im Netz) mesh; (fig: Trick) dodge. **M~ndraht** m wire netting

Maschin|e f -,-n machine; (Flugzeug) plane; (Schreib-) typewriter; **M~e schreiben** type. **m~egeschrieben** a typewritten, typed. **m~ell** a machine … □ adv

by machine. **M~enbau** m mechanical engineering. **M~engewehr** nt machine-gun. **M~enpistole** f sub-machine-gun. **M~erie** f - machinery. **M~eschreiben** nt typing. **M~ist** m -en,-en machinist; (Naut) engineer

Masern pl measles sg

Maserung f -,-en [wood] grain

Maske f -,-n mask; (Theat) make-up. **M~rade** f -,-n disguise; (fig: Heuchelei) masquerade

maskieren vt mask; **sich m~** dress up (als as)

Maskottchen nt -s,- mascot

maskulin a masculine

Maskulinum nt -s,-na (Gram) masculine

Masochis|mus /mazoˈxɪsmʊs/ m - masochism. **M~t** m -en,-en masochist

Maß n -es,-e measure; (Abmessung) measurement; (Grad) degree; (Mäßigung) moderation; **Maß halten** exercise moderation; **in** od **mit Maß[en]** in moderation; **in hohem Maße** to a high degree

Maß² f -,- (SGer) litre [of beer]

Massage /maˈsaːʒə/ f -,-n massage

Massaker nt -s,- massacre

Maßanzug m made-to-measure suit. **M~band** nt (pl -bänder) tape-measure

Masse f -,-n mass; (Culin) mixture; (Menschen-) crowd; **eine M~ Arbeit** (fam) masses of work. **M~nartikel** m mass-produced article. **m~nhaft** adv in huge quantities. **M~nmedien** pl mass media. **M~nproduktion** f mass production. **m~nweise** adv in huge numbers

Masseu|r /maˈsøːɐ/ m -s,-e masseur. **M~rin** f -,-nen, **M~se** /-ˈsøːzə/ f -,-n masseuse

maßgebend a authoritative; (einflussreich) influential. **m~geblich** a decisive, adv -ly.

m~geschneidert *a* made-to-measure. **m~halten†** *vi sep* (haben) NEW Maß halten, *s.* Maß¹

massieren¹ *vt* massage
massieren² (sich) *vr* mass
massig *a* massive
mäßig *a* moderate, *adv* -ly; (mittelmäßig) indifferent. **m~en** *vt* moderate; **sich m~en** moderate; (sich beherrschen) restrain oneself. **M~keit** *f* - moderation. **M~ung** *f* - moderation
massiv *a* solid; (stark) heavy
Maß|krug *m* beer mug. **m~los** *a* excessive; (grenzenlos) boundless; (äußerst) extreme, *adv* -ly. **M~nahme** *f* -,-n measure. **m~regeln** *vt* reprimand. **Maßstab** *m* scale; (Norm & fig) standard. **m~sgerecht**, **m~sgetreu** *a* scale ... □ *adv* to scale
maßvoll *a* moderate
Mast¹ *m* -[e]s,-en pole; (Überland-) pylon; (Naut) mast
Mast² *f* - fattening. **M~darm** *m* rectum
mästen *vt* fatten
Masturb|ation /-'tsi̯o:n/ *f* - masturbation. **m~ieren** *vi* (haben) masturbate
Material *nt* -s,-ien /-i̯ən/ material; (coll) materials *pl*. **M~ismus** *m* - materialism. **m~istisch** *a* materialistic
Mater|ie /ma'te:ri̯ə/ *f* -,-n matter; (Thema) subject. **m~iell** *a* material
Mathe *f* - (fam) maths *sg*
Mathe|matik *f* - mathematics *sg*. **M~matiker** *m* -s,- mathematician. **m~matisch** *a* mathematical
Matinee *f* -,-n (Theat) morning performance
Matratze *f* -,-n mattress
Mätresse *f* -,-n mistress
Matrose *m* -n,-n sailor
Matsch *m* -[e]s mud; (Schnee-) slush. **m~ig** *a* muddy; slushy; (weich) mushy

matt *a* weak; (gedämpft) dim; (glanzlos) dull; (Politur, Farbe) matt; **jdn m~ setzen** checkmate s.o. **M~** *nt* -s (Schach) mate
Matte *f* -,-n mat
Mattglas *nt* frosted glass
Matt|igkeit *f* - weakness; (Müdigkeit) weariness. **M~scheibe** *f* (fam) television screen
Matura *f* - (Aust) ≈ A levels *pl*
Mauer *f* -,-n wall. **m~n** *vt* build □ *vi* (haben) lay bricks. **M~werk** *nt* masonry
Maul *nt* -[e]s, Mäuler (Zool) mouth; **halt's M~!** (fam) shut up! **m~en** *vi* (haben) (fam) grumble. **M~korb** *m* muzzle. **M~tier** *nt* mule. **M~wurf** *m* mole. **M~wurfshaufen**, **M~wurfshügel** *m* molehill
Maurer *m* -s,- bricklayer
Maus *f* -,Mäuse mouse. **M~efalle** *f* mousetrap
mausern (sich) *vr* moult; (fam) turn (zu into)
Maut *f* -,-en (Aust) toll. **M~straße** *f* toll road
maximal *a* maximum
Maximum *nt* -s,-ma maximum
Mayonnaise /majo'nɛ:zə/ *f* -,-n mayonnaise
Mäzen *m* -s,-e patron
Mechan|ik /me'ça:nik/ *f* - mechanics *sg*; (Mechanismus) mechanism. **M~iker** *m* -s,- mechanic. **m~isch** *a* mechanical, *adv* -ly. **m~isieren** *vt* mechanize. **M~ismus** *m* -,-men mechanism
meckern *vi* (haben) bleat; (fam: nörgeln) grumble
Medaille /me'daljə/ *f* -,-n medal. **M~on** /-'jõ:/ *nt* -s,-s medallion (Schmuck) locket
Medikament *nt* -[e]s,-e medicine
Medit|ation /-'tsi̯o:n/ *f* -,-en meditation. **m~ieren** *vi* (haben) meditate
Medium *nt* -s,-ien medium; **die Medien** the media

Medizin f -,-en medicine. **M~er** m -s,- doctor; (*Student*) medical student. **m~isch** a medical; (*heilkräftig*) medicinal

Meer nt -[e]s,-e sea. **M~busen** m gulf. **M~enge** f strait. **M~esspiegel** m sea-level. **M~jungfrau** f mermaid. **M~rettich** m horseradish. **M~schweinchen** nt -s,- guinea-pig

Megaphon, Megafon nt -s,-e megaphone

Mehl nt -[e]s flour. **m~ig** a floury. **M~schwitze** f (*Culin*) roux. **M~speise** f (*Aust*) dessert; (*Kuchen*) pastry. **M~tau** m (*Bot*) mildew

mehr pron & adv more; **nicht m~** no more; (*zeitlich*) no longer; **nichts m~** no more; (*nichts weiter*) nothing else; **nie m~** never again. **m~deutig** a ambiguous. **m~en** vt increase; **sich m~en** increase. **m~ere** pron several. **m~eremal** adv (NEW) **m~ere Mal**, s. **Mal**. **m~eres** pron several things pl. **m~fach** a multiple; (*mehrmalig*) repeated □ adv several times. **M~fahrtenkarte** f book of tickets. **m~farbig** a [multi]coloured. **M~heit** f -,-en majority. **m~malig** a repeated. **m~mals** adv several times. **m~sprachig** a multilingual. **m~stimmig** a (*Mus*) for several voices □ adv **m~stimmig singen** sing in harmony. **M~wertsteuer** f valueadded tax, VAT. **M~zahl** f majority; (*Gram*) plural. **M~zweckpref** multi-purpose

meiden† vt avoid, shun

Meierei f -,-en (*dial*) dairy

Meile f -,-n mile. **M~nstein** m milestone. **M~nweit** adv [for] miles

mein poss pron my. **m~e(r,s)** poss pron mine; **die M~en** od **m~en** pl my family sg

Meineid m perjury; **einen M~ leisten** perjure oneself

meinen vt mean; (*glauben*) think; (*sagen*) say; **gut gemeinter Rat** wel-meant advice; **es gut m~** mean well

meinjerseits adv for my part. **m~etwegen** adv for my sake; (*wegen mir*) because of me, on my account; (*fam: von mir aus*) as far as I'm concerned. **m~etwillen** adv **um m~etwillen** for my sake. **m~ige** poss pron **der/die/das m~ige** mine. **m~s** poss pron mine

Meinung f -,-en opinion; **jdm die M~ sagen** give s.o. a piece of one's mind. **M~sumfrage** f opinion poll

Meise f -,-n (*Zool*) tit

Meißel m -s,- chisel. **m~n** vt/i (*haben*) chisel

meist adv mostly; (*gewöhnlich*) usually. **m~e** a **der/die/das m~e** most; **die m~en Leute** most people; **die m~e Zeit** most of the time; **am m~en** [the] most □ pron **das m~e** most [of it]; **die m~en** most. **m~ens** adv mostly; (*gewöhnlich*) usually

Meister m -s,- master craftsman; (*Könner*) master; (*Sport*) champion. **m~haft** a masterly □ adv in masterly fashion. **m~n** vt master. **M~schaft** f -,-en mastery; (*Sport*) championship. **M~stück, M~werk** nt masterpiece

Melancholie /melaŋko'liː/ f -melancholy. **m~olisch** a melancholy

melden vt report; (*anmelden*) register; (*ankündigen*) announce; **sich m~en** report (**bei** to); (*zum Militär*) enlist; (*freiwillig*) volunteer; (*Teleph*) answer; (*Sch*) put up one's hand; (*von sich hören lassen*) get in touch (**bei** with); **sich krank m~en** (NEW) **sich krankmelden**. **M~ung** f -,-en report; (*Anmeldung*) registration

meliert a mottled; **grau m~es Haar** hair flecked with grey

melken† vt milk

Melod|ie *f* ~-n tune, melody.
m~iös *a* melodious
melodisch *a* melodic; *(melodiös)*
melodious, tuneful
melodramatisch *a* melo-
dramatic, *adv* -ally
Melone *f* ~-n melon; **[schwarze]**
M~ *(fam)* bowler [hat]
Membran *f* ~-en membrane
Memoiren /me'mǫaːrən/ *pl* memoirs
Menge *f* ~-n amount, quantity;
(Menschen-) crowd; *(Math)* set;
eine M~ Geld a lot of money.
m~n *vt* mix
Mensa *f* ~-sen *(Univ)* refectory
Mensch *m* -en,-en human being;
der M~ man; **die M~en** people;
jeder/kein M~ everybody/no-
body. **M~enaffe** *m* ape. **M~en-**
feind *m* misanthropist.
m~enfeindlich *a* antisocial.
M~enfresser *m* -s,- cannibal;
(Zool) man-eater; *(fam)* ogre.
m~enfreundlich *a* philanthropic. **M~enleben** *nt* human life; *(Lebenszeit)* lifetime.
m~enleer *a* deserted. **M~en-**
menge *f* crowd. **M~enraub** *m*
kidnapping. **M~enrechte** *ntpl*
human rights. **m~enscheu** *a* unsociable. **M~enskind** *int (fam)*
good heavens! **M~enverstand** *m*
gesunder M~enverstand common sense. **m~enwürdig** *a* humane, *adv* -ly. **M~heit** *f* - **die**
M~heit mankind, humanity.
m~lich *a* human; *(human)* humane, *adv* -ly. **M~lichkeit** *f* - humanity
Menstrua|tion /-'tsjoːn/ *f* - men-
struation. **m~ieren** *vi (haben)*
menstruate
Mentalität *f* ~-en mentality
Menü *nt* -s,-s menu; *(festes M~)*
set meal
Menuett *nt* -[e]s,-e minuet
Meridian *m* -s,-e meridian
merk|bar *a* noticeable. **M~blatt**
nt [explanatory] leaflet. **m~en** *vt*

notice; **sich** *(dat)* **etw m~en** remember sth. **m~lich** *a* noticeable, *adv* -bly. **M~mal** *nt*
feature
merkwürdig *a* odd, *adv* -ly,
strange, *adv* -ly. **m~erweise** *adv*
oddly enough
mess|bar (meß|bar) *a* measur-
able. **M~becher** *m* *(Culin)*
measure
Messe¹ *f* ~-n *(Relig)* mass;
(Comm) [trade] fair
Messe² *f* ~-n *(Mil)* mess
messen† *vt/i (haben)* measure;
(ansehen) look at; **[bei jdm]** Fieber m~ take s.o.'s temperature;
sich m~ compete **(mit** with);
sich mit jdm m~/nicht m~
können be a/no match for s.o.
Messer *nt* -s,- knife
Messias *m* - Messiah
Messing *nt* -s brass
Messung *f* ~-en measurement
Metabolismus *m* - metabolism
Metall *nt* -s,-e metal. **m~en** *a*
metal; *(metallisch)* metallic.
m~isch *a* metallic
Metallurgie *f* - metallurgy
Metamorphose *f* ~-n metamorphosis
Metaph|er *f* ~-n metaphor. **m~o-**
risch *a* metaphorical, *adv* -ly
Meteor *m* -s,-e meteor. **M~olo-**
gie *f* - meteorology. **m~ologisch**
a meteorological
Meter *m & nt* -s,- metre, *(Amer)*
meter. **M~maß** *nt* tape-measure
Method|e *f* ~-n method. **m~isch**
a methodical
metrisch *a* metric
Metropole *f* ~-n metropolis
metzeln *vt (fig)* massacre
Metzger *m* -s,- butcher. **M~ei** *f*
~-,-en butcher's shop
Meute *f* ~-,-n pack [of hounds]; *(fig:*
Menge) mob
Meuterei *f* ~-,-en mutiny
meutern *vi (haben)* mutiny; *(fam:*
schimpfen) grumble

Mexikan|er(in) *m* -s,- (*f* -,-nen) Mexican. **m~isch** *a* Mexican

Mexiko *nt* -s Mexico

miauen *vi* (*haben*) mew, miaow

mich *pron* (*acc of* **ich**) me; (*refl*) myself

Mieder *nt* -s,- bodice; (*Korsett*) corset

Miene *f* -,-n expression; **M~machen** make as if (**zu** to)

mies *a* (*fam*) lousy; **mir ist m~** I feel rotten

Miet|e *f* -,-n rent; (*Mietgebühr*) hire charge; **zur M~e wohnen** live in rented accommodation. **m~en** *vt* rent (*Haus, Zimmer*); hire (*Auto, Boot, Fernseher*). **M~er(in)** *m* -s,- (*f* -,-nen) tenant. **m~frei** *a* & *adv* rent-free. **M~shaus** *nt* block of rented flats. **M~vertrag** *m* lease. **M~wagen** *m* hire-car. **M~wohnung** *f* rented flat; (*zu vermieten*) flat to let

Mieze *f* -,-n (*fam*) puss[y]

Migräne *f* -,-n migraine

Mikrobe *f* -,-n microbe

Mikro|chip *m* microchip. **M~computer** *m* microcomputer. **M~film** *m* microfilm

Mikro|fon, M~phon *nt* -s,-e microphone. **M~prozessor** *m* -s,-en /-'so:rən/ microprocessor. **M~skop** *nt* -s,-e microscope. **m~skopisch** *a* microscopic

Mikrowelle *f* microwave. **M~ngerät** *nt*, **M~nherd** *m* microwave oven

Milbe *f* -,-n mite

Milch *f* - milk. **M~bar** *f* milk bar. **M~geschäft** *nt* dairy. **M~glas** *nt* opal glass. **m~ig** *a* milky. **M~kuh** *f* dairy cow. **M~mann** *m* (*pl* -männer) milkman. **M~mixgetränk** *nt* milk shake. **M~straße** *f* Milky Way. **M~zahn** *m* milk tooth

mild *a* mild; (*nachsichtig*) lenient; **m~e Gaben** alms. **M~e** *f* - mildness; leniency. **m~ern** *vt* make

milder; (*mäßigen*) moderate; (*lindern*) alleviate, ease; **sich m~ern** become milder; (*sich mäßigen*) moderate; (*nachlassen*) abate; (*Schmerz:*) ease; **m~ernde Umstände** mitigating circumstances. **m~tätig** *a* charitable

Milieu /mi'ljø:/ *nt* -s,-s [social] environment

militant *a* militant

Militär *nt* -s army; (*Soldaten*) troops *pl*; **beim M~** in the army. **m~isch** *a* military

Miliz *f* -,-en militia

Milliarde /mi'ljardə/ *f* -,-n thousand million, billion

Milli|gramm *nt* milligram. **M~meter** *m* & *nt* millimetre. **M~meterpapier** *nt* graph paper

Million /mi'ljo:n/ *f* -,-en million. **M~är** *m* -s,-e millionaire. **M~ärin** *f* -,-nen millionairess

Milz *f* - (*Anat*) spleen

mim|en *vt* (*fam:* vortäuschen) act. **M~ik** *f* - [expressive] gestures and facial expressions *pl*

Mimose *f* -,-n mimosa

minder *a* lesser □ *adv* less; **mehr oder m~** more or less. **M~heit** *f* -,-en minority

minderjährig *a* (*Jur*) under-age; **m~ sein** be under age. **M~e(r)** *m/f* (*Jur*) minor. **M~keit** *f* - (*Jur*) minority

minder|n *vt* diminish; decrease (*Tempo*). **M~ung** *f* - decrease

minderwertig *a* inferior. **M~keit** *f* - inferiority. **M~keitskomplex** *m* inferiority complex

Mindest- *pref* minimum. **m~e** *a* & *pron* **der/die/das M~e** *od* **m~e** the least; **zum M~en** *od* **m~en** at least; **nicht im M~en** *od* **m~en** not in the least. **m~ens** *adv* at least. **M~lohn** *m* minimum wage. **M~maß** *nt* minimum

Mine *f* -,-n mine; (*Bleistift-*) lead; (*Kugelschreiber-*) refill. **M~nfeld** *nt* minefield. **M~nräumboot** *nt* minesweeper

Mineral nt -s,-e & -ien /-jən/ mineral. **m~isch** a mineral. **M~ogie** f - mineralogy.

M~wasser nt mineral water

Miniatur f -,-en miniature

Minigolf nt miniature golf

minimal a minimal

Minimum nt -s,-ma minimum

Minirock m miniskirt

Mini|**ster** m, -s,- minister. **m~steriell** a ministerial. **M~sterium** nt -s,-ien ministry

Minorität f -,-en minority

minus conj, adv & prep (+ gen) minus. **M~** nt - deficit; (Nachteil) disadvantage. **M~zeichen** nt minus [sign]

Minute f -,-n minute

mir pron (dat of **ich**) [to] me; (refl) myself; **mir nichts, dir nichts** without so much as a 'by your leave'

Misch|**ehe** f mixed marriage. **m~en** vt mix; blend ⟨Tee, Kaffee⟩; toss ⟨Salat⟩; shuffle ⟨Karten⟩; **sich m~en** vt mix. **m~en** vir; (Person,) mingle (unter + acc with); **sich m~en** in (+ acc) join in ⟨Gespräch⟩; meddle in ⟨Angelegenheit⟩ □ vi (haben) shuffle the cards. **M~ling** m -s,-e half-caste; (Hund) cross. **M~masch** m -[e]s,-e (fam) hotchpotch. **M~ung** f -,-en mixture; blend

miserabel a abominable; (erbärmlich) wretched

missachten (**mißachten**) vt disregard

Miss|**achtung** (**Miß**|**achtung**) f disregard. **M~behagen** nt [feeling of] unease. **M~bildung** f deformity

missbilligen (**mißbilligen**) vt disapprove of

Miss|**billigung** (**Miß**|**billigung**) f disapproval. **M~brauch** m abuse; (Missbrauch treiben) misuse. **M~brauch treiben mit** abuse

miss|**brauchen** (**miß**|**brauchen**) vt abuse; (vergewaltigen) rape. **m~deuten** vt misinterpret

missen vt do without; **ich möchte es nicht m~** I should not like to be without it

Miss|**erfolg** (**Miß**|**erfolg**) m failure. **M~ernte** f crop failure

Misse|**tat** f misdeed. **M~täter** m (fam) culprit

missfallen (**mißfallen†**) vi (haben) displease (jdm s.o.)

Miss|**fallen** (**Miß**|**fallen**) nt -s displeasure; (Missbilligung) disapproval. **m~gebildet** a deformed. **M~geburt** f freak; (fig) monstrosity. **M~geschick** nt mishap; (Unglück) misfortune. **m~gestimmt** a **m~gestimmt sein** be in a bad mood

miss|**glücken** (**miß**|**glücken**) vi (sein) fail. **m~gönnen** vt begrudge

Miss|**griff** (**Miß**|**griff**) m mistake. **M~gunst** f resentment. **m~günstig** a resentful

misshandeln (**mißhandeln**) vt ill-treat

Miss|**handlung** (**Miß**|**handlung**) f ill-treatment. **M~hellig**|**keit** f -,-en disagreement

Mission f -,-en mission

Missionar(in) m -s,-e (f -,-nen) missionary

Miss|**klang** (**Miß**|**klang**) m discord. **M~kredit** m discredit; in **M~kredit bringen** discredit. **m~lich** a awkward. **m~liebig** a unpopular

misslingen† (**mißlingen†**) vi (sein) fail; **es misslang ihr** she failed. **M~** nt -s failure

Missmut (**Mißmut**) m ill humour. **m~ig** a morose, adv -ly

missraten† (**mißraten†**) vi (sein) turn out badly

Miss|**stand** (**Miß**|**stand**) m abuse; (Zustand) undesirable state of affairs. **M~stimmung** f discord; (Laune) bad mood. **M~ton** m discordant note

misstrauen (**mißtrauen**) vi (haben) jdm/etw m~ mistrust s.o./sth; (Argwohn hegen) distrust s.o./sth

Misstrau|en (Miβtrau|en) nt -s mistrust; (Argwohn) distrust. **M~ensvotum** nt vote of no confidence. **m~isch** a distrustful; (argwöhnisch) suspicious

Miss|verhältnis (Miβ|verhältnis) nt disproportion. **M~verständnis** nt misunderstanding. **m~verstehen†** vt misunderstand. **M~wirtschaft** f mismanagement

Mist m -[e]s manure; (fam) rubbish

Mistel f -,-n mistletoe

Misthaufen m dungheap

mit prep (+ dat) with; (sprechen) to; (mittels) by; (inklusive) including; (bei) at; **mit Bleistift** in pencil; **mit lauter Stimme** in a loud voice; **mit drei Jahren** at the age of three □ adv (auch) as well; **mit anfassen** (fig) lend a hand; **es ist mit das ärmste Land der Welt** it is among the poorest countries in the world

Mitarbeit f collaboration. **m~en** vi sep collaborate (**an** + dat on). **M~er(in)** m(f) collaborator; (Kollege) colleague; (Betriebsangehörige) employee

Mitbestimmung f co-determination

mitbring|en† vt sep bring [along]; **jdm Blumen m~en** bring/(hinbringen) take s.o. flowers. **M~sel** nt -s,- present (brought back from holiday etc)

Mitbürger m fellow citizen

miteinander adv with each other

miterleben vt sep witness

Mitesser m (Med) blackhead

mitfahren† vi sep (sein) go/come along; **mit jdm m~** go with s.o.; (mitgenommen werden) be given a lift by s.o.

mitfühlen vi sep (haben) sympathize. **m~d** a sympathetic; (mitleidig) compassionate

mitgeben† vt sep jdm etw m~ give s.o. sth to take with him

Mitgefühl nt sympathy

mitgehen† vi sep (sein) **mit jdm m~** go with s.o.; **etw m~ lassen** (fam) pinch sth

mitgenommen a worn; **m~ sein** be in a sorry state; (erschöpft) be exhausted

Mitgift f -,-en dowry

Mitglied nt member. **M~schaft** f - membership

mithalten† vi sep (haben) join in; **mit jdm nicht m~ können** not be able to keep up with s.o.

Mithilfe f assistance

mithilfe prep (+ gen) with the aid of

mitkommen† vi sep (sein) come [along] too; (fig: folgen können) keep up; (verstehen) follow

Mitlaut m consonant

Mitleid nt pity, compassion; **M~ erregend** pitiful. **M~enschaft** f in **M~enschaft ziehen** affect. **m~erregend** a = **M~ erregend**, s. Mitleid. **m~ig** a pitying; (mitfühlend) compassionate. **m~slos** a pitiless

mitmachen v sep □ vt take part in; (erleben) go through □ vi (haben) join in

Mitmensch m fellow man

mitnehmen† vt sep take along; (mitfahren lassen) give a lift to; (fig: schädigen) affect badly; (erschöpfen) exhaust; **'zum M~'** 'to take away', (Amer) 'to go'

mitnichten adv not at all

mitreden vi sep (haben) join in [the conversation]; (mit entscheiden) have a say (**bei** in)

mitreißen† vt sep sweep along; (fig: begeistern) carry away; **m~d** rousing

mitsamt prep (+ dat) together with

mitschneiden† vt sep record

mitschreiben† vt sep (haben) take down

Mitschuld f partial blame. **m~ig**
a **m~ig sein** to be partly to blame

Mitschüler(in) m(f) fellow pupil

mitspiel|en vi sep (haben) join in;
(Theat) be in the cast; (beitragen)
play a part; **jdm übel m~en** treat
s.o. badly. **M~er** m fellow player;
(Mitwirkender) participant

Mittag m midday, noon; (Mahlzeit) lunch; (Pause) lunch-break;
heute/gestern M~ at lunch-time today/yesterday; **[zu] M~
essen** have lunch. **m~s** adv at
noon. **heute/gestern m~** (NEW) **heute/gestern M~,** s. **Mittag. M~essen**
nt lunch. **m~s** adv at noon; (als
Mahlzeit) for lunch; **um 12 Uhr
m~s** at noon. **M~spause** f
lunch-hour; (Pause) lunch-break.
M~sschlaf m after-lunch nap.
M~stisch m lunch table; (Essen)
lunch. **M~szeit** f lunch-time

Mittäter|(in) m(f) accomplice.
M~schaft f complicity

Mitte f -,-n middle; (Zentrum)
centre; **die goldene M~** the
golden mean; **M~ Mai** in mid-
May; **in unserer M~** in our
midst

mitteil|en vt sep **jdm etw m~en**
tell s.o. sth; (amtlich) inform s.o.
of sth. **m~sam** a communicative.
M~ung f -,-en communication;
(Nachricht) piece of news

Mittel nt -s,- means sg; (Heil)remedy; (Medikament) medicine;
(M~wert) mean; (Durchschnitt)
average; **M~** pl (Geld-) funds, resources. **m~** pred a medium;
(m~mäßig) middling. **M~alter**
nt Middle Ages pl. **m~alterlich**
a medieval. **m~bar** a indirect,
adv -ly. **M~ding** nt (fig) cross.
m~europäisch a Central European. **M~finger** m middle finger.
m~groß a medium-sized; (Person) of medium height.
M~klasse f middle range.
m~los a destitute. **m~mäßig** a

middling; [nur] **m~mäßig** mediocre. **M~meer** nt Mediterranean. **M~punkt** m centre;
(fig) centre of attention

mittels prep (+ gen) by means of

Mittel|schule f = **Realschule.**
M~smann m (pl -männer).
M~sperson f intermediary, go-
between. **M~stand** m middle
class. **m~ste(r,s)** a middle.
M~streifen m (Auto) central reservation; (Amer) median strip.
M~stürmer m centre-forward.
M~weg m (fig) middle course;
goldener M~weg happy medium. **M~welle** f medium wave.
M~wort nt (pl -wörter) participle

mitten adv **m~ in/auf (dat/acc)**
in the middle of; **m~ unter (dat/
acc)** amidst. **m~durch** adv
[right] through the middle

Mitternacht f midnight

mittler|e(r,s) a middle; (Größe,
Qualität) medium; (durchschnittlich) mean, average.
m~weile adv meanwhile; (seitdem) by now

Mittwoch m -s,-e Wednesday.
m~s adv on Wednesdays

mitunter adv now and again

mitwirk|en vi sep (haben) take
part; (helfen) contribute. **M~ung**
f participation

mix|en vt mix. **M~er** m -s,- (Culin) liquidizer, blender. **M~tur**
f -,-en (Med) mixture

Möbel pl furniture sg. **M~stück**
nt piece of furniture.
M~tischler m cabinet-maker.
M~wagen m removal van

mobil a mobile; (fam: munter)
lively; (nach Krankheit) fit [and
well]; **m~machen** mobilize

Mobile nt -s,-s mobile

Mobiliar nt -s furniture

mobilisier|en vt mobilize.
M~ung f - mobilization

Mobil|machung f - mobilization.
M~telefon nt mobile phone

möblier|en vt furnish; **m~tes
Zimmer** furnished room

mochte, möchte s. mögen
Modalverb nt modal auxiliary
Mode f -,-n fashion; **M~** sein be fashionable
Modell nt -s,-e model; **M~** stehen pose (jdm for s.o.). **m~ieren** vt model
Modenschau f fashion show
Moderator m -s,-en /-'to:rən/, **M~torin** f -,-nen (TV) presenter
modern[1] vi (haben) decay
modern[2] a modern; (modisch) fashionable. **m~isieren** vt modernize
Mode|schmuck m costume jewellery. **M~schöpfer** m fashion designer
Modifi|kation /-'tsjo:n/ f -,-en modification. **m~zieren** vt modify
modisch a fashionable
Modistin f -,-nen milliner
modrig a musty
modulieren vt modulate
Mofa nt -s,-s moped
mogeln vi (haben) (fam) cheat
mögen† vt like; lieber m~ prefer □ v aux ich möchte I'd like; **möchtest du nach Hause?** do you want to go home? **ich mag nicht mehr** I've had enough; **ich hätte weinen m~** I could have cried; **ich mag mich irren** I may be wrong; **wer/was mag das sein?** whoever/whatever can it be? **wie mag es ihm ergangen sein?** I wonder how he got on; **[das] mag sein** that may well be; **mag kommen, was da will** come what may
möglich a possible; **alle m~en** all sorts of; **über alles M~e (m~e) sprechen** talk about all sorts of things; **sein M~stes (m~stes) tun** do one's utmost. **m~erweise** adv possibly. **M~keit** f -,-en possibility. **M~keitsform** f subjunctive. **m~st** adv if possible; **m~st viel/früh** as much/early as possible

Mohammedan|er(in) m -s,- (f -,-nen) Muslim. **m~isch** a Muslim
Mohn m -s poppy; (Culin) poppyseed. **M~blume** f poppy
Möhre, Mohrrübe f -,-n carrot
mokieren (sich) vr make fun (über + acc of)
Mokka m -s mocha; (Geschmack) coffee
Molch m -[e]s,-e newt
Mole f -,-n (Naut) mole
Molekül nt -s,-e molecule
Molkerei f -,-en dairy
Moll nt - (Mus) minor
mollig a cosy; (warm) warm; (rundlich) plump
Moment m -s,-e moment; **im/jeden M~** at the/any moment; **M~[mal]!** just a moment! **m~an** a momentary, adv -ily; (gegenwärtig) at the moment
Momentaufnahme f snapshot
Monarch m -en,-en monarch. **M~ie** f -,-n monarchy
Monat m -s,-e month. **m~elang** adv for months. **m~lich** a & adv monthly. **M~skarte** f monthly season ticket
Mönch m -[e]s,-e monk
Mond m -[e]s,-e moon
mondän a fashionable, adv -bly
Mond|finsternis f lunar eclipse. **m~hell** a moonlit. **M~sichel** f crescent moon. **M~schein** m moonlight
monieren vt criticize
Monitor m -s,-en /-'to:rən/ (Techn) monitor
Monogramm nt -s,-e monogram
Mono|log m -s,-e monologue. **M~pol** nt -s,-e monopoly. **m~polisieren** vt monopolize. **m~ton** a monotonous, adv -ly. **M~tonie** f -,- monotony
Monster nt -s,- monster
monströs a monstrous. **M~osität** f -,-en monstrosity
Monstrum nt -s,-stren monster
Monsun m -s,-e monsoon
Montag m Monday

Montage /mɔn'taːʒə/ f -,-n fitting; (Zusammenbau) assembly; (Film-) editing; (Kunst) montage

montags adv on Mondays

Montanindustrie f coal and steel industry

Monteur /mɔn'tøːɐ/ m -s,-e fitter. **M~anzug** m overalls pl

montieren vt fit; (zusammenbauen) assemble

Monument nt -[e]s,-e monument. **m~al** a monumental

Moor nt -[e]s,-e bog; (Heide-) moor

Moos nt es,-e moss **m~ig** a mossy

Mop m -s,-s (NEW) **Mopp**

Moped nt -s,-s moped

Mopp m -s,-s mop

Mops m -s,-̈e pug [dog]

Moral f - morals pl, (Selbstvertrauen) morale; (Lehre) moral. **m~isch** a moral, adv -ly. **m~isieren** vi (haben) moralize

Morast m -[e]s,-e morass; (Schlamm) mud

Mord m -[e]s,-e murder, (Pol) assassination. **M~anschlag** m murder/assassination attempt. **m~en** vt/i (haben) murder, kill

Mörder m -s,- murderer, (Pol) assassin. **M~in** f -,-nen murderess. **m~isch** a murderous; (fam: schlimm) dreadful

Mords- pref (fam) terrific. **m~mäßig** a (fam) frightful, adv -ly

morgen adv tomorrow; **m~ Abend** (abend)/**Nachmittag** (nachmittag) tomorrow evening/afternoon; **heute/gestern/Montag M~** (NEW) **heute/gestern/Montag M~**, s. **Morgen**

Morgen m -s,- morning; (Maß) ≈ acre; **am M~** in the morning; **heute/gestern/Montag M~** this/yesterday/Monday morning. **M~dämmerung** f dawn. **m~dlich** a morning. **M~grauen** nt -s dawn; **im M~grauen** at dawn. **M~mantel, M~rock** m dressing-gown.

M~rot nt red sky in the morning. **m~s** a in the morning

morgig a tomorrow's; **der m~e Tag** tomorrow

Morphium nt -s morphine

morsch a rotten

Morsealphabet nt Morse code

Mörtel m -s mortar

Mosaik /moza'iːk/ nt -s,-e[n] mosaic

Moschee f -,-n mosque

Mosel f - Moselle. **M~wein** m Moselle [wine]

Moskau nt -s Moscow

Moskito m -s,-s mosquito

Moslem m -s,-s Muslim. **m~lemisch** a Muslim

Most m -[e]s must; (Apfel-) ≈ cider

Mostrich m -s (NGer) mustard

Motel nt -s,-s motel

Motiv nt -s,-e motive; (Kunst) motif. **M~ation** /-'tsjoːn/ f - motivation. **m~ieren** vt motivate

Motor /'moːtɔr, mo'toːɐ/ m -s,-en /-'toːrən/ engine; (Elektro-) motor. **M~boot** nt motor boat

motorisieren vt motorize

Motor|rad nt motor cycle. **M~radfahrer** m motor-cyclist. **M~roller** m motor scooter

Motte f -,-n moth. **M~nkugel** f mothball

Motto nt -s,-s motto

Möwe f -,-n gull

Mücke f -,-n gnat; (kleine) midge; (Stech-) mosquito

mucksen (sich) vr sich nicht **m~** (fam) keep quiet

müd|e a tired; **nicht m~e werden/es m~e sein** not tire of sth; **tired** (etw zu tun of doing sth). **M~igkeit** f - tiredness

Muff m -s,-e muff

muffig a musty; (fam: mürrisch) grumpy

Mühe f -,-n effort; (Aufwand) trouble; **sich** (dat) **M~ geben** make an effort; (sich bemühen) try; **nicht der M~ wert** not worth while; **mit M~ und Not** with great difficulty; (*gerade noch*) only just. **m~los** *a* effortless, *adv* -ly

muhen *vi* (*haben*) moo

mühe|n (sich) *vr* struggle. **m~voll** *a* laborious; (*anstrengend*) arduous

Mühl|e *f* -,-n mill; (*Kaffee-*) grinder. **M~stein** *m* millstone

Müh|sal *f* -,-e (*liter*) toil; (*Mühe*) trouble. **m~sam** *a* laborious, *adv* -ly; (*beschwerlich*) difficult, *adv* with difficulty. **m~selig** *a* laborious, *adv* -ly

Mulde *f* -,-n hollow

Müll *m* -s rubbish, (*Amer*) garbage. **M~abfuhr** *f* refuse collection

Mullbinde *f* gauze bandage

Mülleimer *m* waste bin; (*Mülltonne*) dustbin, (*Amer*) garbage can

Müller *m* -s,- miller

Müll|halde *f* [rubbish] dump. **M~schlucker** *m* refuse chute. **M~tonne** *f* dustbin, (*Amer*) garbage can. **M~wagen** *m* dustcart, (*Amer*) garbage truck

mulmig *a* (*fam*) dodgy; (*Gefühl*) uneasy; **ihm war m~ zumute** he felt uneasy/(*übel*) queasy

multi|national *a* multinational. **M~plikation** /-'tsjo:n/ *f* -,-en multiplication. **m~plizieren** *vt* multiply

Mumie /'mu:mjə/ *f* -,-n mummy

mumifizi̱ert *a* mummified

Mumm *m* -s (*fam*) energy

Mumps *m* - mumps

Mund *m* -[e]s,‿er mouth; **ein M~ voll Suppe** a mouthful of soup; **halt den M~!** be quiet! (*sl*) shut up! **M~art** *f* dialect. **m~artlich** *a* dialectal

Mündel *nt & m* -s,- (*Jur*) ward. **m~sicher** *a* gilt-edged

münden *vi* (*sein*) flow/(*Straße:*) lead (**in** + *acc* into)

mund|faul *a* taciturn. **M~geruch** *m* bad breath. **M~harmonika** *f* mouth-organ

mündig *a* **m~ sein/werden** (*Jur*) be/come of age. **M~keit** *f* - (*Jur*) majority

mündlich *a* verbal, *adv* -ly; **m~e Prüfung** oral

Mund|stück *nt* mouthpiece; (*Zigaretten-*) tip. **m~tot** *a* **m~tot machen** (*fig*) gag

Mündung *f* -,-en (*Fluss-*) mouth; (*Gewehr-*) muzzle

Mund|voll *m* -,- **ein M~voll** (NEW) **ein M~ voll**, s. **Mund**. **M~wasser** *nt* mouthwash. **M~werk** *nt* **ein gutes M~werk haben** (*fam*) be very talkative. **M~winkel** *m* corner of the mouth

Munition /-'tsjo:n/ *f* - ammunition

munkeln *vt/i* (*haben*) talk (**von** of); **es wird gemunkelt** rumour has it (**dass** that)

Münster *nt* -s,- cathedral

munter *a* lively; (*heiter*) merry; **m~ sein** (*wach*) be wide awake/(*aufgestanden, gesund*) up and about; **gesund und m~** fit and well □ *adv* [**immer**] **m~** merrily

Münz|e *f* -,-n coin; (*M~stätte*) mint. **m~en** *vt* mint; **das war auf dich gemünzt** (*fam*) that was aimed at you. **M~fernsprecher** *m* coin-box telephone, payphone. **M~wäscherei** *f* launderette

mürbe *a* crumbly; (*Obst*) mellow; (*Fleisch*) tender; **jdn m~ machen** (*fig*) wear s.o. down. **M~teig** *m* short pastry

Murmel *f* -,-n marble

murmeln *vt/i* (*haben*) murmur; (*undeutlich*) mumble, mutter. **M~** *nt* -s murmur

Murmeltier *nt* marmot

murren *vt/i* (*haben*) grumble

mürrisch *a* surly

Mus *nt* -es purée

Muschel *f* -,-n mussel; (*Schale*) [sea] shell

Museum /mu'ze:ʊm/ *nt* -s,-seen /-'ze:ən/ museum

Musik f - music. **M~alien** /-jən/ pl [printed] music sg. **m~alisch** a musical

Musikbox f juke-box

Musiker(in) m -s,- (f -,-nen) musician

Musik|instrument nt musical instrument. **M~kapelle** f band. **M~pavillon** m bandstand

musisch a artistic

musizieren vi (haben) make music

Muskat m -[e]s nutmeg

Muskel m -s,-n muscle. **M~kater** m stiff and aching muscles pl

Musku|latur f - muscles pl. **m~lös** a muscular

Müsli nt -s muesli

muss (muß) s. **müssen. Muss (Muß)** nt -ein - a must

Muße f - leisure; **mit M~** at leisure

müssen† v aux etw tun m~ have to/(fam) have got to do sth; **ich muss jetzt gehen** I have to or must go now; **ich musste lachen** I had to laugh; **ich muss es wissen** I need to know; **du müsstest es mal versuchen** you ought to or should try it; **muss das sein?** is that necessary?

müßig a idle; (unnütz) futile. **M~gang** m - idleness

musste (mußte), **müsste (müßte)** s. **müssen**

Muster nt -s,- pattern; (Probe) sample; (Vorbild) model. **M~bei-spiel** nt typical example; (Vor-bild) perfect example. **M~betrieb** m model factory. **m~gültig**, **m~haft** a exemplary. **m~n** vt eye; (inspizieren) inspect. **M~schüler(in)** m(f) model pupil. **M~ung** f -,-en inspection; (Mil) medical; (Muster) pattern

Mut m -[e]s courage; **jdm Mut machen** encourage s.o.; **zu M~e sein = zumute sein**, s. **zumute**

Mutation /-'tsio:n/ f -,-en (Biol) mutation

mut|ig a courageous, adv -ly. **m~los** a despondent; (entmutigt) disheartened

mutmaß|en vt presume; (Vermutungen anstellen) speculate. **m~lich** a probable, adv -bly; **der m~liche Täter** the suspect. **M~ung** f -,-en speculation, conjecture

Mutprobe f test of courage

Mutter[1] f -,- mother; **werdende M~** mother-to-be

Mutter[2] f -,-n (Techn) nut

Muttergottes f -,- madonna

Mutter|land nt motherland. **M~leib** m womb

mütterlich a maternal; (für-sorglich) motherly. **m~erseits** adv on one's/the mother's side

Mutter|mal nt birthmark; (dun-kel) mole. **M~schaft** f - motherhood. **m~seelenallein** a & adv all alone. **M~sprache** f mother tongue. **M~tag** m Mother's Day

Mutti f -,-s (fam) mummy

Mutwill|e m wantonness. **m~ig** a wanton, adv -ly

Mütze f -,-n cap; **wollene M~** woolly hat

MwSt. abbr (Mehrwertsteuer) VAT

mysteriös a mysterious, adv -ly

Myst|ik /'mʏstɪk/ f - mysticism. **m~isch** a mystical

myth|isch a mythical. **M~ologie** f - mythology. **M~os** m -,-then myth

N

na int well; **na gut** all right then; **na ja** oh well; **na und?** so what?

Nabe f -,-n hub

Nabel m -s,- navel. **N~schnur** f umbilical cord

nach prep (+ dat) after; (Uhrzeit) past; (Richtung) to; (greifen, rufen, sich sehnen) for; (gemäß) according to; meiner Meinung n~ in my opinion; n~ oben upwards □ adv n~ und n~ gradually, bit by bit; n~ wie vor still

nachäffen vt sep mimic

nachahm|en vt sep imitate. N~ung f -,-en imitation

nacharbeiten vt sep make up for

nacharten vi sep (sein) (+ dat) take after s.o.

Nachbar|(in) m -n,-n (f -,-nen) neighbour. N~haus nt house next door. N~land nt neighbouring country. n~lich a neighbourly; (Nachbar-) neighbouring. N~schaft f - neighbourhood; gute N~schaft neighbourliness

nachbestell|en vt sep reorder. N~ung f repeat order

nachbild|en vt sep copy, reproduce. N~ung f copy, reproduction

nachdatieren vt sep backdate

nachdem conj after; je n~ it depends

nachdenk|en† vi sep (haben) think (über + acc about). N~en nt -s reflection, thought. n~lich a thoughtful, adv -ly

Nachdruck m (pl -e) reproduction; (unveränderter) reprint; (Betonung) emphasis

nachdrücklich a emphatic, adv -ally

nacheifern vi sep (haben) jdm n~ emulate s.o.

nacheilen vi sep (sein) (+ dat) hurry after

nacheinander adv one after the other

Nachfahre m -n,-n descendant

Nachfolg|e f succession. n~en vi sep (sein) (+ dat) follow; (im Amt) succeed. N~er(in) m -s,- (f -,-nen) successor

nachforsch|en vi sep (haben) make enquiries. N~ung f -en enquiry; N~ungen anstellen make enquiries

Nachfrage f (Comm) demand. n~n vi sep (haben) enquire

nachfüllen vt sep refill (Behälter); Wasser n~ fill up with water

nachgeben† v sep □ vi (haben) give way; (sich fügen) give in, yield □ vt jdm Suppe n~ give s.o. more soup

Nachgebühr f surcharge

nachgehen† vi sep (sein) (Uhr:) be slow; jdm/etw n~ follow s.o./ sth; follow up (Spur, Angelegenheit); pursue (Angelegenheit, Tätigkeit); go about (Arbeit)

nachgeraten† vi sep (sein) jdm n~ take after s.o.

Nachgeschmack m after-taste

nachgiebig a indulgent; (gefällig) compliant. N~keit f - indulgence; compliance

nachgrübeln vi sep (haben) ponder (über + acc on)

nachhallen vi sep (haben) reverberate

nachhaltig a lasting

nachhause adv = nach Hause, s. Haus

nachhelfen† vi sep (haben) help

nachher adv later; (danach) afterwards; bis n~! see you later!

Nachhilfeunterricht m coaching

Nachhinein (nachhinein) adv im N~ (n~) afterwards

nachhinken vi sep (sein) (fig) lag behind

nachholen vt sep (später holen) fetch later; (mehr holen) get more; (später machen) do later; (aufholen) catch up on; make up for (Zeit)

nachjagen vi sep (haben) (+ dat) chase after

Nachkomme m -n,-n descendant. n~n† vi sep (sein) follow [later], come later; (Schritt halten) keep up; **etw** ⟨*dat*⟩ **n~n** ⟨*fig*⟩ comply with ⟨*Bitte, Wunsch*⟩; carry out ⟨*Versprechen, Pflicht*⟩. **N~schaft** *f* - descendants *pl*, progeny

Nachkriegszeit *f* post-war period

Nachlass *m* -es,ᵉe ⟨**Nachlaß** *m* -sses,ˉsse⟩ discount; ⟨*of deceased's*⟩ estate

nachlassen† *v sep* □ *vi* ⟨*haben*⟩ decrease; ⟨*Regen, Hitze:*⟩ let up; ⟨*Schmerz:*⟩ ease; ⟨*Sturm:*⟩ abate; ⟨*Augen, Kräfte, Leistungen:*⟩ deteriorate; **er ließ nicht nach [mit Fragen]** he persisted [with his questions] □ *vt* **etw vom Preis n~** take sth off the price

nachlässig *a* careless, *adv* -ly; ⟨*leger*⟩ casual, *adv* -ly; ⟨*unordentlich*⟩ sloppy, *adv* -ily. **N~keit** *f* - carelessness; sloppiness

nachlaufen† *vi sep* ⟨*sein*⟩ (+ *dat*) run after

nachlegen *vt sep* **Holz/Kohlen n~** put more wood/coal on the fire

nachlesen† *vt sep* look up

nachlöse|n *vi sep* ⟨*haben*⟩ pay one's fare on the train/on arrival. **N~schalter** *m* excess-fare office

nachmachen *vt sep* ⟨*später machen*⟩ do later; ⟨*imitieren*⟩ imitate, copy; ⟨*fälschen*⟩ forge; **jdm etw n~** copy sth from s.o.; repeat ⟨*Übung*⟩ after s.o.

Nachmittag *m* afternoon; **heute/ gestern N~** this/yesterday afternoon. **n~** *adv* **heute/gestern n~** NEW **heute/gestern N~**, s. **Nachmittag**. **n~s** *adv* in the afternoon

Nachnahme *f* **etw per N~ schicken** send sth cash on delivery or COD

Nachname *m* surname

Nachporto *nt* excess postage

nachprüfen *vt sep* check, verify

nachrechnen *vt sep* work out; ⟨*prüfen*⟩ check

Nachrede *f* **üble N~** defamation

Nachricht *f* -,-en [piece of] news *sg*; **N~en** news *sg*; **eine N~ hinterlassen** leave a message; **jdm N~ geben** inform, notify s.o. **N~endienst** *m* ⟨*Mil*⟩ intelligence service. **N~ensendung** *f* news bulletin. **N~enwesen** *nt* communications *pl*

nachrücken *vi sep* ⟨*sein*⟩ move up

Nachruf *m* obituary

nachsagen *vt sep* repeat ⟨*said after s.o.*⟩; **jdm Schlechtes/ Gutes n~** speak ill/well of s.o.; **man sagt ihm nach, dass er geizig ist** he is said to be stingy

Nachsaison *f* late season

Nachsatz *m* postscript

nachschicken *vt sep* ⟨*später schicken*⟩ send later; ⟨*hinterher-*⟩ send after ⟨*jdm s.o.*⟩; send on ⟨*Post*⟩ ⟨**jdm** to s.o.⟩

nachschlagen† *v sep* □ *vt* look up □ *vi* ⟨*haben*⟩ **in einem Wörterbuch n~en** consult a dictionary; **jdm n~en** take after s.o. **N~ewerk** *nt* reference book

Nachschlüssel *m* duplicate key

Nachschrift *f* transcript; ⟨*Nachsatz*⟩ postscript

Nachschub *m* ⟨*Mil*⟩ supplies *pl*

nachsehen† *v sep* □ *vt* ⟨*prüfen*⟩ check; ⟨*nachschlagen*⟩ look up; ⟨*hinwegsehen über*⟩ overlook □ *vi* ⟨*haben*⟩ have a look; ⟨*prüfen*⟩ check; **im Wörterbuch n~** consult a dictionary; **jdm/etw n~** gaze after s.o./sth. **N~** *nt* **das N~ haben** ⟨*fam*⟩ go empty-handed

nachsenden† *vt sep* forward ⟨*Post*⟩ ⟨**jdm** to s.o.⟩; **'bitte n~'** 'please forward'

Nachsicht *f* forbearance; ⟨*Milde*⟩ leniency; ⟨*Nachgiebigkeit*⟩ indulgence. **N~ig** *a* forbearing; lenient; indulgent

Nachsilbe *f* suffix

nachsitzen† *vi sep* ⟨*haben*⟩ **n~ müssen** be kept in [after school]; **jdn n~ lassen** give s.o. detention. **N~** *nt* -s ⟨*Sch*⟩ detention

Nachspeise *f* dessert, sweet

Nachspiel nt (fig) sequel

nachspionieren vi sep (haben) jdm n~ spy on s.o.

nachsprechen† vt sep repeat (jdm after s.o.)

nachspülen vt sep rinse

nächst /-çst/ prep (+ dat) next to. n~beste(r,s) a first [available]; (zweitbeste) next best. n~e(r,s) a next; (nächstgelegene) nearest; (Verwandte) closest; n~e Woche next week; in n~er Nähe close by; am n~en be nearest or closest □ pron der/die/das N~e (n~e) the next; der N~e (n~e) bitte next please; als N~es (n~es) next; fürs N~e (n~e) for the time being. N~e(r) m fellow man

nachstehend a following □ adv below

nachstellen v sep □ vt readjust; put back (Uhr) □ vi (haben) (+ dat) pursue

nächste|mal adv das n~emal (NEW) das nächste Mal, s. Mal[1]. N~enliebe f charity. N~ens adv shortly. n~gelegen a nearest. n~liegend a most obvious

nachstreben vi sep (haben) jdm n~ emulate s.o.

nachsuchen vi sep (haben) search; n~ um request

Nacht f -,ꞏe night; über/bei N~ overnight/at night; Montag/morgen N~ Monday/tomorrow night; heute N~ tonight; (letzte Nacht) last night; gestern N~ last night; (vorletzte Nacht) the night before last. n~ adv morgen/heute/gestern n~ (NEW) morgen/heute/gestern N~, s. Nacht. N~dienst m night duty

Nachteil m disadvantage; zum N~ to the detriment (gen of). n~ig a adverse, adv -ly

Nacht|essen nt (SGer) supper. N~falter m moth. N~hemd nt night-dress; (Männer-) nightshirt

Nachtigall f -,-en nightingale

Nachtisch m dessert

Nacht|klub m night-club. N~leben nt night-life

nächtlich a nocturnal, night ...

Nacht|lokal nt night-club. N~mahl nt (Aust) supper

Nachtrag m postscript; (Ergänzung) supplement. n~ent vt sep add; jdm etw n~en walk behind s.o. carrying sth; (fig) bear a grudge against s.o. for sth. n~end a vindictive; n~end sein bear grudges

nachträglich a subsequent, later; (verspätet) belated □ adv later; (nachher) afterwards; (verspätet) belatedly

nachtrauern vi sep (haben) (+ dat) mourn the loss of

Nacht|ruhe f night's rest; angenehme N~ruhe! sleep well! n~s adv at night; 2 Uhr n~s 2 o'clock in the morning. N~schicht f night-shift. N~tisch m bedside table. N~tischlampe f bedside lamp. N~topf m chamber-pot. N~wächter m night-watchman. N~zeit f night-time

Nachuntersuchung f check-up

nachwachsen† vi sep (sein) grow again

Nachwahl f by-election

Nachweis m -es,-e proof. n~bar a demonstrable. n~ent vt sep prove; (aufzeigen) show; (vermitteln) give details of; jdm nichts n~en können have no proof against s.o. n~lich a demonstrable, adv -bly

Nachwelt f posterity

Nachwirkung f after-effect

Nachwort nt (pl -e) epilogue

Nachwuchs m new generation; (fam: Kinder) offspring. N~spieler m young player

nachzahlen vt/i sep (haben) pay extra; (später zahlen) pay later; Steuern n~ pay tax arrears

nachzählen vt/i sep (haben) count again; (prüfen) check
Nachzahlung f extra/later payment; (Gehalts-) back-payment
nachzeichnen vt sep copy
Nachzügler m -s,- late-comer; (Zurückgebliebener) straggler
Nacken m -s,- nape or back of the neck
nackt a naked; (bloß, kahl) bare; (Wahrheit) plain. **N∼heit** f - nakedness, nudity. **N∼kultur** f nudism. **N∼schnecke** f slug
Nadel f -,-n needle; (Häkel-) hook; (Schmuck-, Hut-) pin. **N∼arbeit** f needlework. **N∼baum** m conifer. **N∼kissen** nt pincushion. **N∼stich** m stitch; (fig) pinprick. **N∼wald** m coniferous forest
Nagel m -s,- nail. **N∼bürste** f nail-brush. **N∼feile** f nail-file. **N∼haut** f cuticle. **N∼lack** m nail varnish. **n∼n** vt nail. **N∼neu** a brand-new. **N∼schere** f nail scissors pl
nagen vt/i (haben) gnaw (an + dat at); **n∼d** (fig) nagging
Nagetier nt rodent
nah a, adv & prep = **nahe**; **von nah und fern** from far and wide
Näharbeit f sewing; **eine N∼** a piece of sewing
Nahaufnahme f close-up
nahe a (näher, nächst) nearby; (zeitlich) imminent; (eng) close; **der N∼ Osten** the Middle East; **in n∼r Zukunft** in the near future; **von n∼m** [from] close to; **n∼ sein** be close (dat to); **den Tränen n∼** close to tears □ adv near, close; (verwandt) closely; **n∼ daran sein, etw zu tun** nearly do sth; **n∼ liegen** be close; (fig) be highly likely; **n∼ liegende Lösung** obvious solution; **n∼ legen** (fig) recommend (dat to); **jdm n∼ legen, etw zu tun** urge s.o. to do sth; **jdm n∼ stehen** (fig) be close to s.o.; **etw**

(dat) **n∼ kommen** (fig) come close to sth; **jdm n∼ kommen** (fig) get close to s.o.; **jdm n∼ gehen** (fig) affect s.o. deeply; **jdm zu n∼ treten** (fig) offend s.o. □ prep (+ dat) near [to], close to
Nähe f - nearness, proximity; **aus der N∼** [from] close to; **in der N∼** near or close by; **in der N∼ der Kirche** near the church
nahebei adv near or close by
nahe|gehen vi sep (sein) (NEW) n∼ gehen, s. nahe.
n∼kommen vi sep (sein) (NEW) n∼ kommen, s. nahe. **n∼legen** vt sep (NEW) n∼ legen, s. nahe. **n∼liegen** vi sep (haben) (NEW) n∼ liegen, s. nahe. **n∼liegend** a (NEW) n∼ liegend, s. nahe
nahen vi (sein) (liter) approach
nähen vt/i (haben) sew; (anfertigen) make; (Med) stitch [up]
näher a closer; (Weg) shorter; (Einzelheiten) further □ adv closer; (genauer) more closely; **n∼ kommen** come closer, approach; (fig) get closer (dat to); **sich n∼ erkundigen** make further enquiries; **n∼an** (+ acc/dat) nearer [to], closer to □ prep (+ dat) nearer [to], closer to. **N∼e[s]** nt [further] details pl. **n∼kommen** vi sep (sein) (NEW) n∼ kommen, s. näher. **n∼n (sich)** vr approach
nahestehen vi sep (haben) (NEW) nahe stehen, s. nahe
nahezu adv almost
Nähgarn nt [sewing] cotton
Nahkampf m close combat
Näh|maschine f sewing machine. **N∼nadel** f sewing-needle
nähren vt feed; (fig) nurture; **sich n∼ von** live on □ vi (haben) be nutritious
nahrhaft a nutritious
Nährstoff m nutrient
Nahrung f - food, nourishment. **N∼smittel** nt food
Nährwert m nutritional value

Naht f -,-e seam; (Med) suture. n~los a seamless

Nahverkehr m local service. N~szug m local train

Nähzeug nt sewing; (Zubehör) sewing kit

naiv /na'i:f/ a naïve, adv -ly. N~ität -/vi'te:t/ f naïvety

Name m -ns,-n name; im N~n (+ gen) in the name of; (handeln) on behalf of; das Kind beim rechten N~n nennen (fam) call a spade a spade. N~nlos a nameless; (unbekannt) unknown, anonymous. N~ns adv by the name of □ prep (+ gen) on behalf of. N~nstag m name-day. N~nsvetter m namesake. N~nszug m signature. n~ntlich adv by name; (besonders) especially

namhaft a noted; (ansehnlich) considerable; n~ machen name

nämlich adv (und zwar) namely; (denn) because

nanu int hallo

Napf m -[e]s,-e bowl

Narbe f -,-n scar

Narkose f -,-n general anaesthetic. N~arzt m anaesthetist. N~mittel nt anaesthetic

Narkot|ikum nt -s,-ka narcotic; (Narkosemittel) anaesthetic. n~isieren vt anaesthetize

Narr m -en,-en fool; zum N~en haben od halten make a fool of. n~en vt fool. n~ensicher a foolproof. N~heit f -,-en folly

Närr|in f -,-nen fool. n~isch a foolish; (fam: verrückt) crazy (auf + acc about)

Narzisse f -,-n narcissus; gelbe N~ daffodil

nasal a nasal

nasch|en vt/i (haben) nibble (an + dat at); wer hat vom Kuchen genascht? who's been at the cake? n~haft a sweet-toothed

Nase f -,-n nose; an der N~ herumführen (fam) dupe

näseln vi (haben) speak through one's nose; n~d nasal

Nasen|bluten nt -s nosebleed. N~loch nt nostril. N~rücken m bridge of the nose

Naseweis m -es,-e (fam) know-all

Nashorn nt rhinoceros

nass (naß) a (nasser, nassest) wet

Nässe f - wet; (Nasssein) wetness. n~n vt wet

nasskalt (naßkalt) a cold and wet

Nation /na'tsjo:n/ f -,-en nation. n~al a national. N~alhymne f national anthem. N~alismus m - nationalism. N~alität f -,-en nationality. N~alsozialismus m National Socialism. N~alspieler m international

Natrium nt -s sodium

Natron nt -s doppeltkohlensaures N~ bicarbonate of soda

Natter f -,-n snake; (Gift-) viper

Natur f -,-en nature; von N~ aus by nature. N~alien /-jan/ pl natural produce sg. n~alisieren vt naturalize. N~alisierung f -,-en naturalization

Naturell nt -s,-e disposition

Natur|erscheinung f natural phenomenon. n~farben a natural[-coloured]. N~forscher m naturalist. N~kunde f natural history. N~lehrpfad m nature trail

natürlich a natural □ adv naturally; (selbstverständlich) of course. N~keit f - naturalness

natur|rein a pure. N~schutz m nature conservation; unter N~schutz stehen be protected. N~schutzgebiet nt nature reserve. N~wissenschaft f [natural] science. N~wissenschaftler m scientist. n~wissenschaftlich a scientific; (Sch) science …

nautisch a nautical

Navigation /-'tsjo:n/ f - navigation

Nazi *m* **-s,-s** Nazi

n.Chr. *abbr* (**nach Christus**) AD

Nebel *m* **-s,-** fog; (*leicht*) mist. **n~haft** *a* hazy. **N~horn** *nt* foghorn. **n~ig** *a* = neblig

neben *prep* (+ *dat/acc*) next to, beside; (+ *dat*) (*außer*) apart from; **n~ mir** next to me. **n~an** *adv* next door

Neben|anschluss (**Neben-anschluß**) *m* (*Teleph*) extension. **N~ausgaben** *fpl* incidental expenses

nebenbei *adv* in addition; (*beiläufig*) casually; **n~ bemerkt** incidentally

Neben|bemerkung *f* passing remark. **N~beruf** *m* second job. **N~beschäftigung** *f* spare-time occupation. **N~buhler(in)** *m* (*f* -,-nen) rival

nebeneinander *adv* next to each other, side by side

Neben|eingang *m* side entrance. **N~fach** *nt* (*Univ*) subsidiary subject. **N~fluss** (**N~fluß**) *m* tributary. **N~gleis** *nt* siding. **N~haus** *nt* house next door

nebenher *adv* in addition. **n~gehen†** *vi sep* (*sein*) walk alongside

nebenhin *adv* casually

Neben|höhle *f* sinus. **N~kosten** *pl* additional costs. **N~mann** *m* (*pl* -männer) person next to one. **N~produkt** *nt* by-product. **N~rolle** *f* supporting role; (*Kleine*) minor role; **eine N~rolle spielen** (*fig*) be unimportant. **N~sache** *f* unimportant matter. **n~sächlich** *a* unimportant. **N~satz** *m* subordinate clause. **N~straße** *f* minor road; (*Seiten-*) side street. **N~verdienst** *m* additional earnings *pl*. **N~wirkung** *f* side-effect. **N~zimmer** *nt* room next door

neblig *a* foggy; (*leicht*) misty

nebst *prep* (+ *dat*) [together] with

Necessaire /nese'sε:ɐ̯/ *nt* **-s,-s** toilet bag; (*Näh-, Nagel-*) set

neck|en *vt* tease. **N~erei** *f* - teasing. **n~isch** *a* teasing; (*kess*) saucy

nee *adv* (*fam*) no

Neffe *m* **-n,-n** nephew

negativ *a* negative. **N~** *nt* **-s,-e** (*Phot*) negative

Neger *m* **-s,-** Negro

nehmen† *vt* take (*dat* from); **sich** (*dat*) **etw n~** take sth; help oneself to (*Essen*); **jdn zu sich n~** have s.o. to live with one

Neid *m* **-[e]s** envy, jealousy. **n~en** *vt* **jdm den Erfolg n~** be jealous of s.o.'s success. **n~isch** *a* envious, jealous (**auf** + *acc* of); **auf jdn n~isch sein** envy s.o.

neig|en *vt* incline; (*zur Seite*) tilt; (*beugen*) bend; **sich n~en** incline; (*Boden:*) slope; (*Person:*) bend (**über** + *acc* over) □ *vi* (*haben*) **n~en zu** (*fig*) have a tendency towards; be prone to (*Krankheit*); incline towards (*Ansicht*); **dazu n~en, etw zu tun** tend to do sth. **N~ung** *f* -,-en inclination; (*Gefälle*) slope; (*fig*) tendency; (*Hang*) leaning; (*Herzens-*) affection

nein *adv, N~** *nt* **-s** no

Nektar *m* **-s** nectar

Nelke *f* **-,-n** carnation; (*Feder-*) pink; (*Culin*) clove

nenn|en† *vt* call; (*taufen*) name; (*angeben*) give; (*erwähnen*) mention; **sich n~en** call oneself. **n~enswert** *a* significant. **N~ung** *f* -,-en mention; (*Sport*) entry. **N~wert** *m* face value

Neofaschismus *m* neofascism

Neon *nt* **-s** neon. **N~beleuchtung** *f* fluorescent lighting

neppen *vt* (*fam*) rip off

Nerv *m* **-s,-en** /-f-/ nerve; **jdm N~en verlieren** lose control of oneself. **n~en** *vt* **jdn n~en** (*sl*) get on s.o.'s nerves. **N~enarzt** *m* neurologist. **n~enaufreibend** *a* nerve-racking. **N~enbündel** *nt* (*fam*) bundle of nerves. **N~en-kitzel** *m* (*fam*) thrill. **N~en-system** *nt* nervous system. **N~enzusammenbruch** *m* nervous breakdown

nervös *a* nervy, edgy; (*Med*) nervous; **n~ sein** be on edge

Nervosität *f* - nerviness, edginess

Nerz *m* -es,-e mink

Nessel *f* -,-n nettle

Nessessär *nt* -s,-s = Necessaire

Nest *nt* -[e]s,-er nest; (*fam: Ort*) small place

nesteln *vi* (*haben*) fumble (**an** + *dat* with)

Nesthäkchen *nt* -s,- (*fam*) baby of the family

nett *a* nice, *adv* -ly; (*freundlich*) kind, *adv* -ly

netto *adv* net. **N~gewicht** *nt* net weight

Netz *nt* -es,-e net; (*Einkaufs-*) string bag; (*Spinnen-*) web; (*auf Landkarte*) grid; (*System*) network; (*Electr*) mains *pl*. **N~haut** *f* retina. **N~karte** *f* area season ticket. **N~werk** *nt* network

neu *a* new; (*modern*) modern; **wie neu** as good as new; **das ist mir neu** it's news to me; **aufs N~e (n~e)** [once] again; **von n~em** all over again *o* again *o* adv newly; (*gerade erst*) only just; (*erneut*) again; **etw neu schreiben/streichen** rewrite/repaint sth; **neu vermähltes Paar** newly-weds *pl*. **N~ankömmling** *m* -s,-e newcomer. **N~anschaffung** *f* recent acquisition. **n~artig** *a* new [kind of]. **N~auflage** *f* new edition; (*unverändert*) reprint. **N~bau** *m* (*pl* -ten) new house/building

Neu|e(r) *m/f* new person, newcomer; (*Schüler*) new boy/girl. **N~e(s)** *nt* das **N~e** the new; **etwas N~es** something new; (*Neuigkeit*) a piece of news; **was gibt's N~es?** what's the news?

neuer|dings *adv* [just] recently. **n~lich** *a* renewed, new *o adv* again. **N~ung** *f* -,-en innovation

neuest|e(r,s) *a* newest; (*letzte*) latest; **seit n~em** just recently. **N~e** *nt* **das N~e** the latest thing: (*Neuigkeit*) the latest news *sg*

neugeboren *a* newborn

Neugier, Neugierde *f* - curiosity; (*Wissbegierde*) inquisitiveness

neugierig *a* curious (**auf** + *acc* about), *adv* -ly; (*wissbegierig*) inquisitive, *adv* -ly

Neuheit *f* -,-en novelty; (*Neusein*) newness; **die letzte N~** the latest thing

Neuigkeit *f* -,-en piece of news; **N~en** news *sg*

Neujahr *nt* New Year's Day; **über N~** over the New Year

neulich *adv* the other day

Neu|ling *m* -s,-e novice. **n~modisch** *a* newfangled. **N~mond** *m* new moon

neun *inv a*, **N~** *f* -,-en nine. **n~malkluge(r)** *m* (*fam*) clever Dick. **n~te(r,s)** *a* ninth. **n~zehn** *inv a* nineteen. **n~zehnte(r,s)** *a* nineteenth. **n~zig** *inv a* ninety. **n~zigste(r,s)** *a* ninetieth

Neuralgie *f* -,-n neuralgia

neureich *a* nouveau riche

Neurologe *m* -n,-n neurologist

Neurolse *f* -,-n neurosis. **n~tisch** *a* neurotic

Neuschnee *m* fresh snow

Neuseeland *nt* -s New Zealand

neuste(r,s) *a* = **neueste(r,s)**

neutral *a* neutral. **n~isieren** *vt* neutralize. **N~ität** *f* - neutrality

Neutrum *nt* -s,-tra neuter noun

neu|vermählt *a* (NEW)**n~ ver-mählt**, *s.* **neu**. **N~zeit** *f* modern times *pl*

nicht *adv* not; **ich kann n~** I cannot *or* can't; **er ist n~ gekommen** he hasn't come; **n~ mehr/besser als** no more/better than; **bitte n~!** please don't! n~ berühren! do not touch! **du kommst doch auch, ~ [wahr]?** you are coming too, aren't you? **du kennst ihn doch, n~?** you know him, don't you?

Nichtachtung f disregard; (Geringschätzung) disdain

Nichte f -,-n niece

nichtig a trivial; (Jur) [null and] void

Nichtraucher m non-smoker. **N~abteil** nt non-smoking compartment

nichts pron & a nothing; n~ anderes/Besseres nothing else/better; n~ mehr no more; **ich weiß n~** I know nothing or don't know anything; **n~ ahnend** unsuspecting; **n~ sagend** meaningless; (uninteressant) nondescript. **N~** nt - nothingness; (fig: Leere) void; (Person) nonentity. **n~ahnend** a ᴺᴱᵂ **n~ahnend**, s. nichts

Nichtschwimmer m nonswimmer

nichtsdesto|trotz adv all the same. **n~weniger** adv nevertheless

nichts|nutzig a good-for-nothing; (fam: unartig) naughty. **n~sagend** a ᴺᴱᵂ **n~ sagend**, s. nichts. **N~tun** nt -s idleness

Nickel nt -s nickel

nicken vi (haben) nod. **N~** nt -s nod

Nickerchen nt -s,-, (fam) nap; **ein N~ machen** have forty winks

nie adv never

nieder a low □ adv down. **n~brennen†** vt/i sep (sein) burn down. **N~deutsch** nt Low German. **N~gang** m (fig) decline. **n~gedrückt** a (fig) depressed. **n~gehen†** vi sep (sein) come down. **n~geschlagen** a dejected, despondent. **N~geschlagenheit** f - dejection, despondency. **N~kunft** f -,ᵉe confinement. **N~lage** f defeat

Niederlande (die) pl the Netherlands

Niederländ|er m -s,- Dutchman; **die N~er** the Dutch pl. **N~erin** f -,-nen Dutchwoman. **n~isch** a Dutch

nieder|lassen† vt sep let down; **sich n~lassen** settle; (sich setzen) sit down. **N~lassung** f -,-en settlement; (Zweigstelle) branch. **n~legen** vt sep put or lay down; resign (Amt); **die Arbeit n~legen** go on strike; **sich n~legen** lie down. **n~machen**, **n~metzeln** vt sep massacre. **n~reißen†** vt sep tear down. **N~sachsen** nt Lower Saxony. **N~schlag** m precipitation; (Regen) rainfall; (radioaktiver) fallout; (Boxen) knock-down; **n~schlagen†** vt sep knock down; lower (Augen); (unterdrücken) crush. **n~schmettern** vt sep (fig) shatter. **n~schreiben†** vt sep write down. **n~schreien†** vt sep shout down. **n~setzen** vt sep put or set down; **sich n~setzen** sit down. **n~strecken** vt sep fell; (durch Schuss) gun down

niederträchtig a base, vile

Niederung f -,-en low ground

nieder|walzen vt sep flatten. **n~werfen†** vt sep throw down; (unterdrücken) crush; **n~werfen** prostrate oneself

niedlich a pretty; (goldig) sweet; (Amer) cute

niedrig a low; (fig: gemein) base □ adv low

niemals adv never

niemand pron nobody, no one

Niere f -,-n kidney; **künstliche N~** kidney machine

niesel|n vi (haben) drizzle; **es n~t** it is drizzling. **N~regen** m drizzle

niesen vi (haben) sneeze. **N~** nt -s sneezing; (Niesen) sneeze

Niet m & nt -[e]s,e, **Niete**[1] f -,-n rivet; (an Jeans) stud

Niete[2] f -,-n blank; (fam) failure

nieten vt rivet

Nikotin nt -s nicotine

Nil m -[s] Nile. **N∼pferd** nt hippopotamus

nimmer adv (SGer) not any more; **nie und n∼** never. **n∼müde** a tireless. **n∼satt** a insatiable. **N∼wiedersehen** nt auf N∼wiedersehen (fam) for good

nippen vi (haben) take a sip (**an** + dat of)

nirgend|s, n∼wo adv nowhere

Nische f -,-n recess, niche

nisten vi (haben) nest

Nitrat nt -[e]s,-e nitrate

Niveau /ni'vo:/ nt -s,-s level; (geistig, künstlerisch) standard

nix adv (fam) nothing

Nixe f -,-n mermaid

nobel a noble; (fam: luxuriös) luxurious; (fam: großzügig) generous

noch adv still; (zusätzlich) as well; (mit Komparativ) even; **n∼ nicht** not yet; **gerade n∼** only just; **n∼ immer** od **immer n∼** still; **n∼ letzte Woche** only last week; **es ist n∼ viel Zeit** there's plenty of time yet; **wer/was/wo n∼?** who/what/where else? **n∼ jemand/etwas** someone/something else; (Frage) anyone/anything else? **n∼ einmal** again; **n∼ einmal so viel** as much again; **n∼ ein Bier** another beer; **n∼ größer** even bigger; **n∼ so sehr/schön** however much/beautiful □ conj **weder . . . n∼** neither . . . nor

nochmal|ig a further. **n∼s** adv again

Nomad|e m -n,-n nomad. **n∼isch** a nomadic

Nominativ m -s,-e nominative

nominell a nominal, adv -ly

nominier|en vt nominate. **N∼ung** f -,-en nomination

nonchalant /nõʃa'lã:/ a nonchalant, adv -ly

Nonne f -,-n nun. **N∼nkloster** nt convent

Nonstopflug m direct flight

Nord m -[e]s north. **N∼amerika** nt North America. **n∼deutsch** a North German

Norden m -s north; **nach N∼** north

nordisch a Nordic

nördlich a northern; (Richtung) northerly □ adv & prep (+ gen) **n∼ [von] der Stadt** [to the] north of the town

Nordosten m north-east

Nord|pol m North Pole. **N∼see** f - North Sea. **n∼wärts** adv northwards. **N∼westen** m north-west

Nörgelei f -,-en grumbling

nörgeln vi (haben) grumble

Norm f -,-en norm; (Techn) standard; (Soll) quota

normal a normal, adv -ly. **n∼erweise** adv normally. **n∼isieren** vt normalize; **sich n∼isieren** return to normal

normen, normieren vt standardize

Norwe|gen nt -s Norway. **N∼ger(in)** m -s,- (f -,-nen) Norwegian. **n∼gisch** a Norwegian

Nost|algie f - nostalgia. **n∼algisch** a nostalgic

Not f -,-e need; (Notwendigkeit) necessity; (Entbehrung) hardship; (seelisch) trouble; **Not leiden** be in need, suffer hardship; **Not leidende Menschen** needy people; **mit knapper Not** only just; **zur Not** if need be; (äußerstenfalls) at a pinch

Notar m -s,-e notary public

Not|arzt m emergency doctor. **N∼ausgang** m emergency exit. **N∼behelf** m -[e]s,-e makeshift. **N∼bremse** f emergency brake. **N∼dienst** m **N∼dienst haben** be on call. **n∼dürftig** a scant; (behelfsmäßig) makeshift

Note f -,-n note; (Zensur) mark; **ganze/halbe N∼** (Mus) semibreve/minim, (Amer) whole/half

note; N~n lesen read music;
persönliche N~ personal touch.
N~nblatt nt sheet of music.
N~nschlüssel m clef.
N~nständer m music-stand
Notfall m emergency; im N~ in
an emergency; (notfalls) if need
be; **für den N~** just in case. **n~s**
adv if need be
not|gedrungen adv of necessity.
N~groschen m nest-egg
notieren vt note down; (Comm)
quote; **sich** (dat) etw n~ make a
note of sth
nötig a necessary; **n~ haben**
need; **das N~ste** the essentials
pl ● adv urgently. **n~en** vt force;
(auffordern) press; **laßt euch
nicht n~en** help yourselves.
n~enfalls adv if need be.
N~ung f · coercion
Notiz f -,-en note; (Zeitungs-)
item; **[keine] N~ nehmen** von
take [no] notice of. **N~buch** nt
notebook. **N~kalender** m diary
Not|lage f plight. **n~landen** vi
(sein) make a forced landing.
N~landung f forced landing.
n~leidend a (NEW) Not leidend,
s. Not. **N~lösung** f stopgap.
N~lüge f white lie
notorisch a notorious
Not|ruf m emergency call; (Naut,
Aviat) distress call; (Nummer)
emergency services number.
N~signal nt distress signal.
N~stand m state of emergency.
N~unterkunft f emergency ac-
commodation. **N~wehr** f · (Jur)
self-defence
notwendig a necessary; (uner-
lässlich) essential ● adv urgently.
N~keit f -,-en necessity
Notzucht f (Jur) rape
Nougat /'nu:gat/ m & nt -s nougat
Novelle f -,-n novella; (Pol)
amendment
November m -s,- November
Novität f -,-en novelty
Novize m -n,-n, **Novizin** f -,-nen
(Relig) novice

Nu m im Nu (fam) in a flash
Nuance /'nyã:sə/ f -,-n nuance;
(Spur) shade
nüchtern a sober; (sachlich) mat-
ter-of-fact; (schmucklos) bare;
(ohne Würze) bland; **auf n~en
Magen** on an empty stomach
● adv soberly
Nudel f -,-n piece of pasta; **N~n**
pasta sg; (Band-) noodles.
N~holz nt rolling-pin
Nudist m -en,-en nudist
nuklear a nuclear
null inv a zero, nought; (Teleph)
O; (Sport) nil; (Tennis) love; **no
Fehler** no mistakes; **n~ und
nichtig** (Jur) null and void. **N~**
f -,-en nought, zero; (fig: Person)
nonentity; **drei Grad unter N~**
three degrees below zero.
N~punkt m zero
numerieren vt (NEW) **nummerieren**
numerisch a numerical
Nummer f -,-n number; (Ausgabe) issue; (Darbietung) item;
(Zirkus-) act; (Größe) size.
n~ieren vt number. **N~nschild**
nt number-/(Amer) license-plate
nun adv now; (na) well; (halt) just;
von nun an from now on; nun
gut! very well then! **das Leben
ist nun mal so** life's like that
nur adv only, just; **wo kann sie
nur sein?** wherever can she be?
alles, was ich nur will everything I could possibly want; **er
soll es nur versuchen!**
(drohend) just let him try!
könnte/hätte ich nur ...! if
only I could/had ...! **nur Geduld!** just be patient!
Nürnberg nt -s Nuremberg
nuscheln vt/i (haben) mumble
Nuss f -,-e (Nuß f -,-sse) nut.
N~baum m walnut tree.
N~knacker m · nutcrackers
pl. **N~schale** f nutshell
Nüstern fpl nostrils
Nut f -,-en, **Nute** f -,-n groove
Nutte f -,-n (sl) tart (sl)

Nutz zu N~e machen = **zunutze machen**, s. **zunutze**. **n~bar** a usable; **n~bar machen** utilize; cultivate ⟨Boden⟩. **n~bringend** a profitable, useful. **n~bly**

nütze a zu etwas/nichts n~ sein be useful/useless

nutzen vt use, utilize; (aus-) take advantage of □ vi (haben) = **nützen**. N~ m -s benefit; (Comm) profit; N~ ziehen aus benefit from; von N~ sein be useful

nützen vi (haben) be useful or of use (dat to); ⟨Mittel:⟩ be effective; **nichts n~** be useless or no use; **was nützt mir das?** what good is that to me? □ vt = **nutzen**

Nutzholz nt timber

nützlich a useful; **sich n~ machen** make oneself useful. **N~keit** f - usefulness

nutz|los a useless; ⟨vergeblich⟩ vain. **N~losigkeit** f - uselessness. **N~nießer** m -s,- beneficiary. **N~ung** f - use, utilization

Nylon /ˈnaɪlɔn/ nt -s nylon

Nymphe /ˈnʏmfə/ f -,-n nymph

O

o int o ja/nein! oh yes/no! o weh! oh dear!

Oase f -,-n oasis

ob conj whether; **ob reich, ob arm** rich or poor; **ob sie wohl krank ist?** I wonder whether she is ill; **und ob!** (fam) you bet!

Obacht f O~ geben pay attention; O~ geben auf (+ acc) look after; O~! look out!

Obdach nt -[e]s shelter. **o~los** a homeless. **o~lose(r)** m/f homeless person; **die O~losen** the homeless pl

Obduktion /-ˈtsɪoːn/ f -,-en postmortem

O-Beine ntpl (fam) bow-legs, bandy legs. **O-beinig**, **o-beinig** a bandy-legged

oben adv at the top; (auf der Oberseite) on top; (eine Treppe hoch) upstairs; (im Text) above; **da o~** up there; **o~ im Norden** up in the north; **siehe o~** see above; **o~ auf** (+ acc/dat) on top of; **nach o~** up[wards]; (die Treppe hinauf) upstairs; **von o~** from above/upstairs; **von o~ unten** from top to bottom/⟨Person⟩ to toe; **jdn von o~ bis unten mustern** look s.o. up and down; **o~ erwähnt** od **genannt** above-mentioned. **o~an** adv at the top. **o~auf** adv on top; **o~auf sein** (fig) be cheerful. **o~drein** adv on top of that. **o~erwähnt** od **o~genannt** a (NEW) **o~ erwähnt** od **o~ genannt**, s. **oben**. **o~hin** adv casually

Ober m -s,- waiter

Ober|arm m upper arm. **O~arzt** m ≈ senior registrar. **O~befehlshaber** m commander-in-chief. **O~begriff** m generic term. **O~deck** nt upper deck. **O~e(r,s)** a upper; ⟨höhere⟩ higher. **O~fläche** f surface. **o~flächlich** a superficial, adv -ly. **O~geschoss** (O~geschoß) nt upper storey. **o~halb** adv & prep (+ gen) above; **o~halb vom Dorf** od **des Dorfes** above the village. **O~hand** f **die O~hand gewinnen** gain the upper hand. **O~haupt** nt (fig) head. **O~haus** nt (Pol) upper house; (in GB) House of Lords. **O~hemd** nt [man's] shirt

Oberin f -,-nen matron; (Relig) mother superior

oberirdisch a surface . . . □ adv above ground. **O~kellner** m head waiter. **O~kiefer** m upper jaw. **O~körper** m upper part of the body. **O~leutnant** m lieutenant. **O~licht** nt overhead light; (Fenster) skylight; (über

Tür) fanlight. O~**lippe** *f* upper lip

Obers *nt* - *(Aust)* cream

Ober|schenkel *m* thigh. O~**schicht** *f* upper class. O~**schule** *f* grammar school. O~**schwester** *f (Med)* sister. O~**seite** *f* upper/*(rechte Seite)* right side

Oberst *m* -en & -s,-en colonel

oberste(r,s) *a* top; *(höchste)* highest; *(Befehlshaber, Gerichtshof)* supreme; *(wichtigste)* first

Ober|stimme *f* treble. O~**stufe** *f* upper school. O~**teil** *nt* top. O~**weite** *f* chest/*(der Frau)* bust size

obgleich *conj* although

Obhut *f* - care; **in guter O~ sein** be well looked after

obig *a* above

Objekt *nt* -[e]s,-e object; *(Haus, Grundstück)* property; O~ **der Forschung** subject of research

Objektiv *nt* -s,-e lens. o~*a* objective, *adv* -ly. O~**ität** *f* -objectivity

Oblate *f* -,-n *(Relig)* wafer

obliga|t *a (fam)* inevitable. O~**tion** /-'tsjo:n/ *f* -,-en obligation; *(Comm)* bond. o~**torisch** *a* obligatory

Obmann *m (pl* -männer) [jury] foreman; *(Sport)* representative

Oboe /o'bo:ə/ *f* -,-e oboe

Obrigkeit *f* - authorities *pl*

obschon *conj* although

Observatorium *nt* -s,-ien observatory

obskur *a* obscure; *(zweifelhaft)* dubious

Obst *nt* -es *(coll)* fruit. O~**baum** *m* fruit-tree. O~**garten** *m* orchard. O~**händler** *m* fruiterer. O~**kuchen** *m* fruit flan. O~**salat** *m* fruit salad

obszön *a* obscene. O~**ität** *f* -,-en obscenity

O-Bus *m* trolley bus

obwohl *conj* although

Ochse *m* -n,-n ox. o~**n** *vi (haben)* *(fam)* swot. O~**nschwanzsuppe** *f* oxtail soup

öde *a* desolate; *(unfruchtbar)* barren; *(langweilig)* dull. **Öde** *f* - desolation; barrenness; dullness; *(Gegend)* waste

oder *conj* or; **du kennst ihn doch, o~?** you know him, don't you?

Ofen *m* -s,- stove; *(Heiz-)* heater; *(Back-)* oven; *(Techn)* furnace

offen *a* open, *adv* -ly; *(Haar)* loose; *(Flamme)* naked; *(o~ herzig)* frank, *adv* -ly; *(o~ gezeigt)* overt, *adv* -ly; *(unentschieden)* unsettled; o~**e Stelle** vacancy; **Tag der o~en Tür** open day; **Wein o~ verkaufen** sell wine by the glass; o~**bleiben** remain open; o~**halten** hold open *(Tür)*; keep open *(Mund, Augen)*; o~**lassen** leave open; leave vacant *(Stelle)*; o~**stehen** be open; *(Rechnung:)* be outstanding; **jdm** o~**stehen** *(fig)* be open to s.o.; *adv* o~ **gesagt od gestanden** to be honest. o~**bar** *a* obvious □ *adv* apparently. o~**baren** *vt* reveal. O~**barung** *f* -,-en revelation. o~**bleiben†** *vi sep (sein)* NEW o~ **bleiben, s. offen.** o~**halten†** *vt sep* NEW o~ **halten, s. offen.** O~**heit** *f* - frankness, openness. o~**herzig** *a* frank, *adv* -ly. O~**herzigkeit** *f* - frankness. o~**kundig** *a* manifest, *adv* -ly. o~**lassen†** *vt sep* NEW o~ **lassen, s. offen.** o~**sichtlich** *a* obvious, *adv* -ly

offensiv *a* offensive. O~**e** *f* -,-n offensive

offenstehen† *vi sep (haben)* NEW **offen stehen, s. offen**

öffentlich *a* public, *adv* -ly. Ö~**keit** *f* - public; **an die Ö~keit gelangen** become public; **in aller Ö~keit** in public, publicly

Offerte *f* -,-n *(Comm)* offer

offiziell *a* official, *adv* -ly

Offizier *m* -s,-e *(Mil)* officer

öffn|en *vt/i* (haben) open; **sich ö~en** open. **Ö~er** *m* -s,- opener. **Ö~ung** *f* -,-en opening. **Ö~ungszeiten** *fpl* opening hours

oft *adv* often

öfter *adv* quite often. **ö~e(r,s)** *a* frequent; **des Ö~en (ö~en)** frequently. **ö~s** *adv* (fam) quite often

oftmals *adv* often

oh *int* oh!

ohne *prep* (+ *acc*) without; **o~ mich!** count me out! **oben o~** topless; **nicht o~** sein (fam) be not bad; (nicht harmlos) be quite nasty □ *conj* **o~ zu überlegen** without thinking; **o~ dass ich es merkte** without my noticing it. **o~dies** *adv* anyway. **o~gleichen** *pred a* unparalleled; **eine Frechheit o~gleichen** a piece of unprecedented insolence. **o~hin** *adv* anyway

Ohn|macht *f* -,-en faint; (fig) powerlessness; **in O~macht fallen** faint. **o~mächtig** *a* unconscious; (fig) powerless; **o~mächtig werden** faint

Ohr *nt* -[e]s,-en ear; **übers Ohr hauen** (fam) cheat

Öhr *nt* -[e]s,-e eye

ohren|betäubend *a* deafening. **O~schmalz** *nt* ear-wax. **O~schmerzen** *mpl* earache *sg.* **O~sessel** *m* wing-chair. **O~tropfen** *mpl* ear drops

Ohrfeige *f* slap in the face; **jdm eine O~ geben** slap s.o.'s face. **o~n** *vt* **jdn o~n** slap s.o.'s face

Ohr|läppchen *nt* -s,- ear-lobe. **O~ring** *m* ear-ring. **O~wurm** *m* earwig

oje *int* oh dear!

okay /o'ke:/ *a & adv* (fam) OK

okkult *a* occult

Öko|logie *f* - ecology. **ö~logisch** *a* ecological. **Ö~nomie** *f* - economy; (Wissenschaft) economics *sg.* **ö~nomisch** *a* economic; (sparsam) economical

Oktave *f* -,-n octave

Oktober *m* -s,- October

Okular *nt* -s,-e eyepiece

okulieren *vt* graft

ökumenisch *a* ecumenical

Öl *nt* -[e]s,-e oil; **in Öl malen** paint in oils. **Ölbaum** *m* olivetree. **ölen** *vt* oil; **wie ein geölter Blitz** (fam) like greased lightning. **Ölfarbe** *f* oil-paint. **Ölfeld** *nt* oilfield. **Ölgemälde** *nt* oil-painting. **ölig** *a* oily

Olive *f* -,-n olive. **O~nöl** *nt* olive oil. **o~grün** *a* olive[-green]

öll *a* (fam) old; (fam: hässlich) nasty

Ölmessstab (Ölmeßstab) *m* dipstick. **Ölsardinen** *fpl* sardines in oil. **Ölstand** *m* oil-level. **Öltanker** *m* oil-tanker. **Ölteppich** *m* oil-slick

Olympiade *f* -,-n Olympic Games *pl,* Olympics *pl*

Olymp|iasieger(in) /o'lvmpia-/ *m(f)* Olympic champion. **o~isch** *a* Olympic; **O~ische Spiele** Olympic Games

Ölzeug *nt* oilskins *pl*

Oma *f* -,-s (fam) granny

Omelett *nt* -[e]s,-e & -s omelette

Omen *nt* -s,- omen

ominös *a* ominous

Omnibus *m* bus; (Reise-) coach

onanieren *vi* (haben) masturbate

Onkel *m* -s,- uncle

Opa *m* -s,-s (fam) grandad

Opal *m* -s,-e opal

Oper *f* -,-n opera

Operation /-'tsjo:n/ *f* -,-en operation. **O~ssaal** *m* operating theatre

Operette *f* -,-n operetta

operieren *vt* operate on (Patient, Herz); **sich o~ lassen** have an operation □ *vi* (haben) operate

Opern|glas *nt* opera-glasses *pl.* **O~haus** *nt* opera-house. **O~sänger(in)** *m(f)* opera-singer

Opfer *nt* -s,- sacrifice; (eines Unglücks) victim; **ein O~ bringen** make a sacrifice;

jdm/etw zum O~ fallen fall victim to s.o./sth. O~t vt sacrifice. O~ung f -,-en sacrifice

Opium nt -s opium

opponieren vi (haben) o~ gegen oppose

Opportunist m -en,-en opportunist. o~isch a opportunist

Opposition /-'tsio:n/ f - opposition. O~spartei f opposition party

Optik f - optics sg, (fam: Objektiv) lens. O~er m -s,- optician

optimal a optimum

Optimismus m - optimism. O~t m -en,-en optimist. o~tisch a optimistic, adv -ally

Optimum nt -s,-ma optimum

Option /ɔp'tsio:n/ f -,-en option

optisch a optical, (Eindruck) visual

Orakel nt -s,- oracle

Orange /o'rã:ʒə/ f -,-n orange. o~ inv a orange. O~ade /orã'ʒa:də/ f -,-n orangeade. O~nmarmelade f (orange) marmalade. O~nsaft m orange juice

Oratorium nt -s,-ien oratorio

Orchester /ɔr'kɛstɐ/ nt -s,- orchestra. o~rieren vt orchestrate

Orchidee /ɔrçi'de:ə/ f -,-n orchid

Orden m -s,- (Ritter-, Kloster-) order; (Auszeichnung) medal, decoration; jdm einen O~ verleihen decorate s.o. O~stracht f (Relig) habit

ordentlich a neat. tidy; (anständig) respectable; (ordnungsgemäß, fam: richtig) proper; (Mitglied, Versammlung) ordinary; (fam: gut) decent; (fam: gehörig) good ● adv neatly, tidily; respectably; properly; (fam: gut, gehörig) well; (sehr) very; (regelrecht) really

Order f -,-s & -n order

ordinär a common

Ordination /-'tsio:n/ f -,-en (Relig) ordination; (Aust) surgery. o~ieren vt (Relig) ordain

ordnen vt put in order; (aufräumen) tidy; (an-) arrange; **sich zum Zug o~** form a procession. O~er m -s,- steward; (Akten-) file

Ordnung f - order; O~ halten keep order; in O~ machen tidy up; in O~ bringen put in order; (aufräumen) tidy; (reparieren) mend; (fig) put right; in O~ sein be in order; (ordentlich sein) be tidy; (fig) be all right; ich bin mit dem Magen od meine Magen ist nicht ganz in O~ I have a slight stomach upset; [geht] in O~! OK! o~sgemäß a proper, adv -ly. O~sstrafe f (Jur) fine. o~swidrig a improper, adv -ly

Ordonnanz, Ordonanz f -,-en (Mil) orderly

Organ nt -s,-e organ; (fam: Stimme) voice

Organisation /-'tsio:n/ f -,-en organization. O~sator m -s,-en /-'to:rən/ organizer

organisch a organic, adv -ally

organisieren vt organize; (fam: beschaffen) get (hold of)

Organismus m -,-men organism; (System) system. O~t m -en,-en organist

Organspenderkarte f donor card

Orgasmus m -,-men orgasm

Orgel f -,-n (Mus) organ. O~pfeife f organ-pipe

Orgie /'ɔrgiə/ f -,-n orgy

Orient /'o:riɛnt/ m -s Orient. o~talisch a Oriental

orientieren vt inform (über + acc about); **sich o~en** get one's bearings, orientate oneself; (unterrichten) inform oneself (über + acc about). O~ung f - orientation; die O~ung verlieren lose one's bearings

original a original. O~ nt -s,-e original; (Person) character. O~ität f - originality. O~übertragung f live transmission

originell a original; (*eigenartig*) unusual

Orkan m -s,-e hurricane

Ornament nt -[e]s,-e ornament

Ornat m -[e]s,-e robes pl

Ornithologie f - ornithology

Ort m -[e]s,-e place; (*Ortschaft*) [small] town; **am Ort** locally; **am Ort des Verbrechens** at the scene of the crime; **an Ort und Stelle** in the right place; (*sofort*) on the spot. **o~en** vt locate

ortho|dox a orthodox. **O~graphie, O~grafie** f - spelling. **o~graphisch, o~grafisch** a spelling ... **O~päde** m -n,-n orthopaedic specialist. **o~pädisch** a orthopaedic

örtlich a local, adv -ly. **Ö~keit** f -,-en locality

Ortschaft f -,-en [small] town; (*Dorf*) village; **geschlossene O~** (*Auto*) built-up area

orts|fremd a o~fremd sein be a stranger. **O~gespräch** nt (*Teleph*) local call. **O~name** m place-name. **O~sinn** m sense of direction. **O~verkehr** m local traffic. **O~zeit** f local time

Öse f -,-n eyelet; (*Schlinge*) loop; **Haken und Öse** hook and eye

Ost m -[e]s east. **o~deutsch** a Eastern/(*Pol*) East German

Osten m -s east; **nach O~** east

ostentativ a pointed, adv -ly

Osteopath m -en,-en osteopath

Oster|ei /'o:stɐʔaj/ nt Easter egg. **O~fest** nt Easter. **O~glocke** f daffodil. **O~montag** m Easter Monday. **O~n** nt -,-: Easter; **frohe O~n!** happy Easter!

Österreich nt -s Austria. **Ö~er** m, -s,-. **Ö~erin** f -,-nen Austrian. **ö~isch** a Austrian

östlich a eastern; (*Richtung*) easterly □ adv & prep (+ gen) **ö~ [von] der Stadt** [to the] east of the town

Ost|see f Baltic [Sea]. **o~wärts** adv eastwards

oszillieren vi(haben) oscillate

Otter[1] m -s,- otter

Otter[2] f -,-n adder

Ouvertüre /uver'tyːrə/ f -,-n overture

oval a oval. **O~** nt -s,-e oval

Ovation /-'tsioːn/ f -,-en ovation

Ovulation /-'tsioːn/ f -,-en ovulation

Oxid, Oxyd nt -[e]s,-e oxide

Ozean m -s,-e ocean

Ozon nt -s ozone. **O~loch** nt hole in the ozone layer. **O~schicht** f ozone layer

P

paar pron inv **ein p~** a few; **ein p~ Mal** a few times; **alle p~ Tage** every few days. **P~** nt -[e]s,-e pair; (*Ehe-, Liebes-, Tanz-*) couple. **p~en** vt mate; (*verbinden*) combine; **sich p~en** mate. **p~mal** adv **ein p~mal** NEW **ein p~ Mal**, s. paar. **P~ung** f -,-en mating. **p~weise** adv in pairs, in twos

Pacht f -,-en lease; (*P~summe*) rent. **p~en** vt lease

Pächter m -s,- lessee; (*eines Hofes*) tenant

Pachtvertrag m lease

Pack[1] m -[e]s,-e bundle

Pack[2] nt -[e]s (sl) rabble

Päckchen nt -s,- package, small packet

pack|en vt/i (haben) pack; (*ergreifen*) seize; (*fig: fesseln*) grip; **p~ dich!** (sl) beat it! **P~en** m -s,- bundle. **P~end** a (*fig*) gripping. **P~papier** nt [strong] wrapping paper. **P~ung** f -,-en packet; (*Med*) pack

Pädagog|e m -n,-n educationalist; (*Lehrer*) teacher. **P~ik** f - educational science. **p~isch** a educational

Paddel nt -s,- paddle. **P~boot** nt
canoe. **p~n** vt/i (haben/sein)
paddle. **P~sport** m canoeing

Page /'pa:ʒə/ m -n,-n page

Paillette /paj'jɛtə/ f -,-n sequin

Paket nt -[e]s,-e packet; (Post-)
parcel

Pakistan nt -s Pakistan.
P~aner(in) m -s,- (f-,-nen) Pakistani. **p~anisch** a Pakistani

Pakt m -[e]s,-e pact

Palast m -[e]s,ːe palace

Palästina nt -s Palestine. **P~i-**
nenser(in) m -s,- (f-,-nen) Palestinian. **p~inensisch** a
Palestinian

Palette f -,-n palette

Palme f -,-n palm[-tree]; jdn auf
die **P~e bringen** (fam) drive s.o.
up the wall. **P~sonntag** m Palm
Sunday

Pampelmuse f -,-n grapefruit

Panier|mehl nt (Culin)
breadcrumbs pl. **p~t** a (Culin)
breaded

Panik f - panic; in **P~ geraten**
panic

panisch a **p~e Angst** panic

Panne f -,-n breakdown; (Reifen-)
flat tyre; (Missgeschick) mishap.
P~ndienst m breakdown service

Panorama nt -s panorama

panschen vt adulterate □ vi
(haben) splash about

Panther, Panter m -s,- panther

Pantine f -,-n [wooden] clog

Pantoffel m -s,-n slipper; (ohne
Ferse) mule. **P~held** m (fam)
henpecked husband

Pantomime[1] f -,-n mime

Pantomime[2] m -n,-n mime artist

pantschen vt/i = panschen

Panzer m -s,- armour; (Mil) tank;
(Zool) shell. **p~n** vt armourplate.
P~schrank m safe

Papa /'papa, pa'pa:/ m -s,-s daddy

Papagei m -s & -en,-en parrot

Papier nt -[e]s,-e paper. **P~korb**
m waste-paper basket.

P~schlange f streamer.
P~waren fpl stationery sg

Pappe f - cardboard; (dial: Kleister) glue

Pappel f -,-n poplar

pappen vt/i (haben) (fam) stick

papper a (fam) sticky

Papp|karton m, **P~schachtel** f
cardboard box

Paprika m -s,-[s] [sweet] pepper;
(Gewürz) paprika

Papst m -[e]s,ːe pope

päpstlich a papal

Parade f -,-n parade

Paradeiser m -s,- (Aust) tomato

Paradies nt -es,-e paradise.
p~isch a heavenly

Paradox nt -es,-e paradox. **p~** a
paradoxical

Paraffin nt -s paraffin

Paragraph, Paragraf m -en,-en
section

parallel a & adv parallel. **P~e** f
-,-n parallel

Paranuss (Paranuß) f Brazil
nut

Parasit m -en,-en parasite

parat a ready

Pärchen nt -s,- pair; (Liebes-)
couple

Parcours /par'ku:ɡ/ m -,-
/-[s],-s/ (Sport) course

Pardon /par'dõ:/ int sorry!

Parfüm nt -s,-e & -s perfume,
scent. **P~iert** a perfumed, scented

parieren[1] vt parry

parieren[2] vi (haben) (fam) obey

Parität f - parity; (in Ausschuss)
equal representation

Park m -s,-s park. **p~en** vt/i
(haben) park. **P~en** nt -s parking; 'P~en verboten' 'no parking'

Parkett nt -[e]s,-e parquet floor;
(Theat) stalls pl

Park|haus nt multi-storey car
park. **P~lücke** f parking space.

P~platz m car park, (Amer)

parking-lot; (für ein Auto) parking space; (Autobahn-) lay-by. **P~scheibe** f parking-disc. **P~schein** m car-park ticket. **P~uhr** f parking-meter. **P~verbot** nt parking ban; **'P~verbot'** 'no parking'

Parlament nt-[e]s,-e parliament. **p~arisch** a parliamentary

Parodie f -,-n parody. **p~ren** vt parody

Parole f -,-n slogan; (Mil) password

Part m -s,-s (Theat, Mus) part

Partei f -,-en (Pol, Jur) party; (Miet-) tenant; **für jdn P~ ergreifen** take s.o.'s part. **p~isch** a biased. **p~los** a independent

Parterre /par'tɛr/ nt -s,-s ground floor; (Amer) first floor; (Theat) rear stalls pl. **p~** adv on the ground floor

Partie f -,-n part; (Tennis, Schach) game; (Golf) round; (Comm) batch; **eine gute P~ machen** marry well

Partikel[1] nt -s,- particle

Partikel[2] f -,-n (Gram) particle

Partitur f -,-en (Mus) full score

Partizip nt -s,-ien /-jən/ participle; **erstes/zweites P~** present/past participle

Partner|(in) m -s,- (f -,-nen) partner. **P~schaft** f -,-en partnership. **P~stadt** f twin town

Party /'pa:ṭi/ f -,-s party

Parzelle f -,-n plot [of ground]

Pass m -es,ë (Paß m -sses,ë-sse) passport; (Geog, Sport) pass

passabel a passable

Passage /pa'sa:ʒə/ f -,-n passage; (Einkaufs-) shopping arcade

Passagier /pasa'ʒi:ɐ/ m -s,-e passenger

Passamt (Paßamt) nt passport office

Passant(in) m -en,-en (f -,-nen) passer-by

Passbild (Paßbild) nt passport photograph

Passe f -,-n yoke

passen vi (haben) fit; (geeignet sein) be right (für for); (Sport) pass the ball; (aufgeben) pass; **p~ zu** go [well] with; (übereinstimmen) match; **jdm p~** fit s.o.; (gelegen sein) suit s.o.; **seine Art passt mir nicht** I don't like his manner; **[ich] passe** pass. **p~d** a suitable; (angemessen) appropriate; (günstig) convenient; (übereinstimmend) matching

passier|bar a passable. **p~en** vt pass; cross (Grenze); (Culin) rub through a sieve □ vi (sein) happen (jdm to s.o.); **es ist ein Unglück p~t** there has been an accident. **P~schein** m pass

Passion f -,-en passion. **p~iert** a very keen (Jäger, Angler)

passiv a passive. **P~** nt -s,-e (Gram) passive

Pass|kontrolle (Paßkontrolle) f passport control. **P~straße** f pass

Paste f -,-n paste

Pastell nt -[e]s,-e pastel. **P~farbe** f pastel colour

Pastete f -,-n [individual] pie; (Königin-) vol-au-vent. **P~e** f -,-n pie; (Gänseleber-) pâté

pasteurisieren /pastøri'zi:rən/ vt pasteurize

Pastille f -,-n pastille

Pastinake f -,-n parsnip

Pastor m -s,-en /-'to:rən/ pastor

Pate m -n,-n godfather; (fig) sponsor; **P~n** godparents. **P~nkind** nt godchild. **P~nschaft** f - sponsorship. **P~nsohn** m godson

Patent nt -[e]s,-e patent; (Offiziers-) commission. **p~** a (fam) clever, ingenious; (Person) resourceful. **p~ieren** vt patent

Patentochter f god-daughter

Pater m -s,- (Relig) Father

pathetisch a emotional □ adv with emotion

Patholog|e m -n,-n pathologist. **p~isch** a pathological, adv -ly

Pathos nt - emotion, feeling

Patience /pa'sjã:s/ f -,-n patience

Patient(in) /pa'tsjɛnt(ɪn)/ m -en, -en (f -,-nen) patient

Patin f -,-nen godmother

Patriot(in) m -en,-en (f -,-nen) patriot. p~isch a patriotic. P~ismus m - patriotism

Patrone f -,-n cartridge

Patrouille /pa'trʊljə/ f -,-n patrol. p~ieren /-'ji:rən/ vi (haben/sein) patrol

Patsch|e f in der P~e sitzen (fam) be in a jam. p~en vi (haben/sein) splash □ vt slap. p~naß (p~naß) a (fam) soaking wet

Patt nt -s stalemate

Patz|er m -s,- (fam) slip. p~ig a (fam) insolent

Pauk|e f -,-n kettledrum; auf die P~e hauen (fam) have a good time; (prahlen) boast. p~en vt/i (haben) cram; swot. P~er m -s,- (fam: Lehrer) teacher

pausbäckig a chubby-cheeked

pauschal a all-inclusive; (einheitlich) flat-rate; (fig) sweeping (Urteil); p~e Summe lump sum □ adv in a lump sum; (fig) wholesale. P~e f -,-n lump sum. P~reise f package tour. P~summe f lump sum

Pause[1] f -,-n break; (beim Sprechen) pause; (Theat) interval; (im Kino) intermission; (Mus) rest; P~ machen have a break

Pause[2] f -,-n tracing. p~n vt trace

pausenlos a incessant, adv -ly

pausieren vi (haben) have a break; (ausruhen) rest

Pauspapier nt tracing-paper

Pavian m -s,-e baboon

Pavillon /'pavɪljõ/ m -s,-s pavilion

Pazifik m -s Pacific [Ocean]. p~sch a Pacific

Pazifist m -en,-en pacifist

Pech nt -s pitch; (Unglück) bad luck; P~ haben be unlucky.

p~schwarz a pitch-black; (Haare, Augen) jet-black. P~strähne f run of bad luck. P~vogel m (fam) unlucky devil

Pedal nt -s,-e pedal

Pedant m -en,-en pedant. p~isch a pedantic, adv -ally

Pediküre f -,-n pedicure

Pegel m -s,- level; (Gerät) water-level indicator. P~stand m [water] level

peilen vt take a bearing on; über den Daumen gepeilt (fam) at a rough guess

Pein f -(liter) torment. p~igen vt torment

peinlich a embarrassing, awkward; (genau) scrupulous, adv -ly; es war mir sehr p~ I was very embarrassed

Peitsche f -,-n whip. p~n vt whip; (fig) lash □ vi (sein) lash (an + acc against). P~nhieb m lash

pekuniär a financial, adv -ly

Pelikan m -s,-e pelican

Pell|e f -,-n skin. p~en vt peel; shell (Ei); sich p~en peel. P~kartoffeln fpl potatoes boiled in their skins

Pelz m -es,-e fur. P~mantel m fur coat

Pendel nt -s,- pendulum. p~n vi (haben) swing □ vi (sein) commute. P~verkehr m shuttle-service; (für Pendler) commuter traffic

Pendler m -s,- commuter

penetrant a penetrating; (fig) obtrusive, adv -ly

penibel a fastidious, fussy; (pedantisch) pedantic

Penis m -,-se penis

Penne f -,-n (fam) school. p~n vi (haben) (fam) sleep. P~r m -s,- (sl) tramp

Pension /pã'zjo:n/ f -,-en pension; (Hotel) guest-house; bei voller/halber P~ with full/half board. P~är(in) m (f -,-nen)

pensioner. **P~at** nt -[e]s,-e boarding-school. **p~ieren** vt retire. **p~iert** a retired. **P~ierung** f - retirement

Pensum nt -s [allotted] work

Peperoni f -,- chilli

per prep (+ acc) by; per Luftpost by airmail

perfekt a perfect, adv -ly; **p~ sein** (Vertrag:) be settled

Perfekt nt -s (Gram) perfect

Perfektion /-'tsjo:n/ f - perfection

perforiert a perforated

Pergament nt -[e]s,-e parchment. **P~papier** nt grease-proof paper

Periode f -,-n period. **p~isch** a periodic, adv -ally

Perle f -,-n pearl; (Glas-, Holz-) bead; (Sekt-) bubble; (fam: Hilfe) treasure. **p~en** vi (haben) bubble. **P~mutt** nt -s, **P~mutter** f - & nt -s mother-of-pearl

perplex a (fam) perplexed

Perserkatze f Persian cat

Persien /-jən/ nt -s Persia. **p~isch** a Persian

Person f -,-en person; (Theat) character; **ich für meine P~** [I] for my part; **für vier P~en** for four people

Personal nt -s personnel, staff. **P~ausweis** m identity card. **P~chef** m personnel manager. **P~ien** /-jən/ pl personal particulars. **P~mangel** m staff shortage. **P~pronomen** nt personal pronoun

Personen|kraftwagen m private car. **P~zug** m stopping train

personifizieren vt personify

persönlich a personal □ adv personally, in person. **P~keit** f -,-en personality

Perspektive f -,-n perspective; (Zukunfts-) prospect

Perücke f -,-n wig

pervers a [sexually] perverted. **P~ion** f -,-en perversion

Pessimis|mus m - pessimism. **P~t** m -en,-en pessimist. **p~tisch** a pessimistic, adv -ally

Pest f - plague

Petersilie /-jə/ f - parsley

Petroleum /-leum/ nt -s paraffin, (Amer) kerosene

Petze f -,-n (fam) sneak. **p~n** vi (haben) (fam) sneak

Pfad m -[e]s,-e path. **P~finder** m -s,- [Boy] Scout. **P~finderin** f -,-nen [Girl] Guide

Pfahl m -[e]s,-e stake, post

Pfalz (die) - the Palatinate

Pfand nt -[e]s,-er pledge; (beim Spiel) forfeit; (Flaschen-) deposit

pfänden vt (Jur) seize. **P~erspiel** nt game of forfeits

Pfand|haus nt pawnshop. **P~leiher** m -s,- pawnbroker

Pfändung f -,-en (Jur) seizure

Pfanne f -,-n [frying-]pan. **P~kuchen** m pancake; (Berliner P~kuchen) doughnut

Pfarr|er m -s,- vicar, parson; (katholischer) priest. **P~haus** nt vicarage

Pfau m -[e]s,-en peacock

Pfeffer m -s pepper. **P~kuchen** m gingerbread. **P~minzbonbon** m & nt -[pepper]mint. **P~minze** f -(Bot) peppermint. **P~minztee** m [pepper]mint tea. **p~n** vt pepper; (fam: schmeißen) chuck. **P~streuer** m -s,- pepperpot

Pfeif|e f -,-n whistle; (Tabak-, Orgel-) pipe. **p~en** vt/i (haben) whistle; (als Signal) blow the whistle; **ich p~e darauf!** (fam) I couldn't care less [about it]!

Pfeil m -[e]s,-e arrow

Pfeiler m -s,- pillar; (Brücken-) pier

Pfennig m -s,-e pfennig; **10 P~** 10 pfennigs

Pferch m -[e]s,-e [sheep] pen. **p~en** vt (fam) cram (in + acc into)

Pferd nt -[e]s,-e horse; **zu P~e** on horseback; **das P~ beim**

Schwanz aufzäumen put the cart before the horse. **P~erennen** nt horse-race; (als Sport) [horse-]racing. **P~eschwanz** m horse's tail; (Frisur) pony-tail. **P~estall** m stable. **P~estärke** f horsepower. **P~ewagen** m horse-drawn cart

Pfiff m -[e]s,-e whistle; **P~ haben** (fam) have style

Pfifferling m -s,-e chanterelle

pfiffig a smart

Pfingst|en nt -s Whitsun. **P~montag** m Whit Monday. **P~rose** f peony

Pfirsich m -s,-e peach. **p~farben** a peach[-coloured]

Pflanz|e f -,-n plant. **p~en** vt plant. **P~enfett** nt vegetable fat. **p~lich** a vegetable; (Mittel) herbal. **P~ung** f -,-en plantation

Pflaster nt -s,- pavement; (Heft-) plaster. **p~n** vt pave. **P~stein** m paving-stone

Pflaume f -,-n plum

Pflege f - care; (Kranken-) nursing; in **P~ nehmen** look after; (Admin) foster (Kind). **p~bedürftig** a in need of care. **P~eltern** pl foster-parents. **P~kind** nt foster-child. **p~leicht** a easy-care. **P~mutter** f foster-mother. **p~n** vt look after, care for; nurse (Kranke); cultivate (Künste, Freundschaft). **P~r(in)** m -s,- (f -,-nen) nurse; (Tier-) keeper

Pflicht f -,-en duty; (Sport) compulsory exercise/routine. **p~bewusst** (**p~bewußt**) a conscientious, adv -ly. **p~eifrig** a zealous, adv -ly. **P~fach** nt (Sch) compulsory subject. **P~gefühl** nt sense of duty. **p~gemäß** a due □ adv duly

Pflock m -[e]s,-e peg

pflücken vt pick

Pflug m -[e]s,-e plough

pflügen vt/i (haben) plough

Pforte f -,-n gate

Pförtner m -s,- porter

Pfosten m -s,- post

Pfote f -,-n paw

Pfropfen m -s,- stopper; (Korken) cork. **p~** vt graft (auf + acc on [to]); (fam: pressen) cram (in + acc into)

pfui int ugh; **p~ schäm dich!** you should be ashamed of yourself!

Pfund nt -[e]s,-e & - pound

Pfusch|arbeit f (fam) shoddy work. **p~en** vi (haben) (fam) botch one's work. **P~er** m -s,- (fam) shoddy worker. **P~erei** f -,-en (fam) botch-up

Pfütze f -,-n puddle

Phänomen nt -s,-e phenomenon. **p~al** a phenomenal

Phantasie f -,-n imagination; **P~n** fantasies; (Fieber-) hallucinations. **p~los** a unimaginative. **p~ren** vi (haben) fantasize; (im Fieber) be delirious. **p~voll** a imaginative, adv -ly

phant|astisch a fantastic, adv -ally. **P~om** nt -s,-e phantom

pharma|zeutisch a pharmaceutical. **P~zie** f - pharmacy

Phase f -,-n phase

Philanthrop m -en,-en philanthropist. **p~isch** a philanthropic

Philolo|ge m -n,-n teacher/student of language and literature. **P~gie** f - [study of] language and literature

Philosoph m -en,-en philosopher. **P~ie** f -,-n philosophy. **p~ieren** vi (haben) philosophize. **philosophisch** a philosophical, adv -ly

phlegmatisch a phlegmatic

Phobie f -,-n phobia

Phonet|ik f - phonetics sg. **p~isch** a phonetic, adv -ally

Phonotypistin f -,-nen audio typist

Phosphor m -s phosphorus

Photo nt, **Photo-** = Foto, Foto-

Phrase f -,-n empty phrase

Physik f - physics sg. **p~alisch** a physical

Physiker(in) m -s,- (f -,-nen) physicist

Physio|logie f - physiology. **P~therapie** f physiotherapy

physisch a physical, adv -ly

Pianist(in) m -en,-en (f -,-nen) pianist

Pickel m -s,- pimple, spot; (Spitzhacke) pick. **p~ig** a spotty

picken vt/i (haben) peck (nach at); (fam: nehmen) pick (aus out of); (Aust fam: kleben) stick

Picknick nt -s,-s picnic. **p~en** vi (haben) picnic

piep[s]|en vi (haben) ⟨Vogel:⟩ cheep; ⟨Maus:⟩ squeak; (Techn) bleep. **P~er** m -s,- bleeper

Pier m -s,-e [harbour] pier

Pietät /pie'tɛːt/ f - reverence. **p~los** a irreverent, adv -ly

Pigment nt -[e]s,-e pigment. **P~ierung** f - pigmentation

Pik nt -s,-s (Karten) spades pl

pikant a piquant; (gewagt) racy

piken vt (fam) prick

pikiert a offended, hurt

piksen vt (fam) prick

Pilger|(in) m -s,- (f -,-nen) pilgrim. **P~fahrt** f pilgrimage. **p~n** vi (sein) make a pilgrimage

Pille f -,-n pill

Pilot m -en,-en pilot

Pilz m -es,-e fungus; (essbarer) mushroom; **wie P~e aus dem Boden schießen** (fig) mushroom

pingelig a (fam) fussy

Pinguin m -s,-e penguin

Pinie /-jə/ f -,-n stone-pine

pink pred a shocking pink

pinkeln vi (haben) (fam) pee

Pinsel m -s,- [paint]brush

Pinzette f -,-n tweezers pl

Pionier m -s,-e (Mil) sapper; (fig) pioneer. **P~arbeit** f pioneering work

Pirat m -en,-en pirate

pirschen vi (haben) **p~ auf** (+ acc) stalk □ vr **sich p~** creep (an + acc up to)

pissen vi (haben) (sl) piss

Piste f -,-n (Ski-) run, piste; (Renn-) track; (Aviat) runway

Pistole f -,-n pistol

pitschnass (pitschnaß) a (fam) soaking wet

pittoresk a picturesque

Pizza f -,-s pizza

Pkw /'peːkaveː/ m -s,-s (= Personenkraftwagen) [private] car

placieren /-'siːrən/ vt = platzieren

Plackerei f - (fam) drudgery

plädieren vi (haben) plead (für for); **auf Freispruch p~** (Jur) ask for an acquittal

Plädoyer /plɛdoa'jeː/ nt -s,-s (Jur) closing speech; (fig) plea

Plage f -,-n [hard] labour; (Mühe) trouble; (Belästigung) nuisance. **p~n** vt torment, plague; (bedrängen) pester; **sich p~** struggle; (arbeiten) work hard

Plagiat nt -[e]s,-e plagiarism. **p~ieren** vt plagiarize

Plakat nt -[e]s,-e poster

Plakette f -,-n badge

Plan m -[e]s,:e plan

Plane f -,-n tarpaulin; (Boden-) groundsheet

planen vt/i (haben) plan

Planet m -en,-en planet

planieren vt level. **P~raupe** f bulldozer

Planke f -,-n plank

plan|los a unsystematic, adv -ally. **p~mäßig** a systematic; (Ankunft) scheduled □ adv systematically; (nach Plan) according to plan; (ankommen) on schedule

Plansch|becken nt paddling pool. **p~en** vi (haben) splash about

Plantage /plan'taːʒə/ f -,-n plantation

Planung f - planning

Plapper|maul nt (fam) chatterbox. **p~n** vi (haben) chatter □ vt talk (Unsinn)

plärren vi (haben) bawl; (Radio:) blare

Plasma nt -s plasma

Plastik¹ f -,-en sculpture

Plastik² nt -s plastic. **p~isch** a three-dimensional; (formbar) plastic; (anschaulich) graphic, adv -ally; **p~ische Chirurgie** plastic surgery

Platane f -,-n plane [tree]

Plateau /pla'to:/ nt -s,-s plateau

Platin nt -s platinum

Platitüde f -,-n (NEW) **Plattitüde**

platonisch a platonic

platschen vi (sein) splash

plätschern vi (haben) splash; (Bach:) babble □ vi (sein) (Bach:) babble along

platt a & adv flat; **p~ sein** (fam) be flabbergasted. **P~** nt -[s] (Lang) Low German

Plättbrett nt ironing-board

Platte f -,-n slab; (Druck-) plate; (Metall-, Glas-) sheet; (Fliese) tile; (Koch-) hotplate; (Tisch-) top; (Auszieh-) leaf; (Schall-) record, disc; (zum Servieren) [flat] dish, platter; **kalte P~** assorted cold meats and cheeses pl

Plätt|eisen nt iron. **p~en** vt/i (haben) iron

Plattenspieler m record-player

Platt|form f -,-en platform. **P~füße** mpl flat feet. **P~heit** f -,-en platitude

Plattitüde f -,-n platitude

Platz m -es,-e place; (von Häusern umgeben) square; (Sitz-) seat; (Sport-) ground; (Fußball-) pitch; (Tennis-) court; (Golf-) course; (freier Raum) room, space; **P~ nehmen** take a seat; **P~ machen/lassen** make/leave room; **vom P~ stellen** (Sport) send off. **P~angst** f agoraphobia; (Klaustrophobie) claustrophobia. **P~anweiserin** f -,-nen usherette

Plätzchen nt -s,- spot; (Culin) biscuit

platzen vi (sein) burst; (auf-) split; (fam: scheitern) fall through;

(Verlobung:) be off; **vor Neugier p~** be bursting with curiosity

platzieren vt place, put; **sich p~** (Sport) be placed

Platz|karte f seat reservation ticket. **P~konzert** nt open-air concert. **P~mangel** m lack of space. **P~patrone** f blank. **P~regen** m downpour. **P~verweis** m (Sport) sending off. **P~wunde** f laceration

Plauderei f -,-en chat

plaudern vi (haben) chat

Plausch m -[e]s,-e (SGer) chat. **p~en** vi (haben) (SGer) chat

plausibel a plausible

plazieren vt (NEW) **platzieren**

pleite a (fam) **p~ sein** be broke: (Firma:) be bankrupt; **p~ gehen** (NEW) **P~ gehen**, s. **Pleite**. **P~** f -,-n (fam) bankruptcy; (Misserfolg) flop; **P~ gehen** od **machen** go bankrupt

plissiert a [finely] pleated

Plombe f -,-n seal; (Zahn-) filling. **p~ieren** vt seal; fill (Zahn)

plötzlich a sudden, adv -ly

plump a plump; (ungeschickt) clumsy, adv -ily

plumpsen vi (sein) (fam) fall

Plunder m -s (fam) junk, rubbish

plündern vt/i (haben) loot

Plunderstück nt Danish pastry

Plural m -s,-e plural

plus adv, conj & prep (+ dat) plus. **P~** nt -- surplus; (Gewinn) profit (Vorteil) advantage, plus. **P~punkt** m (Sport) point; (fig) plus. **P~quamperfekt** nt pluperfect. **P~zeichen** nt plus sign

Po m -s,-s (fam) bottom

Pöbel m -s mob, rabble. **p~haft** a loutish

pochen vi (haben) knock, (Herz:) pound; **p~ auf** (+ acc) (fig) insist on

pochieren /pɔ'ʃi:rən/ vt poach

Pocken pl smallpox sg

Podest nt -[e]s,-e rostrum

Podium nt -s,-ien /-jən/ platform; (*Podest*) rostrum

Poesie /poˈziː/ f - poetry

poetisch a poetic

Pointe /ˈpoɛ̃ːtə/ f -,-n point (*of a joke*)

Pokal m -s,-e goblet; (*Sport*) cup

pökeln vt (*Culin*) salt

Poker nt -s poker

Pol m -s,-e pole. **p~ar** a polar

polarisieren vt polarize

Polarstern m pole-star

Pole m, -n, Pole. **P~n** nt -s Poland

Police /poˈliːsə/ f -,-n policy

Polier m -s,-e foreman

polieren vt polish

Polin f -,-nen Pole

Politesse f -,-n (*woman*) traffic warden

Politik f - politics sg; (*Vorgehen, Maßnahme*) policy

Polit|iker(in) m -s,- (f, -,-nen) politician. **p~isch** a political, adv -ly

Politur f -,-en polish

Polizei f - police pl. **P~beamte(r)** m police officer. **p~lich** a police ... □ adv by the police; (*sich anmelden*) with the police. **P~streife** f police patrol. **P~stunde** f closing time. **P~wache** f police station

Polizist m -en,-en policeman. **P~in** f -,-nen policewoman

Pollen m -s pollen

polnisch a Polish

Polohemd nt -s polo shirt

Polster nt -s,- pad; (*Kissen*) cushion; (*Möbel*) upholstery; (*fam: Rücklage*) reserves pl. **P~er** m -s,- upholsterer. **P~möbel** pl upholstered furniture sg. **p~n** vt pad; upholster (*Möbel*). **P~ung** f - padding; upholstery

Polter|abend m wedding-eve party. **p~n** vi (*haben*) thump bang; (*schelten*) bawl □ vi (*sein*) crash down; (*gehen*) clump [along]; (*fahren*) rumble [along]

Polyäthylen nt -s polythene

Polyester m -s polyester

Polyp m -en,-en polyp; (*sl: Polizist*) copper; **P~en** adenoids pl

Pomeranze f -,-n Seville orange

Pommes pl (*fam*) French fries

Pommes frites /pɔmˈfriːt/ pl chips; (*dünner*) French fries

Pomp m -s pomp

Pompon /põˈpõː/ m -s,-s pompon

pompös a ostentatious, adv -ly

Pony[1] m -s,-s pony

Pony[2] m -s,-s fringe

Pop m -[s] pop. **P~musik** f pop music

Popo m -s,-s (*fam*) bottom

popul|är a popular. **P~arität** f - popularity

Pore f -,-n pore

Porno|graphie, **Pornografie** f - pornography. **p~graphisch**, **p~grafisch** a pornographic

porös a porous

Porree m -s leeks pl; **eine Stange P~** a leek

Portal nt -s,-e portal

Portemonnaie /portmoˈneː/ nt -s,-s purse

Portier /porˈtjeː/ m -s,-s doorman, porter

Portion /-ˈtsjoːn/ f -,-en helping, portion

Portmonee nt -s,-s = **Portemonnaie**

Porto nt -s postage. **p~frei** adv post free, post paid

Porträt /porˈtrɛ/ nt -s,-s portrait. **p~ieren** vt paint a portrait of

Portugal nt -s Portugal

Portugies|e m -n,-n, **P~in** f -,-nen Portuguese. **p~isch** a Portuguese

Portwein m port

Porzellan nt -s china, porcelain

Posaune f -,-n trombone

Pose f -,-n pose

posieren vi (*haben*) pose

Position /-ˈtsjoːn/ f -,-en position

positiv a positive, adv -ly. **P~** nt -s,-e (Phot) positive

Posse f -,-n (Theat) farce. **P~n** m -s,- prank; **P~n** pl tomfoolery sg

Possessivpronomen nt possessive pronoun

possierlich a cute

Post f - post office; (Briefe) mail, post; **mit der P~** by post

postalisch a postal

Post|amt nt post office. **P~anweisung** f postal money order. **P~bote** m postman

Posten m -s,- post; (Wache) sentry; (Waren-) batch; (Rechnungs-) item, entry; **P~ stehen** stand guard; **nicht auf dem P~** (fam) under the weather

Poster nt & m -s,- poster

Postfach nt post-office or PO box

postieren vt post, station; **sich p~** station oneself

Post|karte f postcard. **p~lagernd** adv poste restante. **P~leitzahl** f postcode, (Amer) Zip code. **P~scheckkonto** nt ≈ National Girobank account. **P~stempel** m postmark

postum a posthumous, adv -ly

post|wendend adv by return of post. **P~wertzeichen** nt [postage] stamp

Poten|tial /-'tsiaːl/ nt -s,-e = Potenzial. **p~tiell** /-'tsiɛl/ a = potenziell

Potenz f -,-en potency; (Math & fig) power. **P~ial** nt -s,-e potential. **p~iell** a potential, adv -ly

Pracht f - magnificence, splendour. **P~exemplar** nt magnificent specimen

prächtig a magnificent, adv -ly; (prima) splendid, adv -ly

prachtvoll a magnificent, adv -ly

Prädikat nt -[e]s,-e rating; (Comm) grade; (Gram) predicate. **p~iv** a (Gram) predicative, adv -ly. **P~swein** m high-quality wine

prägen vt stamp (auf + acc on); emboss (Leder, Papier); mint (Münze); coin (Wort, Ausdruck); (fig) shape. **P~stempel** m die

pragmatisch a pragmatic, adv -ally

prägnant a succinct, adv -ly

prähistorisch a prehistoric

prahl|en vi (haben) boast, brag (mit about). **p~erisch** a boastful, adv -ly

Prakti|k f -,-en practice. **P~kant(in)** m -en,-en (f -,-nen) trainee

Prakti|kum nt -s,-ka practical training. **p~sch** a practical; (nützlich) handy; (tatsächlich) virtual; **p~scher Arzt** general practitioner □ adv practically; (in der Praxis) in practice; **p~sch arbeiten** do practical work. **p~zieren** vt/i (haben) practise; (anwenden) put into practice; (fam: bekommen) get

Praline f -,-n chocolate; **Schachtel P~n** box of chocolates

prall a bulging; (dick) plump; (Sonne) blazing □ adv **p~ gefüllt** full to bursting. **p~en** vi (sein) **p~ auf** (+ acc)/gegen collide with, hit; (Sonne:) blaze down on

Prämie /-jə/ f -,-n premium; (Preis) award

prämi|ieren vt award a prize to

Pranger m -s,- pillory

Pranke f -,-n paw

Präparat nt -[e]s,-e preparation. **p~ieren** vt prepare; (zerlegen) dissect; (ausstopfen) stuff

Präposition /-'tsioːn/ f -,-en preposition

Präsens nt - (Gram) present

präsentieren vt present; **sich p~** present itself/(Person:) oneself

Präsenz f - presence

Präservativ nt -s,-e condom

Präsident(in) m -en,-en (f -,-nen) president. **P~schaft** f - presidency

Präsidium nt -s presidency; (*Gremium*) executive committee; (*Polizei-*) headquarters pl

prasseln vi (haben) (*Regen:*) beat down; (*Feuer:*) crackle □ vi (sein) **p~ auf** (+ acc)/**gegen** beat down on/beat against

prassen vi (haben) live extravagantly; (*schmausen*) feast

Präteritum nt -s imperfect

präventiv a a preventive

Praxis f -,-xen practice; (*Erfahrung*) practical experience; (*Arzt-*) surgery; **in der P~** in practice

Präzedenzfall m precedent

präzis[e] a precise, adv -ly

Präzision f - precision

predigen vt/i (haben) preach. **P~er** m -s,- preacher. **P~t** f -,-en sermon

Preis m -es,-e price; (*Belohnung*) prize; **um jeden/keinen P~** at any/not at any price. **P~ausschreiben** nt competition

Preiselbeere f (Bot) cowberry; (*Culin*) ≈ cranberry

preisen† vt praise; **sich glücklich p~** count oneself lucky

preisgeben† vt sep abandon (*dat* to); reveal (*Geheimnis*)

preis|gekrönt a award-winning. **P~gericht** nt jury. **p~günstig** a reasonably priced □ adv at a reasonable price. **P~lage** f price range. **p~lich** a price ... □ adv in price. **P~richter** m judge. **P~schild** nt price-tag. **P~träger(in)** m(f) prize-winner. **p~wert** a reasonable, adv -bly; (*billig*) inexpensive, adv -ly

prekär a difficult; (*heikel*) delicate

Prell|bock m buffers pl. **p~en** vt bounce; (*verletzen*) bruise; (*fam: betrügen*) cheat. **P~ung** f -,-en bruise

Premiere /prəˈmjeːrə/ f -,-n première

Premierminister(in) /prəˈmjeː-/ m(f) Prime Minister

Presse f -,-n press. **p~n** vt press; **sich p~n** press (**an** + acc against)

pressieren vi (haben) (SGer) be urgent

Pressluft (**Preßluft**) f compressed air. **P~bohrer** m pneumatic drill

Prestige /presˈtiːʒə/ nt -s prestige

Preuße m -n,-n Prussia. **p~isch** a Prussian

prickeln vi (haben) tingle

Priester m -s,- priest

prima inv a first-class, first-rate; (*fam: toll*) fantastic, adv fantastically well

primär a primary, adv -ily

Primel f -,-n primula; (*Garten-*) polyanthus

primitiv a primitive

Prinz m -en,-en prince. **P~essin** f -,-nen princess

Prinzip nt -s,-ien /-jən/ principle; **im/aus P~** in/on principle. **p~iell** a (*Frage*) of principle □ adv on principle; (*im Prinzip*) in principle

Priorität f -,-en priority

Prise f -,-n P~ Salz pinch of salt

Prisma nt -s,-men prism

privat a private, adv -ly; (*persönlich*) personal. **P~adresse** f home address. **p~isieren** vt privatize

Privat|leben nt private life. **P~lehrer** m private tutor. **P~lehrerin** f governess. **P~patient(in)** m(f) private patient

Privileg nt -[e]s,-ien /-jən/ privilege. **p~iert** a privileged

pro prep (+ dat) per. **Pro** nt -das Pro und Kontra the pros and cons pl

Probe f -,-n test, trial; (*Menge, Muster*) sample; (*Theat*) rehearsal; **auf die P~ stellen** put to the test; **ein Auto P~ fahren** test-drive a car. **P~fahrt** f test drive. **p~n** vt/i (haben) (Theat) rehearse. **p~weise** adv on a trial basis. **P∼zeit** *f* probationary period

probieren *vt/i* (*haben*) try; (*kosten*) taste; (*proben*) rehearse

Problem *nt* -s,-e problem. **p∼atisch** *a* problematic

problemlos *a* problem-free □ *adv* without any problems

Produkt *nt* -[e]s,-e product

Produk|tion /-'tsjo:n/ *f* -,-en production. **p∼tiv** *a* productive. **P∼tivität** *f* - productivity

Produ|zent *m* -en,-en producer. **p∼zieren** *vt* produce; **sich p∼zieren** (*fam*) show off

professionell *a* professional, *adv* -ly

Professor *m* -s,-en /-'so:rən/ professor

Profi *m* -s,-s (*Sport*) professional

Profil *nt* -s,-e profile; (*Reifen-*) tread; (*fig*) image. **p∼iert** *a* (*fig*) distinguished

Profit *m* -[e]s,-e profit. **p∼ieren** *vi* (*haben*) profit (**von** from)

Prognose *f* -,-n forecast; (*Med*) prognosis

Programm *nt* -s,-e programme; (*Computer-*) program; (*TV*) channel; (*Comm: Sortiment*) range. **p∼ieren** *vt/i* (*haben*) (*computer*) program. **P∼ierer(in)** *m* -s,- (*f* -,-nen) [computer] programmer

progressiv *a* progressive

Projekt *nt* -[e]s,-e project

Projektor *m* -s,-en /-'to:rən/ projector

projizieren *vt* project

Proklam|ation /-'tsjo:n/ *f* -,-en proclamation. **p∼ieren** *vt* proclaim

Prolet *m* -en,-en boor. **P∼ariat** *nt* -[e]s proletariat. **P∼arier** /-iɐ/ *m* -s,- proletarian

Prolog *m* -s,-e prologue

Promenade *f* -,-n promenade. **P∼nmischung** *f* (*fam*) mongrel

Promille *pl* (*fam*) alcohol level *sg* in the blood; **zu viel P∼ haben** (*fam*) be over the limit

prominen|t *a* prominent. **P∼z** *f* - prominent figures *pl*

Promiskuität *f* - promiscuity

promovieren *vi* (*haben*) obtain one's doctorate

prompt *a* prompt, *adv* -ly; (*fam: natürlich*) of course

Pronomen *nt* -s,- pronoun

Propag|anda *f* - propaganda; (*Reklame*) publicity. **p∼ieren** *vt* propagate

Propeller *m* -s,- propeller

Prophet *m* -en,-en prophet. **p∼isch** *a* prophetic

prophezei|en *vt* prophesy. **P∼ung** *f* -,-en prophecy

Proportion /-'tsjo:n/ *f* -,-en proportion. **p∼al** *a* proportional. **p∼iert** *a* **gut p∼iert** well proportioned

Prosa *f* - prose

prosaisch *a* prosaic, *adv* -ally

prosit *int* cheers!

Prospekt *m* -[e]s,-e brochure; (*Comm*) prospectus

prost *int* cheers!

Prostituierte *f* -n,-n prostitute. **P∼tion** /-'tsjo:n/ *f* - prostitution

Protest *m* -[e]s,-e protest

Protestant|(in) *m* -en,-en (*f* -,-nen) (*Relig*) Protestant. **p∼isch** *a* (*Relig*) Protestant

protestieren *vi* (*haben*) protest

Prothese *f* -,-n artificial limb; (*Zahn-*) denture

Protokoll *nt* -s,-e record; (*Sitzungs-*) minutes *pl*; (*diplomatisches*) protocol; (*Strafzettel*) ticket

Prototyp *m* -s,-en prototype

protz|en *vi* (*haben*) show off (**mit etw** sth). **p∼ig** *a* ostentatious

Proviant *m* -s provisions *pl*

Provinz *f* -,-en province. **p∼iell** *a* provincial

Provision *f* -,-en (*Comm*) commission

provisorisch *a* provisional, *adv* -ly, temporary, *adv* -ily

Provokation /-'tsjo:n/ f -,-en provocation

provozieren vt provoke. **p~d** a provocative, adv -ly

Prozedur f -,-en [lengthy] business

Prozent nt -[e]s,-e & - per cent; 5 **P~** 5 per cent. **P~satz** m percentage. **p~ual** a percentage . . .

Prozess m -es,-e (Prozeß m -sses,-sse) process; (Jur) lawsuit; (Kriminal-) trial

Prozession f -,-en procession

prüde a prudish

prüf|en vt test/(über-) check (auf + acc for); audit (Bücher); (Sch) examine. **p~ender Blick** searching look. **P~er** m -s,- inspector; (Buch-) auditor; (Sch) examiner. **P~ling** m -s,-e examination candidate. **P~ung** f -,-en examination; (Test) test; (Bücher-) audit; (fig) trial

Prügel m -s,- cudgel; **P~** pl hiding sg, beating sg. **P~ei** f -,-en brawl, fight. **p~n** vt beat, thrash; **sich p~n** fight, brawl

Prunk m -[e]s magnificence, splendour. **p~en** vi (haben) show off (mit etw sth). **p~voll** a magnificent, adv -ly

prusten vi (haben) splutter; (schnauben) snort

Psalm m -s,-en psalm

Pseudonym nt -s,-e pseudonym

pst int shush!

Psychi|ater m -s,- psychiatrist. **P~atrie** f - psychiatry. **p~a-trisch** a psychiatric

psychisch a psychological, adv -ly; (Med) mental, adv -ly

Psycho|analyse f psychoanalysis. **P~loge** m -n,-n psychologist. **P~logie** f - psychology. **p~logisch** a psychological, adv -ly

Pubertät f - puberty

publik a **p~ werden/machen** become/make public

Publi|kum nt -s public; (Zuhörer) audience; (Zuschauer) spectators pl. **p~zieren** vt publish

Pudding m -s,-s blancmange; (im Wasserbad gekocht) pudding

Pudel m -s,- poodle

Puder m & (fam) nt -s,- powder; (Körper-) talcum [powder]. **P~dose** f [powder] compact. **p~n** vt powder. **P~zucker** m icing sugar

Puff[1] m -[e]s,-̈e push, poke

Puff[2] m & nt -s,-s (sl) brothel

puffen vt (fam) poke □ vi (sein) puff along

Puffer m -s,- (Rail) buffer; (Culin) pancake. **P~zone** f buffer zone

Pulli m -s,-s jumper. **P~over** m -s,- jumper; (Herren-) pullover

Puls m -es pulse. **P~ader** f artery. **p~ieren** vi (haben) pulsate

Pult nt -[e]s,-e desk; (Lese-) lectern

Pulver nt -s,- powder. **p~ig** a powdery. **p~isieren** vt pulverize

Pulver|kaffee m instant coffee. **P~schnee** m powder snow

pummelig a (fam) chubby

Pump m auf **P~** (fam) on tick

Pumpe f -,-n pump. **p~n** vt/i (haben) pump; (fam: leihen) lend; [sich (dat)] etw **p~n** (fam: borgen) borrow sth

Pumps /pœmps/ pl court shoes

Punkt m -[e]s,-e dot; (Tex) spot; (Geom, Sport & fig) point; (Gram) full stop, period; **P~ sechs Uhr** at six o'clock sharp; **nach P~en siegen** win on points. **p~iert** a (Linie, Note) dotted

pünktlich a punctual, adv -ly. **P~keit** f - punctuality

Punsch m -[e]s,-e [hot] punch

Pupille f -,-n (Anat) pupil

Puppe f -,-n doll; (Marionette) puppet; (Schaufenster-, Schneider-) dummy; (Zool) chrysalis

pur a pure; (fam: bloß) sheer; **Whisky pur** neat whisky

Püree *nt* -s,-s purée; (*Kartoffel-*) mashed potatoes *pl*

puritanisch *a* puritanical

purpurrot *a* crimson

Purzel|baum *m* (*fam*) somersault. **p~n** *vi* (*sein*) (*fam*) tumble

pusseln *vi* (*haben*) (*fam*) potter

Puste *f* - (*fam*) breath; **aus der P~** out of breath. **p~n** *vt/i* (*haben*) (*fam*) blow

Pute *f* -,-n turkey; (*Henne*) turkey hen. **P~r** *m* -s,- turkey cock

Putsch *m* -[e]s,-e coup

Putz *m* -es plaster; (*Staat*) finery. **p~en** *vt* clean; (*Ausf*) dry-clean; (*zieren*) adorn; **sich p~en** dress up; **sich** (*dat*) **die Zähne/Nase p~en** clean one's teeth/blow one's nose. **P~frau** *f* cleaner, charwoman. **p~ig** *a* (*fam*) amusing, cute; (*seltsam*) odd. **P~macherin** *f* -,-nen milliner

Puzzlespiel /'pazl-/ *nt* jigsaw

Pyramide *f* -,-n pyramid

Q

Quacksalber *m* -s,- quack

Quadrat *nt* -[e]s,-e square. **q~isch** *a* square. **Q~meter** *m* & *nt* square metre

quaken *vi* (*haben*) quack; (*Frosch:*) croak

quäken *vi* (*haben*) screech; (*Baby:*) whine

Quäker(in) *m* -s,- (*f* -,-nen) Quaker

Qual *f* -,-en torment; (*Schmerz*) agony

quälen *vt* torment; (*foltern*) torture; (*bedrängen*) pester; **sich q~** torment oneself; (*leiden*) suffer; (*sich mühen*) struggle. **q~d** *a* agonizing

Quälerei *f* -,-en torture; (*Qual*) agony

Quälgeist *m* (*fam*) pest

Qualifi|kation /-'tsio:n/ *f* -,-en qualification. **q~zieren** *vt* qualify; **sich q~zieren** qualify. **q~ziert** *a* qualified; (*fähig*) competent; (*Arbeit*) skilled

Qualität *f* -,-en quality

Qualle *f* -,-n jellyfish

Qualm *m* -s [thick] smoke. **q~en** *vi* (*haben*) smoke

qualvoll *a* agonizing

Quantität *f* -,-en quantity

Quantum *nt* -s,-ten quantity; (*Anteil*) share, quota

Quarantäne *f* - quarantine

Quark *m* -s quark, ≈ curd cheese; (*fam: Unsinn*) rubbish

Quartal *nt* -s,-e quarter

Quartett *nt* -[e]s,-e quartet

Quartier *nt* -s,-e accommodation; (*Mil*) quarters *pl*; **ein Q~ suchen** look for accommodation

Quarz *m* -es quartz

quasseln *vi* (*haben*) (*fam*) jabber

Quaste *f* -,-n tassel

Quatsch *m* -[e]s (*fam*) nonsense, rubbish; **Q~ machen** (*Unfug machen*) fool around; (*etw falsch machen*) do a silly thing. **q~en** (*fam*) *vi* (*haben*) talk; (*schwatzen*) natter; (*Wasser, Schlamm:*) squelch □ *vt* talk. **q~nass** (*q~naß*) *a* (*fam*) soaking wet

Quecksilber *nt* mercury

Quelle *f* -,-n spring; (*Fluss- & fig*) source. **q~n†** *vi* (*sein*) well [up]/(*fließen*) pour (**aus** from); (*aufquellen*) swell; (*hervortreten*) bulge

quengeln *vi* (*fam*) whine; (*Baby:*) grizzle

quer *adv* across, crosswise; (*schräg*) diagonally; **q~ gestreift** horizontally striped

Quere *f* - der **Q~ nach** across, crosswise; **jdm in die Q~ kommen** get in s.o.'s way

querfeldein *adv* across country

quer|gestreift *a* (NEW) **q~ gestreift**, *s.* **quer**. **q~köpfig** *a* (*fam*) awkward. **Q~latte** *f* cross-

bar. **Q~schiff** nt transept.
Q~schnitt m cross-section.
Q~schnittsgelähmt a paraplegic. **Q~straße** f side-street;
die erste Q~straße links the
first turning on the left.
Q~verweis m cross-reference

quetsch|en vt squash; (drücken)
squeeze; (zerdrücken) crush; (Culin) mash; **sich q~en in** (+ acc)
squeeze into; **sich** (dat) **den Arm
q~en** bruise one's arm. **Q~ung**
f -,-en, **Q~wunde** f bruise

Queue /køː/ nt -s,-s cue

quicklebendig a very lively

quieken vi (haben) squeal;
(Maus:) squeak

quietschen vi (haben) squeal;
(Tür, Dielen:) creak

Quintett nt -[e]s,-e quintet

Quirl m -[e]s,-e blender with a
star-shaped head. **q~en** vt mix

quitt a **q~ sein** (fam) be quits

Quitte f -,-n quince

quittieren vt receipt (Rechnung);
sign for (Geldsumme, Sendung);
(reagieren auf) greet (mit with);
den Dienst q~ resign

Quittung f -,-en receipt

Quiz /kvɪs/ nt -,- quiz

Quote f -,-n proportion

R

Rabatt m -[e]s,-e discount

Rabatte f -,-n (Hort) border

Rabattmarke f trading stamp

Rabbiner m -s,- rabbi

Rabe m -n,-n raven. **r~nschwarz**
a pitch-black

rabiat a violent, adv -ly; (wütend)
furious, adv -ly

Rache f - revenge, vengeance

Rachen m -s,- pharynx; (Maul)
jaws pl

rächen vt avenge; **sich r~** take
revenge (**an** + dat on); (Fehler,
Leichtsinn:) cost s.o. dear

Räcker m -s,- (fam) rascal

Rad nt -[e]s,ِer wheel; (Fahr-) bicycle, (fam) bike; **Rad fahren**
cycle

Radar m & nt -s radar

Radau m -s (fam) din, racket

radebrechen vt/i (haben)
[Deutsch/Englisch] r~ speak
broken German/English

radeln vi (sein) (fam) cycle

Rädelsführer m ringleader

radfahr|en† vi sep (sein)
(NEW) **Rad fahren**, s. **Rad**.

R~er(in) m(f) -s,- (f -,-nen) cyclist

radier|en vt/i (haben) rub out;
(Kunst) etch. **R~gummi** m eraser, rubber. **R~ung** f -,-en
etching

Radieschen /-'diːsçən/ nt -s,-
radish

radikal a radical, adv -ly; (drastisch) drastic, adv -ally. **R~e(r)**
m/f (Pol) radical

Radio nt -s,-s radio

radioaktiv a radioactive. **R~ität**
f - radioactivity

Radioapparat m radio [set]

Radius m -,-ien /-jən/ radius

Rad|kappe f hub-cap. **R~ler** m
-s,- cyclist; (Getränk) shandy.
R~weg m cycle track

raff|en vt grab; (kräuseln) gather;
(kürzen) condense. **r~gierig** a
avaricious

Raffin|ade f - refined sugar.
R~erie f -,-n refinery. **R~esse** f
-,-n refinement; (Schlauheit) cunning. **r~ieren** vt refine. **r~iert** a
ingenious, adv -ly; (durchtrieben)
crafty, adv -ily

Rage /'raːʒə/ f - (fam) fury

ragen vi (haben) rise [up]

Rahm m -s (SGer) cream

rahmen vt frame. **R~** m -s,-
frame; (fig) framework; (Grenze)
limits pl; (einer Feier) setting

Rain m -[e]s,-e grass verge

räkeln v = rekeln

Rakete f -,-n rocket; (Mil) missile

Rallye /'rali/ *nt* -s,-s rally
rammen *vt* ram
Rampe *f* -,-n ramp; ⟨*Theat*⟩ front
of the stage. **R~nlicht** *nt* im
R~nlicht stehen ⟨*fig*⟩ be in the
limelight
ramponier|en *vt* ⟨*fam*⟩ damage;
⟨*ruinieren*⟩ ruin; **r~t** battered
Ramsch *m* -[e]s junk. **R~laden**
m junk-shop
ran *adv* = **heran**
Rand *m* -[e]s,ˆer edge; ⟨*Teller-,
Gläser-, Brillen-*⟩ rim; ⟨*Zier-*⟩ border, edging; ⟨*Buch-, Brief-*⟩ margin; ⟨*Stadt-*⟩ outskirts *pl*; ⟨*Ring*⟩
ring; **am R~e des Ruins** on the
brink of ruin; **am R~e erwähnen** mention in passing; **zu
R~e kommen mit** = **zurande
kommen mit**, *s.* **zurande**. **außer
R~ und Band** ⟨*fam: ausgelassen*⟩ very boisterous
randalieren *vi* ⟨*haben*⟩ rampage
Rand|bemerkung *f* marginal
note. **R~streifen** *m* ⟨*Auto*⟩ hard
shoulder
Rang *m* -[e]s,ˆe rank; ⟨*Theat*⟩ tier;
erster/zweiter R~ ⟨*Theat*⟩
dress/upper circle; **ersten R~es**
first-class
rangieren /raŋ'ʒi:rən/ *vt* shunt
□ *vi* ⟨*haben*⟩ rank ⟨*vor* + *dat* be-
fore⟩; **an erster Stelle r~** come
first
Rangordnung *f* order of importance; ⟨*Hierarchie*⟩ hierarchy
Ranke *f* -,-n tendril; ⟨*Trieb*⟩ shoot
ranken (sich) *vr* ⟨*Bot*⟩ trail; ⟨*in die
Höhe*⟩ climb; **sich r~ um** twine
around
Ranzen *m* -s,- ⟨*Sch*⟩ satchel
ranzig *a* rancid
Rappe *m* -n,-n black horse
rappeln *v* ⟨*fam*⟩ □ *vi* ⟨*haben*⟩
rattle □ *vr* **sich r~** pick oneself
up; ⟨*fig*⟩ rally
Raps *m* -es ⟨*Bot*⟩ rape
rar *a* rare; **er macht sich rar**
⟨*fam*⟩ we don't see much of him.
R~ität *f* -,-en rarity

rasant *a* fast; ⟨*schnittig, schick*⟩
stylish □ *adv* fast; stylishly
rasch *a* quick, *adv* -ly
rascheln *vi* ⟨*haben*⟩ rustle
Rasen *m* -s,- lawn
rasen *vi* ⟨*sein*⟩ tear [along]; ⟨*Puls:*⟩
race; ⟨*Zeit:*⟩ fly; **gegen eine
Mauer r~** career into a wall □ *vi*
⟨*haben*⟩ rave; ⟨*Sturm:*⟩ rage; **vor
Begeisterung r~** go wild with
enthusiasm. **r~d** *a* furious; ⟨*to-
bend*⟩ raving; ⟨*Sturm, Durst*⟩ raging; ⟨*Schmerz*⟩ excruciating;
⟨*Beifall*⟩ tumultuous □ *adv* terribly
Rasenmäher *m* lawn-mower
Raserei *f* - speeding; ⟨*Toben*⟩
frenzy
Rasier|apparat *m* razor. **r~en** *vt*
shave; **sich r~en** shave.
R~klinge *f* razor blade. **R~pin-
sel** *m* shaving-brush. **R~wasser**
nt aftershave [lotion]
Raspel *f* -,-n rasp; ⟨*Culin*⟩ grater.
r~n *vt* grate
Rasse *f* -,-n race. **R~hund** *m* pedigree dog
Rassel *f* -,-n rattle. **r~n** *vi* ⟨*haben*⟩
rattle; ⟨*Schlüssel:*⟩ jangle; ⟨*Kette:*⟩
clank □ *vi* ⟨*sein*⟩ rattle [along]
Rassen|diskriminierung *f* ra-
cial discrimination. **R~tren-
nung** *f* racial segregation
Rassepferd *nt* thoroughbred
rassisch *a* racial
Rassis|mus *m* - racism. **r~tisch**
a racist
Rast *f* -,-en rest. **r~en** *vi* ⟨*haben*⟩
rest. **R~haus** *nt* motorway restaurant. **r~los** *a* restless, *adv* -ly;
⟨*ununterbrochen*⟩ ceaseless, *adv*
-ly. **R~platz** *m* picnic area.
R~stätte *f* motorway restaurant
[and services]
Rasur *f* -,-en shave
Rat¹ *m* -[e]s [piece of] advice;
guter Rat good advice; **sich** ⟨*dat*⟩
keinen Rat wissen not know
what to do; **zu Rat[e] ziehen** =
zurate ziehen, *s.* **zurate**

Rat² m -[e]s,-̈e (Admin) council; (Person) councillor

Rate f -,-n instalment

raten† vt guess; (empfehlen) advise □ vi (haben) guess; **jdm r~** advise s.o.

Ratenzahlung f payment by instalments

Rat|geber m -s,- adviser; (Buch) guide. **R~haus** nt town hall

ratifizier|en vt ratify. **R~ung** f -,-en ratification

Ration /ra'tsi̯o:n/ f -,-en ration; **eiserne R~** iron rations pl. **r~al** a rational, adv -ly. **r~alisieren** vt/i (haben) rationalize. **r~ell** a efficient, adv -ly. **r~ieren** vt ration

rat|los a helpless, adv -ly; **r~los sein** not know what to do. **r~sam** pred a advisable; (klug) prudent. **R~schlag** m piece of advice. **R~schläge** pl advice sg

Rätsel nt -s,- riddle; (Kreuzwort-) puzzle; (Geheimnis) mystery. **r~haft** a puzzling, mysterious. **r~n** vi (haben) puzzle

Ratte f -,-n rat

rattern vi (haben) rattle □ vi (sein) rattle [along]

rau a rough, adv -ly; (unfreundlich) gruff, adv -ly; (Klima, Wind) harsh, raw; (Landschaft) rugged; (heiser) husky; (Hals) sore

Raub m -[e]s robbery; (Menschen-) abduction; (Beute) loot, booty. **r~en** vt steal; (Menschen) abduct; **jdm etw r~en** rob s.o. of sth

Räuber m -s,- robber

Raub|mord m robbery with murder. **R~tier** nt predator. **R~überfall** m robbery. **R~vogel** m bird of prey

Rauch m -[e]s smoke. **r~en** vt/i (haben) smoke. **R~en** nt -s smoking; 'R~en verboten' 'no smoking'. **R~er** m -s,-smoker. **R~erabteil** nt smoking compartment

Räucher|lachs m smoked salmon. **r~n** vt (Culin) smoke

Rauch|fang m (Aust) chimney. **r~ig** a smoky. **R~verbot** nt smoking ban

räudig a mangy

rauf adv = herauf, hinauf

rauf|en vt pull; **sich** (dat) **die Haare r~en** (fig) tear one's hair □ vr/i (haben) [sich] r~en fight. **R~erei** f -,-en fight

rauh a (NEW) **rau**

rau|haarig a wire-haired. **R~heit** f - (s. rau) roughness; gruffness; harshness; ruggedness

rauh|haarig a (NEW) **rauhaarig**.

R~reif m (NEW) **Raureif**

Raum m -[e]s, Räume room; (Gebiet) area; (Welt-) space

räumen vt clear; (Wohnung) evacuate (Gebäude, Gebiet, Mil Stellung); (bringen) put (in/auf + acc into/on); (holen) get (aus out of); beiseite r~ move/put to one side; **aus dem Weg r~** (fam) get rid of

Raum|fahrer m astronaut. **R~fahrt** f space travel. **R~fahrzeug** nt spacecraft. **R~flug** m space flight. **R~inhalt** m volume

räumlich a spatial. **R~keiten** fpl rooms

Raum|pflegerin f cleaner. **R~schiff** nt spaceship

Räumung f - (s. räumen) clearing; vacating; evacuation. **R~sverkauf** m clearance/closing-down sale

raunen vt/i (haben) whisper

Raupe f -,-n caterpillar

Raureif m hoar-frost

raus adv = heraus, hinaus

Rausch m -[e]s, Räusche intoxication; (fig) exhilaration; **einen R~haben** be drunk

rauschen vi (haben) (Wasser, Wind:) rush; (Bäume Blätter:) rustle □ vi (sein) rush [along]; **aus dem Zimmer r~** sweep out of the room. **r~d** *a* rushing; rustling; *(Applaus)* tumultuous

Rauschgift *nt* [narcotic] drug; *(coll)* drugs *pl.* **R~süchtige(r)** *m/f* drug addict

räuspern (sich) *vr* clear one's throat

rausschmeiß|en† *vt sep (fam)* throw out; *(entlassen)* sack. **R~er** *m* -s,- *(fam)* bouncer

Raute *f* -,-n diamond

Razzia *f* -,-ien /-jən/ [police] raid

Reagenzglas *nt* test-tube

reagieren *vi (haben)* react *(auf +* acc *to)*

Reaktion /-'tsjo:n/ *f* -,-en reaction. **r~är** *a* reactionary

Reaktor *m* -s,-en /-'to:rən/ reactor

real *a* real; *(gegenständlich)* tangible; *(realistisch)* realistic, *adv* -ally. **r~isieren** *vt* realize

Realis|mus *m* - realism. **R~t** *m* -en,-en realist. **r~tisch** *a* realistic, *adv* -ally

Realität *f* -,-en reality

Realschule *f* ≈ secondary modern school

Rebe *f* -,-n vine

Rebell *m* -en,-en rebel. **r~ieren** *vi (haben)* rebel. **R~ion** *f* -,-en rebellion

rebellisch *a* rebellious

Rebhuhn *nt* partridge

Rebstock *m* vine

Rechen *m* -s- rake. **r~** *vt/i (haben)* rake

Rechen|aufgabe *f* arithmetical problem; *(Sch)* sum. **R~fehler** *m* arithmetical error. **R~maschine** *f* calculator

Rechenschaft *f* - **R~** ablegen give account *(über +* acc *of)*; **jdn zur R~ ziehen** call s.o. to account

recherchieren /reʃer'ʃi:rən/ *vt/i (haben)* investigate; *(Journ)* research

rechnen *vi (haben)* do arithmetic; *(schätzen)* reckon; *(zählen)* count

(zu among; *auf +* acc on*)*; **r~ mit** reckon with; *(erwarten)* expect; **gut r~ können** be good at figures □ *vt* calculate, work out; do *(Aufgabe)*; *(dazu-)* add *(zu* to*)*; *(fig)* count *(zu* among*)*. **R~ nt** -s arithmetic

Rechner *m* -s,- calculator; *(Computer)* computer; **ein guter R~ sein** be good at figures

Rechnung *f* -,-en bill, *(Amer)* check; *(Comm)* invoice; *(Berechnung)* calculation; **R~ führen über** *(+* acc*)* keep account of; **etw** *(dat)* **R~ tragen** *(fig)* take sth into account. **R~sjahr** *nt* financial year. **R~sprüfer** *m* auditor

Recht *nt* -[e]s,-e law; *(Berechtigung)* right *(auf +* acc to*)*; **im R~ sein** be in the right; **R~ haben/behalten** be right; **R~ bekommen** be proved right; **jdm R~ geben** agree with s.o.; **mit** *od* **zu R~** rightly; **von R~s wegen** by right; *(eigentlich)* by rights

recht *a* right; *(wirklich)* real; **ich habe keine r~e Lust** I don't really feel like it; **es jdm r~ machen** please s.o.; **jdm r~ sein** be all right with s.o.; **r~ haben/behalten/bekommen** ⟨NEW⟩ **Recht haben/behalten/bekommen**, *s.* **Recht**; **jdm r~ geben** ⟨NEW⟩ **jdm Recht geben** □ *adv* correctly; *(ziemlich)* quite; *(sehr)* very; **r~ vielen Dank** many thanks

Recht|e *f* -n,-[n] right side; *(Hand)* right hand; *(Boxen)* right; **die R~e** *(Pol)* the right; **zu meiner R~en** on my right. **r~e(r,s)** *a* right; *(Pol)* right-wing; **r~e Masche** plain stitch. **R~e(r)** *m/f* **der/die R~e** the right man/woman; **du bist mir der/die R~e!** you're a fine one! **R~e(s)** *nt* **das R~e** the right thing; **etwas R~es lernen** learn something useful; **nach dem**

R~en sehen see that everything is all right

Rechteck nt -[e]s,-e rectangle. r~ig a rectangular

rechtfertigen vt justify; **sich r~en** justify oneself. **R~ung** f -,- justification

recht|haberisch a opinionated. r~lich a legal, adv -ly. r~mäßig a legitimate, adv -ly.

rechts adv on the right; (bei Stoff) on the right side; von/nach r~ from/to the right; zwei r~, zwei links stricken knit two, purl two. **R~anwalt** m, **R~anwältin** f lawyer

rechtschaffen a upright; (ehrlich) honest, adv -ly; r~ müde thoroughly tired

rechtschreib|en vi (infonly) spell correctly. **R~fehler** m spelling mistake. **R~ung** f - spelling

Rechts|händer(in) m -s,- (f -,-nen) right-hander. r~händig a & adv right-handed r~kräftig a legal, adv -ly. **R~streit** m law suit. **R~verkehr** m driving on the right. r~widrig a illegal, adv -ly. **R~wissenschaft** f jurisprudence

recht|winklig a right-angled. r~zeitig a & adv in time

Reck nt -[e]s,-e horizontal bar

recken vt stretch; **sich r~** stretch; **den Hals r~** crane one's neck

Redakteur /redak'tø:g/ m -s,-e editor; (Radio, TV) editor

Redaktion /-'tsjo:n/ f -,-en editing; (Radio, TV) production; (Abteilung) editorial/production department. r~ell a editorial

Rede f -,-n speech; zur R~stellen demand an explanation from; davon ist keine R~ there's no question of it; nicht der R~ wert not worth mentioning. r~gewandt a eloquent, adv -ly.

reden vi/t (haben) talk (von about; mit to); (eine Rede halten) speak □ vt talk; speak ⟨Wahrheit⟩; kein

Wort r~ not say a word. R~sart f saying; (Phrase) phrase

Redewendung f idiom

redigieren vt edit

redlich a honest, adv -ly

Red|ner m -s,- speaker. r~selig a talkative

reduzieren vt reduce

Reeder m -s,- shipowner. R~ei f -,-en shipping company

reell a real; (ehrlich) honest, adv -ly; (Preis, Angebot) fair

Refer|at nt -[e]s,-e report; (Abhandlung) paper; (Abteilung) section. **R~ent(in)** m -en,-en (f -,-nen) speaker; (Sachbearbeiter) expert. **R~enz** f -,-en reference. r~ieren vi (haben) deliver a paper; (berichten) report (über + acc on)

reflektieren vt/i (haben) reflect (über + acc on)

Reflex m -es,-e reflex; (Widerschein) reflection. **R~ion** f -,-en reflection. r~iv a reflexive. **R~ivpronomen** nt reflexive pronoun

Reform f -,-en reform. **R~ation** /-'tsjo:n/ f - (Relig) Reformation

Reform|haus nt health-food shop. r~ieren vt reform

Refrain /rə'frɛ̃:/ m -s,-s refrain

Regal nt -s,-e [set of] shelves pl

Regatta f -,-ten regatta

rege a active; (lebhaft) lively; (geistig) alert; (Handel) brisk □ adv actively

Regel f -,-n rule; (Monats-) period; in der R~ as a rule. r~mäßig a regular, adv -ly. r~n vt regulate; direct ⟨Verkehr⟩; (erledigen) settle. r~recht a real, proper □ adv really. **R~ung** f -,-en regulation; settlement. r~widrig a irregular, adv -ly

regen vt move; **sich r~** move; (wach werden) stir

Regen m -s,- rain. **R~bogen** m rainbow. **R~bogenhaut** f iris

Regener|ation /-'tsjo:n/ f - regeneration. **r~ieren** vt regenerate; **sich r~ieren** regenerate

Regen|mantel m raincoat. **R~schirm** m umbrella. **R~tag** m rainy day. **R~tropfen** m raindrop. **R~wetter** nt wet weather. **R~wurm** m earthworm

Regie /re'ʒi:/ f - direction; **R~ führen** direct

regier|en vt/i (haben) govern, rule; ⟨Monarch:⟩ reign [over]; ⟨Gram⟩ take. **r~end** a ruling; reigning. **R~ung** f -,-en government; ⟨Herrschaft⟩ rule; ⟨eines Monarchen⟩ reign

Regime /re'ʒi:m/ nt -s,- /-mə/ regime

Regiment[1] nt -[e]s,-er regiment

Regiment[2] nt -[e]s,-e rule

Region f -,-en region. **r~al** a regional, adv -ly

Regisseur /reʒɪ'søːʁ/ m -s,-e director

Register nt -s,- register; ⟨Inhaltsverzeichnis⟩ index; ⟨Orgel⟩ stop

registrier|en vt register; ⟨Techn⟩ record. **R~kasse** f cash register

Regler m -s,- regulator

reglos a & adv motionless

regn|en vi (haben) rain; **es r~et** it is raining. **r~erisch** a rainy

regul|är a normal, adv -ly; ⟨rechtmäßig⟩ legitimate, adv -ly. **r~ieren** vt regulate

Regung f -,-en movement; ⟨Gefühls⟩ emotion. **r~slos** a & adv motionless

Reh nt -[e]s,-e roe-deer; ⟨Culin⟩ venison

Rehabilitation /-'tsjo:n/ f - rehabilitation. **r~ieren** vt rehabilitate

Rehbock m roebuck

Reib|e f -,-n grater. **r~en†** vt rub; ⟨Culin⟩ grate; **blank r~en** polish □ vi (haben) rub. **R~ereien** fpl (fam) friction sg. **R~ung** f - friction. **r~ungslos** a (fig) smooth, adv -ly

reich a rich ⟨an + dat in⟩, adv -ly; ⟨r~haltig⟩ abundant, adv -ly; **Arm und Reich** und **r~** rich and poor

Reich nt -[e]s,-e empire; ⟨König-⟩ kingdom; ⟨Bereich⟩ realm

Reich|e(r) m/f rich man/woman; **die R~en** the rich pl

reichen vt hand; ⟨anbieten⟩ offer □ vi (haben) be enough; ⟨in der Länge⟩ be long enough; **r~ bis** zu reach [up to]; ⟨sich erstrecken⟩ extend to; **mit dem Geld r~** have enough money; **mir reicht's!** I've had enough!

reich|haltig a extensive, large ⟨Mahlzeit⟩ substantial. **r~lich** a ample; ⟨Vorrat⟩ abundant, plentiful; **eine r~liche Stunde** a good hour □ adv amply; abundantly; ⟨fam: sehr⟩ very. **R~tum** m -s,-tümer wealth ⟨an + dat of⟩. **R~tümer** riches. **R~weite** f reach; ⟨Techn, Mil⟩ range

Reif m -[e]s ⟨hoar⟩frost

reif a ripe; ⟨fig⟩ mature; **r~ für** ready for. **R~e** f - ripeness; ⟨fig⟩ maturity. **r~en** vi (sein) ripen; ⟨Wein, Käse & fig⟩ mature

Reif|en m -s,- hoop; ⟨Arm-⟩ bangle; ⟨Auto-⟩ tyre. **R~druck** m tyre pressure. **R~panne** f puncture, flat tyre

Reifeprüfung f ≈ A levels pl

reiflich a careful, adv -ly

Reihe f -,-n row; ⟨Anzahl & Math⟩ series; **der R~ nach** in turn; **außer der R~** out of turn; **wer ist an der** od **kommt an die R~?** whose turn is it? **r~n** (sich) vr **sich r~n an** (+ acc) follow. **R~nfolge** f order. **R~nhaus** nt terraced house. **r~nweise** adv in rows; ⟨fam⟩ in large numbers

Reiher m -s,- heron

Reim m -[e]s,-e rhyme. **r~en** vt rhyme; **sich r~en** rhyme

rein[1] a pure; ⟨sauber⟩ clean; ⟨Unsinn, Dummheit⟩ sheer; **ins R~e (r~e) schreiben** make a fair copy of; **ins R~e (r~e) bringen**

(fig) sort out □ *adv* purely; *(fam)* absolutely

rein² *adv* = **herein, hinein**

Reineclaude /rɛːnəˈkloːdə/ *f* -,-n greengage

Reinfall *m* *(fam)* let-down; *(Misserfolg)* flop. **r~en†** *vi sep (sein)* fall in; *(fam)* be taken in **(auf** + *acc* by)

Rein|gewinn *m* net profit. **R~heit** *f* · purity

reinigen *vt* clean; *(chemisch)* dry-clean. **R~ung** *f* -,-en cleaning; *(chemische)* dry-cleaning; *(Geschäft)* dry cleaner's

Reinkarnation /reˈɪnkarnaˈtsjoːn/ *f* -,-en reincarnation

reinlegen *vt sep* put in; *(fam)* dupe; *(betrügen)* take for a ride

reinlich *a* clean. **R~keit** *f* - cleanliness

Rein|machefrau *f* cleaner. **R~schrift** *f* fair copy. **r~seiden** a pure silk

Reis *m* -es rice

Reise *f* -,-n journey; *(See-)* voyage; *(Urlaubs-, Geschäfts-)* trip. **R~andenken** *nt* souvenir. **R~büro** *nt* travel agency. **R~bus** *m* coach. **R~führer** *m* tourist guide. *(Buch)* guide. **R~gesellschaft** *f* tourist group. **R~leiter(in)** *m(f)* courier. **r~n** *vi* travel. **R~nde(r)** *m/f* traveller. **R~pass** *m* *(-paß)* *m* passport. **R~scheck** *m* traveller's cheque. **R~unternehmer, R~veranstalter** *m* -s,- tour operator. **R~ziel** *nt* destination

Reisig *nt* -s brushwood

Reißaus *m* **R~ nehmen** *(fam)* run away

Reißbrett *nt* drawing-board

reißen† *vt* tear; *(weg-)* snatch; *(töten)* kill; **Witze r~** crack jokes; **aus dem Schlaf r~** awaken rudely; **an sich** *(acc)* **r~** snatch; seize *(Macht)*; **mit sich r~** sweep away; **sich r~ um** *(fam)* fight for; *(gern mögen)* be keen on; **hin und her gerissen sein** *(fig)* be torn

□ *vi (sein)* tear; *(Seil, Faden:)* break □ *vi (haben)* **r~ an** (+ *dat)* pull at. **r~d** a raging; *(Tier)* ferocious; *(Schmerz)* violent

Reißer *m* -s,- *(fam)* thriller; *(Erfolg)* big hit. **r~isch** a *(fam)* sensational

Reiß|nagel *m* = **R~zwecke. R~verschluss (R~verschluß)** *m* zip [fastener]. **R~wolf** *m* shredder. **R~zwecke** *f* -,-n drawing-pin, *(Amer)* thumbtack

reiten† *vt/i (sein)* ride. **R~er(in)** *m* -s,- *(f* -,-nen) rider. **R~hose** *f* riding breeches *pl.* **R~pferd** *nt* saddle-horse. **R~schule** *f* riding-school. **R~weg** *m* bridle-path

Reiz *m* -es,-e stimulus; *(Anziehungskraft)* attraction, appeal; *(Charme)* charm. **r~bar** a irritable. **R~barkeit** *f* - irritability. **r~en** *vt* provoke; *(Med)* irritate; *(interessieren, locken)* appeal to, attract; arouse *(Neugier)*; *(beim Kartenspiel)* bid. **r~end** a charming, *adv* -ly; *(entzückend)* delightful. **R~ung** *f* -,-en *(Med)* irritation. **r~voll** a attractive

rekapitulieren *vt/i (haben)* recapitulate

rekeln (sich) *vr* stretch; *(lümmeln)* sprawl

Reklamation /-'tsjoːn/ *f* -,-en *(Comm)* complaint

Reklame *f* -,-n advertising, publicity; *(Anzeige)* advertisement; *(TV, Radio)* commercial; **R~e machen** advertise **(für etw** sth). **r~ieren** *vt* complain about; *(fordern)* claim □ *vi (haben)* complain

rekonstru|ieren *vt* reconstruct. **R~ktion** /-'tsjoːn/ *f* -,-en reconstruction

Rekonvaleszenz *f* - convalescence

Rekord *m* -[e]s,-e record

Rekrut *m* -en,-en recruit. **r~ieren** *vt* recruit

Rek|tor *m* -s,-en /-'to:rən/ (*Sch*) head[master]; (*Univ*) vice-chancellor. **R~torin** *f* -,-nen head, headmistress; vice-chancellor

Relais /rə'lɛː/ *nt* -, /-s/, -s,-s/ (*Electr*) relay

relativ *a* relative, *adv* -ly. **R~pronomen** *nt* relative pronoun

relevan|t *a* relevant (**für** to). **R~z** *f* - relevance

Relief /rə'lief/ *nt* -s,-s relief

Religi|on *f* -,-en religion; (*Sch*) religious education. **r~ös** *a* religious

Reling *f* -,-s (*Naut*) rail

Reliquie /re'li:kviə/ *f* -,-n relic

Remouladensoße /remu'la:dən-/ *f* ≈ tartar sauce

rempeln *vt* jostle; (*stoßen*) push

Ren *nt* -s,-s reindeer

Reneklode *f* -,-n greengage

Renn|auto *nt* racing car. **R~bahn** *f* race-track; (*Pferde-*) racecourse. **R~boot** *nt* speedboat. **r~en†** *vt/i* (*sein*) run; **um die Wette r~en** have a race. **R~en** *nt* -s,- race. **R~pferd** *nt* racehorse. **R~sport** *m* racing. **R~wagen** *m* racing car

renom|miert *a* renowned; (*Hotel, Firma*) of repute

renovier|en *vt* renovate; redecorate (*Zimmer*). **R~ung** *f* - renovation; redecoration

rentabel *a* profitable, *adv* -bly

Rente *f* -,-n pension; **in R~ gehen** (*fam*) retire. **R~nversicherung** *f* pension scheme

Rentier *nt* reindeer

rentieren (sich) *vr* be profitable; (*sich lohnen*) be worth while

Rentner(in) *m* -s,- (*f* -,-nen) [old-age] pensioner

Reparatur *f* -,-en repair. **R~werkstatt** *f* repair workshop; (*Auto*) garage

reparieren *vt* repair, mend

repatriieren *vt* repatriate

Repertoire /reper'tǒa:ɐ̯/ *nt* -s,-s repertoire

Reportage /-'ta:ʒə/ *f* -,-n report

Reporter(in) *m* -s,- (*f* -,-nen) reporter

repräsent|ativ *a* representative (**für** of); (*eindrucksvoll*) imposing; (*Prestige verleihend*) prestigious. **r~ieren** *vt* represent □ *vi* (*haben*) perform official/social duties

Repress|alie /-liə/ *f* -,-n reprisal. **r~iv** *a* repressive

Reprodu|ktion /-'tsjoːn/ *f* -,-en reproduction. **r~zieren** *vt* reproduce

Reptil *nt* -s,-ien /-jən/ reptile

Republik *f* -,-en republic. **r~anisch** *a* republican

requirieren *vt* (*Mil*) requisition

Requisiten *pl* (*Theat*) properties, (*fam*) props

Reservat *nt* -[e]s,-e reservation

Reserve *f* -,-n reserve; (*Mil, Sport*) reserves *pl*. **R~rad** *nt* spare wheel. **R~spieler** *m* reserve. **R~tank** *m* reserve tank

reservier|en *vt* reserve; **r~en lassen** book. **r~t** *a* reserved. **R~ung** *f* -,-en reservation

Reservoir /rezɐ'vǒa:ɐ̯/ *nt* -s,-s reservoir

Resid|enz *f* -,-en residence. **r~ieren** *vi* (*haben*) reside

Resign|ation /-'tsjo:n/ *f* - resignation. **r~ieren** *vi* (*haben*) (*fig*) give up. **r~iert** *a* resigned, *adv* -ly

resolut *a* resolute, *adv* -ly

Resolution /-'tsjo:n/ *f* -,-en resolution

Resonanz *f* -,-en resonanance; (*fig*: *Widerhall*) response

Respekt /-sp-, -ʃp-/ *m* -[e]s respect (**vor** + *dat* for). **r~abel** *a* respectable. **r~ieren** *vt* respect

respekt|los *a* disrespectful, *adv* -ly. **r~voll** *a* respectful, *adv* -ly

Ressort /rɛ'so:ɐ̯/ *nt* -s,-s department

Rest m -[e]s,-e remainder; rest; **R~e** remains; (Essens-) leftovers

Restaurant /rɛstoˈrãː/ nt -s,-s restaurant

Restaur|ation /rɛstaura'tsjoːn/ f - restoration. **r~ieren** vt restore

Rest|betrag m balance. **r~lich** a remaining. **r~los** a utter, adv -ly

Resultat nt -[e]s,-e result

Retorte f -,-n (Chem) retort. **R~nbaby** nt (fam) test-tube baby

rett|en vt save (vor + dat from); (aus Gefahr befreien) rescue; **sich r~en** save oneself; (flüchten) escape. **R~er** m -s,- rescuer; (fig) saviour

Rettich m -s,-e white radish

Rettung f -,-en rescue; (fig) salvation; **jds letzte R~** s.o.'s last hope. **R~sboot** nt lifeboat. **R~sdienst** m rescue service. **R~sgürtel** m lifebelt. **r~slos** adv hopelessly. **R~sring** m lifebelt. **R~swagen** m ambulance

retuschieren vt (Phot) retouch

Reu|e f - remorse; (Relig) repentance. **r~en** vt fill with remorse; **es reut mich nicht** I don't regret it. **r~ig** a penitent. **r~mütig** a contrite, adv -ly

Revanche /re'vãːʃə/ f -,-n revenge; **R~e fordern** (Sport) ask for a return match. **r~ieren (sich)** vr take revenge; (sich erkenntlich zeigen) reciprocate (mit with); **sich für eine Einladung r~ieren** return an invitation

Revers /re'veːɐ/ nt -,- /-[s],-s/ lapel

revidieren vt revise; (prüfen) check

Revier nt -s,-e district; (Zool & fig) territory; (Polizei-) [police] station

Revision f -,-en revision; (Prüfung) check; (Bücher-) audit; (Jur) appeal

Revolte f -,-n revolt

Revolution /-'tsjoːn/ f -,-en revolution. **r~är** a revolutionary. **r~ieren** vt revolutionize

Revolver m -s,- revolver

Revue /rə'vyː/ f -,-n revue

Rezen|sent m -en,-en reviewer. **r~sieren** vt review. **R~sion** f -,-en review

Rezept nt -[e]s,-e prescription; (Culin) recipe

Rezeption /-'tsjoːn/ f -,-en reception

Rezession f -,-en recession

rezitieren vt recite

R-Gespräch nt reverse-charge call, (Amer) collect call

Rhabarber m -s rhubarb

Rhapsodie f -,-n rhapsody

Rhein m -s Rhine. **R~land** nt -s Rhineland. **R~wein** m hock

Rhetorik f - rhetoric. **r~sch** a rhetorical

Rheuma nt -s rheumatism. **r~a-tisch** a rheumatic. **R~atismus** m - rheumatism

Rhinozeros nt -[ses],-se rhinoceros

rhyth|misch /'rʏt-/ a rhythmic[al], adv -ally. **R~mus** m -,-men rhythm

Ribisel f -,-n (Aust) redcurrant

richten vt direct (auf + acc at); address (Frage, Briefe) (an + acc to); aim, train (Waffe) (auf + acc at); (einstellen) set; (vorbereiten) prepare; (reparieren) mend; (hin-richten) execute; (SGer: ordentlich machen) tidy; **in die Höhe r~** raise [up]; **das Wort an jdn r~** address s.o.; **sich r~** be directed (auf + acc at; gegen against); (Blick:) turn (auf + acc on); **sich r~ nach** comply with (Vorschrift, jds Wünschen); fit in with (jds Plänen); (befolgen) go by; (abhängen) depend on □ vi (haben) **r~ über** (+ acc) judge

Richter m -s,- judge

Richtfest nt topping-out ceremony

richtig a right, correct; (*wirklich, echt*) real; **das R~e** (r~e) the right thing □*adv* correctly; really; **r~ stellen** put right (*Uhr*); (*fig*) correct (*Irrtum*); **die Uhr geht r~** the clock is right. **R~keit** f - correctness. **r~stellen** vt *sep* (NEW) **r~ stellen**, *s.* richtig

Richtlinien fpl guidelines

Richtung f -,-en direction; (*fig*) trend

riechen† vt/i (haben) smell (**nach** of; **an etw** dat sth)

Riegel m -s,- bolt; (*Seife*) bar

Riemen m -s,- strap; (*Ruder*) oar

Riese m -n,-n giant

rieseln vi (sein) trickle; (*Schnee:*) fall lightly

Riesen|erfolg m huge success. **r~groß** a huge, enormous

riesig a huge; (*gewaltig*) enormous □*adv* (fam) terribly

Riff nt -[e]s,-e reef

rigoros a rigorous, strict

Rille f -,-n groove

Rind nt -es,-er ox; (*Kuh*) cow; (*Stier*) bull; (*R~fleisch*) beef. **R~er** cattle pl

Rinde f -,-n bark; (*Käse-*) rind; (*Brot-*) crust

Rinderbraten m roast beef

Rind|fleisch nt beef. **R~vieh** nt cattle pl; (*fam: Idiot*) idiot

Ring m -[e]s,-e ring

ringeln (sich) vr curl; (*Schlange:*) coil itself (**um** round)

ring|en† vi (haben) wrestle; (*fig*) struggle (**um/nach** for) □vt wring (*Hände*). **R~en** nt -s wrestling. **R~er** m -s,- wrestler. **R~kampf** m wrestling match; (*als Sport*) wrestling. **R~richter** m referee

rings adv **r~ im Kreis** in a circle; **r~ um** jdn/etw all around s.o./sth. **r~herum, r~um** adv all around

Rinn|e f -,-n channel; (*Dach-*) gutter. **r~en**† vi (sein) run; (*Sand:*) trickle. **R~stein** m gutter

Rippe f -,-n rib. **R~nfellentzündung** f pleurisy. **R~nstoß** m dig in the ribs

Risiko nt -s,-s & -ken risk; **ein R~ eingehen** take a risk

risk|ant a risky. **r~ieren** vt risk

Riss m -es,-e (Riß m -sses,-sse) tear; (*Mauer-*) crack; (*fig*) rift

rissig a cracked; (*Haut*) chapped

Rist m -[e]s,-e instep

Ritt m -[e]s,-e ride

Ritter m -s,- knight. **r~lich** a chivalrous, adv -ly. **R~lichkeit** f - chivalry

rittlings adv astride

Ritu|al nt -s,-e ritual. **r~ell** a ritual

Ritz m -es,-e scratch. **R~e** f -,-n crack; (*Fels-*) cleft; (*zwischen Betten, Vorhängen*) gap. **r~en** vt scratch

Rival|e m -n,-n, **R~in** f -,-nen rival. **r~isieren** vi (haben) compete (**mit** with). **r~isierend** a rival . . **R~ität** f -,-en rivalry

Robbe f -,-n seal. **r~n** vi (sein) crawl

Robe f -,-n gown; (*Talar*) robe

Roboter m -s,- robot

robust a robust

röcheln vi (haben) breathe stertorously

Rochen m -s,- (Zool) ray

Rock¹ m -[e]s,-e skirt; (*Jacke*) jacket

Rock² m -[s] (Mus) rock

Rodel|bahn f toboggan run. **r~n** vi (sein/haben) toboggan. **R~schlitten** m toboggan

roden vt clear (*Land*); grub up (*Stumpf*)

Rogen m -s,- [hard] roe

Roggen m -s rye

roh a rough; (*ungekocht*) raw; (*Holz*) bare; (*brutal*) brutal; **r~e Gewalt** brute force □adv roughly; brutally. **R~bau** m -[e]s,-ten shell. **R~heit** f -,-en brutality. **R~kost** f raw [vegetarian] food. **R~ling** m -s,-e brute. **R~material** nt raw material. **R~öl** nt crude oil

Rohr nt -[e]s,-e pipe; (Geschütz-) barrel; (Bot) reed; (Zucker-, Bambus-) cane

Röhr|chen nt -s,- [drinking] straw; (Auto, fam) breathalyser (P). **R~e** f -,-n tube; (Radio-) valve; (Back-) oven

Rohstoff m raw material

Rokoko nt -s rococo

Rolladen m (NEW) **Rolladen**

Rollbahn f taxiway; (Start-/Landebahn) runaway

Rolle f -,-n roll; (Garn-) reel; (Draht-) coil; (Techn) roller; (Seil-) pulley; (Wäsche-) mangle; (Lauf-) castor; (Schrift-) scroll; (Theat) part, role; **das spielt keine R~** (fig) that doesn't matter. **r~n** vt roll; (auf-) roll up; roll out (Teig); put through the mangle (Wäsche); **sich r~n** roll; (sich ein-) curl up ○ vi (sein) roll; (Flugzeug:) taxi ○ vi (haben) (Donner:) rumble. **R~r** m -s,- scooter

Roll|feld nt airfield. **R~kragen** m polo-neck. **R~laden** m roller shutter. **R~mops** m rollmop[s] sg

Rollo nt -s,-s [roller] blind

Roll|schuh m roller-skate. **R~schuh laufen** roller-skate. **R~splitt** m -s loose chippings pl. **R~stuhl** m wheelchair. **R~treppe** f escalator

Rom nt -s Rome

Roman m -s,-e novel. **r~isch** a Romanesque; (Sprache) Romance. **R~schriftsteller(in)** m(f) novelist

Romant|ik f - romanticism. **r~isch** a romantic, adv -ally

Romanze f -,-n romance

Römer(in) m -s,- (f -,-nen) Roman. **r~isch** a Roman

Rommé, Rommee /'rɔmeː/ nt -s rummy

röntgen vt X-ray. **R~aufnahme** f, **R~bild** nt X-ray. **R~strahlen** mpl X-rays

rosa inv a, **R~** nt -[s],- pink

Rose f -,-n rose. **R~nkohl** m [Brussels] sprouts pl. **R~nkranz** m (Relig) rosary. **R~nmontag** m Monday before Shrove Tuesday

Rosette f -,-n rosette

rosig a rosy

Rosine f -,-n raisin

Rosmarin m -s rosemary

Ross nt -es,-er (Roß nt -sses,-sser) horse. **R~kastanie** f horse-chestnut

Rost1 m -[e]s,-e grating; (Kamin-) grate; (Brat-) grill

Rost2 m -[e]s rust. **r~en** vi (haben) rust; **nicht r~end** stainless

rösten vt roast; toast (Brot). **R~er** m -s,- toaster

rostfrei a stainless

rostig a rusty

rot a (röter, rötest), **Rot** nt -s,-; **rot; rot werden** turn red; (erröten) go red, blush

Rotation /-'tsioːn/ f -,-en rotation

Röte f - redness; (Scham-) blush

Röteln pl German measles sg

röten vt redden; **sich r~** turn red

rothaarig a red-haired

rotieren vi (haben) rotate

Rot|kehlchen nt -s,- robin. **R~kohl** m red cabbage

rötlich a reddish

Rot|licht nt red light. **R~wein** m red wine

Roulade /ru'laːdə/ f -,-n beef olive. **R~leau** /-'loː/ nt -s,-s [roller] blind

Route /'ruːtə/ f -,-n route

Routin|e /ru'tiːnə/ f -,-n routine; (Erfahrung) experience. **r~emäßig** a routine ... □ adv routinely. **r~iert** a experienced

Rowdy /'raʊdi/ m -s,-s hooligan

Rübe f -,-n beet; **rote R~** beetroot; **gelbe R~** (SGer) carrot

rüber adv = herüber, hinüber

Rubin m -s,-e ruby

Rubrik f -,-en column; (Kategorie) category

Ruck m -[e]s,-e jerk

Rückantwort f reply

ruckartig a jerky, adv -ily

rück|bezüglich a (Gram) reflexive. **R~blende** f flashback. **R~blick** m (fig) review (**auf** + acc of). **r~blickend** adv in retrospect. **r~datieren** vt (inf & pp only) backdate

rücken vt/i (sein/haben) move; **an etw** (dat) **r~** move sth

Rücken m -s,-; back; (Buch-) spine; (Berg-) ridge. **R~lehne** f back. **R~mark** nt spinal cord. **R~schwimmen** nt backstroke. **R~wind** m following wind; (Aviat) tail wind

rückerstatten vt (inf & pp only) refund

Rückfahr|karte f return ticket. **R~t** f return journey

Rück|fall m relapse. **r~fällig** a **r~fällig werden** (Jur) re-offend.

R~flug m return flight. **R~frage** f [further] query. **r~fragen** vi (haben) (inf & pp only) check (**bei** with). **R~gabe** f return. **R~gang** m decline; (Preis-) drop, fall. **r~gängig** a **r~gängig machen** cancel; break off (Verlobung). **R~grat** nt -[e]s, -e spine, backbone. **R~halt** m (fig) support. **R~hand** f backhand. **R~kehr** f return. **R~lagen** fpl reserves. **R~licht** nt rearlight. **r~lings** adv backwards; (von hinten) from behind. **R~reise** f return journey

Rucksack m rucksack

Rück|schau f review. **R~schlag** m (Sport) return; (fig) set-back. **R~schluss** m (**R~schluß**) m conclusion. **R~schritt** m (fig) retrograde step. **r~schrittlich** a retrograde. **R~seite** f back; (einer Münze) reverse

Rücksicht f -,-en consideration; **R~ nehmen auf** (+ acc) show consideration for; (berücksichtigen) take into consideration. **R~nahme** f -consideration. **r~slos** a inconsiderate, adv -ly; (schonungslos) ruthless, adv -ly. **r~svoll** a considerate, adv -ly

Rück|sitz m back seat; (Sozius) pillion. **R~spiegel** m rear-view mirror. **R~spiel** nt return match. **R~sprache** f consultation; **R~sprache nehmen mit** consult. **R~stand** m (Chem) residue; (Arbeits-) backlog; **im R~stand sein** be behind. **r~ständig** a (fig) backward. **R~stau** m (Auto) tailback. **R~strahler** m -s,- reflector. **R~tritt** m resignation; (Fahrrad) back pedalling. **r~vergüten** vt (inf & pp only) refund. **R~wanderer** m repatriate

rückwärt|ig a back …, rear … **r~s** adv backwards. **R~sgang** m reverse [gear]

Rückweg m way back

ruckweise adv jerkily

rück|wirkend a retrospective, adv -ly. **R~wirkung** f retrospective force; **mit R~wirkung vom** backdated to. **R~zahlung** f repayment. **R~zug** m retreat

Rüde m -n,-n [male] dog

Rudel nt -s,- herd; (Wolfs-) pack; (Löwen-) pride

Ruder nt -s,- oar; (Steuer-) rudder; **am R~** (Naut & fig) at the helm. **R~boot** nt rowing boat. **R~er** m -s,- oarsman. **r~n** vt/i (haben/sein) row

Ruf m -[e]s,-e call; (laut) shout; (Telefon) telephone number; (Ansehen) reputation; **Künstler von Ruf** artist of repute. **r~en†** vt/i (haben) call (**nach** for); **r~en lassen** send for

Rüffel m -s,- (fam) telling-off. **r~n** vt (fam) tell off

Ruf|name m forename by which one is known. **R~nummer** f telephone number. **R~zeichen** nt dialling tone

Rüge f -,-n reprimand. **r~n** vt reprimand; (kritisieren) criticize

Ruhe f - rest; (Stille) quiet; (Frieden) peace; (innere) calm; (Gelassenheit) composure; **die R~ bewahren** keep calm; **in R~ lassen** leave in peace; **sich zur R~ setzen** retire; **R~ [da]!** quiet! **R~gehalt** nt [retirement] pension. **r~los** a restless, adv -ly. **r~n** vi (haben) rest (**auf** + dat on); (Arbeit, Verkehr:) have stopped; **hier ruht ...** here lies ... **R~pause** f rest, break. **R~stand** m retirement, **in den R~stand treten** retire; **im R~stand** retired. **R~störung** f disturbance of the peace. **R~tag** m day of rest; 'Montag R~tag' 'closed on Mondays'

ruhig a quiet, adv -ly; (erholsam) restful; (friedlich) peaceful, adv -ly; (unbewegt, gelassen) calm, adv -ly; **r~ bleiben** remain calm; **sehen Sie sich r~ um** you're welcome to look round; **man kann r~ darüber sprechen** there's no harm in talking about it

Ruhm m -[e]s fame; (Ehre) glory

rühmen vt praise; **sich r~** boast (gen about)

ruhmreich a glorious

Ruhr f - (Med) dysentery

Rühr|ei nt scrambled eggs pl. **r~en** vt move; stir; (Culin) stir; **r~en** move; **zu Tränen r~en** move to tears; **r~t euch!** (Mil) at ease! □ vi (haben) stir; **r~en an** (+ acc) touch; (fig) touch on; **r~en von** (fig) come from. **r~end** a touching, adv -ly

rühr|ig a active. **r~selig** a sentimental. **R~ung** f - emotion

Ruin m -s ruin. **R~e** f -,-n ruin; ruins pl (gen of). **r~ieren** vt ruin

rülpsen vi (haben) (fam) belch

Rum m -s rum

rum adv = **herum**

Rumän|ien /-jən/ nt -s Romania. **r~isch** a Romanian

Rummel m -s (fam) hustle and bustle; (Jahrmarkt) funfair. **R~platz** m fairground

rumoren vi (haben) make a noise; (Magen:) rumble

Rumpel|kammer f junk-room. **r~n** vi (haben/sein) rumble

Rumpf m -[e]s,ᵉe body, trunk; (Schiffs-) hull; (Aviat) fuselage

rümpfen vt **die Nase r~** turn up one's nose (**über** + acc at)

rund a round □ adv approximately; **r~ um** [a]round. **R~blick** m panoramic view. **R~brief** m circular [letter]

Runde f -,-n round; (Kreis) circle; (eines Polizisten) beat; (beim Rennen) lap; **eine R~ Bier** a round of beer. **r~n** vt round; **sich r~n** become round; (Backen:) fill out

Rund|fahrt f tour. **R~frage** f poll

Rundfunk m radio; **im R~** on the radio. **R~gerät** nt radio [set]

Rund|gang m round; (Spaziergang) walk (**durch** round). **r~heraus** adv straight out. **r~herum** adv all around. **r~lich** a rounded; (Person) plump. **R~reise** f [circular] tour. **R~schreiben** nt circular. **r~um** adv all round. **R~ung** f -,-n curve. **r~weg** adv (ablehnen) flatly

runter adv = **herunter**, **hinunter**

Runzel f -,-n wrinkle. **r~n** vt **die Stirn r~n** frown

runzlig a wrinkled

Rüpel m -s,- (fam) lout. **r~haft** a (fam) loutish

rupfen vt pull out; pluck (Geflügel); (fam: schröpfen) fleece

ruppig a rude, adv -ly

Rüsche f -,-n frill

Ruß m -es soot

Russe m -n,-n Russian

Rüssel m -s,- (Zool) trunk

ruß|en vi (haben) smoke. **r~ig** a sooty

Russ|in f -,-nen Russian. **r~isch** a Russian. **R~isch** nt -[s] (Lang) Russian

Russland (Rußland) nt -s Russia

rüsten vi (haben) prepare (zu/für for) □ vr sich r~ get ready; gerüstet sein be ready

rüstig a sprightly

rustikal a rustic

Rüstung f -,-en armament; (Harnisch) armour. **R~skontrolle** f arms control

Rute f -,-n twig; (Angel-, Wünschel-) rod; (zur Züchtigung) birch; (Schwanz) tail

Rutsch m -[e]s,-e slide. **R~bahn** f slide. **R~e** f -,-n chute. **r~en** vt slide; (rücken) move □ vi (sein) slide; (aus-, ab-) slip; (Auto) skid; (rücken) move [along]. **r~ig** a slippery

rütteln vt shake □ vi (haben) **r~ an** (+ dat) rattle

S

Saal m -[e]s,Säle hall; (Theat) auditorium; (Kranken-) ward

Saat f -,-en seed; (Säen) sowing; (Gesätes) crop. **S~gut** nt seed

sabbern vi (haben) (fam) slobber; (Baby:) dribble; (reden) jabber

Säbel m -s,- sabre

Sabo|tage /zabo'ta:ʒə/ f - sabotage. **S~teur** /-'tø:ɐ/ m -s,-e saboteur. **s~tieren** vt sabotage

Sach|bearbeiter m expert. **S~buch** nt non-fiction book. **s~dienlich** a relevant

Sache f -,-n matter, business; (Ding) thing; (fig) cause; zur S~ kommen come to the point

Sach|gebiet nt (fig) area, field. **s~gemäß** a proper, adv -ly. **S~kenntnis** f expertise. **s~kundig** a expert, adv -ly. **s~lich** a factual, adv -ly; (nüchtern) matter-of-fact, adv -ly; (objektiv) objective, adv -ly; (schmucklos) functional

sächlich a (Gram) neuter

Sachse m -n,-n Saxon. **S~n** nt -s Saxony

sächsisch a Saxon

sacht a gentle, adv -ly

Sach|verhalt m -[e]s facts pl. **s~verständig** a expert, adv -ly. **S~verständige(r)** mf expert

Sack m -[e]s,-e sack; mit **S~und Pack** with all one's belongings

sacken vi (sein) sink; (zusammen-) go down; (Person:) slump

Sack|gasse f cul-de-sac; (fig) impasse. **S~leinen** nt sacking

Sadis|mus m - sadism. **S~t** m -en,-en sadist. **s~tisch** a sadistic, adv -ally

säen vt/i (haben) sow

Safe /ze:f/ m -s,-s safe

Saft m -[e]s,-e juice; (Bot) sap. **s~ig** a juicy; (Wiese) lush; (Preis, Rechnung) hefty; (Witz) coarse. **s~los** a dry

Sage f -,-n legend

Säge f -,-n saw. **S~mehl** nt sawdust

sagen vt say; (mitteilen) tell; (bedeuten) mean; das hat nichts zu **s~** it doesn't mean anything; ein viel **s~der Blick** a meaningful look

sägen vt/i (haben) saw

sagenhaft a legendary; (fam: unglaublich) fantastic, adv -ally. **Säge|späne** mpl wood shavings. **S~werk** nt sawmill

Sahne f - cream. **S~bonbon** & nt ≈ toffee. **s~ig** a creamy

Saison /zε'zõ:/ f -,-s season

Saite f -,-n (Mus, Sport) string. **S~ninstrument** nt stringed instrument

Sakko m & nt -s,-s sports jacket

Sakrament nt -[e]s,-e sacrament

Sakrileg nt -s,-e sacrilege

Sakristan|an m -s,-e verger. **S~ei** f -,-en vestry

Salat m -[e]s,-e salad; **ein Kopf S~** a lettuce. **S~soße** f salad-dressing

Salbe f -,-n ointment

Salbei m -s & f -,- sage

salben vt anoint

Saldo m -s,-dos & -den balance

Salon /za'lõ:/ m -s,-s salon; (Naut) saloon

salopp a casual, adv -ly; (Benehmen) informal, adv -ly; (Ausdruck) slangy

Salto m -s,-s somersault

Salut m -[e]s,-e salute. **s~ieren** vi (haben) salute

Salve f -,-n volley; (Geschütz-) salvo, (von Gelächter) burst

Salz nt -es,-e salt. **s~en†** vt salt. **S~fass** (**S~faß**) nt salt-cellar. **s~ig** a salty. **S~kartoffeln** fpl boiled potatoes. **S~säure** f hydrochloric acid

Samen m -s,- seed; (Anat) semen, sperm

sämig a (Culin) thick

Sämling m -s,-e seedling

Sammel|becken nt reservoir. **S~begriff** m collective term. **s~n** vt/i (haben) collect; (suchen, versammeln) gather; **sich s~n** gather; (sich versammeln) gather; (sich fassen) collect oneself. **S~name** m collective noun

Samm|ler(in) m -s,-(f -,-nen) collector. **S~lung** f -,-en collection; (innere) composure

Samstag m -s,-e Saturday. **s~s** adv on Saturdays

samt prep (+ dat) together with □ adv **s~ und sonders** without exception

Samt m -[e]s velvet. **s~ig** a velvety

sämtlich indef pron inv all. **s~e(r,s)** indef pron all the; **s~e**

Werke complete works; **meine s~en Bücher** all my books

Sanatorium nt -s,-ien sanatorium

Sand m -[e]s sand

Sandal|e f -,-n sandal. **S~ette** f -,-n high-heeled sandal

Sand|bank f sandbank. **S~burg** f sand-castle. **s~ig** a sandy. **S~kasten** m sand-pit. **S~kuchen** m Madeira cake. **S~papier** nt sandpaper. **S~stein** m sandstone

sanft a gentle, adv -ly. **s~mütig** a meek

Sänger(in) m -s,-(f -,-nen) singer

sanieren vt clean up; redevelop (Gebiet); (modernisieren) modernize; make profitable (Industrie, Firma); **sich s~** become profitable

sanitär a sanitary

Sanität|er m -s,- first-aid man; (Fahrer) ambulance man; (Mil) medical orderly. **S~swagen** m ambulance

Sanktion /zaŋk'tsjo:n/ f -,-en sanction. **s~ieren** vt sanction

Saphir m -s,-e sapphire

Sardelle f -,-n anchovy

Sardine f -,-n sardine

Sarg m -[e]s,-e coffin

Sarkas|mus m - sarcasm. **s~tisch** a sarcastic, adv -ally

Satan m -s Satan; (fam: Teufel) devil. **s~isch** a satanic

Satellit m -en,-en satellite. **S~enfernsehen** nt satellite television

Satin /za'tɛ̃/ m -s satin

Satire f -,-n satire. **s~isch** a satirical, adv -ly

satt a full; (Farbe) rich; **s~ sein** have had enough [to eat]; **sich s~ essen** eat as much as one wants; **s~ machen** feed; (Speise:) be filling; **etw s~ haben** (fam) be fed up with sth

Sattel m -s,- saddle. **s~n** vt saddle. **S~schlepper** m tractor unit. **S~zug** m articulated lorry

sättigen vt satisfy; (Chem & fig) saturate □ vi (haben) be filling. **s~d** a filling

Satz m -es,-̈e sentence; (Teil-) clause; (These) proposition; (Math) theorem; (Mus) movement; (Tennis, Zusammengehöriges) set; (Boden-) sediment; (Kaffee-) grounds pl; (Steuer-, Zins-) rate; (Druck-) setting; (Schrift-) type; (Sprung) leap, bound. **S~aussage** f predicate. **S~gegenstand** m subject. **S~zeichen** nt punctuation mark

Sau f -,Säue sow; (sl: schmutziger Mensch) dirty pig

sauber a clean; (ordentlich) neat, adv -ly; (anständig) decent, adv -ly; (fam: nicht anständig) fine; **s~ halten** keep clean; **s~ machen** clean. **s~halten**† vt sep NEW **s~ halten**, s. **sauber**. **S~keit** f -cleanliness; neatness; decency

säuberlich a neat, adv -ly

saubermachen† vt/i sep (haben) NEW **sauber machen**, s. **sauber**

säuber|n vt clean; (befreien) rid/ (Pol) purge (von of). **S~ungsaktion** f (Pol) purge

Sauce /'zo:sə/ f -,-n sauce; (Braten-) gravy

Saudi-Arabien /-jən/ nt -s Saudi Arabia

sauer a sour; (Chem) acid; (eingelegt) pickled; (schwer) hard; **saurer Regen** acid rain; **s~ sein** (fam) be annoyed

Sauerei f -,-en = **Schweinerei**

Sauerkraut nt sauerkraut

säuerlich a slightly sour

Sauer|stoff m oxygen

saufen† vt/i (haben) drink; (sl) booze

Säufer m -s,- (sl) boozer

saugen† vt/i (haben) suck; (staub-) vacuum, hoover; sich **voll Wasser s~** soak up water

säugen vt suckle

Sauger m -s,- [baby's] dummy, (Amer) pacifier; (Flaschen-) teat

Säugetier nt mammal

saugfähig a absorbent

Säugling m -s,-e infant

Säule f -,-n column

Saum m -[e]s,Säume hem; (Rand) edge

säumen[1] vt hem; (fig) line

säumen[2] vi (haben) delay. **s~ig** a dilatory

Sauna f -,-nas & -nen sauna

Säure f -,-n acidity; (Chem) acid

säuseln vi (haben) rustle [softly]

sausen vi (haben) rush; (Ohren:) buzz □ vi (sein) rush [along]

Sauwetter nt (sl) lousy weather

Saxophon, Saxofon nt -s,-e saxophone

SB- /ɛs'be:-/ pref (= **Selbstbedienung**) self-service ...

S-Bahn f city and suburban railway

sch int shush! (fort) shoo!

Schabe f -,-n cockroach

schaben vt/i (haben) scrape

schäbig a shabby, adv -ily

Schablone f -,-n stencil; (Muster) pattern; (fig) stereotype

Schach nt -s chess; **S~!** check! **in S~ halten** (fig) keep in check. **S~brett** nt chessboard

schachern vi (haben) haggle

Schachfigur f chess-man

schachmatt a **s~ setzen** checkmate; **s~!** checkmate!

Schachspiel nt game of chess

Schacht m -[e]s,-̈e shaft

Schachtel f -,-n box; (Zigaretten-) packet

Schachzug m move

schade a **s~ sein** be a pity or shame: **zu s~ für** too good for; **[wie] s~!** [what a] pity or shame!

Schädel m -s,- skull. **S~bruch** m fractured skull

schaden vi (haben) (+ dat) damage; (nachteilig sein) hurt; **das schadet nichts** that doesn't matter. **S~** m -s,-̈ damage; (Defekt) defect; (*Nachteil*) disadvantage; **zu S~ kommen** be hurt. **S~ersatz** *m* damages *pl.* **S~freude** *f* malicious glee. **s~froh** *a* gloating

schadhaft *a* defective

schädig|en *vt* damage, harm. **S~ung** *f* -,-en damage

schädlich *a* harmful

Schädling *m* -s,-e pest. **S~bekämpfungsmittel** *nt* pesticide

Schaf *nt* -[e]s,-e sheep; (*fam: Idiot*) idiot. **S~bock** *m* ram

Schäfchen *nt* -s,- lamb

Schäfer *m* -s,- shepherd. **S~hund** *m* sheepdog; **Deutscher S~hund** German shepherd, alsatian

Schaffell *nt* sheepskin

schaffen†1 *vt* create; (*herstellen*) establish; make (*Platz*); **wie geschaffen für** made for

schaffen2 *v* (*reg*) □ *vt* manage (to do); pass (*Prüfung*); catch (*Zug*); (*bringen*) take; **jdm zu~ machen** trouble s.o.; **sich** (*dat*) **zu ~ machen** busy oneself (**an** + *dat* with) □ *vi* (*haben*) (*SGer: arbeiten*) work. **S~** *nt* -s work

Schaffner *m* -s,- conductor; (*Zug-*) ticket-inspector

Schaffung *f* - creation

Schaft *m* -[e]s,⁻e shaft; (*Gewehr-*) stock; (*Stiefel-*) leg. **S~stiefel** *m* high boot

Schal *m* -s,-s scarf

schal *a* insipid; (*abgestanden*) flat; (*fig*) stale

Schale *f* -,-n skin; (*abgeschält*) peel; (*Eier-, Nuss-, Muschel-*) shell; (*Schüssel*) dish

schälen *vt* peel; **sich s~** peel

schalkhaft *a* mischievous, *adv* -ly

Schall *m* -[e]s sound. **S~dämpfer** *m* silencer. **s~dicht** *a* soundproof. **s~en** *vi* (*haben*) ring out; (*nachhallen*) resound; **s~end lachen** roar with laughter. **S~mauer** *f* sound barrier. **S~platte** *f* record, disc

schalt|en *vt* switch □ *vi* (*haben*) switch;/(*Ampel:*) turn (**auf** + *acc* to); (*Auto*) change gear; (*fam: begreifen*) catch on. **S~er** *m* -s,- switch; (*Post-, Bank-*) counter; (*Fahrkarten-*) ticket window. **S~hebel** *m* switch; (*Auto*) gear lever. **S~jahr** *nt* leap year. **S~kreis** *m* circuit; (*Auto*) gear change. **S~ung** *f* -,-en circuit; (*Auto*) gear change

Scham *f* - shame; (*Anat*) private parts *pl*; **falsche S~** false modesty

schämen (**sich**) *vr* be ashamed; **schämt euch!** you should be ashamed of yourselves!

scham|haft *a* modest, *adv* -ly; (*schüchtern*) bashful, *adv* -ly. **s~los** *a* shameless, *adv* -ly

Schampon *nt* -s shampoo. **s~ieren** *vt* shampoo

Schande *f* - disgrace, shame; **S~ machen** (+ *dat*) bring shame on; **zu S~n machen/werden** = **zuschanden machen/werden**, *s. zuschanden*

schänd|en *vt* dishonour; (*fig*) defile; (*Relig*) desecrate; (*sexuell*) violate. **s~lich** *a* disgraceful, *adv* -ly. **S~ung** *f* -,-en defilement, desecration; violation

Schänke *f* -,-n = **Schenke**

Schanktisch *m* bar

Schanze *f* -,-n [ski-]jump

Schar *f* -,-en crowd; (*Vogel-*) flock; **in [hellen] S~en** in droves

Scharade *f* -,-n charade

scharen *vt* **um sich s~** gather round one; **sich s~ um** flock round. **s~weise** *adv* in droves

scharf *a* (**schärfer, schärfst**) sharp; (*stark*) strong; (*stark gewürzt*) hot; (*Geruch*) pungent; (*Frost, Wind, Augen, Verstand*) keen; (*streng*) harsh; (*Galopp, Ritt*) hard; (*Munition*) live; (*Hund*) fierce; **s~ einstellen** (*Phot*) focus; **s~ sein** (*Phot*) be in focus; **s~ sein auf** (+ *acc*) (*fam*) be keen on □ *adv* sharply; (*hinsehen, nachdenken, bremsen,* *reiten* hard; (*streng*) harshly; s~ **schießen** fire live ammunition

Scharfblick *m* perspicacity

Schärfe *f* - (s. **scharf**) sharpness; strength; hotness; pungency; keenness; harshness. **s~n** *vt* sharpen

scharf|machen *vt sep* (*fam*) incite. **S~richter** *m* executioner. **S~schütze** *m* marksman. **s~sichtig** *a* perspicacious. **S~sinn** *m* astuteness. **s~sinnig** *a* astute, *adv* -ly

Scharlach *m* -s scarlet fever

Scharlatan *m* -s,-e charlatan

Scharnier *nt* -s,-e hinge

Schärpe *f* -,-n sash

scharren *vi* (*haben*) scrape; (*Huhn*) scratch; (*Pferd:*) paw the ground □ *vt* scrape

Schart|e *f* -,-n nick. **s~ig** *a* jagged

Schaschlik *m* & *nt* -s,-s kebab

Schatten *m* -s,- shadow; (*schattige Stelle*) shade; **im S~** in the shade. **s~haft** *a* shadowy. **S~riss** (**S~riß**) *m* silhouette. **S~seite** *f* shady side; (*fig*) disadvantage

schattier|en *vt* shade. **S~ung** *f* -,-en shading; (*fig:* **Variante**) shade

schattig *a* shady

Schatz *m* -es,-e treasure; (*Freund, Freundin*) sweetheart; (*Anrede*) darling

Schätzchen *nt* -s,- darling

schätzen *vt* estimate; (*taxieren*) value; (*achten*) esteem; (*würdigen*) appreciate; (*fam:* *vermuten*) reckon; **sich glücklich s~** consider oneself lucky

Schätzung *f* -,-en estimate; (*Taxierung*) valuation. **s~sweise** *adv* approximately

Schau *f* -,-en show; **zur S~ stellen** display. **S~ bild** *nt* diagram

Schauder *m* -s shiver; (*vor Abscheu*) shudder. **s~haft** *a* dreadful, *adv* -ly. **s~n** *vi* (*haben*) shiver;

(*vor Abscheu*) shudder; **mich s~te** I shivered/shuddered

schauen *vi* (*haben*) (*SGer, Aust*) look; see, **dass** make sure that

Schauer *m* -s,- shower; (*Schauder*) shiver. **S~ge-schichte** *f* horror story. **s~lich** *a* ghastly. **s~n** *vi* (*haben*) shiver; **mich s~te** I shivered

Schaufel *f* -,-n shovel; (*Kehr-*) dustpan. **s~n** *vt* shovel; (*graben*) dig

Schaufenster *nt* shop-window. **S~bummel** *m* window-shopping. **S~puppe** *f* dummy

Schaukasten *m* display case

Schaukel *f* -,-n swing. **s~n** *vt* rock □ *vi* (*haben*) rock; (*auf einer Schaukel*) swing; (*schwanken*) sway. **S~pferd** *nt* rocking-horse. **S~stuhl** *m* rocking-chair

schaulustig *a* curious

Schaum *m* -[e]s foam; (*Seifen-*) lather; (*auf Bier*) froth; (*als Frisier-, Rasiermittel*) mousse

schäumen *vi* (*haben*) foam, froth; (*Seife:*) lather

Schaum|gummi *m* foam rubber. **s~ig** *a* frothy; **s~ig rühren** (*Culin*) cream. **S~krone** *f* white crest; (*auf Bier*) head. **S~speise** *f* mousse. **S~stoff** *m* [synthetic] foam. **S~wein** *m* sparkling wine

Schauplatz *m* scene

schaurig *a* dreadful, *adv* -ly; (*unheimlich*) eerie, *adv* eerily

Schauspiel *nt* play; (*Anblick*) spectacle. **S~er** *m* actor. **S~erin** *f* actress. **s~ern** *vi* (*haben*) act; (*sich verstellen*) play-act

Scheck *m* -s,-s cheque, (*Amer*) check. **S~buch**, **S~heft** *nt* cheque-book. **S~karte** *f* cheque card

Scheibe *f* -,-n disc; (*Schieß-*) target; (*Glas-*) pane; (*Brot-, Wurst-*) slice. **S~nwaschanlage** *f* windscreen washer. **S~nwischer** *m* -s,- windscreen-wiper

Scheich *m* -s,-e & -s sheikh

Scheide f -,-n sheath; (Anat) vagina

scheid|en† vt separate; (unterscheiden) distinguish; dissolve (Ehe); **sich s∼en lassen** get divorced; **sich s∼en** diverge; (Meinungen:) differ □ vi (sein) leave; (voneinander) part. **S∼ung** f -,-en divorce

Schein m -[e]s,-e light; (Anschein) appearance; (Bescheinigung) certificate; (Geld-) note; **etw nur zum S∼ tun** only pretend to do sth. **s∼bar** a apparent, adv -ly. **s∼en†** vi (haben) shine; (den Anschein haben) seem, appear; **mir s∼t** it seems to me

scheinheilig a hypocritical, adv -ly. **S∼keit** f hypocrisy

Scheinwerfer m -s,- floodlight; (Such-) searchlight; (Auto) headlight; (Theat) spotlight

Scheiß-, scheiß- pref (vulg) bloody. **S∼e** f - (vulg) shit. **s∼en†** vi (haben) (vulg) shit

Scheit nt -[e]s,-e log

Scheitel m -s,- parting. **s∼n** vt part (Haar)

scheitern vi (sein) fail

Schelle f -,-n bell. **s∼n** vi (haben) ring

Schellfisch m haddock

Schelm m -s,-e rogue. **s∼isch** a mischievous, adv -ly

Schelte f - scolding. **s∼n†** vi (haben) grumble (über + acc about); **mit jdm s∼n** scold s.o. □ vt scold; (bezeichnen) call

Schema nt -s,-mata model, pattern; (Gesellschafts-) class; (Skizze) diagram

Schemel m -s,- stool

Schenke f -,-n tavern

Schenkel m -s,- thigh; (Geom) side

schenken vt give [as a present]; **jdm Vertrauen/Glauben s∼** trust/believe s.o.; **sich (dat) etw s∼** give sth a miss

scheppern vi (haben) clank

Scherbe f -,-n [broken] piece

Schere f -,-n scissors pl; (Techn) shears pl; (Hummer-) claw. **s∼n†** vt shear; crop (Haar); clip (Hund)

scheren² vt (reg) (fam) bother; **sich nicht s∼ um** not care about; **scher dich zum Teufel!** go to hell!

Scherenschnitt m silhouette

Scherereien fpl (fam) trouble sg

Scherz m -es,-e joke; **im/zum S∼** as a joke. **s∼en** vi (haben) joke. **S∼frage** f riddle. **s∼haft** a humorous

scheu a shy, adv -ly; (Tier) timid; **s∼ werden** (Pferd:) shy; **s∼ machen** startle. **S∼** f - shyness; timidity; (Ehrfurcht) awe

scheuchen vt shoo

scheuen vt be afraid of; (meiden) shun; **keine Mühe/Kosten s∼** spare no effort/expense; **sich s∼** be afraid (vor + dat of); shrink (etw zu tun from doing sth) □ vi (haben) (Pferd:) shy

Scheuer|lappen m floor-cloth. **s∼n** vt scrub; (mit Scheuerpulver) scour; (reiben) rub; **[wund] s∼n** chafe □ vi (haben) rub, chafe. **S∼tuch** nt floor-cloth

Scheuklappen fpl blinkers

Scheune f -,-n barn

Scheusal nt -s,-e monster

scheußlich a horrible, adv -bly

Schi m -s,-er ski; **S∼ fahren** od **laufen** ski

Schicht f -,-en layer; (Geol) stratum; (Gesellschafts-) class; (Arbeits-) shift. **S∼arbeit** f shift work. **s∼en** vt stack [up]

schick a stylish, adv -ly; (Frau) chic; (fam: prima) great. **S∼** m -[e]s style

schicken vt/i (haben) send; **s∼ nach** send for; **sich s∼ in** (+ acc) resign oneself to

schicklich a fitting, proper

Schicksal nt -s,-e fate. **s∼haft** a fateful. **S∼sschlag** m misfortune

Schieb|edach nt (Auto) sun-roof. **s∼en†** vt push; (gleitend) slide;

(fam: handeln mit) traffic in; **etw s~en auf** (+ acc) (fig) put sth down to; shift (Schuld, Verantwortung) on to □vi (haben) push. **S~er** m -s, -(Person) black marketeer. **S~etür** f sliding door. **S~ung** f -,-en (fam) illicit deal; (Betrug) rigging, fixing
Schieds|gericht nt panel of judges; (Jur) arbitration tribunal. **S~richter** m referee; (Tennis) umpire; (Jur) arbitrator
schief a crooked; (unsymmetrisch) lopsided; (geneigt) slanting, sloping; (nicht senkrecht) leaning; (Winkel) oblique; (fig) false; (mißtrauisch) suspicious □adv not straight; **jdn s~ ansehen** look at s.o. askance; **s~ gehen** (fam) go wrong
Schiefer m -s slate
schief|gehen† vi sep (sein) (NEW) **s~ gehen,** s. **schief.** **s~lachen (sich)** vr sep double up with laughter
schielen vi (haben) squint
Schienbein nt shin; (Knochen) shinbone
Schiene f -,-n rail; (Gleit-) runner; (Med) splint. **s~n** vt (Med) put in a splint
schier¹ adv almost
schier² a pure; (Fleisch) lean
Schieß|bude f shooting-gallery. **s~en†** vt shoot; fire (Kugel); score (Tor) □vi (haben) shoot, fire (**auf** + acc at) □vi (sein) shoot (Luft); (strömen) gush; **in die Höhe s~en** shoot up. **S~erei** f -,-en shooting. **S~scheibe** f target. **S~stand** m shooting-range
Schi|fahren nt skiing. **S~er(in)** m(f) skier
Schiff nt -[e]s,-e ship; (Kirchen-) nave; (Seiten-) aisle
Schiffahrt f (NEW) **Schifffahrt**
schiff|bar a navigable. **S~bau** m shipbuilding. **S~bruch** m shipwreck. **s~brüchig** a shipwrecked. **S~chen** nt -s,-

small boat; (Tex) shuttle. **S~er** m -s,- skipper. **S~fahrt** f shipping
Schikan|e f -,-n harassment; **mit allen S~en** (fam) with every refinement. **s~ieren** vt harass; (tyrannisieren) bully
Schi|laufen nt -s skiing. **S~läufer(in)** m(f) -s,- (f -,-nen) skier
Schild¹ m -[e]s,-e shield; **etw im S~e führen** (fam) be up to sth
Schild² nt -[e]s,-er sign; (Namens-, Nummern-) plate; (Mützen-) badge; (Etikett) label
Schilddrüse f thyroid gland
schildern vt describe. **S~ung** f -,-en description
Schild|kröte f tortoise; (See-) turtle. **S~patt** nt -[e]s tortoiseshell
Schilf nt -[e]s reeds pl
schillern vi (haben) shimmer
Schimmel m -s,- mould; (Pferd) white horse. **s~ig** a mouldy. **s~n** vi (haben/sein) go mouldy
Schimmer m -s gleam; (Spur) glimmer. **s~n** vi (haben) gleam
Schimpanse m -n,-n chimpanzee
schimpfen vi (haben) grumble (**mit** at; **über** + acc about); scold (**mit jdm** s.o.) □vt call. **S~name** m term of abuse. **S~wort** nt (pl -wörter) swear-word; (Beleidigung) insult
schind|en† vt work or drive hard; (quälen) ill-treat; **sich s~en** slave [away]; **Eindruck s~en** (fam) try to impress. **S~er** m -s,- slave-driver. **S~erei** f -,-en slave-driving; (Plackerei) hard slog
Schinken m -s,- ham. **S~speck** m bacon
Schippe f -,-n shovel. **s~n** vt shovel
Schirm m -[e]s,-e umbrella; (Sonnen-) sunshade; (Lampen-) shade; (Augen-) visor; (Mützen-) peak; (Ofen-, Bild-) screen; (fig: Schutz) shield. **S~herr** m patron. **S~herrschaft** f patronage. **S~mütze** f peaked cap

schizophren a schizophrenic. **S~ie** f schizophrenia

Schlacht f -,-en battle

schlachten vt slaughter, kill

Schlachter, Schlächter m -s,- (NGer) butcher

Schlacht|feld nt battlefield. **S~haus** nt, **S~hof** m abattoir. **S~platte** f plate of assorted cooked meats and sausages. **S~schiff** nt battleship

Schlacke f -,-n slag

Schlaf m -[e]s sleep; **im S~** in one's sleep. **S~anzug** m pyjamas pl, (Amer) pajamas pl. **S~couch** f sofa bed

Schläfe f -,-n (Anat) temple

schlafen† vi (haben) sleep; (fam: nicht aufpassen) be asleep; **s~ gehen** go to bed; **er schläft noch** he is still asleep. **S~szeit** f bedtime

Schläfer(in) m -s,- (f -,-nen) sleeper

schlaff a limp, adv -ly; (Seil) slack; (Muskel) flabby

Schlaf|lied nt lullaby. **s~los** a sleepless. **S~losigkeit** f insomnia. **S~mittel** nt sleeping drug

schläfrig a sleepy, adv -ily

Schlaf|saal m dormitory. **S~sack** m sleeping-bag. **S~tablette** f sleeping-pill. **s~trunken** a [still] half asleep. **S~wagen** m sleeping-car, sleeper. **s~wandeln** vi (haben/sein) sleep-walk. **S~zimmer** nt bedroom

Schlag m -[e]s,-̈e blow; (Faust-) punch; (Herz-, Puls-, Trommel-) beat; (einer Uhr) chime; (Glocken-, Gong- & Med) stroke; (elektrischer) shock; (Portion) helping; (Art) type; (Aust) whipped cream; **S~e bekommen** get a beating; **S~ auf S~** in rapid succession. **S~ader** f artery. **S~anfall** m stroke. **s~artig** a sudden, adv -ly. **S~baum** m barrier

Schlägel m -s,- mallet; (Trommel-) stick

schlagen† vt hit, strike; (fällen) fell; knock ⟨Loch, Nagel⟩ (in + acc into); (prügeln, besiegen) beat; (Culin) whisk ⟨Eiweiß⟩; whip ⟨Sahne⟩; (legen) throw; (wickeln) wrap; (hinzufügen) add (zu to); **sich s~** fight; **sich geschlagen geben** admit defeat ◻ vi (haben) beat; ⟨Tür:⟩ bang; ⟨Uhr:⟩ strike; (melodisch) chime; **mit den Flügeln s~** flap its wings; **um sich s~** lash out; **es schlug sechs** the clock struck six ◻ vi (sein) ⟨Flammen:⟩ (acc) **s~** ⟨Blitz, Kugel:⟩ strike eth; **s~ an** (+ acc) knock against; **nach jdm s~** (fig) take after s.o. **s~d** a (fig) conclusive, adv -ly

Schlager m -s,- popular song; (Erfolg) hit

Schläger m -s,- racket; (Tischtennis-) bat; (Golf-) club; (Hockey-) stick; (fam: Raufbold) thug. **S~ei** f -,-en fight, brawl

schlag|fertig a quick-witted. **S~instrument** nt percussion instrument. **S~loch** nt pot-hole. **S~sahne** f whipped cream; (ungeschlagen) whipping cream. **S~seite** f (Naut) list. **S~stock** m truncheon. **S~wort** nt (pl -worte) slogan. **S~zeile** f headline. **S~zeug** nt (Mus) percussion. **S~zeuger** m -s,- percussionist; (in Band) drummer

schlaksig a gangling

Schlamassel m & nt -s (fam) mess

Schlamm m -[e]s mud. **s~ig** a muddy

Schlampe f -,-n (fam) slut. **s~en** vi (haben) (fam) be sloppy (bei in). **S~erei** f -,-en (fam) sloppiness; (Unordnung) mess. **s~ig** a slovenly; (Arbeit) sloppy ◻ adv in a slovenly way; sloppily

Schlange f -,-n snake; (Menschen-, Auto-) queue; **S~ stehen** queue, (Amer) stand in line

schlängeln (sich) vr wind; (Person:) weave (durch through)

Schlangen|biss (**Schlangen-biß**) *m* snakebite. **S~linie** *f* wavy line

schlank *a* slim. **S~heit** *f* slimness. **S~heitskur** *f* slimming diet

schlapp *a* tired; (*schlaff*) limp, *adv* -ly. **S~e** *f* -,-n (*fam*) hose[pipe]

schlau *a* clever, *adv* -ly; (*gerissen*) crafty, *adv* -ily; **ich werde nicht s~ daraus** I can't make head or tail of it

Schlauch *m* -[e]s,**Schläuche** tube; (*Wasser-*) hose[pipe]. **S~boot** *nt* rubber dinghy. **s~en** *vt* (*fam*) exhaust

Schlaufe *f* -,-n loop

schlecht *a* bad; (*böse*) wicked; (*un-zulänglich*) poor; **s~ werden** go bad; (*Wetter:*) turn bad; **s~er werden** get worse; **s~ aussehen** look bad/(*Person:*) unwell; **mir ist s~** I feel sick; **s~ machen** (*fam*) run down □ *adv* badly; poorly; (*kaum*) not really. **s~gehen†** *vi sep* (*sein*) NEW **s~ gehen**, s. **gehen**. **s. gehen**. (NEW) **s~ gelaunt** *a* (NEW) **s~ gelaunt**, s. **gelaunt**. **s~hin** *adv* quite simply. **S~igkeit** *f* - wickedness. **s~machen** *vt sep* (NEW) **s~ machen**, s. **schlecht**

schlecken *vt/i* (*haben*) lick (**an etw dat** sth); (*auf-*) lap up

Schlegel *m* -s,- (*SGer: Keule*) leg; (*Hühner-*) drumstick; (*Techn, Mus*) (NEW) **Schlägel**

schleichen† *vi* (*sein*) creep; (*langsam gehen/fahren*) crawl □ *vr* **sich s~** creep. **s~d** *a* creeping; (*Krankheit*) insidious

Schleier *m* -s,- veil; (*fig*) haze. **s~haft** *a* **es ist mir s~haft** (*fam*) it's a mystery to me

Schleife *f* -,-n bow; (*Fliege*) bow-tie; (*Biegung*) loop

schleifen¹ *vt* (*reg*) □ *vt* drag; (*zer-stören*) raze to the ground □ *vi* (*haben*) trail, drag

schleifen†² *vt* grind; (*schärfen*) sharpen; cut (*Edelstein, Glas*); (*drillen*) drill

Schleim *m* -[e]s slime; (*Anat*) mucus; (*Med*) phlegm. **s~ig** *a* slimy

schlemm|en *vi* (*haben*) feast □ *vt* feast on. **S~er** *m* -s,- gourmet

schlendern *vi* (*sein*) stroll

schlenkern *vt/i* (*haben*) swing; **s~ mit** swing; dangle (*Beine*)

Schlepp|dampfer *m* tug. **S~e** *f* -,-n train. **s~en** *vt* drag; (*tragen*) carry; (*ziehen*) tow; (*widerrechtlich*) drag oneself; (*sich hinziehen*) drag on; **sich s~en mit** carry. **s~end** *a* slow, *adv* -ly. **S~er** *m* -s,- tug; (*Traktor*) tractor. **S~kahn** *m* barge. **S~lift** *m* T-bar lift. **S~tau** *nt* tow-rope; **ins S~tau nehmen** take in tow

Schleuder *f* -,-n catapult; (*Wäsche-*) spin-drier. **s~n** *vt* hurl; spin (*Wäsche*); extract (*Honig*) □ *vi* (*sein*) skid; **ins S~n geraten** skid. **S~preise** *mpl* knock-down prices. **S~sitz** *m* ejector seat

schleunigst *adv* hurriedly; (*sofort*) at once

Schleuse *f* -,-n lock; (*Sperre*) sluice[-gate]. **s~n** *vt* steer

Schliche *mpl* tricks; **jdm auf die S~ kommen** (*fam*) get on to s.o.

schlicht *a* plain, *adv* -ly; (*einfach*) simple, *adv* -ply

schlicht|en *vt* settle □ *vi* (*haben*) arbitrate. **S~ung** *f* - settlement; (*Jur*) arbitration

Schlick *m* -[e]s silt

Schließe *f* -,-n clasp; (*Schnalle*) buckle

schließen† *vt* close (*ab-*) lock; fasten (*Kleid, Verschluss*); (*stilllegen*) close down; (*beenden, folgern*) conclude; enter (*in Vertrag*); **sich s~** close; **in die Arme s~** embrace; **etw s~ an** (+ *acc*) connect sth to; **sich s~ an** (+ *acc*) follow □ *vi* (*haben*) close, (*den Betrieb einstellen*) close down; (*den Schlüssel drehen*) turn the key; (enden, folgern) conclude; s~ lassen auf (+ acc) suggest

Schließ|fach nt locker. s~lich adv finally, in the end; (immerhin) after all. S~ung f -,-en closure

Schliff m -[e]s cut; (Schleifen) cutting; (fig) polish; der letzte S~ the finishing touches pl

schlimm a bad, adv -ly; s~er werden get worse; nicht so s~! it doesn't matter! s~stenfalls adv if the worst comes to the worst

Schlinge f -,-n loop; (Henkers-) noose; (Med) sling; (Falle) snare

Schlingel m -s,- (fam) rascal

schling|en† vt wind, wrap; tie (Knoten); sich s~en um coil around □ vi (haben) bolt one's food. S~pflanze f climber

Schlips m -es,-e tie

Schlitten m -s,- sledge; (Rodel-) toboggan; (Pferde-) sleigh; S~ fahren toboggan

schlittern vi (haben/ sein) slide

Schlittschuh m skate; S~ laufen skate. S~läufer(in) m(f) -s,- (f -,-nen) skater

Schlitz m -es,-e slit; (für Münze) slot; (Jacken-) vent; (Hosen-) flies pl. s~en vt slit

Schloss nt -es,¨-er (Schloß nt -sses,¨-sser) lock; (Vorhänge-) padlock; (Verschluss) clasp; (Gebäude) castle; (Palast) palace

Schlosser m -s,- locksmith; (Auto-) mechanic; (Maschinen-) fitter

Schlot m -[e]s,-e chimney

schlottern vi (haben) shake, tremble; (Kleider:) hang loose

Schlucht f -,-en ravine, gorge

schluchz|en vi (haben) sob. S~er m -s,- sob

Schluck m -[e]s,-e mouthful; (klein) sip

Schluckauf m -s hiccups pl

schlucken vt/i (haben) swallow. S~ m -s hiccups pl

schlud|ern vi (haben) be sloppy (bei in). s~rig a sloppy, adv -ily; (Arbeit) slipshod

Schlummer m -s slumber. s~n vi (haben) slumber

Schlund m -[e]s [back of the] throat; (fig) mouth

schlüpf|en vi (sein) slip; [aus dem Ei] s~en hatch. S~er m -s,- knickers pl. s~rig a slippery; (anstößig) smutty

schlurfen vi (sein) shuffle

schlürfen vt/i (haben) slurp

Schluss m -es,¨-e (Schluß m -sses, -sse) end; (S~folgerung) conclusion; zum S~ finally; S~ machen stop (mit etw sth); finish (mit jdm with s.o.)

Schlüssel m -s,- key; (Schrauben-) spanner; (Geheim-) code; (Mus) clef. S~bein nt collar-bone. S~bund m & nt bunch of keys. S~loch nt keyhole. S~ring m key-ring

Schlussfolgerung (Schlußfolgerung) f conclusion

schlüssig a conclusive, adv -ly; sich (dat) s~ werden make up one's mind

Schluss|licht (Schluß|licht) nt rear-light. S~verkauf m [end of season] sale

Schmach f - disgrace

schmachten vi (haben) languish

schmächtig a slight

schmackhaft a tasty

schmal a narrow; (dünn) thin; (schlank) slender; (karg) meagre

schmälern vt diminish; (herabsetzen) belittle

Schmalz¹ nt -es lard; (Ohren-) wax

Schmalz² m -es (fam) schmaltz. s~ig a (fam) schmaltzy, slushy

schmarotz|en vi (haben) be parasitic (auf + acc on); (Person:) sponge (bei on). S~er m -s,- parasite; (Person) sponger

Schmarren *m* -s, (*Aust*) pancake [torn into strips]; (*fam*: *Unsinn*) rubbish

schmatzen *vi* (*haben*) eat noisily

schmausen *vi* (*haben*) feast

schmecken *vi* (*haben*) taste (**nach** *of*); [**gut**] s~ taste good; **hat es dir geschmeckt?** did you enjoy it? □ *vt* taste

Schmeichelei *f* -,-en flattery; (*Kompliment*) compliment

schmeichel|haft *a* complimentary, flattering. **s~n** *vi* (*haben*) (+ *dat*) flatter

schmeißen *vt/i* (*haben*) s~ [**mit**] (*fam*) chuck

Schmeißfliege *f* bluebottle

schmelz|en *vt/i* (*sein*) melt; smelt (*Erze*). **S~wasser** *nt* melted snow and ice

Schmerbauch *m* (*fam*) paunch

Schmerz *m* -es,-en pain; (*Kummer*) grief; **S~en haben** be in pain. **s~en** *vt* hurt; (*fig*) grieve □ *vi* (*haben*) hurt, be painful. **S~ensgeld** *nt* compensation for pain and suffering. **s~haft** *a* painful. **s~lich** *a* (*fig*) painful; (*traurig*) sad, *adv* -ly. **s~los** *a* painless, *adv* -ly. **s~stillend** *a* pain-killing; **s~stillendes Mittel** analgesic, pain-killer. **S~tablette** *f* pain-killer

Schmetterball *m* (*Tennis*) smash

Schmetterling *m* -s,-e butterfly

schmettern *vt* hurl; (*Tennis*) smash; (*singen*) sing; (*spielen*) blare out □ *vi* (*haben*) sound; (*Trompeten:*) blare

Schmied *m* -[e]s,-e blacksmith

Schmiede *f* -,-n forge. **S~eisen** *nt* wrought iron. **s~n** *vt* forge; (*fig*) hatch; **Pläne s~n** make plans

schmieg|en *vt* press; **sich s~en an** (+ *acc*) nestle or snuggle up to; (*Kleid:*) cling. **s~sam** *a* supple

Schmier|e *f* -,-n grease; (*Schmutz*) mess. **s~en** *vt* lubricate; (*streichen*) spread; (*schlecht schreiben*) scrawl; (*sl*: *bestechen*) bribe □ *vi* (*haben*) smudge;

(*schreiben*) scrawl. **S~fett** *nt* grease. **S~geld** *nt* (*fam*) bribe. **s~ig** *a* greasy; (*schmutzig*) grubby; (*anstößig*) smutty; (*Person:*) slimy. **S~mittel** *nt* lubricant

Schminke *f* -,-n make-up. **s~n** *vt* make up; **sich s~n** put on make-up; **sich** (*dat*) **die Lippen s~n** put on lipstick

schmirgel|n *vt* sand down. **S~papier** *nt* emery-paper

schmökern *vt/i* (*haben*) (*fam*) read

schmollen *vi* (*haben*) sulk; (*s~d den Mund verziehen*) pout

schmoren *vt/i* (*haben*) braise; (*fam*: *schwitzen*) roast. **S~topf** *m* casserole

Schmuck *m* -[e]s jewellery; (*Verzierung*) ornament, decoration

schmücken *vt* decorate, adorn; **sich s~** adorn oneself

schmuck|los *a* plain. **S~stück** *nt* piece of jewellery; (*fig*) jewel

schmuddelig *a* grubby

Schmuggel *m* -s smuggling. **s~n** *vt* smuggle. **S~ware** *f* contraband

Schmuggler *m* -s,- smuggler

schmunzeln *vi* (*haben*) smile

schmusen *vi* (*haben*) cuddle

Schmutz *m* -es dirt; **in den S~ ziehen** (*fig*) denigrate. **s~en** *vi* (*haben*) get dirty. **S~fleck** *m* dirty mark. **s~ig** *a* dirty

Schnabel *m* -s,- beak, bill; (*eines Kruges*) lip; (*Tülle*) spout

Schnake *f* -,-n mosquito; (*Kohl-*) daddy-long-legs

Schnalle *f* -,-n buckle. **s~n** *vt* strap; (*zu-*) buckle; **den Gürtel enger s~n** tighten one's belt

schnalzen *vi* (*haben*) **mit der Zunge/den Fingern s~** click one's tongue/snap one's fingers

schnapp|en *vt* grab □ *vi* (*sein*) **nach** snap at; gasp for (*Luft*) □ *vt* snatch, grab; (*fam*: *festnehmen*) nab. **S~schloss** (**S~schloß**) *nt* spring lock. **S~schuss (S~schuß)** m snapshot

Schnaps m -es,¨-e schnapps

schnarchen vi (haben) snore

schnarren vi (haben) rattle; ⟨Klingel:⟩ buzz

schnattern vi (haben) cackle

schnauben vi (haben) snort □ vt **sich** (dat) **die Nase s~** blow one's nose

schnaufen vi (haben) puff, pant

Schnauze f -,-n muzzle; ⟨eines Kruges⟩ lip; ⟨Tülle⟩ spout

schnäuzen (sich) vr blow one's nose

Schnecke f -,-n snail; ⟨Nackt-⟩ slug; ⟨Spirale⟩ scroll; ⟨Gebäck⟩ ≈ Chelsea bun. **S~nhaus** nt snailshell

Schnee m -s snow; ⟨Eier-⟩ beaten egg-white. **S~ball** m snowball. **S~besen** m whisk. **S~brille** f snow-goggles pl. **S~fall** m snowfall. **S~flocke** f snowflake. **S~glöckchen** nt -s,- snowdrop. **S~kette** f snow chain. **S~mann** m (pl -männer) snowman. **S~pflug** m snowplough. **S~schläger** m whisk. **S~sturm** m snowstorm, blizzard. **S~wehe** f -,-n snowdrift

Schneid m -[e]s ⟨SGer⟩ courage

Schneide f -,-n ⟨cutting⟩ edge; ⟨Klinge⟩ blade

schneiden† vt cut; ⟨in Scheiben⟩ slice; ⟨kreuzen⟩ cross; ⟨nicht beachten⟩ cut dead; **Gesichter s~** pull faces; **sich s~** cut oneself; ⟨über-⟩ intersect; **sich** ⟨dat/acc⟩ **in den Finger s~** cut one's finger. **s~d** a cutting; ⟨kalt⟩ biting

Schneider m -s,- tailor. **S~in** f -,-nen dressmaker. **s~n** vt make ⟨Anzug, Kostüm⟩

Schneidezahn m incisor

schneidig a dashing, adv -ly

schneien vi (haben) snow; **es schneit** it is snowing

Schneise f -,-n path; ⟨Feuer-⟩ firebreak

schnell a quick; ⟨Auto, Tempo⟩ fast □ adv quickly; ⟨in s~em Tempo⟩ fast; ⟨bald⟩ soon; **mach s~!** hurry up! **s~en** vi (sein) **in die Höhe s~en** shoot up. **S~igkeit** f - rapidity; ⟨Tempo⟩ speed. **S~imbiss** m snackbar. **S~kochtopf** m pressure-cooker. **S~reinigung** f express cleaners. **s~stens** adv as quickly as possible. **S~zug** m express [train]

schnetzeln vt cut into thin strips

schneuzen (sich) vr ⟨NEW⟩ **schnäuzen (sich)**

schnippen vt flick

schnippisch a pert, adv -ly

Schnipsel m & nt -s,- scrap

Schnitt m -[e]s,-e cut; ⟨Film-⟩ cutting; ⟨S~muster⟩ ⟨paper⟩ pattern; **im S~** ⟨durchschnittlich⟩ on average

Schnitte f -,-n slice ⟨of bread⟩; ⟨belegt⟩ open sandwich

schnittig a stylish; ⟨stromlinienförmig⟩ streamlined

Schnitt|käse m hard cheese. **S~lauch** m chives pl. **S~muster** nt ⟨paper⟩ pattern. **S~punkt** m [point of] intersection. **S~wunde** f cut

Schnitzel nt -s,- scrap; ⟨Culin⟩ escalope. **s~n** vt shred

schnitzen vt/i (haben) carve. **S~er** m -s,- carver; ⟨fam: Fehler⟩ blunder. **S~erei** f -,-en carving

schnodderig a ⟨fam⟩ brash

schnöde a despicable, adv -bly; ⟨verächtlich⟩ contemptuous, adv -ly

Schnorchel m -s,- snorkel

Schnörkel m -s,- flourish; ⟨Kunst⟩ scroll. **s~ig** a ornate

schnorren vt/i (haben) ⟨fam⟩ scrounge

schnüffeln vi (haben) sniff ⟨an etw dat sth⟩; ⟨fam: spionieren⟩ snoop [around]

Schnuller m -s,- [baby's] dummy, ⟨Amer⟩ pacifier

schnupf|en *vt* sniff; **Tabak s~en** take snuff. **S~en** *m* -s,- [head] cold. **S~tabak** *m* snuff

schnuppern *vt/i* (haben) sniff (**an etw** *dat* sth)

Schnur *f* -,-̈e string; (Kordel) cord; (Besatz:) braid; (Electr) flex; **eine S~** a piece of string

Schnür|chen *nt* -s,- **wie am S~chen** (fam) like clockwork. **s~en** *vt* tie; lace [up] (Schuhe)

schnurgerade *a & adv* dead straight

Schnurr|bart *m* moustache. **s~en** *vi* (haben) hum; (Katze:) purr

Schnür|schuh *m* lace-up shoe. **S~senkel** *m* -s,- [shoe-]lace

schnurstracks *adv* straight

Schock *m* -[e]s,-e shock. **s~en** *vt* (fam) shock; **geschockt sein** be shocked. **s~ieren** *vt* shock; **s~ierend** shocking

Schöffe *m* -n,-n lay judge

Schokolade *f* - chocolate

Scholle *f* -,-n clod [of earth]; (Eis-) [ice-]floe; (Fisch) plaice

schon *adv* already; (allein) just; (sogar) even; (ohnehin) anyway; **s~ einmal** once; (jemals) ever; **s~ immer/oft/wieder** always/often/again; **hast du ihn s~ gesehen?** have you seen him yet? **s~ der Gedanke daran** the mere thought of it; **s~ deshalb** for that reason alone; **das ist s~ möglich** that's quite possible; **ja s~, aber** well yes, but; **nun geh/komm s~!** go/come on then!

schön *a* beautiful; (Wetter) fine; (angenehm, nett) nice; (gut) good; (fam: beträchtlich) pretty; **s~en Dank!** thank you very much! **na s~** all right then □ *adv* beautifully; nicely; (gut) well; **s~ langsam** nice and slowly

schonen *vt* spare; (gut behandeln) look after; **sich s~** take things easy. **s~d** *a* gentle, *adv* -tly

Schönheit *f* -,-en beauty. **S~sfehler** *m* blemish. **S~skonkurrenz** *f*, **S~swettbewerb** *m* beauty contest

schönmachen *vt sep* smarten up; **sich s~** make oneself look nice

Schonung *f* -,-en gentle care; (nach Krankheit) rest; (Baum-) plantation. **s~slos** a ruthless, *adv* -ly

Schonzeit *f* close season

schöpf|en *vt* scoop [up]; ladle (Suppe); **Mut s~en** take heart; **frische Luft s~en** get some fresh air. **S~er** *m* -s,- creator; (Kelle) ladle. **s~erisch** a creative. **S~kelle** f, **S~löffel** *m* ladle. **S~ung** f -,-en creation

Schoppen *m* -s,- (SGer) ≈ pint

Schorf *m* -[e]s scab

Schornstein *m* chimney. **S~feger** *m* -s,- chimney-sweep

Schoß *m* -es,-̈e lap; (Frack-) tail

Schößling (**Schößling**) *m* -s,-e (Bot) shoot

Schote *f* -,-n pod; (Erbse) pea

Schotte *m* -n,-n Scot, Scotsman

Schotter *m* -s gravel; (für Gleise) ballast

schott|isch a Scottish, Scots. **S~land** *nt* -s Scotland

schraffieren *vt* hatch

schräg *a* diagonal, *adv* -ly; (geneigt) sloping; **s~ halten** tilt. **S~e** f -,-n slope. **S~strich** *m* oblique stroke

Schramme *f* -,-n scratch. **s~n** *vt* scrape, scratch

Schrank *m* -[e]s,-̈e cupboard; (Kleider-) wardrobe; (Akten-, Glas-) cabinet

Schranke *f* -,-n barrier

Schraube *f* -,-n screw; (Schiffs-) propeller. **s~n** *vt* screw; (drehen) turn; **sich in die Höhe s~n** spiral upwards. **S~nmutter** *f* nut. **S~nschlüssel** *m* spanner. **S~nzieher** *m* -s,- screwdriver

Schraubstock *m* vice

Schrebergarten m ≈ allotment

Schreck m -[e]s,-e fright; **jdm einen S~ einjagen** give s.o. a fright. **S~en** m -s,- fright; (*Entsetzen*) horror. **s~en** vt (*reg*) frighten; (*auf-*) startle □ vi (*sein*) **in die Höhe s~en** start up

Schreck|gespenst nt spectre. **s~haft** a easily frightened; (*nervös*) jumpy. **s~lich** a terrible, adv -bly. **S~schuss** (**S~schuß**) m warning shot

Schrei m -[e]s,-e cry, shout; (*gellend*) scream; (*fam*) **der letzte S~** (*fam*) the latest thing

Schreib|block m writing-pad. **s~en†** vt/i (haben) write; (*auf der Maschine*) type; **richtig/falsch s~en** spell right/wrong; **sich s~en** (*Wort:*) be spelt; (*korrespondieren*) correspond; **krank s~en** (NEW) **krankschreiben**. **S~en** nt -s,- writing; (*Brief*) letter. **S~fehler** m spelling mistake. **S~heft** nt exercise book. **S~kraft** f clerical assistant; (*für Maschineschreiben*) typist. **S~maschine** f typewriter. **S~papier** nt writing-paper. **S~schrift** f script. **S~tisch** m desk. **S~ung** f -,-en spelling. **S~waren** fpl stationery sg. **S~weise** f spelling

schreien† vt/i (haben) cry; (*gellend*) scream; (*rufen, laut sprechen*) shout; **zum S~ sein** (*fam*) be a scream. **s~d** a (*fig*) glaring; (*grell*) garish

Schreiner m -s,- joiner

schreiten† vi (sein) walk

Schrift f -,-en writing; (*Druck-*) type; (*Abhandlung*) paper; **die Heilige S~** the Scriptures pl. **S~führer** m secretary. **s~lich** a written □ adv in writing. **S~sprache** f written language. **S~steller(in)** m -s,- (f -,-nen) writer. **S~stück** nt document. **S~zeichen** nt character

schrill a shrill, adv -y

Schritt m -[e]s,-e step; (*Entfernung*) pace; (*Gangart*) walk; (*der Hose*) crotch; **im S~** in step; (*langsam*) at walking pace; **S~ halten mit** (*fig*) keep pace with. **S~macher** m -s,- pace-maker. **s~weise** adv step by step

schroff a precipitous, adv -ly; (*abweisend*) brusque, adv -ly; (*unvermittelt*) abrupt, adv -ly; (*Gegensatz*) stark

schröpfen vt (*fam*) fleece

Schrot m & nt -[e]s coarse meal; (*Blei-*) small shot. **s~en** vt grind coarsely. **S~flinte** f shotgun

Schrott m -[e]s scrap[-metal]; **zu S~ fahren** (*fam*) write off. **S~platz** m scrap-yard. **s~reif** a ready for the scrap-heap

schrubb|en vt/i (haben) scrub. **S~er** m -s,- [long-handled] scrubbing-brush

Schrull|e f -,-n whim; **alte S~e** (*fam*) old crone. **s~ig** a cranky

schrumpfen vi (sein) shrink; (*Obst:*) shrivel

schrump[e]lig a wrinkled

Schrunde f -,-n crack; (*Spalte*) crevasse

Schub m -[e]s,-e (*Phys*) thrust; (*S~fach*) drawer; (*Menge*) batch. **S~fach** nt drawer. **S~karre** f, **S~karren** m wheelbarrow. **S~lade** f drawer

Schubs m -es,-e push, shove. **s~en** vt push, shove

schüchtern a shy, adv -ly; (*zaghaft*) tentative, adv -ly. **S~heit** f -shyness

Schuft m -[e]s,-e (*pej*) swine. **s~en** vi (haben) (*fam*) slave away

Schuh m -[e]s,-e shoe. **S~anzieher** m -s,- shoehorn. **S~band** nt (pl -bänder) shoe-lace. **S~creme** f shoe-polish. **S~löffel** m shoehorn. **S~macher** m -s,- shoemaker; (*zum Flicken*) [shoe]mender. **S~werk** nt shoes pl

Schul|abgänger m -s,- school-leaver. **S~arbeiten,** **S~aufgaben** fpl homework sg. **S~buch** nt school-book

Schuld f -,-en guilt; (Verantwortung) blame; (Geld-) debt; **S~en machen** get into debt; **S~ haben** be to blame (**an** + dat for); **jdm S~ geben** blame s.o.; **sich** (dat) **etwas zu S~en kommen lassen = sich etwas zuschulden kommen lassen,** s. **zuschulden** □ **s~ sein** to be to blame (**an** + dat for); **s~ geben** (NEW) **S~ haben/jdm S~ geben,** s. **Schuld. s~en** vt owe

schuldig a guilty (gen of); (gebührend) due; **jdm etw s~ sein** owe s.o. sth. **S~keit** f - duty

schuld|los a innocent. **S~ner** m -s,- debtor. **S~spruch** m guilty verdict

Schule f -,-n school; **in der/die S~** at/to school. **s~n** vt train

Schüler(in) m -s,- (f -,-nen) pupil. **S~lotse** m pupil acting as crossing warden

schul|frei a **s~freier Tag** day without school; **wir haben morgen s~frei** there's no school tomorrow. **S~hof** m [school] playground. **S~jahr** nt school year; (Klasse) form. **S~junge** m schoolboy. **S~kind** nt schoolchild. **S~leiter(in)** m(f) head [teacher]. **S~mädchen** nt schoolgirl. **S~stunde** f lesson

Schulter f -,-n shoulder. **S~blatt** nt shoulder-blade. **s~n** vt shoulder. **S~tuch** nt shawl

Schulung f - training

schummeln vi (haben) (fam) cheat

Schund m -[e]s trash. **S~roman** m trashy novel

Schuppe f -,-n scale; **S~n** pl dandruff sg. **s~n** (sich) vr flake [off]

Schuppen m -s,- shed

Schur f - shearing

Schür|eisen nt poker. **s~en** vt poke; (fig) stir up

schürf|en vt mine; (sich) (dat) **das Knie s~en** graze one's knee □ vi (haben) **s~en nach** prospect for. **S~wunde** f abrasion, graze

Schürhaken m poker

Schurke m -n,-n villain

Schürze f -,-n apron. **s~n** vt (raffen) gather [up]; tie (Knoten); purse (Lippen). **S~njäger** m (fam) womanizer

Schuss m -es,-̈e (Schuß m -sses, -̈sse) shot; (kleine Menge) dash

Schüssel f -,-n bowl; (TV) dish

schusselig a (fam) scatter-brained

Schuss|fahrt f (Schußfahrt) f (Ski) schuss. **S~waffe** f firearm

Schuster m -s,- = **Schuhmacher**

Schutt m -[e]s rubble. **S~ablade-platz** m rubbish dump

Schüttel|frost m shivering fit. **s~n** vt shake; **sich s~n** shake oneself/itself; (vor Ekel) shudder; **jdm die Hand s~n** shake s.o.'s hand

schütten vt pour; (kippen) tip; (ver-) spill □ vi (haben) **es schüttet** it is pouring [with rain]

Schutthaufen m pile of rubble

Schutz m -es protection; (Zuflucht) shelter; (Techn) guard; **S~ suchen** take refuge; **unter dem S~ der Dunkelheit** under cover of darkness. **S~anzug** m protective suit. **S~blech** nt mudguard. **S~brille** goggles pl

Schütze m -n,-n marksman; (Tor-) scorer; (Astr) Sagittarius; **guter S~** good shot

schützen vt protect/(Zuflucht gewähren) shelter (**vor** + dat from) □ vi (haben) give protection/shelter (**vor** + dat from). **s~d** a protective, adv -ly

Schützenfest nt fair with shooting competition

Schutz|engel m guardian angel. **S~heilige(r)** m/f patron saint

Schützling m -s,-e charge; (Protegé) protégé

schutz|los *a* defenceless, help-
less. **S~mann** *m* (*pl* **-männer** *or*
-leute) policeman. **S~umschlag**
m dust-jacket

Schwaben *nt* -s Swabia

schwäbisch *a* Swabian

schwach *a* (**schwächer,
schwächst**) weak, (*nicht
gut; gering*) poor, *adv* -ly; (*leicht*)
faint, *adv* -ly

Schwäche *f* -,-n weakness. **s~n**
vt weaken

Schwach|heit *f* - weakness.
S~kopf *m* (*fam*) idiot

schwäch|lich *a* delicate. **S~ling**
m -s,-e weakling

Schwachsinn *m* mental deficiency. **s~ig** *a* mentally deficient;
(*fam*) idiotic

Schwächung *f* - weakening

schwafeln (*fam/vi*) (*haben*) waffle
□ *vt* talk

Schwager *m* -s,⸚ brother-in-law

Schwägerin *f* -,-nen sister-in-
law

Schwalbe *f* -,-n swallow

Schwall *m* -[e]s torrent

Schwamm *m* -[e]s,⸚e sponge;
(*SGer: Pilz*) fungus; (*essbar*)
mushroom. **s~ig** *a* spongy; (*aufgedunsen*) bloated

Schwan *m* -[e]s,⸚e swan

schwanen *vi* (*haben*) (*fam*) **mir
schwante, dass** I had a nasty
feeling that

schwanger *a* pregnant

schwängern *vt* make pregnant

Schwangerschaft *f* -,-en preg-
nancy

Schwank *m* -[e]s,⸚e (*Theat*) farce

schwank|en *vi* (*haben*) sway;
(*Boot:*) rock; (*sich ändern*) fluc-
tuate; (*unentschieden sein*) be undecided □ (*sein*) stagger. **S~ung**
f -,-en fluctuation

Schwanz *m* -es,⸚e tail

schwänzen *vt* (*fam*) skip; **die
Schule s~** play truant

Schwarm *m* -[e]s,⸚e swarm;
(*Fisch-*) shoal; (*fam: Liebe*) idol

schwärmen *vi* (*haben*) swarm;
s~ für (*fam*) adore; (*verliebt sein*)
have a crush on; **s~ von** (*fam*)
rave about

Schwarte *f* -,-n (*Speck-*) rind;
(*fam: Buch*) tome

schwarz *a* (**schwärzer, schwär-
zest**) black; (*fam: illegal*) illegal,
adv -ly; **s~er Markt** black market; **s~ gekleidet** dressed in
black; **s~ auf weiß** in black and
white; **s~ sehen** (*fig*) be pessim-
istic; **ins S~e treffen** score a
bull's-eye. **S~** *nt* -[e]s,- black.
S~arbeit *f* moonlighting. **s~ar-
beiten** *vi sep* (*haben*) moonlight.
S~brot *nt* black bread. **S~e(r)**
m/f black

Schwärze *f* - blackness. **s~n** *vt*
blacken

Schwarz|fahrer *m* fare-dodger.
S~handel *m* black market (**mit**
in). **S~händler** *m* black marketeer. **S~markt** *m* black market.
s~sehen† *vi sep* (*haben*) watch
television without a licence;
(*fig* NEW) **s~ sehen**, s. **schwarz**.
S~wald *m* Black Forest. **s~weiß**
a black and white

Schwatz *m* -es (*fam*) chat

schwatzen, schwätzen (*SGer*) *vi*
(*haben*) chat; (*klatschen*) gossip;
(*Sch*) talk [in class] □ *vt* talk

schwatzhaft *a* garrulous

Schwebe f -**in der S~** (*fig*) undecided. **S~bahn** *f* cable railway.
s~n *vi* (*haben*) float; (*fig*) be undecided; (*Verfahren:*) be pending;
in Gefahr s~n be in danger
□ (*sein*) float

Schwed|e *m* -n,-n Swede. **S~en**
nt -s Sweden. **S~in** *f* -,-nen
Swede. **s~isch** *a* Swedish

Schwefel *m* -s sulphur. **S~säure**
f sulphuric acid

schweigen† *vi* (*haben*) be silent;
ganz zu s~ von to say nothing
of, let alone. **S~** *nt* -s silence; **zum
S~ bringen** silence. **s~d** *a*
silent, *adv* -ly

schweigsam a silent; (*wortkarg*) taciturn

Schwein nt -[e]s,-e pig; (*Culin*) pork; (*sl*) (*schmutziger Mensch*) dirty pig; (*Schuft*) swine; **S~haben** (*fam*) be lucky. **S~braten** m roast pork. **S~efleisch** nt pork. **S~ehund** m (*sl*) swine. **S~erei** f -,-en (*sl*) [dirty] mess; (*Gemeinheit*) dirty trick. **S~stall** m pigsty. **S~isch** a lewd. **S~sleder** nt pigskin

Schweiß m -es sweat

schweiß|en vt weld. **S~er** m -s,- welder

Schweiz (die) - Switzerland. **S~er** a & m -s,-, **S~erin** f -,-nen Swiss. **s~erisch** a Swiss

schwelen vi (*haben*) smoulder

schwelgen vi (*haben*) feast; **s~ in** (+ *dat*) wallow in

Schwelle f -,-n threshold; (*Eisenbahn-*) sleeper

schwell|en† vi (*sein*) swell. **S~ung** f -,-en swelling

Schwemme f -,-n watering-place; (*fig: Überangebot*) glut. **S~n** vt wash; **an Land s~n** wash up

Schwenk m -[e]s swing. **s~en** vt swing; (*schwingen*) wave; (*spülen*) rinse; **in Butter s~en** toss in butter □ vi (*sein*) turn

schwer a heavy; (*schwierig*) difficult; (*mühsam, streng*) hard; (*ernst*) serious; (*schlimm*) bad; 3 **Pfund s~ sein** weigh 3 pounds □ adv heavily; with difficulty; (*mühsam, streng*) hard; (*schlimm, sehr*) badly, seriously; **s~ krank/verletzt** seriously ill/injured; **s~ arbeiten** work hard; **s~ hören** be hard of hearing; **etw s~ nehmen** take sth seriously; **jdm s~ fallen** be hard for s.o.; **es jdm s~ machen** make it or things difficult for s.o.; **sich s~ tun** have difficulty (*mit* with); **s~ zu sagen** difficult or hard to say

Schwere f - heaviness; (*Gewicht*) weight; (*Schwierigkeit*) difficulty;

(*Ernst*) gravity. **S~losigkeit** f - weightlessness

schwer|fallen† vi sep (*sein*) NEW **s~ fallen**, s. **schwer**. **s~fällig** a ponderous, adv -ly; (*unbeholfen*) clumsy, adv -ily. **S~gewicht** nt heavyweight. **S~hörig** a hörig **sein** be hard of hearing. **S~kraft** f (*Phys*) gravity. **s~krank** a NEW **s~ krank**, s. **schwer**. **s~lich** adv hardly. **s~machen** vt sep NEW **s~ machen**, s. **schwer**. **s~mütig** a melancholic. **s~nehmen†** vt sep NEW **s~ nehmen**, s. **schwer**. **S~punkt** m centre of gravity; (*fig*) emphasis

Schwert nt -[e]s,-er sword. **S~lilie** f iris

schwer|tun† (sich) vr sep NEW **s~ tun** (sich), s. **schwer**. **S~verbrecher** m serious offender. **s~verdaulich** a NEW **s~ verdaulich**, s. **verdaulich**. **s~verletzt** a NEW **s~ verletzt**, s. **schwer**. **s~wiegend** a weighty

Schwester f -,-n sister; (*Kranken-*) nurse. **s~lich** a sisterly

Schwieger|eltern pl parents-in-law. **S~mutter** f mother-in-law. **S~sohn** m son-in-law. **S~tochter** f daughter-in-law. **S~vater** m father-in-law

Schwiele f -,-n callus

schwierig a difficult. **S~keit** f -,-en difficulty

Schwimm|bad nt swimming-baths pl. **S~becken** nt swimming-pool. **s~en†** vt/i (*sein/haben*) swim; (*auf dem Wasser treiben*) float. **S~er** m -s,- swimmer; (*Techn*) float. **S~weste** f life-jacket

Schwindel m -s dizziness, vertigo; (*fam: Betrug*) fraud; (*Lüge*) lie. **S~anfall** m dizzy spell. **s~frei a s~frei sein** have a good head for heights. **s~n** vi (*haben*) (*lügen*) lie; **mir od mich s~t** I feel dizzy

schwinden† *vi* (*sein*) dwindle; (*vergehen*) fade; (*nachlassen*) fail

Schwindl|er *m* -s,- liar; (*Betrüger*) fraud, con-man. **s~ig** *a* dizzy; **mir ist** *od* **wird s~ig** I feel dizzy

schwing|en† *vi* (*haben*) swing; (*Phys*) oscillate; (*vibrieren*) vibrate □ *vt* swing; wave (*Fahne*); (*drohend*) brandish. **S~tür** *f* swing-door. **S~ung** *f* -,-en oscillation; vibration

Schwips *m* -es,-e **einen S~ haben** (*fam*) be tipsy

schwirren *vi* (*haben/sein*) buzz; (*surren*) whirr

Schwitz|e *f* -,-n (*Culin*) roux. **s~en** *vi* (*haben*) sweat; **es ist** *od* **mich s~t** I am hot □ *vt* (*Culin*) sweat

schwören† *vt/i* (*haben*) swear (**auf** + *acc* by); **Rache s~** swear revenge

schwul *a* (*fam: homosexuell*) gay

schwül *a* close. **S~e** *f* - closeness

schwülstig *a* bombastic, *adv* -ally

Schwung *m* -[e]s,-e swing; (*Bogen*) sweep; (*Schnelligkeit*) momentum; (*Kraft*) vigour; (*Feuer*) verve; (*fam: Anzahl*) batch; **in S~ kommen** gather momentum; (*fig*) get going. **s~haft** *a* brisk, *adv* -ly. **s~los** *a* dull. **s~voll** *a* vigorous, *adv* -ly; (*Bogen, Linie*) sweeping; (*mitreißend*) spirited, lively

Schwur *m* -[e]s,-e vow; (*Eid*) oath. **S~gericht** *nt* jury [court]

sechs *inv a*, **S~** *f* -,-en six; (*Sch*) ≈ fail mark. **s~eckig** *a* hexagonal. **s~te(r,s)** *a* sixth

sech|zehn *inv a* sixteen. **s~zehnte(r,s)** *a* sixteenth. **s~zig** *inv a* sixty. **s~zigste(r,s)** *a* sixtieth

sedieren *vt* sedate

See¹ *m* -s,-n /'ze:ən/ lake

See² *f* - sea; **an die/der See** to/at the seaside; **auf See** at sea. **S~bad** *nt* seaside resort. **S~fahrt** *f* [sea] voyage;

(*Schifffahrt*) navigation. **S~gang** *m* **schwerer S~gang** rough sea. **S~hund** *m* seal. **s~krank** *a* seasick

Seele *f* -,-n soul. **s~nruhig** *a* calm, *adv* -ly

seelisch *a* psychological, *adv* -ly; (*geistig*) mental, *adv* -ly

Seelsorger *m* -s,- pastor

See|luft *f* sea air. **S~macht** *f* maritime power. **S~mann** *m* (*pl* -**leute**) seaman, sailor. **S~not** *f* **in S~not** in distress. **S~räuber** *m* pirate. **S~reise** *f* [sea] voyage. **S~rose** *f* water-lily. **S~sack** *m* kitbag. **S~stern** *m* starfish. **S~tang** *m* seaweed. **s~tüchtig** *a* seaworthy. **S~weg** *m* sea route; **auf dem S~weg** by sea. **S~zunge** *f* sole

Segel *nt* -s,- sail. **S~boot** *nt* sailing-boat. **S~fliegen** *nt* gliding. **S~flieger** *m* glider pilot. **S~flugzeug** *nt* glider. **s~n** *vt/i* (*sein/haben*) sail. **S~schiff** *nt* sailing-ship. **S~sport** *m* sailing. **S~tuch** *nt* canvas

Segen *m* -s blessing. **s~sreich** *a* beneficial; (*gesegnet*) blessed

Segler *m* -s,- yachtsman

Segment *nt* -[e]s,-e segment

segnen *vt* bless; **gesegnet mit** blessed with

sehen *vt* see; watch (*Fernsehsendung*); **jdn/etw wieder s~** see s.o./sth again; **sich s~ lassen** show oneself □ *vi* (*haben*) see; (*blicken*) look (**auf** + *acc* at); (*Augen*) show (**aus** above); **gut/schlecht s~** have good/bad eyesight; **vom S~ kennen** know by sight; **s~ nach** keep an eye on; (*betreuen*) look after; (*suchen*) look for; **darauf s~, dass** see [to it] that. **s~swert**, **s~swürdig** *a* worth seeing. **S~swürdigkeit** *f* -,-en sight

Sehkraft *f* sight, vision

Sehne *f* -,-n tendon; (*eines Bogens*) string

sehnen (**sich**) *vr* long (**nach** for)

sehnig a sinewy; (zäh) stringy

sehn|lich[st] a (Wunsch) dearest □ adv longingly. **s~sucht** f - longing (nach for). **s~süchtig** a longing, adv -ly; (Wunsch) dearest

sehr adv very; (mit Verb) very much; **so s~, dass** so much that

seicht a shallow

seid s. **sein**¹; **ihr s~** you are

Seide f -,-n silk

Seidel nt -s,- beer-mug

seiden a silk ... **S~papier** nt tissue paper. **S~raupe** f silk-worm. **s~weich** a silky-soft

seidig a silky

Seife f -,-n soap. **S~npulver** nt soap powder. **S~nschaum** m lather

seifig a soapy

seihen vt strain

Seil nt -[e]s,-e rope; (Draht-) cable. **S~bahn** f cable railway. **s~springen** vi (sein) (inf & pp only) skip. **S~tänzer(in)** m(f) tightrope walker

sein†¹ vi (sein) be; **er ist Lehrer** he is a teacher; **sei still!** be quiet! **mir ist kalt/schlecht** I am cold/feel sick; **wie dem auch sei** be that as it may; **etw s~ lassen** leave sth; (aufhören mit) stop sth □ v aux have; (angekommen/gestorben) **s~** have arrived/died; **er war/wäre gefallen** he had/ would have fallen; **es ist/war viel zu tun/nichts zu sehen** there is/was a lot to be done/nothing to be seen

sein² poss pron his; (Ding, Tier) its; (nach man) one's; **sein Glück versuchen** try one's luck. **s~e(r,s)** poss pron his; (nach man) one's own; **das S~e** od **seine tun** do one's share. **s~erseits** adv for his part. **s~erzeit** adv in those days. **s~etwegen** adv for his sake; (wegen ihm) because of him, on his account. **s~etwillen** adv **um s~etwillen** for his sake. **s~ige** poss pron **der/die/das s~ige** his

sein|lassen† vt sep (NEW) sein lassen, s. sein¹

seins poss pron his; (nach man) one's own

seit conj & prep (+ dat) since; **s~wann?** since when? **s~ einiger Zeit** for some time [past]; **ich wohne s~ zehn Jahren hier** I've lived here for ten years. **s~dem** conj since □ adv since then

Seite f -,-n side; (Buch-) page; **S~an S~** side by side; **zur S~ legen/treten** put/step aside; **jds starke S~** s.o.'s strong point; **auf der einen/anderen S~** (fig) on the one/other hand; **von S~n (s~n)** (+ gen) = **vonseiten**

seitens prep (+ gen) on the part of

Seiten|schiff nt [side] aisle. **S~sprung** m infidelity; **einen S~sprung machen** be unfaithful. **S~stechen** nt -s (Med) stitch. **S~straße** f side-street. **S~streifen** m verge; (Autobahn-) hard shoulder

seither adv since then

seit|lich a side ... □ adv at/on the side; **s~lich von** to one side of □ prep (+ gen) to one side of. **s~wärts** adv on/to one side; (zur Seite) sideways

Sekret nt -[e]s,-e secretion

Sekret|är m -s,-e secretary; (Schrank) bureau. **S~ariat** nt -[e]s,-e secretary's office. **S~ärin** f -,-nen secretary

Sekt m -[e]s [German] sparkling wine

Sekte f -,-n sect

Sektion f /'tsjo:n/ f -,-en section; (Sezierung) autopsy

Sektor m -s,-en /-'to:rən/ sector

Sekundant m -en,-en (Sport) second

sekundär a secondary

Sekunde f -,-n second

selber pron (fam) = **selbst**

selbst pron oneself; **ich/du/er/ sie s~** I myself/you yourself/ he himself/she herself; **wir/ihr/sie s~** we ourselves/you yourselves/they themselves; **ich schneide mein Haar s~** I cut my own hair; **von s~** of one's own accord; (*automatisch*) automatically; **s~ gemacht** home-made □ *adv* even. **S~achtung** *f* self-esteem, self-respect

selbständig *a* = **selbstständig**. **S~keit** *f* = **Selbstständigkeit**

Selbstaufopferung *f* self-sacrifice

Selbstbedienung *f* self-service **S~srestaurant** *nt* self-service restaurant, cafeteria

Selbst|befriedigung *f* masturbation. **S~beherrschung** *f* self-control. **S~bestimmung** *f* self-determination. **s~bewusst** (**s~bewußt**) *a* self-confident. **S~bewusstsein** (**S~bewußtsein**) *nt* self-confidence. **S~bildnis** *nt* self-portrait. **S~erhaltung** *f* self-preservation. **s~gefällig** *a* self-satisfied, smug, *adv* -ly. **s~gemacht** *a* (NEW)= **gemacht**, s. **selbst**. **s~gerecht** *a* self-righteous. **S~gespräch** *nt* soliloquy; **S~gespräche führen** talk to oneself. **s~haftend** *a* self-adhesive. **s~herrlich** *a* autocratic, *adv* -ally. **S~hilfe** *f* self-help. **s~klebend** *a* self-adhesive. **S~kostenpreis** *m* cost price. **S~laut** *m* vowel. **s~los** *a* selfless, *adv* -ly. **S~mitleid** *nt* self-pity. **S~mord** *m* suicide. **S~mörder(in)** *m(f)* suicide. **s~mörderisch** *a* suicidal. **S~porträt** *nt* self-portrait. **s~sicher** *a* self-assured. **S~sicherheit** *f* self-assurance. **s~ständig** *a* independent, *adv* -ly; self-employed. **sich s~ständig machen** set up on one's own. **S~ständigkeit** *f* independence. **S~süchtig** *a* selfish, *adv* -ly. **S~tanken** *nt* self-service (*for petrol*). **s~tätig** *a*

automatic, *adv* -ally. **S~versorgung** *f* self-catering

selbstverständlich *a* natural, *adv* -ly; **etw für s~ halten** take sth for granted; **das ist s~** that goes without saying; **s~!** of course! **S~keit** *f* - matter of course; **das ist eine S~keit** that goes without saying

Selbst|verteidigung *f* self-defence. **S~vertrauen** *nt* self-confidence. **S~verwaltung** *f* self-government. **s~zufrieden** *a* complacent, *adv* -ly

selig *a* blissfully happy; (*Relig*) blessed; (*verstorben*) late. **S~keit** *f* - bliss

Sellerie *m* -s,-s & *f* -, -celeriac; (*Stangen-*) celery

selten *a* rare □ *adv* rarely, seldom; (*besonders*) exceptionally. **S~heit** *f* -,-en rarity

Selterswasser *nt* seltzer [water]

seltsam *a* odd, *adv* -ly, strange, *adv* -ly. **s~erweise** *adv* oddly/strangely enough

Semester *nt* -s,- (*Univ*) semester

Semikolon *nt* -s,-s semicolon

Seminar *nt* -s,-e seminar; (*Institut*) department; (*Priester-*) seminary

Semmel *f* -,-n [bread] roll. **S~brösel** *pl* breadcrumbs

Senat *m* -[e]s,-e senate. **S~or** *m* -s,-en /-'to:rən/ senator

senden†1 *vt* send

sende|n2 *vt* (*reg*) broadcast; (*über Funk*) transmit, send. **S~r** *m* -s,- [broadcasting] station; (*Anlage*) transmitter. **S~reihe** *f* series

Sendung *f* -,-en consignment, shipment; (*Auftrag*) mission; (*Radio, TV*) programme

Senf *m* -s mustard

sengend *a* scorching

senil *a* senile. **S~ität** *f* - senility

Senior *m* -s,-en /-'o:rən/ senior; **S~en** senior citizens. **S~enheim** *nt* old people's home.

S~enteller *m* senior citizen's menu

Senke *f* -,-n dip, hollow

Senkel *m* -s,- [shoe-]lace

senken *vt* lower; bring down ⟨*Fieber, Preise*⟩; bow ⟨*Kopf*⟩; **sich s~** come down, fall ⟨*absinken*⟩ subside; ⟨*abfallen*⟩ slope down

senkrecht *a* vertical, *adv* -ly. **S~e** *f* -n,-n perpendicular

Sensation /-'tsjo:n/ *f* -,-en sensation. **s~ell** *a* sensational, *adv* -ly

Sense *f* -,-n scythe

sensib|el *a* sensitive, *adv* -ly. **S~i-lität** *f* - sensitivity

sentimental *a* sentimental. **S~i-tät** *f* - sentimentality

separat *a* separate, *adv* -ly

September *m* -s,- September

Serenade *f* -,-n serenade

Serie /'ze:rjə/ *f* -,-n series; ⟨*Briefmarken*⟩ set; ⟨*Comm, Tennis*⟩ range.
S~nnummer *f* serial number

seriös *a* respectable, *adv* -bly; ⟨*zuverlässig*⟩ reliable, *adv* -bly; ⟨*ernstgemeint*⟩ serious

Serpentine *f* -,-n winding road; ⟨*Kehre*⟩ hairpin bend

Serum *nt* -s,**Sera** serum

Service[1] /zɛr'vi:s/ *nt* -[s], /-'vi:s[əs]/ dinner/tea service, set

Service[2] /'zø:gvis/ *m & nt* -s /-'vɪs/ ⟨*Comm, Tennis*⟩ service

servier|en *vt/i* ⟨*haben*⟩ serve.
S~erin *f* -,-nen waitress.
S~wagen *m* trolley

Serviette *f* -,-n napkin, serviette

Servus *int* ⟨*Aust*⟩ cheerio; ⟨*Begrüßung*⟩ hallo

Sessel *m* -s,- armchair. **S~bahn** *f*, **S~lift** *m* chair-lift

sesshaft (**seßhaft**) *a* settled; **s~ werden** settle down

Set /zɛt/ *nt & m* -[s],-s set; ⟨*Deckchen*⟩ place-mat

setz|en *vt* put; ⟨*abstellen*⟩ set down; ⟨*hin-*⟩ sit down ⟨*Kind*⟩; move ⟨*Spielstein*⟩; ⟨*pflanzen*⟩ plant; ⟨*schreiben, wetten*⟩ put; **sich s~en** sit down; ⟨*sinken*⟩

settle □ *vi* ⟨*sein*⟩ leap □ *vi* ⟨*haben*⟩
s~en auf (+ *acc*) back. **S~ling** *m* -s,-e seedling

Seuche *f* -,-n epidemic

seufz|en *vi* ⟨*haben*⟩ sigh. **S~er** *m* -s,- sigh

Sex /zɛks/ *m* -[es] sex. **s~istisch** *a* sexist

Sexualität *f* - sexuality. **s~ell** *a* sexual, *adv* -ly

sexy /'zɛksi/ *inv a* sexy

sezieren *vt* dissect

Shampoo /ʃam'pu:/, **Shampoon** /ʃam'po:n/ *nt* -s shampoo

siamesisch *a* Siamese

sich *refl pron* oneself; ⟨*mit er/sie/es*⟩ himself/herself/itself; ⟨*mit sie pl*⟩ themselves; ⟨*mit Sie*⟩ yourself; ⟨*pl*⟩ yourselves; ⟨*einander*⟩ each other; **s~ kennen** know oneself/⟨*einander*⟩ each other; **s~ waschen** have a wash; **s~** ⟨*dat*⟩ **die Zähne putzen/die Haare kämmen** clean one's teeth/comb one's hair; **s~** ⟨*dat*⟩ **das Bein brechen** break a leg; **s~ wundern/schämen** be surprised/ashamed; **s~ gut lesen/verkaufen** read/sell well; **von s~ aus** of one's own accord

Sichel *f* -,-n sickle

sicher *a* safe; ⟨*gesichert*⟩ secure; ⟨*gewiss*⟩ certain; ⟨*zuverlässig*⟩ reliable; sure ⟨*Urteil, Geschmack*⟩; steady ⟨*Hand*⟩; ⟨*selbstbewusst*⟩ self-confident; **sich** ⟨*dat*⟩ **etw** ⟨*gen*⟩ **sein** be sure of sth; **bist du s~?** are you sure? □ *adv* safely; securely; certainly; self-confidently; ⟨*wahrscheinlich*⟩ most probably; **er kommt s~** he is sure to come; **s~!** certainly! **s~gehen†** *vi sep* ⟨*sein*⟩ ⟨*fig*⟩ be sure

Sicherheit *f* - safety; ⟨*Pol, Psych, Comm*⟩ security; ⟨*Gewissheit*⟩ certainty; ⟨*Zuverlässigkeit*⟩ reliability; ⟨*des Urteils, Geschmacks*⟩ surety; ⟨*Selbstbewusstsein*⟩ self-confidence. **S~sgurt** *m* safety-belt; ⟨*Auto*⟩ seat-belt. **s~shalber**

sicherlich / **Sintflut**

adv to be on the safe side. **S~sna-del** *f* safety-pin

sicherlich *adv* certainly; *(wahrscheinlich)* most probably

sicher|n *vt* secure; *(garantieren)* safeguard; *(schützen)* protect; put the safety-catch on *(Pistole)*; **sich** *(dat)* **etw s~** secure sth. **s~stellen** *vt sep* safeguard; *(beschlagnahmen)* seize. **S~ung** *f* -,-en safeguard, protection; *(Gewehr-)* safety-catch; *(Electr)* fuse

Sicht *f* - view; *(S~weite)* visibility; **in S~ kommen** come into view; **auf lange S~** in the long term. **s~bar** *a* visible, *adv* -bly. **s~en** *vt* sight; *(durchsehen)* sift through. **s~lich** *a* obvious, *adv* -ly. **S~vermerk** *m* visa. **S~weite** *f* visibility; **in/außer S~weite** within/out of sight

sickern *vi (sein)* seep

sie *pron (nom) (sg)* she; *(Ding, Tier)* it; *(pl)* they; *(acc) (sg)* her; *(Ding, Tier)* it; *(pl)* them

Sie *pron* you; **gehen/warten Sie!** go/wait!

Sieb *nt* -[e]s,-e sieve; *(Tee-)* strainer. **s~en¹** *vt* sieve, sift

sieben² *inv a*, **S~** *f* -,-en seven. **S~sachen** *fpl (fam)* belongings. **s~te(r,s)** *a* seventh

sieb|te(r,s) *a* seventh. **s~zehn** *inv a* seventeen. **s~zehnte(r,s)** *a* seventeenth. **s~zig** *inv a* seventy. **s~zigste(r,s)** *a* seventieth

siede|n *vt/i (haben)* boil; **s~nd heiß** boiling hot. **S~punkt** *m* boiling point

Siedl|er *m* -s,- settler. **S~ung** *f* -,-en [housing] estate; *(Niederlassung)* settlement

Sieg *m* -[e]s,-e victory

Siegel *nt* -s,- seal. **S~ring** *m* signet-ring

sieg|en *vi (haben)* win. **S~er(in)** *m* -s,- *(f -,-nen)* winner. **s~reich** *a* victorious

siezen *vt* jdn **s~** call s.o. 'Sie'

Signal *nt* -s,-e signal. **s~isieren** *vt* signal

signieren *vt* sign

Silbe *f* -,-n syllable. **S~ntrennung** *f* word-division

Silber *nt* -s silver. **S~hochzeit** *f* silver wedding. **s~n** *a* silver. **S~papier** *nt* silver paper

Silhouette /zi'lyɛtə/ *f* -,-n silhouette

Silizium *nt* -s silicon

Silo *m & nt* -s,-s silo

Silvester *nt* -s New Year's Eve

simpel *a* simple, *adv* -ply; *(einfältig)* simple-minded

Simplex *nt* -,-e simplex

Sims *m & nt* -es,-e ledge; *(Kamin-)* mantelpiece

Simul|ant *m* -en,-en malingerer. **s~ieren** *vt* feign; *(Techn)* simulate □ *vi (haben)* pretend; *(sich krank stellen)* malinger

simultan *a* simultaneous, *adv* -ly

sind *s.* **sein**'; **wir/sie s~** we/they are

Sinfonie *f* -,-n symphony

singen† *vt/i (haben)* sing

Singular *m* -s,-e singular

Singvogel *m* songbird

sinken† *vi (sein)* sink; *(nieder-)* drop; *(niedriger werden)* go down, fall; **den Mut s~ lassen** lose courage

Sinn *m* -[e]s,-e sense; *(Denken)* mind; *(Zweck)* point; **im S~ haben** have in mind; **in gewissem S~e** in a sense; **es hat keinen S~** it is pointless; **nicht bei S~en sein** be out of one's mind. **S~bild** *nt* symbol. **s~en†** *vi (haben)* think; **auf Rache s~en** plot one's revenge

sinnlich *a* sensory; *(sexuell)* sensual; *(Genüsse)* sensuous. **S~keit** *f* - sensuality; sensuousness

sinn|los *a* senseless, *adv* -ly; *(zwecklos)* pointless, *adv* -ly. **s~voll** *a* meaningful; *(vernünftig)* sensible, *adv* -bly

Sintflut *f* flood

Siphon /ˈziːfɒ/ m -s,-s siphon
Sipp|e f -,-n clan. S~**schaft** f clan; (Pack) crowd
Sirene f -,-n siren
Sirup m -s,-e syrup; (schwarzer) treacle
Sitte f -,-n custom; **S~n** manners. **s~nlos** a immoral
sittlich a moral, adv -ly. **S~keit** f -morality. **S~keitsverbrecher** m sex offender
sittsam a well-behaved; (züchtig) demure, adv -ly
Situa|tion /-ˈtsi̯oːn/ f -,-en situation. **s~iert** a gut/schlecht **s~iert** well/badly off
Sitz m -es,-e seat; (Passform) fit
sitzen† vi (haben) sit; (sich befinden) be; (passen) fit; (fam: treffen) hit home; [im Gefängnis] **s~** (fam) be in jail; **s~bleiben** remain seated; (Sch) stay or be kept down; (nicht heiraten) be left on the shelf; **s~bleiben auf** (+ dat) be left with; **jdn s~ lassen** let s.o. sit down; (fam) (Sch) keep s.o. down; (nicht heiraten) jilt s.o.; (im Stich lassen) leave s.o. in the lurch. **s~bleiben†** vi sep (sein) NEW **s~ bleiben**, s. **sitzen**. **s~d** a seated; (Tätigkeit) sedentary. **s~lassen†** vt sep NEW **s~ lassen**, s. **sitzen**
Sitz|gelegenheit f seat. **S~platz** m seat. **S~ung** f -,-en session
Sizilien /-i̯ən/ nt -s Sicily
Skala f -,-len scale; (Reihe) range
Skalpell nt -s,-e scalpel
skalpieren vt scalp
Skandal m -s,-e scandal. **s~ös** a scandalous
skandieren vt scan ⟨Verse⟩; chant ⟨Parolen⟩
Skandinav|ien /-i̯ən/ nt -s Scandinavia. **s~isch** a Scandinavian
Skat m -s skat
Skelett nt -[e]s,-e skeleton
Skep|sis f - scepticism. **s~tisch** a sceptical, adv -ly; (misstrauisch) doubtful, adv -ly

Ski /ʃiː/ m -s,-er ski; **Ski fahren** od **laufen** ski. **S~fahrer(in)**, **S~läufer(in)** m(f) -s,- (f -,-nen) skier. **S~sport** m skiing
Skizz|e f -,-n sketch. **s~enhaft** a sketchy, adv -ily. **s~ieren** vt sketch
Sklav|e m -n,-n slave. **S~erei** f -slavery. **S~in** f -,-nen slave. **s~isch** a slavish, adv -ly
Skorpion m -s,-e scorpion; (Astr) Scorpio
Skrupel m -s,- scruple. **s~los** a unscrupulous
Skulptur f -,-en sculpture
skurril a absurd, adv -ly
Slalom m -s,-s slalom
Slang /slɛŋ/ m -s slang
Slaw|e m -n,-n, **S~in** f -,-nen Slav. **s~isch** a Slav; (Lang) Slavonic
Slip m -s,-s briefs pl
Smaragd m -[e]s,-e emerald
Smoking m -s,-s dinner jacket, (Amer) tuxedo
Snob m -s,-s snob. **S~ismus** m -snobbery **s~istisch** a snobbish
so adv so; (so sehr) so much; (auf diese Weise) like this/that; (solch) such; (fam: sowieso) anyway; (fam: umsonst) free; (fam: ungefähr) about; **nicht:** so **schnell/viel** not so fast/much; **so gut/bald wie** as good/soon as; **so ein Mann** a man like that; **so ein Zufall!** what a coincidence! **so nicht** not like that; **mir ist so, als ob** I feel as if; **so oder so** in any case; **eine Stunde oder so** an hour or so; **so um zehn Mark** (fam) about ten marks; **[es ist] gut** so that's fine; **so, das ist geschafft** there, that's done; **so?** really? **so kommt doch!** come on then! □ conj (also) so; (dann) then; **so gern ich auch käme** as much as I would like to come; **so dass** (daß) = sodass
sobald conj as soon as
Söckchen nt -s,- [ankle] sock
Socke f -,-n sock

Sockel *m* -s,- plinth, pedestal

Socken *m* -s,- sock

Soda *nt* -s soda

sodass *conj* so that

Sodawasser *nt* soda water

Sodbrennen *nt* -s heartburn

soeben *adv* just [now]

Sofa *nt* -s,-s settee, sofa

sofern *adv* provided [that]

sofort *adv* at once, immediately; *(auf der Stelle)* instantly. **s∼ig** *a* immediate

Software /'zɔftvɛː:ɐ/ *f* - software

sogar *adv* even

sogenannt *a* so-called

sogleich *adv* at once

Sohle *f* -,-n sole; *(Tal-)* bottom

Sohn *m* -[e]s,ˉe son

Sojabohne *f* soya bean

solange *conj* as long as

solch *inv pron* such; **s∼ ein(e)** such a; **s∼ einer/eine/eins** one/(*Person*) someone like that; **s∼e(r,s)** *pron* such; **ein s∼er Mann/eine s∼e Frau** a man/ woman like that; **ich habe s∼e Angst** I am so afraid □ *(substantivisch)* **ein s∼er/eine s∼e/ein s∼es** one/(*Person*) someone like that; **s∼e** (*pl*) those; *(Leute)* people like that

Sold *m* -[e]s (*Mil*) pay

Soldat *m* -en,-en soldier

Söldner *m* -s,- mercenary

solidarisch *a* **∼e Handlung** act of solidarity; **sich ∼ erklären** declare one's solidarity

Solidarität *f* - solidarity

solide *a* solid, *adv* -ly; *(haltbar)* sturdy, *adv* -ily; *(sicher)* sound, *adv* -ly; *(anständig)* respectable, *adv* -bly

Solist(in) *m* -en,-en (*f* -,-nen) soloist

Soll *nt* -s (*Comm*) debit; *(Produktions-)* quota

sollen *v aux* **er soll warten** he is to wait; *(möge)* let him wait; **was soll ich machen?** what shall I do? **du sollst nicht lügen** you

shouldn't tell lies; **du sollst nicht töten** (*liter*) thou shalt not kill; **ihr sollt jetzt still sein!** will you be quiet now! **du solltest dich schämen** you ought to *or* should be ashamed of yourself; **es hat nicht sein s∼** it was not to be; **ich hätte es nicht tun s∼** I ought not to *or* should not have done it; **er soll sehr nett/reich sein** he is supposed to be very nice/rich; **sollte es regnen, so ...** if it should rain then ...; **das soll man nicht [tun]** you're not supposed to do that]; **soll ich [mal versuchen]?** shall I [try]? **soll er doch!** let him! **was soll's?** so what!

Solo *nt* -s,-los & -li solo. **s∼** *adv* solo

somit *adv* therefore, so

Sommer *m* -s,- summer. **S∼ferien** *pl* summer holidays. **s∼lich** *a* summery; *(Sommer-)* summer ... □ *adv* **s∼lich warm** as warm as summer. **S∼schlussverkauf** (**S∼schlußverkauf**) *m* summer sale. **S∼sprossen** *fpl* freckles. **s∼sprossig** *a* freckled

Sonate *f* -,-n sonata

Sonde *f* -,-n probe

Sonder|angebot *nt* special offer. **s∼bar** *a* odd, *adv* -ly. **S∼fahrt** *f* special excursion. **S∼fall** *m* special case. **s∼gleichen** *adv* **eine Gemeinheit/Grausamkeit s∼gleichen** unparalleled meanness/cruelty. **s∼lich** *a* particular, *adv* -ly; *(sonderbar)* odd, *adv* -ly. **S∼ling** *m* -s,-e crank. **S∼marke** *f* special stamp

sondern *conj* but; **nicht nur ... s∼ auch** not only ... but also

Sonder|preis *m* special price. **S∼schule** *f* special school. **S∼zug** *m* special train

sondieren *vt* sound out

Sonett *nt* -[e]s,-e sonnet

Sonnabend *m* -s,-e Saturday. **s∼s** *adv* on Saturdays

Sonne f ~,-n sun. **s~n (sich)** vr sun oneself; (fig) bask (**in** + dat **in**)

Sonnen|aufgang m sunrise. **s~baden** vi (haben) sunbathe. **S~bank** f sun-bed. **S~blume** f sunflower. **S~brand** m sunburn. **S~brille** f sun-glasses pl. **S~energie** f solar energy. **S~finsternis** f solar eclipse. **S~milch** f sun-tan lotion. **S~öl** nt sun-tan oil. **S~schein** m sunshine. **S~schirm** m sunshade. **S~stich** m sunstroke. **S~uhr** f sundial. **S~untergang** m sunset. **S~wende** f solstice

sonnig a sunny

Sonntag m -s,-e Sunday. **s~s** adv on Sundays

sonst adv (gewöhnlich) usually; (im Übrigen) apart from that; (andernfalls) otherwise, or [else]; **wer/was/wie/wo s~?** who/what/how/where else? **s~ niemand/nichts** no one/nothing else; **s~ noch jemand/ etwas?** anyone/anything else? **s~ noch Fragen?** any more questions? **s~ jemand** od **wer** someone/(fragend, verneint) anyone else; (irgendjemand) [just] anyone; **s~ wie** some/(fragend, verneint) any other way; **s~ wo** somewhere/(fragend, verneint) anywhere else; (irgendwo) [just] anywhere. **s~ig** a other. **s~je-mand** pron (NEW) **s~ jemand**. **s~** sonst. **s~ wer** pron (NEW) **s~ wer**, s. sonst. **s~ wie** adv (NEW) **s~ wie**, s. sonst. **s~ wo** adv (NEW) **s~ wo**, s. sonst

sooft conj whenever

Sopran m -s,-e soprano

Sorge f ~,-n worry (**um** about); (Fürsorge) care; **in S~ sein** be worried; **sich** (dat) **S~n machen** worry; **keine S~!** don't worry! **s~n** vi (haben) **s~n für** look after, care for; (vorsorgen) provide for; (sich kümmern) see to;

dafür **s~n, dass** see [to it] or make sure that □ or **sich s~n** worry. **s~nfrei** a carefree. **s~nvoll** a worried, adv -ly. **s~recht** nt (Jur) custody

Sorg|falt f -care. **s~fältig** a careful, adv -ly. **s~los** a careless, adv -ly; (unbekümmert) carefree. **s~sam** a careful, adv -ly

Sorte f -,-n kind, sort; (Comm) brand

sort|ieren vt sort [out]; (Comm) grade. **S~iment** nt -[e]s,-e range

sosehr conj however much

Soße f -,-n sauce; (Braten-) gravy; (Salat-) dressing

Souffl|eur /zu'fløːɐ̯/ m -s,-e, **S~euse** /-ˈøːzə/ f -,-n prompter. **s~ieren** vi (haben) prompt

Souvenir /zuvəˈniːɐ̯/ nt -s,-s souvenir

souverän /zuvəˈrɛːn/ a sovereign; (fig: überlegen) expert adv -ly. **S~ität** f -sovereignty

soviel conj however much; **s~ ich weiß** as far as I know □ adv (NEW) **so viel**, s. viel

soweit conj as far as; (insoweit) [in] so far as □ adv (NEW) **so weit**, s. weit

sowenig conj however little □ adv (NEW) **so wenig**, s. wenig

sowie conj as well as; (sobald) as soon as

sowieso adv anyway, in any case

sowjet|isch a Soviet. **S~union** f - Soviet Union

sowohl adv **s~ ... als** od **wie auch** ...... as well as ...; **s~ er als auch seine Frau** both he and his wife

sozial a social, adv -ly; (Einstellung, Beruf) caring. **S~arbeit** f social work. **S~arbeiter(in)** m(f) social worker. **S~demokrat** m social democrat. **S~hilfe** f social security

Sozialis|mus m - socialism. **S~t** m -en,-en socialist. **s~tisch** a socialist

Sozial|versicherung f National Insurance. **S~wohnung** f ≈ council flat

Sozio|loge m -n,-n sociologist. **S~ogie** f -,-co sociology.

Sozius m -,-se (Comm) partner; (Beifahrersitz) pillion

sozusagen adv so to speak

Spachtel m -s,- & f-,-n spatula

Spagat m -[e]s,-e (Aust) string; **S~ machen** do the splits pl

Spaghetti, Spagetti pl spaghetti sg

spähen vi (haben) peer

Spalier nt -s,-e trellis; **S~ stehen** line the route

Spalt m -[e]s,-e crack; (im Vorhang) chink

Spalte| f -,-n crack, crevice; (Gletscher-) crevasse; (Druck-) column; (Orangen-) segment. **s~en**† vt split; sich **s~en** split. **S~ung** f -,-en splitting; (Kluft) split; (Phys) fission

Span m -[e]s,-e [wood] chip; (Hobel-) shaving

Spange f -,-n clasp; (Haar-) slide; (Zahn-) brace; (Arm-) bangle

Span|ien /-jən/ nt -s Spain. **S~ier** m -s,-, **S~ierin** f -,-nen Spaniard. **s~isch** a Spanish. **S~isch** nt -[s] (Lang) Spanish

Spann m -[e]s instep

Spanne f -,-n span; (Zeit-) space; (Comm) margin

spann|en vt stretch; put up (Leine); (straffen) tighten; (an-) harness (an + acc to); den Hahn **s~en** cock the gun; zu **s~en** tighten □ vi (haben) be too tight. **s~end** a exciting. **S~er** m -s,- (fam) Peeping Tom. **S~ung** f -,-en tension; (Erwartung) suspense; (Electr) voltage

Spar|buch nt savings book. **S~büchse** f money-box. **s~en** vt/i (haben) save; (sparsam sein) economize (**mit/an** + dat on); sich (dat) **die Mühe s~en** save oneself the trouble. **S~er** m -s,- saver

Spargel m -s,- asparagus

Spar|kasse f savings bank. **S~konto** nt deposit account

spärlich a sparse, adv -ly; (dürftig) meagre; (knapp) scanty, adv -ily

sparsam a economical, adv -ly; (Person) thrifty. **S~keit** f - economy; thrift

Sparschwein nt piggy bank

spartanisch a Spartan

Sparte f -,-n branch; (Zeitungs-) section; (Rubrik) column

Spaß m -es,-e fun; (Scherz) joke; **im/aus/zum S~** for fun; **S~ machen** be fun; (Person-) be joking; es macht mir keinen **S~** I don't enjoy it; viel **S~!** have a good time! **s~en** vi (haben) joke. **s~ig** a amusing, funny. **S~vogel** m joker

Spast|iker m -s,- spastic. **s~isch** a spastic

spät a & adv late; **wie s~ ist es?** what time is it? zu **s~** too late; zu **s~ kommen** be late. **s~abends** adv late at night

Spatel m -s,- & f-,-n spatula

Spaten m -s,- spade

später a later; (zukünftig) future □ adv later

spätestens adv at the latest

Spatz m -en,-en sparrow

Spätzle pl (Culin) noodles

spazieren vi (sein) stroll; **s~ gehen** go for a walk. **s~gehen**† vi sep (sein) [NEW]→ **s~ gehen**, s. spazieren

Spazier|gang m walk; einen **S~gang machen** go for a walk. **S~gänger(in)** m -s,- (f -,-nen) walker. **S~stock** m walking-stick

Specht m -[e]s,-e woodpecker

Speck m -s bacon; (fam: Fettpolster) fat. **s~ig** a greasy

Spedi|teur /ʃpedi'tøːɐ̯/ m -s,-e haulage/(für Umzüge) removals contractor. **S~tion** f -/-'tsjoːn/ f

-,-en carriage, haulage; (*Firma*) haulage/(*für Umzüge*) removals firm

Speer m -[e]s,-e spear; (*Sport*) javelin

Speiche f -,-n spoke

Speichel m -s saliva

Speicher m -s,- warehouse; (*dial: Dachboden*) attic; (*Computer*) memory. s∼n vt store

speien† vt spit; (*erbrechen*) vomit

Speise f -,-n food; (*Gericht*) dish; (*Pudding*) blancmange. **S∼eis** ntice-cream. **S∼kammer** f larder. **S∼karte** f menu. s∼n vi (*haben*) eat; **zu Abend** s∼n have dinner □ vt feed. **S∼röhre** f oesophagus. **S∼saal** m dining-room. **S∼wagen** m dining-car

Spektakel m -s (*fam*) noise

spektakulär a spectacular

Spektrum nt -s,-tra spectrum

Spekulant m -en,-en speculator. **S∼ation** /-'tsjo:n/ f -,-en speculation. s∼**ieren** vi (*haben*) speculate; s∼**ieren auf** (+ *acc*) (*fam*) hope to get

Spelze f -,-n husk

spendabel a generous

Spende f -,-n donation. s∼n vt donate; give (*Blut, Schatten*); Beifall s∼n applaud. **S∼r** m -s,- donor; (*Behälter*) dispenser

spendieren vt pay for; **jdm etw/ ein Bier** s∼ treat s.o. to sth/stand s.o. a beer

Spengler m -s,- (*SGer*) plumber

Sperling m -s,-e sparrow

Sperre f -,-n barrier; (*Verbot*) ban; (*Comm*) embargo. s∼n vt close; (*ver-*) block; (*verbieten*) ban; cut off (*Strom, Telefon*); stop (*Scheck, Kredit*); s∼n in (+ *acc*) put in (*Gefängnis, Käfig*); **sich** s∼n balk (**gegen** at); **gesperrt gedruckt** (*Typ*) spaced

Sperr|holz nt plywood. s∼**ig** a bulky. **S∼müll** m bulky refuse. **S∼stunde** f closing time

Spesen pl expenses

spezial|isieren (sich) vr specialize (**auf** + *acc* in). **S∼ist** m -en,-en specialist. **S∼ität** f -,-en speciality

speziell a special, adv -ly

spezifisch a specific, adv -ally

Sphäre /'sfɛːrə/ f -,-n sphere

spicken vt (*Culin*) lard; **gespickt mit** (fig) full of □ vi (*haben*) (*fam*) crib (**bei** from)

Spiegel m -s,- mirror; (*Wasser-, Alkohol-*) level. **S∼bild** nt reflection. **S∼ei** nt fried egg. s∼n vt reflect; **sich** s∼n be reflected □ vi (*haben*) reflect [the light]; (*glänzen*) gleam. **S∼ung** f -,-en reflection

Spiel nt -[e]s,-e game; (*Spielen*) playing; (*Glücks-*) gambling; (*Schau-*) play; (*Satz*) set; **ein** S∼ Karten a pack/(*Amer*) deck of cards; **auf dem** S∼ **stehen** be at stake; **aufs** S∼ **setzen** risk. **S∼art** f variety. **S∼automat** m fruit machine. **S∼bank** f casino. **S∼dose** f musical box. s∼**en** vt/i (*haben*) play; (*im Glücksspiel*) gamble; (*vortäuschen*) act; (*Roman:*) be set (**in** + *dat* in); s∼**en mit** (fig) toy with. s∼**end** a (*mühelos*) effortless, adv -ly

Spieler|(in) m -s,- (f -,-nen) player; (*Glücks-*) gambler. **S∼ei** f -,-en amusement; (*Kleinigkeit*) trifle

Spiel|feld nt field, pitch. **S∼gefährte** m, **S∼gefährtin** f playmate. **S∼karte** f playing-card. **S∼marke** f chip. **S∼plan** m programme. **S∼platz** m playground. **S∼raum** m (fig) scope; (*Techn*) clearance. **S∼regeln** fpl rules [of the game]. **S∼sachen** fpl toys. **S∼verderber** m -s,- spoilsport. **S∼waren** fpl toys. **S∼warengeschäft** nt toyshop. **S∼zeug** nt toy; (*S∼sachen*) toys pl

Spieß m -es,-e spear; (*Brat-*) spit; (*für Schaschlik*) skewer; (*Fleisch-*) kebab; **den** S∼ **umkehren** turn the tables on s.o.

S~bürger *m* [petit] bourgeois. **S~bürgerlich** *a* bourgeois. **s~en** *vt* **etw auf etw** (*acc*) **s~en** spear sth with sth. **S~er** *m* -s,- [petit] bourgeois. **s~ig** *a* bourgeois. **S~ruten** *fpl* **S~ruten laufen** run the gauntlet

Spike[s]reifen /ˈʃpaɪk[s]-/ *m* studded tyre

Spinat *m* -s spinach

Spind *m* & *nt* -[e]s,-e locker

Spindel *f* -,-n spindle

Spinne *f* -,-n spider

spinn|en *vt/i* (*haben*) spin; **er spinnt** (*fam*) he's crazy. **S~ennetz** *nt* spider's web. **S~[en]gewebe** *nt*, **S~webe** *f* -,-n cobweb

Spion *m* -s,-e spy

Spionage /ʃpioˈnaːʒə/ *f* - espionage, spying; **S~ treiben** spy. **S~abwehr** *f* counter-espionage

spionieren *vi* (*haben*) spy

Spionin *f* -,-nen [woman] spy

Spiral|e *f* -,-n spiral. **s~ig** *a* spiral

Spiritis|mus *m* - spiritualism. **s~tisch** *a* spiritualist

Spirituosen *pl* spirits

Spiritus *m* - alcohol; (*Brenn-*) methylated spirits *pl.* **S~kocher** *m* spirit stove

Spital *nt* -s,ˈer (*Aust*) hospital

spitz *a* pointed; (*scharf*) sharp; (*schrill*) shrill; (*Winkel*) acute; **s~e Bemerkung** dig. **S~bube** *m* scoundrel; (*Schlingel*) rascal. **s~bübisch** *a* mischievous, *adv* -ly

Spitze *f* -,-n point; (*oberer Teil*) top; (*vorderer Teil*) front; (*Pfeil-, Finger-, Nasen-*) tip; (*Schuh-, Strumpf-*) toe; (*Zigarren-, Zigaretten-*) holder; (*Höchstleistung*) maximum; (*Tex*) lace; (*fam: Anspielung*) dig; **an der S~ liegen** be in the lead

Spitzel *m* -s,- informer

spitzen *vt* sharpen; purse (*Lippen*); prick up (*Ohren*); **sich**

s~ auf (+ *acc*) (*fam*) look forward to. **S~geschwindigkeit** *f* top speed

spitz|findig *a* over-subtle. **S~hacke** *f* pickaxe. **S~name** *m* nickname

Spleen /ʃpliːn/ *m* -s,-e obsession; **einen S~ haben** be crazy. **s~ig** *a* eccentric

Splitter *m* -s,- splinter. **s~n** *vi* (*sein*) shatter. **s~[faser]nackt** *a* (*fam*) stark naked

sponsern *vt* sponsor

spontan *a* spontaneous, *adv* -ly

sporadisch *a* sporadic, *adv* -ally

Spore *f* -,-n (*Biol*) spore

Sporn *m* -[e]s, **Sporen** spur; **einem Pferd die Sporen geben** spur a horse

Sport *m* -[e]s sport; (*Hobby*) hobby. **S~art** *f* sport. **S~fest** *nt* sports day. **S~ler** *m* -s,- sportsman. **S~lerin** *f* -,-nen sportswoman. **s~lich** *a* sports ...; (*fair*) sporting, *adv* -ly; (*flott, schlank*) sporty. **S~platz** *m* sports ground. **S~verein** *m* sports club. **S~wagen** *m* sports car; (*Kinder-*) push-chair, (*Amer*) stroller

Spott *m* -[e]s mockery. **s~billig** *a* & *adv* dirt cheap

spötteln *vi* (*haben*) mock; **s~ über** (+ *acc*) poke fun at

spotten *vi* (*haben*) mock; **s~ über** (+ *acc*) make fun of; (*höhnend*) ridicule

spöttisch *a* mocking, *adv* -ly

Sprach|e *f* -,-n language; (*Sprechfähigkeit*) speech; **zur S~e bringen** bring up. **S~fehler** *m* speech defect. **S~labor** *nt* language laboratory. **s~lich** *a* linguistic, *adv* -ally. **s~los** *a* speechless

Spray /ʃpreː/ *nt* & *m* -s,-s spray. **S~dose** *f* aerosol [can]

Sprech|anlage *f* intercom. **S~chor** *m* chorus; **im S~chor rufen** chant

sprechen† vi (haben) speak/(sich unterhalten) talk (**über** + acc/**von** about/of); **Deutsch/Englisch s~** speak German/English □ vt speak; (sagen, aufsagen) say; pronounce (Urteil); **schuldig s~** find guilty; **jdn s~** speak to s.o.; **Herr X ist nicht zu s~** Mr X is not available

Sprecher(in) m -s,- (f -,-nen) speaker; (Radio, TV) announcer; (Wortführer) spokesman, f spokeswoman

Sprechstunde f consulting hours pl; (Med) surgery. **S~nhilfe** f (Med) receptionist

Sprechzimmer nt consulting room

spreizen vt spread

Sprengel m -s,- parish

sprengen vt blow up; blast (Felsen); (fig) burst; (begießen) water; (mit Sprenger) sprinkle; dampen (Wäsche). **S~er** m -s,- sprinkler. **S~kopf** m warhead. **S~körper** m explosive device. **S~stoff** m explosive

Spreu f -chaff

Sprich|wort nt (pl -wörter) proverb. **s~wörtlich** a proverbial

sprießen† vi (sein) sprout

Springbrunnen m fountain

springen† vi (sein) jump; (Schwimmsport) dive; (Ball·) bounce; (spritzen) spurt; (zer·) break; (rissig werden) crack; (SGer· laufen) run. **S~er** m -s,- jumper; (Kunst·) diver; (Schach) knight. **S~reiten** nt show-jumping. **S~seil** nt skipping-rope

Sprint m -s,-s sprint

Sprit m -s (fam) petrol

Spritze f -,-n syringe; (Injektion) injection; (Feuer·) hose. **s~n** vt spray; (be·, ver·) splash; (Culin) pipe; (Fett·) spit □ vi (sein) splash; (hervor·) spurt; (fam: laufen) dash. **S~er** m -s,- splash; (Schuss) dash. **s~ig** a lively;

(Wein, Komödie) sparkling. **S~tour** f (fam) spin

spröde a brittle; (trocken) dry; (rissig) chapped; (Stimme) harsh; (abweisend) aloof

Spross m -es,-e (Spröß m -sses, -sse) shoot

Sprosse f -,-n rung. **S~nkohl** m (Aust) Brussels sprouts pl

Sprössling (Sprößling) m -s,-e (fam) offspring

Sprotte f -,-n sprat

Spruch m -[e]s,¨e saying; (Denk·) motto; (Zitat) quotation. **S~band** nt (pl -bänder) banner

Sprudel m -s,- sparkling mineral water. **s~n** vi (haben/sein) bubble

Sprüh|dose f aerosol [can]. **s~en** vt spray □ vi (sein) (Funken:) fly; (fig) sparkle. **S~regen** m fine drizzle

Sprung m -[e]s,¨e jump, leap; (Schwimmsport) dive; (fam: Katzen·) stone's throw; (Riss) crack; **auf einen S~** (fam) for a moment. **S~brett** nt springboard. **s~haft** a erratic; (plötzlich) sudden, adv -ly. **S~schanze** f ski-jump. **S~seil** nt skipping-rope

Spucke f -spit. **s~n** vt/i (haben) spit; (sich übergeben) be sick

Spuk m -[e]s,-e [ghostly] apparition. **s~en** vi (haben) (Geist:) walk; **in diesem Haus s~t es** this house is haunted

Spülbecken nt sink

Spule f -,-n spool

Spüle f -,-n sink unit; (Becken) sink

spulen vt spool

spül|en vt rinse; (schwemmen) wash; **Geschirr s~en** wash up □ vi (haben) flush [the toilet]. **S~kasten** m cistern. **S~mittel** nt washing-up liquid. **S~tuch** nt dishcloth

Spur f -,-en track; (Fahr·) lane; (Fährte) trail; (Anzeichen) trace·

(Hinweis) lead; **keine** od **nicht die S~** (fam) not in the least

spürbar a a noticeable, adv -bly

spuren vi (haben) (fam) toe the line

spüren vt feel; (seelisch) sense. **S~hund** m tracker dog

spurlos adv without trace

spurten vi (sein) put on a spurt; (fam: laufen) sprint

sputen (sich) vr hurry

Staat m -[e]s,-en state; (Land) country; (Putz) finery. **s~lich** a state ... □ adv by the state

Staatsangehörig|e(r) m/f national. **S~keit** f - nationality

Staats|anwalt m state prosecutor. **S~beamte(r)** m civil servant. **S~besuch** m state visit. **S~bürger(in)** m(f) national. **S~mann** m (pl -männer) statesman. **S~streich** m coup

Stab m -[e]s,-e rod; (Gitter-) bar (Sport) baton; (Mitarbeiter-) team; (Mil) staff

Stäbchen ntpl chopsticks

Stabhochsprung m pole-vault

stabil a stable; (gesund) robust; (solide) sturdy, adv -ily. **s~isieren** vt stabilize; **sich s~isieren** stabilize. **S~ität** f - stability

Stachel m -s,- spine; (Gift-) sting; (Spitze) spike. **S~beere** f gooseberry. **S~draht** m barbed wire. **s~ig** a prickly. **S~schwein** nt porcupine

Stadion nt -s,-ien stadium

Stadium nt -s,-ien stage

Stadt f -,-e town; (Groß-) city

Städt|chen nt -s,- small town. **s~isch** a urban; (kommunal) municipal

Stadt|mauer f city wall. **S~mitte** f town centre. **S~plan** m street map. **S~teil** m district. **S~zentrum** nt town centre

Staffel f -,-n team; (S~lauf) relay; (Mil) squadron

Staffelei f -,-en easel

Staffel|lauf m relay race. **s~n** vt stagger; (abstufen) grade

Stagnation /-'tsjo:n/ f - stagnation. **s~ieren** vi (haben) stagnate

Stahl m -s steel. **S~beton** m reinforced concrete

Stall m -[e]s,-e stable; (Kuh-) shed; (Schweine-) sty; (Hühner-) coop; (Kaninchen-) hutch

Stamm m -[e]s,-e trunk; (Sippe) tribe; (Kern) core; (Wort-) stem. **S~baum** m family tree; (eines Tieres) pedigree

stammeln vt/i (haben) stammer

stammen vi (haben) come/(zeitlich) date (von/aus from); **das Zitat stammt von Goethe** the quotation is from Goethe

Stamm|gast m regular. **S~halter** m son and heir

Stamm|kundschaft f regulars pl. **S~lokal** nt favourite pub. **S~tisch** m table reserved for the regulars; (Treffen) meeting of the regulars

stampf|en vi (haben) stamp; (Maschine:) pound; **mit den Füßen s~en** stamp one's feet □ vi (sein) tramp □ vt pound; mash (Kartoffeln). **S~kartoffeln** fpl mashed potatoes

Stand m -[e]s,-e standing position; (Zustand) state; (Spiel-) score; (Höhe) level; (gesellschaftlich) class; (Verkaufs-) stall; (Messe-) stand; (Taxi-) rank; **auf den neuesten S~ bringen** update; **in S~ halten/setzen** = instand halten/setzen, **s. instand**; **im/außer S~e sein** = imstande/außerstande sein, **s. imstande, außerstande**; **zu S~e bringen/kommen** = zustande bringen/kommen, **s. zustande**

Standard m -s,-s standard. **s~isieren** vt standardize

Standarte f -,-n standard

Standbild nt statue

Ständchen nt -s,- serenade; **jdm ein S~ bringen** serenade s.o.

Ständer m -s,- stand; (Geschirr-, Platten-) rack; (Kerzen-) holder

Standes|amt nt registry office. **S~beamte(r)** m registrar. **S~unterschied** m class distinction

stand|haft a steadfast, adv -ly. **s~halten†** vi sep (haben) stand firm; **etw** (dat) **s~halten** stand up to sth

ständig a constant, adv -ly; (fest) permanent, adv -ly

Stand|licht nt sidelights pl. **S~ort** m position; (Geschäft-) location; (Mil) garrison. **S~pauke** f (fam) dressing-down. **S~punkt** m point of view. **S~spur** f hard shoulder. **S~uhr** f grandfather clock

Stange f -,-n bar; (Holz-) pole; (Gardinen-) rail; (Hühner-) perch; (Zimt-) stick; **von der S~** (fam) off the peg

Stängel m -s,- stalk, stem

Stangen|bohne f runner bean. **S~brot** nt French bread

Stanniol nt -s tin foil. **S~papier** nt silver paper

stanzen vt stamp; (aus-) stamp out; punch (Loch)

Stapel m -s,- stack, pile; **vom S~ laufen** be launched. **S~lauf** m launch[ing]. **s~n** vt stack or pile up; **sich s~n** pile up

stapfen vi (sein) tramp, trudge

Star[1] m -[e]s,-e starling

Star[2] m -[e]s (Med) (grauer) **S~** cataract; **grüner S~** glaucoma

Star[3] m -s,-s (Theat, Sport) star

stark a (stärker, stärkst) strong; (Motor) powerful; (Verkehr, Regen) heavy; (Hitze, Kälte) severe; (groß) big; (schlimm) bad; (dick) thick; (korpulent) stout □ adv strongly; heavily; badly; (sehr) very much

Stärke f -,-n (s. stark) strength; power; thickness; stoutness; (Größe) size; (Mais-, Wäsche-)

starch. **S~mehl** nt cornflour. **s~n** vt strengthen; starch (Wäsche); **sich s~n** fortify oneself. **S~ung** f -,-en strengthening; (Erfrischung) refreshment

starr a rigid, adv -ly; (steif) stiff, adv -ly; (Blick) fixed; (unbeugsam) inflexible, adv -bly

starren vi (haben) stare; **vor Schmutz s~** be filthy

starr|köpfig a stubborn. **S~sinn** m obstinacy. **s~sinnig** a obstinate, adv -ly

Start m -s,-s start; (Aviat) take-off. **S~bahn** f runway. **s~en** vi (sein) start; (Aviat) take off; (aufbrechen) set off; (teilnehmen) compete □ vt start; (fig) launch

Station /-'tsjo:n/ f -,-en station; (Haltestelle) stop; (Abschnitt) stage; (Med) ward; **S~ machen** break one's journey; **bei freier S~** all found. **s~är** adv as an in-patient. **s~ieren** vt station

statisch a static

Statist(in) m -en,-en (f -,-nen) (Theat) extra

Statistik f -,-en statistics sg; (Aufstellung) statistics pl. **s~sch** a statistical, adv -ly

Stativ nt -s,-e (Phot) tripod

statt prep (+ gen) instead of; **an seiner s~** in his place; **an Kindes s~ annehmen** adopt; **s~ dessen** NEW **s~dessen** □ conj **s~ etw zu tun** instead of doing sth. **s~dessen** adv instead

Stätte f -,-n place

statt|finden† vi sep (haben) take place. **s~haft** a permitted

stattlich a imposing; (beträchtlich) considerable

Statue /'ʃta:tuə/ f -,-n statue

Statur f - build, stature

Status m - status. **S~symbol** nt status symbol

Statut nt -[e]s,-en statute

Stau m -[e]s,-s congestion; (Auto) [traffic] jam; (Rück-) tailback

Staub m -[e]s dust; S~ wischen dust; S~ saugen vacuum, hoover

Staubecken nt reservoir

staub|en vi (haben) raise dust; **es s~t** it's dusty. **s~ig** a dusty. **s~saugen** vt/i (haben) vacuum, hoover. **S~sauger** m vacuum cleaner, Hoover (P). **S~tuch** nt duster

Staudamm m dam

Staude f -,-n shrub

stauen vt dam up; **sich s~** accumulate; ⟨Autos:⟩ form a tailback

staunen vi (haben) be amazed or astonished. **S~** nt -s amazement, astonishment

Stau|see m reservoir. **S~ung** f -,-en congestion; ⟨Auto⟩ [traffic] jam

Steak /ʃteːk, steːk/ nt -s,-s steak

stechen† vt stick (in + acc in); ⟨verletzen⟩ prick; ⟨mit Messer⟩ stab; ⟨Insekt:⟩ sting; ⟨Mücke:⟩ bite; ⟨gravieren⟩ engrave □ vi (haben) prick; ⟨Insekt:⟩ sting; ⟨Mücke:⟩ bite; ⟨mit Stechuhr⟩ clock in/out; **in See s~** put to sea. **s~d** a stabbing; ⟨Geruch⟩ pungent

Stech|ginster m gorse. **S~kahn** m punt. **S~mücke** f mosquito. **S~palme** f holly. **S~uhr** f time clock

Steck|brief m 'wanted' poster. **S~dose** f socket. **s~en** vt put; ⟨mit Nadel, Reißzwecke⟩ pin; ⟨pflanzen⟩ plant □ vi (haben) be ⟨fest:⟩ be stuck; **s~ bleiben** get stuck; **den Schlüssel s~ lassen** leave the key in the lock; **hinter etw** ⟨dat⟩ **s~en** ⟨fig⟩ be behind sth

Stecken m -s,- ⟨SGer⟩ stick **stecken|bleiben†**   vi (sein) NEW **s~ bleiben**, s. **stecken**. **s~lassen†** vt sep NEW **s~ lassen**, s. **stecken**. **S~pferd** nt hobby-horse

Steck|er m -s,- ⟨Electr⟩ plug. **S~ling** m -s,-e cutting. **S~nadel** f pin. **S~rübe** f swede

Steg m -[e]s,-e foot-bridge; ⟨Boots-⟩ landing-stage; ⟨Brillen-⟩ bridge. **S~reif** m aus dem **S~reif** extempore

stehen† vi (haben) stand; ⟨sich befinden⟩ be; ⟨still-⟩ be stationary; ⟨Maschine, Uhr:⟩ have stopped; **s~ bleiben** remain standing; ⟨Gebäude:⟩ be left standing; ⟨anhalten⟩ stop; ⟨Motor:⟩ stall; ⟨Zeit:⟩ stand still; **s~ lassen** leave [standing]; **sich** ⟨dat⟩ **einen Bart s~ lassen** grow a beard; **vor dem Ruin s~** face ruin; **zu jdm/etw s~** ⟨fig⟩ stand by s.o./sth; **gut s~** ⟨Getreide, Aktien:⟩ be doing well; ⟨Chancen:⟩ be good; **jdm [gut] s~** suit s.o.; **sich gut s~** be on good terms; **es steht 3 zu 1** the score is 3–1; **es steht schlecht um ihn** he is in a bad way. **S~** nt -s standing; **zum S~ bringen/kommen** bring/come to a standstill. **s~bleiben†** vi sep (sein) NEW **s~ bleiben**, s. **stehen**. **s~d** a standing; ⟨sich nicht bewegend⟩ stationary; ⟨Gewässer⟩ stagnant. **s~lassen†** vt sep NEW **s~ lassen**, s. **stehen**

Steh|lampe f standard lamp. **S~leiter** f step-ladder

stehlen† vt/i (haben) steal; **sich s~** steal, creep

Steh|platz m standing place. **S~vermögen** nt stamina, staying-power

steif a stiff, adv -ly. **S~heit** f - stiffness

Steig|bügel m stirrup. **S~eisen** nt crampon

steigen† vi (sein) climb; ⟨hochgehen⟩ rise, go up; ⟨Schulden, Spannung:⟩ mount; **s~ auf** (+ acc) climb on [to] ⟨Stuhl⟩; climb ⟨Berg, Leiter⟩; get on ⟨Pferd, Fahrrad⟩; **s~ in** (+ acc) climb into; get in ⟨Auto⟩; get on ⟨Bus, Zug⟩; **s~ aus** climb out of; get out

of (*Bett, Auto*); get off (*Bus, Zug*);
einen Drachen s~ lassen fly a
kite; **s~de Preise** rising prices
steiger|n vt increase; **sich s~**
increase; (*sich verbessern*) improve. **S~ung** f -,-en increase;
improvement; (*Gram*) comparison
Steigung f -,-en gradient; (*Hang*)
slope
steil a steep, adv -ly. **S~küste** f
cliffs pl
Stein m -[e]s,-e stone; (*Ziegel-*)
brick; (*Spiel-*) piece. **s~alt** a
ancient. **S~bock** m ibex; (*Astr*)
Capricorn. **S~bruch** m quarry.
S~garten m rockery. **S~gut** nt
earthenware. **s~hart** a rockhard. **s~ig** a stony. **s~igen** vt
stone. **S~kohle** f [hard] coal.
s~reich a (*fam*) very rich.
S~schlag m rock fall
Stelle f -,-n place; (*Fleck*) spot;
(*Abschnitt*) passage; (*Stellung*)
job, post; (*Büro*) office; (*Behörde*)
authority; **kahle S~** bare patch;
auf der S~ immediately; **an
deiner S~** in your place
stellen vt put; (*aufrecht*) stand; set
(*Wecker, Aufgabe*); ask (*Frage*);
make (*Antrag, Forderung,
Diagnose*); zur Verfügung s~
provide; **lauter/leiser s~** turn
up/down; **kalt/warm s~** chill/
keep hot; **sich s~** [go and] stand;
give oneself up (*der Polizei* to
the police); **sich tot/schlafend
s~** pretend to be dead/asleep;
gut gestellt sein be well off
Stellen|anzeige f job advertisement. **S~vermittlung** f employment agency. **s~weise** adv in
places
Stellung f -,-en position; (*Arbeit*)
job; **S~ nehmen** make a statement (**zu** on). **s~slos** a jobless.
S~suche f job-hunting
stellvertret|end a deputy ...
☐ adv as a deputy; **s~end für jdn**
on s.o.'s behalf. **S~er** m deputy
Stellwerk nt signal-box

Stelzen fpl stilts. **S~** vi (*sein*) stalk
stemmen vt press; lift (*Gewicht*);
sich s~ gegen brace oneself
against
Stempel m -s,- stamp; (*Post-*) postmark; (*Präge-*) die; (*Feingehalts-*)
hallmark. **s~n** vt stamp;
hallmark (*Silber*); cancel (*Marke*)
Stengel m -s,- (NEW) **Stängel**
Steno f - (*fam*) shorthand
Steno|gramm nt -[e]s,-e shorthand text. **S~graphie** f -,-n shorthand. **S~grafie** f - shorthand. **s~graphieren,
s~grafieren** vt take down in
shorthand ☐ vi (*haben*) do shorthand. **S~typistin** f -,-nen shorthand typist
Steppdecke f quilt
Steppe f -,-n steppe
Stepptanz (Steptanz) m tapdance
sterben vi (*sein*) die (**an** + *dat*
of); **im S~ liegen** be dying
sterblich a mortal. **S~e(r)** m/f
mortal. **S~keit** f - mortality
stereo adv in stereo. **S~anlage** f
stereo [system]
stereotyp a stereotyped
steril a sterile. **s~isieren** vt sterilize. **s~ität** f - sterility
Stern m -[e]s,-e star. **S~bild** nt
constellation. **S~chen** nt -s,- asterisk. **S~kunde** f astronomy.
S~schnuppe f -,-n shooting star.
S~warte f -,-n observatory
stetig a steady, adv -ily
stets adv always
Steuer[1] nt -s,- steering-wheel;
(*Naut*) helm; **am S~** at the wheel
Steuer[2] f -,-n tax
Steuer|bord nt -[e]s starboard
[side]. **S~erklärung** f tax return. **s~frei** a & adv tax-free.
S~mann m (pl -leute) helmsman; (*beim Rudern*) cox. **s~n** vt
steer; (*Aviat*) pilot; (*Techn*) control ☐ vi (*haben*) be at the wheel/
(*Naut*) helm ☐ vi (*sein*) head (**nach**
for). **s~pflichtig** a taxable.
S~rad nt steering-wheel.

S~ruder nt helm. S~ung f ~-
steering; (Techn) controls pl.
S~zahler m -s,- taxpayer

Stewardess /'stju:ɛdɛs/ f ~,-en
(Stewardeß f ~,-ssen) air hostess, stewardess

Stich m -[e]s,-e prick; (Messer-)
stab; (S~wunde) stab wound;
(Bienen-) sting; (Mücken-) bite;
(Schmerz) stabbing pain; (Näh-)
stitch; (Kupfer-) engraving; (Kartenspiel) trick; S~ ins Rötliche
tinge of red; jdn im S~ lassen
leave s.o. in the lurch; (Gedächtnis:) fail s.o. S~eln vi
(haben) make snide remarks

Stich|flamme f jet of flame.
s~haltig a valid. S~probe f
spot check. S~wort nt (pl
-wörter) headword; (pl -worte)
(Theat) cue; S~worte notes

stick|en vt/i (haben) embroider.
S~erei f - embroidery

stickig a stuffy

Stickstoff m nitrogen

Stief|bruder m stepbrother

Stiefel m -s,- boot

Stief|kind nt stepchild.
S~mutter f stepmother.
S~mütterchen nt -s,- pansy.
S~schwester f stepsister.
S~sohn m stepson. S~tochter f
stepdaughter. S~vater m step-
father

Stiege f ~,-n stairs pl

Stiel m -[e]s,-e handle; (Blumen-,
Gläser-) stem; (Blatt-) stalk

Stier m -[e]s,-e bull; (Astr) Taurus

stieren vi (haben) stare

Stier|kampf m bullfight

Stift¹ m -[e]s,-e pin; (Nagel) tack;
(Blei-) pencil; (Farb-) crayon

Stift² nt -[e]s,-e [endowed] foundation. s~en vt endow; (spenden)
donate; create (Unheil, Verwirrung); bring about (Frieden).
S~er m -s,- founder; (Spender)
donor. S~ung f ~,-en foundation;
(Spende) donation

Stigma nt -s (fig) stigma

Stil m -[e]s,-e style; **in großem
S~** in style. s~isieren vt stylize.
s~istisch a stylistic, adv -ally

still a quiet, adv -ly; (reglos, ohne
Kohlensäure) still; (heimlich) secret, adv -ly; der S~e Ozean the
Pacific; im S~en (s~en) secretly; (bei sich) inwardly. S~e f
- quiet; (Schweigen) silence

Stilleben nt S~ Stilleben

stillegen vt sep (NEW) stilllegen

stillen vt satisfy; quench (Durst);
stop (Schmerzen, Blutung);
breast-feed (Kind)

still|halten† vt sep (haben) keep
still. S~leben nt still life.
s~legen vt sep close down. S~le-
gung f ~,-en closure

Stillschweigen nt silence. s~d a
silent, adv -ly; (fig) tacit, adv -ly

still|sitzen† vt sep (haben) sit
still. S~stand m standstill; zum
S~stand bringen/kommen
stop. s~stehen† vt sep (haben)
stand still; (anhalten) stop; (Verkehr:) be at a standstill

Stil|möbel pl reproduction furni-
ture sg. s~voll a stylish, adv -ly

Stimm|bänder ntpl vocal cords.
s~berechtigt a entitled to vote.
S~bruch m er ist im S~bruch
his voice is breaking

Stimme f ~,-n voice; (Wahl-) vote

stimmen vi (haben) be right;
(wählen) vote; stimmt das? is
that right/(wahr) true? □ vt tune;
jdn traurig/fröhlich s~ make
s.o. feel sad/happy

Stimm|enthaltung f abstention.
s~recht nt right to vote

Stimmung f ~,-en mood; (Atmosphäre) atmosphere. s~svoll a
full of atmosphere

Stimmzettel m ballot-paper

stimulieren vt stimulate

stink|en vi (haben) smell/(stark)
stink (nach of). S~tier nt skunk

Stipendium nt -s,-ien scholarship; (Beihilfe) grant

Stirn f -,-en forehead; **die S~
bieten** (+ dat) (fig) defy. **S~
runzeln** nt -s frown

stöbern vi (haben) rummage

stochern vi (haben) **s~ in** (+ dat)
poke ⟨Feuer⟩; pick at ⟨Essen⟩; pick
⟨Zähne⟩

Stock¹ m -[e]s,¨e stick; ⟨Ski-⟩ pole;
⟨Bienen-⟩ hive; ⟨Rosen-⟩ bush;
⟨Reb-⟩ vine

Stock² m -[e]s,- storey, floor.
S~bett nt bunk-beds pl. **s~dun-
kel** a (fam) pitch-dark

stock|en vi (haben) stop; ⟨Ver-
kehr:⟩ come to a standstill; ⟨Per-
son:⟩ falter. **s~end** a hesitant,
adv -ly. **s~taub** a (fam) stone-
deaf. **S~ung** f -,-en hold-up

Stockwerk nt storey, floor

Stoff m -[e]s,-e substance; ⟨Tex⟩
fabric, material; ⟨Thema⟩ subject
[matter]; ⟨Gesprächs-⟩ topic.
S~tier nt soft toy. **S~wechsel** m
metabolism

stöhnen vi (haben) groan, moan

stoisch a stoic, adv -ally

Stola f -,-len stole

Stollen m -s,- gallery; ⟨Kuchen⟩
stollen

stolpern vi (sein) stumble; **s~
über** (+ acc) trip over

stolz a proud (**auf** + acc of), adv
-ly. **S~** m -es pride

stolzieren vi (sein) strut

stopfen vt stuff; ⟨stecken⟩ put;
⟨ausbessern⟩ darn □ vi (haben) be
constipating; ⟨fam: essen⟩ guzzle

Stopp m -s,-s stop. **s~** int stop!

stoppel|ig a stubbly. **S~n** fpl
stubble sg

stopp|en vt stop; ⟨Sport⟩ time □ vi
(haben) stop. **S~schild** nt stop
sign. **S~uhr** f stop-watch

Stöpsel m -s,- plug; ⟨Flaschen-⟩
stopper

Storch m -[e]s,¨e stork

Store /ʃtoːɐ/ m -s,-s net curtain

stören vt disturb; disrupt ⟨Rede,
Sitzung⟩; jam ⟨Sender⟩;

⟨missfallen⟩ bother; **stört es Sie,
wenn ich rauche?** do you mind
if I smoke? □ vi (haben) be a nuisance; **entschuldigen Sie, dass
ich störe** I'm sorry to bother you

stornieren vt cancel

störrisch a stubborn, adv -ly

Störung f -,-en ⟨s. stören⟩ disturbance; disruption; ⟨Med⟩
trouble; ⟨Radio⟩ interference;
technische S~ technical fault

Stoß m -es,¨e push, knock; ⟨mit
Ellbogen⟩ dig; ⟨Hörner-⟩ butt; ⟨mit
Waffe⟩ thrust; ⟨Schwimm-⟩
stroke; ⟨Ruck⟩ jolt; ⟨Erd-⟩ shock;
⟨Stapel⟩ stack, pile. **S~dämpfer**
m -s,- shock absorber

stoßen vt push, knock; ⟨mit
Füßen⟩ kick; ⟨mit Kopf, Hörnern⟩
butt; ⟨an-⟩ poke, nudge; ⟨treiben⟩
thrust; **sich s~** knock oneself;
sich ⟨dat⟩ **den Kopf s~** hit one's
head □ vi (haben) push; **s~ an** (+
acc) knock against; ⟨angrenzen⟩
adjoin □ vi (sein) **s~ gegen** knock
against; bump into ⟨Tür⟩; **s~ auf**
(+ acc) bump into; ⟨entdecken⟩
come across; strike ⟨Öl⟩; ⟨fig⟩
meet with ⟨Ablehnung⟩

Stoß|stange f bumper. **S~ver-
kehr** m rush-hour traffic.
S~zahn m tusk. **S~zeit** f rush-
hour

stottern vt/i (haben) stutter,
stammer

Str. abbr ⟨Straße⟩ St

Straf|anstalt f prison. **S~arbeit**
f ⟨Sch⟩ imposition. **s~bar** a pun-
ishable; **sich s~bar machen**
commit an offence

Strafe f -,-n punishment; ⟨Jur &
fig⟩ penalty; ⟨Geld-⟩ fine;
⟨Freiheits-⟩ sentence. **s~n** vt punish

straff a tight, taut. **s~en** vt
tighten; **sich s~en** tighten

Strafgesetz nt criminal law

sträf|lich a criminal, adv -ly.
S~ling m -s,-e prisoner

Straf|mandat m ⟨Auto⟩ [park-
ing/speeding] ticket. **S~porto** nt

excess postage. **S~predigt** *f* (*fam*) lecture. **S~raum** *m* penalty area. **S~stoss** (**S~stoß**) *m* penalty. **S~tat** *f* crime. **S~zettel** *m* (*fam*) = **S~mandat**

Strahl *m* -[e]s,-en ray; (*einer Taschenlampe*) beam; (*Wasser-*) jet. **s~en** *vi* (*haben*) shine; (*funkeln*) sparkle; (*lächeln*) beam. **S~enbehandlung** *f* radiotherapy. **s~end** *a* shining; sparkling; beaming; radiant (*Schönheit*). **S~entherapie** *f* radiotherapy. **S~ung** *f* - radiation

Strähne *f* -,-n strand. **s~ig** *a* straggly

stramm *a* tight, *adv* -ly; (*kräftig*) sturdy; (*gerade*) upright

Strampel|höschen /-sç-/ *nt* -s,- rompers *pl.* **s~n** *vi* (*haben*) (*Baby:*) kick

Strand *m* -[e]s,-e beach. **s~en** *vi* (*sein*) run aground; (*fig*) fail. **S~korb** *m* wicker beach-chair. **S~promenade** *f* promenade

Strang *m* -[e]s,-e rope

Strapaz|e *f* -,-n strain. **s~ieren** *vt* be hard on; tax (*Nerven, Geduld*). **s~ierfähig** *a* hard-wearing. **s~iös** *a* exhausting

Strass *m* - & -es (**Straß** *m* - & -sses) paste

Straße *f* -,-n road; (*in der Stadt auch*) street; (*Meeres-*) strait; **auf der S~** in the road/street. **S~nbahn** *f* tram, (*Amer*) streetcar. **S~nkarte** *f* road-map. **S~nlaterne** *f* street lamp. **S~nsperre** *f* road-block

Strat|egie *f* -,-n strategy. **s~egisch** *a* strategic, *adv* -ally

sträuben *vt* ruffle up (*Federn*); **sich s~** (*Fell, Haar:*) stand on end; (*fig*) resist

Strauch *m* -[e]s, Sträucher bush

straucheln *vi* (*sein*) stumble

Strauß¹ *m* -es, Sträuße bunch [of flowers]; (*Buket*) bouquet

Strauß² *m* -es,-e ostrich

Strebe *f* -,-n brace, strut

streben *vi* (*haben*) strive (**nach** for) □ *vi* (*sein*) head (**nach/zu** for)

Strebler *m* -s,- pushy person; (*Sch*) swot. **s~sam** *a* industrious

Strecke *f* -,-n stretch, section; (*Entfernung*) distance; (*Rail*) line; (*Route*) route

strecken *vt* stretch; (*aus-*) stretch out; (*gerade machen*) straighten; (*Culin*) thin down; **sich s~** stretch; (*sich aus-*) stretch out; **den Kopf aus dem Fenster s~** put one's head out of the window

Streich *m* -[e]s,-e prank, trick; **jdm einen S~ spielen** play a trick on s.o.

streicheln *vt* stroke

streichen† *vt* spread; (*weg-*) smooth; (*an-*) paint; (*aus-*) delete; (*kürzen*) cut □ *vi* (*haben*) **s~ über** (+ *acc*) stroke

Streicher *m* -s,- string-player; **die S~** the strings

Streichholz *nt* match. **S~schachtel** *f* matchbox

Streich|instrument *nt* stringed instrument. **S~käse** *m* cheese spread. **S~orchester** *nt* string orchestra. **S~ung** *f* -,-en deletion; (*Kürzung*) cut

Streife *f* -,-n patrol

streifen *vt* brush against; (*berühren*) touch; (*verletzen*) graze; (*fig*) touch on (*Thema*); (*über-*) slip (**über** + *acc* over); **mit dem Blick s~** glance at □ *vi* (*sein*) roam

Streifen *m* -s,- stripe; (*Licht-*) streak; (*auf der Fahrbahn*) line; (*schmales Stück*) strip

Streifenwagen *m* patrol car. **s~ig** *a* streaky. **S~schuss** (**S~schuß**) *m* glancing shot; (*Wunde*) graze

Streik *m* -s,-s strike; **in den S~ treten** go on strike. **S~brecher** *m* strike-breaker, (*pej*) scab. **s~en** *vi* (*haben*) strike; (*fam*) refuse; (*versagen*) pack up. **S~ende(r)** *m* striker. **S~posten** *m* picket

Streit m -[e]s,-e quarrel; (*Auseinandersetzung*) dispute. **s~en†** vr/i (*haben*) [**sich**] **s~en** quarrel. **s~ig** a jdm etw **s~ig machen** dispute s.o.'s right to sth. **S~igkeiten** fpl quarrels. **S~kräfte** fpl armed forces. **s~süchtig** a quarrelsome

streng a strict; adv -ly; (*Blick, Ton*) stern, adv -ly; (*rau, nüchtern*) severe, adv -ly; (*Geschmack*) sharp; **s~ genommen** strictly speaking. **S~e** f - strictness; sternness; severity. **s~genommen** adv (NEW) **s~ genommen**, s. **streng**. **s~gläubig** a strict; (*orthodox*) orthodox. **s~stens** adv strictly

Stress m -es,-e (**Streß** m -sses,-sse) stress

stressig a (*fam*) stressful

streuen vt spread; (*ver-*) scatter; sprinkle (*Zucker, Salz*); **die Straßen s~** grit the roads

streunen vi (*sein*) roam; **s~der Hund** stray dog

Strich m -[e]s,-e line; (*Feder-, Pinsel-*) stroke; (*Morse-, Gedanken-*) dash; **gegen den S~** the wrong way; (*fig*) against the grain. **S~kode** m bar code. **S~punkt** m semicolon

Strick m -[e]s,-e cord; (*Seil*) rope; (*fam: Schlingel*) rascal

strick|en vt/i (*haben*) knit. **S~jacke** f cardigan. **S~leiter** f rope-ladder. **S~nadel** f knitting-needle. **S~waren** fpl knitwear sg. **S~zeug** nt knitting

striegeln vt groom

strikt a strict, adv -ly

strittig a contentious

Stroh nt -[e]s straw. **S~blumen** fpl everlasting flowers. **S~dach** nt thatched roof. **s~gedeckt** a thatched. **S~halm** m straw

Strolch m -[e]s,-e (*fam*) rascal

Strom m -[e]s,-e river; (*Menschen-, Auto-, Blut-*) stream; (*Tränen-*) flood; (*Schwall*) torrent; (*Electr*) current, power;

gegen den S~ (*fig*) against the tide; **es regnet in Strömen** it is pouring with rain. **s~abwärts** adv downstream. **s~aufwärts** adv upstream

strömen vi (*sein*) flow; (*Menschen, Blut:*) stream, pour; **s~der Regen** pouring rain

Strom|kreis m circuit. **s~linienförmig** a streamlined. **S~sperre** f power cut

Strömung f -,-en current

Strophe f -,-n verse

strotzen vi (*haben*) be full (vor + dat of); **vor Gesundheit s~d** bursting with health

Strudel m -s,- whirlpool; (*SGer Culin*) strudel

Struktur f -,-en structure; (*Tex*) texture

Strumpf m -[e]s,-e stocking; (*Knie-*) sock. **S~band** nt (pl **-bänder**) suspender, (*Amer*) garter. **S~bandgürtel** m suspender/(*Amer*) garter belt. **S~halter** m = **S~band**. **S~hose** f tights pl, (*Amer*) pantyhose

Strunk m -[e]s,-e stalk; (*Baum-*) stump

struppig a shaggy

Stube f -,-n room. **s~nrein** a house-trained

Stuck m -s stucco

Stück nt -[e]s,-e piece; (*Zucker-*) lump; (*Seife*) tablet; (*Theater-*) play; (*Gegenstand*) item; (*Exemplar*) specimen; **20 S~ Vieh** 20 head of cattle; **ein S~** (*Entfernung*) some way; **aus freien S~en** voluntarily. **S~chen** nt -s,- [little] bit. **s~weise** adv bit by bit; (*einzeln*) singly

Student(in) m -en,-en (f -,-nen) student. **s~isch** a student ...

Studie f -/-ja/ f -,-n study

studier|en vt/i (*haben*) study. **S~zimmer** nt study

Studio nt -s,-s studio

Studium nt -s,-ien studies pl

Stufe f -,-n step; (Treppen-) stair; (Raketen-) stage; (Niveau) level. **s∼n** vt terrace; (staffeln) grade

Stuhl m -[e]s,⁻e chair; (Med) stools pl. **S∼gang** m bowel movement

stülpen vt put (über + acc over)

stumm a dumb; (schweigsam) silent, adv -ly

Stummel m -s,- stump; (Zigaretten-) butt; (Bleistift-) stub

Stümper m -s,- bungler. **s∼haft** a incompetent, adv -ly

stumpf a blunt; (Winkel) obtuse; (glanzlos) dull; (fig) apathetic, adv -ally. **S∼** m -[e]s,⁻e stump

Stumpfsinn m apathy; (Langweiligkeit) tedium. **s∼ig** a apathetic, adv -ally; (langweilig) tedious

Stunde f -,-n hour; (Sch) lesson

stunden vt jdm eine Schuld s∼ give s.o. time to pay a debt

Stunden|kilometer mpl kilometres per hour. **s∼lang** adv for hours. **S∼lohn** m hourly rate. **S∼plan** m timetable. **s∼weise** adv by the hour

stündlich a & adv hourly

Stups m -es,-e nudge; (Schubs) push. **s∼en** vt nudge; (schubsen) push. **S∼nase** f snub nose

stur a pigheaded; (phlegmatisch) stolid, adv -ly; (unbeirrbar) dogged, adv -ly

Sturm m -[e]s,⁻e gale; (schwer) storm; (Mil) assault

stürm|en vi (haben) (Wind:) blow hard; es s∼t it's blowing a gale □ vi (sein) rush □ vt storm; (bedrängen) besiege. **S∼er** m -s,- forward. **s∼isch** a stormy; (Überfahrt) rough; (fig) tumultuous, adv -ly; (ungestüm) tempestuous, adv -ly

Sturz m -es,⁻e [heavy] fall; (Preis-, Kurs-) sharp drop; (Pol) overthrow

stürzen vi (sein) fall [heavily]; (in die Tiefe) plunge; (Preise, Kurse:) drop sharply; (Regierung:) fall; (eilen) rush □ vt throw;

(umkippen) turn upside down; turn out (Speise, Kuchen); (Pol) overthrow, topple; **sich s∼** throw oneself (aus/in + acc out of/into); **sich s∼ auf** (+ acc) pounce on

Sturz|flug m (Aviat) dive. **S∼helm** m crash-helmet

Stute f -,-n mare

Stütze f -,-n support; (Kopf-, Arm-) rest

stutzen vi (haben) stop short □ vt trim; (Hort) cut back; (kupieren) crop

stützen vt support; (auf-) rest; **sich s∼ auf** (+ acc) lean on; (beruhen) be based on

Stutzer m -s,- dandy

stutzig a puzzled; (misstrauisch) suspicious

Stützpunkt m (Mil) base

Subjekt nt -[e]s,-e subject. **s∼iv** a subjective, adv -ly

Subskription /-'tsio:n/ f -,-en subscription

Substantiv nt -s,-e noun

Substanz f -,-en substance

subtil a subtle, adv -tly

subtra|hieren vt subtract. **S∼ktion** /-'tsio:n/ f -,-en subtraction

Subvention /-'tsio:n/ f -,-en subsidy. **s∼ieren** vt subsidize

subversiv a subversive

Suche f - search; **auf der S∼e nach** looking for. **s∼en** vt look for; (intensiv) search for; seek (Hilfe, Rat), '**Zimmer gesucht**' 'room wanted' □ vi (haben) look, search (nach for). **S∼er** m -s,- (Phot) viewfinder

Sucht f -,⁻e addiction; (fig) mania

süchtig a addicted. **S∼e(r)** m/f addict

Süd m -[e]s south. **S∼afrika** nt South Africa. **S∼amerika** nt South America. **s∼deutsch** a South German

Süden m -s south; **nach S∼** south

Süd|frucht f tropical fruit. **s~lich** a southern; ⟨Richtung⟩ southerly □ adv & prep (+ gen) **s~lich [von] der Stadt** [to the] south of the town. **S~osten** m south-east. **S~pol** m South Pole. **s~wärts** adv southwards. **S~westen** m south-west

süffisant a smug, adv -ly

suggerieren vt suggest (dat to)

Suggest|ion /-'tjo:n/ f -,-en suggestion. **s~iv** a suggestive

Sühne f -,-n atonement; ⟨Strafe⟩ penalty. **s~n** vt atone for

Sultan|ine f -,-n sultana

Sülze f -,-n [meat] jelly; ⟨Schweinskopf⟩ brawn

Summe f -,-n sum

summ|en vi (haben) hum; ⟨Biene:⟩ buzz □ vt hum. **S~er** m -s,- buzzer

summieren (sich) vr add up; ⟨sich häufen⟩ increase

Sumpf m -[e]s,-e marsh, swamp. **s~ig** a marshy

Sünd|e f -,-n sin. **S~enbock** m scapegoat. **S~er(in)** m -s,- ⟨f -,-nen⟩ sinner. **s~haft** a sinful. **s~igen** vi (haben) sin

super inv a ⟨fam⟩ great. **S~lativ** m -s,-e superlative. **S~markt** m supermarket

Suppe f -,-n soup. **S~nlöffel** m soup-spoon. **S~nteller** m soup-plate. **S~nwürfel** m stock cube

Surf|brett /'sœ:gf-/ nt surfboard. **S~en** nt -s surfing

surren vi (haben) whirr

süß a sweet, adv -ly. **S~e** f - sweetness. **s~en** vt sweeten. **S~igkeit** f -,-en sweet. **s~lich** a sweetish; ⟨fig⟩ sugary. **S~speise** f sweet. **S~stoff** m sweetener. **S~waren** fpl confectionery sg, sweets pl. **S~wasser-** pref freshwater . . .

Sylvester nt -s = Silvester

Symbol nt -s,-e symbol. **S~ik** f - symbolism. **s~isch** a symbolic, adv -ally. **s~isieren** vt symbolize

Sym|metrie f - symmetry. **s~metrisch** a symmetrical, adv -ly

Sympathie f -,-n sympathy

sympath|isch a agreeable; ⟨Person⟩ likeable. **s~isieren** vi (haben) be sympathetic (mit to)

Symphonie f -,-n = Sinfonie

Symptom nt -s,-e symptom. **s~atisch** a symptomatic

Synagoge f -,-n synagogue

synchronisieren /zvnkroni'zi:-ran/ vt synchronize; dub ⟨Film⟩

Syndikat nt -[e]s,-e syndicate

Syndrom nt -s,-e syndrome

synonym a synonymous, adv -ly. **S~** nt -s,-e synonym

Syntax /'zvntaks/ f - syntax

Synthe|se f -,-n synthesis. **S~tik** nt -s synthetic material. **s~tisch** a synthetic, adv -ally

Syrien /-jan/ nt -s Syria

System nt -s,-e system. **s~atisch** a systematic, adv -ally

Szene f -,-n scene. **S~rie** f - scenery

T

Tabak m -s,-e tobacco

Tabelle f -,-n table; ⟨Sport⟩ league table

Tablett nt -[e]s,-s tray

Tablette f -,-n tablet

tabu a taboo. **T~** nt -s,-s taboo

Tacho m -s,-s, **Tachometer** m & nt speedometer

Tadel m -s,- reprimand; ⟨Kritik⟩ censure; ⟨Sch⟩ black mark. **t~los** a impeccable, adv -bly. **t~n** vt reprimand; censure. **t~nswert** a reprehensible

Tafel f -,-n ⟨Tisch, Tabelle⟩ table; ⟨Platte⟩ slab; ⟨Anschlag-, Hinweis-⟩ board; ⟨Gedenk-⟩ plaque; ⟨Schiefer-⟩ slate; ⟨Wand-⟩ blackboard; ⟨Bild-⟩ plate; ⟨Schokolade⟩ bar. **t~n** vi (haben) feast

Täfelung f - panelling

Tag m -[e]s,-e day; **Tag für Tag** day by day; **am T~e** in the daytime; **eines T~es** one day; **unter T~e** underground; **es wird Tag** it is getting light; **guten T~** good morning/afternoon!; **zu T~e treten** od **kommen/ bringen** = zutage treten od kommen/bringen, s. zutage. **t~aus** adv **t~aus, t~ein** day in, day out

Tage|buch nt diary. **t~lang** adv for days

tagen vi (haben) meet; ⟨Gericht:⟩ sit; **es tagt** day is breaking

Tages|anbruch m daybreak. **T~ausflug** m day trip. **T~decke** f bedspread. **T~karte** f day ticket; ⟨Speise-⟩ menu of the day. **T~licht** nt daylight. **T~mutter** f child-minder. **T~ordnung** f agenda. **T~rückfahrkarte** f day return [ticket]. **T~zeit** f time of the day. **T~zeitung** f daily [news]paper

täglich a & adv daily; **zweimal t~** twice a day

tags adv by day; **t~ zuvor/darauf** the day before/after

tagsüber adv during the day

tag|täglich a daily □ adv every single day. **T~traum** m daydream. **T~undnachtgleiche** f -,-n equinox. **T~ung** f -,-en meeting; ⟨Konferenz⟩ conference

Taill|e /'talja/ f -,-n waist. **t~iert** /ta'ji:ɐt/ a fitted

Takt m -[e]s,-e tact; ⟨Mus⟩ bar; ⟨Tempo⟩ time; ⟨Rhythmus⟩ rhythm; **im T~** in time [to the music]. **T~gefühl** nt tact

Takt|ik f -,-en tactics pl. **t~isch** a tactical, adv -ly

takt|los a tactless, adv -ly. **T~losigkeit** f - tactlessness. **T~stock** m baton. **t~voll** a tactful, adv -ly

Tal nt -[e]s,-er valley

Talar m -s,-e robe; ⟨Univ⟩ gown

Talent nt -[e]s,-e talent. **t~iert** a talented

Talg m -s tallow; ⟨Culin⟩ suet

Talsperre f dam

Tampon /tam'põ:/ m -s,-s tampon

Tang m -s seaweed

Tangente f -,-n tangent; ⟨Straße⟩ bypass

Tank m -s,-s tank. **t~en** vt fill up with ⟨Benzin⟩ □ vi (haben) fill up with petrol; ⟨Aviat⟩ refuel; **ich muss t~en** I need petrol. **T~er** m -s,- tanker. **T~stelle** f petrol/ ⟨Amer⟩ gas station. **T~wart** m -[e]s,-e petrol-pump attendant

Tanne f -,-n fir [tree]. **T~nbaum** m fir tree; ⟨Weihnachtsbaum⟩ Christmas tree. **T~nzapfen** m fir cone

Tante f -,-n aunt

Tantiemen /tan'tje:mən/ pl royalties

Tanz m -es,-e dance. **t~en** vt/i (haben) dance

Tänzer(in) m -s,- (f -,-nen) dancer

Tanz|lokal nt dance-hall. **T~musik** f dance music

Tapete f -,-n wallpaper. **T~nwechsel** m (fam) change of scene

tapezier|en vt paper. **T~er** m -s,- paperhanger, decorator

tapfer a brave, adv -ly. **T~keit** f - bravery

tappen vi (sein) walk hesitantly; ⟨greifen⟩ grope (**nach** for)

Tarif m -s,-e rate; ⟨Verzeichnis⟩ tariff

tarn|en vt disguise; ⟨Mil⟩ camouflage; **sich t~en** disguise/camouflage oneself. **T~ung** f - disguise; camouflage

Tasche f -,-n bag; ⟨Hosen-, Mantel-⟩ pocket. **T~nbuch** nt paper-back. **T~ndieb** m pickpocket. **T~ngeld** nt pocket-money. **T~nlampe** f torch, ⟨Amer⟩ flashlight. **T~nmesser** nt penknife. **t~ntuch** nt handkerchief

Tasse f -,-n cup

Tastatur f -,-en keyboard

tast|bar a palpable. **T~e** f -,-n key; ⟨Druck-⟩ push-button. **t~en**

Tat vi (haben) feel, grope (**nach** for) □ vt key in (Daten); **sich t~en** feel one's way (zu to). **t~end** a tentative, adv -ly

Tat f -,-en action; (Helden-) deed; (Straf-) crime; **in der Tat** indeed; **auf frischer Tat ertappt** caught in the act. **t~enlos** adv passively

Täter(in) m -s,- (f -,-nen) culprit; (Jur) offender

tätig a active, adv -ly; t~ **sein** work. **T~keit** f -,-en activity; (Funktionieren) action; (Arbeit) work, job

Tatkraft f energy

tätlich a physical, adv -ly; t~**werden** become violent. **T~keiten** fpl violence sg

Tatort m scene of the crime

tätowier|en vt tattoo. **T~ung** f -,-en tattooing; (Bild) tattoo

Tatsache f fact. **T~nbericht** m documentary

tatsächlich a actual, adv -ly

tätscheln vt pat

Tatze f -,-n paw

Tau¹ m -[e]s dew

Tau² nt -[e]s,-e rope

taub a deaf; (gefühllos) numb; (Nuss) empty; (Gestein) worthless

Taube f -,-n pigeon; (Turtel-& fig) dove. **T~nschlag** m pigeon-loft

Taub|heit f - deafness; (Gefühllosigkeit) numbness. t~**stumm** a deaf and dumb

tauch|en vt dip, plunge; (unter-) duck □ vi (haben/sein) (ab)dive; plunge (in + acc into); (auf-) appear (aus out of). **T~er** m -s,- diver. **T~eranzug** m diving-suit. **T~sieder** m -s,- [small, portable] immersion heater

tauen vi (sein) melt, thaw □ impers **es taut** it is thawing

Tauf|becken nt font. **T~e** f -,-en christening, baptism. t~**en** vt christen, baptize. **T~pate** m godfather. **T~stein** m font

taug|en vi (haben) **etwas/nichts t~en** be good/no good; **zu etw**

t~n/nicht t~n be good/no good for sth. **T~nichts** m -es,-e goodfor-nothing

tauglich a suitable; (Mil) fit. **T~keit** f - suitability; fitness

Taumel m -s daze; **wie im T~** in a daze. t~**n** vi (sein) stagger

Tausch m -[e]s,-e exchange; (fam) swap. **t~en** vt exchange/(handeln) barter (**gegen** for); **die Plätze t~en** change places □ vi (haben) swap (**mit etw** sth; **mit jdm** with s.o.)

täuschen vt deceive, fool; betray (Vertrauen); **sich t~** delude oneself; (sich irren) be mistaken □ vi (haben) be deceptive; (Ähnlichkeit) striking □ a deceptive. **t~d** a deceptive; (Ähnlichkeit) striking

Tausch|geschäft nt exchange. **T~handel** m barter; (T~geschäft) exchange

Täuschung f -,-en deception; (Irrtum) mistake; (Illusion) delusion

tausend inv a one/a thousand. **T~** nt -s,-e thousand; **T~e od T~e** von thousands of. **T~füßler** m -s,- centipede. t~**ste(r,s)** a thousandth. **T~stel** nt -s,- thousandth

Tau|tropfen m dewdrop. **T~wetter** nt thaw. **T~ziehen** nt -s tug of war

Taxe f -,-n charge; (Kur-) tax; (Taxi) taxi

Taxi nt -s,-s taxi, cab

taxieren vt estimate/(im Wert) value (**auf** + acc at); (fam: mustern) size up

Taxi|fahrer m taxi driver. **T~stand** m taxi rank

Teakholz /ˈtiːk-/ nt teak

Team /tiːm/ nt -s,-s team

Techni|k f -,-en technology; (Methode) technique. **T~ker** m -s,- technician. t~**sch** a technical, adv -ly; (technologisch) technological, adv -ly; **T~sche Hochschule** Technical University

Techno|logie f -,-n technology. t~**logisch** a technological

Teckel m -s,- dachshund

Teddybär m teddy bear
Tee m -s,-s tea. **T~beutel** m tea-bag. **T~kanne** f teapot. **T~kessel** m kettle. **T~löffel** m tea-spoon
Teer m -s tar. **t~en** vt tar
Tee|sieb nt tea-strainer. **T~tasse** f teacup. **T~wagen** m [tea] trolley
Teich m -[e]s,-e pond
Teig m -[e]s,-e pastry; (Knet-) dough; (Rühr-) mixture; (Pfannkuchen-) batter. **T~rolle** f, **T~roller** m rolling-pin. **T~waren** fpl pasta sg
Teil m -[e]s,-e part; (Bestand-) component; (Jur) party; der vordere **T~** the front part; zum **T~** partly; zum großen/größten **T~** for the most part □ m & nt -[e]s (Anteil) share; sein[en] **T~beitragen** do one's share; ich für mein[en] **T~** for my part □ nt -[e]s,-e part; (Ersatz-) spare part; (Anbau-) unit
teil|bar a divisible. **T~chen** nt -s,- particle. **t~en** vt divide; (auf-) share out; (gemeinsam haben) share; (Pol) partition 〈Land〉; sich (dat) etw [mit jdm] **t~en** share sth [with s.o.]; sich **t~en** divide; (sich gabeln) fork; 〈Vorhang:〉 open; 〈Meinungen:〉 differ □ vi (haben) share
teilhab|en† vi sep (haben) share (an etw dat sth). **T~er** m -s,- (Comm) partner
Teilnahm|e f - participation; (innere) interest; (Mitgefühl) sympathy. **t~slos** a apathetic, adv -ally
teilnehm|en† vi sep (haben) **t~en an** (+ dat) take part in; (mitfühlen) share [in]. **T~er(in)** m -s,- (f -,-nen) participant; (an Wettbewerb) competitor
teil|s adv partly. **T~ung** f -,-en division; (Pol) partition. **t~weise** a partial □ adv partially, partly; (manchmal) in some

cases. **T~zahlung** f part-payment; (Rate) instalment. **T~zeitbeschäftigung** f part-time job
Teint /tɛ̃/ m -s,-s complexion
Telefax nt fax
Telefon nt -s,-e [tele]phone. **T~anruf** m, **T~at** nt -[e]s,-e [tele]phone call. **T~buch** nt [tele]phone book. **t~ieren** vi (haben) [tele]phone
telefon|isch a [tele]phone ... □ adv by [tele]phone. **T~ist(in)** m -en,-en (f -,-nen) telephonist. **T~karte** f phone card. **T~nummer** f [tele]phone number. **T~zelle** f [tele]phone box
Telegraf m -en,-en telegraph. **T~enmast** m telegraph pole. **t~ieren** vi (haben) send a telegram. **t~isch** a telegraphic □ adv by telegram
Telegramm nt -s,-e telegram
Telegraph m -en,-en = **Telegraf**
Teleobjektiv nt telephoto lens
Telepathie f - telepathy
Telephon nt -s,-e = **Telefon**
Teleskop nt -s,-e telescope. **t~isch** a telescopic
Telex nt -,-[e] telex. **t~en** vt telex
Teller m -s,- plate
Tempel m -s,- temple
Temperament nt -s,-e temperament; (Lebhaftigkeit) vivacity. **t~los** a dull. **t~voll** a vivacious; (Pferd) spirited
Temperatur f -,-en temperature
Tempo nt -s,-s speed; (Mus: pl -pi) tempo; **T~!** hurry up!
Tend|enz f -,-en trend; (Neigung) tendency. **t~ieren** vi (haben) tend (zu towards)
Tennis nt - tennis. **T~platz** m tennis-court. **T~schläger** m tennis-racket
Tenor m -s,-̈e (Mus) tenor
Teppich m -s,-e carpet. **T~boden** m fitted carpet

Termin *m* -s,-e date; (*Arzt-*) appointment; **[letzter] T∼** deadline. **T∼kalender** *m* [appointments] diary

Terminologie *f* -,-n terminology

Terpentin *nt* -s turpentine

Terrain /tɛˈrɛ̃/ *nt* -s,-s terrain

Terrasse *f* -,-n terrace

Terrier /ˈtɛrɪə/ *m* -s,- terrier

Terrine *f* -,-n tureen

Territorium *nt* -s,-ien territory

Terror *m* -s terror. **t∼isieren** *vt* terrorize. **T∼ismus** *m* - terrorism. **T∼ist** *m* -en,-en terrorist

Terzett *nt* -[e]s,-e [vocal] trio

Tesafilm (P) *m* ≈ Sellotape (P)

Test *m* -[e]s,-s & -e test

Testament *nt* -[e]s,-e will; **Altes/ Neues T∼** Old/New Testament. **T∼svollstrecker** *m* -s,- executor

testen *vt* test

Tetanus *m* - tetanus

teuer *a* expensive, *adv* -ly; (*lieb*) dear; **wie t∼?** how much? **T∼ung** *f* -,-en rise in prices

Teufel *m* -s,- devil; **zum T∼!** (*sl*) damn [it]! **T∼skreis** *m* vicious circle

teuflisch *a* fiendish

Text *m* -[e]s,-e text; (*Passage*) passage; (*Bild-*) caption; (*Lied-*) lyrics *pl*, words *pl*; (*Opern-*) libretto. **T∼er** *m* -s,- copy-writer; (*Schlager-*) lyricist

Textil|ien /-jən/ *pl* textiles; (*Textilwaren*) textile goods. **T∼industrie** *f* textile industry

Textverarbeitungssystem *nt* word processor

TH *abbr* = Technische Hochschule

Theater *nt* -s,- theatre; (*fam: Getue*) fuss, to-do; **T∼ spielen** act; (*fam*) put on an act. **T∼kasse** *f* box-office. **T∼stück** *nt* play

theatralisch *a* theatrical, *adv* -ly

Theke *f* -,-n bar; (*Ladentisch*) counter

Thema *nt* -s,-men subject; (*Mus*) theme

Themse *f* - Thames

Theolo|ge *m* -n,-n theologian. **T∼gie** *f* - theology

theor|etisch *a* theoretical, *adv* -ly. **T∼ie** *f* -,-n theory

Therapeut|(in) *m* -en,-en (*f* -,-nen) therapist. **t∼isch** *a* therapeutic

Therapie *f* -,-n therapy

Thermal|bad *nt* thermal bath; (*Ort*) thermal spa. **T∼quelle** *f* thermal spring

Thermometer *nt* -s,- thermometer

Thermosflasche (P) *f* Thermos flask (P)

Thermostat *m* -[e]s,-e thermostat

These *f* -,-n thesis

Thrombose *f* -,-n thrombosis

Thron *m* -[e]s,-e throne. **t∼en** *vi* (*haben*) sit [in state]. **T∼folge** *f* succession. **T∼folger** *m* -s,- heir to the throne

Thunfisch *m* tuna

Thymian *m* -s thyme

Tick *m* -s,-s (*fam*) quirk; **einen T∼haben** be crazy

ticken *vi* (*haben*) tick

tief *a* deep; (*t∼ liegend, niedrig*) low; (*t∼gründig*) profound; **t∼er Teller** soup-plate; **im t∼sten Winter** in the depths of winter □ *adv* deep; low; (*sehr*) deeply, profoundly; (*schlafen*) soundly; **t∼ greifend** (*fig*) radical, *adv* -ly; **t∼ schürfend** (*fig*) profound. **T∼** *nt* -s,-s (*Meteorol*) depression. **T∼bau** *m* civil engineering. **T∼e** *f* -,-n depth

Tief|ebene *f* [lowland] plain. **T∼garage** *f* underground car park. **t∼gekühlt** *a* [deep-]frozen. **t∼greifend** *a* NEW t∼ greifend, s. tief. **t∼gründig** *a* (*fig*) profound

Tief|kühl|fach *nt* freezer compartment. **T∼kost** *f* frozen food. **T∼truhe** *f* deep-freeze

Tief|land nt lowlands pl. **T~punkt** m (fig) low. **t~schür-** fend a (NEW) **t~ schürfend**, s. **tief. t~sinnig** (fig) profound; (trübsinnig) melancholy. **T~** **stand** m (fig) low

Tiefsttemperatur f minimum temperature

Tier nt -[e]s,-e animal. **T~arzt** m, **T~ärztin** f vet, veterinary sur- geon. **T~garten** m zoo. **t~isch** a animal ...; (fig: roh) bestial. **T~kreis** m zodiac. **T~kreis- zeichen** nt sign of the zodiac. **T~kunde** f zoology. **T~quä- lerei** f cruelty to animals

Tiger m -s,- tiger

tilgen vt pay off (Schuld); (strei- chen) delete; (fig: auslöschen) wipe out

Tinte f -,-n ink. **T~nfisch** m squid

Tipp (**Tip**) m -s,-s (fam) tip

tipp|en vt (fam) type □ vi (haben) (berühren) touch (**auf/an etw** acc sth); (fam: Maschine schreiben) type; (**t~en auf** + acc) (fam: wetten) bet on. **T~fehler** m (fam) typing error. **T~schein** m pools/lottery coupon

tipptopp a (fam) immaculate, adv -ly

Tirol nt -s [the] Tyrol

Tisch m -[e]s,-e table; (Schreib-) desk; **nach T~** after the meal. **T~decke** f table-cloth. **T~gebet** nt grace. **T~ler** m -s,- joiner; (Möbel-) cabinet-maker. **T~rede** f after-dinner speech. **T~tennis** nt table tennis. **T~tuch** nt table- cloth

Titel m -s,- title. **T~rolle** f title- role

Toast /to:st/ m -[e]s,-e toast; (Scheibe) piece of toast; **einen T~ ausbringen** propose a toast (**auf** + acc to). **T~er** m -s,- toaster

tob|en vi (haben) rave; (Sturm:) rage; (Kinder:) play boisterously □ vi (sein) rush. **t~süchtig** a rav- ing mad

Tochter f -,- daughter. **T~ge- sellschaft** f subsidiary

Tod m -es death. **t~blass** (**t~blaß**) a deathly pale. **t~ernst** a deadly serious, adv -ly

Todes|angst f mortal fear. **T~an- zeige** f death announcement; (Zeitungs-) obituary. **T~fall** m death. **T~opfer** nt fatality, casu- alty. **T~strafe** f death penalty. **T~urteil** nt death sentence

Tod|feind m mortal enemy. **t~krank** a dangerously ill

tödlich a fatal, adv -ly; (Gefahr) mortal, adv -ly; (groß) deadly; **t~gelangweilt** bored to death

tod|müde a dead tired. **t~sicher** a (fam) dead certain □ adv for sure. **T~sünde** f deadly sin. **t~unglücklich** a desperately unhappy

Toilette /tǫa'lɛtə/ f -,-n toilet. **T~npapier** nt toilet paper

toler|ant a tolerant. **T~anz** f - tolerance. **t~ieren** vt tolerate

toll a crazy, mad; (fam: prima) fantastic; (schlimm) awful □ adv beautifully; (sehr) very; (schlimm) badly. **t~en** vi (ha- ben/sein) romp. **t~kühn** a fool- hardy. **t~patschig** a clumsy, adv -ily. **T~wut** f rabies. **t~wütig** a rabid

tolpatschig a (NEW) **tollpatschig**

Tölpel m -s,- fool

Tomate f -,-n tomato. **T~nmark** nt tomato purée

Tombola f -,-s raffle

Ton[1] m -[e]s clay

Ton[2] m -[e]s,-e tone; (Klang) sound; (Note) note; (Betonung) stress; (Farb-) shade; **der gute Ton** (fig) good form. **T~ab- nehmer** m -s,- pick-up. **T~ange- bend** a (fig) leading. **T~art** f tone [of voice]; (Mus) key. **T~- band** nt (pl -bänder) tape. **T~bandgerät** nt tape recorder

tönen vi (haben) sound □ vt tint

Ton|fall m tone [of voice]: (Ak-zent) intonation. **T~leiter** f scale. **t~los** a toneless, adv -ly

Tonne f -,-n barrel, cask: (Müll-) bin; (Maß) tonne, metric ton

Topf m -[e]s,-̈e pot; (Koch-) pan

Topfen m -s (Aust) ≈ curd cheese

Töpfer|(in) m -s,- (f-,-nen) potter. **T~ei** f -,-en pottery

Töpferwaren fpl pottery sg

Topf|lappen m oven-cloth. **T~pflanze** f potted plant

Tor¹ m -en,-en fool

Tor² nt -[e]s,-e gate; (Einfahrt) gateway; (Sport) goal. **T~bogen** m archway

Torf m -s peat

Torheit f -,-en folly

Torhüter m -s,- goalkeeper

töricht a foolish, adv -ly

torkeln vi (sein/haben) stagger

Tornister m -s,- knapsack; (Sch) satchel

torp|edieren vt torpedo. **T~edo** m -s,-s torpedo

Torpfosten m goal-post

Torte f -,-n gateau; (Obst-) flan

Tortur f -,-en torture

Torwart m -s,-e goalkeeper

tosen vi (haben) roar; ⟨Sturm:⟩ rage

tot a dead; **tot geboren** stillborn; **sich tot stellen** pretend to be dead; **einen t~en Punkt haben** (fig) be at a low ebb

total a total, adv -ly. **t~itär** a totalitarian. **T~schaden** m ≈ write-off

Tote(r) m/f dead man/woman; (Todesopfer) fatality; **die T~n** the dead pl

töten vt kill

toten|blass (**totenblaß**) a deathly pale. **T~gräber** m -s,-grave-digger. **T~kopf** m skull. **T~schein** m death certificate. **T~stille** f deathly silence

tot|fahren† vt sep run over and kill. **t~geboren**, **s. tot. t~lachen (sich)** vt sep (fam) be in stitches

Toto nt & m -s football pools pl.

T~schein m pools coupon

tot|schießen† vt sep shoot dead. **T~schlag** m (Jur) manslaughter. **t~schlagen**† vt sep kill. **t~schweigen**† vt sep (fig) hush up. **t~stellen (sich)** vr s. tot

Tötung f -,-en killing; **fahrlässige T~** (Jur) manslaughter

Toupet /tu'pe:/ nt -s,-s toupee. **t~ieren** vt back-comb

Tour /tu:ɐ/ f -,-en tour; (Ausflug) trip; (Auto-) drive; (Rad-) ride; (Strecke) distance; (Techn) revolution; (fam: Weise) way; **auf vollen T~en** at full speed; (fam) flat out

Touris|mus /tu'rɪsmʊs/ m - tourism. **T~t** m -en,-en tourist

Tournee /tʊr'ne:/ f -,-n tour

Trab m -s trot

Trabant m -en,-en satellite

traben vi (haben/sein) trot

Tracht f -,-en [national] costume; **eine T~Prügel** a good hiding

trachten vi (haben) strive (**nach** for); **jdm nach dem Leben t~** be out to kill s.o

trächtig a pregnant

Tradition /-'tsjo:n/ f -,-en tradition. **t~ell** a traditional, adv -ly

Trafik f -,-en (Aust) tobacconist's

Trag|bahre f stretcher. **t~bar** a portable; (Kleidung) wearable; (erträglich) bearable

träge a sluggish, adv -ly; (faul) lazy, adv -ly; (Phys) inert

tragen† vt carry; (an/aufhaben) wear; (fig) bear □ vi (haben) carry; **gut t~** ⟨Baum:⟩ produce a good crop; **schwer t~** carry a heavy load; (fig) be deeply affected (**an** + dat by). **t~d** a (Techn) load-bearing; (trächtig) pregnant

Träger m -s,- porter; (Inhaber) bearer; (eines Ordens) holder; (Bau-) beam; (Stahl-) girder; (Achsel-) [shoulder] strap.

T~kleid nt pinafore dress

Trag|etasche f carrier bag. **T~fläche** f (Aviat) wing; (Naut) hydrofoil. **T~flächenboot,** **T~flügelboot** nt hydrofoil

Trägheit f - sluggishness; (Faulheit) laziness; (Phys) inertia

Trag|ik f - tragedy. **t~isch** a tragic, adv -ally

Tragödie /-jə/ f -,-n tragedy

Tragweite f range; (fig) consequence

Train|er /'trɛːnɐ/ m -s,- trainer; (Tennis-) coach. **t~ieren** vt/i (haben) train

Training /'trɛːnɪŋ/ nt -s training. **T~anzug** m tracksuit. **T~schuhe** mpl trainers

Trakt m -[e]s,-e section; (Flügel) wing

traktieren vi (haben) mit Schlä- gen/Tritten **t~** hit/kick

Traktor m -s,-en /-'to:rən/ trac- tor

trampeln vi (haben) stamp one's feet □ vi (sein) trample (**auf** + acc on) □ vt trample

trampen /'trɛmpən/ vi (sein) (fam) hitch-hike

Trance /'trɑ̃:sə/ f -,-n trance

Tranchier|messer /trɑ̃'ʃiːɐ-/ nt carving-knife. **t~en** vt carve

Träne f -,-n tear. **t~n** vi (haben) water. **T~ngas** nt tear-gas

Tränke f -,-n watering-place; (Trog) drinking-trough. **t~n** vt water (Pferd); (nässen) soak (mit with)

Trans|aktion f transaction. **T~fer** m -s,-s transfer. **T~for- mator** m -s,-en /-'to:rən/ trans- former. **T~fusion** f -,-en [blood] transfusion

Transistor m -,-en /-'to:rən/ transistor

Transit /tran'zi:t/ m -s transit

transitiv a transitive, adv -ly

Transparent nt -[e]s,-e banner; (Bild) transparency

transpirieren vi (haben) per- spire

Transplantation /-'tsjo:n/ f -,-en transplant

Transport m -[e]s,-e transport; (Güter-) consignment. **t~ieren** vt transport. **T~mittel** nt means of transport

Trapez nt -es,-e trapeze; (Geom) trapezium

Tratsch m -[e]s (fam) gossip. **t~en** vi (haben) (fam) gossip

Tratte f -,-n (Comm) draft

Traube f -,-n bunch of grapes; (Beere) grape; (fig) cluster. **T~n- zucker** m glucose

trauen vi (haben) (+ dat) trust; ich traute kaum meinen Augen I could hardly believe my eyes □ vt (haben) marry; **sich t~** dare (etw zu tun [to] do sth); venture (in + acc/aus into/out of)

Trauer f - mourning; (Schmerz) grief (um for); **T~ tragen** be [dressed] in mourning. **T~fall** m bereavement. **T~feier** f funeral service. **T~marsch** m funeral march. **t~n** vi (haben) grieve; **t~n um** mourn [for]. **T~spiel** nt tragedy. **T~weide** f weeping wil- low

traulich a cosy, adv -ily

Traum m -[e]s, Träume dream

Trau|ma nt -s,-men trauma. **t~matisch** a traumatic

träumen vt/i (haben) dream

traumhaft a dreamlike; (schön) fabulous, adv -ly

traurig a sad, adv -ly; (erbärm- lich) sorry. **T~keit** f - sadness

Trau|ring m wedding-ring. **T~schein** m marriage certific- ate. **T~ung** f -,-en wedding [cere- mony]

Treck m -s,-s trek

Trecker m -s,-s tractor

Treff nt -s,-s (Karten) spades pl

treff|en vt hit; (Blitz:) strike; (fig: verletzen) hurt; (zusammenkom- men mit) meet; take (Maßnahme); **sich t~en** meet (**mit jdm** s.o.); **sich gut t~en** be convenient; **es**

traf sich, dass it so happened that; **es gut/schlecht t~en** be lucky/unlucky t~en hit the target; **t~en auf** (+ acc) meet; (fig) meet with. **T~en** nt -s,- meeting. **t~end** a apt, adv -ly; ⟨Ähnlichkeit⟩ striking. **T~er** m -s,- hit; ⟨Los⟩ winner. **T~punkt** m meeting-place

treiben† vt drive; (sich befassen mit) do; carry on (Gewerbe); indulge in (Luxus); get up to (Unfug); **Handel t~** trade; **Blüten/Blätter t~** come into flower/leaf; **zur Eile t~** hurry [up]; **was treibt ihr da?** (fam) what are you up to? ⟷ vi (sein) drift; (schwimmen) float ⟷ vi (haben) sprout. (Bot) sprout. **T~ ~** nt -s activity; (Getriebe) bustle

Treib|haus nt hothouse. **T~hauseffekt** m greenhouse effect. **T~holz** nt driftwood. **T~riemen** m transmission belt. **T~sand** m quicksand. **T~stoff** m fuel

Trend m -s,-s trend

trenn|bar a separable. **t~en** vt separate/(abmachen) detach (von from); divide, split (Wort); **sich t~en** separate; (auseinander gehen) part; **sich t~en von** leave; (fortgeben) part with. **T~ung** f -,-en separation; ⟨Silben-⟩ division. **T~ungsstrich** m hyphen. **T~wand** f partition

trepp|ab adv downstairs. **t~auf** adv upstairs

Treppe f -,-n stairs pl; (Außen-) steps pl; **eine T~** a flight of stairs/steps. **T~nflur** m landing. **T~ngeländer** nt banisters pl. **T~nhaus** nt stairwell. **T~nstufe** f stair, step

Tresor m -s,-e safe

Tresse f -,-n braid

Treteimer m pedal bin

treten† vi (sein/haben) step; (versehentlich) tread; (ausschlagen) kick (nach at); **in Verbindung** **t~** get in touch ⟷ vt tread; (mit Füßen) kick

treu a faithful, adv -ly; (fest) loyal, adv -ly. **T~e** f - faithfulness; loyalty; (eheliche) fidelity. **T~händer** m -s,- trustee. **t~herzig** a trusting, adv -ly; (arglos) innocent, adv -ly. **t~los** a disloyal, adv -ly; (untreu) unfaithful

Tribüne f -,-n platform; (Zuschauer-) stand

Tribut m -[e]s,-e tribute; (Opfer) toll

Trichter m -s,- funnel; (Bomben-) crater

Trick m -s,-s trick. **T~film** m cartoon. **t~reich** a clever

Trieb m -[e]s,-e drive, urge; (Instinkt) instinct; (Bot) shoot. **T~täter, T~verbrecher** m sex offender. **T~werk** nt (Aviat) engine; (Uhr-) mechanism

trief|en† vi (haben) drip; (nass sein) be dripping (von/vor + dat with). **t~nass** (t~naß) a dripping wet

triftig a valid

Trigonometrie f - trigonometry

Trikot¹ /tri'ko:/ m -s (Tex) jersey

Trikot² nt -s,-s (Sport) jersey; (Fußball-) shirt

Trimester nt -s,- term

Trimm-dich nt -s keep-fit

trimmen vt trim; (fam) train; tune (Motor); **sich t~** keep fit

trink|bar a drinkable. **t~en†** vt/i (haben) drink. **T~er(in)** m -s,-/f -,-nen) alcoholic. **T~geld** nt tip. **T~halm** m [drinking-]straw. **T~spruch** m toast. **T~wasser** nt drinking-water

Trio nt -s,-s trio

trippeln vi (sein) trip along

trist a dreary

Tritt m -[e]s,-e step; (Fuß-) kick. **T~brett** nt step. **T~leiter** f stepladder

Triumph m -s,-e triumph. **t~ieren** vi (haben) rejoice; **t~ieren über** (+ acc) triumph over. **t~ierend** *a* triumphant, *adv* -ly

trocken *a* dry, *adv* drily. **T~haube** *f* drier. **T~heit** *f* -,-en dryness; ⟨*Dürre*⟩ drought. **t~legen** *vt sep* change ⟨*Baby*⟩; drain ⟨*Sumpf*⟩. **T~milch** *f* powdered milk

trockn|en *vt/i* ⟨*sein*⟩ dry. **T~er** *m* -s,- drier

Troddel *f* -,-n tassel

Trödel *m* -s ⟨*fam*⟩ junk. **T~laden** *m* ⟨*fam*⟩ junk-shop. **T~markt** *m* ⟨*fam*⟩ flea market. **t~n** *vi* ⟨*haben*⟩ dawdle

Trödler *m* -s,- ⟨*fam*⟩ slowcoach; ⟨*Händler*⟩ junk-dealer

Trog *m* -[e]s,̈e trough

Trommel *f* -,-n drum. **T~fell** *nt* ear-drum. **t~n** *vi* ⟨*haben*⟩ drum

Trommler *m* -s,- drummer

Trompete *f* -,-n trumpet. **T~r** *m* -s,- trumpeter

Tropen *pl* tropics

Tropf *m* -[e]s,-e ⟨*Med*⟩ drip

tröpfeln *vt/i* ⟨*sein/haben*⟩ drip; **es tröpfelt** it's spitting with rain

tropfen *vt/i* ⟨*sein/haben*⟩ drip. **T~** *m* -s,- drop; ⟨*fallend*⟩ drip. **t~weise** *adv* drop by drop

tropf|nass (**tropfnaß**) *a* dripping wet. **T~stein** *m* stalagmite; ⟨*hängend*⟩ stalactite

Trophäe /tro'fɛːə/ *f* -,-n trophy

tropisch *a* tropical

Trost *m* -[e]s,-e consolation, comfort

tröst|en *vt* console, comfort; **sich t~en** console oneself. **t~lich** *a* comforting

trost|los *a* desolate; ⟨*elend*⟩ wretched; ⟨*reizlos*⟩ dreary. **T~preis** *m* consolation prize. **t~reich** *a* comforting

Trott *m* -s amble; ⟨*fig*⟩ routine

Trottel *m* -s,- ⟨*fam*⟩ idiot

trotten *vi* ⟨*sein*⟩ traipse; ⟨*Tier:*⟩ amble

Trottoir /trɔ'tŏaːɐ/ *nt* -s,-s pavement, ⟨*Amer*⟩ sidewalk

trotz *prep* (+ *gen*) despite, in spite of. **T~** *m* -es defiance. **t~dem** *adv* nevertheless. **t~en** *vi* ⟨*haben*⟩ (+ *dat*) defy. **t~ig** *a* defiant, *adv* -ly; ⟨*Kind*⟩ stubborn

trübe *a* dull; ⟨*Licht*⟩ dim; ⟨*Flüssigkeit*⟩ cloudy; ⟨*fig*⟩ gloomy

Trubel *m* -s bustle

trüben *vt* dull; make cloudy ⟨*Flüssigkeit*⟩; ⟨*fig*⟩ spoil; strain ⟨*Verhältnis*⟩; **sich t~** ⟨*Flüssigkeit:*⟩ become cloudy; ⟨*Himmel:*⟩ cloud over; ⟨*Augen:*⟩ dim; ⟨*Verhältnis, Erinnerung:*⟩ deteriorate

Trüb|sal *f* - misery; **T~sal blasen** ⟨*fam*⟩ mope. **t~selig** *a* miserable; ⟨*trübe*⟩ gloomy, *adv* -ily. **T~sinn** *m* melancholy. **t~sinnig** *a* melancholy

Trugbild *nt* illusion

trügen† *vt* deceive □ *vi* ⟨*haben*⟩ be deceptive. **t~erisch** *a* false; ⟨*täuschend*⟩ deceptive

Trugschluss (**Trugschluß**) *m* fallacy

Truhe *f* -,-n chest

Trümmer *pl* rubble *sg*; ⟨*T~teile*⟩ wreckage *sg*, ⟨*fig*⟩ ruins. **T~haufen** *m* pile of rubble

Trumpf *m* -[e]s,̈e trump ⟨*card*⟩. **T~ sein** be trumps. **t~en** *vt/i* ⟨*haben*⟩ play trumps

Trunk *m* -[e]s drink. **T~enbold** *m* -[e]s,-e drunkard. **T~enheit** *f* - drunkenness; **T~enheit am Steuer** drunken driving. **T~sucht** *f* alcoholism

Trupp *m* -s,-s group; ⟨*Mil*⟩ squad. **T~e** *f* -,-n ⟨*Mil*⟩ unit; ⟨*Theat*⟩ troupe; **T~en** *pl* troops

Truthahn *m* turkey

Tschech|e *m* -n,-n, **T~in** *f* -,-nen Czech. **t~isch** *a* Czech. **T~oslowakei (die)** - Czechoslovakia

tschüs, tschüss *int* bye, cheerio

Tuba *f* -,-ben ⟨*Mus*⟩ tuba

Tube *f* -,-n tube

Tuberkulose *f* - tuberculosis

Tuch[1] *nt* -[e]s,̈er cloth; ⟨*Hals-, Kopf-*⟩ scarf; ⟨*Schulter-*⟩ shawl

Tuch² nt -[e]s,-e (*Stoff*) cloth

tüchtig a competent; (*reichlich, beträchtlich*) good; (*groß*) big □ adv competently; (*ausreichend*) well; (*regnen, schneien*) hard. **T~keit** f - competence

Tück|e f -,-n malice; **T~en haben** be temperamental; (*gefährlich sein*) be treacherous. **t~isch** a malicious, adv -ly; (*gefährlich*) treacherous

tüfteln vi (haben) (*fam*) fiddle (**an** + dat with); (*geistig*) puzzle (**an** + dat over)

Tugend f -,-en virtue. **t~haft** a virtuous

Tülle f -,-n spout

Tulpe f -,-n tulip

tummeln (sich) vr romp [about]; (*sich beeilen*) hurry [up]

Tümmler m -s,- porpoise

Tumor m -s,-en /-'mo:rən/ tumour

Tümpel m -s,- pond

Tumult m -[e]s,-e commotion; (*Aufruhr*) riot

tun† vt do; take (*Schritt, Blick*); work (*Wunder*); (*bringen*) put (**in** + acc into); **sich tun** happen; **jdm etwas tun** hurt s.o.; **viel zu tun haben** have a lot to do; **das tut man nicht** it isn't done; **das tut nichts** it doesn't matter □ vi (haben) act (**als ob** as if); **überrascht tun** pretend to be surprised; **er tut nur so** he's just pretending; **jdm/etw gut tun do** s.o./sth good; **zu tun haben** have things/work to do; **[es] zu tun haben mit** have to deal with; **[es] mit dem Herzen zu tun haben** have heart trouble. **Tun** nt -s actions pl

Tünche f -,-n whitewash; (*fig*) veneer. **t~n** vt whitewash

Tunesien /-jən/ nt -s Tunisia

Tunfisch m = Thunfisch

Tunke f -,-n sauce. **t~n** vt/i (haben) (*fam*) dip (**in** + acc into)

Tunnel m -s,- tunnel

tupf|en vt dab □ vi (haben) **t~en an/auf** (+ acc) touch. **T~en** m -s,- spot. **T~er** m -s,- spot; (*Med*) swab

Tür f -,-en door

Turban m -s,-e turban

Turbine f -,-n turbine

turbulen|t a turbulent. **T~z** f -,-en turbulence

Türk|e m -n,-n Turk. **T~ei (die)** Turkey. **T~in** f -,-nen Turk

türkis inv a turquoise. **T~** m -es,-e turquoise

türkisch a Turkish

Turm m -[e]s,-e tower; (*Schach*) rook, castle

Türm|chen nt -s,- turret. **t~en** vt pile [up]; **sich t~en** pile up □ vi (sein) (*fam*) escape

Turmspitze f spire

turn|en vi (haben) do gymnastics. **T~en** nt -s gymnastics sg; (*Sch*) physical education, (*fam*) gym. **T~er(in)** m -s,- (f -,-nen) gymnast. **T~halle** f gymnasium

Turnier nt -s,-e tournament; (*Reit-*) show

Turnschuhe mpl gym shoes; (*Trainingsschuhe*) trainers

Türschwelle f doorstep, threshold

Tusch m -[e]s,-e fanfare

Tusche f -,-n [drawing] ink; (*Wasserfarbe*) watercolour

tuscheln vt/i (haben) whisper

Tüte f -,-n bag; (*Comm*) packet; (*Eis-*) cornet; **in die T~ blasen** (*fam*) be breathalysed

tuten vi (haben) hoot; (*Schiff:*) sound its hooter; (*Sirene:*) sound

TÜV m - ≈ MOT [test]

Typ m -s,-en type; (*fam: Kerl*) bloke. **T~e** f -,-n type; (*fam: Person*) character

Typhus m - typhoid

typisch a typical, adv -ly (**für** of)

Typographie, Typografie f - typography

Typus m -, Typen type

Tyrann *m* -en,-en tyrant. **T~ei** *f*
- tyranny. **t~isch** *a* tyrannical.
t~isieren *vt* tyrannize

U

u.a. *abbr* (**unter anderem**)
amongst other things
U-Bahn *f* underground, (*Amer*)
subway
übel *a* bad; (*hässlich*) nasty, *adv*
-ily; **mir ist/wird ü~** I feel sick;
etw ü~nehmen take sth amiss;
jdm etw ü~ nehmen hold sth
against s.o. **Ü~** *nt* -s,- evil. **Ü~**
keit *f* - nausea. **ü~nehmen†** *vt*
sep (NEW) **ü~ nehmen**, *s*. **übel**.
Ü~täter *m* culprit
üben *vt/i* (*haben*) practise; **sich**
in etw (*dat*) **ü~** practise sth
über *prep* (+ *dat/acc*) over; (*höher*
als) above; (*betreffend*) about;
⟨*Buch*, *Vortrag*⟩ on; ⟨*Scheck*,
Rechnung⟩ for; ⟨*quer*⟩ across;
ü~ Köln fahren go via Cologne;
ü~ Ostern over Easter; **die**
Woche ü~ during the week;
heute ü~ eine Woche a week
today; **Fehler ü~ Fehler** mistake after mistake □ *adv* **ü~ und**
ü~ all over; **jdm ü~ sein** be
better/(*stärker*) stronger than
s.o. □ *a* (*fam*) **ü~ sein** be left
over; **etw ü~ sein** be fed up with
sth
überall *adv* everywhere
überanstrengen *vt insep* overtax; strain ⟨*Augen*⟩; **sich ü~** overexert oneself
überarbeit|en *vt insep* revise;
sich ü~en overwork. **Ü~ung** *f*
- revision; overwork
überaus *adv* extremely
überbewerten *vt insep* overrate
überbieten† *vt insep* outbid; (*fig*)
outdo; (*übertreffen*) surpass
Überblick *m* overall view; (*Ab-*
riss) summary

überblicken *vt insep* overlook;
(*abschätzen*) assess
überbringen† *vt insep* deliver
überbrücken *vt insep* (*fig*) bridge
überdauern *vt insep* survive
überdenken† *vt insep* think over
überdies *adv* moreover
überdimensional *a* oversized
Überdosis *f* overdose
Überdruss *m* -es (**Überdruß** *m*
-sses) surfeit; **bis zum Ü~** ad
nauseam
überdrüssig *a* **ü~ sein/werden**
be/grow tired (*gen* of)
übereignen *vt insep* transfer
übereilt *a* over-hasty, *adv* -ily
übereinander *adv* one on top
of/above the other; ⟨*sprechen*⟩
about each other; **die Arme/**
Beine ü~ schlagen fold one's
arms/cross one's legs. **ü~**
schlagen† *vt sep* (NEW) **ü~**
schlagen, *s*. **übereinander**
übereinkomen† *vi sep* (*sein*)
agree. **Ü~kunft** *f* - agreement.
ü~stimmen *vi sep* (*haben*) agree;
⟨*Zahlen*⟩ tally; ⟨*Ansichten*⟩ coincide; ⟨*Farben*⟩ match. **Ü~**
stimmung *f* agreement
überempfindlich *a* over-sensi-
tive; (*Med*) hypersensitive
überfahren† *vt insep* run over
Überfahrt *f* crossing
Überfall *m* attack; (*Bank-*) raid
überfallen† *vt insep* attack; raid
⟨*Bank*⟩; (*bestürmen*) bombard
(**mit** with); (*überkommen*) come
over; (*fam: besuchen*) surprise
überfällig *a* overdue
überfliegen† *vt insep* fly over;
(*lesen*) skim over
überflügeln *vt insep* outstrip
Überfluss (**Überfluß**) *m* abundance; (*Wohlstand*) affluence
überflüssig *a* superfluous
überfluten *vt insep* flood
überfordern *vt insep* overtax
überführ|en *vt insep* transfer;
(*Jur*) convict (*gen* of). **Ü~ung** *f*

transfer; (Straße) flyover; (Fußgänger-) foot-bridge

überfüllt a overcrowded

Übergabe f (s. **übergeben**) handing over; transfer

Übergang m crossing; (Wechsel) transition. **Ü~stadium** nt transitional stage

übergeben† vt insep hand over; (übereignen) transfer; **sich ü~** be sick

übergehen†1 vi sep (sein) pass (**an** + acc to); (überwechseln) go over (**zu** to); (werden zu) turn (**in** + acc into); **zum Angriff ü~** start the attack

übergehen†2 vt insep (fig) pass over; (nicht beachten) ignore; (auslassen) leave out

Übergewicht nt excess weight; (fig) predominance; **Ü~ haben** be overweight

übergießen† vt insep **mit Wasser ü~** pour water over

überglücklich a overjoyed

über|greifen† vi sep (haben) spread (**auf** + acc to). **Ü~griff** m infringement

über|groß a outsize; (übertrieben) exaggerated. **Ü~größe** f outsize

überhaben† vt sep have on; (fam: satthaben) be fed up with

überhand adv **ü~ nehmen** increase alarmingly. **ü~nehmen†** vi sep (haben) NEW **ü~ nehmen**, s. **überhand**

überhängen v sep □ vi† (haben) overhang □ vt (reg) sich (dat) etw **ü~** sling over one's shoulder (Gewehr); put round one's shoulders (Jacke)

überhäufen vt insep inundate (**mit** with)

überhaupt adv (im Allgemeinen) altogether; (eigentlich) anyway; (überdies) besides; **ü~ nicht/nichts** not/nothing at all

überheblich a arrogant, adv -ly. **Ü~keit** f - arrogance

überhol|en vt insep overtake; (reparieren) overhaul. **ü~t** a outdated. **Ü~ung** f -,-en overhaul. **Ü~verbot** nt 'Ü~verbot' 'no overtaking'

überhören vt insep fail to hear; (nicht beachten) ignore

überirdisch a supernatural

überkochen vi sep (sein) boil over

überladen† vt insep overload □ a over-ornate

überlassen† vt insep **jdm etw ü~** leave sth to s.o.; (geben) let s.o. have sth; **sich seinem Schmerz ü~** abandon oneself to one's grief; **sich (dat) selbst ü~ sein** be left to one's own devices

überlasten vt insep overload; overtax (Person)

Überlauf m overflow

überlaufen†1 vi sep (sein) overflow; (Mil, Pol) desert

überlaufen†2 vt insep **jdn ü~** (Gefühl:) come over s.o. □ a overrun; (Kursus) over-subscribed

Überläufer m defector

überleben vt/i insep (haben) survive. **Ü~de(r)** m/f survivor

überlegen†1 vt sep put over

überlegen2 v insep □ vt [**sich** dat] **ü~** think over, consider; **es sich** (dat) **anders ü~** change one's mind □ vi (haben) think, reflect; **ohne zu ü~** without thinking

überlegen3 a superior; (herablassend) supercilious, adv -ly. **Ü~heit** f - superiority

Überlegung f -,-en reflection

überliefer|n vt insep hand down. **Ü~ung** f tradition

überlisten vt insep outwit

überm prep = **über dem**

Über|macht f superiority. **ü~mächtig** a superior; (Gefühl) overpowering

übermannen vt insep overcome

Über|maß nt excess. **ü~mäßig** a excessive, adv -ly

Übermensch m superman. **ü~lich** a superhuman

übermitteln vt insep convey; (senden) transmit

übermorgen adv the day after tomorrow

übermüdet a overtired

Über|mut m high spirits pl. **ü~mütig** a high-spirited □ adv in high spirits

übern prep = über den

übernächst|e(r,s) a next ... but one; **ü~es Jahr** the year after next

übernacht|en vi insep (haben) stay overnight. **Ü~ung** f -,-en overnight stay; **Ü~ung und Frühstück** bed and breakfast

Übernahme f - taking over; (Comm) take-over

übernatürlich a supernatural

übernehmen† vt insep take over; (annehmen) take on; sich **ü~** overdo things; (finanziell) overreach oneself

überprüf|en vt insep check. **Ü~ung** f check

überqueren vt insep cross

überragen vt insep tower above; (fig) surpass. **ü~d** a outstanding

überrasch|en vt insep surprise. **ü~end** a surprising, adv -ly; (unerwartet) unexpected, adv -ly. **Ü~ung** f -,-en surprise

überreden vt insep persuade

überreichen vt insep present

überreizt a overwrought

überrennen† vt insep overrun

Überreste mpl remains

überrrumpeln vt insep take by surprise

übers prep = über das

Überschall- pref supersonic

überschatten vt insep overshadow

überschätzen vt insep overestimate

Überschlag m rough estimate; (Sport) somersault

überschlagen†1 vt sep cross ⟨Beine⟩

überschlagen†2 vt insep calculate roughly; (auslassen) skip; sich **ü~** somersault; ⟨Ereignisse:⟩ happen fast □ a tepid

überschnappen vi sep (sein) (fam) go crazy

überschneiden† (sich) vr insep intersect, cross; (zusammenfallen) overlap

überschreiben† vt insep entitle; (übertragen) transfer

überschreiten† vt insep cross; (fig) exceed

Überschrift f heading; (Zeitungs-) headline

Über|schuss (**Überschuß**) m surplus. **ü~schüssig** a surplus

überschütten vt insep **ü~ mit** cover with; (fig) shower with

überschwänglich a effusive, adv -ly

überschwemm|en vt insep flood; (fig) inundate. **Ü~ung** f -,-en flood

überschwenglich a (NEW) **überschwänglich**

Übersee in/nach **Ü~** overseas; **aus/von Ü~** from overseas. **Ü~dampfer** m ocean liner. **ü~isch** a overseas

übersehen† vt insep look out over; (abschätzen) assess; (nicht sehen) overlook, miss; (ignorieren) ignore

übersenden† vt insep send

übersetzen¹ vt sep (haben/sein) cross [over]

übersetz|en² vt insep translate. **Ü~er(in)** m -s, (f -,-nen) translator. **Ü~ung** f -,-en translation

Übersicht f overall view; (Abriss) summary; (Tabelle) table. **ü~lich** a clear, adv -ly

übersied|eln vi sep (sein), **übersied|eln** vi insep (sein) move (nach to). **Ü~lung** f move

übersinnlich a supernatural

überspannt a exaggerated; (verschroben) eccentric

überspielen vt insep (fig) cover up; **auf Band ü~** tape

überspitzt a exaggerated

überspringen† vt insep jump [over]; (auslassen) skip

überstehen†¹ vi sep (haben) project, jut out

überstehen†² vt insep come through; get over ⟨Krankheit⟩; (überleben) survive

übersteigen† vt insep climb [over]; (fig) exceed

überstimmen vt insep outvote

überstreifen vt sep slip on

Überstunden fpl overtime sg; **Ü~ machen** work overtime

überstürzen vt insep rush; **sich ü~en** ⟨Ereignisse:⟩ happen fast; ⟨Worte:⟩ tumble out. **ü~t** a hasty, adv -ily

übertölpeln vt insep dupe

übertönen vt insep drown [out]

übertrag|bar a transferable; (Med) infectious. **ü~en†** vt insep transfer; (übergeben) assign (dat to); (Techn, Med) transmit; (Radio, TV) broadcast; (übersetzen) translate; (anwenden) apply (**auf** + acc to) ⟨a transferred, figurative. **Ü~ung** f -,-en transfer; transmission; broadcast; translation, application

übertreffen† vt insep surpass; (übersteigen) exceed; **sich selbst ü~** excel oneself

übertreib|en† vt insep exaggerate; (zu weit treiben) overdo. **Ü~ung** f -,-en exaggeration

übertret|en†¹ vi sep (sein) step over the line; (Pol) go over/(Relig) convert (**zu** to)

übertret|en†² vt insep infringe; break ⟨Gesetz⟩. **Ü~ung** f -,-en infringement; breach

übertrieben a exaggerated; (übermäßig) excessive, adv -ly

übervölkert a overpopulated

übervorteilen vt insep cheat

überwachen vt insep supervise; (kontrollieren) monitor; (bespitzeln) keep under surveillance

überwachsen a overgrown

überwältigen vt insep overpower; (fig) overwhelm. **ü~d** a overwhelming

überweis|en† vt insep transfer; refer ⟨Patienten⟩. **Ü~ung** f transfer; (ärztliche) referral

überwerfen†¹ vt sep throw on ⟨Mantel⟩

überwerfen†² (sich) vr insep fall out (**mit** with)

überwiegen† v insep □ vi (haben) predominate. □ vt outweigh. **ü~d** a predominant, adv -ly

überwind|en† vt insep overcome; **sich ü~en** force oneself. **Ü~ung** f effort

Überwurf m wrap; (Bett-) bedspread

Über|zahl f majority. **ü~zählig** a spare

überzeug|en vt insep convince; **sich [selbst] ü~en** satisfy oneself. **Ü~end** a convincing, adv -ly. **Ü~ung** f -,- conviction

überziehen†¹ vt sep put on

überziehen†² vt insep cover; overdraw ⟨Konto⟩

Überzug m cover; (Schicht) coating

üblich a usual; (gebräuchlich) customary

U-Boot nt submarine

übrig a remaining; (andere) other; **alles Ü~e (ü~e)** [all] the rest; **im Ü~en (ü~en)** besides; (ansonsten) apart from that; **ü~ sein** od **bleiben** be left [over]; **ü~ haben** od **behalten** have sth left [over]; **etw ü~ lassen** leave sth [over]; **uns blieb nichts anderes ü~** we had no choice. **ü~behalten†** vt sep NEW **ü~ behalten,** s. übrig. **ü~bleiben†** vi insep NEW **ü~ bleiben,** s. übrig. **ü~ens** adv by the way. **ü~lassen†** vt sep NEW **ü~ lassen,** s. übrig

Übung f -,-en exercise; (Üben) practice; **außer** od **aus der Ü~** out of practice

UdSSR f - USSR

Ufer nt -s,- shore; (Fluss-) bank

Uhr f -,-en clock; (Armband-) watch; (Zähler) meter; **um ein U~** at one o'clock; **wie viel U~ ist es?** what's the time? **U~armband** nt watch-strap. **U~macher** m -s,- watch and clockmaker. **U~werk** nt clock/watch mechanism. **U~zeiger** m [clock-/watch-]hand. **U~zeigersinn** m **im/entgegen dem U~zeigersinn** clockwise/anticlockwise. **U~zeit** f time

Uhu m -s,-s eagle owl

UKW abbr (Ultrakurzwelle) VHF

Ulk m -s fun; (Streich) trick. **u~en** vi (haben) joke. **u~ig** a funny; (seltsam) odd. **adv -ly**

Ulme f -,-n elm

Ultimatum nt -s,-ten ultimatum

Ultrakurzwelle f very high frequency

Ultraschall m ultrasound

ultraviolett a ultraviolet

um prep (+ acc) [a]round; (Uhrzeit) at; (bitten, kämpfen) for; (streiten) over; (sich sorgen) about; (betrügen) out of; (bei Angabe einer Differenz) by; **um [... herum]** around, [round] about; **Tag um Tag** day after day; **einen Tag um den andern** every other day; **um seinetwillen** for his sake ○adv (ungefähr) around, about; **um sein** (fam) be over; (Zeit) be up ○conj **um zu** to; (Absicht) [in order] to; **zu müde, um zu ...** too tired to ...; **um so besser** (NEW) **umso besser**, s. **umso**

umändern vt sep alter

umarbeiten vt sep alter; (bearbeiten) revise

umarm|en vt insep embrace, hug. **U~ung** f -,-en embrace, hug

Umbau m rebuilding; conversion (zu into). **u~en** vt sep rebuild; convert (zu into)

umbild|en vt sep change; (umgestalten) reorganize; reshuffle (Kabinett). **U~ung** f reorganization; (Pol) reshuffle

umbinden† vt sep put on

umblättern v sep ○vt turn [over] ○vi (haben) turn the page

umblicken (sich) vr sep look round; (zurück) look back

umbringen† vt sep kill; **sich u~** kill oneself

Umbruch m (fig) radical change

umbuchen v sep ○vt change; (Comm) transfer ○vi (haben) change one's booking

umdrehen v sep ○vt turn round/(wenden) over; (Schlüssel); (umkrempeln) turn inside out; **sich u~** turn round; (im Liegen) turn over ○vi (haben/sein) turn back

Umdrehung f turn; (Motor-) revolution

umeinander adv around each other; **sich u~ sorgen** worry about each other

umfahren†1 vt sep run over

umfahren†2 vt insep go round; bypass (Ort)

umfallen† vt sep (sein) fall over; (Person:) fall down

Umfang m girth; (Geom) circumference; (Größe) size; (Ausmaß) extent; (Mus) range

umfangen† vt insep embrace; (fig) envelop

umfangreich a extensive; (dick) big

umfassen vt insep consist of, comprise; (umgeben) surround. **u~d** a comprehensive

Umfrage f survey, poll

umfüllen vt sep transfer

umfunktionieren vt sep convert

Umgang m [social] contact; (Umgehen) dealing (mit with). **U~ haben mit** associate with

umgänglich a sociable

Umgangs|formen *fpl* manners. **U~sprache** *f* colloquial language. **u~sprachlich** *a* colloquial, *adv* -ly

umgeb|en† *vt/i insep* (haben) surround □ *a* **u~en von** surrounded by. **U~ung** □ *f* -,-en surroundings *pl*

umgehen†1 *vi sep* (sein) go round; **u~ mit** treat, handle; (verkehren) associate with; **in dem Schloss geht es im Gespenst um** the castle is haunted

umgehen†2 *vt insep* avoid; (nicht beachten) evade; (Straße:) bypass

umgehend *a* immediate, *adv* -ly

Umgehungsstraße *f* bypass

umgekehrt *a* inverse; (Reihenfolge) reverse; **es war u~** it was the other way round □ *adv* conversely; **und u~** and vice versa

umgraben† *vt sep* dig [over]

umhaben† *vt sep* have on

Umhang *m* cloak

umhauen† *vt sep* knock down; (fällen) chop down

umher *adv* **sel y** = all around. **u~gehen†** *vi sep* (sein) walk about

umhören (sich) *vr sep* ask around

Umkehr *f* - turning back. **u~en** *v sep* □ *vi* (sein) turn back □ *vt* turn round; turn inside out □ *vt* (fig) reverse. **U~ung** *f* - reversal

umkippen *v sep* □ *vt* tip over; (versehentlich) knock over □ *vi* (sein) fall over; (Boot:) capsize; (fam: ohnmächtig werden) faint

Umkleide|kabine *f* changing-cubicle. **u~n** (sich) *vr sep* change. **U~raum** *m* changing-room

umknicken *v sep* □ *vt* bend; (falten) fold □ *vi* bend; (mit dem Fuß) go over on one's ankle

umkommen† *vi sep* (sein) perish; **u~ lassen** waste (Lebensmittel)

Umkreis *m* surroundings *pl*; **im U~ von** within a radius of

umkreisen *vt insep* circle; (Astr) revolve around; (Satellit:) orbit

umkrempeln *vt sep* turn up; (von innen nach außen) turn inside out; (ändern) change radically

Umlauf *m* circulation; (Astr) revolution. **U~bahn** *f* orbit

Umlaut *m* umlaut

umlegen *vt sep* lay *or* put down; flatten (Getreide); turn down (Kragen); put on (Schal); throw (Hebel); (verlegen) transfer; (fam: niederschlagen) knock down; (töten) kill

umleiten *vt sep* divert. **U~ung** *f* diversion

umliegend *a* surrounding

umpflanzen *vt sep* transplant

umrahmen *vt insep* frame

umranden *vt insep* edge

umräumen *vt sep* rearrange

umrechn|en *vt sep* convert. **U~ung** *f* conversion

umreißen†1 *vt sep* tear down; knock down (Person)

umreißen†2 *vt insep* outline

umringen *vt insep* surround

Umriss (**Umriß**) *m* outline

umrühren *vt/i sep* (haben) stir

ums *pron* = **um das**; **u~ Leben kommen** lose one's life

Umsatz *m* (Comm) turnover

umschalten *vt/i sep* (haben) switch over; **auf Rot u~** (Ampel:) change to red

Umschau *f* **U~ halten nach** look out for. **u~en** (sich) *vr sep* look round/(zurück) back

Umschlag *m* cover; (Schutz-) jacket; (Brief-) envelope; (Med) compress; (Hosen-) turn-up; (Wechsel) change. **u~en†** *v sep* □ *vt* turn up; turn over (Seite); (fällen) chop down □ *vi* (sein) topple over; (Boot:) capsize; (Wetter:) change; (Wind:) veer

umschließen† *vt insep* enclose

umschnallen *vt sep* buckle on

umschreiben†1 *vt sep* rewrite

umschreib|en² vt insep define; (anders ausdrücken) paraphrase. **U~ung** f definition; paraphrase

umschulen vt sep retrain; (Sch) transfer to another school

Umschweife pl keine **U~ machen** come straight out with it; **ohne U~** straight out

Umschwung m (fig) change; (Pol) U-turn

umsehen† (sich) vr sep look round; (zurück) look back; **sich u~ nach** look for

umsein† vi sep (sein) (NEW) **um sein, s. um**

umseitig a & adv overleaf

umsetzen vt sep move; (umpflanzen) transplant; (Comm) sell

Umsicht f circumspection. **u~ig** a circumspect, adv -ly

umsied|eln v sep □ vt resettle □ vi (sein) move. **U~lung** f resettlement

umso conj ~ **besser/mehr** all the better/more; **je mehr, ~ besser** the more the better

umsonst adv in vain; (grundlos) without reason; (gratis) free

umspringen† vi sep (sein) change; (Wind:) veer; **übel u~ mit** treat badly

Umstand m circumstance; (Tatsache) fact; (Aufwand) fuss; (Mühe) trouble; **unter U~en** possibly; **U~e machen** make a fuss; **jdm U~e machen** put s.o. to trouble; **in andern U~en** pregnant

umständlich a laborious, adv -ly; (kompliziert) involved; (Person) fussy

Umstands|kleid nt maternity dress. **U~wort** nt (pl -wörter) adverb

umstehen† vi insep surround

Umstehende pl bystanders

umsteigen† vi sep (sein) change

umstellen¹ vt insep surround

umstell|en² vt sep rearrange; transpose (Wörter); (anders einstellen) reset; (Techn) convert; (ändern) change; **sich u~en** adjust. **U~ung** f rearrangement; transposition; resetting; conversion; change; adjustment

umstimmen vt sep **jdn u~** change s.o.'s mind

umstoßen† vt sep knock over; (fig) overturn; upset (Plan)

umstritten a controversial; (ungeklärt) disputed

umstülpen vt sep turn upside down; (von innen nach außen) turn inside out

Um|sturz m coup. **u~stürzen** v sep □ vt overturn; (Pol) overthrow □ vi (sein) fall over

umtaufen vt sep rename

Umtausch m exchange. **u~en** vt sep change; exchange (**gegen** for)

umwälzend a revolutionary

umwandeln vt sep convert; (fig) transform

umwechseln vt sep change

Umweg m detour. **auf U~en** (fig) in a roundabout way

Umwelt f environment. **u~freundlich** a environmentally friendly. **U~schutz** m protection of the environment. **U~schützer** m environmentalist

umwenden† vt sep turn over; **sich u~** turn round

umwerfen† vt sep knock over; (fig) upset (Plan); (fam) bowl over (Person)

umziehen† v sep □ vi (sein) move □ vt change; **sich u~** change

umzingeln vt insep surround

Umzug m move; (Prozession) procession

unabänderlich a irrevocable; (Tatsache) unalterable

unabhängig a independent, adv -ly; **u~ davon, ob** irrespective of whether. **U~keit** f - independence

unabkömmlich pred a busy

unablässig a incessant, adv -ly
unabsehbar a incalculable
unabsichtlich a unintentional,
  adv -ly
unachtsam a careless, adv -ly.
  U∼keit f - carelessness
unangebracht a inappropriate
unangemeldet a unexpected,
  adv -ly
unangemessen a inappropriate,
  adv -ly
unangenehm a unpleasant, adv
  -ly; ⟨peinlich⟩ embarrassing
Unannehmlichkeiten   fpl
  trouble sg
unansehnlich a shabby; ⟨Person⟩
  plain
unanständig a indecent, adv -ly
unantastbar a inviolable
unappetitlich a unappetizing
Unart f -,-en bad habit. **u∼ig** a
  naughty
unauffällig a inconspicuous, adv
  -ly, unobtrusive, adv -ly
unauffindbar a **u∼ sein** be nowhere to be found
unaufgefordert adv without
  being asked
unauf|haltsam a inexorable, adv
  -bly. **u∼hörlich** a incessant, adv
  -ly
unaufmerksam a inattentive
unaufrichtig a insincere
unausbleiblich a inevitable
unausgeglichen a unbalanced;
  ⟨Person⟩ unstable
unaus|löschlich a ⟨fig⟩ indelible,
  adv -bly. **u∼sprechlich** a indescribable, adv -bly. **u∼stehlich** a
  insufferable
unbarmherzig a merciless, adv
  -ly
unbeabsichtigt a unintentional,
  adv -ly
unbedacht a rash, adv -ly
unbedenklich a harmless □ adv
  without hesitation
unbedeutend a insignificant;
  ⟨geringfügig⟩ slight, adv -ly

unbedingt a absolute, adv -ly;
  nicht u∼ not necessarily
unbefangen a natural, adv -ly;
  ⟨unparteiisch⟩ impartial
unbefriedigend a unsatisfactory. **u∼t** a dissatisfied
unbefugt a unauthorized □ adv
  without authorization
unbegreiflich a incomprehensible
unbegrenzt a unlimited □ adv in-
  definitely
unbegründet a unfounded
Unbehag|en n unease; ⟨körper-
  lich⟩ discomfort. **u∼lich** a uncomfortable, adv -bly
unbeholfen a awkward, adv -ly
unbekannt a unknown; ⟨nicht
  vertraut⟩ unfamiliar. **U∼e(r)** m/f
  stranger
unbekümmert a unconcerned;
  ⟨unbeschwert⟩ carefree
unbeliebt a unpopular. **U∼heit** f
  unpopularity
unbemannt a unmanned
unbemerkt a & adv unnoticed
unbenutzt a unused
unbequem a uncomfortable, adv
  -bly; ⟨lästig⟩ awkward
unberechenbar a unpredictable
unberechtigt a unjustified; ⟨un-
  befugt⟩ unauthorized
unberufen int touch wood!
unberührt a untouched; ⟨fig⟩ virgin; ⟨Landschaft⟩ unspoilt
unbescheiden a presumptuous
unbeschrankt a unguarded
unbeschränkt a unlimited □ adv
  without limit
unbeschreiblich a indescribable, adv -bly
unbeschwert a carefree
unbesiegbar a invincible
unbesiegt a undefeated
unbesonnen a rash, adv -ly
unbespielt a blank
unbeständig a inconsistent;
  ⟨Wetter⟩ unsettled
unbestechlich a incorruptible

unbestimmt a indefinite; ⟨Alter⟩ indeterminate; ⟨ungewiss⟩ uncertain; ⟨unklar⟩ vague □ adv vaguely

unbestreitbar a indisputable, adv -bly

unbestritten a undisputed □ adv indisputably

unbeteiligt a indifferent; u~ an (+ dat) not involved in

unbetont a unstressed

unbewacht a unguarded

unbewaffnet a unarmed

unbeweglich a & adv motionless, still

unbewohnt a uninhabited

unbewusst (unbewußt) a unconscious, adv -ly

unbezahlbar a priceless

unbezahlt a unpaid

unbrauchbar a useless

und conj and; u~ so weiter and so on; nach und nach bit by bit

Undank m ingratitude. **u~bar** a ungrateful; ⟨nicht lohnend⟩ thankless. **U~barkeit** f ingratitude

undefinierbar a indefinable

undenk|bar a unthinkable. **u~lich** a seit u~lichen Zeiten from time immemorial

undeutlich a indistinct, adv -ly; ⟨vage⟩ vague, adv -ly

undicht a leaking; u~e Stelle leak

Unding nt absurdity

undiplomatisch a undiplomatic. adv -ally

unduldsam a intolerant

undurch|dringlich a impenetrable; ⟨Miene⟩ inscrutable. **u~führbar** a impracticable

undurch|lässig a impermeable. **u~sichtig** a opaque; ⟨fig⟩ doubtful

uneben a uneven, adv -ly. **U~heit** f -,-en unevenness; ⟨Buckel⟩ bump

unecht a false; u~er Schmuck/Pelz imitation jewellery/fur

unehelich a illegitimate

unehr|enhaft a dishonourable, adv -bly. **u~lich** a dishonest, adv -ly. **U~lichkeit** f dishonesty

uneinig a ⟨fig⟩ divided; [sich ⟨dat⟩] u~ sein disagree. **U~keit** f disagreement; ⟨Streit⟩ discord

uneins a ~ sein be at odds

unempfindlich a insensitive ⟨gegen⟩ to; ⟨widerstandsfähig⟩ tough; ⟨Med⟩ immune

unendlich a infinite, adv -ly; ⟨endlos⟩ endless, adv -ly. **U~keit** f - infinity

unentbehrlich a indispensable

unentgeltlich a free, ⟨Arbeit⟩ unpaid □ adv free of charge; ⟨arbeiten⟩ without pay

unentschieden a undecided; ⟨Sport⟩ drawn; u~ spielen draw. U~ nt -s,- draw

unentschlossen a indecisive; ⟨unentschieden⟩ undecided. **U~heit** f indecision

unentwegt a persistent adv -ly ⟨unaufhörlich⟩ incessant, adv -ly

unerbittlich a implacable, adv -bly; ⟨Schicksal⟩ inexorable

unerfahren a inexperienced. **U~heit** f - inexperience

unerfreulich a unpleasant, adv -ly

unergründlich a unfathomable

unerhört a enormous, adv -ly; ⟨empörend⟩ outrageous, adv -ly

unerklärlich a inexplicable

unerlässlich (unerläßlich) a essential

unerlaubt a unauthorized □ adv without permission

unermesslich (unermeßlich) a immense, adv -ly

unermüdlich a tireless, adv -ly

unersättlich a insatiable

unerschöpflich a inexhaustible

unerschütterlich a unshakeable

unerschwinglich a prohibitive

unersetzlich a irreplaceable; ⟨Verlust⟩ irreparable

unerträglich *a* unbearable, *adv* -bly

unerwartet *a* unexpected, *adv* -ly

unerwünscht *a* unwanted; *(Besuch)* unwelcome

unfähig *a* incompetent; **u~, etw zu tun** incapable of doing sth; *(nicht in der Lage)* unable to do sth. **U~keit** *f* incompetence; inability *(zu* to)

unfair *a* unfair, *adv* -ly

Unfall *m* accident. **U~flucht** *f* failure to stop after an accident. **U~station** *f* casualty department

unfassbar (unfaßbar) *a* incomprehensible; *(unglaublich)* unimaginable

unfehlbar *a* infallible. **U~keit** *f* infallibility

unfolgsam *a* disobedient

unförmig *a* shapeless

unfreiwillig *a* involuntary, *adv* -ily; *(unbeabsichtigt)* unintentional, *adv* -ly

unfreundlich *a* unfriendly; *(unangenehm)* unpleasant, *adv* -ly. **U~keit** *f* unfriendliness; unpleasantness

Unfriede[n] *m* discord

unfruchtbar *a* infertile, *(fig)* unproductive. **U~keit** *f* infertility

Unfug *m* -s mischief; *(Unsinn)* nonsense

Ungar|(in) *m* -n,-n *(f* -,-nen*)* Hungarian. **u~isch** *a* Hungarian. **U~n** *nt* -s Hungary

ungastlich *a* inhospitable

ungeachtet *prep* (+ *gen)* in spite of; **dessen u~** notwithstanding [this]. **ungebärdig** *a* unruly. **ungebeugt** *a (Gram)* uninflected. **ungebraucht** *a* unused. **ungebührlich** *a* improper, *adv* -ly. **ungedeckt** *a* uncovered; *(Sport)* unmarked; *(Tisch)* unlaid

Ungeduld *f* impatience. **u~ig** *a* impatient, *adv* -ly

ungeeignet *a* unsuitable

ungefähr *a* approximate, *adv* -ly, rough, *adv* -ly

ungefährlich *a* harmless

ungehalten *a* angry, *adv* -ily

ungeheuer *a* enormous, *adv* -ly. **U~** *nt* -s,- monster

ungeheuerlich *a* outrageous

ungehobelt *a* uncouth

ungehörig *a* improper, *adv* -ly; *(frech)* impertinent, *adv* -ly

ungehorsam *a* disobedient. **U~** *m* disobedience

ungeklärt *a* unsolved; *(Frage)* unsettled; *(Ursache)* unknown

ungeladen *a* unloaded; *(Gast)* uninvited

ungelegen *a* inconvenient. **U~heiten** *fpl* trouble *sg*

ungelernt *a* unskilled. **ungemein** *a* tremendous, *adv* -ly

ungemütlich *a* uncomfortable, *adv* -bly; *(unangenehm)* unpleasant, *adv* -ly

ungenau *a* inaccurate, *adv* -ly; *(vage)* vague, *adv* -ly. **U~igkeit** *f* -,-en inaccuracy

ungeniert /'ʊnʒeniːɐ̯t/ *a* uninhibited □ *adv* openly

ungenießbar *a* inedible; *(Getränk)* undrinkable. **ungenügend** *a* inadequate, *adv* -ly; *(Sch)* unsatisfactory. **ungepflegt** *a* neglected; *(Person)* unkempt. **ungerade** *a (Zahl)* odd

ungerecht *a* unjust, *adv* -ly. **U~igkeit** *f* -,-en injustice

ungern *adv* reluctantly

ungesalzen *a* unsalted

ungeschehen *a* **u~ machen** undo

Ungeschick|lichkeit *f* clumsiness. **u~t** *a* clumsy, *adv* -ily

ungeschminkt *a* without make-up; *(Wahrheit)* unvarnished. **ungeschrieben** *a* unwritten. **ungesehen** *a & adv* unseen. **ungesellig** *a* unsociable. **ungesetzlich** *a* illegal, *adv* -ly. **ungestört** *a* undisturbed. **ungestraft** *adv* with impunity. **ungestüm** *a* impetuous, *adv* -ly. **ungesund** *a* unhealthy. **ungesüßt** *a* unsweetened. **ungetrübt** *a* perfect

Ungetüm *nt* -s,-e monster

ungewiss (**ungewiß**) *a* uncertain; **im Ungewissen** (**ungewissen**) **sein/lassen** be/leave in the dark. **U~heit** *f* uncertainty

ungewöhnlich *a* unusual, *adv* -ly. **ungewohnt** *a* unaccustomed; (*nicht vertraut*) unfamiliar. **ungewollt** *a* unintentional, *adv* -ly; (*Schwangerschaft*) unwanted

Ungeziefer *nt* -s vermin

ungezogen *a* naughty, *adv* -ily. **ungezwungen** *a* informal, *adv* -ly; (*natürlich*) natural, *adv* -ly

ungläubig *a* incredulous

unglaublich *a* incredible, *adv* -bly, unbelievable, *adv* -bly

ungleich *a* unequal, *adv* -ly; (*verschieden*) different. **U~heit** *f* - inequality. **u~mäßig** *a* uneven, *adv* -ly

Unglück *nt* -s,-e misfortune; (*Pech*) bad luck; (*Missgeschick*) mishap; (*Unfall*) accident; **U~ bringen** be unlucky. **u~lich** *a* unhappy, *adv* -ily; (*ungünstig*) unfortunate, *adv* -ly. **u~licherweise** *adv* unfortunately. **u~selig** *a* unfortunate. **U~sfall** *m* accident

ungültig *a* invalid; (*Jur*) void

ungünstig *a* unfavourable, *adv* -bly; (*unpassend*) inconvenient, *adv* -ly

ungut *a* (*Gefühl*) uneasy; **nichts für u~!** no offence!

unhandlich *a* unwieldy

Unheil *nt* -s disaster; **U~ anrichten** cause havoc

unheilbar *a* incurable, *adv* -bly

unheimlich *a* eerie; (*gruselig*) creepy; (*fam: groß*) terrific □ *adv* eerily; (*fam: sehr*) terribly

unhöflich *a* rude, *adv* -ly. **U~keit** *f* rudeness

unhörbar *a* inaudible, *adv* -bly

unhygienisch *a* unhygienic

Uni *f* -,-s (*fam*) university

uni /y'ni:/ *inv a* plain

Uniform *f* -,-en uniform

uninteress|ant *a* uninteresting. **u~iert** *a* uninterested; (*unbeteiligt*) disinterested

Union *f* -,-en union

universal *a* universal

universell *a* universal, *adv* -ly

Universität *f* -,-en university

Universum *nt* -s universe

unkenntlich *a* unrecognizable. **U~nis** *f* ignorance

unklar *a* unclear; (*ungewiss*) uncertain; (*vage*) vague, *adv* -ly; **im U~en** (**u~en**) **sein/lassen** be/leave in the dark. **U~heit** *f* -,-en uncertainty

unklug *a* unwise, *adv* -ly

unkompliziert *a* uncomplicated

Unkosten *pl* expenses

Unkraut *nt* -s weed; (*coll*) weeds *pl*; **U~ jäten** weed. **U~vertilgungsmittel** *nt* weed-killer

unkultiviert *a* uncultured

unlängst *adv* recently

unlauter *a* dishonest; (*unfair*) unfair

unleserlich *a* illegible, *adv* -bly

unleugbar *a* undeniable, *adv* -bly

unlogisch *a* illogical, *adv* -ly

unlös|bar *a* (*fig*) insoluble. **u~lich** *a* (*Chem*) insoluble

unlustig *a* listless, *adv* -ly

unmäßig *a* excessive, *adv* -ly; (*äußerst*) extreme, *adv* -ly

Unmenge *f* enormous amount/(*Anzahl*) number

Unmensch *m* (*fam*) brute. **u~lich** *a* inhuman; (*entsetzlich*) appalling, *adv* -ly

unmerklich *a* imperceptible, *adv* -bly

unmissverständlich (**unmißverständlich**) *a* unambiguous, *adv* -ly; (*offen*) unequivocal, *adv* -ly

unmittelbar *a* immediate, *adv* -ly; (*direkt*) direct, *adv* -ly

unmöbliert *a* unfurnished

unmodern *a* old-fashioned

unmöglich *a* impossible, *adv* -bly. **U~keit** *f* - impossibility

Unmoral *f* immorality. **u~isch** *a* immoral, *adv* -ly

unmündig *a* under-age

Unmut *m* displeasure

unnachahmlich *a* inimitable

unnachgiebig *a* intransigent

unnatürlich *a* unnatural, *adv* -ly

unnormal *a* abnormal, *adv* -ly

unnötig *a* unnecessary, *adv* -ly

unnütz *a* useless □ *adv* needlessly

unord|entlich *a* untidy, *adv* -ily ⟨*nachlässig*⟩ sloppy, *adv* -ily. **U~nung** *f* disorder; ⟨*Durcheinander*⟩ muddle

unorganisiert *a* disorganized

unorthodox *a* unorthodox □ *adv* in an unorthodox manner

unparteiisch *a* impartial, *adv* -ly

unpassend *a* inappropriate, *adv* -ly; ⟨*Moment*⟩ inopportune

unpässlich (**unpäßlich**) *a* indisposed

unpersönlich *a* impersonal

unpraktisch *a* impractical

unpünktlich *a* unpunctual □ *adv* late

unrasiert *a* unshaven

Unrast *f* restlessness

unrealistisch *a* unrealistic, *adv* -ally

unrecht *a* wrong, *adv* -ly □ *n* jdm u~ tun do s.o. an injustice; u~ haben/geben, s. Unrecht. U~ *nt* wrong; zu U~ wrongly; jdm U~ geben disagree with s.o. u~mäßig *a* unlawful, *adv* -ly

unregelmäßig *a* irregular, *adv* -ly. **U~keit** *f* irregularity

unreif *a* unripe; ⟨*fig*⟩ immature

unrein *a* impure; ⟨*Luft*⟩ polluted; ⟨*Haut*⟩ bad; **ins U~e** (**u~e**) **schreiben** make a rough draft of

unrentabel *a* unprofitable, *adv* -bly

unrichtig *a* incorrect

Unruh|e *f* -,-n restlessness; ⟨*Erregung*⟩ agitation; ⟨*Besorgnis*⟩ anxiety; **U~en** ⟨*Pol*⟩ unrest *sg*. **u~ig** *a* restless, *adv* -ly; ⟨*Meer*⟩ agitated; ⟨*laut*⟩ noisy, *adv* -ily; ⟨*besorgt*⟩ anxious, *adv* -ly

uns *pron* ⟨*acc/dat* of **wir**⟩ us; ⟨*refl*⟩ ourselves; ⟨*einander*⟩ each other; **ein Freund von uns** a friend of ours

unsagbar, **unsäglich** *a* indescribable, *adv* -bly

unsanft *a* rough, *adv* -ly

unsauber *a* dirty; ⟨*nachlässig*⟩ sloppy, *adv* -ily; ⟨*unlauter*⟩ dishonest, *adv* -ly

unschädlich *a* harmless

unscharf *a* blurred

unschätzbar *a* inestimable

unscheinbar *a* inconspicuous

unschicklich *a* improper, *adv* -ly

unschlagbar *a* unbeatable

unschlüssig *a* undecided

Unschuld *f* - innocence; ⟨*Jungfräulichkeit*⟩ virginity. **u~ig** *a* innocent, *adv* -ly

unselbstständig, **unselbständig** *a* dependent □ *adv* **u~ denken** not think for oneself

unser *poss pron* our. **u~e(r,s)** *poss pron* ours. **u~erseits** *adv* for our part. **u~twegen** *adv* for our sake; ⟨*wegen uns*⟩ because of us, on our account. **u~twillen** *adv* **um u~twillen** for our sake

unsicher *a* unsafe; ⟨*ungewiss*⟩ uncertain; ⟨*nicht zuverlässig*⟩ unreliable; ⟨*Schritte, Hand*⟩ unsteady; ⟨*Person*⟩ insecure □ *adv* unsteadily. **U~heit** *f* uncertainty; unreliability; insecurity

unsichtbar *a* invisible

Unsinn *m* nonsense. **u~ig** *a* nonsensical, absurd

Unsitt|e *f* bad habit. **u~lich** *a* indecent, *adv* -ly

unsportlich *a* not sporty; ⟨*unfair*⟩ unsporting, *adv* -ly

uns|re(r,s) *poss pron* = **unsere(r,s)**. **u~rige** *poss pron* **der/die/das u~rige** ours

unsterblich a immortal. **U~keit** f immortality

unstet a restless, adv -ly; (unbeständig) unstable

Unstimmigkeit f -,-en inconsistency; (Streit) difference

Unsumme f vast sum

unsymmetrisch a not symmetrical

unsympathisch a unpleasant; **er ist mir u~** I don't like him

untätig a idle, adv idly. **U~keit** f - idleness

untauglich a unsuitable; (Mil) unfit

unteilbar a indivisible

unten adv at the bottom; (auf der Unterseite) underneath; (eine Treppe tiefer) downstairs; (im Text) below; **hier/da u~** down here/there; **nach u~** down [-wards]; (die Treppe hinunter) downstairs; **siehe u~** see below

unter prep (+ dat/acc) under; (niedriger als) below; (inmitten, zwischen) among; **u~ anderem** among other things; **u~ der Woche** during the week; **u~ sich** by themselves; **u~ uns gesagt** between ourselves

Unter|arm m forearm. **U~bewusstsein (U~bewußtsein)** nt subconscious

unterbieten† vt insep undercut; beat (Rekord)

unterbinden† vt insep stop

unterbleiben† vi insep (sein) cease; **es hat zu u~** it must stop

unterbrech|en† vt insep interrupt; break (Reise). **U~ung** f -,-en interruption, break

unterbreiten vt insep present

unterbringen† vt sep put; (beherbergen) put up

unterdessen adv in the meantime

unterdrück|en vt insep suppress; oppress (Volk). **U~ung** f - suppression; oppression

untere(r,s) a lower

untereinander adv one below the other; (miteinander) among ourselves/yourselves/themselves

unterernähr|t a undernourished. **U~ung** f malnutrition

Unterfangen nt -s,- venture

Unterführung f underpass; (Fußgänger-) subway

Untergang m (Astr) setting; (Naut) sinking; (Zugrundegehen) disappearance; (der Welt) end

Untergebene(r) m/f subordinate

untergehen† vi sep (sein) (Astr) set; (versinken) go under; (Schiff:) go down, sink; (zugrunde gehen) disappear; (Welt:) come to an end

untergeordnet a subordinate

Untergeschoss (Untergeschoß) nt basement

untergraben† vt insep (fig) undermine

Untergrund m foundation; (Hintergrund) background; (Pol) underground. **U~bahn** f underground [railway]. (Amer) subway

unterhaken vt sep **jdn u~** take s.o.'s arm; **untergehakt arm in arm**

unterhalb adv & prep (+ gen) below

Unterhalt m maintenance

unterhalt|en† vt insep maintain; (ernähren) support; (betreiben) run; (erheitern) entertain; **sich u~en** talk; (sich vergnügen) enjoy oneself. **U~sam** a entertaining. **U~ung** f -,-en maintenance; (Gespräch) conversation; (Zeitvertreib) entertainment

unterhandeln vi insep (haben) negotiate

Unter|haus nt (Pol) lower house; (in UK) House of Commons. **U~hemd** nt vest. **U~holz** nt undergrowth. **U~hose** f underpants pl. **u~irdisch** a & adv underground

unterjochen vt insep subjugate

Unterkiefer *m* lower jaw

unter|kommen† *vi sep (sein)* find accommodation; *(eine Stellung finden)* get a job. **u~kriegen** *vt sep (fam)* get down

Unterkunft *f* -,⸗künfte accommodation

Unterlage *f* pad; **U~n** papers

Unterlass (**Unterlaß**) *m* ohne **U~** incessantly

unterlass|en† *vt insep* etw **u~en** refrain from [doing] sth; **es u~en, etw zu tun** fail *or* omit to do sth. **U~ung** *f* -,-en omission

unterlaufen† *vi insep (sein)* occur; **mir ist ein Fehler u~** I made a mistake

unterlegen¹ *vt sep* put underneath

unterlegen² *a* inferior; *(Sport)* losing; **zahlenmäßig u~** outnumbered *(dat* by). **U~e(r)** *m/f* loser

Unterleib *m* abdomen

unterliegen† *vi insep (sein)* lose *(dat* to); *(unterworfen sein)* be subject *(dat* to)

Unterlippe *f* lower lip

unterm *prep* = unter dem

Untermiete *f* **zur U~ wohnen** be a lodger. **U~r(in)** *m(f)* lodger

unterminieren *vt insep* undermine

untern *prep* = unter den

unternehm|en† *vt insep* undertake; take *(Schritte)*; **etw/nichts u~en** do sth/nothing. **U~en** *nt* -s,- undertaking, enterprise *(Betrieb)* concern. **u~end** *a* enterprising. **U~er** *m* -s,- employer; *(Bau-)* contractor; *(Industrieller)* industrialist. **U~ung** *f* -,-en undertaking; *(Comm)* venture. **u~ungslustig** *a* enterprising; *(abenteuerlustig)* adventurous

Unteroffizier *m* non-commissioned officer

unterordnen *vt sep* subordinate; **sich u~** accept a subordinate role

Unterredung *f* -,-en talk

Unterricht *m* -[e]s teaching; *(Privat-)* tuition; *(U~sstunden)* lessons *pl*; **U~ geben/nehmen** give/have lessons

unterrichten *vt/i insep (haben)* teach; *(informieren)* inform; **sich u~** inform oneself

Unterrock *m* slip

unters *prep* = unter das

untersagen *vt insep* forbid

Untersatz *m* mat; *(mit Füßen)* stand; *(Gläser-)* coaster

unterschätzen *vt insep* underestimate

unterscheid|en† *vt/i insep (haben)* distinguish; *(auseinanderhalten)* tell apart; **sich u~en** differ. **U~ung** *f* -,-en distinction

Unterschied *m* -[e]s,-e difference; *(Unterscheidung)* distinction; **im U~ zu ihm** unlike him. **u~lich** *a* different; *(wechselnd)* varying; **das ist u~lich** it varies. **u~slos** *a* equal, adv -ly

unterschlag|en† *vt insep* embezzle; *(verheimlichen)* suppress. **U~ung** *f* -,-en embezzlement; suppression

Unterschlupf *m* -[e]s shelter; *(Versteck)* hiding-place

unterschreiben† *vt/i insep (haben)* sign

Unter|schrift *f* signature; *(Bild-)* caption. **U~seeboot** *nt* submarine. **U~setzer** *m* -s,- = Untersatz

untersetzt *a* stocky

Unterstand *m* shelter

unterste(r,s) *a* lowest, bottom

unterstehen†¹ *vi sep (haben)* shelter

unterstehen†² *v insep* □ *vi (haben)* be answerable *(dat* to); *(unterliegen)* be subject *(dat* to) □ *vr sich u~* dare; **untersteh dich!** don't you dare!

unterstellen¹ *vt sep* put underneath; *(abstellen)* store; **sich u~** shelter

unterstellen² vt insep place under the control (dat of); (annehmen) assume; (fälschlich zuschreiben) impute (dat to)

unterstreichen† vt insep underline

unterstütz|en vt insep support; (helfen) aid. **U~ung** f -,-en support; (finanziell) aid; (regelmäßiger Betrag) allowance; (Arbeitslosen-) benefit

untersuch|en vt insep examine; (Jur) investigate; (prüfen) test; (überprüfen) check; (durchsuchen) search. **U~ung** f -,-en examination; investigation; test; check; search. **U~ungshaft** f detention on remand; **in U~ungshaft** on remand. **U~ungsrichter** m examining magistrate

Untertan m -s & -en,-en subject

Untertasse f saucer

untertauchen v sep □ vt duck □ vi (sein) go under; (fig) disappear

Unterteil nt bottom (part)

unterteilen vt insep subdivide; (aufteilen) divide

Untertitel m subtitle

Unterton m undertone

untervermieten vt/i insep (haben) sublet

unterwandern vt insep infiltrate

Unterwäsche f underwear

Unterwasser- pref underwater

unterwegs adv on the way; (außer Haus) out; (verreist) away

unterweisen† vt insep instruct

Unterwelt f underworld

unterwerfen† vt insep subjugate; **sich u~** submit (dat to); **etw** (dat) **unterworfen sein** be subject to sth

unterwürfig a obsequious, adv -ly

unterzeichnen vt insep sign

unterziehen†¹ vt sep put on underneath (Culin) fold in

unterziehen†² vt insep einer Untersuchung/Überprüfung **u~** examine/ check sth; **sich**

einer Operation/Prüfung **u~** have an operation/take a test

Untier nt monster

untragbar a intolerable

untrennbar a inseparable

untreu a disloyal; (in der Ehe) unfaithful. **U~e** f disloyalty; infidelity

untröstlich a inconsolable

untrüglich a infallible

Untugend f bad habit

unüberlegt a rash, adv -ly

unüber|sehbar a obvious; (groß) immense. **u~troffen** a unsurpassed

unum|gänglich a absolutely necessary. **u~schränkt** a absolute. **u~wunden** adv frankly

ununterbrochen a incessant, adv -ly

unveränderlich a invariable; (gleichbleibend) unchanging

unverändert a unchanged

unverantwortlich a irresponsible, adv -bly

unverbesserlich a incorrigible

unverbindlich a non-committal; (Comm) not binding □ adv without obligation

unverblümt a blunt □ adv -ly

unverdaulich a indigestible

unver|einbar a incompatible. **u~geßlich** (**u~geßlich**) a unforgettable. **u~gleichlich** a incomparable

unver|hältnismäßig adv disproportionately. **u~heiratet** a unmarried. **u~hofft** a unexpected, adv -ly. **u~hohlen** a undisguised □ adv openly. **u~käuflich** a not for sale; (Muster) free

unverkennbar a unmistakable, adv -bly

unverletzt a unhurt

unvermeidlich a inevitable

unver|mindert a & adv undiminished. **u~mittelt** a abrupt, adv -ly. **u~mutet** a unexpected, adv -ly

Unver|nunft f folly. **u~nünftig** a foolish, adv -ly

unverschämt a insolent, adv -ly; (fam: ungeheuer) outrageous, adv -ly. **U~heit** f -,-en insolence

unver|sehens adv suddenly. **u~sehrt** a unhurt; (unbeschädigt) intact. **u~söhnlich** a irreconcilable; (Gegner) implacable

unverständ|lich a incomprehensible; (undeutlich) indistinct. **U~nis** nt lack of understanding

unverträglich a incompatible; (Person) quarrelsome; (unbekömmlich) indigestible

unverwandt a fixed, adv -ly

unver|wundbar a invulnerable. **u~wüstlich** a indestructible; (Person, Humor) irrepressible; (Gesundheit) robust. **u~zeihlich** a unforgivable

unverzüglich a immediate, adv -ly

unvollendet a unfinished

unvollkommen a imperfect; (unvollständig) incomplete. **U~heit** f -,-en imperfection

unvollständig a incomplete

unvor|bereitet a unprepared. **u~eingenommen** a unbiased. **u~hergesehen** a unforeseen

unvorsichtig a careless, adv -ly. **U~keit** f - carelessness

unvorstellbar a unimaginable, adv -bly

unvorteilhaft a unfavourable; (nicht hübsch) unattractive; (Kleid, Frisur) unflattering

unwahr a untrue. **U~heit** f -,-en untruth. **u~scheinlich** a unlikely; (unglaublich) improbable; (fam: groß) incredible, adv -bly

unweigerlich a inevitable, adv -bly

unweit adv & prep (+ gen) not far; **u~ vom Fluss od des Flusses** not far from the river

unwesentlich a unimportant □ adv slightly

Unwetter nt -s,- storm

unwichtig a unimportant

unwider|legbar a irrefutable. **u~ruflich** a irrevocable, adv -bly. **u~stehlich** a irresistible

Unwille m displeasure. **u~ig** a angry, adv -ily; (widerwillig) reluctant, adv -ly. **u~kürlich** a involuntary, adv -ily; (instinktiv) instinctive, adv -ly

unwirklich a unreal

unwirksam a ineffective

unwirsch a irritable, adv -bly

unwirtlich a inhospitable

unwirtschaftlich a uneconomic, adv -ally

unwissen|d a ignorant. **U~heit** f - ignorance

unwohl a unwell; (unbehaglich) uneasy. **U~sein** nt -s indisposition

unwürdig a unworthy (gen of); (würdelos) undignified

Unzahl f vast number. **unzählig** a innumerable, countless

unzerbrechlich a unbreakable

unzerstörbar a indestructible

unzertrennlich a inseparable

Unzucht f sexual offence; **gewerbsmäßige U~** prostitution

unzüchtig a indecent, adv -ly; (Schriften) obscene

unzufrieden a dissatisfied; (innerlich) discontented. **U~heit** f dissatisfaction; (Pol) discontent

unzulänglich a inadequate, adv -ly

unzulässig a inadmissible

unzumutbar a unreasonable

unzurechnungsfähig a insane. **U~keit** f insanity

unzusammenhängend a incoherent

unzutreffend a inapplicable; (falsch) incorrect

unzuverlässig a unreliable

unzweckmäßig a unsuitable, adv -bly

unzweideutig a unambiguous

üppig a luxuriant, adv -ly; ⟨*überreichlich*⟩ lavish, adv -ly; ⟨*Busen, Figur*⟩ voluptuous

uralt a ancient

Uran nt -s uranium

Uraufführung f first performance

urbar a u~ machen cultivate

Ureinwohner mpl native inhabitants

Urenkel m great-grandson; ⟨pl⟩ great-grandchildren

Urgroß|mutter f great-grandmother. U~vater m great-grandfather

Urheber m -s,- originator; ⟨*Verfasser*⟩ author. U~recht nt copyright

Urin m -s,-e urine

Urkunde f -,-n certificate; ⟨*Dokument*⟩ document

Urlaub m -s holiday; ⟨*Mil, Admin*⟩ leave; auf U~ on holiday/leave; U~ haben be on holiday/leave. U~er(in) m -s,- ⟨f -,-nen⟩ holiday-maker. U~sort m holiday resort

Urne f -,-n urn; ⟨*Wahl-*⟩ ballot-box

Ursache f cause; ⟨*Grund*⟩ reason; keine U~! don't mention it!

Ursprung m origin

ursprünglich a original, adv -ly; ⟨*anfänglich*⟩ initial, adv -ly; ⟨*natürlich*⟩ natural

Urteil nt -s,-e judgement; ⟨*Meinung*⟩ opinion; ⟨U~sspruch⟩ verdict; ⟨*Strafe*⟩ sentence. u~en vi ⟨*haben*⟩ judge. U~svermögen nt [power of] judgement

Urwald m primeval forest; ⟨*tropischer*⟩ jungle

urwüchsig a natural; ⟨*derb*⟩ earthy

Urzeit f primeval times pl; seit U~en from time immemorial

USA pl USA sg

usw. abbr (und so weiter) etc.

Utensilien /-jən/ ntpl utensils

utopisch a Utopian

V

vage /'va:gə/ a vague, adv -ly

Vakuum /'va:kuʊm/ nt -s vacuum. v~verpackt a vacuum-packed

Vanille /va'nɪljə/ f -vanilla

vari|abel /va'rja:bəl/ a variable. V~ante f -,-n variant. V~ation /-'tsjo:n/ f -,-en variation. /-'tsjo:n/ f -,-en vary

Vase /'va:zə/ f -,-n vase

Vater m -s,: father. V~land nt fatherland

väterlich a paternal; ⟨*fürsorglich*⟩ fatherly. v~erseits adv on one's/the father's side

Vater|schaft f -fatherhood; ⟨*Jur*⟩ paternity. V~unser nt -s,- Lord's Prayer

Vati m -s,-s ⟨fam⟩ daddy

v. Chr. abbr ⟨vor Christus⟩ BC

Vegetar|ier(in) /vege'ta:rjɐ, -jərɪn/ m(f) -s,- ⟨f -,-nen⟩ vegetarian. v~isch a vegetarian

Vegetation /vegeta'tsjo:n/ f -,-en vegetation

Veilchen nt -s,-n violet

Vene /'ve:nə/ f -,-n vein

Venedig /ve'ne:dɪç/ nt -s Venice

Ventil /vɛn'ti:l/ nt -s,-e valve. V~ator m -s,-en /-'to:rən/ fan

verabred|en vt arrange; sich [mit jdm] v~en arrange to meet [s.o.]. V~ung f -,-en arrangement; ⟨*Treffen*⟩ appointment

verabreichen vt administer

verabscheuen vt detest, loathe

verabschieden vt say goodbye to; ⟨*aus dem Dienst*⟩ retire; pass ⟨*Gesetz*⟩; sich v~ say goodbye

verachten vt despise. v~swert a contemptible

verächtlich a contemptuous, adv -ly; ⟨*unwürdig*⟩ contemptible

Verachtung f -contempt

verallgemeiner|n vt/i (haben) generalize. **V~ung** f -,-en generalization

veralte|n vi (sein) become obsolete. **v~t** a obsolete

Veranda /ve'randa/ f -,-den veranda

veränder|lich a changeable; (Math) variable. **v~n** vt change; **sich v~n** change; (beruflich) change one's job. **V~ung** f change

verängstigt a frightened, scared

verankern vt anchor

veranlag|t a künstlerisch/musikalisch v~t sein have an artistic/a musical bent; **praktisch v~t** practically minded. **V~ung** f -,-en disposition; (Neigung) tendency; (künstlerisch) bent

veranlass|en vt (reg) arrange for; (einleiten) institute; **jdn v~en** prompt s.o. (zu to). **V~ung** f reason; **auf meine V~ung** at my suggestion; (Befehl) on my orders

veranschaulichen vt illustrate

veranschlagen vt (reg) estimate

veranstalt|en vt organize; hold, give (Party); make (Lärm). **V~er** m -s,- organizer. **V~ung** f -,-en event

verantwort|en vt take responsibility for; **sich v~en** answer (für for). **v~lich** a responsible; **v~lich machen** hold responsible. **V~ung** f -responsibility. **v~ungsbewusst** (v~ungsbewußt) a responsible, adv -ly. **v~ungslos** a irresponsible, adv -bly. **v~ungsvoll** a responsible

verarbeiten vt use; (Techn) process; (verdauen & fig) digest; **v~ zu** make into

verärgern vt annoy

verarmt a impoverished

verästeln (sich) vr branch out

verausgaben (sich) vr spend all one's money; (körperlich) wear oneself out

veräußern vt sell

Verb /vɛrp/ nt -s,-en verb. **v~al** /vɛr'baːl/ a verbal, adv -ly

Verband m -[e]s,-e association; (Mil) unit; (Med) bandage; (Wund-) dressing. **V~szeug** nt first-aid kit

verbann|en vt exile; (fig) banish. **V~ung** f - exile

verbarrikadieren vt barricade

verbeißen† vt suppress; **ich konnte mir kaum das Lachen v~** I could hardly keep a straight face

verbergen† vt hide; **sich v~** hide

verbesser|n vt improve; (berichtigen) correct. **V~ung** f -,-en improvement; correction

verbeugen (sich) vr bow. **V~ung** f bow

verbeulen vt dent

verbiegen† vt bend; **sich v~** bend

verbieten† vt forbid; (Admin) prohibit, ban

verbilligen vt reduce [in price]. **v~t** a reduced

verbind|en† vt connect (mit to); (zusammenfügen) join; (verknüpfen) combine; (in Verbindung bringen) associate; (Med) bandage; dress (Wunde); **sich v~** combine; (sich zusammentun) join together; **jdm die Augen v~** blindfold s.o.; **jdm verbunden sein** (fig) be obliged to s.o. **v~lich** a friendly; (bindend) binding. **V~keit** f -,-en friendliness; **V~keiten** obligations; (Comm) liabilities

Verbindung f connection; (Verknüpfung) combination; (Kontakt) contact; (Vereinigung) association; **chemische V~** chemical compound; **in V~ stehen/sich in V~ setzen** be/get in touch

verbissen a grim, adv -ly; (zäh) dogged, adv -ly

verbitten† vt **sich (dat) etw v~** not stand for sth

verbitter|n vt make bitter. **v~t** a bitter. **V~ung** f - bitterness

verblassen vi (sein) fade

verbläuen vt (fam) beat up

Verbleib m -s whereabouts pl. **v~en†** vi (sein) remain

verbleichen† vi (sein) fade

verbleit a ⟨Benzin⟩ leaded

verbleuen vt (NEW) **verbläuen**

verblüff|en vt amaze, astound. **V~ung** f - amazement

verblühen vi (sein) wither, fade

verbluten vi (sein) bleed to death

verborgen¹ a hidden

verborgen² vt lend

Verbot nt -[e]s,-e ban. **v~en** a forbidden; ⟨Admin⟩ prohibited; 'Rauchen v~en' 'no smoking'

Verbrauch m -[e]s consumption. **v~en** vt use; consume ⟨Lebensmittel⟩; ⟨erschöpfen⟩ use up, exhaust. **V~er** m -s,- consumer. **v~t** a worn; ⟨Luft⟩ stale

verbrechen† vt (fam) perpetrate. **V~** nt -s,- crime

Verbrecher m -s,- criminal. **v~isch** a criminal

verbreit|en vt spread; **sich v~en** spread. **v~ern** vt widen; **sich v~ern** widen. **v~et** a widespread. **V~ung** f - spread; ⟨Verbreiten⟩ spreading

verbrenn|en† vt/i (sein) burn; cremate ⟨Leiche⟩. **V~ung** f -,-en burning; cremation; ⟨Wunde⟩ burn

verbringen† vt spend

verbrühen vt scald

verbuchen vt enter; (fig) notch up ⟨Erfolg⟩

verbünd|en (sich) vr form an alliance. **V~ete(r)** m/f ally

verbürgen vt guarantee; **sich v~ für** vouch for

verbüßen vt serve ⟨Strafe⟩

Verdacht m -[e]s suspicion; **in** or **im V~ haben** suspect

verdächtig a suspicious, adv -ly. **v~en** vt suspect ⟨gen of⟩. **V~te(r)** m/f suspect

verdamm|en vt condemn; ⟨Relig⟩ damn. **V~nis** f - damnation. **v~t**

a & adv (sl) damned; **v~t!** damn!

verdampfen vt/i (sein) evaporate

verdanken vt owe ⟨dat to⟩

verdau|en vt digest. **v~lich** a digestible; **schwer v~lich** indigestible. **V~ung** f - digestion

Verdeck nt -[e]s,-e hood; ⟨Oberdeck⟩ top deck. **v~en** vt cover; ⟨verbergen⟩ hide, conceal

verdenken† vt **das kann man ihm nicht v~** you can't blame him for it

verderb|en† vt/i (sein) spoil ⟨Lebensmittel⟩ go bad □ vt spoil; ⟨zerstören⟩ ruin; ⟨moralisch⟩ corrupt; **ich habe mir den Magen verdorben** I have an upset stomach. **V~en** nt -s ruin. **v~lich** a perishable; ⟨schädlich⟩ pernicious

verdeutlichen vt make clear

verdichten vt compress; **sich v~** ⟨Nebel⟩ thicken

verdien|en vt/i (haben) earn; (fig) deserve. **V~er** m -s,- wage-earner

Verdienst¹ m -[e]s earnings pl

Verdienst² nt -[e]s,-e merit

verdient a a well-deserved; ⟨Person⟩ of outstanding merit. **v~ermaßen** adv deservedly

verdoppeln vt double; (fig) redouble; **sich v~** double

verdorben a spoilt, ruined; ⟨Magen⟩ upset; ⟨moralisch⟩ corrupt; ⟨verkommen⟩ depraved

verdorren vi (sein) wither

verdrängen vt force out; (fig) displace; ⟨psychisch⟩ repress

verdreh|en vt twist; roll ⟨Augen⟩; (fig) distort. **v~t** a (fam) crazy

verdreifachen vt treble, triple

verdreschen† vt (fam) thrash

verdrießlich a morose, adv -ly

verdrücken vt crumple; ⟨fam: essen⟩ polish off; **sich v~** ⟨fam⟩ slip away

Verdruss m -es ⟨Verdruß m -sses⟩ annoyance

verdunk|eln vt darken; black out ⟨Zimmer⟩; **sich v~eln** darken. **V~[e]lung** f - black-out

verdünnen *vt* dilute; **sich v∼** taper off

verdunst|en *vi* (sein) evaporate. **V∼ung** *f* - evaporation

verdursten *vi* (sein) die of thirst

verdutzt *a* baffled

veredeln *vt* refine; (*Hort*) graft

verehr|en *vt* revere; (*Relig*) worship; (*bewundern*) admire; (*schenken*) give. **V∼er(in)** *m* -s, ⟨*f* -,-nen⟩ admirer. **V∼ung** *f* - veneration; worship; admiration

vereidigen *vt* swear in

Verein *m* -s,-e society; (*Sport*-) club

vereinbar *a* compatible. **v∼en** *vt* arrange; **nicht zu v∼en** incompatible. **V∼ung** *f* -,-en agreement

vereinen *vt* unite; **sich v∼** unite

vereinfachen *vt* simplify

vereinheitlichen *vt* standardize

vereinig|en *vt* unite; merge (*Firmen*); **wieder v∼en** reunite; reunify (*Land*); **sich v∼en** unite; **V∼te Staaten [von Amerika]** United States *sg* (of America). **V∼ung** *f* -,-en union; (*Organisation*) organization

vereinsamt *a* lonely

vereinzelt *a* isolated □ *adv* occasionally

vereist *a* frozen; (*Straße*) icy

vereiteln *vt* foil, thwart

vereitert *a* septic

verenden *vi* (sein) die

verengen *vt* restrict; **sich v∼** narrow; (*Pupille:*) contract

vererb|en *vt* leave (*dat* to); (*Biol* & *fig*) pass on (*dat* to). **V∼ung** *f* - heredity

verewigen *vt* immortalize; **sich v∼** (*fam*) leave one's mark

verfahren† *vi* (sein) proceed; **v∼ mit** deal with □ *vr* sich v∼ lose one's way □ *a* muddled. **V∼nt** -s, procedure; (*Techn*) process; (*Jur*) proceedings *pl*

Verfall *m* decay; (*eines Gebäudes*) dilapidation; (*körperlich & fig*)

decline; (*Ablauf*) expiry. **v∼en†** *vi* (sein) decay; (*Person, Sitten:*) decline; (*ablaufen*) expire; **v∼en in** (+ *acc*) lapse into; **v∼en auf** (+ *acc*) hit on (*Idee*); **jdm/etw v∼en sein** be under the spell of s.o./sth; be addicted to (*Alkohol*)

verfälschen *vt* falsify; adulterate (*Wein, Lebensmittel*)

verfänglich *a* awkward

verfärben (sich) *vr* change colour; (*Stoff:*) discolour

verfass|en *vt* write; (*Jur*) draw up; (*entwerfen*) draft. **V∼er** *m* -s, author. **V∼ung** *f* (*Pol*) constitution; (*Zustand*) state

verfaulen *vi* (sein) rot, decay

verfechten† *vt* advocate

verfehlen *vt* miss

verfeinde|n (sich) *vr* become enemies; **v∼t sein** be enemies

verfeinern *vt* refine; (*verbessern*) improve

verfilmen *vt* film

verfilzt *a* matted

verflieg|en *vi* (sein) evaporate; (*Zeit:*) fly

verflixt *a* (*fam*) awkward; (*verdammt*) blessed; **v∼!** damn!

verfluch|en *vt* curse. **v∼t** *a* & *adv* (*fam*) damned; **v∼t!** damn!

verflüchtigen (sich) *vr* evaporate

verflüssigen *vt* liquefy

verfolg|en *vt* pursue; (*folgen*) follow; (*bedrängen*) pester; (*Pol*) persecute; **strafrechtlich v∼en** prosecute. **V∼er** *m* -s, pursuer. **V∼ung** *f* - pursuit; persecution

verfrachten *vt* ship

verfrüht *a* premature

verfügbar *a* available

verfüg|en *vt* order; (*Jur*) decree □ *vi* (*haben*) **v∼en über** (+ *acc*) have at one's disposal. **V∼ung** *f* -,-en order; (*Jur*) decree; **jdm zur V∼ung stehen/stellen** be/place at s.o.'s disposal

verführ|en vt seduce; ⟨verlocken⟩ tempt. **V~er** m seducer. **v~erisch** a seductive; tempting. **V~ung** f seduction; temptation

vergammelt a rotten; ⟨Gebäude⟩ decayed; ⟨Person⟩ scruffy

vergangen a past; ⟨letzte⟩ last. **V~heit** f - past; ⟨Gram⟩ past tense

vergänglich a transitory

vergas|en vt gas. **V~er** m -s, carburettor

vergeb|en† vt award (**an** + dat to); ⟨weggeben⟩ give away; ⟨verzeihen⟩ forgive. **v~ens** adv in vain. **v~lich** a futile, vain □ adv in vain. **V~ung** f -forgiveness

vergehen† vi (sein) pass; **v~ vor** (+ dat) nearly die of; **sich v~** violate (**gegen etw** sth); ⟨sexuell⟩ sexually assault (**an jdm** s.o.). **V~** nt -s,- offence

vergelt|en† vt repay. **V~ung** f retaliation; ⟨Rache⟩ revenge. **V~ungsmaßnahme** f reprisal

vergessen† vt forget; ⟨liegen lassen⟩ leave behind. **V~heit** f oblivion; **in V~heit geraten** be forgotten

vergesslich (vergeßlich) a forgetful. **V~keit** f - forgetfulness

vergeuden vt waste, squander

vergewaltig|en vt rape. **V~ung** f -,-en rape

vergewissern (sich) vr make sure (**gen** of)

vergießen† vt spill; shed ⟨Tränen, Blut⟩

vergift|en vt poison. **V~ung** f -,-en poisoning

Vergissmeinnicht (Vergißmeinnicht) nt -[e]s,-[e] forget-me-not

vergittert a barred

verglasen vt glaze

Vergleich m -[e]s,-e comparison; ⟨Jur⟩ settlement. **v~bar** a comparable. **v~en†** vt compare (**mit** with/to). **v~sweise** adv comparatively

vergnüg|en (sich) vr enjoy oneself. **V~en** nt -s,- pleasure; ⟨Spaß⟩ fun; **viel V~en!** have a good time! **v~lich** a enjoyable. **v~t** a cheerful, adv -ly; ⟨zufrieden⟩ happy, adv -ily; ⟨vergnüglich⟩ enjoyable. **V~ungen** fpl entertainments

vergolden vt gild; ⟨plattieren⟩ gold-plate

vergönnen vt grant

vergöttern vt idolize

vergraben† vt bury

vergreifen† (sich) vr **sich v~an** (+ dat) assault; ⟨stehlen⟩ steal

vergriffen a out of print

vergrößer|n vt enlarge; ⟨Linse:⟩ magnify; ⟨vermehren⟩ increase; ⟨erweitern⟩ extend; expand ⟨Geschäft⟩; **sich v~n** grow bigger; ⟨Firma:⟩ expand; ⟨zunehmen⟩ increase. **V~ung** f -,-en magnification; increase; expansion; ⟨Phot⟩ enlargement. **V~ungsglas** nt magnifying glass

Vergünstigung f -,-en privilege

vergüt|en vt pay for; **jdm etw v~en** reimburse s.o. for sth. **V~ung** f -,-en remuneration; ⟨Erstattung⟩ reimbursement

verhaft|en vt arrest. **V~ung** f -,-en arrest

verhalten† (sich) vr behave; ⟨handeln⟩ act; ⟨beschaffen sein⟩ be; **sich still v~** keep quiet. **V~** nt -s behaviour, conduct

Verhältnis nt -ses,-se relationship; ⟨Liebes⟩ affair; ⟨Math⟩ ratio; **V~se** circumstances; ⟨Bedingungen⟩ conditions; **über seine V~se leben** live beyond one's means. **v~mäßig** adv comparatively, relatively

verhand|eln vt discuss; ⟨Jur⟩ try □ vi ⟨haben⟩ negotiate; **v~eln gegen** ⟨Jur⟩ try. **V~lung** f ⟨Jur⟩ trial; **V~lungen** negotiations

verhängen vt cover; ⟨fig⟩ impose

Verhängnis nt -ses fate, doom. **v~voll** a fatal, disastrous

verharmlosen vt play down

verharren vi (haben) remain

verhärten vt/i (sein) harden; **sich v~** harden

verhasst (verhaßt) a hated

verhätscheln vt spoil, pamper

verhauen† vt (fam) beat; make a mess of ⟨Prüfung⟩

verheerend a devastating; (fam) terrible

verhehlen vt conceal

verheilen vi (sein) heal

verheimlichen vt keep secret

verheirat|en (sich) vr get married (mit to); **sich wieder v~en** remarry. **v~et** a married

verhelfen† vt (haben) jdm zu etw v~ help s.o. get sth

verherrlichen vt glorify

verhexen vt bewitch; **es ist wie verhext** (fam) there is a jinx on it

verhinder|n vt prevent; **v~t sein** be unable to come. **V~ung** f prevention

verhöhnen vt deride

Verhör nt -s,-e interrogation; ins **V~ nehmen** interrogate. **v~en** vt interrogate; **sich v~en** mishear

verhüllen vt cover; (fig) disguise. **v~d** a euphemistic, adv -ally

verhungern vi (sein) starve

verhüt|en vt prevent. **V~ung** f - prevention. **V~ungsmittel** nt contraceptive

verhutzelt a wizened

verirren (sich) vr get lost

verjagen vt chase away

verjüngen vt rejuvenate; **sich v~** taper

verkalkt a (fam) senile

verkalkulieren (sich) vr miscalculate

Verkauf m sale; **zum V~** for sale. **v~en** vt sell; **zu v~en** for sale

Verkäufer(in) m(f) seller; (im Geschäft) shop assistant

Verkehr m -s traffic; (Kontakt) contact; (Geschlechts-) intercourse; **aus dem V~ ziehen** take

out of circulation. **v~en** vi (haben) operate; ⟨Bus, Zug:⟩ run; (Umgang haben) associate, mix (mit with); ⟨Gast sein⟩ visit (bei jdm s.o.); frequent (in einem Lokal a restaurant); brieflich **v~en** correspond □ vt ins **Gegenteil v~en** turn round

Verkehrs|ampel f traffic lights pl. **V~büro** nt = **V~verein**. **V~funk** m [radio] traffic information. **V~unfall** m road accident. **V~verein** m tourist office. **V~zeichen** nt traffic sign

verkehrt a wrong, adv -ly; **v~ herum** adv the wrong way round; (links) inside out

verkennen† vt misjudge

verklagen vt sue (auf + acc for)

verkleid|en vt disguise; (Techn) line; **sich v~en** disguise oneself; (für Kostümfest) dress up. **V~ung** f -,-en disguise; (Kostüm) fancy dress; (Techn) lining

verkleiner|n vt reduce [in size]. **V~ung** f - reduction. **V~ungsform** f diminutive

verklemmt a jammed; (psychisch) inhibited

verkneifen† vt sich (dat) etw v~ do without sth; (verbeißen) suppress sth

verknittern vt/i (sein) crumple

verknüpfen vt knot together; (verbinden) connect, link; (zugleich tun) combine

verkomment vi (sein) be neglected; ⟨sittlich:⟩ go to the bad; ⟨verfallen⟩ decay; ⟨Haus:⟩ fall into disrepair; ⟨Gegend:⟩ become rundown; ⟨Lebensmittel:⟩ go bad □ a neglected; ⟨sittlich⟩ depraved; ⟨Haus⟩ dilapidated; ⟨Gegend⟩ rundown

verkörper|n vt embody, personify. **V~ung** f -,-en embodiment, personification

verkraften vt cope with

verkrampft a (fig) tense

verkriechen† (sich) vr hide

verkrümmt a crooked, bent

verkrüppelt *a* crippled; ⟨*Glied*⟩ deformed

verkühl|en (sich) *vr* catch a chill. **V~ung** *f* -,-en chill

verkümmer|n *vi* ⟨*sein*⟩ waste-/⟨*Pflanze:*⟩ wither away. **v~t** *a* stunted

verkünd|en *vt* announce; pronounce ⟨*Urteil*⟩. **v~igen** *vt* announce; ⟨*predigen*⟩ preach

verkürzen *vt* shorten; ⟨*verringern*⟩ reduce; ⟨*abbrechen*⟩ cut short; while away ⟨*Zeit*⟩

verladen† *vt* load

Verlag *m* -[e]s,-e publishing firm

verlangen *vt* ask for; ⟨*fordern*⟩ demand; ⟨*berechnen*⟩ charge; **am Telefon verlangt werden** be wanted on the telephone. **V~** *nt* -s desire; ⟨*Bitte:*⟩ request; **auf V~** on demand

verlänger|n *vt* extend; lengthen ⟨*Kleid*⟩; ⟨*zeitlich*⟩ prolong; renew ⟨*Pass, Vertrag*⟩; ⟨*Culin*⟩ thin down. **V~ung** *f* -,-en extension; renewal. **V~ungsschnur** *f* extension cable

verlangsamen *vt* slow down

Verlass (Verlaß) *m* **auf ihn ist kein V~** you cannot rely on him

verlassen† *vt* leave; ⟨*im Stich lassen*⟩ desert; **sich v~ auf** (+ *acc*) rely or depend on □ *a* deserted. **V~heit** *f* - desolation

verlässlich (verläßlich) *a* reliable

Verlauf *m* course; **im V~** (+ *gen*) in the course of. **v~en†** *vi* ⟨*sein*⟩ run; ⟨*ablaufen*⟩ go; ⟨*zerlaufen*⟩ melt; **gut v~en** go [off] well □ *vr* **sich v~en** lose one's way; ⟨*Menge:*⟩ disperse; ⟨*Wasser:*⟩ drain away

verleben *vt* spend

verlegen *vt* move; ⟨*verschieben*⟩ postpone; ⟨*vor-*⟩ bring forward; ⟨*verlieren*⟩ mislay; ⟨*versperren*⟩ block; ⟨*legen*⟩ lay ⟨*Teppich, Rohre*⟩; ⟨*veröffentlichen*⟩ publish; **sich v~ auf** (+ *acc*) take up ⟨*Beruf, Fach*⟩; resort to ⟨*Taktik,*

Bitten⟩ □ *a* embarrassed; **nie v~ um** never at a loss for. **V~heit** *f* - embarrassment

Verleger *m* -s,- publisher

verleih|en† *vt* lend; ⟨*gegen Gebühr*⟩ hire out; ⟨*überreichen*⟩ award, confer; ⟨*fig*⟩ give

verleiten *vt* induce/⟨*verlocken*⟩ tempt **(zu** to)

verlernen *vt* forget

verlesen† *vt* read out; **ich habe mich v~** I misread it

verlesen†2 *vt* sort out

verletz|en *vt* injure; ⟨*kränken*⟩ hurt; ⟨*verstoßen gegen*⟩ infringe; violate ⟨*Grenze*⟩. **v~end** *a* hurtful, wounding. **v~lich** *a* vulnerable. **V~te(r)** *m/f* injured person; ⟨*bei Unfall*⟩ casualty. **V~ung** *f* -,-en injury; ⟨*Verstoß*⟩ infringement; violation

verleugnen *vt* deny; disown ⟨*Freund*⟩

verleumd|en *vt* slander; ⟨*schriftlich*⟩ libel. **v~erisch** *a* slanderous; libellous. **V~ung** *f* -,-en slander; ⟨*schriftlich*⟩ libel

verlieben (sich) *vr* fall in love **(in** + *acc* with); **verliebt sein** be in love **(in** + *acc* with)

verlier|en† *vt* lose; shed ⟨*Laub*⟩; **sich v~en** disappear; ⟨*Weg:*⟩ peter out □ *vi* ⟨*haben*⟩ lose **(an etw** *dat* sth). **V~er** *m* -s,- loser

verlob|en (sich) *vr* get engaged **(mit** to); **v~t sein** be engaged. **V~te** *f* fiancée. **V~te(r)** *m* fiancé. **V~ung** *f* -,-en engagement

verlock|en *vt* tempt; **v~end** tempting. **V~ung** *f* -,-en temptation

verlogen *a* lying

verloren *a* lost; **v~e Eier** poached eggs; **v~ gehen** get lost. **v~gehen†** *vi* sep ⟨*sein*⟩ NEW **v~ gehen**, *s.* **verloren**

verlos|en *vt* raffle. **V~ung** *f* -,-en raffle; ⟨*Ziehung*⟩ draw

verlottert *a* run-down; ⟨*Person*⟩ scruffy; ⟨*sittlich*⟩ dissolute

Verlust m -[e]s,-e loss
vermachen vt leave, bequeath
Vermächtnis nt -ses,-se legacy
vermähl|en (sich) vr marry.
V~ung f -,-en marriage
vermehren vt increase; propagate (Pflanzen); **sich** v~ increase; (sich fortpflanzen) breed, multiply
vermeiden† vt avoid
vermeintlich a supposed, adv -ly
Vermerk m -[e]s,-e note. v~en note [down]; **übel** v~en take amiss
vermessen|en† vt measure; survey (Gelände) □ a presumptuous. V~enheit f - presumption. V~ung f measurement; (Land-) survey
vermiet|en vt let, rent [out]; hire out (Boot, Auto); **zu** v~en to let; (Boot:) for hire. V~er m landlord. V~erin f landlady
vermindern vt reduce, lessen. V~ung f - reduction, decrease
vermischen vt mix; **sich** v~ mix
vermissen vt miss
vermisst (vermißt) a missing. V~e(r) m missing person; (Mil) soldier
vermittel|n vi (haben) mediate □ vt arrange; (beschaffen) find; place (Arbeitskräfte); impart (Wissen); convey (Eindruck). v~s prep (+ gen) by means of
Vermittl|er m -s,- agent; (Schlichter) mediator. V~ung f -,-en arrangement; (Agentur) agency; (Teleph) exchange; (Schlichtung) mediation
vermögen† vt be able (zu to). V~ nt -s,- fortune. V~d a wealthy
vermut|en vt suspect; (glauben) presume. v~lich a probable □ adv presumably. V~ung f -,-en supposition; (Verdacht) suspicion; (Mutmaßung) conjecture
vernachlässig|en vt neglect. V~ung f - neglect

vernehm|en† vt hear; (verhören) question; (Jur) examine. V~ung f -,-en questioning
verneig|en (sich) vr bow. V~ung f -,-en bow
vernein|en vt answer in the negative; (ablehnen) reject. v~end a negative. V~ung f -,-en negative answer; (Gram) negative
vernicht|en vt destroy; (ausrotten) exterminate. v~end a devastating; (Niederlage) crushing. V~ung f - destruction; extermination
Vernunft f - reason; V~ annehmen see reason
vernünftig a reasonable, sensible; (fair: ordentlich) decent □ adv sensibly; (fam) properly
veröffentlich|en vt publish. V~ung f -,-en publication
verordn|en vt prescribe (dat for). V~ung f -,-en prescription; (Verfügung) decree
verpachten vt lease [out]
verpack|en vt pack; (einwickeln) wrap. V~ung f packaging; wrapping
verpassen vt miss; (fam: geben) give
verpfänden vt pawn
verpflanzen vt transplant
verpfleg|en vt feed: **sich selbst** v~en cater for oneself. V~ung f - board; (Essen) food; **Unterkunft und** V~ung board and lodging
verpflicht|en vt oblige; (einstellen) engage; (Sport) sign; **sich** v~en undertake/(versprechen) promise (zu to); (vertraglich) sign a contract; **jdm** v~et **sein** be indebted to s.o. V~ung f -,-en obligation, commitment
verpfuschen vt make a mess of
verpönt a v~ **sein** be frowned upon
verprügeln vt beat up, thrash
Verputz m -es plaster. v~en vt plaster; (fam: essen) polish off

Verrat m -[e]s betrayal, treachery. v~en† vt betray; give away ⟨Geheimnis⟩; (fam: sagen) tell; sich v~en give oneself away

Verräter m -s, -. traitor. v~isch a treacherous; (fig) revealing

verräuchert a smoky

verrech|nen vt settle; clear ⟨Scheck⟩; sich v~nen make a mistake; (fig) miscalculate. V~nungsscheck m crossed cheque

verregnet a spoilt by rain; ⟨Tag⟩ rainy, wet

verreisen vi (sein) go away; **verreist sein** be away

verreißen† vt (fam) pan, slate

verrenken vt dislocate; **sich v~** contort oneself

verricht|en vt perform, do; say ⟨Gebet⟩. V~ung f -, -en task

verriegeln vt bolt

verringer|n vt reduce; sich v~n decrease. V~ung f - reduction; decrease

verrost|en vi (sein) rust. v~et a rusty

verrücken vt move

verrückt a crazy, mad; v~ werden/machen go/drive crazy. V~e(r) m/f lunatic. V~heit f -, -en madness; ⟨Torheit⟩ folly

Verruf m disrepute. v~en a disreputable

verrühren vt mix

verrunzelt a wrinkled

verrutschen† vi slip

Vers /fɛrs/ m -es, -e verse

versag|en vi (haben) fail □ vt jdm/sich etw v~en deny s.o./oneself sth. V~en nt -s, - failure. V~er m -s, - failure

versalzen† vt put too much salt in/on; (fig) spoil

versamm|eln vt assemble; sich v~eln assemble, meet. V~lung f assembly, meeting

Versand m -[e]s dispatch. V~haus nt mail-order firm

versäum|en vt miss; lose ⟨Zeit⟩; (unterlassen) neglect; [es] v~en, etw zu tun fail or neglect to do sth. V~nis nt -ses, -se omission

verschaffen vt get; sich ⟨dat⟩ v~ obtain; gain ⟨Respekt⟩

verschämt a bashful, coy. **-ly**

verschandeln vt spoil

verschärf|en vt intensify; tighten ⟨Kontrolle⟩; increase ⟨Tempo⟩; aggravate ⟨Lage⟩; sich v~ intensify; increase; ⟨Lage:⟩ worsen

verschätzen (sich) vr sich v~ in (+ dat) misjudge

verschenken vt give away

verscheuchen vt shoo/(jagen) chase away

verschicken vt send; (Comm) dispatch

verschieb|en† vt move; (aufschieben) put off, postpone; (sl: handeln mit) traffic in; sich v~en move, shift; (verrutschen) slip; ⟨zeitlich⟩ be postponed. V~ung f shift; postponement

verschieden a different; v~e (pl) different; (mehrere) various; V~es (v~es) some things; (dieses und jenes) various things; die v~sten Farben a whole variety of colours; das ist v~ it varies □ adv differently; v~ groß/lang of different sizes/lengths. v~artig a diverse. V~heit f - difference; (Vielfalt) diversity. v~tlich adv several times

verschimmel|n vi (sein) go mouldy. v~t a mouldy

verschlafen† vi (haben) oversleep □ vt sleep through ⟨Tag⟩; (versäumen) miss ⟨Zug, Termin⟩; sich v~ oversleep □ a sleepy; noch v~ still half asleep

Verschlag m -[e]s, -̈e shed

verschlag|en† vt lose ⟨Seite⟩; jdm die Sprache/den Atem v~ leave s.o. speechless/take s.o.'s breath away; nach X v~ werden end up in X □ a sly, adv -ly

verschlechter|n vt make worse; **sich v~n** get worse, deteriorate. **V~ung** f -,-en deterioration

verschleier|n vt veil; (fig) hide

Verschleiß m -es wear and tear; (Verbrauch) consumption. **v~en†** vt/i (sein) wear out

verschleppen vt carry off; (entführen) abduct; spread (Seuche); neglect (Krankheit); (hinausziehen) delay

verschleudern vt sell at a loss; (verschwenden) squander

verschließen† vt close; (abschließen) lock; (einschließen) lock up

verschlimmer|n vt make worse; aggravate (Lage); **sich v~n** get worse, deteriorate. **V~ung** f -,-en deterioration

verschlingen† vt intertwine; (fressen) devour; (fig) swallow

verschlissen a worn

verschlossen a reserved. **V~heit** f - reserve

verschlucken vt swallow; **sich v~** choke (an + dat on)

Verschluss m -es,-̈e (Verschluß m -sses,-̈sse) fastener, clasp; (Fenster-, Koffer-) catch; (Flaschen-) top; (luftdicht) seal; (Phot) shutter; **unter V~** under lock and key

verschlüsselt a coded

verschmähen vt spurn

verschmelzen† vt/i (sein) fuse

verschmerzen vt get over

verschmutz|en vt pollute; (Luft □ vi (sein) get dirty. **V~ung** f - pollution

verschnaufen vi/r (haben) [sich] **v~** get one's breath

verschneit a snow-covered

verschnörkelt a ornate

verschnüren vt tie up

verschollen a missing

verschonen vt spare

verschönern vt brighten up; (verbessern) improve

verschossen a faded

verschrammt a scratched

verschränken vt cross

verschreiben† vt prescribe; **sich v~** make a slip of the pen

verschrie[e]n a notorious

verschroben a eccentric

verschrotten vt scrap

verschulden vt be to blame for. **V~** nt -s fault

verschuldet a **v~ sein** be in debt

verschütten vt spill; (begraben) bury

verschweigen† vt conceal, hide

verschwend|en vt waste. **v~erisch** a extravagant, adv -ly; (üppig) lavish, adv -ly. **V~ung** f - extravagance; (Vergeudung) waste

verschwiegen a discreet; (Ort) secluded. **V~heit** f - discretion

verschwimmen† vi (sein) become blurred

verschwinden† vi (sein) disappear; [mal] **v~** (fam) spend a penny. **V~** nt -s disappearance

verschwommen a blurred

verschwör|en† (sich) vr conspire. **V~ung** f -,-en conspiracy

versehen† vt perform; hold (Posten); keep (Haushalt); **v~ mit** provide with; **sich v~** make a mistake; **ehe man sich's versieht** before you know where you are. **V~** nt -s,- oversight; (Fehler) slip; **aus V~** by mistake. **v~tlich** adv by mistake

Versehrte(r) m disabled person

versenden† vt send [out]

versengen vt singe; (stärker) scorch

versenken vt sink; **sich v~ in** (+ acc) immerse oneself in

versessen a keen (auf + acc on)

versetz|en vt move; transfer (Person); (Sch) move up; (verpfänden) pawn; (verkaufen) sell; (vermischen) blend; (antworten) reply; **jdn v~en** (fam: warten lassen) stand s.o. up; **jdm einen Stoß/Schreck v~en** give s.o. a

push/fright; **jdm in Angst/Er-
staunen v~n** frighten/aston-
ish s.o.; **sich in jds Lage v~n**
put oneself in s.o.'s place. **V~ung**
f -,-en move; transfer; (*Sch*) move
to a higher class

verseuch|en *vt* contaminate.
V~ung *f* - contamination

versicher|n *vt* insure; (*bekräf-
tigen*) affirm; **jdm v~n** assure s.o
(**dass** that). **V~ung** *f* -,-en insurance; assurance

versiegeln *vt* seal

versiegen *vi* (*sein*) dry up

versiert /vɛrˈʒiːɐt/ *a* experienced

versilbert *a* silver-plated

versinken† (*sein*) sink; **in Gedanken versunken** lost in
thought

Version /vɛrˈzjoːn/ *f* -,-en version

Versmaß /ˈfɛrs-/ *nt* metre

versöhn|en *vt* reconcile; **sich
v~en** become reconciled.
v~lich *a* conciliatory. **V~ung** *f*
-,-en reconciliation

versorg|en *vt* provide, supply
(**mit** with); provide for (*Familie*); (*betreuen*) look after; keep
(*Haushalt*). **V~ung** *f* - provision,
supply; (*Betreuung*) care

verspät|en (sich) *vr* be late. **v~et**
a late; (*Zug*) delayed; (*Dank,
Glückwunsch*) belated □ *adv* late;
belatedly. **V~ung** *f* - lateness;
V~ung haben be late

versperren *vt* block; bar (*Weg*)

verspiel|en *vt* gamble away. **sich
v~en** play a wrong note. **v~t** *a*
playful, *adv* -ly

verspotten *vt* mock, ridicule

versprech|en† *vt* promise; **sich
v~en** make a slip of the tongue;
sich (*dat*) **viel v~en von** have
high hopes of; **ein viel v~ender
Anfang** a promising start. **V~en**
nt -s,- promise. **V~ungen** *fpl* pro-
mises

verspüren *vt* feel

verstaatlich|en *vt* nationalize.
V~ung *f* - nationalization

Verstand *m* -[e]s mind; (*Vernunft*) reason; **den V~ verlieren**
go out of one's mind. **v~esmäßig**
a rational, *adv* -ly

verständig *a* sensible, *adv* -bly;
(*klug*) intelligent, *adv* -ly. **v~en**
vt notify, inform; **sich v~en** communicate; (*sich verständlich
machen*) make oneself understood; (*sich einigen*) reach agreement. **V~ung** *f* - notification;
communication; (*Einigung*)
agreement

verständlich *a* comprehensible,
adv -bly; (*deutlich*) clear, *adv* -ly;
(*begreiflich*) understandable;
leicht v~ easily understood;
sich v~ machen make oneself
understood. **v~erweise** *adv*
understandably

Verständnis *nt* -ses understanding. **v~los** *a* uncomprehending,
adv -ly. **v~voll** *a* understanding,
adv -ly

verstärk|en *vt* strengthen, rein-
force; (*steigern*) intensify, increase; amplify (*Ton*); **sich v~en**
intensify. **V~er** *m* -s,- amplifier.
V~ung *f* - reinforcement; increase; amplification; (*Truppen*)
reinforcements *pl*

verstaubt *a* dusty

verstauchen *vt* sprain

verstauen *vt* stow

Versteck *nt* -[e]s,-e hiding-place;
V~ spielen play hide-and-seek.
v~en *vt* hide; **sich v~en** hide.
v~t *a* hidden; (*heimlich*) secret;
(*verstohlen*) furtive, *adv* -ly

versteh|en† *vt* understand;
(*können*) know; **falsch v~** misunderstand; **sich v~** understand
one another; (*auskommen*) get on;
das versteht sich von selbst
that goes without saying

versteif|en *vt* stiffen; **sich v~**
stiffen; (*fig*) insist (**auf** + *acc* on)

versteiger|n *vt* auction. **V~ung**
f auction

versteinert *a* fossilized

verstell|bar a adjustable. **v~en**
vt adjust; (versperren) block; (verändern) disguise; **sich v~en** pretend. **V~ung** f - pretence
versteuern vt pay tax on
verstiegen a (fig) extravagant
verstimm|t a disgruntled;
(Magen) upset; (Mus) out of tune.
V~ung f - ill humour; (Magen-)
upset
verstockt a stubborn, adv -ly
verstohlen a furtive, adv -ly
verstopf|en vt plug; (versperren)
block; **v~t** blocked; (Person) con-
stipated. **V~ung** f -,-en blockage; (Med) constipation
verstorben a late, deceased.
V~e(r) m/f deceased
verstört a bewildered
Verstoß m infringement. **v~en†**
vt disown □ vi (haben) **v~en
gegen** contravene, infringe; offend against (Anstand)
verstreichen† vt spread □ vi
(sein) pass
verstreuen vt scatter
verstümmeln vt mutilate; garble
(Text)
verstummen vi (sein) fall silent;
(Gespräch, Lärm:) cease
Versuch m -[e]s,-e attempt; (Experiment) experiment. **v~en** vt/i
(haben) try; **sich v~en in** (+ dat)
try one's hand at; **v~t sein** be
tempted (zu to). **V~skaninchen**
nt (fig) guinea-pig. **v~sweise**
adv as an experiment. **V~ung** f
-,-en temptation
versündigen (sich) vr sin (an +
dat against)
vertagen vt adjourn; (aufschieben) postpone; **sich v~** adjourn
vertauschen vt exchange;
(verwechseln) mix up
verteidig|en vt defend. **V~er** m
-s,- defender; (Jur) defence counsel. **V~ung** f -,-en defence
verteil|en vt distribute; (zuteilen)
allocate; (ausgeben) hand out;
(verstreichen) spread; **sich v~en**

spread out. **V~ung** f - distribu-
tion; allocation
vertief|en vt deepen; **v~t sein in**
(+ acc) be engrossed in. **V~ung**
f -,-en hollow, depression
vertikal /verti'ka:l/ a vertical,
adv -ly
vertilgen vt exterminate; kill [off]
(Unkraut); (fam: essen) demolish
vertippen (sich) vr make a typing mistake
vertonen vt set to music
Vertrag m -[e]s,-̈e contract; (Pol)
treaty
vertragen† vt tolerate, stand;
take (Kritik, Spaß); **sich v~** get
on; (passen) go (mit with); **sich
wieder v~** make it up □ a worn
vertraglich a contractual
verträglich a good-natured; (bekömmlich) digestible
vertrauen vi (haben) trust
(jdm/etw s.o./sth; **auf +** acc in).
V~ nt -s trust, confidence (zu in);
im V~ in confidence. **V~smann**
m (pl -leute) representative;
(Sprecher) spokesman. **v~svoll** a
trusting, adv -ly. **v~swürdig** a
trustworthy
vertraulich a confidential, adv
-ly; (intim) familiar, adv -ly
vertraut a intimate; (bekannt)
familiar; **sich v~ machen mit**
familiarize oneself with. **V~heit**
f - intimacy; familiarity
vertreib|en† vt drive away; drive
out (Feind); (Comm) sell; **sich
(dat) die Zeit v~en** pass the
time. **V~ung** f - expulsion
vertret|en† vt represent; (ein-
springen für) stand in or deputize
for; (verfechten) support; hold
(Meinung); **sich (dat) den Fuß
v~en** twist one's ankle; **sich
(dat) die Beine v~en** stretch
one's legs. **V~er** m -s,- representative; deputy; (Arzt-) locum; (Verfechter) supporter, advocate.
V~ung f -,-en representation;
(Person) deputy; (eines Arztes) locum; (Handels-) agency

Vertrieb *m* -[e]s (*Comm*) sale.
V∼ene(r) *m/f* displaced person
vertrocknen *vi* (sein) dry up
vertrösten *vt* **jdn auf später v∼** put s.o. off until later
vertun† *vt* waste; **sich v∼** (*fam*) make a mistake
vertuschen *vt* hush up
verübeln *vt* **jdm etw v∼** hold sth against s.o.
verüben *vt* commit
verunglimpfen *vt* denigrate
verunglücken *vi* (sein) be involved in an accident; (*fam: missglücken*) go wrong; **tödlich v∼** be killed in an accident
verunreinigen *vt* pollute; (*verseuchen*) contaminate; (*verschmutzen*) soil
verunstalten *vt* disfigure
veruntreuen *vt* embezzle.
V∼ung *f* -,-en embezzlement
verursachen *vt* cause
verurteil|en *vt* condemn; (*Jur*) convict (**wegen** of); sentence (**zum Tode** to death). **V∼ung** *f* - condemnation; (*Jur*) conviction
vervielfachen *vt* multiply
vervielfältigen *vt* duplicate
vervollkommnen *vt* perfect
vervollständigen *vt* complete
verwachsen *a* deformed
verwählen (sich) *vr* misdial
verwahren *vt* keep; (*verstauen*) put away; **sich v∼** (*fig*) protest
verwahrlost *a* neglected; (*Haus*) dilapidated; (*sittlich*) depraved
Verwahrung *f* - keeping; **in V∼ nehmen** take into safe keeping
verwaist *a* orphaned
verwalt|en *vt* administer; (*leiten*) manage; govern (*Land*). **V∼er** *m* -s,- administrator; manager.
V∼ung *f* -,-en administration; management; government
verwand|eln *vt* transform, change (**in** + *acc* into) **sich v∼eln** change, turn (**in** + *acc* into). **V∼lung** *f* transformation

verwandt *a* related (**mit** to).
V∼e(r) *m/f* relative. **V∼schaft** *f* - relationship; (*Menschen*) relatives *pl*
verwarn|en *vt* warn, caution.
V∼ung *f* warning, caution
verwaschen *a* washed out, faded
verwechs|eln *vt* mix up, confuse; (*halten für*) mistake (**mit** for).
V∼lung *f* -,-en mix-up
verwegen *a* audacious, *adv* -ly
Verwehung *f* -,-en [snow-]drift
verweichlicht *a* (*fig*) soft
verweiger|n *vt/i* (haben) refuse (**jdm etw** s.o. sth); **den Gehorsam v∼** refuse to obey. **V∼ung** *f* refusal
verweilen *vi* (haben) stay
Verweis *m* -es,-e reference (**auf** + *acc* to); (*Tadel*) reprimand; **v∼en†** *vt* refer (**auf/an** + *acc* to); (*tadeln*) reprimand; **von der Schule v∼en** expel
verwelken *vi* (sein) wilt
verwend|en† *vt* use; spend (*Zeit, Mühe*). **V∼ung** *f* use
verwerf|en† *vt* reject; **sich v∼en** warp. **v∼lich** *a* reprehensible
verwert|en *vt* utilize, use; (*Comm*) exploit. **V∼ung** *f* - utilization; exploitation
verwesen *vi* (sein) decompose
verwick|eln *vt* involve (**in** + *acc* in); **sich v∼eln** get tangled up; **in etw** (*acc*) **v∼elt sein** (*fig*) be involved or mixed up in sth.
v∼elt *a* complicated
verwildern *vi* run wild; (*Garten*) overgrown; (*Aussehen*) unkempt
verwinden† *vt* (*fig*) get over
verwirken *vt* forfeit
verwirklichen *vt* realize; **sich v∼** be realized
verwirr|en *vt* tangle up; (*fig*) confuse; **sich v∼en** get tangled; (*fig*) become confused. **v∼t** *a* confused. **V∼ung** *f* - confusion
verwischen *vt* smudge
verwittert *a* weathered; (*Gesicht*) weather-beaten

verwitwet *a* widowed
verwöhn|en *vt* spoil. **v~t** *a* spoilt; (*anspruchsvoll*) discriminating
verworren *a* confused
verwund|bar *a* vulnerable. **v~en** *vt* wound
verwunder|lich *a* surprising. **v~n** *vt* surprise; **sich v~n** be surprised. **V~ung** *f* - surprise
Verwund|ete(r) *m* wounded soldier; **die V~eten** the wounded *pl*. **V~ung** *f* -,-en wound
verwünsch|en *vt* curse. **v~t** *a* confounded
verwüst|en *vt* devastate, ravage. **V~ung** *f* -,-en devastation
verzagen *vi* (*haben*) lose heart
verzählen (sich) *vr* miscount
verzärteln *vt* mollycoddle
verzauber|n *vt* bewitch; (*fig*) enchant; **v~n in** (+ *acc*) turn into
Verzehr *m* -s consumption. **v~en** *vt* eat; (*aufbrauchen*) use up; **sich v~en** (*fig*) pine away
verzeich|nen *vt* list; (*registrieren*) register. **V~nis** *nt* -ses, -se list; (*Inhalts-*) index
verzeih|en† *vt* forgive; **v~en Sie!** excuse me! **V~ung** *f* - forgiveness; **um V~ung** bitten apologize; **V~ung!** sorry! (*bei Frage*) excuse me!
verzerren *vt* distort; contort (*Gesicht*); pull (*Muskel*)
Verzicht *m* -[e]s renunciation (**auf** + *acc* of). **v~en** *vi* (*haben*) do without; **v~en auf** (+ *acc*) give up; renounce (*Recht, Erbe*)
verziehen† *vt* pull out of shape; (*verwöhnen*) spoil; **sich v~** lose shape; (*Holz:*) warp; (*verschwinden*) disappear; (*Nebel:*) disperse; (*Gesicht*) pass; **das Gesicht v~** pull a face □ *vi* (*sein*) move [away]
verzier|en *vt* decorate. **V~ung** *f* -,-en decoration
verzinsen *vt* pay interest on

verzöger|n *vt* delay; (*verlangsamen*) slow down; **sich v~n** be delayed. **V~ung** *f* -,-en delay
verzollen *vt* pay duty on; **haben Sie etwas zu v~?** have you anything to declare?
verzück|t *a* ecstatic, *adv* -ally. **V~ung** *f* - rapture, ecstasy
Verzug *m* delay; **in V~** in arrears
verzweif|eln *vi* (*sein*) despair. **v~elt** *a* desperate, *adv* -ly; **v~elt sein** be in despair; (*ratlos*) be desperate. **V~ung** *f* - despair; (*Ratlosigkeit*) desperation
verzweigen (sich) *vr* branch [out]
verzwickt *a* (*fam*) tricky
Veto /'ve:to/ *nt* -s,-s veto
Vetter *m* -s,-n cousin. **V~nwirtschaft** *f* nepotism
vgl. *abbr* (**vergleiche**) cf.
Viadukt /vja'dʊkt/ *nt* -[e]s,-e viaduct
vibrieren /vi'bri:rən/ *vi* (*haben*) vibrate
Video /'vi:deo/ *nt* -s,-s video. **V~kassette** *f* video cassette. **V~recorder** /-rɛkɔrdə/ *m* -s,-video recorder
Vieh *nt* -[e]s livestock; (*Rinder*) cattle *pl*; (*fam: Tier*) creature. **v~isch** *a* brutal, *adv* -ly
viel *pron* a great deal/(*fam*) a lot of; (*pl*) many, (*fam*) a lot of; (*substantivisch*) **v~[es]** much, (*fam*) a lot; **nicht/so/wie/zu v~** not/so/how/too much/ (*pl*) many; **v~e** *pl* many; **das v~e Geld/Lesen** all that money/reading □ *adv* much, (*fam*) a lot; **v~mehr/weniger** much more/less; **v~zu groß/klein/viel** much *or* far too big/small/much; **so v~ wie möglich** as much as possible; **so/zu v~ arbeiten** work so/too much
vieldeutig *a* ambiguous. **v~erlei** *inv* *a* many kinds of □ *pron* many things. **v~fach** *a* multiple □ *adv* many times; (*fam: oft*) frequently. **V~falt** *f* - diversity,

[great] variety. **v~fältig** a diverse, varied

vielleicht adv perhaps; maybe; (fam: wirklich) really

vielmals adv very much; **danke v~!** thank you very much!

viel|mehr adv rather; (im Gegenteil) on the contrary. **v~sagend** a (NEW)~ **sagend**, s. sagen

vielseitig a varied; (Person) versatile □ adv widely. **v~begabt** versatile. **V~keit** f · versatility

vielversprechend a (NEW)~ **viel versprechend**, s. versprechen

vier inv a, **V~** f ·,**-en** four; (Sch) ≈ fair. **V~eck** nt ·[e]s,**-e** oblong, rectangle; (Quadrat) square. **v~eckig** a oblong, rectangular; square. **v~fach** a quadruple. **V~linge** mpl quadruplets

viertel /'firtəl/ inv a a quarter; **eine v~ Million** a quarter of a million; **um v~ neun** at [a] quarter past eight; **um drei v~ neun** at [a] quarter to nine; **= eine Viertelstunde**. **V~** nt ·s,**-** quarter; (Wein) quarter litre; **V~ vor/nach sechs** [a] quarter to/past six; **um V~/drei V~ neun** (NEW)**um V~/drei V~ neun**, s. viertel. **V~finale** nt quarter-final. **V~jahr** nt three months pl; (Comm) quarter. **v~jährlich** a & adv quarterly. **v~n** vt quarter. **V~note** f crotchet, (Amer) quarter note. **V~stunde** f quarter of an hour

vier|zehn /'fir-/ inv a a fourteen. **v~zehnte(r,s)** a fourteenth. **v~zig** inv a a forty. **v~zigste(r,s)** a fortieth

Villa /'vɪla/ f ·,**-len** villa

violett /vjo'lɛt/ a a violet

Vio|line /vjo'li:nə/ f ·,**-n** violin. **V~linschlüssel** m treble clef. **V~loncello** f ·[ɔn'tʃɛlo/ nt cello

Virtuose /vɪr'tuo:zə/ m ·n,**-n** virtuoso

Virus /'vi:rʊs/ nt ·,**-ren** virus

Visier /vi'zi:ɐ/ nt ·s,**-e** visor

Vision /vi'zjo:n/ f ·,**-en** vision

Visite /vi'zi:tə/ f ·,**-n** round; **V~ machen** do one's round

visuell /vi'zyɛl/ a visual, adv -ly

Visum /'vi:zʊm/ nt ·s,**-sa** visa

vital /vi'ta:l/ a vital; (Person) energetic. **V~ität** f · vitality

Vitamin /vita'mi:n/ nt ·s,**-e** vitamin

Vitrine /vi'tri:nə/ f ·,**-n** display cabinet/(im Museum) case

Vizepräsident /'fi:tsə-/ m vice president

Vogel m ·s,** ̈** bird; **einen V~ haben** (fam) have a screw loose. **V~scheuche** f ·,**-n** scarecrow

Vokab|el /vo'ka:bəln/ fpl vocabulary sg. **V~ular** nt ·s,**-e** vocabulary

Vokal /vo'ka:l/ m ·s,**-e** vowel

Volant /vo'lã:/ m ·s,**-s** flounce; (Auto) steering-wheel

Volk nt ·[e]s,** ̈er** people sg; (Bevölkerung) people pl; (Bienen-) colony

Völker|kunde f · ethnology. **V~mord** m genocide. **V~recht** nt international law

Volks|abstimmung f plebiscite. **V~fest** nt public festival. **V~hochschule** f adult education classes pl/(Gebäude) centre. **V~lied** nt folk-song. **V~tanz** m folk-dance. **v~tümlich** a a popular. **V~wirt** m economist. **V~wirtschaft** f economics sg. **V~zählung** f [national] census

voll a full (von od mit of); (Haar) thick; (Erfolg, Ernst) complete; (Wahrheit) whole; **v~ machen** fill up; **v~ tanken** fill up with petrol; **die Uhr schlug v~** (fam) the clock struck the hour □ adv (ganz) completely; (arbeiten) fulltime; (auszahlen) in full; **v~ und ganz** completely

vollauf adv fully, completely

Voll|beschäftigung f full employment. **V~blut** nt thoroughbred

vollbringen† vt insep accomplish work (Wunder)

vollende|n vt insep complete. v~t a perfect, adv -ly. v~te Gegenwart/Vergangenheit perfect/pluperfect

vollends adv completely

Vollendung f completion; (Vollkommenheit) perfection

voller inv a full of; v~ Angst/Freude filled with fear/joy; v~ Flecken covered with stains

Völlerei f - gluttony

Volleyball /'vɔli-/ m volleyball

vollführen vt insep perform

vollfüllen vt sep fill up

Vollgas nt V~ geben put one's foot down; mit V~ flat out

völlig a complete, adv -ly

volljährig a v~ sein (Jur) be of age. V~keit f - (Jur) majority

Vollkaskoversicherung f fully comprehensive insurance

vollkommen a perfect, adv -ly; (völlig) complete, adv -ly. V~heit f - perfection

Voll|kornbrot nt wholemeal bread. V~macht f -,-en authority; (Jur) power of attorney. V~mond m full moon. V~pension f full board. V~schlank a with a fuller figure

vollständig a complete, adv -ly

vollstrecken vt insep execute; carry out (Urteil)

volltanken vi sep (haben) (NEW) voll tanken, s. voll

Volltreffer m direct hit

vollzählig a complete; sind wir v~? are we all here?

vollziehen† vt insep carry out; perform (Handlung); consummate (Ehe); sich v~ take place

Volt /vɔlt/ nt -[s],- volt

Volumen /vo'lu:mən/ nt -s,- volume

vom prep = von dem; vom Rauchen from smoking

von prep (+ dat) of; (über) about; (Ausgangspunkt, Ursache) from;

(beim Passiv) by; Musik von Mozart music by Mozart; einer von euch one of you; von hier/heute an from here/today; von mir aus I don't mind

voneinander adv from each other; (abhängig) on each other

vonseiten prep (+ gen) on the part of

vonstatten adv v~ gehen take place; gut v~ gehen go [off] well

vor prep (+ dat/acc) in front of; (zeitlich, Reihenfolge) before; (+ dat) (bei Uhrzeit) to; (warnen, sich fürchten/schämen) of; (schützen, davonlaufen) from; (Respekt haben) for; vor Angst/Kälte zittern tremble with fear/cold; vor drei Tagen/Jahren three days/years ago; vor sich (acc) hin murmeln mumble to oneself; vor allen Dingen above all □ adv forward; vor und zurück backwards and forwards

Vor|abend m eve. V~ahnung f premonition

voran adv at the front; (voraus) ahead; (vorwärts) forward. v~gehen† vi sep (sein) lead the way; (Fortschritte machen) make progress; jdm/etw v~gehen precede s.o./sth. v~kommen† vi sep (sein) make progress; (fig) get on

Vor|anschlag m estimate. V~anzeige f advance notice. V~arbeit f preliminary work. V~arbeiter m foreman

voraus adv ahead (dat of); (vorn) at the front; (vorwärts) forward □ im Voraus (voraus) in advance. v~bezahlen vt sep pay in advance. v~gehen† vi sep (sein) go on ahead; jdm/etw v~gehen precede s.o./sth. V~sage f -,-n prediction. v~sagen vt sep predict. v~sehen† vt sep foresee

voraussetz|en vt sep take for granted; (erfordern) require; vorausgesetzt, dass provided that.

V~ung f -,-en assumption; (*Erfordernis*) prerequisite; **unter der V~ung, dass** on condition that

Voraussicht f foresight; **aller V~** nach in all probability. **v~lich** a anticipated, expected □ adv probably

Vorbehalt m -[e]s,-e reservation. v~en† vt sep sich (dat) v~en reserve (*Recht*); **jdm v~en sein/ bleiben** be left to s.o. **v~los** a unreserved, adv -ly

vorbei adv past (**an** jdm/etw s.o./sth); (*zu Ende*) over. v~fahren† vi sep (sein) drive/go past. v~gehen† vi sep (sein) go past; (*verfehlen*) miss; (*vergehen*) pass; (*fam: besuchen*) drop in (**bei** on). v~kommen† vi sep (sein) pass/(*v~können*) get past (**an** jdm/etw s.o./sth); (*fam: besuchen*) drop in (**bei** on)

vorbereit|en vt sep prepare; prepare for (*Reise*); **sich v~en** prepare [oneself] (**auf** + acc for). V~ung f -,-en preparation

vorbestellen vt sep order/(*im Theater, Hotel*) book in advance

vorbestraft a v~ sein have a [criminal] record

vorbeug|en v sep □ vt bend forward; **sich v~en** bend or lean forward □ vi (*haben*) prevent (etw dat sth); **v~end** preventive. V~ung f - prevention

Vorbild nt model. v~lich a exemplary, model □ adv in an exemplary manner

vorbringen† vt sep put forward; offer (*Entschuldigung*)

vordatieren vt sep post-date

Vorder|bein nt foreleg. v~e(r,s) a front. V~grund m foreground. V~mann m (pl -männer) person in front; **jdn zum V~mann bringen** (fam) lick into shape; (*aufräumen*) tidy up. V~rad nt front wheel. V~seite f front; (*einer Münze*) obverse. v~ste(r,s) a front, first. V~teil nt front

vor|**drängeln (sich)** vr sep (fam) jump the queue. **v~drängen (sich)** vr sep push forward. **v~dringen**† vi sep (sein) advance

vor|**ehelich** a pre-marital. **v~eilig** a rash, adv -ly

voreingenommen a biased, prejudiced. V~heit f - bias

vorenthalten† vt sep withhold

vorerst adv for the time being

Vorfahr m -en,-en ancestor

vorfahren† vi sep (sein) drive up; (*vorwärts-*) move forward; (*voraus-*) drive on ahead

Vorfahrt f right of way; '**V~ beachten**' 'give way'. V~straße f ≈ major road

Vorfall m incident. **v~en**† vi sep (sein) happen

vorfinden† vt sep find

Vorfreude f [happy] anticipation

vorführ|en vt sep present, show; (*demonstrieren*) demonstrate; (*aufführen*) perform. V~ung f presentation; demonstration; performance

Vor|**gabe** f (Sport) handicap. V~gang m occurrence; (*Techn*) process. V~gänger(in) m -s,- (f -,-nen) predecessor. V~garten m front garden

vorgeben† vt sep pretend

vor|**gefasst** (**vor**|**gefaßt**) a preconceived; (*Ansicht*). **v~gefertigt** a prefabricated

vorgehen† vi sep (sein) go forward; (*voraus-*) go on ahead; (*Uhr:*) be fast; (*vordringlich sein*) take precedence; (*verfahren*) act, proceed; (*geschehen*) happen, go on. V~ nt -s action

vor|**geschichtlich** a prehistoric. V~geschmack m foretaste. V~gesetzte(r) m/f superior. **v~gestern** adv the day before yesterday; **v~gestern Abend/ Nacht** the evening/night before last

vorhaben† vt sep propose, intend (**zu** to); **etw v~** have sth planned

nichts v~ have no plans. **V~** *nt* -s,- plan; (*Projekt*) project

vorhalt|en† *v sep* □ *vt* hold up; **jdm etw v~en** reproach s.o. for sth □ *vi* (*haben*) last. **V~ungen** *fpl* **jdm V~ungen machen** reproach s.o. (**wegen** for)

Vorhand *f* (*Sport*) forehand

vorhanden *a* existing; **v~ sein** exist; (*verfügbar sein*) be available. **V~sein** *nt* -s existence

Vorhang *m* curtain

Vorhängeschloss (**Vorhänge-schloß**) *nt* padlock

vorher *adv* before[hand]

vorhergehend *a* previous

vorherig *a* prior; (*vorhergehend*) previous

Vorherrsch|aft *f* supremacy. **v~en** *vi sep* (*haben*) predominate. **v~end** *a* predominant

Vorher|sage *f* -,-n prediction; (*Wetter-*) forecast. **v~sagen** *vt sep* predict; forecast (*Wetter*). **v~sehen†** *vt sep* foresee

vorhin *adv* just now

vorige(r,s) *a* last, previous

Vor|kämpfer *m* (*fig*) champion. **V~kehrungen** *fpl* precautions. **V~kenntnisse** *fpl* previous knowledge *sg*

vorkommen† *vi sep* (*sein*) happen; (*vorhanden sein*) occur; (*nach vorn kommen*) come forward; (*hervorkommen*) come out; (*zu sehen sein*) show; **jdm bekannt/verdächtig v~** seem familiar/suspicious to s.o.; **sich** (*dat*) **dumm/alt v~** feel stupid/old. **V~** *nt* -s,- occurrence; (*Geol*) deposit

Vorkriegszeit *f* pre-war period

vorlad|en† *vt sep* (*Jur*) summons. **V~ung** *f* summons

Vorlage *f* model; (*Muster*) pattern; (*Gesetzes-*) bill

vorlassen† *vt sep* admit; **jdn v~** (*fam*) let s.o. pass; (*den Vortritt lassen*) let s.o. go first

Vor|lauf *m* (*Sport*) heat. **V~läufer** *m* forerunner. **v~läufig** *a* provisional, *adv* -ly; (*zunächst*) for the time being. **v~laut** *a* forward. **V~leben** *nt* past

vorlegen *vt sep* put on (*Kette*); (*unterbreiten*) present; (*zeigen*) show; **jdm Fleisch v~en** serve s.o. with meat. **V~er** *m* -s,- mat; (*Bett-*) rug

vorles|en† *vt sep* read [out]; **jdm v~en** read to s.o. **V~ung** *f* lecture

vorletzt|e(r,s) *a* last ... but one; (*Silbe*) penultimate; **v~es Jahr** the year before last

vorlieb *do v~ nehmen* make do (**mit** with). **v~nehmen†** *vt sep* (NEW) **v~ nehmen**, *s.* **vorlieb**

Vorliebe *f* preference

vorliegen† *vt sep* (*haben*) be present/(*vorhanden*) available; (*bestehen*) exist, be; **es muss ein Irrtum v~** there must be some mistake. **v~d** *a* present; (*Frage*) at issue

vorlügen† *vt sep* lie (*dat* to)

vorm *prep* = **vor dem**

vormachen *vt sep* put up; put on (*Kette*); push (*Riegel*); (*zeigen*) demonstrate; **jdm etwas v~** (*fam:täuschen*) kid s.o.

Vormacht *f* supremacy

vormals *adv* formerly

Vormarsch *m* (*Mil & fig*) advance

vormerken *vt sep* make a note of; (*reservieren*) reserve

Vormittag *m* morning; **gestern/heute** v~ yesterday/this morning. **v~** *adv* **gestern/heute** v~ gestern/heute v~, *s.* **Vormittag**. **v~s** *adv* in the morning

Vormund *m* -[e]s,-munde & -münder guardian

vorn *adv* at the front; **nach v~** to the front; **von v~** from the front/(*vom Anfang*) beginning; **von v~ anfangen** start afresh

Vorname *m* first name

vorne adv = **vorn**

vornehm a distinguished; (elegant) smart, adv -ly

vornehmen† vt sep carry out; **sich** (dat) v~, **etw zu tun** plan/ (beschließen) resolve to do sth

vorn|herein adv **von v~herein** from the start. **V~über** adv forward

Vor|ort m suburb. **V~rang** m priority, precedence (**vor** + dat over). **V~rat** m -[e]s,-e supply, stock (**an** + dat of). v~**rätig** a available; **v~rätig haben** have in stock. **V~ratskammer** f larder. **V~raum** m ante-room. **V~recht** nt privilege. **V~richtung** f device

vorrücken vt/i sep (sein) move forward; (Mil) advance

Vorrunde f qualifying round

vors prep = **vor das**

vorsagen vt/i sep (haben) recite; **jdm [die Antwort] v~** tell s.o. the answer

Vor|satz m resolution. v~**sätzlich** a deliberate, adv -ly; (Jur) premeditated

Vorschau f preview; (Film-) trailer

Vorschein m **zum V~kommen** appear

vorschießen† vt sep advance (Geld)

Vorschlag m suggestion, proposal. v~**en†** vt sep suggest, propose

vorschnell a rash, adv -ly

vorschreiben† vt sep lay down; dictate (dat to); **vorgeschriebene Dosis** prescribed dose

Vorschrift f regulation; (Anweisung) instruction; **jdm V~en machen** tell s.o. what to do; **Dienst nach V~** work to rule. v~**smäßig** a correct, adv -ly

Vorschule f nursery school

Vorschuss (**Vorschuß**) m advance

vorschützen vt sep plead [as an excuse]; feign (Krankheit)

vorseh|en† v sep □ vt intend (**für/als** for/as); (planen) plan; v~**en** be careful (**vor** + dat of) □ vi (haben) peep out. **V~ung** f -providence

vorsetzen vt sep move forward; **jdm etw v~** serve s.o. sth

Vorsicht f care; (bei Gefahr) caution; **V~!** careful! (auf Schild) 'caution'. v~**ig** a careful, adv -ly; cautious, adv -ly. v~**shalber** adv to be on the safe side. **V~smaßnahme** f precaution

Vorsilbe f prefix

Vorsitz m chairmanship; **den V~ führen** be in the chair. **v~en†** vi sep (haben) preside (dat over). **V~ende(r)** m/f chairman

Vorsorge f **V~ treffen** take precautions; make provisions (**für** for). **v~n** vi sep (haben) provide (**für** for). **V~untersuchung** f check-up

vorsorglich adv as a precaution

Vorspeise f starter

Vorspiel nt prelude. v~**en** v sep □ vt perform/ (Mus) play (dat for) □ vi (haben) audition

vorsprechen† v sep □ vt recite; (zum Nachsagen) say (dat to) □ vi (haben) (Theat) audition; **bei jdm v~** call on s.o.

vorspringen† vi sep (sein) jut out; **v~des Kinn** prominent chin

Vor|sprung m projection; (Fels-) ledge; (Vorteil) lead (**vor** + dat over). **V~stadt** f suburb. v~**städtisch** a suburban. **V~stand** m board [of directors]; (Vereins-) committee; (Partei-) executive

vorsteh|en† vi sep (haben) project, protrude; **einer Abteilung v~en** be in charge of a department; **v~end** protruding; (Augen) bulging. **V~er** m -s,- head; (Gemeinde-) chairman

vorstell|bar a imaginable, conceivable. **v∼en** vt sep put forward (*Bein, Uhr*); (*darstellen*) represent; (*bekanntmachen*) introduce; **sich v∼en** introduce oneself; (*als Bewerber*) go for an interview; **sich** (*dat*) **etw v∼en** imagine sth. **V∼ung** f introduction; (*bei Bewerbung*) interview; (*Aufführung*) performance; (*Idee*) idea; (*Phantasie*) imagination. **V∼ungsgespräch** nt interview.

Vorstoß m advance

Vorstrafe f previous conviction

Vortag m day before

vortäuschen vt sep feign, fake

Vorteil m advantage. **v∼haft** a advantageous, adv -ly; (*Kleidung, Farbe*) flattering

Vortrag m -[e]s,-̈e talk; (*wissenschaftlich*) lecture; (*Klavier-, Gedicht-*) recital. **v∼en†** vt sep perform; (*aufsagen*) recite; (*singen*) sing; (*darlegen*) present (*dat* to); express (*Wunsch*)

vortrefflich a excellent, adv -ly

vortreten† vi sep (*sein*) step forward, (*hervor-*) protrude

Vortritt m precedence; **jdm den V∼ lassen** let s.o. go first

vorüber adv **v∼ sein** be over; **an etw** (*dat*) **v∼ sein** sth. **v∼gehen†** vi sep (*sein*) walk past; (*vergehen*) pass. **v∼gehend** a temporary, adv -ily

Vor|urteil nt prejudice. **V∼verkauf** m advance booking

vorverlegen vt sep bring forward

Vor|wahl[nummer] f dialling code. **V∼wand** m -[e]s,-̈e pretext; (*Ausrede*) excuse

vorwärts adv forward[s]; **v∼ kommen** make progress; (*fig*) get on or ahead. **v∼kommen†** vi sep (*sein*) (NEW) **v∼ kommen, s. vorwärts**

vorweg adv beforehand; (*vorn*) in front; (*voraus*) ahead. **v∼nehmen†** vt sep anticipate

vorweisen† vt sep show

vorwerfen† vt sep throw (*dat* to); **jdm etw v∼** reproach s.o. with sth; (*beschuldigen*) accuse s.o. of sth

vorwiegend adv predominantly

Vorwort nt (pl -worte) preface

Vorwurf m reproach; **jdm Vorwürfe machen** reproach s.o. **v∼svoll** a reproachful, adv -ly

Vorzeichen nt sign; (*fig*) omen

vorzeigen vt sep show

vorzeitig a premature, adv -ly

vorziehen† vt sep pull forward; draw (*Vorhang*); (*vorverlegen*) bring forward; (*lieber mögen*) prefer; (*bevorzugen*) favour

Vor|zimmer nt ante-room; (*Büro*) outer office. **V∼zug** m preference; (*gute Eigenschaft*) merit, virtue; (*Vorteil*) advantage

vorzüglich a excellent, adv -ly

vorzugsweise adv preferably

vulgär /vʊl'gɛːɐ̯/ a vulgar □ adv in a vulgar way

Vulkan /vʊl'kaːn/ m -s,-e volcano

W

Waage f -,-n scales pl; (*Astr*) Libra. **w∼recht** a horizontal, adv -ly

Wabe f -,-n honeycomb

wach a awake; (*aufgeweckt*) alert; **w∼ werden** wake up

Wache f -,-n guard; (*Posten*) sentry; (*Dienst*) guard duty; (*Naut*) watch; (*Polizei*-) station; **W∼ halten** keep watch; **W∼ stehen** stand guard. **w∼en** vi (*haben*) be awake; **w∼en über** (+ *acc*) watch over. **W∼hund** m guard-dog

Wacholder m -s juniper

Wachposten m sentry

Wachs nt -es wax

wachsam a vigilant, adv -ly. **W∼keit** f - vigilance

wachsen†¹ vi (*sein*) grow

wachs|en² vt (reg) wax. **W~figur** f waxwork. **W~tuch** nt oil-cloth

Wachstum nt -s growth

Wächter m -s,- guard; ⟨Park-⟩ keeper; ⟨Parkplatz-⟩ attendant

Wacht|meister m [police] constable. **W~posten** m sentry

Wachturm m watch-tower

wackel|ig a wobbly; ⟨Stuhl⟩ rickety; ⟨Person⟩ shaky. **W~kontakt** m loose connection. **w~n** vi ⟨haben⟩ wobble; ⟨zittern⟩ shake □ vi ⟨sein⟩ totter

wacklig a = **wackelig**

Wade f -,-n ⟨Anat⟩ calf

Waffe f -,-n weapon; **W~n** arms

Waffel f -,-n waffle; ⟨Eis-⟩ wafer

Waffen|ruhe f cease-fire. **W~schein** m firearms licence. **W~stillstand** m armistice

Wagemut m daring. **w~ig** a daring, adv -ly

wagen vt risk; **es w~, etw zu tun** dare [to] do sth; **sich w~** ⟨gehen⟩ venture

Wagen m -s,- cart; ⟨Eisenbahn-⟩ carriage, coach; ⟨Güter-⟩ wagon; ⟨Kinder-⟩ pram; ⟨Auto⟩ car. **W~heber** m -s,- jack

Waggon /va'gõ:/ m -s,-s wagon

waghalsig a daring, adv -ly

Wagnis nt -ses,-se risk

Wagon /va'gõ:/ m -s,-s = Waggon

Wahl f -,-en choice; ⟨Pol, Admin⟩ election; ⟨geheime⟩ ballot; **zweite W~** ⟨Comm⟩ seconds pl

wähl|en vt/i ⟨haben⟩ choose; ⟨Pol, Admin⟩ elect; ⟨stimmen⟩ vote; ⟨Teleph⟩ dial; **jdn wieder w~** re-elect s.o. **W~er(in)** m -s,- (f -,-nen) voter. **w~erisch** a choosy, fussy

Wahl|fach nt optional subject. **w~frei** a optional. **W~kampf** m election campaign. **W~kreis** m constituency. **W~lokal** nt polling-station. **w~los** a indiscriminate, adv -ly. **W~recht** nt [right to] vote

Wählscheibe f ⟨Teleph⟩ dial

Wahl|spruch m motto. **W~urne** f ballot-box

Wahn m -[e]s delusion; ⟨Manie⟩ mania

wähnen vt believe

Wahnsinn m madness. **w~ig** a mad, insane; ⟨fam: unsinnig⟩ crazy; ⟨fam: groß⟩ terrible; **w~ig werden** go mad □ adv ⟨fam⟩ terribly. **W~ige(r)** m/f maniac

wahr a true; ⟨echt⟩ real; **w~ werden** come true; **du kommst doch, nicht w~?** you are coming, aren't you?

wahren vt keep; ⟨verteidigen⟩ safeguard; **den Schein w~** keep up appearances

während vi ⟨haben⟩ last

während prep (+ gen) during □ conj while; ⟨wohingegen⟩ whereas. **w~dessen** adv in the meantime

wahrhaben vt **etw nicht w~wollen** refuse to admit sth

wahrhaftig adv really, truly

Wahrheit f -,-en truth. **w~sgemäß** a truthful, adv -ly

wahrnehm|bar a perceptible. **w~en†** vt sep notice; ⟨nutzen⟩ take advantage of; exploit ⟨Vorteil⟩; look after ⟨Interessen⟩. **W~ung** f -,-en perception

wahrsag|en v sep □ vt predict □ vi ⟨haben⟩ **jdm w~en** tell s.o.'s fortune. **W~erin** f -,-nen fortune-teller

wahrscheinlich a probable, adv -bly. **W~keit** f - probability

Währung f -,-en currency

Wahrzeichen nt symbol

Waise f -,-n orphan. **W~nhaus** nt orphanage. **W~nkind** nt orphan

Wal m -[e]s,-e whale

Wald m -[e]s,-er wood; ⟨groß⟩ forest. **w~ig** a wooded

Wal|iser m -s,- Welshman. **w~isch** a Welsh

Wall m -[e]s,-e mound; ⟨Mil⟩ rampart

Wallfahr|er(in) m(f) pilgrim. **W~t** f pilgrimage

Walnuss (Walnuß) f walnut

Walze f -,-n roller. **w~n** vt roll

wälzen vt roll; pore over (Bücher); mull over (Probleme); **sich w~** roll [about]; (schlaflos) toss and turn

Walzer m -s,- waltz

Wand f -,¨e wall; (Trenn-) partition; (Seite) side; (Fels-) face

Wandel m -s change. **w~bar** a changeable. **w~n** vi (sein) stroll **□** vt change. **w~n** sich w~n change

Wander|er m -s,-, **W~in** f -,-nen hiker, rambler. **w~n** vi (sein) hike, ramble; (ziehen) travel; (gemächlich gehen) wander; (ziellos) roam. **W~schaft** f - travels pl. **W~ung** f -,-en hike, ramble; (länger) walking tour. **W~weg** m footpath

Wandgemälde nt mural

Wandlung f -,-en change, transformation

Wand|malerei f mural. **W~tafel** f blackboard. **W~teppich** m tapestry

Wange f -,-n cheek

wankelmütig a fickle. **w~en** vi (haben) sway; (Person:) stagger; (fig) waver **□** vi (sein) stagger

wann adv when

Wanne f -,-n tub

Wanze f -,-n bug

Wappen nt -s,- coat of arms. **W~kunde** f heraldry

war, wäre s. **sein[1]**

Ware f -,-n article; (Comm) commodity; (coll) merchandise. **W~n** goods. **W~nhaus** nt department store. **W~nprobe** f sample. **W~nzeichen** nt trademark

warm a (wärmer, wärmst) warm; (Mahlzeit) hot; **w~ machen** heat **□** adv warmly; **w~ essen** have a hot meal

Wärme f - warmth; (Phys) heat; **10 Grad W~e** 10 degrees above

zero. **w~en** vt warm; heat (Essen, Wasser). **W~flasche** f hot-water bottle

warmherzig a warm-hearted

Warn|blinkanlage f hazard [warning] lights pl. **w~en** vt/i (haben) warn (vor + dat of). **W~ung** f -,-en warning

Warteliste f waiting list

warten vi (haben) wait (auf + acc for); auf sich (acc) w~ lassen take one's/its time **□** vt service

Wärter(in) m -s,- (f -,-nen) keeper; (Museums-) attendant; (Gefängnis-) warder; (Amer) guard; (Kranken-) orderly

Warte|raum, W~saal m waiting-room. **W~zimmer** m (Med) waiting-room

Wartung f - (Techn) service

warum adv why

Warze f -,-n wart

was pron what; **was für [ein]?** what kind of [a]? **was für ein Pech!** what bad luck! **das gefällt dir, was?** you like that, don't you? **□** rel pron that; **alles, was ich brauche** all [that] I need **□** indef pron (fam: etwas) something; (fragend, verneint) anything; **was zu essen** something to eat; **so was Ärgerliches!** what a nuisance! **□** adv (fam) (warum) why; (wie) how

wasch|bar a washable. **W~becken** nt wash-basin. **W~beutel** m sponge-bag

Wäsche f - washing; (Unter-) underwear; **in der W~** in the wash

waschecht a colour-fast; (fam) genuine

Wäsche|klammer f clothes-peg. **W~leine** f clothes-line

waschen† vt wash; sich w~ have a wash; **sich** (dat) **die Hände w~** wash one's hands; **W~ und Legen** shampoo and set **□** vi (haben) do the washing

Wäscherei f -,-en laundry

Wäsche|schleuder f spin-drier.
W~trockner m tumble-drier
Wasch|küche f laundry-room.
W~lappen m face-flannel;
(fam: Feigling) sissy. **W~maschine** f
washing machine. **W~mittel** nt
detergent. **W~pulver** nt washing-powder. **W~raum** m washroom. **W~salon** m launderette.
W~zettel m blurb
Wasser nt -s water; (Haar-) lotion;
ins W~ fallen (fam) fall
through; **mir lief das W~ im
Mund zusammen** my mouth
was watering. **W~ball** m beachball; (Spiel) water polo. **w~dicht**
a watertight; (Kleidung)
waterproof. **W~fall** m waterfall.
W~farbe f water-colour.
W~hahn m tap, (Amer) faucet.
W~kasten m cistern. **W~kraft**
f water-power. **W~kraftwerk** nt
hydroelectric power-station.
W~leitung f water-main; **aus
der W~leitung** from the tap.
W~mann m (Astr) Aquarius
wässern vt soak; (begießen) water
□ vi (haben) water
Wasser|scheide f watershed.
W~ski m -s water-skiing.
W~stoff m hydrogen.
W~straße f waterway. **W~
waage** f spirit-level. **W~werfer**
m -s,- water-cannon. **W~zeichen**
nt watermark
wässrig (wäßrig) a watery
waten vi (sein) wade
watscheln vi (sein) waddle
Watt[1] nt -[e]s mud-flats pl
Watt[2] nt -s,- (Phys) watt
Watte f -,-n cotton wool. **w~iert** a
padded; (gesteppt) quilted
WC /ve'tse:/ nt -s,-s WC
web|en vt/i (haben) weave. **W~er**
m -s,- weaver. **W~stuhl** m loom
Wechsel m -s,- change; (Tausch)
exchange; (Comm) bill of exchange. **W~geld** nt change.
w~haft a changeable. **W~jahre**
npl menopause sg. **W~kurs** m

exchange rate. **w~n** vt change;
(tauschen) exchange □ vi (haben)
change; (ab-) alternate; (verschieden sein) vary. **w~nd** a
changing; (verschieden) varying.
w~seitig a mutual, adv -ly.
W~strom m alternating current. **W~stube** f bureau de
change. **w~weise** adv alternately. **W~wirkung** f interaction
weck|en vt wake [up]; (fig)
awaken □ vi (haben) (Wecker:) go
off. **W~er** m -s,- alarm [clock]
wedeln vi (haben) wave; **mit dem
Schwanz w~** wag its tail
weder conj **w~ ... noch** neither
... nor

Weg m -[e]s,-e way; (Fuß-) path;
(Fahr-) track; (Gang) errand; **auf
dem Weg** on the way (nach to);
sich auf den Weg machen set
off; **im Weg sein** be in the way;
zu W~e bringen = **zuwege
bringen**, s. **zuwege**
weg adv away, off; (verschwunden)
gone; **weg sein** be away; (gegangen/verschwunden) have gone;
(fam: schlafen) be asleep; **Hände
weg!** hands off! **w~bleiben**† vi
sep (sein) stay away.
w~bringen† vt sep take away
wegen prep (+ gen) because of;
(um ... willen) for the sake of;
(bezüglich) about
weg|fahren† vi sep (sein) go away;
(abfahren) leave. **w~fallen**† vi
sep (sein) be dropped/(ausgelassen) omitted; (entfallen) no
longer apply; (aufhören) cease.
w~geben† vt sep give away; send
to the laundry (Wäsche).
w~gehen† vi sep (sein) leave, go
away; (ausgehen) go out; (Fleck:)
come out. **w~jagen** vt sep chase
away. **w~kommen**† vi sep (sein)
get away; (verloren gehen) disappear; **schlecht w~kommen**
(fam) get a raw deal. **w~lassen**†
vt sep let go; (auslassen) omit.
w~laufen† vi sep (sein) run
away. **w~machen** vt sep remove.

w~nehmen† *vt sep* take away.
w~räumen *vt sep* put away;
⟨*entfernen*⟩ clear away. **w~schicken** *vt sep* send away; ⟨*abschicken*⟩ send off. **w~tun†** *vt sep* put away; ⟨*wegwerfen*⟩ throw away
Wegweiser *m* -s,- signpost
weg|werfen† *vt sep* throw away.
w~ziehen† *v sep* □ *vt* pull away □ *vi* ⟨*sein*⟩ move away
weh *a* sore; **weh tun** hurt; ⟨*Kopf, Rücken.*⟩ ache; **jdm weh tun** hurt s.o. □ *int* **oh weh!** oh dear!
wehe *int* alas; **w~ [dir/euch]!** ⟨*drohend*⟩ don't you dare!
wehen *vt* ⟨*haben*⟩ blow; ⟨*flattern*⟩ flutter □ *vi* blow
Wehen *fpl* contractions; **in den W~liegen** be in labour
weh|leidig *a* soft; ⟨*weinerlich*⟩ whining. **w~mut** *f* wistfulness. **w~mütig** *a* wistful, *adv* -ly
Wehr¹ *nt* -[e]s,-e weir
Wehr² *f* sich zur W~ setzen resist. **W~dienst** *m* military service. **W~dienstverweigerer** *m* -s,- conscientious objector
wehren (sich) *vr* resist; ⟨*gegen Anschuldigung*⟩ protest; ⟨*sich sträuben*⟩ refuse
wehr|los *a* defenceless. **W~macht** *f* armed forces *pl*. **W~pflicht** *f* conscription
Weib *nt* -[e]s,-er woman; ⟨*Ehe-*⟩ wife. **W~chen** *nt* -s,- ⟨*Zool*⟩ female. **W~erheld** *m* womanizer. **w~isch** *a* effeminate. **w~lich** *a* feminine; ⟨*Biol*⟩ female. **W~lichkeit** *f* - femininity
weich *a* soft, *adv* -ly; ⟨*gar*⟩ done; ⟨*Ei*⟩ soft-boiled; ⟨*Mensch*⟩ soft-hearted; **w~ werden** ⟨*fig*⟩ relent
Weiche *f* -,-n ⟨*Rail*⟩ points *pl*
weichen¹ *vi* ⟨*sein*⟩ ⟨*reg*⟩ soak
weichen†² *vi* ⟨*sein*⟩ give way ⟨*dat* to⟩; **nicht von jds Seite w~** not leave s.o.'s side
Weich|heit *f* - softness. **w~herzig** *a* soft-hearted. **w~lich** *a* soft; ⟨*Charakter*⟩ weak. **W~spüler** *m*

-s,- ⟨*Tex*⟩ conditioner. **W~tier** *nt* mollusc
Weide¹ *f* -,-n ⟨*Bot*⟩ willow
Weide² *f* -,-n pasture. **w~n** *vt/i* ⟨*haben*⟩ graze; **sich w~n an** (+ *dat*) enjoy; ⟨*schadenfroh*⟩ gloat over
weiger|n (sich) *vr* refuse.
W~ung *f* -,-en refusal
Weihe *f* -,-n consecration; ⟨*Priester-*⟩ ordination. **w~n** *vt* consecrate; ⟨*zum Priester*⟩ ordain; ⟨*dedicate* (*Kirche*) ⟨*dat* to⟩
Weiher *m* -s,- pond
Weihnacht|en *nt* -s & *pl* Christmas. **w~lich** *a* Christmassy. **W~sbaum** *m* Christmas tree. **W~sfest** *nt* Christmas. **W~slied** *nt* Christmas carol. **W~smann** *m* (*pl* -männer) Father Christmas. **W~stag** *m* erster/zweiter **W~stag** Christmas Day/Boxing Day
Weih|rauch *m* incense. **W~wasser** *nt* holy water
weil *conj* because; ⟨*da*⟩ since
Weile *f* - while
Wein *m* -[e]s,-e wine; ⟨*Bot*⟩ vines *pl*; ⟨*Trauben*⟩ grapes *pl*. **W~bau** *m* wine-growing. **W~beere** *f* grape. **W~berg** *m* vineyard. **W~brand** *m* -[e]s brandy
wein|en *vt/i* ⟨*haben*⟩ cry, weep. **w~erlich** *a* tearful, *adv* -ly
Wein|glas *nt* wineglass. **W~karte** *f* wine-list. **W~keller** *m* wine-cellar. **W~lese** *f* grape harvest. **W~liste** *f* wine-list. **W~probe** *f* wine-tasting. **W~rebe** *f* vine. **W~stock** *m* vine. **W~stube** *f* wine-bar. **W~traube** *f* bunch of grapes; ⟨*W~beere*⟩ grape
weise *a* wise, *adv* -ly
Weise *f* -,-n way; ⟨*Melodie*⟩ tune; **auf diese W~** in this way
weisen† *vt* show; **von sich w~** ⟨*fig*⟩ reject □ *vi* ⟨*haben*⟩ point (**auf** + *acc* at)

Weisheit f -,-en wisdom.
W~zahn m wisdom tooth

weiß a, **W~** nt -,- white

weissag|en vt/i insep (haben)
prophesy. **W~ung** f -,-en prophecy

Weiß|brot nt white bread.
W~e(r) m/f white man/woman.
w~en vt whitewash. **W~wein** m
white wine

Weisung f -,-en instruction; (Befehl) order

weit a wide; (ausgedehnt) extensive; (lang) long □ adv widely;
(offen, öffnen) wide; (lang) far;
von w~em from a distance; **bei
w~em** by far; **w~ und breit** far
and wide; **ist es noch w~?** is it
much further? **so w~ wie möglich** as far as possible; **ich bin so
w~** I'm ready; **es ist so w~** the
time has come; **zu w~ gehen**
(fig) go too far; **w~ verbreitet**
widespread; **w~ blickend** (fig)
far-sighted; **w~ reichende
Folgen** far-reaching consequences. **w~aus** adv far.
W~blick m (fig) far-sightedness.
w~blickend a = **w~ blickend**,
s. weit

Weite f -,-n expanse; (Entfernung)
distance; (Größe) width. **w~n** vt
widen; stretch (Schuhe); sich
w~n widen; stretch; (Pupille) dilate

weiter a further □ adv further;
(außerdem) in addition; (an-
schließend) then; **etw w~tun** go
on doing sth; **w~ nichts/nie-
mand** nothing/no one else; **und
so w~** and so on. **w~arbeiten** vi
sep (haben) go on working

weiter|e(r,s) a further; **im w~en
Sinne** in a wider sense; **ohne
w~es** just like that; (leicht)
easily; **bis auf w~es** until
further notice; (vorläufig) for the
time being

weiter|erzählen vt sep go on
with; (w~sagen) repeat.
w~fahren† vi sep go on.

w~geben† vt sep pass on.
w~gehen† vi sep (sein) go on.
w~hin adv (immer noch) still; (in
Zukunft) in future; (außerdem)
furthermore; **etw w~hin tun** go
on doing sth. **w~kommen†** vi sep
(sein) get on. **w~machen** vi sep
(haben) carry on. **w~sagen** vt sep
pass on; (verraten) repeat

weit|gehend a extensive □ adv to
a large extent. **w~hin** adv a long
way; (fig) widely. **w~läufig** a
spacious; (entfernt) distant, adv
-ly; (ausführlich) lengthy, adv at
length. **w~reichend** a = **w~
reichend**, s. weit. **w~schweifig**
a long-winded. **w~sichtig** a
long-sighted; (fig) far-sighted.
W~sprung m long jump.
w~verbreitet a = **w~ verbreitet**, s. weit

Weizen m -s wheat

welch inv pron what; **w~ ein(e)**
what a. **w~e(r,s)** pron which; um
w~e Zeit? at what time? □ rel
pron which; (Person) who □ indef
pron some; (fragend) any; **was
für w~e?** what sort of?

welk a wilted; (Laub) dead. **w~en**
vi (haben) wilt; (fig) fade

Wellblech nt corrugated iron

Welle f -,-n wave; (Techn) shaft.
W~nlänge f wavelength.
W~nlinie f wavy line. **W~en-
reiter** nt surfing. **W~ensittich**
m -s,-e budgerigar. **w~ig** a wavy

Welt f -,-en world; **auf der W~**
in the world; **auf die od zur W~
kommen** be born. **W~all** nt universe. **w~berühmt** a world-fam-
ous. **w~fremd** a unworldly.
w~gewandt a sophisticated.
W~kugel f globe. **w~lich** a
worldly; (nicht geistlich) secular

Weltmeister|(in) m(f) world
champion. **W~schaft** f world
championship

Weltraum m space. **W~fahrer** m
astronaut

Welt|rekord m world record.
w~weit a & adv world-wide

wem pron (dat of **wer**) to whom

wen pron (acc of **wer**) whom

Wende f -,-n change. **W~kreis** m (Geog) tropic

Wendeltreppe f spiral staircase

wenden¹ vt (reg) turn; **sich zum Guten w~** take a turn for the better □ vi (haben) turn [round]

wenden†² (& reg) vt turn; **sich w~** turn; **sich an jdn w~** turn/(schriftlich) write to s.o.

Wend|epunkt m (fig) turning-point. **w~ig** a nimble; (Auto) manœuvrable. **W~ung** f -,-en turn; (Biegung) bend; (Veränderung) change; **eine W~ung zum Besseren/Schlechteren** a turn for the better/worse

wenig pron little; few; **so/zu w~** so/too little/(pl) few; **w~e** pl few □ adv little; (kaum) not much; **so/zu w~ verdienen** earn so/too little; **so w~ wie möglich** as little as possible. **w~er** pron less; (pl) fewer; **immer w~er** less and less □ adv & conj less. **w~ste(r,s)** pron least; **am w~sten** least [of all]. **w~stens** adv at least

wenn conj if; (sobald) when; **immer w~** whenever; **w~ auch** even though; **außer w~** unless; **w~ auch** even though

wer pron who; (fam: jemand) someone; (fragend) anyone; **ist da wer?** is anyone there?

Werbe|agentur f advertising agency. **w~n**† vt recruit; attract (Kunden, Besucher) □ vi (haben) **w~n für** advertise; canvass for (Partei); **w~n um** try to attract (Besucher); court (Frau, Gunst). **W~spot** -sp-/ m -s,-s commercial

Werbung f - advertising

werden† vi (sein) become; (müde, alt, länger) get, grow; (blind, wahnsinnig) go; **blass w~** turn pale; **krank w~** fall ill; **es wird warm/dunkel** it is getting warm/dark; **mir wurde**

schlecht/schwindlig I felt sick/dizzy; **er will Lehrer w~** he wants to be a teacher; **was ist aus ihm geworden?** what has become of him? □ v aux (Zukunft) shall; **wir w~ sehen** we shall see; **es wird bald regnen** it's going to rain soon; **würden Sie so nett sein?** would you be so kind? □ (Passiv; pp **worden**) be; **geliebt/geboren w~** be loved/born; **es wurde gemunkelt** it was rumoured

werfen† vt throw; cast (Blick, Schatten); **sich w~** (Holz:) warp □ vi (haben) **w~mit** throw

Werft f -,-en shipyard

Werk nt -[e]s,-e work; (Fabrik) works sg, factory; (Trieb-) mechanism. **W~ent** nt -s (Sch) handicraft. **W~statt** f -,-en workshop; (Auto-) garage; (Künstler-) studio. **W~tag** m weekday. **w~tags** adv on weekdays. **w~tätig** a working. **W~unterricht** m (Sch) handicraft

Werkzeug nt tool; (coll) tools pl. **W~maschine** f machine tool

Wermut m -s vermouth

wert a viel/50 Mark **w~** worth a lot/50 marks; **nichts w~ sein** be worthless; **jds/etw** (gen) **w~ sein** be worthy of s.o./sth. **W~** m -[e]s,-e value; (Nenn-) denomination; **im W~ von worth**; **w~ legen auf** (+ acc) set great store by. **w~en** vt rate

Wert|gegenstand m object of value; **W~gegenstände** valuables. **w~los** a worthless. **W~minderung** f depreciation. **W~papier** nt (Comm) security. **W~sachen** fpl valuables. **w~voll** a valuable

Wesen nt -s,- nature; (Lebe-) being; (Mensch) creature

wesentlich a essential; (grundlegend) fundamental; (erheblich) considerable; **im W~en (w~en)**

essentially □ adv considerably, much

weshalb adv why

Wespe f -,-n wasp

wessen pron (gen of **wer**) whose

westdeutsch a West German

Weste f -,-n waistcoat, (Amer) vest

Westen m -s west; **nach W~** west

Western m -[s],- western

Westfalen nt -s Westphalia

Westindien nt West Indies pl

west|lich a western; (Richtung) westerly □ adv & prep (+ gen) **w~lich [von] der Stadt** [to the] west of the town. **W~wärts** adv westwards

weswegen adv why

wett a **w~ sein** be quits

Wett|bewerb m -s,-e competition. **W~büro** nt betting shop

Wette f -,-n bet; **um die W~ laufen** race (**mit jdm** s.o.)

wetteifern vi (haben) compete

wetten vt/i (haben) bet (**auf** + acc on); **mit jdm w~** have a bet with s.o.

Wetter nt -s,- weather; (Un-) storm. **W~bericht** m weather report. **W~hahn** m weathercock. **W~lage** f weather conditions pl. **W~vorhersage** f weather forecast. **W~warte** f -,-n meteorological station

Wett|kampf m contest. **W~kämpfer(in)** m(f) competitor. **W~lauf** m race. **w~machen** vt sep make up for. **W~rennen** nt race. **W~streit** m contest

wetzen vt sharpen □ vi (sein) (fam) dash

Whisky m -s whisky

wichsen vt polish

wichtig a important; **w~ nehmen** take seriously; **W~keit** f -importance. **w~tuerisch** a self-important

Wicke f -,-n sweet pea

Wickel m -s,- compress

wick|eln vt wind; (ein-) wrap; (bandagieren) bandage; **ein Kind frisch w~eln** change a baby. **W~ler** m -s,- curler

Widder m -s,- ram; (Astr) Aries

wider prep (+ acc) against; (entgegen) contrary to; **w~ Willen** against one's will

widerfahren† vi insep (sein) **jdm w~** happen to s.o.

widerhallen vi sep (haben) echo

widerlegen vt insep refute

wider|lich a repulsive; (unangenehm) nasty, adv -ily. **w~rechtlich** a unlawful, adv -ly. **W~rede** f contradiction; **keine W~rede!** don't argue!

widerrufen† vt/i insep (haben) retract; revoke (Befehl)

Widersacher m -s,- adversary

widersetzen (sich) vr insep resist (**jdm/etw** s.o./sth)

wider|sinnig a absurd. **w~spenstig** a unruly; (störrisch) stubborn

widerspiegeln vt sep reflect; **sich w~** be reflected

widersprechen† vi insep (haben) contradict (**jdm/etw** s.o./sth)

Widerspruch m contradiction; (Protest) protest. **w~sprüchlich** a contradictory. **w~spruchslos** adv without protest

Widerstand m resistance; **W~ leisten** resist. **w~sfähig** a resistant; (Bot) hardy

widerstehen† vi insep (haben) resist (**jdm/etw** s.o./sth); (anwidern) be repugnant (**jdm** to s.o.)

widerstreben vi insep (haben) **es widerstrebt mir** I am reluctant (**zu** to). **W~** nt -s reluctance. **w~d** a reluctant, adv -ly

widerwärtig a disagreeable, unpleasant; (ungünstig) adverse

Widerwille m aversion, repugnance. **w~ig** a reluctant, adv -ly

widm|en vt dedicate (dat to); (verwenden) devote (dat to); **sich**

w~en (+ dat) devote oneself to.
W~ung f -,-en dedication
widrig a adverse, unfavourable
wie adv how; wie viel how
much/(pl) many; um wie viel
Uhr? at what time? wie viele?
how many? wie ist Ihr Name?
what is your name? wie ist das
Wetter? what is the weather
like? □ conj as; (gleich wie) like;
(sowie) as well as; (als) when, as;
genau wie du just like you; so
gut/reich wie as good/rich as;
nichts wie nothing but; größer
wie ich (fam) bigger than me
wieder adv again; er ist w~ da he
is back; jdn/etw w~ erkennen
recognize s.o./sth; eine Tätigkeit w~ aufnehmen resume an
activity; etw w~ verwenden/
verwerten reuse/recycle sth;
etw w~ gutmachen make up
for (Schaden); redress (Unrecht);
(bezahlen) pay for sth
Wiederaufbau m reconstruc-
tion. w~en vt sep NEW wieder
aufbauen, s. aufbauen
wieder|aufnehmen† vt sep
NEW w~ aufnehmen, s. wieder.
W~aufrüstung f rearmament
wieder|bekommen† vt sep get
back. w~beleben vt sep
NEW w~ beleben, s. beleben.
W~belebung f - resuscitation.
w~bringen† vt sep bring back.
w~erkennen† vt sep NEW w~
erkennen, s. wieder. W~gabe f
(s. w~geben) return; portrayal;
rendering; reproduction. w~
geben† vt sep give back, return;
(darstellen) portray; (ausdrück-
en, übersetzen) render; (zitieren)
quote; (Techn) reproduce.
W~geburt f reincarnation
wiedergutmach|en vt sep
NEW w~ gutmachen, s. wie-
der. W~ung f - reparation; (Entschädigung) compensation

wiederher|stellen vt sep re-
establish; restore (Gebäude); restore to health (Kranke); w~ge-
stellt sein be fully recovered.
W~stellung f re-establishment;
restoration; (Genesung) recovery
wiederholen[1] vt sep get back
wiederhol|en[2] vt insep repeat;
(Sch) revise; sich w~en recur;
(Person:) repeat oneself. w~t a
repeated, adv -ly. W~ung f -,-en
repetition; (Sch) revision
Wieder|hören nt auf W~hören!
goodbye! W~käuer m -s,- ruminant. W~kehr f - return;
(W~holung) recurrence. w~
kehren vi sep (sein) return; (sich
wiederholen) recur. w~kom-
men† vi sep (sein) come back
wiedersehen vt sep NEW wieder
sehen, s. sehen. W~ nt -s,- reunion; auf W~! goodbye!
wiederum adv again; (andererseits) on the other hand
wiedervereinig|en vt sep NEW
wieder vereinigen, s. vereinigen. W~ung f reunification
wieder|verheiraten (sich) vr sep
NEW w~ verheiraten (sich),
s. verheiraten. w~verwendent†
vt sep NEW w~ verwenden, s.
wieder. w~verwerten vt
sep NEW w~ verwerten, s.
wieder. w~wählen vt sep NEW
w~ wählen, s. wählen
Wiege f -,-n cradle
wiegen[1] vt/i (haben) weigh
wiegen[2] vt (reg) rock; sich w~
sway; (schaukeln) rock. W~lied
nt lullaby
wiehern vi (haben) neigh
Wien nt -s Vienna. W~er a Viennese; W~er Schnitzel Wiener
schnitzel □ m -s,- Viennese □ f -,-
≈ frankfurter. w~erisch a Viennese
Wiese f -,-n meadow
Wiesel nt -s,- weasel
wieso adv why

wieviel pron (NEW) **wie viel**, s. **wie**. **W~e(r,s)** a which; **der W~te ist heute?** what is the date today?

wieweit adv how far

wild a wild, adv -ly; (Stamm) savage; **w~er Streik** wildcat strike; **w~ wachsen** grow wild. **W~** -[e]s game; (Rot-) deer; (Culin) venison. **W~dieb** m poacher. **W~e(r)** m/f savage

Wilder|er m -s,- poacher. **w~n** vt/i (haben) poach

wildfremd a totally strange; **w~e Leute** total strangers

Wild|heger m -s, gamekeeper. **W~hüter** m -s,- gamekeeper. **W~leder** nt suede. **w~ledern** a suede. **W~nis** f - wilderness. **W~schwein** nt wild boar. **W~westfilm** m western

Wille m -ns will; **letzter W~** will; **seinen W~n durchsetzen** get one's [own] way; **mit W~n** intentionally

willen prep (+ gen) **um ... w~** for the sake of ...

Willens|kraft f will-power. **w~stark** a strong-willed

willig a willing, adv -ly

willkommen a welcome; **w~ heißen** welcome. **W~** nt -s welcome

willkürlich a arbitrary, adv -ily

wimmeln vi (haben) swarm

wimmern vi (haben) whimper

Wimpel m -s,- pennant

Wimper f -,-n [eye]lash; **nicht mit der W~ zucken** (fam) not bat an eyelid. **W~ntusche** f mascara

Wind m -[e]s,-e wind

Winde f -,-n (Techn) winch

Windel f -,-n nappy, (Amer) diaper

winden† vt wind; make (Kranz); **in die Höhe w~** winch up; **sich w~** wind (um round); (sich krümmen) writhe

Wind|hund m greyhound. **w~ig** a windy. **W~mühle** f windmill. **W~pocken** fpl chickenpox sg.

W~schutzscheibe f windscreen, (Amer) windshield. **w~still** a calm. **W~stille** f calm. **W~stoß** m gust of wind. **W~surfen** nt windsurfing

Windung f -,-en bend; (Spirale) spiral

Wink m -[e]s,-e sign; (Hinweis) hint

Winkel m -s,- angle; (Ecke) corner. **W~messer** m -s,- protractor

winken vi (haben) wave; **jdm w~** wave/(herbei) beckon to s.o.

winseln vi (haben) whine

Winter m -s,- winter. **w~lich** a wintry; (Winter-) winter ... **W~schlaf** m hibernation; **W~schlaf halten** hibernate. **W~sport** m winter sports pl

Winzer m -s,- winegrower

winzig a tiny, minute

Wipfel m -s,- [tree-]top

Wippe f -,-n see-saw. **w~n** vi (haben) bounce; (auf Wippe) play on the see-saw

wir pron we; **wir sind es** it's us

Wirbel m -s,- eddy; (Drehung) whirl; (Trommel-) roll; (Anat) vertebra; (Haar-) crown; (Aufsehen) fuss. **w~n** vt/i (sein/haben) whirl. **W~säule** f spine. **W~sturm** m cyclone. **W~tier** nt vertebrate. **W~wind** m whirlwind

wird s. **werden**

wirken vi (haben) have an effect (**auf** + acc on); (zur Geltung kommen) be effective; (tätig sein) work; (scheinen) seem □ vt (Tex) knit; **Wunder w~** work miracles

wirklich a real, adv -ly. **W~keit** f -,-en reality

wirksam a effective, adv -ly. **W~keit** f - effectiveness

Wirkung f -,-en effect. **w~slos** a ineffective, adv -ly. **w~svoll** a effective, adv -ly

wirr a tangled; (Haar) tousled; (verwirrt, verworren) confused. **W~warr** m -s tangle; (fig) confusion; (von Stimmen) hubbub

Wirt m -[e]s,-e landlord. **W~in** f -,-nen landlady

Wirtschaft f -,-en economy; (Gast-) restaurant; (Kneipe) pub. **w~en** vi (haben) manage one's finances; (sich betätigen) busy oneself; **sie kann nicht w~** she's a bad manager. **W~erin** f -,-nen housekeeper. **w~lich** a economic, (sparsam) economical, adv -ly. **W~sgeld** nt housekeeping [money]. **W~s-prüfer** m auditor

Wirtshaus nt inn; (Kneipe) pub

Wisch m -[e]s,-e (fam) piece of paper

wisch|en vt/i (haben) wipe; wash (Fußboden) □ vi (sein) slip; (Maus:) scurry. **W~lappen** m cloth; (Aufwisch-) floor-cloth

wispern vt/i (haben) whisper

wissen† vt/i (haben) know; **weißt du noch?** do you remember? **ich wüsste gern...** I should like to know...; **nichts w~ wollen von** not want anything to do with. **W~** nt -s knowledge; **meines W~s** to my knowledge

Wissenschaft f -,-en science. **W~ler** m -s,- academic; (Natur-) scientist. **w~lich** a academic, adv -ally; scientific, adv -ally

wissen|swert a worth knowing. **w~tlich** a deliberate □ adv knowingly

witter|n vt scent; (ahnen) sense. **W~ung** f - scent; (Wetter) weather

Witwe f -,-n widow. **W~r** m -s,- widower

Witz m -es,-e joke; (Geist) wit. **W~bold** m -[e]s,-e joker. **w~ig** a funny; (geistreich) witty

wo adv where; (als) when; (irgendwo) somewhere; **wo immer** wherever □ conj seeing that; (obwohl) although; (wenn) if

woanders adv somewhere else

wobei adv how; (relativ) during the course of which

Woche f -,-n week. **W~nende** nt weekend. **W~nkarte** f weekly ticket. **w~nlang** adv for weeks. **W~ntag** m day of the week; (Werktag) weekday. **w~ntags** adv on weekdays

wöchentlich a & adv weekly

Wodka m -s vodka

wodurch adv how; (relativ) through/(Ursache) by which; (Folge) as a result of which

wofür adv what ... for; (relativ) for which

Woge f -,-n wave

wogegen adv what ... against; (relativ) against which □ conj whereas. **woher** adv where from; **woher weißt du das?** how do you know that? **wohin** adv where [to]; **wohin gehst du?** where are you going? **wohingegen** conj whereas

wohl adv well; (vermutlich) probably; (etwa) about; (zwar) perhaps; **w~ kaum** hardly; **w~ oder übel** willy-nilly; **sich w~ fühlen** feel well/(behaglich) comfortable; **jdm w~ tun** do s.o. good; **der ist w~ verrückt!** he must be mad! **W~** nt -[e]s welfare, well-being; **auf jds W~ trinken** drink s.o.'s health; **zum W~** (+ gen) for the good of; **zum W~!** cheers!

wohlauf a **w~ sein** be well

Wohl|befinden nt well-being. **W~behagen** nt feeling of well-being. **w~behalten** a safe, adv -ly. **W~ergehen** nt -s welfare. **w~erzogen** a well brought-up

Wohlfahrt f - welfare. **W~sstaat** m Welfare State

Wohl|gefallen nt -s pleasure. **W~geruch** m fragrance. **w~gesinnt** a well disposed (dat towards). **w~habend** a prosperous, well-to-do. **w~ig** a comfortable, adv -bly. **w~klingend** a melodious. **w~riechend** a fragrant. **w~schmeckend** a tasty

Wohlstand m prosperity. **W~sgesellschaft** f affluent society

Wohltat f [act of] kindness; (Annehmlichkeit) treat; (Genuss) bliss

Wohltät|er m benefactor. **w~ig** a charitable

wohl|tuend a agreeable, adv -bly. **w~tun†** vi sep (haben) (NEW) **w~ tun**, s. **wohl**. **w~verdient** a well-deserved. **w~weislich** adv deliberately

Wohlwollen nt -s goodwill; (Gunst) favour. **w~d** a benevolent, adv -ly

Wohn|anhänger m = **Wohnwagen**. **W~block** m block of flats. **w~en** vi (haben) live; (vorübergehend) stay. **W~gegend** f residential area. **w~haft** a resident. **W~haus** nt [dwelling-]house. **W~heim** nt hostel; (Alten-) home. **w~lich** a comfortable, adv -bly. **W~mobil** nt -s,-e camper. **W~ort** m place of residence. **W~raum** m living space; (Zimmer) living-room. **W~sitz** m place of residence

Wohnung f -,-en flat, (Amer) apartment; (Unterkunft) accommodation. **W~snot** f housing shortage

Wohn|wagen m caravan, (Amer) trailer. **W~zimmer** nt living-room

wölb|en vt curve; arch (Rücken). **W~ung** f -,-en curve; (Archit) vault

Wolf m -[e]s,¨e wolf; (Fleisch-) mincer; (Reiß-) shredder

Wolke f -,-n cloud. **W~nbruch** m cloudburst. **W~nkratzer** m skyscraper. **w~nlos** a cloudless. **w~ig** a cloudy

Woll|decke f blanket. **W~e** f -,-n wool

wollen†1 vt/i (haben) & v aux want; **etw tun w~** want to do sth; (beabsichtigen) be going to do sth; **ich will nach Hause** I want to go

home; **wir wollten gerade gehen** we were just going; **ich wollte, ich könnte dir helfen** I wish I could help you; **der Motor will nicht anspringen** the engine won't start

wollen2 a woollen. **w~ig** a woolly. **W~sachen** fpl woollens

wollüstig a sensual, adv -ly

womit adv what ... with; (relativ) with which. **womöglich** adv possibly. **wonach** adv what ... after/(suchen) for/(riechen) of; (relativ) after/for/of which

Wonne f -,-n bliss; (Freude) joy. **w~ig** a sweet

woran adv what ... on/(denken, sterben) of; (relativ) on/of which; **woran hast du ihn erkannt?** how did you recognize him? **worauf** adv what ... on/(warten) for; (relativ) on/for which; (woraufhin) whereupon. **woraufhin** adv whereupon. **woraus** adv what ... from; (relativ) from which. **worin** adv what ... in; (relativ) in which

Wort nt -[e]s,¨er & -e word; **jdm ins W~fallen** interrupt s.o.; **ein paar W~e sagen** say a few words. **w~brüchig** a **w~brüchig werden** break one's word

Wörterbuch nt dictionary

Wort|führer m spokesman. **w~getreu** a & adv word-for-word. **w~gewandt** a eloquent, adv -ly. **w~karg** a taciturn. **W~laut** m wording

wörtlich a literal, adv -ly; (wortgetreu) word-for-word

wort|los a silent ○ adv without a word. **W~schatz** m vocabulary. **W~spiel** nt pun, play on words. **W~wechsel** m exchange of words; (Streit) argument. **w~wörtlich** a & adv = **wörtlich**

worüber adv what ... over/(lachen, sprechen) about; (relativ) over/about which. **worum** adv what ... round/(bitten, kämpfen) for; (*relativ*) round/for which; **worum geht es?** what is it about? **worunter** *adv* what ... under/ (*wozwischen*) among; (*relativ*) under/among which. **wovon** *adv* what ... from/(*sprechen*) about; (*relativ*) from/about which. **wovor** *adv* what ... in front of; (*sich fürchten*) what ... of; (*relativ*) in front of which; of which. **wozu** *adv* what ... to/(*brauchen, benutzen*) for; (*relativ*) to/for which; **wozu?** what for?

Wrack *nt* **-s,-s** wreck

wringen† *vt* wring

wuchern *vi* (*haben/sein*) grow profusely. **W~preis** *m* extortionate price. **W~ung** *f* **-,-en** growth

Wuchs *m* **-es** growth; (*Gestalt*) stature

Wucht *f* - force. **w~en** *vt* heave. **w~ig** *a* massive

wühlen *vi* (*haben*) rummage; (*in der Erde*) burrow □ *vt* dig

Wulst *m* **-[e]s,·e** bulge; (*Fett-*) roll. **w~ig** *a* bulging; (*Lippen*) thick

wund *a* sore; **w~ reiben** chafe; **sich w~ liegen** get bedsores. **W~brand** *m* gangrene

Wunde *f* **-,-n** wound

Wunder *nt* **-s,-** wonder, marvel; (*übernatürliches*) miracle; **kein W~!** no wonder! **w~bar** *a* miraculous; (*herrlich*) wonderful, *adv* -ly, marvellous, *adv* -ly. **W~kind** *nt* infant prodigy. **w~lich** *a* odd, *adv* -ly. **w~n** *vt* surprise; **sich w~n** be surprised (**über** + *acc* at). **w~schön** *a* beautiful, *adv* -ly. **w~voll** *a* wonderful, *adv* -ly

Wundstarrkrampf *m* tetanus

Wunsch *m* **-[e]s,·e** wish; (*Verlangen*) desire; (*Bitte*) request

wünschen *vt* want; wish (*dat*) **etw w~** want sth; (*bitten um*) ask for sth; **jdm Glück/gute Nacht w~** wish s.o. luck/good night; **ich wünschte, ich könnte ... I** wish I could ...; **Sie w~?** can I help you? **zu w~ übrig lassen** leave

something to be desired. **w~swert** *a* desirable

Wunsch|konzert *nt* musical request programme. **W~traum** *m* (*fig*) dream

wurde, würde *s.* **werden**

Würde *f* **-,-n** dignity; (*Ehrenrang*) honour. **w~los** *a* undignified. **W~nträger** *m* dignitary. **w~voll** *a* dignified □ *adv* with dignity

würdig *a* dignified; (*wert*) worthy. **w~en** *vt* recognize; (*schätzen*) appreciate; **keines Blickes w~en** not deign to look at

Wurf *m* **-[e]s,·e** throw; (*Junge*) litter

Würfel *m* **-s,-** cube; (*Spiel-*) dice; (*Zucker-*) lump. **w~n** *vi* (*haben*) throw the dice; **w~n um** play dice for □ *vt* throw; (*in Würfel schneiden*) dice. **W~zucker** *m* cube sugar

Wurfgeschoss (**Wurfgeschoß**) *nt* missile

würgen *vt* choke □ *vi* (*haben*) retch; choke (**an** + *dat* on)

Wurm *m* **-[e]s,·er** worm; (*Made*) maggot. **w~en** *vi* (*haben*) **jdn w~en** (*fam*) rankle [with s.o.]. **w~stichig** *a* worm-eaten

Wurst *f* **-,·e** sausage; **das ist mir W~** (*fam*) I couldn't care less

Würstchen *nt* **-s,-** small sausage; **Frankfurter W~** frankfurter

Würze *f* **-,-n** spice; (*Aroma*) aroma

Wurzel *f* **-,-n** root; **W~n schlagen** take root. **w~n** *vi* (*haben*) root

würz|en *vt* season. **w~ig** *a* tasty; (*aromatisch*) aromatic; (*pikant*) spicy

wüst *a* chaotic; (*wirr*) tangled; (*öde*) desolate; (*wild*) wild, *adv* -ly; (*schlimm*) terrible, *adv* -bly

Wüste *f* **-,-n** desert

Wut *f* - rage, fury. **W~anfall** *m* fit of rage

wüten vi (haben) rage. **w~d** a furious, adv -ly; **w~d machen** infuriate

X

x /ıks/ inv a (Math) x; (fam) umpteen. **X-Beine** ntpl knock-knees. **x-beinig**, **X-beinig** a knock-kneed. **x-beliebig** a (fam) any; **eine x-beliebige Zahl** any number [you like]. **x-mal** adv (fam) umpteen times; **zum x-ten Mal** for the umpteenth time

Y

Yoga /'jo:ga/ m & nt -[s] yoga

Z

Zack|e f -,-n point; (Berg-) peak; (Gabel-) prong. **z~ig** a jagged; (gezackt) serrated; (fam: schneidig) smart, adv -ly

zaghaft a timid, adv -ly; (zögernd) tentative, adv -ly

zäh a tough; (hartnäckig) tenacious, adv -ly; (zähflüssig) viscous; (schleppend) sluggish, adv -ly. **z~flüssig** a viscous; (Verkehr) slow-moving. **Z~igkeit** f - toughness; tenacity

Zahl f -,-en number; (Ziffer, Betrag) figure

zahl|bar a payable. **z~en** vt/i (haben) pay; (bezahlen) pay for; **bitte z~en!** the bill please!

zählen vt/i (haben) count; z~ zu (fig) be one/(pl) some of; z~ auf (+ acc) count on/vt count; z~ zu add to; (fig) count among; **die Stadt zählt 5000 Einwohner** the town has 5000 inhabitants

zahlenmäßig a numerical, adv -ly

Zähler m -s,- meter

Zahl|grenze f fare-stage. **Z~karte** f paying-in slip. **z~los** a countless. **z~reich** a numerous; (Anzahl, Gruppe) large □ adv in large numbers. **Z~ung** f -,-en payment; **in Z~ung nehmen** take in part-exchange

Zählung f -,-en count

zahlungsunfähig a insolvent

Zahlwort nt (pl -wörter) numeral

zahm a tame

zähmen vt tame; (fig) restrain

Zahn m -[e]s,-e tooth; (am Zahnrad) cog. **Z~arzt** m, **Z~ärztin** f dentist. **Z~belag** m plaque. **Z~bürste** f toothbrush. **z~en** vi (haben) be teething. **Z~fleisch** nt gums pl. **z~los** a toothless. **Z~pasta** f toothpaste. **Z~rad** nt cog-wheel. **Z~schmelz** m enamel. **Z~schmerzen** mpl toothache sg. **Z~spange** f brace. **Z~stein** m tartar. **Z~stocher** m -s,- toothpick

Zange f -,-n pliers pl; (Kneif-) pincers pl; (Kohlen-, Zucker-) tongs pl; (Geburts-) forceps pl

Zank m -[e]s squabble. **z~en** vr sich z~en squabble □ vi (haben) scold (mit jdm s.o.)

zänkisch a quarrelsome

Zäpfchen nt -s,- (Anat) uvula; (Med) suppository

Zapfen m -s,- (Bot) cone; (Stöpsel) bung; (Eis-) icicle. z~ vt tap, draw. **Z~streich** m (Mil) tattoo

Zapf|hahn m tap. **Z~säule** f petrol-pump

zappel|ig a fidgety; (nervös) jittery. z~n vi (haben) wriggle; (Kind:) fidget

zart a delicate, adv -ly; (weich, zärtlich) tender, adv -ly; (sanft) gentle, adv -ly. **Z~gefühl** nt tact. **Z~heit** f - delicacy; tenderness; gentleness

zärtlich a tender, adv -ly; (liebe-voll) loving, adv -ly. **Z~keit** f -,-en tenderness; (Liebkosung) caress

Zauber m -s magic; (Bann) spell. **Z~er** m -s,- magician. **z~haft** a enchanting. **Z~künstler** m conjuror. **Z~kunststück** nt = **Z~trick**. **z~n** vi (haben) do magic; (Zaubertricks ausführen) do conjuring tricks □ vt produce as if by magic. **Z~stab** m magic wand. **Z~trick** m conjuring trick

zaudern vi (haben) delay; (zögern) hesitate

Zaum m -[e]s,Zäume bridle; im **Z~ halten** (fig) restrain

Zaun m -[e]s,Zäune fence. **Z~könig** m wren

z.B. abbr (zum Beispiel) e.g.

Zebra nt -s,-s zebra. **Z~streifen** m zebra crossing

Zeche f -,-n bill; (Bergwerk) pit

zechen vi (haben) (fam) drink

Zeder f -,-n cedar

Zeh m -[e]s,-en toe. **Z~e** f -,-n toe; (Knoblauch-) clove. **Z~ennagel** m toenail

zehn inv a, **Z~** f -,-en ten. **z~te(r, s)** a tenth. **Z~tel** nt -s,- tenth

Zeichen nt -s,- sign; (Signal) signal. **Z~setzung** f - punctuation. **Z~trickfilm** m cartoon [film]

zeichn|en vt/i (haben) draw; (kenn-) mark; (unter-) sign. **Z~er** m -s,- draughtsman. **Z~ung** f -,-en drawing; (auf Fell) markings pl

Zeige|finger m index finger. **z~n** vt show; sich **z~n** appear; (sich herausstellen) become clear; **das wird sich z~n** we shall see □ vi (haben) point (**auf** + acc to). **Z~r** m -s,- pointer; (Uhr-) hand

Zeile f -,-n line; (Reihe) row

Zeit f prep (+ gen) **z~ meines/ seines Lebens** all my/his life

Zeit f -,-en time; sich (dat) **Z~ lassen** take one's time; **es hat Z~** there's no hurry; **mit der Z~** in time; **in nächster Z~** in the near future; **die erste Z~** at first; **von Z~ zu Z~** from time to time; **zur Z~** (rechtzeitig) in time; (derzeit) at present; **eine Z~ lang** for a time or while; [ach] du **liebe Z~!** (fam) good heavens!

Zeit|alter nt age, era. **Z~arbeit** f temporary work. **Z~bombe** f time bomb. **z~gemäß** a modern, up-to-date. **Z~genosse** m, **Z~genossin** f contemporary. **z~genössisch** a contemporary. **z~ig** a & adv early. **Z~lang** f **eine Z~lang** (NEW) **eine Z~ lang**, s. **Zeit**. **z~lebens** adv all one's life

zeitlich a (Dauer) in time; (Folge) chronological. □ adv **z~ be-grenzt** for a limited time

zeit|los a timeless. **Z~lupe** f slow motion. **Z~punkt** m time. **z~raubend** a time-consuming. **Z~raum** m period. **Z~schrift** f magazine, periodical

Zeitung f -,-en newspaper. **Z~spapier** nt newspaper

Zeit|verschwendung f waste of time. **Z~vertreib** m pastime; **zum Z~vertreib** to pass the time. **z~weilig** a temporary □ adv temporarily; (hin und wie-der) at times. **z~weise** adv at times. **Z~wort** nt (pl -wörter) verb. **Z~zünder** m time fuse

Zelle f -,-n cell; (Telefon-) box

Zelt nt -[e]s,-e tent; (Fest-) marquee. **z~en** vi (haben) camp. **Z~en** nt -s camping. **Z~plane** f tarpaulin. **Z~platz** m campsite

Zement m -[e]s cement. **z~ieren** vt cement

zen|sieren vt (Sch) mark; censor (Presse, Film). **Z~sur** f -,-en (Sch) mark, (Amer) grade; (Presse-) censorship

Zentimeter m & nt centimetre. **Z~maß** nt tape-measure

Zentner m -s,- [metric] hundred-weight (50 kg)

zentral a central. **adv** -ly. **Z∼e f**
-,-n central office; (*Partei*-) headquarters pl; (*Teleph*) exchange.
Z∼heizung f central heating.
z∼isieren vt centralize
Zentrum nt -s,-tren centre
zerbrech|en† vt/i (sein) break;
sich (dat) **den Kopf z∼en** rack
one's brains. **z∼lich** a fragile
zerdrücken vt crush; mash (*Kartoffeln*)
Zeremonie f -,-n ceremony
Zeremoniell nt -s,-e ceremonial.
z∼ a ceremonial, adv -ly
Zerfall m disintegration; (*Verfall*)
decay. **z∼en†** vi (sein) disin-
tegrate; (*verfallen*) decay; **in drei
Teile z∼en** be divided into three
parts
zerfetzen vt tear to pieces
zerfließen† vi (sein) melt; (*Tinte*:)
run
zergehen† vi (sein) melt; (*sich
auflösen*) dissolve
zergliedern vt dissect
zerkleinern vt chop/(*schneiden*)
cut up; (*mahlen*) grind
zerknirscht a contrite
zerknüllen vt crumple [up]
zerkratzen vt scratch
zerlassen† vt melt
zerlegen vt take to pieces, dismantle; (*zerschneiden*) cut up;
(*tranchieren*) carve
zerlumpt a ragged
zermalmen vt crush
zermürben vt (fig) wear down.
Z∼ungskrieg m war of attrition
zerplatzen vi (sein) burst
zerquetschen vt squash; crush;
mash (*Kartoffeln*)
Zerrbild nt caricature
zerreißen† vt tear; (*in Stücke*)
tear up; break (*Faden, Seil*) □ vi
(sein) tear; break
zerren vt drag; pull (*Muskel*) □ vi
(haben) pull (**an** + dat at)
zerrinnen† vi (sein) melt
zerrissen a torn

zerrütten vt ruin, wreck; shatter
(*Nerven*); **zerrüttete Ehe** broken
marriage
zerschlagen† vt smash; smash up
(*Möbel*); **sich z∼** (fig) fall
through; (*Hoffnung*:) be dashed
□ a (*erschöpft*) worn out
zerschmettern vt/i (sein) smash
zerschneiden† vt cut; (*in Stücke*)
cut up
zersetzen vt corrode; undermine
(*Moral*); **sich z∼** decompose
zersplittern vi (sein) splinter;
(*Glas*:) shatter □ vt shatter
zerspringen† vi (sein) shatter;
(*bersten*) burst
Zerstäub|er m -s,- atomizer
zerstör|en vt destroy; (*zunichte
machen*) wreck. **Z∼er** m -s,- des-
troyer. **Z∼ung f** destruction
zerstreu|en vt scatter; disperse
(*Menge*); dispel (*Zweifel*); **sich
z∼en** (*sich unterhalten*)
amuse oneself. **z∼t** a absent-
minded, adv -ly. **Z∼ung f** -,-en
(*Unterhaltung*) entertainment
zerstückeln vt cut up into pieces
zerteilen vt divide up
Zertifikat nt -[e]s,-e certificate
zertreten† vt stamp on; (*zerdrücken*) crush
zertrümmern vt smash [up];
wreck (*Gebäude, Stadt*)
zerzaus|en vt tousle. **z∼t** a dis-
hevelled; (*Haar*) tousled
Zettel m -s,- piece of paper; (*Notiz*)
note; (*Bekanntmachung*) notice;
(*Reklame*-) leaflet
Zeug nt -s (fam) stuff; (*Sachen*)
things pl; (*Ausrüstung*) gear;
dummes Z∼ nonsense; **das Z∼
haben zu** have the makings of
Zeuge m -n,-n witness. **z∼n** vi
(haben) testify; **z∼n von** (fig)
show □ vt father. **Z∼naussage f**
testimony. **Z∼nstand** m witness
box/(*Amer*) stand
Zeugin f -,-nen witness
Zeugnis nt -ses,-se certificate;
(*Sch*) report; (*Referenz*) reference; (*fig: Beweis*) evidence

Zickzack m -[e]s,-e zigzag
Ziege f -,-n goat
Ziegel m -s,- brick; ⟨Dach-⟩ tile. **Z~stein** m brick
ziehen† vt pull; ⟨sanfter; zücken; zeichnen⟩ draw; ⟨heraus-⟩ pull out; extract ⟨Zahn⟩; raise ⟨Hut⟩; put on ⟨Bremse⟩; move ⟨Schachfigur⟩; put up ⟨Leine, Zaun⟩; ⟨dehnen⟩ stretch; make ⟨Grimasse, Scheitel⟩; ⟨züchten⟩ breed; grow ⟨Rosen, Gemüse⟩; **nach sich z~** ⟨fig⟩ entail □ vr **sich z~** ⟨sich erstrecken⟩ run; ⟨sich verziehen⟩ warp □ vi (haben) pull ⟨an + dat on/at⟩; ⟨Tee, Ofen:⟩ draw; ⟨Culin:⟩ simmer; **es zieht** there is a draught; **solche Filme z~ nicht mehr** like that are no longer popular □ vi (sein) ⟨um-⟩ move ⟨nach to⟩; ⟨Menge:⟩ march; ⟨Vögel:⟩ migrate; ⟨Wolken, Nebel:⟩ drift. **Z~** nt -s ache
Ziehharmonika f accordion
Ziehung f -,-en draw
Ziel nt -[e]s,-e destination; ⟨Sport⟩ finish; ⟨Z~scheibe & Mil⟩ target; ⟨Zweck⟩ aim, goal. **z~bewusst** (z~bewußt) a purposeful, adv -ly. **z~en** vi (haben) aim ⟨auf + acc at⟩. **z~end** a ⟨Gram⟩ transitive. **z~los** a aimless, adv -ly. **Z~scheibe** f target; ⟨fig⟩ butt. **z~strebig** a single-minded, adv -ly
ziemen (sich) vr be seemly
ziemlich a ⟨fam⟩ fair □ adv rather, fairly; ⟨fast⟩ pretty well
Zier|de f -,-n ornament. **z~en** vt adorn; **sich z~en** make a fuss; ⟨sich bitten lassen⟩ need coaxing. **z~lich** a dainty, adv -ily; ⟨fein⟩ delicate, adv -ly; ⟨Frau⟩ petite
Ziffer f -,-n figure, digit; ⟨Zahlzeichen⟩ numeral. **Z~blatt** nt dial
zig inv a ⟨fam⟩ umpteen
Zigarette f -,-n cigarette
Zigarre f -,-n cigar
Zigeuner(in) m -s,- (f -,-nen) gypsy

Zimmer nt -s,- room. **Z~mädchen** nt chambermaid. **Z~mann** m (pl -leute) carpenter. **z~n** vt make □ vi do carpentry. **Z~nachweis** m accommodation bureau. **Z~pflanze** f house plant
zimperlich a squeamish; ⟨wehleidig⟩ soft; ⟨prüde⟩ prudish
Zimt m -[e]s cinnamon
Zink nt -s zinc
Zinke f -,-n prong; ⟨Kamm-⟩ tooth
Zinn nt -[e]s tin; ⟨Gefäße⟩ pewter
Zins|en mpl interest sg; **Z~en tragen** earn interest. **Z~eszins** m -es,-en compound interest. **Z~fuß, Z~satz** m interest rate
Zipfel m -s,- corner; ⟨Spitze⟩ point; ⟨Wurst-⟩ [tail-]end
zirka adv about
Zirkel m -s,- ⟨pair of⟩ compasses pl; ⟨Gruppe⟩ circle
Zirkulation /-'tsio:n/ f -,-en circulation. **z~ieren** vi (sein) circulate
Zirkus m -,-se circus
zirpen vi (haben) chirp
zischen vi (haben) hiss; ⟨Fett:⟩ sizzle □ vt hiss
Zitat nt -[e]s,-e quotation. **z~ieren** vt/i (haben) quote; ⟨rufen⟩ summon
Zitr|onat nt -[e]s candied lemon-peel. **Z~one** f -,-n lemon. **Z~onenlimonade** f lemonade
zittern vi (haben) tremble; ⟨vor Kälte⟩ shiver; ⟨beben⟩ shake
zittrig a shaky, adv -ily
Zitze f -,-n teat
zivil a civilian; ⟨Ehe, Recht, Luftfahrt⟩ civil; ⟨mäßig⟩ reasonable. **Z~** nt -s civilian clothes pl. **Z~courage** /-kura:-zǝ/ f - courage of one's convictions. **Z~dienst** m community service
Zivili|sation /-'tsio:n/ f -,-en civilization. **z~sieren** vt civilize. **z~siert** a civilized □ adv in a civilized manner
Zivilist m -en,-en civilian

zögern vi (haben) hesitate. Z~ nt -s hesitation. **z~d** a hesitant, adv -ly

Zoll[1] m -[e]s, -inch

Zoll[2] m -[e]s,¨e [customs] duty; (Behörde) customs pl. **Z~abfertigung** f customs clearance. **Z~beamte(r)** m customs officer. **z~frei** a & adv duty-free. **Z~kontrolle** f customs check

Zone f -,-n zone

Zoo m -s,-s zoo

Zoo|loge /tsoo'lo:gə/ m -n,-n zoologist. **Z~logie** f - zoology. **z~logisch** a zoological

Zopf m -[e]s,¨e plait

Zorn m -[e]s anger. **z~ig** a angry, adv -ily

zotig a smutty, dirty

zottig a shaggy

z.T. abbr (zum Teil) partly

zu prep (+ dat) to; (dazu) with; (zeitlich, preislich) at; (Zweck) for; (über) about; zu . . . hin towards; zu Hause at home; zu Fuß/Pferde on foot/horseback; zu beiden Seiten on both sides; zu Ostern at Easter; zu diesem Zweck for this purpose; zu meinem Erstaunen/Entsetzen to my surprise/horror; zu Dutzenden by the dozen; eine Marke zu 60 Pfennig a 60-pfennig stamp; das Stück zu zwei Mark at two marks each; wir waren zu dritt/viert there were three/four of us; es steht 5 zu 3 the score is 5-3; zu etw werden turn into sth □ adv (allzu) too; (Richtung) towards; (geschlossen) closed; (an Schalter, Hahn) off; zu sein be closed; zu groß/viel/weit too big/much/far; nach dem Fluss zu towards the river; Augen zu! close your eyes! Tür zu! shut the door! nur zu! go on! macht zu! (fam) hurry up! □ conj to; etwas zu essen something to eat; nicht zu glauben unbelievable; zu erörternde

Probleme problems to be discussed

zuallererst adv first of all. **z~letzt** adv last of all

Zubehör nt -s accessories pl

zubereit|en vt sep prepare. **Z~ung** f - preparation; (in Rezept) method

zubilligen vt sep grant

zubinden vt sep tie [up]

zubringen vt sep spend. **Z~er** m -s,- access road; (Bus) shuttle

Zucchini /tsu'ki:ni/ pl courgettes

Zucht f -,-en breeding; (Pflanzen-) cultivation; (Art, Rasse) breed; (von Pflanzen) strain; (Z~farm) farm; (Pferde-) stud; (Disziplin) discipline

zücht|en vt breed; cultivate, grow (Rosen, Gemüse). **Z~er** m -s,- breeder; grower

Zuchthaus nt prison

züchtigen vt chastise

Züchtung f -,-en breeding (Pflanzen-) cultivation; (Art, Rasse) breed; (von Pflanzen) strain

zucken vi (haben) twitch; (sich z~d bewegen) jerk; (Blitz:) flash; (Flamme:) flicker □ vt die Achseln z~ shrug one's shoulders

zücken vt draw (Messer)

Zucker m -s sugar. **Z~dose** f sugar basin. **Z~guss** (**Z~guß**) m icing. **z~krank** a diabetic. **Z~krankheit** f diabetes. **z~n** vt sugar. **Z~rohr** nt sugar cane. **Z~rübe** f sugar beet. **z~süß** a sweet; (fig) sugary. **Z~watte** f candyfloss. **Z~zange** f sugar tongs pl

zuckrig a sugary

zudecken vt sep cover up; (im Bett) tuck up; cover (Topf)

zudem adv moreover

zudrehen vt sep turn off; jdm den Rücken z~ turn one's back on s.o.

zudringlich a pushing, (fam) pushy

zudrücken vt sep press or push shut; close (Augen)

zueinander adv to one another; z~ passen go together; z~ halten (fig) stick together. z~halten† vi sep (haben) (NEW) z~ halten, s. zueinander

zuerkennen† vt sep award (dat to)

zuerst adv first; (anfangs) at first; mit dem Kopf z~ head first

zufahr|en† vi sep (sein) z~en auf (+ acc) drive towards. Z~t f access; (Einfahrt) drive

Zufall m chance; (Zusammentreffen) coincidence; durch Z~ by chance/coincidence. z~en† vi sep (sein) close, shut; jdm z~en (Aufgabe:) fall/(Erbe:) go to s.o.

zufällig a chance, accidental □ adv by chance; ich war z~ da I happened to be there

Zuflucht f refuge; (Schutz) shelter. Z~sort f refuge

zufolge prep (+ dat) according to

zufrieden a contented, adv -ly; (befriedigt) satisfied; sich z~ geben be satisfied; jdn z~ lassen leave s.o. in peace; jdn z~ stellen satisfy s.o.; z~stellend satisfactory. z~geben† (sich) vt sep (NEW) z~ geben (sich), s. zufrieden. Z~heit f -, contentment; satisfaction. z~lassen† vt sep (NEW) z~ lassen, s. zufrieden. z~stellen vt sep (NEW) z~ stellen, s. zufrieden. z~stellend a (NEW) z~ stellend, s. zufrieden

zufrieren† vi sep (sein) freeze over

zufügen vt sep inflict (dat on); do (Unrecht) (dat to)

Zufuhr f -supply

zuführen vt sep □ vt supply □ vi (haben) z~ auf (+ acc) lead to

Zug m -[e]s, ·̈e train; (Kolonne) column; (Um-) procession; (Mil) platoon; (Vogelschar) flock; (Ziehen, Zugkraft) pull; (Wandern, Ziehen) migration; (Schluck, Luft-) draught; (Atem-) breath;

(beim Rauchen) puff; (Schach-) move; (beim Schwimmen, Rudern) stroke; (Gesichts-) feature; (Wesens-) trait; etw in vollen Zügen genießen enjoy sth to the full; in einem Zug[e] at one go

Zugabe f (Geschenk) [free] gift; (Mus) encore

Zugang m access

zugänglich a accessible; (Mensch:) approachable; (fig) amenable (dat/für to)

Zugbrücke f drawbridge

zugeben† vt sep add; (gestehen) admit; (erlauben) allow. zugebenermaßen adv admittedly

zugegen a z~ sein be present

zugehen† vi sep (sein) close; jdm z~ be sent to s.o.; z~ auf (+ acc) go towards; dem Ende z~ draw to a close; (Vorräte:) run low; auf der Party ging es lebhaft zu the party was pretty lively

Zugehörigkeit f - membership

Zügel m -s, - rein

zugelassen a registered

zügel|los a unrestrained, adv -ly; (sittenlos) licentious. z~n vt rein in; (fig) curb

Zuge|ständnis nt concession. z~stehen† vt sep grant

zugetan a fond (dat of)

zugig a draughty

zügig a quick, adv -ly

Zug|kraft f pull; (fig) attraction. z~kräftig a effective; (anreizend) popular; (Titel) catchy

zugleich adv at the same time

Zug|luft f draught. Z~pferd nt draught-horse; (fam) draw

zugreifen† vi sep (haben) grab it/ them; (bei Tisch) help oneself; (bei Angebot) jump at it; (helfen) lend a hand

zugrunde adv z~ richten destroy; z~ gehen be destroyed; (Ehe:) founder; (sterben) die; z~ liegen form the basis (dat of)

zugucken vi sep (haben) = zusehen

zugunsten *prep* (+ *gen*) in favour of; (*Sammlung*) in aid of

zugute *adv* jdm/etw z~ **kommen** benefit s.o./sth; **jdm seine Jugend z~ halten** make allowances for s.o.'s youth

Zugvogel *m* migratory bird

zuhalten *v sep* □ *vt* keep closed; (*bedecken*) cover; **sich** (*dat*) **die Nase z~** hold one's nose □ *vi* (*haben*) **z~ auf** (+ *acc*) head for

Zuhälter *m* -s,- pimp

zuhause *adv* = **zu Hause**, s. **Haus**. **Z~** *nt* -s,- home

zuhör|en *vi sep* (*haben*) listen (*dat* to). **Z~er(in)** *m(f)* listener

zujubeln *vi sep* (*haben*) jdm z~ cheer s.o.

zukehren *vt sep* turn (*dat* to)

zukleben *vt sep* seal

zuknallen *vt/i sep* (*sein*) slam

zuknöpfen *vt sep* button up

zukommen *vi sep* (*sein*) z~ **auf** (+ *acc*) come towards; (*sich nähern*) approach; **z~ lassen** send (jdm s.o.); devote (*Pflege*) (*dat* to); **jdm z~** be s.o.'s right

Zukunft *f* - future. **zukünftig** *a* future □ *adv* in future

zulächeln *vi sep* (*haben*) smile (*dat* at)

Zulage *f* -,-n extra allowance

zulangen *vi sep* (*haben*) help oneself; **tüchtig z~** tuck in

zulassen† *vt sep* allow, permit; (*teilnehmen lassen*) admit; (*Admin*) license, register; (*geschlossen lassen*) leave closed; leave unopened (*Brief*)

zulässig *a* permissible

Zulassung *f* -,-en admission; registration; (*Lizenz*) licence

zulaufen† *vi sep* (*sein*) z~ **auf** (+ *acc*) run towards; **spitz z~en** taper to a point

zulegen *vt sep* add; **sich** (*dat*) **etw z~** get sth; grow (*Bart*)

zuleide *adv* jdm etwas z~ **tun** hurt s.o.

zuletzt *adv* last; (*schließlich*) in the end; **nicht z~** not least

zuliebe *adv* jdm/etw z~ for the sake of s.o./sth

zum *prep* = **zu dem**; **zum Spaß** for fun; **etw zum Lesen** sth to read

zumachen *v sep* □ *vt* close, shut; do up (*Jacke*); seal (*Umschlag*); turn off (*Hahn*); (*stilllegen*) close down □ *vi* (*haben*) close, shut; (*stillgelegt werden*) close down

zumal *adv* especially □ *conj* especially since

zumeist *adv* for the most part

zumindest *adv* at least

zumutbar *a* reasonable

zumute *adv* **mir ist traurig/elend z~** I feel sad/wretched; **mir ist nicht danach z~** I don't feel like it

zumut|en *vt sep* jdm etw z~en ask or expect sth of s.o.; **sich** (*dat*) **zu viel z~en** overdo things. **Z~ung** *f* - imposition; **eine Z~ung sein** be unreasonable

zunächst *adv* first [of all]; (*anfangs*) at first; (*vorläufig*) for the moment □ *prep* (+ *dat*) nearest to

Zunahme *f* -,-n increase

Zuname *m* surname

zünd|en *vt/i* (*haben*) ignite; **z~ende Rede** rousing speech. **Z~er** *m* -s,- detonator, fuse. **Z~holz** *nt* match. **Z~kerze** *f* sparking-plug. **Z~schlüssel** *m* ignition key. **Z~schnur** *f* fuse. **Z~ung** *f* -,-en ignition

zunehmen† *vt sep* (*haben*) increase (**an** + *dat* in); (*Mond:*) wax; (*an Gewicht*) put on weight. **z~d** *a* increasing, *adv* -ly

Zuneigung *f* - affection

Zunft *f* -,-̈e guild

zünftig *a* proper, *adv* -ly

Zunge *f* -,-n tongue. **Z~nbrecher** *m* tongue-twister

zunichte *a* z~ **machen** wreck; **z~ werden** come to nothing

zunicken vi sep (haben) nod (dat to)

zunutze a sich (dat) etw z~ machen make use of sth; (ausnutzen) take advantage of sth

zuoberst adv right at the top

zuordnen vt sep assign (dat to)

zupfen vt/i (haben) pluck (an + dat at); pull out (Unkraut)

zur prep = zu der; **zur Schule/ Arbeit** to school/work; **zur Zeit** at present

zurande adv z~ kommen mit (fam) cope with

zurate adv z~ ziehen consult

zurechnungsfähig a of sound mind

zurecht|finden† (sich) vr sep find one's way. z~kommen† vi sep (sein) cope (mit with); (rechtzeitig kommen) be in time. z~legen vt sep put out ready; sich (dat) eine Ausrede z~legen have an excuse all ready. z~machen vt sep get ready; sich z~machen get ready. z~weisen† vt sep reprimand. **Z~weisung** f reprimand

zureden vi sep (haben) jdm z~ try to persuade s.o.

zurichten vt sep prepare; (beschädigen) damage; (verletzen) injure

zuriegeln vt sep bolt

zurück adv back; Berlin, hin und z~ return to Berlin. z~behalten† vt sep keep back; be left with (Narbe). z~bekommen† vt sep get back; **20 Pfennig z~bekommen** get 20 pfennigs change. z~bleiben† vi sep (sein) stay behind; (nicht mithalten) lag behind. z~blicken vi sep (haben) look back. z~bringen† vt sep bring back; (wieder hinbringen) take back. z~erobern vt sep recapture; (fig) regain. z~erstatten vt sep refund. z~fahren† v sep □ vt drive back □ vi (sein) return, go back; (im Auto) drive back; (z~weichen) recoil. z~finden† vi sep (haben) find

one's way back. z~führen v sep □ vt take back; (fig) attribute (auf + acc to) □ vi (haben) lead back. z~geben† vt sep give back, return. z~geblieben a retarded. z~gehen† vi sep (sein) go back, return; (abnehmen) go down; z~gehen auf (+ acc) (fig) go back to

zurückgezogen a secluded. **Z~heit** f – seclusion

zurückhalt|en† vt sep hold back; (abhalten) stop; sich z~en restrain oneself. z~end a reserved. **Z~ung** f – reserve

zurück|kehren vi sep (sein) return. z~kommen† vi sep (sein) come back, return; (ankommen) get back; z~kommen auf (+ acc) (fig) come back to. z~lassen† vt sep leave behind; (z~kehren lassen) allow back. z~legen vt sep (sparen) put by; cover (Strecke). z~lehnen vt sep lean back. z~liegen† vi sep (haben) be in the past; (Sport) be behind; das liegt lange zurück that was long ago. z~melden (sich) vr sep report back. z~nehmen† vt sep take back. z~rufen† vt/i sep (haben) call back. z~scheuen vi sep (sein) shrink (vor + dat from). z~schicken vt sep send back. z~schlagen† v sep □ vt (haben) hit back □ vt hit back; (abwehren) beat back; (umschlagen) turn back. z~schneiden† vt sep cut back. z~schrecken† vi sep (sein) shrink back, recoil; (fig) shrink (vor + dat from). z~setzen v sep □ vt reverse, back; (herabsetzen) reduce; (fig) neglect □ vi (haben) reverse, back. z~stellen vt sep put back; (fig) put aside; (aufschieben) postpone. z~stoßen† v sep □ vt push back □ vi (sein) reverse, back. z~treten† vi sep (sein) step back;

(vom Amt) resign; (verzichten) withdraw. z~**weichen**† vi sep (sein) draw back; (z~schrecken) shrink back. z~**weisen**† vt sep turn away; (fig) reject. z~**werfen**† vt throw back; (reflektieren) reflect. z~**zahlen** vt sep pay back. z~**ziehen**† vt sep draw back; (fig) withdraw; **sich** z~**ziehen** withdraw; (vom Beruf) retire; (Mil) retreat

Zuruf m shout. z~**en**† vt sep shout (dat to)

zurzeit adv at present

Zusage f -,-n acceptance; (Versprechen) promise. z~**n** v sep □ vt promise □ vi (haben) accept; **jdm** z~**n** appeal to s.o.

zusammen adv together; (insgesamt) altogether; z~ **sein** be together. Z~**arbeit** f co-operation. z~**arbeiten** vi sep (haben) co-operate. z~**bauen** vt sep assemble. z~**beißen**† vt sep **die Zähne** z~**beißen** clench/(fig) grit one's teeth. z~**bleiben**† vi sep (sein) stay together. z~**brechen**† vi sep (sein) collapse. z~**bringen**† vt sep bring together; (beschaffen) raise. Z~**bruch** m collapse; (Nerven- & fig) breakdown. z~**fahren**† vi sep (sein) collide; (z~zucken) start. z~**fallen**† vi sep (sein) collapse; (zeitlich) coincide. z~**falten** vt sep fold up. z~**fassen** vt sep summarize, sum up. Z~**fassung** f summary. z~**fügen** vt sep fit together. z~**führen** vt sep bring together. z~**gehören** vi sep (haben) belong together; (z~passen) go together. z~**gesetzt** a (Gram) compound. z~**halten**† v sep □ vt hold together; (beisammenhalten) keep together □ vi (haben) (fig) stick together. Z~**hang** m connection; (Kontext) context. z~**hängen**† vi sep (haben) be connected. z~**hanglos** a incoherent, adv -ly. z~**klappen** v sep □ vt fold

up □ vi (sein) collapse. z~**kommen**† vi sep (sein) meet; (sich ansammeln) accumulate. Z~**kunft** f -,-e meeting. z~**laufen**† vi sep (sein) gather; (Flüssigkeit:) collect; (Linien:) converge. z~**leben** vi sep (haben) live together. z~**legen** v sep □ vt put together; (z~falten) fold up; (vereinigen) amalgamate; pool (Geld) □ vi (haben) club together. z~**nehmen**† vt sep gather up; summon up (Mut); collect (Gedanken); **sich** z~**nehmen** pull oneself together. z~**passen** vi sep (haben) go together, match; (Personen:) be well matched. Z~**prall** m collision. z~**prallen** vi sep (sein) collide. z~**rechnen** vt sep add up. z~**reißen** (sich) vr sep (fam) pull oneself together. z~**rollen** vt sep roll up; **sich** z~**rollen** curl up. z~**schlagen**† vt sep smash up; (prügeln) beat up. z~**schließen** (sich) vr sep join together; (Firmen:) merge. Z~**schluss** (Z~**schluß**) m union; (Comm) merger. z~**schreiben**† vt sep write as one word

zusammensein† vi sep (sein) (NEW) zusammen sein, s. zusammen. Z~ nt -s get-together

zusammensetzen vt sep put together; (Techn) assemble; **sich** z~**en** sit [down] together; (bestehen) be made up (aus from). Z~**ung** f -,-en composition; (Techn) assembly; (Wort) compound

zusammen|stellen vt sep put together; (gestalten) compile. Z~**stoß** m collision; (fig) clash. z~**stoßen**† vi sep (sein) collide. z~**treffen**† vi sep (sein) meet; (zeitlich) coincide. Z~**treffen** nt meeting; coincidence. z~**zählen** vt sep add up. z~**ziehen**† v sep □ vt draw together; (addieren) add up; (konzentrieren) mass; **sich** z~**ziehen** contract; (Gewitter:) gather □ vi (sein) move in together; move in (**mit** with).

z~**zucken** vi sep (sein) start; (vor Schmerz) wince

Zusatz m addition; (Jur) rider; (Lebensmittel-) additive. **Z~gerät** nt attachment. **zusätzlich** a additional □ adv in addition

zuschanden adv z~ **machen** ruin, wreck; z~ **werden** be wrecked or ruined; z~ **fahren** wreck

zuschauen vi sep (haben) watch. **Z~er(in)** m -s, - (f -,-nen) spectator; (TV) viewer. **Z~erraum** m auditorium

zuschicken† vt sep send (dat to)

Zuschlag m surcharge; (D-Zug-) supplement. **z~en**† v sep □ vt shut; (heftig) slam; (bei Auktion) knock down (**jdm** to s.o.) □ vi (haben) hit out; (Feind:) strike □ vi (haben) slam shut. **z~pflichtig** a (Zug) for which a supplement is payable

zuschließen† v sep □ vt lock □ vi (haben) lock up

zuschneiden† vt sep cut out; cut to (Holz)

zuschreiben† vt sep attribute (dat to); **jdm die Schuld** z~ blame s.o.

Zuschrift f letter; (auf Annonce) reply

zuschulden adv **sich** (dat) **etwas** z~ **kommen lassen** do wrong

Zuschuss (**Zuschuß**) m contribution; (staatlich) subsidy

zusehen† vi sep (haben) watch; z~, **dass** see [to it] that

zusehends adv visibly

zusein† vi sep (sein) (NEW) **zu sein**, s. **zu**

zusenden† vt sep send (dat to)

zusetzen v sep □ vt add; (einbüßen) lose □ vi (haben) **jdm** z~ pester s.o.; (Hitze:) take it out of s.o.

zusicher|n vt sep promise. **Z~ung** f promise.

Zuspätkommende(r) m/f latecomer

zuspielen vt sep (Sport) pass

zuspitzen (**sich**) vr sep (fig) become critical

zusprechen† v sep vt award (**jdm** s.o.); **jdm Trost/Mut** z~ comfort/encourage s.o. □ vi (haben) **dem Essen** z~ eat heartily

Zustand m condition, state

zustande adv z~ **bringen/kommen** bring/come about

zuständig a competent; (verantwortlich) responsible. **Z~keit** f - competence; responsibility

zustehen† vi sep (haben) **jdm** z~ be s.o.'s right; (Urlaub:) be due to s.o.; **es steht ihm nicht zu** he is not entitled to it; (gebührt) it is not for him (**zu** to)

zusteigen† vi sep (sein) get on; **noch jemand zugestiegen?** tickets please; (im Bus) any more fares please?

zustellen vt sep block; (bringen) deliver. **Z~ung** f delivery

zusteuern v sep □ vi (sein) head (**auf** + acc for) □ vt contribute

zustimm|en vi sep (haben) agree; (billigen) approve (dat of). **Z~ung** f consent; approval

zustoßen† vi sep (sein) happen (dat to)

Zustrom m influx

zutage adv z~ **treten** od **kommen/bringen** come/bring to light

Zutat f (Culin) ingredient

zuteil|en vt sep allocate; assign (Aufgabe). **Z~ung** f allocation

zutiefst adv deeply

zutrag|en† vt sep carry/(fig) report (dat to); **sich** z~ happen

zutrau|en vt sep **jdm etw** z~ believe s.o. capable of sth. **Z~en** nt -s confidence. **z~lich** a trusting, adv -ly; (Tier) friendly

zutreffen† vi sep (haben) be correct; z~ **auf** (+ acc) apply to. **z~d** a applicable (**auf** + acc to); (richtig) correct, adv -ly

trinken† vi sep (haben) **jdm z~** drink to s.o.

Zutritt m admittance

zuunterst adv right at the bottom

zuverlässig a reliable, adv -bly. **Z~keit** f reliability

Zuversicht f confidence. **z~lich** a confident, adv -ly

zuviel pron & adv (NEW) **zu viel, s. viel**

zuvor adv before; (erst) first

zuvorkommen† vi sep (sein) (+ dat) anticipate; **jdm z~** beat s.o. to it. **z~d** a obliging, adv -ly

Zuwachs m -es increase

zuwege adv **z~ bringen** achieve

zuweilen adv now and then

zuweisen† vt sep assign; (zuteilen) allocate

zuwenden† vt sep turn (dat to); **sich z~en** (+ dat) turn to; (fig) devote oneself to. **Z~ung** f donation; (Fürsorge) care

zuwenig pron & adv (NEW) **zu wenig, s. wenig**

zuwerfen† vt sep slam (Tür); **jdm etw z~** throw s.o. sth; give s.o. (Blick, Lächeln)

zuwider adv **jdm z~ sein** be repugnant to s.o. □ prep (+ dat) contrary to. **z~handeln** vi sep (haben) contravene (etw dat sth)

zuzahlen vt sep pay extra

zuziehen† v sep □ vt pull tight; draw (Vorhänge); (hinzu-) call in; **sich** (dat) **etw z~** contract (Krankheit); sustain (Verletzung); incur (Zorn) □ vi (sein) move into the area

zuzüglich prep (+ gen) plus

Zwang m -[e]s,ˉe compulsion; (Gewalt) force; (Verpflichtung) obligation

zwängen vt squeeze

zwanglos a informal, adv -ly; (Benehmen) free and easy. **Z~igkeit** f informality

Zwangsjacke f straitjacket. **Z~lage** f predicament. **z~läufig** a inevitable, adv -bly

zwanzig inv a twenty. **z~ste(r,s)** a twentieth

zwar adv admittedly; **und z~** to be precise

Zweck m -[e]s,-e purpose; (Sinn) point; **es hat keinen Z~** there is no point. **z~dienlich** a appropriate; (Information) relevant. **z~los** a pointless. **z~mäßig** a suitable, adv -ly; (praktisch) functional, adv -ly. **z~s** prep (+ gen) for the purpose of

zwei inv a two. **Z~** f -,-en two; (Sch) ≈ B. **Z~bettzimmer** nt twin-bedded room

zweideutig a ambiguous, adv -ly. (schlüpfrig) suggestive, adv -ly. **Z~keit** f -,-en ambiguity

zweierlei inv a two kinds of □ pron two things. **z~fach** a double

Zweifel m -s,- doubt. **z~haft** a doubtful; (fragwürdig) dubious. **z~los** adv undoubtedly. **z~n** vi (haben) doubt (an etw dat sth)

Zweig m -[e]s,-e branch. **Z~geschäft** nt branch. **Z~stelle** f branch [office]

Zweikampf m duel. **z~mal** adv twice. **z~reihig** a (Anzug) double-breasted. **z~sprachig** a bilingual

zweit adv **zu z~** in twos; **wir waren zu z~** there were two of us. **z~beste(r,s)** a second-best. **z~e(r,s)** a second

zweiteilig a two-piece; (Film, Programm) two-part. **z~tens** adv secondly

zweitklassig a second-class

Zwerchfell nt diaphragm

Zwerg m -[e]s,-e dwarf

Zwetsch[g]e f -,-n quetsche

Zwickel m -s,- gusset

zwicken vt/i (haben) pinch

Zwieback m -[e]s,-e rusk

Zwiebel f -,-n onion; (Blumen-)bulb

Zwielicht nt half-light; (Dämmerlicht) twilight. **z~ig** a shady

Zwie|spalt m conflict. z~spältig a conflicting. Z~tracht f - discord

Zwilling m -s,-e twin; Z~e (Astr) Gemini

zwingen† vt force; **sich z~** force oneself. z~d a compelling

Zwinger m -s,- run; (Zucht-) kennels pl

zwinkern vi (haben) blink; (als Zeichen) wink

Zwirn m -[e]s button thread

zwischen prep (+ dat/acc) between; (unter) among[st]. Z~bemerkung f interjection. Z~ding nt (fam) cross. z~durch adv in between; (in der Z~zeit) in the meantime; (ab und zu) now and again. Z~fall m incident. Z~händler m middleman.

Z~landung f stopover. Z~raum m gap, space. Z~ruf m interjection. Z~stecker m adaptor. Z~wand f partition. Z~zeit f in der Z~zeit in the meantime

Zwist m -[e]s,-e discord; (Streit) feud. Z~igkeiten fpl quarrels

zwitschern vi (haben) chirp

zwo inv a two

zwölf inv a twelve. z~te(r,s) a twelfth

zwote(r,s) a second

Zyklus m -,-klen cycle

Zylind|er m -s,- cylinder; (Hut) top hat. z~risch a cylindrical

Zyn|iker m -s,- cynic. z~isch a cynical, adv -ly. Z~ismus m - cynicism

Zypern nt -s Cyprus

Zypresse f -,-n cypress

Zyste /'tsʏstə/ f -,-n cyst

Numbers/Zahlen

Cardinal numbers/Kardinalzahlen

0	zero	**null**
1	one	**eins**
2	two	**zwei**
3	three	**drei**
4	four	**vier**
5	five	**fünf**
6	six	**sechs**
7	seven	**sieben**
8	eight	**acht**
9	nine	**neun**
10	ten	**zehn**
11	eleven	**elf**
12	twelve	**zwölf**
13	thirteen	**dreizehn**
14	fourteen	**vierzehn**
15	fifteen	**fünfzehn**
16	sixteen	**sechzehn**
17	seventeen	**siebzehn**
18	eighteen	**achtzehn**
19	nineteen	**neunzehn**
20	twenty	**zwanzig**
21	twenty-one	**einundzwanzig**
30	thirty	**dreißig**
40	forty	**vierzig**
50	fifty	**fünfzig**
60	sixty	**sechzig**
70	seventy	**siebzig**
80	eighty	**achtzig**
90	ninety	**neunzig**
100	a hundred	**hundert**
101	a hundred and one	**huderteins**

1,000	a thousand	**tausend**
10,000	ten thousand	**zehntausend**
100,000	a hundred thousand	**hunderttausend**
1,000,000	a million	**eine Million**

Ordinal numbers/Ordinalzahlen

1st	first	**erster/erste/erstes**
2nd	second	**zweiter/zweite/zweites**
3rd	third	**dritter/dritte/drittes**
4th	fourth	**vierter/vierte/viertes**
5th	fifth	**fünfter/fünfte/fünftes**
6th	sixth	**sechster/sechste/sechstes**
7th	seventh	**siebter/siebte/siebtes**
8th	eighth	**achter/achte/achtes**
9th	ninth	**neunter/neunte/neuntes**
10th	tenth	**zehnter/zehnte/zehntes**
11th	eleventh	**elfter/elfte/elftes**
20th	twentieth	**zwanzigster/zwanzigste/zwanzigstes**

Phrasefinder/Sprachführer

Key phrases

yes, please
no, thank you
sorry!
you're welcome
I don't understand

Nützliche Redewendungen

ja bitte
nein danke
Entschuldigung!
nichts zu danken
ich verstehe das nicht

Meeting people

hello/goodbye
how are you?

fine, thank you
see you later!

Wir lernen uns kennen

hallo!/auf Wiedersehen!
wie geht es Ihnen?/wie geht's?
danke, gut
bis nachher!

Asking questions

do you speak English/
German?
what's your name?
where are you from?

how much is it?
how far is it?

Fragen

sprechen Sie/sprichst du Englisch/
Deutsch?
wie heißen Sie?/wie heißt du?
woher kommen Sie?/woher
kommst du?
wie viel kostet das?
wie weit ist es?

Statements about yourself

my name is…
I'm English
I don't speak German/
English very well
I'm here on holiday
I live near Manchester/Hamburg

Alles über mich

ich heiße…
ich bin Engländer/Engländerin
ich kann nicht gut Deutsch/
Englisch sprechen
ich bin auf Urlaub hier
ich wohne in der Nähe von
Manchester/Hamburg

Emergencies

can you help me, please?
I'm lost
call an ambulance
get the police/a doctor
watch out!

Im Notfall

können Sie mir bitte helfen?
ich habe mich verlaufen
rufen Sie einen Krankenwagen
holen Sie die Polizei/einen Arzt
Vorsicht!

❶ Going Places

On the road

where's the nearest garage (for repairs)/petrol station (*Amer* filling station)?

what's the best way to get there?

I've got a puncture

I'd like to hire a bike/car

where can I park around here?

there's been an accident

my car's broken down

the car won't start

Auf der Straße

wo ist die nächste Werkstatt/Tankstelle?

wie komme ich am besten dorthin?

ich habe eine Reifenpanne

ich möchte ein Rad/Auto mieten

wo kann man hier parken?

es ist ein Unfall passiert

mein Auto hat eine Panne

der Wagen springt nicht an

By rail

where can I buy a ticket?

what time is the next train to York/Berlin?

do I have to change?

can I take my bike on the train?

which platform for the train to Bath/Cologne?

the train is arriving on platform 2

there's a train to London at 10 o'clock

a single/return to Birmingham/Frankfurt, please

I'd like a cheap day return/an all-day ticket

I'd like to reserve a seat

Mit der Bahn

wo kann ich eine Fahrkarte kaufen?

wann geht der nächste Zug nach York/Berlin?

muss ich umsteigen?

kann ich mein Rad im Zug mitnehmen?

von welchem Bahnsteig fährt der Zug nach Bath/Köln ab?

der Zug fährt auf Gleis 2 ein

es gibt einen Zug nach London um zehn Uhr

einmal einfach/eine Rückfahrkarte nach Birmingham/Frankfurt, bitte

ich möchte eine Tagesrückfahrkarte/Tageskarte

ich möchte einen Platz reservieren

At the airport | Am Flughafen

when's the next flight to Paris/Rome? — wann geht der nächste Flug nach Paris/Rom?

what time do I have to check in? — um wie viel Uhr muss ich einchecken?

where do I check in? — wo checkt man ein?

I'd like to confirm/cancel my flight — ich möchte meinen Flug bestätigen/stornieren

can I change my booking? — kann ich umbuchen?

I'd like a window seat/an aisle seat — ich möchte einen Fensterplatz/Platz am Gang

Asking how to get there | Nach dem Weg fragen

could you tell me the way to the castle? — können Sie mir bitte sagen, wie ich zum Schloss komme?

how long will it take me to walk there? — wie lange werde ich zu Fuß brauchen?

how far is it from here? — wie weit ist das von hier?

which bus do I take for the cathedral? — mit welchem Bus komme ich zum Dom?

where does this bus go? — wohin fährt dieser Bus?

where do I get the bus for…? — wo fährt der Bus nach… ab?

does this bus/train go to…? — fährt dieser Bus/Zug nach…?

which bus goes to…? — welcher Bus fährt nach…?

where do I get off? — wo muss ich aussteigen?

how much is the fare to the town centre (Amer center)? — was kostet es ins Stadtzentrum?

what time is the last bus? — wann fährt der letzte Bus?

how do I get to the airport? — wie komme ich zum Flughafen?

where's the nearest underground (Amer subway) station? — wo ist die nächste U-Bahn-Station?

is this the turning for…? — ist das die Abzweigung nach…?

take the first turning right — nehmen Sie die erste Straße rechts

····································

❷ Keeping in touch

On the phone	Am Telefon
where can I buy a phone card?	wo kann man Telefonkarten kaufen?
may I use your phone?	darf ich Ihr Telefon benutzen?
do you have a mobile?	haben Sie ein Handy?
what is the code for Leipzig/Sheffield?	wie ist die Vorwahl von Leipzig/Sheffield?
I'd like to make a phone call	ich möchte gern telefonieren
I'd like to reverse the charges (*Amer* call collect)	ich möchte ein R-Gespräch anmelden
the line's engaged (*Amer* busy)	es ist besetzt
there's no answer	es meldet sich niemand
hello, this is Natalie	hallo, hier spricht Natalie
can I speak to Simon, please?	kann ich bitte Simon sprechen?
who's calling?	wer ist am Apparat?
sorry, I must have the wrong number	Entschuldigung, ich habe mich verwählt
just a moment, please	einen Augenblick bitte
please hold the line	bleiben sie bitte am Apparat
please tell him/her I called	richten Sie ihm/ihr bitte aus, dass ich angerufen habe
can I leave a message for Eva?	kann ich eine Nachricht für Eva hinterlassen?
I'll try again later	Ich versuche es später noch einmal
please tell her that Danielle called	sagen Sie ihr bitte, dass Danielle angerufen hat
can he/she ring me back?	kann er/sie mich zurückrufen?
my home number is…	meine Privatnummer ist…
my office number is…	meine Nummer im Büro ist…
my fax number is…	meine Faxnummer ist…
can I send a fax from here?	kann ich von hier faxen?
we were cut off	wir sind unterbrochen worden

Writing | Schreiben

can you give me your address?

können Sie mir Ihre/kannst du mir deine Adresse geben?

where is the nearest post office?

wo ist die nächste Post?

two one-mark stamps

zwei Briefmarken zu einer Mark

I'd like a stamp for a letter to Germany/Italy

ich hätte gern eine Briefmarke für einen Brief nach Deutschland/Italien

can I have stamps for two postcards to England/ the USA, please?

kann ich bitte Briefmarken für zwei Postkarten nach England/in die USA haben?

I'd like to send a parcel/ a telegram

ich möchte ein Paket abschicken/ein Telegramm aufgeben

On line | Online

are you on the Internet?

hast du Zugang zum Internet?

what's your e-mail address?

wie ist deine E-Mail-Adresse?

we could send it by e-mail

wir könnten es per E-Mail schicken

I'll e-mail it to you on Thursday

ich schicke es Ihnen am Donnerstag per E-Mail

I've looked for it on the Internet

ich habe es im Internet gesucht

he found the information surfing the net

er hat die Information beim Surfen im Internet gefunden

Meeting up | Verabredungen

what shall we do this evening?

was machen wir heute Abend?

where shall we meet?

wo treffen wir uns?

see you outside the cinema at 6 o'clock

ich treffe dich um sechs Uhr vor dem Kino

do you fancy joining in?

hast du Lust mitzumachen?

I can't today, I'm busy

ich kann heute nicht, ich habe keine Zeit

❸ Food and drink

Booking a restaurant

can you recommend a good restaurant?

I'd like to reserve a table for four

a reservation for tomorrow evening at eight o'clock

I booked a table for two

Vorbestellungen

können Sie uns/mir ein gutes Restaurant empfehlen?

ich möchte einen Tisch für vier Personen bestellen

eine Vorbestellung für morgen Abend um acht Uhr

ich habe einen Tisch für zwei Personen bestellt

Ordering

could we see the menu/ wine list, please?

do you have a vegetarian/ children's menu?

could we have some more bread/chips?

could I have the bill (*Amer* check), please?

we'd like something to drink first

a bottle/glass of mineral water, please

as a starter… to follow… and for dessert…

a black/white coffee

we'd like to pay separately

Wir möchten bestellen

können wir bitte die Speisekarte/Weinkarte haben?

haben Sie vegetarische Gerichte/Kinderportionen?

noch etwas Brot/noch Pommes frites, bitte

die Rechnung bitte

wir hätten gern erst etwas zu trinken

eine Flasche/ein Glas Mineralwasser bitte

als Vorspeise… als Hauptgericht… und zum Nachtisch…

einen Kaffee ohne Milch/ einen Kaffee mit Milch

wir möchten getrennt bezahlen

Reading a menu

starters

soups/salads

main dishes

Die Speisekarte

Vorspeisen

Suppen/Salate

Hauptgerichte

dish of the day	Tagesgericht
seafood	Meeresfrüchte
choice of vegetables	Gemüse nach Wahl
meat/game/poultry	Fleischgerichte/Wild/Geflügel
side dish	Beilage
desserts	Nachspeisen
drinks	Getränke

Any complaints?

Beschwerden

there's a mistake in the bill (Amer check)	die Rechnung stimmt nicht
the meat isn't cooked/is burnt	das Fleisch ist nicht durch/ist angebrannt
that's not what I ordered	das habe ich nicht bestellt
I asked for a small/large portion	ich habe eine kleine/große Portion bestellt
when can we order?	wann können wir bestellen?
we are still waiting for our drinks	wir warten immer noch auf unsere Getränke
my coffee is cold	mein Kaffee ist kalt
the wine is not chilled	der Wein ist nicht kalt genug

Food shopping

Lebensmittel einkaufen

where is the nearest supermarket?	wo ist der nächste Supermarkt?
is there a baker's/greengrocer near here?	gibt es eine Bäckerei/einen Gemüsehändler in der Nähe?
can I have a carrier bag, please?	kann ich bitte eine Tragetasche haben?
how much is it?	was kostet das?
I'll have that one/this jam	ich nehme den/die/das da/diese Marmelade
a loaf of bread, please	ein Brot bitte

❹ Places to stay

Camping

we're looking for a campsite	wir suchen einen Campingplatz
this is a list of local campsites	in diesem Campingführer stehen alle hiesigen Campingplätze
can we pitch our tent here?	können wir hier zelten?
can we park our caravan here?	können wir unseren Wohnwagen hier parken?
do you have space for a caravan/tent?	haben Sie Platz für einen Wohnwagen/ein Zelt?
are there shopping facilities?	gibt es Einkaufsmöglichkeiten?
how much is it per night?	was kostet es pro Nacht?
we go on a camping holiday every year	wir machen jedes Jahr Campingurlaub

At the hotel / Im Hotel

I'd like a double/single room with bath	ich möchte ein Doppelzimmer/Einzelzimmer mit Bad
we have a reservation in the name of Milnes	wir haben auf den Namen Milnes reservieren lassen
I reserved two rooms	ich habe zwei Zimmer reservieren lassen
for three nights, from Friday to Sunday	für drei Nächte, von Freitag bis Sonntag
how much does the room cost?	was kostet das Zimmer?
I'd like to see the room first, please	ich möchte das Zimmer erst sehen, bitte
what time is breakfast?	wann gibt es Frühstück?
can I leave this in the safe?	kann ich das im Safe lassen?
bed and breakfast	Zimmer mit Frühstück
we'd like to stay another night	wir möchten noch eine Nacht bleiben
please call me at 7:30	bitte wecken Sie mich um 7:30

are there any messages for me? | hat jemand eine Nachricht für mich hinterlassen?

Hostels

Heime und Jugendherbergen

could you tell me where the youth hostel is? | können Sie mir sagen, wo die Jugendherberge ist?

what time does the hostel close? | um wie viel Uhr macht das Heim zu?

I spent the night in a youth hostel | ich habe in einer Jugendherberge übernachtet

the hostel we're staying in is great value | unser Wohnheim ist sehr preiswert

I'm staying in a youth hostel | ich wohne in einer Jugendherberge

I know a really good youth hostel in Dublin | ich kenne eine sehr gute Jugendherberge in Dublin

I'd like to go backpacking in Australia | ich würde gern in Australien mit dem Rucksack herum reisen

Rooms to let

Zimmer zu vermieten

I'm looking for a room with a reasonable rent | ich suche ein preiswertes Zimmer

I'd like to rent an apartment for three weeks | ich möchte eine Wohnung für drei Wochen mieten

where do I find out about rooms to let? | wo kann man sich nach Fremdenzimmern erkundigen?

what's the weekly rent for the flat? | was kostet die Wohnung pro Woche?

I'm staying with friends at the moment | ich wohne zur Zeit bei Freunden

I rent an apartment on the outskirts of town | ich habe eine Wohnung am Stadtrand gemietet

the room's fine—I'll take it | das Zimmer ist gut— ich nehme es

➎ Shopping and money

At the bank	In der Bank
I'd like to change some money	ich möchte gern Geld wechseln
I want to change 100 marks into pounds	ich möchte 100 Mark in Pfund wechseln
do you take Eurocheques?	nehmen Sie Euroschecks?
what's the exchange rate today?	wie steht der Wechselkurs heute?
I prefer traveller's cheques (*Amer* traveler's checks) to cash	mir sind Reiseschecks lieber als Bargeld
I'd like to transfer some money from my account	ich möchte Geld von meinem Konto überweisen
I'll get some money from the cash machine	ich hole mir Geld vom Automaten
a £50 cheque (*Amer* check)	ein Scheck über 50 Pfund
can I cash this cheque (*Amer* check) here?	kann ich diesen Scheck hier einlösen?
can I get some cash with my credit card?	kann ich auf meine Kreditkarte Bargeld bekommen?

Finding the right shop	Das richtige Geschäft finden
where's the main shopping district?	wo ist das Haupteinkaufsviertel?
is the shopping centre (*Amer* mall) far from here?	ist das Einkaufszentrum weit von hier?
where's a good place to buy sunglasses/shoes?	wo kauft man am besten Schuhe/eine Sonnenbrille?
where can I buy batteries/postcards?	wo kann ich Batterien/Postkarten kaufen?
where's the nearest chemist (*Amer* drugstore)?	wo ist die nächste Drogerie?
what time do the shops open/close?	um wie viel Uhr machen die Läden auf/zu?
where did you get those?	wo hast du die her?
I'm looking for a present for my mother	ich suche ein Geschenk für meine Mutter

Are you being served?

how much does that cost?	was kostet das?
can I try it on?	kann ich es anprobieren?
can you keep it for me?	können Sie es mir zurücklegen?
could you gift-wrap it for me, please?	können Sie es bitte in Geschenkpapier einwickeln?
please wrap it up well	verpacken Sie es bitte gut
can I pay by credit card/ cheque (*Amer* check)?	kann ich mit Kreditkarte/ Scheck zahlen?
do you have this in another colour?	haben Sie das in einer anderen Farbe?
I'm just looking	ich sehe mich nur um
a receipt, please	eine Quittung bitte
I need a bigger size	ich brauche die nächste Größe
I take a size…	ich habe Größe…
it doesn't suit me	das steht mir nicht

Werden Sie schon bedient?

Changing things

can I have a refund?	kann ich mein Geld zurückbekommen?
can you mend it for me?	können Sie es mir reparieren?
can I speak to the manager?	kann ich den Geschäftsführer/ die Geschäftsführerin sprechen?
it doesn't work	es funktioniert nicht
I'd like to change the dress	ich möchte das Kleid umtauschen
I bought this here yesterday	ich habe das gestern hier gekauft

Umtauschen

➏ Sport and leisure

Keeping fit | Wir halten uns fit

Keeping fit	Wir halten uns fit
where can we play football/squash?	wo kann man Fußball/Squash spielen?
is there a local sports centre (*Amer* center)?	gibt es hier ein Sportzentrum?
what's the charge per day?	was muss man pro Tag zahlen?
is there a reduction for children/a student discount?	gibt es eine Ermäßigung für Kinder/Studenten?
where can we go swimming/play tennis?	wo kann man schwimmen gehen/Tennis spielen?
do you have to be a member?	muss man Mitglied sein?
I play tennis on Mondays	ich spiele jeden Montag Tennis
I would like to go fishing/riding	ich würde gern angeln gehen/reiten
I want to do aerobics	ich will Aerobic machen
I love swimming/playing baseball	ich schwimme gern/spiele gern Baseball
we want to hire skis/snowboards	wir wollen Skier/Snowboards mieten

Watching sport | Zuschauen

Watching sport	Zuschauen
is there a football match on Saturday?	gibt es am Samstag ein Fußballspiel?
who's playing?	wer spielt?
which teams are playing?	welche Mannschaften spielen?
where can I get tickets?	wo kann man Karten bekommen?
can you get me a ticket?	kannst du mir eine Karte besorgen?
I'd like to see a rugby/football match	ich würde gern ein Rugbyspiel/Fußballspiel sehen
my favourite (*Amer* favorite) team is Bayern	ich bin ein Bayern-Fan
let's watch the match on TV	sehen wir uns das Spiel im Fernsehen an

Going to the cinema/theatre/club

Wir gehen ins Kino/Theater/in einen Club

what's on at the cinema (*Amer* at the movies)?	was läuft im Kino?
what's on at the theatre?	was wird im Theater gespielt?
how long is the performance?	wie lange dauert die Vorstellung?
when does the box office open/close?	wann macht die Kasse auf/zu?
what time does the performance start?	um wie viel Uhr fängt die Aufführung an?
when does the film (*Amer* movie) finish?	wann ist der Film aus?
are there any tickets left?	gibt es noch Karten?
how much are the tickets?	was kosten die Karten?
where can I get a programme (*Amer* program)?	wo kann man ein Programm kaufen?
I want to book tickets for tonight	ich möchte für heute Abend Karten bestellen
I'd rather have seats in the stalls	Plätze im Parkett wären mir lieber
we'd like to go to a club	wir wollen in einen Club gehen
I go clubbing every weekend	ich gehe am Wochenende immer in Clubs

Hobbies

Hobbys

do you have any hobbies?	hast du irgendwelche Hobbys?
what do you do at the weekend?	was macht ihr am Wochenende?
I like yoga/listening to music	ich mache gern Yoga/höre gern Musik
I spend a lot of time surfing the Net	ich surfe viel im Internet
I read a lot	ich lese viel
I collect comics	ich sammle Comichefte

❼ Good timing

Telling the time	Uhrzeit
could you tell me the time?	können Sie mir sagen, wie spät es ist?
what time is it?	wie viel Uhr ist es?
it's 2 o'clock	es ist zwei Uhr
at about 8 o'clock	gegen acht Uhr
at 9 o'clock tomorrow	morgen um neun Uhr
from 10 o'clock onwards	ab zehn Uhr
the meeting starts at 8 p.m.	die Besprechung fängt um zwanzig Uhr an
at 5 o'clock in the morning/afternoon	um fünf Uhr morgens/um fünf Uhr nachmittags (um siebzehn Uhr)
at exactly 1 o'clock	um Punkt eins
it's five past…/quarter past…	es ist fünf nach…/Viertel nach…
it's half past one	es ist halb zwei
it's twenty-five to one	es ist fünf nach halb eins
it's quarter to/five to one	es ist Viertel vor/fünf vor eins
a quarter of an hour	eine Viertelstunde
three quarters of an hour	eine Dreiviertelstunde

Days and date	Wochentage und Datum
Sunday, Monday, Tuesday, Wednesday, Thursday, Friday, Saturday	Sonntag, Montag, Dienstag, Mittwoch, Donnerstag, Freitag, Samstag/Sonnabend
January, February, March, April, May, June, July, August, September, October, November, December	Januar, Februar, März, April, Mai, Juni, Juli, August, September, Oktober, November, Dezember
what's the date?	der Wievielte ist heute?
it's the second of June	heute ist der zweite Juni
we meet up every Monday	wir treffen uns jeden Montag

she comes on Tuesdays	sie kommt immer dienstags
we're going away in August	wir verreisen im August
I forgot it was the first of April today	ich habe ganz vergessen, dass heute der erste April ist
on November 8th	am achten November
about the 8th of June	um den 8. Juni
put it in your diary	notiere es dir in deinem Terminkalender

Public holidays and special days

Feste und Feiertage

Bank holiday	gesetzlicher Feiertag
New Year's Day (Jan 1)	Neujahr
Epiphany (Jan 6)	Heilige Drei Könige
St Valentine's Day (Feb 14)	Valentinstag
Shrove Tuesday	Fastnachtsdienstag/ Faschingsdienstag
Ash Wednesday	Aschermittwoch
Mothering Sunday/Mother's Day	Muttertag
Palm Sunday	Palmsonntag
Maundy Thursday	Gründonnerstag
Good Friday	Karfreitag
Easter Day	Ostersonntag
Easter Monday	Ostermontag
May Day (May 1)	der Erste Mai
Father's Day	Vatertag
Day of German Unity (Oct 3)	Tag der Deutschen Einheit
First Sunday in Advent	erster Advent
St Nicholas' Day (Dec 6)	Nikolaus
Christmas Eve	Heiligabend
Christmas Day (Dec 25)	erster Weihnachtstag
Boxing Day (Dec 26)	zweiter Weihnachtstag
New Year's Eve (Dec 31)	Silvester

Weights & measures/Maße u. Gewichte

Length/Längenmaße

inches/Zoll	0.39	3.9	7.8	11.7	15.6	19.7	39
cm/zentimeter	1	10	20	30	40	50	100

Distance/Entfernungen

miles/Meilen	0.62	6.2	12.4	18.6	24.9	31	62
km/Kilometer	1	10	20	30	40	50	100

Weight/Gewichte

pounds/Pfund	2.2	22	44	66	88	110	220
kg/Kilogramm	1	10	20	30	40	50	100

Capacity/Hohlmaße

gallons/Gallonen	0.22	2.2	4.4	6.6	8.8	11	22
litres/Liter	1	10	20	30	40	50	100

Temperature/Temperatur

°C	0	5	10	15	20	25	30	37	38	40
°F	32	41	50	59	68	77	86	98.4	100	104

Clothing and shoe sizes

Women's clothing sizes/Damengrößen

UK	8	10	12	14	16	18	
US	6	8	10	12	14	16	
Continent		36	38	40	42	44	46

Men's clothing sizes/Herrengrößen

UK/US	36	38	40	42	44	46
Continent	46	48	50	52	54	56

Men's and women's shoes/Schuhgrößen

UK women	4	5	6	7	7.5	8			
UK men				6	7	8	9	10	11
US		6.5	7.5	8.5	9.5	10.5	11.5	12.5	13.5	14.5
Continent		37	38	39	40	41	42	43	44	45

A

a /ə, *betont* eɪ/ (*vor einem Vokal* **an**) *indef art* ein(e); (*each*) pro; **not a** kein(e)

aback /ə'bæk/ *adv* **be taken ∼** verblüfft sein

abandon /ə'bændən/ *vt* verlassen; (*give up*) aufgeben □n Hingabe *f*. **∼ed** *a* verlassen; (*behaviour*) hemmungslos

abase /ə'beɪs/ *vt* demütigen

abashed /ə'bæʃt/ *a* beschämt, verlegen

abate /ə'beɪt/ *vi* nachlassen

abattoir /'æbətwɑ:(r)/ *n* Schlachthof *m*

abb|ey /'æbɪ/ *n* Abtei *f*. **∼ot** /-ət/ *n* Abt *m*

abbreviat|e /ə'bri:vɪeɪt/ *vt* abkürzen. **∼ion** /-'eɪʃn/ *n* Abkürzung *f*

abdicat|e /'æbdɪkeɪt/ *vi* abdanken. **∼ion** /-'keɪʃn/ *n* Abdankung *f*

abdom|en /'æbdəmən/ *n* Unterleib *m*. **∼inal** /-'dɒmɪnl/ *a* Unterleibs-

abduct /əb'dʌkt/ *vt* entführen. **∼ion** /-ʌkʃn/ *n* Entführung *f*. **∼or** *n* Entführer *m*

aberration /æbə'reɪʃn/ *n* Abweichung *f*; (*mental*) Verwirrung *f*

abet /ə'bet/ *vt* (*pt/pp* **abetted**) **aid and ∼** (*Jur*) Beihilfe leisten (+ *dat*)

abeyance /ə'beɪəns/ *n* **in ∼** [zeitweilig] außer Kraft; **fall into ∼** außer Kraft kommen

abhor /əb'hɔ:(r)/ *vt* (*pt/pp* **abhorred**) verabscheuen. **∼rence** /-'hɒrəns/ *n* Abscheu *f*. **∼rent** /-'hɒrənt/ *a* abscheulich

abid|e /ə'baɪd/ *vt* (*pt/pp* **abided**) (*tolerate*) aushalten; ausstehen (*person*) □ *vi* **∼e by** sich halten an (+ *acc*). **∼ing** *a* bleibend

ability /ə'bɪlətɪ/ *n* Fähigkeit *f*; (*talent*) Begabung *f*

abject /'æbdʒekt/ *a* erbärmlich; (*humble*) demütig

ablaze /ə'bleɪz/ *a* in Flammen; **be ∼** in Flammen stehen

able /'eɪbl/ *a* (**-r, -st**) fähig; **be ∼ to do sth** etw tun können. **∼-'bodied** *a* körperlich gesund; (*Mil*) tauglich

ably /'eɪblɪ/ *adv* gekonnt

abnormal /æb'nɔ:ml/ *a* anormal; (*Med*) abnorm. **∼ity** /-'mælətɪ/ *n* Abnormität *f*. **∼ly** *adv* ungewöhnlich

aboard /ə'bɔ:d/ *adv* & *prep* an Bord (+ *gen*)

abode /ə'bəʊd/ *n* Wohnsitz *m*

abol|ish /ə'bɒlɪʃ/ *vt* abschaffen. **∼ition** /æbə'lɪʃn/ *n* Abschaffung *f*

abominable /ə'bɒmɪnəbl/ *a*, **-bly** *adv* abscheulich

abominate /ə'bɒmɪneɪt/ *vt* verabscheuen

aborigines /æbə'rɪdʒəni:z/ *npl* Ureinwohner *pl*

abort /ə'bɔ:t/ *vt* abtreiben. **∼ion** /-ɔ:ʃn/ *n* Abtreibung *f*; **have an ∼ion** eine Abtreibung vornehmen lassen. **∼ive** /-tɪv/ *a* (*attempt*) vergeblich

abound /ə'baʊnd/ *vi* reichlich vorhanden sein; **∼ in** reich sein an (+ *dat*)

about /ə'baʊt/ *adv* umher, herum; (*approximately*) ungefähr; **be ∼** (*in circulation*) umgehen; (*in existence*) vorhanden sein; **be up and ∼** auf den Beinen sein; **be ∼ to do sth** im Begriff sein, etw zu tun; **there are a lot ∼** es gibt viele; **there was no one ∼** es war kein Mensch da; **run/play ∼** herumlaufen/-spielen □ *prep* um (+ *acc*) [.. herum]; (*concerning*) über (+ *acc*); **what is it ∼?** worum geht es? (*book*) wovon handelt es? **I know nothing ∼ it** ich weiß nichts davon; **talk/know ∼** reden/wissen von

about: **∼-'face** *n*, **'turn ∼** Kehrtwendung *f*

above /əˈbʌv/ *adv* oben □ *prep* über (+ *dat/acc*); **∼ all** vor allem

above: **∼'board** *a* legal. **∼-mentioned** *a* oben erwähnt

abrasion /əˈbreɪʒn/ *n* Schürfwunde *f*

abrasive /əˈbreɪsɪv/ *a* Scheuer-; (*remark*) verletzend □ *n* Scheuermittel *nt*; (*Techn*) Schleifmittel *nt*

abreast /əˈbrest/ *adv* nebeneinander; **keep ∼ of** Schritt halten mit

abridge /əˈbrɪdʒ/ *vt* kürzen

abroad /əˈbrɔːd/ *adv* im Ausland; **go ∼** ins Ausland fahren

abrupt /əˈbrʌpt/ *a*, **-ly** *adv* abrupt; (*sudden*) plötzlich; (*curt*) schroff

abscess /ˈæbsɪs/ *n* Abszess *m*

abscond /əbˈskɒnd/ *vi* entfliehen

absence /ˈæbsəns/ *n* Abwesenheit *f*

absent[1] /ˈæbsənt/ *a*, **-ly** *adv* abwesend; **be ∼** fehlen

absent[2] /æbˈsent/ *vt* **∼ oneself** fernbleiben

absentee /æbsənˈtiː/ *n* Abwesende(r) *m/f*

absent-minded /æbsəntˈmaɪndɪd/ *a*, **-ly** *adv* geistesabwesend; (*forgetful*) zerstreut

absolute /ˈæbsəluːt/ *a*, **-ly** *adv* absolut

absolution /æbsəˈluːʃn/ *n* Absolution *f*

absolve /əbˈzɒlv/ *vt* lossprechen

absorb /əbˈsɔːb/ *vt* absorbieren, aufsaugen; **∼ed in** vertieft in (+ *acc*). **∼ent** /-ənt/ *a* saugfähig

absorption /əbˈsɔːpʃn/ *n* Absorption *f*

abstain /əbˈsteɪn/ *vi* sich enthalten (**from** *gen*); **∼ from voting** sich der Stimme enthalten

abstemious /əbˈstiːmɪəs/ *a* enthaltsam

abstention /əbˈstenʃn/ *n* (*Pol*) [Stimm]enthaltung *f*

abstinence /ˈæbstɪnəns/ *n* Enthaltsamkeit *f*

abstract /ˈæbstrækt/ *a* abstrakt □ *n* (*summary*) Abriss *m*

absurd /əbˈsɜːd/ *a*, **-ly** *adv* absurd. **∼ity** *n* Absurdität *f*

abundan|ce /əˈbʌndəns/ *n* Fülle *f* (**of** an + *dat*). **∼t** *a* reichlich

abuse[1] /əˈbjuːz/ *vt* missbrauchen; (*insult*) beschimpfen

abus|e[2] /əˈbjuːs/ *n* Missbrauch *m*; (*insults*) Beschimpfungen *pl*. **∼ive** /-ɪv/ *a* ausfallend

abut /əˈbʌt/ *vi* (*pt/pp* **abutted**) angrenzen (**on to** an + *acc*)

abysmal /əˈbɪzml/ *a* (*fam*) katastrophal

abyss /əˈbɪs/ *n* Abgrund *m*

academic /ækəˈdemɪk/ *a*, **-ally** *adv* akademisch □ *n* Akademiker(in) *m(f)*

academy /əˈkædəmɪ/ *n* Akademie *f*

accede /əkˈsiːd/ *vi* **∼ to** zustimmen (+ *dat*); besteigen (*throne*)

accelerat|e /əkˈseləreɪt/ *vt* beschleunigen □ *vi* die Geschwindigkeit erhöhen. **∼ion** /-ˈreɪʃn/ *n* Beschleunigung *f*. **∼or** *n* (*Auto*) Gaspedal *nt*

accent[1] /ˈæksənt/ *n* Akzent *m*

accent[2] /ækˈsent/ *vt* betonen

accentuate /əkˈsentjueɪt/ *vt* betonen

accept /əkˈsept/ *vt* annehmen; (*fig*) akzeptieren □ *vi* zusagen. **∼able** /-əbl/ *a* annehmbar.

~ance *n* Annahme *f*; (*of invitation*) Zusage *f*

access /'ækses/ *n* Zugang *m*; (*road*) Zufahrt *f*. ~ible /ək'sesəbl/ *a* zugänglich

accession /ək'seʃn/ *n* (*to throne*) Thronbesteigung *f*

accessor|y /ək'sesərɪ/ *n* (*Jur*) Mitschuldige(r) *m/f*; ~ies *pl* (*fashion*) Accessoires *pl*; (*Techn*) Zubehör *nt*

accident /'æksɪdənt/ *n* Unfall *m*; (*chance*) Zufall *m*; by ~ zufällig; (*unintentionally*) versehentlich. ~al /-'dentl/ *a*, ~ly *adv* zufällig; (*unintentional*) versehentlich

acclaim /ə'kleɪm/ *n* Beifall *m* □ *vt* feiern (as als)

acclimate /'æklɪmeɪt/ *vt* (*Amer*) = acclimatize

acclimatize /ə'klaɪmətaɪz/ *vt* become □d sich akklimatisieren

accolade /'ækəleɪd/ *n* Auszeichnung *f*

accommodat|e /ə'kɒmədeɪt/ *vt* unterbringen; (*oblige*) entgegenkommen (+ *dat*). ~ing *a* entgegenkommend. ~ion /-'deɪʃn/ *n* (*rooms*) Unterkunft *f*

accompan|iment /ə'kʌmpənɪmənt/ *n* Begleitung *f*. ~ist *n* (*Mus*) Begleiter(in) *m(f)*

accompany /ə'kʌmpənɪ/ *vt* (*pt/pp* -ied) begleiten

accomplice /ə'kʌmplɪs/ *n* Komplize/-zin *m/f*

accomplish /ə'kʌmplɪʃ/ *vt* erfüllen (*task*); (*achieve*) erreichen. ~ed *a* fähig. ~ment *n* Fertigkeit *f*; (*achievement*) Leistung *f*

accord /ə'kɔ:d/ *n* (*treaty*) Abkommen *nt*; of one ~ einmütig; of one's own ~ aus eigenem Antrieb □ *vt* gewähren. ~ance *n* in ~ance with entsprechend (+ *dat*)

according /ə'kɔ:dɪŋ/ *adv* ~ to nach (+ *dat*). ~ly *adv* entsprechend

accordion /ə'kɔ:dɪən/ *n* Akkordeon *nt*

accost /ə'kɒst/ *vt* ansprechen

account /ə'kaʊnt/ *n* Konto *nt*; (*bill*) Rechnung *f*; (*description*) Darstellung *f*; (*report*) Bericht *m*; ~s *pl* (*Comm*) Bücher *pl*; on ~ of wegen (+ *gen*); on no ~ auf keinen Fall; on this ~ deshalb; on my ~ meinetwegen; of no ~ ohne Bedeutung; take into ~ in Betracht ziehen, berücksichtigen □ *vi* ~ for Rechenschaft ablegen für; (*explain*) erklären

accountant /ə'kaʊntənt/ *n* Buchhalter(in) *m(f)*; (*chartered*) Wirtschaftsprüfer *m*; (*for tax*) Steuerberater *m*

accoutrements /ə'ku:trəmənts/ *npl* Ausrüstung *f*

accredited /ə'kredɪtɪd/ *a* akkreditiert

accrue /ə'kru:/ *vi* sich ansammeln

accumulat|e /ə'kju:mjʊleɪt/ *vt* ansammeln, anhäufen □ *vi* sich ansammeln, sich anhäufen. ~ion /-'leɪʃn/ *n* Ansammlung *f*, Anhäufung *f*. ~or *n* (*Electr*) Akkumulator *m*

accura|cy /'ækʊrəsɪ/ *n* Genauigkeit *f*. ~te /-rət/ *a*, ~ly *adv* genau

accusation /ækju:'zeɪʃn/ *n* Anklage *f*

accusative /ə'kju:zətɪv/ *a* & *n* ~ [case] (*Gram*) Akkusativ *m*

accuse /ə'kju:z/ *vt* (*Jur*) anklagen (of *gen*); ~ s.o. of doing sth jdn beschuldigen, etw getan zu haben. ~d *n* the ~d der/die Angeklagte

accustom /ə'kʌstəm/ *vt* gewöhnen (to an + *dat*); grow or get ~ed to sich gewöhnen an (+ *acc*). ~ed *a* gewohnt

ace /eɪs/ *n* (*Cards, Sport*) Ass *nt*

ache /eɪk/ *n* Schmerzen *pl* □ *vi* weh tun, schmerzen

achieve /ə'tʃi:v/ *vt* leisten; (*gain*) erzielen; (*reach*) erreichen. ~ment *n* (*feat*) Leistung *f*

acid /'æsɪd/ *a* sauer; (*fig*) beißend □ *n* Säure *f*. ~ity /ə'sɪdɪtɪ/ *n*

Säure *f.* ~**'rain** *n* saurer Regen *m*

acknowledge /ək'nɒlɪdʒ/ *vt* anerkennen; (*admit*) zugeben; erwidern (*greeting*); ~ **receipt of** den Empfang bestätigen (+ *gen*). ~**ment** /-ənt/ *n* Anerkennung *f.*; (*of letter*) Empfangsbestätigung *f*

acne /'ækni/ *n* Akne *f*

acorn /'eɪkɔːn/ *n* Eichel *f*

acoustic /ə'kuːstɪk/ *a*, **-ally** *adv* akustisch. ~**s** *npl* Akustik *f*

acquaint /ə'kweɪnt/ *vt* ~ **s.o. with** jdn bekannt machen mit; **be** ~**ed with** kennen; vertraut sein mit (*fact*). ~**ance** *n* Bekanntschaft *f*; (*person*) Bekannte(r) *m/f*; **make s.o.'s** ~**ance** jdn kennen lernen

acquiesce /ækwɪ'es/ *vi* einwilligen (**to** in + *acc*). ~**nce** *n* Einwilligung *f*

acquire /ə'kwaɪə(r)/ *vt* erwerben

acquisition /ækwɪ'zɪʃn/ *n* Erwerb *m*; (*thing*) Erwerbung *f.* ~**ive** /ə'kwɪzɪtɪv/ *a* habgierig

acquit /ə'kwɪt/ *vt* (*pt/pp* **acquitted**) freisprechen; ~ **oneself well** seiner Aufgabe gerecht werden. ~**tal** *n* Freispruch *m*

acre /'eɪkə(r)/ *n* ≈ Morgen *m*

acrid /'ækrɪd/ *a* scharf

acrimon|ious /ækrɪ'məʊniəs/ *a* bitter. ~**y** /'ækrɪmənɪ/ *n* Bitterkeit *f*

acrobat /'ækrəbæt/ *n* Akrobat(in) *m(f).* ~**ic** /-'bætɪk/ *a* akrobatisch

across /ə'krɒs/ *adv* hinüber/herüber; (*wide*) breit; (*not lengthwise*) quer; (*in crossword*) waagerecht; **come** ~ **sth** auf etw (*acc*) stoßen; **go** ~ hinübergehen; **bring** ~ herüberbringen □ *prep* über (+ *acc*); (*crosswise*) quer über (+ *acc/dat*); (*on the other side of*) auf der anderen Seite (+ *gen*)

act /ækt/ *n* Tat *f*; (*action*) Handlung *f*; (*law*) Gesetz *nt*; (*Theat*) Akt *m*; (*Item*) Nummer *f*; **put on**

an ~ (*fam*) sich verstellen □ *vi* handeln; (*behave*) sich verhalten; (*Theat*) spielen; (*pretend*) sich verstellen; ~ **as** fungieren als □ *vt* spielen (*role*). ~**ing** *a* (*deputy*) stellvertretend □ *n* (*Theat*) Schauspielerei *f.* ~**ing profession** *n* Schauspielerberuf *m*

action /'ækʃn/ *n* Handlung *f*; (*deed*) Tat *f*; (*Mil*) Einsatz *m*; (*Jur*) Klage *f*; (*effect*) Wirkung *f*; (*Techn*) Mechanismus *m*; **out of** ~ (*machine:*) außer Betrieb; **take** ~ handeln; **killed in** ~ gefallen. ~ **'replay** *n* (*TV*) Wiederholung *f*

activate /'æktɪveɪt/ *vt* betätigen; (*Chem, Phys*) aktivieren

activ|e /'æktɪv/ *a*, **-ly** *adv* aktiv; **on** ~ **service** im Einsatz. ~**ity** /-'tɪvɪtɪ/ *n* Aktivität *f*

act|or /'æktə(r)/ *n* Schauspieler *m.* ~**ress** *n* Schauspielerin *f*

actual /'æktʃʊəl/ *a*, **-ly** *adv* eigentlich; (*real*) tatsächlich. ~**ity** /-'ælətɪ/ *n* Wirklichkeit *f*

acumen /'ækjʊmən/ *n* Scharfsinn *m*

acupuncture /'ækjʊ-/ *n* Akupunktur *f*

acute /ə'kjuːt/ *a* scharf; (*angle*) spitz; (*illness*) akut. ~**ly** *adv* sehr

AD *abbr* (*Anno Domini*) n.Chr.

ad /æd/ *n* (*fam*) = advertisement

adamant /'ædəmənt/ *a* **be** ~ **that** darauf bestehen, dass

adapt /ə'dæpt/ *vt* anpassen; bearbeiten (*play*) □ *vi* sich anpassen. ~**ability** /-ə'bɪlɪtɪ/ *n* Anpassungsfähigkeit *f.* ~**able** /-əbl/ *a* anpassungsfähig

adaptation /ædæp'teɪʃn/ *n* (*Theat*) Bearbeitung *f*

adapter, adaptor /ə'dæptə(r)/ *n* (*Techn*) Adapter *m*; (*Electr*) (*two-way*) Doppelstecker *m*

add /æd/ *vt* hinzufügen; (*Math*) addieren □ *vi* zusammenzählen, addieren; ~ **to** hinzufügen *zu*; (*fig: increase*) steigern; (*compound*) verschlimmern. ~ **up** *vt* zusammenzählen ⟨*figures*⟩ □ *vi* zusammenzählen, addieren; ~ **up to** machen; **it doesn't ~ up** ⟨*fig*⟩ da stimmt etwas nicht

adder /'ædə(r)/ *n* Kreuzotter *f*

addict /'ædɪkt/ *n* Süchtige(r) *m/f*

addict|ed /ə'dɪktɪd/ *a* süchtig; **~ed to drugs** drogensüchtig. **~ion** /-ɪkʃn/ *n* Sucht *f*. **~ive** /-ɪv/ *a* **be ~ive** zur Süchtigkeit führen

addition /ə'dɪʃn/ *n* Hinzufügung *f*; ⟨*Math*⟩ Addition *f*; ⟨*thing added*⟩ Ergänzung *f*; **in ~** zusätzlich. **~al** *a*, **-ly** *adv* zusätzlich

additive /'ædɪtɪv/ *n* Zusatz *m*

address /ə'dres/ *n* Adresse *f*, Anschrift *f*; ⟨*speech*⟩ Ansprache *f*; ⟨*on*⟩ Anrede *f* □ *vt* adressieren ⟨**to an** + *acc*⟩; ⟨*speak to*⟩ sprechen zu (+ *dat*) ⟨*meeting*⟩. **~ee** /ædre'siː/ *n* Empfänger *m*

adenoids /'ædənɔɪdz/ *npl* [Rachen]polypen *pl*

adept /'ædept/ *a* geschickt (**at in** + *dat*)

adequate /'ædɪkwət/ *a*, **-ly** *adv* ausreichend

adhere /əd'hɪə(r)/ *vi* kleben/⟨*fig*⟩ festhalten (**to an** + *dat*). **~nce** *n* Festhalten *nt*

adhesive /əd'hiːsɪv/ *a* klebend □ *n* Klebstoff *m*

adjacent /ə'dʒeɪsnt/ *a* angrenzend

adjective /'ædʒɪktɪv/ *n* Adjektiv *nt*

adjoin /ə'dʒɔɪn/ *vt* angrenzen an (+ *acc*). **~ing** *a* angrenzend

adjourn /ə'dʒɜːn/ *vt* vertagen ⟨**until** auf + *acc*⟩ □ *vi* sich vertagen. **~ment** *n* Vertagung *f*

adjudicate /ə'dʒuːdɪkeɪt/ *vi* entscheiden; ⟨*in competition*⟩ Preisrichter sein

adjust /ə'dʒʌst/ *vt* einstellen; ⟨*alter*⟩ verstellen □ *vi* sich anpassen (**to** *dat*). **~able** /-əbl/ *a* verstellbar. **~ment** *n* Einstellung *f*; Anpassung *f*

ad lib /æd'lɪb/ *adv* aus dem Stegreif □ *vi* ⟨*pt/pp* **ad libbed**⟩ ⟨*fam*⟩ improvisieren

administer /əd'mɪnɪstə(r)/ *vt* verwalten; verabreichen ⟨*medicine*⟩

administrat|ion /ədmɪnɪ'streɪʃn/ *n* Verwaltung *f*; ⟨*Pol*⟩ Regierung *f*. **~or** /əd'mɪnɪstreɪtə(r)/ *n* Verwaltungsbeamte(r) *m* /-beamtin *f*

admirable /'ædmərəbl/ *a* bewundernswert

admiral /'ædmərəl/ *n* Admiral *m*

admiration /ædmə'reɪʃn/ *n* Bewunderung *f*

admire /əd'maɪə(r)/ *vt* bewundern. **~r** *n* Verehrer(in) *m(f)*

admissable /əd'mɪsəbl/ *a* zulässig

admission /əd'mɪʃn/ *n* Eingeständnis *nt*; ⟨*entry*⟩ Eintritt *m*

admit /əd'mɪt/ *vt* ⟨*pt/pp* **admitted**⟩ ⟨*let in*⟩ hereinlassen; ⟨*acknowledge*⟩ zugeben; **~ to sth** etw zugeben. **~tance** *n* Eintritt *m*. **~tedly** *adv* zugegebenermaßen

admoni|sh /əd'mɒnɪʃ/ *vt* ermahnen. **~tion** /ædmə'nɪʃn/ *n* Ermahnung *f*

ado /ə'duː/ *n* **without more ~** ohne weiteres

adolescen|ce /ædə'lesns/ *n* Jugend *f*, Pubertät *f*. **~t** *a* Jugend-; ⟨*boy, girl*⟩ halbwüchsig □ *n* Jugendliche(r) *m/f*

adopt /ə'dɒpt/ *vt* adoptieren; ergreifen ⟨*measure*⟩; ⟨*Pol*⟩ annehmen ⟨*candidate*⟩. **~ion** /-ɒpʃn/ *n* Adoption *f*. **~ive** /-ɪv/ *a* Adoptiv-

ador|able /ə'dɔːrəbl/ *a* bezaubernd. **~ation** /ædə'reɪʃn/ *n* Anbetung *f*

adore /ə'dɔː(r)/ *vt* ⟨*worship*⟩ anbeten; ⟨*fam: like*⟩ lieben

adorn /ə'dɔːn/ *vt* schmücken. **~ment** *n* Schmuck *m*

adrenalin /ə'drenəlɪn/ *n* Adrenalin *nt*

Adriatic /ˌeɪdrɪˈætɪk/ *a & n* ~ [Sea] Adria *f*

adrift /əˈdrɪft/ *a*, **be** ~ treiben; **come** ~ sich losreißen

adroit /əˈdrɔɪt/ *a*, **-ly** *adv* gewandt, geschickt

adulation /ædjʊˈleɪʃn/ *n* Schwärmerei *f*

adult /ˈædʌlt/ *n* Erwachsene(r) *m/f*

adulterate /əˈdʌltəreɪt/ *vt* verfälschen; panschen (*wine*)

adultery /əˈdʌltərɪ/ *n* Ehebruch *m*

advance /ədˈvɑːns/ *n* Fortschritt *m*; (*Mil*) Vorrücken *nt*; (*payment*) Vorschuss *m*; **in** ~ im Voraus □ *vi* vorankommen; (*Mil*) vorrücken; (*make progress*) Fortschritte machen □ *vt* fördern (*cause*); vorbringen (*idea*); vorschießen (*money*). ~ **booking** *n* Kartenvorverkauf *m*. ~ **d** *a* fortgeschritten; (*progressive*) fortschrittlich. ~**ment** *n* Förderung *f*; (*promotion*) Beförderung *f*

advantage /ədˈvɑːntɪdʒ/ *n* Vorteil *m*; **take** ~ **of** ausnutzen. ~**ous** /ædvənˈteɪdʒəs/ *a* vorteilhaft

advent /ˈædvent/ *n* Ankunft *f*; A~ (*season*) Advent *m*

adventur|e /ədˈventʃə(r)/ *n* Abenteuer *nt*. ~**er** *n* Abenteurer *m*. ~**ous** /-rəs/ *a* abenteuerlich; (*person*) abenteuerlustig

adverb /ˈædvɜːb/ *n* Adverb *nt*

adversary /ˈædvəsərɪ/ *n* Widersacher *m*

advers|e /ˈædvɜːs/ *a* ungünstig. ~**ity** /ədˈvɜːsɪtɪ/ *n* Not *f*

advert /ˈædvɜːt/ *n* (*fam*) = **advertisement**

advertise /ˈædvətaɪz/ *vt* Reklame machen für; (*by small ad*) inserieren □ *vi* Reklame machen; inserieren; ~ **for** per Anzeige suchen

advertisement /ədˈvɜːtɪsmənt/ *n* Anzeige *f*; (*publicity*) Reklame *f*; (*small ad*) Inserat *nt*

advertis|er /ˈædvətaɪzə(r)/ *n* Inserent *m*. ~**ing** *n* Werbung *f* □ *attrib* Werbe-

advice /ədˈvaɪs/ *n* Rat *m*. ~ **note** *n* Benachrichtigung *f*

advisable /ədˈvaɪzəbl/ *a* ratsam

advis|e /ədˈvaɪz/ *vt* raten (s.o. jdm); (*counsel*) beraten; (*inform*) benachrichtigen. ~**e** s.o. **against sth** jdm von etw abraten □ *vi* raten. ~**er** *n* Berater/in *m(f)*. ~**ory** /-ərɪ/ *a* beratend

advocate¹ /ˈædvəkət/ *n* [Rechts]anwalt *m*/-anwältin *f*; (*supporter*) Befürworter *m*

advocate² /ˈædvəkeɪt/ *vt* befürworten

aerial /ˈeərɪəl/ *a* Luft-. □ *n* Antenne *f*

aerobics /eəˈrəʊbɪks/ *n* Aerobic *nt*

aero|drome /ˈeərədrəʊm/ *n* Flugplatz *m*. ~**plane** *n* Flugzeug *nt*

aerosol /ˈeərəsɒl/ *n* Spraydose *f*

aesthetic /iːsˈθetɪk/ *a* ästhetisch

afar /əˈfɑː(r)/ *adv* **from** ~ aus der Ferne

affable /ˈæfəbl/ *a*, **-bly** *adv* freundlich

affair /əˈfeə(r)/ *n* Angelegenheit *f*, Sache *f*; (*scandal*) Affäre *f*; [love-]~ [Liebes]verhältnis *nt*

affect /əˈfekt/ *vt* sich auswirken auf (+ *acc*); (*concern*) betreffen; (*move*) rühren; (*pretend*) vortäuschen. ~**ation** /æfekˈteɪʃn/ *n* Affektiertheit *f*. ~**ed** *a* affektiert

affection /əˈfekʃn/ *n* Liebe *f*. ~**ate** /-ət/ *a*, **-ly** *adv* liebevoll

affiliated /əˈfɪlieɪtɪd/ *a* angeschlossen (**to** *dat*)

affinity /əˈfɪnɪtɪ/ *n* Ähnlichkeit *f*; (*attraction*) gegenseitige Anziehung *f*

affirm /əˈfɜːm/ *vt* behaupten; (*Jur*) eidesstattlich erklären

affirmative /əˈfɜːmətɪv/ *a* bejahend □ *n* Bejahung *f*

affix /əˈfɪks/ *vt* anbringen (**to** *dat*); (*stick*) aufkleben (**to** auf +

acc) setzen ⟨*signature*⟩ (to unter + *acc*)

afflict /əˈflɪkt/ *vt* be ~ed with behaftet sein mit. ~**ion** /-ɪkʃn/ *n* Leiden *nt*

affluen|ce /ˈæfluəns/ *n* Reichtum *m*. ~**t** *a* wohlhabend. ~**t society** *n* Wohlstandsgesellschaft *f*

afford /əˈfɔːd/ *vt* ⟨*provide*⟩ gewähren; **be able to** ~ **sth** sich (*dat*) etw leisten können. ~**able** /-əbl/ *a* erschwinglich

affray /əˈfreɪ/ *n* Schlägerei *f*

affront /əˈfrʌnt/ *n* Beleidigung *f* □ *vt* beleidigen

afield /əˈfiːld/ *adv* further ~ weiter weg

afloat /əˈfləʊt/ *a* be ~ ⟨*ship*⟩: flott sein; **keep** ~ ⟨*person*⟩: sich über Wasser halten

afoot /əˈfʊt/ *a* im Gange

aforesaid /əˈfɔːsed/ *a* ⟨*Jur*⟩ oben erwähnt

afraid /əˈfreɪd/ *a* be ~ Angst haben (of vor + *dat*); **I'm** ~ **not** leider nicht; **I'm** ~ **so** [ja] leider; **I'm** ~ **I can't help you** ich kann Ihnen leider nicht helfen

afresh /əˈfreʃ/ *adv* von vorne

Africa /ˈæfrɪkə/ *n* Afrika *nt*. ~**n** *a* afrikanisch □ *n* Afrikaner(in) *m(f)*

after /ˈɑːftə(r)/ *adv* danach □ *prep* nach (+ *dat*); ~ **that** danach; ~ **all** schließlich; **the day** ~ **tomorrow** übermorgen; **be** ~ aus sein auf (+ *acc*) □ *conj* nachdem

after: ~**effect** *n* Nachwirkung *f*. ~**math** /-mɑːθ/ *n* Auswirkungen *pl*. ~**noon** *n* Nachmittag *m*; **good** ~**noon!** guten Tag! ~**sales service** *n* Kundendienst *m*. ~**shave** *n* Rasierwasser *nt*. ~**thought** *n* nachträglicher Einfall *m*. ~**wards** *adv* nachher

again /əˈɡen/ *adv* wieder; ⟨*once more*⟩ noch einmal; ⟨*besides*⟩ außerdem; ~ **and** ~ immer wieder

against /əˈɡenst/ *prep* gegen (+ *acc*)

age /eɪdʒ/ *n* Alter *nt*; ⟨*era*⟩ Zeitalter *nt*; ~**s** ⟨*fam*⟩ ewig; **under** ~ minderjährig; **of** ~ volljährig; **two years of** ~ zwei Jahre alt □ *v* ⟨*pres p* ageing⟩ □ *vt* älter machen □ *vi* altern; ⟨*mature*⟩ reifen

aged[1] /eɪdʒd/ *a* ~ **two** zwei Jahre alt

aged[2] /ˈeɪdʒɪd/ *a* betagt □ **the** ~ *pl* die Alten

ageless /ˈeɪdʒlɪs/ *a* ewig jung

agency /ˈeɪdʒənsɪ/ *n* Agentur *f*; ⟨*office*⟩ Büro *nt*; **have the** ~ **for** die Vertretung haben für

agenda /əˈdʒendə/ *n* Tagesordnung *f*; **on the** ~ auf dem Programm

agent /ˈeɪdʒənt/ *n* Agent(in) *m(f)*; ⟨*Comm*⟩ Vertreter(in) *m(f)*; ⟨*substance*⟩ Mittel *nt*

aggravat|e /ˈæɡrəveɪt/ *vt* verschlimmern; ⟨*fam: annoy*⟩ ärgern. ~**ion** /-ˈveɪʃn/ *n* ⟨*fam*⟩ Ärger *m*

aggregate /ˈæɡrɪɡət/ *a* gesamt □ *n* Gesamtzahl *f*; ⟨*sum*⟩ Gesamtsumme *f*

aggress|ion /əˈɡreʃn/ *n* Aggression *f*. ~**ive** /-sɪv/ *a*, **-ly** *adv* aggressiv. ~**iveness** *n* Aggressivität *f*. ~**or** *n* Angreifer(in) *m(f)*

aggrieved /əˈɡriːvd/ *a* verletzt

aggro /ˈæɡrəʊ/ *n* ⟨*fam*⟩ Ärger *m*

aghast /əˈɡɑːst/ *a* entsetzt

agil|e /ˈædʒaɪl/ *a* flink, behände; ⟨*mind*⟩ wendig. ~**ity** /əˈdʒɪlətɪ/ *n* Flinkheit *f*, Behändigkeit *f*

agitat|e /ˈædʒɪteɪt/ *vt* bewegen; ⟨*shake*⟩ schütteln □ *vi* ⟨*fig*⟩ ~ **for** agitieren für. ~**ed** *a*, **-ly** *adv* erregt. ~**ion** /-ˈteɪʃn/ *n* Erregung *f*; ⟨*Pol*⟩ Agitation *f*. ~**or** *n* Agitator *m*

agnostic /æɡˈnɒstɪk/ *n* Agnostiker *m*

ago /əˈɡəʊ/ *adv* vor (+ *dat*); **a month** ~ vor einem Monat; **a long time** ~ vor langer Zeit; **hov long** ~ **is it?** wie lange ist es he

agog /əˈɡɒɡ/ *a* gespannt

agoniz|e /'æɡənaɪz/ vi [innerlich]
ringen. **~ing** a qualvoll

agony /'æɡənɪ/ n Qual f; **be in ~**
furchtbare Schmerzen haben

agree /ə'ɡriː/ vt vereinbaren; (admit) zugeben; **~ to do sth** sich
bereit erklären, etw zu tun □ vi
(people, figures:) übereinstimmen; (reach agreement) sich einigen; (get on) gut miteinander
auskommen; (consent) einwilligen (to in + acc); **I ~** der Meinung bin ich auch; **~ with s.o.**
jdm zustimmen; (food:) jdm bekommen; **~ with sth** (approve of)
mit etw einverstanden sein

agreeable /ə'ɡriːəbl/ a angenehm; **be ~** einverstanden sein
(to mit)

agreed /ə'ɡriːd/ a vereinbart

agreement /ə'ɡriːmənt/ n Übereinstimmung f; (consent) Einwilligung f; (contract) Abkommen
nt; **reach ~** sich einigen

agricultur|al /æɡrɪ'kʌltʃərəl/ a
landwirtschaftlich. **~e** /'æɡrɪ-
kʌltʃə(r)/ n Landwirtschaft f

aground /ə'ɡraʊnd/ a gestrandet;
run ~ (ship:) stranden

ahead /ə'hed/ adv straight ~
geradeaus; **be ~ of s.o./sth** vor
jdm/etw sein; (fig) voraus sein;
draw ~ nach vorne ziehen; **go
on ~** vorangehen, vorauskom-
men; **go ~!** (fam) bitte! **look/
plan ~** vorausblicken/-planen

aid /eɪd/ n Hilfe f; (financial) Unterstützung f; **in ~ of** zugunsten
(+ gen) □ vt helfen (+ dat)

aide /eɪd/ n Berater m

Aids /eɪdz/ n Aids nt

ail|ing /'eɪlɪŋ/ a kränkelnd.
~ment n Leiden nt

aim /eɪm/ n Ziel nt; **take ~** zielen
□ vt richten (at auf + acc); □ vi
zielen (at auf + acc); **~ to do sth**
beabsichtigen, etw zu tun. **~less**
a, **-ly** adv ziellos

air /eə(r)/ n Luft f; (tune) Melodie
f; (expression) Miene f; (appearance) Anschein m; **be on the**

~ (programme:) gesendet
werden; (person:) senden, auf
Sendung sein. **~ on ~** vornehm tun; **by ~** auf dem Luftweg;
(airmail) mit Luftpost □ vt lüften;
vorbringen (views)

air: **~-bed** n Luftmatratze f. **~-
conditioned** a klimatisiert. **~-
conditioning** n Klimaanlage f.
~craft n Flugzeug nt. **~fare**
Flugpreis m. **~field** n Flugplatz
m. **~ force** n Luftwaffe f. **~
freshener** n Raumspray nt.
~gun n Luftgewehr nt. **~ hostess** n Stewardess f. **~ letter** n
Aerogramm nt. **~line** n Flugge-
sellschaft f. **~lock** n Luftblase f.
~mail n Luftpost f. **~man** n
Flieger m. **~plane** n (Amer) Flugzeug nt. **~ pocket** n Luftloch nt.
~port n Flughafen m. **~raid** n
Luftangriff m. **~-raid shelter** n
Luftschutzbunker m. **~ship** n
Luftschiff nt. **~ ticket** n Flugschein m. **~tight** a luftdicht. **~
traffic** n Luftverkehr m. **~
traffic controller** n Fluglotse m.
~worthy a flugtüchtig

airy /'eərɪ/ a (ier,-iest) luftig;
(manner) nonchalant

aisle /aɪl/ n Gang m

ajar /ə'dʒɑː(r)/ a angelehnt

akin /ə'kɪn/ a **~ to** verwandt mit;
(similar) ähnlich (to dat)

alabaster /'æləbɑːstə(r)/ n Alabaster m

alacrity /ə'lækrɪtɪ/ n Bereitfer-
tigkeit f

alarm /əlɑːm/ n Alarm m; (device)
Alarmanlage f; (clock) Wecker m;
(fear) Unruhe f □ vt erschrecken;
alarmieren. **~ clock** n Wecker m

alas /ə'læs/ int ach!

album /'ælbəm/ n Album nt

alcohol /'ælkəhɒl/ n Alkohol m.
~ic /-'hɒlɪk/ a alkoholisch □ n
Alkoholiker(in) m(f). **~ism** n Al-
koholismus m

alcove /'ælkəʊv/ n Nische f

alert /ə'lɜ:t/ *a* aufmerksam □*n* Alarm *m*; **on the ~** auf der Hut □*vt* alarmieren

algae /'ældʒi:/ *npl* Algen *pl*

algebra /'ældʒɪbrə/ *n* Algebra *f*

Algeria /æl'dʒɪərɪə/ *n* Algerien *nt*

alias /'eɪlɪəs/ *n* Deckname *m* □*adv* alias

alibi /'ælɪbaɪ/ *n* Alibi *nt*

alien /'eɪlɪən/ *a* fremd □*n* Ausländer(in) *m(f)*

alienat|e /'eɪlɪəneɪt/ *vt* entfremden. **~ion** /-'neɪʃn/ *n* Entfremdung *f*

alight[1] /ə'laɪt/ *vi* aussteigen (**from** aus); ⟨*bird:*⟩ sich niederlassen

alight[2] *a* **be ~** brennen; **set ~** anzünden

align /ə'laɪn/ *vt* ausrichten. **~ment** *n* Ausrichtung *f*; **out of ~ment** nicht richtig ausgerichtet

alike /ə'laɪk/ *a & adv* ähnlich; *(same)* gleich; **look ~** sich *(dat)* ähnlich sehen

alimony /'ælɪmənɪ/ *n* Unterhalt *m*

alive /ə'laɪv/ *a* lebendig; **be ~** leben; **be ~ with** wimmeln von

alkali /'ælkəlaɪ/ *n* Base *f*, Alkali *nt*

all /ɔ:l/ *a* alle *pl*; *(whole)* ganz; **~ [the] children** alle Kinder; **~ our children** alle unsere Kinder; **~ the others** alle anderen; **~ day** den ganzen Tag; **~ the wine** der ganze Wein; **for ~ that** *(nevertheless)* trotzdem; **in ~ innocence** in aller Unschuld □*pron* alle *pl*; *(everything)* alles; **~ of you/them** Sie/sie alle; **~ of the town** die ganze Stadt; **not at ~** gar nicht; **in ~** insgesamt; **~ in** alles in allem; **most of ~** am meisten; **once and for ~** ein für alle Mal □*adv* ganz; **~ but** fast; **~ at once** auf einmal; **~ too soon** viel zu früh; **~ the same** *(nevertheless)* trotzdem; **the better** umso besser; **be ~ in** *(fam)* völlig

erledigt sein; **four ~** *(Sport)* vier zu vier

allay /ə'leɪ/ *vt* zerstreuen

allegation /ælɪ'geɪʃn/ *n* Behauptung *f*

allege /ə'ledʒ/ *vt* behaupten. **~d** *a* **-ly** *adv* angeblich

allegiance /ə'li:dʒəns/ *n* Treue *f*

allegor|ical /ælɪ'gɒrɪk/ *a* allegorisch. **~y** /'ælɪgərɪ/ *n* Allegorie *f*

allerg|ic /ə'lɜ:dʒɪk/ *a* allergisch (**to** gegen). **~y** /'ælədʒɪ/ *n* Allergie *f*

alleviate /ə'li:vɪeɪt/ *vt* lindern

alley /'ælɪ/ *n* Gasse *f*; *(for bowling)* Bahn *f*

alliance /ə'laɪəns/ *n* Verbindung *f*; *(Pol)* Bündnis *nt*

allied /'ælaɪd/ *a* alliiert; *(fig: related)* verwandt (**to** mit)

alligator /'ælɪgeɪtə(r)/ *n* Alligator *m*

allocat|e /'æləkeɪt/ *vt* zuteilen; *(share out)* verteilen. **~ion** /-'keɪʃn/ *n* Zuteilung *f*

allot /ə'lɒt/ *vt* (*pt/pp* **allotted**) zuteilen (**s.o. sth**). **~ment** *n* ≈ Schrebergarten *m*

allow /ə'laʊ/ *vt* erlauben; *(give)* geben; *(grant)* gewähren; *(reckon)* rechnen; *(agree, admit)* zugeben; **~ for** berücksichtigen; **s.o. to do sth** jdm erlauben, etw zu tun; **be ~ed to do sth** etw tun dürfen

allowance /ə'laʊəns/ *n* [finanzielle] Unterstützung *f*; **~ for petrol** Benzingeld *nt*; **make ~s for** berücksichtigen

alloy /'ælɔɪ/ *n* Legierung *f*

allude /ə'lu:d/ *vi* anspielen (**to** auf + *acc*)

allure /æ'ljʊə(r)/ *n* Reiz *m*

allusion /ə'lu:ʒn/ *n* Anspielung *f*

ally[1] /'ælaɪ/ *n* Verbündete(r) *m/f*; **the Allies** *pl* die Alliierten

ally[2] /ə'laɪ/ *vt* (*pt/pp* **-ied**) verbinden; **~ oneself with** sich verbünden mit

almighty /ɔːlˈmaɪtɪ/ a allmächtig; (fam: big) Riesen- □ n the A ~ der Allmächtige

almond /ˈɑːmənd/ n (Bot) Mandel f

almost /ˈɔːlməʊst/ adv fast, beinahe

alms /ɑːmz/ npl (liter) Almosen pl

alone /əˈləʊn/ a & adv allein; **leave me** ~ lass mich in Ruhe; **leave that** ~! lass die Finger davon! **let** ~ ganz zu schweigen von

along /əˈlɒŋ/ prep entlang (+ acc); ~ **the river** den Fluss entlang □ adv ~ **with** zusammen mit; **all** ~ die ganze Zeit; **come** ~ komm doch; **I'll bring it** ~ ich bringe es mit; **move** ~ weitergehen

along'side adv daneben □ prep neben (+ dat)

aloof /əˈluːf/ a distanziert

aloud /əˈlaʊd/ adv laut

alphabet /ˈælfəbet/ n Alphabet nt. ~**ical** /-ˈbetɪkl/ a, **-ly** adv alphabetisch

alpine /ˈælpaɪn/ a alpin; **A**~ Alpen-

Alps /ælps/ npl Alpen pl

already /ɔːlˈredɪ/ adv schon

Alsace /ælˈsæs/ n Elsass nt

Alsatian /ælˈseɪʃn/ n (dog) [deutscher] Schäferhund m

also /ˈɔːlsəʊ/ adv auch

altar /ˈɔːltə(r)/ n Altar m

alter /ˈɔːltə(r)/ vt ändern □ vi sich verändern. ~**ation** /-ˈreɪʃn/ n Änderung f

alternate¹ /ˈɔːltəneɪt/ vi [sich] abwechseln □ vt abwechseln

alternate² /ɔːlˈtɜːnət/ a, **-ly** adv abwechselnd; (Amer: alternative) **on** ~ **days** jeden zweiten Tag

'alternating current n Wechselstrom m

alternative /ɔːlˈtɜːnətɪv/ a andere(r,s) □ n Alternative f. ~**ly** adv oder aber

although /ɔːlˈðəʊ/ conj obgleich, obwohl

altitude /ˈæltɪtjuːd/ n Höhe f

altogether /ɔːltəˈgeðə(r)/ adv insgesamt; (on the whole) alles in allem

altruistic /æltruːˈɪstɪk/ altruistisch

aluminium /æljʊˈmɪnɪəm/ n, (Amer) **aluminium** /əˈluː-mɪnəm/ n Aluminium nt

always /ˈɔːlweɪz/ adv immer

am /æm/ see **be**

a.m. abbr (ante meridiem) vormittags

amalgamate /əˈmælgəmeɪt/ vt vereinigen; (Chem) amalgamieren □ vi sich vereinigen; (Chem) sich amalgamieren

amass /əˈmæs/ vt anhäufen

amateur /ˈæmətə(r)/ n Amateur m □ attrib Amateur-; (Theat) Laien-. ~**ish** a laienhaft

amaze /əˈmeɪz/ vt erstaunen. ~**d** a erstaunt. ~**ment** n Erstaunen nt

amazing /əˈmeɪzɪŋ/ a, **-ly** adv erstaunlich

ambassador /æmˈbæsədə(r)/ n Botschafter m

amber /ˈæmbə(r)/ n Bernstein m □ a (colour) gelb

ambidextrous /æmbɪˈdekstrəs/ a **be** ~ mit beiden Händen gleich geschickt sein

ambience /ˈæmbɪəns/ n Atmosphäre f

ambigu|ity /æmbɪˈgjuːətɪ/ n Zweideutigkeit f. ~**ous** /-ˈbɪgjʊəs/ a, **-ly** adv zweideutig

ambition /æmˈbɪʃn/ n Ehrgeiz m; (aim) Ambition f. ~**ous** /-ʃəs/ a ehrgeizig

ambivalent /æmˈbɪvələnt/ a zwiespältig; **be/feel** ~ im Zwiespalt sein

amble /ˈæmbl/ vi schlendern

ambulance /ˈæmbjʊləns/ n Krankenwagen m. ~**man** n Sanitäter m

ambush /'æmbʊʃ/ n Hinterhalt m □ vt aus dem Hinterhalt überfallen

amen /ɑː'men/ int amen

amenable /ə'miːnəbl/ a ~ to zugänglich (to dat)

amend /ə'mend/ vt ändern. ~ment n Änderung f. ~s npl make ~s for sth etw wieder gutmachen

amenities /ə'miːnɪtɪz/ npl Einrichtungen pl

America /ə'merɪkə/ n Amerika nt. ~n a amerikanisch □n Amerikaner(in) m(f). ~nism n Amerikanismus m

amiable /'eɪmɪəbl/ a liebenswürdig

amicable /'æmɪkəbl/ a, -bly adv freundschaftlich; (agreement) gütlich

amid[st] /ə'mɪd[st]/ prep inmitten (+ gen)

amiss /ə'mɪs/ a be ~ nicht stimmen □ adv not come ~ nicht unangebracht sein; take sth ~ etw übel nehmen

ammonia /ə'məʊnɪə/ n Ammoniak nt

ammunition /æmjʊ'nɪʃn/ n Munition f

amnesia /æm'niːzɪə/ n Amnesie f

amnesty /'æmnəstɪ/ n Amnestie f

among[st] /ə'mʌŋ[st]/ prep unter (+ dat/acc); ~ yourselves untereinander

amoral /eɪ'mɒrəl/ a amoralisch

amorous /'æmərəs/ a zärtlich

amount /ə'maʊnt/ n Menge f; (sum of money) Betrag m; (total) Gesamtsumme f □ vi ~ to sich belaufen auf (+ acc); (fig) hinauslaufen auf (+ acc)

amp /æmp/ n Ampere nt

amphibian /æm'fɪbɪən/ n Amphibie f. ~ous /-ɪəs/ a amphibisch

amphitheatre /'æmfɪ-/ n Amphitheater nt

ample /'æmpl/ a (-r, -st), -ly adv reichlich; (large) füllig

amplif|ier /'æmplɪfaɪə(r)/ n Verstärker m. ~y /-faɪ/ vt (pt/pp -ied) weiter ausführen; verstärken (sound)

amputat|e /'æmpjʊteɪt/ vt amputieren. ~ion /-'teɪʃn/ n Amputation f

amuse /ə'mjuːz/ vt amüsieren, belustigen; (entertain) unterhalten. ~ment n Belustigung f; Unterhaltung f. ~ment arcade n Spielhalle f

amusing /ə'mjuːzɪŋ/ a amüsant

an /ən, betont æn/ see a

anaem|ia /ə'niːmɪə/ n Blutarmut f, Anämie f. ~ic a blutarm

anaesthesia /ænəs'θiːzɪə/ n Betäubung f

anaesthetic /ænəs'θetɪk/ n Narkosemittel nt, Betäubungsmittel nt; under [an] ~ in Narkose; give s.o. an ~ jdm eine Narkose geben

anaesthet|ist /ə'niːsθətɪst/ n Narkosearzt m. ~ize /-taɪz/ vt betäuben

analog[ue] /'ænəlɒg/ a Analog-

analogy /ə'nælədʒɪ/ n Analogie f

analyse /'ænəlaɪz/ vt analysieren

analysis /ə'næləsɪs/ n Analyse f

analyst /'ænəlɪst/ n Chemiker(in) m(f); (Psych) Analytiker m

analytical /ænə'lɪtɪkl/ a analytisch

anarch|ist /'ænəkɪst/ n Anarchist m. ~y n Anarchie f

anathema /ə'næθəmə/ n Gräuel m

anatom|ical /ænə'tɒmɪkl/ a, -ly adv anatomisch. ~y /ə'nætəmɪ/ n Anatomie f

ancest|or /'ænsestə(r)/ n Vorfahr m. ~ry n Abstammung f

anchor /'æŋkə(r)/ n Anker m □ vi ankern □ vt verankern

anchovy /'æntʃəvɪ/ n Sardelle f

ancient /'eɪnʃənt/ a alt

ancillary /ˈænsɪlərɪ/ a Hilfs-

and /ənd, *betont* ænd/ conj und; ~ **so on** und so weiter; **six hundred ~ two** sechshundertzwei; **more ~ more** immer mehr; **nice ~ warm** schön warm; **try ~ come** versuche zu kommen

anecdote /ˈænɪkdəʊt/ n Anekdote f

anew /əˈnjuː/ adv von neuem

angel /ˈeɪndʒl/ n Engel m. ~**ic** /ænˈdʒelɪk/ a engelhaft

anger /ˈæŋɡə(r)/ n Zorn m □ vt zornig machen

angle[1] /ˈæŋɡl/ n Winkel m; **at an ~** schräg Standpunkt m; **at an ~** schräg

angle[2] vi angeln; ~ **for** (fig) fischen nach. ~**r** n Angler m

Anglican /ˈæŋɡlɪkən/ a anglika-nisch □ n Anglikaner(in) m(f)

Anglo-Saxon /æŋɡləʊˈsæksn/ a angelsächsisch □ n Angelsäch-sisch nt

angry /ˈæŋɡrɪ/ a (-ier,-iest), **-ily** adv zornig; **be ~ with** böse sein auf (+ acc)

anguish /ˈæŋɡwɪʃ/ n Qual f

angular /ˈæŋɡjʊlə(r)/ a eckig; (features) kantig

animal /ˈænɪml/ n Tier nt □ a tie-risch

animate[1] /ˈænɪmət/ a lebendig

animate[2] /ˈænɪmeɪt/ vt beleben. ~**d** a lebhaft. ~**ion** /-ˈmeɪʃn/ n Lebhaftigkeit f

animosity /ænɪˈmɒsɪtɪ/ n Feind-seligkeit f

aniseed /ˈænɪsiːd/ n Anis m

ankle /ˈæŋkl/ n [Fuß]knöchel m

annex /əˈneks/ vt annektieren

annex[e] /ˈæneks/ n Nebenge-bäude nt; (extension) Anbau m

annihilate /əˈnaɪəleɪt/ vt ver-nichten. ~**ion** /-ˈleɪʃn/ n Ver-nichtung f

anniversary /ænɪˈvɜːsərɪ/ n Jah-restag m

annotate /ˈænəteɪt/ vt kommen-tieren

announce /əˈnaʊns/ vt bekannt geben; (over loudspeaker) durch-sagen; (at reception) ankündigen; (Radio, TV) ansagen; (in news-paper) anzeigen. ~**ment** n Be-kanntgabe f, Bekanntmachung f; Durchsage f; Ansage f; Anzeige f. ~**r** n Ansager(in) m(f)

annoy /əˈnɔɪ/ vt ärgern; (pester) belästigen; **get ~ed** sich ärgern. ~**ance** n Ärger m. ~**ing** a ärger-lich

annual /ˈænjʊəl/ a, **-ly** adv jährlich □ n (Bot) einjährige Pflanze f; (book) Jahresalbum nt

annuity /əˈnjuːɪtɪ/ n [Leib]rente f

annul /əˈnʌl/ vt (pt/pp annulled) annullieren

anoint /əˈnɔɪnt/ vt salben

anomaly /əˈnɒmlɪ/ n Anomalie f

anonymous /əˈnɒnɪməs/ a, **-ly** adv anonym

anorak /ˈænəræk/ n Anorak m

anorexia /ænəˈreksɪə/ n Mager-sucht f

another /əˈnʌðə(r)/ a & pron ein anderer/eine andere/ein ande-res; (additional) noch ein(e); ~ [one] noch einer/eine/eins; ~ **day** an einem anderen Tag; **in ~ way** auf andere Weise; ~ **time** ein andermal; **one ~** einander

answer /ˈɑːnsə(r)/ n Antwort f; (solution) Lösung f □ vt antworten (s.o. jdm); be-antworten (question, letter); ~ **the door/telephone** an die Tür/ ans Telefon gehen □ vi antworten; (Teleph) sich melden; ~ **back** eine freche Antwort geben; ~ **for** verantwortlich sein für. ~**able** /-əbl/ a verantwort-lich. ~**ing machine** n (Teleph) Anrufbeantworter m

ant /ænt/ n Ameise f

antagonis|m /ænˈtæɡənɪzm/ n Antagonismus m. ~**tic** /-ˈnɪstɪk/ a feindselig

antagonize /æn'tægənaɪz/ vt gegen sich aufbringen

Antarctic /ænt'ɑːktɪk/ n Antarktis f

antelope /'æntɪləʊp/ n Antilope f

antenatal /ænti'neɪtl/ a ~ care Schwangerschaftsfürsorge f

antenna /æn'tenə/ n Fühler m; (Amer: aerial) Antenne f

ante-room /'ænti-/ n Vorraum m

anthem /'ænθəm/ n Hymne f

anthology /æn'θɒlədʒi/ n Anthologie f

anthropology /ænθrə'pɒlədʒi/ n Anthropologie f

anti-'aircraft /ænti-/ a Flugabwehr-

antibiotic /æntibaɪ'ɒtɪk/ n Antibiotikum nt

'antibody n Antikörper m

anticipat|e /æn'tɪsɪpeɪt/ vt vorhersehen; (forestall) zuvorkommen (+ dat); (expect) erwarten. ~ion /-'peɪʃn/ n Erwartung f

anti'climax n Enttäuschung f

anti'clockwise a & adv gegen den Uhrzeigersinn

antics /'æntɪks/ npl Mätzchen pl

anti'cyclone n Hochdruckgebiet nt

antidote /'æntɪdəʊt/ n Gegengift nt

'antifreeze n Frostschutzmittel nt

antipathy /æn'tɪpəθi/ n Abneigung f, Antipathie f

antiquarian /ænti'kweərɪən/ a antiquarisch. ~ **bookshop** n Antiquariat nt

antiquated /'æntɪkweɪtɪd/ a veraltet

antique /æn'tiːk/ a antik □n Antiquität f. ~ **dealer** n Antiquitätenhändler m

antiquity /æn'tɪkwəti/ n Altertum nt

anti-Semitic /æntɪsɪ'mɪtɪk/ a antisemitisch

anti'septic a antiseptisch □n Antiseptikum nt

anti'social a asozial; (fam) ungesellig

antithesis /æn'tɪθəsɪs/ n Gegensatz m

antlers /'æntləz/ npl Geweih nt

anus /'eɪnəs/ n After m

anvil /'ænvɪl/ n Amboss m

anxiety /æŋ'zaɪəti/ n Sorge f

anxious /'æŋkʃəs/ a, -ly adv ängstlich; (worried) besorgt; **be ~ to do sth** etw gerne machen wollen

any /'eni/ a irgendein(e); pl irgendwelche; (every) jede(r,s); pl alle; (after negative) kein(e); pl keine; ~ **colour/number you like** eine beliebige Farbe/Zahl; **have you ~ wine/apples?** haben Sie Wein/Äpfel? **for ~ reason** aus irgendeinem Grund □pron [irgend]einer/eine/eins; pl [irgend]welche; (some) welche(r,s); pl welche; (all) alle pl; (negative) keiner/keine/keins; pl keine; **I don't want ~ of it** ich will nichts davon; **there aren't ~** es gibt keine; **I need wine/apples/money—have we ~?** ich brauche Wein/Äpfel/Geld—haben wir welchen/welche/welches? □adv noch; ~ **quicker/slower** noch schneller/langsamer; **is it ~ better?** geht es etwas besser? **would you like ~ more?** möchten Sie noch [etwas]? **I can't eat ~ more** ich kann nichts mehr essen; **I can't go ~ further** ich kann nicht mehr weiter

'anybody pron [irgend]jemand; (after negative) niemand; ~ **can do that** das kann jeder

'anyhow adv jedenfalls; (nevertheless) trotzdem; (badly) irgendwie

'anyone pron = anybody

'anything pron [irgend]etwas; (after negative) nichts; (everything) alles '**anyway** adv jedenfalls; (in any case) sowieso

'**anywhere** adv irgendwo; (after negative) nirgendwo; (be, live) überall; **I'd go** ~ ich würde überallhin gehen

apart /ə'pɑːt/ adv auseinander; **live** ~ getrennt leben; ~ **from** abgesehen von

apartment /ə'pɑːtmənt/ n Zimmer nt; (Amer: flat) Wohnung f

apathy /'æpəθɪ/ n Apathie f

ape /eɪp/ n [Menschen]affe m □ vt nachäffen

aperitif /ə'perətiːf/ n Aperitif m

aperture /'æpətʃə(r)/ n Öffnung f; (Phot) Blende f

apex /'eɪpeks/ n Spitze f; (fig) Gipfel m

apiece /ə'piːs/ adv pro Person; (thing) pro Stück

apologetic /əpɒlə'dʒetɪk/ a, -ally adv entschuldigend; **be** ~ sich entschuldigen

apologize /ə'pɒlədʒaɪz/ vi sich entschuldigen (to bei)

apology /ə'pɒlədʒɪ/ n Entschuldigung f

apostle /ə'pɒsl/ n Apostel m

apostrophe /ə'pɒstrəfɪ/ n Apostroph m

appal /ə'pɔːl/ vt (pt/pp appalled) entsetzen. ~**ling** a entsetzlich

apparatus /æpə'reɪtəs/ n Apparatur f; (Sport) Geräte pl; (single piece) Gerät nt

apparel /ə'pærəl/ n Kleidung f

apparent /ə'pærənt/ a offenbar; (seeming) scheinbar. ~**ly** adv offenbar, anscheinend

apparition /æpə'rɪʃn/ n Erscheinung f

appeal /ə'piːl/ n Appell m, Aufruf m; (request) Bitte f; (attraction) Reiz m; (Jur) Berufung f □ vi appellieren (to an + acc); (ask) bitten (for um); (be attractive) zusagen (to dat); (Jur) Berufung einlegen. ~**ing** a ansprechend

appear /ə'pɪə(r)/ vi erscheinen; (seem) scheinen; (Theat) auftreten. ~**ance** n Erscheinen nt; (look) Aussehen nt; **to all** ~**ances** allem Anschein nach

appease /ə'piːz/ vt beschwichtigen

append /ə'pend/ vt nachtragen; setzen (signature) (to unter + acc). ~**age** /-ɪdʒ/ n Anhängsel nt

appendicitis /əpendɪ'saɪtɪs/ n Blinddarmentzündung f

appendix /ə'pendɪks/ n (pl -ices /-ɪsiːz/) (of book) Anhang m □ (pl -es) (Anat) Blinddarm m

appertain /æpə'teɪn/ vi ~ **to** betreffen

appetite /'æpɪtaɪt/ n Appetit m

appetizing /'æpɪtaɪzɪŋ/ a appetitlich

applaud /ə'plɔːd/ vt/i Beifall klatschen (+ dat). ~**se** n Beifall m

apple /'æpl/ n Apfel m

appliance /ə'plaɪəns/ n Gerät nt

applicable /'æplɪkəbl/ a anwendbar (to auf + acc); (on form) **not** ~ nicht zutreffend

applicant /'æplɪkənt/ n Bewerber(in) m(f)

application /æplɪ'keɪʃn/ n Anwendung f; (request) Antrag m; (for job) Bewerbung f; (diligence) Fleiß m

applied /ə'plaɪd/ a angewandt

apply /ə'plaɪ/ vt (pt/pp -ied) auftragen (paint); anwenden (force, rule) □ vi zutreffen (to auf + acc); ~ **for** beantragen; sich bewerben um (job)

appoint /ə'pɔɪnt/ vt ernennen; (fix) festlegen; **well** ~**ed** gut ausgestattet. ~**ment** n Ernennung f; (meeting) Verabredung f; (at doctor's, hairdresser's) Termin m; (job) Posten m; **make an** ~**ment** sich anmelden

apposite /'æpəzɪt/ a treffend

appraise /ə'preɪz/ vt abschätzen

appreciable /ə'priːʃəbl/ *a* merklich; (*considerable*) beträchtlich

appreciat|e /ə'priːʃɪeɪt/ *vt* zu schätzen wissen; (*be grateful for*) dankbar sein für; (*enjoy*) schätzen; (*understand*) verstehen □ *vi* (*increase in value*) im Wert steigen. **∼ion** /-'eɪʃn/ *n* (*gratitude*) Dankbarkeit *f*; **in ∼ion** als Dank (**of** für). **∼ive** /-ətɪv/ *a* dankbar

apprehend /æprɪ'hend/ *vt* festnehmen

apprehens|ion /æprɪ'henʃn/ *n* Festnahme *f*; (*fear*) Angst *f*. **∼ive** /-sɪv/ *a* ängstlich

apprentice /ə'prentɪs/ *n* Lehrling *m*. **∼ship** *n* Lehre *f*

approach /ə'prəʊtʃ/ *vi* näherkommen *nt*; (*of time*) Nahen *nt*; (*access*) Zugang *m*; (*road*) Zufahrt *f* □ *vi* sich nähern; (*time:*) nahen □ *vt* sich nähern (+ *dat*); (*with request*) herantreten an (+ *acc*); (*set about*) sich heranmachen an (+ *acc*). **∼able** /-əbl/ *a* zugänglich

approbation /æprə'beɪʃn/ *n* Billigung *f*

appropriate¹ /ə'prəʊprɪət/ *a* angebracht, angemessen

appropriate² /ə'prəʊprɪeɪt/ *vt* sich (*dat*) aneignen

approval /ə'pruːvl/ *n* Billigung *f*; **on ∼** zur Ansicht

approv|e /ə'pruːv/ *vt* billigen □ *vi* **∼e of sth/s.o.** mit etw/jdm einverstanden sein. **∼ing** *a*, **-ly** *adv* anerkennend

approximate¹ /ə'prɒksɪmeɪt/ *vi* **∼ to** nahe kommen (+ *dat*)

approximate² /ə'prɒksɪmət/ *a*, ungefähr. **-ly** *adv* ungefähr, etwa

approximation /əprɒksɪ'meɪʃn/ *n* Schätzung *f*

apricot /'eɪprɪkɒt/ *n* Aprikose *f*

April /'eɪprəl/ *n* April *m*; **make an ∼ fool** of in den April schicken

apron /'eɪprən/ *n* Schürze *f*

apropos /'æprəpəʊ/ *adv* ∼ [**of**] betreffs (+ *gen*)

apt /æpt/ *a*, **-ly** *adv* passend; (*pupil*) begabt; **be ∼ to do sth** dazu neigen, etw zu tun

aptitude /'æptɪtjuːd/ *n* Begabung *f*

aqualung /'ækwəlʌŋ/ *n* Tauchgerät *nt*

aquarium /ə'kweərɪəm/ *n* Aquarium *nt*

Aquarius /ə'kweərɪəs/ *n* (*Astr*) Wassermann *m*

aquatic /ə'kwætɪk/ *a* Wasser-

Arab /'ærəb/ *a* arabisch □ *n* Araber(in) *m(f)*. **∼ian** /ə'reɪbɪən/ *a* arabisch

Arabic /'ærəbɪk/ *a* arabisch

arable /'ærəbl/ *a* ∼ **land** Ackerland *nt*

arbitrary /'ɑːbɪtrəri/ *a*, **-ily** *adv* willkürlich

arbitrat|e /'ɑːbɪtreɪt/ *vi* schlichten. **∼ion** /-'treɪʃn/ *n* Schlichtung *f*

arc /ɑːk/ *n* Bogen *m*

arcade /ɑː'keɪd/ *n* Laubengang *m*; (*shops*) Einkaufspassage *f*

arch /ɑːtʃ/ *n* Bogen *m*; (*of foot*) Gewölbe *nt* □ *vt* ∼ **its back** (*cat:*) einen Buckel machen

archaeological /ɑːkɪə'lɒdʒɪkl/ *a* archäologisch

archaeolog|ist /ɑːkɪ'ɒlədʒɪst/. *n* Archäologe *m*/-login *f*. **∼y** *n* Archäologie *f*

archaic /ɑː'keɪɪk/ *a* veraltet

arch'bishop /ɑːtʃ-/ *n* Erzbischof *m*

arch-'enemy *n* Erzfeind *m*

archer /'ɑːtʃə(r)/ *n* Bogenschütze *m*. **∼y** *n* Bogenschießen *nt*

architect /'ɑːkɪtekt/ *n* Architekt(in) *m(f)*. **∼ural** /ɑː'kɪtektʃərəl/ *a*, **-ly** *adv* architektonisch

architecture /'ɑːkɪtektʃə(r)/ *n* Architektur *f*

archives /'ɑːkaɪvz/ *npl* Archiv *nt*

archway /'ɑːtʃweɪ/ *n* Torbogen *m*

Arctic /'ɑ:ktɪk/ a arktisch □ n **the ~** die Arktis

ardent /'ɑ:dənt/ a, **-ly** adv leidenschaftlich

ardour /'ɑ:də(r)/ n Leidenschaft f

arduous /'ɑ:djʊəs/ a mühsam

are /ɑ:(r)/ see **be**

area /'eərɪə/ n (surface) Fläche f; (Geom) Flächeninhalt m; (region) Gegend f; (fig) Gebiet nt. **~ code** n Vorwahlnummer f

arena /ə'ri:nə/ n Arena f

aren't /ɑ:nt/ = **are not**. See be

Argentina /ɑ:dʒən'ti:nə/ n Argentinien nt

Argentin|e /'ɑ:dʒəntaɪn/, **~ian** /-'tɪnɪən/ a argentinisch

argue /'ɑ:gju:/ vi streiten (about über + acc); (two people:) sich streiten; (debate) diskutieren; **don't ~!** keine Widerrede! □ vt (debate) diskutieren; (reason) ~ **that** argumentieren, dass

argument /'ɑ:gjʊmənt/ n Streit m, Auseinandersetzung f; (reasoning) Argument nt; **have an ~** sich streiten. **~ative** /-'mentətɪv/ a streitlustig

aria /'ɑ:rɪə/ n Arie f

arid /'ærɪd/ a dürr

Aries /'eəri:z/ n (Astr) Widder m

arise /ə'raɪz/ vi (pt **arose**, pp **arisen**) sich ergeben (**from** aus)

aristocracy /ærɪ'stɒkrəsɪ/ n Aristokratie f

aristocrat /'ærɪstəkræt/ n Aristokrat(in) m(f). **~ic** /-'krætɪk/ a aristokratisch

arithmetic /ə'rɪθmətɪk/ n Rechnen nt

ark /ɑ:k/ n Noah's A ~ die Arche Noah

arm /ɑ:m/ n Arm m; (of chair) Armlehne f; **~s** pl (weapons) Waffen pl; (Heraldry) Wappen nt; **up in ~s** (fam) empört □ vt bewaffnen

armament /'ɑ:məmənt/ n Bewaffnung f; **~s** pl Waffen pl

armchair n Sessel m

armed /ɑ:md/ a bewaffnet; **~ forces** Streitkräfte pl

armistice /'ɑ:mɪstɪs/ n Waffenstillstand m

armour /'ɑ:mə(r)/ n Rüstung f. **~ed** a Panzer-

armpit n Achselhöhle f

army /'ɑ:mɪ/ n Heer nt; (specific) Armee f; **join the ~** zum Militär gehen

aroma /ə'rəʊmə/ n Aroma nt, Duft m. **~tic** /ærə'mætɪk/ a aromatisch

arose /ə'rəʊz/ see **arise**

around /ə'raʊnd/ adv [all] ~ rings herum; **he's not ~** er ist nicht da; **look/turn ~** sich umsehen/umdrehen; **travel ~** herumreisen □ prep um (+ acc) ... herum (approximately) gegen

arouse /ə'raʊz/ vt aufwecken; (excite) erregen

arrange /ə'reɪndʒ/ vt arrangieren; anordnen (furniture, books); (settle) abmachen; **I have ~d to go there** ich habe abgemacht, dass ich dahingehe. **~ment** n Anordnung f; (agreement) Vereinbarung f; (of flowers) Gesteck nt; **make ~ments** Vorkehrungen treffen

arrears /ə'rɪəz/ npl Rückstände pl; **in ~** im Rückstand

arrest /ə'rest/ n Verhaftung f; **under ~** verhaftet □ vt verhaften

arrival /ə'raɪvl/ n Ankunft f; **new ~s** pl Neuankömmlinge pl

arrive /ə'raɪv/ vi ankommen; ~ **at** (fig) gelangen zu

arrogan|ce /'ærəgəns/ n Arroganz f. **~t a, -ly** adv arrogant

arrow /'ærəʊ/ n Pfeil m

arse /ɑ:s/ n (vulg) Arsch m

arsenic /'ɑ:sənɪk/ n Arsen nt

arson /'ɑ:sn/ n Brandstiftung f. **~ist** /-sənɪst/ n Brandstifter m

art /ɑ:t/ n Kunst f; **work of ~** Kunstwerk nt; **~s and crafts** pl

Kunstgewerbe *nt*; A~s *pl* (*Univ*) Geisteswissenschaften *pl*

artery /'ɑːtəri/ *n* Schlagader *f*, Arterie *f*

artful /'ɑːtfl/ *a* gerissen

'art gallery *n* Kunstgalerie *f*

arthritis /ɑː'θraɪtɪs/ *n* Arthritis *f*

artichoke /'ɑːtɪtʃəʊk/ *n* Artischocke *f*

article /'ɑːtɪkl/ *n* Artikel *m*; (*object*) Gegenstand *m*; ~ **of clothing** Kleidungsstück *nt*

articulate[1] /ɑː'tɪkjʊlət/ *a* deutlich; **be** ~ sich gut ausdrücken können

articulate[2] /ɑː'tɪkjʊleɪt/ *vt* aussprechen. ~**d lorry** *n* Sattelzug *m*

artifice /'ɑːtɪfɪs/ *n* Arglist *f*

artificial /ɑːtɪ'fɪʃl/ *a*, **-ly** *adv* künstlich

artillery /ɑː'tɪləri/ *n* Artillerie *f*

artist /'ɑːtɪst/ *n* Künstler(in) *m(f)*

artiste /ɑː'tiːst/ *n* (*Theat*) Artist(in) *m(f)*

artistic /ɑː'tɪstɪk/ *a*, **-ally** *adv* künstlerisch

artless /'ɑːtlɪs/ *a* unschuldig

as /æz/ *conj* (*because*) da; (*when*) als; (*while*) während □ *prep* als; **as a child/foreigner** als Kind/Ausländer □ *adv* as well auch; **as soon as** sobald; **as much as** so viel wie; **as quick as** so schnell wie du; **as you know** wie Sie wissen; **as far as I'm concerned** was mich betrifft

asbestos /æz'bestɒs/ *n* Asbest *m*

ascend /ə'send/ *vi* [auf]steigen □ *vt* besteigen (*throne*)

Ascension /ə'senʃn/ *n* (*Relig*) [Christi] Himmelfahrt *f*

ascent /ə'sent/ *n* Aufstieg *m*

ascertain /æsə'teɪn/ *vt* ermitteln

ascribe /ə'skraɪb/ *vt* zuschreiben (**to** *dat*)

ash[1] /æʃ/ *n* (*tree*) Esche *f*

ash[2] *n* Asche *f*

ashamed /ə'ʃeɪmd/ *a* beschämt; **be** ~ sich schämen (**of** über + *acc*)

ashore /ə'ʃɔː(r)/ *adv* an Land

ash: ~**tray** *n* Aschenbecher *m*. A~ **Wednesday** *n* Aschermittwoch *m*

Asia /'eɪʃə/ *n* Asien *nt*. ~**n** *a* asiatisch □ *n* Asiat(in) *m(f)*. ~**tic** /eɪʃɪ'ætɪk/ *a* asiatisch

aside /ə'saɪd/ *adv* beiseite; ~ **from** (*Amer*) außer (+ *dat*)

ask /ɑːsk/ *vt/i* fragen; stellen (*question*); (*invite*) einladen; ~ **for** bitten um; verlangen (*s.o.*); ~ **after** sich erkundigen nach; ~ **s.o. in** jdn hereinbitten; ~ **s.o. to do sth** jdn bitten, etw zu tun

askance /ə'skɑːns/ *adv* **look** ~ **at** schief ansehen

askew /ə'skjuː/ *a & adv* schief

asleep /ə'sliːp/ *a* **be** ~ schlafen; **fall** ~ einschlafen

asparagus /ə'spærəgəs/ *n* Spargel *m*

aspect /'æspekt/ *n* Aspekt *m*

aspersions /ə'spɜːʃnz/ *npl* **cast** ~ **on** schlecht machen

asphalt /'æsfælt/ *n* Asphalt *m*

asphyxia /æ'sfɪksɪə/ *n* Erstickung *f*. ~**te** /æ'sfɪksɪeɪt/ *vt/i* ersticken. ~**tion** /-'eɪʃn/ *n* Erstickung *f*

aspirations /æspə'reɪʃnz/ *npl* Streben *nt*

aspire /ə'spaɪə(r)/ *vi* ~ **to** streben nach

ass /æs/ *n* Esel *m*

assail /ə'seɪl/ *vt* bestürmen. ~**ant** *n* Angreifer(in) *m(f)*

assassin /ə'sæsɪn/ *n* Mörder(in) *m(f)*. ~**ate** *vt* ermorden. ~**ation** /-'neɪʃn/ *n* [politischer] Mord *m*

assault /ə'sɔːlt/ *n* (*Mil*) Angriff *m*; (*Jur*) Körperverletzung *f* □ *vt* [tätlich] angreifen

assemble /ə'sembl/ *vi* sich versammeln □ *vt* versammeln; (*Techn*) montieren

assembly /ə'sembli/ *n* Versammlung *f*; (*Sch*) Andacht *f*; (*Techn*) Montage *f*. ~ **line** *n* Fließband *nt*

assent /ə'sent/ n Zustimmung f
□ vi zustimmen (**to** dat)

assert /ə'sɜ:t/ vt behaupten; ~
oneself sich durchsetzen. ~**ion**
/-ʃn/ n Behauptung f. ~**ive**
/-tɪv/ a be ~**ive** sich durchsetzen
können

assess /ə'ses/ vt bewerten; (fig &
for tax purposes) einschätzen;
schätzen (value). ~**ment** n Einschätzung f; (of tax) Steuerbe-
scheid m

asset /'æset/ n Vorteil m; ~**s** pl
(money) Vermögen nt; (Comm)
Aktiva pl

assiduous /ə'sɪdjʊəs/ a, **-ly** adv
fleißig

assign /ə'saɪn/ vt zuweisen (**to**
dat). ~**ment** n (task) Aufgabe f

assimilate /ə'sɪmɪleɪt/ vt aufnehmen; (integrate) assimilieren

assist /ə'sɪst/ vt/i helfen (+ dat).
~**ance** n Hilfe f. ~**ant** a Hilfs-
□ n Assistent(in) m(f); (in shop)
Verkäufer(in) m(f)

associate¹ /ə'səʊʃɪeɪt/ vt verbinden; (Psych) assoziieren □ vi
~ **with** verkehren mit. ~**ion**
/-'eɪʃn/ n Verband m. **A**~**ion**
football n Fußball m

associate² /ə'səʊʃɪət/ a assozi-
iert □ n Kollege m/-gin f

assort|ed /ə'sɔ:tɪd/ a gemischt.
~**ment** n Mischung f

assume /ə'sju:m/ vt annehmen;
übernehmen (office); ~**ing that**
angenommen, dass

assumption /ə'sʌmpʃn/ n Annahme f; **on the** ~ in der Annahme (**that** dass)

assurance /ə'ʃʊərəns/ n Versicherung f; (confidence) Selbstsicherheit f

assure /ə'ʃʊə(r)/ vt versichern
(s.o. jdm); **I** ~ **you** [**of that**] das
versichere ich Ihnen. ~**d** a sicher

asterisk /'æstərɪsk/ n Sternchen
nt

astern /ə'stɜ:n/ adv achtern

asthma /'æsmə/ n Asthma nt.
~**tic** /-'mætɪk/ a asthmatisch

astonish /ə'stɒnɪʃ/ vt erstaunen.
~**ing** a erstaunlich. ~**ment** n Erstaunen nt

astound /ə'staʊnd/ vt in Erstaunen setzen

astray /ə'streɪ/ adv **go** ~ verloren
gehen; (person:) sich verlieren;
(fig) vom rechten Weg ab-
kommen; **lead** ~ verleiten

astride /ə'straɪd/ adv rittlings
□ prep rittlings auf (+ dat/acc)

astringent /ə'strɪndʒənt/ a ad-
stringierend; (fig) beißend

astrolog|er /ə'strɒlədʒə(r)/ n
Astrologe m/-gin f. ~**y** n Astro-
logie f

astronaut /'æstrənɔ:t/ n Astro-
naut(in) m(f)

astronom|er /ə'strɒnəmə(r)/ n
Astronom m. ~**ical** /æstrə-
'nɒmɪkl/ a astronomisch. ~**y** n
Astronomie f

astute /ə'stju:t/ a scharfsinnig.
~**ness** n Scharfsinn m

asylum /ə'saɪləm/ n Asyl nt;
[**lunatic**] ~ Irrenanstalt f

at /ət, betont æt/ prep an (+ dat/
acc); (with town) in; (price) zu;
(speed) mit; **at the station** am
Bahnhof; **at the beginning/end**
am Anfang/Ende; **at home** zu
Hause; **at John's** bei John; **at
work/the hairdresser's** bei der
Arbeit/beim Friseur; **at school/
the office** in der Schule/im Büro;
at a party/wedding auf einer
Party/Hochzeit; **at one o'clock**
um ein Uhr; **at Christmas/Eas-
ter** zu Weihnachten/Ostern; **at
the age of** im Alter von; **not at
all** gar nicht; **at times** manchmal; **two at a time** zwei auf einmal; **good/bad at languages**
gut/schlecht in Sprachen

ate /et/ see **eat**

atheist /'eɪθɪɪst/ n Atheist(in)
m(f)

athlet|e /'æθli:t/ n Athlet(in)
m(f). ~**ic** /-'letɪk/ a sportlich.
~**ics** /-'letɪks/ n Leichtathletik f

Atlantic /ət'læntɪk/ a & n the ~ [Ocean] der Atlantik

atlas /'ætləs/ n Atlas m

atmospher|e /'ætməsfɪə(r)/ n Atmosphäre f. ~ic /-'ferɪk/ a atmosphärisch

atom /'ætəm/ n Atom m. ~ bomb n Atombombe f

atomic /ə'tɒmɪk/ a Atom-

atone /ə'təʊn/ vi büßen (for für). ~ment n Buße f

atrocious /ə'trəʊʃəs/ a abscheulich

atrocity /ə'trɒsətɪ/ n Gräueltat f

attach /ə'tætʃ/ vt befestigen (to an + dat); beimessen (importance) (to dat). be ~ed to (fig) hängen an (+ dat)

attaché /ə'tæʃeɪ/ n Attaché m. ~ case n Aktenkoffer m

attachment /ə'tætʃmənt/ n Bindung f; (tool) Zubehörteil nt; (additional) Zusatzgerät nt

attack /ə'tæk/ n Angriff m; (Med) Anfall m □ vt/i angreifen. ~er n Angreifer m

attain /ə'teɪn/ vt erreichen; (get) erlangen. ~able /-əbl/ a erreichbar

attempt /ə'tempt/ n Versuch m □ vt versuchen

attend /ə'tend/ vt anwesend sein bei; (go regularly to) besuchen; (take part in) teilnehmen an (+ dat); (accompany) begleiten; (doctor:) behandeln □ vi anwesend sein; (pay attention) aufpassen; ~ to sich kümmern um; (in shop) bedienen. ~ance n Anwesenheit f; (number) Besucherzahl f. ~ant n Wärter(in) m(f); (in car park) Wächter m

attention /ə'tenʃn/ n Aufmerksamkeit f; ~! (Mil) stillgestanden! pay ~ aufpassen; pay ~ to beachten, achten auf (+ acc); need ~ reparaturbedürftig sein; for the ~ of zu Händen von

attentive /ə'tentɪv/ a, -ly adv aufmerksam

attest /ə'test/ vt/i ~ [to] bezeugen

attic /'ætɪk/ n Dachboden m

attire /ə'taɪə(r)/ n Kleidung f □ vt kleiden

attitude /'ætɪtjuːd/ n Haltung f

attorney /ə'tɜːnɪ/ n (Amer: lawyer) Rechtsanwalt m; power of ~ Vollmacht f

attract /ə'trækt/ vt anziehen; erregen (attention); ~ s.o.'s attention jds Aufmerksamkeit auf sich (acc) lenken. ~ion /-kʃn/ n Anziehungskraft f; (charm) Reiz m; (thing) Attraktion f. ~ive /-tɪv/ a, -ly adv attraktiv

attribute¹ /'ætrɪbjuːt/ n Attribut nt

attribut|e² /ə'trɪbjuːt/ vt zuschreiben (to dat). ~ive /-tɪv/ a, -ly adv attributiv

attrition /ə'trɪʃn/ n war of ~ Zermürbungskrieg m

aubergine /'əʊbəʒiːn/ n Aubergine f

auburn /'ɔːbən/ a kastanienbraun

auction /'ɔːkʃn/ n Auktion f Versteigerung f □ vt versteigern. ~eer /-ʃə'nɪə(r)/ n Auktionator m

audacious /ɔː'deɪʃəs/ a, -ly adv verwegen. ~ty /-'dæsɪtɪ/ n Verwegenheit f; (impudence) Dreistigkeit f

audible /'ɔːdəbl/ a, -bly adv hörbar

audience /'ɔːdɪəns/ n Publikum nt; (Theat, TV) Zuschauer pl; (Radio) Zuhörer pl; (meeting) Audienz f

audio /'ɔːdɪəʊ/: ~ typist n Phonotypistin f. ~ visual a audiovisuell

audit /'ɔːdɪt/ n Bücherrevision f □ vt (Comm) prüfen

audition /ɔː'dɪʃn/ n (Theat) Vorsprechen nt; (Mus) Vorspielen nt (for singer) Vorsingen nt □ vi vorsprechen; vorspielen; vorsingen

auditor /'ɔ:dɪtə(r)/ n Buchprüfer m

auditorium /ɔ:dɪ'tɔ:rɪəm/ n Zuschauerraum m

augment /ɔ:g'ment/ vt vergrößern

augur /'ɔ:gə(r)/ vi ~ **well/ill** etwas/nichts Gutes verheißen

august /ɔ:'gʌst/ a hoheitsvoll

August /'ɔ:gəst/ n August m

aunt /ɑ:nt/ n Tante f

au pair /əʊ'peə(r)/ n ~ **[girl]** Aupairmädchen nt

aura /'ɔ:rə/ n Fluidum nt

auspices /'ɔ:spɪsɪz/ npl (protection) Schirmherrschaft f

auspicious /ɔ:'spɪʃəs/ a günstig; (occasion) freudig

auster|e /ɒ'stɪə(r)/ a streng; (simple) nüchtern. ~**ity** /-'terɑ:tɪ/ n Strenge f; (hardship) Entbehrung f

Australia /ɒ'streɪlɪə/ n Australien nt. ~**n** a australisch □ n Australier(in) m(f)

Austria /'ɒstrɪə/ n Österreich nt. ~**n** a österreichisch □ n Österreicher(in) m(f)

authentic /ɔ:'θentɪk/ a echt, authentisch. ~**ate** vt beglaubigen. ~**ity** /-'tɪsɑtɪ/ n Echtheit f

author /'ɔ:θə(r)/ n Schriftsteller m, Autor m; (of document) Verfasser m

authoritarian /ɔ:θɒrɪ'teərɪən/ a autoritär

authoritative /ɔ:'θɒrɪtətɪv/ a maßgebend; **be ~** Autorität haben

authority /ɔ:'θɒrɪtɪ/ n Autorität f; (public) Behörde f; **in ~** verantwortlich

authorization /ɔ:θərɑɪ'zeɪʃn/ n Ermächtigung f

authorize /'ɔ:θərɑɪz/ vt ermächtigen ⟨s.o.⟩; genehmigen ⟨sth⟩

autobi|ography /ɔ:tə-/ n Autobiographie f

autocratic /ɔ:tə'krætɪk/ a autokratisch

autograph /'ɔ:tə-/ n Autogramm nt

automatic /ɔ:tə'mætɪk/ a, **-ally** adv automatisch □ n (car) Fahrzeug nt mit Automatikgetriebe; (washing machine) Waschautomat m

automation /ɔ:tə'meɪʃn/ n Automation f

automobile /'ɔ:təməbi:l/ n Auto nt

autonom|ous /ɔ:'tɒnəməs/ a autonom. ~**y** n Autonomie f

autopsy /'ɔ:tɒpsɪ/ n Autopsie f

autumn /'ɔ:təm/ n Herbst m. ~**al** /-'tʌmnl/ a herbstlich

auxiliary /ɔ:g'zɪlɪərɪ/ a Hilfs- □ n Helfer(in) m(f), Hilfskraft f

avail /ə'veɪl/ n **to no ~** vergeblich □ vi ~ **oneself of** Gebrauch machen von

available /ə'veɪləbl/ a verfügbar; (obtainable) erhältlich

avalanche /'ævəlɑ:nʃ/ n Lawine f

avaric|e /'ævərɪs/ n Habsucht f. ~**ious** /-'rɪʃəs/ a habgierig, habsüchtig

avenge /ə'vendʒ/ vt rächen

avenue /'ævənju:/ n Allee f

average /'ævərɪdʒ/ a Durchschnitts-, durchschnittlich □ n Durchschnitt m; **on ~** im Durchschnitt, durchschnittlich □ vt durchschnittlich schaffen □ vi ~ **out at** im Durchschnitt ergeben

avers|e /ə'vɜ:s/ a **not be ~e to** sth etw (dat) nicht abgeneigt sein. ~**ion** /-ʃn/ n Abneigung f (**to** gegen)

avert /ə'vɜ:t/ vt abwenden

aviary /'eɪvɪərɪ/ n Vogelhaus nt

aviation /eɪvɪ'eɪʃn/ n Luftfahrt f

avid /'ævɪd/ a gierig (**for** nach); (keen) eifrig

avocado /ævə'kɑ:dəʊ/ n Avocado f

avoid /ə'vɔɪd/ vt vermeiden; ~ **s.o.** jdm aus dem Weg gehen.

~able /-əbl/ a vermeidbar.
~ance n Vermeidung f

await /ə'weɪt/ vt warten auf (+
acc)

awake /ə'weɪk/ a wach; **wide ~**
hellwach □vi (pt **awoke**, pp
awoken) erwachen

awaken /ə'weɪkn/ vt wecken □ vi
erwachen. **~ing** n Erwachen nt

award /ə'wɔ:d/ n Auszeichnung
f; (prize) Preis m □ vt zuerkennen
(**to s.o.** dat); verleihen (prize)

aware /ə'weə(r)/ a **become ~** gewahr werden (**of** gen); **be ~ that**
wissen, dass. **~ness** n Bewusstsein nt

awash /ə'wɒʃ/ a **be ~** unter
Wasser stehen

away /ə'weɪ/ adv weg, fort; (absent) abwesend; **be ~** nicht da
sein; **far ~** weit weg; **four kilometres ~** vier Kilometer
entfernt; **play ~** (Sport) auswärts
spielen; **go/stay ~** weggehen/
bleiben. **~ game** n Auswärtsspiel
nt

awe /ɔ:/ n Ehrfurcht f

awful /'ɔ:fl/ a, **-ly** adv furchtbar

awhile /ə'waɪl/ adv eine Weile

awkward /'ɔ:kwəd/ a schwierig;
(clumsy) ungeschickt; (embarrassing) peinlich; (inconvenient)
ungünstig. **~ly** adv ungeschickt;
(embarrassedly) verlegen

awning /'ɔ:nɪŋ/ n Markise f

awoke(n) /ə'wəʊk(n)/ see **awake**

awry /ə'raɪ/ adv schief

axe /æks/ n Axt f □ vt (pres p ax-
ing) streichen; (dismiss) entlassen

axis /'æksɪs/ n (pl **axes** /-si:z/)
Achse f

axle /'æksl/ n (Techn) Achse f

ay[e] /aɪ/ adv ja □ n Jastimme f

B

B /bi:/ n (Mus) H nt

BA abbr of **Bachelor of Arts**

babble /'bæbl/ vi plappern;
(stream:) plätschern

baboon /bə'bu:n/ n Pavian m

baby /'beɪbɪ/ n Baby nt; (Amer,
fam) Schätzchen f

baby: **~ carriage** n (Amer) Kinderwagen m. **~ish** a kindisch.
~-minder n Tagesmutter f. **~-
sit** vi babysitten. **~-sitter** n
Babysitter m

bachelor /'bætʃələ(r)/ n Junggeselle m; **B ~ of Arts/Science**
Bakkalaureus Artium/Scienti-
um

bacillus /bə'sɪləs/ n (pl **-lli**) Bazillus m

back /bæk/ n Rücken m; (reverse)
Rückseite f; (of chair) Rü-
ckenlehne f; (Sport) Verteidiger
m; **at/**(Auto) **in the ~** hinten; **on
the ~** auf der Rückseite; **~ to
front** verkehrt; **at the ~ of beyond** am Ende der Welt □ a Hin-
ter- □ adv zurück; **~ here/there**
hier/da hinten; **~ at home** zu
Hause; **go/pay ~** zurückgehen/
-zahlen □ vt (support) unterstützen; (with money) finanzieren; (Auto) zurücksetzen;
(Betting) [Geld] setzen auf (+
acc); (cover the back of) mit einer
Verstärkung versehen □ vi (Auto)
zurücksetzen. **~ down** vi klein
beigeben. **~ in** vi rückwärts hi-
neinfahren. **~ out** vi rückwärts
hinaus-/herausfahren; (fig) aussteigen (**of** aus). **~ up** vt unterstützen; (confirm) bestätigen □ vi
(Auto) zurücksetzen

back: **~ache** n Rückenschmerzen
pl. **~biting** n gehässiges Gerede
nt. **~bone** n Rückgrat nt. **~chat**
n Widerrede f. **~comb** vt tou-
pieren. **~date** vt rückdatieren;
~dated to rückwirkend von. **~
'door** n Hintertür f

backer /'bækə(r)/ n Geldgeber m

back: **~fire** vi (Auto) fehlzünden;
(fig) fehlschlagen. **~ground** n
Hintergrund m; **family
~ground** Familienverhältnisse
pl. **~hand** n (Sport) Rückhand f.

~handed a ⟨compliment⟩ zweifelhaft. **~hander** n ⟨Sport⟩ Rückhandschlag m; ⟨fam: bribe⟩ Schmiergeld nt

backing /'bækɪŋ/ n ⟨support⟩ Unterstützung f; ⟨material⟩ Verstärkung f

back: **~lash** n ⟨fig⟩ Gegenschlag m. **~log** n Rückstand m ⟨of an + dat⟩. **~'seat** n Rücksitz m. **~side** n ⟨fam⟩ Hintern m. **~stage** adv hinter der Bühne. **~stroke** n Rückenschwimmen nt. **~up** n Unterstützung f; ⟨Amer: traffic jam⟩ Stau m

backward /'bækwəd/ a zurückgeblieben; ⟨country⟩ rückständig □ adv rückwärts. **~s** rückwärts; **~s and forwards** hin und her

back: **~water** n ⟨fig⟩ unbenührtes Fleckchen nt. **~'yard** n Hinterhof m; **not in my ~ yard** ⟨fam⟩ nicht vor meiner Haustür

bacon /'beɪkn/ n [Schinken]speck m

bacteria /bæk'tɪərɪə/ npl Bakterien pl

bad /bæd/ a ⟨worse, worst⟩ schlecht; ⟨serious⟩ schwer, schlimm; ⟨naughty⟩ unartig; **~ language** gemeine Ausdrucksweise f; **feel ~** sich schlecht fühlen; ⟨feel guilty⟩ ein schlechtes Gewissen haben; **go ~** schlecht werden

bade /bæd/ see bid²

badge /bædʒ/ n Abzeichen nt

badger /'bædʒə(r)/ n Dachs m □ vt plagen

badly /'bædlɪ/ adv schlecht; ⟨seriously⟩ schwer; **~ off** schlecht gestellt; **~ behaved** unerzogen; **want ~** sich ⟨dat⟩ sehnsüchtig wünschen; **need ~** dringend brauchen

bad-'mannered a mit schlechten Manieren

badminton /'bædmɪntən/ n Federball m

bad-'tempered a schlecht gelaunt

baffle /'bæfl/ vt verblüffen

bag /bæg/ n Tasche f; ⟨of paper⟩ Tüte f; ⟨pouch⟩ Beutel m; **~s** of ⟨fam⟩ jede Menge □ vt ⟨fam: reserve⟩ in Beschlag nehmen

baggage /'bægɪdʒ/ n [Reise]gepäck nt

baggy /'bægɪ/ a ⟨clothes⟩ ausgebeult

'bagpipes npl Dudelsack m

bail /beɪl/ n Kaution f; **on ~** gegen Kaution □ vt **~ s.o. out** jdn gegen Kaution freibekommen; ⟨fig⟩ jdm aus der Patsche helfen. **~ out** ⟨Naut⟩ ausschöpfen □ vi ⟨Aviat⟩ abspringen

bailiff /'beɪlɪf/ n Gerichtsvollzieher m; ⟨of estate⟩ Gutsverwalter m

bait /beɪt/ n Köder m □ vt mit einem Köder versehen; ⟨fig: torment⟩ reizen

bake /beɪk/ vt/i backen

baker /'beɪkə(r)/ n Bäcker m; **~'s [shop]** Bäckerei f. **~y** n Bäckerei f

baking /'beɪkɪŋ/ n Backen m. **~-powder** n Backpulver nt. **~-tin** n Backform f

balance /'bæləns/ n ⟨equilibrium⟩ Gleichgewicht nt, Balance f; ⟨scales⟩ Waage f; ⟨Comm⟩ Saldo m; ⟨outstanding sum⟩ Restbetrag m; **[bank] ~** Kontostand m; **in the ~** ⟨fig⟩ in der Schwebe □ vt balancieren; ⟨equalize⟩ ausgleichen; ⟨Comm⟩ abschließen ⟨books⟩ □ vi balancieren; ⟨fig & Comm⟩ sich ausgleichen. **~d** a ausgewogen. **~ sheet** n Bilanz f

balcony /'bælkənɪ/ n Balkon m

bald /bɔːld/ a ⟨-er, -est⟩ kahl; ⟨person⟩ kahlköpfig; **go ~** eine Glatze bekommen

balderdash /'bɔːldədæʃ/ n Unsinn m

bald|ing /'bɔːldɪŋ/ a **be ~ing** eine Glatze bekommen. **~ly** adv unverblümt. **~ness** n Kahlköpfigkeit f

bale /beɪl/ n Ballen m

baleful /'beɪlfl/ a, -ly adv böse

balk /bɔ:lk/ vt vereiteln □ vi ~ **at** zurückschrecken vor (+ dat)

Balkans /'bɔ:lknz/ npl Balkan m

ball¹ /bɔ:l/ n Ball m; (Billiards, Croquet) Kugel f; (of yarn) Knäuel s & nt; on the ~ (fam) auf Draht

ball² n (dance) Ball m

ballad /'bæləd/ n Ballade f

ballast /'bæləst/ n Ballast m

ball-'bearing n Kugellager nt

ballerina /bælə'ri:nə/ n Ballerina f

ballet /'bæleɪ/ n Ballett nt. ~-dancer n Ballettänzer(in) m(f)

ballistic /bə'lɪstɪk/ a ballistisch. ~s n Ballistik f

balloon /bə'lu:n/ n Luftballon m; (Aviat) Ballon m

ballot /'bælət/ n [geheime] Wahl f; (on issue) [geheime] Abstimmung f. ~-box n Wahlurne f. ~-paper n Stimmzettel m

ball: ~-point ['pen] n Kugelschreiber m. ~room n Ballsaal m

balm /ba:m/ n Balsam m

balmy /'ba:mɪ/ a (-ier, -iest) a sanft; (fam: crazy) verrückt

Baltic /'bɔ:ltɪk/ a & n the ~ [Sea] die Ostsee

balustrade /bælə'streɪd/ n Balustrade f

bamboo /bæm'bu:/ n Bambus m

bamboozle /bæm'bu:zl/ vt (fam) übers Ohr hauen

ban /bæn/ n Verbot nt □ vt (pt/pp banned) verbieten

banal /bə'nɑ:l/ a banal. ~ity /-'ælətɪ/ n Banalität f

banana /bə'nɑ:nə/ n Banane f

band /bænd/ n Band nt; (stripe) Streifen m; (group) Schar f; (Mus) Kapelle f □ vi ~ **together** sich zusammenschließen

bandage /'bændɪdʒ/ n Verband m; (for support) Bandage f □ vt verbinden; bandagieren (limb)

b. & b. abbr of **bed and breakfast**

bandit /'bændɪt/ n Bandit m

band: ~**stand** n Musikpavillon m. ~**wagon** n jump on the ~wagon (fig) sich einer erfolgreichen Sache anschließen

bandy¹ /'bændɪ/ vt (pt/pp -ied) wechseln (words)

bandy² a (-ier, -iest) be ~ O-Beine haben. ~**legged** a O-beinig

bang /bæŋ/ n (noise) Knall m; (blow) Schlag m □ adv go ~ knallen □ int bums! peng! □ vt knallen; (shut noisily) zuknallen; (strike) schlagen auf (+ acc); ~ one's head sich (dat) den Kopf stoßen (on an + acc) □ vi schlagen; (door:) zuknallen

banger /'bæŋə(r)/ n (firework) Knallfrosch m; (fam: sausage) Wurst f; old ~ (fam: car) Klapperkiste f

bangle /'bæŋgl/ n Armreifen m

banish /'bænɪʃ/ vt verbannen

banisters /'bænɪstəz/ npl [Treppen]geländer nt

banjo /'bændʒəʊ/ n Banjo nt

bank¹ /bæŋk/ n (of river) Ufer nt; (slope) Hang m □ vi (Aviat) in die Kurve gehen

bank² n Bank f □ vt einzahlen; ~ **with** ein Konto haben bei. ~ **on** vt sich verlassen auf (+ acc)

bank account n Bankkonto nt

banker /'bæŋkə(r)/ n Bankier m

bank: ~ **holiday** n gesetzlicher Feiertag m. ~**ing** n Bankwesen nt. ~**note** n Banknote f

bankrupt /'bæŋkrʌpt/ a bankrott; go ~ Bankrott machen □ n Bankrotteur m □ vt Bankrott machen. ~**cy** n Bankrott m

banner /'bænə(r)/ n Banner nt; (carried by demonstrators) Transparent nt, Spruchband nt

banns /bænz/ npl (Relig) Aufgebot nt

banquet /'bæŋkwɪt/ n Bankett nt

banter /'bæntə(r)/ n Spöttelei f

bap /bæp/ n weiches Brötchen nt

baptism /'bæptɪzm/ n Taufe f

Baptist /'bæptɪst/ n Baptist(in) m(f)

baptize /bæp'taɪz/ vt taufen

bar /ba:(r)/ n Stange f; (of cage) [Gitter]stab m; (of gold) Barren m; (of chocolate) Tafel f; (of soap) Stück nt; (long) Riegel m; (café) Bar f; (counter) Theke f; (Mus) Takt m; (fig: obstacle) Hindernis nt; **parallel ~s** (Sport) Barren m; **be called to the ~** (Jur) als plädierender Anwalt zugelassen werden; **behind ~s** (fam) hinter Gittern □ vt (pt/pp barred) versperren (way, door); ausschließen (person) □ prep außer; **~ none** ohne Ausnahme

barbarian /ba:'beərɪən/ n Barbar m

barbar|ic /ba:'bærɪk/ a barbarisch. **~ity** n Barbarei f. **~ous** /'ba:bərəs/ a barbarisch

barbecue /'ba:bɪkju:/ n Grill m; (party) Grillfest nt □ vt (im Freien) grillen

barbed /ba:bd/ a **~ wire** Stacheldraht m

barber /'ba:bə(r)/ n [Herren]friseur m

barbiturate /ba:'bɪtjʊrət/ n Barbiturat nt

'bar code n Strichkode m

bare /beə(r)/ a (-r, -st) nackt, bloß; (tree) kahl; (empty) leer; (mere) bloß □ vt entblößen; fletschen (teeth)

bare: **~back** adv ohne Sattel. **~faced** a schamlos. **~foot** adv barfuß. **~headed** a mit unbedecktem Kopf

barely /'beəlɪ/ adv kaum

bargain /'ba:gɪn/ n (agreement) Geschäft nt; (good buy) Gelegenheitskauf m; **into the ~** noch dazu; **make a ~** sich einigen (□ vi handeln; (haggle) feilschen; **~ for** (expect) rechnen mit

barge /ba:dʒ/ n Lastkahn m; (towed) Schleppkahn m □ vi **~ in** (fam) hereinplatzen

baritone /'bærɪtəʊn/ n Bariton m

bark¹ /ba:k/ n (of tree) Rinde f

bark² n Bellen nt □ vi bellen

barley /'ba:lɪ/ n Gerste f

bar: **~maid** n Schankmädchen nt. **~man** n Barmann m

barmy /'ba:mɪ/ a (fam) verrückt

barn /ba:n/ n Scheune f

barometer /bə'rɒmɪtə(r)/ n Barometer nt

baron /'bærn/ n Baron m. **~ess** n Baronin f

baroque /bə'rɒk/ a barock □ n Barock nt

barracks /'bærəks/ npl Kaserne f

barrage /'bæra:ʒ/ n (in river) Wehr nt; (Mil) Sperrfeuer nt; (fig) Hagel m

barrel /'bærl/ n Fass nt; (of gun) Lauf m; (of cannon) Rohr nt. **~organ** n Drehorgel f

barren /'bærn/ a unfruchtbar; (landscape) öde

barricade /bærɪ'keɪd/ n Barrikade f □ vt verbarrikadieren

barrier /'bærɪə(r)/ n Barriere f; (across road) Schranke f; (Rail) Sperre f; (fig) Hindernis nt

barring /'ba:rɪŋ/ prep **~ accidents** wenn alles gut geht

barrister /'bærɪstə(r)/ n [plädierender] Rechtsanwalt m

barrow /'bærəʊ/ n Karre f, Karren m. **~ boy** n Straßenhändler m

barter /'ba:tə(r)/ vt tauschen (for gegen)

base /beɪs/ n Fuß m; (fig) Basis f; (Mil) Stützpunkt m □ a gemein; (metal) unedel □ vt stützen (on auf + acc); **be ~d on** basieren auf (+ dat)

base: **~ball** n Baseball m. **~less** a unbegründet. **~ment** n Kellergeschoss nt. **~ment flat** n Kellerwohnung f

bash /bæʃ/ n Schlag m; **have a ~!** (fam) probier es mal! □ vt hauen; (dent) einbeulen; **~ed in** a verbeult

bashful /'bæʃfl/ a, -ly adv
schüchtern

basic /'beɪsɪk/ a Grund-;
(fundamental) grundlegend; (essential) wesentlich; (unadorned)
einfach; **the ~s** das Wesentliche.
~ally adv grundsätzlich

basil /'bæzl/ n Basilikum nt

basilica /bə'zɪlɪkə/ n Basilika f

basin /'beɪsn/ n Becken nt; (for
washing) Waschbecken nt; (for
food) Schüssel f

basis /'beɪsɪs/ n (pl -ses /-siːz/)
Basis f

bask /bɑːsk/ vi sich sonnen

basket /'bɑːskɪt/ n Korb m. **~ball**
n Basketball m

Basle /bɑːl/ n Basel nt

bass /beɪs/ a Bass-; **~ voice**
Bassstimme f □ n Bass m; (person) Bassist m

bassoon /bə'suːn/ n Fagott nt

bastard /'bɑːstəd/ n (sl) Schuft m

baste¹ /beɪst/ vt (sew) heften

baste² vt (Culin) begießen

bastion /'bæstɪən/ n Bastion f

bat¹ /bæt/ n Schläger m; **off one's
own ~** (fam) auf eigene Faust
□ vt (pt/pp batted) schlagen; **not
~ an eyelid** (fig) nicht mit der
Wimper zucken

bat² n (Zool) Fledermaus f

batch /bætʃ/ n (of people) Gruppe
f; (of papers) Stoß m; (of goods)
Sendung f; (of bread) Schub m

bated /'beɪtɪd/ a **with ~ breath**
mit angehaltenem Atem

bath /bɑːθ/ n (pl ~s /bɑːðz/) Bad
nt; (tub) Badewanne f; **~s** pl Ba-
deanstalt f; **have a ~** baden
□ vt/i baden

bathe /beɪð/ n Bad nt □ vt/i
baden. **~r** n Badende(r) m/f

bathing /'beɪðɪŋ/ n Baden nt. **~
cap** n Bademütze f. **~costume**
n Badeanzug m

bath: **~mat** n Bademate f.
~robe n (Amer) Bademantel m.
~room n Badezimmer nt. **~
towel** n Badetuch nt

baton /'bætn/ n (Mus) Taktstock
m; (Mil) Stab m

battalion /bə'tælɪən/ n Bataillon
nt

batten /'bætn/ n Latte f

batter /'bætə(r)/ n (Culin) flüs-
siger Teig m □ vt schlagen. **~ed** a
(car) verbeult; (wife) misshandelt

battery /'bætərɪ/ n Batterie f

battle /'bætl/ n Schlacht f; (fig)
Kampf m □ vi (fig) kämpfen (for
um)

battle: **~axe** n (fam) Drachen m.
~field n Schlachtfeld nt. **~ship**
n Schlachtschiff nt

batty /'bætɪ/ a (fam) verrückt

Bavaria /bə'veərɪə/ n Bayern nt.
~n a bayrisch □ n Bayer(in) m(f)

bawdy /'bɔːdɪ/ a (-ier, -iest) derb

bawl /bɔːl/ vt/i brüllen

bay¹ /beɪ/ n (Geog) Bucht f; (Archit) Erker m

bay² n **keep at ~** fern halten

bay³ n (horse) Braune(r) m

bay⁴ n (Bot) [echter] Lorbeer m.
~leaf n Lorbeerblatt nt

bayonet /'beɪənet/ n Bajonett nt

bay 'window n Erkerfenster nt

bazaar /bə'zɑː(r)/ n Basar m

BC abbr (before Christ) v. Chr.

be /biː/ vi (pres am, are, is, pl are;
pt was, pl were; pp been) sein;
(lie) liegen; (stand) stehen; (cost)
kosten; **he is a teacher** er ist
Lehrer; **be quiet!** sei still! **I am
cold/hot** mir ist kalt/heiß; **how
are you?** wie geht es Ihnen? **I am
well** mir geht es gut; **there is/
are** es gibt; **what do you want
to be?** was willst du werden? **I
have been to Vienna** ich bin in
Wien gewesen; **has the postman
been?** war der Briefträger schon
da? **it's hot, isn't it?** es ist heiß,
nicht [wahr]? **you are coming
too, aren't you?** du kommst mit,
nicht [wahr]? **it's yours, is it?**
das gehört also Ihnen? **yes he is/I
am** ja; (negating previous statement) doch; **three and three are**

six drei und drei macht sechs □ *v aux* ~ **reading/going** lesen/ gehen; **I am coming/staying ich komme/bleibe; what is he doing?** was macht er? **I am being lazy** ich faulenze; **I was thinking of you** ich dachte an dich; **you were going to . . .** du wolltest . . .; **I am to stay ich soll bleiben; you are not to . . .** du darfst nicht . . .; **you are to do that immediately** das musst du sofort machen □ *passive* werden; **be attacked/deceived** überfallen/betrogen werden

beach /biːtʃ/ *n* Strand *m*. ~**wear** *n* Strandkleidung *f*

beacon /ˈbiːkn/ *n* Leuchtfeuer *nt*; (*Naut, Aviat*) Bake *f*

bead /biːd/ *n* Perle *f*

beak /biːk/ *n* Schnabel *m*

beaker /ˈbiːkə(r)/ *n* Becher *m*

beam /biːm/ *n* Balken *m*; (*of light*) Strahl *m* □ *vi* strahlen. ~**ing** *a* [freuden]strahlend

bean /biːn/ *n* Bohne *f*; **spill the** ~**s** (*fam*) alles ausplaudern

bear[1] /beə(r)/ *n* Bär *m*

bear[2] *v* (*pt* bore, *pp* borne) tragen; (*endure*) ertragen; gebären (*child*); ~ **right** sich rechts halten. ~**able** /-əbl/ *a* erträglich

beard /biəd/ *n* Bart *m*. ~**ed** *a* bärtig

bearer /ˈbeərə(r)/ *n* Träger *m*; (*of news, cheque*) Überbringer *m*; (*of passport*) Inhaber(in) *m(f)*

bearing /ˈbeərɪŋ/ *n* Haltung *f*; (*Techn*) Lager *nt*; **have a** ~ **on** von Belang sein für; **get one's** ~**s** sich orientieren; **lose one's** ~**s** die Orientierung verlieren

beast /biːst/ *n* Tier *nt*; (*fam: person*) Biest *nt*

beastly /ˈbiːstlɪ/ *a* (-ier, -iest) (*fam*) scheußlich; (*person*) gemein

beat /biːt/ *n* Schlag *m*; (*of policeman*) Runde *f*; (*rhythm*) Takt *m* □ *vt/i* (*pt* beat, *pp* beaten) schlagen; (*thrash*) verprügeln;

klopfen (*carpet*); (*hammer*) hämmern (**on** an + *acc*); ~ **a retreat** (*Mil*) sich zurückziehen; ~ **it!** (*fam*) hau ab! ~ **s me** (*fam*) das begreife ich nicht. ~ **up** *vt* zusammenschlagen

beat|en /ˈbiːtn/ *a* **off the** ~**en track** abseits. ~**ing** *n* Prügel *pl*

beautician /bjuːˈtɪʃn/ *n* Kosmetikerin *f*

beauti|ful /ˈbjuːtɪfl/ *a*, **-ly** *adv* schön. ~**fy** /-faɪ/ *vt* (*pt/pp* -ied) verschönern

beauty /ˈbjuːtɪ/ *n* Schönheit *f*. ~ **parlour** *n* Kosmetiksalon *m*. ~ **spot** *n* Schönheitsfleck *m*; (*place*) landschaftlich besonders reizvolles Fleckchen *nt*

beaver /ˈbiːvə(r)/ *n* Biber *m*

became /bɪˈkeɪm/ *see* become

because /bɪˈkɒz/ *conj* weil □ *adv* ~ **of** wegen (+ *gen*)

beckon /ˈbekn/ *vt/i* ~ **[to]** herbeiwinken

become /bɪˈkʌm/ *vt/i* (*pt* became, *pp* become) werden. ~**ing** *a* (*clothes*) kleidsam

bed /bed/ *n* Bett *nt*; (*layer*) Schicht *f*; (*of flowers*) Beet *nt*; **in** ~ im Bett; **go to** ~ ins *od* zu Bett gehen; ~ **and breakfast** Zimmer mit Frühstück. ~**clothes** *npl*, ~**ding** *n* Bettzeug *nt*

bedlam /ˈbedləm/ *n* Chaos *nt*

bedpan *n* Bettpfanne *f*

bedraggled /bɪˈdrægld/ *a* nass und verschmutzt

bed: ~**ridden** *a* bettlägerig. ~**room** *n* Schlafzimmer *nt*

bedside *n* **at his** ~ an seinem Bett. ~ **lamp** *n* Nachttischlampe *f*. ~ **rug** *n* Bettvorleger *m*. ~ **table** *n* Nachttisch *m*

bed: ~**sitter** *n*, ~**sitting-room** *n* Wohnschlafzimmer *nt*. ~**spread** *n* Tagesdecke *f*. ~**time** *n* **at** ~**time** vor dem Schlafengehen

bee /biː/ *n* Biene *f*

beech /biːtʃ/ *n* Buche *f*

beef /biːf/ n Rindfleisch nt.
~burger n Hamburger m
bee: **~hive** n Bienenstock m. **~keeper** n Imker(in) m(f).
~keeping n Bienenzucht f. **~line** n **make a ~line for** (fam) zusteuern auf (+ acc)

been /biːn/ see be

beer /bɪə(r)/ n Bier nt.

beet /biːt/ n (Amer: beetroot) rote Bete f; **[sugar] ~** Zuckerrübe f

beetle /ˈbiːtl/ n Käfer m

beetroot n rote Bete f

before /bɪˈfɔː(r)/ prep vor (+ dat/acc); **the day ~ yesterday** vorgestern; (already) schon; **~ long** bald □ adv vorher; (already) schon; **never ~** noch nie; **~ that** davor □ conj (time) ehe, bevor. **~hand** adv vorher, im Voraus

befriend /bɪˈfrend/ vt sich anfreunden mit

beg /beg/ v (pt/pp begged) □ vi betteln □ vt (entreat) anflehen; (ask) bitten (for um)

began /bɪˈɡæn/ see begin

beggar /ˈbeɡə(r)/ n Bettler(in) m(f); (fam) Kerl m

begin /bɪˈɡɪn/ vt/i (pt began, pp begun, pres p beginning) anfangen, beginnen; **to ~ with** anfangs. **~ner** n Anfänger(in) m(f). **~ning** n Anfang m, Beginn m

begonia /bɪˈɡəʊnɪə/ n Begonie f

begrudge /bɪˈɡrʌdʒ/ vt ~ s.o. sth jdm etw missgönnen

beguile /bɪˈɡaɪl/ vt betören

begun /bɪˈɡʌn/ see begin

behalf /bɪˈhɑːf/ n **on ~ of** im Namen von; **on my ~** meinetwegen

behave /bɪˈheɪv/ vi sich verhalten; **~ oneself** sich benehmen

behaviour /bɪˈheɪvjə(r)/ n Verhalten nt; **good/bad ~** gutes/schlechtes Benehmen nt; **~ pattern** Verhaltensweise f

behead /bɪˈhed/ vt enthaupten

beheld /bɪˈheld/ see behold

behind /bɪˈhaɪnd/ prep hinter (+ dat/acc); **be ~ sth** hinter etw

(dat) stecken □ adv hinten; (late) im Rückstand; **a long way ~** weit zurück; **in the car ~** im Wagen dahinter □ n (fam) Hintern m. **~hand** adv im Rückstand

behold /bɪˈhəʊld/ vt (pt/pp beheld) (liter) sehen

beholden /bɪˈhəʊldn/ a verbunden (to dat)

beige /beɪʒ/ a beige

being /ˈbiːɪŋ/ n Dasein nt; **living ~** Lebewesen nt; **come into ~** entstehen

belated /bɪˈleɪtɪd/ a, **-ly** adv verspätet

belch /beltʃ/ vi rülpsen □ vt **~ out** ausstoßen (smoke)

belfry /ˈbelfrɪ/ n Glockenstube f; (tower) Glockenturm m

Belgian /ˈbeldʒən/ a belgisch □ n Belgier(in) m(f)

Belgium /ˈbeldʒəm/ n Belgien nt

belief /bɪˈliːf/ n Glaube m

believable /bɪˈliːvəbl/ a glaubhaft

believe /bɪˈliːv/ vt/i glauben (s.o. jdm; **in** an + acc). **~r** n (Relig) Gläubige(r) m/f

belittle /bɪˈlɪtl/ vt herabsetzen

bell /bel/ n Glocke f; (on door) Klingel f

belligerent /bɪˈlɪdʒərənt/ a Krieg führend; (aggressive) streitlustig

bellow /ˈbeləʊ/ vt/i brüllen

bellows /ˈbeləʊz/ npl Blasebalg m

belly /ˈbelɪ/ n Bauch m

belong /bɪˈlɒŋ/ vi gehören (to dat); (be member) angehören (to dat). **~ings** npl Sachen pl

beloved /bɪˈlʌvɪd/ a geliebt □ n Geliebte(r) m/f

below /bɪˈləʊ/ prep unter (+ dat/acc) □ adv unten; (Naut) unter Deck

belt /belt/ n Gürtel m; (area) Zone f; (Techn) Riemen m □ vi (fam: rush) rasen □ vt (fam: hit) hauen

bemused /bɪˈmjuːzd/ a verwirrt

bench /bentʃ/ n Bank f; (work-) Werkbank f; the B ~ (Jur) ≈ die Richter pl

bend /bend/ n Biegung f; (in road) Kurve f; round the ~ (fam) verrückt □ v (pt/pp bent) □ vt biegen; beugen (arm, leg) □ vi sich bücken; (thing:) sich biegen; (road:) eine Biegung machen. ~ **down** vi sich bücken. ~ **over** vi sich vornüberbeugen

beneath /bɪˈniːθ/ prep unter (+ dat/acc); ~ **him** (fig) unter seiner Würde; ~ **contempt** unter aller Würde □ adv darunter

benediction /benɪˈdɪkʃn/ n (Relig) Segen m

benefactor /ˈbenɪfæktə(r)/ n Wohltäter(in) m(f)

beneficial /benɪˈfɪʃl/ a nützlich

beneficiary /benɪˈfɪʃərɪ/ n Begünstigte(r) m/f

benefit /ˈbenɪfɪt/ n Vorteil m; (allowance) Unterstützung f; (insurance) Leistung f; **sickness** ~ Krankengeld nt □ v (pt/pp -fited, pres p -fiting) □ vt nützen (+ dat) □ vi profitieren (from von)

benevolen|ce /bɪˈnevələns/ n Wohlwollen nt. ~**t** a, -ly adv wohlwollend

benign /bɪˈnaɪn/ a, -ly adv gütig; (Med) gutartig

bent /bent/ see bend □ a (person) gebeugt; (distorted) verbogen; (fam:dishonest) korrupt; be ~ on doing sth darauf erpicht sein, etw zu tun □ n Hang m, Neigung f (for zu); **artistic** ~ künstlerische Ader f

be|queath /bɪˈkwiːð/ vt vermachen (to dat). ~**quest** /-ˈkwest/ n Vermächtnis nt

bereave|d /bɪˈriːvd/ n the ~**d** pl die Hinterbliebenen. ~**ment** n Trauerfall m; (state) Trauer f

bereft /bɪˈreft/ a ~ **of** beraubt (+ gen)

beret /ˈbereɪ/ n Baskenmütze f

Berne /bɜːn/ n Bern nt

berry /ˈberɪ/ n Beere f

berserk /bəˈsɜːk/ a **go** ~ wild werden

berth /bɜːθ/ n (on ship) [Schlaf-]koje f; (ship's anchorage) Liegeplatz m; **give a wide** ~ **to** (fam) einen großen Bogen machen um □ vi anlegen

beseech /bɪˈsiːtʃ/ vt (pt/pp beseeched or besought) anflehen

beside /bɪˈsaɪd/ prep neben (+ dat/acc); ~ **oneself** außer sich (dat)

besides /bɪˈsaɪdz/ prep außer (+ dat) □ adv außerdem

besiege /bɪˈsiːdʒ/ vt belagern

besought /bɪˈsɔːt/ see beseech

bespoke /bɪˈspəʊk/ a (suit) maßgeschneidert

best /best/ a & n beste(r,s); **the** ~ der/die/das Beste; **at** ~ bestenfalls; **all the** ~! alles Gute! **do one's** ~ sein Bestes tun; **the** ~ **part of a year** fast ein Jahr; **to the** ~ **of my knowledge** so viel ich weiß; **make the** ~ **of it** das Beste daraus machen □ adv am besten; **as** ~ **I could** so gut ich konnte. ~**man** n ≈ Trauzeuge m

bestow /bɪˈstəʊ/ vt schenken (on dat)

best-seller n Bestseller m

bet /bet/ n Wette f □ v (pt/pp bet or betted) □ vt ~ **s.o. £5** mit jdm um £5 wetten □ vi wetten; ~ **on** [Geld] setzen auf (+ acc)

betray /bɪˈtreɪ/ vt verraten. ~**al** n Verrat m

better /ˈbetə(r)/ a besser; **get** ~ sich bessern; (after illness) sich erholen □ adv besser; ~ **off** besser dran; **not** ~ **liber nicht; all the** ~ umso besser; **the sooner the** ~ je eher, desto besser; **think** ~ **of sth** sich eines Besseren besinnen; **you'd** ~ **stay** du bleibst am besten hier □ vt verbessern; (do better than) übertreffen; ~ **oneself** sich verbessern

'betting shop n Wettbüro nt

between /bɪ'twiːn/ *prep* zwischen (+ *dat/acc*); ~ **you and me** unter uns; ~ **us** (*together*) zusammen □ *adv* [**in**] ~ dazwischen

beverage /'bevərɪdʒ/ *n* Getränk *nt*

bevy /'bevɪ/ *n* Schar *f*

beware /bɪ'weə(r)/ *vi* sich in Acht nehmen (**of** vor + *dat*); ~ **of the dog!** Vorsicht, bissiger Hund!

bewilder /bɪ'wɪldə(r)/ *vt* verwirren. ~**ment** *n* Verwirrung *f*

bewitch /bɪ'wɪtʃ/ *vt* verzaubern; (*fig*) bezaubern

beyond /bɪ'jɒnd/ *prep* über (+ *acc*) ... hinaus; (*further*) weiter als; ~ **reach** außer Reichweite; ~ **doubt** ohne jeden Zweifel; **it's** ~ **me** (*fam*) das geht über meinen Horizont □ *adv* darüber hinaus

bias /'baɪəs/ *n* Voreingenommenheit *f*; (*preference*) Vorliebe *f*; (*Jur*) Befangenheit *f*; **cut on the** ~ schräg geschnitten □ *vt* (*pt/pp* biased) (*influence*) beeinflussen. ~**ed** *a* voreingenommen; (*Jur*) befangen

bib /bɪb/ *n* Lätzchen *nt*

Bible /'baɪbl/ *n* Bibel *f*

biblical /'bɪblɪkl/ *a* biblisch

bibliography /bɪblɪ'ɒɡrəfɪ/ *n* Bibliographie *f*

bicarbonate /baɪ'kɑːbənɪt/ *n* ~ **of soda** doppeltkohlensaures Natron *nt*

bicker /'bɪkə(r)/ *vi* sich zanken

bicycle /'baɪsɪkl/ *n* Fahrrad *nt* □ *vi* mit dem Rad fahren

bid¹ /bɪd/ *n* Gebot *nt*; (*attempt*) Versuch *m* □ *vt/i* (*pt/pp* bid, *pres p* bidding) bieten (**for** auf + *acc*); (*Cards*) reizen

bid² *vt* (*pt* bade *or* bid, *pp* bidden *or* bid, *pres p* bidding) heißen; ~ **s.o. welcome** jdn willkommen heißen

bidder /'bɪdə(r)/ *n* Bieter(in) *m(f)*

bide /baɪd/ *vt* ~ **one's time** den richtigen Moment abwarten

biennial /baɪ'enɪəl/ *a* zweijährlich; (*lasting two years*) zweijährig

bier /bɪə(r)/ *n* [Toten]bahre *f*

bifocals /baɪ'fəʊklz/ *npl* [**pair of**] ~ Bifokalbrille *f*

big /bɪɡ/ *a* (bigger, biggest) groß □ *adv* **talk** ~ (*fam*) angeben

bigam|ist /'bɪɡəmɪst/ *n* Bigamist *m*. ~**y** *n* Bigamie *f*

big-headed *a* (*fam*) eingebildet

bigot /'bɪɡət/ *n* Eiferer *m*. ~**ed** *a* engstirnig

bigwig *n* (*fam*) hohes Tier *nt*

bike /baɪk/ *n* (*fam*) [Fahr]rad *nt*

bikini /bɪ'kiːnɪ/ *n* Bikini *m*

bilberry /'bɪlbərɪ/ *n* Heidelbeere *f*

bile /baɪl/ *n* Galle *f*

bilingual /baɪ'lɪŋɡwəl/ *a* zweisprachig

bilious /'bɪljəs/ *a* (*Med*) ~ **attack** verdorbener Magen *m*

bill¹ /bɪl/ *n* Rechnung *f*; (*poster*) Plakat *nt*; (*Pol*) Gesetzentwurf *m*; (*Amer: note*) Banknote *f*. ~ **of exchange** Wechsel *m* □ *vt* eine Rechnung schicken (+ *dat*)

bill² *n* (*break*) Schnabel *m*

billet /'bɪlɪt/ *n* (*Mil*) Quartier *nt* □ *vt* (*pt/pp* billeted) einquartieren (**on** bei)

billfold *n* (*Amer*) Brieftasche *f*

billiards /'bɪljədz/ *n* Billard *nt*

billion /'bɪljən/ *n* (*thousand million*) Milliarde *f*; (*million million*) Billion *f*

billy-goat /'bɪlɪ-/ *n* Ziegenbock *m*

bin /bɪn/ *n* Mülleimer *m*; (*for bread*) Kasten *m*

bind /baɪnd/ *vt* (*pt/pp* bound) binden (**to** an + *acc*); (*bandage*) verbinden; (*Jur*) verpflichten; (*cover the edge of*) einfassen. ~**ing** *a* verbindlich □ *n* Einband *m*; (*braid*) Borte *f*; (*on ski*) Bindung *f*

binge /bɪndʒ/ *n* (*fam*) **go on the** ~ eine Sauftour machen

binoculars /bɪˈnɒkjʊləz/ *npl* [pair of] ~ Fernglas *nt*

bio|'chemistry /baɪəʊ-/ *n* Biochemie *f.* ~**degradable** /-dɪˈgreɪdəbl/ *a* biologisch abbaubar

biograph|er /baɪˈɒgrəfə(r)/ *n* Biograph(in) *m(f).* ~**y** *n* Biographie *f*

biological /baɪəˈlɒdʒɪkl/ *a* biologisch

biolog|ist /baɪˈɒlədʒɪst/ *n* Biologe *m.* ~**y** *n* Biologie *f*

birch /bɜːtʃ/ *n* Birke *f;* (*whip*) Rute *f*

bird /bɜːd/ *n* Vogel *m;* (*fam: girl*) Mädchen *nt;* **kill two ~s with one stone** zwei Fliegen mit einer Klappe schlagen

Biro (P) /'baɪrəʊ/ *n* Kugelschreiber *m*

birth /bɜːθ/ *n* Geburt *f*

birth: ~ **certificate** *n* Geburtsurkunde *f.* ~**control** *n* Geburtenregelung *f.* ~**day** *n* Geburtstag *m.* ~**mark** *n* Muttermal *nt.* ~**rate** *n* Geburtenziffer *f* ~**right** *n* Geburtsrecht *nt*

biscuit /'bɪskɪt/ *n* Keks *m*

bisect /baɪˈsekt/ *vt* halbieren

bishop /'bɪʃəp/ *n* Bischof *m;* (*Chess*) Läufer *m*

bit¹ /bɪt/ *n* Stückchen *nt;* (*for horse*) Gebiss *nt;* (*Techn*) Bohreinsatz *m;* **a** ~ ein bisschen; ~ **by** ~ nach und nach; **a** ~ **of bread** ein bisschen Brot; **do one's** ~ sein Teil tun

bit² *see* **bite**

bitch /bɪtʃ/ *n* Hündin *f;* (*sl*) Luder *nt.* ~**y** *a* gehässig

bit|e /baɪt/ *n* Biss *m;* (*insect*) Stich *m;* (*mouthful*) Bissen *m* □ *vt/i* (*pt* **bit**, *pp* **bitten**) beißen; (*insect.*) stechen; kauen (*one's nails*). ~**ing** *a* beißend

bitten /'bɪtn/ *see* **bite**

bitter /'bɪtə(r)/ *a,* -**ly** *adv* bitter; **cry** ~**ly** bitterlich weinen; ~**ly cold** bitterkalt □ *n* bitteres Bier *nt.* ~**ness** *n* Bitterkeit *f*

bitty /'bɪtɪ/ *a* zusammengestoppelt

bizarre /bɪˈzɑː(r)/ *a* bizarr

blab /blæb/ *vi* (*pt/pp* **blabbed**) alles ausplaudern

black /blæk/ *a* (-**er**, -**est**) schwarz; **be** ~**and blue** grün und blau sein □ *n* Schwarz *nt;* (*person*) Schwarze(r) *m/f* □ *vt* schwärzen; boykottieren (*goods*). ~ **out** *vt* verdunkeln □ *vi* (*lose consciousness*) das Bewusstsein verlieren

black: ~**berry** *n* Brombeere *f.* ~**bird** *n* Amsel *f.* ~**board** *n* (*Sch*) [Wand]tafel *f.* ~**currant** *n* schwarze Johannisbeere *f*

blacken *vt/i* schwärzen

black: ~**eye** *n* blaues Auge *nt.* **B~ Forest** *n* Schwarzwald *m.* ~ **ice** *n* Glatteis *nt.* ~**leg** *n* Streikbrecher *m.* ~**list** *vt auf* die schwarze Liste setzen. ~**mail** *n* Erpressung *f* □ *vt* erpressen. ~**mailer** *n* Erpresser(in) *m(f).* ~ **'market** *n* schwarzer Markt *m.* ~**out** *n* Verdunkelung *f;* **have a** ~**out** (*Med*) das Bewusstsein verlieren. ~ **'pudding** *n* Blutwurst *f.* ~**smith** *n* [Huf]schmied *m*

bladder /'blædə(r)/ *n* (*Anat*) Blase *f*

blade /bleɪd/ *n* Klinge *f;* (*of grass*) Halm *m*

blame /bleɪm/ *n* Schuld *f* □ *vt* die Schuld geben (+ *dat*); **no one is to** ~ keiner ist daran. ~**less** *a* schuldlos

blanch /blɑːntʃ/ *vi* blass werden □ *vt* (*Culin*) blanchieren

blancmange /bləˈmɒnʒ/ *n* Pudding *m*

bland /blænd/ *a* (-**er**, -**est**) mild

blank /blæŋk/ *a* leer; (*look*) ausdruckslos □ *n* Lücke *f;* (*cartridge*) Platzpatrone *f.* ~ **'cheque** *n* Blankoscheck *m*

blanket /'blæŋkɪt/ *n* Decke *f;* **wet** ~ (*fam*) Spielverderber(in) *m(f)*

blank 'verse *n* Blankvers *m*

blare /bleə(r)/ *vt/i* schmettern

blasé /'blɑːzeɪ/ *a* blasiert

blaspheme /blæsˈfiːm/ vi lästern
blasphem|ous /ˈblæsfəməs/ a
[gottes]lästerlich. ~y n [Gottes]-
lästerung f

blast /blɑːst/ n (gust) Luftstoß m;
(sound) Schmettern nt; (of horn)
Tuten nt □ sprengen □ int (sl)
verdammt. ~ed a (sl) verdammt

blast: ~furnace n Hochofen m.
~-off n (of missile) Start m

blatant /ˈbleɪtənt/ a offensichtlich

blaze /bleɪz/ n Feuer nt □ vi
brennen

blazer /ˈbleɪzə(r)/ n Blazer m

bleach /bliːtʃ/ n Bleichmittel n
□ vt/i bleichen

bleak /bliːk/ a (-er, -est) öde; (fig)
trostlos

bleary-eyed /ˈblɪərɪ-/ a mit trüben (on waking up) verschlafe-
nen Augen

bleat /bliːt/ vi blöken; (goat:) meckern

bleed /bliːd/ v (pt/pp bled) vi
bluten □ vt entlüften ⟨radiator⟩

bleep /bliːp/ n Piepton m □ vi
piepsen □ vt mit dem Piepser
rufen. ~er n Piepser m

blemish /ˈblemɪʃ/ n Makel m

blend /blend/ n Mischung f □ vt
mischen □ vi sich vermischen.
~er n (Culin) Mixer m

bless /bles/ vt segnen. ~ed /-
sɪd/ a heilig; (sl) verflixt. ~ing n
Segen m

blew /bluː/ see blow[2]

blight /blaɪt/ n (Bot) Brand m □ vt
(spoil) vereiteln

blind /blaɪnd/ a blind; (corner)
unübersichtlich; ~ man/
woman Blinde/r m/f □ n
[roller] Rouleau f □ vt blenden

blind: ~ 'alley n Sackgasse f.
~fold n & adv mit verbundenen
Augen □ n Augenbinde f □ vt die
Augen verbinden (+ dat). ~ly
adv blindlings. ~ness n
Blindheit f

blink /blɪŋk/ vi blinzeln; ⟨light:⟩
blinken

blinkers /ˈblɪŋkəz/ npl Scheuklappen pl

bliss /blɪs/ n Glückseligkeit f.
~ful a glücklich

blister /ˈblɪstə(r)/ n (Med) Blase f
□ vi ⟨paint:⟩ Blasen werfen

blitz /blɪts/ n Luftangriff m; (fam)
Großaktion f

blizzard /ˈblɪzəd/ n Schneesturm
m

bloated /ˈbləʊtɪd/ a aufgedunsen

blob /blɒb/ n Klecks m

bloc /blɒk/ n (Pol) Block m

block /blɒk/ n Block m; (of wood)
Klotz m; (of flats) [Wohn]block m
□ vt blockieren. ~ up zustopfen

blockade /blɒˈkeɪd/ n Blockade f
□ vt blockieren

blockage /ˈblɒkɪdʒ/ n Verstopfung f

block: ~head n (fam) Dummkopf
m. ~letters npl Blockschrift f

bloke /bləʊk/ n (fam) Kerl m

blonde /blɒnd/ a blond □ n Blon-
dine f

blood /blʌd/ n Blut nt

blood: ~count n Blutbild nt. ~
curdling a markerschütternd. ~
donor n Blutspender m. ~group
n Blutgruppe f. ~hound n
Bluthund m. ~poisoning n
Blutvergiftung f. ~pressure n
Blutdruck m. ~relative n Bluts-
verwandte(r) m/f. ~shed n Blut-
vergießen nt. ~shot a
blutunterlaufen. ~sports npl
Jagdsport m. ~stained a
blutbefleckt. ~stream n Blut-
bahn f. ~test n Blutprobe f.
~thirsty a blutdürstig. ~trans-
fusion n Blutübertragung f. ~
vessel n Blutgefäß nt

bloody /ˈblʌdɪ/ a (-ier, -iest) blutig; (sl) verdammt. ~-minded a
(sl) stur

bloom /bluːm/ n Blüte f □ vi blühen

bloom|er /'bluːmə(r)/ n (fam) Schnitzer m. **~ing** a (fam) verdammt

blossom /'blɒsəm/ n Blüte f □ vi blühen. **~ out** vi (fig) aufblühen

blot /blɒt/ n [Tinten]klecks m; (fig) Fleck m □ vt (pt/pp **blotted**) löschen. **~ out** vt (fig) auslöschen

blotch /blɒtʃ/ n Fleck m. **~y** a fleckig

'blotting-paper n Löschpapier nt

blouse /blaʊz/ n Bluse f

blow[1] /bləʊ/ n Schlag m

blow[2] v (pt blew, pp blown) □ vt blasen; (fam; squander) verpulvern; **~ one's nose** sich (dat) die Nase putzen □ vi blasen; (fuse:) durchbrennen. **~ away** vt wegblasen □ vi wegfliegen. **~ down** vt umwehen □ vi umfallen. **~ out** vt (extinguish) ausblasen. **~ over** vi umfallen; (fig: die down) sich vorübergehen. **~ up** vt (inflate) aufblasen; (enlarge) vergrößern; (shatter by explosion) sprengen □ vi explodieren

blow: **~-dry** vt föhnen. **~fly** n Schmeißfliege f. **~-lamp** n Lötlampe f

blown /bləʊn/ see blow[2]

'blowtorch n (Amer) Lötlampe f

blowy /'bləʊɪ/ a windig

bludgeon /'blʌdʒn/ vt (fig) zwingen

blue /bluː/ a (-r, -st) blau; feel ~ deprimiert sein □ n Blau nt; have the ~s deprimiert sein; out of the ~ aus heiterem Himmel

blue: **~bell** n Sternhyazinthe f. **~berry** n Heidelbeere f. **~bottle** n Schmeißfliege f. **~ film** n Pornofilm m. **~print** n (fig) Vorbild nt

bluff /blʌf/ n Bluff m □ vi bluffen

blunder /'blʌndə(r)/ n Schnitzer m □ vi einen Schnitzer machen

blunt /blʌnt/ a stumpf; (person) geradeheraus. **~ly** adv unverblümt, geradeheraus

blur /blɜː(r)/ n it's all a ~ alles ist verschwommen □ vt (pt/pp **blurred**) verschwommen machen; **~red** verschwommen

blurb /blɜːb/ n Klappentext m

blurt /blɜːt/ vt **~ out** herausplatzen mit

blush /blʌʃ/ n Erröten nt □ vi erröten

bluster /'blʌstə(r)/ n Großtuerei f. **~y** a windig

boar /bɔː(r)/ n Eber m

board /bɔːd/ n Brett nt; (for notices) schwarzes Brett nt; (committee) Ausschuss m; (of directors) Vorstand m; **on ~** an Bord; **full ~** Vollpension f; **~ and lodging** Unterkunft und Verpflegung; **go by the ~** (fam) unter den Tisch fallen □ vt einsteigen in (+ acc); (Naut, Aviat) besteigen □ vi an Bord gehen; **~ with** in Pension wohnen bei. **~ up** vt mit Brettern verschlagen

boarder /'bɔːdə(r)/ n Pensionsgast m; (Sch) Internatsschüler(in) m(f)

board: **~-game** n Brettspiel nt. **~ing-house** n Pension f. **~ing-school** n Internat nt

boast /bəʊst/ vi sich rühmen (+ gen) □ vi prahlen (about mit). **~ful** a, **-ly** adv prahlerisch

boat /bəʊt/ n Boot nt; (ship) Schiff nt. **~er** n (hat) flacher Strohhut m

bob /bɒb/ n Bubikopf m □ vt (pt/pp **bobbed**) (curtsy) **~ up and down** sich auf und ab bewegen

bobbin /'bɒbɪn/ n Spule f

bob-sleigh n Bob m

bode /bəʊd/ vi **~ well/ill** etwas/nichts Gutes verheißen

bodice /'bɒdɪs/ n Mieder nt

bodily /'bɒdɪlɪ/ a körperlich □ adv (forcibly) mit Gewalt

body /'bɒdɪ/ n Körper m; (corpse) Leiche f; (organization) Körperschaft f; **the main ~** der Hauptanteil. **~guard** n Leibwächter m. **~work** n (Auto) Karosserie f

bog /bɒg/ n Sumpf m □ vt (pt/pp **bogged**) **get ~ged down** stecken bleiben

boggle /'bɒgl/ vi **the mind ~s** es ist kaum vorstellbar

bogus /'bəʊgəs/ a falsch

boil¹ /bɔɪl/ n Furunkel m

boil² n **bring/come to the ~** zum Kochen bringen/kommen □ vt/i kochen; **~ed potatoes** Salzkartoffeln pl. **~ down** vi (fig) hinauslaufen (**to** auf + acc). **~ over** vi überkochen. **~ up** vt aufkochen

boiler /'bɔɪlə(r)/ n Heizkessel m. **~suit** n Overall m

'boiling point n Siedepunkt m

boisterous /'bɔɪstərəs/ a übermütig

bold /bəʊld/ a (-er, -est), **-ly** adv kühn; (Typ) fett. **~ness** n Kühnheit f

bollard /'bɒlɑːd/ n Poller m

bolster /'bəʊlstə(r)/ n Nackenrolle f □ vt **~ up** Mut machen (+ dat)

bolt /bəʊlt/ n Riegel m; (Techn) Bolzen m; **nuts and ~s** Schrauben und Muttern pl □ vt schrauben (**to** an + acc); verriegeln ⟨door⟩; hinunterschlingen ⟨food⟩ □ vi abhauen; ⟨horse:⟩ durchgehen □ adv **~upright** aufkerzengerade

bomb /bɒm/ n Bombe f □ vt bombardieren

bombard /bɒm'bɑːd/ vt beschießen; (fig) bombardieren

bombastic /bɒm'bæstɪk/ a bombastisch

bomb|er /'bɒmə(r)/ n (Aviat) Bomber m; (person) Bombenleger(in) m(f). **~shell** n **be a ~shell** (fig) wie eine Bombe einschlagen

bond /bɒnd/ n (fig) Band nt; (Comm) Obligation f; **be in ~** unter Zollverschluss stehen

bondage /'bɒndɪdʒ/ n (fig) Sklaverei f

bone /bəʊn/ n Knochen m; (of fish) Gräte f □ vt von den

Knochen lösen ⟨meat⟩; entgräten ⟨fish⟩. **~-'dry** a knochentrocken

bonfire /'bɒn-/ n Gartenfeuer nt; (celebratory) Freudenfeuer m

bonnet /'bɒnɪt/ n Haube f

bonus /'bəʊnəs/ n Prämie f; (gratuity) Gratifikation f; (fig) Plus nt

bony /'bəʊnɪ/ a (-ier, -iest) knochig; (fish) grätig

boo /buː/ int buh! □ vt ausbuhen □ vi buhen

boob /buːb/ n (fam: mistake) Schnitzer m □ vi (fam) einen Schnitzer machen

book /bʊk/ n Buch nt; (of tickets) Heft nt; **keep the ~s** (Comm) die Bücher führen □ vt/i buchen; (reserve) [vor]bestellen; (for offence) aufschreiben. **~able** /-əbl/ a im Vorverkauf erhältlich

book: **~case** n Bücherregal nt. **~ends** npl Bücherstützen pl. **~ing-office** n Fahrkartenschalter m. **~keeping** n Buchführung f. **~let** n Broschüre f. **~maker** n Buchmacher m. **~mark** n Lesezeichen nt. **~seller** n Buchhändler(in) m(f). **~shop** n Buchhandlung f. **~stall** n Bücherstand m. **~worm** n Bücherwurm m

boom /buːm/ n (Comm) Hochkonjunktur f; (upturn) Aufschwung m □ vi dröhnen; (fig) blühen

boon /buːn/ n Segen m

boor /bʊə(r)/ n Flegel m. **~ish** a flegelhaft

boost /buːst/ n Auftrieb m □ vt Auftrieb geben (+ dat). **~er** n (Med) Nachimpfung f

boot /buːt/ n Stiefel m; (Auto) Kofferraum m

booth /buːð/ n Bude f; (cubicle) Kabine f

booty /'buːtɪ/ n Beute f

booze /buːz/ n (fam) Alkohol m □ vi (fam) saufen

border /'bɔːdə(r)/ n Rand m; (frontier) Grenze f; (in garden) Rabatte f □ vi **~ on** grenzen an

(+ acc). ~line n Grenzlinie f.
~line case n Grenzfall m

bore¹ /bɔː(r)/ see bear²

bore² vt/i (Techn) bohren

bor|e³ n (of gun) Kaliber nt; (person) langweiliger Mensch m; (thing) langweilige Sache f □ vt langweilen; be ~ed sich langweilen. ~edom n Langeweile f. ~ing a langweilig

born /bɔːn/ pp be ~ geboren werden □ a geboren

borne /bɔːn/ see bear²

borough /ˈbʌrə/ n Stadtgemeinde f

borrow /ˈbɒrəʊ/ vt [sich (dat)] borgen od leihen (from von)

bosom /ˈbʊzm/ n Busen m

boss /bɒs/ n (fam) Chef m □ vt herumkommandieren. ~y a herrschsüchtig

botanical /bəˈtænɪkl/ a botanisch

botan|ist /ˈbɒtənɪst/ n Botaniker(in) m(f). ~y n Botanik f

botch /bɒtʃ/ vt verpfuschen

both /bəʊθ/ a & pron beide; ~[of] the children beide Kinder; ~ of them beide [von ihnen] □ adv ~ men and women sowohl Männer als auch Frauen

bother /ˈbɒðə(r)/ n Mühe f; (minor trouble) Ärger m □ int (fam) verflixt! □ vt belästigen; (disturb) stören □ vi sich kümmern (about um); don't ~ nicht nötig

bottle /ˈbɒtl/ n Flasche f □ vt auf Flaschen abfüllen; (preserve) einmachen. ~ up vt (fig) in sich (dat) aufstauen

bottle: ~neck n (fig) Engpass m. ~opener n Flaschenöffner m

bottom /ˈbɒtəm/ a unterste(r,s) □ n (of container) Boden m; (of river) Grund m; (of page, hill) Fuß m; (buttocks) Hintern m; at the ~ unten; get to the ~ of sth (fig) hinter etw (acc) kommen. ~less a bodenlos

bough /baʊ/ n Ast m

bought /bɔːt/ see buy

boulder /ˈbəʊldə(r)/ n Felsblock m

bounce /baʊns/ vi [auf]springen; (cheque:) (fam) nicht gedeckt sein □ vt aufspringen lassen (ball)

bouncer /ˈbaʊnsə(r)/ n (fam) Rausschmeißer m

bouncing /ˈbaʊnsɪŋ/ a ~ baby strammer Säugling m

bound¹ /baʊnd/ n Sprung m □ vi springen

bound² see bind □ a ~ for (ship) mit Kurs auf (+ acc); be ~ to do sth etw bestimmt machen; (obliged) verpflichtet sein, etw zu machen

boundary /ˈbaʊndri/ n Grenze f

boundless a grenzenlos

bounds /baʊndz/ npl (fig) Grenzen pl; out of ~ verboten

bouquet /buˈkeɪ/ n [Blumen]strauß m; (of wine) Bukett nt

bourgeois /ˈbʊəʒwɑː/ a (pej) spießbürgerlich

bout /baʊt/ n (Med) Anfall m; (Sport) Kampf m

bow¹ /bəʊ/ n (weapon & Mus) Bogen m; (knot) Schleife f

bow² /baʊ/ n Verbeugung f □ vi sich verbeugen □ vt neigen (head)

bow³ /baʊ/ n (Naut) Bug m

bowel /ˈbaʊəl/ n Darm m; ~ movement Stuhlgang m. ~s pl Eingeweide pl; (digestion) Verdauung f

bowl¹ /bəʊl/ n Schüssel f; (shallow) Schale f; (of pipe) Kopf m; (of spoon) Schöpfteil m

bowl² /bəʊl/ n Kugel f □ vt/i werfen. ~ over vt umwerfen

bow-legged /bəʊˈlegd/ a O-beinig

bowler¹ /ˈbəʊlə(r)/ n (Sport) Werfer m

bowler² n ~ [hat] Melone f

bowling /ˈbəʊlɪŋ/ n Kegeln nt. ~alley n Kegelbahn f

bowls /bəʊlz/ n Bowlsspiel nt

bow-'tie /baʊ-/ n Fliege f

box[1] /bɒks/ n Schachtel f; (wooden) Kiste f; (cardboard) Karton m; (Theat) Loge f

box[2] vt/i (Sport) boxen; ~ s.o.'s ears jdn ohrfeigen

boxer /'bɒksə(r)/ n Boxer m. ~ing n Boxen nt. B~ing Day n zweiter Weihnachtstag m

box: ~-office n (Theat) Kasse f. ~-room n Abstellraum m

boy /bɔɪ/ n Junge m

boycott /'bɔɪkɒt/ n Boykott m □ vt boykottieren

boy: ~friend n Freund m. ~ish a jungenhaft

bra /brɑː/ n BH m

brace /breɪs/ n Strebe f, Stütze f; (dental) Zahnspange f; ~ npl Hosenträger mpl □ vt ~ oneself sich stemmen (against gegen); (fig) sich gefasst machen (for auf + acc)

bracelet /'breɪslɪt/ n Armband nt

bracing /'breɪsɪŋ/ a stärkend

bracken /'brækn/ n Farnkraut nt

bracket /'brækɪt/ n Konsole f; (group) Gruppe f; (Typ) round/square ~ runde/eckige Klammern □ vt einklammern

brag /bræg/ vi (pt/pp bragged) prahlen (about mit)

braid /breɪd/ n Borte f

braille /breɪl/ n Blindenschrift f

brain /breɪn/ n Gehirn nt; ~s (fig) Intelligenz f

brain: ~child n geistiges Produkt m. ~less a dumm. ~wash vt einer Gehirnwäsche unterziehen. ~wave n Geistesblitz m

brainy /'breɪnɪ/ a (-ier, -iest) klug

braise /breɪz/ vt schmoren

brake /breɪk/ n Bremse f □ vt/i bremsen. ~light n Bremslicht nt

bramble /'bræmbl/ n Brombeerstrauch m

bran /bræn/ n Kleie f

branch /brɑːntʃ/ n Ast m; (fig) Zweig m; (Comm) Zweigstelle f; (shop) Filiale f □ vi sich gabeln.

~ off vi abzweigen. ~ out vi ~ out into sich verlegen auf (+ acc)

brand /brænd/ n Marke f; (on animal) Brandzeichen nt □ vt mit dem Brandeisen zeichnen (animal); (fig) brandmarken als

brandish /'brændɪʃ/ vt schwingen

brand-new a nagelneu

brandy /'brændɪ/ n Weinbrand m

brash /bræʃ/ a nassforsch

brass /brɑːs/ n Messing nt; (Mus) Blech nt; get down to ~ tacks (fam) zur Sache kommen; top ~ (fam) hohe Tiere pl. ~ band n Blaskapelle f

brassière /'bræzɪə(r)/ n Büstenhalter m

brassy /'brɑːsɪ/ a (-ier, -iest) (fam) ordinär

brat /bræt/ n (pej) Balg nt

bravado /brə'vɑːdəʊ/ n Forschheit f

brave /breɪv/ a (-r, -st), -ly adv tapfer □ vt die Stirn bieten (+ dat). ~ry /-ərɪ/ n Tapferkeit f

bravo /brɑː'vəʊ/ int bravo!

brawl /brɔːl/ n Schlägerei f □ vi sich schlagen

brawn /brɔːn/ n (Culin) Sülze f

brawny /'brɔːnɪ/ a muskulös

bray /breɪ/ vi iahen

brazen /'breɪzn/ a unverschämt

brazier /'breɪzɪə(r)/ n Kohlenbecken nt

Brazil /brə'zɪl/ n Brasilien nt. ~ian a brasilianisch. ~ nut n Paranuss f

breach /briːtʃ/ n Bruch m; (Mil & fig) Bresche f; ~ of contract Vertragsbruch m □ vt durchbrechen; brechen (contract)

bread /bred/ n Brot nt; slice of ~ and butter Butterbrot nt

bread: ~crumbs npl Brotkrümel pl; (Culin) Paniermehl nt. ~line n be on the ~line gerade genug zum Leben haben

breadth /bredθ/ n Breite f

'**bread-winner** *n* Brotverdiener *m*

break /breɪk/ *n* Bruch *m*; (*interval*) Pause *f*; (*interruption*) Unterbrechung *f*; (*fam: chance*) Chance *f* □ *v* (*pt* **broke**, *pp* **broken**) □ *vt* brechen; (*smash*) zerbrechen; (*damage*) kaputtmachen (*fam*); (*interrupt*) unterbrechen; ~ **one's arm** sich (*dat*) den Arm brechen □ *vi* brechen; (*day:*) anbrechen; (*storm:*) losbrechen; (*thing:*) kaputtgehen (*fam*); (*rope, thread:*) reißen; (*news:*) bekannt werden; **his voice is** ~**ing** er ist im Stimmbruch. ~ **away** *vi* sich losreißen/(*fig*) sich absetzen (**from** von). ~ **down** *vi* zusammenbrechen; (*Techn*) eine Panne haben; (*negotiations:*) scheitern □ *vt* aufbrechen (*door*); aufgliedern (*figures*). ~ **in** *vi* einbrechen. ~ **off** *vt/i* abbrechen; lösen (*engagement*). ~ **out** *vi* ausbrechen. ~ **up** *vt* zerbrechen □ *vi* (*crowd:*) sich zerstreuen; (*marriage, couple:*) auseinandergehen; (*Sch*) Ferien bekommen

break|able /'breɪkəbl/ *a* zerbrechlich. ~**age** /-ɪdʒ/ *n* Bruch *m*. ~**down** *n* (*Techn*) Panne *f*; (*Med*) Zusammenbruch *m*; (*of figures*) Aufgliederung *f*. ~**er** *n* (*wave*) Brecher *m*

breakfast /'brekfəst/ *n* Frühstück *nt*

break: ~**through** *n* Durchbruch *m*. ~**water** *n* Buhne *f*

breast /brest/ *n* Brust *f*. ~**bone** *n* Brustbein *nt*. ~**feed** *vt* stillen. ~**stroke** *n* Brustschwimmen *nt*

breath /breθ/ *n* Atem *m*; **out of** ~ außer Atem; **under one's** ~ vor sich (*acc*) hin

breathalyse /'breθəlaɪz/ *vt* ins Röhrchen blasen lassen. ~**r (P)** *n* Röhrchen *nt*. ~**r test** *n* Alcotest (P) *m*

breathe /briːð/ *vt/i* atmen. ~ **in** *vt/i* einatmen. ~ **out** *vt/i* ausatmen

breath|er /'briːðə(r)/ *n* Atempause *f*. ~**ing** *n* Atmen *nt*

breath /breθ-/: ~**less** *a* atemlos. ~**-taking** *a* atemberaubend. ~ **test** *n* Alcotest (P) *m*

bred /bred/ *see* **breed**

breeches /'brɪtʃɪz/ *npl* Kniehose *f*; (*for riding*) Reithose *f*

breed /briːd/ *n* Rasse *f* □ *v* (*pt/pp* **bred**) □ *vt* züchten; (*give rise to*) erzeugen □ *vi* sich vermehren. ~**er** *n* Züchter *m*. ~**ing** *n* Zucht *f*; (*fig*) [gute] Lebensart *f*

breeze /briːz/ *n* Lüftchen *nt*; (*Naut*) Brise *f*. ~**y** *a* [leicht] windig

brevity /'brevɪtɪ/ *n* Kürze *f*

brew /bruː/ *n* Gebräu *nt* □ *vt* brauen; kochen (*tea*) □ *vi* (*fig*) sich zusammenbrauen. ~**er** *n* Brauer *m*. ~**ery** *n* Brauerei *f*

bribe /braɪb/ *n* (*money*) Bestechungsgeld *nt* □ *vt* bestechen. ~**ry** /-ərɪ/ *n* Bestechung *f*

brick /brɪk/ *n* Ziegelstein *m*, Backstein *m* □ *vt* ~ **up** zumauern

'**bricklayer** *n* Maurer *m*

bridal /'braɪdl/ *a* Braut-

bride /braɪd/ *n* Braut *f*. ~**groom** *n* Bräutigam *m*. ~**smaid** *n* Brautjungfer *f*

bridge[1] /brɪdʒ/ *n* Brücke *f*; (*of nose*) Nasenrücken *m*; (*of spectacles*) Steg *m* □ *vt* (*fig*) überbrücken

bridge[2] *n* (*Cards*) Bridge *nt*

bridle /'braɪdl/ *n* Zaum *m*. ~**path** *n* Reitweg *m*

brief[1] /briːf/ *a* (-**er**, -**est**) kurz; **be** ~ (*person.*) sich kurz fassen

brief[2] *n* Instruktionen *pl*; (*Jur: case*) Mandat *nt* □ *vt* instruktionen geben (+ *dat*); (*Jur*) beauftragen. ~**case** *n* Aktentasche *f*

brief|ing /'briːfɪŋ/ *n* Informationsgespräch *nt*. ~**ly** *adv* kurz. ~**ness** *n* Kürze *f*

briefs /briːfs/ *npl* Slip *m*

brigad|e /brɪˈgeɪd/ *n* Brigade *f*. ∼**ier** /-əˈdɪə(r)/ *n* Brigadegeneral *m*

bright /braɪt/ *a* (-er, -est), -ly *adv* hell; (*day*) heiter; ∼ **red** hellrot

bright|en /ˈbraɪtn/ *v* ∼**en [up]** □*vt* aufheitern □*vi* sich aufheitern. ∼**ness** *n* Helligkeit *f*

brilliance /ˈbrɪljəns/ *n* Glanz *m*; (*of person*) Genialität *f*

brilliant /ˈbrɪljənt/ *a*, -ly *adv* glänzend; (*person*) genial

brim /brɪm/ *n* Rand *m*; (*of hat*) Krempe *f* □*vi* (*pt/pp* brimmed) ∼ **over** überfließen

brine /braɪn/ *n* Salzwasser *nt*; (*Culin*) [Salz]lake *f*

bring /brɪŋ/ *vt* (*pt/pp* brought) bringen; ∼ **them with you** bring sie mit; **I can't b**∼ **myself to do it** ich bringe es nicht fertig. ∼ **about** *vt* verursachen. ∼ **along** *vt* mitbringen. ∼ **back** *vt* zurückbringen. ∼ **down** *vt* herunterbringen; senken (*price*). ∼ **off** *vt* vollbringen. ∼ **on** *vt* (*cause*) verursachen. ∼ **out** *vt* herausbringen. ∼ **round** *vt* vorbeibringen; (*persuade*) überreden; wieder zum Bewusstsein bringen (*unconscious person*). ∼ **up** *vt* heraufbringen; (*vomit*) erbrechen; aufziehen (*children*); erwähnen (*question*)

brink /brɪŋk/ *n* Rand *m*

brisk /brɪsk/ *a* (-er, -est), -ly *adv* lebhaft; (*quick*) schnell

bristl|e /ˈbrɪsl/ *n* Borste *f*. ∼**ly** *a* borstig

Brit|ain /ˈbrɪtn/ *n* Großbritannien *nt*. ∼**ish** *a* britisch; the ∼**ish** die Briten *pl*. ∼**on** *n* Brite *m*/Britin *f*

Brittany /ˈbrɪtənɪ/ *n* die Bretagne

brittle /ˈbrɪtl/ *a* brüchig, spröde

broach /brəʊtʃ/ *vt* anzapfen; anschneiden (*subject*)

broad /brɔːd/ *a* (-er, -est) breit; (*hint*) deutlich; **in** ∼ **daylight** in

hellichten Tag. ∼ **beans** *npl* dicke Bohnen *pl*

broadcast *n* Sendung *f* □*vt/i* (*pt/pp* -cast) senden. ∼**er** *n* Rundfunk- und Fernsehpersönlichkeit *f*. ∼**ing** *n* Funk und Fernsehen *pl*

broaden /ˈbrɔːdn/ *vt* verbreitern; (*fig*) erweitern □*vi* sich verbreitern

broadly /ˈbrɔːdlɪ/ *adv* breit; ∼ **speaking** allgemein gesagt

broad'minded *a* tolerant

brocade /brəˈkeɪd/ *n* Brokat *m*

broccoli /ˈbrɒkəlɪ/ *n inv* Brokkoli *pl*

brochure /ˈbrəʊʃə(r)/ *n* Broschüre *f*

brogue /brəʊg/ *n* (*shoe*) Wanderschuh *m*; **Irish** ∼ irischer Akzent *m*

broke /brəʊk/ *see* **break** □*a* (*fam*) pleite

broken /ˈbrəʊkn/ *see* **break** □*a* zerbrochen; (*fam*) kaputt; ∼ **English** gebrochenes Englisch *nt*. ∼**-hearted** *a* untröstlich

broker /ˈbrəʊkə(r)/ *n* Makler *m*

brolly /ˈbrɒlɪ/ *n* (*fam*) Schirm *m*

bronchitis /brɒŋˈkaɪtɪs/ *n* Bronchitis *f*

bronze /brɒnz/ *n* Bronze *f*

brooch /brəʊtʃ/ *n* Brosche *f*

brood /bruːd/ *n* Brut *f* □*vi* brüten; (*fig*) grübeln

brook[1] /brʊk/ *n* Bach *m*

brook[2] *vt* dulden

broom /bruːm/ *n* Besen *m*; (*Bot*) Ginster *m*. ∼**stick** *n* Besenstiel *m*

broth /brɒθ/ *n* Brühe *f*

brothel /ˈbrɒθl/ *n* Bordell *m*

brother /ˈbrʌðə(r)/ *n* Bruder *m*

brother: ∼**-in-law** *n* (*pl* -s-in-law) Schwager *m*. ∼**ly** *a* brüderlich

brought /brɔːt/ *see* **bring**

brow /braʊ/ *n* Augenbraue *f*; (*forehead*) Stirn *f*; (*of hill*) [Berg]kuppe *f* 'browbeat vt (pt -beat, pp -beaten) einschüchtern

brown /braʊn/ a (-er, -est) braun; ~ 'paper Packpapier nt □ n Braun nt □ vt bräunen □ vi braun werden

Brownie /'braʊnɪ/ n Wichtel m

browse /braʊz/ vi (read) schmökern; (in shop) sich umsehen

bruise /bruːz/ n blauer Fleck m □ vt beschädigen ⟨fruit⟩; ~ one's arm sich (dat) den Arm quetschen

brunch /brʌntʃ/ n Brunch m

brunette /bruː'net/ n Brünette f

Brunswick /'brʌnzwɪk/ n Braunschweig nt

brunt /brʌnt/ n the ~ of die volle Wucht (+ gen)

brush /brʌʃ/ n Bürste f; (with handle) Handfeger m; (for paint, pastry) Pinsel m; (bushes) Unterholz nt; (fig: conflict) Zusammenstoß m □ vt bürsten putzen ⟨teeth⟩; ~ against streifen [gegen]; ~ aside (fig) abtun. ~ off vt abbürsten; (reject) zurückweisen. ~ up vt/i (fig) ~ up [on] auffrischen

brusque /brʊsk/ a, -ly adv brüsk

Brussels /'brʌslz/ n Brüssel nt. ~ sprouts npl Rosenkohl m

brutal /'bruːtl/ a, -ly adv brutal. ~ity /-'tælɪtɪ/ n Brutalität f

brute /bruːt/ n Unmensch m. ~ force n rohe Gewalt f

B.Sc. abbr of Bachelor of Science

bubble /'bʌbl/ n [Luft]blase f □ vi sprudeln

buck[1] /bʌk/ n (deer & Gym) Bock m; (rabbit) Rammler m □ vi ⟨horse:⟩ bocken. ~ up vi (fam) sich aufheitern; (hurry) sich beeilen

buck[2] n (Amer, fam) Dollar m

buck[3] n pass the ~ die Verantwortung abschieben

bucket /'bʌkɪt/ n Eimer m

buckle /'bʌkl/ n Schnalle f □ vt zuschnallen □ vi sich verbiegen

bud /bʌd/ n Knospe f □ vi (pt/pp budded) knospen

Buddhis|m /'bʊdɪzm/ n Buddhismus m. ~t a buddhistisch □ n Buddhist(in) m(f)

buddy /'bʌdɪ/ n (fam) Freund m

budge /bʌdʒ/ vt bewegen □ vi sich [von der Stelle] rühren

budgerigar /'bʌdʒərɪgɑː(r)/ n Wellensittich m

budget /'bʌdʒɪt/ n Budget nt; (Pol) Haushaltsplan m; (money available) Etat m □ vi (pt/pp budgeted) ~ for sth etw einkalkulieren

buff /bʌf/ a (colour) sandfarben □ n Sandfarbe f; (Amer, fam) Fan m □ vt polieren

buffalo /'bʌfələʊ/ n (inv or pl -es) Büffel m

buffer /'bʌfə(r)/ n (Rail) Puffer m; old ~ (fam) alter Knacker m; ~ zone Pufferzone f

buffet[1] /'bʊfeɪ/ n Büfett nt, (on station) Imbissstube f

buffet[2] /'bʌfɪt/ vt (pt/pp buffeted) hin und her werfen

buffoon /bə'fuːn/ n Narr m

bug /bʌg/ n Wanze f; (fam: virus) Bazillus m; (fam: device) Abhörgerät nt, (fam) Wanze f □ vt (pt/pp bugged) (fam) verwanzen ⟨room⟩; abhören ⟨telephone⟩; (Amer: annoy) ärgern

buggy /'bʌgɪ/ n [Kinder]sportwagen m

bugle /'bjuːgl/ n Signalhorn nt

build /bɪld/ n (of person) Körperbau m □ vt/i (pt/pp built) bauen. ~ on vt anbauen (to an + acc). ~ up vt aufbauen □ vi zunehmen; (traffic:) sich stauen

builder /'bɪldə(r)/ n Bauunternehmer m

building /'bɪldɪŋ/ n Gebäude nt. ~ site n Baustelle f. ~ society n Bausparkasse f

built /bɪlt/ *see* build. **~in** *a* eingebaut. **~in** 'cupboard *n* Einbauschrank *m*. **~up area** *n* bebautes Gebiet *nt*; (*Auto*) geschlossene Ortschaft *f*

bulb /bʌlb/ *n* [Blumen]zwiebel *f*; (*Electr*) [Glüh]birne *f*

bulbous /'bʌlbəs/ *a* bauchig

Bulgaria /bʌl'geərɪə/ *n* Bulgarien *nt*

bulge /bʌldʒ/ *n* Ausbauchung *f* □ *vi* sich ausbauchen. **~ing** *a* prall; (*eyes*) hervorquellend; **~ing with** prall gefüllt mit

bulk /bʌlk/ *n* Masse *f*; (*greater part*) Hauptteil *m*; **in ~** en gros; (*loose*) lose. **~y** *a* sperrig; (*large*) massig

bull /bʊl/ *n* Bulle *m*, Stier *m*

'bulldog *n* Bulldogge *f*

bulldozer /'bʊldəʊzə(r)/ *n* Planierraupe *f*

bullet /'bʊlɪt/ *n* Kugel *f*

bulletin /'bʊlɪtɪn/ *n* Bulletin *nt*

'bullet-proof *a* kugelsicher

'bullfight *n* Stierkampf *m*. **~er** *n* Stierkämpfer *m*

'bullfinch *n* Dompfaff *m*

bullion /'bʊlɪən/ *n* **gold ~** Barrengold *nt*

bullock /'bʊlək/ *n* Ochse *m*

bull: **~ring** *n* Stierkampfarena *f*. **~'s-eye** *n* **score a ~'s-eye** ins Schwarze treffen

bully /'bʊlɪ/ *n* Tyrann *m* □ *vt* tyrannisieren

bum[1] /bʌm/ *n* (*sl*) Hintern *m*

bum[2] *n* (*Amer, fam*) Landstreicher *m*

bumble-bee /'bʌmbl-/ *n* Hummel *f*

bump /bʌmp/ *n* Bums *m*; (*swelling*) Beule *f*; (*in road*) holprige Stelle *f* □ *vt* stoßen; **~ into** stoßen gegen; (*meet*) zufällig treffen. **~ off** *vt* (*fam*) um die Ecke bringen

bumper /'bʌmpə(r)/ *a* Rekord- □ *n* (*Auto*) Stoßstange *f*

bumpkin /'bʌmpkɪn/ *n* **country ~** Tölpel *m*

bumptious /'bʌmpʃəs/ *a* aufgeblasen

bumpy /'bʌmpɪ/ *a* holperig

bun /bʌn/ *n* Milchbrötchen *nt*; (*hair*) [Haar]knoten *m*

bunch /bʌntʃ/ *n* (*of flowers*) Strauß *m*; (*of radishes, keys*) Bund *m*; (*of people*) Gruppe *f*; **~ of grapes** [ganze] Weintraube *f*

bundle /'bʌndl/ *n* Bündel *nt* □ *vt* **~ [up]** bündeln

bung /bʌŋ/ *vt* (*fam*) (*throw*) schmeißen. **~ up** *vt* (*fam*) verstopfen

bungalow /'bʌŋgələʊ/ *n* Bungalow *m*

bungle /'bʌŋgl/ *vt* verpfuschen

bunion /'bʌnjən/ *n* (*Med*) Ballen *m*

bunk /bʌŋk/ *n* [Schlaf]koje *f*. **~beds** *npl* Etagenbett *nt*

bunker /'bʌŋkə(r)/ *n* Bunker *m*

bunkum /'bʌŋkəm/ *n* Quatsch *m*

bunny /'bʌnɪ/ *n* (*fam*) Kaninchen *nt*

buoy /bɔɪ/ *n* Boje *f*. **~ up** *vt* (*fig*) stärken

buoyancy /'bɔɪənsɪ/ *n* Auftrieb *m*. **~t** *a* **be ~t** schwimmen; (*water:*) gut tragen

burden /'bɜːdn/ *n* Last *f* □ *vt* belasten. **~some** /-səm/ *a* lästig

bureau /'bjʊərəʊ/ *n* (*pl* **-x** /-əʊz/ *or* **~s**) (*desk*) Sekretär *m*; (*office*) Büro *nt*

bureaucracy /bjʊə'rɒkrəsɪ/ *n* Bürokratie *f*

bureaucrat /'bjʊərəkræt/ *n* Bürokrat *m*. **~ic** /-'krætɪk/ *a* bürokratisch

burger /'bɜːgə(r)/ *n* Hamburger *m*

burglar /'bɜːglə(r)/ *n* Einbrecher *m*. **~ alarm** *n* Alarmanlage *f*

burglar|ize /'bɜːgləraɪz/ *vt* (*Amer*) einbrechen in (+ *acc*). **~y** *n* Einbruch *m*

burgle /'bɜːgl/ *vt* einbrechen in (+ *acc*); **they have been ~d** bei ihnen ist eingebrochen worden

Burgundy /'bɜ:gəndɪ/ n Burgund nt; b~ (wine) Burgunder m

burial /'berɪəl/ n Begräbnis nt

burlesque /bɜ:'lesk/ n Burleske f

burly /'bɜ:lɪ/ a (-ier, -iest) stämmig

Burm|a /'bɜ:mə/ n Birma nt. ~ese /-'mi:z/ a birmanisch

burn /bɜ:n/ n Verbrennung f; (on skin) Brandwunde f; (on material) Brandstelle f □ v (pt/pp burnt or burned) □ vt verbrennen □ vi brennen; (food:) anbrennen. ~ **down** vt/i niederbrennen

burnish /'bɜ:nɪʃ/ vt polieren

burnt /bɜ:nt/ see burn

burp /bɜ:p/ vi (fam) aufstoßen

burrow /'bʌrəʊ/ n Bau m □ vi wühlen

bursar /'bɜ:sə(r)/ n Rechnungsführer m. ~**y** n Stipendium nt

burst /bɜ:st/ n Bruch m; (surge) Ausbruch m □ v (pt/pp burst) □ vt platzen machen □ vi platzen; (bud:) aufgehen; ~ **into tears** in Tränen ausbrechen

bury /'berɪ/ vt (pt/pp -ied) begraben; (hide) vergraben

bus /bʌs/ n [Auto]bus m □ vt/i (pt/pp bussed) mit dem Bus fahren

bush /bʊʃ/ n Strauch m; (land) Busch m. ~**y** a (-ier, -iest) buschig

busily /'bɪzɪlɪ/ adv eifrig

business /'bɪznɪs/ n Angelegenheit f; (Comm) Geschäft nt; on ~ geschäftlich; he has no ~ er hat kein Recht (to zu); mind one's own ~ sich um seine eigenen Angelegenheiten kümmern; that's none of your ~ das geht Sie nichts an. ~**like** a geschäftsmäßig. ~**man** n Geschäftsmann m

busker /'bʌskə(r)/ n Straßenmusikant m

'bus-stop n Bushaltestelle f

bust¹ /bʌst/ n Büste f. ~ **size** n Oberweite f

bust² /bʌst/ a kaputt; **go** ~ Pleite gehen □ v (pt/pp busted or bust) (fam) □ vt kaputtmachen □ vt kaputtgehen

bustl|e /'bʌsl/ n Betrieb m, Getriebe nt □ vi. ~**e about** geschäftig hin und her laufen. ~**ing** a belebt

'bust-up n (fam) Streit m, Krach m

busy /'bɪzɪ/ a (-ier, -iest) beschäftigt; (day) voll; (street) belebt; (with traffic) stark befahren; (Amer Teleph) besetzt; **be** ~ zu tun haben □ vt ~ **oneself** sich beschäftigen (with mit)

'busybody n Wichtigtuer(in) m(f)

but /bʌt, unbetont bət/ conj aber; (after negative) sondern □ prep außer (+ dat); ~ **for** (without) ohne (+ acc); **the last** ~ **one** der/die/das vorletzte; **the next** ~ **one** der/die/das übernächste □ adv nur

butcher /'bʊtʃə(r)/ n Fleischer m, Metzger m; ~**'s [shop]** Fleischerei f, Metzgerei f □ vt [ab]schlachten

butler /'bʌtlə(r)/ n Butler m

butt /bʌt/ n (of gun) [Gewehr]kolben m; (fig: target) Zielscheibe f; (of cigarette) Stummel m; (for water) Regentonne f □ vt mit dem Kopf stoßen □ vi. ~ **in** unterbrechen

butter /'bʌtə(r)/ n Butter f □ vt mit Butter bestreichen. ~ **up** vt (fam) schmeicheln (+ dat)

butter- ~**cup** a Butterblume f, Hahnenfuß m. ~**fly** n Schmetterling m

buttocks /'bʌtəks/ npl Gesäß nt

button /'bʌtn/ n Knopf m □ vt [up] zuknöpfen □ vi geknöpft werden. ~**hole** n Knopfloch nt

buttress /'bʌtrɪs/ n Strebepfeiler m; **flying** ~ Strebebogen m

buxom /'bʌksəm/ a drall

buy /baɪ/ n Kauf m □ vt (pt/pp **bought**) kaufen. **~er** n Käufer(in) m(f)

buzz /bʌz/ n Summen nt □ vi summen. **~ off** vi (fam) abhauen

buzzard /ˈbʌzəd/ n Bussard m

buzzer /ˈbʌzə(r)/ n Summer m

by /baɪ/ prep (close to) bei (+ dat); (next to) neben (+ dat/acc); (past) an (+ dat)... vorbei; (to the extent of) um (+ acc); (at the latest) bis; (by means of) durch; by Mozart/Dickens von Mozart/Dickens; **~ oneself** allein; **~ the sea** am Meer; **~ car/bus** mit dem Auto/Bus; **~ sea** mit dem Schiff; **~ day/night** bei Tag/Nacht; **~ the hour** pro Stunde; **~ the metre** meterweise; **six metres ~ four** sechs mal vier Meter; **win ~ a length** mit einer Länge Vorsprung gewinnen; **miss the train ~ a minute** den Zug um eine Minute verpassen □ adv **~ and ~** mit der Zeit; **~ and large** im Großen und Ganzen; **put ~** beiseite legen; **go/pass ~** vorbeigehen

bye /baɪ/ int (fam) tschüs

by: **~-election** n Nachwahl f. **~gone** a vergangen. **~law** n Verordnung f. **~pass** n Umgehungsstraße f; (Med) Bypass m □ vt umfahren. **~-product** n Nebenprodukt m. **~road** n Nebenstraße f. **~stander** n Zuschauer(in) m(f)

Byzantine /brˈzæntaɪn/ a byzantinisch

C

cab /kæb/ n Taxi nt; (of lorry, train) Führerhaus nt

cabaret /ˈkæbəreɪ/ n Kabarett nt

cabbage /ˈkæbɪdʒ/ n Kohl m

cabin /ˈkæbɪn/ n Kabine f; (hut) Hütte f

cabinet /ˈkæbɪnɪt/ n Schrank m; **[display]** ~ Vitrine f; (TV, Radio) Gehäuse nt; **C~** (Pol) Kabinett nt. **~-maker** n Möbeltischler m

cable /ˈkeɪbl/ n Kabel nt; (rope) Tau nt; **~ railway** n Seilbahn f; **~ television** n Kabelfernsehen nt

cache /kæʃ/ n Versteck nt; **~ of arms** Waffenlager nt

cackle /ˈkækl/ vi gackern

cactus /ˈkæktəs/ n (pl -ti /-taɪ/ or -tuses) Kaktus m

caddie /ˈkædɪ/ n Caddie m

caddy /ˈkædɪ/ n **[tea-]~** Teedose f

cadet /kəˈdet/ n Kadett m

cadge /kædʒ/ vt/i (fam) schnorren

Caesarean /sɪˈzeəriən/ a & n **[section]** Kaiserschnitt m

café /ˈkæfeɪ/ n Café nt

cafeteria /kæfəˈtɪərɪə/ n Selbstbedienungsrestaurant nt

caffeine /ˈkæfiːn/ n Koffein nt

cage /keɪdʒ/ n Käfig m

cagey /ˈkeɪdʒɪ/ a (fam) **be ~** mit der Sprache nicht herauswollen

cajole /kəˈdʒəʊl/ vt gut zureden (+ dat)

cake /keɪk/ n Kuchen m; (of soap) Stück nt. **~d** a verkrustet (with mit)

calamity /kəˈlæmətɪ/ n Katastrophe f

calcium /ˈkælsɪəm/ n Kalzium nt

calculat|e /ˈkælkjʊleɪt/ vt berechnen; (estimate) kalkulieren. **~ing** a (fig) berechnend. **~ion** /-ˈleɪʃn/ n Rechnung f, Kalkulation f. **~or** n Rechner m

calendar /ˈkælɪndə(r)/ n Kalender m

calf[1] /kɑːf/ n (pl **calves**) Kalb nt

calf[2] n (pl **calves**) (Anat) Wade f

calibre /ˈkælɪbə(r)/ n Kaliber nt

calico /ˈkælɪkəʊ/ n Kattun m

call /kɔːl/ n Ruf m; (Teleph) Anruf m; (visit) Besuch m; **be on ~** ⟨doctor:⟩ Bereitschaftsdienst haben

call □ *vt* rufen; *(Teleph)* anrufen; *(wake)* wecken; *(strike)* *(name)* nennen; **be ~ed** heißen □ *vi* rufen; **~ [in** *or* **round]** vorbeikommen. **~ back** *vt* zurückrufen □ *vi* noch einmal vorbeikommen. **~ for** *vt* rufen nach; *(demand)* verlangen; *(fetch)* abholen. **~ off** *vt* zurückrufen *(dog)*; *(cancel)* absagen. **~ on** *vt* bitten (**for** um); *(appeal to)* appellieren an (+ *acc*); *(visit)* besuchen. **~ out** *vt* rufen; aufrufen *(names)* □ *vi* rufen. **~ up** *vt (Mil)* einberufen; *(Teleph)* anrufen

call: **~box** *n* Telefonzelle *f.* **~er** *n* Besucher *m*; *(Teleph)* Anrufer *m.* **~ing** *n* Berufung *f*

callous /ˈkæləs/ *a* gefühllos

'call-up *n (Mil)* Einberufung *f*

calm /kɑ:m/ *a* (-er, -est), **-ly** *adv* ruhig □ *n* Ruhe *f* □ *vt* ~ **[down]** beruhigen □ *vi* ~ **down** sich beruhigen. **~ness** *n* Ruhe *f*; *(of sea)* Stille *f*

calorie /ˈkælərɪ/ *n* Kalorie *f*

calves /kɑ:vz/ *npl see* **calf**[1] & [2]

camber /ˈkæmbə(r)/ *n* Wölbung *f*

came /keɪm/ *see* **come**

camel /ˈkæml/ *n* Kamel *nt*

camera /ˈkæmərə/ *n* Kamera *f.* **~man** *n* Kameramann *m*

camouflage /ˈkæməflɑ:ʒ/ *n* Tarnung *f* □ *vt* tarnen

camp /kæmp/ *n* Lager *nt* □ *vi* campen; *(Mil)* kampieren

campaign /kæmˈpeɪn/ *n* Feldzug *m*; *(Comm, Pol)* Kampagne *f* □ *vi* kämpfen; *(pol)* im Wahlkampf arbeiten

camp: **~bed** *n* Feldbett *nt.* **~er** *n* Camper *m*; *(Auto)* Wohnmobil *nt.* **~ing** *n* Camping *nt.* **~site** *n* Campingplatz *m*

campus /ˈkæmpəs/ *n* (*pl* **-puses**) *(Univ)* Campus *m*

can[1] /kæn/ *n (for petrol)* Kanister *m*; *(tin)* Dose *f*, Büchse *f*; **a ~ of beer** eine Dose Bier □ *vt* in Dosen *od* Büchsen konservieren

can[2] /kæn, *unbetont* kən/ *v aux* (*pres* **can**; *pt* **could**) können; **I cannot/can't go** ich kann nicht gehen; **he could not go** er konnte nicht gehen; **if I could go** wenn ich gehen könnte

Canad|a /ˈkænədə/ *n* Kanada *nt.* **~ian** /kəˈneɪdɪən/ *a* kanadisch □ *n* Kanadier(in) *m(f)*

canal /kəˈnæl/ *n* Kanal *m*

Canaries /kəˈneərɪz/ *npl* Kanarische Inseln *pl*

canary /kəˈneərɪ/ *n* Kanarienvogel *m*

cancel /ˈkænsl/ *vt/i (pt/pp* **cancelled**) absagen; entwerten *(stamp)*; *(annul)* rückgängig machen; *(Comm)* stornieren; bestellen *(newspaper)*; **be ~led** ausfallen. **~lation** /-ə'leɪʃn/ *n* Absage *f*

cancer /ˈkænsə(r)/ *n*, & *(Astr)* **C~** Krebs *m.* **~ous** /-rəs/ *a* krebsig

candelabra /kændə'lɑ:brə/ *n* Armleuchter *m*

candid /ˈkændɪd/ *a*, **-ly** *adv* offen

candidate /ˈkændɪdət/ *n* Kandidat(in) *m(f)*

candied /ˈkændɪd/ *a* kandiert

candle /ˈkændl/ *n* Kerze *f.* **~stick** *n* Kerzenständer *m*, Leuchter *m*

candour /ˈkændə(r)/ *n* Offenheit *f*

candy /ˈkændɪ/ *n (Amer)* Süßigkeiten *pl*; **[piece of]** ~ Bonbon *m.* **~floss** /-flɒs/ *n* Zuckerwatte *f*

cane /keɪn/ *n* Rohr *nt*; *(stick)* Stock *m* □ *vt* mit dem Stock züchtigen

canine /ˈkeɪnaɪn/ *a* Hunde-. **~tooth** *n* Eckzahn *m*

canister /ˈkænɪstə(r)/ *n* Blechdose *f*

cannabis /ˈkænəbɪs/ *n* Haschisch *m*

canned /kænd/ *a* Dosen-, Büchsen-; ~ **music** *(fam)* Musik *f* aus der Konserve

cannibal /ˈkænɪbl/ *n* Kannibale *m.* **~ism** /-bəlɪzm/ *n* Kannibalismus *m*

cannon /'kænən/ n Kanone f.
~ball n Kanonenkugel f

cannot /'kænɒt/ see **can²**

canny /'kænɪ/ a schlau

canoe /kə'nu:/ n Paddelboot nt;
(Sport) Kanu nt □ vi paddeln;
(Sport) Kanu fahren

canon /'kænən/ n Kanon m; (person) Kanonikus m. **~ize** /-aɪz/ vt
kanonisieren

'can-opener n Dosenöffner m,
Büchsenöffner m

canopy /'kænəpɪ/ n Baldachin m

cant /kænt/ n Heuchelei f

can't /kɑ:nt/ = cannot. See **can²**

cantankerous /kæn'tæŋkərəs/ a
zänkisch

canteen /kæn'ti:n/ n Kantine f; **~
of cutlery** Besteckkasten m

canter /'kæntə(r)/ n Kanter m □ vi
kantern

canvas /'kænvəs/ n Segeltuch nt;
(Art) Leinwand f; (painting) Gemälde nt

canvass /'kænvəs/ vi um Stimmen werben

canyon /'kænjən/ n Cañon m

cap /kæp/ n Kappe f, Mütze f;
(nurse's) Haube f; (top, lid)
Verschluss m □ vt (pt/pp capped)
(fig) übertreffen

capability /keɪpə'bɪlətɪ/ n Fähigkeit f

capable /'keɪpəbl/ a, **-bly** adv
fähig; **be ~ of doing sth** fähig
sein, etw zu tun

capacity /kə'pæsətɪ/ n Fassungsvermögen f; (ability) Fähigkeit
f; **in my ~ as** in meiner Eigenschaft als

cape¹ /keɪp/ n (cloak) Cape nt

cape² n (Geog) Kap nt

caper¹ /'keɪpə(r)/ vi herumspringen

caper² n (Culin) Kaper f

capital /'kæpɪtl/ a (letter) groß □ n
(town) Hauptstadt f; (money) Kapital nt; (letter) Großbuchstabe m

capital|ism /'kæpɪtəlɪzm/ n Kapitalismus m. **~ist** /-ɪst/ a kapitalistisch □ n Kapitalist m. **~ize**
/-aɪz/ vi **~ize on** (fig) Kapital
schlagen aus. **~ 'letter** n Großbuchstabe m. **~ 'punishment** n
Todesstrafe f

capitulat|e /kə'pɪtjʊleɪt/ vi kapitulieren. **~ion** /-'leɪʃn/ n Kapitulation f

capricious /kə'prɪʃəs/ a launisch

Capricorn /'kæprɪkɔ:n/ n (Astr)
Steinbock m

capsize /kæp'saɪz/ vi kentern □ vt
zum Kentern bringen

capsule /'kæpsju:l/ n Kapsel f

captain /'kæptɪn/ n Kapitän m;
(Mil) Hauptmann m □ vt anführen (team)

caption /'kæpʃn/ n Überschrift f;
(of illustration) Bildtext m

captivate /'kæptɪveɪt/ vt bezaubern

captive /'kæptɪv/ a **hold/take
~e** gefangen halten/nehmen □ n
Gefangene(r) m/f. **~ity** /-'tɪvətɪ/
n Gefangenschaft f

capture /'kæptʃə(r)/ n Gefangennahme f □ vt gefangen nehmen;
(ein)fangen (animal); (Mil) einnehmen (town)

car /kɑ:(r)/ n Auto nt, Wagen m;
by ~ mit dem Auto od Wagen

carafe /kə'ræf/ n Karaffe f

caramel /'kærəmel/ n Karamell
m

carat /'kærət/ n Karat nt

caravan /'kærəvæn/ n Wohnwagen m; (procession) Karawane
f

carbohydrate /kɑ:bə'haɪdreɪt/ n
Kohlenhydrat nt

carbon /'kɑ:bən/ n Kohlenstoff
m; (paper) Kohlepapier nt; (copy)
Durchschlag m

carbon: **~ copy** n Durchschlag m.
~ di'oxide n Kohlendioxid nt; (in
drink) Kohlensäure f. **~ paper** n
Kohlepapier nt

carburettor /ˈkɑːbjuˈretə(r)/ n Vergaser m

carcass /ˈkɑːkəs/ n Kadaver m

card /kɑːd/ n Karte f

'cardboard n Pappe f, Karton m. ~ 'box n Pappschachtel f; (large) [Papp]karton m

'card-game n Kartenspiel m

cardiac /ˈkɑːdiæk/ a Herz-

cardigan /ˈkɑːdɪgən/ n Strickjacke f

cardinal /ˈkɑːdɪnl/ a Kardinal-; ~ number Kardinalzahl f □ n (Relig) Kardinal m

card 'index n Kartei f

care /keə(r)/ n Sorgfalt f; (caution) Vorsicht f; (protection) Obhut f; (looking after) Pflege f; (worry) Sorge f. ~ of (on letter abbr c/o) bei; take ~ vorsichtig sein; take into ~ in Pflege nehmen; take ~ of sich kümmern um □ vi ~ about sich kümmern um; ~ for (like) mögen; (look after) betreuen; I don't ~ das ist mir gleich

career /kəˈrɪə(r)/ n Laufbahn f; (profession) Beruf m □ vi rasen

care: ~free a sorglos. ~ful a, -ly adv sorgfältig; (cautious) vorsichtig. ~less a, -ly adv nachlässig. ~lessness n Nachlässigkeit f

caress /kəˈres/ n Liebkosung f □ vt liebkosen

'caretaker n Hausmeister m

'car ferry n Autofähre f

cargo /ˈkɑːgəʊ/ n (pl -es) Ladung f

Caribbean /kærɪˈbiːən/ n the ~ die Karibik

caricature /ˈkærɪkətjʊə(r)/ n Karikatur f □ vt karikieren

caring /ˈkeərɪŋ/ a (parent) liebevoll; (profession, attitude) sozial

carnage /ˈkɑːnɪdʒ/ n Gemetzel m

carnal /ˈkɑːnl/ a fleischlich

carnation /kɑːˈneɪʃn/ n Nelke f

carnival /ˈkɑːnɪvl/ n Karneval m

carnivorous /kɑːˈnɪvərəs/ a Fleisch fressend

carol /ˈkærl/ n [Christmas] ~ Weihnachtslied nt

carp¹ /kɑːp/ n inv Karpfen m

carp² □ vi nörgeln; ~ at herumnörgeln an (+ dat)

'car park n Parkplatz m; (multistorey) Parkhaus nt; (underground) Tiefgarage f

carpent|er /ˈkɑːpɪntə(r)/ n Zimmermann m; (joiner) Tischler m. ~ry n Tischlerei f

carpet /ˈkɑːpɪt/ n Teppich m □ vt mit Teppich auslegen

carriage /ˈkærɪdʒ/ n Kutsche f; (Rail) Wagen m; (of goods) Beförderung f; (cost) Frachtkosten pl; (bearing) Haltung f. ~way n Fahrbahn f

carrier /ˈkærɪə(r)/ n Träger(in) m(f); (Comm) Spediteur m; ~ [bag] Tragetasche f

carrot /ˈkærət/ n Möhre f, Karotte f

carry /ˈkærɪ/ vt/i (pt/pp -ied) tragen; be carried away (fam) hingerissen sein. ~ off vt wegtragen; gewinnen (prize). ~ on vi weitermachen; ~ on at (fam) herumnörgeln an (+ dat); ~ on with (fam) eine Affäre haben mit □ vt führen; (continue) fortführen. ~ out vt hinaus-/heraustragen; (perform) ausführen

'carry-cot n Babytragetasche f

cart /kɑːt/ n Karren m; put the ~ before the horse das Pferd beim Schwanz aufzäumen □ vt karren; (fam: carry) schleppen

cartilage /ˈkɑːtɪlɪdʒ/ n (Anat) Knorpel m

carton /ˈkɑːtn/ n [Papp]karton m; (for drink) Tüte f; (of cream, yoghurt) Becher m

cartoon /kɑːˈtuːn/ n Karikatur f; (joke) Witzzeichnung f; (strip) Comic Strips pl; (film) Zeichentrickfilm m; (Art) Karton m. ~ist n Karikaturist m

cartridge /'kɑːtrɪdʒ/ n Patrone f; (for film, typewriter ribbon) Kassette f; (of record player) Tonabnehmer m

carve /kɑːv/ vt schnitzen; (in stone) hauen; (Culin) aufschneiden

carving /'kɑːvɪŋ/ n Schnitzerei f. **~-knife** n Tranchiermesser nt

'car wash n Autowäsche f; (place) Autowaschanlage f

case[1] /keɪs/ n Fall m; **in any ~** auf jeden Fall; **just in ~** für alle Fälle; **in ~ he comes** falls er kommt

case[2] n Kasten m; (crate) Kiste f; (for spectacles) Etui nt; (suitcase) Koffer m; (for display) Vitrine f

cash /kæʃ/ n Bargeld nt; **pay [in] ~ [in]** bar bezahlen; **~ on delivery** per Nachnahme □ vt einlösen (cheque). **~ desk** n Kasse f

cashier /kæ'ʃɪə(r)/ n Kassierer(in) m(f)

'cash register n Registrierkasse f

casino /kə'siːnəʊ/ n Kasino nt

cask /kɑːsk/ n Fass nt

casket /'kɑːskɪt/ n Kasten m; (Amer: coffin) Sarg m

casserole /'kæsərəʊl/ n Schmortopf m; (stew) Eintopf m

cassette /kə'set/ n Kassette f. **~ recorder** n Kassettenrecorder m

cast /kɑːst/ n (throw) Wurf m; (mould) Form f; (model) Abguss m; (Theat) Besetzung f; **[plaster] ~** (Med) Gipsverband m □ vt (pt/pp **cast**) (throw) werfen; (shed) abwerfen; (give up vote) abgeben; (metal, Theat) besetzen (role); **~ a glance** at einen Blick werfen auf (+ acc). **~ off** vi (Naut) ablegen □ vt (Knitting) abketten. **~ on** vt (Knitting) anschlagen

castanets /kæstə'nets/ npl Kastagnetten pl

castaway /'kɑːstəweɪ/ n Schiffbrüchige(r) m/f

caste /kɑːst/ n Kaste f

cast 'iron n Gusseisen nt

cast-'iron a gusseisern

castle /'kɑːsl/ n Schloss nt; (fortified) Burg f; (Chess) Turm m

'cast-offs npl abgelegte Kleidung f

castor /'kɑːstə(r)/ n (wheel) [Lauf]rolle f

castor sugar n Streuzucker m

castrat|**e** /kæ'streɪt/ vt kastrieren. **~ion** n -eɪʃn/ Kastration f

casual /'kæzʊəl/ a, **-ly** adv (chance) zufällig; (offhand) lässig; (informal) zwanglos; (not permanent) Gelegenheits-; (not wear) Freizeitbekleidung f

casualty /'kæzʊəltɪ/ n [Todes]opfer nt; (injured person) Verletzte(r) m/f; **~ [department]** Unfallstation f

cat /kæt/ n Katze f

catalogue /'kætəlɒg/ n Katalog m □ vt katalogisieren

catalyst /'kætəlɪst/ n (Chem & fig) Katalysator m

catalytic /kætə'lɪtɪk/ a **~ converter** (Auto) Katalysator m

catapult /'kætəpʌlt/ n Katapult nt □ vt katapultieren

cataract /'kætərækt/ n (Med) grauer Star m

catarrh /kə'tɑː(r)/ n Katarrh m

catastroph|**e** /kə'tæstrəfɪ/ n Katastrophe f. **~ic** /kætə'strɒfɪk/ a katastrophal

catch /kætʃ/ n (of fish) Fang m; (fastener) Verschluss m; (on door) Klinke f; (fam: snag) Haken m □ v (pt/pp **caught**) □ vt fangen; (be in time for) erreichen; (travel by) fahren mit; (become infected with) bekommen (illness); **~ a cold** sich erkälten; **~ sight of** erblicken; **~ s.o. stealing** jdn beim Stehlen erwischen; **~ one's finger in the door** sich (dat) den Finger in der Tür [ein]klemmen □ vi (burn) anbrennen; (get stuck) klemmen. **~ on** vi (fam) (understand) kapieren; (become popular) sich durchsetzen

~ up *vt* einholen □ *vi* aufholen; **~ up with** einholen (*s.o.*); nachholen (*work*)

catching /'kætʃɪŋ/ *a* ansteckend

catch: **~-phrase** *n*, **~-word** *n* Schlagwort *nt*

catchy /'kætʃɪ/ *a* (**-ier, -iest**) einprägsam

catechism /'kætɪkɪzm/ *n* Katechismus *m*

categor|ical /kætɪ'gɒrɪkl/ *a*, **-ly** *adv* kategorisch. **~y** /'kætɪgərɪ/ *n* Kategorie *f*

cater /keɪtə(r)/ *vi* **~ for** beköstigen; (*firm:*) das Essen liefern für (*party*); (*fig*) eingestellt sein auf (+ *acc*). **~ing** *n* (*trade*) Gaststättengewerbe *nt*

caterpillar /'kætəpɪlə(r)/ *n* Raupe *f*

cathedral /kə'θiːdrl/ *n* Dom *m*, Kathedrale *f*

Catholic /'kæθəlɪk/ *a* katholisch □ *n* Katholik(in) *m(f)*. **C ~ism** /kə'θɒlɪsɪzm/ *n* Katholizismus *m*

catkin /'kætkɪn/ *n* (*Bot*) Kätzchen *nt*

cattle /'kætl/ *npl* Vieh *nt*

catty /'kætɪ/ *a* (**-ier, -iest**) boshaft

caught /kɔːt/ *see* **catch**

cauldron /'kɔːldrən/ *n* [großer] Kessel *m*

cauliflower /'kɒlɪ-/ *n* Blumenkohl *m*

cause /kɔːz/ *n* Ursache *f*; (*reason*) Grund *m*; **good ~** gute Sache *f* □ *vt* verursachen; **~ s.o. to do sth** jdn veranlassen, etw zu tun

'causeway *n* [Insel]damm *m*

caustic /'kɔːstɪk/ *a* ätzend; (*fig*) beißend

cauterize /'kɔːtəraɪz/ *vt* kauterisieren

caution /'kɔːʃn/ *n* Vorsicht *f*; (*warning*) Verwarnung *f* □ *vt* (*Jur*) verwarnen

cautious /'kɔːʃəs/ *a*, **-ly** *adv* vorsichtig

cavalry /'kævəlrɪ/ *n* Kavallerie *f*

cave /keɪv/ *n* Höhle *f* □ *vi* **~ in** einstürzen

cavern /'kævən/ *n* Höhle *f*

caviare /'kævɪɑː(r)/ *n* Kaviar *m*

caving /'keɪvɪŋ/ *n* Höhlenforschung *f*

cavity /'kævətɪ/ *n* Hohlraum *m*; (*in tooth*) Loch *nt*

cavort /kə'vɔːt/ *vi* tollen

cease /siːs/ *n* **without ~** unaufhörlich □ *vt/i* aufhören. **~fire** *n* Waffenruhe *f*. **~less** *a*, **-ly** *adv* unaufhörlich

cedar /'siːdə(r)/ *n* Zeder *f*

cede /siːd/ *vt* abtreten (**to an** + *acc*)

ceiling /'siːlɪŋ/ *n* [Zimmer]decke *f*; (*fig*) oberste Grenze *f*

celebrat|e /'selɪbreɪt/ *vt/i* feiern. **~ed** *a* berühmt (**for** wegen). **~ion** /-'breɪʃn/ *n* Feier *f*

celebrity /sɪ'lebrətɪ/ *n* Berühmtheit *f*

celery /'selərɪ/ *n* [Stangen]sellerie *m & f*

celiba|cy /'selɪbəsɪ/ *n* Zölibat *nt*. **~te** *a* **be ~te** im Zölibat leben

cell /sel/ *n* Zelle *f*

cellar /'selə(r)/ *n* Keller *m*

cellist /'tʃelɪst/ *n* Cellist(in) *m(f)*

cello /'tʃeləʊ/ *n* Cello *nt*

Celsius /'selsɪəs/ *a* Celsius

Celt /kelt/ *n* Kelte *m*/ Keltin *f*. **~ic** *a* keltisch

cement /sɪ'ment/ *n* Zement *m*; (*adhesive*) Kitt *m* □ *vt* zementieren; (*stick*) kitten

cemetery /'semɪtrɪ/ *n* Friedhof *m*

censor /'sensə(r)/ *n* Zensor *m* □ *vt* zensieren. **~ship** *n* Zensur *f*

censure /'senʃə(r)/ *n* Tadel *m* □ *vt* tadeln

census /'sensəs/ *n* Volkszählung *f*

cent /sent/ *n* (*coin*) Cent *m*

centenary /sen'tiːnərɪ/ *n*, (*Amer*) **centennial** /sen'tenɪəl/ *n* Hundertjahrfeier *f*

center /'sentə(r)/ *n* (*Amer*) = **centre**

centi|grade /'sentɪ-/ *a* Celsius; 5° ~ 5° Celsius. **~metre** *m* Zentimeter *m* & *nt*. **~pede** /-pi:d/ *n* Tausendfüßler *m*

central /'sentrəl/ *a*, **-ly** *adv* zentral. ~ **'heating** *n* Zentralheizung *f*. **~ize** *vt* zentralisieren. **~reser'vation** *n* (*Auto*) Mittelstreifen *m*

centre /'sentə(r)/ *n* Zentrum *nt*; (*middle*) Mitte *f* □ *v* (*pt/pp* **centred**) □ *vt* zentrieren; □ *vi* (*fig*) sich drehen um. **~'forward** *n* Mittelstürmer *m*

centrifugal /sentrɪ'fju:gl/ *a* ~ **force** Fliehkraft *f*

century /'sentʃərɪ/ *n* Jahrhundert *nt*

ceramic /sɪ'ræmɪk/ *a* Keramik-. **~s** *n* Keramik *f*

cereal /'sɪərɪəl/ *n* Getreide *nt*; (*breakfast food*) Frühstücksflocken *pl*

cerebral /'serɪbrl/ *a* Gehirn-

ceremon|ial /serɪ'məʊnɪəl/ *a*, **-ly** *adv* zeremoniell, feierlich □ *n* Zeremoniell *nt*. **~ious** /-ɪəs/ *a*, **-ly** *adv* förmlich

ceremony /'serɪmənɪ/ *n* Zeremonie *f*, Feier *f*; **without** ~ ohne weitere Umstände

certain /'sɜ:tn/ *a* sicher; (*not named*) gewiss; **for** ~ mit Bestimmtheit; **make** ~ (*check*) sich vergewissern (**that** dass); (*ensure*) dafür sorgen (**that** dass); **he is** ~ **to win** er wird ganz bestimmt siegen. **~ly** *adv* bestimmt, sicher; **~ly not!** auf keinen Fall! **~ty** *n* Sicherheit *f*, Gewissheit *f*; **it's a ~ty** es ist sicher

certificate /sə'tɪfɪkət/ *n* Bescheinigung *f*; (*Jur*) Urkunde *f*; (*Sch*) Zeugnis *nt*

certify /'sɜ:tɪfaɪ/ *vt* (*pt/pp* **-ied**) bescheinigen; (*declare insane*) für geisteskrank erklären

cessation /se'seɪʃn/ *n* Ende *nt*

cesspool /'ses-/ *n* Senkgrube *f*

cf. *abbr* (*compare*) vgl.

chafe /tʃeɪf/ *vt* wund reiben

chaff /tʃɑ:f/ *n* Spreu *f*

chaffinch /'tʃæfɪntʃ/ *n* Buchfink *m*

chain /tʃeɪn/ *n* Kette *f* □ *vt* ketten (**to** an + *acc*). ~ **up** *vt* anketten

chain: ~ **re'action** *n* Kettenreaktion *f*. **~-smoker** *n* Kettenraucher *m*. ~ **store** *n* Kettenladen *m*

chair /tʃeə(r)/ *n* Stuhl *m*; (*Univ*) Lehrstuhl *m*; (*Adm*) Vorsitzende(r) *m/f* □ *vt* den Vorsitz führen bei. **~-lift** *n* Sessellift *m*. **~man** *n* Vorsitzende(r) *m/f*

chalet /'ʃæleɪ/ *n* Chalet *nt*

chalice /'tʃælɪs/ *n* (*Relig*) Kelch *m*

chalk /tʃɔ:k/ *n* Kreide *f*. **~y** *a* kreidig

challeng|e /'tʃælɪndʒ/ *n* Herausforderung *f*; (*Mil*) Anruf *m* □ *vt* herausfordern; (*Mil*) anrufen; (*fig*) anfechten (*statement*). **~er** *n* Herausforderer *m*. **~ing** *a* herausfordernd; (*demanding*) anspruchsvoll

chamber /'tʃeɪmbə(r)/ *n* Kammer *f*; **~s** *pl* (*Jur*) [Anwalts]büro *nt*; **C~ of Commerce** Handelskammer *f*

chamber: **~maid** *n* Zimmermädchen *nt*. **~music** *n* Kammermusik *f*. **~pot** *n* Nachttopf *m*

chamois[1] /'ʃæmwɑ:/ *n inv* (*animal*) Gämse *f*

chamois[2] /'ʃæmɪ/ *n* ~ **[-leather]** Ledertuch *nt*

champagne /ʃæm'peɪn/ *n* Champagner *m*

champion /'tʃæmpɪən/ *n* (*Sport*) Meister(in) *m(f)*; (*of cause*) Verfechter *m* □ *vt* sich einsetzen für. **~ship** *n* (*Sport*) Meisterschaft *f*

chance /tʃɑ:ns/ *n* Zufall *m*; (*prospect*) Chancen *pl*; (*likelihood*) Aussicht *f*; (*opportunity*) Gelegenheit *f*; **by** ~ zufällig; **take a** ~ ein Risiko eingehen; **give s.o. a** ~ jdm eine Chance geben □ *attrib* zufällig □ *vt* ~ **it** es riskieren

chancellor /'tʃɑːnsələ(r)/ n
Kanzler m; (Univ) Rektor m; **C~
of the Exchequer** Schatzkanzler
m

chancy /'tʃɑːnsɪ/ a riskant

chandelier /ʃændə'lɪə(r)/ n
Kronleuchter m

change /tʃeɪndʒ/ n Veränderung
f; (alteration) Änderung f;
(money) Wechselgeld nt; **for a ~**
zur Abwechslung □ vt wechseln;
(alter) ändern; (exchange) um-
tauschen (**for** gegen); (transform)
verwandeln; trocken legen
⟨baby⟩; **~ one's clothes** sich
umziehen; (**~ trains**) umsteigen
□ vi sich verändern; (**~ clothes**)
sich umziehen; (**~ trains**) umsteigen; **all ~!** alles aussteigen!

changeable /'tʃeɪndʒəbl/ a wech-
selhaft

'changing-room n Umkleide-
raum m

channel /'tʃænl/ n Rinne f;
(Radio, TV) Kanal m; (fig) Weg m;
the [English] C~ der Ärmelkanal; **the C~ Islands** die Kanal-
inseln □ vt (pt/pp **channelled**)
leiten; (fig) lenken

chant /tʃɑːnt/ n liturgischer Gesang m □ vt singen; (demonstrators:) skandieren

chaos /'keɪɒs/ n Chaos nt. **~tic**
/-'ɒtɪk/ a chaotisch

chap /tʃæp/ n (fam) Kerl m

chapel /'tʃæpl/ n Kapelle f

chaperon /'ʃæpərəʊn/ n An-
standsdame f □ vt begleiten

chaplain /'tʃæplɪn/ n Geist-
liche(r) m

chapped /tʃæpt/ a ⟨skin⟩ aufgesprungen

chapter /'tʃæptə(r)/ n Kapitel nt

char¹ /tʃɑː(r)/ n (fam) Putzfrau f

char² vt (pt/pp **charred**) (burn)
verkohlen

character /'kærɪktə(r)/ n
Charakter m; (in novel, play) Gestalt f; (Typ) Schriftzeichen nt;
out of ~ uncharakteristisch;
quite a ~ (fam) ein Original

characteristic /kærɪktə'rɪstɪk/ a,
-ally adv charakteristisch (**of**
für) □ n Merkmal nt

characterize /'kærɪktəraɪz/ vt
charakterisieren

charade /ʃə'rɑːd/ n Scharade f

charcoal /'tʃɑː-/ n Holzkohle f

charge /tʃɑːdʒ/ n (price) Gebühr
f; (Electr) Ladung f; (attack) Angriff m; (Jur) Anklage f; **free of
~** kostenlos; **be in ~** verantwortlich sein (**of** für); **take ~** die Aufsicht übernehmen (**of** über + acc)
□ vt berechnen ⟨fee⟩; (Electr)
laden; (attack) angreifen; (Jur)
anklagen (**with** gen); **~ s.o. for
sth** jdm etw berechnen □ vi
(attack) angreifen

chariot /'tʃærɪət/ n Wagen m

charisma /kə'rɪzmə/ n Charisma
nt. **~tic** /kærɪz'mætɪk/ a char-
ismatisch

charitable /'tʃærɪtəbl/ a wohltä-
tig; (kind) wohlwollend

charity /'tʃærətɪ/ n Nächsten-
liebe f; (organization) wohltätige
Einrichtung f; **for ~** für
Wohltätigkeitszwecke; **live on ~**
von Almosen leben

charlatan /'ʃɑːlətən/ n Scharlatan m

charm /tʃɑːm/ n Reiz m; (of person) Charme f; (object) Amulett
nt □ vt bezaubern. **~ing** a, **-ly** adv
reizend; ⟨person, smile⟩ charmant

chart /tʃɑːt/ n Karte f; (table) Tabelle f

charter /'tʃɑːtə(r)/ n **~ [flight]**
Charterflug m □ vt chartern; **~ed
accountant** Wirtschaftsprü-
fer(in) m(f)

charwoman /'tʃɑː-/ n Putzfrau f

chase /tʃeɪs/ n Verfolgungsjagd
f □ vt jagen, verfolgen. **~ away** or
off vt wegjagen

chasm /'kæzm/ n Kluft f

chassis /'ʃæsɪ/ n (pl **chassis**
/-sɪz/) Chassis nt

chaste /tʃeɪst/ a keusch

chastise /tʃæ'staɪz/ vt züchtigen

chastity /'tʃæstɪtɪ/ n Keuschheit f

chat /tʃæt/ n Plauderei f; **have a ~ with** plaudern mit □ vi (pt/pp **chatted**) plaudern. **~ show** n Talkshow f

chatter /'tʃætə(r)/ n Geschwätz nt □ vi schwatzen; (child:) plappern; ⟨teeth:⟩ klappern. **~box** n (fam) Plappermaul nt

chatty /'tʃætɪ/ a (-ier, -iest) geschwätzig

chauffeur /'ʃəʊfə(r)/ n Chauffeur m

chauvin|ism /'ʃəʊvɪnɪzm/ n Chauvinismus m. **~ist** n Chauvinist m; **male ~ist** (fam) Chauvi m

cheap /tʃiːp/ a & adv (-er, -est), **-ly** adv billig. **~en** vt entwürdigen; **~en oneself** sich erniedrigen

cheat /tʃiːt/ n Betrüger(in) m(f); (at games) Mogler m □ vt betrügen □ vi (at games) mogeln (fam)

check¹ /tʃek/ a (squared) kariert □ n Karo nt

check² n Überprüfung f; (inspection) Kontrolle f; (Chess) Schach nt; (Amer: bill) Rechnung f; (Amer: cheque) Scheck m; (Amer: tick) Haken m; **keep a ~ on** kontrollieren □ vt [über]prüfen; (inspect) kontrollieren; (restrain) hemmen; (stop) aufhalten □ vi [go and] ~ nachsehen. **~ in** vi sich anmelden; (Aviat) einchecken □ vt abfertigen; einchecken. **~ out** vi sich abmelden. **~ up** vi prüfen, kontrollieren. **~ up on** vt überprüfen

checked /tʃekt/ a kariert. **~ers** n (Amer) Damespiel nt

check: **~mate** int schachmatt! **~-out** n Kasse f. **~room** n (Amer) Garderobe f. **~-up** n (Med) [Kontroll]untersuchung f

cheek /tʃiːk/ n Backe f; (impudence) Frechheit f. **~y a**, **-ily** adv frech

cheep /tʃiːp/ vi piepen

cheer /tʃɪə(r)/ n Beifallsruf m; **three ~s** ein dreifaches Hoch (for auf + acc); **~s!** prost! (goodbye) tschüs! □ vt zujubeln (+ dat) □ vi jubeln. **~ up** vt aufmuntern; aufheitern □ vi munterer werden. **~ful** a, **-ly** adv fröhlich. **~fulness** n Fröhlichkeit f

cheerio /tʃɪərɪ'əʊ/ int (fam) tschüs!

cheerless a trostlos

cheese /tʃiːz/ n Käse m. **~cake** n Käsekuchen m

cheetah /'tʃiːtə/ n Gepard m

chef /ʃef/ n Koch m

chemical /'kemɪkl/ a, **-ly** adv chemisch □ n Chemikalie f

chemist /'kemɪst/ n (pharmacist) Apotheker(in) m(f); (scientist) Chemiker(in) m(f); **~'s [shop]** Drogerie f; (dispensing) Apotheke f. **~ry** n Chemie f

cheque /tʃek/ n Scheck m. **~book** n Scheckbuch nt. **~ card** n Scheckkarte f

cherish /'tʃerɪʃ/ vt lieben; (fig) hegen

cherry /'tʃerɪ/ n Kirsche f □ attrib Kirsch-

cherub /'tʃerəb/ n Engelchen nt

chess /tʃes/ n Schach nt

chess: **~board** n Schachbrett nt. **~man** n Schachfigur f

chest /tʃest/ n Brust f; (box) Truhe f

chestnut /'tʃesnʌt/ n Esskastanie f, Marone f; (horse-) [Ross]kastanie f

chest of 'drawers n Kommode f

chew /tʃuː/ vt kauen. **~ing-gum** n Kaugummi m

chic /ʃiːk/ a schick

chick /tʃɪk/ n Küken nt

chicken /'tʃɪkɪn/ n Huhn nt □ attrib Hühner- □ a (fam) feige □ vi **~ out** (fam) kneifen. **~pox** n Windpocken pl

chicory /'tʃɪkərɪ/ n Chicorée f; (in coffee) Zichorie f

chief /tʃiːf/ a Haupt– □ n Chef m; (of tribe) Häuptling m. ~ly adv hauptsächlich

chilblain /'tʃɪlbleɪn/ n Frostbeule f

child /tʃaɪld/ n (pl ~ren) Kind nt

child: ~birth n Geburt f. ~hood n Kindheit f. ~ish a kindisch. ~less a kinderlos. ~like a kindlich. ~minder n Tagesmutter f

children /'tʃɪldrən/ npl see child

Chile /'tʃɪlɪ/ n Chile nt

chill /tʃɪl/ n Kälte f; (illness) Erkältung f □ vt kühlen

chilli /'tʃɪlɪ/ n (pl -es) Chili m

chilly /'tʃɪlɪ/ a kühl; I felt ~ mich fröstelte [es]

chime /tʃaɪm/ vi läuten; (clock:) schlagen

chimney /'tʃɪmnɪ/ n Schornstein m. ~pot n Schornsteinaufsatz m. ~sweep n Schornsteinfeger m

chimpanzee /tʃɪmpæn'ziː/ n Schimpanse m

chin /tʃɪn/ n Kinn nt

china /'tʃaɪnə/ n Porzellan nt

Chin|a China nt. ~ese /-'niːz/ a chinesisch □ n (Lang) Chinesisch nt; the ~ese pl die Chinesen. ~ese 'lantern n Lampion m

chink[1] /tʃɪŋk/ n (slit) Ritze f

chink[2] n Geklirr nt □ vi klirren; (coins:) klimpern

chip /tʃɪp/ n (fragment) Span m; (in china, paintwork) angeschlagene Stelle f; (Computing, Gambling) Chip m; ~s pl (Culin) Pommes frites pl; (Amer: crisps) Chips pl □ vt (pt/pp chipped) (damage) anschlagen. ~ped a angeschlagen

chiropodist /kɪ'rɒpədɪst/ n Fußpfleger(in) m(f). ~y n Fußpflege f

chirp /tʃɜːp/ vi zwitschern; (cricket:) zirpen. ~y a (fam) munter

chisel /'tʃɪzl/ n Meißel m □ vt/i (pt/pp chiselled) meißeln

chit /tʃɪt/ n Zettel m

chivalrous /'ʃɪvlrəs/ a, ~ly adv ritterlich. ~ry n Ritterlichkeit f

chives /tʃaɪvz/ npl Schnittlauch m

chlorine /'klɔːriːn/ n Chlor m

chloroform /'klɒrəfɔːm/ n Chloroform nt

chocolate /'tʃɒkələt/ n Schokolade f; (sweet) Praline f

choice /tʃɔɪs/ n Wahl f; (variety) Auswahl f □ a auserlesen

choir /'kwaɪə(r)/ n Chor m. ~boy n Chorknabe m

choke /tʃəʊk/ n (Auto) Choke m □ vt würgen; (to death) erwürgen □ vi sich verschlucken; ~ on [fast] ersticken an (+ dat)

cholera /'kɒlərə/ n Cholera f

cholesterol /kə'lestərɒl/ n Cholesterin nt

choose /tʃuːz/ vt/i (pt chose, pp chosen) wählen; (select) sich (dat) aussuchen; ~ to do/go [freiwillig] tun/gehen; as you ~ wie Sie wollen

choos[e]y /'tʃuːzi/ a (fam) wählerisch

chop /tʃɒp/ n (blow) Hieb m; (Culin) Kotelett nt □ vt (pt/pp chopped) hacken. ~ down vt abhacken; fällen (tree). ~ off vt abhacken

chop|per /'tʃɒpə(r)/ n Beil nt; (fam) Hubschrauber m. ~py a kabbelig

'chopsticks npl Essstäbchen pl

choral /'kɔːrəl/ a Chor–; ~ society Gesangverein m

chord /kɔːd/ n (Mus) Akkord m

chore /tʃɔː(r)/ n lästige Pflicht f; [household] ~s Hausarbeit f

choreography /kɒrɪ'ɒgrəfɪ/ n Choreographie f

chortle /'tʃɔːtl/ n [vor Lachen] glucksen

chorus /'kɔːrəs/ n Chor m; (of song) Refrain m

chose, chosen /tʃəʊz, 'tʃəʊzn/ see choose

Christ /kraɪst/ n Christus m

christen /'krɪsn/ vt taufen. **~ing** n Taufe f

Christian /'krɪstʃən/ a christlich □ n Christ(in) m(f). **~ity** /-stɪ'ænətɪ/ n Christentum nt. **~ name** n Vorname m

Christmas /'krɪsməs/ n Weihnachten nt. **~ card** n Weihnachtskarte f. **~ 'Day** n erster Weihnachtstag m. **~ 'Eve** n Heiligabend m. **~ tree** n Weihnachtsbaum m

chrome /krəum/ n, **chromium** /'krəumɪəm/ n Chrom nt

chromosome /'krəuməsəum/ n Chromosom nt

chronic /'krɒnɪk/ a chronisch

chronicle /'krɒnɪkl/ n Chronik f

chronological /krɒnə'lɒdʒɪkl/ a, **-ly** adv chronologisch

chrysalis /'krɪsəlɪs/ n Puppe f

chrysanthemum /krɪ'sæn-θəməm/ n Chrysantheme f

chubby /'tʃʌbɪ/ a (-ier, -iest) mollig

chuck /tʃʌk/ vt (fam) schmeißen. **~ out** vt (fam) rausschmeißen

chuckle /'tʃʌkl/ vi in sich (acc) hineinlachen

chum /tʃʌm/ n Freund(in) m(f)

chunk /tʃʌŋk/ n Stück nt

church /tʃɜ:tʃ/ n Kirche f. **~yard** n Friedhof m

churlish /'tʃɜ:lɪʃ/ a unhöflich

churn /tʃɜ:n/ n Butterfass nt; (for milk) Milchkanne f □ vt **~ out** am laufenden Band produzieren

chute /ʃu:t/ n Rutsche f; (for rubbish) Müllschlucker m

CID abbr (**Criminal Investigation Department**) Kripo f

cider /'saɪdə(r)/ n Apfelwein m

cigar /sɪ'gɑ:(r)/ n Zigarre f

cigarette /sɪgə'ret/ n Zigarette f

cine-camera /'sɪnɪ-/ n Filmkamera f

cinema /'sɪnɪmə/ n Kino nt

cinnamon /'sɪnəmən/ n Zimt m

cipher /'saɪfə(r)/ n (code) Chiffre f; (numeral) Ziffer f; (fig) Null f

circle /'sɜ:kl/ n Kreis m; (Theat) Rang m □ vt umkreisen □ vi kreisen

circuit /'sɜ:kɪt/ n Runde f; (racetrack) Rennbahn f; (Electr) Stromkreis m. **~ous** /sə'kju:ɪtəs/ a **~ route** Umweg m

circular /'sɜ:kjulə(r)/ a kreisförmig □ n Rundschreiben nt. **~ 'saw** n Kreissäge f. **~ 'tour** n Rundfahrt f

circulat|e /'sɜ:kjuleɪt/ vt in Umlauf setzen □ vi zirkulieren. **~ion** /-'leɪʃn/ n Kreislauf m; (of newspaper) Auflage f

circumcis|e /'sɜ:kəmsaɪz/ vt beschneiden. **~ion** /-'sɪʒn/ n Beschneidung f

circumference /sə'kʌmfərəns/ n Umfang m

circumspect /'sɜ:kəmspekt/ a, **-ly** adv umsichtig

circumstance /'sɜ:kəmstəns/ n Umstand m; **~s** pl Umstände pl; (financial) Verhältnisse pl

circus /'sɜ:kəs/ n Zirkus m

CIS abbr (**Commonwealth of Independent States**) GUS f

cistern /'sɪstən/ n (tank) Wasserbehälter m; (of WC) Spülkasten m

cite /saɪt/ vt zitieren

citizen /'sɪtɪzn/ n Bürger(in) m(f). **~ship** n Staatsangehörigkeit f

citrus /'sɪtrəs/ n **~ [fruit]** Zitrusfrucht f

city /'sɪtɪ/ n [Groß]stadt f

civic /'sɪvɪk/ a Bürger-

civil /'sɪvl/ a bürgerlich; (aviation, defence) zivil; (polite) höflich. **~ engi'neering** n Hoch- und Tiefbau m

civilian /sɪ'vɪljən/ a Zivil-; in **~ clothes** in Zivil □ n Zivilist m

civility /sɪ'vɪlətɪ/ n Höflichkeit f

civiliz|ation /sɪvəlaɪ'zeɪʃn/ n Zivilisation f. **~e** /'sɪvəlaɪz/ vt zivilisieren

civil: ~ **'servant** n Beamte(r) m/Beamtin f. **C~ 'Service** n Staatsdienst m

clad /klæd/ a gekleidet (**in** in + acc)

claim /kleɪm/ n Anspruch m; (application) Antrag m; (demand) Forderung f; (assertion) Behauptung f □ vt beanspruchen; (apply for) beantragen; (demand) fordern; (assert) behaupten; (collect) abholen. **ant** n Antragsteller m

clairvoyant /kleə'vɔɪənt/ n Hellseher(in) m(f)

clam /klæm/ n Klaffmuschel f

clamber /'klæmbə(r)/ vi klettern

clammy /'klæmɪ/ a (-ier, -iest) feucht

clamour /'klæmə(r)/ n Geschrei nt □ vi ~ **for** schreien nach

clamp /klæmp/ n Klammer f □ vt [ein]spannen □ vi ~ **down** (fam) durchgreifen; ~ **down on** vorgehen gegen

clan /klæn/ n Clan m

clandestine /klæn'destɪn/ a geheim

clang /klæŋ/ n Schmettern nt. ~**er** n (fam) Schnitzer m

clank /klæŋk/ vi klirren

clap /klæp/ n **give s.o. a** ~ jdm Beifall klatschen; ~ **of thunder** Donnerschlag m □ vt/i (pt/pp clapped) Beifall klatschen (+ dat); ~ **one's hands** [in die Hände] klatschen

claret /'klærət/ n roter Bordeaux m

clari|fication /klærɪfɪ'keɪʃn/ n Klärung f. ~**fy** /'klærɪfaɪ/ vt/i (pt/pp -ied) klären

clarinet /klærɪ'net/ n Klarinette f

clarity /'klærətɪ/ n Klarheit f

clash /klæʃ/ n Geklirr nt; (fig) Konflikt m □ vi klirren; (colours:) sich beißen; (events:) ungünstig zusammenfallen

clasp /klɑːsp/ n Verschluss m □ vt ergreifen; (hold) halten

class /klɑːs/ n Klasse f; **travel first/second** ~ erster/zweiter Klasse reisen □ vt einordnen

classic /'klæsɪk/ a klassisch □ n Klassiker m; ~**s** pl (Univ) Altphilologie f. ~**al** a klassisch

classi|fication /klæsɪfɪ'keɪʃn/ n Klassifikation f. ~**fy** /'klæsɪfaɪ/ vt (pt/pp -ied) klassifizieren

'classroom n Klassenzimmer nt

classy /'klɑːsɪ/ a (-ier, -iest) (fam) schick

clatter /'klætə(r)/ n Geklapper nt □ vi klappern

clause /klɔːz/ n Klausel f; (Gram) Satzteil m

claustrophobia /klɔːstrə'fəʊbɪə/ n Klaustrophobie f, (fam) Platzangst m

claw /klɔː/ n Kralle f; (of bird of prey & Techn) Klaue f; (of crab, lobster) Schere f □ vt kratzen

clay /kleɪ/ n Lehm m; (pottery) Ton m

clean /kliːn/ a (-er, -est) sauber □ adv glatt □ vt sauber machen; putzen (shoes, windows); ~ **one's teeth** sich die Zähne putzen; **have sth** ~**ed** etw reinigen lassen. ~ **up** vt sauber machen

cleaner /'kliːnə(r)/ n Putzfrau f; (substance) Reinigungsmittel nt; [dry] ~'s chemische Reinigung f

cleanliness /'klenlɪnɪs/ n Sauberkeit f

cleanse /klenz/ vt reinigen. ~**r** n Reinigungsmittel nt

clean-shaven a glatt rasiert

cleansing cream /'klenz-/ n Reinigungscreme f

clear /klɪə(r)/ a (-er, -est), **-ly** adv klar; (obvious) eindeutig; (distinct) deutlich; (conscience) rein; (without obstacles) frei; **make sth** ~ etw klarmachen (**to** dat) □ adv **stand** ~ zurücktreten; **keep** ~ **of** aus dem Wege gehen (+ dat) □ vt räumen; abräumen (table); (acquit) freisprechen; ~ (authorize) genehmigen; (jump over) überspringen; **~ one's throat** sich räuspern □ *vi* (*fog:*) sich auflösen. **~ away** *vi* wegräumen. **~ off** *vi* (*fam*) abhauen. **~ out** *vt* ausräumen □ *vi* (*fam*) abhauen. **~ up** *vt* (*tidy*) aufräumen; (*solve*) aufklären □ *vi* (*weather:*) sich aufklären

clearance /'klɪərəns/ *n* Räumung *f*; (*authorization*) Genehmigung *f*; (*customs*) [Zoll]abfertigung *f*; (*Techn*) Spielraum *m*. **~ sale** *n* Räumungsverkauf *m*

clear|ing /'klɪərɪŋ/ *n* Lichtung *f*. **~ way** *n* (*Auto*) Straße *f* mit Halteverbot

cleavage /'kliːvɪdʒ/ *n* Spaltung *f*; (*woman*"s) Dekolleté *nt*

clef /klef/ *n* Notenschlüssel *m*

cleft /kleft/ *n* Spalte *f*

clemen|cy /'klemənsɪ/ *n* Milde *f*. **~t** *a* mild

clench /klentʃ/ *vt* **~ one's fist** die Faust ballen; **~ one's teeth** die Zähne zusammenbeißen

clergy /'klɜːdʒɪ/ *n pl* Geistlichkeit *f*. **~man** *n* Geistliche(r) *m*

cleric /'klerɪk/ *n* Geistliche(r) *m*. **~al** *a* Schreib-; (*Relig*) geistlich

clerk /klɑːk/, *Amer:* /klɜːk/ *n* Büroangestellte(r) *m/f*; (*Amer: shop assistant*) Verkäufer(in) *m(f)*

clever /'klevə(r)/ *a* (**-er, -est**), **-ly** *adv* klug; (*skilful*) geschickt

cliché /'kliːʃeɪ/ *n* Klischee *nt*

click /klɪk/ *vi* klicken

client /'klaɪənt/ *n* Kunde *m*/ Kundin *f*; (*Jur*) Klient(in) *m(f)*

clientele /kliːɒn'tel/ *n* Kundschaft *f*

cliff /klɪf/ *n* Kliff *nt*

climat|e /'klaɪmət/ *n* Klima *nt*. **~ic** /-'mætɪk/ *a* klimatisch

climax /'klaɪmæks/ *n* Höhepunkt *m*

climb /klaɪm/ *n* Aufstieg *m* □ *vt* besteigen (*mountain*); steigen auf (+ *acc*) (*ladder, tree*) □ *vi* klettern; (*rise*) steigen; (*road:*) ansteigen.

~ down *vi* hinunter-/heruntersteigen; (*from ladder, tree*) heruntersteigen; (*fam*) nachgeben

climber /'klaɪmə(r)/ *n* Bergsteiger *m*; (*plant*) Kletterpflanze *f*

clinch /klɪntʃ/ *vt* perfekt machen (*deal*) □ *vi* (*boxing*) clinchen

cling /klɪŋ/ *vi* (*pt/pp* clung) sich klammern (**to** an + *acc*); (*stick*) haften (**to** an + *dat*). **~ film** *n* Sichtfolie *f* mit Hafteffekt

clinic /'klɪnɪk/ *n* Klinik *f*. **~al** *a*, **-ly** *adv* klinisch

clink /klɪŋk/ *n* Klirren *nt*; (*fam: prison*) Knast *m* □ *vi* klirren

clip[1] /klɪp/ *n* Klammer *f*; (*jewellery*) Klipp *m* □ *vt* (*pt/pp* **clipped**) anklammern (**to** an + *acc*)

clip[2] *n* (*extract*) Ausschnitt *m* □ *vt* schneiden; knipsen (*ticket*). **~board** *n* Klemmbrett *nt*. **~pers** *npl* Schere *f*. **~ping** *n* (*extract*) Ausschnitt *m*

clique /kliːk/ *n* Clique *f*

cloak /kləʊk/ *n* Umhang *m*. **~room** *n* Garderobe *f*; (*toilet*) Toilette *f*

clobber /'klɒbə(r)/ *n* (*fam*) Zeug *nt* □ *vt* (*fam: hit, defeat*) schlagen

clock /klɒk/ *n* Uhr *f*; (*fam: speedometer*) Tacho *m* □ *vi* **~ in/out** stechen

clock: **~ tower** *n* Uhrenturm *m*. **~wise** *a* & *adv* im Uhrzeigersinn. **~work** *n* Uhrwerk *nt*; (*of toy*) Aufziehmechanismus *m*; **like ~work** (*fam*) wie am Schnürchen

clod /klɒd/ *n* Klumpen *m*

clog /klɒg/ *n* Holzschuh *m* □ *vt/i* (*pt/pp* **clogged**) **~ [up]** verstopfen

cloister /'klɔɪstə(r)/ *n* Kreuzgang *m*

close[1] /kləʊs/ *a* (**-r, -st**) nah[e] (**to** dat); (*friend*) eng; (*weather*) schwül; **have a ~ shave** (*fam*) mit knapper Not davonkommen

□ *adv* nahe; **~ by** nicht weit weg □ *n* ⟨street⟩ Sackgasse *f*

close² /kləʊz/ *n* Ende *nt*; **draw to a ~** sich dem Ende nähern □ *vt* zumachen, schließen; ⟨bring to an end⟩ beenden; sperren ⟨road⟩ □ *vi* sich schließen; ⟨shop:⟩ schließen, zumachen; ⟨end⟩ enden. **~ down** *vt* schließen; stilllegen ⟨factory⟩ □ *vi* schließen; ⟨factory:⟩ stillgelegt werden

closed 'shop /kləʊzd-/ *n* ≈ Gewerkschaftszwang *m*

closely /ˈkləʊslɪ/ *adv* eng, nah[e]; ⟨with attention⟩ genau

close season /ˈkləʊs-/ *n* Schonzeit *f*

closet /ˈklɒzɪt/ *n* ⟨Amer⟩ Schrank *m*

close-up /ˈkləʊs-/ *n* Nahaufnahme *f*

closure /ˈkləʊʒə(r)/ *n* Schließung *f*; ⟨of factory⟩ Stilllegung *f*; ⟨of road⟩ Sperrung *f*

clot /klɒt/ *n* [Blut]gerinnsel *nt*; ⟨fam: idiot⟩ Trottel *m* □ *vi* ⟨pt/pp **clotted**⟩ ⟨blood:⟩ gerinnen

cloth /klɒθ/ *n* Tuch *nt*

clothe /kləʊð/ *vt* kleiden

clothes /kləʊðz/ *npl* Kleider *pl*. **~-brush** *n* Kleiderbürste *f*. **~-line** *n* Wäscheleine *f*

clothing /ˈkləʊðɪŋ/ *n* Kleidung *f*

cloud /klaʊd/ *n* Wolke *f* □ *vi* **~ over** sich bewölken. **~burst** *n* Wolkenbruch *m*

cloudy /ˈklaʊdɪ/ *a* (-ier, -iest) wolkig, bewölkt; ⟨liquid⟩ trübe

clout /klaʊt/ *n* ⟨fam⟩ Schlag *m*; ⟨influence⟩ Einfluss *m* □ *vt* ⟨fam⟩ hauen

clove /kləʊv/ *n* [Gewürz]nelke *f*; **~ of garlic** Knoblauchzehe *f*

clover /ˈkləʊvə(r)/ *n* Klee *m*. **~ leaf** *n* Kleeblatt *nt*

clown /klaʊn/ *n* Clown *m* □ *vi* **~ [about]** herumalbern

club /klʌb/ *n* Klub *m*; ⟨weapon⟩ Keule *f*; ⟨Sport⟩ Schläger *m*; **~s** *pl* ⟨Cards⟩ Kreuz *nt*, Treff *nt* □ *v*

⟨pt/pp **clubbed**⟩ □ *vt* knüppeln □ *vi* **~ together** zusammenlegen

cluck /klʌk/ *vi* glucken

clue /kluː/ *n* Anhaltspunkt *m*; ⟨in crossword⟩ Frage *f*; **I haven't a ~** ⟨fam⟩ ich habe keine Ahnung

clump /klʌmp/ *n* Gruppe *f*

clumsiness /ˈklʌmzɪnɪs/ *n* Ungeschicklichkeit *f*

clumsy /ˈklʌmzɪ/ *a* (-ier, -iest), **-ily** *adv* ungeschickt; ⟨unwieldy⟩ unförmig

clung /klʌŋ/ *see* **cling**

cluster /ˈklʌstə(r)/ *n* Gruppe *f*; ⟨of flowers⟩ Büschel *nt* □ *vi* sich scharen ⟨round um⟩

clutch /klʌtʃ/ *n* Griff *m*; ⟨Auto⟩ Kupplung *f*; **be in s.o.'s ~es** ⟨fam⟩ in jds Klauen sein □ *vt* festhalten; ⟨grab⟩ ergreifen □ *vi* **~ at** greifen nach

clutter /ˈklʌtə(r)/ *n* Kram *m* □ *vt* **~ [up]** vollstopfen

c/o *abbr* (**care of**) bei

coach /kəʊtʃ/ *n* [Reise]bus *m*; ⟨Rail⟩ Wagen *m*; ⟨horse-drawn⟩ Kutsche *f*; ⟨Sport⟩ Trainer *m* □ *vt* Nachhilfestunden geben (+ *dat*); ⟨Sport⟩ trainieren

coagulate /kəʊˈæɡjʊleɪt/ *vi* gerinnen

coal /kəʊl/ *n* Kohle *f*

coalition /kəʊəˈlɪʃn/ *n* Koalition *f*

'coal-mine *n* Kohlenbergwerk *nt*

coarse /kɔːs/ *a* (-r, -st), **-ly** *adv* grob

coast /kəʊst/ *n* Küste *f* □ *vi* ⟨freewheel⟩ im Freilauf fahren; ⟨Auto⟩ im Leerlauf fahren. **~al** *a* Küsten-. **~er** *n* ⟨mat⟩ Untersatz *m*

coast-: **~guard** *n* Küstenwache *f*. **~line** *n* Küste *f*

coat /kəʊt/ *n* Mantel *m*; ⟨of animal⟩ Fell *nt*; ⟨of paint⟩ Anstrich *m*; **~ of arms** Wappen *nt* □ *vt* überziehen; ⟨with paint⟩ streichen. **~-hanger** *n* Kleiderbügel *m*. **~-hook** *n* Kleiderhaken *m*

coating /'kəʊtɪŋ/ n Überzug m, Schicht f; (of paint) Anstrich m

coax /kəʊks/ vt gut zureden (+ dat)

cob /kɒb/ n (of corn) [Mais]kolben m

cobble¹ /'kɒbl/ n Kopfstein m; ~s pl Kopfsteinpflaster nt

cobble² vt flicken. ~r m Schuster m

'cobblestones npl = cobbles

cobweb /'kɒb–/ n Spinnengewebe nt

cocaine /kə'keɪn/ n Kokain nt

cock /kɒk/ n Hahn m; (any male bird) Männchen nt. ~ its ~ ears die Ohren spitzen; ~ the gun den Hahn spannen. ~ and-'bull story n (fam) Lügengeschichte f

cockerel /'kɒkərəl/ n [junger] Hahn m

cock-'eyed a (fam) schief; (absurd) verrückt

cockle /'kɒkl/ n Herzmuschel f

cockney /'kɒknɪ/ n (dialect) Cockney nt; (person) Cockney m

cock: ~'pit n (Aviat) Cockpit nt. ~roach /-rəʊtʃ/ n Küchenschabe f. ~tail n Cocktail m. ~-up n (sl) make a ~-up Mist bauen (of bei)

cocky /'kɒkɪ/ a (-ier, -iest) (fam) eingebildet

cocoa /'kəʊkəʊ/ n Kakao m

coconut /'kəʊkənʌt/ n Kokosnuss f

cocoon /kə'ku:n/ n Kokon m

cod /kɒd/ n inv Kabeljau m

COD abbr (cash on delivery) per Nachnahme

coddle /'kɒdl/ vt verhätscheln

code /kəʊd/ n Kode m; (Computing) Code m; (set of rules) Kodex m. ~d a verschlüsselt

coedu'cational /kəʊ–/ a gemischt. ~ school n Koedukationsschule f

coerc|e /kəʊ'ɜ:s/ vt zwingen. ~ion /-'ɜ:ʃn/ n Zwang m

coe'xist vi koexistieren. ~ence n Koexistenz f

coffee /'kɒfɪ/ n Kaffee m

coffee: ~-grinder n Kaffeemühle f. ~-pot n Kaffeekanne f. ~-table n Couchtisch m

coffin /'kɒfɪn/ n Sarg m

cog /kɒg/ n (Techn) Zahn m

cogent /'kəʊdʒənt/ a überzeugend

cog-wheel n Zahnrad nt

cohabit /kəʊ'hæbɪt/ vi (Jur) zusammenleben

coherent /kəʊ'hɪərənt/ a zusammenhängend; (comprehensible) verständlich

coil /kɔɪl/ n Rolle f; (Electr) Spule f; (one ring) Windung f □ vt ~[up] zusammenrollen

coin /kɔɪn/ n Münze f □ vt prägen

coincide /kəʊɪn'saɪd/ vi zusammenfallen; (agree) übereinstimmen

coinciden|ce /kəʊ'ɪnsɪdəns/ n Zufall m. ~tal /-'dentl/ a, -ly adv zufällig

coke /kəʊk/ n Koks m

Coke (P) n (drink) Cola f

colander /'kʌləndə(r)/ n (Culin) Durchschlag m

cold /kəʊld/ a (-er, -est) kalt; I am or feel ~ mir ist kalt □ n Kälte f; (Med) Erkältung f

cold: ~-'blooded a kaltblütig. ~hearted a kaltherzig. ~ly adv (fig) kalt, kühl. ~ness n Kälte f

coleslaw /'kəʊlslɔ:/ n Krautsalat m

colic /'kɒlɪk/ n Kolik f

collaborat|e /kə'læbəreɪt/ vi zusammenarbeiten (with mit); ~e on sth mitarbeiten an etw. ~ion /-'reɪʃn/ n Zusammenarbeit f, Mitarbeit f; (with enemy) Kollaboration f. ~or n Mitarbeiter(in) m(f); Kollaborateur m

collaps|e /kə'læps/ n Zusammenbruch m; Einsturz m □ vi zusammenbrechen; (roof, building:)

einstürzen. **~ible** *a* zusammenklappbar

collar /'kɒlə(r)/ *n* Kragen *m*; (*for animal*) Halsband *nt.* **~bone** *n* Schlüsselbein *nt*

colleague /'kɒliːg/ *n* Kollege *m*/Kollegin *f*

collect /kə'lekt/ *vt* sammeln; (*fetch*) abholen; einsammeln (*tickets*); einziehen (*taxes*) □ *vi* sich [an]sammeln □ *adv* **call ~** (*Amer*) ein R-Gespräch führen. **~ed** /-ɪd/ *a* gesammelt; (*calm*) gefasst

collection /kə'lekʃn/ *n* Sammlung *f*; (*in church*) Kollekte *f*; (*of post*) Leerung *f*; (*designer's*) Kollektion *f*

collective /kə'lektɪv/ *a* gemeinsam; (*Pol*) kollektiv. **~ noun** *n* Kollektivum *nt*

collector /kə'lektə(r)/ *n* Sammler(in) *m(f)*

college /'kɒlɪdʒ/ *n* College *nt*

collide /kə'laɪd/ *vi* zusammenstoßen

colliery /'kɒlɪərɪ/ *n* Kohlengrube *f*

collision /kə'lɪʒn/ *n* Zusammenstoß *m*

colloquial /kə'ləʊkwɪəl/ *a*, **-ly** *adv* umgangssprachlich. **~ism** *n* umgangssprachlicher Ausdruck *m*

Cologne /kə'ləʊn/ *n* Köln *nt*

colon /'kəʊlən/ *n* Doppelpunkt *m*; (*Anat*) Dickdarm *m*

colonel /'kɜːnl/ *n* Oberst *m*

colonial /kə'ləʊnɪəl/ *a* Kolonial-. **colon|ize** /'kɒlənaɪz/ *vt* kolonisieren. **~y** *n* Kolonie *f*

colossal /kə'lɒsl/ *a* riesig

colour /'kʌlə(r)/ *n* Farbe *f*; (*complexion*) Gesichtsfarbe *f*; (*race*) Hautfarbe *f*; **~s** *pl* (*flag*) Fahne *f*; **off ~** (*fam*) nicht ganz auf der Höhe □ *vt* färben; **~ [in]** ausmalen □ *vi* (*blush*) erröten

colour: **~ bar** *n* Rassenschranke *f*. **~-blind** *a* farbenblind. **~ed** *a*

farbig □ *n* (*person*) Farbige(r) *m/f.* **~-fast** *a* farbecht. **~ film** *n* Farbfilm *m.* **~ful** *a* farbenfroh. **~less** *a* farblos. **~ photo-[graph]** *n* Farbaufnahme *f.* **~ television** *n* Farbfernsehen *nt*

colt /kəʊlt/ *n* junger Hengst *m*

column /'kɒləm/ *n* Säule *f*; (*of soldiers, figures*) Kolonne *f*; (*Typ*) Spalte *f*; (*Journ*) Kolumne *f.* **~ist** /-nɪst/ *n* Kolumnist *m*

coma /'kəʊmə/ *n* Koma *nt*

comb /kəʊm/ *n* Kamm *m* □ *vt* kämmen; (*search*) absuchen; **~ one's hair** sich (*dat*) [die Haare] kämmen

combat /'kɒmbæt/ *n* Kampf *m* □ *vt* (*pt/pp* **combated**) bekämpfen

combination /kɒmbɪ'neɪʃn/ *n* Verbindung *f*; (*for lock*) Kombination *f*

combine[1] /kəm'baɪn/ *vt* verbinden □ *vi* sich verbinden; (*people:*) sich zusammenschließen

combine[2] /'kɒmbaɪn/ *n* (*Comm*) Konzern *m*. **~ [harvester]** *n* Mähdrescher *m*

combustion /kəm'bʌstʃn/ *n* Verbrennung *f*

come /kʌm/ *vi* (*pt* **came**, *pp* **come**) kommen; (*reach*) reichen (**to** an + *acc*); **that ~s to £10** das macht £10; **~ into money** zu Geld kommen; **~ true** wahr werden; **~ in two sizes** in zwei Größen erhältlich sein; **the years to ~** die kommenden Jahre; **how ~?** (*fam*) wie das? **~ about** *vi* geschehen. **~ across** *vi* herüberkommen; (*fig*) klar werden □ *vt* stoßen auf (+ *acc*). **~ apart** *vi* sich auseinander nehmen lassen; (*accidentally*) auseinander gehen. **~ away** *vi* weggehen; (*thing:*) abgehen. **~ back** *vi* zurückkommen. **~ by** *vi* vorbeikommen □ *vt* (*obtain*) bekommen. **~ in** *vi* hereinkommen. **~ off** *vi* abgehen; (*take* place) stattfinden; (succeed) klappen (fam). ~ **out** vi herauskommen; (book:) erscheinen; (stain:) herausgehen. ~ **round** vi vorbeikommen; (after fainting) [wieder] zu sich kommen; (change one's mind) es sich umstimmen lassen. ~ **to** vi [wieder] zu sich kommen. ~ **up** vi heraufkommen; (plant:) aufgehen; (reach) reichen (to bis); ~ **up with** sich (dat) einfallen lassen

'**come-back** n Comeback nt

comedian /kə'miːdɪən/ n Komiker m

'**come-down** n Rückschritt m

comedy /'kɒmədɪ/ n Komödie f

comet /'kɒmɪt/ n Komet m

come-uppance /kʌm'ʌpəns/ n **get one's** ~ (fam) sein Fett abkriegen

comfort /'kʌmfət/ n Bequemlichkeit f; (consolation) Trost m □ vt trösten

comfortable /'kʌmfətəbl/ a, **-bly** adv bequem

'**comfort station** n (Amer) öffentliche Toilette f

comfy /'kʌmfɪ/ a (fam) bequem

comic /'kɒmɪk/ a komisch □ n Komiker m; (periodical) Comic-Heft nt. ~**al** a, **-ly** adv komisch. ~ **strip** n Comic Strips pl

coming /'kʌmɪŋ/ a kommend □ n Kommen nt; ~**s and goings** Kommen und Gehen nt

comma /'kɒmə/ n Komma nt

command /kə'mɑːnd/ n Befehl m; (Mil) Kommando nt; (mastery) Beherrschung f □ vt befehlen (+ dat); kommandieren (army)

commandeer /kɒmən'dɪə(r)/ vt beschlagnahmen

commander /kə'mɑːndə(r)/ n Befehlshaber m; (of unit) Kommandeur m; (of ship) Kommandant m. ~**ing** a (view) beherrschend. ~**ing officer** n Befehlshaber m. ~**ment** n Gebot nt

commemorat|e /kə'meməreɪt/ vt gedenken (+ gen). ~**ion** /-'reɪʃn/

n Gedenken nt. ~**ive** /-ətɪv/ a Gedenk-

commence /kə'mens/ vt/i anfangen, beginnen. ~**ment** n Anfang m, Beginn m

commend /kə'mend/ vt loben; (recommend) empfehlen (to dat). ~**able** /-əbl/ a lobenswert. ~**ation** /kɒmen'deɪʃn/ n Lob nt

commensurate /kə'menʃərət/ a angemessen; **be** ~ **with** entsprechen (+ dat)

comment /'kɒment/ n Bemerkung f; **no** ~! kein Kommentar! □ vi sich äußern (on zu); ~ **on** (Journ) kommentieren

commentary /'kɒməntrɪ/ n Kommentar m; [**running**] ~ (Radio, TV) Reportage f

commentat|e /'kɒmənteɪt/ vi ~**e on** kommentieren. ~**or** n Kommentator m; (Sport) Reporter m

commerce /'kɒmɜːs/ n Handel m

commercial /kə'mɜːʃl/ a, **-ly** adv kommerziell □ n (Radio, TV) Werbespot m. ~**ize** vt kommerzialisieren

commiserate /kə'mɪzəreɪt/ vi sein Mitleid ausdrücken (**with** dat)

commission /kə'mɪʃn/ n (order for work) Auftrag m; (body of people) Kommission f; (payment) Provision f; (Mil) [Offiziers]patent nt; **out of** ~ außer Betrieb □ vt beauftragen (s.o.); in Auftrag geben (thing); (Mil) zum Offizier ernennen

commissionaire /kəmɪʃə'neə(r)/ n Portier m

commissioner /kə'mɪʃənə(r)/ n Kommissar m; ~ **for oaths** Notar m

commit /kə'mɪt/ vt (pt/pp **committed**) begehen; (entrust) anvertrauen (to dat); (consign) einweisen (to in + acc); ~ **one-self** sich festlegen; (involve oneself) sich engagieren; ~ **sth to memory** sich (dat) etw einprägen. ~**ment** n Verpflichtung

†

f; (involvement) Engagement nt.
~ted a engagiert

committee /kə'mɪtɪ/ n Ausschuss m, Komitee nt

commodity /kə'mɒdətɪ/ n Ware f

common /'kɒmən/ a (-er, -est) gemeinsam; (frequent) häufig; (ordinary) gewöhnlich; (vulgar) ordinär □ n Gemeindeland nt; **have in ~** gemeinsam haben; **House of C~s** Unterhaus nt. **~er** n Bürger(in) m/f

common: ~ **law** n Gewohnheitsrecht nt. ~**ly** adv allgemein. C~ **'Market** n Gemeinsamer Markt m. ~**place** a häufig. ~**room** n Aufenthaltsraum m. ~ **'sense** n gesunder Menschenverstand m

commotion /kə'məʊʃn/ n Tumult m

communal /'kɒmjunl/ a gemeinschaftlich

communicable /kə'mju:nɪkəbl/ a (disease) übertragbar

communicate /kə'mju:nɪkeɪt/ vt mitteilen (to dat); übertragen (disease) □ vi sich verständigen; (be in touch) Verbindung haben

communication /kə,mju:nɪ-'keɪʃn/ n Verständigung f; (contact) Verbindung f; (of disease) Übertragung f; (message) Mitteilung f; ~s pl (technology) Nachrichtenwesen nt. ~ **cord** n Notbremse f

communicative /kə'mju:nɪkətɪv/ a mitteilsam

Communion /kə'mju:nɪən/ n [Holy] ~ das [heilige] Abendmahl; (Roman Catholic) die [heilige] Kommunion

communiqué /kə'mju:nɪkeɪ/ n Kommuniqué nt

Communis|m /'kɒmjʊnɪzm/ n Kommunismus m. ~**t** /-ɪst/ a kommunistisch □ n Kommunist(in) m/f

community /kə'mju:nətɪ/ n Gemeinschaft f; local ~ Gemeinde

f. ~ **centre** n Gemeinschaftszentrum nt

commute /kə'mju:t/ vi pendeln □ vt (Jur) umwandeln. ~**r** n Pendler(in) m/f

compact¹ /kəm'pækt/ a kompakt

compact² /'kɒmpækt/ n Puderdose f. ~ **disc** n CD f

companion /kəm'pænjən/ n Begleiter(in) m/f. ~**ship** n Gesellschaft f

company /'kʌmpənɪ/ n Gesellschaft f; (firm) Firma f; (Mil) Kompanie f; (fam: guests) Besuch m. ~ **car** n Firmenwagen m

comparable /'kɒmpərəbl/ a vergleichbar

comparative /kəm'pærətɪv/ a vergleichend; (relative) relativ □ n (Gram) Komparativ m. ~**ly** adv verhältnismäßig

compare /kəm'peə(r)/ vt vergleichen (with/to mit) □ vi sich vergleichen lassen

comparison /kəm'pærɪsn/ n Vergleich m

compartment /kəm'pɑ:tmənt/ n Fach nt; (Rail) Abteil nt

compass /'kʌmpəs/ n Kompass m. ~**es** npl pair of ~es Zirkel m

compassion /kəm'pæʃn/ n Mitleid nt. ~**ate** /-ʃənət/ a mitfühlend

compatible /kəm'pætəbl/ a vereinbar; (drugs) verträglich; (Techn) kompatibel; **be ~** (people:) [gut] zueinander passen

compatriot /kəm'pætrɪət/ n Landsmann m /-männin f

compel /kəm'pel/ vt (pt/pp compelled) zwingen

compensat|e /'kɒmpənseɪt/ vt entschädigen □ vi ~**e for** (fig) ausgleichen. ~**ion** /-'seɪʃn/ n Entschädigung f; (fig) Ausgleich m

compère /'kɒmpeə(r)/ n Conférencier m

compete /kəm'pi:t/ vi konkurrieren; (take part) teilnehmen (in an + dat)

competen|ce /'kɒmpɪtəns/ n
Tüchtigkeit f; (ability) Fähigkeit
f; (Jur) Kompetenz f. **~t** a tüchtig; fähig; (Jur) kompetent

competition /kɒmpə'tɪʃn/ n Kon-
kurrenz f; (contest) Wettbewerb
m; (in newspaper) Preisaus-
schreiben nt

competitive /kəm'petɪtɪv/ a
(Comm) konkurrenzfähig

competitor /kəm'petɪtə(r)/ n
Teilnehmer m; (Comm) Konkur-
rent m

compile /kəm'paɪl/ vt zusammenstellen; verfassen (dictionary)

complacen|cy /kəm'pleɪsənsɪ/ n
Selbstzufriedenheit f. **~t** a, **~tly**
adv selbstzufrieden

complain /kəm'pleɪn/ vi klagen
(about/of über + acc);
(formally) sich beschweren. **~t** n
Klage f; (formal) Beschwerde f;
(Med) Leiden nt

complement1 /'kɒmplɪmənt/ n
Ergänzung f; **full ~** volle Anzahl
f

complement2 /'kɒmplɪment/ vt
ergänzen; **~ each other** sich ergänzen. **~ary** /-'mentri/ a sich
ergänzend; **be ~ary** sich ergänzen

complete /kəm'pli:t/ a vollständig; (finished) fertig; (utter) völlig
□ vt vervollständigen; (finish)
abschließen; (fill in) ausfüllen.
~ly adv völlig

completion /kəm'pli:ʃn/ n Ver-
vollständigung f; (end) Abschluss m

complex /'kɒmpleks/ a komplex
□ n Komplex m

complexion /kəm'plekʃn/ n
Teint m; (colour) Gesichtsfarbe
f; (fig) Aspekt m

complexity /kəm'pleksətɪ/ n
Komplexität f

compliance /kəm'plaɪəns/ n Einverständnis nt; **in ~ with** gemäß
(+ dat)

complicat|e /'kɒmplɪkeɪt/ vt
komplizieren. **~ed** a kompliziert. **~ion** /-'keɪʃn/ n Komplikation f

complicity /kəm'plɪsətɪ/ n Mittä-
terschaft f

compliment /'kɒmplɪmənt/ n
Kompliment nt; **~s** pl Grüße pl
□ vt ein Kompliment machen (+
dat). **~ary** /-'mentri/ a schmei-
chelhaft; (given free) Frei-

comply /kəm'plaɪ/ vi (pt/pp -ied)
~ with nachkommen (+ dat)

component /kəm'pəunənt/ a & n
[part] Bestandteil m, Teil nt

compose /kəm'pəuz/ vt verfassen; (Mus) komponieren; **~
oneself** sich fassen; **be ~d of** sich
zusammensetzen aus. **~d** a
(calm) gefasst. **~r** n Komponist
m

composition /kɒmpə'zɪʃn/ n
Komposition f; (essay) Aufsatz m

compost /'kɒmpɒst/ n Kompost
m

composure /kəm'pəuʒə(r)/ n
Fassung f

compound1 /kəm'paund/ vt
(make worse) verschlimmern

compound2 /'kɒmpaund/ a zu-
sammengesetzt; (fracture) kompliziert □ n (Chem) Verbindung f;
(Gram) Kompositum nt; (enclosure) Einfriedigung f. **~ 'interest**
n Zinseszins m

comprehen|d /kɒmprɪ'hend/ vt
begreifen, verstehen; (include)
umfassen. **~sible** a, **-bly** adv
verständlich. **~sion** /-'henʃn/ n
Verständnis nt

comprehensive /kɒmprɪ'hensɪv/
a & n umfassend. **~ [school]** Ge-
samtschule f. **~ insurance** n
(Auto) Vollkaskoversicherung f

compress1 /'kɒmpres/ n Kompresse f

compress2 /kəm'pres/ vt zusam-
menpressen; **~ed air** Druckluft
f

comprise /kəm'praɪz/ vt umfassen, bestehen aus

compromise /'kɒmprəmaɪz/ n Kompromiss m □ vt kompromittieren (person) □ vi einen Kompromiss schließen

compulsion /kəm'pʌlʃn/ n Zwang m. **~ive** /-sɪv/ a zwanghaft; **~ive eating** Esszwang m. **~ory** /-sərɪ/ a obligatorisch; **~ory subject** Pflichtfach nt

compunction /kəm'pʌŋkʃn/ n Gewissensbisse pl

comput|er /kəm'pju:tə(r)/ n Computer m. **~erize** vt computerisieren (data); auf Computer umstellen (firm). **~ing** n Computertechnik f

comrade /'kɒmreɪd/ n Kamerad m; (Pol) Genosse m/Genossin f. **~ship** n Kameradschaft f

con¹ /kɒn/ see **pro**

con² n (fam) Schwindel m □ vt (pt/pp conned) (fam) beschwindeln

concave /'kɒŋkeɪv/ a konkav

conceal /kən'si:l/ vt verstecken; (keep secret) verheimlichen

concede /kən'si:d/ vt zugeben; (give up) aufgeben

conceit /kən'si:t/ n Einbildung f. **~ed** a eingebildet

conceivable /kən'si:vəbl/ a denkbar

conceive /kən'si:v/ vt (Biol) empfangen; (fig) sich (dat) ausdenken □ vi schwanger werden. **~ of** (fig) sich (dat) vorstellen

concentrat|e /'kɒnsəntreɪt/ vt konzentrieren □ vi sich konzentrieren. **~ion** /-'treɪʃn/ n Konzentration f. **~ion camp** n Konzentrationslager nt

concept /'kɒnsept/ n Begriff m. **~ion** /kən'sepʃn/ n Empfängnis f; (idea) Vorstellung f

concern /kən'sɜ:n/ n Angelegenheit f; (worry) Sorge f; (Comm) Unternehmen nt □ vt (be about, affect) betreffen; (worry) kümmern; **be ~ed about** besorgt sein um; **~ oneself with** sich beschäftigen mit; **as far as I am ~ed** was

mich angeht od betrifft. **~ing** prep bezüglich (+ gen)

concert /'kɒnsət/ n Konzert nt; **in ~** im Chor. **~ed** /kən'sɜ:tɪd/ a gemeinsam

concertina /kɒnsə'ti:nə/ n Konzertina f

'concertmaster n (Amer) Konzertmeister m

concerto /kən'tʃeətəʊ/ n Konzert nt

concession /kən'seʃn/ n Zugeständnis nt; (Comm) Konzession f; (reduction) Ermäßigung f. **~ary** /a (reduced) ermäßigt

conciliation /kənsɪlɪ'eɪʃn/ n Schlichtung f

concise /kən'saɪs/ a, **-ly** adv kurz

conclude /kən'klu:d/ vt/i schließen

conclusion /kən'klu:ʒn/ n Schluss m; **in ~** abschließend, zum Schluss

conclusive /kən'klu:sɪv/ a schlüssig

concoct /kən'kɒkt/ vt zusammenstellen; (fig) fabrizieren. **~ion** /-ɒkʃn/ n Zusammenstellung f; (drink) Gebräu nt

concourse /'kɒŋkɔ:s/ a Halle f

concrete /'kɒŋkri:t/ a konkret □ n Beton m □ vt betonieren

concur /kən'kɜ:(r)/ vi (pt/pp concurred) übereinstimmen

concurrently /kən'kʌrəntlɪ/ adv gleichzeitig

concussion /kən'kʌʃn/ n Gehirnerschütterung f

condemn /kən'dem/ vt verurteilen; (declare unfit) für untauglich erklären. **~ation** /kɒndem'neɪʃn/ n Verurteilung f

condensation /kɒnden'seɪʃn/ n Kondensation f

condense /kən'dens/ vt zusammenfassen; (Phys) kondensieren □ vi sich kondensieren. **~d milk** n Kondensmilch f

condescend /kɒndɪ'send/ vi herablassen (to zu). **~ing** a, **-ly** adv herablassend

condiment /'kɒndɪmənt/ n Gewürz nt

condition /kən'dɪʃn/ n Bedingung f; (state) Zustand m; ~s pl Verhältnisse pl; on ~ that unter der Bedingung, dass □ vt (Psych) konditionieren. ~al a bedingt; be ~al on abhängig von □ n (Gram) Konditional m. ~er n Haarkur f; (for fabrics) Weichspüler m

condolences /kən'dəʊlənsɪz/ npl Beileid nt

condom /'kɒndəm/ n Kondom nt

condominium /kɒndə'mɪnɪəm/ n (Amer) ≈ Eigentumswohnung f

condone /kən'dəʊn/ vt hinwegsehen über (+ acc)

conducive /kən'dju:sɪv/ a förderlich (to dat)

conduct¹ /'kɒndʌkt/ n Verhalten nt; (Sch) Betragen nt.

conduct² /kən'dʌkt/ vt führen; (Phys) leiten; (Mus) dirigieren. ~or n Dirigent m; (of bus) Schaffner m; (Phys) Leiter m. ~ress n Schaffnerin f

cone /kəʊn/ n Kegel m; (Bot) Zapfen m; (for ice-cream) [Eis]tüte f; (Auto) Leitkegel m

confectioner /kən'fekʃənə(r)/ n Konditor m. ~y n Süßwaren pl

confederation /kənfedə'reɪʃn/ n Bund m; (Pol) Konföderation f

confer /kən'fɜ:(r)/ v (pt/pp conferred) □ vt verleihen (on dat) □ vi sich beraten

conference /'kɒnfərəns/ n Konferenz f

confess /kən'fes/ vt/i gestehen; (Relig) beichten. ~ion /-eʃn/ n Geständnis nt; (Relig) Beichte f. ~ional /-eʃənl/ n Beichtstuhl m. ~or n Beichtvater m

confetti /kən'fetɪ/ n Konfetti nt

confide /kən'faɪd/ vt anvertrauen □ vi ~ in s.o. sich jdm anvertrauen

confidence /'kɒnfɪdəns/ n (trust) Vertrauen nt; (self-assurance)

Selbstvertrauen nt; (secret) Geheimnis nt; in ~ im Vertrauen. ~ trick n Schwindel m

confident /'kɒnfɪdənt/ a, -ly adv zuversichtlich; (self-assured) selbstsicher

confidential /kɒnfɪ'denʃl/ a, -ly adv vertraulich

confine /kən'faɪn/ vt beschränken auf (+ acc); be ~d to bed das Bett hüten müssen. ~d a (narrow) eng. ~ment n Haft f

confines /'kɒnfaɪnz/ npl Grenzen pl

confirm /kən'fɜ:m/ vt bestätigen; (Relig) konfirmieren; (Roman Catholic) firmen. ~ation /kɒnfə'meɪʃn/ n Bestätigung f; Konfirmation f; Firmung f. ~ed a eingefleischt; ~ed bachelor Junggeselle m

confiscate /'kɒnfɪskeɪt/ vt beschlagnahmen. ~ion /-'keɪʃn/ n Beschlagnahme f

conflict¹ /'kɒnflɪkt/ n Konflikt m

conflict² /kən'flɪkt/ vi im Widerspruch stehen (with zu). ~ing a widersprüchlich

conform /kən'fɔ:m/ vi (person:) sich anpassen; (thing:) entsprechen (to dat). ~ist n Konformist m

confounded /kən'faʊndɪd/ a (fam) verflixt

confront /kən'frʌnt/ vt konfrontieren. ~ation /kɒnfrən'teɪʃn/ n Konfrontation f

confuse /kən'fju:z/ vt verwirren; (mistake for) verwechseln (with mit). ~ing a verwirrend. ~ion /-ju:ʒn/ n Verwirrung f; (muddle) Durcheinander nt

congeal /kən'dʒi:l/ vi fest werden; (blood:) gerinnen

congenial /kən'dʒi:nɪəl/ a angenehm

congenital /kən'dʒenɪtl/ a angeboren

congested /kən'dʒestɪd/ a verstopft; (with people) überfüllt

~ion /- estʃn/ n Verstopfung f; Überfüllung f

congratulat|e /kən'grætjuleɪt/ vt gratulieren (+ dat) (on zu). ~ions /-'leɪʃnz/ npl Glückwünsche pl; ~ions! [ich] gratuliere!

congregat|e /'kɒŋgrɪgeɪt/ vi sich versammeln. ~ion /-'geɪʃn/ n (Relig) Gemeinde f

congress /'kɒŋgres/ n Kongress m. ~man n Kongressabgeordnete(r) m

conical /'kɒnɪkl/ a kegelförmig

conifer /'kɒnɪfə(r)/ n Nadelbaum m

conjecture /kən'dʒektʃə(r)/ n Mutmaßung f □ vt/i mutmaßen

conjugal /'kɒndʒʊgl/ a ehelich

conjugat|e /'kɒndʒʊgeɪt/ vt konjugieren. ~ion /-'geɪʃn/ n Konjugation f

conjunction /kən'dʒʌŋkʃn/ n Konjunktion f; in ~ with zusammen mit

conjunctivitis /kəndʒʌŋktɪ-'vaɪtɪs/ n Bindehautentzündung f

conjur|e /'kʌndʒə(r)/ vi zaubern □ vt ~e up heraufbeschwören. ~or n Zauberkünstler m

conk /kɒŋk/ vi ~ out (fam) (machine:) kaputtgehen; (person:) zusammenklappen

conker /'kɒŋkə(r)/ n (fam) Kastanie f

'con-man n (fam) Schwindler m

connect /kə'nekt/ vt verbinden (to mit); (Electr) anschließen (to an + acc); (Electr) verbunden sein; (train:) Anschluss haben (with an + acc); be ~ed with zu tun haben mit; (be related to) verwandt sein mit

connection /kə'nekʃn/ n Verbindung f; (Rail, Electr) Anschluss m; in ~ with in Zusammenhang mit. ~s npl Beziehungen pl

conniv|ance /kə'naɪvəns/ n stillschweigende Duldung f. ~e vi ~e at stillschweigend dulden

connoisseur /kɒnə'sɜ:(r)/ n Kenner m

connotation /kɒnə'teɪʃn/ n Assoziation f

conquer /'kɒŋkə(r)/ vt erobern; (fig) besiegen. ~or n Eroberer m

conquest /'kɒŋkwest/ n Eroberung f

conscience /'kɒnʃəns/ n Gewissen nt

conscientious /kɒnʃɪ'enʃəs/ a, -ly adv gewissenhaft. ~ objector n Kriegsdienstverweigerer m

conscious /'kɒnʃəs/ a, -ly adv bewusst; [fully] ~ bei [vollem] Bewusstsein; be/become ~ of sth sich (dat) etw (gen) bewusst sein/werden. ~ness n Bewusstsein nt

conscript¹ /'kɒnskrɪpt/ n Einberufene(r) m

conscript² /kən'skrɪpt/ vt einberufen. ~ion /-ɪpʃn/ n allgemeine Wehrpflicht f

consecrat|e /'kɒnsɪkreɪt/ vt weihen; einweihen (church). ~ion /-'kreɪʃn/ n Weihe f; Einweihung f

consecutive /kən'sekjʊtɪv/ a aufeinander folgend. -ly adv fortlaufend

consensus /kən'sensəs/ n Übereinstimmung f

consent /kən'sent/ n Einwilligung f, Zustimmung f □ vi einwilligen (to in + acc), zustimmen (to dat)

consequen|ce /'kɒnsɪkwəns/ n Folge f; (importance) Bedeutung f. ~t a daraus folgend. ~tly adv folglich

conservation /kɒnsə'veɪʃn/ n Erhaltung f, Bewahrung f. ~ist n Umweltschützer m

conservative /kən'sɜ:vətɪv/ a konservativ; (estimate) vorsichtig. C~ (Pol) a konservativ □ n Konservative(r) m/f

conservatory /kən'sɜ:vətrɪ/ n Wintergarten m

conserve /kən'sɜːv/ vt erhalten, bewahren; sparen ⟨energy⟩

consider /kən'sɪdə(r)/ vt erwägen; ⟨think over⟩ sich ⟨dat⟩ überlegen; ⟨take into account⟩ berücksichtigen; ⟨regard as⟩ betrachten als; ~ **doing sth** erwägen, etw zu tun. **~able** /-əbl/ a, **-bly** adv erheblich

consider|ate /kən'sɪdərət/ a, **-ly** adv rücksichtsvoll. **~ation** /-'reɪʃn/ n Erwägung f; ⟨thoughtfulness⟩ Rücksicht f; ⟨payment⟩ Entgelt nt; **take into ~ation** berücksichtigen. **~ing** prep wenn man bedenkt (**that** dass); **~ing the circumstances** unter den Umständen

consign /kən'saɪn/ vt übergeben (**to** dat). **~ment** n Lieferung f

consist /kən'sɪst/ vi **~ of** bestehen aus

consisten|cy /kən'sɪstənsɪ/ n Konsequenz f; ⟨density⟩ Konsistenz f. **~t** a konsequent; ⟨unchanging⟩ gleichbleibend; **be ~t with** entsprechen (+ dat). **~tly** adv konsequent; ⟨constantly⟩ ständig

consolation /kɒnsə'leɪʃn/ n Trost m. **~ prize** n Trostpreis m

console /kən'səʊl/ vt trösten

consolidate /kən'sɒlɪdeɪt/ vt konsolidieren

consonant /'kɒnsənənt/ n Konsonant m

consort /kən'sɔːt/ n Gemahl(in) m(f)

conspicuous /kən'spɪkjʊəs/ a auffällig

conspiracy /kən'spɪrəsɪ/ n Verschwörung f

conspire /kən'spaɪə(r)/ vi sich verschwören

constable /'kʌnstəbl/ n Polizist m

constant /'kɒnstənt/ a, **-ly** adv beständig; ⟨continuous⟩ ständig

constellation /kɒnstə'leɪʃn/ n Sternbild nt

consternation /kɒnstə'neɪʃn/ n Bestürzung f

constipat|ed /'kɒnstɪpeɪtɪd/ a verstopft. **~ion** /-'peɪʃn/ n Verstopfung f

constituency /kən'stɪtjʊənsɪ/ n Wahlkreis m

constituent /kən'stɪtjʊənt/ n Bestandteil m; ⟨Pol⟩ Wähler(in) m(f)

constitute /'kɒnstɪtjuːt/ vt bilden. **~ion** /-'tjuːʃn/ n ⟨Pol⟩ Verfassung f; ⟨of person⟩ Konstitution f. **~ional** /-'tjuːʃənl/ a Verfassungs- □ n Verdauungsspaziergang m

constrain /kən'streɪn/ vt zwingen. **~t** n Zwang m; ⟨restriction⟩ Beschränkung f; ⟨strained manner⟩ Gezwungenheit f

constrict /kən'strɪkt/ vt einengen

construct /kən'strʌkt/ vt bauen. **~ion** /-ʌkʃn/ n Bau m; ⟨Gram⟩ Konstruktion f; ⟨interpretation⟩ Deutung f; **under ~ion** im Bau. **~ive** /-ɪv/ a konstruktiv

construe /kən'struː/ vt deuten

consul /'kɒnsl/ n Konsul m. **~ate** /'kɒnsjʊlət/ n Konsulat nt

consult /kən'sʌlt/ vt ⟨um Rat⟩ fragen; konsultieren ⟨doctor⟩; nachschlagen in (+ dat) ⟨book⟩. **~ant** n Berater m; ⟨Med⟩ Chefarzt m. **~ation** /kɒnsl'teɪʃn/ n Beratung f; ⟨Med⟩ Konsultation f

consume /kən'sjuːm/ vt verzehren; ⟨use⟩ verbrauchen. **~r** n Verbraucher m. **~r goods** npl Konsumgüter pl

consummat|e /'kɒnsəmeɪt/ vt vollziehen. **~ion** /-'meɪʃn/ n Vollzug m

consumption /kən'sʌmpʃn/ n Konsum m; ⟨use⟩ Verbrauch m

contact /'kɒntækt/ n Kontakt m; ⟨person⟩ Kontaktperson f □ vt sich in Verbindung setzen mit. **~ lenses** npl Kontaktlinsen pl

contagious /kən'teɪdʒəs/ a direkt übertragbar

contain /kən'teɪn/ vt enthalten; (control) beherrschen. **~er** n Behälter m; (Comm) Container m

contaminat|e /kən'tæmɪneɪt/ vt verseuchen. **~ion** /-'neɪʃn/ n Verseuchung f

contemplat|e /'kɒntəmpleɪt/ vt betrachten; (meditate) nachdenken über (+ acc); **~e doing sth** daran denken, etw zu tun. **~ion** /-'pleɪʃn/ n Betrachtung f; Nachdenken nt

contemporary /kən'tempərərɪ/ a zeitgenössisch □ n Zeitgenosse m/ -genossin f

contempt /kən'tempt/ n Verachtung f; **beneath ~** verabscheuungswürdig; **~ of court** Missachtung f des Gerichts. **~ible** /-əbl/ a verachtenswert. **~uous** /-tjʊəs/ a, **-ly** adv verächtlich

contend /kən'tend/ vi kämpfen (with mit) □ vt (assert) behaupten. **~er** n Bewerber(in) m(f); (Sport) Wettkämpfer(in) m(f)

content1 /'kɒntent/ n & contents pl Inhalt m

content2 /kən'tent/ a zufrieden □ n to one's heart's **~** nach Herzenslust □ vt **~ oneself** sich begnügen (with mit). **~ed** a, **-ly** adv zufrieden

contention /kən'tenʃn/ n (assertion) Behauptung f

contentment /kən'tentmənt/ n Zufriedenheit f

contest1 /'kɒntest/ n Kampf m; (competition) Wettbewerb m

contest2 /kən'test/ vt (dispute) bestreiten; (Jur) anfechten; (Pol) kandidieren in (+ dat). **~ant** n Teilnehmer m

context /'kɒntekst/ n Zusammenhang m

continent /'kɒntɪnənt/ n Kontinent m

continental /kɒntɪ'nentl/ a Kontinental-. **~ breakfast** n kleines

Frühstück nt. **~ quilt** n Daunendecke f

contingen|cy /kən'tɪndʒənsɪ/ n Eventualität f. **~t a be ~t upon** abhängen von □ n (Mil) Kontingent nt

continual /kən'tɪnjʊəl/ a, **-ly** adv dauernd

continuation /kən'tɪnjʊ'eɪʃn/ n Fortsetzung f

continue /kən'tɪnju:/ vt fortsetzen; **~ doing** or **to do sth** fortfahren, etw zu tun; **to be ~d** Fortsetzung folgt □ vi weitergehen; (doing sth) weitermachen; (speaking) fortfahren; (weather:) anhalten

continuity /kɒntɪ'nju:ətɪ/ n Kontinuität f

continuous /kən'tɪnjʊəs/ a, **-ly** adv anhaltend, ununterbrochen

contort /kən'tɔ:t/ vt verzerren. **~ion** /-ɔ:ʃn/ n Verzerrung f

contour /'kɒntʊə(r)/ n Kontur f; (line) Höhenlinie f

contraband /'kɒntrəbænd/ n Schmuggelware f

contracep|tion /kɒntrə'sepʃn/ n Empfängnisverhütung f. **~tive** /-tɪv/ a empfängnisverhütend □ n Empfängnisverhütungsmittel nt

contract1 /'kɒntrækt/ n Vertrag m

contract2 /kən'trækt/ vi sich zusammenziehen □ vt zusammenziehen; sich (dat) zuziehen (illness). **~ion** /-ækʃn/ n Zusammenziehung f; (abbreviation) Abkürzung f; (in childbirth) Wehe f. **~or** n Unternehmer m

contradict /kɒntrə'dɪkt/ vt widersprechen (+ dat). **~ion** /-ɪkʃn/ n Widerspruch m. **~ory** /-ərɪ/ a widersprüchlich

contra-flow /'kɒntrə-/ n Umleitung f [auf die entgegengesetzte Fahrbahn]

contralto /kən'træltəʊ/ n Alt m; (singer) Altistin f

contraption /kən'træpʃn/ n (fam) Apparat m

contrary¹ /'kɒntrəri/ a & adv entgegengesetzt; ~ **to** entgegen (+ dat) □ n Gegenteil nt; **on the** ~ im Gegenteil

contrary² /kən'treəri/ a widerspenstig

contrast¹ /'kɒntrɑ:st/ n Kontrast m

contrast² /kən'trɑ:st/ vt gegenüberstellen (with dat) □ vi einen Kontrast bilden (with zu). ~ing a gegensätzlich; (colour) Kontrast-

contraven|e /kɒntrə'vi:n/ vt verstoßen gegen. ~tion /-'venʃn/ n Verstoß m (of gegen)

contribut|e /kən'trɪbju:t/ vt/i beitragen; beisteuern (money); (donate) spenden. ~ion /kɒntrɪ'bju:ʃn/ n Beitrag m; (donation) Spende f. ~or n Beitragende(r) m/f

contrite /kən'traɪt/ a reuig

contrivance /kən'traɪvəns/ n Vorrichtung f

contrive /kən'traɪv/ vt verfertigen; ~ **to do sth** es fertig bringen, etw zu tun

control /kən'trəʊl/ n Kontrolle f; (mastery) Beherrschung f; (Techn) Regler m; ~s pl (of car, plane) Steuerung f; **get out of** ~ außer Kontrolle geraten □ vt (pt/pp **controlled**) kontrollieren; (restrain) unter Kontrolle halten; ~ **oneself** sich beherrschen

controvers|ial /kɒntrə'vɜ:ʃl/ a umstritten. ~**y** /'kɒntrəvɜ:ʃɪ/ n Kontroverse f

conundrum /kə'nʌndrəm/ n Rätsel nt

conurbation /kɒnɜ:'beɪʃn/ n Ballungsgebiet nt

convalesce /kɒnvə'les/ vi sich erholen. ~**nce** n Erholung f

convalescent /kɒnvə'lesnt/ a be ~ noch erholungsbedürftig sein. ~ **home** n Erholungsheim nt

convector /kən'vektə(r)/ n ~ [heater] Konvektor m

convene /kən'vi:n/ vt einberufen □ vi sich versammeln

convenience /kən'vi:nɪəns/ n Bequemlichkeit f; [public] ~ öffentliche Toilette f; **with all modern** ~**s** mit allem Komfort

convenient /kən'vi:nɪənt/ a, ~**ly** adv günstig; **be** ~ **for s.o.** jdm gelegen sein od jdm passen; **if it is** ~ **[for you]** wenn es Ihnen passt

convent /'kɒnvənt/ n [Nonnen]-kloster nt

convention /kən'venʃn/ n (custom) Brauch m, Sitte f; (agreement) Konvention f; (assembly) Tagung f. ~**al** a, -**ly** adv konventionell

converge /kən'vɜ:dʒ/ vi zusammenlaufen

conversant /kən'vɜ:sənt/ a ~ **with** vertraut mit

conversation /kɒnvə'seɪʃn/ n Gespräch nt; (Sch) Konversation f

converse¹ /kən'vɜ:s/ vi sich unterhalten

converse² /'kɒnvɜ:s/ n Gegenteil nt. ~**ly** adv umgekehrt

conversion /kən'vɜ:ʃn/ n Umbau m; (Relig) Bekehrung f; (calculation) Umrechnung f

convert¹ /'kɒnvɜ:t/ n Bekehrte(r) m/f, Konvertit m

convert² /kən'vɜ:t/ vt bekehren (person); (change) umwandeln (into in + acc); umbauen (building); (calculate) umrechnen; (Techn) umstellen. ~**ible** /-əbl/ a verwandelbar □ n (Auto) Kabriolett nt

convex /'kɒnveks/ a konvex

convey /kən'veɪ/ vt befördern; vermitteln (idea, message). ~**ance** n Beförderung f; (vehicle) Beförderungsmittel nt. ~**or belt** n Förderband nt

convict¹ /'kɒnvɪkt/ n Sträfling m

convict² /kən'vɪkt/ *vt* verurteilen (**of** wegen). **~ion** /-ɪkʃn/ *n* Verurteilung *f*; (*belief*) Überzeugung *f*; **previous ~ion** Vorstrafe *f*

convinc|e /kən'vɪns/ *vt* überzeugen. **~ing** *a*, **-ly** *adv* überzeugend

convivial /kən'vɪvɪəl/ *a* gesellig

convoluted /'kɒnvəlu:tɪd/ *a* verschlungen; (*fig*) verwickelt

convoy /'kɒnvɔɪ/ *n* Konvoi *m*

convuls|e /kən'vʌls/ *vt* **be ~ed** sich krümmen (**with** vor + *dat*). **~ion** /-ʌlʃn/ *n* Krampf *m*

coo /ku:/ *vi* gurren

cook /kʊk/ *n* Koch *m*/ Köchin *f* □ *vt/i* kochen; **is it ~ed?** ist es gar? • **the books** (*fam*) die Bilanz frisieren. **~book** *n* (*Amer*) Kochbuch *nt*

cooker /'kʊkə(r)/ *n* [Koch]herd *m*; (*apple*) Kochapfel *m*. **~y** *n* Kochen *nt*. **~y book** *n* Kochbuch *nt*

cookie /'kʊkɪ/ *n* (*Amer*) Keks *m*

cool /ku:l/ *a* (**-er, -est**), **-ly** *adv* kühlen □ *n* Kühle *f* □ *vt* kühlen □ *vi* abkühlen. **~box** *n* Kühlbox *f*. **~ness** *n* Kühle *f*

coop /ku:p/ *n* [Hühner]stall *m* □ *vt* **~ up** einsperren

co-operate /kəʊ'ɒpəreɪt/ *vi* zusammenarbeiten. **~ion** /-'reɪʃn/ *n* Kooperation *f*

co-operative /kəʊ'ɒpərətɪv/ *a* hilfsbereit □ *n* Genossenschaft *f*

co-opt /kəʊ'ɒpt/ *vt* hinzuwählen

co-ordinat|e /kəʊ'ɔ:dɪneɪt/ *vt* koordinieren. **~ion** /-'neɪʃn/ *n* Koordination *f*

cop /kɒp/ *n* (*fam*) Polizist *m*

cope /kəʊp/ *vi* (*fam*) zurechtkommen; **~ with** fertig werden mit

copious /'kəʊpɪəs/ *a* reichlich

copper¹ /'kɒpə(r)/ *n* Kupfer *nt*; **~s** *pl* Kleingeld *nt* □ *a* kupfern

copper² /'kɒpə(r)/ *n* (*fam*) Polizist *m*

copper 'beech *n* Blutbuche *f*

coppice /'kɒpɪs/ *n*, **copse** /kɒps/ *n* Gehölz *nt*

copulate /'kɒpjʊleɪt/ *vi* sich begatten

copy /'kɒpɪ/ *n* Kopie *f*; (*book*) Exemplar *nt* □ *vt* (*pt/pp* **-ied**) kopieren; (*imitate*) nachmachen; (*Sch*) abschreiben

copy: **~right** *n* Copyright *nt*. **~writer** *n* Texter *m*

coral /'kɒrl/ *n* Koralle *f*

cord /kɔ:d/ *n* Schnur *f*; (*fabric*) Cordsamt *m*; **~s** *pl* Cordhose *f*

cordial /'kɔ:dɪəl/ *a*, **-ly** *adv* herzlich □ *n* Fruchtsirup *m*

cordon /'kɔ:dn/ *n* Kordon *m* □ *vt* **~ off** absperren

corduroy /'kɔ:dərɔɪ/ *n* Cordsamt *m*

core /kɔ:(r)/ *n* Kern *m*; (*of apple, pear*) Kernegehäuse *nt*

cork /kɔ:k/ *n* Kork *m*; (*for bottle*) Korken *m*. **~screw** *n* Korkenzieher *m*

corn¹ /kɔ:n/ *n* Korn *nt*; (*Amer: maize*) Mais *m*

corn² /kɔ:n/ *n* (*Med*) Hühnerauge *nt*

cornea /'kɔ:nɪə/ *n* Hornhaut *f*

corned beef /kɔ:nd'bi:f/ *n* Cornedbeef *nt*

corner /'kɔ:nə(r)/ *n* Ecke *f*; (*bend*) Kurve *f*; (*football*) Eckball *m* □ *vt* (*fig*) in die Enge treiben; (*Comm*) monopolisieren (*market*). **~stone** *n* Eckstein *m*

cornet /'kɔ:nɪt/ *n* (*Mus*) Kornett *nt*; (*for ice-cream*) [Eis]tüte *f*

corn: **~flour** *n*, (*Amer*) **~starch** *n* Stärkemehl *nt*

corny /'kɔ:nɪ/ *a* (*fam*) abgedroschen

coronary /'kɒrənərɪ/ *a* & *n* **~ [thrombosis]** Koronarthrombose *f*

coronation /kɒrə'neɪʃn/ *n* Krönung *f*

coroner /'kɒrənə(r)/ *n* Beamte *m*, der verdächtige Todesfälle untersucht

coronet /'kɒrənet/ *n* Adelskrone *f*

corporal[1] /'kɔːpərəl/ n (Mil) Stabsunteroffizier m

corporal[2] a körperlich; ~ **punishment** körperliche Züchtigung f

corporate /'kɔːpərət/ a gemeinschaftlich

corporation /kɔːpə'reɪʃn/ n Körperschaft f; (of town) Stadtverwaltung f

corps /kɔː(r)/ n (pl corps /kɔːz/) Korps nt

corpse /kɔːps/ n Leiche f

corpulent /'kɔːpjʊlənt/ a korpulent

corpuscle /'kɔːpʌsl/ n Blutkörperchen nt

correct /kə'rekt/ a, **-ly** adv richtig; (proper) korrekt □ vt verbessern; (Sch, Typ) korrigieren. **~ion** /-ekʃn/ n Verbesserung f; (Typ) Korrektur f

correlation /kɒrə'leɪʃn/ n Wechselbeziehung f

correspond /kɒrɪ'spɒnd/ vi entsprechen (to dat); (two things:) sich entsprechen; (write) korrespondieren. **~ence** n Briefwechsel m; (Comm) Korrespondenz f. **~ent** n Korrespondent(in) m(f). **~ing**, **-ly** adv entsprechend

corridor /'kɒrɪdɔː(r)/ n Gang m; (Pol, Aviat) Korridor m

corroborate /kə'rɒbəreɪt/ vt bestätigen

corrolde /kə'rəʊd/ vt zerfressen □ vi rosten. **~sion** /-'rəʊʒn/ n Korrosion f

corrugated /'kɒrəgeɪtɪd/ a gewellt. **~ iron** n Wellblech nt

corrupt /kə'rʌpt/ a korrupt □ vt korrumpieren; (spoil) verderben. **~ion** /-ʌpʃn/ n Korruption f

corset /'kɔːsɪt/ n & -s pl Korsett nt

Corsica /'kɔːsɪkə/ n Korsika nt

cortège /kɔː'teɪʒ/ n [funeral] ~ Leichenzug m

cosh /kɒʃ/ n Totschläger m

cosmetic /kɒz'metɪk/ a kosmetisch □ n ~s pl Kosmetika pl

cosmic /'kɒzmɪk/ a kosmisch

cosmonaut /'kɒzmənɔːt/ n Kosmonaut(in) m(f)

cosmopolitan /kɒzmə'pɒlɪtən/ a kosmopolitisch

cosmos /'kɒzmɒs/ n Kosmos m

cosset /'kɒsɪt/ vt verhätscheln

cost /kɒst/ n Kosten pl; ~s pl (Jur) Kosten; at all ~s um jeden Preis; I learnt to my ~ es hat mich teuer zu stehen gekommen □ vt (pt/pp cost) kosten; it ~ me £20 es hat mich £20 gekostet □ vt (pt/pp costed) ~ [out] die Kosten kalkulieren für

costly /'kɒstlɪ/ a (-ier, -iest) teuer

cost: ~ **of 'living** n Lebenshaltungskosten pl. ~ **price** n Selbstkostenpreis m

costume /'kɒstjuːm/ n Kostüm nt; (national) Tracht f. ~ **jewellery** n Modeschmuck m

cosy /'kəʊzɪ/ a (-ier, -iest) gemütlich □ n (tea-, egg-) Wärmer m

cot /kɒt/ n Kinderbett nt; (Amer: camp-bed) Feldbett nt

cottage /'kɒtɪdʒ/ n Häuschen n. ~ **'cheese** n Hüttenkäse m

cotton /'kɒtn/ n Baumwolle f; (thread) Nähgarn nt □ a baumwollen □ vi ~ **on** (fam) kapieren

cotton 'wool n Watte f

couch /kaʊtʃ/ n Liege f

couchette /kuː'ʃet/ n (Rail) Liegeplatz m

cough /kɒf/ n Husten m □ vi husten. ~ **up** vt/i husten; (fam: pay) blechen

'cough mixture n Hustensaft m

could /kʊd, unbetont kəd/ see can[2]

council /'kaʊnsl/ n Rat m; (Admin) Stadtverwaltung f; (rural) Gemeindeverwaltung f. ~ **house** n ≈ Sozialwohnung f

councillor /'kaʊnsələ(r)/ n Stadtverordnete(r) m/f

'council tax n Gemeindesteuer f

counsel /'kaʊnsl/ n Rat m; (Jur) Anwalt m □vt (pt/pp **counselled**) beraten. **~lor** n Berater(in) m(f)

count¹ /kaʊnt/ n Graf m

count² n Zählung f; **keep ~** zählen □vt/i zählen. **~ on** vt rechnen auf (+ acc)

countenance /'kaʊntənəns/ n Gesicht nt □vt dulden

counter¹ /'kaʊntə(r)/ n (in shop) Ladentisch m; (in bank) Schalter m; (in café) Theke f; (Games) Spielmarke f

counter² adv **~ to** gegen (+ acc) □a Gegen- □vt/i kontern

counter·act vt entgegenwirken (+ dat)

'**counter-attack** n Gegenangriff m

counter-'espionage n Spionageabwehr f

'**counterfeit** /-fɪt/ a gefälscht □n Fälschung f □vt fälschen

'**counterfoil** n Kontrollabschnitt m

'**counterpart** n Gegenstück nt

counter-pro'ductive a be ~ das Gegenteil bewirken

'**countersign** vt gegenzeichnen

countess /'kaʊntɪs/ n Gräfin f

countless /'kaʊntlɪs/ a unzählig

countrified /'kʌntrɪfaɪd/ a ländlich

country /'kʌntrɪ/ n Land nt; (native land) Heimat f; (countryside) Landschaft f; **in the ~** auf dem Lande. **~man** n [fellow] **~man** Landsmann m. **~side** n Landschaft f

county /'kaʊntɪ/ n Grafschaft f

coup /kuː/ n (Pol) Staatsstreich m

couple /'kʌpl/ n Paar nt; a **~ of** (two) zwei □vt verbinden; (Rail) koppeln

coupon /'kuːpɒn/ n Kupon m; (voucher) Gutschein m; (entry form) Schein m

courage /'kʌrɪdʒ/ n Mut m. **~ous** /kə'reɪdʒəs/ a, **-ly** adv mutig

courgettes /kʊə'ʒets/ npl Zucchini pl

courier /'kʊrɪə(r)/ n Bote m; (diplomatic) Kurier m; (for tourists) Reiseleiter(in) m(f)

course /kɔːs/ n (Naut, Sch) Kurs m; (Culin) Gang m; (for golf) Platz m; **~ of treatment** (Med) Kur f; **of ~** natürlich, selbstverständlich; **in the ~ of** im Lauf[e] (+ gen)

court /kɔːt/ n Hof m; (Sport) Platz m; (Jur) Gericht nt □vt werben um; herausfordern (danger)

courteous /'kɜːtɪəs/ a, **-ly** adv höflich

courtesy /'kɜːtəsɪ/ n Höflichkeit f

court: ~ 'martial n (pl **~s martial**) Militärgericht nt. **~ shoes** npl Pumps pl. **~yard** n Hof m

cousin /'kʌzn/ n Vetter m, Cousin m; (female) Kusine f

cove /kəʊv/ n kleine Bucht f

cover /'kʌvə(r)/ n Decke f; (of cushion) Bezug m; (of umbrella) Hülle f; (of typewriter) Haube f; (of book, lid) Deckel m; (of magazine) Umschlag m; (protection) Deckung f, Schutz m; **take ~** Deckung nehmen; **under separate ~** mit separater Post □vt bedecken; beziehen (cushion); decken (costs, needs); zurücklegen (distance); (Journ) berichten über (+ acc); (insure) versichern. **~ up** vt zudecken; (fig) vertuschen

coverage /'kʌvərɪdʒ/ n (Journ) Berichterstattung f (**of** über + acc)

cover: ~ charge n Gedeck nt. **~ing** n Decke f; (for floor) Belag m. **~-up** n Vertuschung f

covet /'kʌvɪt/ vt begehren

cow /kaʊ/ n Kuh f

coward /'kaʊəd/ n Feigling m. **~ice** /-ɪs/ n Feigheit f. **~ly** a feige

'**cowboy** n Cowboy m; (fam) unsolider Handwerker m

cower /'kauə(r)/ vi sich
[ängstlich] ducken

'cowshed n Kuhstall m

cox /kɒks/ n, **coxswain** /'kɒksn/
n Steuermann m

coy /kɔɪ/ a (-er, -est) gespielt
schüchtern

crab /kræb/ n Krabbe f. **~apple**
n Holzapfel m

crack /kræk/ n Riss m; (in china,
glass) Sprung m; (noise) Knall m;
(fam: joke) Witz m; (fam: attempt)
Versuch m □ a (fam) erstklassig
□ vt knacken (nut, code); einen
Sprung machen in (+ acc) (china,
glass); (fam) reißen (joke); (fam)
lösen (problem) □ vi (china,
glass): springen; (whip:) knallen.
~ down vi (fam) durchgreifen

cracked /krækt/ a gesprungen;
(rib) angebrochen; (fam: crazy)
verrückt

cracker /'krækə(r)/ n (biscuit)
Kräcker m; (firework)
Knallkörper m; **[Christmas] ~**
Knallbonbon m. **~s a be ~s** (fam)
einen Knacks haben

crackle /'krækl/ vi knistern

cradle /'kreɪdl/ n Wiege f

craft[1] /krɑːft/ n inv (boat) [Was-
ser]fahrzeug nt

craft[2] n Handwerk nt; (technique)
Fertigkeit f. **~sman** n
Handwerker m

crafty /'krɑːftɪ/ a (-ier, -iest), -ily
adv gerissen

crag /kræg/ n Felszacken m. **~gy**
a felsig; (face) kantig

cram /kræm/ v (pt/pp crammed)
□ vt hineinstopfen (into in +
acc); vollstopfen (with mit) □ vi
(for exams) pauken

cramp /kræmp/ n Krampf m.
~ed a eng

crampon /'kræmpən/ n Steig-
eisen nt

cranberry /'krænbərɪ/ n (Culin)
Preiselbeere f

crane /kreɪn/ n Kran m; (bird)
Kranich m □ vt **~ one's neck** den
Hals recken

crank[1] /kræŋk/ n (fam) Exzentriker m

crank[2] n (Techn) Kurbel f.
~shaft n Kurbelwelle f

cranky /'kræŋkɪ/ a exzentrisch;
(Amer: irritable) reizbar

cranny /'krænɪ/ n Ritze f

crash /kræʃ/ n (noise) Krach m;
(Auto) Zusammenstoß m; (Aviat)
Absturz m □ vi krachen (into
gegen); (cars:) zusammenstoßen;
(plane:) abstürzen □ vt einen Unfall haben mit (car)

crash: ~course n Schnellkurs m.
~helmet n Sturzhelm m. **~**
landing n Bruchlandung f

crate /kreɪt/ n Kiste f

crater /'kreɪtə(r)/ n Krater m

crav|e /kreɪv/ vi **~e for** sich
sehnen nach. **~ing** n Gelüst nt

crawl /krɔːl/ n (Swimming) Kraul
nt; **do the ~** kraulen; **at a ~** im
Kriechtempo □ vi kriechen;
(baby:) krabbeln; **~ with** wimmeln von. **~er lane** n (Auto)
Kriechspur f

crayon /'kreɪən/ n Wachsstift m;
(pencil) Buntstift m

craze /kreɪz/ n Mode f

crazy /'kreɪzɪ/ a (-ier, -iest) verrückt; **be ~ about** verrückt sein
nach

creak /kriːk/ n Knarren nt □ vi
knarren

cream /kriːm/ n Sahne f; (Cosmetic, Med, Culin) Creme f □ a
(colour) cremefarben □ vt (Culin)
cremig rühren. **~ 'cheese** n ≈
Quark m. **~y** a sahnig; (smooth)
cremig

crease /kriːs/ n Falte f; (unwanted) Knitterfalte f □ vt falten;
(accidentally) zerknittern □ vi
knittern. **~-resistant** a knitter-
frei

creat|e /kriːˈeɪt/ vt schaffen. **~ion**
/-'eɪʃn/ n Schöpfung f. **~ive**
/-tɪv/ a schöpferisch. **~or** n
Schöpfer m

creature /'kri:tʃə(r)/ n Geschöpf nt

crèche /kreʃ/ n Kinderkrippe f

credentials /krɪ'denʃlz/ npl Beglaubigungsschreiben nt

credibility /kredə'bɪlɪtɪ/ n Glaubwürdigkeit f

credible /'kredəbl/ a glaubwürdig

credit /'kredɪt/ n Kredit m; (honour) Ehre f □ vt glauben; ~ s.o. with sth (Comm) jdm ein Gut-haben zuschreiben; (fig) jdm etw zu-schreiben. ~able /-əbl/ a lobenswert

credit: ~ card n Kreditkarte f. ~or n Gläubiger m

creed /kri:d/ n Glaubensbekenntnis nt

creek /kri:k/ n enge Bucht f; (Amer: stream) Bach m

creep /kri:p/ vi (pt/pp crept) schleichen □ n (fam) fieser Kerl m; it gives me the ~s es ist mir unheimlich. ~er n Kletterpflanze f. ~y a gruselig

cremat|e /krɪ'meɪt/ vt ein-äschern. ~ion /-eɪʃn/ n Ein-äscherung f

crematorium /kremə'tɔ:rɪəm/ n Krematorium nt

crêpe /kreɪp/ n Krepp m. ~ paper n Kreppapier nt

crept /krept/ see creep

crescent /'kresənt/ n Halbmond m

cress /kres/ n Kresse f

crest /krest/ n Kamm m; (coat of arms) Wappen nt

Crete /kri:t/ n Kreta nt

crevasse /krɪ'væs/ n [Gletscher]-spalte f

crevice /'krevɪs/ n Spalte f

crew /kru:/ n Besatzung f; (gang) Bande f. ~ cut n Bürstenschnitt m

crib[1] /krɪb/ n Krippe f

crib[2] /krɪb/ vt/i (pt/pp cribbed) (fam) abschreiben

crick /krɪk/ n ~ in the neck steifes Genick nt

cricket[1] /'krɪkɪt/ n (insect) Grille f

cricket[2] n Kricket nt. ~er n Kricketspieler m

crime /kraɪm/ n Verbrechen nt; (rate) Kriminalität f

criminal /'krɪmɪnl/ a kriminell, verbrecherisch; (law, court) Straf- □ n Verbrecher m

crimson /'krɪmzn/ a purpurrot

cringe /krɪndʒ/ vi sich [ängstlich] ducken

crinkle /'krɪŋkl/ vt/i knittern

cripple /'krɪpl/ n Krüppel m □ vt zum Krüppel machen; (fig) lahmlegen. ~d a verkrüppelt

crisis /'kraɪsɪs/ n (pl -ses /-si:z/) Krise f

crisp /'krɪsp/ a (-er, -est) knusprig. ~bread n Knäckebrot nt. ~s npl Chips pl

criss-cross /'krɪs-/ a schräg ge-kreuzt

criterion /kraɪ'tɪərɪən/ n (pl -ria /-rɪə/) Kriterium nt

critic /'krɪtɪk/ n Kritiker m. ~al a kritisch. ~ally adv kritisch; ~ally ill schwer krank

criticism /'krɪtɪsɪzm/ n Kritik f

criticize /'krɪtɪsaɪz/ vt kritisieren

croak /krəʊk/ vi krächzen; (frog:) quaken

crochet /'krəʊʃeɪ/ n Häkelarbeit f □ vt/i häkeln. ~hook n Häkelnadel f

crock /krɒk/ n (fam) old ~ (person) Wrack m; (car) Klapperkiste f

crockery /'krɒkərɪ/ n Geschirr nt

crocodile /'krɒkədaɪl/ n Krokodil nt

crocus /'krəʊkəs/ n (pl -es) Krokus m

crony /'krəʊnɪ/ n Kumpel m

crook /krʊk/ n (stick) Stab m; (fam: criminal) Schwindler m, Gauner m

crooked /'krʊkɪd/ a schief; (bent) krumm; (fam: dishonest) unehrlich

crop /krɒp/ n Feldfrucht f; (harvest) Ernte f; (of bird) Kropf m □ v (pt/pp **cropped**) □ vt stutzen □ vi ~ **up** (fam) zur Sprache kommen; (occur) dazwischenkommen

croquet /ˈkrəʊkeɪ/ n Krocket nt

croquette /krəʊˈket/ n Krokette f

cross /krɒs/ a, **-ly** adv (annoyed) böse (**with** auf + acc); **talk at ~ purposes** aneinander vorbeireden □ n Kreuz nt; (Bot, Zool) Kreuzung f; **on the ~** schräg □ vt kreuzen (cheque, animals); überqueren (road); ~ **oneself** sich bekreuzigen; ~ **one's arms** die Arme verschränken; ~ **one's legs** die Beine übereinanderschlagen; **keep one's fingers ~ed for s.o.** jdm die Daumen drücken; **it ~ed my mind** es fiel mir ein □ vi (go across) hinübergehen/-fahren; (lines:) sich kreuzen. ~ **out** vt durchstreichen

cross: ~**bar** n Querlatte f; (on bicycle) Stange f. ~'**country** n (Sport) Crosslauf m. ~-ex'**amine** vt ins Kreuzverhör nehmen. ~-exami'**nation** n Kreuzverhör nt. ~-**eyed** a schielend; **be ~-eyed** schielen. ~**fire** n Kreuzfeuer nt. ~**ing** n Übergang m; (sea journey) Überfahrt f. ~'**reference** n Querverweis m. ~**roads** n [Straßen]kreuzung f. ~-**section** n Querschnitt m. ~**stitch** n Kreuzstich m. ~**wise** adv quer. ~**word** n ~**word** [puzzle] Kreuzworträtsel nt

crotchet /ˈkrɒtʃɪt/ n Viertelnote f

crotchety /ˈkrɒtʃɪtɪ/ a griesgrämig

crouch /kraʊtʃ/ vi kauern

crow /krəʊ/ n Krähe f; **as the ~ flies** Luftlinie f □ vi krähen. ~**bar** n Brechstange f

crowd /kraʊd/ n [Menschen]menge f □ vi sich drängen. ~**ed** /ˈkraʊdɪd/ a [gedrängt] voll

crown /kraʊn/ n Krone f □ vt krönen; überkronen (tooth)

crucial /ˈkruːʃl/ a höchst wichtig; (decisive) entscheidend (**to** für)

crucifix /ˈkruːsɪfɪks/ n Kruzifix nt

cruci|**fixion** /kruːsɪˈfɪkʃn/ n Kreuzigung f. ~**fy** /-faɪ/ vt (pt/pp -**ied**) kreuzigen

crude /kruːd/ a (-r, -st) (raw) roh

cruel /ˈkruːəl/ a (**crueller**, **cruellest**), **-ly** adv grausam (**to** gegen). ~**ty** n Grausamkeit f; ~**ty to animals** Tierquälerei f

cruise /kruːz/ n Kreuzfahrt f □ vi kreuzen; (car:) fahren. ~**er** n (Mil) Kreuzer m; (motor boat) Kajütboot nt. ~**ing speed** n Reisegeschwindigkeit f

crumb /krʌm/ n Krümel m

crumble /ˈkrʌmbl/ vt/i krümeln; (collapse) einstürzen. ~**ly** a krümelig

crumple /ˈkrʌmpl/ vt zerknittern □ vi knittern

crunch /krʌntʃ/ n (fam) **when it comes to the ~** wenn es [wirklich] drauf ankommt □ vt mampfen □ vi knirschen

crusade /kruːˈseɪd/ n Kreuzzug m; (fig) Kampagne f. ~**r** n Kreuzfahrer m; (fig) Kämpfer m

crush /krʌʃ/ n (crowd) Gedränge nt □ vt zerquetschen; zerknittern (clothes); (fig: subdue) niederschlagen

crust /krʌst/ n Kruste f

crutch /krʌtʃ/ n Krücke f

crux /krʌks/ n (fig) springender Punkt m

cry /kraɪ/ n Ruf m; (shout) Schrei m; **a far ~ from** (fig) weit entfernt von □ vi (pt/pp **cried**) (weep) weinen; (baby:) schreien; (call) rufen

crypt /krɪpt/ n Krypta f. ~**ic** a rätselhaft

crystal /ˈkrɪstl/ n Kristall m; (glass) Kristall nt. ~**lize** vi [sich] kristallisieren

cub /kʌb/ n (Zool) Junge(s) nt; C~ [Scout] Wölfling m

Cuba /'kju:bə/ n Kuba nt

cubby-hole /'kʌbɪ-/ n Fach nt

cub|e /kju:b/ n Würfel m. ~ic a ein Kubik-

cubicle /'kju:bɪkl/ n Kabine f

cuckoo /'kuku:/ n Kuckuck m. ~ clock n Kuckucksuhr f

cucumber /'kju:kʌmbə(r)/ n Gurke f

cuddl|e /'kʌdl/ vt herzen □ vi ~e up to sich kuscheln an (+ acc). ~y a kuschelig. ~y 'toy n Plüschtier nt

cudgel /'kʌdʒl/ n Knüppel m

cue1 /kju:/ n Stichwort nt

cue2 n (Billiards) Queue m

cuff /kʌf/ n Manschette f; (Amer: turn-up) [Hosen]aufschlag m; (blow) Klaps m; off the ~ (fam) aus dem Stegreif □ vt einen Klaps geben (+ dat). ~-link n Manschettenknopf m

cul-de-sac /'kʌldəsæk/ n Sackgasse f

culinary /'kʌlɪnərɪ/ a kulinarisch

cull /kʌl/ vt pflücken (flowers); (kill) ausmerzen

culminat|e /'kʌlmɪneɪt/ vi gipfeln (in in + dat). ~ion /-'neɪʃn/ n Gipfelpunkt m

culottes /kju:'lɒts/ npl Hosenrock m

culprit /'kʌlprɪt/ n Täter m

cult /kʌlt/ n Kult m

cultivate /'kʌltɪveɪt/ vt anbauen (crop); bebauen (land)

cultural /'kʌltʃərəl/ a kulturell

culture /'kʌltʃə(r)/ n Kultur f. ~d a kultiviert

cumbersome /'kʌmbəsəm/ a hinderlich; (unwieldy) unhandlich

cumulative /'kju:mjolətɪv/ a kumulativ

cunning /'kʌnɪŋ/ a listig □ n List f

cup /kʌp/ n Tasse f; (prize) Pokal m

cupboard /'kʌbəd/ n Schrank m

Cup 'Final n Pokalendspiel nt

Cupid /'kju:pɪd/ n Amor m

curable /'kjuərəbl/ a heilbar

curate /'kjuərət/ n Vikar m; (Roman Catholic) Kaplan m

curator /kjuə'reɪtə(r)/ n Kustos m

curb /kɜ:b/ vt zügeln

curdle /'kɜ:dl/ vi gerinnen

cure /kjuə(r)/ n [Heil]mittel nt □ vt heilen; (salt) pökeln; (smoke) räuchern; gerben (skin)

curfew /'kɜ:fju:/ n Ausgangssperre f

curio /'kjuərɪəu/ n Kuriosität f

curiosity /kjuərɪ'ɒsətɪ/ n Neugier f; (object) Kuriosität f

curious /'kjuərɪəs/ a, -ly adv neugierig; (strange) merkwürdig, seltsam

curl /kɜ:l/ n Locke f □ vt locken □ vi sich locken. ~ up vi sich zusammenrollen

curler /'kɜ:lə(r)/ n Lockenwickler m

curly /'kɜ:lɪ/ a (-ier, -iest) lockig

currant /'kʌrənt/ n (dried) Korinthe f

currency /'kʌrənsɪ/ n Geläufigkeit f; (money) Währung f; foreign ~ Devisen pl

current /'kʌrənt/ a augenblicklich, gegenwärtig; (in general use) geläufig, gebräuchlich □ n Strömung f; (Electr) Strom m. ~ af-fairs or events npl Aktuelle(s) nt. ~ly adv zurzeit

curriculum /kə'rɪkjuləm/ n Lehrplan m. ~ vitae /-'vi:taɪ/ n Lebenslauf m

curry /'kʌrɪ/ n Curry nt & m; (meal) Currygericht nt □ vt (pt/pp -ied) ~ favour sich einschmeicheln (with bei)

curse /kɜ:s/ n Fluch m □ vt verfluchen □ vi fluchen

cursory /'kɜ:sərɪ/ a flüchtig

curt /kɜ:t/ a, -ly adv barsch

curtail /kɜː'teɪl/ vt abkürzen
curtain /'kɜːtn/ n Vorhang m
curtsy /'kɜːtsɪ/ n Knicks m □vi
(pt/pp -ied) knicksen
curve /kɜːv/ n Kurve f □ vi einen
Bogen machen; ~ **to the right/**
left nach rechts/links biegen.
~d a gebogen
cushion /'kʊʃn/ n Kissen nt □ vt
dämpfen; (protect) beschützen
cushy /'kʊʃɪ/ a (-ier, -iest) (fam)
bequem
custard /'kʌstəd/ n Vanillesoße f
custodian /kʌ'stəʊdɪən/ n Hüter
m
custody /'kʌstədɪ/ n Obhut f; (of
child) Sorgerecht nt; (imprisonment) Haft f
custom /'kʌstəm/ n Brauch m;
(habit) Gewohnheit f; (Comm)
Kundschaft f. ~ary a üblich;
(habitual) gewohnt. ~er n Kunde
m/Kundin f
customs /'kʌstəmz/ npl Zoll m. ~
officer n Zollbeamte(r) m
cut /kʌt/ n Schnitt m; (Med)
Schnittwunde f; (reduction) Kürzung f; (in price) Senkung f; ~
[of meat] [Fleisch]stück nt □ vt/i
(pt/pp cut, pres p cutting)
schneiden; (mow) mähen; abheben (cards); (reduce) kürzen;
senken (price); ~ **one's finger**
sich in den Finger schneiden; ~
s.o.'s hair jdm die Haare schneiden; ~ **short** abkürzen. ~ **back**
vt zurückschneiden; (fig) einschränken, kürzen. ~ **down** vt
fällen; (fig) einschränken. ~ **off**
vt abschneiden; (disconnect)
abstellen; **be** ~ **off** (Teleph)
unterbrochen werden. ~ **out** vt
ausschneiden; (delete) streichen;
be ~ **out for** (fam) geeignet sein
zu. ~ **up** vt zerschneiden; (slice)
aufschneiden
'cut-back n Kürzung f, Einschränkung f
cute /kjuːt/ a (-r, -st) (fam) niedlich
cut 'glass n Kristall nt

cuticle /'kjuːtɪkl/ n Nagelhaut f
cutlery /'kʌtlərɪ/ n Besteck nt
cutlet /'kʌtlɪt/ n Kotelett nt
'cut-price a verbilligt
cutting /'kʌtɪŋ/ a (remark) bissig
□ n (from newspaper) Ausschnitt
m; (of plant) Ableger m
CV abbr of curriculum vitae
cyclamen /'sɪkləmən/ n Alpen-
veilchen n
cycle /'saɪkl/ n Zyklus m; (bicycle) [Fahr]rad □ vi mit dem
Rad fahren. ~**ing** n Radfahren nt.
~**ist** n Radfahrer(in) m(f)
cyclone /'saɪkləʊn/ n Wirbelsturm m
cylind|er /'sɪlɪndə(r)/ n Zylinder
m. ~**rical** /-'lɪndrɪkl/ a zylind-
risch
cymbals /'sɪmblz/ npl (Mus) Becken nt
cynic /'sɪnɪk/ n Zyniker m. ~**al**
a, -**ly** adv zynisch. ~**ism** /-sɪzm/
n Zynismus m
cypress /'saɪprəs/ n Zypresse f
Cyprus /'saɪprəs/ n Zypern nt
cyst /sɪst/ n Zyste f. ~**itis**
/-'taɪtɪs/ n Blasenentzündung f
Czech /tʃek/ a tschechisch □ n
Tscheche m/ Tschechin f
Czechoslovak /tʃekə'sləʊvæk/
a tschechoslowakisch. ~**ia**
/-'vækɪə/ n die Tschechoslowa-
kei. ~**ian** /-'vækɪən/ a tschechoslowakisch

D

dab /dæb/ n Tupfer m; (of butter)
Klecks m; **a** ~ **of** ein bisschen □ vt
(pt/pp dabbed) abtupfen; be-
tupfen (with mit)
dabble /'dæbl/ vi ~ **in sth** (fig)
sich nebenbei mit etw befassen
dachshund /'dækshʊnd/ n Dackel m
dad[dy] /'dæd[ɪ]/ n (fam) Vati m

daddy-'long-legs n [Kohl]-schnake f; (*Amer: spider*) Weberknecht m

daffodil /'dæfədɪl/ n Osterglocke f, gelbe Narzisse f

daft /dɑːft/ a (-er, -est) dumm

dagger /'dægə(r)/ n Dolch m; (*Typ*) Kreuz nt; **be at ~s drawn** (*fam*) auf Kriegsfuß stehen

dahlia /'deɪlɪə/ n Dahlie f

daily /'deɪlɪ/ a & adv täglich □ n (*newspaper*) Tageszeitung f; (*fam: cleaner*) Putzfrau f

dainty /'deɪntɪ/ a (-ier, -iest) zierlich

dairy /'deərɪ/ n Molkerei f; (*shop*) Milchgeschäft nt. **~ cow** n Milchkuh f. **~ products** pl Milchprodukte pl

dais /'deɪɪs/ n Podium nt

daisy /'deɪzɪ/ n Gänseblümchen nt

dale /deɪl/ n (*liter*) Tal nt

dally /'dælɪ/ vi (pt/pp -ied) trödeln

dam /dæm/ n [Stau]damm m □ vt (pt/pp **dammed**) eindämmen

damag|e /'dæmɪdʒ/ n Schaden m (**to** an + dat); **~es** pl (Jur) Schadenersatz m □ vt beschädigen; (*fig*) beeinträchtigen. **~ing** a schädlich

damask /'dæməsk/ n Damast m

dame /deɪm/ n (*liter*) Dame f; (*Amer sl*) Weib nt

damn /dæm/ a, int & adv (*fam*) verdammt □ **I don't care or give a ~** (*fam*) ich schere mich einen Dreck darum □ vt verdammen. **~ation** /-'neɪʃn/ n Verdammnis f □ int (*fam*) verdammt!

damp /dæmp/ a (-er, -est) feucht □ n Feuchtigkeit f □ vt = **dampen**

damp|en vt anfeuchten; (*fig*) dämpfen. **~ness** n Feuchtigkeit f

dance /dɑːns/ n Tanz m; (*function*) Tanzveranstaltung f □ vt/i tanzen. **~-hall** n Tanzlokal nt. **~ music** n Tanzmusik f

dancer /'dɑːnsə(r)/ n Tänzer(in) m(f)

dandelion /'dændɪlaɪən/ n Löwenzahn m

dandruff /'dændrʌf/ n Schuppen pl

Dane /deɪn/ n Däne m/Dänin f; **Great ~** [deutsche] Dogge f

danger /'deɪndʒə(r)/ n Gefahr f; **in/out of ~** in/außer Gefahr. **~ous** /-rəs/ a, **-ly** adv gefährlich; **~ously ill** schwer erkrankt

dangle /'dæŋgl/ vi baumeln □ vt baumeln lassen

Danish /'deɪnɪʃ/ a dänisch. **~ pastry** n Hefeteilchen nt, Plunderstück nt

dank /dæŋk/ a (-er, -est) naßkalt

Danube /'dænjuːb/ n Donau f

dare /deə(r)/ n Mutprobe f □ vt/i (*challenge*) herausfordern (**to** zu); **~ [to] do sth** [es] wagen, etw zu tun; **I ~ say!** das mag wohl sein! **~devil** n Draufgänger m

daring /'deərɪŋ/ a verwegen □ n Verwegenheit f

dark /dɑːk/ a (-er, -est) dunkel; **~ blue/brown** dunkelblau/-braun; **~ horse** (*fig*) stilles Wasser nt; **keep sth ~** (*fig*) etw geheim halten □ n Dunkelheit f; **after ~** nach Einbruch der Dunkelheit; **in the ~** im Dunkeln; **keep in the ~** (*fig*) im Dunkeln lassen

dark|en /'dɑːkn/ vt verdunkeln □ vi dunkler werden. **~ness** n Dunkelheit f

'dark-room n Dunkelkammer f

darling /'dɑːlɪŋ/ a allerliebst □ n Liebling m

darn /dɑːn/ vt stopfen. **~ing-needle** n Stopfnadel f

dart /dɑːt/ n Pfeil m; (*Sewing*) Abnäher m; **~s** sg (*game*) [Wurf]pfeil m □ vi flitzen

dash /dæʃ/ n (*Typ*) Gedankenstrich m; (*in Morse*) Strich m; **a**

~ **of milk** ein Schuss Milch; **make a** ~ losstürzen **(for** auf + *acc***)** ○ **vi** rennen □ *vt* schleudern. ~ **off** *vi* losstürzen □ *vt* **(***write quickly***)** hinwerfen

'**dashboard** *n* Armaturenbrett *nt*

dashing /'dæʃɪŋ/ *a* schneidig

data /'deɪtə/ *npl & sg* Daten *pl.* ~ **processing** *n* Datenverarbeitung *f*

date[1] /deɪt/ *n* (*fruit*) Dattel *f*

date[2] *n* Datum *nt*; (*fam*) Verabredung *f*; **to** ~ bis heute; **out of** ~ überholt; (*expired*) ungültig; **be up to** ~ auf dem Laufenden sein □ *vt/i* datieren; (*Amer, fam:* go out with) ausgehen mit; ~ **back to** zurückgehen auf (+ *acc*)

dated /'deɪtɪd/ *a* altmodisch

'**date-line** *n* Datumsgrenze *f*

dative /'deɪtɪv/ *a & n* (*Gram*) [**case**] Dativ *m*

daub /dɔːb/ *vt* beschmieren **(with** mit); schmieren (*paint*)

daughter /'dɔːtə(r)/ *n* Tochter *f.* ~**in-law** *n* (*pl* ~**s-in-law**) Schwiegertochter *f*

daunt /dɔːnt/ *vt* entmutigen; **nothing** ~**ed** unverzagt. ~**less** *a* furchtlos

dawdle /'dɔːdl/ *vi* trödeln

dawn /dɔːn/ *n* Morgendämmerung *f*; **at** ~ bei Tagesanbruch □ *vi* anbrechen; **it** ~**ed on me** (*fig*) es ging mir auf

day /deɪ/ *n* Tag *m*; ~ **by** ~ Tag für Tag; ~ **after** ~ Tag um Tag; **these** ~**s** heutzutage; **in those** ~**s** zu der Zeit; **it's had its** ~ (*fam*) es hat ausgedient

day: ~**break** *n* **at** ~**break** bei Tagesanbruch *m.* ~**dream** *n* Tagtraum *m* □ *vi* [mit offenen Augen] träumen. ~**light** *n* Tageslicht *nt.* ~ **re'turn** *n* (*ticket*) Tagesrückfahrkarte *f.* ~**time** *n* **in the** ~**time** am Tage

daze /deɪz/ *n* **in a** ~ wie benommen. ~**d** *a* benommen

dazzle /'dæzl/ *vt* blenden

deacon /'diːkn/ *n* Diakon *m*

dead /ded/ *a* tot; (*flower*) verwelkt; (*numb*) taub; ~ **body** Leiche *f*; **be** ~ **on time** auf die Minute pünktlich kommen; ~ **centre** genau in der Mitte □ *adv* ~ **tired** todmüde; ~ **slow** sehr langsam; ~ **stop** stehen bleiben □ *n* **the** ~ *pl* die Toten; **in the** ~ **of night** mitten in der Nacht

deaden /'dedn/ *vt* dämpfen (*sound*); betäuben (*pain*)

dead: ~'**end** *n* Sackgasse *f.* ~ '**heat** *n* totes Rennen *nt.* ~'**line** *n* [letzter] Termin *m.* ~'**lock** *n* **reach** ~'**lock** (*fig*) sich festfahren

deadly /'dedlɪ/ *a* (**-ier, -iest**) tödlich; (*fam: dreary*) sterbenslangweilig; ~ **sins** *pl* Todsünden *pl*

deaf /def/ *a* (**-er, -est**) taub; ~ **and dumb** taubstumm. ~-**aid** *n* Hörgerät *nt*

deafen /'defn/ *vt* betäuben; (*permanently*) taub machen. ~**ening** *a* ohrenbetäubend. ~**ness** *n* Taubheit *f*

deal /diːl/ *n* (*transaction*) Geschäft *nt*; **whose** ~? (*Cards*) wer gibt? **a good or great** ~ eine Menge; **get a raw** ~ (*fam*) schlecht wegkommen □ *v* (*pt/pp* **dealt**) □ *vt* (*Cards*) geben. ~ **out** austeilen; ~ **s.o. a blow** jdm einen Schlag versetzen □ *vi* ~ **in** handeln mit; ~ **with** zu tun haben mit; (*handle*) sich befassen mit; (*cope with*) fertig werden mit; (*be about*) handeln von; **that's been dealt with** das ist schon erledigt

dealer /'diːlə(r)/ *n* Händler *m*; (*Cards*) Kartengeber *m.* ~**ings** *npl* **have** ~**ings with** zu tun haben mit

dean /diːn/ *n* Dekan *m*

dear /dɪə(r)/ *a* (**-er, -est**) lieb; (*expensive*) teuer; (*in letter*) liebe(r,s)/ (*formal*) sehr geehrte(r,s) □ *n* Liebe(r) *m/f* □ *int* **oh** ~! oje! ~**ly** *adv* (*love*) sehr; (*pay*) teuer

dearth /dɜːθ/ n Mangel m (of an + dat)

death /deθ/ n Tod m; **three ~s** drei Todesfälle. **~ certificate** n Sterbeurkunde f. **~ duty** n Erbschaftssteuer f

deathly a **~ silence** Totenstille f □ adv **~ pale** totenblass

death: ~ penalty n Todesstrafe f. **~'s head** n Totenkopf m. **~-trap** n Todesfalle f

debar /dɪˈbɑː(r)/ vt ⟨pt/pp debarred⟩ ausschließen

debase /dɪˈbeɪs/ vt erniedrigen

debatable /dɪˈbeɪtəbl/ a strittig

debate /dɪˈbeɪt/ n Debatte f □ vt/i debattieren

debauchery /dɪˈbɔːtʃərɪ/ n Ausschweifung f

debility /dɪˈbɪlətɪ/ n Entkräftung f

debit /ˈdebɪt/ n Schuldbetrag m; **~ [side]** Soll nt □ vt ⟨pt/pp debited⟩ (Comm) belasten; abbuchen ⟨sum⟩

debris /ˈdebriː/ n Trümmer pl

debt /det/ n Schuld f; **in ~** verschuldet. **~or** n Schuldner m

début /ˈdeɪbuː/ n Debüt nt

decade /ˈdekeɪd/ n Jahrzehnt nt

decaden|ce /ˈdekədəns/ n Dekadenz f. **~t** a dekadent

decaffeinated /dɪˈkæfɪneɪtɪd/ a koffeinfrei

decant /dɪˈkænt/ vt umfüllen. **~er** n Karaffe f

decapitate /dɪˈkæpɪteɪt/ vt köpfen

decay /dɪˈkeɪ/ n Verfall m; ⟨rot⟩ Verwesung f; ⟨of tooth⟩ Zahnfäule f □ vi verfallen; ⟨rot⟩ verwesen; ⟨tooth:⟩ schlecht werden

decease /dɪˈsiːs/ n Ableben nt. **~d** a verstorben □ n the **~d** der/die Verstorbene

deceit /dɪˈsiːt/ n Täuschung f. **~ful** a, **-ly** adv unaufrichtig

deceive /dɪˈsiːv/ vt täuschen; ⟨be unfaithful to⟩ betrügen

December /dɪˈsembə(r)/ n Dezember m

decency /ˈdiːsənsɪ/ n Anstand m

decent /ˈdiːsnt/ a, **-ly** adv anständig

decentralize /diːˈsentrəlaɪz/ vt dezentralisieren

decept|ion /dɪˈsepʃn/ n Täuschung f; ⟨fraud⟩ Betrug m. **~ive** /-tɪv/ a, **-ly** adv täuschend

decibel /ˈdesɪbel/ n Dezibel nt

decide /dɪˈsaɪd/ vt entscheiden □ vi sich entscheiden (on für)

decided /dɪˈsaɪdɪd/ a, **-ly** adv entschieden

deciduous /dɪˈsɪdjuəs/ a **~ tree** Laubbaum m

decimal /ˈdesɪml/ a Dezimal- □ n Dezimalzahl f. **~ 'point** n Komma nt. **~ system** n Dezimalsystem nt

decimate /ˈdesɪmeɪt/ vt dezimieren

decipher /dɪˈsaɪfə(r)/ vt entziffern

decision /dɪˈsɪʒn/ n Entscheidung f; ⟨firmness⟩ Entschlossenheit f

decisive /dɪˈsaɪsɪv/ a ausschlaggebend; ⟨firm⟩ entschlossen

deck¹ /dek/ vt schmücken

deck² n (Naut) Deck nt; **on ~** an Deck; **top ~** ⟨of bus⟩ Oberdeck nt; **~ of cards** (Amer) [Karten]spiel nt. **~-chair** n Liegestuhl m

declaration /dekləˈreɪʃn/ n Erklärung f

declare /dɪˈkleə(r)/ vt erklären; angeben ⟨goods⟩; **anything to ~?** etwas zu verzollen?

declension /dɪˈklenʃn/ n Deklination f

decline /dɪˈklaɪn/ n Rückgang m; (in health) Verfall m □ vt ablehnen; (Gram) deklinieren □ vi ablehnen; ⟨fall⟩ sinken; ⟨decrease⟩ nachlassen

decode /diːˈkəʊd/ vt entschlüsseln

decompos|e /ˌdiːkəmˈpəʊz/ vi sich zersetzen

décor /ˈdeɪkɔː(r)/ n Ausstattung f

decorat|e /ˈdekəreɪt/ vt (adorn) schmücken; verzieren (cake); (paint) streichen; (wallpaper) tapezieren; (award medal to) einen Orden verleihen (+ dat). ~**ion** /-ˈreɪʃn/ n Verzierung f; (medal) Orden m; ~**ions** pl Schmuck m. ~**ive** /-rətɪv/ a dekorativ. ~**or** n painter and ~or m Maler und Tapezierer m

decorous /ˈdekərəs/ a, -ly adv schamhaft

decorum /dɪˈkɔːrəm/ n Anstand m

decoy¹ /ˈdiːkɔɪ/ n Lockvogel m

decoy² /dɪˈkɔɪ/ vt locken

decrease¹ /ˈdiːkriːs/ n Verringerung f; (in number) Rückgang m; be on the ~ zurückgehen

decrease² /dɪˈkriːs/ vt verringern; herabsetzen (price) □ vi sich verringern; (price:) sinken

decree /dɪˈkriː/ n Erlass m □ vt (pt/pp **decreed**) verordnen

decrepit /dɪˈkrepɪt/ a altersschwach

dedicat|e /ˈdedɪkeɪt/ vt widmen; (Relig) weihen. ~**ed** a hingebungsvoll; (person) aufopfernd. ~**ion** /-ˈkeɪʃn/ n Hingabe f; (in book) Widmung f

deduce /dɪˈdjuːs/ vt folgern (from aus)

deduct /dɪˈdʌkt/ vt abziehen

deduction /dɪˈdʌkʃn/ n Abzug m; (conclusion) Folgerung f

deed /diːd/ n Tat f; (Jur) Urkunde f

deem /diːm/ vt halten für

deep /diːp/ a (-er, -est), -ly adv tief; **go off the** ~ **end** (fam) auf die Palme gehen □ adv tief

deepen /ˈdiːpn/ vt vertiefen □ vi tiefer werden; (fig) sich vertiefen

deep-ˈfreeze n Gefriertruhe f; (upright) Gefrierschrank m

deer /dɪə(r)/ n inv Hirsch m; (roe) Reh nt

deface /dɪˈfeɪs/ vt beschädigen

defamat|ion /defəˈmeɪʃn/ n Verleumdung f. ~**ory** /dɪˈfæmətərɪ/ a verleumderisch

default /dɪˈfɔːlt/ n (Jur) Nichtzahlung f; (failure to appear) Nichterscheinen nt; (Sport) kampflos gewinnen □ vi nicht zahlen; nicht erscheinen

defeat /dɪˈfiːt/ n Niederlage f; (defeating) Besiegung f; (rejection) Ablehnung f □ vt besiegen; ablehnen; (frustrate) vereiteln

defect¹ /dɪˈfekt/ n (Pol) überlaufen

defect² /ˈdiːfekt/ n Fehler m; (Techn) Defekt m. ~**ive** /dɪˈfektɪv/ a fehlerhaft; (Techn) defekt

defence /dɪˈfens/ n Verteidigung f. ~**less** a wehrlos

defend /dɪˈfend/ vt verteidigen; (justify) rechtfertigen. ~**ant** n (Jur) Beklagte(r) m/f; (in criminal court) Angeklagte(r) m/f

defensive /dɪˈfensɪv/ a defensiv □ n Defensive f

defer /dɪˈfɜː(r)/ vt (pt/pp **deferred**) (postpone) aufschieben; ~ **to s.o.** sich jdm fügen

deferen|ce /ˈdefərəns/ n Ehrerbietung f. ~**tial** /-ˈrenʃl/ a, -ly adv ehrerbietig

defian|ce /dɪˈfaɪəns/ n Trotz m; in ~**ce of** zum Trotz (+ dat). ~**t** a, -ly adv aufsässig

deficien|cy /dɪˈfɪʃnsɪ/ n Mangel m. ~**t** a mangelhaft; **he is** ~**t in** ... ihm mangelt es an ... (dat)

deficit /ˈdefɪsɪt/ n Defizit nt

defile /dɪˈfaɪl/ vt (fig) schänden

define /dɪˈfaɪn/ vt bestimmen; definieren (word)

definite /ˈdefɪnɪt/ a, -ly adv bestimmt; (certain) sicher

definition /defɪˈnɪʃn/ n Definition f; (Phot, TV) Schärfe f

definitive /dɪˈfɪnətɪv/ a endgültig; (authoritative) maßgeblich

deflat|e /dɪ'fleɪt/ vt die Luft auslassen aus. **~ion** /-eɪʃn/ n (Comm) Deflation f

deflect /dɪ'flekt/ vt ablenken

deform|ed /dɪ'fɔ:md/ a missgebildet. **~ity** n Missbildung f

defraud /dɪ'frɔ:d/ vt betrügen (**of** um)

defray /dɪ'freɪ/ vt bestreiten

defrost /di:'frɒst/ vt entfrosten; abtauen (fridge); auftauen (food)

deft /deft/ a (**-er, -est**), **-ly** adv geschickt. **~ness** n Geschicklichkeit f

defunct /dɪ'fʌŋkt/ a aufgelöst; (law) außer Kraft gesetzt

defuse /di:'fju:z/ vt entschärfen

defy /dɪ'faɪ/ vt (pt/pp **-ied**) trotzen (+ dat); widerstehen (+ dat) (attempt)

degenerate¹ /dɪ'dʒenəreɪt/ vi degenerieren; **~ into** (fig) ausarten in (+ acc)

degenerate² /dɪ'dʒenərət/ a degeneriert

degrading /dɪ'greɪdɪŋ/ a entwürdigend

degree /dɪ'gri:/ n Grad m; (Univ) akademischer Grad m; **20 ~s** 20 Grad

dehydrate /di:'haɪdreɪt/ vt Wasser entziehen (+ dat). **~d** /-ɪd/ a ausgetrocknet

de-ice /di:'aɪs/ vt enteisen

deign /deɪn/ vi **~ to do sth** sich herablassen, etw zu tun

deity /'di:ɪtɪ/ n Gottheit f

dejected /dɪ'dʒektɪd/ a, **-ly** adv niedergeschlagen

delay /dɪ'leɪ/ n Verzögerung f; (of train, aircraft) Verspätung f; **without ~** unverzüglich □ vt aufhalten; (postpone) aufschieben; **be ~ed** (person:) aufgehalten werden; (train, aircraft:) Verspätung haben □ vi zögern

delegate¹ /'delɪgət/ n Delegierte(r) m/f

delegat|e² /'delɪgeɪt/ vt delegieren. **~ion** /-'geɪʃn/ n Delegation f

delet|e /dɪ'li:t/ vt streichen. **~ion** /-i:ʃn/ n Streichung f

deliberate¹ /dɪ'lɪbərət/ a, **-ly** adv absichtlich; (slow) bedächtig

deliberat|e² /dɪ'lɪbəreɪt/ vt/i überlegen. **~ion** /-'reɪʃn/ n Überlegung f; **with ~ion** mit Bedacht

delicacy /'delɪkəsɪ/ n Feinheit f; Zartheit f; (food) Delikatesse f

delicate /'delɪkət/ a fein; (fabric, health) zart; (situation) heikel; (mechanism) empfindlich

delicatessen /delɪkə'tesn/ n Delikatessengeschäft nt

delicious /dɪ'lɪʃəs/ a köstlich

delight /dɪ'laɪt/ n Freude f □ vt entzücken □ vi **~ in** sich erfreuen an (+ dat). **~ed** a hocherfreut; **be ~ed** sich sehr freuen. **~ful** a reizend

delinquen|cy /dɪ'lɪŋkwənsɪ/ n Kriminalität f. **~t** a straffällig □ n Straffällige(r) m/f

deli|rious /dɪ'lɪrɪəs/ a **be ~rious** im Delirium sein. **~rium** /-rɪəm/ n Delirium nt

deliver /dɪ'lɪvə(r)/ vt liefern; zustellen (post, newspaper); halten (speech); überbringen (message); versetzen (blow); (set free) befreien; **~ a baby** ein Kind zur Welt bringen. **~ance** n Erlösung f. **~y** n Lieferung f; (of post) Zustellung f; (Med) Entbindung f; **cash on ~y** per Nachnahme

delta /'deltə/ n Delta nt

delude /dɪ'lu:d/ vt täuschen; **~ oneself** sich (dat) Illusionen machen

deluge /'delju:dʒ/ n Flut f; (heavy rain) schwerer Guss m □ vt überschwemmen

delusion /dɪ'lu:ʒn/ n Täuschung f

de luxe /də'lʌks/ a Luxus-

delve /delv/ vi hineingreifen (**into** in + acc); (fig) eingehen (**into** auf + acc)

demand /dɪ'mɑːnd/ n Forderung f; (Comm) Nachfrage f; in ~ gefragt; on ~ auf Verlangen □ vt verlangen, fordern (of/from von). ~ing a anspruchsvoll

demarcation /diːmɑː'keɪʃn/ n Abgrenzung f

demean /dɪ'miːn/ vt ~ oneself sich erniedrigen

demeanour /dɪ'miːnə(r)/ n Verhalten nt

demented /dɪ'mentɪd/ a verrückt

demise /dɪ'maɪz/ n Tod m

demister /diː'mɪstə(r)/ n (Auto) Defroster m

demo /'deməʊ/ n (pl ~s) (fam) Demonstration f

demobilize /diː'məʊbɪlaɪz/ vt (Mil) entlassen

democracy /dɪ'mɒkrəsɪ/ n Demokratie f

democrat /'deməkræt/ n Demokrat m. ~ic /-'krætɪk/ a, ~ally adv demokratisch

demolish /dɪ'mɒlɪʃ/ vt abbrechen; (destroy) zerstören. ~lition /demə'lɪʃn/ n Abbruch m

demon /'diːmən/ n Dämon m

demonstrat|e /'demənstreɪt/ vt beweisen; vorführen ⟨appliance⟩ □ vi (Pol) demonstrieren. ~ion /-'streɪʃn/ n Vorführung f; (Pol) Demonstration f

demonstrative /dɪ'mɒnstrətɪv/ a (Gram) demonstrativ; be ~ seine Gefühle zeigen

demonstrator /'demənstreɪtə(r)/ n Vorführer m; (Pol) Demonstrant m

demoralize /dɪ'mɒrəlaɪz/ vt demoralisieren

demote /dɪ'məʊt/ vt degradieren

demure /dɪ'mjʊə(r)/ a, ~ly adv sittsam

den /den/ n Höhle f; (room) Bude f

denial /dɪ'naɪəl/ n Leugnen nt; official ~ Dementi nt

denigrate /'denɪɡreɪt/ vt herabsetzen

denim /'denɪm/ n Jeansstoff m; ~s pl Jeans pl

Denmark /'denmɑːk/ n Dänemark m

denomination /dɪnɒmɪ'neɪʃn/ n (Relig) Konfession f; (money) Nennwert m

denote /dɪ'nəʊt/ vt bezeichnen

denounce /dɪ'naʊns/ vt denunzieren; (condemn) verurteilen

dens|e /dens/ a (-r, -st), -ly adv dicht; (fam: stupid) blöd[e]. ~ity n Dichte f

dent /dent/ n Delle f, Beule f □ vt einbeulen; ~ed /-ɪd/ verbeult

dental /'dentl/ a Zahn-; (treatment) zahnärztlich. ~ floss /flɒs/ n Zahnseide f. ~ surgeon n Zahnarzt m

dentist /'dentɪst/ n Zahnarzt m/-ärztin f. ~ry n Zahnmedizin f

denture /'dentʃə(r)/ n Zahnprothese f; ~s pl künstliches Gebiss nt

denude /dɪ'njuːd/ vt entblößen

denunciation /dɪnʌnsɪ'eɪʃn/ n Denunziation f; (condemnation) Verurteilung f

deny /dɪ'naɪ/ vt (pt/pp -ied) leugnen; (officially) dementieren; ~ s.o. sth jdm etw verweigern

deodorant /diː'əʊdərənt/ n Deodorant nt

depart /dɪ'pɑːt/ vi abfahren; (Aviat) abfliegen; (go away) weggehen/-fahren; (deviate) abweichen (from von)

department /dɪ'pɑːtmənt/ n Abteilung f; (Pol) Ministerium nt. ~ store n Kaufhaus nt

departure /dɪ'pɑːtʃə(r)/ n Abfahrt f; (Aviat) Abflug m; (from rule) Abweichung f; new ~ Neuerung f

depend /dɪ'pend/ vi abhängen (on von); (rely) sich verlassen (on auf + acc); it all ~s das kommt darauf an. ~able /-əbl/ a zuverlässig. ~ant n Abhängige(r) m/f. ~ence n Abhängigkeit f. ~ent a abhängig (on von)

depict /dɪ'pɪkt/ vt darstellen

depilatory /dɪ'pɪlətərɪ/ n Enthaarungsmittel nt

deplete /dɪ'pli:t/ vt verringern

deplor|able /dɪ'plɔːrəbl/ a bedauerlich. ~e vt bedauern

deploy /dɪ'plɔɪ/ vt (Mil) einsetzen □ vi sich aufstellen

depopulate /diː'pɒpjʊleɪt/ vt entvölkern

deport /dɪ'pɔːt/ vt deportieren, ausweisen. ~ation /dɪːpɔː'teɪʃn/ n Ausweisung f

deportment /dɪ'pɔːtmənt/ n Haltung f

depose /dɪ'pəʊz/ vt absetzen

deposit /dɪ'pɒzɪt/ n Anzahlung f; (against damage) Kaution f; (on bottle) Pfand nt; (sediment) Bodensatz m; (Geol) Ablagerung f □ vt (pt/pp deposited) legen; (for safety) deponieren; (Geol) ablagern. ~ account n Sparkonto nt

depot /'depəʊ/ n Depot nt; (Amer: railway station) Bahnhof m

deprav|e /dɪ'preɪv/ vt verderben. ~ed a verkommen. ~ity /-'prævətɪ/ n Verderbtheit f

deprecate /'deprəkeɪt/ vt missbilligen

depreciat|e /dɪ'priːʃɪeɪt/ vi an Wert verlieren. ~ion /-'eɪʃn/ n Wertminderung f; (Comm) Abschreibung f

depress /dɪ'pres/ vt deprimieren; (press down) herunterdrücken. ~ed a deprimiert; ~ed area Notstandsgebiet nt. ~ing a deprimierend. ~ion /-'eʃn/ n Vertiefung f; (Med) Depression f; (Meteorol) Tief nt

deprivation /deprɪ'veɪʃn/ n Entbehrung f

deprive /dɪ'praɪv/ vt entziehen; ~ s.o. of sth jdm etw entziehen. ~d a benachteiligt

depth /depθ/ n Tiefe f; in ~ gründlich; in the ~s of winter im tiefsten Winter

deputation /depjʊ'teɪʃn/ n Abordnung f

deputize /'depjʊtaɪz/ vi ~ for vertreten

deputy /'depjʊtɪ/ n Stellvertreter m □ attrib stellvertretend

derail /dɪ'reɪl/ vt be ~ed entgleisen. ~ment n Entgleisung f

deranged /dɪ'reɪndʒd/ a geistesgestört

derelict /'derəlɪkt/ a verfallen; (abandoned) verlassen

deri|de /dɪ'raɪd/ vt verhöhnen. ~sion /-'rɪʒn/ n Hohn m

derisive /dɪ'raɪsɪv/ a, -ly adv höhnisch

derisory /dɪ'raɪsərɪ/ a höhnisch; (offer) lächerlich

derivation /derɪ'veɪʃn/ n Ableitung f

derivative /dɪ'rɪvətɪv/ a abgeleitet □ n Ableitung f

derive /dɪ'raɪv/ vt/i (obtain) gewinnen (from aus); be ~d from (word:) hergeleitet sein aus

dermatologist /dɜːmə'tɒlədʒɪst/ n Hautarzt m /-ärztin f

derogatory /dɪ'rɒgətrɪ/ a abfällig

derrick /'derɪk/ n Bohrturm m

derv /dɜːv/ n Diesel[kraftstoff] m

descend /dɪ'send/ vt/i hinunter-/herunterhehen; (vehicle, lift:) hinunter-/herunterfahren; be ~ed from abstammen von. ~ant n Nachkomme m

descent /dɪ'sent/ n Abstieg m; (lineage) Abstammung f

describe /dɪ'skraɪb/ vt beschreiben

description /dɪ'skrɪpʃn/ n Beschreibung f; (sort) Art f. ~tive /-tɪv/ a beschreibend; (vivid) anschaulich

desecrat|e /'desɪkreɪt/ vt entweihen. ~ion /-'kreɪʃn/ n Entweihung f

desert¹ /'dezət/ n Wüste f □ a Wüsten-; ~ island verlassene Insel f

desert² /dɪ'zɜːt/ vt verlassen □ vi desertieren. ~ed a verlassen.

~er n (Mil) Deserteur m. ~ion /-ɜ:ʃn/ n Fahnenflucht f

deserts /dɪ'zɜ:ts/ npl get one's ~ seinen verdienten Lohn bekommen

deserv|e /dɪ'zɜ:v/ vt verdienen. ~edly /-ɪdlɪ/ adv verdientermaßen. ~ing a verdienstvoll; ~ing cause guter Zweck m

design /dɪ'zaɪn/ n Entwurf m; (pattern) Muster nt; (construction) Konstruktion f; (aim) Absicht f □ vt entwerfen; (construct) konstruieren; be ~ed for bestimmt sein für

designat|e /'dezɪgneɪt/ vt bezeichnen; (appoint) ernennen. ~ion /-'neɪʃn/ n Bezeichnung f

designer /dɪ'zaɪnə(r)/ n Designer m; (Techn) Konstrukteur m; (Theat) Bühnenbildner m

desirable /dɪ'zaɪrəbl/ a wünschenswert; (sexually) begehrenswert

desire /dɪ'zaɪə(r)/ n Wunsch m; (longing) Verlangen nt (for nach); (sexual) Begierde f □ vt [sich (dat)] wünschen; (sexually) begehren

desk /desk/ n Schreibtisch m; (Sch) Pult nt; (Comm) Kasse f; (in hotel) Rezeption f

desolat|e /'desələt/ a trostlos. ~ion /-'leɪʃn/ n Trostlosigkeit f

despair /dɪ'speə(r)/ n Verzweiflung f; in ~ verzweifelt □ vi verzweifeln

desperat|e /'despərət/ a, -ly adv verzweifelt; (urgent) dringend; be ~e (criminal:) zu Äußersten entschlossen sein; be ~e for dringend brauchen. ~ion /-'reɪʃn/ n Verzweiflung f; in ~ion aus Verzweiflung

despicable /dɪ'spɪkəbl/ a verachtenswert

despise /dɪ'spaɪz/ vt verachten

despite /dɪ'spaɪt/ prep trotz (+ gen)

despondent /dɪ'spɒndənt/ a niedergeschlagen

despot /'despɒt/ n Despot m

dessert /dɪ'zɜ:t/ n Dessert nt, Nachtisch m. ~spoon n Dessertlöffel m

destination /destɪ'neɪʃn/ n [Reise]ziel nt; (of goods) Bestimmungsort m

destine /'destɪn/ vt bestimmen

destiny /'destɪnɪ/ n Schicksal nt

destitute /'destɪtju:t/ a völlig mittellos

destroy /dɪ'strɔɪ/ vt zerstören; (totally) vernichten. ~er n (Naut) Zerstörer m

destruc|tion /dɪ'strʌkʃn/ n Zerstörung f; Vernichtung f. -tive /-tɪv/ a zerstörerisch; (fig) destruktiv

detach /dɪ'tætʃ/ vt abnehmen; (tear off) abtrennen. ~able /-əbl/ a abnehmbar. ~ed a (fig) distanziert; ~ed house Einzelhaus nt

detachment /dɪ'tætʃmənt/ n Distanz f; (objectivity) Abstand m; (Mil) Sonderkommando nt

detail /'di:teɪl/ n Einzelheit f, Detail nt; in ~ ausführlich □ vt einzeln aufführen; (Mil) abkommandieren. ~ed a ausführlich

detain /dɪ'teɪn/ vt aufhalten; (police:) in Haft behalten; (take into custody) in Haft nehmen. ~ee /di:teɪ'ni:/ n Häftling m

detect /dɪ'tekt/ vt entdecken; (perceive) wahrnehmen. ~ion /-ekʃn/ n Entdeckung f

detective /dɪ'tektɪv/ n Detektiv m. ~ story n Detektivroman m

detector /dɪ'tektə(r)/ n Suchgerät nt; (for metal) Metalldetektor m

detention /dɪ'tenʃn/ n Haft f; (Sch) Nachsitzen nt

deter /dɪ'tɜ:(r)/ vt (pt/pp deterred) abschrecken; (prevent) abhalten

detergent /dɪ'tɜ:dʒənt/ n Waschmittel nt

deteriorat|e /dɪ'tɪərɪəreɪt/ vi sich verschlechtern. **~ion** /-'reɪʃn/ n Verschlechterung f

determination /dɪtɜːmɪ'neɪʃn/ n Entschlossenheit f

determine /dɪ'tɜːmɪn/ vt bestimmen; **~ to** (resolve) sich entschließen zu. **~d** a entschlossen

deterrent /dɪ'terənt/ n Abschreckungsmittel nt

detest /dɪ'test/ vt verabscheuen. **~able** /-əbl/ a abscheulich

detonat|e /'detəneɪt/ vt zünden □ vi explodieren. **~or** n Zünder m

detour /'diːtʊə(r)/ n Umweg m; (for traffic) Umleitung f

detract /dɪ'trækt/ vi **~ from** beeinträchtigen

detriment /'detrɪmənt/ n **to the ~** zum Schaden (**of** gen). **~al** /-'mentl/ a schädlich (**to** dat)

deuce /djuːs/ n (Tennis) Einstand m

devaluation /diːvæljʊ'eɪʃn/ n Abwertung f

de'value vt abwerten (currency)

devastat|e /'devəsteɪt/ vt verwüsten. **~ed** /-ɪd/ a (fam) erschüttert. **~ing** a verheerend. **~ion** /-'steɪʃn/ n Verwüstung f

develop /dɪ'veləp/ vt entwickeln; bekommen (illness); erschließen (area) □ vi sich entwickeln (**into** zu). **~er** n [**property**] **~er** Bodenspekulant m

de'veloping country n Entwicklungsland nt

development /dɪ'veləpmənt/ n Entwicklung f

deviant /'diːvɪənt/ a abweichend

deviat|e /'diːvɪeɪt/ vi abweichen. **~ion** /-'eɪʃn/ n Abweichung f

device /dɪ'vaɪs/ n Gerät nt; (fig) Mittel nt; **leave s.o. to his own ~s** jdn sich (dat) selbst überlassen

devil /'devl/ n Teufel m. **~ish** a teuflisch

devious /'diːvɪəs/ a verschlagen; **~ route** Umweg m

devise /dɪ'vaɪz/ vt sich (dat) ausdenken

devoid /dɪ'vɔɪd/ a **~ of** ohne

devolution /diːvə'luːʃn/ n Dezentralisierung f; (of power) Übertragung f

devot|e /dɪ'vəʊt/ vt widmen (**to** dat). **~ed** a, **-ly** adv ergeben; (care) liebevoll; **be ~ed to** s.o. sehr an jdm hängen. **~ee** /devə'tiː/ n Anhänger(in) m(f)

devotion /dɪ'vəʊʃn/ n Hingabe f; **~s** pl (Relig) Andacht f

devour /dɪ'vaʊə(r)/ vt verschlingen

devout /dɪ'vaʊt/ a fromm

dew /djuː/ n Tau m

dexterity /dek'sterətɪ/ n Geschicklichkeit f

diabet|es /daɪə'biːtiːz/ n Zuckerkrankheit f. **~ic** /-'betɪk/ a zuckerkrank □ n Zuckerkranke(r) m/f, Diabetiker(in) m(f)

diabolical /daɪə'bɒlɪkl/ a teuflisch

diagnose /daɪəg'nəʊz/ vt diagnostizieren

diagnosis /daɪəg'nəʊsɪs/ n (pl **-oses** /-siːz/) Diagnose f

diagonal /daɪ'ægənl/ a, **-ly** adv diagonal □ n Diagonale f

diagram /'daɪəgræm/ n Diagramm nt

dial /'daɪəl/ n (of clock) Zifferblatt nt; (Techn) Skala f; (Teleph) Wählscheibe f □ vt/i (pt/pp dialled) (Teleph) wählen; **~ direct** durchwählen

dialect /'daɪəlekt/ n Dialekt m

dialling: **~ code** n Vorwahlnummer f. **~ tone** n Amtszeichen nt

dialogue /'daɪəlɒg/ n Dialog m

'dial tone n (Amer, Teleph) Amtszeichen nt

diameter /daɪ'æmɪtə(r)/ n Durchmesser m

diametrically /daɪə'metrɪkəlɪ/ adv ~ **opposed** genau entgegengesetzt (**to** dat)

diamond /'daɪəmənd/ n Diamant m; (cut) Brillant m; (shape) Raute f; ~s pl (Cards) Karo nt

diaper /'daɪəpə(r)/ n (Amer) Windel f

diaphragm /'daɪəfræm/ n (Anat) Zwerchfell nt; (Phot) Blende f

diarrhoea /daɪə'rɪːə/ n Durchfall m

diary /'daɪərɪ/ n Tagebuch nt; (for appointments) [Termin]kalender m

dice /daɪs/ n inv Würfel m □ vt (Culin) in Würfel schneiden

dicey /'daɪsɪ/ a (fam) riskant

dictate /dɪk'teɪt/ vt/i diktieren. ~ion /-eɪʃn/ n Diktat nt

dictator /dɪk'teɪtə(r)/ n Diktator m. ~ial /-'tɔːrɪəl/ a diktatorisch. ~ship n Diktatur f

diction /'dɪkʃn/ n Aussprache f

dictionary /'dɪkʃənrɪ/ n Wörterbuch nt

did /dɪd/ see do

didactic /dɪ'dæktɪk/ a didaktisch

diddle /'dɪdl/ vt (fam) übers Ohr hauen

didn't /'dɪdnt/ = did not

die¹ /daɪ/ n (Techn) Prägestempel m; (metal mould) Gussform f

die² vi (pres p dying) sterben (of an + dat); (plant, animal:) eingehen; (flower:) verwelken; **be dying to do sth** (fam) darauf brennen, etw zu tun; **be dying for sth** (fam) sich nach etw sehnen. ~ **down** vi nachlassen; (fire:) herunterbrennen. ~ **out** vi aussterben

diesel /'diːzl/ n Diesel m. ~ **engine** n Dieselmotor m

diet /'daɪət/ n Kost f; (restricted) Diät f; (for slimming) Schlankheitskur f; **be on a** ~ Diät leben; eine Schlankheitskur machen □ vi diät leben; eine Schlankheitskur machen

dietician /daɪə'tɪʃn/ n Diätassistent(in) m(f)

differ /'dɪfə(r)/ vi sich unterscheiden; (disagree) verschiedener Meinung sein

differen|ce /'dɪfrəns/ n Unterschied m; (disagreement) Meinungsverschiedenheit f. ~**t** a andere(r,s); (various) verschiedene; **be** ~**t** anders sein (**from** als)

differential /dɪfə'renʃl/ a Differenzial-. □ n Unterschied m; (Techn) Differenzial nt

differentiate /dɪfə'renʃɪeɪt/ vt/i unterscheiden (**between** + dat)

differently /'dɪfrəntlɪ/ adv anders

difficult /'dɪfɪkəlt/ a schwierig, schwer. ~**y** n Schwierigkeit f

diffiden|ce /'dɪfɪdəns/ n Zaghaftigkeit f. ~**t** a zaghaft

diffuse¹ /dɪ'fjuːs/ a ausgebreitet; (wordy) langatmig

diffuse² /dɪ'fjuːz/ vt (Phys) streuen

dig /dɪg/ n (poke) Stoß m; (remark) spitze Bemerkung f; (Archaeol) Ausgrabung f; ~s pl (fam) möbliertes Zimmer nt □ vt/i (pt/pp **dug**, pres p **digging**) graben; umgraben (garden); ~ **s.o. in the ribs** jdm einen Rippenstoß geben. ~ **out** vt ausgraben. ~ **up** vt ausgraben; umgraben (garden); aufreißen (street)

digest¹ /'daɪdʒest/ n Kurzfassung f

digest² /dɪ'dʒest/ vt verdauen. ~**ible** a verdaulich. ~**ion** /-estʃn/ n Verdauung f

digger /'dɪgə(r)/ n (Techn) Bagger m

digit /'dɪdʒɪt/ n Ziffer f; (finger) Finger m; (toe) Zehe f

digital /'dɪdʒɪtl/ a Digital-; ~ **clock** Digitaluhr f

dignified /'dɪgnɪfaɪd/ a würdevoll

dignitary /'dɪgnɪtərɪ/ n Würdenträger m

dignity /'dɪgnɪtɪ/ n Würde f

digress /daɪ'gres/ vi abschweifen.
~ion /-eʃn/ n Abschweifung f

dike /daɪk/ n Deich m; (ditch)
Graben m

dilapidated /dɪ'læpɪdeɪtɪd/ a
baufällig

dilate /daɪ'leɪt/ vt erweitern □ vi
sich erweitern

dilatory /'dɪlətərɪ/ a langsam

dilemma /dɪ'lemə/ n Dilemma nt

dilettante /dɪlɪ'tæntɪ/ n Dilet-
tant(in) m(f)

diligenc|e /'dɪlɪdʒəns/ n Fleiß m.
~t a, **-ly** adv fleißig

dill /dɪl/ n Dill m

dilly-dally /'dɪlɪdælɪ/ vi (pt/pp
-ied) (fam) trödeln

dilute /daɪ'luːt/ vt verdünnen

dim /dɪm/ a (**dimmer, dimmest**)
-ly adv (weak) schwach; (dark)
trüb[e]; (indistinct) undeutlich;
(fam: stupid) dumm, (fam) doof
□ vi (pt/pp **dimmed**) □ vt dämpfen
□ vi schwächer werden

dime /daɪm/ n (Amer)
Zehncentstück nt

dimension /daɪ'menʃn/ n Dimension f; **~s** pl Maße pl

diminish /dɪ'mɪnɪʃ/ vt verringern □ vi sich verringern

diminutive /dɪ'mɪnjʊtɪv/ a winzig □ n Verkleinerungsform f

dimple /'dɪmpl/ n Grübchen nt

din /dɪn/ n Krach m, Getöse nt

dine /daɪn/ vi speisen. **~r** n Spei-
sende(r) m/f; (Amer: restaurant)
Esslokal nt

dinghy /'dɪŋgɪ/ n Dinghi nt; (inflatable) Schlauchboot nt

dingy /'dɪndʒɪ/ a (**-ier, -iest**) trübe

dining /'daɪnɪŋ/: **~car** n Speisewagen m. **~room** n Esszimmer
nt. **~table** n Esstisch m

dinner /'dɪnə(r)/ n Abendessen
nt; (at midday) Mittagessen nt;
(formal) Essen nt. **~jacket** n
Smoking m

dinosaur /'daɪnəsɔː(r)/ n Dinosaurier m

dint /dɪnt/ n **by ~ of** durch (+
acc)

diocese /'daɪəsɪs/ n Diözese f

dip /dɪp/ n (in ground) Senke f;
(Culin) Dip m; **go for a ~** kurz
schwimmen gehen □ v (pt/pp
dipped) vt [ein]tauchen; **~ one's
headlights** (Auto) [die
Scheinwerfer] abblenden □ vi
sich senken

diphtheria /dɪf'θɪərɪə/ n Diphtherie f

diphthong /'dɪfθɒŋ/ n Diphthong m

diploma /dɪ'pləʊmə/ n Diplom nt

diplomacy /dɪ'pləʊməsɪ/ n Dip-
lomatie f

diplomat /'dɪpləmæt/ n Diplomat
m. **~ic** /-'mætɪk/ a, **-ally** adv dip-
lomatisch

'dip-stick n (Auto) Ölmessstab m

dire /'daɪə(r)/ a (**-r, -st**) bitter;
(situation, consequences) furchtbar

direct /dɪ'rekt/ a & adv direkt □ vt
(aim) richten (at auf / (fig) an +
acc); (control) leiten; (order)
anweisen; **~ s.o.** (show the way)
jdm den Weg sagen; **~ a
film/play** bei einem
Film/Theaterstück Regie
führen. **~ 'current** n Gleich-
strom m

direction /dɪ'rekʃn/ n Richtung
f; (control) Leitung f; (of play,
film) Regie f; **~s** pl Anweisungen
pl; **~s for use** Gebrauchsanweisung f

directly /dɪ'rektlɪ/ adv direkt; (at
once) sofort □ conj (fam) sobald

director /dɪ'rektə(r)/ n (Comm)
Direktor m; (of play, film) Regisseur m

directory /dɪ'rektərɪ/ n Ver-
zeichnis nt; (Teleph) Telefonbuch
nt

dirt /dɜːt/ n Schmutz m; (soil)
Erde f; **~ cheap** (fam) spottbillig

dirty /'dɜːtɪ/ a (-ier, -iest) schmutzig □ vt schmutzig machen

dis|a'bility /dɪs-/ n Behinderung f. **~abled** /dɪ'seɪbld/ a (körper)behindert

disad'van|tage n Nachteil m; **at a ~tage** im Nachteil. **~taged** a benachteiligt. **~tageous** a nachteilig

disaf'fected a unzufrieden; (disloyal) illoyal

disa'gree vi nicht übereinstimmen (with mit); **I ~** ich bin anderer Meinung; **we ~** wir sind verschiedener Meinung; **oysters ~ with me** Austern bekommen mir nicht

disa'greeable a unangenehm

disa'greement n Meinungsverschiedenheit f

disap'pear vi verschwinden. **~ance** n Verschwinden nt

disap'point vt enttäuschen. **~ment** n Enttäuschung f

disap'proval n Missbilligung f

disap'prove vi dagegen sein; **~ of** missbilligen

dis'arm vt entwaffnen □ vi (Mil) abrüsten. **~ament** n Abrüstung f. **~ing** a entwaffnend

disar'ray n Unordnung f

disast|er /dɪ'zɑːstə(r)/ n Katastrophe f; (accident) Unglück nt. **~rous** /-rəs/ a katastrophal

dis'band vt auflösen □ vi sich auflösen

disbe'lief n Ungläubigkeit f; **in ~** ungläubig

disc /dɪsk/ n Scheibe f; (record) [Schall]platte f; (CD) CD f

discard /dɪ'skɑːd/ vt ablegen; (throw away) wegwerfen

discern /dɪ'sɜːn/ vt wahrnehmen. **~ible** a wahrnehmbar. **~ing** a anspruchsvoll

'discharge¹ n Ausstoßen nt; (Naut, Electr) Entladung f; (dismissal) Entlassung f; (Jur) Freispruch m; (Med) Ausfluss m

dis'charge² vt ausstoßen; (Naut, Electr) entladen; (dismiss) entlassen; (Jur) freisprechen (accused); **~ a duty** sich einer Pflicht entledigen

disciple /dɪ'saɪpl/ n Jünger m; (fig) Schüler m

disciplinary /'dɪsɪplɪnərɪ/ a disziplinarisch

discipline /'dɪsɪplɪn/ n Disziplin f □ vt Disziplin beibringen (+ dat); (punish) bestrafen

disc jockey n Diskjockey m

dis'claim vt abstreiten. **~er** n Verzichterklärung f

dis'clos|e vt enthüllen. **~ure** n Enthüllung f

disco /'dɪskəʊ/ n (fam) Disko f

dis'colour vt verfärben □ vi sich verfärben

dis'comfort n Beschwerden pl; (fig) Unbehagen nt

disconcert /dɪskən'sɜːt/ vt aus der Fassung bringen

discon'nect vt trennen; (Electr) ausschalten; (cut supply) abstellen

disconsolate /dɪs'kɒnsələt/ a untröstlich

discon'tent n Unzufriedenheit f. **~ed** a unzufrieden

discon'tinue vt einstellen; (Comm) nicht mehr herstellen

'discord n Zwietracht f; (Mus & fig) Missklang m. **~ant** /dɪ'skɔː-dənt/ a **a ~ant note** Missklang m

discothèque /'dɪskətek/ n Diskothek f

'discount¹ n Rabatt m

dis'count² vt außer Acht lassen

dis'courage vt entmutigen; (dissuade) abraten (+ dat)

'discourse n Rede f

dis'courteous a, **-ly** adv unhöflich

discover /dɪ'skʌvə(r)/ vt entdecken. **~y** n Entdeckung f

dis'credit n Misskredit m □ vt in Misskredit bringen

discreet /dɪˈskriːt/ a, **-ly** adv diskret

discrepancy /dɪˈskrepənsɪ/ n Diskrepanz f

discretion /dɪˈskreʃn/ n Diskretion f; (judgement) Ermessen nt

discriminat|e /dɪˈskrɪmɪneɪt/ vi unterscheiden (between zwischen + dat); ~e against diskriminieren. ~ing a anspruchsvoll. ~ion /-ˈneɪʃn/ n Diskriminierung f; (quality) Urteilskraft f

discus /ˈdɪskəs/ n Diskus m

discuss /dɪˈskʌs/ vt besprechen; (examine critically) diskutieren. ~ion /-ʌʃn/ n Besprechung f; Diskussion f

disdain /dɪsˈdeɪn/ n Verachtung f □ vt verachten. ~ful a verächtlich

disease /dɪˈziːz/ n Krankheit f. ~d a krank

disem'bark vi an Land gehen

disen'chant vt ernüchtern. ~ment n Ernüchterung f

disen'gage vt losmachen; ~ the clutch (Auto) auskuppeln

disen'tangle vt entwirren

dis'favour n Ungnade f; (disapproval) Missfallen nt

dis'figure vt entstellen

dis'gorge vt ausspeien

dis'grace n Schande f; in ~ in Ungnade □ vt Schande machen (+ dat). ~ful a schändlich

disgruntled /dɪsˈɡrʌntld/ a verstimmt

disguise /dɪsˈɡaɪz/ n Verkleidung f; in ~ verkleidet □ vt verkleiden; verstellen (voice); (conceal) verhehlen

disgust /dɪsˈɡʌst/ n Ekel m; in ~ empört □ vt anekeln; (appal) empören. ~ing a eklig; (appalling) abscheulich

dish /dɪʃ/ n Schüssel f; (shallow) Schale f; (small) Schälchen nt; (food) Gericht nt. ~ out vt austeilen. ~ up vt auftragen

'dishcloth n Spültuch nt

dis'hearten vt entmutigen. ~ing a entmutigend

dishevelled /dɪˈʃevld/ a zerzaust

dis'honest a, **-ly** adv unehrlich. ~y n Unehrlichkeit f

dis'honour n Schande f □ vt entehren; nicht honorieren (cheque). ~able, -bly adv unehrenhaft

'dishwasher n Geschirrspülmaschine f

disil'lusion vt ernüchtern. ~ment n Ernüchterung f

disin'fect vt desinfizieren. ~ant n Desinfektionsmittel nt

disin'herit vt enterben

disin'tegrate vi zerfallen

disin'terested a unvoreingenommen; (uninterested) uninteressiert

dis'jointed a unzusammenhängend

disk /dɪsk/ n = disc

dis'like n Abneigung f □ vt nicht mögen

dislocate /ˈdɪsləkeɪt/ vt ausrenken; ~ one's shoulder sich (dat) den Arm auskugeln

dis'lodge vt entfernen

dis'loyal a, **-ly** adv illoyal. ~ty n Illoyalität f

dismal /ˈdɪzməl/ a trüb[e]; (person) trübselig; (fam: poor) kläglich

dismantle /dɪsˈmæntl/ vt auseinander nehmen; (take down) abbauen

dis'may n Bestürzung f. ~ed a bestürzt

dis'miss vt entlassen; (reject) zurückweisen. ~al n Entlassung f; Zurückweisung f

dis'mount vi absteigen

diso'bedien|ce n Ungehorsam m. ~t a ungehorsam

diso'bey vt/i nicht gehorchen (+ dat); nicht befolgen (rule)

dis'order n Unordnung f; (Med) Störung f. ~ly a unordentlich;

~**ly conduct** ungebührliches Benehmen *nt*

dis'organized *a* unorganisiert

dis'orientate *vt* verwirren; **be ~d** die Orientierung verloren haben

dis'own *vt* verleugnen

disparaging /dɪ'spærɪdʒɪŋ/ *a*, -**ly** *adv* abschätzig

disparity /dɪ'spærətɪ/ *n* Ungleichheit *f*

dispassionate /dɪ'spæʃənət/ *a*, -**ly** *adv* gelassen; (*impartial*) unparteiisch

dispatch /dɪ'spætʃ/ *n* (*Comm*) Versand *m*; (*Mil*) Nachricht *f*; (*report*) Bericht *m*; **with ~** prompt □ *vt* [ab]senden; (*deal with*) erledigen; (*kill*) töten. ~-**rider** *n* Meldefahrer *m*

dispel /dɪ'spel/ *vt* (*pt/pp* **dispelled**) vertreiben

dispensable /dɪ'spensəbl/ *a* entbehrlich

dispensary /dɪ'spensərɪ/ *n* Apotheke *f*

dispense /dɪ'spens/ *vt* austeilen; **~ with** verzichten auf (+ *acc*). **~r** *n* Apotheker(in) *m(f)*; (*device*) Automat *m*

dispers|al /dɪ'spɜːsl/ *n* Zerstreuung *f*. **~e** /dɪ'spɜːs/ *vt* zerstreuen □ *vi* sich zerstreuen

dispirited /dɪ'spɪrɪtɪd/ *a* entmutigt

dis'place *vt* verschieben; **~d person** Vertriebene(r) *m/f*

display /dɪ'spleɪ/ *n* Ausstellung *f*; (*Comm*) Auslage *f*; (*performance*) Vorführung *f* □ *vt* zeigen; ausstellen (*goods*)

dis'please *vt* missfallen (+ *dat*)

dis'pleasure *n* Missfallen *nt*

disposable /dɪ'spəʊzəbl/ *a* Wegwerf-; (*income*) verfügbar

disposal /dɪ'spəʊzl/ *n* Beseitigung *f*; **be at s.o.'s ~** jdm zur Verfügung stehen

dispose /dɪ'spəʊz/ *vi* **~ of** beseitigen; (*deal with*) erledigen; **be**

---

well ~d wohlgesinnt sein (**to** *dat*)

disposition /dɪspə'zɪʃn/ *n* Veranlagung *f*; (*nature*) Wesensart *f*

disproportionate /dɪsprə'pɔːʃənət/ *a*, -**ly** *adv* unverhältnismäßig

dis'prove *vt* widerlegen

dispute /dɪ'spjuːt/ *n* Disput *m*; (*quarrel*) Streit *m* □ *vt* bestreiten

disqualifi'cation *n* Disqualifikation *f*

dis'qualify *vt* disqualifizieren; **~ s.o. from driving** jdm den Führerschein entziehen

disquieting /dɪs'kwaɪətɪŋ/ *a* beunruhigend

disre'gard *n* Nichtbeachtung *f* □ *vt* nicht beachten, ignorieren

disre'pair *n* **fall into ~** verfallen

dis'reputable *a* verrufen

disre'pute *n* Verruf *m*

disre'spect *n* Respektlosigkeit *f*. **~ful** *a*, -**ly** *adv* respektlos

disrupt /dɪs'rʌpt/ *vt* stören. **~ion** /-ʌpʃn/ *n* Störung *f*. **~ive** /-tɪv/ *a* störend

dissatis'faction *n* Unzufriedenheit *f*

dis'satisfied *a* unzufrieden

dissect /dɪ'sekt/ *vt* zergliedern; (*Med*) sezieren. **~ion** /-ekʃn/ *n* Zergliederung *f*; (*Med*) Sektion *f*

disseminat|e /dɪ'semɪneɪt/ *vt* verbreiten. **~ion** /-'neɪʃn/ *n* Verbreitung *f*

dissent /dɪ'sent/ *n* Nichtübereinstimmung *f* □ *vi* nicht übereinstimmen

dissertation /dɪsə'teɪʃn/ *n* Dissertation *f*

dis'service *n* schlechter Dienst *m*

dissident /'dɪsɪdənt/ *n* Dissident *m*

dis'similar *a* unähnlich (**to** *dat*)

dissociate /dɪ'səʊʃɪeɪt/ *vt* trennen; **~ oneself** sich distanzieren (**from** von)

dissolute /'dɪsəluːt/ *a* zügellos; (*life*) ausschweifend

dissolution /dɪsə'lu:ʃn/ n Auflösung f

dissolve /dɪ'zɒlv/ vt auflösen □ vi sich auflösen

dissuade /dɪ'sweɪd/ vt abbringen (**from** von)

distance /'dɪstəns/ n Entfernung f; **long/short** ~ lange/kurze Strecke f; **in the/from a** ~ in/aus der Ferne

distant /'dɪstənt/ a fern; (aloof) kühl; (relative) entfernt

dis'taste n Abneigung f. ~ful a unangenehm

distend /dɪ'stend/ vi sich [auf]blähen

distil /dɪ'stɪl/ vt (pt/pp distilled) brennen; (Chem) destillieren. ~lation /-'leɪʃn/ n Destillation f. ~lery /-ərɪ/ n Brennerei f

distinct /dɪ'stɪŋkt/ a deutlich; (different) verschieden. ~ion /-ɪŋkʃn/ n Unterschied m; (Sch) Auszeichnung f. ~ive /-tɪv/ a kennzeichnend; (unmistakable) unverwechselbar. ~ly adv deutlich

distinguish /dɪ'stɪŋgwɪʃ/ vt/i unterscheiden; (make out) erkennen; ~ **oneself** sich auszeichnen. ~ed a angesehen; (appearance) distinguiert

distort /dɪ'stɔ:t/ vt verzerren; (fig) verdrehen. ~ion /-ɔ:ʃn/ n Verzerrung f; (fig) Verdrehung f

distract /dɪ'strækt/ vt ablenken. ~ed /-ɪd/ a [völlig] aufgelöst. ~ion /-ækʃn/ n Ablenkung f; (despair) Verzweiflung f

distraught /dɪ'strɔ:t/ a [völlig] aufgelöst

distress /dɪ'stres/ n Kummer m; (pain) Schmerz m; (poverty, danger) Not f □ vt Kummer/Schmerz bereiten (+ dat); (sadden) bekümmern; (shock) erschüttern. ~ing a schmerzlich; (shocking) erschütternd. ~ **signal** n Notsignal nt

distribut|e /dɪ'strɪbju:t/ vt verteilen; (Comm) vertreiben. ~ion /-'bju:ʃn/ n Verteilung f; Vertrieb m. ~or n Verteiler m

district /'dɪstrɪkt/ n Gegend f; (Admin) Bezirk m. ~ **nurse** n Gemeindeschwester f

dis'trust n Misstrauen nt □ vt misstrauen (+ dat). ~ful a misstrauisch

disturb /dɪ'stɜ:b/ vt stören; (perturb) beunruhigen; (touch) anrühren. ~ance n Unruhe f; (interruption) Störung f. ~ed a beunruhigt; [mentally] ~ed geistig gestört. ~ing a beunruhigend

dis'used a stillgelegt; (empty) leer

ditch /dɪtʃ/ n Graben m □ vt (fam: abandon) fallen lassen (plan); wegschmeißen (thing)

dither /'dɪðə(r)/ vi zaudern

ditto /'dɪtəʊ/ n dito; (fam) ebenfalls

divan /dɪ'væn/ n Polsterbett nt

dive /daɪv/ n [Kopf]sprung m; (Aviat) Sturzflug m; (fam: place) Spelunke f □ vi einen Kopfsprung machen; (when in water) tauchen; (Aviat) einen Sturzflug machen; (fam: rush) stürzen

diver /'daɪvə(r)/ n Taucher m; (Sport) [Kunst]springer m

diverg|e /daɪ'vɜ:dʒ/ vi auseinander gehen. ~gent /-ənt/ a abweichend

diverse /daɪ'vɜ:s/ a verschieden

diversify /daɪ'vɜ:sɪfaɪ/ vt/i (pt/pp -ied) variieren; (Comm) diversifizieren

diversion /daɪ'vɜ:ʃn/ n Umleitung f; (distraction) Ablenkung f

diversity /daɪ'vɜ:sətɪ/ n Vielfalt f

divert /daɪ'vɜ:t/ vt umleiten; ablenken (attention); (entertain) unterhalten

divest /daɪ'vest/ vt sich entledigen (of + gen); (fig) entkleiden

divide /dɪ'vaɪd/ *vt* teilen; *(separate)* trennen; *(Math)* dividieren (by durch) □ *vi* sich teilen

dividend /'dɪvɪdend/ *n* Dividende *f*

divine /dɪ'vaɪn/ *a* göttlich

diving /'daɪvɪŋ/ *n* (Sport) Kunstspringen *nt.* ~**board** *n* Sprungbrett *nt.* ~**suit** *n* Taucheranzug *m*

divinity /dɪ'vɪnɪtɪ/ *n* Göttlichkeit *f*; *(subject)* Theologie *f*

divisible /dɪ'vɪzɪbl/ *a* teilbar (by durch)

division /dɪ'vɪʒn/ *n* Teilung *f*; *(separation)* Trennung *f*; *(Math, Mil)* Division *f*; *(Parl)* Hammelsprung *m*; *(line)* Trennlinie *f*; *(group)* Abteilung *f*

divorce /dɪ'vɔːs/ *n* Scheidung *f* □ *vt* sich scheiden lassen von. ~**d** *a* geschieden; **get** ~**d** sich scheiden lassen

divorcee /dɪvɔː'siː/ *n* Geschiedene(r) *m/f*

divulge /daɪ'vʌldʒ/ *vt* preisgeben

DIY *abbr* of **do-it-yourself**

dizziness /'dɪzɪnɪs/ *n* Schwindel *m*

dizzy /'dɪzɪ/ *a* (-ier, -iest) schwindlig; **I feel** ~ mir ist schwindlig

do /duː/ *n* (*pl* dos *or* do's) *(fam)* Veranstaltung *f* □ *v* (3 sg pres tense **does**; *pt* did; *pp* **done**) □ *vt/i* tun, machen; *(be suitable)* passen; *(be enough)* reichen, genügen; *(cook)* kochen; *(clean)* putzen; *(Sch: study)* durchnehmen; *(fam: cheat)* beschwindeln (out of um); **do without** ausgekommen ohne; **do away with** abschaffen; **be done** *(Culin)* gar sein; **well done!** *(Culin)* gut gemacht! *(Culin)* gut durchgebraten; **done in** *(fam)* kaputt, fertig; **done for** *(fam)* verloren, erledigt; **do the flowers** die Blumen arrangieren; **do the potatoes** die Kartoffeln schälen; **do the washing up** abwaschen,

spülen; **do one's hair** sich frisieren; **do well/badly** gut/schlecht abschneiden; **how is he doing?** wie geht es ihm? **this won't do** das geht nicht; **are you doing anything today?** haben Sie heute etwas vor? **I could do with a spanner** ich könnte einen Schraubenschlüssel gebrauchen □ *v aux* **do you speak German?** sprechen Sie Deutsch? **yes, I do** ja; *(emphatic)* doch; **no, I don't** nein; **I don't smoke** ich rauche nicht; **don't you/doesn't he?** nicht [wahr]? **so do I** ich auch; **do come in** kommen Sie doch herein; **how do you do?** guten Tag. **do in** *vt (fam)* um die Ecke bringen. **do up** *vt (fasten)* zumachen; *(renovate)* renovieren; *(wrap)* einpacken

docile /'dəʊsaɪl/ *a* fügsam

dock¹ /dɒk/ *n* (Jur) Anklagebank *f*

dock² *n* Dock *nt* □ *vi* anlegen, docken □ *vt* docken. ~**er** *n* Hafenarbeiter *m.* ~**yard** *n* Werft *f*

doctor /'dɒktə(r)/ *n* Arzt *m* / Ärztin *f*; *(Univ)* Doktor *m* □ *vt* kastrieren; *(spay)* sterilisieren. ~**ate** /-ət/ *n* Doktorwürde *f*

doctrine /'dɒktrɪn/ *n* Lehre *f*, Doktrin *f*

document /'dɒkjumənt/ *n* Dokument *nt.* ~**ary** /-'mentərɪ/ *a* Dokumentar- □ *n* Dokumentarbericht *m*; *(film)* Dokumentarfilm *m*

doddery /'dɒdərɪ/ *a (fam)* tatterig

dodge /dɒdʒ/ *n (fam)* Trick *m*, Kniff *m* □ *vt/i* ausweichen (+ *dat)*; ~ **out of the way** zur Seite springen

dodgems /'dɒdʒəmz/ *npl* Autoskooter *pl*

dodgy /'dɒdʒɪ/ *a* (-ier, -iest) *(fam)* *(awkward)* knifflig; *(dubious)* zweifelhaft

doe /dəʊ/ *n* Ricke *f*; *(rabbit)* [Kaninchen]weibchen *nt*

does /dʌz/ *see* do

doesn't /'dʌznt/ = does not

dog /dɒg/ *n* Hund *m* □ *vt (pt/pp*
dogged) verfolgen

dog: ~**biscuit** *n* Hundekuchen
m. ~**collar** *n* Hundehalsband *nt;*
(Relig, fam) Kragen *m* eines
Geistlichen. ~**eared** *a* be ~
eared Eselsohren haben

dogged /'dɒgɪd/ *a,* **-ly** *adv* beharrlich

dogma /'dɒgmə/ *n* Dogma *nt.*
~**tic** /-'mætɪk/ *a* dogmatisch

'dogsbody /*n* (*fam*) Mädchen *nt*
für alles

doily /'dɔɪlɪ/ *n* Deckchen *nt*

do-it-yourself /'du:ɪtjə'self/ *n*
Heimwerken *nt.* ~ **shop** *n*
Heimwerkerladen *m*

doldrums /'dɒldrəmz/ *npl* be in
the ~ niedergeschlagen sein;
(business:) danieder liegen

dole /dəʊl/ *n (fam)* Stempelgeld
nt; be on the ~ arbeitslos sein
□ *vt* ~ out austeilen

doleful /'dəʊlfl/ *a,* **-ly** *adv* trauervoll

doll /dɒl/ *n* Puppe *f* □ *vt (fam)* ~
oneself up sich herausputzen

dollar /'dɒlə(r)/ *n* Dollar *m*

dollop /'dɒləp/ *n (fam)* Klecks *m*

dolphin /'dɒlfɪn/ *n* Delphin *m*

domain /də'meɪn/ *n* Gebiet *nt*

dome /dəʊm/ *n* Kuppel *m*

domestic /də'mestɪk/ *a* häuslich;
(Pol) Innen-; *(Comm)* Binnen-. ~
animal *n* Haustier *nt*

domesticated /də'mestɪkeɪtɪd/ *a*
häuslich; *(animal)* zahm

domestic: ~ **flight** *n* Inlandflug
m. ~ **'servant** *n* Hausangestell-
te(r) *m/f*

dominant /'dɒmɪnənt/ *a*
vorherrschend

dominat|e /'dɒmɪneɪt/ *vt* be-
herrschen □ *vi* dominieren;
~**e over** beherrschen. ~**ion**
/-'neɪʃn/ *n* Vorherrschaft *f*

domineer /dɒmɪ'nɪə(r)/ *vi* ~
over tyrannisieren. ~**ing** *a*
herrschsüchtig

dominion /də'mɪnjən/ *n*
Herrschaft *f*

domino /'dɒmɪnəʊ/ *n (pl* **-es**)
Dominostein *m;* ~**es** *sg (game)*
Domino *nt*

don[1] /dɒn/ *vt (pt/pp* **donned)**
(liter) anziehen

don[2] *n* [Universitäts]dozent *m*

donat|e /dəʊ'neɪt/ *vt* spenden.
~**ion** /-eɪʃn/ *n* Spende *f*

done /dʌn/ *see* do

donkey /'dɒŋkɪ/ *n* Esel *m;* ~**'s**
years *(fam)* eine Ewigkeit. ~
work *n* Routinearbeit *f*

donor /'dəʊnə(r)/ *n* Spender(in)
m(f)

don't /dəʊnt/ = do not

doodle /'du:dl/ *vi* kritzeln

doom /du:m/ *n* Schicksal *nt;*
(ruin) Verhängnis *nt* □ *vt* be ~**ed**
to failure zum Scheitern verur-
teilt sein

door /dɔː(r)/ *n* Tür *f;* out of ~**s**
im Freien

door: ~**man** *n* Portier *m.* ~**mat**
n [Fuß]abtreter *m.* ~**step** *n*
Türschwelle *f;* on the ~**step** vor
der Tür. ~**way** *n* Türöffnung *f*

dope /dəʊp/ *n (fam)* Drogen *pl;*
(fam: information) Infor-
mationen *pl;* (*fam: idiot*) Trottel
m □ *vt* betäuben; *(Sport)* dopen

dopey /'dəʊpɪ/ *a (fam)* benommen; *(stupid)* blöd[e]

dormant /'dɔːmənt/ *a* ruhend

dormer /'dɔːmə(r)/ *n* ~ [win-
dow] Mansardenfenster *nt*

dormitory /'dɔːmɪtərɪ/ *n* Schlaf-
saal *m*

dormouse /'dɔː-/ *n* Haselmaus *f*

dosage /'dəʊsɪdʒ/ *n* Dosierung *f*

dose /dəʊs/ *n* Dosis *f*

doss /dɒs/ *vi (sl)* pennen. ~**er** *n*
Penner *m.* ~**house** *n* Penne *f*

dot /dɒt/ *n* Punkt *m;* on the ~
pünktlich

dote /dəʊt/ *vi* ~ **on** vernarrt sein
in (+ *acc*)

dotted /'dɒtɪd/ *a* ~ **line** punk-
tierte Linie *f;* be ~ **with** bestreut
sein mit

dotty /'dɒtɪ/ a (-ier, -iest) (fam)
verdreht

double /'dʌbl/ a & adv doppelt;
⟨bed, chin⟩ Doppel-; ⟨flower⟩ gefüllt □ n das Doppelte; ⟨person⟩
Doppelgänger m; ~s pl (Tennis)
Doppel nt; **at the** ~ im Laufschritt □ vt verdoppeln; ⟨fold⟩ falten □ vi sich verdoppeln. ~ **back**
vi zurückgehen. ~ **up** vi sich
krümmen (**with** vor + dat)

double: ~'**bass** n Kontrabass m.
~-**breasted** a zweireihig. ~
'**cross** vt ein Doppelspiel treiben
mit. ~-**decker** n Doppeldecker
m. ~ '**Dutch** n (fam) Kauderwelsch nt. ~-**glazing** n Dop-
pelverglasung f. ~'**room** n
Doppelzimmer nt

doubly /'dʌblɪ/ adv doppelt

doubt /daʊt/ n Zweifel m □ vt
bezweifeln. ~**ful, -ly** adv zweifelhaft; ⟨disbelieving⟩ skeptisch.
~**less** adv zweifellos

dough /dəʊ/ n [fester] Teig m;
⟨fam: money⟩ Pinke f. ~**nut** n
Berliner [Pfannkuchen] m,
Krapfen m

douse /daʊs/ vt übergießen; aus-
gießen ⟨flames⟩

dove /dʌv/ n Taube f. ~**tail** n
(Techn) Schwalbenschwanz m

dowdy /'daʊdɪ/ a (-ier, -iest)
unschick

down[1] /daʊn/ n ⟨feathers⟩
Daunen pl

down[2] adv unten; ⟨with move-
ment⟩ nach unten; **go** ~ herunter-
gehen; **come** ~ herunterkommen; ~ **there** da unten; **£50**
~ **£50** Anzahlung; ~! ⟨to dog⟩
Platz! ~ **with . . . !** nieder mit . . . !
□ prep ~ **the** road/stairs die
Straße/Treppe hinunter; ~ **the**
river den Fluss abwärts; **be** ~ **the**
pub (fam) in der Kneipe sein
□ vt (fam) ⟨drink⟩ runterkippen; ~
tools die Arbeit niederlegen

down: ~-**and-'out** n Penner m.
~**cast** a niedergeschlagen. ~**fall**
n Sturz m; ⟨ruin⟩ Ruin m.

~'**grade** vt niedriger einstufen
~-'**hearted** a entmutigt. ~'**hill**
adv bergab. ~ **payment** n Anzahlung f. ~**pour** n Platzregen m.
~**right** a & adv ausgesprochen.
~'**stairs** adv unten; ⟨go⟩ nach unten □ a /'~-/ im Erdgeschoss.
~'**stream** adv stromabwärts. ~
to-'earth a sachlich. ~**town** adv
(Amer) im Stadtzentrum.
~**trodden** a unterdrückt.
~**ward** a nach unten; ⟨slope⟩
abfallend □ adv ~[s] abwärts,
nach unten

downy /'daʊnɪ/ a (-ier, -iest)
flaumig

dowry /'daʊrɪ/ n Mitgift f

doze /dəʊz/ n Nickerchen nt □ vi
dösen. ~ **off** vi einnicken

dozen /'dʌzn/ n Dutzend nt

Dr abbr of **doctor**

draft[1] /drɑːft/ n Entwurf m;
(Comm) Tratte f; (Amer Mil) Ein-
berufung f □ vt entwerfen; (Amer
Mil) einberufen

draft[2] n (Amer) = **draught**

drag /dræg/ n (fam) Klotz m am
Bein; **in** ~ (fam) ⟨man⟩ als Frau
gekleidet □ vt (pt/pp **dragged**)
schleppen; absuchen ⟨river⟩. ~
on vi sich in die Länge ziehen

dragon /'drægən/ n Drache m. ~
fly n Libelle f

'**drag show** n Transvestitenshow
f

drain /dreɪn/ n Abfluss m; ⟨under-
ground⟩ Kanal m; **the** ~**s** die Ka-
nalisation □ vt entwässern
⟨land⟩; ablassen ⟨liquid⟩; das
Wasser ablassen aus ⟨tank⟩;
abgießen ⟨vegetables⟩; austrinken
⟨glass⟩ □ vi ~ [**away**] ablaufen;
leave sth to ~ etw abtropfen
lassen

drain|age /'dreɪnɪdʒ/ n Kanali-
sation f; ⟨of land⟩ Dränage f.
~**ing board** n Abtropfbrett n.
~**pipe** n Abflussrohr nt

drake /dreɪk/ n Enterich m

drama /'drɑːmə/ n Drama nt;
⟨quality⟩ Dramatik f

…atic /drə'mætɪk/ a, **-ally** dramatisch

…at**ist** /'dræmətɪst/ n Dramatiker m. **~ize** vt für die Bühne bearbeiten; (fig) dramatisieren

…k /dræŋk/ see **drink**

…pe /dreɪp/ n (Amer) Vorhang m; vt drapieren

…ic /'dræstɪk/ a, **-ally** adv drastisch

draught /drɑːft/ n [Luft]zug m; **~er** (game) Damestein nt; **there is a ~** es zieht

draught: **~ beer** n Bier nt vom Fass. **~sman** n technischer Zeichner m

draughty /'drɑːftɪ/ a zugig; **it's ~** es zieht

draw /drɔː/ n Attraktion f; (Sport) Unentschieden nt; (in lottery) Ziehung f □ vt (pt **drew**, pp **drawn**) □ vt ziehen; (attract) anziehen; zeichnen (picture); abheben (money); holen (water); **~ the curtains** die Vorhänge zuziehen/ (back) aufziehen; **~ lots** losen (**for** um) □ vi (tea:) ziehen; (Sport) unentschieden spielen. **~ back** vt zurückziehen □ vi (recoil) zurückweichen. **~ in** vt einziehen □ vi einfahren; (days:) kürzer werden. **~ out** vt herausziehen; abheben (money) □ vi ausfahren; (days:) länger werden. **~ up** vt aufsetzen (document); herrücken (chair); **~ oneself up** sich aufrichten □ vi [an]halten

draw: **~back** n Nachteil m. **~bridge** n Zugbrücke f

drawer /drɔː(r)/ n Schublade f

drawing /'drɔːɪŋ/ n Zeichnung f

drawing: **~-board** n Reißbrett nt. **~-pin** n Reißzwecke f. **~-room** n Wohnzimmer nt

drawl /drɔːl/ n schleppende Aussprache f

drawn /drɔːn/ see **draw**

dread /dred/ n Furcht f (**of** vor + dat) □ vt fürchten. **~ful** a, **-fully** adv fürchterlich

dream /driːm/ n Traum m □ attrib Traum- □ vt/i (pt/pp **dreamt** /dremt/ or **dreamed**) träumen (**about/of** von)

dreary /'drɪərɪ/ a (**-ier, -iest**) trüb[e]; (boring) langweilig

dredge /dredʒ/ vt/i baggern. **~r** n [Nass]bagger m

dregs /dregz/ npl Bodensatz m

drench /drentʃ/ vt durchnässen

dress /dres/ n Kleid nt; (clothing) Kleidung f □ vt anziehen; (decorate) schmücken; (Culin) anmachen; (Med) verbinden; **~ oneself, get ~ed** sich anziehen □ vi sich anziehen. **~ up** vi sich schön anziehen; (in disguise) sich verkleiden (**as** als)

dress: **~ circle** n (Theat) erster Rang m. **~er** n (furniture) Anrichte f; (Amer: dressing-table) Frisiertisch m

dressing n (Culin) Soße f; (Med) Verband m

dressing: **~'down** n (fam) Standpauke f. **~-gown** n Morgenmantel m. **~-room** n Ankleidezimmer nt; (Theat) [Künstler]garderobe f. **~-table** n Frisiertisch m

dress: **~maker** n Schneiderin f. **~making** n Damenschneiderei f. **~ rehearsal** n Generalprobe f

dressy /'dresɪ/ a (**-ier, -iest**) schick

drew /druː/ see **draw**

dribble /'drɪbl/ vi sabbern; (Sport) dribbeln

dried /draɪd/ a getrocknet; **~ fruit** n Dörrobst nt

drier /'draɪə(r)/ n Trockner m

drift /drɪft/ n Abtrieb f; (of snow) Schneewehe f; (meaning) Sinn m □ vi treiben; (off course) abtreiben; (snow:) Wehen bilden; (fig:person:) sich treiben lassen; **~ apart** (persons:) sich auseinander leben. **~wood** n Treibholz nt

drill /drɪl/ n Bohrer m; (Mil) Drill m □ vt/i bohren (**for** nach); (Mil) drillen

drily /ˈdraɪlɪ/ adv trocken

drink /drɪŋk/ n Getränk nt; (alcoholic) Drink m; (alcohol) Alkohol m; **have a ~** etwas trinken □ vt/i (pt **drank**, pp **drunk**) trinken. **~ up** vt/i austrinken

drink|able /ˈdrɪŋkəbl/ a trinkbar. **~er** n Trinker m

'drinking-water n Trinkwasser nt

drip /drɪp/ n Tropfen nt; (drop) Tropfen m; (Med) Tropf m; (fam: person) Niete f □ vi (pt/pp **dripped**) tropfen. **~-dry** a bügelfrei. **~ping** n Schmalz nt

drive /draɪv/ n [Auto]fahrt f; (entrance) Einfahrt f; (energy) Elan m; (Psych) Trieb m; (Pol) Aktion f; (Sport) Treibschlag m; (Techn) Antrieb m □ v (pt **drove**, pp **driven**) □ vt treiben; fahren (car); (Sport: hit) schlagen; (Techn) antreiben; **~ s.o. mad** (fam) jdn verrückt machen; **what are you driving at?** (fam) worauf willst du hinaus? □ vi fahren. **~ away** vt vertreiben □ vi abfahren. **~ in** vi hinein-/hereinfahren. **~ off** vi vertreiben □ vi abfahren. **~ on** vi weiterfahren. **~ up** vi vorfahren

'drive-in a **~ cinema** Autokino nt

drivel /ˈdrɪvl/ n (fam) Quatsch m

driven /ˈdrɪvn/ see **drive**

driver /ˈdraɪvə(r)/ n Fahrer/in m(f); (of train) Lokführer m

driving /ˈdraɪvɪŋ/ a (rain) peitschend; (force) treibend

driving: ~ lesson n Fahrstunde f. **~ licence** n Führerschein m. **~ school** n Fahrschule f. **~ test** Fahrprüfung f; **take one's ~ test** den Führerschein machen

drizzle /ˈdrɪzl/ n Nieselregen m □ vi nieseln

drone /drəʊn/ n Drohne f; (sound) Brummen m

droop /druːp/ vi herabhängen; (flowers:) die Köpfe hängen lassen

drop /drɒp/ n Tropfen m; (fall) Fall m; (in price, temperature) Rückgang m □ v (pt/pp **dropped**) □ vt fallen lassen; abwerfen (bomb); (omit) auslassen; (give up) aufgeben □ vi fallen; (fall lower) sinken; (wind:) nachlassen. **~ in** vi vorbeikommen. **~ off** vt absetzen (person) □ vi abfallen; (fall asleep) einschlafen. **~ out** vi herausfallen; (give up) aufgeben

'drop-out n Aussteiger m

droppings /ˈdrɒpɪŋz/ npl Kot m

drought /draʊt/ n Dürre f

drove /drəʊv/ see **drive**

droves /drəʊvz/ npl **in ~** in Scharen

drown /draʊn/ vi ertrinken □ vt ertränken; übertönen (noise); **be ~ed** ertrinken

drowsy /ˈdraʊzɪ/ a schläfrig

drudgery /ˈdrʌdʒərɪ/ n Plackerei f

drug /drʌg/ n Droge f □ vt (pt/pp **drugged**) betäuben

drug: ~ addict n Drogenabhängige(r) m/f. **~gist** n (Amer) Apotheker m. **~store** n (Amer) Drogerie f; (dispensing) Apotheke f

drum /drʌm/ n Trommel f; (for oil) Tonne f □ v (pt/pp **drummed**) □ vi trommeln □ vt **~sth into s.o.** (fam) jdm etw einbläuen. **~mer** n Trommler m; (in pop-group) Schlagzeuger m. **~stick** n Trommelschlegel m; (Culin) Keule f

drunk /drʌŋk/ see **drink** □ a betrunken; **get ~** sich betrinken □ n Betrunkene(r) m

drunk|ard /ˈdrʌŋkəd/ n Trinker m. **~en** a betrunken; **~en driving** Trunkenheit f am Steuer

dry /draɪ/ a (**drier**, **driest**) trocken □ vt/i trocknen; **one's eyes** sich dat die Tränen abwischen. **~ up** vi austrocknen;

〈*fig*〉 versiegen □ *vt* austrocknen; abtrocknen 〈*dishes*〉

dry: ~'**clean** *vt* chemisch reinigen. ~'**cleaner's** *n* 〈*shop*〉 chemische Reinigung *f*. ~**ness** *f*. Trockenheit *f*

dual /'dju:əl/ *a* doppelt

dual: ~ '**carriageway** *n* ≈ Schnellstraße *f*. ~'**purpose** *a* zweifach verwendbar

dub /dʌb/ *vt* (*pt/pp* **dubbed**) synchronisieren 〈*film*〉; kopieren 〈*tape*〉; 〈*name*〉 benennen

dubious /'dju:bɪəs/ *a* zweifelhaft; **be** ~ **about** Zweifel haben über (+ *acc*)

duchess /'dʌtʃɪs/ *n* Herzogin *f*

duck /dʌk/ *n* Ente *f* □ *vt* (*in water*) untertauchen; ~**one's head** den Kopf einziehen □ *vi* sich ducken. ~**ling** *n* Entchen *nt*; 〈*Culin*〉 Ente *f*

duct /dʌkt/ *n* Rohr *nt*; 〈*Anat*〉 Gang *m*

dud /dʌd/ *a* 〈*fam*〉 nutzlos; 〈*coin*〉 falsch; 〈*cheque*〉 ungedeckt; 〈*forged*〉 gefälscht □ *n* 〈*fam*〉 〈*banknote*〉 Blüte *f*; 〈*Mil: shell*〉 Blindgänger *m*

due /dju:/ *a* angemessen; **be** ~ fällig sein; 〈*baby:*〉 erwartet werden; 〈*train:*〉 planmäßig ankommen; ~ **to** 〈*owing to*〉 wegen (+ *gen*); **be** ~ **to** zurückzuführen sein auf (+ *acc*); **in** ~ **course** im Laufe der Zeit; 〈*write*〉 zu gegebener Zeit □ *adv* ~ **west** genau westlich

duel /'dju:əl/ *n* Duell *nt*

dues /dju:z/ *npl* Gebühren *pl*

duet /dju:'et/ *n* Duo *nt*; 〈*vocal*〉 Duett *nt*

dug /dʌg/ *see* **dig**

duke /dju:k/ *n* Herzog *m*

dull /dʌl/ *a* (**-er, -est**) 〈*overcast, not bright*〉 trüb[e]; 〈*not shiny*〉 matt; 〈*sound*〉 dumpf; 〈*boring*〉 langweilig; 〈*stupid*〉 schwerfällig □ *vt* betäuben; abstumpfen 〈*mind*〉

duly /'dju:lɪ/ *adv* ordnungsgemäß

dumb /dʌm/ *a* (**-er, -est**) stumm; 〈*fam: stupid*〉 dumm. ~**founded** *a* sprachlos

dummy /'dʌmɪ/ *n* 〈*tailor's*〉 [Schneider]puppe *f*; 〈*for baby*〉 Schnuller *m*; 〈*Comm*〉 Attrappe *f*

dump /dʌmp/ *n* Abfallhaufen *m*; 〈*for refuse*〉 Müllhalde *f*, Deponie *f*; 〈*fam: town*〉 Kaff *nt*; **be down in the** ~**s** 〈*fam*〉 deprimiert sein □ *vt* abladen; 〈*fam: put down*〉 hinwerfen 〈**on** auf *+ acc*〉

dumpling /'dʌmplɪŋ/ *n* Kloß *m*, Knödel *m*

dunce /dʌns/ *n* Dummkopf *m*

dune /dju:n/ *n* Düne *f*

dung /dʌŋ/ *n* Mist *m*

dungarees /dʌŋgə'ri:z/ *npl* Latzhose *f*

dungeon /'dʌndʒən/ *n* Verlies *nt*

dunk /dʌŋk/ *vt* eintunken

duo /'dju:əʊ/ *n* Paar *nt*; 〈*Mus*〉 Duo *nt*

dupe /dju:p/ *n* Betrogene(r) *m/f* □ *vt* betrügen

duplicate¹ /'dju:plɪkət/ *a* Zweit-□ *n* Doppel *nt*; 〈*document*〉 Duplikat *nt*; **in** ~ in doppelter Ausfertigung *f*

duplicat|e² /'dju:plɪkeɪt/ *vt* kopieren; 〈*do twice*〉 zweimal machen. ~**or** *n* Vervielfältigungsapparat *m*

durable /'djʊərəbl/ *a* haltbar

duration /djʊə'reɪʃn/ *n* Dauer *f*

duress /djʊə'res/ *n* Zwang *m*

during /'djʊərɪŋ/ *prep* während (+ *gen*)

dusk /dʌsk/ *n* [Abend]dämmerung *f*

dust /dʌst/ *n* Staub *m* □ *vt* abstauben; 〈*sprinkle*〉 bestäuben (**with** mit) □ *vi* Staub wischen

dust: ~**bin** *n* Mülltonne *f*. ~**cart** *n* Müllwagen *m*. ~**er** *n* Staubtuch *nt*. ~**jacket** *n* Schutzumschlag *m*. ~**man** *n* Müllmann *m*. ~**pan** *n* Kehrschaufel *f*

dusty /'dʌstɪ/ *a* (**-ier, -iest**) staubig

Dutch /dʌtʃ/ a holländisch; go ~ (fam) getrennte Kasse machen □ n (Lang) Holländisch nt; the ~ pl die Holländer. ~man n Holländer m

dutiable /'dju:tɪəbl/ a zollpflichtig

dutiful /'dju:tɪfl/ a, -ly adv pflichtbewusst; (obedient) gehorsam

duty /'dju:tɪ/ n Pflicht f; (task) Aufgabe f; (tax) Zoll m; be on ~ Dienst haben. ~-free a zollfrei

duvet /'du:veɪ/ n Steppdecke f

dwarf /dwɔ:f/ n (pl -s or dwarves) Zwerg m

dwell /dwel/ vi (pt/pp dwelt) (liter) wohnen. ~ on (fig) verweilen bei. ~ing n Wohnung f

dwindle /'dwɪndl/ vi abnehmen, schwinden

dye /daɪ/ n Farbstoff m □ vt (pres p dyeing) färben

dying /'daɪɪŋ/ see die[2]

dynamic /daɪ'næmɪk/ a dynamisch. ~s n Dynamik f

dynamite /'daɪnəmaɪt/ n Dynamit nt

dynamo /'daɪnəməʊ/ n Dynamo m

dynasty /'dɪnəstɪ/ n Dynastie f

dysentery /'dɪsntrɪ/ n Ruhr f

dyslex|ia /dɪs'leksɪə/ n Legasthenie f. ~ic a legasthenisch; be ~ic Legastheniker sein

E

each /i:tʃ/ a & pron jede(r,s); (per) je; ~ other einander; £1 ~ £1 pro Person; (for thing) pro Stück

eager /'i:gə(r)/ a, -ly adv eifrig; be ~ to do sth etw gerne machen wollen. ~ness n Eifer m

eagle /'i:gl/ n Adler m

ear[1] /ɪə(r)/ n (of corn) Ähre f

ear[2] /ɪə(r)/ n Ohr nt. ~ache n Ohrenschmerzen pl. ~-drum n Trommelfell nt

earl /ɜ:l/ n Graf m

early /'ɜ:lɪ/ a & adv (-ier, -iest) früh; (reply) baldig; be ~ früh dran sein; ~ in the morning früh am Morgen

earmark vt ~ for bestimmen für

earn /ɜ:n/ vt verdienen

earnest /'ɜ:nɪst/ a, -ly adv ernsthaft □ n in ~ im Ernst

earnings /'ɜ:nɪŋz/ npl Verdienst m

ear: ~phones npl Kopfhörer pl. ~-ring n Ohrring m; (clip-on) Ohrklips m. ~shot n within/out of ~shot in/außer Hörweite

earth /ɜ:θ/ n Erde f; (of fox) Bau m; where/what on ~? wo/was in aller Welt? □ vt (Electr) erden

earthenware /'ɜ:θn-/ n Tonwaren f

earthly /'ɜ:θlɪ/ a irdisch; be no ~ use (fam) völlig nutzlos sein

'earthquake n Erdbeben nt

earthy /'ɜ:θɪ/ a erdig; (coarse) derb

earwig /'ɪəwɪg/ n Ohrwurm m

ease /i:z/ n Leichtigkeit f; at ~! (Mil) rührt euch! be or feel ill at ~ ein ungutes Gefühl haben □ vt erleichtern; lindern (pain) □ vi (pain:) nachlassen; (situation:) sich entspannen

easel /'i:zl/ n Staffelei f

easily /'i:zɪlɪ/ adv leicht, mit Leichtigkeit

east /i:st/ n Osten m; to the ~ of östlich von □ a Ost-, ost- □ adv nach Osten

Easter /'i:stə(r)/ n Ostern nt □ attrib Oster-. ~ egg n Osterei nt

east|erly /'i:stəlɪ/ a östlich. ~ern a östlich. ~ward[s] /-wəd[z]/ adv nach Osten

easy /'i:zɪ/ a (-ier, -iest) leicht; take it ~ (fam) sich schonen; take it ~! beruhige dich! go ~

with (*fam*) sparsam umgehen mit

easy: ~ **chair** *n* Sessel *m*. ~**'going** *a* gelassen; **too**~**going** lässig

eat /iːt/ *vt/i* (*pt* **ate,** *pp* **eaten**) essen; (*animal:*) fressen. ~ **up** *vt* aufessen

eat|able /'iːtəbl/ *a* genießbar. ~**er** *n* (*apple*) Essapfel *m*

eau-de-Cologne /əʊdəkə'ləʊn/ *n* Kölnisch Wasser *nt*

eaves /iːvz/ *npl* Dachüberhang *m*. ~**drop** *vi* (*pt/pp* ~ **dropped**) [heimlich] lauschen; ~**drop on** belauschen

ebb /eb/ *n* (*tide*) Ebbe *f*; **at a low** ~ (*fig*) auf einem Tiefstand □ *vi* zurückgehen; (*fig*) verebben

ebony /'ebənɪ/ *n* Ebenholz *nt*

ebullient /ɪ'bʌlɪənt/ *a* überschwänglich

EC *abbr* (**European Community**) EG *f*

eccentric /ɪk'sentrɪk/ *a* exzentrisch □ *n* Exzentriker *m*

ecclesiastical /ɪkliːzɪ'æstɪkl/ *a* kirchlich

echo /'ekəʊ/ *n* (*pl* **-es**) Echo *nt*, Widerhall *m* □ *v* (*pt/pp* **echoed**, *pres p* **echoing**) □ *vt* zurückwerfen; (*imitate*) nachsagen □ *vi* widerhallen (**with** von)

eclipse /ɪ'klɪps/ *n* (*Astr*) Finsternis *f* □ *vt* (*fig*) in den Schatten stellen

ecological /iːkə'lɒdʒɪkl/ *a* ökologisch. ~**y** /iːˈkɒlədʒɪ/ *n* Ökologie *f*

economic /iːkə'nɒmɪk/ *a* wirtschaftlich. ~**al** *a* sparsam. ~**ally** *adv* wirtschaftlich; (*thriftly*) sparsam. ~**s** *n* Volkswirtschaft *f*

economist /ɪ'kɒnəmɪst/ *n* Volkswirt *m*; (*Univ*) Wirtschaftswissenschaftler *m*

economize /ɪ'kɒnəmaɪz/ *vi* sparen (**on** an + *dat*)

economy /ɪ'kɒnəmɪ/ *n* Wirtschaft *f*; (*thrift*) Sparsamkeit *f*

ecstasy /'ekstəsɪ/ *n* Ekstase *f*

ecstatic /ɪk'stætɪk/ *a*, **-ally** *adv* ekstatisch

ecu /'eɪkjuː/ *n* Ecu *m*

ecumenical /iːkjuː'menɪkl/ *a* ökumenisch

eczema /'eksɪmə/ *n* Ekzem *nt*

eddy /'edɪ/ *n* Wirbel *m*

edge /edʒ/ *n* Rand *m*; (*of table, lawn*) Kante *f*; (*of knife*) Schneide *f*; **on** ~ (*fam*) nervös; **have the** ~ **on** (*fam*) etwas besser sein als □ *vt* einfassen. ~ **forward** *vi* sich nach vorn schieben

edging /'edʒɪŋ/ *n* Einfassung *f*

edgy /'edʒɪ/ *a* (*fam*) nervös

edible /'edɪbl/ *a* essbar

edict /'iːdɪkt/ *n* Erlass *m*

edifice /'edɪfɪs/ *n* [großes] Gebäude *nt*

edify /'edɪfaɪ/ *vt* (*pt/pp* **-ied**) bauen. ~**ing** *a* erbaulich

edit /'edɪt/ *vt* (*pt/pp* **edited**) redigieren; herausgeben (*anthology, dictionary*); schneiden (*film, tape*)

edition /ɪ'dɪʃn/ *n* Ausgabe *f*; (*impression*) Auflage *f*

editor /'edɪtə(r)/ *n* Redakteur *m*; (*of anthology, dictionary*) Herausgeber *m*; (*of newspaper*) Chefredakteur *m*; (*of film*) Cutter(in) *m(f)*

editorial /edɪ'tɔːrɪəl/ *a* redaktionell, Redaktions- □ *n* (*Journ*) Leitartikel *m*

educate /'edjʊkeɪt/ *vt* erziehen; **be** ~**d at X** auf die X-Schule gehen. ~**d** *a* gebildet

education /edjʊ'keɪʃn/ *n* Erziehung *f*; (*culture*) Bildung *f*. ~**al** *a* pädagogisch; (*visit*) kulturell

eel /iːl/ *n* Aal *m*

eerie /'ɪərɪ/ *a* (**-ier, -iest**) unheimlich

effect /ɪ'fekt/ *n* Wirkung *f*, Effekt *m*; **in** ~ in Wirklichkeit; **take** ~ in Kraft treten □ *vt* bewirken

effective /ɪ'fektɪv/ *a*, **-ly** *adv* wirksam, effektiv; (*striking*) wirkungsvoll, effektvoll; (*actual*) tatsächlich. ~**ness** *n* Wirksamkeit *f*

effeminate /ɪˈfemɪnət/ a unmännlich

effervescent /efəˈvesnt/ a sprudelnd

efficiency /ɪˈfɪʃənsɪ/ n Tüchtigkeit f; (of machine, organization) Leistungsfähigkeit f

efficient /ɪˈfɪʃənt/ a tüchtig; ⟨machine, organization⟩ leistungsfähig; ⟨method⟩ rationell. **~ly** adv gut; ⟨function⟩ rationell

effigy /ˈefɪdʒɪ/ n Bildnis nt

effort /ˈefət/ n Anstrengung f; **make an ~** sich (dat) Mühe geben. **~less a, -ly** adv mühelos

effrontery /ɪˈfrʌntərɪ/ n Unverschämtheit f

effusive /ɪˈfjuːsɪv/ a, **-ly** adv überschwänglich

e.g. abbr (**exempli gratia**) z.B.

egalitarian /ɪɡælɪˈteərɪən/ a egalitär

egg¹ /eɡ/ vt **~on** (fam) anstacheln

egg² n Ei nt. **~-cup** n Eierbecher m. **~shell** n Eierschale f. **~timer** n Eieruhr f

ego /ˈiːɡəʊ/ n Ich nt. **~centric** /-ˈsentrɪk/ a egozentrisch. **~ism** n Egoismus m. **~ist** n Egoist m. **~tism** n Ichbezogenheit f. **~tist** n ichbezogener Mensch m

Egypt /ˈiːdʒɪpt/ n Ägypten nt. **~ian** /ɪˈdʒɪpʃn/ a ägyptisch □ n Ägypter(in) m(f)

eiderdown /ˈaɪdə-/ n (quilt) Daunendecke f

eight /eɪt/ a acht □ n Acht f; (boat) Achter m. **~'teen** a achtzehn. **~'teenth** a achtzehnte(r,s)

eighth /eɪtθ/ a achte(r,s) □ n Achtel nt

eightieth /ˈeɪtɪɪθ/ a achtzigste(r,s)

eighty /ˈeɪtɪ/ a achtzig

either /ˈaɪðə(r)/ a & pron ~ [of them] einer von [den] beiden; (both) beide; on ~ side auf beiden Seiten □ adv I don't ~ ich auch nicht □ conj ~ ... or entweder ... oder

eject /ɪˈdʒekt/ vt hinauswerfen

eke /iːk/ vt ~ out strecken; (increase) ergänzen; ~ out a living sich kümmerlich durchschlagen

elaborate¹ /ɪˈlæbərət/ a, **-ly** adv kunstvoll; (fig) kompliziert

elaborate² /ɪˈlæbəreɪt/ vi ausführlicher sein; ~ on näher ausführen

elapse /ɪˈlæps/ vi vergehen

elastic /ɪˈlæstɪk/ a elastisch □ n Gummiband nt. ~ **band** n Gummiband nt

elasticity /ɪlæsˈtɪsətɪ/ n Elastizität f

elated /ɪˈleɪtɪd/ a überglücklich

elbow /ˈelbəʊ/ n Ellbogen m

elder¹ /ˈeldə(r)/ n Holunder m

elder² /ˈeldə(r)/ a ältere(r,s) □ n the **~er** der/die Ältere. **~erly** a ält. **~est** a älteste(r,s) □ n the **~est** der/die Älteste

elect /ɪˈlekt/ a the president ~ der designierte Präsident □ vt wählen; ~ **to do** sth sich dafür entscheiden, etw zu tun. **~ion** /-ekʃn/ n Wahl f

elector /ɪˈlektə(r)/ n Wähler(in) m(f). **~al** a Wahl-; **~al roll** Wählerverzeichnis nt. **~ate** /-rət/ n Wählerschaft f

electric /ɪˈlektrɪk/ a, **-ally** adv elektrisch

electrical /ɪˈlektrɪkl/ a elektrisch; ~ **engineering** Elektrotechnik f

electric: ~ **blanket** n Heizdecke f. ~ **fire** n elektrischer Heizofen m

electrician /ɪlekˈtrɪʃn/ n Elektriker m

electricity /ɪlekˈtrɪsətɪ/ n Elektrizität f; (supply) Strom m

electrify /ɪˈlektrɪfaɪ/ vt (pt/pp -ied) elektrifizieren. **~ing** a (fig) elektrisierend

electrocute /ɪˈlektrəkjuːt/ vt durch einen elektrischen Schlag töten; (execute) auf dem elektrischen Stuhl hinrichten

rode /ɪˈlektrəʊd/ n Elektrode f

ectron /ɪˈlektrɒn/ n Elektron nt

lectronic /ɪlekˈtrɒnɪk/ a elektronisch. **~s** n Elektronik f

elegance /ˈelɪɡəns/ n Eleganz f

elegant /ˈelɪɡənt/ a, **-ly** adv elegant

elegy /ˈelɪdʒɪ/ n Elegie f

element /ˈelɪmənt/ n Element nt. **~ary** /-ˈmentərɪ/ a elementar

elephant /ˈelɪfənt/ n Elefant m

elevat|e /ˈelɪveɪt/ vt heben; (fig) erheben. **~ion** /-ˈveɪʃn/ n Erhebung f

elevator /ˈelɪveɪtə(r)/ n (Amer) Aufzug m, Fahrstuhl m

eleven /ɪˈlevn/ a elf □n Elf f. **~th** a elfte(r,s); **at the ~th hour** (fam) in letzter Minute

elf /elf/ n (pl **elves**) Elfe f

elicit /ɪˈlɪsɪt/ vt herausbekommen

eligible /ˈelɪdʒəbl/ a berechtigt; **~ young man** gute Partie f

eliminate /ɪˈlɪmɪneɪt/ vt ausschalten; (excrete) ausscheiden

élite /eɪˈliːt/ n Elite f

ellip|se /ɪˈlɪps/ n Ellipse f. **~tical** a elliptisch

elm /elm/ n Ulme f

elocution /eləˈkjuːʃn/ n Sprecherziehung f

elongate /ˈiːlɒŋɡeɪt/ vt verlängern

elope /ɪˈ əʊp/ vi durchbrennen (fam)

eloquen|ce /ˈeləkwəns/ n Beredsamkeit f. **~t** a, **-ly** adv beredt

else /els/ adv sonst; **who ~?** wer sonst? **nothing ~** sonst nichts; **or ~** oder; (otherwise) sonst; **someone/somewhere ~** jemand/irgendwo anders; **anyone ~** jeder andere; (as question) sonst noch jemand? **anything ~** alles andere; (as question) sonst noch etwas? **~where** adv woanders

elucidate /ɪˈluːsɪdeɪt/ vt erläutern

elude /ɪˈluːd/ vt entkommen (+ dat); (avoid) ausweichen (+ dat)

elusive /ɪˈluːsɪv/ a **be ~** schwer zu fassen sein

emaciated /ɪˈmeɪsɪeɪtɪd/ a abgezehrt

emanate /ˈeməneɪt/ vi ausgehen (from von)

emancipat|ed /ɪˈmænsɪpeɪtɪd/ a emanzipiert. **~ion** /-ˈpeɪʃn/ n Emanzipation f; (of slaves) Freilassung f

embalm /ɪmˈbɑːm/ vt einbalsamieren

embankment /ɪmˈbæŋkmənt/ n Böschung f; (of railway) Bahndamm m

embargo /emˈbɑːɡəʊ/ n (pl **-es**) Embargo nt

embark /ɪmˈbɑːk/ vi sich einschiffen; **~ on** anfangen mit. **~ation** /embɑːˈkeɪʃn/ n Einschiffung f

embarrass /ɪmˈbærəs/ vt in Verlegenheit bringen. **~ed** a verlegen. **~ing** a peinlich. **~ment** n Verlegenheit f

embassy /ˈembəsɪ/ n Botschaft f

embedded /ɪmˈbedɪd/ a **be deeply ~ in** tief stecken in (+ dat)

embellish /ɪmˈbelɪʃ/ vt verzieren; (fig) ausschmücken

embers /ˈembəz/ npl Glut f

embezzle /ɪmˈbezl/ vt unterschlagen. **~ment** n Unterschlagung f

embitter /ɪmˈbɪtə(r)/ vt verbittern

emblem /ˈembləm/ n Emblem nt

embodiment /ɪmˈbɒdɪmənt/ n Verkörperung f

embody /ɪmˈbɒdɪ/ vt (pt/pp **-ied**) verkörpern; (include) enthalten

emboss /ɪmˈbɒs/ vt prägen

embrace /ɪmˈbreɪs/ n Umarmung f □vt umarmen; (fig) umfassen □vi sich umarmen

embroider /ɪmˈbrɔɪdə(r)/ vt besticken; sticken (design); (fig)

ausschmücken □ *vi* sticken. **~y** *n*
Stickerei *f*

embroil /ɪm'brɔɪl/ *vt* become
~ed in sth in etw (*acc*) verwickelt werden

embryo /'embrɪəʊ/ *n* Embryo *m*

emerald /'emərəld/ *n* Smaragd *m*

emer|ge /ɪ'mɜːdʒ/ *vi* auftauchen
(**from** aus); (*become known*) sich
herausstellen; (*come into being*)
entstehen. **~gence** /-əns/ *n* Auftauchen *nt*; Entstehung *f*

emergency /ɪ'mɜːdʒənsɪ/ *n* Notfall *m*; **in an ~** im Notfall. **~ exit**
n Notausgang *m*

emery-paper /'emərɪ-/ *n* Schmirgelpapier *nt*

emigrant /'emɪgrənt/ *n* Auswanderer *m*

emigrat|e /'emɪgreɪt/ *vi* auswandern. **~ion** /-'greɪʃn/ *n* Auswanderung *f*

eminent /'emɪnənt/ *a*, **-ly** *adv*
eminent

emission /ɪ'mɪʃn/ *n* Ausstrahlung *f*; (*of pollutant*) Emission *f*

emit /ɪ'mɪt/ *vt* (*pt/pp* **emitted**)
ausstrahlen (*light, heat*); ausstoßen (*smoke, fumes, cry*)

emotion /ɪ'məʊʃn/ *n* Gefühl *nt*.
~al *a* emotional; **become ~al**
sich erregen

emotive /ɪ'məʊtɪv/ *a* emotional

empath|ize /'empəθaɪz/ *vi* **~ize
with** s.o. sich in jdn einfühlen.
~y *n* Einfühlungsvermögen *nt*

emperor /'empərə(r)/ *n* Kaiser *m*

emphasis /'emfəsɪs/ *n* Betonung
f

emphasize /'emfəsaɪz/ *vt* betonen

emphatic /ɪm'fætɪk/ *a*, **-ally** *adv*
nachdrücklich

empire /'empaɪə(r)/ *n* Reich *nt*

empirical /ɪm'pɪrɪkl/ *a* empirisch

employ /ɪm'plɔɪ/ *vt* beschäftigen;
(*appoint*) einstellen; (*fig*)
anwenden. **~ee** /emplɔɪ'iː/ *n* Beschäftigte *m/f*; (*in contrast to

employer) Arbeitnehmer *m*. **~er**
n Arbeitgeber *m*. **~ment** *n* Beschäftigung *f*; (*work*) Arbeit *f*.
~ment agency *n* Stellenvermittlung *f*

empower /ɪm'paʊə(r)/ *vt* ermächtigen

empress /'emprɪs/ *n* Kaiserin *f*

empties /'emptɪz/ *npl* leere
Flaschen *pl*

emptiness /'emptɪnɪs/ *n* Leere *f*

empty /'emptɪ/ *a* leer □ *vt* leeren;
ausleeren (*container*) □ *vi* sich
leeren

emulate /'emjʊleɪt/ *vt* nacheifern
(+ *dat*)

emulsion /ɪ'mʌlʃn/ *n* Emulsion *f*

enable /ɪ'neɪbl/ *vt* **~ s.o. to** es jdm
möglich machen, zu

enact /ɪ'nækt/ *vt* (*Theat*) aufführen

enamel /ɪ'næml/ *n* Email *nt*; (*on
teeth*) Zahnschmelz *m*; (*paint*)
Lack *m* □ *vt* (*pt/pp* **enamelled**)
emaillieren

enamoured /ɪ'næməd/ *a* **be ~ of**
sehr angetan sein von

enchant /ɪn'tʃɑːnt/ *vt* bezaubern.
~ing *a* bezaubernd. **~ment** *n*
Zauber *m*

encircle /ɪn'sɜːkl/ *vt* einkreisen

enclave /'enkleɪv/ *n* Enklave *f*

enclos|e /ɪn'kləʊz/ *vt* einschließen; (*in letter*) beilegen (**with**
dat). **~ure** /-ʒə(r)/ *n* (*at zoo*)
Gehege *nt*; (*in letter*) Anlage *f*

encompass /ɪn'kʌmpəs/ *vt* umfassen

encore /'ɒŋkɔ:(r)/ *n* Zugabe *f*
□ *int* bravo!

encounter /ɪn'kaʊntə(r)/ *n* Begegnung *f*; (*battle*) Zusammenstoß *m* □ *vt* begegnen (+ *dat*);
(*fig*) stoßen auf (+ *acc*)

encourag|e /ɪn'kʌrɪdʒ/ *vt* ermutigen; (*promote*) fördern. **~ement** *n* Ermutigung *f*. **~ing** *a*
ermutigend

encroach /ɪn'krəʊtʃ/ *vi* **~ on**
eindringen in (+ *acc*) (*land*); beanspruchen (*time*)

encumb|er /ɪn'kʌmbə(r)/ vt belasten (with mit). ∼**rance** /-rəns/ n Belastung f

encyclopaed|ia /ɪnsaɪklə'piːdɪə/ n Enzyklopädie f, Lexikon nt. ∼**ic** a enzyklopädisch

end /end/ n Ende nt; (purpose) Zweck m; in the ∼ schließlich; **at the ∼ of May** Ende Mai; **on ∼** hochkant; **for days on ∼** tagelang; **make ∼s meet** (fam) [gerade] auskommen; **no ∼ of** (fam) unheimlich viel(e) □ vt beenden □ vi enden; ∼ **up in** (fam: arrive at) landen in (+ dat)

endanger /ɪn'deɪndʒə(r)/ vt gefährden

endear|ing /ɪn'dɪərɪŋ/ a liebenswert. ∼**ment** n term of ∼**ment** Kosewort nt

endeavour /ɪn'devə(r)/ n Bemühung f □ vi sich bemühen (**to** zu)

ending /'endɪŋ/ n Schluss m, Ende nt; (Gram) Endung f

endive /'endaɪv/ n Endivie f

endless /'endlɪs/ a, **-ly** adv endlos

endorse /ɪn'dɔːs/ vt (Comm) indossieren; (confirm) bestätigen. ∼**ment** n (Comm) Indossament nt; (fig) Bestätigung f; (on driving licence) Strafvermerk m

endow /ɪn'daʊ/ vt stiften; **be ∼ed with** (fig) haben. ∼**ment** n Stiftung f

endur|able /ɪn'djʊərəbl/ a erträglich. ∼**ance** /-rəns/ n Durchhaltevermögen nt; **beyond** ∼**ance** unerträglich

endur|e /ɪn'djʊə(r)/ vt ertragen □ vi (lange) bestehen. ∼**ing** a dauernd

enemy /'enəmɪ/ n Feind m □ attrib feindlich

energetic /enə'dʒetɪk/ a tatkräftig; **be** ∼ voller Energie sein

energy /'enədʒɪ/ n Energie f

enforce /ɪn'fɔːs/ vt durchsetzen. ∼**d** a unfreiwillig

engage /ɪn'geɪdʒ/ vt einstellen (staff); (Theat) engagieren; (Auto)

einlegen (gear) □ vi sich beteiligen (**in** an + dat); (Techn) ineinander greifen. ∼**d** a besetzt; (person) beschäftigt; (to be married) verlobt; **get** ∼**d** sich verloben (**to** mit). ∼**ment** n Verlobung f; (appointment) Verabredung f; (Mil) Gefecht nt

engaging /ɪn'geɪdʒɪŋ/ a einnehmend

engender /ɪn'dʒendə(r)/ vt (fig) erzeugen

engine /'endʒɪn/ n Motor m; (Naut) Maschine f; (Rail) Lokomotive f; (of jet-plane) Triebwerk nt. ∼**-driver** n Lokomotivführer m

engineer /endʒɪ'nɪə(r)/ n Ingenieur m; (service, installation) Techniker m; (Naut) Maschinist m; (Amer) Lokomotivführer m □ vt (fig) organisieren. ∼**ing** n [mechanical] ∼**ing** Maschinenbau m

England /'ɪŋglənd/ n England nt

English /'ɪŋglɪʃ/ a englisch; **the** ∼ **Channel** der Ärmelkanal □ n (Lang) Englisch nt; **in** ∼ auf Englisch; **into** ∼ ins Englische; **the** ∼ pl die Engländer. ∼**man** n Engländer m. ∼**woman** n Engländerin f

engrav|e /ɪn'greɪv/ vt eingravieren. ∼**ing** n Stich m

engross /ɪn'grəʊs/ vt **be** ∼**ed in** vertieft sein in (+ acc)

engulf /ɪn'gʌlf/ vt verschlingen

enhance /ɪn'hɑːns/ vt verschönern; (fig) steigern

enigma /ɪ'nɪgmə/ n Rätsel nt. ∼**tic** /enɪg'mætɪk/ a rätselhaft

enjoy /ɪn'dʒɔɪ/ vt genießen; ∼ **oneself** sich amüsieren; ∼ **cooking/painting** gern kochen/malen; **I** ∼**ed it** es hat mir gut gefallen; (food:) geschmeckt. ∼**able** /-əbl/ a angenehm, nett. ∼**ment** n Vergnügen nt

enlarge /ɪn'lɑːdʒ/ vt vergrößern □ vi ∼ **upon** sich näher auslassen über (+ acc). ~ment n Vergrößerung f

enlighten /ɪn'laɪtn/ vt aufklären. ~ment n Aufklärung f

enlist /ɪn'lɪst/ vt (Mil) einziehen; ~ s.o.'s help jdn zur Hilfe heranziehen □ vi sich melden

enliven /ɪn'laɪvn/ vt beleben

enmity /'enmɪtɪ/ n Feindschaft f

enormity /ɪ'nɔːmətɪ/ n Ungeheuerlichkeit f

enormous /ɪ'nɔːməs/ a, -ly adv riesig

enough /ɪ'nʌf/ a, adv & n genug; be ~ reichen; **funnily** ~ komischerweise; **I've had** ~! (fam) jetzt reicht's mir aber!

enquire /ɪn'kwaɪə(r)/ vi sich erkundigen (**about** nach) □ vt sich erkundigen f; (investigation) Untersuchung f

enrage /ɪn'reɪdʒ/ vt wütend machen

enrich /ɪn'rɪtʃ/ vt bereichern; (improve) anreichern

enrol /ɪn'rəʊl/ v (pt/pp -rolled) □ vt einschreiben □ vi sich einschreiben. ~ment n Einschreibung f

ensemble /ɒn'sɒmbl/ n (clothing & Mus) Ensemble nt

ensign /'ensaɪn/ n Flagge f

enslave /ɪn'sleɪv/ vt versklaven

ensue /ɪn'sjuː/ vi folgen; (result) sich ergeben (**from** aus)

ensure /ɪn'ʃʊə(r)/ vt sicherstellen; ~ **that** dafür sorgen, dass

entail /ɪn'teɪl/ vt erfordelich machen; **what does it** ~? was ist damit verbunden?

entangle /ɪn'tæŋgl/ vt **get** ~d sich verfangen (**in** in + dat); (fig) sich verstricken (**in** in + acc)

enter /'entə(r)/ vt eintreten; ⟨vehicle:⟩ einfahren in (+ acc); einreisen in (+ acc) ⟨country⟩; (register) eintragen; sich anmelden zu (competition) □ vi eintreten;

⟨vehicle:⟩ einfahren; (Theat) auftreten; (register as competitor) sich anmelden; (take part) sich beteiligen (**in** an + dat)

enterprise /'entəpraɪz/ n Unternehmen nt; (quality) Unternehmungsgeist m. ~ing a unternehmend

entertain /entə'teɪn/ vt unterhalten; (invite) einladen; (to meal) bewirten ⟨guest⟩; (fig) in Erwägung ziehen □ vi unterhalten; (have guests) Gäste haben. ~er n Unterhalter m. ~ment n Unterhaltung f

enthral /ɪn'θrɔːl/ vt (pt/pp enthralled) **be** ~led gefesselt sein (**by** von)

enthuse /ɪn'θjuːz/ vi ~ **over** schwärmen von

enthusias|m /ɪn'θjuːzɪæzm/ n Begeisterung f. ~t n Enthusiast m. ~tic /-'æstɪk/ a, -ally adv begeistert

entice /ɪn'taɪs/ vt locken. ~ment n Anreiz m

entire /ɪn'taɪə(r)/ a ganz. ~ly adv ganz, völlig. ~ty /-rətɪ/ n in its ~ty in seiner Gesamtheit

entitle /ɪn'taɪtl/ vt berechtigen; ~d ... mit dem Titel ...; **be** ~d **to sth das** Recht auf etw (acc) haben. ~ment n Berechtigung f; (claim) Anspruch m (**to** auf + acc)

entity /'entɪtɪ/ n Wesen nt

entomology /entə'mɒlədʒɪ/ n Entomologie f

entourage /'ɒntʊrɑːʒ/ n Gefolge nt

entrails /'entreɪlz/ npl Eingeweide pl

entrance¹ /ɪn'trɑːns/ vt bezaubern

entrance² /'entrəns/ n Eintritt m; (Theat) Auftritt m; (way in) Eingang m; (for vehicle) Einfahrt f. ~ **examination** n Aufnahmeprüfung f. ~ **fee** n Eintrittsgebühr f

entrant /'entrənt/ n Teilnehmer(in) m(f)

entreat /ɪn'triːt/ vt anflehen (for um)

entrench /ɪn'trentʃ/ vt be ~ed in verwurzelt sein in (+ dat)

entrust /ɪn'trʌst/ vt ~ s.o. with sth, ~ sth to s.o. jdm etw anvertrauen

entry /'entrɪ/ n Eintritt m; (into country) Einreise f; (on list) Eintrag m; no ~ Zutritt/ (Auto) Einfahrt verboten. ~ form n Anmeldeformular nt. ~ visa n Einreisevisum nt

enumerate /ɪ'njuːməreɪt/ vt aufzählen

enunciate /ɪ'nʌnsɪeɪt/ vt [deutlich] aussprechen; (state) vorbringen

envelop /ɪn'veləp/ vt (pt/pp enveloped) einhüllen

envelope /'envələʊp/ n [Brief]umschlag m

enviable /'envɪəbl/ a beneidenswert

envious /'envɪəs/ a, -ly adv neidisch (of auf + acc)

environment /ɪn'vaɪərənmənt/ n Umwelt f

environmental /ɪnvaɪərən'mentl/ a Umwelt-. ~ist n Umweltschützer m. ~ly adv ~ly friendly umweltfreundlich

envisage /ɪn'vɪzɪdʒ/ vt sich (dat) vorstellen

envoy /'envɔɪ/ n Gesandte(r) m

envy /'envɪ/ n Neid m □ vt (pt/pp -ied) ~ s.o. sth jdn um etw beneiden

enzyme /'enzaɪm/ n Enzym nt

epic /'epɪk/ a episch □ n Epos nt

epidemic /epɪ'demɪk/ n Epidemie f

epilepsy /'epɪlepsɪ/ n Epilepsie f. ~tic /-'leptɪk/ a epileptisch □ n Epileptiker(in) m(f)

epilogue /'epɪlɒg/ n Epilog m

episode /'epɪsəʊd/ n Episode f; (instalment) Folge f

epistle /ɪ'pɪsl/ n (liter) Brief m

epitaph /'epɪtɑːf/ n Epitaph nt

epithet /'epɪθet/ n Beiname m

epitom|e /ɪ'pɪtəmɪ/ n Inbegriff m. ~ize vt verkörpern

epoch /'iːpɒk/ n Epoche f. ~making a epochemachend

equal /'iːkwl/ a gleich (to dat); be ~ to a task einer Aufgabe gewachsen sein □ n Gleichgestellte(r) m/f □ vt (pt/pp equalled) gleichen (+ dat); (fig) gleichkommen (+ dat). ~ity /ɪ'kwɒlətɪ/ n Gleichheit f

equalize /'iːkwəlaɪz/ vt/i ausgleichen. ~r n (Sport) Ausgleich[streffer] m

equally /'iːkwəlɪ/ adv gleich; (divide) gleichmäßig; (just as) genauso

equanimity /ekwə'nɪmətɪ/ n Gleichmut f

equat|e /ɪ'kweɪt/ vt gleichsetzen (with mit). ~ion /-eɪʒn/ n (Math) Gleichung f

equator /ɪ'kweɪtə(r)/ n Äquator m. ~ial /ekwə'tɔːrɪəl/ a Äquator-

equestrian /ɪ'kwestrɪən/ a Reit-

equilibrium /iːkwɪ'lɪbrɪəm/ n Gleichgewicht nt

equinox /'iːkwɪnɒks/ n Tagundnachtgleiche f

equip /ɪ'kwɪp/ vt (pt/pp equipped) ausrüsten; (furnish) ausstatten. ~ment n Ausrüstung f; Ausstattung f

equitable /'ekwɪtəbl/ a gerecht

equity /'ekwətɪ/ n Gerechtigkeit f

equivalent /ɪ'kwɪvələnt/ a gleichwertig; (corresponding) entsprechend □ n Äquivalent nt; (value) Gegenwert m; (counterpart) Gegenstück nt

equivocal /ɪ'kwɪvəkl/ a zweideutig

era /'ɪərə/ n Ära f, Zeitalter nt

eradicate /ɪ'rædɪkeɪt/ vt ausrotten

erase /ɪ'reɪz/ vt ausradieren; (from tape) löschen; (fig) auslöschen. **~r** n Radiergummi m

erect /ɪ'rekt/ a aufrecht □ vt errichten. **~ion** /-ekʃn/ n Errichtung f; (building) Bau m; (Biol) Erektion f

ermine /'ɜːmɪn/ n Hermelin m

ero|de /ɪ'rəʊd/ vt (water.) auswaschen; (acid:) angreifen. **~sion** /-əʊʒn/ n Erosion f

erotic /ɪ'rɒtɪk/ a erotisch. **~ism** /-tɪsɪzm/ n Erotik f

err /ɜː(r)/ vi sich irren; (sin) sündigen

errand /'erənd/ n Botengang m

erratic /ɪ'rætɪk/ a unregelmäßig; (person) unberechenbar

erroneous /ɪ'rəʊnɪəs/ a falsch; (belief, assumption) irrig. **~ly** adv fälschlich; irrigerweise

error /'erə(r)/ n Irrtum m; (mistake) Fehler m; **in ~** irrtümlicherweise

erudit|e /'eruːdaɪt/ a gelehrt. **~ion** /-'dɪʃn/ n Gelehrsamkeit f

erupt /ɪ'rʌpt/ vi ausbrechen. **~ion** /-ʌpʃn/ n Ausbruch m

escalat|e /'eskəleɪt/ vt/i eskalieren. **~ion** /-'leɪʃn/ n Eskalation f. **~or** n Rolltreppe f

escapade /'eskəpeɪd/ n Eskapade f

escape /ɪ'skeɪp/ n Flucht f; (from prison) Ausbruch m; **have a narrow ~** gerade noch davonkommen □ vi flüchten; (prisoner:) ausbrechen; entkommen (from aus; from s.o. jdm); (gas:) entweichen □ vt **~ notice** unbemerkt bleiben; **the name ~s me** der Name entfällt mir

escapism /ɪ'skeɪpɪzm/ n Flucht f vor der Wirklichkeit, Eskapismus m

escort[1] /'eskɔːt/ n (of person) Begleiter m; (Mil) Eskorte f; **under ~** unter Bewachung

escort[2] /ɪ'skɔːt/ vt begleiten; (Mil) eskortieren

Eskimo /'eskɪməʊ/ n Eskimo m

esoteric /esə'terɪk/ a esoterisch

especial /ɪ'speʃl/ a besondere(r,s). **~ly** adv besonders

espionage /'espɪənɑːʒ/ n Spionage f

essay /'eseɪ/ n Aufsatz m

essence /'esns/ n Wesen nt; (Chem, Culin) Essenz f; **in ~** im Wesentlichen

essential /ɪ'senʃl/ a wesentlich; (indispensable) unentbehrlich □ n **the ~s** das Wesentliche; (items) das Nötigste. **~ly** adv im Wesentlichen

establish /ɪ'stæblɪʃ/ vt gründen; (form) bilden; (prove) beweisen. **~ment** n (firm) Unternehmen nt

estate /ɪ'steɪt/ n Gut nt; (possessions) Besitz m; (after death) Nachlass m; (housing) [Wohn]siedlung f. **~ agent** n Immobilienmakler m. **~ car** n Kombi[wagen] m

esteem /ɪ'stiːm/ n Achtung f □ vt hochschätzen

estimate[1] /'estɪmət/ n Schätzung f; (Comm) [Kosten]voranschlag m; **at a rough ~** grob geschätzt

estimate[2] /'estɪmeɪt/ vt schätzen. **~ion** /-'meɪʃn/ n Einschätzung f; (esteem) Achtung f; **in my ~ion** meiner Meinung nach

estuary /'estjʊərɪ/ n Mündung f

etc. /et'setərə/ abbr (et cetera) und so weiter, usw.

etching /'etʃɪŋ/ n Radierung f

eternal /ɪ'tɜːnl/ a, **-ly** adv ewig

eternity /ɪ'tɜːnətɪ/ n Ewigkeit f

ether /'iːθə(r)/ n Äther m

ethic /'eθɪk/ n Ethik f. **~al** a ethisch; (morally correct) moralisch einwandfrei. **~s** n Ethik f

Ethiopia /iːθɪ'əʊpɪə/ n Äthiopien nt

ethnic /'eθnɪk/ a ethnisch

etiquette /'etɪket/ n Etikette f

etymology /etɪ'mɒlədʒɪ/ n Etymologie f

eucalyptus /ˌjuːkəˈlɪptəs/ n Eukalyptus m

eulogy /ˈjuːlədʒɪ/ n Lobrede f

euphemis|m /ˈjuːfəmɪzm/ n Euphemismus m. **~tic** /-ˈmɪstɪk/ a, **-ally** adv verhüllend

euphoria /juːˈfɔːrɪə/ n Euphorie f

Euro /ˈjʊərəʊ/ n Euro m. **~cheque** n Euroscheck m. **~passport** n Europaß m

Europe /ˈjʊərəp/ n Europa nt

European /jʊərəˈpiːən/ a europäisch; **~ Community** Europäische Gemeinschaft f □ n Europäer(in) m(f)

evacuate /ɪˈvækjʊeɪt/ vt evakuieren; räumen ⟨building, area⟩. **~ion** /-ˈeɪʃn/ n Evakuierung f; Räumung f

evade /ɪˈveɪd/ vt sich entziehen (+ dat); hinterziehen ⟨taxes⟩; **~ the issue** ausweichen

evaluate /ɪˈvæljʊeɪt/ vt einschätzen

evange|lical /iːvænˈdʒelɪkl/ a evangelisch. **~list** /ɪˈvændʒəlɪst/ n Evangelist m

evaporat|e /ɪˈvæpəreɪt/ vi verdunsten. **~ed milk** Kondensmilch f, Dosenmilch f. **~ion** /-ˈreɪʃn/ n Verdampfung f

evasion /ɪˈveɪʒn/ n Ausweichen nt; **~ of taxes** Steuerhinterziehung f

evasive /ɪˈveɪsɪv/ a, **-ly** adv ausweichend; **be ~** ausweichen

eve /iːv/ n ⟨liter⟩ Vorabend m

even /ˈiːvn/ a ⟨level⟩ eben; ⟨same, equal⟩ gleich; ⟨regular⟩ gleichmäßig; ⟨number⟩ gerade; **get ~ with** ⟨fam⟩ es jdm heimzahlen □ adv sogar, selbst; **~ so** trotzdem; **not ~** nicht einmal □ vt **~ the score** ausgleichen. **~ up** vt ausgleichen □ vi sich ausgleichen

evening /ˈiːvnɪŋ/ n Abend m; **this ~** heute Abend; **in the ~** abends, am Abend. **~ class** n Abendkurs m

evenly /ˈiːvnlɪ/ adv gleichmäßig

event /ɪˈvent/ n Ereignis nt; ⟨function⟩ Veranstaltung f; ⟨Sport⟩ Wettbewerb m; **in the ~ of** im Falle (+ gen); **in the ~** wie es sich ergab. **~ful** a ereignisreich

eventual /ɪˈventjʊəl/ a **his ~ success** der Erfolg, der ihm schließlich zuteil wurde. **~ity** /-ˈælətɪ/ n Eventualität f, Fall m. **~ly** adv schließlich

ever /ˈevə(r)/ adv je[mals]; **~** not nie; **for ~** für immer; **hardly ~** fast nie; **~ since** seitdem; **~ so** ⟨fam⟩ sehr, furchtbar ⟨fam⟩

evergreen n immergrüner Strauch m/ ⟨tree⟩ Baum m

everlasting a ewig

every /ˈevrɪ/ a jede(r,s); **~ one** jede(r,s) Einzelne; **~ other day** jeden zweiten Tag

every|body pron jeder[mann]; alle pl. **~day** a alltäglich. **~one** pron jeder[mann]; alle pl. **~thing** pron alles. **~where** adv überall

evict /ɪˈvɪkt/ vt [aus der Wohnung] hinausweisen. **~ion** /-ɪkʃn/ n Ausweisung f

eviden|ce /ˈevɪdəns/ n Beweise pl; ⟨Jur⟩ Beweismaterial nt; ⟨testimony⟩ Aussage f; **give ~** aussagen. **~t** a, **-ly** adv offensichtlich

evil /ˈiːvl/ a böse □ n Böse nt

evocative /ɪˈvɒkətɪv/ a **be ~ of** heraufbeschwören

evoke /ɪˈvəʊk/ vt heraufbeschwören

evolution /iːvəˈluːʃn/ n Evolution f

evolve /ɪˈvɒlv/ vt entwickeln □ vi sich entwickeln

ewe /juː/ n Schaf nt

exacerbate /ekˈsæsəbeɪt/ vt verschlimmern; verschärfen ⟨situation⟩

exact /ɪgˈzækt/ a, **-ly** adv genau; **not ~ly** nicht gerade □ vt erzwingen. **~ing** a anspruchsvoll. **~itude** /-ɪtjuːd/ n, **~ness** n Genauigkeit f

exaggerat|e /ɪgˈzædʒəreɪt/ vt/i übertreiben. **~ion** /-ˈreɪʃn/ n Übertreibung f

exalt /ɪgˈzɔːlt/ vt erheben; (praise) preisen

exam /ɪgˈzæm/ n (fam) Prüfung f

examination /ɪgzæmɪˈneɪʃn/ n Untersuchung f; (Sch) Prüfung f

examine /ɪgˈzæmɪn/ vt untersuchen; (Sch) prüfen; (Jur) verhören. **~r** n (Sch) Prüfer m

example /ɪgˈzɑːmpl/ n Beispiel n (of für); **for ~** zum Beispiel; **make an ~ of** ein Exempel statuieren an (+ dat)

exasperat|e /ɪgˈzæspəreɪt/ vt zur Verzweiflung treiben. **~ion** /-ˈreɪʃn/ n Verzweiflung f

excavat|e /ˈekskəveɪt/ vt ausschachten; (Archaeol) ausgraben. **~ion** /-ˈveɪʃn/ n Ausgrabung f

exceed /ɪkˈsiːd/ vt übersteigen. **~ingly** adv äußerst

excel /ɪkˈsel/ v (pt/pp excelled) vi sich auszeichnen □ vt ~ **oneself** sich selbst übertreffen

excellen|ce /ˈeksələns/ n Vorzüglichkeit f. **E~cy** n (title) Exzellenz f. **~t** a, **-ly** adv ausgezeichnet, vorzüglich

except /ɪkˈsept/ prep außer (+ dat); **~ for** abgesehen von □ vt ausnehmen. **~ing** prep außer (+ dat)

exception /ɪkˈsepʃn/ n Ausnahme f; **take ~ to** Anstoß nehmen an (+ dat). **~al** a, **-ly** adv außergewöhnlich

excerpt /ˈeksɜːpt/ n Auszug m

excess /ɪkˈses/ n Übermaß nt (of an + dat); (surplus) Überschuss m; **~es** pl Exzesse pl; **in ~ of** über (+ dat)

excess 'fare /ˈekses-/ n Nachlösegebühr f

excessive /ɪkˈsesɪv/ a, **-ly** adv übermäßig

exchange /ɪksˈtʃeɪndʒ/ n Austausch m; (Teleph) Fernsprechamt nt; (Comm) [Geld]wechsel m; **[stock] ~** Börse f; **in ~** dafür □ vt austauschen (for gegen); tauschen (places, greetings, money). **~ rate** n Wechselkurs m

exchequer /ɪksˈtʃekə(r)/ n (Pol) Staatskasse f

excise[1] /ˈeksaɪz/ n ~ **duty** Verbrauchssteuer f

excise[2] /ekˈsaɪz/ vt herausschneiden

excitable /ɪkˈsaɪtəbl/ a [leicht] erregbar

excit|e /ɪkˈsaɪt/ vt aufregen; (cause) erregen. **~ed** a, **-ly** adv aufgeregt; **get ~ed** sich aufregen. **~ement** n Aufregung f; Erregung f. **~ing** a aufregend; (story) spannend

exclaim /ɪkˈskleɪm/ vt/i ausrufen

exclamation /ekskləˈmeɪʃn/ n Ausruf m. **~ mark** n, (Amer) **~ point** n Ausrufezeichen nt

exclu|de /ɪkˈskluːd/ vt ausschließen. **~ding** prep ausschließlich (+ gen). **~sion** /-ʒn/ n Ausschluss m

exclusive /ɪkˈskluːsɪv/ a, **-ly** adv ausschließlich; (select) exklusiv; **~ of** ausschließlich (+ gen)

excommunicate /ekskəˈmjuːnɪkeɪt/ vt exkommunizieren

excrement /ˈekskrɪmənt/ n Kot m

excrete /ɪkˈskriːt/ vt ausscheiden

excruciating /ɪkˈskruːʃieɪtɪŋ/ a grässlich

excursion /ɪkˈskɜːʃn/ n Ausflug m

excusable /ɪkˈskjuːzəbl/ a entschuldbar

excuse[1] /ɪkˈskjuːs/ n Entschuldigung f; (pretext) Ausrede f

excuse[2] /ɪkˈskjuːz/ vt entschuldigen; **~ from** freistellen von; **~ me!** Entschuldigung!

ex-di'rectory a be **~** nicht im Telefonbuch stehen

execute /'eksɪkjuːt/ vt ausführen; (put to death) hinrichten

execution /eksɪ'kjuːʃn/ n (see execute) Ausführung f; Hinrichtung f. **~er** n Scharfrichter m

executive /ɪg'zekjʊtɪv/ a leitend □ n leitende(r) Angestellte(r) m/f; (Pol) Exekutive f

executor /ɪg'zekjʊtə(r)/ n (Jur) Testamentsvollstrecker m

exemplary /ɪg'zemplərɪ/ a beispielhaft; (as a warning) exemplarisch

exemplify /ɪg'zemplɪfaɪ/ vt (pt/pp -ied) veranschaulichen

exempt /ɪg'zempt/ a befreit □ vt befreien (from von). **~ion** /-empʃn/ n Befreiung f

exercise /'eksəsaɪz/ n Übung f; physical ~ körperliche Bewegung f; take ~ sich bewegen □ vt (use) ausüben; bewegen ⟨horse⟩; spazieren führen ⟨dog⟩ □ vi sich bewegen. **~ book** n [Schul]heft nt

exert /ɪg'zɜːt/ vt ausüben; **~ one-self** sich anstrengen. **~ion** /-ɜːʃn/ n Anstrengung f

exhale /eks'heɪl/ vt/i ausatmen

exhaust /ɪg'zɔːst/ n Auspuff m; (pipe) Auspuffrohr nt; (fumes) Abgase pl □ vt erschöpfen. **~ed** a erschöpft. **~ing** a anstrengend. **~ion** /-ɔːstʃn/ n Erschöpfung f. **~ive** /-ɪv/ a (fig) erschöpfend

exhibit /ɪg'zɪbɪt/ n Ausstellungsstück nt; (Jur) Beweisstück nt □ vt ausstellen; (fig) zeigen

exhibition /eksɪ'bɪʃn/ n Ausstellung f; (Univ) Stipendium nt. **~ist** n Exhibitionist(in) m(f)

exhibitor /ɪg'zɪbɪtə(r)/ n Aussteller m

exhilarat|ed /ɪg'zɪləreɪtɪd/ a beschwingt. **~ing** a berauschend. **~ion** /-'reɪʃn/ n Hochgefühl nt

exhort /ɪg'zɔːt/ vt ermahnen

exhume /ɪg'zjuːm/ vt exhumieren

exile /'eksaɪl/ n Exil nt; (person) im Exil Lebende(r) m/f □ vt ins Exil schicken

exist /ɪg'zɪst/ vi bestehen, existieren. **~ence** /-əns/ n Existenz f; **be in ~ence** existieren

exit /'eksɪt/ n Ausgang m; (Auto) Ausfahrt f; (Theat) Abgang m □ vi (Theat) abgehen. **~ visa** n Ausreisevisum nt

exonerate /ɪg'zɒnəreɪt/ vt entlasten

exorbitant /ɪg'zɔːbɪtənt/ a übermäßig hoch

exorcize /'eksɔːsaɪz/ vt austreiben

exotic /ɪg'zɒtɪk/ a exotisch

expand /ɪk'spænd/ vt ausdehnen; (explain better) weiter ausführen □ vi sich ausdehnen; (Comm) expandieren; **~ on** (fig) weiter ausführen

expans|e /ɪk'spæns/ n Weite f. **~ion** /-ænʃn/ n Ausdehnung f; (Techn, Pol, Comm) Expansion f. **~ive** /-ɪv/ a mitteilsam

expatriate /eks'pætrɪət/ n be an ~ im Ausland leben

expect /ɪk'spekt/ vt erwarten; (suppose) annehmen; **I ~ so** wahrscheinlich; **we ~ to arrive on Monday** wir rechnen damit, dass wir am Montag ankommen

expectan|cy /ɪk'spektənsɪ/ n Erwartung f. **~t** a, **-ly** adv erwartungsvoll; **~t mother** werdende Mutter f

expectation /ekspek'teɪʃn/ n Erwartung f; **~ of life** Lebenserwartung f

expedient /ɪk'spiːdɪənt/ a zweckdienlich

expedite /'ekspɪdaɪt/ vt beschleunigen

expedition /ekspɪ'dɪʃn/ n Expedition f. **~ary** a (Mil) Expeditions-

expel /ɪk'spel/ vt (pt/pp expelled) ausweisen (from aus); (from school) von der Schule verweisen

expend /ɪkˈspend/ vt aufwenden.
~able /-əbl/ a entbehrlich

expenditure /ɪkˈspendɪtʃə(r)/ n
Ausgaben pl

expense /ɪkˈspens/ n Kosten pl;
business ~s pl Spesen pl; **at my
~** auf meine Kosten; **at the ~ of**
(fig) auf Kosten (+ gen)

expensive /ɪkˈspensɪv/ a, **-ly** adv
teuer

experience /ɪkˈspɪərɪəns/ n Erfahrung f; (event) Erlebnis nt □ vt
erleben. **~d** a erfahren

experiment /ɪkˈsperɪmənt/ n Versuch m, Experiment nt □ /-ment/
vi experimentieren. **~al**
/-ˈmentl/ a experimentell

expert /ˈekspɜːt/ a, **-ly** adv fachmännisch □ n Fachmann m, Experte m

expertise /eksˈpɜːˈtiːz/ n Sachkenntnis f; (skill) Geschick nt

expire /ɪkˈspaɪə(r)/ vi ablaufen

expiry /ɪkˈspaɪərɪ/ n Ablauf m. **~
date** n Verfallsdatum nt

explain /ɪkˈspleɪn/ vt erklären

explana|tion /ekspləˈneɪʃn/ n Erklärung f. **~tory** /ɪkˈsplænətərɪ/
a erklärend

expletive /ɪkˈspliːtɪv/ n
Kraftausdruck m

explicit /ɪkˈsplɪsɪt/ a, **-ly** adv
deutlich

explode /ɪkˈspləʊd/ vi explodieren □ vt zur Explosion bringen

exploit[1] /ˈeksplɔɪt/ n [Helden]tat
f

exploit[2] /ɪkˈsplɔɪt/ vt ausbeuten.
~ation /eksplɔɪˈteɪʃn/ n Ausbeutung f

explora|tion /ekspləˈreɪʃn/ n Erforschung f. **~tory** /ɪkˈsplɒrətərɪ/ a Probe-

explore /ɪkˈsplɔː(r)/ vt erforschen. **~r** n Forschungsreisende(r) m

explos|ion /ɪkˈspləʊʒn/ n Explosion f. **~ive** /-sɪv/ a explosiv □ n
Sprengstoff m

exponent /ɪkˈspəʊnənt/ n Vertreter m

export[1] /ˈekspɔːt/ n Export m,
Ausfuhr f

export[2] /ɪkˈspɔːt/ vt exportieren,
ausführen. **~er** n Exporteur m

expos|e /ɪkˈspəʊz/ vt freilegen; (to
danger) aussetzen (**to** dat); (reveal) aufdecken; (Phot) belichten.
~ure /-ʒə(r)/ n Aussetzung f;
(Med) Unterkühlung f; (Phot) Belichtung f; **24 ~ures** 24 Aufnahmen

expound /ɪkˈspaʊnd/ vt erläutern

express /ɪkˈspres/ a ausdrücklich; (purpose) fest □ adv (send)
per Eilpost □ n (train) Schnellzug
m □ vt ausdrücken; **~ oneself**
sich ausdrücken. **~ion** /-ʃn/ n
Ausdruck m. **~ive** /-ɪv/ a
ausdrucksvoll. **~ly** adv ausdrücklich

expulsion /ɪkˈspʌlʃn/ n Ausweisung f; (Sch) Verweisung f von
der Schule

expurgate /ˈekspɜːgeɪt/ vt zensieren

exquisite /ekˈskwɪzɪt/ a erlesen

ex-serviceman n Veteran m

extempore /ɪkˈstempərɪ/ adv
(speak) aus dem Stegreif

extend /ɪkˈstend/ vt verlängern;
(stretch out) ausstrecken; (enlarge) vergrößern □ vi sich ausdehnen; (table:) sich ausziehen
lassen

extension /ɪkˈstenʃn/ n Verlängerung f; (to house) Anbau m;
(Teleph) Nebenanschluss m;
~ 7 Apparat 7

extensive /ɪkˈstensɪv/ a weit;
(fig) umfassend. **-ly** adv viel

extent /ɪkˈstent/ n Ausdehnung f;
(scope) Ausmaß nt, Umfang m; **to
a certain ~** in gewissem Maße

extenuating /ɪkˈstenjʊeɪtɪŋ/ a
mildernd

exterior /ɪkˈstɪərɪə(r)/ a äußere(r,s) □ n **the ~** das Äußere

exterminat|e /ɪk'stɜːmɪneɪt/ vt ausrotten. **~ion** /-'neɪʃn/ n Ausrottung f

external /ɪk'stɜːnl/ a äußere(r,s); **for ~ use only** (Med) nur äußerlich. **~ly** adv äußerlich

extinct /ɪk'stɪŋkt/ a ausgestorben; (volcano) erloschen. **~ion** /-ɪŋkʃn/ n Aussterben nt

extinguish /ɪk'stɪŋgwɪʃ/ vt löschen. **~er** n Feuerlöscher m

extol /ɪk'stəʊl/ vt (pt/pp extolled) preisen

extort /ɪk'stɔːt/ vt erpressen. **~ion** /-ʃn/ n Erpressung f

extortionate /ɪk'stɔːʃənət/ a übermäßig hoch

extra /'ekstrə/ a zusätzlich □ adv extra; (especially) besonders; **~ strong** extrastark □ n (Theat) Statist(in) m(f); (Auto) Extras pl

extract¹ /'ekstrækt/ n Auszug m; (Culin) Extrakt m

extract² /ɪk'strækt/ vt herausziehen; ziehen (tooth); (fig) erzwingen. **~or** [fan] n Entlüfter m

extradit|e /'ekstrədaɪt/ vt (Jur) ausliefern. **~ion** /-'dɪʃn/ n (Jur) Auslieferung f

extra-marital a außerehelich

extraordinary /ɪk'strɔːdɪnərɪ/ a, **-ily** adv außerordentlich; (strange) seltsam

extravagan|ce /ɪk'strævəgəns/ n Verschwendung f; **an ~ce** ein Luxus m. **~t** a verschwenderisch; (exaggerated) extravagant

extrem|e /ɪk'striːm/ a äußerste(r,s); (fig) extrem □ n Extrem nt; **in the ~e** im höchsten Grade. **~ely** adv äußerst. **~ist** n Extremist m

extremit|y /ɪk'stremɪtɪ/ n (distress) Not f; **the ~ies** pl die Extremitäten pl

extricate /'ekstrɪkeɪt/ vt befreien

extrovert /'ekstrəvɜːt/ n extravertierter Mensch m

exuberant /ɪg'zjuːbərənt/ a überglücklich

exude /ɪg'zjuːd/ vt absondern; (fig) ausstrahlen

exult /ɪg'zʌlt/ vi frohlocken

eye /aɪ/ n Auge nt; (of needle) Öhr nt; (for hook) Öse f; **keep an ~ on** aufpassen auf (+ acc); **see ~ to ~** einer Meinung sein □ vt (pt/pp eyed, pres p ey[e]ing) ansehen

eye: ~ball n Augapfel m. **~brow** n Augenbraue f. **~lash** n Wimper f. **~let** /-lɪt/ n Öse f. **~lid** n Augenlid nt. **~shadow** n Lidschatten m. **~sight** n Sehkraft f. **~sore** n (fam) Schandfleck m. **~tooth** n Eckzahn m. **~witness** n Augenzeuge m

F

fable /'feɪbl/ n Fabel f

fabric /'fæbrɪk/ n Stoff m; (fig) Gefüge nt

fabrication /fæbrɪ'keɪʃn/ n Erfindung f

fabulous /'fæbjʊləs/ a (fam) phantastisch

façade /fə'sɑːd/ n Fassade f

face /feɪs/ n Gesicht nt; (grimace) Grimasse f; (surface) Fläche f; (of clock) Zifferblatt nt; **pull ~s** Gesichter schneiden; **in the ~ of** angesichts (+ gen); **on the ~ of it** allem Anschein nach □ vt/i gegenüberstehen (+ dat); **~ north** (house:) nach Norden liegen; **~ me!** sieh mich an! **~ the fact that** sich damit abfinden, dass; **~ up to s.o.** jdm die Stirn bieten

face: ~flannel n Waschlappen m. **~less** a anonym. **~lift** n Gesichtsstraffung f

facet /'fæsɪt/ n Facette f; (fig) Aspekt m

facetious /fə'siːʃəs/ a, **-ly** adv spöttisch

'face value n Nennwert m

facial /'feɪʃl/ a Gesichts-

facile /'fæsaɪl/ a oberflächlich

facilitate /fə'sɪlɪteɪt/ vt erleichtern

facilit|y /fə'sɪlɪtɪ/ n Leichtigkeit f; ⟨skill⟩ Gewandtheit f; **~ies** pl Einrichtungen pl

facing /'feɪsɪŋ/ n Besatz m

facsimile /fæk'sɪməlɪ/ n Faksimile nt

fact /fækt/ n Tatsache f; **in ~** tatsächlich; ⟨actually⟩ eigentlich

faction /'fækʃn/ n Gruppe f

factor /'fæktə(r)/ n Faktor m

factory /'fæktərɪ/ n Fabrik f

factual /'fæktʃʊəl/ a, **-ly** adv sachlich

faculty /'fækəltɪ/ n Fähigkeit f; ⟨Univ⟩ Fakultät f

fad /fæd/ n Fimmel m

fade /feɪd/ vi verblassen; ⟨material:⟩ verbleichen; ⟨sound:⟩ abklingen; ⟨flower:⟩ verwelken. **~ in/out** vt ⟨Radio, TV⟩ ein-/ausblenden

fag /fæg/ n ⟨chore⟩ Plage f; ⟨fam: cigarette⟩ Zigarette f; ⟨Amer sl⟩ Homosexuelle(r) m

fagged /fægd/ a **~ out** ⟨fam⟩ völlig erledigt

Fahrenheit /'færənhaɪt/ a Fahrenheit

fail /feɪl/ n **without ~** unbedingt ● vi ⟨attempt:⟩ scheitern; ⟨grow weak⟩ nachlassen; ⟨break down⟩ versagen; ⟨in exam⟩ durchfallen; **~ to do** sth etw nicht tun; **he ~ed to break the record** es gelang ihm nicht, den Rekord zu brechen ● vt nicht bestehen ⟨exam⟩; durchfallen lassen ⟨candidate⟩; ⟨disappoint⟩ enttäuschen; **words ~ me** ich weiß nicht, was ich sagen soll

failing /'feɪlɪŋ/ n Fehler m ● prep **~ that** andernfalls

failure /'feɪljə(r)/ n Misserfolg m; ⟨breakdown⟩ Versagen nt; ⟨person:⟩ Versager m

faint /feɪnt/ a (-er, -est), **-ly** adv schwach; **I feel~** mir ist schwach ● n Ohnmacht f ● vi ohnmächtig werden

faint: ~'hearted a zaghaft. **~ness** n Schwäche f

fair[1] /feə(r)/ n Jahrmarkt m; ⟨Comm⟩ Messe f

fair[2] a (-er, -est) ⟨hair⟩ blond; ⟨skin⟩ hell; ⟨weather⟩ heiter; ⟨just⟩ gerecht, fair; ⟨quite good⟩ ziemlich gut; ⟨Sch⟩ genügend; **a ~ amount** ziemlich viel ● adv **play ~** fair sein. **~ly** adv gerecht; ⟨rather⟩ ziemlich. **~ness** n Blondheit f; Helle f; Gerechtigkeit f; ⟨Sport⟩ Fairness f

fairy /'feərɪ/ n Elfe f; **good/ wicked ~** gute/böse Fee f. **~ story, ~tale** n Märchen nt

faith /feɪθ/ n Glaube m; ⟨trust⟩ Vertrauen nt (**in** zu); **in good ~** in gutem Glauben

faithful /'feɪθfl/ a, **-ly** adv treu; ⟨exact⟩ genau; **Yours ~ly** Hochachtungsvoll. **~ness** n Treue f; Genauigkeit f

'faith-healer n Gesundbeter(in) m(f)

fake /feɪk/ a falsch ● n Fälschung f; ⟨person⟩ Schwindler m ● vt fälschen; ⟨pretend⟩ vortäuschen

falcon /'fɔːlkən/ n Falke m

fall /fɔːl/ n Fall m; ⟨heavy⟩ Sturz m; ⟨in prices⟩ Fallen nt; ⟨Amer: autumn⟩ Herbst m; **have a ~** fallen ● vi ⟨pt **fell**, pp **fallen**⟩ fallen; ⟨heavily⟩ stürzen; ⟨night:⟩ anbrechen; **~in** sich verlieben; **~ back on** zurückgreifen auf (+ acc); **~ for s.o.** ⟨fam⟩ sich in jdn verlieben; **~ for sth** ⟨fam⟩ auf etw (acc) hereinfallen. **~ about** vi ⟨with laughter⟩ sich vor Lachen⟩ kringeln. **~ down** vi umfallen; ⟨thing:⟩ herunterfallen; ⟨building:⟩ einstürzen. **~ in** vi hineinfallen; ⟨collapse⟩ einfallen; ⟨Mil⟩ antreten; **~ in with** sich anschließen (+ dat). **~ off** vi herunterfallen; *(diminish)* abnehmen. ~ **out** *vi* herausfallen; *(hair:)* ausfallen; *(quarrel)* sich überwerfen. ~ **over** *vi* hinfallen. ~ **through** *vi* durchfallen; *(plan:)* ins Wasser fallen

fallacy /'fæləsɪ/ *n* Irrtum *m*

fallible /'fæləbl/ *a* fehlbar

'fall-out *n* [radioaktiver] Niederschlag *m*

fallow /'fæləʊ/ *a* **lie ~** brachliegen

false /fɔːls/ *a* falsch; *(artificial)* künstlich; ~ **start** *(Sport)* Fehlstart *m*. ~**hood** *n* Unwahrheit *f*. ~**ly** *adv* falsch. ~**ness** *n* Falschheit *f*

false 'teeth *npl* [künstliches] Gebiss *nt*

falsify /'fɔːlsɪfaɪ/ *vt (pt/pp -ied)* fälschen; *(misrepresent)* verfälschen

falter /'fɔːltə(r)/ *vi* zögern; *(stumble)* straucheln

fame /feɪm/ *n* Ruhm *m*. ~**d** *a* berühmt

familiar /fə'mɪljə(r)/ *a* vertraut; *(known)* bekannt; **too ~** familiär. ~**ity** /-lɪ'ærətɪ/ *n* Vertrautheit *f*. ~**ize** *vt* vertraut machen **(with** mit)

family /'fæməlɪ/ *n* Familie *f*

family: ~ **al'lowance** *n* Kindergeld *nt*. ~ **'doctor** *n* Hausarzt *m*. ~ **'life** *n* Familienleben *nt*. ~ **'planning** *n* Familienplanung *f*. ~ **'tree** *n* Stammbaum *m*

famine /'fæmɪn/ *n* Hungersnot *f*

famished /'fæmɪʃt/ *a* sehr hungrig

famous /'feɪməs/ *a* berühmt

fan¹ /fæn/ *n* Fächer *m*; *(Techn)* Ventilator *m* □ *v (pt/pp* **fanned)** □ *vt* fächeln; ~ **oneself** sich fächeln □ *vi* ~ **out** sich fächerförmig ausbreiten

fan² *n (admirer)* Fan *m*

fanatic /fə'nætɪk/ *n* Fanatiker *m*. ~**al**, **-ly** *adv* fanatisch. ~**ism** /-sɪzm/ *n* Fanatismus *m*

'fan belt *n* Keilriemen *m*

fanciful /'fænsɪfl/ *a* phantastisch; *(imaginative)* phantasiereich

fancy /'fænsɪ/ *n* Phantasie *f*; **have a ~ to** Lust haben, zu; **I have taken a real ~ to him** er hat es mir angetan □ *a* ausgefallen; ~ **cakes and biscuits** Feingebäck *nt* □ *vt (believe)* meinen; *(imagine)* sich *(dat)* einbilden; *(fam: want)* Lust haben auf (+ *acc*); ~ **that!** stell dir vor! *(really)* tatsächlich! ~ **'dress** *n* Kostüm *nt*

fanfare /'fænfeə(r)/ *n* Fanfare *f*

fang /fæŋ/ *n* Fangzahn *m*; *(of snake)* Giftzahn *m*

fan: ~ **heater** *n* Heizlüfter *m*. ~**light** *n* Oberlicht *nt*

fanta|size /'fæntəsaɪz/ *vi* phantasieren. ~**tic** /-'tæstɪk/ *a* phantastisch. ~**y** *n* Phantasie *f*; *(Mus)* Fantasie *f*

far /fɑː(r)/ *adv* weit; *(much)* viel; **by ~** bei weitem; ~ **away** weit weg; **as ~ as I know** soviel ich weiß; **as ~ as the church** bis zur Kirche □ *a* **at the ~ end** am anderen Ende; **the F~ East** der Ferne Osten

farc|e /fɑːs/ *n* Farce *f*. ~**ical** *a* lächerlich

fare /feə(r)/ *n* Fahrpreis *m*; *(money)* Fahrgeld *nt*; *(food)* Kost *f*; ~ **air** ~ Flugpreis *m*. ~**-dodger** /-dɒdʒə(r)/ *n* Schwarzfahrer *m*

farewell /feə'wel/ *int (liter)* lebe wohl! □ *n* Lebewohl *nt*; ~ **dinner** *n* Abschiedsessen *nt*

far-'fetched *a* weit hergeholt; **be ~** an den Haaren herbeigezogen sein

farm /fɑːm/ *n* Bauernhof *m* □ *vi* Landwirtschaft betreiben □ *vt* bewirtschaften *(land)*. ~**er** *n* Landwirt *m*

farm: ~**house** *n* Bauernhaus *nt*. ~**ing** *n* Landwirtschaft *f*. ~**yard** *n* Hof *m*

far: ~·'**reaching** a weit reichend. ~·'**sighted** a (fig) umsichtig; (Amer: long-sighted) weitsichtig

fart /fɑːt/ n (vulg) Furz m □ vi (vulg) furzen

farther /'fɑːðə(r)/ adv weiter; ~ **off** weiter entfernt □ a **at the** ~ **end** am anderen Ende

fascinat|e /'fæsɪneɪt/ vt faszinieren. ~**ing** a faszinierend. ~**ion** /-'neɪʃn/ n Faszination f

fascis|m /'fæʃɪzm/ n Faschismus m. ~**t** n Faschist m □ a faschistisch

fashion /'fæʃn/ n Mode f; (manner) Art f □ vt machen; (mould) formen. ~**able** /-əbl/ a, ~**bly** adv modisch; **be** ~**able** Mode sein

fast¹ /fɑːst/ a & adv (-er, -est) schnell; (firm) fest; (colour) waschecht; **be** ~ (clock:) vorgehen; **be** ~ **asleep** fest schlafen

fast² n Fasten nt □ vi fasten

fastback n (Auto) Fließheck nt

fasten /'fɑːsn/ vt zumachen; (fix) befestigen (**to** an + dat); ~ **one's seatbelt** sich anschnallen. ~**er** n, ~**ing** n Verschluss m

fastidious /fə'stɪdɪəs/ a wählerisch; (particular) penibel

fat /fæt/ a (fatter, fattest) dick; ⟨meat⟩ fett □ n Fett nt

fatal /'feɪtl/ a tödlich; (error) verhängnisvoll. ~**ism** /-təlɪzm/ n Fatalismus m. ~**ist** /-təlɪst/ n Fatalist m. ~**ity** /fə'tælətɪ/ n Todesopfer nt. ~**ly** /-təlɪ/ adv tödlich

fate /feɪt/ n Schicksal nt. ~**ful** a verhängnisvoll

'**fat-head** n (fam) Dummkopf m

father /'fɑːðə(r)/ n Vater m; **F~ Christmas** der Weihnachtsmann □ vt zeugen

father: ~**hood** n Vaterschaft f. ~-**in-law** n (pl ~**s-in-law**) Schwiegervater m. ~**ly** a väterlich

fathom /'fæðəm/ n (Naut) Faden m □ vt verstehen; ~ **out** ergründen

fatigue /fə'tiːg/ n Ermüdung f □ vt ermüden

fatten /'fætn/ vt mästen (animal). ~**ing** a **cream is** ~**ing** Sahne macht dick

fatty /'fætɪ/ a fett; (foods) fetthaltig

fatuous /'fætjʊəs/ a, ~**ly** adv albern

faucet /'fɔːsɪt/ n (Amer) Wasserhahn m

fault /fɔːlt/ n Fehler m; (Techn) Defekt m; (Geol) Verwerfung f; **at** ~ **im Unrecht; find** ~ **with** etwas auszusetzen haben an (+ dat); **it's your** ~ du bist schuld □ vt etwas auszusetzen haben an (+ dat). ~**less** a, ~**ly** adv fehlerfrei

faulty /'fɔːltɪ/ a fehlerhaft

fauna /'fɔːnə/ n Fauna f

favour /'feɪvə(r)/ n Gunst f; **I am in** ~ ich bin dafür; **do s.o. a** ~ jdm einen Gefallen tun □ vt begünstigen; (prefer) bevorzugen. ~**able** /-əbl/ a, ~**bly** adv günstig; (reply) positiv

favourit|e /'feɪvərɪt/ a Lieblings- □ n Liebling m; (Sport) Favorit(in) m(f). ~**ism** n Bevorzugung f

fawn¹ /fɔːn/ a rehbraun □ n Hirschkalb nt

fawn² vi sich einschmeicheln (**on** bei)

fax /fæks/ n Fax nt □ vt faxen (s.o. jdm). ~ **machine** n Faxgerät nt

fear /fɪə(r)/ n Furcht f, Angst f (**of** vor + dat); **no** ~! (fam) keine Angst! □ vt/i fürchten

fear|ful /'fɪəfl/ a besorgt; (awful) furchtbar. ~**less** a, ~**ly** adv furchtlos. ~**some** /-səm/ a Furcht erregend

feas|ibility /fiːzə'bɪlətɪ/ n Durchführbarkeit f. ~**ible** a durchführbar; (possible) möglich

feast /fiːst/ n Festmahl nt; (Relig) Fest nt □ vi ~ [**on**] schmausen

feat /fiːt/ n Leistung f

feather /ˈfeðə(r)/ n Feder f

feature /ˈfiːtʃə(r)/ n Gesichtszug m; (quality) Merkmal nt; (Journ) Feature nt □ vt darstellen; (film:) in der Hauptrolle zeigen. ~ **film** n Hauptfilm m

February /ˈfebruərɪ/ n Februar m

feckless /ˈfeklɪs/ a verantwortungslos

fed /fed/ see **feed** □ a be ~ **up** (fam) die Nase voll haben (with von)

federal /ˈfedərəl/ a Bundes-

federation /fedəˈreɪʃn/ n Föderation f

fee /fiː/ n Gebühr f; (professional) Honorar nt

feeble /ˈfiːbl/ a (-r, -st), -bly adv schwach

feed /fiːd/ n Futter nt; (for baby) Essen nt □ v (pt/pp fed) □ vt füttern; (support) ernähren; (into machine) eingeben; speisen (computer) □ vi sich ernähren (on von)

feedback n Feedback nt

feel /fiːl/ v (pt/pp felt) □ vt fühlen; (experience) empfinden; (think) meinen □ vi sich fühlen; ~ **soft/hard** sich weich/hart anfühlen; I ~ **hot/ill** mir ist heiß/schlecht; I don't ~ **like it** ich habe keine Lust dazu. ~**er** n Fühler m. ~**ing** n Gefühl nt; no hard ~**ings** nichts für ungut

feet /fiːt/ see **foot**

feign /feɪn/ vt vortäuschen

feint /feɪnt/ n Finte f

feline /ˈfiːlaɪn/ a Katzen-; (catlike) katzenartig

fell¹ /fel/ vt fällen

fell² see **fall**

fellow /ˈfeləʊ/ n (of society) Mitglied nt; (fam: man) Kerl m

fellow: ~-**countryman** n Landsmann m. ~ **men** pl Mitmenschen pl. ~**ship** n Kameradschaft f; (group) Gesellschaft f

felony /ˈfelənɪ/ n Verbrechen nt

felt¹ /felt/ see **feel**

felt² /felt/ n Filz m. ~-**[tipped]** 'pen n Filzstift m

female /ˈfiːmeɪl/ a weiblich □ n Weibchen nt; (pej: woman) Weib nt

feminine /ˈfemɪnɪn/ a weiblich □ n (Gram) Femininum nt. ~**inity** /-ˈnɪnɪtɪ/ n Weiblichkeit f. ~**ist** a feministisch □ n Feminist(in) m(f)

fence /fens/ n Zaun m; (fam: person) Hehler m □ vi (Sport) fechten □ vt ~**e in** einzäunen. ~**er** n Fechter m. ~**ing** n Zaun m; (Sport) Fechten nt

fend /fend/ vi ~ **for oneself** sich allein durchschlagen. ~ **off** vt abwehren

fender /ˈfendə(r)/ n Kaminvorsetzer m; (Naut) Fender m; (Amer: wing) Kotflügel m

fennel /ˈfenl/ n Fenchel m

ferment¹ /ˈfɜːment/ n Erregung f

ferment² /fəˈment/ vi gären □ vt gären lassen. ~**ation** /fɜːmenˈteɪʃn/ n Gärung f

fern /fɜːn/ n Farn m

ferocious /fəˈrəʊʃəs/ a wild. ~**ity** /-ˈrɒsətɪ/ n Wildheit f

ferret /ˈferɪt/ n Frettchen nt

ferry /ˈferɪ/ n Fähre f □ vt ~ [**across**] übersetzen

fertile /ˈfɜːtaɪl/ a fruchtbar. ~**ity** /fɜːˈtɪlətɪ/ n Fruchtbarkeit f

fertilize /ˈfɜːtəlaɪz/ vt befruchten; düngen (land). ~**r** n Dünger m

fervent /ˈfɜːvənt/ a leidenschaftlich

fervour /ˈfɜːvə(r)/ n Leidenschaft f

fester /ˈfestə(r)/ vi eitern

festival /ˈfestɪvl/ n Fest nt; (Mus, Theat) Festspiele pl

festive /ˈfestɪv/ a festlich; ~ **season** Festzeit. f. ~**ities** /-ˈstɪvɪtɪz/ npl Feierlichkeiten pl

festoon /feˈstuːn/ vt behängen (with mit)

fetch /fetʃ/ vt holen; (collect) abholen; (be sold for) einbringen

fetching /ˈfetʃɪŋ/ a anziehend

fête /feɪt/ n Fest nt □ vt feiern

fetish /ˈfetɪʃ/ n Fetisch m

fetter /ˈfetə(r)/ vt fesseln

fettle /ˈfetl/ n **in fine ~** in bester Form

feud /fjuːd/ n Fehde f

feudal /ˈfjuːdl/ a Feudal-

fever /ˈfiːvə(r)/ n Fieber nt. **~ish** a fiebrig; (fig) fieberhaft

few /fjuː/ a (-er, -est) wenige; **every ~ days** alle paar Tage □ n **a ~** ein paar; **quite a ~** ziemlich viele

fiancé /fɪˈɒnseɪ/ n Verlobte(r) m. **fiancée** n Verlobte f

fiasco /fɪˈæskəʊ/ n Fiasko nt

fib /fɪb/ n kleine Lüge; **tell a ~** schwindeln

fibre /ˈfaɪbə(r)/ n Faser f

fickle /ˈfɪkl/ a unbeständig

fiction /ˈfɪkʃn/ n Erfindung f; **[works of] ~** Erzählungsliteratur f. **~al** a erfunden

fictitious /fɪkˈtɪʃəs/ a [frei] erfunden

fiddle /ˈfɪdl/ n (fam) Geige f; (cheating) Schwindel m □ vi herumspielen (**with** mit) □ vt (fam) frisieren (accounts); (arrange) arrangieren

fiddly /ˈfɪdlɪ/ a knifflig

fidelity /fɪˈdelətɪ/ n Treue f

fidget /ˈfɪdʒɪt/ vi zappeln. **~y** a zappelig

field /fiːld/ n Feld nt; (meadow) Wiese f; (subject) Gebiet nt

field: **~ events** npl Sprung- und Wurfdisziplinen pl. **~glasses** npl Feldstecher m. **F~ 'Marshal** n Feldmarschall m. **~work** n Feldforschung f

fiend /fiːnd/ n Teufel m. **~ish** a teuflisch

fierce /fɪəs/ a (-r, -st), **-ly** adv wild; (fig) heftig. **~ness** n Wildheit f; (fig) Heftigkeit f

fiery /ˈfaɪərɪ/ a (-ier, -iest) feurig

fifteen /fɪfˈtiːn/ a fünfzehn □ n Fünfzehn f. **~th** a fünfzehnte(r,s)

fifth /fɪfθ/ a fünfte(r,s)

fiftieth /ˈfɪftɪɪθ/ a fünfzigste(r,s)

fifty /ˈfɪftɪ/ a fünfzig

fig /fɪg/ n Feige f

fight /faɪt/ n Kampf m; (brawl) Schlägerei f; (between children, dogs) Rauferei f □ v (pt/pp **fought**) □ vt kämpfen gegen; (fig) bekämpfen □ vi kämpfen; (brawl) sich schlagen; (children, dogs) sich raufen. **~er** n Kämpfer m; (Aviat) Jagdflugzeug nt. **~ing** n Kampf m

figment /ˈfɪgmənt/ n **~ of the imagination** Hirngespinst nt

figurative /ˈfɪgjərətɪv/ a, **-ly** adv bildlich, übertragen

figure /ˈfɪgə(r)/ n (digit) Ziffer f; (number) Zahl f; (sum) Summe f; (carving, sculpture, woman's) Figur f; (form) Gestalt f; (illustration) Abbildung f. **~ of speech** Redefigur f; **good at ~s** gut im Rechnen □ vi (appear) erscheinen □ vt (Amer: think) glauben. **~ out** vt ausrechnen

figure: **~head** n Galionsfigur f; (fig) Repräsentationsfigur f. **~ skating** n Eiskunstlauf m

filament /ˈfɪləmənt/ n Faden m; (Electr) Glühfaden m

filch /fɪltʃ/ vt (fam) klauen

file¹ /faɪl/ n Akte f; (for documents) [Akten]ordner m □ vt ablegen (documents); (Jur) einreichen

file² n (line) Reihe f; **in single ~** im Gänsemarsch

file³ n (Techn) Feile f □ vt feilen

filigree /ˈfɪlɪgriː/ n Filigran nt

filings /ˈfaɪlɪŋz/ npl Feilspäne pl

fill /fɪl/ n **eat one's ~** sich satt essen □ vt füllen; plombieren (tooth) □ vi sich füllen. **~ in** vt auffüllen; ausfüllen (form). **~ out** vt ausfüllen (form). **~ up** vi sich füllen □ vt vollfüllen; (Auto) volltanken; ausfüllen (form)

fillet /'fɪlɪt/ n Filet nt □ vt (pt/pp **filleted**) entgräten

filling /'fɪlɪŋ/ n Füllung f; (of tooth) Plombe f. ~ **station** n Tankstelle f

filly /'fɪlɪ/ n junge Stute f

film /fɪlm/ n Film m □ vt/i (Culin) [cling] ~ Klarsichtfolie f □ vt/i filmen; verfilmen ⟨book⟩. ~ **star** n Filmstar m

filter /'fɪltə(r)/ n Filter m □ vt filtern. ~ **through** vi durchsickern. ~ **tip** n Filter m; (cigarette) Filterzigarette f

filth /fɪlθ/ n Dreck m. ~**y** a (-ier, -iest) dreckig

fin /fɪn/ n Flosse f

final /'faɪnl/ a letzte(r,s); (conclusive) endgültig. ~ **result** Endresultat nt □ n (Sport) Finale nt, Endspiel nt; ~**s** pl (Univ) Abschlussprüfung f

finale /fɪ'nɑːlɪ/ n Finale nt

finalist /'faɪnəlɪst/ n Finalist(in) m(f). ~**ity** /-'nælətɪ/ n Endgültigkeit f

finalize /'faɪnəlaɪz/ vt endgültig festlegen. ~**ly** adv schließlich

finance /'faɪnæns/ n Finanz f □ vt finanzieren

financial /faɪ'nænʃl/ a, **-ly** adv finanziell

finch /fɪntʃ/ n Fink m

find /faɪnd/ n Fund m □ vt (pt/pp **found**) finden; (establish) feststellen; **go and** ~ holen; **try to** ~ suchen; ~ **guilty** (Jur) schuldig sprechen. ~ **out** vt herausfinden; (learn) erfahren □ vi (enquire) sich erkundigen

findings /'faɪndɪŋz/ npl Ergebnisse pl

fine¹ /faɪn/ n Geldstrafe f □ vt zu einer Geldstrafe verurteilen

fine² a (-r, -st), **-ly** adv fein; (weather) schön; **he's** ~ es geht ihm gut □ adv gut; **cut it** ~ (fam) sich (dat) wenig Zeit lassen. ~ **arts** npl schöne Künste pl

finery /'faɪnərɪ/ n Putz m, Staat m

finesse /fɪ'nes/ n Gewandtheit f

finger /'fɪŋgə(r)/ n Finger m □ vt anfassen

finger: ~**mark** n Fingerabdruck m. ~**nail** n Fingernagel m. ~**print** n Fingerabdruck m. ~**tip** n Fingerspitze f; **have sth at one's** ~**tips** etw im kleinen Finger haben

finicky /'fɪnɪkɪ/ a knifflig; (choosy) wählerisch

finish /'fɪnɪʃ/ n Schluss m; (Sport) Finish nt; (line) Ziel nt; (of product) Ausführung f □ vt beenden; (use up) aufbrauchen; ~ **one's drink** austrinken; ~ **reading** zu Ende lesen □ vi fertig werden; (performance:) zu Ende sein; (runner:) durchs Ziel gehen

finite /'faɪnaɪt/ a begrenzt

Finland /'fɪnlənd/ n Finnland nt

Finn /fɪn/ n Finne m/ Finnin f. ~**ish** a finnisch

fiord /fjɔːd/ n Fjord m

fir /fɜː(r)/ n Tanne f

fire /'faɪə(r)/ n Feuer nt; (forest, house) Brand m; **be on** ~ brennen; **catch** ~ Feuer fangen; **set** ~ **to** anzünden; ⟨arsonist:⟩ in Brand stecken; **under** ~ unter Beschuss □ vt brennen ⟨pottery⟩; abfeuern ⟨shot⟩; schießen mit ⟨gun⟩; (fam: dismiss) feuern □ vi schießen (**at** auf + acc); ⟨engine:⟩ anspringen

fire: ~ **alarm** n Feueralarm m; (apparatus) Feuermelder m. ~**arm** n Schusswaffe f. ~**brigade** n Feuerwehr f. ~**engine** n Löschfahrzeug nt. ~**escape** n Feuertreppe f. ~ **extinguisher** n Feuerlöscher m. ~**man** n Feuerwehrmann m. ~**place** n Kamin m. ~**side** n **by** or **at the** ~**side** am Kamin. ~ **station** n Feuerwache f. ~**wood** n Brennholz nt. ~**work** n Feuerwerkskörper m; ~**works** pl (display) Feuerwerk nt

'firing squad n Erschießungskommando nt

firm[1] /fɜ:m/ n Firma f

firm[2] a (-er, -est), -ly adv fest; (resolute) entschlossen; (strict) streng

first /fɜ:st/ a & n erste(r,s); at ~ zuerst; who's ~? wer ist der Erste? at ~ sight auf den ersten Blick; for the ~ time zum ersten Mal; from the ~ von Anfang an □ adv zuerst; (firstly) erstens

first: ~ 'aid n erste Hilfe. ~'aid kit n Verbandkasten m. ~class a erstklassig; (Rail) erster Klasse. □ /-'-/ adv (travel) erster Klasse. ~ e'dition n Erstausgabe f. ~floor n erster Stock; (Amer: groundfloor) Erdgeschoss nt. ~ly adv erstens. ~name n Vorname m. ~rate a erstklassig

fish /fɪʃ/ n Fisch m □ vt/i fischen; (with rod) angeln. ~ out vt herausfischen

fish: ~bone n Gräte f. ~erman n Fischer m. ~farm n Fischzucht f. ~finger n Fischstäbchen n

fishing /'fɪʃɪŋ/ n Fischerei f. ~boat n Fischerboot nt. ~rod n Angel[rute] f

fish: ~monger /-mʌŋgə(r)/ n Fischhändler m. ~slice n Fischheber m. ~y a Fisch-; (fam: suspicious) verdächtig

fission /'fɪʃn/ n (Phys) Spaltung f

fist /fɪst/ n Faust f

fit[1] /fɪt/ n (attack) Anfall m

fit[2] a (fitter, fittest) (suitable) geeignet; (healthy) gesund; (Sport) fit; ~ to eat essbar; keep ~ sich fit halten; see ~ es für angebracht halten (to zu)

fit[3] n (of clothes) Sitz m; be a good ~ gut passen □ vt (pt/pp fitted) □ vi (be the right size) passen □ vt anbringen (to an + dat); (install) einbauen; (clothes:) passen (+ dat); ~ with versehen mit. ~ in vi hineinpassen; (adapt) sich einfügen (with in + acc) □ vt (accommodate) unterbringen

fit|ful /'fɪtfl/ a, -ly adv (sleep) unruhig. ~ment n Einrichtungsgegenstand m; (attachment) Zusatzgerät nt. ~ness n Eignung f; [physical] ~ness Gesundheit f; (Sport) Fitness f. ~ted a eingebaut; (garment) tailliert

fitted: ~ 'carpet n Teppichboden m. ~ 'cupboard n Einbauschrank m. ~ 'kitchen n Einbauküche f. ~ 'sheet n Spannlaken nt

fitter /'fɪtə(r)/ n Monteur m

fitting /'fɪtɪŋ/ a passend □ n (of clothes) Anprobe f; (of shoes) Weite f; (Techn) Zubehörteil nt; ~s pl Zubehör nt. ~room n Anprobekabine f

five /faɪv/ a fünf □ n Fünf f. ~r n Fünfpfundschein m

fix /fɪks/ n (sl: drugs) Fix m; be in a ~ (fam) in der Klemme sitzen □ vt befestigen (to an + dat); (arrange) festlegen; (repair) reparieren; (Phot) fixieren; ~ a meal (Amer) Essen machen

fixation /fɪk'seɪʃn/ n Fixierung f

fixed /'fɪkst/ a fest

fixture /'fɪkstʃə(r)/ n (Sport) Veranstaltung f; ~s and fittings zu einer Wohnung gehörende Einrichtungen pl

fizz /fɪz/ vi sprudeln

fizzle /'fɪzl/ vi ~ out verpuffen

fizzy /'fɪzɪ/ a sprudelnd. ~ drink n Brause[limonade] f

flabbergasted /'flæbəgɑːstɪd/ a be ~ platt sein (fam)

flabby /'flæbɪ/ a schlaff

flag[1] /flæg/ n Fahne f; (Naut) Flagge f □ vt (pt/pp flagged) ~ down anhalten (taxi)

flag[2] vi (pt/pp flagged) ermüden

flagon /'flægən/ n Krug m

flag-pole n Fahnenstange f

flagrant /'fleɪgrənt/ a flagrant

flagstone n [Pflaster]platte f

flair /fleə(r)/ n Begabung f

flake /fleɪk/ n Flocke f □ vi ~ [off] abblättern

flaky /'fleɪkɪ/ *a* blättrig. **~ pastry** *n* Blätterteig *m*

flamboyant /flæm'bɔɪənt/ *a* extravagant

flame /fleɪm/ *n* Flamme *f*

flammable /'flæməbl/ *a* feuergefährlich

flan /flæn/ *n* [**fruit**] **~** Obsttorte *f*

flank /flæŋk/ *n* Flanke *f* □ *vt* flankieren

flannel /'flænl/ *n* Flanell *m*; (*for washing*) Waschlappen *m*

flannelette /flænə'let/ *n* (*Tex*) Biber *m*

flap /flæp/ *n* Klappe *f*; **in a ~** (*fam*) aufgeregt □ *v* (*pt/pp* **flapped**) *vi* flattern; (*fam*) sich aufregen □ *vt* **~ its wings** mit den Flügeln schlagen

flare /fleə(r)/ *n* Leuchtsignal *nt*. □ *vi* **~ up** aufflodern; (*fam: get angry*) aufbrausen. **~d** *a* (*garment*) ausgestellt

flash /flæʃ/ *n* Blitz *m*; **in a ~** (*fam*) im Nu □ *vi* blitzen; (*repeatedly*) blinken; **~ past** vorbeirasen □ *vt* aufleuchten lassen; **~ one's headlights** die Lichthupe betätigen

flash: **~back** *n* Rückblende *f*. **~bulb** *n* (*Phot*) Blitzbirne *f*. **~er** *n* (*Auto*) Blinker *m*. **~light** *n* (*Phot*) Blitzlicht *nt*; (*Amer*) Taschenlampe *f*. **~y** *a* auffällig

flask /flɑːsk/ *n* Flasche *f*; (*Chem*) Kolben *m*; (*vacuum* ~) Thermosflasche (P) *f*

flat /flæt/ *a* (**flatter, flattest**) flach; (*surface*) eben; (*refusal*) glatt; (*beer*) schal; (*battery*) verbraucht/ (*Auto*) leer; (*tyre*) platt; (*Mus*) **A ~** As *nt*; **B ~** B *nt* □ *n* Wohnung *f*; (*Mus*) Erniedrigungszeichen *nt*; (*fam: puncture*) Reifenpanne *f*

flat: **~ 'feet** *npl* Plattfüße *pl*. **~ fish** *n* Plattfisch *m*. **~ly** *adv* (*refuse*) glatt. **~ rate** *n* Einheitspreis *m*

flatten /'flætn/ *vt* platt drücken

flatter /'flætə(r)/ *vt* schmeicheln (+ *dat*). **~y** *n* Schmeichelei *f*

flat 'tyre *n* Reifenpanne *f*

flatulence /'flætjʊləns/ *n* Blähungen *pl*

flaunt /flɔːnt/ *vt* prunken mit

flautist /'flɔːtɪst/ *n* Flötist(in) *m(f)*

flavour /'fleɪvə(r)/ *n* Geschmack *m* □ *vt* abschmecken. **~ing** *n* Aroma *nt*

flaw /flɔː/ *n* Fehler *m*. **~less** *a* tadellos; (*complexion*) makellos

flax /flæks/ *n* Flachs *m*. **~en** *a* flachsblond

flea /fliː/ *n* Floh *m*. **~ market** *n* Flohmarkt *m*

fleck /flek/ *n* Tupfen *m*

fled /fled/ *see* **flee**

flee /fliː/ *v* (*pt/pp* **fled**) *vi* fliehen (**from** vor + *dat*) □ *vt* flüchten aus

fleece /fliːs/ *n* Vlies *nt* □ *vt* (*fam*) schröpfen. **~y** *a* flauschig

fleet /fliːt/ *n* Flotte *f*; (*of cars*) Wagenpark *m*

fleeting /'fliːtɪŋ/ *a* flüchtig

Flemish /'flemɪʃ/ *a* flämisch

flesh /fleʃ/ *n* Fleisch *nt*; **in the ~** (*fam*) in Person. **~y** *a* fleischig

flew /fluː/ *see* **fly**[2]

flex[1] /fleks/ *vt* anspannen (*muscle*)

flex[2] *n* (*Electr*) Schnur *f*

flexibility /fleksə'bɪlətɪ/ *n* Biegsamkeit *f*; (*fig*) Flexibilität *f*. **~le** *a* biegsam; (*fig*) flexibel

flexitime /'fleksɪ-/ *n* Gleitzeit *f*

flick /flɪk/ *vt* schnippen. **~ through** *vi* schnell durchblättern

flicker /'flɪkə(r)/ *vi* flackern

flier /'flaɪə(r)/ *n* = **flyer**

flight[1] /flaɪt/ *n* (*fleeing*) Flucht *f*; **take ~** die Flucht ergreifen

flight[2] *n* (*flying*) Flug *m*; **~ of stairs** Treppe *f*

flight: **~ path** *n* Flugschneise *f*. **~ recorder** *n* Flugschreiber *m*

flighty /ˈflaɪtɪ/ a (-ier, -iest) flatterhaft

flimsy /ˈflɪmzɪ/ a (-ier, -iest) dünn; ⟨excuse⟩ fadenscheinig

flinch /flɪntʃ/ vi zurückzucken

fling /flɪŋ/ n have a ~ ⟨fam⟩ sich austoben □ vt (pt/pp flung) schleudern

flint /flɪnt/ n Feuerstein m

flip /flɪp/ vt/i schnippen; ~ **through** durchblättern

flippant /ˈflɪpənt/ a, -ly adv leichtfertig

flipper /ˈflɪpə(r)/ n Flosse f

flirt /flɜːt/ n kokette Frau f □ vi flirten

flirtat|ion /flɜːˈteɪʃn/ n Flirt m. ~ious /-ʃəs/ a kokett

flit /flɪt/ vi (pt/pp flitted) flattern

float /fləʊt/ n Schwimmer m; (in procession) Festwagen m; (money) Wechselgeld m □ vi ⟨thing:⟩ schwimmen; ⟨person:⟩ sich treiben lassen; (in air) schweben; (Comm) floaten

flock /flɒk/ n Herde f; (of birds) Schwarm m □ vi strömen

flog /flɒg/ vt (pt/pp flogged) auspeitschen; ⟨fam: sell⟩ verkloppen

flood /flʌd/ n Überschwemmung f; ⟨fig⟩ Flut f; **be in** ~ ⟨river:⟩ Hochwasser führen □ vt überschwemmen □ vi ⟨river:⟩ über die Ufer treten

floodlight n Flutlicht nt □ vt (pt/pp floodlit) anstrahlen

floor /flɔː(r)/ n Fußboden m; (storey) Stock m □ vt (baffle) verblüffen

floor: ~ **board** n Dielenbrett nt. ~**cloth** n Scheuertuch nt. ~**polish** n Bohnerwachs nt. ~ **show** n Kabarettvorstellung f

flop /flɒp/ n ⟨fam⟩ (failure) Reinfall m; (Theat) Durchfall m □ vi (pt/pp flopped) ⟨fam⟩ (fail) durchfallen; ~ **down** sich plumpsen lassen

floppy /ˈflɒpɪ/ a schlapp. ~ **disc** n Diskette f

flora /ˈflɔːrə/ n Flora f

floral /ˈflɔːrl/ a Blumen-

florid /ˈflɒrɪd/ a ⟨complexion⟩ gerötet; ⟨style⟩ blumig

florist /ˈflɒrɪst/ n Blumenhändler(in) m(f)

flounce /flaʊns/ n Volant m □ vi ~ **out** hinausstolzieren

flounder[1] /ˈflaʊndə(r)/ vi zappeln

flounder[2] n (fish) Flunder f

flour /ˈflaʊə(r)/ n Mehl nt

flourish /ˈflʌrɪʃ/ n große Geste f; (scroll) Schnörkel m □ vi gedeihen; ⟨fig⟩ blühen □ vt schwenken

floury /ˈflaʊərɪ/ a mehlig

flout /flaʊt/ vt missachten

flow /fləʊ/ n Fluss m; (of traffic, blood) Strom m □ vi fließen

flower /ˈflaʊə(r)/ n Blume f □ vi blühen

flower: ~**bed** n Blumenbeet nt. ~**ed** a geblümt. ~**pot** n Blumentopf m. ~**y** a blumig

flown /fləʊn/ see **fly**[2]

flu /fluː/ n ⟨fam⟩ Grippe f

fluctuat|e /ˈflʌktjʊeɪt/ vi schwanken. ~**ion** /-ˈeɪʃn/ n Schwankung f

fluent /ˈfluːənt/ a, -ly adv fließend

fluff /flʌf/ n Fusseln pl; (down) Flaum m. ~**y** a (-ier, -iest) flauschig

fluid /ˈfluːɪd/ a flüssig, ⟨fig⟩ veränderlich □ n Flüssigkeit f

fluke /fluːk/ n [glücklicher] Zufall m

flung /flʌŋ/ see **fling**

flunk /flʌŋk/ vt/i ⟨Amer, fam⟩ durchfallen (in + dat)

fluorescent /flʊəˈresnt/ a fluoreszierend; ~ **lighting** Neonbeleuchtung f

fluoride /ˈflʊəraɪd/ n Fluor nt

flurry /ˈflʌrɪ/ n (snow) Gestöber nt; ⟨fig⟩ Aufregung f

flush /flʌʃ/ n (blush) Erröten nt □ vi rot werden □ vt spülen □ a in einer Ebene (**with** mit); ⟨fam: affluent⟩ gut bei Kasse

flustered /'flʌstəd/ a nervös

flute /fluːt/ n Flöte f

flutter /'flʌtə(r)/ n Flattern nt □ vi flattern

flux /flʌks/ n **in a state of ~** im Fluss

fly¹ /flaɪ/ n (pl **flies**) Fliege f

fly² v (pt **flew**, pp **flown**) □ vi fliegen; (flag:) wehen; (rush) sausen □ vt fliegen; führen (flag)

fly³ n & **flies** pl (on trousers) Hosenschlitz m

flyer /'flaɪə(r)/ n Flieger(in) m(f); (Amer: leaflet) Flugblatt nt

flying: ~ **'buttress** n Strebebogen m. ~ **'saucer** n fliegende Untertasse f. ~ **'visit** n Stippvisite f

fly: ~ **leaf** n Vorsatzblatt nt. ~**over** n Überführung f

foal /fəʊl/ n Fohlen nt

foam /fəʊm/ n Schaum m; (synthetic) Schaumstoff m □ vi schäumen. ~ **'rubber** n Schaumgummi m

fob /fɒb/ vt (pt/pp **fobbed**) ~ **sth off** etw andrehen (**on s.o.** jdm); ~ **s.o. off** jdn abspeisen (**with** mit)

focal /'fəʊkl/ a Brenn-

focus /'fəʊkəs/ n Brennpunkt m; **in** ~ scharf eingestellt □ v (pt/pp **focused** or **focussed**) □ vt einstellen (**on auf** + acc); (fig) konzentrieren (**on auf** + acc); □ vi (fig) sich konzentrieren (**on auf** + acc)

fodder /'fɒdə(r)/ n Futter nt

foe /fəʊ/ n Feind m

foetus /'fiːtəs/ n (pl **-tuses**) Fötus m

fog /fɒg/ n Nebel m

foggy /'fɒgɪ/ a (**foggier, foggiest**) neblig

'fog-horn n Nebelhorn nt

fogy /'fəʊgɪ/ n **old** ~ alter Knacker m

foible /'fɔɪbl/ n Eigenart f

foil¹ /fɔɪl/ n Folie f; (Culin) Alufolie f

foil² vt (thwart) vereiteln

foil³ n (Fencing) Florett nt

foist /fɔɪst/ vt andrehen (**on s.o.** jdm)

fold¹ /fəʊld/ n (for sheep) Pferch m

fold² n Falte f; (in paper) Kniff m □ vt falten; ~ **one's arms** die Arme verschränken □ vi sich falten lassen; (fail) eingehen. ~ **up** vt zusammenfalten; zusammenklappen (chair) □ vi sich zusammenfalten/-klappen lassen; (fam) (business:) eingehen

fold|er /'fəʊldə(r)/ n Mappe f. ~**ing** a Klapp-

foliage /'fəʊlɪɪdʒ/ n Blätter pl; (of tree) Laub nt

folk /fəʊk/ npl Leute pl

folk: ~**dance** n Volkstanz m. ~**lore** n Folklore f. ~**song** n Volkslied nt

follow /'fɒləʊ/ vt/i folgen (+ dat); (pursue) verfolgen; (in vehicle) nachfahren (+ dat); ~ **suit** (fig) dasselbe tun. ~ **up** vt nachgehen (+ dat)

follow|er /'fɒləʊə(r)/ n Anhänger(in) m(f). ~**ing** a folgend □ n Folgende(s) nt; (supporters) Anhängerschaft f □ prep im Anschluss an (+ acc)

folly /'fɒlɪ/ n Torheit f

fond /fɒnd/ a (**-er, -est**), **-ly** adv liebevoll; **be** ~ **of** gern haben; gern essen (food)

fondle /'fɒndl/ vt liebkosen

fondness /'fɒndnɪs/ n Liebe f (**for** zu)

font /fɒnt/ n Taufstein m

food /fuːd/ n Essen nt; (for animals) Futter nt; (groceries) Lebensmittel pl

food: ~ **mixer** n Küchenmaschine f. ~ **poisoning** n Lebensmittelvergiftung f. ~ **processor** n Küchenmaschine f. ~ **value** n Nährwert m

fool¹ /fuːl/ n (Culin) Fruchtcreme f

fool² n Narr m; **you are a** ~ du bist dumm; **make a** ~ **of oneself**

sich lächerlich machen □ *vt* hereinlegen □ *vi* ~ **around** herumalbern

'**fool**|**hardy** *a* tollkühn. ~**ish** *a*, -**ly** *adv* dumm. ~**ishness** *n* Dummheit *f*. ~**proof** *a* narrensicher

foot /fʊt/ *n* (*pl* **feet**) Fuß *m*; (*measure*) Fuß *m* (30,48 cm); (*of bed*) Fußende *nt*; **on** ~ zu Fuß; **on one's feet** auf den Beinen; **put one's** ~ **in it** (*fam*) ins Fettnäpfchen treten

foot: ~**-and-'mouth disease** *n* Maul- und Klauenseuche *f*. ~**ball** *n* Fußball *m*. ~**baller** *n* Fußballspieler *m*. ~**ball pools** *npl* Fußballtoto *nt*. ~**brake** *n* Fußbremse *f*. ~**bridge** *n* Fußgängerbrücke *f*. ~**hills** *npl* Vorgebirge *nt*. ~**hold** *n* Halt *m*. ~**ing** *n* Halt *m*; (*fig*) Basis *f*. ~**lights** *npl* Rampenlicht *nt*. ~**man** *n* Lakai *m*. ~**note** *n* Fußnote *f*. ~**path** *n* Fußweg *m*. ~**print** *n* Fußabdruck *m*. ~**step** *n* Schritt *m*; **follow in s.o.'s** ~**steps** (*fig*) in jds Fußstapfen treten. ~**stool** *n* Fußbank *f*. ~**wear** *n* Schuhwerk *nt*

for /fə(r), *betont* fɔː(r)/ *prep* für (+ *acc*); ⟨*send, long*⟩ nach; ⟨*ask, fight*⟩ um; **what** ~? wozu? ~ **supper** zum Abendessen; ~ **nothing** umsonst; ~ **all that** trotz allem; ~ **this reason** aus diesem Grund; ~ **a month** einen Monat; **I have lived here** ~ **ten years** ich wohne seit zehn Jahren hier □ *conj* denn

forage /'fɒrɪdʒ/ *n* Futter *nt* □ *vi* ~ **for** suchen nach

forbade /fə'bæd/ *see* **forbid**

forbear|ance /fɔː'beərəns/ *n* Nachsicht *f*. ~**ing** *a* nachsichtig

forbid /fə'bɪd/ *vt* (*pt* **forbade**, *pp* **forbidden**) verbieten (s.o. jdm). ~**ding** *a* bedrohlich; (*stern*) streng

force /fɔːs/ *n* Kraft *f*; (*of blow*) Wucht *f*; (*violence*) Gewalt *f*; **in**

~ **gültig**; (*in large numbers*) in großer Zahl; **come into** ~ in Kraft treten; **the** ~**s** *pl* die Streitkräfte *pl* □ *vt* zwingen; (*break open*) aufbrechen; ~ **sth on s.o.** jdm etw aufdrängen

forced /fɔːst/ *a* gezwungen; ~ **landing** Notlandung *f*

force: ~'**feed** *vt* (*pt/pp* **-fed**) zwangsernähren. ~**ful** *a*, -**ly** *adv* energisch

forceps /'fɔːseps/ *n inv* Zange *f*

forcible /'fɔːsɪbl/ *a* gewaltsam. ~**y** *adv* mit Gewalt

ford /fɔːd/ *n* Furt *f* □ *vt* durchwaten; (*in vehicle*) durchfahren

fore /fɔː(r)/ *a* vordere(r,s) □ *n* **to the** ~ im Vordergrund

fore: ~**arm** *n* Unterarm *m*. ~**boding** /-'bəʊdɪŋ/ *n* Vorahnung *f*. ~**cast** *n* Voraussage *f*; (*for weather*) Vorhersage *f* □ *vt* (*pt/pp* ~**cast**) voraussagen, vorhersagen. ~**court** *n* Vorhof *m*. ~**fathers** *npl* Vorfahren *pl*. ~**finger** *n* Zeigefinger *m*. ~**front** *n* **be in the** ~**front** führend sein. ~**gone** *a* **be a** ~**gone conclusion** von vornherein feststehen. ~**ground** *n* Vordergrund *m*. ~**head** /'fɒrɪd/ *n* Stirn *f*. ~**hand** *n* Vorhand *f*

foreign /'fɒrən/ *a* ausländisch; (*country*) fremd; **he is** ~ **er** ist Ausländer. ~ **currency** *n* Devisen *pl*. ~**er** *n* Ausländer(in) *m(f)*. ~ **language** *n* Fremdsprache *f*

Foreign: ~ **Office** *n* ≈ Außenministerium *nt*. ~ '**Secretary** *n* ≈ Außenminister *m*

fore: ~**leg** *n* Vorderbein *nt*. ~**man** *n* Vorarbeiter *m*. ~**most** *a* führend □ *adv* **first** and ~**most** zuallererst. ~**name** *n* Vorname *m*

forensic /fə'rensɪk/ *a* ~ **medicine** Gerichtsmedizin *f*

forerunner *n* Vorläufer *m*

fore'see *vt* (*pt* **-saw**, *pp* **-seen**) voraussehen, vorhersehen. ~**able** /-əbl/ *a* **in the** ~**able future** in absehbarer Zeit

'**foresight** n Weitblick m

forest /'fɒrɪst/ n Wald m. **~er** n Förster m

fore'stall vt zuvorkommen (+ dat)

forestry /'fɒrɪstrɪ/ n Forstwirtschaft f

'**foretaste** n Vorgeschmack m

fore'tell vt (pt/pp -told) vorhersagen

forever /fə'revə(r)/ adv für immer

fore'warn vt vorher warnen

foreword /'fɔ:wɜ:d/ n Vorwort nt

forfeit /'fɔ:fɪt/ n (in game) Pfand nt □ vt verwirken

forgave /fə'geɪv/ see **forgive**

forge¹ /fɔ:dʒ/ n ~ **ahead** (fig) Fortschritte machen

forge² n Schmiede f □ vt schmieden; (counterfeit) fälschen. **~r** n Fälscher m. **~ry** n Fälschung f

forget /fə'get/ vt/i (pt -got, pp -gotten) vergessen; verlernen (language, skill). **~ful** a vergesslich. **~fulness** n Vergesslichkeit f. **~-me-not** n Vergissmeinnicht nt

forgive /fə'gɪv/ vt (pt -gave, pp -given) ~ **s.o. for sth** jdm etw vergeben od verzeihen. **~ness** n Vergebung f, Verzeihung f

forgo /fɔ:'gəʊ/ vt (pt -went, pp -gone) verzichten auf (+ acc)

forgot(ten) /fə'gɒt(n)/ see **forget**

fork /fɔ:k/ n Gabel f; (in road) Gabelung f □ vi (road): sich gabeln; ~ **right** rechts abzweigen. ~ **out** vt (fam) blechen

fork-lift 'truck n Gabelstapler m

forlorn /fə'lɔ:n/ a verlassen; (hope) schwach

form /fɔ:m/ n Form f; (document) Formular nt; (bench) Bank f; (Sch) Klasse f □ vt formen (into zu); (create) bilden □ vi sich bilden; (idea:) Gestalt annehmen

formal /'fɔ:ml/ a, **-ly** adv formell, förmlich. **~ity** /-'mælətɪ/ n

Förmlichkeit f; (requirement) Formalität f

format /'fɔ:mæt/ n Format nt

formation /fɔ:'meɪʃn/ n Formation f

formative /'fɔ:mətɪv/ a ~ **years** Entwicklungsjahre pl

former /'fɔ:mə(r)/ a ehemalig; **the** ~ der/die/das Erstere. **~ly** adv früher

formidable /'fɔmɪdəbl/ a gewaltig

formula /'fɔ:mjʊlə/ n (pl **-ae** /-li:/ or **-s**) Formel f

formulate /'fɔ:mjʊleɪt/ vt formulieren

forsake /fə'seɪk/ vt (pt **-sook** /-sʊk/, pp **-saken**) verlassen

fort /fɔ:t/ n (Mil) Fort nt

forte /'fɔ:teɪ/ n Stärke f

forth /fɔ:θ/ adv **back and** ~ hin und her; **and so** ~ und so weiter

forth'coming a bevorstehend; (fam: communicative) mitteilsam. **~right** a direkt. **~'with** adv umgehend

fortieth /'fɔ:tɪɪθ/ a vierzigste(r,s)

fortification /fɔ:tɪfɪ'keɪʃn/ n Befestigung f

fortify /'fɔ:tɪfaɪ/ vt (pt/pp **-ied**) befestigen; (fig) stärken

fortitude /'fɔ:tɪtjuːd/ n Standhaftigkeit f

fortnight /'fɔ:t-/ n vierzehn Tage pl. **~ly** a vierzehntäglich □ adv alle vierzehn Tage

fortress /'fɔ:trɪs/ n Festung f

fortuitous /fɔ:'tju:ɪtəs/ a, **-ly** adv zufällig

fortunate /'fɔ:tʃʊnət/ a glücklich; **be** ~ Glück haben. **~ly** adv glücklicherweise

fortune /'fɔ:tʃuːn/ n Glück nt; (money) Vermögen nt. **~-teller** n Wahrsagerin f

forty /'fɔ:tɪ/ a vierzig; **have** ~ **winks** (fam) ein Nickerchen machen □ n Vierzig f

forum /'fɔ:rəm/ n Forum nt

forward /ˈfɔːwəd/ adv vorwärts; (to the front) nach vorn □ a Vorwärts-; (presumptuous) anmaßend □ n (Sport) Stürmer m □ vt nachsenden (letter). **~s** adv vorwärts

fossil /ˈfɒsl/ n Fossil nt. **~ized** a versteinert

foster /ˈfɒstə(r)/ vt fördern; in Pflege nehmen ⟨child⟩. **~child** n Pflegekind nt. **~mother** n Pflegemutter f

fought /fɔːt/ see **fight**

foul /faʊl/ a (-er, -est) widerlich; ⟨language⟩ unflätig; **~ play** (Jur) Mord m □ n (Sport) Foul nt □ vt verschmutzen; (obstruct) blockieren; (Sport) foulen. **~smelling** a übel riechend

found[1] /faʊnd/ see **find**

found[2] vt gründen

foundation /faʊnˈdeɪʃn/ n (basis) Grundlage f; ⟨charitable⟩ Stiftung f; **~s** pl Fundament nt. **~stone** n Grundstein m

founder[1] /ˈfaʊndə(r)/ n Gründer(in) m(f)

founder[2] vi ⟨ship:⟩ sinken; (fig) scheitern

foundry /ˈfaʊndrɪ/ n Gießerei f

fountain /ˈfaʊntɪn/ n Brunnen m. **~pen** n Füllfederhalter m

four /fɔː(r)/ a vier □ n Vier f

four: **~poster** n Himmelbett nt. **~some** /ˈfɔːsəm/ n **in a ~some** zu viert. **~teen** a vierzehn □ n Vierzehn f. **~teenth** a vierzehnte(r,s)

fourth /fɔːθ/ a vierte(r,s)

fowl /faʊl/ n Geflügel nt

fox /fɒks/ n Fuchs m □ vt (puzzle) verblüffen

foyer /ˈfɔɪeɪ/ n Foyer nt; (in hotel) Empfangshalle f

fraction /ˈfrækʃn/ n Bruchteil m; (Math) Bruch m

fracture /ˈfræktʃə(r)/ n Bruch m □ vt/i brechen

fragile /ˈfrædʒaɪl/ a zerbrechlich

fragment /ˈfrægmənt/ n Bruchstück nt, Fragment nt. **~ary** a bruchstückhaft

fragran|ce /ˈfreɪgrəns/ n Duft m. **~t** a duftend

frail /freɪl/ a (-er, -est) gebrechlich

frame /freɪm/ n Rahmen m; (of spectacles) Gestell nt; (Anat) Körperbau m; **~ of mind** Gemütsverfassung f □ vt einrahmen; (fig) formulieren; (sl) ein Verbrechen anhängen (+ dat). **~work** n Gerüst nt; (fig) Gerippe nt

franc /fræŋk/ n (French, Belgian) Franc m; (Swiss) Franken m

France /frɑːns/ n Frankreich nt

franchise /ˈfræntʃaɪz/ n (Pol) Wahlrecht nt; (Comm) Franchise nt

frank[1] /fræŋk/ vt frankieren

frank[2] a, **-ly** adv offen

frankfurter /ˈfræŋkfɜːtə(r)/ n Frankfurter f

frantic /ˈfræntɪk/ a, **-ally** adv verzweifelt; **be ~** außer sich (dat) sein (with vor)

fraternal /frəˈtɜːnl/ a brüderlich

fraud /frɔːd/ n Betrug m; (person) Betrüger(in) m(f). **~ulent** /-julənt/ a betrügerisch

fraught /frɔːt/ a **~ with danger** gefahrvoll

fray[1] /freɪ/ n Kampf m

fray[2] vt/i ausfransen

freak /friːk/ n Missbildung f; (person) Missgeburt f; (phenomenon) Ausnahmeerscheinung f □ a anormal. **~ish** a anormal

freckle /ˈfrekl/ n Sommersprosse f. **~d** a sommersprossig

free /friː/ a (a **freer**, **freest**) frei; ⟨ticket, copy, time⟩ Frei-; (lavish) freigebig; **~ [of charge]** kostenlos; **set ~** freilassen; (rescue) befreien; **you are ~ to ...** es steht Ihnen frei, zu ... □ vt (pt/pp **freed**) freilassen; (rescue) befreien; (disentangle) freibekommen

free: ~**dom** n Freiheit f. ~**hand** adv aus freier Hand. ~**hold** n [freier] Grundbesitz m. ~**kick** n Freistoß m. ~**lance** a & adv freiberuflich. ~**ly** adv frei; (voluntarily) freiwillig; (generously) großzügig. **F~mason** n Freimaurer m. **F~masonry** n Freimaurerei f. ~**range** a ~**range eggs** Landeier pl. ~ **'sample** n Gratisprobe f. ~**style** n Freistil m. ~**way** n (Amer) Autobahn f. ~**'wheel** vi im Freilauf fahren

freeze /fri:z/ vt (pt **froze**, pp **frozen**) einfrieren; stoppen (wages) □ vi gefrieren; it's ~**ing** es friert

freezer /'fri:zə(r)/ n Gefriertruhe f; (upright) Gefrierschrank m. ~**ing** a eiskalt □ n below ~**ing** unter Null

freight /freɪt/ n Fracht f. ~**er** n Frachter m. ~ **train** n (Amer) Güterzug m

French /frentʃ/ a französisch □ n (Lang) Französisch nt; **the** ~ pl die Franzosen

French: ~ **'beans** npl grüne Bohnen pl. ~ **'bread** n Stangenbrot m. ~**'fries** npl Pommes frites pl. ~**man** n Franzose m. ~**'window** n Terrassentür f. ~**woman** n Französin f

frenzied /'frenzɪd/ a rasend

frenzy /'frenzɪ/ n Raserei f

frequency /'fri:kwənsɪ/ n Häufigkeit f; (Phys) Frequenz f

frequent[1] /'fri:kwənt/ a, ~**ly** adv häufig

frequent[2] /frɪ'kwent/ vt regelmäßig besuchen

fresco /'freskəʊ/ n Fresko nt

fresh /freʃ/ a (-er, -est), ~**ly** adv frisch; (new) neu; (Amer: cheeky) frech

freshen /'freʃn/ vi (wind:) auffrischen. ~ **up** vi auffrischen □ vi sich frisch machen

freshness /'freʃnɪs/ n Frische f

'freshwater a Süßwasser-

fret /fret/ vi (pt/pp **fretted**) sich grämen. ~**ful** a weinerlich

'fretsaw n Laubsäge f

friar /'fraɪə(r)/ n Mönch m

friction /'frɪkʃn/ n Reibung f; (fig) Reibereien pl

Friday /'fraɪdeɪ/ n Freitag m

fridge /frɪdʒ/ n Kühlschrank m

fried /fraɪd/ see **fry**[2] □ a gebraten; ~ **egg** Spiegelei nt

friend /frend/ n Freund(in) m(f). ~**liness** n Freundlichkeit f. ~**ly** a (-ier, -iest) freundlich; ~**ly with** befreundet mit. ~**ship** n Freundschaft f

frieze /fri:z/ n Fries m

fright /fraɪt/ n Schreck m

frighten /'fraɪtn/ vt Angst machen (+ dat); (startle) erschrecken; **be** ~**ed** Angst haben (**of** or + dat). ~**ing** a Angst erregend

frightful /'fraɪtfl/ a, ~**ly** adv schrecklich

frigid /'frɪdʒɪd/ a frostig; (Psych) frigide. ~**ity** /-'dʒɪdɪtɪ/ n Frostigkeit f; Frigidität f

frill /frɪl/ n Rüsche f; (paper) Manschette f. ~**y** a rüschenbesetzt

fringe /frɪndʒ/ n Fransen pl; (of hair) Pony m; (fig: edge) Rand m. ~ **benefits** npl zusätzliche Leistungen pl

frisk /frɪsk/ vi herumspringen □ vt (search) durchsuchen, (fam) filzen

frisky /'frɪskɪ/ a (-ier, -iest) lebhaft

fritter /'frɪtə(r)/ vt ~ **[away]** verplempern (fam)

frivolity /frɪ'vɒlɪtɪ/ n Frivolität f. ~**ous** /'frɪvələs/ a, ~**ly** adv frivol, leichtfertig

frizzy /'frɪzɪ/ a kraus

fro /frəʊ/ see **to**

frock /frɒk/ n Kleid nt

frog /frɒg/ n Frosch m. ~**man** n Froschmann m. ~**spawn** n Froschlaich m

frolic /'frɒlɪk/ vi (pt/pp **frolick-ed**) herumtollen

from /frɒm/ prep von (+ dat); (out of) aus (+ dat); (according to) nach (+ dat); ~ **Monday** ab Montag; ~ **that day** seit dem Tag

front /frʌnt/ n Vorderseite f; (of building) Fassade f; (of garment) Vorderteil nt; (sea-) Strandpromenade f; (Mil, Pol, Meteorol) Front f; **in** ~ **of** vor; **in** or **at the** ~ vorne; **to the** ~ nach vorne □ a vordere(r, s); (page, row) erste(r,s); (tooth, wheel) Vorder-

frontal /'frʌntl/ a Frontal-

front: ~ **'door** n Haustür f. ~ **'garden** n Vorgarten m

frontier /frʌntɪə(r)/ n Grenze f

front-wheel 'drive n Vorderradantrieb m

frost /frɒst/ n Frost m; (hoar-) Raureif m; **ten degrees of** ~ zehn Grad Kälte. ~**bite** n Erfrierung f. ~**bitten** a erfroren

frost|ed /'frɒstɪd/ a ~**ed glass** Mattglas nt. ~**ing** n (Amer Culin) Zuckerguss m. ~**y** a, **-ily** adv frostig

froth /frɒθ/ n Schaum m □ vi schäumen. ~**y** a schaumig

frown /fraʊn/ n Stirnrunzeln nt □ vi die Stirn runzeln; ~ **on** missbilligen

froze /frəʊz/ see **freeze**

frozen /'frəʊzn/ see **freeze** □ a gefroren; (Culin) tiefgekühlt; **I'm** ~ (fam) mir ist eiskalt. ~ **food** n Tiefkühlkost f

frugal /'fru:gl/ a, **-ly** adv sparsam; (meal) frugal

fruit /fru:t/ n Frucht f; (collectively) Obst nt. ~ **cake** n englischer [Tee]kuchen m

fruit|erer /'fru:tərə(r)/ n Obsthändler m. ~**ful** a fruchtbar

fruition /fru:'ɪʃn/ n **come to** ~ sich verwirklichen

fruit: ~ **juice** n Obstsaft m. ~**less** a, **-ly** adv fruchtlos. ~ **machine** n Spielautomat m. ~ **salad** n Obstsalat m

fruity /'fru:tɪ/ a fruchtig

frumpy /'frʌmpɪ/ a unmodisch

frustrat|e /frʌ'streɪt/ vt vereiteln; (psych) frustrieren. ~**ing** a frustrierend. ~**ion** /-eɪʃn/ n Frustration f

fry[1] /fraɪ/ n inv **small** ~ (fig) kleine Fische pl

fry[2] /fraɪ/ vt/i (pt/pp **fried**) (in der Pfanne) braten. ~**ing-pan** n Bratpfanne f

fuck /fʌk/ vt/i (vulg) ficken. ~**ing** a (vulg) Scheiß-

fuddy-duddy /'fʌdɪdʌdɪ/ n (fam) verknöcherter Kerl m

fudge /fʌdʒ/ n weiche Karamellen pl

fuel /'fju:əl/ n Brennstoff m; (for car) Kraftstoff m; (for aircraft) Treibstoff m

fugitive /'fju:dʒətɪv/ n Flüchtling m

fugue /fju:g/ n (Mus) Fuge f

fulfil /fʊl'fɪl/ vt (pt/pp **-filled**) erfüllen. ~**ment** n Erfüllung f

full /fʊl/ a & adv (-er, -est) voll; (detailed) ausführlich; (skirt) weit; ~ **of** voll von (+ dat), voller (+ gen); **at** ~ **speed** in voller Fahrt □ n **in** ~ vollständig

full: ~ **'moon** n Vollmond m. ~**-scale** a (model) in Originalgröße; (rescue, alert) groß angelegt. ~ **'stop** n Punkt m. ~**-time** a ganztägig □ adv ganztags

fully /'fʊlɪ/ adv völlig; (in detail) ausführlich

fulsome /'fʊlsəm/ a übertrieben

fumble /'fʌmbl/ vi herumfummeln (with an + dat)

fume /fju:m/ vi vor Wut schäumen

fumes /fju:mz/ npl Dämpfe pl; (from car) Abgase pl

fumigate /'fju:mɪgeɪt/ vt ausräuchern

fun /fʌn/ n Spaß m; **for** ~ aus od zum Spaß; **make** ~ **of** sich lustig machen über (+ acc); **have** ~! viel Spaß!

function /'fʌŋkʃn/ n Funktion f; (event) Veranstaltung f □ vi funktionieren; (serve) dienen als (as als). ~al a zweckmäßig

fund /fʌnd/ n Fonds m; (fig) Vorrat m; ~s pl Geldmittel pl □ vt finanzieren

fundamental /fʌndə'mentl/ a grundlegend; (essential) wesentlich

funeral /'fju:nərl/ n Beerdigung f; (cremation) Feuerbestattung f. **funeral:** ~ directors pl, (Amer) ~ home n Bestattungsinstitut nt. ~ march n Trauermarsch m. ~ parlour n (Amer) Bestattungsinstitut nt. ~ service n Trauergottesdienst m

'funfair n Jahrmarkt m, Kirmes f

fungus /'fʌŋgəs/ n (pl -gi -gaɪ/) Pilz m

funicular /fju:'nɪkjʊlə(r)/ n Seilbahn f

funnel /'fʌnl/ n Trichter m; (on ship, train) Schornstein m

funnily /'fʌnɪlɪ/ adv komisch; ~ enough komischerweise

funny /'fʌnɪ/ a (-ier, -iest) komisch. ~**bone** n (fam) Musikantenknochen m

fur /fɜ:(r)/ n Fell nt; (for clothing) Pelz m; (in kettle) Kesselstein m. ~ 'coat n Pelzmantel m

furious /'fjʊərɪəs/ a, -ly adv wütend (with auf + acc)

furnace /'fɜ:nɪs/ n (Techn) Ofen m

furnish /'fɜ:nɪʃ/ vt einrichten; (supply) liefern. ~ed a ~ed room möbliertes Zimmer nt. ~ings npl Einrichtungsgegenstände pl

furniture /'fɜ:nɪtʃə(r)/ n Möbel pl

furred /fɜ:d/ a (tongue) belegt

furrow /'fʌrəʊ/ n Furche f

furry /'fɜ:rɪ/ a (animal) Pelz-; (toy) Plüsch-

further /'fɜ:ðə(r)/ a weitere(r,s); at the ~ end am anderen Ende;

until ~ notice bis auf weiteres □ adv weiter; ~ off weiter entfernt □ vt fördern

further: ~ edu'cation n Weiterbildung f. ~'more adv überdies

furthest /'fɜ:ðɪst/ a am weitesten entfernt □ adv am weitesten

furtive /'fɜ:tɪv/ a, -ly adv verstohlen

fury /'fjʊərɪ/ n Wut f

fuse[1] /fju:z/ n (of bomb) Zünder m; (cord) Zündschnur f

fuse[2] n (Electr) Sicherung f □ vt/i verschmelzen; **the lights have** ~**d** die Sicherung [für das Licht] ist durchgebrannt. ~**box** n Sicherungskasten m

fuselage /'fju:zəla:ʒ/ n (Aviat) Rumpf m

fusion /'fju:ʒn/ n Verschmelzung f, Fusion f

fuss /fʌs/ n Getue nt; **make a** ~ of verwöhnen; (caress) liebkosen □ vi Umstände machen

fussy /'fʌsɪ/ a (-ier, -iest) wählerisch; (particular) penibel

fusty /'fʌstɪ/ a moderig

futile /'fju:taɪl/ a zwecklos. ~**ity** /-'tɪlətɪ/ n Zwecklosigkeit f

future /'fju:tʃə(r)/ a zukünftig □ n Zukunft f; (Gram) [erstes] Futur nt; ~ **perfect** zweites Futur nt; **in** ~ in Zukunft

futuristic /fju:tʃə'rɪstɪk/ a futuristisch

fuzz /fʌz/ n **the** ~ (sl) die Bullen pl

fuzzy /'fʌzɪ/ a (-ier, -iest) (hair) kraus; (blurred) verschwommen

G

gab /gæb/ n (fam) **have the gift of the** ~ gut reden können

gabble /'gæbl/ vi schnell reden

gable /'geɪbl/ n Giebel m

gad /gæd/ vi (pt/pp gadded) ~ **about** dauernd ausgehen

gadget /'gædʒɪt/ n [kleines] Gerät nt

Gaelic /'geɪlɪk/ n Gälisch nt

gaffe /gæf/ n Fauxpas m

gag /gæg/ n Knebel m; (joke) Witz m; (Theat) Gag m □ vt (pt/pp gagged) knebeln

gaiety /'geɪətɪ/ n Fröhlichkeit f

gaily /'geɪlɪ/ adv fröhlich

gain /geɪn/ n Gewinn m; (increase) Zunahme f □ vt gewinnen; (obtain) erlangen; ~ **weight** zunehmen □ vi (clock:) vorgehen. ~**ful** a ~**ful employment** Erwerbstätigkeit f

gait /geɪt/ n Gang m

gala /'gɑːlə/ n Fest nt; **swimming** ~ Schwimmfest n □ attrib Gala-

galaxy /'gæləksɪ/ n Galaxie f; **the G~** die Milchstraße

gale /geɪl/ n Sturm m

gall /gɔːl/ n Galle f; (impudence) Frechheit f

gallant /'gælənt/ a, -**ly** adv tapfer; (chivalrous) galant. ~**ry** n Tapferkeit f

'gall-bladder n Gallenblase f

gallery /'gælərɪ/ n Galerie f

galley /'gælɪ/ n (ship's kitchen) Kombüse f; ~ **[proof]** [Druck]-fahne f

gallivant /'gælɪvænt/ vi (fam) ausgehen

gallon /'gælən/ n Gallone f (= 4,5 l; Amer = 3,785 l)

gallop /'gæləp/ n Galopp m □ vi galoppieren

gallows /'gæləʊz/ n Galgen m

'gallstone n Gallenstein m

galore /gə'lɔː(r)/ adv in Hülle und Fülle

galvanize /'gælvənaɪz/ vt galvanisieren

gambit /'gæmbɪt/ n Eröffnungs-manöver nt

gamble /'gæmbl/ n (risk) Risiko nt □ vi [um Geld] spielen; ~ **on** (rely) sich verlassen auf (+ acc). ~**r** n Spieler(in) m(f)

game /geɪm/ n Spiel nt; (animals, birds) Wild nt; ~**s** (Sch) Sport m □ a (brave) tapfer; (willing) bereit (for zu). ~**keeper** n Wildhüter m

gammon /'gæmən/ n [geräu-cherter] Schinken m

gamut /'gæmət/ n Skala f

gander /'gændə(r)/ n Gänserich m

gang /gæŋ/ n Bande f; (of work-men) Kolonne f □ vi ~ **up** sich zusammenrotten (**on** gegen)

gangling /'gæŋglɪŋ/ a schlaksig

gangrene /'gæŋgriːn/ n Wund-brand m

gangster /'gæŋstə(r)/ n Gangster m

gangway /'gæŋweɪ/ n Gang m; (Naut, Aviat) Gangway f

gaol /dʒeɪl/ n Gefängnis nt □ vt ins Gefängnis sperren. ~**er** n Ge-fängniswärter m

gap /gæp/ n Lücke f; (interval) Pause f; (difference) Unterschied m

gape /geɪp/ vi gaffen; ~ **at** an-starren. ~**ing** a klaffend

garage /'gærɑːʒ/ n Garage f; (for repairs) Werkstatt f; (for petrol) Tankstelle f

garb /gɑːb/ n Kleidung f

garbage /'gɑːbɪdʒ/ n Müll m. ~ **can** n (Amer) Mülleimer m

garbled /'gɑːbld/ a verworren

garden /'gɑːdn/ n Garten m; **[public]** ~**s** pl [öffentliche] An-lagen pl □ vi im Garten arbeiten. ~**er** n Gärtner(in) m(f). ~**ing** n Gartenarbeit f

gargle /'gɑːgl/ n (liquid) Gurgel-wasser nt □ vi gurgeln

gargoyle /'gɑːgɔɪl/ n Wasser-speier m

garish /'geərɪʃ/ a grell

garland /'gɑːlənd/ n Girlande f

garlic /'gɑːlɪk/ n Knoblauch m

garment /'gɑːmənt/ n Kleidungsstück nt

garnet /'gɑːnɪt/ n Granat m

garnish /'gɑːnɪʃ/ n Garnierung f □ vt garnieren

garret /'gærɪt/ n Dachstube f

garrison /'gærɪsn/ n Garnison f

garrulous /'gærʊləs/ a geschwätzig

garter /'gɑːtə(r)/ n Strumpfband nt; (Amer: suspender) Strumpfhalter m

gas /gæs/ n Gas nt; (Amer fam: petrol) Benzin nt □ v (pt/pp gassed) □ vt vergasen □ vi (fam) schwatzen. ~ **cooker** n Gasherd m. ~ '**fire** n Gasofen m

gash /gæʃ/ n Schnitt m; (wound) klaffende Wunde f □ vt ~ **one's arm** sich (dat) den Arm aufschlitzen

gasket /'gæskɪt/ n (Techn) Dichtung f

gas: ~ **mask** n Gasmaske f. ~ **meter** n Gaszähler m

gasoline /'gæsəliːn/ n (Amer) Benzin nt

gasp /gɑːsp/ vi keuchen; (in surprise) hörbar die Luft einziehen f

'**gas station** n (Amer) Tankstelle f

gastric /'gæstrɪk/ a Magen-. ~ '**flu** n Darmgrippe f. ~ '**ulcer** n Magengeschwür nt

gastronomy /gæ'strɒnəmɪ/ n Gastronomie f

gate /geɪt/ n Tor nt; (to field) Gatter nt; (barrier) Schranke f; (at airport) Flugsteig m

gâteau /'gætəʊ/ n Torte f

gate: ~**crasher** n ungeladener Gast m. ~**way** n Tor nt

gather /'gæðə(r)/ vt sammeln; (pick) pflücken; (conclude) folgern (from aus); (Sewing) kräuseln; ~ **speed** schneller werden □ vi sich versammeln; (storm:) sich zusammenziehen. ~ **in** family ~**ing** Familientreffen nt

gaudy /'gɔːdɪ/ a (-ier, -iest) knallig

gauge /geɪdʒ/ n Stärke f; (Rail) Spurweite f; (device) Messinstrument nt □ vt messen; (estimate) schätzen

gaunt /gɔːnt/ a hager

gauntlet /'gɔːntlɪt/ n run the ~ Spießruten laufen

gauze /gɔːz/ n Gaze f

gave /geɪv/ see give

gawky /'gɔːkɪ/ a (-ier, -iest) schlaksig

gawp /gɔːp/ vi (fam) glotzen; ~ at anglotzen

gay /geɪ/ a (-er, -est) fröhlich; (fam) homosexuell, (fam) schwul

gaze /geɪz/ n [langer] Blick m □ vi sehen; ~ at ansehen

gazelle /gə'zel/ n Gazelle f

GB abbr of **Great Britain**

gear /gɪə(r)/ n Ausrüstung f; (Techn) Getriebe nt; (Auto) Gang m; in ~ mit eingelegtem Gang; **change** ~ schalten □ vt anpassen (to dat)

gear: ~**box** n (Auto) Getriebe nt. ~**lever** n, (Amer) ~**shift** n Schalthebel m

geese /giːs/ see **goose**

geezer /'giːzə(r)/ n (sl) Typ m

gel /dʒel/ n Gel nt

gelatine /'dʒelətɪn/ n Gelatine f

gelignite /'dʒelɪgnaɪt/ n Gelatinedynamit nt

gem /dʒem/ n Juwel nt

Gemini /'dʒemɪnaɪ/ n (Astr) Zwillinge pl

gender /'dʒendə(r)/ n (Gram) Geschlecht nt

gene /dʒiːn/ n Gen nt

genealogy /dʒiːnɪ'ælədʒɪ/ n Genealogie f

general /'dʒenrəl/ a allgemein □ n General m; in ~ im Allgemeinen. ~ e'**lection** n allgemeine Wahlen pl

generaliz|ation /dʒenrəlaɪ'zeɪʃn/ n Verallgemeinerung f. ~**e** /'dʒenrəlaɪz/ vi verallgemeinern

generally /'dʒenrəlɪ/ adv im Allgemeinen

general prac'titioner n praktischer Arzt m

generate /'dʒenəreɪt/ vt erzeugen

generation /dʒenə'reɪʃn/ n Generation f

generator /'dʒenəreɪtə(r)/ n Generator m

generic /dʒɪ'nerɪk/ a ~ **term** Oberbegriff m

generosity /dʒenə'rɒsɪtɪ/ n Großzügigkeit f

generous /'dʒenərəs/ a, -ly adv großzügig

genetic /dʒɪ'netɪk/ a genetisch. ~ **engineering** n Gentechnologie f. ~s n Genetik f

Geneva /dʒɪ'niːvə/ n Genf nt

genial /'dʒiːnɪəl/ a, -ly adv freundlich

genitals /'dʒenɪtlz/ pl [äußere] Geschlechtsteile pl

genitive /'dʒenɪtɪv/ a & n ~ **[case]** Genitiv m

genius /'dʒiːnɪəs/ n (pl -uses) Genie nt; (quality) Genialität f

genocide /'dʒenəsaɪd/ n Völkermord m

genre /'ʒɑ̃rə/ n Gattung f, Genre nt

gent /dʒent/ n (fam) Herr m; the ~s sg die Herrentoilette f

genteel /dʒen'tiːl/ a vornehm

gentle /'dʒentl/ a (-r, -st) sanft

gentleman /'dʒentlmən/ n Herr m; (well-mannered) Gentleman m

gentleness /'dʒentlnɪs/ n Sanftheit f. ~ly adv sanft

genuine /'dʒenjuɪn/ a echt; (sincere) aufrichtig. ~ly adv (honestly) ehrlich

genus /'dʒiːnəs/ n (Biol) Gattung f

geographical /dʒɪə'græfɪkl/ a, -ly adv geographisch. ~y /dʒɪ'ɒgrəfɪ/ n Geographie f, Erdkunde f

geological /dʒɪə'lɒdʒɪkl/ a, -ly adv geologisch

geologist /dʒɪ'ɒlədʒɪst/ n Geologe m/-gin f. ~y n Geologie f

geometric(al) /dʒɪə'metrɪk(l)/ a geometrisch. ~y /dʒɪ'ɒmətrɪ/ n Geometrie f

geranium /dʒə'reɪnɪəm/ n Geranie f

geriatric /dʒerɪ'ætrɪk/ a geriatrisch □ n geriatrischer Patient m. ~s n Geriatrie f

germ /dʒɜːm/ n Keim m; ~s pl (fam) Bazillen pl

German /'dʒɜːmən/ a deutsch □ n (person) Deutsche(r) m/f; (Lang) Deutsch nt; **in** ~ auf Deutsch; **into** ~ ins Deutsche

Germanic /dʒə'mænɪk/ a germanisch

German: ~ **measles** n Röteln pl. ~ **shepherd [dog]** n [deutscher] Schäferhund m

Germany /'dʒɜːmənɪ/ n Deutschland nt

germinate /'dʒɜːmɪneɪt/ vi keimen

gesticulate /dʒe'stɪkjʊleɪt/ vi gestikulieren

gesture /'dʒestʃə(r)/ n Geste f

get /get/ v (pt/pp got, pp Amer also gotten, pres p getting) □ vt bekommen; (fam) kriegen; (procure) besorgen; (buy) kaufen; (fetch) holen; (take) bringen; (on telephone) erreichen; (fam: understand) kapieren; machen ⟨meal⟩; ~ **s.o. to do sth** jdn dazu bringen, etw zu tun □ vi (become) werden; ~ **to** kommen zu/nach ⟨town⟩; (reach) erreichen; ~ **dressed** sich anziehen; ~ **married** heiraten. ~ **at** vt herankommen an (+ acc); **what are you ~ting at?** worauf willst du hinaus? ~ **away** vi (leave) wegkommen; (escape) entkommen. ~ **back** vi zurückkommen □ vt (recover) zurückbekommen; **one's own back** sich revanchieren. ~ **by** vi vorbeikommen; (manage) sein Auskommen haben. ~ **down** vi heruntersteigen; ~ **down to** sich [heran]machen an

(+ *acc*) □ *vt* (*depress*) deprimieren. ~ **in** *vi* einsteigen □ *vt* (*fetch*) hereinholen. ~ **off** *vi* (*dismount*) absteigen; (*from bus*) aussteigen; (*leave*) wegkommen; (*Jur*) freigesprochen werden □ *vt* (*remove*) abbekommen. ~ **on** *vi* (*mount*) aufsteigen; (*to bus*) einsteigen; (*be on good terms*) gut auskommen (**with** mit); (*make progress*) Fortschritte machen; **how are you ~ting on?** wie geht's? ~ **out** *vi* herauskommen; (*of car*) aussteigen; ~ **out of** (*avoid doing*) sich drücken um □ *vt* herausholen; (*cork, stain*). ~ **over** *vi* hinübersteigen □ *vt* (*fig*) hinwegkommen über (+ *acc*). ~ **round** *vi* herumkommen; **I never ~ round to it** ich komme nie dazu □ *vt* herumkriegen; (*avoid*) umgehen. ~ **through** *vi* durchkommen. ~ **up** *vi* aufstehen

get: ~**away** *n* Flucht *f*. ~**up** *n* Aufmachung *f*

geyser /'giːzə(r)/ *n* Durchlauferhitzer *m*; (*Geol*) Geysir *m*

ghastly /'gɑːstlɪ/ *a* (**-ier**, **-iest**) grässlich; (*pale*) blass

gherkin /'gɜːkɪn/ *n* Essiggurke *f*

ghetto /'getəu/ *n* Getto *nt*

ghost /gəust/ *n* Geist *m*, Gespenst *nt*. ~**ly** *a* geisterhaft

ghoulish /'guːlɪʃ/ *a* makaber

giant /'dʒaɪənt/ *n* Riese *m* □ *a* riesig

gibberish /'dʒɪbərɪʃ/ *n* Kauderwelsch *nt*

gibe /dʒaɪb/ *n* spöttische Bemerkung *f* □ *vi* spotten (**at** über + *acc*)

giblets /'dʒɪblɪts/ *npl* Geflügelklein *nt*

giddiness /'gɪdɪnɪs/ *n* Schwindel *m*

giddy /'gɪdɪ/ *a* (**-ier**, **-iest**) schwindlig; **I feel ~** mir ist schwindlig

gift /gɪft/ *n* Geschenk *nt*; (*to charity*) Gabe *f*; (*talent*) Begabung *f*. ~**ed** /-ɪd/ *a* begabt. ~**wrap** *vt* als Geschenk einpacken

gig /gɪg/ *n* (*fam*, *Mus*) Gig *m*

gigantic /dʒaɪˈgæntɪk/ *a* riesig, riesengroß

giggle /'gɪgl/ *n* Kichern *nt* □ *vi* kichern

gild /gɪld/ *vt* vergolden

gills /gɪlz/ *npl* Kiemen *pl*

gilt /gɪlt/ *a* vergoldet □ *n* Vergoldung *f*. ~**edged** /-ɪd/ *a* (*Comm*) mündelsicher

gimmick /'gɪmɪk/ *n* Trick *m*

gin /dʒɪn/ *n* Gin *m*

ginger /'dʒɪndʒə(r)/ *a* rotblond; (*cat*) rot □ *n* Ingwer *m*. ~**bread** *n* Pfefferkuchen *m*

gingerly /'dʒɪndʒəlɪ/ *adv* vorsichtig

gipsy /'dʒɪpsɪ/ *n* = **gypsy**

giraffe /dʒɪ'rɑːf/ *n* Giraffe *f*

girder /'gɜːdə(r)/ *n* (*Techn*) Träger *m*

girdle /'gɜːdl/ *n* Bindegürtel *m*; (*corset*) Hüfthalter *m*

girl /gɜːl/ *n* Mädchen *nt*; (*young woman*) junge Frau *f*. ~**friend** *n* Freundin *f*. ~**ish** *a*, **-ly** *adv* mädchenhaft

giro /'dʒaɪərəu/ *n* Giro *nt*; (*cheque*) Postscheck *m*

girth /gɜːθ/ *n* Umfang *m*; (*for horse*) Bauchgurt *m*

gist /dʒɪst/ *n* **the ~** das Wesentliche

give /gɪv/ *n* Elastizität *f* □ *v* (*pt* **gave**, *pp* **given**) □ *vt* geben/(*as present*) schenken (**to** *dat*); (*donate*) spenden; (*lecture*) halten; (*one's name*) angeben □ *vi* geben; (*yield*) nachgeben. ~ **away** *vt* verschenken; (*betray*) verraten; (*distribute*) verteilen; ~ **away the bride** ≈ Brautführer sein. ~ **back** *vt* zurückgeben. ~ **in** *vi* einreichen □ *vi* (*yield*) nachgeben. ~ **off** *vt* abgeben. ~ **up** *vt*/*i* aufgeben; ~ **oneself up** sich stellen.

~ way vi nachgeben; (Auto) die Vorfahrt beachten

given /'gɪvn/ see **give** □ a **~ name** Vorname m

glacier /'glæsɪə(r)/ n Gletscher m

glad /glæd/ a froh (**of** über + acc). **~ den** /'glædn/ vt erfreuen

glade /gleɪd/ n Lichtung f

gladly /'glædlɪ/ adv gern(e)

glamorous /'glæmərəs/ a glanzvoll; (film star) glamourös

glamour /'glæmə(r)/ n [betörender] Glanz m

glance /glɑːns/ n [flüchtiger] Blick m □ vi **~ at** einen Blick werfen auf (+ acc). **~ up** vi aufblicken

gland /glænd/ n Drüse f

glandular /'glændjʊlə(r)/ a Drüsen-

glare /gleə(r)/ n grelles Licht nt; (look) ärgerlicher Blick m □ vi **~ at** böse ansehen

glaring /'gleərɪŋ/ a grell; (mistake) krass

glass /glɑːs/ n Glas nt; (mirror) Spiegel m; **~es** pl (spectacles) Brille f. **~y** a glasig

glaze /gleɪz/ n Glasur f □ vt verglasen; (Culin, Pottery) glasieren

glazier /'gleɪzɪə(r)/ n Glaser m

gleam /gliːm/ n Schein m □ vi glänzen

glean /gliːn/ vi Ähren lesen □ vt (learn) erfahren

glee /gliː/ n Frohlocken nt. **~ful** a, **-ly** adv frohlockend

glen /glen/ n [enges] Tal nt

glib /glɪb/ a, **-ly** adv (pej) gewandt

glid|e /glaɪd/ vi gleiten; (through the air) schweben. **~er** n Segelflugzeug m nt. **~ing** n Segelfliegen nt

glimmer /'glɪmə(r)/ n Glimmen nt □ vi glimmen

glimpse /glɪmps/ n **catch a ~ of** flüchtig sehen □ vt flüchtig sehen

glint /glɪnt/ n Blitzen nt □ vi blitzen

glisten /'glɪsn/ vi glitzern

glitter /'glɪtə(r)/ vi glitzern

gloat /gləʊt/ vi schadenfroh sein; **~ over** sich weiden an (+ dat)

global /'gləʊbl/ a, **-ly** adv global

globe /gləʊb/ n Kugel f; (map) Globus m

gloom /gluːm/ n Düsterkeit f; (fig) Pessimismus m

gloomy /'gluːmɪ/ a (-ier, -iest), **-ily** adv düster; (fig) perssimistisch

glori|fy /'glɔːrɪfaɪ/ vt (pt/pp -ied) verherrlichen; **a ~ied waitress** eine bessere Kellnerin f

glorious /'glɔːrɪəs/ a herrlich; (deed, hero) glorreich

glory /'glɔːrɪ/ n Ruhm m; (splendour) Pracht f □ vi **~ in** sich ergehen in

gloss /glɒs/ n Glanz m □ a Glanz- □ vi **~ over** beschönigen

glossary /'glɒsərɪ/ n Glossar nt

glossy /'glɒsɪ/ a (-ier, -iest) glänzend

glove /glʌv/ n Handschuh m. **~ compartment** n (Auto) Handschuhfach nt

glow /gləʊ/ n Glut f; (of candle) Schein m □ vi glühen; (candle:) scheinen. **~ing** a glühend; (account) begeistert

glow-worm n Glühwürmchen nt

glucose /'gluːkəʊs/ n Traubenzucker m, Glukose f

glue /gluː/ n Klebstoff m □ vt (pres p **gluing**) kleben (**to** an + acc)

glum /glʌm/ a (**glummer, glummest**), **-ly** adv niedergeschlagen

glut /glʌt/ n Überfluss m (**of** an + dat); **~ of fruit** Obstschwemme f

glutton /'glʌtən/ n Vielfraß m. **~ous** /-əs/ a gefräßig. **~y** n Gefräßigkeit f

gnarled /nɑːld/ a knorrig; (hands) knotig

gnash /næʃ/ vt **~ one's teeth** mit den Zähnen knirschen

gnat /næt/ n Mücke f

gnaw /nɔː/ vt/i nagen (**at** an + dat)

gnome /nəʊm/ n Gnom m

go /gəʊ/ n (pl **goes**) Energie f; (attempt) Versuch m; **on the go** auf Trab; **at one go** auf einmal; **it's your go** du bist dran; **make a go of it** Erfolg haben □ vi (pt **went**, pp **gone**) gehen; (in vehicle) fahren; (leave) weggehen; (on journey) abfahren; (time:) vergehen; (vanish) verschwinden; (fail) versagen; (become) werden; (belong) kommen; **go swimming/shopping** schwimmen/einkaufen gehen; **where are you going?** wo gehst du hin? **it's all gone** es ist nichts mehr übrig; **I am not going to** ich werde es nicht tun; **'to go'** (Amer) 'zum Mitnehmen'. **go away** vi weggehen/-fahren. **go back** vi zurückgehen/-fahren. **go by** vi vorbeigehen/-fahren; (time:) vergehen. **go down** vi hinuntergehen/-fahren; (sun, ship:) untergehen; (prices:) fallen; (temperature, swelling:) zurückgehen. **go for** vt holen; (fam: attack) losgehen auf (+ acc). **go in** vi hineingehen/-fahren. **go in for** teilnehmen an (+ dat) (competition); (take up) sich verlegen auf (+ acc). **go off** vi weggehen/-fahren; (alarm:) klingeln; (gun, bomb:) losgehen; (go bad) schlecht werden; **go off well** gut verlaufen. **go on** vi weitergehen/-fahren; (continue) weitermachen; (talking) fortfahren; (happen) vorgehen; **go on at** (fam) herumnörgeln an (+ dat). **go out** vi ausgehen; (leave) hinausgehen/-fahren. **go over** vi hinübergehen/-fahren □ vt (check) durchgehen. **go round** vi herumgehen/-fahren; (visit) vorbeigehen; (turn) sich drehen; (be enough) reichen. **go through** vi durchgehen/-fahren □ vt (suffer)

durchmachen; (check) durchgehen. **go under** vi untergehen; (fail) scheitern. **go up** vi hinaufgehen/-fahren; (lift:) hochfahren; (prices:) steigen. **go without** vt verzichten auf (+ acc) □ vi darauf verzichten

goad /gəʊd/ vt anstacheln (into zu); (taunt) reizen

go-ahead a fortschrittlich; (enterprising) grünes Licht nt

goal /gəʊl/ n Ziel nt; (sport) Tor nt. **~keeper** n Torwart m. **~post** n Torpfosten m

goat /gəʊt/ n Ziege f

gobble /'gɒbl/ vt hinunterschlingen

go-between n Vermittler(in) m(f)

goblet /'gɒblɪt/ n Pokal m; (glass) Kelchglas nt

goblin /'gɒblɪn/ n Kobold m

God, god /gɒd/ n Gott m

god: **~child** n Patenkind nt. **~daughter** n Patentochter f. **~dess** n Göttin f. **~father** n Pate m. **G~forsaken** a gottverlassen. **~mother** n Patin f. **~parents** npl Paten pl. **~send** n Segen m. **~son** n Patensohn m

goggle /'gɒgl/ vi (fam) **~ at** anglotzen. **~s** npl Schutzbrille f

going /'gəʊɪŋ/ a (price, rate) gängig; (concern) gut gehend □ n **it is hard** ~ es ist schwierig; **while the** ~ **is good** solange es noch geht. **~s-'on** npl [seltsame] Vorgänge pl

gold /gəʊld/ n Gold nt □ a golden

golden /'gəʊldn/ a golden. **~ 'handshake** n hohe Abfindungssumme f. **~ 'wedding** n goldene Hochzeit f

gold: **~fish** n inv Goldfisch m. **~mine** n Goldgrube f. **~plated** a vergoldet. **~smith** n Goldschmied m

golf /gɒlf/ n Golf nt

golf: **~club** n Golfklub m; (implement) Golfschläger m. **~course**

n Golfplatz *m*. **~er** *m* Golfspieler(in) *m(f)*

gondo|la /'gɒndələ/ *n* Gondel *f*. **~lier** /-'lɪə(r)/ *n* Gondoliere *m*

gone /gɒn/ *see* **go**

gong /gɒŋ/ *n* Gong *m*

good /gʊd/ *a* (**better, best**) gut; (*well-behaved*) brav, artig; ~ **at** gut in (+ *dat*); **a ~ deal** ziemlich viel; **as ~ as** so gut wie; (*almost*) fast; ~ **morning/evening** guten Morgen/Abend; ~ **afternoon** guten Tag; ~ **night** gute Nacht □ *n* the ~ das Gute; **for ~** für immer; **do s.o.** ~ jdm gut tun; **it's no ~** es ist nutzlos; (*hopeless*) da ist nichts zu machen; **be up to no ~** nichts Gutes im Schilde führen

goodbye /gʊd'baɪ/ *int* auf Wiedersehen; (*Teleph, Radio*) auf Wiederhören

good: **~-for-nothing** *a* nichtsnutzig □ *n* Taugenichts *m*. **G~ 'Friday** *n* Karfreitag *m*. **~-'looking** *a* gut aussehend. **~-'natured** *a* gutmütig

goodness /'gʊdnɪs/ *n* Güte *f*; **my ~!** du meine Güte! **thank ~!** Gott sei Dank!

goods /gʊdz/ *npl* Waren *pl*. ~ **train** *n* Güterzug *m*

good'will *n* Wohlwollen *nt*; (*Comm*) Goodwill *m*

goody /'gʊdɪ/ *n* (*fam*) Gute(r) *m/f*. **~-goody** *n* Musterknabe *m*

gooey /'guːɪ/ *a* (*fam*) klebrig

goof /guːf/ *vi* (*fam*) einen Schnitzer machen

goose /guːs/ *n* (*pl* **geese**) Gans *f*

gooseberry /'gʊzbərɪ/ *n* Stachelbeere *f*

goose /guːs/: **~flesh** *n*, **~pimples** *npl* Gänsehaut *f*

gore[1] /gɔː(r)/ *n* Blut *nt*

gore[2] *vt* mit den Hörnern aufspießen

gorge /gɔːdʒ/ *n* (*Geog*) Schlucht *f* □ *vt* **~ oneself** sich vollessen

gorgeous /'gɔːdʒəs/ *a* prachtvoll; (*fam*) herrlich

gorilla /gə'rɪlə/ *n* Gorilla *m*

gormless /'gɔːmlɪs/ *a* (*fam*) doof

gorse /gɔːs/ *n inv* Stechginster *m*

gory /'gɔːrɪ/ *a* (**-ier, -iest**) blutig; (*story*) blutrünstig

gosh /gɒʃ/ *int* (*fam*) Mensch!

go-'slow *n* Bummelstreik *m*

gospel /'gɒspl/ *n* Evangelium *nt*

gossip /'gɒsɪp/ *n* Klatsch *m*; (*person*) Klatschbase *f* □ *vi* klatschen. **~y** *a* geschwätzig

got /gɒt/ *see* **get**; **have ~** haben; **have ~ to** müssen; **have ~ to do sth** etw tun müssen

Gothic /'gɒθɪk/ *a* gotisch

gotten /'gɒtn/ *see* **get**

gouge /gaʊdʒ/ *vt* **~ out** aushöhlen

goulash /'guːlæʃ/ *n* Gulasch *nt*

gourmet /'gʊəmeɪ/ *n* Feinschmecker *m*

gout /gaʊt/ *n* Gicht *f*

govern /'gʌvn/ *vt/i* regieren; (*determine*) bestimmen. **~ess** *n* Gouvernante *f*

government /'gʌvnmənt/ *n* Regierung *f*. **~al** /-'mentl/ *a* Regierungs-

governor /'gʌvənə(r)/ *n* Gouverneur *m*; (*on board*) Vorstandsmitglied *nt*; (*of prison*) Direktor *m*; (*fam: boss*) Chef *m*

gown /gaʊn/ *n* [elegantes] Kleid *nt*; (*Univ, Jur*) Talar *m*

GP *abbr of* **general practitioner**

grab /græb/ *vt* (*pt/pp* **grabbed**) ergreifen; ~ **[hold of]** packen

grace /greɪs/ *n* Anmut *f*; (*before meal*) Tischgebet *nt*; (*Relig*) Gnade *f*; **with good ~** mit Anstand; **say ~** [vor dem Essen] beten; **three days' ~** drei Tage Frist. **~ful** *a*, **-ly** *adv* anmutig

gracious /'greɪʃəs/ *a* gnädig; (*elegant*) vornehm

grade /greɪd/ *n* Stufe *f*; (*Comm*) Güteklasse *f*; (*Sch*) Note *f*; (*Amer, Sch: class*) Klasse *f*; (*Amer*) =

gradient □ vt einstufen; (Comm) sortieren. ~ crossing n (Amer) Bahanübergang m

gradient /'greɪdɪənt/ n Steigung f; (downward) Gefälle nt

gradual /'grædʒʊəl/ a, -ly adv allmählich

graduate¹ /'grædʒʊət/ n Akademiker(in) m(f)

graduate² /'grædʒʊeɪt/ vi (Univ) sein Examen machen. □ a abgestuft; (container) mit Maßeinteilung

graffiti /grə'fiːti/ npl Graffiti pl

graft /grɑːft/ n (Bot) Pfropfreis nt; (Med) Transplantat nt; (fam: hard work) Plackerei f □ vt (Bot) aufpfropfen; (Med) übertragen

grain /greɪn/ n (sand, salt, rice) Korn nt; (cereals) Getreide nt; (in wood) Maserung f; against the ~ (fig) gegen den Strich

gram /græm/ n Gramm nt

grammar /'græmə(r)/ n Grammatik f. ~ school n ≈ Gymnasium nt

grammatical /grə'mætɪkl/ a, -ly adv grammatisch

granary /'grænəri/ n Getreidespeicher m

grand /grænd/ a (-er, -est) großartig

grandad /'grændæd/ n (fam) Opa m

'grandchild n Enkelkind nt

'granddaughter n Enkelin f

grandeur /'grændʒə(r)/ n Pracht f

'grandfather n Großvater m. ~ clock n Standuhr f

grandiose /'grændɪəʊs/ a grandios

grand: ~mother n Großmutter f. ~parents npl Großeltern pl. ~ pi'ano n Flügel m. ~son n Enkel m. ~stand n Tribüne f

granite /'grænɪt/ n Granit m

granny /'grænɪ/ n (fam) Oma f

grant /grɑːnt/ n Subvention f; (Univ) Studienbeihilfe f □ vt gewähren; (admit) zugeben; take

sth for ~ed etw als selbstverständlich hinnehmen

granular /'grænjʊlə(r)/ a körnig

granulated /'grænjʊleɪtɪd/ a ~ sugar Kristallzucker m

granule /'grænjuːl/ n Körnchen nt

grape /greɪp/ n [Wein]traube f; bunch of ~s [ganze] Weintraube

grapefruit /'greɪp-/ n invar Grapefruit f, Pampelmuse f

graph /grɑːf/ n Kurvendiagramm nt

graphic /'græfɪk/ a, -ally adv grafisch; (vivid) anschaulich. ~s n (in design) grafische Gestaltung f

'graph paper n Millimeterpapier nt

grapple /'græpl/ vi ringen

grasp /grɑːsp/ n Griff m □ vt ergreifen; (understand) begreifen. ~ing a habgierig

grass /grɑːs/ n Gras nt; (lawn) Rasen m; at the ~ roots an der Basis. ~hopper n Heuschrecke f. ~land n Weideland nt

grassy /'grɑːsɪ/ a grasig

grate¹ /greɪt/ n Feuerrost m; (hearth) Kamin m

grate² vt (Culin) reiben; ~ one's teeth mit den Zähnen knirschen

grateful /'greɪtfl/ a, -ly adv dankbar (to dat)

grater /'greɪtə(r)/ n (Culin) Reibe f

gratify /'grætɪfaɪ/ vt (pt/pp -ied) befriedigen. ~ing a erfreulich

grating /'greɪtɪŋ/ n Gitter nt

gratis /'grɑːtɪs/ adv gratis

gratitude /'grætɪtjuːd/ n Dankbarkeit f

gratuitous /grə'tjuːɪtəs/ a (uncalled for) überflüssig

gratuity /grə'tjuːətɪ/ n (tip) Trinkgeld nt

grave¹ /greɪv/ a (-r, -st), -ly adv ernst; ~ly ill schwer krank

grave² n Grab nt. ~digger n Totengräber m

gravel /'grævl/ n Kies m

grave: ~**stone** n Grabstein m. ~**yard** n Friedhof m

gravitate /'græviteit/ vi gravitieren

gravity /'grævəti/ n Ernst m; (force) Schwerkraft f

gravy /'greivi/ n [Braten]soße f

gray /grei/ a (Amer) = grey

graze[1] /greiz/ vi (animal:) weiden

graze[2] n Schürfwunde f □ vt (car) streifen; (knee) aufschürfen

grease /gri:s/ n Fett nt; (lubricant) Schmierfett nt □ vt einfetten; (lubricate) schmieren. ~**proof 'paper** n Pergamentpapier nt

greasy /'gri:si/ a (-ier, -iest) fettig

great /greit/ a (-er, -est) groß; (fam: marvellous) großartig

great: ~'**aunt** n Großtante f. **G~ 'Britain** n Großbritannien nt. ~'**grandchildren** npl Urenkel pl. ~'**grandfather** n Urgroßvater m. ~'**grandmother** n Urgroßmutter f

great|**ly** /'greitli/ adv sehr. ~**ness** n Größe f

great-'uncle n Großonkel m

Greece /gri:s/ n Griechenland nt

greed /gri:d/ n [Hab]gier f

greedy /'gri:di/ a (-ier, -iest), -ily adv gierig; **don't be** ~ sei nicht so unbescheiden

Greek /gri:k/ a griechisch □ n Grieche m/Griechin f; (Lang) Griechisch nt

green /gri:n/ a (-er, -est) grün; (fig) unerfahren □ n Grün nt; (grass) Wiese f; ~s pl Kohl m; **the G~s** pl (Pol) die Grünen pl

greenery /'gri:nəri/ n Grün nt

'**greenfly** n Blattlaus f

greengage /'gri:ngeidʒ/ n Reneklode f

green: ~**grocer** n Obst- und Gemüsehändler m. ~**house** n Gewächshaus nt. ~**house effect** n Treibhauseffekt m

Greenland /'gri:nlənd/ n Grönland nt

greet /gri:t/ vt grüßen; (welcome) begrüßen. ~**ing** n Gruß m; (welcome) Begrüßung f. ~**ings card** n Glückwunschkarte f

gregarious /gri'geəriəs/ a gesellig

grenade /gri'neid/ n Granate f

grew /gru:/ see **grow**

grey /grei/ a (-er, -est) grau □ n Grau nt □ vi grau werden. ~**hound** n Windhund m

grid /grid/ n Gitter nt; (on map) Gitternetz nt; (Electr) Überlandleitungsnetz nt

grief /gri:f/ n Trauer f; **come to** ~ scheitern

grievance /'gri:vəns/ n Beschwerde f

grieve /gri:v/ vt betrüben □ vi trauern (for um)

grievous /'gri:vəs/ a, -ly adv schwer

grill /gril/ n Gitter nt; (Culin) Grill m; **mixed** ~ Gemischtes nt vom Grill □ vt/i grillen; (interrogate) [streng] verhören

grille /gril/ n Gitter nt

grim /grim/ a (grimmer, grimmest), -ly adv ernst; (determination) verbissen

grimace /gri'meis/ n Grimasse f □ vi Grimassen schneiden

grime /graim/ n Schmutz m

grimy /'graimi/ a (-ier, -iest) schmutzig

grin /grin/ n Grinsen nt □ vi (pt/pp grinned) grinsen

grind /graind/ n (fam: hard work) Plackerei f □ vt (pt/pp ground) mahlen; (smooth, sharpen) schleifen; (Amer: mince) durchdrehen; ~ **one's teeth** mit den Zähnen knirschen

grip /grip/ n Griff m; (bag) Reisetasche f □ vt (pt/pp gripped) ergreifen; (hold) festhalten; fesseln (interest)

gripe /graip/ vi (sl: grumble) meckern

gripping /'gripiŋ/ a fesselnd

grisly /'grɪzlɪ/ a (-ier, -iest) grausig

gristle /'grɪsl/ n Knorpel m

grit /grɪt/ n [grober] Sand m; (for roads) Streugut nt; (courage) Mut m □ vt (pt/pp gritted) streuen (road); ~ **one's teeth** die Zähne zusammenbeißen

grizzle /'grɪzl/ vi quengeln

groan /grəʊn/ n Stöhnen nt □ vi stöhnen

grocer /'grəʊsə(r)/ n Lebensmittelhändler m; ~**'s [shop]** Lebensmittelgeschäft nt. ~**ies** pl Lebensmittel pl

groggy /'grɒgɪ/ a schwach; (unsteady) wackelig [auf den Beinen]

groin /grɔɪn/ n (Anat) Leiste f

groom /gruːm/ n Bräutigam m; (for horse) Pferdepfleger(in) m(f) □ vt striegeln (horse)

groove /gruːv/ n Rille f

grope /grəʊp/ vi tasten (for nach)

gross /grəʊs/ a (-er, -est) fett; (coarse) derb; (glaring) grob; (Comm) brutto; (salary, weight) Brutto- □ n inv Gros nt. ~**ly** adv (very) sehr

grotesque /grəʊ'tesk/ a, -**ly** adv grotesk

grotto /'grɒtəʊ/ n (pl -es) Grotte f

grotty /'grɒtɪ/ a, (fam) mies

ground¹ /graʊnd/ see **grind**

ground² n Boden m; (terrain) Gelände nt; (reason) Grund m; (Amer, Electr) Erde f. ~**s** pl (park) Anlagen pl; (of coffee) Satz m □ vi (ship:) auflaufen □ vt aus dem Verkehr ziehen (aircraft); (Amer, Electr) erden

ground: ~ **floor** n Erdgeschoss nt. ~**ing** n Grundlage f. ~**less** a grundlos. ~'**meat** n Hackfleisch nt. ~**sheet** n Bodenplane f. ~**work** n Vorarbeiten pl

group /gruːp/ n Gruppe f □ vt gruppieren □ vi sich gruppieren

grouse¹ /graʊs/ n inv schottisches Moorschneehuhn nt

grouse² vi (fam) meckern

grovel /'grɒvl/ vi (pt/pp grovelled) kriechen. ~**ling** a kriecherisch

grow /grəʊ/ v (pt **grew**, pp **grown**) □ vi wachsen; (become) werden; (increase) zunehmen □ vt anbauen; ~ **one's hair** sich (dat) die Haare wachsen lassen. ~ **up** vi aufwachsen; (town:) entstehen

growl /graʊl/ n Knurren nt □ vi knurren

grown /grəʊn/ see **grow**. ~-**up** a erwachsen □ n Erwachsene(r) m/f

growth /grəʊθ/ n Wachstum nt; (increase) Zunahme f; (Med) Gewächs nt

grub /grʌb/ n (larva) Made f; (fam: food) Essen nt

grubby /'grʌbɪ/ a (-ier, -iest) schmuddelig

grudge /grʌdʒ/ n Groll m; **bear s.o. a ~** einen Groll gegen jdn hegen □ vt ~**e** s.o. **sth** jdm etw missgönnen. ~**ing** a, -**ly** adv widerwillig

gruelling /'gruːəlɪŋ/ a strapaziös

gruesome /'gruːsəm/ a grausig

gruff /grʌf/ a, -**ly** adv barsch

grumble /'grʌmbl/ vi schimpfen (at mit)

grumpy /'grʌmpɪ/ a (-ier, -iest) griesgrämig

grunt /grʌnt/ n Grunzen nt □ vi grunzen

guarantee /gærən'tiː/ n Garantie f; (document) Garantieschein m □ vt garantieren; garantieren für (quality, success); **be** ~**ed** (product:) Garantie haben. ~**or** n Bürge m

guard /gɑːd/ n Wache f; (security) Wächter m; (on train) ≈ Zugführer m; (Techn) Schutz m; **be on** ~ Wache stehen; **on one's** ~ auf der Hut sein □ vt bewachen; (protect) schützen □ vi ~ **against** sich hüten vor (+ dat). ~**dog** n Wachhund m

guarded /'gɑːdɪd/ a vorsichtig

guardian /'gɑ:dɪən/ n Vormund m

guerrilla /gə'rɪlə/ n Guerillakämpfer m. ~ **warfare** n Partisanenkrieg m

guess /ges/ n Vermutung f □ vt erraten □ vi raten; (Amer: believe) glauben. ~**work** n Vermutung f

guest /gest/ n Gast m. ~**house** n Pension f

guffaw /gʌ'fɔ:/ n derbes Lachen nt □ vi derb lachen

guidance /'gaɪdəns/ n Führung f, Leitung f; (advice) Beratung f

guide /gaɪd/ n Führer(in) m(f); (book) Führer m; [**Girl**] **G**~ Pfadfinderin f □ vt führen, leiten. ~**book** n Führer m

guided /'gaɪdɪd/ a ~ **missile** Fernlenkgeschoss nt; ~ **tour** Führung f

guide: ~**dog** n Blindenhund m. ~**lines** npl Richtlinien pl

guild /gɪld/ n Gilde f, Zunft f

guile /gaɪl/ n Arglist f

guillotine /'gɪləti:n/ n Guillotine f; (for paper) Papierschneidemaschine f

guilt /gɪlt/ n Schuld f. ~**ily** adv schuldbewusst

guilty /'gɪltɪ/ a (-ier, -iest) a schuldig (of gen); (look) schuldbewusst; (conscience) schlecht

guinea-pig /'gɪnɪ-/ n Meerschweinchen nt; (person) Versuchskaninchen nt

guise /gaɪz/ n **in the** ~ **of** in Gestalt (+ gen)

guitar /gɪ'tɑ:(r)/ n Gitarre f. ~**ist** n Gitarrist(in) m(f)

gulf /gʌlf/ n (Geog) Golf m; (fig) Kluft f

gull /gʌl/ n Möwe f

gullet /'gʌlɪt/ n Speiseröhre f; (throat) Kehle f

gullible /'gʌlɪbl/ a leichtgläubig

gully /'gʌlɪ/ n Schlucht f; (drain) Rinne f

gulp /gʌlp/ n Schluck m □ vi schlucken □ vt ~ **down** hinunterschlucken

gum[1] /gʌm/ n & -**s** pl (Anat) Zahnfleisch nt

gum[2] n Gummi[harz] nt; (glue) Klebstoff m; (chewing-gum) Kaugummi m □ vt (pt/pp **gummed**) kleben (**to an** + acc). ~**boot** n Gummistiefel m

gummed /gʌmd/ see **gum**[2] □ (label) gummiert

gumption /'gʌmpʃn/ n (fam) Grips m

gun /gʌn/ n Schusswaffe f; (pistol) Pistole f; (rifle) Gewehr nt; (cannon) Geschütz nt □ vt (pt/pp **gunned**) ~ **down** niederschießen

gun: ~**fire** n Geschützfeuer nt. ~**man** bewaffneter Bandit m

gunner /'gʌnə(r)/ n Artillerist m

gun: ~**powder** n Schießpulver nt. ~**shot** n Schuss m

gurgle /'gɜ:gl/ vi gluckern; (of baby) glucksen

gush /gʌʃ/ vi strömen; (enthuse) schwärmen (**over** von). ~ **out** vi herausströmen

gusset /'gʌsɪt/ n Zwickel m

gust /gʌst/ n (of wind) Windstoß m; (Naut) Bö f

gusto /'gʌstəʊ/ n **with** ~ mit Schwung

gusty /'gʌstɪ/ a böig

gut /gʌt/ n Darm m; ~**s** pl Eingeweide pl; (fam: courage) Schneid m □ vt (pt/pp **gutted**) (Culin) ausnehmen; ~**ted by fire** ausgebrannt

gutter /'gʌtə(r)/ n Rinnstein m; (fig) Gosse f; (on roof) Dachrinne f

guttural /'gʌtərl/ a guttural

guy /gaɪ/ n (fam) Kerl m

guzzle /'gʌzl/ vt/i schlingen; (drink) schlürfen

gym /dʒɪm/ n (fam) Turnhalle f; (gymnastics) Turnen nt

gymnasium /dʒɪm'neɪzɪəm/ n Turnhalle f

gymnast /'dʒɪmnæst/ n Turner(in) m(f). ~**ics** /-'næstɪks/ n Turnen nt

gym: ~ **shoes** pl Turnschuhe pl. ~**slip** n (Sch) Trägerkleid nt

gynaecolog|ist /ˌgaɪnɪˈkɒlədʒɪst/ n Frauenarzt m /-ärztin f. ~**y** n Gynäkologie f

gypsy /ˈdʒɪpsɪ/ n Zigeuner(in) m(f)

gyrate /dʒaɪəˈreɪt/ vi sich drehen

H

haberdashery /ˈhæbədæʃərɪ/ n Kurzwaren pl; (Amer) Herrenmoden pl

habit /ˈhæbɪt/ n Gewohnheit f; (Relig: costume) Ordenstracht f; **be in the** ~ die Angewohnheit haben (of zu)

habitable /ˈhæbɪtəbl/ a bewohnbar

habitat /ˈhæbɪtæt/ n Habitat nt

habitation /hæbɪˈteɪʃn/ n **unfit for human** ~ für Wohnzwecke ungeeignet

habitual /həˈbɪtjʊəl/ a gewohnt; (inveterate) gewohnheitsmäßig. ~**ly** adv gewohnheitsmäßig; (constantly) ständig

hack1 /hæk/ n (writer) Schreiberling m; (hired horse) Mietpferd nt

hack2 vt hacken; ~ **to pieces** zerhacken

hackneyed /ˈhæknɪd/ a abgedroschen

'hacksaw n Metallsäge f

had /hæd/ see **have**

haddock /ˈhædək/ n inv Schellfisch m

haemorrhage /ˈhemərɪdʒ/ n Blutung f

haemorrhoids /ˈhemərɔɪdz/ npl Hämorrhoiden pl

hag /hæg/ n old ~ alte Hexe f

haggard /ˈhægəd/ a abgehärmt

haggle /ˈhægl/ vi feilschen (over um)

hail1 /heɪl/ vt begrüßen; herbeirufen (taxi) □ vi ~ **from** kommen aus

hail2 n Hagel m □ vi hageln. ~**stone** n Hagelkorn nt

hair /heə(r)/ n Haar nt; **wash one's** ~ sich (dat) die Haare waschen

hair: ~**brush** n Haarbürste f. ~**cut** n Haarschnitt m; **have a** ~**cut** sich (dat) die Haare schneiden lassen. ~**do** n (fam) Frisur f. ~**dresser** n Friseur m/Friseuse f. ~**drier** n Haartrockner m; (hand-held) Föhn m. ~**grip** n [Haar]klemme f. ~**pin** n Haarnadel f. ~**pin 'bend** n Haarnadelkurve f. ~**raising** a haarsträubend. ~**style** n Frisur f

hairy /ˈheərɪ/ a (-ier, -iest) behaart; (excessively) haarig; (fam; frightening) brenzlig

hake /heɪk/ n inv Seehecht m

hale /heɪl/ a ~ **and hearty** gesund und munter

half /haːf/ n pl **halves** Hälfte f; **cut in** ~ halbieren; **one and a** ~ eineinhalb, anderthalb; ~ **a dozen** ein halbes Dutzend; ~ **an hour** eine halbe Stunde □ a & adv halb; ~ **past two** halb drei; **[at]** ~ **price** zum halben Preis

half: ~**board** n Halbpension f. ~**caste** n Mischling m. ~**'hearted** a lustlos. ~**'hourly** a & adv halbstündlich. ~**'mast** n **at** ~**mast** auf halbmast. ~**measure** n Halbheit f. ~**'term** n schulfreie Tage nach dem halben Trimester. ~**'timbered** a Fachwerk-. ~**'time** n (Sport) Halbzeit f. ~**'way** a **the** ~**way mark/stage** die Hälfte □ adv auf halbem Weg; **get** ~**way** (fig) bis zur Hälfte kommen. ~**wit** n Idiot m

halibut /ˈhælɪbət/ n inv Heilbutt m

hall /hɔːl/ n Halle f; (room) Saal m; (Sch) Aula f; (entrance) Flur m; (mansion) Gutshaus nt. ~ **of residence** (Univ) Studentenheim nt

'hallmark n [Feingehalts]stempel m; (fig) Kennzeichen nt (of für) □ vt stempeln

hallo /hə'ləʊ/ int [guten] Tag! (fam) hallo!

Hallowe'en /hæləʊ'i:n/ n der Tag vor Allerheiligen

hallucination /həlu:sɪ'neɪʃn/ n Halluzination f

halo /'heɪləʊ/ n (pl -es) Heiligenschein m; (Astr) Hof m

halt /hɔ:lt/ n Halt m; **come to a ~** stehen bleiben; (traffic:) zum Stillstand kommen □ vi Halt machen; ~! halt! ~**ing** a, adv -**ly** zögernd

halve /hɑ:v/ vt halbieren; (reduce) um die Hälfte reduzieren

ham /hæm/ n Schinken m

hamburger /'hæmbɜ:gə(r)/ n Hamburger m

hamlet /'hæmlɪt/ n Weiler m

hammer /'hæmə(r)/ n Hammer m □ vt/i hämmern (**at** an + acc)

hammock /'hæmɒk/ n Hängematte f

hamper¹ /'hæmpə(r)/ n Picknickkorb m; [gift] ~ Geschenkkorb m

hamper² vt behindern

hamster /'hæmstə(r)/ n Hamster m

hand /hænd/ n Hand f; (of clock) Zeiger m; (writing) Handschrift f; (worker) Arbeiter(in) m(f); (Cards) Blatt n; **at all ~s** (Naut) alle Mann; **in ~** in der Nähe; **on the one/other ~** einer-/andererseits; **out of ~** außer Kontrolle; (summarily) kurzerhand; **in ~** unter Kontrolle; (available) verfügbar; **give s.o. a ~** jdm behilflich sein □ vt reichen (**to** dat). ~ **in** vt abgeben. ~ **out** vt austeilen. ~ **over** vt überreichen

hand: ~**bag** n Handtasche f. ~**book** n Handbuch nt. ~**brake** n Handbremse f. ~**cuffs** n Handschellen pl. ~**ful** n Handvoll f; **be [quite] a** ~**ful** (fam) nicht leicht zu haben sein

handicap /'hændɪkæp/ n Behinderung f; (Sport & fig) Handikap nt. ~**ped** a **mentally/physically** ~**ped** geistig/körperlich behindert

handi|craft /'hændɪkrɑ:ft/ n Basteln nt; (Sch) Werken nt. ~**work** n Werk nt

handkerchief /'hæŋkətʃɪf/ n (pl ~**s** & **-chieves**) Taschentuch nt

handle /'hændl/ n Griff m; (of door) Klinke f; (of cup) Henkel m; (of broom) Stiel m; **fly off the ~** (fam) aus der Haut fahren □ vt handhaben; (treat) umgehen mit; (touch) anfassen. ~**bars** npl Lenkstange f

hand: ~**luggage** n Handgepäck nt. ~**made** a handgemacht. ~**out** n Prospekt m; (money) Unterstützung f. ~**rail** n Handlauf m. ~**shake** n Händedruck m

handsome /'hænsəm/ a gut aussehend; (generous) großzügig; (large) beträchtlich

hand: ~**stand** n Handstand m. ~**writing** n Handschrift f. ~-**written** a handgeschrieben

handy /'hændɪ/ a (-**ier**, -**iest**) handlich; (person) geschickt; **have/keep a** ~ griffbereit haben/halten. ~**man** n [home] ~**man** Heimwerker m

hang /hæŋ/ vt/i (pt/pp **hung**) hängen; (wallpaper) tapezieren □ vt (pt/pp **hanged**) hängen (criminal); ~ **oneself** sich erhängen □ **get the** ~ **of it** (fam) den Dreh herauskriegen. ~ **about** vi sich herumdrücken. ~ **on** vi sich festhalten (**to** an + dat); (fam: wait) warten. ~ **out** vi heraushängen; (fam: live) wohnen □ vt draußen aufhängen (washing). ~ **up** vt/i aufhängen

hangar /'hæŋə(r)/ n Flugzeughalle f

hanger /'hæŋə(r)/ n [Kleider]bügel m

hang: ~-**glider** n Drachenflieger m. ~-**gliding** n Drachenfliegen

hanker nt. ~**man** n Henker m. ~**over** n (fam) Kater m (fam). ~**up** n (fam) Komplex m

hanker /'hæŋkə(r)/ vi ~ **after sth** sich (dat) etw wünschen

hanky /'hæŋkɪ/ n (fam) Taschentuch nt

hanky-panky /'hæŋkɪ'pæŋkɪ/ n (fam) Mauscheleien pl

haphazard /hæp'hæzəd/ a, -ly adv planlos

happen /'hæpn/ vi geschehen, passieren; **as it** ~**s** zufälligerweise; **I** ~**ed to be there** ich war zufällig da; **what has** ~**ed to him?** was ist mit ihm los? (become of) was ist aus ihm geworden? ~**ing** n Ereignis nt

happi|ly /'hæpɪlɪ/ adv glücklich; (fortunately) glücklicherweise. ~**ness** n Glück nt

happy /'hæpɪ/ a (-ier, -iest) glücklich. ~**-go-'lucky** a sorglos

harass /'hærəs/ vt schikanieren. ~**ed** a abgehetzt. ~**ment** n Schikane f; (sexual) Belästigung f

harbour /'hɑːbə(r)/ n Hafen m □ vt Unterschlupf gewähren (+ dat); hegen (grudge)

hard /hɑːd/ a (-er, -est) hart; (difficult) schwer; ~ **of hearing** schwerhörig □ adv hart; (work) schwer; (pull) kräftig; (rain, snow) stark; **think** ~! denk mal nach! **be** ~ **up** (fam) knapp bei Kasse sein; **be** ~ **done by** (fam) ungerecht behandelt werden

hard: ~**back** n gebundene Ausgabe f. ~**board** n Hartfaserplatte f. ~**-boiled** a hart gekocht

harden /'hɑːdn/ vi hart werden

hard-'hearted a hartherzig

hard|ly /'hɑːdlɪ/ adv kaum; ~**ly ever** kaum [jemals]. ~**ness** n Härte f. ~**ship** n Not f

hard: ~**'shoulder** n (Auto) Randstreifen m. ~**ware** n Haushaltswaren pl; (Computing) Hardware f. ~**'wearing** a strapazierfähig. ~**'working** a fleißig

hardy /'hɑːdɪ/ a (-ier, -iest) abgehärtet; (plant) winterhart

hare /heə(r)/ n Hase m. ~**'lip** n Hasenscharte f

hark /hɑːk/ vi ~! hört! ~ **back** n ~ **back to** (fig) zurückkommen auf (+ acc)

harm /hɑːm/ n Schaden m; **out of** ~**'s way** in Sicherheit; **it won't do any** ~ es kann nichts schaden □ vt ~ **s.o.** jdm etwas antun. ~**ful** a schädlich. ~**less** a harmlos

harmonica /hɑː'mɒnɪkə/ n Mundharmonika f

harmonious /hɑː'məʊnɪəs/ a, -ly adv harmonisch

harmon|ize /'hɑːmənaɪz/ vi (fig) harmonieren. ~**y** n Harmonie f

harness /'hɑːnɪs/ n Geschirr nt; (of parachute) Gurtwerk nt □ vt anschirren (horse); (use) nutzbar machen

harp /hɑːp/ n Harfe f □ vi ~ **on [about]** (fam) herumreiten auf (+ dat). ~**ist** n Harfenist(in) m(f)

harpoon /hɑː'puːn/ n Harpune f

harpsichord /'hɑːpsɪkɔːd/ n Cembalo nt

harrow /'hærəʊ/ n Egge f. ~**ing** a grauenhaft

harsh /hɑːʃ/ a (-er, -est), -ly adv hart; (voice) rau; (light) grell. ~**ness** n Härte f; Rauheit f

harvest /'hɑːvɪst/ n Ernte f □ vt ernten

has /hæz/ see **have**

hash /hæʃ/ n (Culin) Haschee nt; **make a** ~ **of** (fam) verpfuschen

hashish /'hæʃɪʃ/ n Haschisch nt

hassle /'hæsl/ n (fam) Ärger m □ vt schikanieren

haste /heɪst/ n Eile f; **make** ~ sich beeilen

hasten /'heɪsn/ vi sich beeilen (**to** zu); (go quickly) eilen □ vt beschleunigen

hasty /'heɪstɪ/ a (-ier, -iest), -ily adv hastig; (decision) voreilig hat /hæt/ n Hut m; (knitted) Mütze f

hatch¹ /hætʃ/ n (for food) Durchreiche f; (Naut) Luke f

hatch² vi ~[out] ausschlüpfen □ vt ausbrüten

'hatchback n (Auto) Modell nt mit Hecktür

hatchet /'hætʃɪt/ n Beil nt

hate /heɪt/ n Hass m □ vt hassen. ~ful a abscheulich

hatred /'heɪtrɪd/ n Hass m

haughty /'hɔːtɪ/ a (-ier, -iest), -ily adv hochmütig

haul /hɔːl/ n (fish) Fang m; (loot) Beute f □ vt/i ziehen (on an + dat). ~age /-ɪdʒ/ n Transport m. ~ier /-ɪə(r)/ n Spediteur m

haunt /hɔːnt/ n Lieblingsaufenthalt m □ vt umgehen in (+ dat); this house is ~ed in diesem Haus spukt es

have /hæv/ vt (3 sg pres tense has) pt/pp had) haben; bekommen (baby); holen (doctor); ~ a meal/drink etwas essen/trinken; ~ lunch zu Mittag essen; ~ a walk spazieren gehen; ~ a dream träumen; ~ a rest sich ausruhen; ~ a swim schwimmen; ~ sth done etw machen lassen; ~ sth made sich (dat) etw machen lassen; ~ to do sth etw tun müssen; ~ it out with zur Rede stellen; so I ~! tatsächlich! he has [got] two houses er hat zwei Häuser; you have got the money, haven't you? du hast das Geld, nicht [wahr]? □ v aux haben; (with verbs of motion & some others) sein; I ~ seen him ich habe ihn gesehen; he has never been there er ist nie da gewesen. ~ on vt (be wearing) anhaben; (dupe) anführen

haven /'heɪvn/ n (fig) Zuflucht f

haversack /'hævə-/ n Rucksack m

havoc /'hævək/ n Verwüstung f; play ~ with (fig) völlig durcheinander bringen

haw /hɔː/ see hum

hawk¹ /hɔːk/ n Falke m

hawk² vt hausieren mit. ~er n Hausierer m

hawthorn /'hɔː-/ n Hagedorn m

hay /heɪ/ n Heu nt. ~ fever n Heuschnupfen m. ~stack n Heuschober m

haywire a (fam) go ~ verrückt spielen; (plans:) über den Haufen geworfen werden

hazard /'hæzəd/ n Gefahr f; (risk) Risiko m □ vt riskieren. ~ous /-əs/ a gefährlich; (risky) riskant. ~ [warning] lights npl (Auto) Warnblinkanlage f

haze /heɪz/ n Dunst m

hazel /'heɪzl/ n Haselbusch m. ~nut n Haselnuss f

hazy /'heɪzɪ/ a (-ier, -iest) dunstig; (fig) unklar

he /hiː/ pron er

head /hed/ n Kopf m; (chief) Oberhaupt nt; (of firm) Chef(in) m(f); (of school) Schulleiter(in) m(f); (on beer) Schaumkrone f; (of bed) Kopfende nt; 20 ~ of cattle 20 Stück Vieh; ~ first kopfüber □ vt anführen; (Sport) köpfen (ball) □ vi ~ for zusteuern auf (+ acc). ~ache n Kopfschmerzen m pl. ~-dress n Kopfschmuck m

head|er /'hedə(r)/ n Kopfball m; (dive) Kopfsprung m. ~ing n Überschrift f

head: ~lamp n (Auto) Scheinwerfer m. ~land n Landspitze f. ~light n (Auto) Scheinwerfer m. ~line n Schlagzeile f. ~long adv kopfüber. ~master n Schulleiter m. ~mistress n Schulleiterin f. ~on a & adv frontal. ~phones npl Kopfhörer m. ~quarters npl Hauptquartier nt; (Pol) Zentrale f. ~rest n Kopfstütze f. ~room n lichte Höhe f. ~scarf n Kopftuch nt. ~strong a eigenwillig. ~ waiter n Oberkellner m. ~way make ~way Fortschritte machen. ~wind n

Gegenwind m. **~word** n Stichwort nt

heady /'hedɪ/ a berauschend

heal /hi:l/ vt/i heilen

health /helθ/ n Gesundheit f

health: ~farm n Schönheitsfarm f. **~ foods** npl Reformkost f. **~food shop** n Reformhaus nt. **~ insurance** n Krankenversicherung f

healthy /'helθɪ/ a (-ier, -iest), -ily adv gesund

heap /hi:p/ n Haufen m; **~s** (fam) jede Menge □ vt **~ [up]** häufen; **~ed teaspoon** gehäufter Teelöffel

hear /hɪə(r)/ vt/i (pt/pp **heard**) hören; **~,~!** hört, hört! **he would not ~ of it** er ließ es nicht zu

hearing /'hɪərɪŋ/ n Gehör nt; (Jur) Verhandlung f. **~-aid** n Hörgerät nt

'hearsay n **from ~** vom Hörensagen

hearse /hɜːs/ n Leichenwagen m

heart /hɑːt/ n Herz nt; (courage) Mut m; **~s** pl (Cards) Herz nt; **by ~** auswendig

heart: ~ache n Kummer m. **~attack** n Herzanfall m. **~beat** n Herzschlag m. **~break** n Leid nt. **~breaking** a herzzerreißend. **~broken** a untröstlich. **~burn** n Sodbrennen nt. **~en** vt ermutigen. **~felt** a herzlich[st]

hearth /hɑːθ/ n Herd m; (fireplace) Kamin m. **~rug** n Kaminvorleger m

heart|ily /'hɑːtɪlɪ/ adv herzlich; (eat) viel. **~less** a, **-ly** adv herzlos. **~y** a herzlich; (meal) groß; (person) burschikos

heat /hiːt/ n Hitze f; (Sport) Vorlauf m □ vt heiß machen; heizen (room). **~ed** a geheizt; (swimming pool) beheizt; (discussion) hitzig. **~er** n Heizgerät nt; (Auto) Heizanlage f

heath /hiːθ/ n Heide f

heathen /'hiːðn/ a heidnisch □ n Heide m/Heidin f

heather /'heðə(r)/ n Heidekraut nt

heating /'hiːtɪŋ/ n Heizung f

heat: ~stroke n Hitzschlag m. **~wave** n Hitzewelle f

heave /hiːv/ vt/i ziehen; (lift) heben; (fam: throw) schmeißen; **~ a sigh** einen Seufzer ausstoßen

heaven /'hevn/ n Himmel m. **~ly** a himmlisch

heavy /'hevɪ/ a (-ier, -iest), -ily adv schwer; (traffic, rain) stark; (sleep) tief. **~weight** n Schwergewicht nt

Hebrew /'hiːbruː/ a hebräisch

heckle /'hekl/ vt [durch Zwischenrufe] unterbrechen. **~r** n Zwischenrufer m

hectic /'hektɪk/ a hektisch

hedge /hedʒ/ n Hecke f □ vi (fig) ausweichen. **~hog** n Igel m

heed /hiːd/ n **pay ~ to** Beachtung schenken (+ dat) □ vt beachten. **~less** a ungeachtet (of gen)

heel[1] /hiːl/ n Ferse f; (of shoe) Absatz m; **down at ~** heruntergekommen; **take to one's ~s** (fam) Fersengeld geben

heel[2] vi **~ over** (Naut) sich auf die Seite legen

hefty /'heftɪ/ a (-ier, -iest) kräftig; (heavy) schwer

heifer /'hefə(r)/ n Färse f

height /haɪt/ n Höhe f; (of person) Größe f. **~en** vt (fig) steigern

heir /eə(r)/ n Erbe m. **~ess** n Erbin f. **~loom** n Erbstück nt

held /held/ see **hold[2]**

helicopter /'helɪkɒptə(r)/ n Hubschrauber m

hell /hel/ n Hölle f; **go to ~!** (sl) geh zum Teufel! □ int verdammt!

hello /hə'ləʊ/ int [guten] Tag! (fam) hallo!

helm /helm/ n [Steuer]ruder nt; **at the ~** (fig) am Ruder

helmet /'helmɪt/ n Helm m

help /help/ n Hilfe f; (employees) Hilfskräfte pl; **that's no ~** das nützt nichts □ vt/i helfen (s.o.

jdm); ~ **oneself to sth** sich (*dat*)
etw nehmen; ~ **yourself** (*at*
table) greif zu; **I could not ~**
laughing ich musste lachen; **it**
cannot be ~ed es lässt sich nicht
ändern; **I can't ~ it** ich kann
nichts dafür

helper /'helpə(r)/ *n* Helfer(in)
m(f). ~**ful** *a*, **-ly** *adv* hilfsbereit;
(*advice*) nützlich. ~**ing** *n* Portion
f. ~**less** *a*, **-ly** *adv* hilflos

helter-skelter /heltə'skeltə(r)/
adv holterdiepolter □ *n* Rutsch-
bahn *f*

hem /hem/ *n* Saum *m* □ *vt* (*pt/pp*
hemmed) säumen; ~ **in** umzingeln

hemisphere /'hemɪ-/ *n* Hemisphäre *f*

'hem-line *n* Rocklänge *f*

hemp /hemp/ *n* Hanf *m*

hen /hen/ *n* Henne *f*; (*any female*
bird) Weibchen *nt*

hence /hens/ *adv* daher; **five**
years ~ in fünf Jahren. ~**'forth**
adv von nun an

henchman /'hentʃmən/ *n* (*pej*)
Gefolgsmann *m*

'henpecked *a* ~ **husband** Pantof-
felheld *m*

her /hɜː(r)/ *a* ihr □ *pron* (*acc*) sie;
(*dat*) ihr; **I know** ~ ich kenne sie;
give ~ **the money** gib ihr das
Geld

herald /'herəld/ *vt* verkünden.
~**ry** *n* Wappenkunde *f*

herb /hɜːb/ *n* Kraut *nt*

herbaceous /hɜː'beɪʃəs/ *a* kraut-
artig; ~ **border** Staudenrabatte
f

herd /hɜːd/ *n* Herde *f* □ *vt* (*tend*)
hüten; (*drive*) treiben. ~ **to-**
gether *vi* sich zusammendrängen □ *vt* zusammentreiben

here /hɪə(r)/ *adv* hier; (*to this*
place) hierher; **in** ~ hier drinnen;
come/bring ~ herkom-
men/herbringen. ~**after** *adv* im
Folgenden. ~**by** *adv* hiermit

hereditary /hə'redɪtərɪ/ *a* erblich. ~**y** *n* Vererbung *f*

heresy /'herəsɪ/ *n* Ketzerei *f.*
~**tic** *n* Ketzer(in) *m(f)*

here'with *adv* (*Comm*) beiliegend

heritage /'herɪtɪdʒ/ *n* Erbe *nt*

hermetic /hɜː'metɪk/ *a*, **-ally** *adv*
hermetisch

hermit /'hɜːmɪt/ *n* Einsiedler *m*

hernia /'hɜːnɪə/ *n* Bruch *m*, Hernie *f*

hero /'hɪərəʊ/ *n* (*pl* **-es**) Held *m*

heroic /hɪ'rəʊɪk/ *a*, **-ally** *adv* hel-
denhaft

heroin /'herəʊɪn/ *n* Heroin *nt*

heroine /'herəʊɪn/ *n* Heldin *f.*
~**ism** *n* Heldentum *nt*

heron /'hern/ *n* Reiher *m*

herring /'herɪŋ/ *n* Hering *m*; **red**
~ (*fam*) falsche Spur *f.* ~**bone** *n*
(*pattern*) Fischgrätenmuster *nt*

hers /hɜːz/ *poss pron* ihre(r), ihrs;
a friend of ~ ein Freund von ihr;
that is ~ das gehört ihr

her'self *pron* selbst; (*refl*) sich; **by**
~ allein

hesitant /'hezɪtənt/ *a*, **-ly** *adv* zögernd

hesitate /'hezɪteɪt/ *vi* zögern.
~**ion** /-'teɪʃn/ *n* Zögern *nt*;
without ~**ion** ohne zu zögern

het /het/ *a* ~ **up** (*fam*) aufgeregt

hetero'sexual /hetərəʊ-/ *a* heterosexuell

hew /hjuː/ *vt* (*pt* **hewed**, *pp*
hewed *or* **hewn**) hauen

hexagonal /hek'sægənl/ *a* sechs-
eckig

heyday /'heɪ-/ *n* Glanzzeit *f*

hi /haɪ/ *int* he! (*hallo*) Tag!

hiatus /haɪ'eɪtəs/ *n* (*pl* **-tuses**) Lücke *f*

hibernate /'haɪbəneɪt/ *vi* Winterschlaf halten. ~**ion** /-'neɪʃn/
n Winterschlaf *m*

hiccup /'hɪkʌp/ *n* Hick *m*; (*fam:*
hitch) Panne *f*; **have the** ~**s** den
Schluckauf haben □ *vi* hick
machen

hid /hɪd/, **hidden** *see* **hide**²

hide¹ /haɪd/ *n* (*Comm*) Haut *f*;
(*leather*) Leder *nt*

hide[2] v (pt **hid**, pp **hidden**) □ vt verstecken; (keep secret) verheimlichen □ vi sich verstecken. ~-**and-'seek** n play ~**-and-seek** Verstecke spielen

hideous /'hɪdɪəs/ a, -ly adv hässlich; (horrible) grässlich

'hide-out n Versteck nt

hiding[1] /'haɪdɪŋ/ n (fam) give s.o. a ~ jdn verdreschen

hiding[2] n go into ~ untertauchen

hierarchy /'haɪərɑːkɪ/ n Hierarchie f

hieroglyphics /haɪərə'glɪfɪks/ npl Hieroglyphen pl

higgledy-piggledy /hɪgldɪ-'pɪgldɪ/ adv kunterbunt durcheinander

high /haɪ/ a (-er, -est) hoch; attrib hohe(r,s); (meat) angegangen; (wind) stark; (on drugs) high; it's ~ time es ist höchste Zeit □ adv hoch; ~ and low überall □ n Hoch nt; (temperature) Höchsttemperatur f

high: ~**brow** a intellektuell. ~**chair** n Kinderhochstuhl m. ~'-**handed** a selbstherrlich. ~'-**heeled** a hochhackig. ~**jump** n Hochsprung m

'highlight n (fig) Höhepunkt m; ~s pl (in hair) helle Strähnen pl □ vt (emphasize) hervorheben

highly /'haɪlɪ/ adv hoch; **speak** ~ **of** loben; **think** ~ **of** sehr schätzen. ~'**strung** a nervös

Highness /'haɪnɪs/ n Hoheit f

high: ~**rise** a ~**rise flats** pl Wohnturm m. ~ **season** n Hochsaison f. ~ **street** n Hauptstraße f. ~ '**tide** n Hochwasser nt. ~**way** n public ~**way** öffentliche Straße

hijack /'haɪdʒæk/ vt entführen. ~**er** n Entführer m

hike /haɪk/ n Wanderung f □ vi wandern. ~**r** n Wanderer m

hilarious /hɪ'leərɪəs/ a sehr komisch

hill /hɪl/ n Berg m; (mound) Hügel m; (slope) Hang m

hill: ~**billy** n (Amer) Hinterwäldler m. ~**side** n Hang m. ~**y** a hügelig

hilt /hɪlt/ n Griff m; **to the** ~ (fam) voll und ganz

him /hɪm/ pron (acc) ihn; (dat) ihm; **I know** ~ ich kenne ihn; **give** ~ **the money** gib ihm das Geld. ~'**self** pron selbst; (refl) sich; **by** ~**self** allein

hind /haɪnd/ a Hinter-

hinder /'hɪndə(r)/ vt hindern. ~**rance** /-rəns/ n Hindernis nt

hindsight /'haɪnd-/ n **with** ~ rückblickend

Hindu /'hɪnduː/ n Hindu m □ a Hindu-. ~**ism** n Hinduismus m

hinge /hɪndʒ/ n Scharnier nt; (on door) Angel f □ vi ~ **on** (fig) ankommen auf (+ acc)

hint /hɪnt/ n Wink m, Andeutung f; (advice) Hinweis m; (trace) Spur f □ vi ~ **at** anspielen auf (+ acc)

hip /hɪp/ n Hüfte f

hippie /'hɪpɪ/ n Hippie m

hip 'pocket n Gesäßtasche f

hippopotamus /hɪpə'pɒtəməs/ n (pl -**muses** or -**mi** /-maɪ/) Nilpferd nt

hire /'haɪə(r)/ vt mieten (car); leihen (suit); einstellen (person); ~[**out**] vermieten; verleihen □ n Mieten nt; Leihen nt. ~**car** n Leihwagen m

his /hɪz/ a sein □ poss pron seine(r), seins; **a friend of** ~ ein Freund von ihm; **that is** ~ das gehört ihm

hiss /hɪs/ n Zischen nt □ vt/i zischen

historian /hɪ'stɔːrɪən/ n Historiker(in) m(f)

historic /hɪ'stɒrɪk/ a historisch. ~**al** a, -ly adv geschichtlich, historisch

history /'hɪstərɪ/ n Geschichte f

hit /hɪt/ n (blow) Schlag m; (fam: success) Erfolg m; direct ~ Volltreffer m □ vt/i (pt/pp hit, pres p hitting) schlagen; (knock against, collide with, affect) treffen; ~ the target das Ziel treffen; ~ on (fig) kommen auf (+ acc); ~ it off gut auskommen (with mit); ~ one's head on sth sich (dat) den Kopf an etw (dat) stoßen

hitch /hɪtʃ/ n Problem nt; technical ~ Panne f □ vt festmachen (to an + dat); ~ up hochziehen; ~ a lift per Anhalter fahren, (fam) trampen. ~-hiker vi per Anhalter fahren, (fam) trampen. ~-hiker n Anhalter(in) m(f)

hither /ˈhɪðə(r)/ adv hierher; ~ and thither hin und her. ~to adv bisher

hive /haɪv/ n Bienenstock m. ~ off vt (Comm) abspalten

hoard /hɔːd/ n Hort m □ vt horten, hamstern

hoarding /ˈhɔːdɪŋ/ n Bauzaun m; (with advertisements) Reklamewand f

hoar-frost /ˈhɔː-/ n Raureif m

hoarse /hɔːs/ a (-r, -st), -ly adv heiser. ~ness n Heiserkeit f

hoax /həʊks/ n übler Scherz m; (false alarm) blinder Alarm m

hob /hɒb/ n Kochmulde f

hobble /ˈhɒbl/ vi humpeln

hobby /ˈhɒbɪ/ n Hobby nt. ~-horse n (fig) Lieblingsthema nt

hobnailed /ˈhɒb-/ ~ boots pl genagelte Schuhe pl

hock /hɒk/ n [weißer] Rheinwein m

hockey /ˈhɒkɪ/ n Hockey nt

hoe /həʊ/ n Hacke f □ vt (pres p hoeing) hacken

hog /hɒg/ n [Mast]schwein nt □ vt (pt/pp hogged) (fam) mit Beschlag belegen

hoist /hɔɪst/ n Lastenaufzug m □ vt hochziehen; hissen (flag)

hold[1] /həʊld/ n (Naut) Laderaum m

hold[2] n Halt m; (Sport) Griff m; (fig: influence) Einfluss m; get ~ of fassen; (fam: contact) erreichen □ v (pt/pp held) □ vt fassen; (container:) fassen; (believe) meinen; (possess) haben; anhalten (breath:); ~ one's tongue den Mund halten; (weather:) sich halten; not ~ with (fam) nicht einverstanden sein mit. ~ back vt zurückhalten □ vi zögern. ~ on vi (wait) warten; (on telephone) am Apparat bleiben; ~ on to (keep) behalten; (cling to) sich festhalten an (+ dat). ~ out vt hinhalten □ vi (resist) aushalten. ~ up vt hochhalten; (delay) aufhalten; (rob) überfallen

hold|**all** n Reisetasche f. ~er n Inhaber(in) m(f); (container) Halter m. ~-up n Verzögerung f; (attack) Überfall m

hole /həʊl/ n Loch nt

holiday /ˈhɒlədeɪ/ n Urlaub m; (Sch) Ferien pl; (public) Feiertag m; (day off) freier Tag m; go on ~ in Urlaub fahren. ~-maker n Urlauber(in) m(f)

holiness /ˈhəʊlɪnɪs/ n Heiligkeit f

Holland /ˈhɒlənd/ n Holland nt

hollow /ˈhɒləʊ/ a hohl; (promise) leer □ n Vertiefung f; (in ground) Mulde f. ~ out vt aushöhlen

holly /ˈhɒlɪ/ n Stechpalme f

hollyhock n Stockrose f

hologram /ˈhɒləgræm/ n Hologramm nt

holster /ˈhəʊlstə(r)/ n Pistolentasche f

holy /ˈhəʊlɪ/ a (-ier, -est) heilig. H~ Ghost or Spirit n Heiliger Geist m. ~ water n Weihwasser nt. H~ Week n Karwoche f

homage /ˈhɒmɪdʒ/ n Huldigung f; pay ~ to huldigen (+ dat)

home /həʊm/ n Zuhause nt (house) Haus nt; (institution) Heim nt; (native land) Heimat f

□ *adv* at ~ zu Hause; come/go ~
nach Hause kommen/gehen
home: ~ **ad'dress** *n* Heimatan-
schrift *f*. ~ **com'puter** *n* Heim-
computer *m*. ~ **game** *n*
Heimspiel *nt*. ~ **help** *n* Haus-
haltshilfe *f*. ~**land** *n* Heimatland *nt*. ~**less** *a* obdachlos
homely /'həʊmlɪ/ *a* (-ier, -iest) *a*
gemütlich (*Amer:* ugly) unscheinbar
home: ~'**made** *a* selbst gemacht.
H~ **Office** *n* Innenministerium
nt. H~ '**Secretary** Innenminis-
ter *m*. ~**sick** *a* be ~**sick**
Heimweh haben (for nach). ~
sickness *n* Heimweh *nt*. ~'**town**
n Heimatstadt *f*. ~**work** *n* (*Sch*)
Hausaufgaben *pl*
homicide /'hɒmɪsaɪd/ *n* Totschlag *m*; (*murder*) Mord *m*
homoeopath|ic /həʊmɪə'pæθɪk/
a homöopathisch. ~**y** /-'ɒpəθi/ *n*
Homöopathie *f*
homogeneous /hɒmə'dʒiːnɪəs/ *a*
homogen
homo'sexual *a* homosexuell □ *n*
Homosexuelle(r) *m/f*
honest /'ɒnɪst/ *a*, **-ly** *adv* ehrlich.
~**y** *n* Ehrlichkeit *f*
honey /'hʌnɪ/ *n* Honig *m* (*fam:
darling*) Schatz *m*
honey: ~**comb** *n* Honigwabe *f*.
~**moon** *n* Flitterwochen *pl*;
(*journey*) Hochzeitsreise *f*. ~
suckle *n* Geißblatt *nt*
honk /hɒŋk/ *vi* hupen
honorary /'ɒnərərɪ/ *a* ehren-
amtlich; (*member, doctorate*)
Ehren-
honour /'ɒnə(r)/ *n* Ehre *f* □ *vt*
ehren; honorieren (*cheque*).
~**able** /-əbl/ *a*, **-bly** *adv* ehren-
haft
hood /hʊd/ *n* Kapuze *f*; (*of pram*)
[Klapp]verdeck *nt*; (*over cooker*)
Abzugshaube *f*; (*Auto, Amer*)
Kühlerhaube *f*
hoodlum /'huːdləm/ *n* Rowdy *m*
'**hoodwink** *vt* (*fam*) reinlegen

hoof /huːf/ *n* (*pl* ~s *or* hooves)
Huf *m*
hook /hʊk/ *n* Haken *m*; **by** ~ **or**
by crook mit allen Mitteln □ *vt*
festhaken (**to** an + *acc*)
hook|ed /hʊkt/ *a* ~**ed nose** Ha-
kennase *f*; ~**ed on** (*fam*) abhängig von; (*keen on*) besessen von.
~**er** *n* (*Amer, sl*) Nutte *f*
hookey /'hʊkɪ/ *n* **play** ~ (*Amer,
fam*) schwänzen
hooligan /'huːlɪgən/ *n* Rowdy *m*.
~**ism** *n* Rowdytum *nt*
hoop /huːp/ *n* Reifen *m*
hooray /hʊ'reɪ/ *int* & *n* = **hurrah**
hoot /huːt/ *n* Ruf *m*; ~**s of
laughter** schallendes Gelächter
nt □ *vi* (*owl:*) rufen; (*car:*) hupen;
(*jeer*) johlen. ~**er** *n* (*of factory*)
Sirene *f*; (*Auto*) Hupe *f*
hoover /'huːvə(r)/ *n* H~ (P)
Staubsauger *m* □ *vt/i* [staub]-
saugen
hop[1] /hɒp/ *n*, & ~**s** *pl* Hopfen *m*
hop[2] *n* Hüpfer *m*; **catch s.o. on
the** ~ (*fam*) jdm ungelegen kommen □ *vi* (*pt/pp* hopped) hüpfen;
~ **it!** (*fam*) hau ab! ~ **in** *vi* (*fam*)
einsteigen. ~ **out** *vi* (*fam*) aussteigen
hope /həʊp/ *n* Hoffnung *f*; (*prospect*) Aussicht *f* (**of** auf + *acc*)
□ *vt/i* hoffen (**for** auf + *acc*); **I** ~
so hoffentlich
hope|ful /'həʊpfl/ *a* hoffnungs-
voll; **be** ~**ful that** hoffen, dass.
~**fully** *adv* hoffnungsvoll; (*it is
hoped*) hoffentlich. ~**less** *a*, **-ly**
adv hoffnungslos; (*useless*)
nutzlos; (*incompetent*) untauglich
horde /hɔːd/ *n* Horde *f*
horizon /hə'raɪzn/ *n* Horizont *m*.
on the ~ am Horizont
horizontal /hɒrɪ'zɒntl/ *a*, **-ly** *adv*
horizontal. ~'**bar** *n* Reck *nt*
horn /hɔːn/ *n* Horn *nt*; (*Auto*)
Hupe *f*
hornet /'hɔːnɪt/ *n* Hornisse *f*
horny /'hɔːnɪ/ *a* schwielig

horoscope /'hɔrəskəup/ n Horoskop nt

horrible /'hɒrɪbl/ a, **-bly** adv schrecklich

horrid /'hɒrɪd/ a grässlich

horrific /hə'rɪfɪk/ a entsetzlich

horrify /'hɒrɪfaɪ/ vt (pt/pp -ied) entsetzen

horror /'hɒrə(r)/ n Entsetzen nt. ~ **film** n Horrorfilm m

hors-d'oeuvre /ɔː'dɜːvr/ n Vorspeise f

horse /hɔːs/ n Pferd nt. **~back** n on ~ **back** zu Pferde. **~chestnut** n [Ross]kastanie f. **~man** n Reiter m. **~play** n Toben nt. **~power** n Pferdestärke f. **~racing** n Pferderennen nt. **~radish** n Meerrettich m. **~shoe** n Hufeisen nt

horti'cultural /hɔːtɪ-/ a Garten-
'horticulture n Gartenbau m

hose /həʊz/ n (pipe) Schlauch m □ vt ~ **down** abspritzen

hosiery /'həʊʒərɪ/ n Strumpfwaren pl

hospice /'hɒspɪs/ n Heim nt; (for the terminally ill) Sterbeklinik f

hospitable /hɒ'spɪtəbl/ a, **-bly** adv gastfreundlich

hospital /'hɒspɪtl/ n Krankenhaus nt

hospitality /hɒspɪ'tælətɪ/ n Gastfreundschaft f

host[1] /həʊst/ n a ~ **of** eine Menge von

host[2] n Gastgeber m

host[3] n (Relig) Hostie f

hostage /'hɒstɪdʒ/ n Geisel f

hostel /'hɒstl/ n [Wohn]heim nt

hostess /'həʊstɪs/ n Gastgeberin f

hostile /'hɒstaɪl/ a feindlich; (unfriendly) feindselig

hostility /hɒ'stɪlətɪ/ n Feindschaft f; **~ies** pl Feindseligkeiten pl

hot /hɒt/ a (hotter, hottest) heiß; (meal) warm; (spicy) scharf; **I am** or **feel ~** mir ist heiß

'hotbed n (fig) Brutstätte f

hotchpotch /'hɒtʃpɒtʃ/ n Mischmasch m

hotel /həʊ'tel/ n Hotel nt. **~ier** /-ɪə(r)/ n Hotelier m

hot: ~head n Hitzkopf m. **~headed** a hitzköpfig. **~house** n Treibhaus nt. **~ly** adv (fig) heiß, heftig. **~plate** n Tellerwärmer m; (of cooker) Kochplatte f. **~ tap** n Warmwasserhahn m. **~tempered** a jähzornig. **~'waterbottle** n Wärmflasche f

hound /haʊnd/ n Jagdhund m □ vt (fig) verfolgen

hour /'aʊə(r)/ n Stunde f. **~ly** a & adv stündlich; **~ly pay** or **rate** Stundenlohn m

house[1] /haʊs/ n Haus nt; **at my ~** bei mir

house[2] /haʊz/ vt unterbringen

house /haʊs/: **~boat** n Hausboot nt. **~breaking** n Einbruch m. **~hold** n Haushalt m. **~holder** n Hausinhaber(in) f. **~keeper** n Haushälterin f. **~keeping** n Hauswirtschaft f; (money) Haushaltsgeld nt. **~plant** n Zimmerpflanze f. **~trained** a stubenrein. **~warming** n have a **~warming party** Einstand feiern. **~wife** n Hausfrau f. **~work** n Hausarbeit f

housing /'haʊzɪŋ/ n Wohnungen pl; (Techn) Gehäuse nt. **~ estate** n Wohnsiedlung f

hovel /'hɒvl/ n elende Hütte f

hover /'hɒvə(r)/ vi schweben; (be undecided) schwanken; (linger) herumstehen. **~craft** n Luftkissenfahrzeug nt

how /haʊ/ adv wie; **~ do you do?** guten Tag! **~ many** wie viele; **~ much** wie viel; **and ~!** und ob!

how'ever adv (in question) wie; (nevertheless) jedoch, aber; **~ small** wie klein es auch sein mag

howl /haʊl/ n Heulen nt □ vi heulen; (baby:) brüllen. **~er** n (fam) Schnitzer m

hub /hʌb/ n Nabe f; (fig) Mittelpunkt m

hubbub /'hʌbʌb/ n Stimmengewirr n

'hub-cap n Radkappe f

huddle /'hʌdl/ vi ~ **together** sich zusammendrängen

hue¹ /hju:/ n Farbe f

hue² n ~ **and cry** Aufruhr m

huff /hʌf/ n **in a** ~ beleidigt

hug /hʌg/ n Umarmung f □ vt (pt/pp **hugged**) umarmen

huge /hju:dʒ/ a, **-ly** adv riesig

hulking /'hʌlkɪŋ/ a (fam) ungeschlacht

hull /hʌl/ n (Naut) Rumpf m

hullo /hə'ləʊ/ int = hallo

hum /hʌm/ n Summen nt; Brummen nt □ vt/i (pt/pp **hummed**) summen; ⟨motor:⟩ brummen; ~ **and haw** nach den Worten herauswollen

human /'hju:mən/ a menschlich □ n Mensch m. ~ **being** n Mensch m

humane /hju:'meɪn/ a, **-ly** adv human

humanitarian /hju:mænɪ'teərɪən/ a humanitär

humanit|y /hju:'mænətɪ/ n Menschheit f; ~**ies** pl (Univ) Geisteswissenschaften pl

humble /'hʌmbl/ a (**-r**, **-st**), **-bly** adv demütig □ vt demütigen

'humdrum a eintönig

humid /'hju:mɪd/ a feucht. ~**ity** /-'mɪdətɪ/ n Feuchtigkeit f

humiliat|e /hju:'mɪlɪeɪt/ vt demütigen. ~**ion** /-'eɪʃn/ n Demütigung f

humility /hju:'mɪlətɪ/ n Demut f

'humming-bird n Kolibri m

humorous /'hju:mərəs/ a, **-ly** adv humorvoll; ⟨story⟩ humoristisch

humour /'hju:mə(r)/ n Humor m; ⟨mood⟩ Laune f; **have a sense of** ~ Humor haben □ vt ~ **s.o** jdm seinen Willen lassen

hump /hʌmp/ n Buckel m; (of camel) Höcker m □ vt schleppen

hunch /hʌntʃ/ n (idea) Ahnung f

'hunch|back n Bucklige(r) m/f. ~**ed** a ~**ed up** gebeugt

hundred /'hʌndrəd/ a **one/a** ~ [ein]hundert □ n Hundert nt; (written figure) Hundert f. ~**th** a hundertste(r,s) □ n Hundertstel nt. ~**weight** n ≈ Zentner m

hung /hʌŋ/ see **hang**

Hungarian /hʌŋ'geərɪən/ a ungarisch □ n Ungar(in) m(f)

Hungary /'hʌŋgərɪ/ n Ungarn nt

hunger /'hʌŋgə(r)/ n Hunger m. ~**-strike** n Hungerstreik m

hungry /'hʌŋgrɪ/ a (**-ier**, **-iest**), **-ily** adv hungrig; **be** ~ Hunger haben

hunk /hʌŋk/ n [großes] Stück nt

hunt /hʌnt/ n Jagd f; (for criminal) Fahndung f □ vt/i jagen; fahnden nach (criminal); ~ **for** suchen. ~**er** n Jäger m; (horse) Jagdpferd m. ~**ing** n Jagd f

hurdle /'hɜ:dl/ n (Sport & fig) Hürde f. ~**r** n Hürdenläufer(in) m(f)

hurl /hɜ:l/ vt schleudern

hurrah /hʊ'rɑ:/, **hurray** /hʊ'reɪ/ int hurra! □ n Hurra nt

hurricane /'hʌrɪkən/ n Orkan m

hurried /'hʌrɪd/ a, **-ly** adv eilig; (superficial) flüchtig

hurry /'hʌrɪ/ n Eile f; **be in a** ~ es eilig haben □ vi (pt/pp **-ied**) sich beeilen; (go quickly) eilen. ~ **up** vi sich beeilen □ vt antreiben

hurt /hɜ:t/ n Schmerz m □ vt/i (pt/pp **hurt**) weh tun (+ dat); (injure) verletzen; (offend) kränken. ~**ful** a verletzend

hurtle /'hɜ:tl/ vi ~ **along** rasen

husband /'hʌzbənd/ n [Ehe]mann m

hush /hʌʃ/ n Stille f □ vt ~ **up** vertuschen. ~**ed** a gedämpft. ~**'hush** a (fam) streng geheim

husk /hʌsk/ n Spelze f

husky /'hʌskɪ/ a (**-ier**, **-iest**) heiser; (burly) Stämmig

hustle /'hʌsl/ vt drängen □ n Gedränge nt; **~ and bustle** geschäftiges Treiben nt

hut /hʌt/ n Hütte f

hutch /hʌtʃ/ n [Kaninchen]stall m

hybrid /'haɪbrɪd/ a hybrid □ n Hybride f

hydrangea /haɪ'dreɪndʒə/ n Hortensie f

hydrant /'haɪdrənt/ n **[fire] ~** Hydrant m

hydraulic /haɪ'drɔːlɪk/ a, **-ally** adv hydraulisch

hydrochloric /haɪdrə'klɔːrɪk/ **~ acid** Salzsäure f

hydroe'lectric /haɪdrəʊ-/ a hydroelektrisch. **~ power station** n Wasserkraftwerk nt

hydrofoil /'haɪdrə-/ n Tragflügelboot nt

hydrogen /'haɪdrədʒən/ n Wasserstoff m

hyena /haɪ'iːnə/ n Hyäne f

hygien|e /'haɪdʒiːn/ n Hygiene f. **~ic** /haɪ'dʒiːnɪk/ a, **-ally** adv hygienisch

hymn /hɪm/ n Kirchenlied nt. **~book** n Gesangbuch nt

hyphen /'haɪfn/ n Bindestrich m. **~ate** vt mit Bindestrich schreiben

hypno|sis /hɪp'nəʊsɪs/ n Hypnose f. **~tic** /-'nɒtɪk/ a hypnotisch

hypno|tism /'hɪpnətɪzm/ n Hypnotik f. **~tist** /-tɪst/ n Hypnotiseur m. **~tize** vt hypnotisieren

hypochondriac /haɪpə'kɒndriæk/ a hypochondrisch □ n Hypochonder m

hypocrisy /hɪ'pɒkrəsɪ/ n Heuchelei f

hypocrit|e /'hɪpəkrɪt/ n Heuchler(in) m(f). **~ical** /-'krɪtɪkl/ a, **-ly** adv heuchlerisch

hypodermic /haɪpə'dɜːmɪk/ a & n **[syringe]** Injektionsspritze f

hypothe|sis /haɪ'pɒθəsɪs/ n Hypothese f. **~tical** /-ə'θetɪkl/ a, **-ly** adv hypothetisch

hyster|ia /hɪ'stɪərɪə/ n Hysterie f. **~ical** /-'sterɪkl/ a, **-ly** adv hysterisch. **~ics** /hɪ'sterɪks/ npl hysterischer Anfall m

I

I /aɪ/ pron ich

ice /aɪs/ n Eis nt □ vt mit Zuckerguss überziehen ⟨cake⟩

ice: ~ age n Eiszeit f. **~axe** n Eispickel m. **~berg** /-bɜːg/ n Eisberg m. **~box** n (Amer) Kühlschrank m. **~cream** n [Speise]eis nt. **~cream parlour** n Eisdiele f. **~cube** n Eiswürfel m

Iceland /'aɪslənd/ n Island m

ice: ~lolly n Eis nt am Stiel. **~rink** n Eisbahn f

icicle /'aɪsɪkl/ n Eiszapfen m

icing /'aɪsɪŋ/ n Zuckerguss m. **~sugar** n Puderzucker m

icon /'aɪkɒn/ n Ikone f

icy /'aɪsɪ/ a (**-ier, -iest**) **-ily** adv eisig; ⟨road⟩ vereist

idea /aɪ'dɪə/ n Idee f; ⟨conception⟩ Vorstellung f. **I have no ~!** ich habe keine Ahnung!

ideal /aɪ'dɪəl/ a ideal □ n Ideal nt. **~ism** n Idealismus m. **~ist** n Idealist(in) m(f). **~istic** /-'lɪstɪk/ a idealistisch. **~ize** vt idealisieren. **~ly** adv ideal; ⟨in ideal circumstances⟩ idealerweise

identi|fication /aɪdentɪfɪ'keɪʃn/ n Identifizierung f; ⟨proof of identity⟩ Ausweispapiere pl. **~fy** /aɪ'dentɪfaɪ/ vt (pt/pp **-ied**) identifizieren

identity /aɪ'dentətɪ/ n Identität f. **~card** n [Personal]ausweis m

ideological /aɪdɪə'lɒdʒɪkl/ a ideologisch. **~y** /aɪdɪ'ɒlədʒɪ/ n Ideologie f

idiom /'ɪdɪəm/ n [feste] Redewendung f. **~atic** /-'mætɪk/ a, **-ally** adv idiomatisch

idiosyncrasy /ɪdɪə'sɪŋkrəsɪ/ n
Eigenart f

idiot /'ɪdɪət/ n Idiot m. **~ic**
/-'ɒtɪk/ a idiotisch

idle /'aɪdl/ a (-r, -st), **-ly** adv untätig; (lazy) faul; (empty) leer;
(machine) nicht in Betrieb □ vi
faulenzen; (engine:) leer laufen.
~ness n Untätigkeit f; Faulheit
f

idol /'aɪdl/ n Idol nt. **~ize** /'aɪdə-
laɪz/ vt vergöttern

idyllic /ɪ'dɪlɪk/ a idyllisch

i.e. abbr (id est) d.h.

if /ɪf/ conj wenn; (whether) ob; **as
if** als ob

ignite /ɪg'naɪt/ vt entzünden □ vi
sich entzünden

ignition /ɪg'nɪʃn/ n (Auto) Zün-
dung f. **~ key** n Zündschlüssel
m

ignoramus /ɪgnə'reɪməs/ n Igno-
rant m

ignoran|ce /'ɪgnərəns/ n Unwis-
senheit f. **~t** a unwissend; (rude)
ungehobelt

ignore /ɪg'nɔː(r)/ vt ignorieren

ilk /ɪlk/ n (fam) **of that ~** von der
Sorte

ill /ɪl/ a krank; (bad) schlecht;
feel ~ at ease sich unbehaglich
fühlen □ adv schlecht □ n
Schlechte(s) nt; (evil) Übel nt. **~-
advised** a unklug. **~-bred** a
schlecht erzogen

illegal /ɪ'liːgl/ a, **-ly** adv illegal

illegible /ɪ'ledʒəbl/ a, **-bly** adv
unleserlich

illegitima|cy /ɪlɪ'dʒɪtɪməsɪ/ n
Unehelichkeit f. **~te** /-mət/ a unehelich; (claim) unberechtigt

illicit /ɪ'lɪsɪt/ a, **-ly** adv illegal

illitera|cy /ɪ'lɪtərəsɪ/ n Anal-
phabetentum nt. **~te** /-rət/ a be
~te nicht lesen und schreiben
können □ n Analphabet(in) m(f)

illness /'ɪlnɪs/ n Krankheit f

illogical /ɪ'lɒdʒɪkl/ a, **-ly** adv unlogisch

ill-treat /ɪl'triːt/ vt misshandeln.
~ment n Misshandlung f

illuminat|e /ɪ'luːmɪneɪt/ vt be-
leuchten. **~ing** a aufschlussreich. **~ion** /-'neɪʃn/ n
Beleuchtung f

illusion /ɪ'luːʒn/ n Illusion f; **be
under the ~ that** sich (dat) einbilden, dass

illusory /ɪ'luːsərɪ/ a illusorisch

illustrat|e /'ɪləstreɪt/ vt illust-
rieren. **~ion** /-'streɪʃn/ n Illustration f

illustrious /ɪ'lʌstrɪəs/ a berühmt

image /'ɪmɪdʒ/ n Bild nt; (statue)
Standbild nt; (figure) Figur f; (ex-
act likeness) Ebenbild nt; [public]
~ Image nt

imagin|able /ɪ'mædʒɪnəbl/ a vor-
stellbar. **~ary** /-ərɪ/ a eingebildet

imaginat|ion /ɪmædʒɪ'neɪʃn/ n
Phantasie f; (fancy) Einbildung
f. **~ive** /ɪ'mædʒɪnətɪv/ a, **-ly** adv
phantasievoll; (full of ideas) ein-
fallsreich

imagine /ɪ'mædʒɪn/ vt sich (dat)
vorstellen; (wrongly) sich (dat)
einbilden

im'balance n Unausgeglichen-
heit f

imbecile /'ɪmbəsiːl/ n Schwach-
sinnige(r) m/f; (pej) Idiot m

imbibe /ɪm'baɪb/ vt trinken; (fig)
aufnehmen

imbue /ɪm'bjuː/ vt **be ~d with**
erfüllt sein von

imitat|e /'ɪmɪteɪt/ vt nachahmen,
imitieren. **~ion** /-'teɪʃn/ n Nachahmung f, Imitation f

immaculate /ɪ'mækjʊlət/ a, **-ly**
adv tadellos; (Relig) unbefleckt

imma'terial a (unimportant) unwichtig, unwesentlich

imma'ture a unreif

immediate /ɪ'miːdɪət/ a sofortig;
(nearest) nächste(r,s). **~ly** adv sofort; **~ly next to** unmittelbar
neben □ conj sobald

immemorial /ɪmə'mɔːrɪəl/ a
from time ~ seit Urzeiten

immense /ɪ'mens/ *a*, **-ly** *adv* riesig; (*fam*) enorm; (*extreme*) äußerst

immers|e /ɪ'mɜːs/ *vt* untertauchen; **be ~ed in** (*fig*) vertieft sein in (+ *acc*). **~ion** /-ʒ:ʃn/ *n* Untertauchen *nt*. **~ion heater** *m* Heißwasserbereiter *m*

immigrant /'ɪmɪgrənt/ *n* Einwanderer *m*

immigrat|e /'ɪmɪgreɪt/ *vi* einwandern. **~ion** /-'greɪʃn/ *n* Einwanderung *f*

imminent /'ɪmɪnənt/ *a* **be ~** unmittelbar bevorstehen

immobil|e /ɪ'məʊbaɪl/ *a* unbeweglich. **~ize** /-bəlaɪz/ *vt* (*fig*) lähmen; (*Med*) ruhigstellen

immoderate /ɪ'mɒdərət/ *a* übermäßig

immodest /ɪ'mɒdɪst/ *a* unbescheiden

immoral /ɪ'mɒrəl/ *a*, **-ly** *adv* unmoralisch. **~ity** /ɪmə'rælɪtɪ/ *n* Unmoral *f*

immortal /ɪ'mɔːtl/ *a* unsterblich. **~ity** /-'tælɪtɪ/ *n* Unsterblichkeit *f*. **~ize** *vt* verewigen

immovable /ɪ'muːvəbl/ *a* unbeweglich; (*fig*) fest

immune /ɪ'mjuːn/ *a* immun (**to/ from** gegen). **~ system** *n* Abwehrsystem *nt*

immunity /ɪ'mjuːnɪtɪ/ *n* Immunität *f*

immunize /'ɪmjʊnaɪz/ *vt* immunisieren

imp /ɪmp/ *n* Kobold *m*

impact /'ɪmpækt/ *n* Aufprall *m*; (*collision*) Zusammenprall *m*; (*of bomb*) Einschlag *m*; (*fig*) Auswirkung *f*

impair /ɪm'peə(r)/ *vt* beeinträchtigen

impale /ɪm'peɪl/ *vt* aufspießen

impart /ɪm'pɑːt/ *vt* übermitteln (**to** *dat*); vermitteln ⟨*knowledge*⟩

impartial /ɪm'pɑːʃl/ *a* unparteiisch. **~ality** /-ʃɪ'ælɪtɪ/ *n* Unparteilichkeit *f*

impassable /ɪm'pɑːsəbl/ *a* unpassierbar

impasse /æm'pɑːs/ *n* (*fig*) Sackgasse *f*

impassioned /ɪm'pæʃnd/ *a* leidenschaftlich

impassive /ɪm'pæsɪv/ *a*, **-ly** *adv* unbeweglich

impatien|ce /ɪm'peɪʃns/ *n* Ungeduld *f*. **~t** *a*, **-ly** *adv* ungeduldig

impeach /ɪm'piːtʃ/ *vt* anklagen

impeccable /ɪm'pekəbl/ *a*, **-bly** *adv* tadellos

impede /ɪm'piːd/ *vt* behindern

impediment /ɪm'pedɪmənt/ *n* Hindernis *nt*; (*in speech*) Sprachfehler *m*

impel /ɪm'pel/ *vt* (*pt/pp* **impelled**) treiben; **feel ~led** sich genötigt fühlen (**to** zu)

impending /ɪm'pendɪŋ/ *a* bevorstehend

impenetrable /ɪm'penɪtrəbl/ *a* undurchdringlich

imperative /ɪm'perətɪv/ *a* **be ~** dringend notwendig sein □ *n* (*Gram*) Imperativ *m*, Befehlsform *f*

imper'ceptible *a* nicht wahrnehmbar

im'perfect *a* unvollkommen; (*faulty*) fehlerhaft □ *n* (*Gram*) Imperfekt *nt*. **~ion** /-'fekʃn/ *n* Unvollkommenheit *f*; (*fault*) Fehler *m*

imperial /ɪm'pɪərɪəl/ *a* kaiserlich. **~ism** *n* Imperialismus *m*

imperil /ɪm'perəl/ *vt* (*pt/pp* **imperilled**) gefährden

imperious /ɪm'pɪərɪəs/ *a*, **-ly** *adv* herrisch

im'personal *a* unpersönlich

impersonat|e /ɪm'pɜːsəneɪt/ *vt* sich ausgeben als; (*Theat*) nachahmen, imitieren. **~or** *n* Imitator *m*

impertinen|ce /ɪm'pɜːtɪnəns/ *n* Frechheit *f*. **~t** *a* frech

imperturbable /ɪmpə'tɜːbəbl/ *a* unerschütterlich

impervious /ɪm'pɜːvɪəs/ *a* **~ to** (*fig*) unempfänglich für

impetuous /ɪm'petjʊəs/ a, -ly adv ungestüm

impetus /'ɪmpɪtəs/ n Schwung m

impish /'ɪmpɪʃ/ a schelmisch

implacable /ɪm'plækəbl/ a unerbittlich

im'plant[1] vt einpflanzen

'implant[2] n Implantat nt

implement[1] /'ɪmplɪmənt/ n Gerät nt

implement[2] /'ɪmplɪment/ vt ausführen

implicate /'ɪmplɪkeɪt/ vt verwickeln. ~ion /-'keɪʃn/ n Verwicklung f; ~ions pl Auswirkungen pl; by ~ion implizit

implicit /ɪm'plɪsɪt/ a, -ly adv unausgesprochen; (absolute) unbedingt

implore /ɪm'plɔː(r)/ vt anflehen

imply /ɪm'plaɪ/ vt (pt/pp -ied) andeuten; what are you ~ing? was wollen Sie damit sagen?

impo'lite a, -ly adv unhöflich

import[1] /'ɪmpɔːt/ n Import m, Einfuhr f; (importance) Wichtigkeit f; (meaning) Bedeutung f

import[2] /ɪm'pɔːt/ vt importieren, einführen

importan|ce /ɪm'pɔːtns/ n Wichtigkeit f. ~t a wichtig

importer /ɪm'pɔːtə(r)/ n Importeur m

impos|e /ɪm'pəʊz/ vt auferlegen (on dat) □ vi sich aufdrängen (on dat). ~ing a eindrucksvoll. ~ition /ɪmpə'zɪʃn/ n be an ~ition eine Zumutung sein

impossi'bility n Unmöglichkeit f

im'possible a, -bly adv unmöglich

impostor /ɪm'pɒstə(r)/ n Betrüger(in) m(f)

impoten|ce /'ɪmpətəns/ n Machtlosigkeit f; (Med) Impotenz f. ~t a machtlos; (Med) impotent

impound /ɪm'paʊnd/ vt beschlagnahmen

impoverished /ɪm'pɒvərɪʃt/ a verarmt

im'practicable a undurchführbar

im'practical a unpraktisch

impre'cise a ungenau

impregnable /ɪm'pregnəbl/ a uneinnehmbar

impregnate /'ɪmpregneɪt/ vt tränken; (Biol) befruchten

im'press vt beeindrucken; ~ sth [up]on s.o. jdm etw einprägen

impression /ɪm'preʃn/ n Eindruck m; (imitation) Nachahmung f; (imprint) Abdruck m; (edition) Auflage f. ~ism n Impressionismus m

impressive /ɪm'presɪv/ a eindrucksvoll

'imprint[1] n Abdruck m

im'print[2] vt prägen; (fig) einprägen (on dat)

im'prison vt gefangen halten; (put in prison) ins Gefängnis sperren

im'probable a unwahrscheinlich

impromptu /ɪm'promptjuː/ a improvisiert □ adv aus dem Stegreif

im'proper a, -ly adv inkorrekt; (indecent) unanständig

impro'priety n Unkorrektheit f

improve /ɪm'pruːv/ vt verbessern; verschönern (appearance) □ vi sich bessern; ~ [up]on übertreffen. ~ment /-mənt/ n Verbesserung f; (in health) Besserung f

improvise /'ɪmprəvaɪz/ vt/i improvisieren

im'prudent a unklug

impuden|ce /'ɪmpjʊdəns/ n Frechheit f. ~t a, -ly adv frech

impulse /'ɪmpʌls/ n Impuls m; on [an] ~ e impulsiv. ~ive /-'pʌlsɪv/ a, -ly adv impulsiv

impunity /ɪm'pjuːnəti/ n with ~ ungestraft

im'pure a unrein. ~ity n Unreinheit f; ~ities pl Verunreinigungen pl

impute /ɪm'pjuːt/ vt zuschreiben (**to** dat)

in /ɪn/ prep in (+ dat/into) (+ acc); **sit in the garden** im Garten sitzen; **go in the garden** in den Garten gehen; **in May** im Mai; **in the summer/winter** im Sommer/Winter; **in 1992** [im Jahre] 1992; **in the heat** bei dieser Hitze; **in the rain/sun** im Regen/in der Sonne; **in the evening** am Abend; **in the sky** am Himmel; **in the world** auf der Welt; **in the street** auf der Straße; **deaf in one ear** auf einem Ohr taub; **in the army** beim Militär; **in English/German** auf Englisch/Deutsch; **in ink/pencil** mit Tinte/Bleistift; **in a soft/loud voice** mit leiser/lauter Stimme; **in doing this, he** ... indem er das tut, ... er ○ adv (at home) zu Hause; (indoors) drinnen; **he's not in yet** er ist noch nicht da; **all in** alles inbegriffen; (fam: exhausted) kaputt; (fam) **day in, day out** tagaus, tagein; **keep in with s.o.** sich mit jdm gut stellen; **have it in for s.o.** (fam) es auf jdn abgesehen haben; **let oneself in for sth** sich auf etw (acc) einlassen; **send/go in** hineinschicken/-gehen; **come/bring in** hereinkommen/-bringen ○ a (fam: in fashion) in ○ n **the ins and outs** alle Einzelheiten pl

ina'bility n Unfähigkeit f

inac'cessible a unzugänglich

in'accura|cy n Ungenauigkeit f. **~te** a, **-ly** adv ungenau

in'active a untätig. **~tivity** n Untätigkeit f

in'adequate a, **-ly** adv unzulänglich; **feel** ~ sich der Situation nicht gewachsen fühlen

inad'missable a unzulässig

inad'vertent|ly /ɪnəd'vɜːtəntlɪ/ adv versehentlich

inad'visable a nicht ratsam

inane /ɪ'neɪn/ a, **-ly** adv albern

in'animate a unbelebt

in'applicable a nicht zutreffend

inap'propriate a unangebracht

inar'ticulate a undeutlich; **be** ~ sich nicht gut ausdrücken können

inat'tentive a unaufmerksam

in'audible a, **-bly** adv unhörbar

inaugural /ɪ'nɔːgjʊrl/ a Antritts-

inaugurat|e /ɪ'nɔːgjʊreɪt/ vt [feierlich] in sein Amt einführen. **~ion** /-'reɪʃn/ n Amtseinführung f

inau'spicious a ungünstig

inborn /'ɪnbɔːn/ a angeboren

inbred /ɪn'bred/ a angeboren

incalculable /ɪn'kælkjʊləbl/ a nicht berechenbar; (fig) unabsehbar

in'capable a unfähig; **be** ~ **of doing sth** nicht fähig sein, etw zu tun

incapacitate /ɪnkə'pæsɪteɪt/ vt unfähig machen

incarcerate /ɪn'kɑːsəreɪt/ vt einkerkern

incarnat|e /ɪn'kɑːnət/ a **the devil** ~**e** der leibhaftige Satan. **~ion** /-'neɪʃn/ n Inkarnation f

incendiary /ɪn'sendɪərɪ/ a & n [**bomb**] Brandbombe f

incense[1] /'ɪnsens/ n Weihrauch m

incense[2] /ɪn'sens/ vt wütend machen

incentive /ɪn'sentɪv/ n Anreiz m

inception /ɪn'sepʃn/ n Beginn m

incessant /ɪn'sesnt/ a, **-ly** adv unaufhörlich

incest /'ɪnsest/ n Inzest m, Blutschande f

inch /ɪntʃ/ n Zoll m ○ vi ~ **forward** sich ganz langsam vorwärts schieben

inciden|ce /'ɪnsɪdəns/ n Vorkommen nt. **~t** n Zwischenfall m

incidental /ɪnsɪ'dentl/ a nebensächlich; (remark) beiläufig; (expenses) Neben-. **~ly** adv übrigens

incinerat|e /ɪn'sɪnəreɪt/ vt verbrennen. **~or** n Verbrennungsofen m

incipient /ɪnˈsɪpɪənt/ a angehend

incision /ɪnˈsɪʒn/ n Einschnitt m

incisive /ɪnˈsaɪsɪv/ a scharfsinnig

incisor /ɪnˈsaɪzə(r)/ n Schneidezahn m

incite /ɪnˈsaɪt/ vt aufhetzen. **~ment** n Aufhetzung f

inci'vility n Unhöflichkeit f

in'clement a rau

inclination /ɪnklɪˈneɪʃn/ n Neigung f

incline¹ /ɪnˈklaɪn/ vt neigen; **be ~d to do sth** dazu neigen, etw zu tun □ vi sich neigen

incline² /ˈɪnklaɪn/ n Neigung f

inclu|de /ɪnˈkluːd/ vt einschließen; (contain) enthalten; (incorporate) aufnehmen (**in** in + acc). **~ding** prep einschließlich (+ gen). **~sion** /-uːʒn/ n Aufnahme f

inclusive /ɪnˈkluːsɪv/ a Inklusiv-; **~ of** einschließlich (+ gen) □ adv inklusive

incognito /ɪnkɒgˈniːtəʊ/ adv inkognito

inco'herent a, **-ly** adv zusammenhanglos; (incomprehensible) unverständlich

income /ˈɪnkəm/ n Einkommen nt. **~ tax** n Einkommensteuer f

'incoming a ankommend; (mail, call) eingehend. **~ tide** n steigende Flut f

in'comparable a unvergleichlich

incom'patible a unvereinbar; **be ~** (people:) nicht zueinander passen

in'competen|ce n Unfähigkeit f. **~t** a unfähig

incom'plete a unvollständig

incompre'hensible a unverständlich

incon'ceivable a undenkbar

incon'clusive a nicht schlüssig

incongruous /ɪnˈkɒŋɡrʊəs/ a unpassend

inconsequential /ɪnkɒnsɪˈkwenʃl/ a unbedeutend

incon'siderate a rücksichtslos

incon'sisten|t a, **-ly** adv widersprüchlich; (illogical) inkonsequent; **be ~** nicht übereinstimmen

inconsolable /ɪnkənˈsəʊləbl/ a untröstlich

incon'spicuous a unauffällig

continen|ce /ɪnˈkɒntɪnəns/ n Inkontinenz f. **~t** a inkontinent

incon'venien|ce n Unannehmlichkeit f; (drawback) Nachteil m; **put s.o. to ~ce** Umstände machen. **~t** a, **-ly** adv ungünstig; **be ~t for s.o.** jdm nicht passen

incorporate /ɪnˈkɔːpəreɪt/ vt aufnehmen; (contain) enthalten

incor'rect a, **-ly** adv inkorrekt

incorrigible /ɪnˈkɒrɪdʒəbl/ a unverbesserlich

incorruptible /ɪnkəˈrʌptəbl/ a unbestechlich

increase¹ /ˈɪnkriːs/ n Zunahme f; (rise) Erhöhung f; **be on the ~** zunehmen

increase² /ɪnˈkriːs/ vt vergrößern; (raise) erhöhen □ vi zunehmen; (rise) sich erhöhen. **~ing** a, **-ly** adv zunehmend

in'credible a, **-bly** adv unglaublich

incredulous /ɪnˈkredjʊləs/ a ungläubig

increment /ˈɪnkrɪmənt/ n Gehaltszulage f

incriminate /ɪnˈkrɪmɪneɪt/ vt (Jur) belasten

incubat|e /ˈɪŋkjʊbeɪt/ vt ausbrüten. **~ion** /-ˈbeɪʃn/ n Ausbrüten nt. **~ion period** n (Med) Inkubationszeit f. **~or** n (for baby) Brutkasten m

inculcate /ˈɪnkʌlkeɪt/ vt einprägen (**in** dat)

incumbent /ɪnˈkʌmbənt/ a **be ~ on s.o.** jds Pflicht sein

incur /ɪnˈkɜː(r)/ vt (pt/pp incurred) sich (dat) zuziehen; machen (debts) in'curable *a*, -bly *adv* unheilbar

incursion /ɪn'kɜ:ʃn/ *n* Einfall *m*

indebted /ɪn'detɪd/ *a* verpflichtet
(to *dat*)

in'decent *a*, -ly *adv* unanständig

inde'cision *n* Unentschlossenheit *f*

inde'cisive *a* ergebnislos; *(person)* unentschlossen

indeed /ɪn'di:d/ *adv* in der Tat,
tatsächlich; yes ~! allerdings!
I am/do oh doch! very much ~
sehr; thank you very much ~
vielen herzlichen Dank

indefatigable /ɪndɪ'fætɪgəbl/ *a*
unermüdlich

in'definite *a* unbestimmt. ~ly
adv unbegrenzt; *(postpone)* auf
unbestimmte Zeit

indelible /ɪn'delɪbl/ *a*, -bly *adv*
nicht zu entfernen; *(fig)* unauslöschlich

indemni|fy /ɪn'demnɪfaɪ/ *vt*
(pt/pp -ied) versichern; *(compensate)* entschädigen. ~ty *n* Versicherung *f*; Entschädigung *f*

indent /ɪn'dent/ *vt (Typ)* einrücken. ~ation /-'teɪʃn/ *n* Einrückung *f*; *(notch)* Kerbe *f*

inde'penden|ce *n* Unabhängigkeit *f*; *(self-reliance)* Selbständigkeit *f*. ~t *a*, -ly *adv*
unabhängig; selbständig

indescribable /ɪndɪ'skraɪbəbl/ *a*,
-bly *adv* unbeschreiblich

indestructible /ɪndɪ'strʌktəbl/ *a*
unzerstörbar

indeterminate /ɪndɪ'tɜ:mɪnət/ *a*
unbestimmt

index /'ɪndeks/ *n* Register *nt*

index: ~ card *n* Karteikarte *f*. ~
finger *n* Zeigefinger *m*. ~-linked
a (pension) dynamisch

India /'ɪndɪə/ *n* Indien *nt*. ~n *a*
indisch; *(American)* indianisch
□ *n* Inder(in) *m(f)*; *(American)* Indianer(in) *m(f)*

Indian: ~ 'ink *n* Tusche *f*. ~
'summer *n* Nachsommer *m*

indicat|e /'ɪndɪkeɪt/ *vt* zeigen;
(point at) zeigen auf (+ *acc)*;
(hint) andeuten; *(register)* anzeigen □ *vi (Auto)* blinken. ~ion
/-'keɪʃn/ *n* Anzeichen *nt*

indicative /ɪn'dɪkətɪv/ *a* be ~ of
schließen lassen auf (+ *acc)* □ *n*
(Gram) Indikativ *m*

indicator /'ɪndɪkeɪtə(r)/ *n (Auto)*
Blinker *m*

indict /ɪn'daɪt/ *vt* anklagen.
~ment *n* Anklage *f*

in'differen|ce *n* Gleichgültigkeit
f. ~t *a*, -ly *adv* gleichgültig; *(not
good)* mittelmäßig

indigenous /ɪn'dɪdʒɪnəs/ *a*
einheimisch

indi'gest|ible *a* unverdaulich;
(difficult to digest) schwer verdaulich. ~ion *n* Magenverstimmung *f*

indigna|nt /ɪn'dɪgnənt/ *a*, -ly *adv*
entrüstet, empört. ~tion
/-'neɪʃn/ *n* Entrüstung *f*, Empörung *f*

in'dignity *n* Demütigung *f*

indi'rect *a*, -ly *adv* indirekt

indi'screet *a* indiskret

indis'cretion *n* Indiskretion *f*

indiscriminate /ɪndɪ'skrɪmɪnət/
a, -ly *adv* wahllos

indi'spensable *a* unentbehrlich

indisposed /ɪndɪ'spəʊzd/ *a* indisponiert

indisputable /ɪndɪ'spju:təbl/ *a*,
-bly *adv* unbestreitbar

indi'stinct *a*, -ly *adv* undeutlich

indistinguishable /ɪndɪ'stɪŋgwɪʃəbl/ *a* be ~ nicht zu unterscheiden sein; *(not visible)* nicht
erkennbar sein

individual /ɪndɪ'vɪdjʊəl/ *a*, -ly
adv individuell; *(single)* einzeln
□ *n* Individuum *nt*. ~ity /-'ælətɪ/
n Individualität *f*

indi'visible *a* unteilbar

indoctrinate /ɪn'dɒktrɪneɪt/ *vt*
indoktrinieren

indolen|ce /'ɪndələns/ *n* Faulheit
f. ~t *a* faul

indomitable /ɪnˈdɒmɪtəbl/ a unbeugsam

indoor /ˈɪndɔː(r)/ a Innen-; (clothes) Haus-; (plant) Zimmer-; (Sport) Hallen-. **~s** /-ˈdɔːz/ adv im Haus, drinnen; **go ~s** ins Haus gehen

induce /ɪnˈdjuːs/ vt dazu bewegen (**to** zu); (produce) herbeiführen. **~ment** n (incentive) Anreiz m

indulge /ɪnˈdʌldʒ/ vt frönen (+ dat); verwöhnen (child) □ vi **~ in** frönen (+ dat). **~nce** /-əns/ n Nachgiebigkeit f; (leniency) Nachsicht f. **~nt** a [zu] nachgiebig; nachsichtig

industrial /ɪnˈdʌstrɪəl/ a Industrie-; **take ~ action** streiken. **~ist** n Industrielle(r) m. **~ized** a industrialisiert

industr|ious /ɪnˈdʌstrɪəs/ a, **-ly** adv fleißig. **~y** /ˈɪndəstrɪ/ n Industrie f; (zeal) Fleiß m

inebriated /ɪˈniːbrɪeɪtɪd/ a betrunken

in'edible a nicht essbar

inef'fective a, **-ly** adv unwirksam; (person) untauglich

ineffectual /ɪnɪˈfektʃʊəl/ a unwirksam; (person) untauglich

inef'ficient a unfähig; (organization) nicht leistungsfähig; (method) nicht rationell

in'eligible a nicht berechtigt

inept /ɪˈnept/ a ungeschickt

ine'quality n Ungleichheit f

inert /ɪˈnɜːt/ a unbeweglich; (Phys) träge. **~ia** /ɪˈnɜːʃə/ n Trägheit f

inescapable /ɪnɪˈskeɪpəbl/ a unvermeidlich

inestimable /ɪnˈestɪməbl/ a unschätzbar

inevitab|le /ɪnˈevɪtəbl/ a unvermeidlich. **~ly** adv zwangsläufig

ine'xact a ungenau

inex'cusable a unverzeihlich

inexhaustible /ɪnɪgˈzɔːstəbl/ a unerschöpflich

inexorable /ɪnˈeksərəbl/ a unerbittlich

inex'pensive a, **-ly** adv preiswert

inex'perience n Unerfahrenheit f. **~d** a unerfahren

inexplicable /ɪnɪkˈsplɪkəbl/ a unerklärlich

in'fallible a unfehlbar

infam|ous /ˈɪnfəməs/ a niederträchtig; (notorious) berüchtigt. **~y** n Niederträchtigkeit f

infan|cy /ˈɪnfənsɪ/ n frühe Kindheit f; (fig) Anfangsstadium nt. **~t** n Kleinkind nt. **~tile** a kindisch

infantry /ˈɪnfəntrɪ/ n Infanterie f

infatuated /ɪnˈfætʃʊeɪtɪd/ a vernarrt (**with** in + acc)

infect /ɪnˈfekt/ vt anstecken, infizieren; **become ~ed** (wound:) sich infizieren. **~ion** /-ˈfekʃn/ n Infektion f. **~ious** /-ˈfekʃəs/ a ansteckend

infer /ɪnˈfɜː(r)/ vt (pt/pp inferred) folgern (**from** aus); (imply) andeuten. **~ence** /ˈɪnfərəns/ n Folgerung f

inferior /ɪnˈfɪərɪə(r)/ a minderwertig; (in rank) untergeordnet □ n Untergebene(r) m/f

inferiority /ɪnfɪərɪˈɒrətɪ/ n Minderwertigkeit f. **~ complex** n Minderwertigkeitskomplex m

infern|al /ɪnˈfɜːnl/ a höllisch. **~o** n flammendes Inferno nt

in'fertile a unfruchtbar. **~'tility** n Unfruchtbarkeit f

infest /ɪnˈfest/ vt **be ~ed with** befallen sein von; (place) verseucht sein mit

infi'delity n Untreue f

infighting /ˈɪnfaɪtɪŋ/ n (fig) interne Machtkämpfe pl

infiltrate /ˈɪnfɪltreɪt/ vt infiltrieren; (Pol) unterwandern

infinite /ˈɪnfɪnət/ a, **-ly** adv unendlich

infinitesimal /ɪnfɪnɪˈtesɪml/ a unendlich klein

infinitive /ɪnˈfɪnətɪv/ n (Gram)
Infinitiv m

infinity /ɪnˈfɪnɪtɪ/ n Unendlichkeit f

infirm /ɪnˈfɜːm/ a gebrechlich.
~ary n Krankenhaus nt. **~ity** n
Gebrechlichkeit f

inflame /ɪnˈfleɪm/ vt entzünden;
become ~d sich entzünden. **~d**
a entzündet

in'flammable a feuergefährlich

inflammation /ɪnfləˈmeɪʃn/ n
Entzündung f

inflammatory /ɪnˈflæmətrɪ/ a
aufrührerisch

inflatable /ɪnˈfleɪtəbl/ a aufblasbar

inflat|e /ɪnˈfleɪt/ vt aufblasen;
(with pump) aufpumpen. **~ion**
/-eɪʃn/ n Inflation f. **~ionary**
/-eɪʃənərɪ/ a inflationär

in'flexible a starr; (person) unbeugsam

inflexion /ɪnˈflekʃn/ n Tonfall m;
(Gram) Flexion f

inflict /ɪnˈflɪkt/ vt zufügen (on
dat); versetzen (blow) (on dat)

influen|ce /ˈɪnfluəns/ n Einfluss
m □ vt beeinflussen. **~tial**
/-ˈenʃl/ a einflussreich

influenza /ɪnfluˈenzə/ n Grippe f

influx /ˈɪnflʌks/ n Zustrom m

inform /ɪnˈfɔːm/ vt benachrichtigen; (officially) informieren; **~
s.o. of sth** jdm etw mitteilen;
keep s.o. ~ed jdn auf dem Laufenden halten □ vi **~ against** denunzieren

in'formal a, **-ly** adv zwanglos;
(unofficial) inoffiziell. **~mality**
n Zwanglosigkeit f

informant /ɪnˈfɔːmənt/ n Gewährsmann m

informat|ion /ɪnfəˈmeɪʃn/ n Auskunft f; **a piece of ~ion** eine
Auskunft. **~ive** /ɪnˈfɔːmətɪv/ a
aufschlussreich; (instructive)
lehrreich

informer /ɪnˈfɔːmə(r)/ n Spitzel
m; (Pol) Denunziant m

infra-'red /ɪnfrə-/ a infrarot

in'frequent a, **-ly** adv selten

infringe /ɪnˈfrɪndʒ/ vt/i **~ [on]**
verstoßen gegen. **~ment** n Verstoß m

infuriat|e /ɪnˈfjʊərɪeɪt/ vt wütend
machen. **~ing** a ärgerlich; **he is
~ing** er kann einen zur Raserei
bringen

infusion /ɪnˈfjuːʒn/ n Aufguss m

ingenious /ɪnˈdʒiːnɪəs/ a erfinderisch; (thing) raffiniert

ingenuity /ɪndʒɪˈnjuːɪtɪ/ n
Geschicklichkeit f

ingenuous /ɪnˈdʒenjʊəs/ a unschuldig

ingot /ˈɪŋgət/ n Barren m

ingrained /ɪnˈgreɪnd/ a eingefleischt; **be ~** (dirt:) sitzen

ingratiate /ɪnˈgreɪʃɪeɪt/ vt **~oneself** sich einschmeicheln (with
bei)

in'gratitude n Undankbarkeit f

ingredient /ɪnˈgriːdɪənt/ n (Culin) Zutat f

ingrowing /ˈɪngrəʊɪŋ/ a (nail)
eingewachsen

inhabit /ɪnˈhæbɪt/ vt bewohnen.
~ant n Einwohner(in) m(f)

inhale /ɪnˈheɪl/ vt/i einatmen;
(Med & when smoking) inhalieren

inherent /ɪnˈhɪərənt/ a natürlich

inherit /ɪnˈherɪt/ vt erben. **~ance**
/-əns/ n Erbschaft f, Erbe nt

inhibit /ɪnˈhɪbɪt/ vt hemmen.
~ed a gehemmt. **~ion** /-ˈbɪʃn/ n
Hemmung f

inho'spitable a ungastlich

in'human a unmenschlich

inimitable /ɪˈnɪmɪtəbl/ a unnachahmlich

iniquitous /ɪˈnɪkwɪtəs/ a schändlich; (unjust) ungerecht

initial /ɪˈnɪʃl/ a anfänglich, Anfangs- □ n Anfangsbuchstabe m;
my ~s meine Initialen f □ vt
(pt/pp **initialled**) abzeichnen;
(Pol) paraphieren. **~ly** adv anfangs, am Anfang

initiat|e /ɪ'nɪʃɪeɪt/ vt einführen. **~ion** /-'eɪʃn/ n Einführung f

initiative /ɪ'nɪʃɪətɪv/ n Initiative f

inject /ɪn'dʒekt/ vt einspritzen, injizieren. **~ion** /-ekʃn/ n Spritze f, Injektion f

injunction /ɪn'dʒʌŋkʃn/ n gerichtliche Verfügung f

injur|e /'ɪndʒə(r)/ vt verletzen. **~y** n Verletzung f

in'justice n Ungerechtigkeit f; **do s.o. an ~** jdm unrecht tun

ink /ɪŋk/ n Tinte f

inkling /'ɪŋklɪŋ/ n Ahnung f

inlaid /ɪn'leɪd/ a eingelegt

inland /'ɪnlənd/ a Binnen- □ adv landeinwärts. **I ~ Revenue** n ≈ Finanzamt nt

in-laws /'ɪnlɔːz/ npl (fam) Schwiegereltern pl

inlay /'ɪnleɪ/ n Einlegearbeit f

inlet /'ɪnlet/ n schmale Bucht f; (Techn) Zuleitung f

inmate /'ɪnmeɪt/ n Insasse m

inn /ɪn/ n Gasthaus nt

innards /'ɪnədz/ npl (fam) Eingeweide pl

innate /ɪ'neɪt/ a angeboren

inner /'ɪnə(r)/ a innere(r,s). **~most** a innerste(r,s)

'innkeeper n Gastwirt m

innocen|ce /'ɪnəsns/ n Unschuld f. **~t** a unschuldig. **~tly** adv in aller Unschuld

innocuous /ɪ'nɒkjʊəs/ a harmlos

innovat|e /'ɪnəveɪt/ vi neu einführen. **~ion** /-'veɪʃn/ n Neuerung f. **~or** n Neuerer m

innuendo /ɪnjuː'endəʊ/ n (pl -es) [versteckte] Anspielung f

innumerable /ɪ'njuːmərəbl/ a unzählig

inoculat|e /ɪ'nɒkjʊleɪt/ vt impfen. **~ion** /-'leɪʃn/ n Impfung f

inof'fensive a harmlos

in'operable a nicht operierbar

in'opportune a unpassend

inordinate /ɪ'nɔːdɪnət/ a, **-ly** adv übermäßig

inor'ganic a anorganisch

'in-patient n [stationär behandelter] Krankenhauspatient m

input /'ɪnpʊt/ n Input m & nt

inquest /'ɪnkwest/ n gerichtliche Untersuchung f

inquir|e /ɪn'kwaɪə(r)/ vi sich erkundigen (about nach); **~e into** untersuchen □ vt sich erkundigen nach. **~y** n Erkundigung f; (investigation) Untersuchung f

inquisitive /ɪn'kwɪzɪtɪv/ a, **-ly** adv neugierig

inroad /'ɪnrəʊd/ n Einfall m; **make ~s into sth** etw angreifen

in'sane a geisteskrank; (fig) wahnsinnig

in'sanitary a unhygienisch

in'sanity n Geisteskrankheit f

insatiable /ɪn'seɪʃəbl/ a unersättlich

inscri|be /ɪn'skraɪb/ vt eingravieren. **~ption** /-'skrɪpʃn/ n Inschrift f

inscrutable /ɪn'skruːtəbl/ a undurchgründlich; (expression) undurchdringlich

insect /'ɪnsekt/ n Insekt nt. **~icide** /-'sektɪsaɪd/ n Insektenvertilgungsmittel nt

inse'cur|e a nicht sicher; (fig) unsicher. **~ity** n Unsicherheit f

insemination /ɪnsemɪ'neɪʃn/ n Besamung f; (Med) Befruchtung f

in'sensible a (unconscious) bewusstlos

in'sensitive a gefühllos; **~ to** unempfindlich gegen

in'separable a untrennbar; (people) unzertrennlich

insert[1] /'ɪnsɜːt/ n Einsatz m

insert[2] /ɪn'sɜːt/ vt einfügen, einsetzen; einstecken (key); einwerfen (coin). **~ion** /-ɜːʃn/ n (insert) Einsatz m; (in text) Einfügung f

inside /ɪnˈsaɪd/ n Innenseite f; (of house) Innere(s) nt □ attrib Innennen- □ adv innen; (indoors) drinnen; **go ~** hineingehen; **come ~** hereinkommen; **~ out** links [herum]; **know sth ~ out** etw in- und auswendig kennen □ prep **~ [of]** in (+ dat/ (into) + acc)

insidious /ɪnˈsɪdɪəs/ a, **-ly** adv heimtückisch

insight /ˈɪnsaɪt/ n Einblick m (**into** in + acc); (understanding) Einsicht f

insignia /ɪnˈsɪɡnɪə/ npl Insignien pl

insig'nificant a unbedeutend

insin'cere a unaufrichtig

insinuat|e /ɪnˈsɪnjʊeɪt/ vt andeuten. **~ion** /-ˈeɪʃn/ n Andeutung f

insipid /ɪnˈsɪpɪd/ a fade

insist /ɪnˈsɪst/ vi darauf bestehen; **~ on** bestehen auf (+ dat) □ vt **~ that** darauf bestehen, dass. **~ence** n Bestehen nt. **~ent** a, **-ly** adv beharrlich; **be ~ent** darauf bestehen

'insole n Einlegesohle f

insolen|ce /ˈɪnsələns/ n Unverschämtheit f. **~t** a, **-ly** adv unverschämt

in'soluble a unlöslich; (fig) unlösbar

in'solvent a zahlungsunfähig

insomnia /ɪnˈsɒmnɪə/ n Schlaflosigkeit f

inspect /ɪnˈspekt/ vt inspizieren; (test) prüfen; kontrollieren (ticket). **~ion** /-ekʃn/ n Inspektion f. **~or** n Inspektor m; (of tickets) Kontrolleur m

inspiration /ɪnspəˈreɪʃn/ n Inspiration f

inspire /ɪnˈspaɪə(r)/ vt inspirieren; **~ sth in s.o.** jdm etw einflößen

insta'bility n Unbeständigkeit f; (of person) Labilität f

install /ɪnˈstɔːl/ vt installieren; [in ein Amt] einführen (person).

~ation /-stəˈleɪʃn/ n Installation f; Amtseinführung f

instalment /ɪnˈstɔːlmənt/ n (Comm) Rate f; (of serial) Fortsetzung f; (Radio, TV) Folge f

instance /ˈɪnstəns/ n Fall m; (example) Beispiel nt; **in the first ~** zunächst; **for ~** zum Beispiel

instant /ˈɪnstənt/ a sofortig; (Culin) Instant- □ n Augenblick m, Moment m. **~aneous** /-ˈteɪnɪəs/ a unverzüglich, unmittelbar; **death was ~aneous** der Tod trat sofort ein

instant 'coffee n Pulverkaffee m

instantly /ˈɪnstəntlɪ/ adv sofort

instead /ɪnˈsted/ adv statt dessen; **~ of** statt (+ gen), anstelle von; **~ of me** an meiner Stelle; **~ of going** anstatt zu gehen

'instep n Spann m, Rist m

instigat|e /ˈɪnstɪɡeɪt/ vt anstiften; einleiten (proceedings). **~ion** /-ˈɡeɪʃn/ n Anstiftung f; **at his ~ion** auf seine Veranlassung. **~or** n Anstifter(in) m(f)

instil /ɪnˈstɪl/ vt (pt/pp instilled) einprägen (**into** s.o. jdm)

instinct /ˈɪnstɪŋkt/ n Instinkt m. **~ive** /ɪnˈstɪŋktɪv/ a, **-ly** adv instinktiv

institut|e /ˈɪnstɪtjuːt/ n Institut nt □ vt einführen; einleiten (search). **~ion** /-ˈtjuːʃn/ n Institution f; (home) Anstalt f

instruct /ɪnˈstrʌkt/ vt unterrichten; (order) anweisen. **~ion** /-ˌʌkʃn/ n Unterricht m; Anweisung f; **~ions** pl **for use** Gebrauchsanweisung f. **~ive** /-ɪv/ a lehrreich. **~or** n Lehrer(in) m(f); (Mil) Ausbilder m

instrument /ˈɪnstrəmənt/ n Instrument nt. **~al** /-ˈmentl/ a Instrumental-; **be ~al** in eine entscheidende Rolle spielen bei

insu'bordina|te a ungehorsam. **~nation** /-ˈneɪʃn/ n Ungehorsam m; (Mil) Insubordination f

in'sufferable a unerträglich

insuf'ficient *a*, **-ly** *adv* nicht genügend

insular /'ɪnsjʊlə(r)/ *a* (*fig*) engstirnig

insulat|e /'ɪnsjʊleɪt/ *vt* isolieren. **~ing tape** *n* Isolierband *nt*. **~ion** /-'leɪʃn/ *n* Isolierung *f*

insulin /'ɪnsjʊlɪn/ *n* Insulin *nt*

insult¹ /'ɪnsʌlt/ *n* Beleidigung *f*

insult² /ɪn'sʌlt/ *vt* beleidigen

insuperable /ɪn'su:pərəbl/ *a* unüberwindlich

insur|ance /ɪn'ʃʊərəns/ *n* Versicherung *f*. **~e** *vt* versichern

insurrection /ɪnsə'rekʃn/ *n* Aufstand *m*

intact /ɪn'tækt/ *a* unbeschädigt; (*complete*) vollständig

intake *n* Aufnahme *f*

in'tangible *a* nicht greifbar

integral /'ɪntɪgrl/ *a* wesentlich

integrat|e /'ɪntɪgreɪt/ *vt* integrieren □ *vi* sich integrieren. **~ion** /-'greɪʃn/ *n* Integration *f*

integrity /ɪn'tegrəti/ *n* Integrität *f*

intellect /'ɪntəlekt/ *n* Intellekt *m*. **~ual** /-'lektjʊəl/ *a* intellektuell

intelligen|ce /ɪn'telɪdʒəns/ *n* Intelligenz *f*; (*Mil*) Nachrichtendienst *m*; (*information*) Meldungen *pl*. **~t** *a*, **-ly** *adv* intelligent

intelligentsia /ɪntelɪ'dʒentsɪə/ *n* Intelligenz *f*

intelligible /ɪn'telɪdʒəbl/ *a* verständlich

intend /ɪn'tend/ *vt* beabsichtigen; **be ~ed for** bestimmt sein für

intense /ɪn'tens/ *a* intensiv; (*pain*) stark. **~ly** *adv* äußerst; (*study*) angestrengt

intensi|fication /ɪntensɪfɪ'keɪʃn/ *n* Intensivierung *f*. **~fy** /-'tensɪfaɪ/ *v* (*pt/pp* **-ied**) □ *vt* intensivieren □ *vi* zunehmen

intensity /ɪn'tensəti/ *n* Intensität *f*

intensive /ɪn'tensɪv/ *a*, **-ly** *adv* intensiv; **be in ~ care** auf der Intensivstation sein

intent /ɪn'tent/ *a*, **-ly** *adv* aufmerksam; **~ on** (*absorbed in*) vertieft in (+ *acc*); **be ~ on doing** sth fest entschlossen sein, etw zu tun □ *n* Absicht *f*; **to all ~s and purposes** im Grunde

intention /ɪn'tenʃn/ *n* Absicht *f*. **~al** *a*, **-ly** *adv* absichtlich

inter /ɪn'tɜ:(r)/ *vt* (*pt/pp* **interred**) bestatten

inter'action *n* Wechselwirkung *f*

intercede /ɪntə'si:d/ *vi* Fürsprache einlegen (**on behalf of** für)

intercept /ɪntə'sept/ *vt* abfangen

'interchange¹ *n* Austausch *m*; (*Auto*) Autobahnkreuz *nt*

inter'change² *vt* austauschen. **~able** *a* austauschbar

intercom /'ɪntəkɒm/ *n* [Gegen]sprechanlage *f*

'intercourse *n* Verkehr *m*; (*sexual*) Geschlechtsverkehr *m*

interest /'ɪntrəst/ *n* Interesse *nt*; (*Comm*) Zinsen *pl*; **have an ~** (*Comm*) beteiligt sein (**in** an + *dat*) □ *vt* interessieren; **be ~ed** sich interessieren (**in** für). **~ing** *a* interessant. **~ rate** *n* Zinssatz *m*

interfere /ɪntə'fɪə(r)/ *vi* sich einmischen. **~nce** /-əns/ *n* Einmischung *f*; (*Radio, TV*) Störung *f*

interim /'ɪntərɪm/ *a* Zwischen-; (*temporary*) vorläufig □ *n* **in the ~** in der Zwischenzeit

interior /ɪn'tɪərɪə(r)/ *a* innere(r,s), Innen- □ *n* Innere(s) *nt*

interject /ɪntə'dʒekt/ *vt* einwerfen. **~ion** /-ekʃn/ *n* Interjektion *f*; (*remark*) Einwurf *m*

inter'lock *vi* ineinander greifen

interloper /'ɪntələʊpə(r)/ *n* Eindringling *m*

interlude /'ɪntəlu:d/ *n* Pause *f*; (*performance*) Zwischenspiel *nt*

inter'marry *vi* untereinander heiraten; (*different groups:*) Mischehen schließen

intermediary /ɪntə'mi:dɪəri/ *n* Vermittler(in) *m(f)*

intermediate /ɪntə'miːdɪət/ a
Zwischen-

interminable /ɪn'tɜːmɪnəbl/ a
endlos [lang]

intermission /ɪntə'mɪʃn/ n
Pause f

intermittent /ɪntə'mɪtənt/ a in
Abständen auftretend

intern /ɪn'tɜːn/ vt internieren

internal /ɪn'tɜːnl/ a innere(r,s);
⟨matter, dispute⟩ intern. **~ly** adv
innerlich; ⟨deal with⟩ intern

inter'national a international
□n Länderspiel nt;
⟨player⟩ Nationalspieler(in) m(f)

internist /ɪn'tɜːnɪst/ n (Amer) Internist m

internment /ɪn'tɜːnmənt/ n Internierung f

'interplay n Wechselspiel nt

interpolate /ɪn'tɜːpəleɪt/ vt
einwerfen

interpret /ɪn'tɜːprɪt/ vt interpretieren; auslegen ⟨text⟩; deuten
⟨dream⟩; ⟨translate⟩ dolmetschen
□vi dolmetschen. **~ation**
/-'teɪʃn/ n Interpretation f. **~er**
n Dolmetscher(in) m(f)

interre'lated a verwandt; ⟨facts⟩
zusammenhängend

interrogate /ɪn'terəgeɪt/ vt verhören. **~ion** /-'geɪʃn/ n Verhör
nt

interrogative /ɪntə'rɒgətɪv/ a &
n ~ [pronoun] Interrogativpronomen nt

interrupt /ɪntə'rʌpt/ vt/i unterbrechen; **don't ~!** red nicht dazwischen! **~ion** /-ʌpʃn/ n
Unterbrechung f

intersect /ɪntə'sekt/ vi sich
kreuzen; (Geom) sich schneiden.
~ion /-ekʃn/ n Kreuzung f

interspersed /ɪntə'spɜːst/ a ~
with durchsetzt mit

inter'twine vi sich ineinander
schlingen

interval /'ɪntəvl/ n Abstand m;
(Theat) Pause f; (Mus) Intervall
nt; **at hourly ~s** alle Stunde;
bright ~s pl Aufheiterungen pl

interven|e /ɪntə'viːn/ vi eingreifen; (occur) dazwischenkommen. **~tion** /-'venʃn/ n
Eingreifen nt; (Mil, Pol) Intervention f

interview /'ɪntəvjuː/ n (Journ)
Interview nt; (for job) Vorstellungsgespräch nt; go for an ~
sich vorstellen □ vt interviewen;
ein Vorstellungsgespräch führen
mit. **~er** n Interviewer(in) m(f)

intestine /ɪn'testɪn/ n Darm m

intimacy /'ɪntɪməsɪ/ n Vertrautheit f; (sexual) Intimität f

intimate¹ /'ɪntɪmət/ a, **-ly** adv
vertraut; ⟨friend⟩ eng; ⟨sexually⟩
intim

intimate² /'ɪntɪmeɪt/ vt zu verstehen geben; (imply) andeuten

intimidat|e /ɪn'tɪmɪdeɪt/ vt einschüchtern. **~ion** /-'deɪʃn/ n
Einschüchterung f

into /'ɪntə, vor einem Vokal 'ɪntʊ/
prep in (+ acc); go ~ the house
ins Haus [hinein]gehen; be ~
(fam) sich auskennen mit; 7 ~
21 21 [geteilt] durch 7

in'tolerable a unerträglich

in'toleran|ce n Intoleranz f. **~t**
a intolerant

intonation /ɪntə'neɪʃn/ n Tonfall
m

intoxicat|ed /ɪn'tɒksɪkeɪtɪd/ a betrunken; (fig) berauscht. **~ion**
/-'keɪʃn/ n Rausch m

intractable /ɪn'træktəbl/ a widerspenstig; ⟨problem⟩ hartnäckig

intransigent /ɪn'trænsɪdʒənt/ a
unnachgiebig

in'transitive a, **-ly** adv intransitiv

intravenous /ɪntrə'viːnəs/ a, **-ly**
adv intravenös

intrepid /ɪn'trepɪd/ a kühn,
unerschrocken

intricate /'ɪntrɪkət/ a kompliziert

intrigu|e /ɪn'triːg/ n Intrige f □ vt
faszinieren □vi intrigieren.
~ing a faszinierend

intrinsic /ɪnˈtrɪnsɪk/ *a* ~ **value** Eigenwert *m*

introduce /ɪntrəˈdjuːs/ *vt* vorstellen; (*bring in, insert*) einführen

introduct|ion /ɪntrəˈdʌkʃn/ *n* Einführung *f*; (*to person*) Vorstellung *f*; (*to book*) Einleitung *f*. **~ory** /-tərɪ/ *a* einleitend

introspective /ɪntrəˈspɛktɪv/ *a* in sich (*acc*) gerichtet

introvert /ˈɪntrəvɜːt/ *n* introvertierter Mensch *m*

intru|de /ɪnˈtruːd/ *vi* stören. **~der** *n* Eindringling *m*. **~sion** /-uːʒn/ *n* Störung *f*

intuit|ion /ɪntjuːˈɪʃn/ *n* Intuition *f*. **~ive** /-ˈtjuːɪtɪv/ *a*, **-ly** *adv* intuitiv

inundate /ˈɪnəndeɪt/ *vt* überschwemmen

invade /ɪnˈveɪd/ *vt* einfallen in (+ *acc*). **~r** *n* Angreifer *m*

invalid[1] /ˈɪnvəlɪd/ *n* Kranke(r) *m/f*

invalid[2] /ɪnˈvælɪd/ *a* ungültig. **~ate** *vt* ungültig machen

in'valuable *a* unschätzbar; (*person*) unersetzlich

in'variab|le *a* unveränderlich. **~ly** *adv* immer

invasion /ɪnˈveɪʒn/ *n* Invasion *f*

invective /ɪnˈvɛktɪv/ *n* Beschimpfungen *pl*

invent /ɪnˈvɛnt/ *vt* erfinden. **~ion** /-enʃn/ *n* Erfindung *f*. **~ive** /-tɪv/ *a* erfinderisch. **~or** *n* Erfinder *m*

inventory /ˈɪnvəntrɪ/ *n* Bestandsliste *f*; **make an** ~ ein Inventar aufstellen

inverse /ɪnˈvɜːs/ *a*, **-ly** *adv* umgekehrt □ *n* Gegenteil *nt*

invert /ɪnˈvɜːt/ *vt* umkehren. **~ed commas** *npl* Anführungszeichen *pl*

invest /ɪnˈvɛst/ *vt* investieren, anlegen; ~ **in** (*fam: buy*) sich (*dat*) zulegen

investigat|e /ɪnˈvɛstɪgeɪt/ *vt* untersuchen. **~ion** /-ˈgeɪʃn/ *n* Untersuchung *f*

invest|ment /ɪnˈvɛstmənt/ *n* Anlage *f*; **be a good ~ment** (*fig*) sich bezahlt machen. **~or** *n* Kapitalanleger *m*

inveterate /ɪnˈvɛtərət/ *a* Gewohnheits-; (*liar*) unverbesserlich

invidious /ɪnˈvɪdɪəs/ *a* unerfreulich; (*unfair*) ungerecht

invigilate /ɪnˈvɪdʒɪleɪt/ *vi* (*Sch*) Aufsicht führen

invigorate /ɪnˈvɪgəreɪt/ *vt* beleben

invincible /ɪnˈvɪnsəbl/ *a* unbesiegbar

inviolable /ɪnˈvaɪələbl/ *a* unantastbar

in'visible *a* unsichtbar. **~ mending** *n* Kunststopfen *nt*

invitation /ɪnvɪˈteɪʃn/ *n* Einladung *f*

invit|e /ɪnˈvaɪt/ *vt* einladen. **~ing** *a* einladend

invoice /ˈɪnvɔɪs/ *n* Rechnung *f* □ *vt* ~ **s.o.** jdm eine Rechnung schicken

invoke /ɪnˈvəʊk/ *vt* anrufen

in'voluntary *a*, **-ily** *adv* unwillkürlich

involve /ɪnˈvɒlv/ *vt* beteiligen; (*affect*) betreffen; (*implicate*) verwickeln; (*entail*) mit sich bringen; (*mean*) bedeuten; **be ~d in** beteiligt sein an (+ *dat*); (*implicated*) verwickelt sein in (+ *acc*); **get ~d with s.o.** sich mit jdm einlassen. **~d** *a* kompliziert

in'vulnerable *a* unverwundbar; (*position*) unangreifbar

inward /ˈɪnwəd/ *a* innere(r,s). **~ly** *adv* innerlich. **~s** *adv* nach innen

iodine /ˈaɪədiːn/ *n* Jod *nt*

iota /aɪˈəʊtə/ *n* Jota *nt*, (*fam*) Funke *m*

IOU *abbr* (**I owe you**) Schuldschein *m*

Iran /ɪˈrɑːn/ *n* der Iran

Iraq /ɪˈrɑːk/ *n* der Irak

irascible /ɪˈræsəbl/ *a* aufbrausend

irate /aɪˈreɪt/ a wütend

Ireland /ˈaɪələnd/ n Irland nt

iris /ˈaɪərɪs/ n (Anat) Regenbogenhaut f, Iris f; (Bot) Schwertlilie f

Irish /ˈaɪərɪʃ/ a irisch □ n the ~ pl die Iren. ~man n Ire m. ~woman n Irin f

irk /ɜːk/ vt ärgern. ~some /-səm/ a lästig

iron /ˈaɪən/ a Eisen-; (fig) eisern □ n Eisen nt; (appliance) Bügeleisen nt □ vt/i bügeln. ~ out vt ausbügeln

ironic[al] /aɪˈrɒnɪk[l]/ a ironisch

ironing /ˈaɪənɪŋ/ n Bügeln nt; (articles) Bügelwäsche f; **do the** ~ bügeln. ~board n Bügelbrett nt

ironmonger /-mʌŋgə(r)/ n ~'s [shop] Haushaltswarengeschäft nt

irony /ˈaɪərənɪ/ n Ironie f

irradiate /ɪˈreɪdɪeɪt/ vt bestrahlen

irrational /ɪˈræʃənl/ a irrational

irreconcilable /ɪˈrekənsaɪləbl/ a unversöhnlich

irrefutable /ɪrɪˈfjuːtəbl/ a unwiderlegbar

irregular /ɪˈregjʊlə(r)/ a, -ly adv unregelmäßig; (against rules) regelwidrig. ~ity /-ˈlærɪtɪ/ n Unregelmäßigkeit f; Regelwidrigkeit f

irrelevant /ɪˈreləvənt/ a irrelevant

irreparable /ɪˈrepərəbl/ a unersetzlich; **be** ~ nicht wieder gutzumachen sein

irreplaceable /ɪrɪˈpleɪsəbl/ a unersetzlich

irrepressible /ɪrɪˈpresəbl/ a unverwüstlich; **be** ~ (person:) nicht unterzukriegen sein

irresistible /ɪrɪˈzɪstəbl/ a unwiderstehlich

irresolute /ɪˈrezəluːt/ a unentschlossen

irrespective /ɪrɪˈspektɪv/ a ~ of ungeachtet (+ gen)

irresponsible /ɪrɪˈspɒnsəbl/ a, -bly adv unverantwortlich; (person) verantwortungslos

irreverent /ɪˈrevərənt/ a, -ly adv respektlos

irreversible /ɪrɪˈvɜːsəbl/ a unwiderruflich; (Med) irreversibel

irrevocable /ɪˈrevəkəbl/ a, -bly adv unwiderruflich

irrigat|e /ˈɪrɪgeɪt/ vt bewässern. ~ion /-ˈgeɪʃn/ n Bewässerung f

irritability /ɪrɪtəˈbɪlɪtɪ/ n Gereiztheit f

irritable /ˈɪrɪtəbl/ a reizbar

irritant /ˈɪrɪtənt/ n Reizstoff m

irritat|e /ˈɪrɪteɪt/ vt irritieren; (Med) reizen. ~ion /-ˈteɪʃn/ n Ärger m; (Med) Reizung f

is /ɪz/ see be

Islam /ˈɪzlɑːm/ n der Islam. ~ic /-ˈlæmɪk/ a islamisch

island /ˈaɪlənd/ n Insel f. ~er n Inselbewohner(in) m(f)

isle /aɪl/ n Insel f

isolat|e /ˈaɪsəleɪt/ vt isolieren. ~ed a (remote) abgelegen; (single) einzeln. ~ion /-ˈleɪʃn/ n Isoliertheit f; (Med) Isolierung f

Israel /ˈɪzreɪl/ n Israel nt. ~i /ɪzˈreɪlɪ/ a israelisch □ n Israeli m/f

issue /ˈɪʃuː/ n Frage f; (outcome) Ergebnis nt; (of magazine, stamps) Ausgabe f; (offspring) Nachkommen pl; **what is at** ~? worum geht es? **take** ~ **with s.o.** jdm widersprechen □ vt ausgeben; ausstellen (passport); erteilen (order); herausgeben (book); **be** ~**d with sth** etw erhalten □ vi ~ **from** herausströmen aus

isthmus /ˈɪsməs/ n (pl -muses) Landenge f

it /ɪt/ pron es; (m) er; (f) sie; (as direct object) es; (m) ihn; (f) sie; (as indirect object) ihm; (f) ihr; **it is raining** es regnet; **it's me** ich bin's; **who is it?** wer ist da? **of/from it** davon; **with it** damit; **out of it** daraus

Italian /ɪ'tæljən/ a italienisch □ n Italiener(in) m(f); (Lang) Italienisch nt

italic /ɪ'tælɪk/ a kursiv. ~s npl Kursivschrift f; **in** ~s kursiv

Italy /'ɪtəlɪ/ n Italien nt

itch /ɪtʃ/ n Juckreiz m; **I have an** ~ es juckt mich □ vi jucken; **I'm** ~**ing** (fam) es juckt mich (**to** zu). ~**y** a be ~**y** jucken

item /'aɪtəm/ n Gegenstand m; (Comm) Artikel m; (on agenda) Punkt m; (on invoice) Posten m; (act) Nummer f; ~ **[of news]** Nachricht f. ~**ize** vt einzeln aufführen; spezifizieren (bill)

itinerant /aɪ'tɪnərənt/ a Wander-

itinerary /aɪ'tɪnərərɪ/ n [Reise]-route f

its /ɪts/ poss pron sein; (f) ihr

it's = **it is, it has**

itself /ɪt'self/ pron selbst; (refl) sich; **by** ~ von selbst; (alone) allein

ivory /'aɪvərɪ/ n Elfenbein nt □ attrib Elfenbein-

ivy /'aɪvɪ/ n Efeu m

J

jab /dʒæb/ n Stoß m; (fam: injection) Spritze f □ vt (pt/pp jabbed) stoßen

jabber /'dʒæbə(r)/ vi plappern

jack /dʒæk/ n (Auto) Wagenheber m; (Cards) Bube m □ vt ~ **up** (Auto) aufbocken

jackdaw /'dʒækdɔː/ n Dohle f

jacket /'dʒækɪt/ n Jacke f; (of book) Schutzumschlag m. ~ po-**'tato** n in der Schale gebackene Kartoffel f

'jackpot n **hit the** ~ das große Los ziehen

jade /dʒeɪd/ n Jade m

jaded /'dʒeɪdɪd/ a abgespannt

jagged /'dʒægɪd/ a zackig

jail /dʒeɪl/ = **gaol**

jalopy /dʒə'lɒpɪ/ n (fam) Klapperkiste f

jam¹ /dʒæm/ n Marmelade f

jam² /dʒæm/ n Gedränge nt; (Auto) Stau m; (fam. difficulty) Klemme f □ v (pt/pp jammed) □ vt klemmen (**in** in + acc); stören (broadcast) □ vi klemmen

Jamaica /dʒə'meɪkə/ n Jamaika nt

jangle /'dʒæŋgl/ vi klimpern □ vt klimpern mit

janitor /'dʒænɪtə(r)/ n Hausmeister m

January /'dʒænjʊərɪ/ n Januar m

Japan /dʒə'pæn/ n Japan nt. ~**ese** /dʒæpə'niːz/ a japanisch □ n Japaner(in) m(f); (Lang) Japanisch nt

jar¹ /dʒɑː(r)/ n Glas nt; (earthenware) Topf m

jar² /dʒɑː(r)/ v (pt/pp jarred) vi stören □ vt erschüttern

jargon /'dʒɑːgən/ n Jargon m

jaundice /'dʒɔːndɪs/ n Gelbsucht f. ~**d** a (fig) zynisch

jaunt /dʒɔːnt/ n Ausflug m

jaunty /'dʒɔːntɪ/ a (-ier, -iest) -ily adv keck

javelin /'dʒævlɪn/ n Speer m

jaw /dʒɔː/ n Kiefer m; ~**s** pl Rachen m □ vi (fam) quatschen

jay /dʒeɪ/ n Eichelhäher m. ~**walker** n achtloser Fußgänger m

jazz /dʒæz/ n Jazz m. ~**y** a knallig

jealous /'dʒeləs/ a, -**ly** adv eifersüchtig (**of** auf + acc). ~**y** n Eifersucht f

jeans /dʒiːnz/ npl Jeans pl

jeer /dʒɪə(r)/ n Johlen nt □ vi johlen; ~ **at** verhöhnen

jell /dʒel/ vi gelieren

jelly /'dʒelɪ/ n Gelee nt; (dessert) Götterspeise f. ~**fish** n Qualle f

jemmy /'dʒemɪ/ n Brecheisen nt

jeopar|dize /'dʒepədaɪz/ vt gefährden. ~**dy** /-dɪ/ n **in** ~**dy** gefährdet

jerk /dʒɜːk/ n Ruck m □ vt stoßen; (pull) reißen □ vi rucken; (limb, *muscle:*) zucken. **~ily** *adv* ruckweise. **~y** *a* ruckartig

jersey /'dʒɜːzi/ *n* Pullover *m*; (*Sport*) Trikot *nt*; (*fabric*) Jersey *m*

jest /dʒest/ *n* Scherz *m*; **in ~** im Spaß □ *vi* scherzen

jet[1] /dʒet/ *n* (*Miner*) Jett *m*

jet[2] *n* (*of water*) [Wasser]strahl *m*; (*nozzle*) Düse *f*; (*plane*) Düsenflugzeug *nt*

jet: **~-black** *a* pechschwarz. **~-lag** *n* Jet-lag *m*. **~-pro'pelled** *a* mit Düsenantrieb

jettison /'dʒetisn/ *vt* über Bord werfen

jetty /'dʒeti/ *n* Landesteg *m*; (*breakwater*) Buhne *f*

Jew /dʒuː/ *n* Jude *m*/Jüdin *f*

jewel /'dʒuːəl/ *n* Edelstein *m*; (*fig*) Juwel *nt*. **~ler** *n* Juwelier *m*. **~ler's** [**shop**] Juweliergeschäft *nt*. **~lery** *n* Schmuck *m*

Jew|ess /'dʒuːɪs/ *n* Jüdin *f*. **~ish** *a* jüdisch

jib /dʒɪb/ *vi* (*pt/pp* jibbed) (*fig*) sich sträuben (**at** gegen)

jiffy /'dʒɪfi/ *n* (*fam*) **in a ~** in einem Augenblick

jigsaw /'dʒɪgsɔː/ *n* **~** [**puzzle**] Puzzlespiel *nt*

jilt /dʒɪlt/ *vt* sitzen lassen

jingle /'dʒɪŋgl/ *n* (*rhyme*) Verschen *nt* □ *vi* klimpern □ *vt* klimpern mit

jinx /dʒɪŋks/ *n* (*fam*) **it's got a ~ on it** es ist verhext

jitter|s /'dʒɪtəz/ *npl* (*fam*) **have the ~s** nervös sein. **~y** *a* (*fam*) nervös

job /dʒɒb/ *n* Aufgabe *f*; (*post*) Stelle *f*, (*fam*) Job *m*; **be a ~** (*fam*) nicht leicht sein; **it's a good ~ that** es ist [nur] gut, dass. **~ centre** *n* Arbeitsvermittlungsstelle *f*. **~less** *a* arbeitslos

jockey /'dʒɒki/ *n* Jockei *m*

jocular /'dʒɒkjʊlə(r)/ *a*, **-ly** *adv* spaßhaft

jog /dʒɒg/ *n* Stoß *m*; **at a ~** im Dauerlauf □ *v* (*pt/pp* jogged) □ *vt* anstoßen; **~ s.o.'s memory** jds Gedächtnis nachhelfen □ *vi* (*Sport*) joggen. **~ging** *n* Jogging *nt*

john /dʒɒn/ *n* (*Amer, fam*) Klo *nt*

join /dʒɔɪn/ *n* Nahtstelle *f* □ *vt* verbinden (**to** mit); sich anschließen (+ *dat*) (*person*); (*become member of*) beitreten (+ *dat*); eintreten in (+ *acc*) (*firm*) □ *vi* (*roads:*) sich treffen. **~ in** *vi* mitmachen. **~ up** *vi* (*Mil*) Soldat werden □ *vt* zusammenfügen

joiner /'dʒɔɪnə(r)/ *n* Tischler *m*

joint /dʒɔɪnt/ *a*, **-ly** *adv* gemeinsam □ *n* Gelenk *nt*; (*in wood, brickwork*) Fuge *f*; (*Culin*) Braten *m*; (*fam: bar*) Lokal *nt*

joist /dʒɔɪst/ *n* Dielenbalken *m*

jok|e /dʒəʊk/ *n* Scherz *m*; (*funny story*) Witz *m*; (*trick*) Streich *m* □ *vi* scherzen. **~er** *n* Witzbold *m*; (*Cards*) Joker *m*. **~ing** *n* **~ing apart** Spaß beiseite. **~ingly** *adv* im Spaß

jollity /'dʒɒləti/ *n* Lustigkeit *f*

jolly /'dʒɒli/ *a* (**-ier, -iest**) lustig □ *adv* (*fam*) sehr

jolt /dʒəʊlt/ *n* Ruck *m* □ *vt* einen Ruck versetzen (+ *dat*) □ *vi* holpern

Jordan /'dʒɔːdn/ *n* Jordanien *nt*

jostle /'dʒɒsl/ *vt* anrempeln □ *vi* drängeln

jot /dʒɒt/ *n* Jota *nt* □ *vt* (*pt/pp* jotted) **~** [**down**] sich (*dat*) notieren. **~ter** *n* Notizblock *m*

journal /'dʒɜːnl/ *n* Zeitschrift *f*; (*diary*) Tagebuch *nt*. **~ese** /-ə'liːz/ *n* Zeitungsjargon *m*. **~ism** *n* Journalismus *m*. **~ist** *n* Journalist(in) *m(f)*

journey /'dʒɜːni/ *n* Reise *f*

jovial /'dʒəʊvɪəl/ *a* lustig

joy /dʒɔɪ/ *n* Freude *f*. **~ful** *a*, **-ly** *adv* freudig, froh. **~ride** *n* (*fam*) Spritztour *f* [im gestohlenen Auto]

jubil|ant /'dʒuːbɪlənt/ a überglücklich. **~ation** /-'leɪʃn/ n Jubel m

jubilee /'dʒuːbɪliː/ n Jubiläum nt

Judaism /'dʒuːdeɪɪzm/ n Judentum nt

judder /'dʒʌdə(r)/ vi rucken

judge /dʒʌdʒ/ n Richter m; (of competition) Preisrichter m □ vt beurteilen; (estimate) [ein]schätzen □ vi urteilen (by nach). **~ment** n Beurteilung f; (Jur) Urteil nt; (fig) Urteilsvermögen nt

judic|ial /dʒuː'dɪʃl/ a gerichtlich. **~iary** /-ʃərɪ/ n Richterstand m. **~ious** /-ʃəs/ a klug

judo /'dʒuːdəʊ/ n Judo nt

jug /dʒʌg/ n Kanne f; (small) Kännchen nt; (for water, wine) Krug m

juggernaut /'dʒʌgənɔːt/ n (fam) Riesenlaster m

juggle /'dʒʌgl/ vi jonglieren. **~r** n Jongleur m

juice /dʒuːs/ n Saft m. **~ extractor** n Entsafter m

juicy /'dʒuːsɪ/ a (-ier, -iest) saftig; (fam) (story) pikant

juke-box /'dʒuːk-/ n Musikbox f

July /dʒʊ'laɪ/ n Juli m

jumble /'dʒʌmbl/ n Durcheinander nt □ vt **~ [up]** durcheinander bringen. **~ sale** n [Wohltätigkeits]basar m

jumbo /'dʒʌmbəʊ/ n **~ [jet]** Jumbo[jet] m

jump /dʒʌmp/ n Sprung m; (in prices) Anstieg m; (in horse racing) Hindernis nt □ vi springen; (start) zusammenzucken; **make s.o. ~** jdn erschrecken; **~ at** (fig) sofort zugreifen bei (offer); **~ to conclusions** voreilige Schlüsse ziehen □ vt überspringen; **~ the gun** (fig) vorschnell handeln. **~ up** vi aufspringen

jumper /'dʒʌmpə(r)/ n Pullover m, Pulli m

jumpy /'dʒʌmpɪ/ a nervös

junction /'dʒʌŋkʃn/ n Kreuzung f; (Rail) Knotenpunkt m

juncture /'dʒʌŋktʃə(r)/ n **at this ~** zu diesem Zeitpunkt

June /dʒuːn/ n Juni m

jungle /'dʒʌŋgl/ n Dschungel m

junior /'dʒuːnɪə(r)/ a jünger; (in rank) untergeordnet; (Sport) Junioren- □ n Junior m. **~ school** n Grundschule f

juniper /'dʒuːnɪpə(r)/ n Wacholder m

junk /dʒʌŋk/ n Gerümpel nt, Trödel m

junkie /'dʒʌŋkɪ/ n (sl) Fixer m

junk-shop n Trödelladen m

juris|diction /dʒʊərɪs'dɪkʃn/ n Gerichtsbarkeit f. **~prudence** n Rechtswissenschaft f

juror /'dʒʊərə(r)/ n Geschworene(r) m/f

jury /'dʒʊərɪ/ n **the ~** die Geschworenen pl; (for competition) die Jury

just /dʒʌst/ a gerecht □ adv gerade; (only) nur; (simply) einfach; (exactly) genau; **~ as tall** ebenso groß; **~ listen!** hör doch mal! I'm **~ going** ich gehe schon; **~ put it down** stell es nur hin

justice /'dʒʌstɪs/ n Gerechtigkeit f; **do ~ to** gerecht werden (+ dat); **J~ of the Peace** ≈ Friedensrichter m

justifi|able /'dʒʌstɪfaɪəbl/ a berechtigt. **~ly** adv berechtigterweise

justi|fication /dʒʌstɪfɪ'keɪʃn/ n Rechtfertigung f. **~fy** /'dʒʌstɪfaɪ/ vt (pt/pp -ied) rechtfertigen

justly /'dʒʌstlɪ/ adv zu Recht

jut /dʒʌt/ vi (pt/pp jutted) **~ out** vorstehen

juvenile /'dʒuːvənaɪl/ a jugendlich; (childish) kindisch □ n Jugendliche(r) m/f. **~ delinquency** n Jugendkriminalität f

juxtapose /dʒʌkstə'pəʊz/ *vt* nebeneinander stellen

K

kangaroo /kæŋgə'ru:/ *n* Känguru *nt*

karate /kə'rɑːtɪ/ *n* Karate *nt*

kebab /kɪ'bæb/ *n* (Culin) Spießchen *nt*

keel /kiːl/ *n* Kiel *m* □ *vi* ~ **over** umkippen; (Naut) kentern

keen /kiːn/ *a* (-er, -est) (sharp) scharf; (intense) groß; (eager) eifrig, begeistert; ~ **on** (fam) erpicht auf (+ acc); ~ **on s.o.** von jdm sehr angetan; **be** ~ **to do sth** etw gerne machen wollen. ~**ly** *adv* tief. ~**ness** *n* Eifer *m*, Begeisterung *f*

keep /kiːp/ *n* (maintenance) Unterhalt *m*; (of castle) Bergfried *m*; **for** ~**s** für immer □ *v* (pt/pp **kept**) □ *vt* behalten; (store) aufbewahren; (not throw away) aufheben; (support) unterhalten; (detain) aufhalten; freihalten (seat); halten (promise, animals); führen (shop); einhalten (law, rules); ~ **sth hot** etw warm halten; ~ **s.o. from doing sth** jdn davon abhalten, etw zu tun; ~ **s.o. waiting** jdn warten lassen; ~ **sth to oneself** etw nicht weitersagen; **where do you** ~ **the sugar?** wo hast du den Zucker? □ *vi* (remain) bleiben; (food:) sich halten; ~ **left/right** sich links/rechts halten; ~ **doing sth** etw dauernd machen; ~ **on doing sth** etw weitermachen; ~ **in with s.o** sich gut stellen mit. ~ **up** *vi* Schritt halten □ *vt* (continue) weitermachen

keep|er /'kiːpə(r)/ *n* Wärter(in) *m(f)*. ~**ing** *n* Obhut *f*; **be in** ~**ing with** passen zu. ~ **sake** *n* Andenken *nt*

keg /keg/ *n* kleines Faß *nt*

kennel /'kenl/ *n* Hundehütte *f*; ~**s** *pl* (boarding) Hundepension *f*; (breeding) Zwinger *m*

Kenya /'kenjə/ *n* Kenia *nt*

kept /kept/ *see* **keep**

kerb /kɜːb/ *n* Bordstein *m*

kernel /'kɜːnl/ *n* kern *m*

kerosene /'kerəsiːn/ *n* (Amer) Petroleum *nt*

ketchup /'ketʃʌp/ *n* Ketschup *m*

kettle /'ketl/ *n* [Wasser]kessel *m*; **put the** ~ **on** Wasser aufsetzen; **a pretty** ~ **of fish** (fam) eine schöne Bescherung *f*

key /kiː/ *n* Schlüssel *m*; (Mus) Tonart *f*; (of piano, typewriter) Taste *f* □ *vt* ~ **in** eintasten. ~**board** *n* Tastatur *f*; (Mus) Klaviatur *f*. ~**boarder** *n* Tastster(in) *m(f)*. ~**hole** *n* Schlüsselloch *nt*. ~**ring** *n* Schlüsselring *m*

khaki /'kɑːkɪ/ *a* khakifarben □ *n* Khaki *nt*

kick /kɪk/ *n* [Fuß]tritt *m*; **for** ~**s** (fam) zum Spaß □ *vt* treten; ~ **the bucket** (fam) abkratzen □ *vi* (animal) ausschlagen. ~**off** *n* (Sport) Anstoß *m*

kid /kɪd/ *n* Kitz *nt*; (fam: child) Kind *nt* □ *vt* (pt/pp **kidded**) (fam) ~ **s.o.** jdm etwas vormachen. ~ **gloves** *npl* Glacéhandschuhe *pl*

kidnap /'kɪdnæp/ *vt* (pt/pp **-napped**) entführen. ~**per** *n* Entführer *m*. ~**ping** *n* Entführung *f*

kidney /'kɪdnɪ/ *n* Niere *f*. ~ **machine** *n* künstliche Niere *f*

kill /kɪl/ *vt* töten; (fam) totschlagen (time); ~ **two birds with one stone** zwei Fliegen mit einer Klappe schlagen. ~**er** *n* Mörder(in) *m(f)*. ~**ing** *n* Tötung *f*; (murder) Mord *m*

'killjoy *n* Spielverderber *m*

kiln /kɪln/ *n* Brennofen *m*

kilo /'kiːləʊ/ *n* Kilo *nt*

kilo /'kɪlə/-. ~**gram** *n* Kilogramm *nt*. ~**hertz** /-'hɜːts/ *n* Kilohertz

kilt ~**metre** n Kilometer m.
~**watt** n Kilowatt nt

kilt /kɪlt/ n Schottenrock m

kin /kɪn/ n Verwandtschaft f;
next of ~ nächster Verwandter
m/nächste Verwandte f

kind[1] /kaɪnd/ n Art f; (brand,
type) Sorte f; **what** ~ **of?** was
für ein Auto? ~ **of** (fam) irgendwie

kind[2] a (-er, -est) nett; ~ **to animals** gut zu Tieren; ~ **regards**
herzliche Grüße

kindergarten /'kɪndəgɑ:tn/ n
Vorschule f

kindle /'kɪndl/ vt anzünden

kind|ly /'kaɪndlɪ/ a (-ier, -iest)
nett □ adv netterweise; (if you
please) gefälligst. ~**ness** n Güte
f; (favour) Gefallen m

kindred /'kɪndrɪd/ a ~ **spirit**
Gleichgesinnte(r) m/f

kinetic /kɪ'netɪk/ a kinetisch

king /kɪŋ/ n König m; (Draughts)
Dame f. ~**dom** n Königreich nt;
(fig & Relig) Reich nt

king: ~**fisher** n Eisvogel m. ~-
sized a extragroß

kink /kɪŋk/ n Knick m. ~**y** a
(fam) pervers

kiosk /'kiːɒsk/ n Kiosk m

kip /kɪp/ n **have a** ~ (fam)
pennen □ vi (pt/pp **kipped**) (fam)
pennen

kipper /'kɪpə(r)/ n Räucherhe-
ring m

kiss /kɪs/ n Kuss m □ vt/i küssen

kit /kɪt/ n Ausrüstung f; (tools)
Werkzeug nt; (construction ~)
Bausatz m □ vt (pt/pp **kitted**)
~**out** ausrüsten. ~**bag** n Seesack
m

kitchen /'kɪtʃɪn/ n Küche f
□ attrib Küchen-. ~**ette** /kɪtʃɪ-
'net/ n Kochnische f

kitchen: ~ '**garden** n Gemüse-
garten m. ~ '**sink** n Spülbecken
nt

kite /kaɪt/ n Drachen m

kith /kɪθ/ n ~ **and kin** mit
der ganzen Verwandtschaft

kitten /'kɪtn/ n Kätzchen n

kitty /'kɪtɪ/ n (money) [gemein-
same] Kasse f

kleptomaniac /klɛptə'meɪnɪæk/
n Kleptomane m/ -manin f

knack /næk/ n Trick m, Dreh m

knapsack /'næp-/ n Tornister m

knead /ni:d/ vt kneten

knee /ni:/ n Knie nt. ~**cap** n Knie-
scheibe f

kneel /ni:l/ vi (pt/pp **knelt**)
knien; ~ [**down**] sich [nieder-]
knien

knelt /nɛlt/ see **kneel**

knew /nju:/ see **know**

knickers /'nɪkəz/ npl Schlüpfer
m

knick-knacks /'nɪknæks/ npl
Nippsachen pl

knife /naɪf/ n (pl **knives**) Messer
nt □ vt einen Messerstich versetzen (+ dat); (to death) erstechen

knight /naɪt/ n Ritter m; (Chess)
Springer m □ vt adeln

knit /nɪt/ vt/i (pt/pp **knitted**)
stricken; ~ **one, purl one** eine
rechts eine links; ~ **one's brow**
die Stirn runzeln. ~**ting** n Stricken nt; (work) Strickzeug nt.
~**ting-needle** n Stricknadel f.
~**wear** n Strickwaren pl

knives /naɪvz/ npl see **knife**

knob /nɒb/ n Knopf m; (on door)
Knauf m; (small lump) Beule f;
(small piece) Stückchen nt. ~**bly**
a knorrig; (bony) knochig

knock /nɒk/ n Klopfen nt; (blow)
Schlag m; **there was a** ~ **at the
door** es klopfte □ vt anstoßen; (at
door) klopfen an (+ acc); (fam:
criticize) heruntermachen; ~ **a
hole in sth** ein Loch in etw (acc)
schlagen; ~ **one's head** sich (dat)
den Kopf stoßen (**on an** + dat)
□ vi klopfen. ~**about** vt schlagen
□ vi (fam) herumkommen. ~-
down vt herunterwerfen; (with
fist) niederschlagen; (in car)

anfahren; (demolish) abreißen;
(fam: reduce) herabsetzen. ~ **off**
vt herunterwerfen; (fam: steal)
klauen; (fam: complete quickly)
hinhauen □ vi (fam: cease work)
Feierabend machen. ~ **out** vt
ausschlagen; (make unconscious)
bewusstlos schlagen; (Boxing)
k.o. schlagen. ~ **over** vt
umwerfen; (in car) anfahren

knock: ~**down** a ~**down
prices** Schleuderpreise pl. ~**er** n
Türklopfer m. ~**kneed** /-'ni:d/ a
X-beinig. ~**out** n (Boxing) K.o.
m

knot /nɒt/ n Knoten m □ vt (pt/pp
knotted) knoten

knotty /'nɒtɪ/ a (-**ier**, -**iest**) (fam)
verwickelt

know /nəʊ/ vt/i (pt **knew**, pp
known) wissen; kennen (person);
können (language); **get to** ~
kennen lernen □ **in the** ~ (fam)
im Bild

know: ~**all** n (fam) Alleswisser
m. ~**how** n (fam) [Sach]-
kenntnis f. ~**ing** a wissend. ~**in-
gly** adv (intentionally)
wissentlich

knowledge /'nɒlɪdʒ/ n Kenntnis
f (of von/gen); (general) Wissen
nt; (specialized) Kenntnisse pl.
~**able** /-əbl/ a ~**able** viel
wissen

known /nəʊn/ see **know** □ a bekannt

knuckle /'nʌkl/ n [Finger]knö-
chel m; (Culin) Hachse f □ vi ~
under sich fügen; ~ **down** sich
dahinter klemmen

kosher /'kəʊʃə(r)/ a koscher

kowtow /kaʊ'taʊ/ vi Kotau
machen (**to** vor + dat)

kudos /'kju:dɒs/ n (fam) Prestige
nt

L

lab /læb/ n (fam) Labor nt

label /'leɪbl/ n Etikett nt □ vt
(pt/pp **labelled**) etikettieren

laboratory /lə'bɒrətrɪ/ n Labor
nt

laborious /lə'bɔ:rɪəs/ a, -**ly** adv
mühsam

labour /'leɪbə(r)/ n Arbeit f;
(workers) Arbeitskräfte pl; (Med)
Wehen pl; **L~** (Pol) die
Labourpartei □ attrib Labour-
□ vi arbeiten □ vt (fig) sich lange
auslassen über (+ acc). ~**er** n Arbeiter m

'**labour-saving** a arbeitssparend

laburnum /lə'bɜ:nəm/ n Gold-
regen m

labyrinth /'læbərɪnθ/ n Labyrinth nt

lace /leɪs/ n Spitze f; (of shoe)
Schnürsenkel m □ vt schnüren;
~**d with rum** mit einem Schuss
Rum

lacerate /'læsəreɪt/ vt zerreißen

lack /læk/ n Mangel m (of an +
dat) □ vt **I** ~ **the time** mir fehlt
die Zeit □ vi **be** ~**ing** fehlen

lackadaisical /lækə'deɪzɪkl/ a
lustlos

laconic /lə'kɒnɪk/ a, -**ally** adv
lakonisch

lacquer /'lækə(r)/ n Lack m; (for
hair) [Haar]spray m

lad /læd/ n Junge m

ladder /'lædə(r)/ n Leiter f; (in
fabric) Laufmasche f

laden /'leɪdn/ a beladen

ladle /'leɪdl/ n [Schöpf]kelle f □ vt
schöpfen

lady /'leɪdɪ/ n Dame f; (title) Lady
f

lady: ~**bird** n, (Amer) ~**bug** n
Marienkäfer m. ~**like** a damen-
haft

lag[1] /læg/ vi (pt/pp **lagged**) ~ **behind** zurückbleiben; (fig)
nachhinken

lag[2] vt (pt/pp **lagged**) unwickeln
(pipes)

lager /'lɑ:gə(r)/ n Lagerbier nt

lagoon /lə'gu:n/ n Lagune f

laid /leɪd/ see **lay**[3]

lain /leɪn/ see **lie**[2]

lair /leə(r)/ n Lager nt

laity /'leɪətɪ/ n Laienstand m

lake /leɪk/ n See m

lamb /læm/ n Lamm nt

lame /leɪm/ a (-r, -st) lahm

lament /lə'ment/ n Klage f; (song) Klagelied nt □ vt beklagen □ vi klagen. ~able /'læməntəbl/ a beklagenswert

laminated /'læmɪneɪtɪd/ a laminiert

lamp /læmp/ n Lampe f; (in street) Laterne f. ~post n Laternenpfahl m. ~shade n Lampenschirm m

lance /lɑːns/ n Lanze f □ vt (Med) aufschneiden. ~-corporal n Gefreite(r) m

land /lænd/ n Land nt; plot of ~ Grundstück nt □ vt/i landen; ~ s.o. with sth (fam) jdm etw auf halsen

landing /'lændɪŋ/ n Landung f; (top of stairs) Treppenflur m. ~-stage n Landesteg m

land: ~lady n Wirtin f. ~locked a ~locked country Binnenstaat m. ~lord n Wirt m; (of land) Grundbesitzer m; (of building) Hausbesitzer m. ~mark n Erkennungszeichen nt; (fig) Meilenstein m. ~owner n Grundbesitzer m. ~scape /-skeɪp/ n Landschaft f. ~slide n Erdrutsch m

lane /leɪn/ n kleine Landstraße f; (Auto) Spur f; (Sport) Bahn f; 'get in ~' (Auto) 'bitte einordnen'

language /'læŋgwɪdʒ/ n Sprache f; (speech, style) Ausdrucksweise f. ~ laboratory n Sprachlabor nt

languid /'læŋgwɪd/ a, -ly adv träge

languish /'læŋgwɪʃ/ vi schmachten

lank /læŋk/ a (hair) strähnig

lanky /'læŋkɪ/ a (-ier, -iest) schlaksig

lantern /'læntən/ n Laterne f

lap1 /læp/ n Schoß m

lap2 n (Sport) Runde f; (of journey) Etappe f □ vi (pt/pp lapped) plätschern (against gegen)

lap3 vt (pt/pp lapped) ~ up aufschlecken

lapel /lə'pel/ n Revers nt

lapse /læps/ n Fehler m; (moral) Fehltritt m; (of time) Zeitspanne f □ vi (expire) erlöschen; ~ into verfallen in (+ acc)

larceny /'lɑːsənɪ/ n Diebstahl m

lard /lɑːd/ n [Schweine]schmalz nt

larder /'lɑːdə(r)/ n Speisekammer f

large /lɑːdʒ/ a (-r, -st) & adv groß; by and ~ im Großen und Ganzen; at ~ auf freiem Fuß; (in general) im Allgemeinen. ~ly adv großenteils

lark1 /lɑːk/ n (bird) Lerche f

lark2 n (joke) Jux m □ vi ~ about herumalbern

larva /'lɑːvə/ n (pl -vae /-viː/) Larve f

laryngitis /lærɪn'dʒaɪtɪs/ n Kehlkopfentzündung f

larynx /'lærɪŋks/ n Kehlkopf m

lascivious /lə'sɪvɪəs/ a lüstern

laser /'leɪzə(r)/ n Laser m

lash /læʃ/ n Peitschenhieb m; (eyelash) Wimper f □ vt peitschen; (tie) festbinden (to an + acc). ~ out vt um sich schlagen; (spend) viel Geld ausgeben (on für)

lashings /'læʃɪŋz/ npl ~ of (fam) eine Riesenmenge von

lass /læs/ n Mädchen nt

lasso /læ'suː/ n Lasso nt

last1 /lɑːst/ n (for shoe) Leisten m

last2 a & n letzte(r,s); ~ night heute od gestern Nacht; (evening) gestern Abend; at ~ endlich; the ~ time das letzte Mal; for the ~ time zum letzten Mal; the ~ but one der/die/das vorletzte; that's the ~ straw (fam) das schlägt dem Faß den Boden aus □ adv zuletzt; (last time) das letzte Mal;

do sth ~ etw zuletzt *od* als Letztes machen; **he/she went ~** er/sie ging als Letzter/Letzte □ *vi* dauern; *(weather:)* sich halten; *(relationship:)* halten. **~ing** *a* dauerhaft. **~ly** *adv* schließlich, zum Schluss

latch /lætʃ/ *n* [einfache] Klinke *f*; **on the ~** nicht verschlossen

late /leɪt/ *a & adv* (**-r, -st**) spät; *(delayed)* verspätet; *(deceased)* verstorben; **the ~st news** die neuesten Nachrichten; **stay up ~** bis spät aufbleiben; **of ~** in letzter Zeit; **arrive ~** zu spät ankommen; **I am ~** ich komme zu spät *od* habe mich verspätet; **the train is ~** der Zug hat Verspätung. **~comer** *n* Zuspätkommende(r) *m/f*. **~ly** *adv* in letzter Zeit. **~ness** *n* Zuspätkommen *nt*; *(delay)* Verspätung *f*

latent /ˈleɪtnt/ *a* latent

later /ˈleɪtə(r)/ *a & adv* später; **~ on** nachher

lateral /ˈlætərəl/ *a* seitlich

lathe /leɪð/ *n* Drehbank *f*

lather /ˈlɑːðə(r)/ *n* [Seifen]schaum *m* □ *vt* einseifen □ *vi* schäumen

Latin /ˈlætɪn/ *a* lateinisch □ *n* Latein *nt*. **~ A'merica** *n* Lateinamerika *nt*

latitude /ˈlætɪtjuːd/ *n* (Geog) Breite *f*; *(fig)* Freiheit *f*

latter /ˈlætə(r)/ *a & n* **the ~** der/die/das Letztere. **~ly** *adv* in letzter Zeit

lattice /ˈlætɪs/ *n* Gitter *nt*

Latvia /ˈlætvɪə/ *n* Lettland *nt*

laudable /ˈlɔːdəbl/ *a* lobenswert

laugh /lɑːf/ *n* Lachen *nt*; **with a ~** lachend □ *vi* lachen (**at/about** über + *acc*); **~ at s.o.** *(mock)* jdn auslachen. **~able** /-əbl/ *a* lachhaft, lächerlich. **~ing-stock** *n* Gegenstand *m* des Spottes

laughter /ˈlɑːftə(r)/ *n* Gelächter *nt*

launch¹ /lɔːntʃ/ *n* (boat) Barkasse *f*

launch² *n* Stapellauf *m*; *(of rocket)* Abschuss *m*; *(of product)* Lancierung *f* □ *vt* vom Stapel lassen *(ship)*; zu Wasser lassen *(lifeboat)*; abschießen *(rocket)*; starten *(attack)*; (Comm) lancieren *(product)*

launder /ˈlɔːndə(r)/ *vt* waschen. **~ette** /-ˈdret/ *n* Münzwäscherei *f*

laundry /ˈlɔːndrɪ/ *n* Wäscherei *f*; *(clothes)* Wäsche *f*

laurel /ˈlɒrl/ *n* Lorbeer *m*

lava /ˈlɑːvə/ *n* Lava *f*

lavatory /ˈlævətrɪ/ *n* Toilette *f*

lavender /ˈlævəndə(r)/ *n* Lavendel *m*

lavish /ˈlævɪʃ/ *a*, **-ly** *adv* großzügig; *(wasteful)* verschwenderisch; **on a ~ scale** mit viel Aufwand □ *vt* **~ sth on s.o.** jdn mit etw überschütten

law /lɔː/ *n* Gesetz *nt*; *(system)* Recht *nt*; **study ~** Jura studieren; **~ and order** Recht und Ordnung

law: ~-abiding *a* gesetzestreu. **~court** *n* Gerichtshof *m*. **~ful** *a* rechtmäßig. **~less** *a* gesetzlos

lawn /lɔːn/ *n* Rasen *m*. **~-mower** *n* Rasenmäher *m*

'law suit *n* Prozess *m*

lawyer /ˈlɔːjə(r)/ *n* Rechtsanwalt *m* /-anwältin *f*

lax /læks/ *a* lax, locker

laxative /ˈlæksətɪv/ *n* Abführmittel *nt*

laxity /ˈlæksətɪ/ *n* Laxheit *f*

lay¹ /leɪ/ *a* Laien-

lay² *see* **lie²**

lay³ *vt* (pt/pp laid) decken *(table)*; **~ a trap** eine Falle stellen. **~ down** *vt* hinlegen; festlegen *(rules, conditions)*. **~ off** *vt* entlassen *(workers)* □ *vi* *(fam: stop)* aufhören. **~ out** *vt* hinlegen; aufbahren *(corpse)*; anlegen *(garden)*; (Typ) gestalten

lay: ~about *n* Faulenzer *m*. **~ by** *n* Parkbucht *f*; *(on motorway)* Rastplatz *m*

layer /'leɪə(r)/ n Schicht f

layette /leɪ'et/ n Babyausstattung f

lay: ~man n Laie m. **~out** n Anordnung f; (design) Gestaltung f; (Typ) Layout nt. **~-preacher** n Laienprediger m

laze /leɪz/ vi **~about** faulenzen

laziness /'leɪzɪnɪs/ n Faulheit f

lazy /'leɪzɪ/ a (-ier, -iest) faul. **~bones** n Faulenzer m

lb /paund/ abbr (pound) Pfd.

lead¹ /led/ n Blei nt; (of pencil) [Bleistift]mine f

lead² /li:d/ n Führung f; (leash) Leine f; (flex) Schnur f; (clue) Hinweis m, Spur f; (Theat) Hauptrolle f; (distance ahead) Vorsprung m; **be in the ~** in Führung liegen □ vt/i (pt/pp led) führen; leiten (team); (induce) bringen; (at cards) ausspielen; **~ the way** vorangehen; **~ up to sth** (fig) etw (dat) vorangehen. **~ away** vt wegführen

leaded /'ledɪd/ a verbleit

leader /'li:də(r)/ n Führer m; (of expedition, group) Leiter(in) m(f); (of orchestra) Konzertmeister m; (in newspaper) Leitartikel m. **~ship** n Führung f; Leitung f

leading /'li:dɪŋ/ a führend; **~ lady** Hauptdarstellerin f; **~ question** Suggestivfrage f

leaf /li:f/ n (pl **leaves**) Blatt nt; (of table) Ausziehplatte f □ vi **~ through sth** etw durchblättern. **~ let** n Merkblatt nt; (advertising) Reklameblatt nt; (political) Flugblatt nt

league /li:g/ n Liga f; **be in ~ with** unter einer Decke stecken mit

leak /li:k/ n (hole) undichte Stelle f; (Naut) Leck nt; (of gas) Gasausfluss m □ vi undicht sein; (ship:) leck sein, lecken; (liquid:) auslaufen; (gas:) ausströmen □ vt auslaufen lassen; **~ sth to s.o.**

(fig) jdm etw zuspielen. **~y** a undicht; (Naut) leck

lean¹ /li:n/ a (-er, -est) mager

lean² v (pt/pp **leaned** or **leant** /lent/) □ vt lehnen (against/on an + acc) □ vi (person) sich lehnen (against/on an + acc); (not be straight) sich neigen; **~ing against** lehnen an (+ dat); **~ on s.o.** (depend) bei jdm festen Halt finden. **~ back** vi sich zurücklehnen. **~ forward** vi sich vorbeugen. **~ out** vi sich hinauslehnen. **~ over** vi sich vorbeugen

leaning /'li:nɪŋ/ a schief □ n Neigung f

leap /li:p/ n Sprung m □ vi (pt/pp **leapt** /lept/ or **leaped**) springen; **he leapt at it** (fam) er griff sofort zu. **~-frog** n Bockspringen nt. **~ year** n Schaltjahr nt

learn /lɜːn/ vt/i (pt/pp **learnt** or **learned**) lernen; (hear) erfahren; **~ to swim** schwimmen lernen

learn|ed /'lɜːnɪd/ a gelehrt. **~er** n Anfänger m; **~er [driver]** Fahrschüler(in) m(f). **~ing** n Gelehrsamkeit f

lease /li:s/ n Pacht f; (contract) Mietvertrag m; (Comm) Pachtvertrag m □ vt pachten; (let) verpachten

leash /li:ʃ/ n Leine f

least /li:st/ a geringste(r,s); **have ~ time** am wenigsten Zeit haben □ n **the ~** das wenigste; **at ~** wenigstens, mindestens; **not in the ~** nicht im Geringsten □ adv am wenigsten

leather /'leðə(r)/ n Leder nt. **~y** a ledern; (tough) zäh

leave /li:v/ n Erlaubnis f; (holiday) Urlaub m; **on ~** auf Urlaub; **take one's ~** sich verabschieden □ vt (pt/pp **left**) lassen; (go out of, abandon) verlassen; (forget) liegen lassen; (bequeath) vermachen (to dat); **~ it to me!** überlassen Sie es mir! **there is nothing left** es ist nichts mehr übrig □ vi [weg]gehen/-fahren;

⟨train, bus:⟩ abfahren. **~ behind** vt zurücklassen; ⟨forget⟩ liegen lassen. **~ out** vt liegen lassen; ⟨leave outside⟩ draußen lassen; ⟨omit⟩ auslassen

leaves /li:vz/ see **leaf**

Lebanon /'lebənən/ n Libanon m

lecherous /'letʃərəs/ a lüstern

lectern /'lektən/ n [Lese]pult nt

lecture /'lektʃə(r)/ n Vortrag m; ⟨Univ⟩ Vorlesung f; ⟨reproof⟩ Strafpredigt f □ vi einen Vortrag/ eine Vorlesung halten (**on** über + acc) □ vt ~ s.o. jdm eine Strafpredigt halten. **~r** n Vortragende(r) m/f; ⟨Univ⟩ Dozent/in m(f)

led /led/ see **lead**²

ledge /ledʒ/ n Leiste f; ⟨shelf, of window⟩ Sims m; ⟨in rock⟩ Vorsprung m

ledger /'ledʒə(r)/ n Hauptbuch nt

lee /li:/ n ⟨Naut⟩ Lee f

leech /li:tʃ/ n Blutegel m

leek /li:k/ n Stange f Porree; **~s** pl Porree m

leer /lɪə(r)/ n anzügliches Grinsen nt □ vi anzüglich grinsen

lee|**ward** /'li:wəd/ adv nach Lee. **~way** n ⟨fig⟩ Spielraum m

left¹ /left/ see **leave**

left² a /left/ □ adv links; ⟨go⟩ nach links □ n linke Seite f; **on the ~** links; **from/to the ~** von/ nach links; **the ~** ⟨Pol⟩ die Linke

left: **~'handed** a linkshändig. **~ 'luggage [office]** n Gepäckaufbewahrung f. **~overs** npl Reste pl. **~'wing** a ⟨Pol⟩ linke(r,s)

leg /leg/ n Bein nt; ⟨Culin⟩ Keule f; ⟨of journey⟩ Etappe f

legacy /'legəsi/ n Vermächtnis nt, Erbschaft f

legal /'li:gl/ a, **-ly** adv gesetzlich; ⟨matters⟩ rechtlich; ⟨department, position⟩ Rechts-; **be ~** ⟨be gesetzlich⟩ erlaubt sein; **take ~ action** gerichtlich vorgehen

legality /lɪ'gæləti/ n Legalität f

legalize /'li:gəlaɪz/ vt legalisieren

legend /'ledʒənd/ n Legende f. **~ary** a legendär

legible /'ledʒəbl/ a, **-bly** adv leserlich

legion /'li:dʒn/ n Legion f

legislat|**e** /'ledʒɪsleɪt/ vi Gesetze erlassen. **~ion** /-'leɪʃn/ n Gesetzgebung f; ⟨laws⟩ Gesetze pl

legislat|**ive** /'ledʒɪslətɪv/ a gesetzgebend. **~ure** /-tʃə(r)/ n Legislative f

legitimate /lɪ'dʒɪtɪmət/ a rechtmäßig; ⟨justifiable⟩ berechtigt; ⟨child⟩ ehelich

leisure /'leʒə(r)/ n Freizeit f; **at your ~** wenn Sie Zeit haben. **~ly** a gemächlich

lemon /'lemən/ n Zitrone f. **~ade** /-'neɪd/ n Zitronenlimonade f

lend /lend/ vt (pt/pp **lent**) leihen; **~ s.o. sth** jdm etw leihen; **~ a hand** (fig) helfen. **~ing library** n Leihbücherei f

length /leŋθ/ n Länge f; ⟨piece⟩ Stück nt; ⟨of wallpaper⟩ Bahn f; ⟨of time⟩ Dauer f; **at ~** ⟨at last⟩ ausführlich; ⟨at last⟩ endlich

length|**en** /'leŋθən/ vt länger machen □ vi länger werden. **~ways** adv der Länge nach, längs

lengthy /'leŋθɪ/ a (**-ier, -iest**) langwierig

lenien|**ce** /'li:nɪəns/ n Nachsicht f. **~t** a, **-ly** adv nachsichtig

lens /lenz/ n Linse f; ⟨Phot⟩ Objektiv nt; ⟨of spectacles⟩ Glas nt

lent /lent/ see **lend**

Lent n Fastenzeit f

lentil /'lentl/ n ⟨Bot⟩ Linse f

Leo /'li:əʊ/ n ⟨Astr⟩ Löwe m

leopard /'lepəd/ n Leopard m

leotard /'li:əta:d/ n Trikot nt

leper /'lepə(r)/ n Leprakranke(r) m/f; n ⟨Bible & fig⟩ Aussätzige(r) m/f

leprosy /'leprəsi/ n Lepra f

lesbian /'lezbɪən/ a lesbisch □ n Lesbierin f

lesion /'liːʒn/ n Verletzung f

less /les/ a, adv, n & prep weniger; ~ **and** ~ immer weniger; **not any the** ~ um nichts weniger

lessen /'lesn/ vt verringern □ vi nachlassen; (value:) abnehmen

lesser /'lesə(r)/ a geringer(e,s)

lesson /'lesn/ n Stunde f; (in text-book) Lektion f; (Relig) Lesung f; **teach s.o. a** ~ (fig) jdm eine Lehre erteilen

lest /lest/ conj (liter) damit ... nicht

let /let/ vt (pt/pp let, pres p letting) lassen; (rent) vermieten; ~ **alone** (not to mention) geschweige denn; '~ **to** ~' 'zu vermieten'; ~ **us go** gehen wir; ~ **me know** lassen Sie mir Bescheid; ~ **him do it** lass ihn das machen; **just** ~ **him!** soll er doch! ~ **s.o. sleep/win** jdn schlafen/gewinnen lassen; ~ **oneself in for sth** (fam) sich (dat) etw einbrocken. ~ **down** vt hinunter-/herunterlassen; (lengthen) länger machen; ~ **s.o. down** (fam) jdn im Stich lassen (disappoint) jdn enttäuschen. ~ **in** vt hereinlassen. ~ **off** vt abfeuern (gun); hochgehen lassen (firework, bomb); (emit) ausstoßen; (excuse from) befreien von; (not punish) frei ausgehen lassen. ~ **out** vt hinaus-/herauslassen; (make larger) auslassen. ~ **through** vt durchlassen. ~ **up** vi (fam) nachlassen

'let-down n Enttäuschung f, (fam) Reinfall m

lethal /'liːθl/ a tödlich

lethargic /lɪ'θɑːdʒɪk/ a lethargisch. ~**y** /'leθədʒɪ/ n Lethargie f

letter /'letə(r)/ n Brief m; (of alphabet) Buchstabe m; **by** ~ brieflich. ~**box** n Briefkasten m. ~**head** n Briefkopf m. ~**ing** n Beschriftung f

lettuce /'letɪs/ n [Kopf]salat m

'let-up n (fam) Nachlassen nt

leukaemia /luːˈkiːmɪə/ n Leukämie f

level /'levl/ a eben; (horizontal) waagerecht; (in height) auf gleicher Höhe; (spoonful) gestrichen; **draw** ~ **with** gleichziehen mit; **one's** ~ **best** sein Möglichstes □n Höhe f; (fig) Ebene f, Niveau nt; (stage) Stufe f; **on the** ~ (fam) ehrlich □vt (pt/pp levelled) einebnen; (aim) richten (**at** auf + acc)

level- ~ **'crossing** n Bahnübergang m. ~**'headed** a vernünftig

lever /'liːvə(r)/ n Hebel m □vt ~ **up** mit einem Hebel anheben. ~**age** /-rɪdʒ/ n Hebelkraft f

levity /'levɪtɪ/ n Heiterkeit f; (frivolity) Leichtfertigkeit f

levy /'levɪ/ vt (pt/pp levied) erheben (tax)

lewd /ljuːd/ a (-er, -est) anstößig

liab|**ility** /laɪə'bɪlɪtɪ/ n Haftung f; ~**ies** pl Verbindlichkeiten pl

liable /'laɪəbl/ a haftbar; **be** ~ **to do sth** etw leicht tun können

liaise /lɪ'eɪz/ vi (fam) Verbindungsperson sein

liaison /lɪ'eɪzɒn/ n Verbindung f; (affair) Verhältnis nt

liar /'laɪə(r)/ n Lügner(in) m(f)

libel /'laɪbl/ n Verleumdung f □vt (pt/pp libelled) verleumden. ~**lous** a verleumderisch

liberal /'lɪbərl/ a, ~**ly** adv tolerant; (generous) großzügig. **L**~ a (Pol) liberal □n Liberale(r) m/f

liberat|**e** /'lɪbəreɪt/ vt befreien. ~**ed** a (woman) emanzipiert. ~**ion** /-'reɪʃn/ n Befreiung f. ~**or** n Befreier m

liberty /'lɪbətɪ/ n Freiheit f; **take the** ~ **of doing sth** sich (dat) erlauben, etw zu tun; **take liberties** sich (dat) Freiheiten erlauben

Libra /'liːbrə/ n (Astr) Waage f

librarian /laɪ'breərɪən/ n Bibliothekar(in) m(f)

library /'laɪbrərɪ/ n Bibliothek f

Libya /'lɪbɪə/ n Libyen nt

lice /laɪs/ see **louse**

licence /'laɪsns/ n Genehmigung f; (Comm) Lizenz f; (for TV) n Fernsehgebühr f; (for driving) Führerschein m; (for alcohol) Schankkonzession f; (freedom) Freiheit f

license /'laɪsns/ vt eine Genehmigung/(Comm) Lizenz erteilen (+ dat); be ~d (car:) zugelassen sein; (restaurant:) Schankkonzession haben. ~plate n Nummernschild nt

licentious /laɪ'senʃəs/ a lasterhaft

lichen /'laɪkən/ n (Bot) Flechte f

lick /lɪk/ n Lecken nt; a ~ of paint ein bisschen Farbe □vt lecken; (fam: defeat) schlagen

lid /lɪd/ n Deckel m; (of eye) Lid nt

lie[1] /laɪ/ n Lüge f; tell a ~ lügen □vi (pt/pp lied, pres p lying) lügen; ~ to belügen

lie[2] vi (pt lay, pp lain, pres p lying) liegen; **here** ~**s** . . . hier ruht . . . ~ **down** vi sich hinlegen

Liège /lɪ'eɪʒ/ n Lüttich nt

lie-in n **have a** ~ [sich] ausschlafen

lieu /ljuː/ n **in** ~ **of** statt (+ gen)

lieutenant /lef'tenənt/ n Oberleutnant m

life /laɪf/ n (pl **lives**) Leben nt; (biography) Biographie f; **lose one's** ~ ums Leben kommen

life: ~**belt** n Rettungsring m. ~**boat** n Rettungsboot nt. ~**buoy** n Rettungsring m. ~**guard** n Lebensretter m. ~**jacket** n Schwimmweste f. ~**less** a leblos. ~**like** a naturgetreu. ~**line** n Rettungsleine f. ~**long** a lebenslang. ~**preserver** n (Amer) Rettungsring m. ~**size(d)** a (in Lebensgröße. ~**time** n Leben nt; **in s.o.'s** ~ zu jds Lebzeiten; **the chance of a** ~**time** eine einmalige Gelegenheit

lift /lɪft/ n Aufzug m, Lift m; **give s.o. a** ~ jdn mitnehmen; **get a** ~

mitgenommen werden □vt heben; aufheben (restrictions) □vi (fog:) sich lichten. ~ **up** vt hochheben

lift-off n Abheben nt

ligament /'lɪgəmənt/ n (Anat) Band nt

light[1] /laɪt/ a (-er, -est) (not dark) hell; ~ **blue** hellblau □ n Licht nt; (lamp) Lampe f; **in the** ~ **of** (fig) angesichts (+ gen); **have you [got] a** ~? haben Sie Feuer? □ vt (pt/pp **lit** or **lighted**) anzünden (fire, cigarette); (illuminate) beleuchten (lamp); (illuminate) beleuchten. ~ **up** vi (face:) sich erhellen

light[2] a (-er, -est) (not heavy) leicht; ~ **sentence** milde Strafe f □ adv **travel** ~ mit wenig Gepäck reisen

light-bulb n Glühbirne f

lighten[1] /'laɪtn/ vt heller machen □ vi heller werden

lighten[2] vt leichter machen (load)

lighter /'laɪtə(r)/ n Feuerzeug nt

light: ~**headed** a benommen. ~**hearted** a unbekümmert. ~**house** n Leuchtturm m. ~**ing** n Beleuchtung f. ~**ly** adv leicht; (casually) leichthin; **get off** ~**ly** glimpflich davonkommen

lightning /'laɪtnɪŋ/ n Blitz m. ~**conductor** n Blitzableiter m

lightweight a leicht □ n (Boxing) Leichtgewicht nt

like[1] /laɪk/ a ähnlich; (same) gleich □ prep wie; (similar to) ähnlich (+ dat); ~ **this** so; **a man** ~ **that** so ein Mann; **what's he** ~? wie ist er denn? □ conj (fam: as) wie; (Amer: as if) als ob

like[2] vt mögen; **I should/would** ~ ich möchte; **I** ~ **the car** das Auto gefällt mir; **I** ~ **chocolate** ich esse gern Schokolade; ~ **dancing/singing** gern tanzen/singen; **I** ~ **that!** (fam) das ist doch die Höhe! □ n ~**s and dislikes** pl Vorlieben und Abneigungen pl

like|able /'laɪkəbl/ a sympathisch. **~lihood** /-lɪhʊd/ n Wahrscheinlichkeit f. **~ly** a (-ier, -iest) & adv wahrscheinlich; **not ~ly!** (fam) auf gar keinen Fall!

'like-minded a gleich gesinnt

liken /'laɪkən/ vt vergleichen (**to** mit)

like|ness /'laɪknɪs/ n Ähnlichkeit f. **~wise** adv ebenso

liking /'laɪkɪŋ/ n Vorliebe f; **is it to your ~?** gefällt es Ihnen?

lilac /'laɪlək/ n Flieder m □ a fliederfarben

lily /'lɪlɪ/ n. Lilie f. **~ of the valley** n Maiglöckchen nt

limb /lɪm/ n Glied nt

limber /'lɪmbə(r)/ vi **~ up** Lockerungsübungen machen

lime¹ /laɪm/ n (fruit) Limone f; (tree) Linde f

lime² n Kalk m. **~light** n **be in the ~light** im Rampenlicht stehen. **~stone** n Kalkstein m

limit /'lɪmɪt/ n Grenze f; (limitation) Beschränkung f; **that's the ~!** (fam) das ist doch die Höhe! □ vt beschränken (**to** auf + acc). **~ation** /-'teɪʃn/ n Beschränkung f. **~ed** a beschränkt. **~ed company** Gesellschaft f mit beschränkter Haftung

limousine /'lɪməzi:n/ n Limousine f

limp¹ /lɪmp/ n Hinken nt; **have a ~** hinken □ vi hinken

limp² a (-er -est), **-ly** adv schlaff

limpet /'lɪmpɪt/ n **like a ~** (fig) wie eine Klette

limpid /'lɪmpɪd/ a klar

linctus /'lɪŋktəs/ n [**cough**] **~** Hustensirup m

line¹ /laɪn/ n Linie f; (length of rope, cord) Leine f; (Teleph) Leitung f; (of writing) Zeile f; (row) Reihe f; (wrinkle) Falte f; (of business) f; (Amer: queue) Schlange f; **in ~ with** gemäß (+ dat) □ vt

säumen ⟨street⟩. **~ up** vi sich aufstellen □ vt aufstellen

line² vt füttern ⟨garment⟩; (Techn) auskleiden

lineage /'lɪnɪɪdʒ/ n Herkunft f

linear /'lɪnɪə(r)/ a linear

lined¹ /laɪnd/ a (wrinkled) faltig; ⟨paper⟩ liniert

lined² a ⟨garment⟩ gefüttert

linen /'lɪnɪn/ n Leinen nt; (articles) Wäsche f

liner /'laɪnə(r)/ n Passagierschiff nt

linesman n (Sport) Linienrichter m

linger /'lɪŋgə(r)/ vi [zurück]bleiben

lingerie /'læʒərɪ/ n Damenunterwäsche f

linguist /'lɪŋgwɪst/ n Sprachkundige(r) m/f

linguistic /lɪŋ'gwɪstɪk/ a, **-ally** adv sprachlich. **~s** n Linguistik f

lining /'laɪnɪŋ/ n (of garment) Futter nt; (Techn) Auskleidung f

link /lɪŋk/ n (of chain) Glied nt (fig) Verbindung f □ vt verbinden; **~ arms** sich unterhaken

links /lɪŋks/ n or npl Golfplatz m

lino /'laɪnəʊ/ n, **linoleum** /lɪ'nəʊlɪəm/ n Linoleum nt

lint /lɪnt/ n Verbandstoff m

lion /'laɪən/ n Löwe m; **~'s share** (fig) Löwenanteil m. **~ess** n Löwin f

lip /lɪp/ n Lippe f; (edge) Rand m; (of jug) Schnabel m

lip: **~-reading** n Lippenlesen nt. **~-service** n pay **~-service** ein Lippenbekenntnis ablegen (**to** zu). **~stick** n Lippenstift m

liquefy /'lɪkwɪfaɪ/ vt (pt/pp **-ied**) verflüssigen □ vi sich verflüssigen

liqueur /lɪ'kjʊə(r)/ n Likör m

liquid /'lɪkwɪd/ n Flüssigkeit f □ a flüssig

liquidat|e /'lɪkwɪdeɪt/ vt liquidieren. **~ion** /-'deɪʃn/ n Liquidation f

liquidize /'lıkwıdaız/ vt [im Mixer] pürieren. **~r** n (Culin) Mixer m

liquor /'lıkə(r)/ n Alkohol m; (juice) Flüssigkeit f

liquorice /'lıkərıs/ n Lakritze f

'liquor store n (Amer) Spirituosengeschäft nt

lisp /lısp/ n Lispeln nt □ vt/i lispeln

list[1] /lıst/ n Liste f □ vt aufführen

list[2] vi (ship:) Schlagseite haben

listen /'lısn/ vi zuhören (to dat); **~ to the radio** Radio hören. **~er** n Zuhörer(in) m(f); (Radio) Hörer(in) m(f)

listless /'lıstlıs/ a, **-ly** adv lustlos

lit /lıt/ see **light**[1]

litany /'lıtənı/ n Litanei f

literacy /'lıtərəsı/ n Lese- und Schreibfertigkeit f

literal /'lıtərl/ a wörtlich. **-ly** adv buchstäblich

literary /'lıtərərı/ a literarisch

literate /'lıtərət/ a **be ~** lesen und schreiben können

literature /'lıtrətʃə(r)/ n Literatur f; (fam) Informationsmaterial nt

lithe /laıð/ a geschmeidig

Lithuania /lıθjʊ'eınıə/ n Litauen nt

litigation /lıtı'geıʃn/ n Rechtsstreit m

litre /'li:tə(r)/ n Liter m & nt

litter /'lıtə(r)/ n Abfall m; (Zool) Wurf m □ vt **be ~ed with** übersät sein mit. **~-bin** n Abfalleimer m

little /'lıtl/ a klein; (not much) wenig □ adv & n wenig; **a ~** ein bisschen/wenig; **~ by ~** nach und nach

liturgy /'lıtədʒı/ n Liturgie f

live[1] /laıv/ a lebendig; (ammunition) scharf; **~ broadcast** Live-Sendung f; **be ~** (Electr) unter Strom stehen □ adv (Radio, TV) live

live[2] /lıv/ vi leben; (reside) wohnen; **~ up to** gerecht werden

(+ dat). **~ on** vt leben von; (eat) sich ernähren von □ vi weiterleben

livelihood /'laıvlıhʊd/ n Lebensunterhalt m. **~ness** n Lebendigkeit f

lively /'laıvlı/ a (-ier, -iest) lebhaft, lebendig

liven /'laıvn/ v **~ up** vt beleben □ vi lebhaft werden

liver /'lıvə(r)/ n Leber f

lives /laıvz/ see **life**

livestock /'laıv-/ n Vieh nt

livid /'lıvıd/ a (fam) wütend

living /'lıvıŋ/ a lebend □ n **earn one's ~** seinen Lebensunterhalt verdienen; **the ~** pl die Lebenden. **~-room** n Wohnzimmer nt

lizard /'lızəd/ n Eidechse f

load /ləʊd/ n Last f; (quantity) Ladung f; (Electr) Belastung f; **~s of** (fam) jede Menge □ vt laden (goods, gun); beladen (vehicle); **~ a camera** einen Film in eine Kamera einlegen. **~ed** a beladen; (fam: rich) steinreich; **~ed question** Fangfrage f

loaf[1] /ləʊf/ n (pl **loaves**) Brot nt

loaf[2] vi faulenzen

loan /ləʊn/ n Leihgabe f; (money) Darlehen nt; **on ~** geliehen □ vt leihen (to dat)

loath /ləʊθ/ a **be ~ to do sth** etw ungern tun

loath|**e** /ləʊð/ vt verabscheuen. **~ing** n Abscheu m. **~some** a abscheulich

loaves /ləʊvz/ see **loaf**[1]

lobby /'lɒbı/ n Foyer nt; (anteroom) Vorraum m; (Pol) Lobby f

lobe /ləʊb/ n (of ear) Ohrläppchen nt

lobster /'lɒbstə(r)/ n Hummer m

local /'ləʊkl/ a hiesig; (time, traffic) Orts-; **under ~ anaesthetic** unter örtlicher Betäubung; **I'm not ~** ich bin nicht von hier □ n Hiesige(r) m/f; (fam: public house) Stammkneipe f.

~ au'thority n Kommunalbehörde f. **~ call** n (Teleph) Ortsgespräch nt

locality /ləʊ'kælətɪ/ n Gegend f

localized /'ləʊkəlaɪzd/ a lokalisiert

locally /'ləʊkəlɪ/ adv am Ort

locat|e /ləʊ'keɪt/ vt ausfindig machen; **be ~ed** sich befinden. **~ion** /-'keɪʃn/ n Lage f; **filmed on ~ion** als Außenaufnahme gedreht

lock[1] /lɒk/ n (hair) Strähne f

lock[2] n (on door) Schloss nt; (on canal) Schleuse f □ vt abschließen □ vi sich abschließen lassen. **~ in** vt einschließen. **~ out** vt ausschließen. **~ up** vt abschließen; einsperren (person) □ vi zuschließen

locker /'lɒkə(r)/ n Schließfach nt; (Mil) Spind m; (in hospital) kleiner Schrank m

locket /'lɒkɪt/ n Medaillon nt

lock: **~-out** n Aussperrung f. **~smith** n Schlosser m

locomotion /ləʊkə'məʊʃn/ n Fortbewegung f

locomotive /ləʊkə'məʊtɪv/ n Lokomotive f

locum /'ləʊkəm/ n Vertreter(in) m(f)

locust /'ləʊkəst/ n Heuschrecke f

lodge /lɒdʒ/ n (porter's) Pförtnerhaus nt; (masonic) Loge f □ vt (submit) einreichen; (deposit) deponieren □ vi zur Untermiete wohnen (with bei); (become fixed) stecken bleiben. **~r** n Untermieter(in) m(f)

lodging /'lɒdʒɪŋ/ n Unterkunft f; **~s** npl möbliertes Zimmer nt

loft /lɒft/ n Dachboden m

lofty /'lɒftɪ/ a (-ier, -iest) hoch; (haughty) hochmütig

log /lɒg/ n Baumstamm m; (for fire) [Holz]scheit nt; **sleep like a ~** (fam) wie ein Murmeltier schlafen

logarithm /'lɒgərɪðm/ n Logarithmus m

'log-book n (Naut) Logbuch nt

loggerheads /'lɒgə-/ npl **be at ~** (fam) sich in den Haaren liegen

logic /'lɒdʒɪk/ n Logik f. **~al** a, **-ly** adv logisch

logistics /lə'dʒɪstɪks/ npl Logistik f

logo /'ləʊgəʊ/ n Symbol nt, Logo nt

loin /lɔɪn/ n (Culin) Lende f

loiter /'lɔɪtə(r)/ vi herumlungern

loll /lɒl/ vi sich lümmeln

loll|ipop /'lɒlɪpɒp/ n Lutscher m. **~y** n Lutscher m; (fam: money) Moneten pl

London /'lʌndən/ n London nt □ attrib Londoner. **~er** n Londoner(in) m(f)

lone /ləʊn/ a einzeln. **~liness** n Einsamkeit f

lonely /'ləʊnlɪ/ a (-ier, -iest) einsam

lone|r /'ləʊnə(r)/ n Einzelgänger m. **~some** a einsam

long[1] /lɒŋ/ a (-er /'lɒŋgə(r)/, -est /'lɒŋgɪst/) lang; (journey) weit; **a ~ time** lange; **a ~ way** weit; **in the ~ run** auflange Sicht; (in the end) letzten Endes □ adv lange; **all day ~** den ganzen Tag; **not ~ ago** vor kurzem; **before ~** bald; **no ~er** nicht mehr; **as or so ~ as** solange; **so ~!** (fam) tschüs! **will you be ~?** dauert es noch lange [bei dir]? **it won't take ~** es dauert nicht lange

long[2] vi **~ for** sich sehnen nach

long-'distance a Fern-; (Sport) Langstrecken-

longevity /lɒn'dʒevətɪ/ n Langlebigkeit f

'longhand n Langschrift f

longing /'lɒŋɪŋ/ a, **-ly** adv sehnsüchtig □ n Sehnsucht f

longitude /'lɒŋgɪtjuːd/ n (Geog) Länge f

long: **~ jump** n Weitsprung m. **~-life 'milk** n H-Milch f. **~-lived**

/l-ıvd/ a langlebig. **~range** a (Mil, Aviat) Langstrecken-; (forecast) langfristig. **~sighted** a weitsichtig. **~sleeved** a langärmelig. **~suffering** a langmütig. **~term** a langfristig. **~wave** n Langewelle f. **~winded** /-'wındıd/ a langatmig

loo /lu:/ n (fam) Klo nt

look /lʊk/ n Blick m; (appearance) Aussehen nt; **[good]** **~s** pl [gutes] Aussehen nt; **have a ~** at sich (dat) ansehen; **go and have a ~** sieh mal nach □ vi sehen; (search) nachsehen; (seem) aussehen; **don't ~** sieh nicht hin; **~ here!** hören Sie mal! □ **~ at** ansehen; **~ for** suchen; **~ forward to** sich freuen auf (+ acc); **~ in on** vorbeischauen bei; **~ into** (examine) nachsehen (+ dat); **~ like** aussehen wie; **~ on to** (room:) gehen auf (+ acc). **~ after** vt betreuen. **~ down** vi hinuntersehen. **~ down on s.o.** (fig) auf jdn herabsehen. **~ out** vi hinaus-/heraussehen; (take care) aufpassen; **~ out for** Ausschau halten nach; **~ out!** Vorsicht! **~ round** vi sich umsehen. **~ up** vi aufblicken; **~ up to s.o.** (fig) zu jdm aufsehen □ vt nachschlagen (word)

'look-out n Wache f; (prospect) Aussicht f; **be on the ~ for** Ausschau halten nach

loom[1] /lu:m/ n Webstuhl m

loom[2] vi auftauchen; (fig) sich abzeichnen

loony /'lu:nı/ a (fam) verrückt

loop /lu:p/ n Schlinge f; (in road) Schleife f; (on garment) Aufhänger m □ vt schlingen. **~hole** n Hintertürchen nt; (in the law) Lücke f

loose /lu:s/ a (-r, -st), **-ly** adv lose; (not tight enough) locker; (inexact) frei; **be at a ~ end** nichts zu tun haben; **set ~** freilassen; **run ~** frei herumlaufen. **'change** n Kleingeld nt. **~ 'chippings** npl Rollsplit m

loosen /'lu:sn/ vt lockern □ vi sich lockern

loot /lu:t/ n Beute f □ vt/i plündern. **~er** n Plünderer m

lop /lɒp/ vt (pt/pp lopped) stutzen. **~ off** vt abhacken

lop'sided a schief

loquacious /lə'kweıʃəs/ a redselig

lord /lɔ:d/ n Herr m; (title) Lord m; House of L**~**s ≈ Oberhaus nt; the L**~**'s Prayer das Vaterunser; good L**~**! du liebe Zeit!

lore /lɔ:(r)/ n Überlieferung f

lorry /'lɒrı/ n Last[kraft]wagen m

lose /lu:z/ v (pt/pp lost) □ vt verlieren; (miss) verpassen □ vi verlieren; (clock:) nachgehen; **get lost** verloren gehen; (person:) sich verlaufen. **~r** n Verlierer m

loss /lɒs/ n Verlust m; **be at a ~** nicht mehr weiter wissen; **be at a ~ for words** nicht wissen, was man sagen soll

lost /lɒst/ see lose. **~ 'property office** n Fundbüro nt

lot[1] /lɒt/ Los nt; (at auction) Posten m; **draw ~s** losen (forum)

lot[2] n the **~** (everything) alles; **a ~** [of] viel; (many) viele; **~s of** (fam) eine Menge; **it has changed a ~** es hat sich sehr verändert

lotion /'ləʊʃn/ n Lotion f

lottery /'lɒtərı/ n Lotterie f. **~ ticket** n Los nt

loud /laʊd/ a (-er, -est), -ly adv laut; (colours) grell □ adv [out]. **~ 'hailer** n Megaphon nt. **~ 'speaker** n Lautsprecher m

lounge /laʊndʒ/ n Wohnzimmer nt; (in hotel) Aufenthaltsraum m □ vi sich lümmeln. **~ suit** n Straßenanzug m

louse /laʊs/ n (pl lice) Laus f

lousy /'laʊzı/ a (-ier, -iest) (fam) lausig

lout /laʊt/ n Flegel m, Lümmel m. **~ish** a flegelhaft

lovable /'lʌvəbl/ a liebenswert

love /lʌv/ n Liebe f; (Tennis) null; **in** ~ verliebt □ vt lieben; ~ **doing sth** etw sehr gerne machen; **I** ~ **chocolate** ich esse sehr gerne Schokolade. ~**affair** n Liebesverhältnis nt. ~ **letter** n Liebesbrief m

lovely /'lʌvlɪ/ a (-ier, -iest) schön; **we had a** ~ **time** es war sehr schön

lover /'lʌvə(r)/ n Liebhaber m

love: ~**song** n Liebeslied nt. ~ **story** n Liebesgeschichte f

loving /'lʌvɪŋ/ a, -ly adv liebevoll

low /ləʊ/ a (-er, -est) niedrig; (cloud, note) tief; (voice) leise; (depressed) niedergeschlagen □ adv niedrig; (fly, sing) tief; (speak) leise; **feel** ~ deprimiert sein □ n (Meteorol) Tief nt; (fig) Tiefstand m

low: ~**brow** a geistig anspruchslos. ~**cut** a (dress) tief ausgeschnitten

lower /'ləʊə(r)/ a & adv see low □ vt niedriger machen; (let down) herunterlassen; (reduce) senken; ~ **oneself** sich herabwürdigen

low: ~'**fat** a fettarm. ~'**grade** a minderwertig. ~'**lands** /-ləndz/ npl Tiefland nt. ~'**tide** n Ebbe f

loyal /'lɔɪəl/ a, -ly adv treu. ~**ty** n Treue f

lozenge /'lɒzɪndʒ/ n Pastille f

Ltd abbr (Limited) GmbH

lubricant /'lu:brɪkənt/ n Schmiermittel nt

lubricat|e /'lu:brɪkeɪt/ vt schmieren. ~**ion** /-'keɪʃn/ n Schmierung f

lucid /'lu:sɪd/ a klar. ~**ity** /-'sɪdətɪ/ n Klarheit f

luck /lʌk/ n Glück nt; **bad** ~ Pech nt; **good** ~! viel Glück! ~**ily** adv glücklicherweise, zum Glück

lucky /'lʌkɪ/ a (-ier, -iest) glücklich; (day, number) Glücks-; **be** ~ Glück haben; (thing:) Glück bringen. ~ '**charm** n Amulett nt

lucrative /'lu:krətɪv/ a einträglich

ludicrous /'lu:dɪkrəs/ a lächerlich

lug /lʌg/ vt (pt/pp lugged) (fam) schleppen

luggage /'lʌgɪdʒ/ n Gepäck nt

luggage: ~**rack** in Gepäckablage f. ~ **trolley** n Kofferkuli m. ~**van** n Gepäckwagen m

lugubrious /lu:'gu:brɪəs/ a traurig

lukewarm /'lu:k-/ a lauwarm

lull /lʌl/ n Pause f □ vt ~ **to sleep** einschläfern

lullaby /'lʌləbaɪ/ n Wiegenlied nt

lumbago /lʌm'beɪgəʊ/ n Hexenschuss m

lumber /'lʌmbə(r)/ n Gerümpel nt; (Amer: timber) Bauholz nt □ vt ~ **s.o. with sth** jdm etw aufhalsen. ~**jack** n (Amer) Holzfäller m

luminous /'lu:mɪnəs/ a leuchtend; **be** ~ leuchten

lump¹ /lʌmp/ n Klumpen m; (of sugar) Stück nt; (swelling) Beule f; (in breast) Knoten m; (tumour) Geschwulst f; **a** ~ **in one's throat** (fam) ein Kloß im Hals □ vt ~ **together** zusammenfassen

lump² /lʌmp/ vt ~ **it** (fam) sich damit abfinden

lump: ~**sugar** n Würfelzucker m. ~ '**sum** n Pauschalsumme f

lumpy /'lʌmpɪ/ a (-ier, -iest) klumpig

lunacy /'lu:nəsɪ/ n Wahnsinn m

lunar /'lu:nə(r)/ a Mond-

lunatic /'lu:nətɪk/ n Wahnsinnige(r) m/f

lunch /lʌntʃ/ n Mittagessen nt □ vi zu Mittag essen

luncheon /'lʌntʃən/ n Mittagessen nt. ~ **meat** n Frühstücksfleisch nt. ~ **voucher** n Essensbon m

lunch: ~**hour** n Mittagspause f. ~**time** n Mittagszeit f

lung /lʌŋ/ n Lungenflügel m; ~**s** pl Lunge f. ~ **cancer** n Lungenkrebs m

lunge /lʌndʒ/ vi sich stürzen (at auf + acc)

lurch¹ /lɜ:tʃ/ n leave in the ~ (fam) im Stich lassen

lurch² vi schleudern; (person:) torkeln

lure /ljʊə(r)/ n Lockung f; (bait) Köder m □ vt locken

lurid /'lʊərɪd/ a grell; (sensational) reißerisch

lurk /lɜ:k/ vi lauern

luscious /'lʌʃəs/ a lecker, köstlich

lush /lʌʃ/ a üppig

lust /lʌst/ n Begierde f □ vi ~ after gieren nach. **~ful** a lüstern

lustre /'lʌstə(r)/ n Glanz m

lusty /'lʌstɪ/ a (-ier, -iest) kräftig

lute /lu:t/ n Laute f

luxuriant /lʌg'ʒʊərɪənt/ a üppig

luxurious /lʌg'ʒʊərɪəs/ a, -ly adv luxuriös

luxury /'lʌkʃərɪ/ n Luxus m □ attrib Luxus-

lying /'laɪɪŋ/ see lie¹, lie²

lymph gland /'lɪmf-/ n Lymph-drüse f

lynch /lɪntʃ/ vt lynchen

lynx /lɪŋks/ n Luchs m

lyric /'lɪrɪk/ a lyrisch. **~al** a lyrisch; (fam: enthusiastic) schwärmerisch. **~ poetry** n Lyrik f. **~s** npl [Lied]text m

M

mac /mæk/ n (fam) Regenmantel m

macabre /mə'kɑ:brə/ a makaber

macaroni /mækə'rəʊnɪ/ n Makkaroni pl

macaroon /mækə'ru:n/ n Makrone f

mace¹ /meɪs/ n Amtsstab m

mace² n (spice) Muskatblüte f

machinations /mækɪ'neɪʃnz/ pl Machenschaften pl

machine /mə'ʃi:n/ n Maschine f □ vt (sew) mit der Maschine nähen; (Techn) maschinell bearbeiten. **~-gun** n Maschinengewehr nt

machinery /mə'ʃi:nərɪ/ n Maschinerie f

machine tool n Werkzeugmaschine f

machinist /mə'ʃi:nɪst/ n Maschinist m; (on sewing machine) Maschinennäherin f

mackerel /'mækrl/ n inv Makrele f

mackintosh /'mækɪntɒʃ/ n Regenmantel m

mad /mæd/ a (madder, maddest) verrückt; (dog) tollwütig; (fam: angry) böse (at auf + acc)

madam /'mædəm/ n gnädige Frau f

madden /'mædn/ vt (make angry) wütend machen

made /meɪd/ see make; ~ to measure maßgeschneidert

Madeira cake /mə'dɪərə-/ n Sandkuchen m

mad|ly /'mædlɪ/ adv (fam) wahnsinnig. **~man** n Irre(r) m. **~ness** n Wahnsinn m

madonna /mə'dɒnə/ n Madonna f

magazine /mægə'zi:n/ n Zeitschrift f; (Mil, Phot) Magazin nt

maggot /'mægət/ n Made f. **~y** a madig

Magi /'meɪdʒaɪ/ npl the ~ die Heiligen Drei Könige

magic /'mædʒɪk/ n Zauber m; (tricks) Zauberkunst f □ a magisch; (word, wand, flute) Zauber-. **~al** a zauberhaft

magician /mə'dʒɪʃn/ n Zauberer m; (entertainer) Zauberkünstler m

magistrate /'mædʒɪstreɪt/ n ≈ Friedensrichter m

magnanim|ity /mægnə'nɪmətɪ/ n Großmut f. **~ous** /-'nænɪməs/ a großmütig

magnesia /mæg'niːʃə/ n Magnesia f

magnet /'mægnɪt/ n Magnet m. **~ic** /-'netik/ a magnetisch. **~ism** n Magnetismus m. **~ize** vt magnetisieren

magnification /mægnɪfɪ'keɪʃn/ n Vergrößerung f

magnificen|ce /mæg'nɪfɪsəns/ n Großartigkeit f. **~t** a, **-ly** adv großartig

magnify /'mægnɪfaɪ/ vt (pt/pp -ied) vergrößern; (exaggerate) übertreiben. **~ing glass** n Vergrößerungsglas nt

magnitude /'mægnɪtjuːd/ n Größe f; (importance) Bedeutung f

magpie /'mægpaɪ/ n Elster f

mahogany /mə'hɒgənɪ/ n Mahagoni nt

maid /meɪd/ n Dienstmädchen nt; (liter: girl) Maid f; **old ~** (pej) alte Jungfer f

maiden /'meɪdn/ n (liter) Maid f □ a (speech, voyage) Jungfern-. **~ name** n Mädchenname m

mail[1] /meɪl/ n Kettenpanzer m

mail[2] n Post f □ vt mit der Post schicken; (send off) abschicken. **~bag** n Postsack m. **~box** n (Amer) Briefkasten m. **~ing list** n Postversandliste f. **~man** n (Amer) Briefträger m. **~-order firm** n Versandhaus nt

maim /meɪm/ vt verstümmeln

main[1] /meɪn/ n (water, gas, electricity) Hauptleitung f

main[2] n Haupt- □ n **in the ~** im Großen und Ganzen

main: **~land** /-lənd/ n Festland nt. **~ly** adv hauptsächlich. **~stay** n (fig) Stütze f. **~ street** n Hauptstraße f

maintain /meɪn'teɪn/ vt aufrechterhalten; (keep in repair) instand halten; (support) unterhalten; (claim) behaupten

maintenance /'meɪntənəns/ n Aufrechterhaltung f; (care) Instandhaltung f; (allowance) Unterhalt m

maisonette /meɪzə'net/ n Wohnung f [auf zwei Etagen]

maize /meɪz/ n Mais m

majestic /mə'dʒestɪk/ a, **-ally** adv majestätisch

majesty /'mædʒəstɪ/ n Majestät f

major /'meɪdʒə(r)/ a größer □ n (Mil) Major m; (Mus) Dur nt □ vi (Amer) **~ in** als Hauptfach studieren

Majorca /mə'jɔːkə/ n Mallorca nt

majority /mə'dʒɒrətɪ/ n Mehrheit f; **in the ~** in der Mehrzahl

major road n Hauptverkehrsstraße f

make /meɪk/ n (brand) Marke f □ v (pt/pp made) □ vt machen; (force) zwingen; (earn) verdienen; halten (speech); treffen (decision); erreichen (destination) □ vi **~ as if to** Miene machen zu. **~ do** vi zurechtkommen (with mit). **~ for** vi zusteuern auf (+ acc). **~ off** vi sich davonmachen (with mit). **~ out** vt (distinguish) ausmachen; (write out) ausstellen; (assert) behaupten. **~ over** vt überschreiben (to auf + acc). **~ up** vt (constitute) bilden; (invent) erfinden; (apply cosmetics to) schminken; **~ up one's mind** sich entschließen □ vi sich versöhnen; **~ up for sth** wieder gutmachen; **~ up for lost time** verlorene Zeit aufholen

make-believe n Phantasie f

maker /'meɪkə(r)/ n Hersteller m

make: **~ shift** a behelfsmäßig □ n Notbehelf m. **~-up** n Make-up nt

making /'meɪkɪŋ/ n **have the ~s of** das Zeug haben zu

maladjusted /mælə'dʒʌstɪd/ a verhaltensgestört

malaise /mə'leɪz/ n (fig) Unbehagen nt

male /meɪl/ a männlich □ n Mann m; (animal) Männchen nt. ~ **nurse** n Krankenpfleger m. ~ **voice 'choir** n Männerchor m

malevolen|ce /mə'levələns/ n Bosheit f. ~t a boshaft

malfunction /mæl'fʌŋkʃn/ n technische Störung f. (Med) Funktionsstörung f □ vi nicht richtig funktionieren

malice /'mælɪs/ n Bosheit f; **bear s.o.** ~ einen Groll gegen jdn hegen

malicious /mə'lɪʃəs/ a, -**ly** adv böswillig

malign /mə'laɪn/ vt verleumden

malignan|cy /mə'lɪgnənsɪ/ n Bösartigkeit f. ~t a bösartig

malinger /mə'lɪŋgə(r)/ vi simulieren, sich krank stellen. ~**er** n Simulant m

malleable /'mælɪəbl/ a formbar

mallet /'mælɪt/ n Holzhammer m

malnu'trition /mæl-/ n Unterernährung f

mal'practice n Berufsvergehen nt

malt /mɔːlt/ n Malz nt

mal'treat /mæl-/ vt misshandeln. ~**ment** n Misshandlung f

mammal /'mæml/ n Säugetier nt

mammoth /'mæməθ/ a riesig □ n Mammut nt

man /mæn/ n (pl men) Mann m; (mankind) der Mensch; (chess) Figur f; (draughts) Stein m □ vt (pt/pp **manned**) bemannen (ship); bedienen (pump); besetzen (counter)

manacle /'mænəkl/ vt fesseln (**to** an + acc); ~ **d** in Handschellen

manage /'mænɪdʒ/ vt leiten; verwalten (estate); (cope with) fertig werden mit; ~ **to do sth** es schaffen, etw zu tun □ vi zurechtkommen; ~ **on** auskommen mit. ~**able** /-əbl/ a (tool) handlich; (person) fügsam. ~**ment** /-mənt/ n **the** ~**ment** die Geschäftsleitung f

manager /'mænɪdʒə(r)/ n Geschäftsführer m; (of bank) Direktor m; (of estate) Verwalter m; (Sport) [Chef]trainer m. ~**ess** n Geschäftsführerin f. ~**ial** /-'dʒɪərɪəl/ a ~**ial staff** Führungskräfte pl

managing /'mænɪdʒɪŋ/ a ~ **director** Generaldirektor m

mandarin /'mændərɪn/ n [**orange**] Mandarine f

mandat|e /'mændeɪt/ n Mandat nt. ~**ory** /-dətrɪ/ a obligatorisch

mane /meɪn/ n Mähne f

manful /'mænfl/ a, -**ly** adv mannhaft

manger /'meɪndʒə(r)/ n Krippe f

mangle1 /'mæŋgl/ n Wringmaschine f; (for smoothing) Mangel f

mangle2 vt (damage) verstümmeln

mango /'mæŋgəʊ/ n (pl -**es**) Mango f

mangy /'meɪndʒɪ/ a (dog) räudig

man: ~**handle** vt grob behandeln (person). ~**hole** n Kanalschacht m. ~**hole cover** n Kanaldeckel m. ~**hood** n Mannesalter nt; (quality) Männlichkeit f. ~**hour** n Arbeitsstunde f. ~**hunt** n Fahndung f

man|ia /'meɪnɪə/ n Manie f. ~**iac** /-ɪæk/ n Wahnsinnige(r) m/f

manicur|e /'mænɪkjʊə(r)/ n Maniküre f □ vt maniküren. ~**ist** n Maniküre f

manifest /'mænɪfest/ a, -**ly** adv offensichtlich □ vt sich ~ **itself** sich manifestieren

manifesto /mænɪ'festəʊ/ n Manifest nt

manifold /'mænɪfəʊld/ a mannigfaltig

manipulat|e /mə'nɪpjʊleɪt/ vt handhaben; (pej) manipulieren. ~**ion** /-'leɪʃn/ n Manipulation f

man'kind n die Menschheit

manly /'mænlɪ/ a männlich

'**man-made** a künstlich. ~ **fibre** n Kunstfaser f

manner /'mænə(r)/ n Weise f; (kind, behaviour) Art f; **in this** ~ auf diese Weise; **[good/bad]** ~s [gute/schlechte] Manieren pl. ~**ism** n Angewohnheit f

mannish /'mænɪʃ/ a männlich

manœuvrable /mə'nu:vrəbl/ a manövrierfähig

manœuvre /mə'nu:və(r)/ n Manöver nt □ vt/i manövrieren

manor /'mænə(r)/ n Gutshof m; (house) Gutshaus nt

man: ~**power** n Arbeitskräfte pl. ~**servant** n (pl **menservants**) Diener m

mansion /'mænʃn/ n Villa f

'**manslaughter** n Totschlag m

mantelpiece /'mæntl-/ n Kaminsims m & nt

manual /'mænjʊəl/ a Hand- □ n Handbuch nt

manufacture /mænjʊ'fæktʃə(r)/ vt herstellen □ n Herstellung f. ~**r** n Hersteller m

manure /mə'njʊə(r)/ n Mist m

manuscript /'mænjʊskrɪpt/ n Manuskript nt

many /'menɪ/ a viele; ~ **a time** oft □ n a **good/great** ~ sehr viele

map /mæp/ n Landkarte f; (of town) Stadtplan m □ vt (pt/pp **mapped**) ~ **out** (fig) ausarbeiten

maple /'meɪpl/ n Ahorn m

mar /mɑ:(r)/ vt (pt/pp **marred**) verderben

marathon /'mærəθən/ n Marathon m

marauding /mə'rɔ:dɪŋ/ a plündernd

marble /'mɑ:bl/ n Marmor m; (for game) Murmel f

March /mɑ:tʃ/ n März m

march n Marsch m □ vi marschieren □ vt marschieren lassen; ~ **s.o. off** jdn abführen

mare /'meə(r)/ n Stute f

margarine /mɑ:dʒə'ri:n/ n Margarine f

margin /'mɑ:dʒɪn/ n Rand m; (leeway) Spielraum m; (Comm)

Spanne f. ~**al** a, -**ly** adv geringfügig

marigold /'mærɪɡəʊld/ n Ringelblume f

marijuana /mærɪ'hwɑ:nə/ n Marihuana nt

marina /mə'ri:nə/ n Jachthafen m

marinade /mærɪ'neɪd/ n Marinade f □ vt marinieren

marine /mə'ri:n/ a Meeres- □ n Marine f; (sailor) Marineinfanterist m

marionette /mærɪə'net/ n Marionette f

marital /'mærɪtl/ a ehelich. ~ **status** n Familienstand m

maritime /'mærɪtaɪm/ a See-

marjoram /'mɑ:dʒərəm/ n Majoran m

mark¹ /mɑ:k/ n (currency) Mark f

mark² n Fleck m; (sign) Zeichen nt; (trace) Spur f; (target) Ziel nt; (Sch) Note f □ vt markieren; (spoil) beschädigen; (characterize) kennzeichnen; (Sch) korrigieren; (Sport) decken; ~ **time** (Mil) auf der Stelle treten; (fig) abwarten; ~ **my words** das [eine] will ich dir sagen. ~ **out** vt markieren

marked /mɑ:kt/ a, -**ly** /-kɪdlɪ/ adv deutlich; (pronounced) ausgeprägt

marker /'mɑ:kə(r)/ n Marke f; (of exam) Korrektor(in) m(f)

market /'mɑ:kɪt/ n Markt m □ vt vertreiben; (launch) auf den Markt bringen. ~**ing** n Marketing nt. ~ **re'search** n Marktforschung f

marking /'mɑ:kɪŋ/ n Markierung f; (on animal) Zeichnung f

marksman /'mɑ:ksmən/ n Scharfschütze m

marmalade /'mɑ:məleɪd/ n Orangenmarmelade f

marmot /'mɑ:mət/ n Murmeltier nt

maroon /mə'ruːn/ a dunkelrot

marooned /mə'ruːnd/ a (fig) von der Außenwelt abgeschnitten

marquee /maː'kiː/ n Festzelt nt; (Amer: awning) Markise f

marquetry /'maːkɪtrɪ/ n Einlegearbeit f

marquis /'maːkwɪs/ n Marquis m

marriage /'mærɪdʒ/ n Ehe f; (wedding) Hochzeit f. **~able** /-əbl/ a heiratsfähig

married /'mærɪd/ see **marry** □ a verheiratet. **~ life** n Eheleben nt

marrow /'mærəʊ/ n (Anat) Mark nt; (vegetable) Kürbis m

marr|y /'mærɪ/ vt/i (pt/pp **married**); (unite) trauen; get **~ied** heiraten

marsh /maːʃ/ n Sumpf m

marshal /'maːʃl/ n Marschall m; (steward) Ordner m □ vt (pt/pp **marshalled**) (Mil) formieren; (fig) ordnen

marshy /'maːʃɪ/ a sumpfig

marsupial /maː'suːpɪəl/ n Beuteltier nt

martial /'maːʃl/ a kriegerisch. **~ 'law** n Kriegsrecht nt

martyr /'maːtə(r)/ n Märtyrer(in) m(f) □ vt zum Märtyrer machen. **~dom** /-dəm/ n Martyrium nt

marvel /'maːvl/ n Wunder nt □ vi (pt/pp **marvelled**) staunen (at über + acc). **~lous** /-vələs/ a, **-ly** adv wunderbar

Marxis|m /'maːksɪzm/ n Marxismus m. **~t** a marxistisch □ n Marxist(in) m(f)

marzipan /'maːzɪpæn/ n Marzipan nt

mascara /mæ'skaːrə/ n Wimperntusche f

mascot /'mæskət/ n Maskottchen nt

masculin|e /'mæskjʊlɪn/ a männlich □ n (Gram) Maskulinum nt. **~ity** /-'lɪnətɪ/ n Männlichkeit f

mash /mæʃ/ n (fam, Culin) Kartoffelpüree nt □ vt stampfen. **~ed potatoes** npl Kartoffelpüree nt

mask /maːsk/ n Maske f □ vt maskieren

masochis|m /'mæsəkɪzm/ n Masochismus m. **~t** /-ɪst/ n Masochist m

mason /'meɪsn/ n Steinmetz m

Mason n Freimaurer m. **~ic** /mə'sɒnɪk/ a freimaurerisch

masonry /'meɪsnrɪ/ n Mauerwerk nt

masquerade /mæskə'reɪd/ n (fig) Maskerade f □ vi **~ as** (pose) sich ausgeben als

mass¹ /mæs/ n (Relig) Messe f

mass² n Masse f □ vi sich sammeln; (Mil) sich massieren

massacre /'mæsəkə(r)/ n Massaker nt □ vt niedermetzeln

massage /'mæsaːʒ/ n Massage f □ vt massieren

masseu|r /mæ'sɜː(r)/ n Masseur m. **~se** /-'sɜːz/ n Masseuse f

massive /'mæsɪv/ a massiv; (huge) riesig

mass: **~ 'media** npl Massenmedien pl. **~pro'duce** vt in Massenproduktion herstellen. **~ pro'duction** n Massenproduktion f

mast /maːst/ n Mast m

master /'maːstə(r)/ n Herr m; (teacher) Lehrer m; (craftsman, artist) Meister m; (of ship) Kapitän m □ vt meistern; beherrschen (language)

master: **~key** n Hauptschlüssel m. **~ly** a meisterhaft. **~mind** n führender Kopf m □ vt der führende Kopf sein von. **~piece** n Meisterwerk nt. **~y** n (of subject) Beherrschung f

masturbat|e /'mæstəbeɪt/ vi masturbieren. **~ion** /-'beɪʃn/ n Masturbation f

mat /mæt/ n Matte f; (on table) Untersatz m

match¹ /mætʃ/ n Wettkampf m; (in ball games) Spiel nt; (Tennis) Match nt; (marriage) Heirat f; **be a good ~** (colours:) gut zusammenpassen; **be no ~ for s.o.** jdm nicht gewachsen sein □ vt (equal) gleichkommen (+ dat); (be like) passen zu; (find sth similar) etwas Passendes finden zu □ vi zusammenpassen

match² n Streichholz nt. **~box** n Streichholzschachtel f

matching /'mætʃɪŋ/ a [zusammen]passend

mate¹ /meɪt/ n Kumpel m; (assistant) Gehilfe m; (Naut) Maat m; (Zool) Männchen nt; (female) Weibchen nt □ vi sich paaren □ vt paaren

mate² n (Chess) Matt nt

material /mə'tɪərɪəl/ n Material nt; (fabric) Stoff m; **raw ~s** Rohstoffe pl □ a materiell

material|ism /mə'tɪərɪəlɪzm/ n Materialismus m. **~istic** /-'lɪstɪk/ a materialistisch. **~ize** /-laɪz/ vi sich verwirklichen

maternal /mə'tɜːnl/ a mütterlich

maternity /mə'tɜːnətɪ/ n Mutterschaft f. **~ clothes** npl Umstandskleidung f. **~ ward** n Entbindungsstation f

matey /'meɪtɪ/ a (fam) freundlich

mathematic|al /mæθə'mætɪkl/ a, **-ly** adv mathematisch. **~ian** /-mə'tɪʃn/ n Mathematiker(in) m(f)

mathematics /mæθə'mætɪks/ n Mathematik f

maths /mæθs/ n (fam) Mathe f

matinée /'mætɪneɪ/ n (Theat) Nachmittagsvorstellung f

matriculate /mə'trɪkjuleɪt/ vi sich immatrikulieren. **~ion** /-'leɪʃn/ n Immatrikulation f

matrimon|ial /mætrɪ'məʊnɪəl/ a Ehe-. **~y** /'mætrɪmənɪ/ n Ehe f

matrix /'meɪtrɪks/ n (pl **matrices** /-siːz/) n (Techn: mould) Matrize f

matron /'meɪtrən/ n (of hospital) Oberin f; (of school) Hausmutter f. **~ly** a matronenhaft

matt /mæt/ a matt

matted /'mætɪd/ a verfilzt

matter /'mætə(r)/ n (affair) Sache f; (pus) Eiter m; (Phys: substance) Materie f; (money ~s) Geldangelegenheiten pl; **as a ~ of fact** eigentlich; **what is the ~?** was ist los? □ vi wichtig sein; **~ to s.o.** jdm etwas ausmachen; **it doesn't ~** es macht nichts. **~-of-fact** a sachlich

matting /'mætɪŋ/ n Matten pl

mattress /'mætrɪs/ n Matratze f

matur|e /mə'tjʊə(r)/ a reif; (Comm) fällig □ vi reifen; (person:) reifer werden; (Comm) fällig werden □ vt reifen lassen. **~ity** n Reife f; (Comm) Fälligkeit f

maul /mɔːl/ vt übel zurichten

Maundy /'mɔːndɪ/ n **~ Thursday** Gründonnerstag m

mauve /məʊv/ a lila

mawkish /'mɔːkɪʃ/ a rührselig

maxim /'mæksɪm/ n Maxime f

maximum /'mæksɪməm/ a maximal □ n (pl **-ima**) Maximum nt. **~ speed** n Höchstgeschwindigkeit f

may /meɪ/ v aux (nur Präsens) (be allowed to) dürfen; (be possible) können; **may I come in?** darf ich reinkommen? **may he succeed** möge es ihm gelingen; **I may as well stay** am besten bleibe ich hier; **it may be true** es könnte wahr sein

May n Mai m

maybe /'meɪbɪ/ adv vielleicht

'May Day n der Erste Mai

mayonnaise /meɪə'neɪz/ n Mayonnaise f

mayor /'meə(r)/ n Bürgermeister m. **~ess** n Bürgermeisterin f; (wife of mayor) Frau Bürgermeister f

maze /meɪz/ n Irrgarten m; (fig) Labyrinth nt

me /miː/ *pron (acc)* mich; *(dat)* mir; **he knows ∼** er kennt mich; **give ∼ the money** gib mir das Geld; **it's ∼** *(fam)* ich bin es

meadow /ˈmedəʊ/ *n* Wiese *f*

meagre /ˈmiːɡə(r)/ *a* dürftig

meal¹ /miːl/ *n* Mahlzeit *f*; *(food)* Essen *nt*

meal² *n (grain)* Schrot *m*

mealy-mouthed /miːlɪˈmaʊðd/ *a* heuchlerisch

mean¹ /miːn/ *a* (-er, -est) geizig; *(unkind)* gemein; *(poor)* schäbig

mean² *a* mittlere(r,s) □ *n (average)* Durchschnitt *m*; **the golden ∼** die goldene Mitte

mean³ *vt (pt/pp meant)* heißen; *(signify)* bedeuten; *(intend)* beabsichtigen; **I ∼ it** das ist mein Ernst; **∼ well** es gut meinen; **be meant for** *(present:)* bestimmt sein für; *(remark:)* gerichtet sein an *(+ acc)*

meander /mɪˈændə(r)/ *vi* sich schlängeln; *(person:)* schlendern

meaning /ˈmiːnɪŋ/ *n* Bedeutung *f*. **∼ful** *a* bedeutungsvoll. **∼less** *a* bedeutungslos

means /miːnz/ *n* Möglichkeit *f*, Mittel *nt*; **∼ of transport** Verkehrsmittel *nt*; **by ∼ of** durch; **by all ∼!** aber natürlich!; **by no ∼** keineswegs □ *npl (resources)* [Geld]mittel *pl*. **∼ test** *n* Bedürftigkeitsnachweis *m*

meant /ment/ *see* mean³

'meantime *n* **in the ∼** in der Zwischenzeit □ *adv* inzwischen

'meanwhile *adv* inzwischen

measles /ˈmiːzlz/ *n* Masern *pl*

measly /ˈmiːzlɪ/ *a (fam)* mickerig

measurable /ˈmeʒərəbl/ *a* messbar

measure /ˈmeʒə(r)/ *n* Maß *nt*; *(action)* Maßnahme *f* □ *vt/i* messen; **∼ up to** *(fig)* herankommen an *(+ acc)*. **∼d** *a* gemessen. **∼ment** /-mənt/ *n* Maß *nt*

meat /miːt/ *n* Fleisch *nt*. **∼ ball** *n* *(Culin)* Klops *m*. **∼ loaf** *n* falscher Hase *m*

mechan|ic /mɪˈkænɪk/ *n* Mechaniker *m*. **∼ical** *a*, **-ly** *adv* mechanisch. **∼ical engineering** Maschinenbau *m*. **∼ics** *n* Mechanik *f* □ *n pl* Mechanismus *m*

mechan|ism /ˈmekənɪzm/ *n* Mechanismus *m*. **∼ize** *vt* mechanisieren

medal /ˈmedl/ *n* Orden *m*; *(Sport)* Medaille *f*

medallion /mɪˈdælɪən/ *n* Medaillon *nt*

medallist /ˈmedəlɪst/ *n* Medaillengewinner(in) *m(f)*

meddle /ˈmedl/ *vi* sich einmischen (**in** in + *acc*); *(tinker)* herumhantieren (**with** an + *acc*)

media /ˈmiːdɪə/ *see* medium □ *n pl* **the ∼** die Medien □ *n*

median /ˈmiːdɪən/ *a* **∼ strip** *(Amer)* Mittelstreifen *m*

mediat|e /ˈmiːdɪeɪt/ *vi* vermitteln. **∼or** *n* Vermittler(in) *m(f)*

medical /ˈmedɪkl/ *a* medizinisch; *(treatment)* ärztlich □ *n* ärztliche Untersuchung *f*. **∼ insurance** *n* Krankenversicherung *f*. **∼ student** *n* Medizinstudent *m*

medicat|ed /ˈmedɪkeɪtɪd/ *a* medizinisch. **∼ion** /-ˈkeɪʃn/ *n (drugs)* Medikamente *pl*

medicinal /mɪˈdɪsɪnl/ *a* medizinisch; *(plant)* heilkräftig

medicine /ˈmedsən/ *n* Medizin *f*; *(preparation)* Medikament *nt*

medieval /medɪˈiːvl/ *a* mittelalterlich

mediocr|e /miːdɪˈəʊkə(r)/ *a* mittelmäßig. **∼ity** /-ˈɒkrəti/ *n* Mittelmäßigkeit *f*

meditat|e /ˈmedɪteɪt/ *vi* nachdenken (**on** über + *acc*); *(Relig)* meditieren. **∼ion** /-ˈteɪʃn/ *n* Meditation *f*

Mediterranean /medɪtəˈreɪnɪən/ *n* Mittelmeer *nt* □ *a* Mittelmeer-

medium /ˈmiːdɪəm/ *a* mittlere(r,s); *(steak)* medium; **of ∼ size** von mittlerer Größe □ *n (pl* **media)** Medium *nt*; *(means)* Mittel *nt* □ *(pl* **-s)** *(person)* Medium *nt*

medium /~sized a mittelgroß. ~ **wave** n Mittelwelle f

medley /'medlɪ/ n Gemisch nt; (Mus) Potpourri nt

meek /miːk/ a (-er, -est), -ly adv sanftmütig; (unprotesting) widerspruchslos

meet /miːt/ v (pt/pp **met**) □ vt treffen; (by chance) begegnen (+ dat); (at station) abholen; (make the acquaintance of) kennen lernen; stoßen auf (+ acc) (problem); bezahlen (bill); erfüllen (requirements) □ vi sich treffen; (for the first time) sich kennen lernen; ~ **with** stoßen auf (+ acc) (problem); sich treffen mit (person) □ n Jagdtreffen nt

meeting /'miːtɪŋ/ n Treffen nt; (by chance) Begegnung f; (discussion) Besprechung f; (of committee) Sitzung f; (large) Versammlung f

megalomania /megələ'meɪnɪə/ n Größenwahnsinn m

megaphone /'megəfəʊn/ n Megaphon nt

melancholy /'melənkəlɪ/ a melancholisch □ n Melancholie f

mellow /'meləʊ/ a(-er, -est) (fruit) ausgereift; (sound, person) sanft □ vi reifer werden

melodic /mɪ'lɒdɪk/ a melodisch

melodious /mɪ'ləʊdɪəs/ a melodiös

melodrama /'melə-/ n Melodrama nt. ~**tic** /-drə'mætɪk/ a, -ally adv melodramatisch

melody /'melədɪ/ n Melodie f

melon /'melən/ n Melone f

melt /melt/ vt/i schmelzen. ~ **down** vt einschmelzen. ~**ing-pot** n (fig) Schmelztiegel m

member /'membə(r)/ n Mitglied nt; (of family) Angehörige(r) m/f; **M~ of Parliament** Abgeordnete(r) m/f. ~**ship** n Mitgliedschaft f; (members) Mitgliederzahl f

membrane /'membreɪn/ n Membran f

memento /mɪ'mentəʊ/ n Andenken nt

memo /'meməʊ/ n Mitteilung f

memoirs /'memwɑːz/ n pl Memoiren pl

memorable /'memərəbl/ a denkwürdig

memorandum /memə'rændəm/ n Mitteilung f

memorial /mɪ'mɔːrɪəl/ n Denkmal nt. ~ **service** n Gedenkfeier f

memorize /'meməraɪz/ vt sich (dat) einprägen

memory /'memərɪ/ n Gedächtnis nt; (thing remembered) Erinnerung f; (of computer) Speicher m; **from** ~ auswendig; **in** ~ **of** zur Erinnerung an (+ acc)

men /men/ see **man**

menac|e /'menɪs/ n Drohung f; (nuisance) Plage f □ vt bedrohen. ~**ing** a, -**ly** adv drohend

mend /mend/ vt reparieren; (patch) flicken; ausbessern (clothes) □ n **on the** ~ auf dem Weg der Besserung

menfolk n pl Männer pl

menial /'miːnɪəl/ a niedrig

meningitis /menɪn'dʒaɪtɪs/ n Hirnhautentzündung f, Meningitis f

menopause /'menə-/ n Wechseljahre pl

menstruat|e /'menstrʊeɪt/ vi menstruieren. ~**ion** /-'eɪʃn/ n Menstruation f

mental /'mentl/ a, -**ly** adv geistig; (fam: mad) verrückt. ~ **arithmetic** n Kopfrechnen nt. ~ **illness** n Geisteskrankheit f

mentality /men'tælətɪ/ n Mentalität f

mention /'menʃn/ n Erwähnung f □ vt erwähnen; **don't** ~ **it** keine Ursache; bitte

menu /'menjuː/ n Speisekarte f

mercantile /'mɜːkəntaɪl/ a Handels-

mercenary /'mɜːsɪnərɪ/ a geldgierig □ n Söldner m

merchandise /ˈmɜːtʃəndaɪz/ n Ware f

merchant /ˈmɜːtʃənt/ n Kaufmann m; (dealer) Händler m. ~navy n Handelsmarine f

merciful /ˈmɜːsɪfl/ a barmherzig. ~fully adv (fam) glücklicherweise. ~less a, -ly adv erbarmungslos

mercury /ˈmɜːkjʊrɪ/ n Quecksilber nt

mercy /ˈmɜːsɪ/ n Barmherzigkeit f, Gnade f; be at s.o.'s ~ jdm ausgeliefert sein

mere /mɪə(r)/ a, -ly adv bloß

merest /ˈmɪərɪst/ a kleinste(r,s)

merge /mɜːdʒ/ vi zusammenlaufen; (Comm) fusionieren □ vt (Comm) zusammenlegen

merger /ˈmɜːdʒə(r)/ n Fusion f

meridian /məˈrɪdɪən/ n Meridian m

meringue /məˈræŋ/ n Baiser nt

merit /ˈmerɪt/ n Verdienst nt; (advantage) Vorzug m; (worth) Wert m □ vt verdienen

mermaid /ˈmɜːmeɪd/ n Meerjungfrau f

merri|ly /ˈmerɪlɪ/ adv fröhlich. ~ment /-mənt/ n Fröhlichkeit f; (laughter) Gelächter nt

merry /ˈmerɪ/ a (-ier, -iest) fröhlich; ~ Christmas! fröhliche Weihnachten!

merry: ~-go-round n Karussell nt. ~making n Feiern nt

mesh /meʃ/ n Masche f; (size) Maschenweite f; (fig: network) Netz nt

mesmerize /ˈmezməraɪz/ vt hypnotisieren. ~d a (fig) [wie] gebannt

mess /mes/ n Durcheinander nt; (trouble) Schwierigkeiten pl; (something spilt) Bescherung f (fam); (Mil) Messe f; make a ~ of (botch) verpfuschen □ vt ~ up in Unordnung bringen; (botch) verpfuschen □ vi ~ about herumalbern; (tinker) herumspielen (with mit)

message /ˈmesɪdʒ/ n Nachricht f; give s.o. a ~ jdm etwas ausrichten

messenger /ˈmesɪndʒə(r)/ n Bote m

Messiah /mɪˈsaɪə/ n Messias m

Messrs /ˈmesəz/ n pl see Mr; (on letter) ~ Smith Firma Smith

messy /ˈmesɪ/ a (-ier, -iest) schmutzig; (untidy) unordentlich

met /met/ see meet

metabolism /mɪˈtæbəlɪzm/ n Stoffwechsel m

metal /ˈmetl/ n Metall nt □ a Metall-. ~lic /mɪˈtælɪk/ a metallisch. ~lurgy /mɪˈtælədʒɪ/ n Metallurgie f

metamorphosis /metəˈmɔːfəsɪs/ n (pl -phoses /-siːz/) Metamorphose f

metaphor /ˈmetəfə(r)/ n Metapher f. ~ical /-ˈforɪkl/ a, -ly adv metaphorisch

meteor /ˈmiːtɪə(r)/ n Meteor m. ~ic /-ˈɒrɪk/ a kometenhaft

meteorological /miːtɪərə-ˈlɒdʒɪkl/ a Wetter-

meteorolog|ist /miːtɪəˈrɒlədʒɪst/ n Meteorologe m/ -gin f. ~y n Meteorologie f

meter¹ /ˈmiːtə(r)/ n Zähler m

meter² n (Amer) = metre

method /ˈmeθəd/ n Methode f; (Culin) Zubereitung f

methodical /mɪˈθɒdɪkl/ a, -ly adv systematisch, methodisch

Methodist /ˈmeθədɪst/ n Methodist(in) m(f)

meths /meθs/ n (fam) Brennspiritus m

methylated /ˈmeθɪleɪtɪd/ a ~ spirit[s] Brennspiritus m

meticulous /mɪˈtɪkjʊləs/ a, -ly adv sehr genau

metre /ˈmiːtə(r)/ n Meter m & n; (rhythm) Versmaß nt

metric /ˈmetrɪk/ a metrisch

metropolis /mɪˈtrɒpəlɪs/ n Metropole f

metropolitan /metrə'pɒlɪtən/ a haupstädtisch; (*international*) welstädtisch

mettle /'metl/ n Mut m

mew /mju:/ n Miau nt □ vi miauen

Mexican /'meksɪkən/ a mexikanisch □ n Mexikaner(in) m(f). **'Mexico** n Mexiko nt

miaow /mɪ'au/ n Miau nt □ vi miauen

mice /maɪs/ see **mouse**

microbe /'maɪkrəub/ n Mikrobe f

micro /'maɪkrəu/: **~chip** n Mikrochip nt. **~computer** n Mikrocomputer m. **~film** n Mikrofilm m. **~phone** n Mikrofon nt. **~processor** n Mikroprozessor m. **~scope** /-skəup/ n Mikroskop nt. **~scopic** /-'skɒpɪk/ a mikroskopisch. **~wave** n Mikrowelle f. **~wave [oven]** n Mikrowellenherd m

mid /mɪd/ a ~ May Mitte Mai; **in ~ air** in der Luft

midday /mɪd'deɪ/ n Mittag m

middle /'mɪdl/ a mittlere(r,s); the M~ Ages das Mittelalter; the **class[es]** der Mittelstand; the M~ East der Nahe Osten □ n Mitte f; in the ~ of the night mitten in der Nacht

middle: **~-aged** a mittleren Alters. **~-class** a bürgerlich. **~man** n (Comm) Zwischenhändler m

middling /'mɪdlɪŋ/ a mittelmäßig

midge /mɪdʒ/ n [kleine] Mücke f

midget /'mɪdʒɪt/ n Liliputaner(in) m(f)

Midlands /'mɪdləndz/ npl the ~ Mittelengland n

midnight n Mitternacht f

midriff /'mɪdrɪf/ n (fam) Taille f

midst /mɪdst/ n in the ~ of mitten in (+ dat); in our ~ unter uns

mid /mɪd/: **~summer** n Hochsommer m; (solstice) Sommersonnenwende f. **~way** adv auf halbem Wege. **~wife** n Hebamme f. **~wifery** /-wɪfrɪ/ n Geburtshilfe f. **~winter** n Mitte f des Winters

might[1] /maɪt/ v aux I ~ vielleicht; **it ~ be true** es könnte wahr sein; **I ~ as well stay** am besten bleibe ich hier; **he asked if he ~ go** er fragte, ob er gehen dürfte; **you ~ have drowned** du hättest ertrinken können

might[2] n Macht f

mighty /'maɪtɪ/ a (-ier, -iest) mächtig

migraine /'mi:greɪn/ n Migräne f

migrant /'maɪgrənt/ a Wander- □ n (bird) Zugvogel m

migrat|e /maɪ'greɪt/ vi abwandern; (birds:) ziehen. **~ion** /-'greɪʃn/ n Wanderung f; (of birds) Zug m

mike /maɪk/ n (fam) Mikrofon nt

mild /maɪld/ a (-er, -est) mild

mildew /'mɪldju:/ n Schimmel m; (Bot) Mehltau m

mild|ly /'maɪldlɪ/ adv leicht; **to put it ~ly** gelinde gesagt. **~ness** n Milde f

mile /maɪl/ n Meile f (= 1,6 km); **~s too big** (fam) viel zu groß

mile|age /-ɪdʒ/ n Meilenzahl f; (of car) Meilenstand m. **~stone** n Meilenstein m

militant /'mɪlɪtənt/ a militant

military /'mɪlɪtrɪ/ a militärisch. **~ service** n Wehrdienst m

militate /'mɪlɪteɪt/ vi ~ against sprechen gegen

militia /mɪ'lɪʃə/ n Miliz f

milk /mɪlk/ n Milch f □ vt melken

milk: **~man** n Milchmann m. **~shake** n Milchmixgetränk nt. **~tooth** n Milchzahn m

milky /'mɪlkɪ/ a (-ier, -iest) milchig. M~ Way n (Astr) Milchstraße f

mill /mɪl/ n Mühle f; (factory) Fabrik f □ vt/i mahlen; (Techn) fräsen. ~ **about**, ~ **around** vi umherlaufen

millenium /'mɪˈlenɪəm/ n Jahrtausend nt

miller /'mɪlə(r)/ n Müller m

millet /'mɪlɪt/ n Hirse f

milli|gram /'mɪlɪ-/ n Milligramm nt. ~**metre** n Millimeter m & nt

milliner /'mɪlɪnə(r)/ n Modistin f; (man) Hutmacher m. ~**y** n Damenhüte pl

million /'mɪljən/ n Million f; **a** ~ **pounds** eine Million Pfund. ~**aire** /-'neə(r)/ n Millionär m(f)

millstone n Mühlstein m

mime /maɪm/ n Pantomime f □ vt pantomimisch darstellen

mimic /'mɪmɪk/ n Imitator m □ vt (pt/pp **mimicked**) nachahmen. ~**ry** n Nachahmung f

mimosa /mɪˈməʊzə/ n Mimose f

mince /mɪns/ n Hackfleisch nt □ vt (Culin) durchdrehen; **not** ~ **words** kein Blatt vor den Mund nehmen

mince: ~**meat** n Masse f aus Korinthen, Zitronat usw; **make** ~ **meat of** (fig) vernichtend schlagen. ~**pie** n mit 'mincemeat' gefülltes Pastetchen nt

mincer /'mɪnsə(r)/ n Fleischwolf m

mind /maɪnd/ n Geist m; (sanity) Verstand m; **to my** ~ meiner Meinung nach; **give s.o. a piece of one's** ~ jdm gehörig die Meinung sagen; **make up one's** ~ sich entschließen; **be out of one's** ~ nicht bei Verstand sein; **have sth in** ~ an etw (acc) denken; **have a good** ~ **to** große Lust haben, zu; **I have changed my** ~ ich habe es mir anders überlegt □ vt aufpassen auf (+ acc); **I don't** ~ **the noise** der Lärm stört mich nicht; ~ **the step!** Achtung Stufe! □ vi (care) sich kümmern (**about** um); **I don't** ~ mir macht es

nichts aus; **never** ~! macht nichts! **do you** ~ **if?** haben Sie etwas dagegen, wenn? ~ **out** vi aufpassen

mind|ful a ~**ful of** eingedenk (+ gen). ~**less** a geistlos

mine[1] /maɪn/ poss pron meine(r), meins; **a friend of** ~ ein Freund von mir; **that is** ~ das gehört mir

mine[2] n Bergwerk nt; (explosive) Mine f □ vt abbauen; (Mil) verminen. ~ **detector** n Minensuchgerät nt. ~**field** n Minenfeld nt

miner /'maɪnə(r)/ n Bergarbeiter m

mineral /'mɪnərl/ n Mineral nt. ~**ogy** /-'rælədʒɪ/ n Mineralogie f. ~ **water** n Mineralwasser nt

minesweeper /'maɪn-/ n Minenräumboot nt

mingle /'mɪŋgl/ vi ~ **with** sich mischen unter (+ acc)

miniature /'mɪnɪtʃə(r)/ n Kleinod n Miniatur f

mini|bus /'mɪnɪ-/ n Kleinbus m. ~**cab** n Taxi nt

minim /'mɪnɪm/ n (Mus) halbe Note f

minim|al /'mɪnɪml/ a minimal. ~**ize** vt auf ein Minimum reduzieren. ~**um** n (pl -**ima**) Minimum nt □ a Mindest-

mining /'maɪnɪŋ/ n Bergbau m

miniskirt /'mɪnɪ-/ n Minirock m

minister /'mɪnɪstə(r)/ n Minister m; (Relig) Pastor m. ~**erial** /-'stɪərɪəl/ a ministeriell

ministry /'mɪnɪstrɪ/ n (Pol) Ministerium nt; **the** ~ (Relig) das geistliche Amt

mink /mɪŋk/ n Nerz m

minor /'maɪnə(r)/ a kleiner; (less important) unbedeutend □ n Minderjährige(r) m/f; (Mus) Moll nt

minority /maɪˈnɒrɪtɪ/ n Minderheit f; (age) Minderjährigkeit f

minor road n Nebenstraße f

mint[1] /mɪnt/ n Münzstätte f □ a (stamp) postfrisch; **in** ~ **condition** wie neu □ vt prägen

mint² n (herb) Minze f; (sweet) Pfefferminzbonbon m & nt

minuet /'mɪnjʊ'et/ n Menuett nt

minus /'maɪnəs/ prep minus, weniger; (fam: without) ohne □ n ~ [sign] Minuszeichen nt

minute¹ /'mɪnɪt/ n Minute f; in a ~ (shortly) gleich; ~s pl (of meeting) Protokoll nt

minute² /maɪ'nju:t/ a winzig; (precise) genau

mirac|le /'mɪrəkl/ n Wunder nt. ~ulous /-'rækjʊləs/ a wunderbar

mirage /-'mɪrɑ:ʒ/ n Fata Morgana f

mire /'maɪə(r)/ n Morast m

mirror /'mɪrə(r)/ n Spiegel m □ vt widerspiegeln

mirth /mɜ:θ/ n Heiterkeit f

misad'venture /mɪs-/ n Missgeschick nt

misanthropist /mɪ'zænθrəpɪst/ n Menschenfeind m

misappre'hension /mɪs-/ n Missverständnis nt; **be under a ~** sich irren

misbe'hav|e vi sich schlecht benehmen. ~iour n schlechtes Benehmen nt

mis'calcu|late vt falsch berechnen □ vi sich verrechnen. ~'lation n Fehlkalkulation f

'miscarriage n Fehlgeburt f; ~ of justice Justizirrtum m. **mis'carry** vi eine Fehlgeburt haben

miscellaneous /mɪsə'leɪnɪəs/ a vermischt

mischief /'mɪstʃɪf/ n Unfug m; (harm) Schaden m

mischievous /'mɪstʃɪvəs/ a, -ly adv schelmisch; (malicious) boshaft

miscon'ception n falsche Vorstellung f

mis'conduct n unkorrektes Verhalten nt; (adultery) Ehebruch m

miscon'strue vt falsch deuten

mis'deed n Missetat f

misde'meanour n Missetat f

miser /'maɪzə(r)/ n Geizhals m

miserable /'mɪzrəbl/ a, -bly adv unglücklich; (wretched) elend

miserly /'maɪzəlɪ/ adv geizig

misery /'mɪzərɪ/ n Elend nt; (fam: person) Miesepeter m

mis'fire vi fehlzünden; (go wrong) fehlschlagen

'misfit n Außenseiter(in) m(f)

mis'fortune n Unglück nt

mis'givings npl Bedenken pl

mis'guided a töricht

mishap /'mɪshæp/ n Missgeschick nt

misin'form vt falsch unterrichten

misin'terpret vt missdeuten

mis'judge vt falsch beurteilen; (estimate wrongly) falsch einschätzen

mis'lay vt (pt/pp -laid) verlegen

mis'lead vt (pt/pp -led) irreführen. ~ing a irreführend

mis'manage vt schlecht verwalten. ~ment n Misswirtschaft f

misnomer /mɪs'nəʊmə(r)/ n Fehlbezeichnung f

'misprint n Druckfehler m

mis'quote vt falsch zitieren

misrepre'sent vt falsch darstellen

miss /mɪs/ n Fehltreffer m □ vt verpassen; (fail to hit or find) verfehlen; (fail to attend) versäumen; (fail to notice) übersehen; (feel the loss of) vermissen □ vi (fail to hit) nicht treffen. ~ **out** vt auslassen

Miss n (pl -es) Fräulein nt

misshapen /mɪs'ʃeɪpən/ a missgestaltet

missile /'mɪsaɪl/ n [Wurf]geschoss nt; (Mil) Rakete f

missing /'mɪsɪŋ/ a fehlend (lost) verschwunden; (Mil) vermisst; **be ~** fehlen

mission /'mɪʃn/ n Auftrag m; (Mil) Einsatz m; (Relig) Mission f

missionary /'mɪʃənrɪ/ n Missionar(in) m(f)

mis'spell vt (pt/pp **-spelt** or **-spelled**) falsch schreiben

mist /mɪst/ n Dunst m; (fog) Nebel m; (on window) Beschlag m □ vi ~ **up** beschlagen

mistake /mɪ'steɪk/ n Fehler m; **by** ~ aus Versehen □ vt (pt **mistook**, pp **mistaken**) missverstehen; ~ **for** verwechseln mit

mistaken /mɪ'steɪkən/ a falsch; **be** ~ sich irren; ~ **identity** Verwechslung f. ~**ly** adv irrtümlicherweise

mistletoe /'mɪsltəʊ/ n Mistel f

mistress /'mɪstrɪs/ n Herrin f; (teacher) Lehrerin f; (lover) Geliebte f

mis'trust n Misstrauen vt misstrauen (+ dat)

misty /'mɪstɪ/ a (-ier, -iest) dunstig; (foggy) neblig; (fig) unklar

misunder'stand vt (pt/pp -stood) missverstehen. ~**ing** n Missverständnis nt

misuse¹ /mɪs'juːz/ vt missbrauchen

misuse² /mɪs'juːs/ n Missbrauch m

mite /maɪt/ n (Zool) Milbe f; little ~ (child) kleines Ding nt

mitigat|e /'mɪtɪgeɪt/ vt mildern. ~**ing** a mildernd

mitten /'mɪtn/ n Fausthandschuh m

mix /mɪks/ n Mischung f □ vt mischen □ vi sich mischen; ~ **with** (associate with) verkehren mit. ~ **up** vt mischen; (muddle) durcheinander bringen; (mistake for) verwechseln (**with** mit)

mixed /mɪkst/ a gemischt; **be** ~ **up** durcheinander sein

mixer /'mɪksə(r)/ n Mischmaschine f; (Culin) Küchenmaschine f

mixture /'mɪkstʃə(r)/ n Mischung f; (medicine) Mixtur f; (Culin) Teig m

'mix-up n Durcheinander nt; (confusion) Verwirrung f; (mistake) Verwechslung f

moan /məʊn/ n Stöhnen nt □ vi stöhnen; (complain) jammern

moat /məʊt/ n Burggraben m

mob /mɒb/ n Horde f; (rabble) Pöbel m; (fam: gang) Bande f □ vt (pt/pp **mobbed**) herfallen über (+ acc); belagern (celebrity)

mobile /'məʊbaɪl/ a beweglich □ n Mobile nt; (telephone) Handy nt. ~ **'home** n Wohnwagen m. ~ **'phone** n Mobiltelefon nt, Handy nt

mobility /mə'bɪlɪtɪ/ n Beweglichkeit f

mobi|lization /məʊbɪlaɪ'zeɪʃn/ n Mobilisierung f. ~**lize** /'məʊbɪlaɪz/ vt mobilisieren

mocha /'mɒkə/ n Mokka m

mock /mɒk/ a Schein- □ vt verspotten. ~**ery** n Spott m

'mock-up n Modell nt

modal /'məʊdl/ a ~ **auxiliary** Modalverb nt

mode /məʊd/ n [Art und] Weise f; (fashion) Mode f

model /'mɒdl/ n Modell nt; (example) Vorbild nt; [**fashion**] ~ Mannequin nt □ a Modell-; (exemplary) Muster- □ v (pt/pp **modelled**) □ vt formen, modellieren; vorführen (clothes) □ vi Mannequin sein; (for artist) Modell stehen

moderate¹ /'mɒdəreɪt/ vt mäßigen □ vi sich mäßigen

moderate² /'mɒdərət/ a mäßig; (opinion) gemäßigt □ n (Pol) Gemäßigte(r) m/f. ~**ly** adv mäßig; (fairly) einigermaßen

moderation /mɒdə'reɪʃn/ n Mäßigung f; **in** ~ mit Maß[en]

modern /'mɒdn/ a modern. ~ **'languages** npl neuere Sprachen pl

modest /'mɒdɪst/ a bescheiden; (decorous) schamhaft. ~**y** n Bescheidenheit f

modicum /'mɒdɪkəm/ n a ~ of ein bisschen

modif|ication /mɒdɪfɪ'keɪʃn/ n Abänderung f. ~y /'mɒdɪfaɪ/ vt (pt/pp -fied) abändern

modulate /'mɒdjʊleɪt/ vt/i modulieren

moist /mɔɪst/ a (-er, -est) feucht

moisten /'mɔɪsn/ vt befeuchten

moistur|e /'mɔɪstʃə(r)/ n Feuchtigkeit f. ~izer /-aɪzə(r)/ n Feuchtigkeitscreme f

molar /'məʊlə(r)/ n Backenzahn m

molasses /mə'læsɪz/ n (Amer) Sirup m

mole¹ /məʊl/ n Leberfleck m

mole² n (Zool) Maulwurf m

mole³ n (breakwater) Mole f

molecule /'mɒlɪkjuːl/ n Molekül nt

'molehill n Maulwurfshaufen m

molest /mə'lest/ vt belästigen

mollify /'mɒlɪfaɪ/ vt (pt/pp -ied) besänftigen

mollusc /'mɒləsk/ n Weichtier nt

mollycoddle /'mɒlɪkɒdl/ vt verzärteln

molten /'məʊltən/ a geschmolzen

mom /mɒm/ n (Amer fam) Mutti f

moment /'məʊmənt/ n Moment m, Augenblick m; **at the** ~ im Augenblick, augenblicklich. ~ary a vorübergehend

momentous /mə'mentəs/ a bedeutsam

momentum /mə'mentəm/ n Schwung m

monarch /'mɒnək/ n Monarch(in) m(f). ~y n Monarchie f

monast|ery /'mɒnəstrɪ/ n Kloster nt. ~ic /mə'næstɪk/ a Kloster-

Monday /'mʌndeɪ/ n Montag m

money /'mʌnɪ/ n Geld nt

money: ~-**box** n Sparbüchse f. ~-**lender** n Geldverleiher m. ~ **order** n Zahlungsanweisung f

mongrel /'mʌŋgrəl/ n Promenadenmischung f

monitor /'mɒnɪtə(r)/ n (Techn) Monitor m □ vt überwachen (progress); abhören (broadcast)

monk /mʌŋk/ n Mönch m

monkey /'mʌŋkɪ/ n Affe m. ~**nut** n Erdnuss f. ~-**wrench** n (Techn) Engländer m

mono /'mɒnəʊ/ n Mono nt

monocle /'mɒnəkl/ n Monokel nt

monogram /'mɒnəgræm/ n Monogramm nt

monologue /'mɒnəlɒg/ n Monolog m

monopol|ize /mə'nɒpəlaɪz/ vt monopolisieren. ~y n Monopol nt

monosyll|abic /mɒnəsɪ'læbɪk/ a einsilbig. ~**able** /'mɒnəsɪləbl/ n einsilbiges Wort nt

monotone /'mɒnətəʊn/ n **in a** ~ mit monotoner Stimme

monoton|ous /mə'nɒtənəs/ a, -**ly** adv eintönig, monoton; (tedious) langweilig. ~y n Eintönigkeit f, Monotonie f

monsoon /mɒn'suːn/ n Monsun m

monster /'mɒnstə(r)/ n Ungeheuer nt; (cruel person) Unmensch m

monstrosity /mɒn'strɒsətɪ/ n Monstrosität f

monstrous /'mɒnstrəs/ a ungeheuer; (outrageous) ungeheuerlich

montage /mɒn'tɑːʒ/ n Montage f

month /mʌnθ/ n Monat m. ~**ly** a & adv monatlich □ n (periodical) Monatszeitschrift f

monument /'mɒnjʊmənt/ n Denkmal nt. ~**al** /-'mentl/ a (fig) monumental

moo /muː/ n Muh nt □ vi (pt/pp mooed) muhen

mooch /muːtʃ/ vi ~ **about** (fam) herumschleichen

mood /muːd/ n Laune f; **be in a good/bad** ~ gute/schlechte Laune haben

moody /'muːdɪ/ a (-ier, -iest) launisch

moon /muːn/ n Mond m; **over the ~** (fam) überglücklich

moon: ~light n Mondschein m. **~lighting** n (fam) ≈ Schwarzarbeit f. **~lit** a mondhell

moor[1] /mʊə(r)/ n Moor nt

moor[2] vt (Naut) festmachen □ vi anlegen. **~ings** npl (chains) Verankerung f; (place) Anlegestelle f

moose /muːs/ n Elch m

moot /muːt/ a **it's a ~ point** darüber lässt sich streiten □ vt aufwerfen (question)

mop /mɒp/ n Mopp m; **~ of hair** Wuschelkopf m vt (pt/pp **mopped**) wischen. **~ up** vt aufwischen

mope /məʊp/ vi Trübsal blasen

moped /'məʊped/ n Moped nt

moral /'mɒrl/ a, **-ly** adv moralisch, sittlich; (virtuous) tugendhaft □ n Moral f; **~s** pl Moral f

morale /mə'rɑːl/ n Moral f

morality /mə'rælɪt/ n Sittlichkeit f

moralize /'mɒrəlaɪz/ vi moralisieren

morbid /'mɔːbɪd/ a krankhaft; (gloomy) trübe

more /mɔː(r)/ a, adv & n mehr; (in addition) noch; **a few ~** noch ein paar; **any ~** noch etwas; **once ~** noch einmal; **~ or less** mehr oder weniger; **some ~ tea?** noch etwas Tee? **~ interesting** interessanter; **~ [and] ~ quickly** [immer] schneller; **no ~, thank you**, nichts mehr, danke; **no ~ bread** kein Brot mehr; **no ~ apples** keine Äpfel mehr

moreover /mɔː'rəʊvə(r)/ adv außerdem

morgue /mɔːg/ n Leichenschauhaus nt

moribund /'mɒrɪbʌnd/ a sterbend

morning /'mɔːnɪŋ/ n Morgen m; **in the ~** morgens, am Morgen; (tomorrow) morgen früh

Morocco /mə'rɒkəʊ/ n Marokko nt

moron /'mɔːrɒn/ n (fam) Idiot m

morose /mə'rəʊs/ a, **-ly** adv mürrisch

morphine /'mɔːfiːn/ n Morphium nt

Morse /mɔːs/ n **~ [code]** Morsealphabet nt

morsel /'mɔːsl/ n (food) Happen m

mortal /'mɔːtl/ a sterblich; (fatal) tödlich □ n Sterbliche(r) m/f. **~ity** /mɔː'tælətɪ/ n Sterblichkeit f. **~ly** adv tödlich

mortar /'mɔːtə(r)/ n Mörtel m

mortgage /'mɔːgɪdʒ/ n Hypothek f □ vt hypothekarisch belasten

mortify /'mɔːtɪfaɪ/ vt (pt/pp **-ied**) demütigen

mortuary /'mɔːtjʊərɪ/ n Leichenhalle f; (public) Leichenschauhaus nt; (Amer: undertaker's) Bestattungsinstitut nt

mosaic /məʊ'zeɪɪk/ n Mosaik nt

Moscow /'mɒskəʊ/ n Moskau nt

Moselle /məʊ'zel/ n Mosel f; (wine) Moselwein m

mosque /mɒsk/ n Moschee f

mosquito /mɒs'kiːtəʊ/ n (pl **-es**) [Stech]mücke f, Schnake f; (tropical) Moskito m

moss /mɒs/ n Moos nt. **~y** a moosig

most /məʊst/ a der/die/das meiste; (majority) die meisten; **for the ~ part** zum größten Teil □ adv am meisten; (very) höchst; **the ~ interesting day** der interessanteste Tag; **~ unlikely** höchst unwahrscheinlich □ n das meiste; **~ of them** die meisten [von ihnen]; **at [the] ~** höchstens; **~ of the time** die meiste Zeit. **~ly** adv meist

MOT n ≈ TÜV m

motel /məʊ'tel/ n Motel nt

moth /mɒθ/ n Nachtfalter m; **[clothes-]** ~ Motte f
moth: ~ball n Mottenkugel f. ~eaten a mottenzerfressen
mother /ˈmʌðə(r)/ n Mutter f; **M~'s Day** Muttertag m □ vt bemuttern
mother: ~hood n Mutterschaft f. ~-in-law n (pl ~s-in-law) Schwiegermutter f. ~land n Mutterland nt. ~ly a mütterlich. ~-of-pearl n Perlmutter f. ~-to-be n werdende Mutter f. ~ tongue n Muttersprache f
mothproof /mɒθ-/ a mottenfest
motif /məʊˈtiːf/ n Motiv nt
motion /ˈməʊʃn/ n Bewegung f; (proposal) Antrag m □ vt/i ~ [to] s.o. jdm ein Zeichen geben (to zu). ~less a, ~ly adv bewegungslos
motivat|e /ˈməʊtɪveɪt/ vt motivieren. ~ion /-ˈveɪʃn/ n Motivation f
motive /ˈməʊtɪv/ n Motiv nt
motley /ˈmɒtlɪ/ a bunt
motor /ˈməʊtə(r)/ n Motor m; (car) Auto nt □ a Motor-; (Anat) motorisch □ vi [mit dem Auto] fahren
Motorail /ˈməʊtəreɪl/ n Autozug m
motor: ~ bike n (fam) Motorrad nt. ~ boat n Motorboot nt. ~cade /-keɪd/ n (Amer) Autokolonne f. ~ car n Auto nt, Wagen m. ~cycle n Motorrad nt. ~cyclist n Motorradfahrer m. ~ing n Autofahren nt. ~ist n Autofahrer(in) m(f). ~ize vt motorisieren. ~ vehicle n Kraftfahrzeug nt. ~way n Autobahn f
mottled /ˈmɒtld/ a gesprenkelt
motto /ˈmɒtəʊ/ n (pl -es) Motto nt
mould¹ /məʊld/ n (fungus) Schimmel m
mould² n Form f □ vt formen (into zu). ~ing n (Archit) Fries m
mouldy /ˈməʊldɪ/ a schimmelig; (fam: worthless) schäbig

moult /məʊlt/ vi (bird:) sich mausern; (animal:) sich haaren
mound /maʊnd/ n Hügel m; (of stones) Haufen m
mount¹ /maʊnt/ n Berg m
mount² n (animal) Reittier nt; (of jewel) Fassung f; (of photo, picture) Passepartout nt □ vt (get on) steigen auf (+ acc); (on pedestal) montieren auf (+ acc); besteigen (horse); fassen (jewel); aufziehen (photo, picture) □ vi aufsteigen; (tension:) steigen. ~ up vi sich häufen; (add up) sich anhäufen
mountain /ˈmaʊntɪn/ n Berg m
mountaineer /maʊntɪˈnɪə(r)/ n Bergsteiger(in) m(f). ~ing n Bergsteigen nt
mountainous /ˈmaʊntɪnəs/ a bergig, gebirgig
mourn /mɔːn/ vt betrauern □ vi trauern (for um). ~er n Trauernde(r) m/f. ~ful a, ~ly adv trauervoll. ~ing n Trauer f
mouse /maʊs/ n (pl mice) Maus f. ~trap n Mausefalle f
mousse /muːs/ n Schaum m; (Culin) Mousse f
moustache /məˈstɑːʃ/ n Schnurrbart m
mousy /ˈmaʊsɪ/ a graubraun; (person) farblos
mouth¹ /maʊð/ vt ~ sth etw lautlos mit den Lippen sagen
mouth² /maʊθ/ n Mund m; (of animal) Maul nt; (of river) Mündung f
mouth: ~ful n Mundvoll m; (bite) Bissen m. ~organ n Mundharmonika f. ~piece n Mundstück nt; (fig: person) Sprachrohr nt. ~wash n Mundwasser nt
movable /ˈmuːvəbl/ a beweglich
move /muːv/ n Bewegung f; (fig) Schritt m; (moving house) Umzug m; (in board-game) Zug m; **on the** ~ unterwegs; **get a** ~ **on** (fam) sich beeilen □ vt bewegen; (emotionally) rühren; (move along) rücken; (in board-game) ziehen;

(take away) wegnehmen; wegfahren *(car)*; *(rearrange)* umstellen; *(transfer)* versetzen *(person)*; verlegen *(office)*; *(propose)* beantragen; **~ house** umziehen □ *vi* sich bewegen; *(move house)* umziehen; **don't ~!** stillhalten! *(stop)* stillstehen! **~ along** *vt/i* weiterrücken. **~ away** *vt/i* wegrücken; *(move house)* wegziehen. **~ forward** *vt/i* vorrücken; *(vehicle)* vorwärts fahren. **~ in** *vi* einziehen. **~ off** *vi* *(vehicle:)* wegfahren. **~ out** *vi* ausziehen. **~ over** *vt/i* [zur Seite] rücken. **~ up** *vi* aufrücken

movement /'mu:vmənt/ *n* Bewegung *f*; *(Mus)* Satz *m*; *(of clock)* Uhrwerk *nt*

movie /'mu:vɪ/ *n (Amer)* Film *m*; **go to the ~s** ins Kino gehen

moving /'mu:vɪŋ/ *a* beweglich; *(touching)* rührend

mow /məʊ/ *vt (pt mowed, pp mown or mowed)* mähen. **~ down** *vt (destroy)* niedermähen

mower /'məʊə(r)/ *n* Rasenmäher *m*

MP *abbr see* **Member of Parliament**

Mr /'mɪstə(r)/ *n (pl Messrs)* Herr *m*

Mrs /'mɪsɪz/ *n* Frau *f*

Ms /mɪz/ *n* Frau *f*

much /mʌtʃ/ *a, adv & n* viel; **as ~ as** so viel wie; **very ~ loved/interested** sehr geliebt/interessiert

muck /mʌk/ *n* Mist *m*; *(fam: filth)* Dreck *m*. **~ about** *vi* herumalbern; *(tinker)* herumspielen *(with* mit*)*. **~ in** *vi (fam)* mitmachen. **~ out** *vt* ausmisten. **~ up** *vt (fam)* vermasseln; *(make dirty)* schmutzig machen

mucky /'mʌkɪ/ *a (-ier, -iest)* dreckig

mucus /'mju:kəs/ *n* Schleim *m*

mud /mʌd/ *n* Schlamm *m*

muddle /'mʌdl/ *n* Durcheinander *nt*; *(confusion)* Verwirrung *f* □ *vt* **~ [up]** durcheinander bringen

muddy /'mʌdɪ/ *a (-ier, -iest)* schlammig; *(shoes)* schmutzig

'mudguard *n* Kotflügel *m*; *(on bicycle)* Schutzblech *nt*

muesli /'mu:zlɪ/ *n* Müsli *nt*

muff /mʌf/ *n* Muff *m*

muffle /'mʌfl/ *vt* dämpfen *(sound)*; **~ [up]** *(for warmth)* einhüllen *(in* in + *acc)*

muffler /'mʌflə(r)/ *n* Schal *m*; *(Amer, Auto)* Auspufftopf *m*

mufti /'mʌftɪ/ *n* **in ~** in Zivil

mug[1] /mʌg/ *n* Becher *m*; *(for beer)* Bierkrug *m*; *(fam: face)* Visage *f*; *(fam; simpleton)* Trottel *m*

mug[2] *vt (pt/pp mugged)* überfallen. **~ger** *n* Straßenräuber *m*. **~ging** *n* Straßenraub *m*

muggy /'mʌgɪ/ *a (-ier, -iest)* schwül

mule[1] /mju:l/ *n* Maultier *nt*

mule[2] *n (slipper)* Pantoffel *m*

mull /mʌl/ *vt* **~ over** nachdenken über (+ *acc*)

mulled /mʌld/ *a* **~ wine** Glühwein *m*

multi /'mʌltɪ/: **~coloured** *a* vielfarbig, bunt. **~lingual** /-'lɪŋgwəl/ *a* mehrsprachig. **~national** *a* multinational

multiple /'mʌltɪpl/ *a* vielfach; *(with* pl) mehrere □ *n* Vielfache[s] *nt*

multiplication /mʌltɪplɪ'keɪʃn/ *n* Multiplikation *f*

multiply /'mʌltɪplaɪ/ *v (pt/pp -ied)* □ *vt* multiplizieren *(by* mit*)* □ *vi* sich vermehren

multistorey *a* **~ car park** Parkhaus *nt*

mum[1] /mʌm/ *a* **keep ~** *(fam)* den Mund halten

mum[2] *n (fam)* Mutti *f*

mumble /'mʌmbl/ *vt/i* murmeln

mummy[1] /'mʌmɪ/ *n (fam)* Mutti *f*

mummy[2] *n (Archaeol)* Mumie *f*

mumps /mʌmps/ n Mumps m

munch /mʌntʃ/ vt/i mampfen

mundane /mʌn'deɪn/ a banal; (worldly) weltlich

municipal /mju:'nɪsɪpl/ a städtisch

munitions /mju:'nɪʃnz/ npl Kriegsmaterial nt

mural /'mjʊərəl/ n Wandgemälde nt

murder /'mɜ:də(r)/ n Mord m □ vt ermorden; (fam: ruin) verhunzen. **~er** n Mörder m. **~ess** n Mörderin f. **~ous** /-rəs/ a mörderisch

murky /'mɜ:kɪ/ a (-ier, -iest) düster

murmur /'mɜ:mə(r)/ n Murmeln nt □ vt/i murmeln

muscle /'mʌsl/ n Muskel m

muscular /'mʌskjʊlə(r)/ a Muskel-; (strong) muskulös

muse /mju:z/ vi nachsinnen (on über + acc)

museum /mju:'zɪəm/ n Museum nt

mush /mʌʃ/ n Brei m

mushroom /'mʌʃrʊm/ n [essbarer] Pilz m, esp Champignon m □ vi (fig) wie Pilze aus dem Boden schießen

mushy /'mʌʃɪ/ a breiig

music /'mju:zɪk/ n Musik f; (written) Noten pl; **set to** ~ vertonen

musical /'mju:zɪkl/ a musikalisch □ n Musical nt. **~ box** n Spieldose f. **~ instrument** n Musikinstrument nt

'music-hall n Varieté nt

musician /mju:'zɪʃn/ n Musiker(in) m(f)

'music-stand n Notenständer m

Muslim /'mʊzlɪm/ a mohammedanisch □ n Mohammedaner(in) m(f)

muslin /'mʌzlɪn/ n Musselin m

mussel /'mʌsl/ n [Mies]muschel f

must /mʌst/ v aux (nur Präsens) müssen; (with negative) dürfen □ n **a** ~ (fam) ein Muss nt

mustard /'mʌstəd/ n Senf m

muster /'mʌstə(r)/ vt versammeln; aufbringen ⟨strength⟩ □ vi sich versammeln

musty /'mʌstɪ/ a (-ier, -iest) muffig

mutation /mju:'teɪʃn/ n Veränderung f; (Biol) Mutation f

mute /mju:t/ a stumm

muted /'mju:tɪd/ a gedämpft

mutilat|e /'mju:tɪleɪt/ vt verstümmeln. **~ion** /-'leɪʃn/ n Verstümmelung f

mutin|ous /'mju:tɪnəs/ a meuterisch. **~y** n Meuterei f □ vi (pt/pp -ied) meutern

mutter /'mʌtə(r)/ n Murmeln nt □ vt/i murmeln

mutton /'mʌtn/ n Hammelfleisch nt

mutual /'mju:tjʊəl/ a gegenseitig; (fam: common) gemeinsam. **~ly** adv gegenseitig

muzzle /'mʌzl/ n (of animal) Schnauze f; (of firearm) Mündung f; (for dog) Maulkorb m □ vt einen Maulkorb anlegen (+ dat)

my /maɪ/ a mein

myopic /maɪ'ɒpɪk/ a kurzsichtig

myself /maɪ'self/ pron selbst; (refl) mich; **by** ~ allein; **I thought to** ~ ich habe mir gedacht

mysterious /mɪ'stɪərɪəs/ a, -**ly** adv geheimnisvoll; (puzzling) mysteriös, rätselhaft

mystery /'mɪstərɪ/ n Geheimnis nt; (puzzle) Rätsel nt; ~ **[story]** Krimi m

mysti|c[al] /'mɪstɪk[l]/ a mystisch. **~cism** /-sɪzm/ n Mystik f

mystification /mɪstɪfɪ'keɪʃn/ n Verwunderung f

mystified /'mɪstɪfaɪd/ a **be** ~ vor einem Rätsel stehen

mystique /mɪ'sti:k/ n geheimnisvoller Zauber m

myth /mɪθ/ n Mythos m; (fam: untruth) Märchen nt. **~ical** a mythisch; (fig) erfunden

mythology /mɪˈθɒlədʒɪ/ n Mythologie f

N

nab /næb/ vt (pt/pp **nabbed**) (fam) erwischen

nag¹ /næg/ n (horse) Gaul m

nag² vt/i (pp/pp **nagged**) herumnörgeln (s.o. an jdm). **~ging** a (pain) nagend □ n Nörgelei f

nail /neɪl/ n (Anat, Techn) Nagel m; **on the ~** (fam) sofort □ vt nageln (**to** an + acc). **~ down** vt festnageln; (close) zunageln

nail: **~brush** n Nagelbürste f. **~file** n Nagelfeile f. **~ polish** n Nagellack m. **~ scissors** npl Nagelschere f. **~ varnish** n Nagellack m

naïve /naɪˈiːv/ a, **-ly** adv naiv. **~ty** /-əti/ n Naivität f

naked /ˈneɪkɪd/ a nackt; (flame) offen; **with the ~ eye** mit bloßem Auge. **~ness** n Nacktheit f

name /neɪm/ n Name m; (reputation) Ruf m; **by ~** dem Namen nach; **by the ~ of** namens; **call s.o. ~s** (fam) jdn beschimpfen □ vt nennen; (give a name to) einen Namen geben (+ dat); (announce publicly) den Namen bekannt geben von. **~less** a namenlos. **~ly** adv nämlich

name: **~plate** n Namensschild nt. **~sake** n Namensvetter m/Namensschwester f

nanny /ˈnænɪ/ n Kindermädchen nt. **~goat** n Ziege f

nap /næp/ n Nickerchen nt; **have a ~** ein Nickerchen machen □ vi **catch s.o. ~ping** jdn überrumpeln

nape /neɪp/ n **~ [of the neck]** Nacken m

napkin /ˈnæpkɪn/ n Serviette f; (for baby) Windel f

nappy /ˈnæpɪ/ n Windel f

narcotic /naːˈkɒtɪk/ a betäubend □ n Narkotikum nt; (drug) Rauschgift nt

narrat|e /nəˈreɪt/ vt erzählen. **~ion** /-eɪʃn/ n Erzählung f

narrative /ˈnærətɪv/ a erzählend □ n Erzählung f

narrator /nəˈreɪtə(r)/ n Erzähler(in) m(f)

narrow /ˈnærəʊ/ a (-er, -est) schmal; (restricted) eng; (margin, majority) knapp; (fig) beschränkt; **have a ~ escape**, adv **~ly escape** mit knapper Not davonkommen □ vi sich verengen. **~-minded** a engstirnig

nasal /ˈneɪzl/ a nasal; (Med & Anat) Nasen-

nastily /ˈnaːstɪlɪ/ adv boshaft

nasturtium /nəˈstɜːʃəm/ n Kapuzinerkresse f

nasty /ˈnaːstɪ/ a (-ier, -iest) übel; (unpleasant) unangenehm; (unkind) boshaft; (serious) schlimm; **turn ~** gemein werden

nation /ˈneɪʃn/ n Nation f; (people) Volk nt

national /ˈnæʃənl/ a national; (newspaper) überregional; (campaign) landesweit □ n Staatsbürger(in) m(f)

national: **~ 'anthem** n Nationalhymne f. **N~ 'Health Service** n staatlicher Gesundheitsdienst m. **N~ In'surance** n Sozialversicherung f

nationalism /ˈnæʃənəlɪzm/ n Nationalismus m

nationality /næʃəˈnælətɪ/ n Staatsangehörigkeit f

national|ization /næʃənəlaɪˈzeɪʃn/ n Verstaatlichung f. **~ize** /ˈnæʃənəlaɪz/ vt verstaatlichen. **'~ly** /ˈnæʃənəlɪ/ adv landesweit

'nation-wide a landesweit

native /ˈneɪtɪv/ a einheimisch; (innate) angeboren □ n Eingeborene(r) m/f; (local inhabitant) Einheimische(r) m/f; **a ~ of Vienna** ein gebürtiger Wiener

native: ~ **land** n Heimatland nt.
~ **'language** n Muttersprache f
Nativity /nəˈtɪvɪtɪ/ n the ~
Christi Geburt f. ~ **play** n Krippenspiel nt
natter /ˈnætə(r)/ n have a ~
(fam) einen Schwatz halten □ vi
(fam) schwatzen
natural /ˈnætʃrəl/ a, -ly adv natürlich; ~[-coloured] naturfarben
natural: ~ **'gas** n Erdgas nt. ~
'history n Naturkunde f
naturalist /ˈnætʃrəlɪst/ n Naturforscher m
natural|ization /nætʃrəlaɪ-
'zeɪʃn/ n Einbürgerung f. ~**ize**
/ˈnætʃrəlaɪz/ vt einbürgern
nature /ˈneɪtʃə(r)/ n Natur f;
(kind) Art f; by ~ von Natur aus.
~ **reserve** n Naturschutzgebiet
nt
naturism /ˈneɪtʃərɪzm/ n Freikörperkultur f
naught /nɔːt/ n = nought
naughty /ˈnɔːtɪ/ a (-ier, -iest),
-ily adv unartig; (slightly indecent) gewagt
nausea /ˈnɔːzɪə/ n Übelkeit f
nause|ate /ˈnɔːzɪeɪt/ vt anekeln.
~**ating** a ekelhaft. ~ous /-ɪəs/ a
I feel ~ous mir ist übel
nautical /ˈnɔːtɪkl/ a nautisch. ~
mile n Seemeile f
naval /ˈneɪvl/ a Marine-
nave /neɪv/ n Kirchenschiff nt
navel /ˈneɪvl/ n Nabel m
navigable /ˈnævɪgəbl/ a schiffbar
navig|ate /ˈnævɪgeɪt/ vi navigieren □ vt befahren (river). ~**ion**
/-ˈgeɪʃn/ n Navigation f. ~**or** n
Navigator m
navvy /ˈnævɪ/ n Straßenarbeiter
m
navy /ˈneɪvɪ/ n [Kriegs]marine f
□ a ~ [**blue**] marineblau
near /nɪə(r)/ a (-er, -est) nah[e];
the ~**est bank** die nächste Bank
□ adv nahe; ~**by** nicht weit weg;
~ **at hand** in der Nähe; **draw** ~

sich nähern □ prep nahe an (+
dat/acc); in der Nähe von; ~ **to
tears** den Tränen nahe; **go** ~ **[to]**
sth nahe an etw (acc) herangehen
□ vt sich nähern (+ dat)
near: ~**by** a nahe gelegen, nahe
liegend. ~**ly** adv fast, beinahe;
not ~**ly** bei weitem nicht. ~**ness**
n Nähe f. ~ **side** n Beifahrerseite
f. ~**sighted** a (Amer) kurzsichtig
neat /niːt/ a (-er, -est), -ly adv ordrett; (tidy) ordentlich; (clever)
geschickt; (undiluted) pur.
~**ness** n Ordentlichkeit f
necessarily /ˈnesəsərɪlɪ/ adv
notwendigerweise; **not** ~ nicht
unbedingt
necessary /ˈnesəsərɪ/ a nötig,
notwendig
necessit|ate /nɪˈsesɪteɪt/ vt
notwendig machen. ~**y** n
Notwendigkeit f; **she works
from** ~**y** sie arbeitet, weil sie es
nötig hat
neck /nek/ n Hals m; ~ **and** ~
Kopf an Kopf
necklace /ˈneklɪs/ n Halskette f
neck: ~**line** n Halsausschnitt m.
~**tie** n Schlips m
nectar /ˈnektə(r)/ n Nektar m
née /neɪ/ a ~ **Brett** geborene
Brett
need /niːd/ n Bedürfnis nt; (misfortune) Not f; **be in** ~ Not leiden;
be in ~ **of** brauchen; **in case of**
~ notfalls; **if** ~ **be** wenn nötig;
there is a ~ **for** es besteht ein
Bedarf an (+ dat); **there is no** ~
for that das ist nicht nötig; **there
is no** ~ **for you to go** du brauchst
nicht zu gehen □ vt brauchen;
you ~ **not go** du brauchst nicht
zu gehen; ~ **I come?** muss ich
kommen? **I** ~ **to know** ich muss
es wissen; **it** ~**s to be done** es
muss gemacht werden
needle /ˈniːdl/ n Nadel f □ vt (annoy) ärgern

needless /ˈni:dlɪs/ *a*, **-ly** *adv* unnötig; **~ to say** selbstverständlich, natürlich
ˈneedlework *n* Nadelarbeit *f*
needy /ˈni:dɪ/ *a* **(-ier, -iest)** bedürftig
negation /nɪˈgeɪʃn/ *n* Verneinung *f*
negative /ˈnegətɪv/ *a* negativ □ *n* Verneinung *f*; ⟨*photo*⟩ Negativ *nt*
neglect /nɪˈglekt/ *n* Vernachlässigung *f*; **state of ~** verwahrloster Zustand *m* □ *vt* vernachlässigen; ⟨*omit*⟩ versäumen **(to** zu). **~ed** *a* verwahrlost. **~ful** *a* nachlässig; **be ~ful of** vernachlässigen
negligen|ce /ˈneglɪdʒəns/ *n* Nachlässigkeit *f*; ⟨*Jur*⟩ Fahrlässigkeit *f*. **~t** *a*, **-ly** *adv* nachlässig; ⟨*Jur*⟩ fahrlässig
negligible /ˈneglɪdʒəbl/ *a* unbedeutend
negotiable /nɪˈgəʊʃəbl/ *a* ⟨*road*⟩ befahrbar; ⟨*Comm*⟩ unverbindlich; **not ~** nicht übertragbar
negotiat|e /nɪˈgəʊʃɪeɪt/ *vt* aushandeln; ⟨*Auto*⟩ nehmen ⟨*bend*⟩ □ *vi* verhandeln. **~ion** /-ˈeɪʃn/ *n* Verhandlung *f*. **~or** *n* Unterhändler(in) *m(f)*
Negro /ˈni:grəʊ/ *a* Neger- □ *n* (*pl* **-es)** Neger *m*
neigh /neɪ/ *vi* wiehern
neighbour /ˈneɪbə(r)/ *n* Nachbar(in) *m(f)*. **~hood** *n* Nachbarschaft *f*; **in the ~hood of** in der Nähe von; ⟨*fig*⟩ um … herum. **~ing** *a* Nachbar-. **~ly** *a* [gut]nachbarlich
neither /ˈnaɪðə(r)/ *a & pron* keine(r, s) [von beiden] □ *adv* **~… nor** weder … noch □ *conj* auch nicht
neon /ˈni:ɒn/ *n* Neon *nt*. **~ light** *n* Neonlicht *nt*
nephew /ˈnevju:/ *n* Neffe *m*
nepotism /ˈnepətɪzm/ *n* Vetternwirtschaft *f*
nerve /nɜ:v/ *n* Nerv *m*; ⟨*fam: courage*⟩ **Mut** *m*; ⟨*fam: impudence*⟩ Frechheit *f*; **lose one's ~** den Mut verlieren. **~-racking** *a* nervenaufreibend
nervous /ˈnɜ:vəs/ *a*, **-ly** *adv* ⟨*afraid*⟩ ängstlich; ⟨*highly strung*⟩ nervös; ⟨*Anat, Med*⟩ Nerven-; **be ~** Angst haben. **~ ˈbreakdown** *n* Nervenzusammenbruch *m*. **~ness** Ängstlichkeit *f*; ⟨*Med*⟩ Nervosität *f*
nervy /ˈnɜ:vɪ/ *a* **(-ier, -iest)** nervös; ⟨*Amer: impudent*⟩ frech
nest /nest/ *n* Nest *nt* □ *vi* nisten. **~-egg** *n* Notgroschen *m*
nestle /ˈnesl/ *vi* sich schmiegen **(against** an + *acc*)
net[1] /net/ *n* Netz *nt*; ⟨*curtain*⟩ Store *m* □ *vt* (*pt/pp* **netted)** ⟨*catch*⟩ [mit dem Netz] fangen
net[2] *a* netto; ⟨*salary, weight*⟩ Netto- □ *vt* (*pt/pp* **netted)** netto einnehmen; ⟨*yield*⟩ einbringen
ˈnetball *n* ≈ Korbball *m*
Netherlands /ˈneðələndz/ *npl* **the ~** die Niederlande *pl*
netting /ˈnetɪŋ/ *n* **[wire] ~** Maschendraht *m*
nettle /ˈnetl/ *n* Nessel *f*
ˈnetwork *n* Netz *nt*
neuralgia /njʊəˈrældʒə/ *n* Neuralgie *f*
neurolog|ist /njʊəˈrɒlədʒɪst/ *n* Neurologe *m*/ -gin *f*. **~y** *n* Neurologie *f*
neur|osis /njʊəˈrəʊsɪs/ *n* (*pl* **-oses** /-si:z/) Neurose *f*. **~otic** /-ˈrɒtɪk/ *a* neurotisch
neuter /ˈnju:tə(r)/ *a* ⟨*Gram*⟩ sächlich □ *n* ⟨*Gram*⟩ Neutrum *nt* □ *vt* kastrieren; ⟨*spay*⟩ sterilisieren
neutral /ˈnju:trl/ *a* neutral □ *n* **in ~** ⟨*Auto*⟩ im Leerlauf. **~ity** /-ˈtrælətɪ/ *n* Neutralität *f*. **~ize** *vt* neutralisieren
never /ˈnevə(r)/ *adv* nie, niemals; ⟨*fam: not*⟩ nicht; **~ mind** macht nichts; **well I ~!** ja so was! **~-ending** *a* endlos
nevertheless /nevəðəˈles/ *adv* dennoch, trotzdem
new /nju:/ *a* **(-er, -est)** neu

new: ~**born** a neugeboren.
~**comer** n Neuankömmling m.
~**fangled** /-ˈfæŋɡld/ a (pej) neumodisch. ~**laid** a frisch gelegt

newly adv frisch. ~**weds** npl Jungverheiratete pl

new: ~ **'moon** n Neumond m.
~**ness** n Neuheit f

news /njuːz/ n Nachricht f;
(Radio, TV) Nachrichten pl;
piece of ~ Neuigkeit f

news: ~**agent** n Zeitungshändler m. ~ **bulletin** n Nachrichtensendung f. ~**caster** n Nachrichtensprecher(in) m(f). ~**flash** n Kurzmeldung f. ~**letter** n Mitteilungsblatt nt. ~**paper** n Zeitung f; (material) Zeitungspapier nt. ~**reader** n Nachrichtensprecher(in) m(f)

newt /njuːt/ n Molch m

New: ~ **Year's Day** n Neujahr nt.
~ **Year's Eve** n Silvester m. ~
Zealand /ˈziːlənd/ n Neuseeland nt

next /nekst/ a & n nächste(r, s);
who's ~? wer kommt als Nächster dran? **the** ~ **best** das nächstbeste; ~ **door** nebenan;
my ~ **of kin** mein nächster Verwandter; ~ **to nothing** fast gar nichts; **the week after** ~ übernächste Woche □ adv als Nächstes; ~ **to** neben

NHS abbr see National Health Service

nib /nɪb/ n Feder f

nibble /ˈnɪbl/ vt/i knabbern (at an + dat)

nice /naɪs/ a (-r, -st) nett; (day, weather) schön; (food) gut; (distinction) fein. ~**ly** adv nett; (well) gut. ~**ties** /ˈnaɪsətɪz/ npl Feinheiten pl

niche /niːʃ/ n Nische f; (fig) Platz m

nick /nɪk/ n Kerbe f; (fam: prison) Knast m; (fam: police station) Revier nt; **in the** ~ **of time** gerade noch rechtzeitig; **in good** ~ (fam) in gutem Zustand □ vt

einkerben; (steal) klauen; (fam: arrest) schnappen

nickel /ˈnɪkl/ n Nickel nt; (Amer) Fünfcentstück nt

'nickname n Spitzname m

nicotine /ˈnɪkətiːn/ n Nikotin nt

niece /niːs/ n Nichte f

Nigeria /naɪˈdʒɪərɪə/ n Nigeria nt. ~**n** a nigerianisch □ n Nigerianer(in) m(f)

niggardly /ˈnɪɡədlɪ/ a knauserig

niggling /ˈnɪɡlɪŋ/ a gering; (petty) kleinlich; (pain) quälend

night /naɪt/ n Nacht f; (evening) Abend m; **at** ~ nachts; **Monday** ~ Montag Nacht/Abend

night: ~**cap** n Schlafmütze f; (drink) Schlaftrunk m. ~**club** n Nachtklub m. ~**dress** n Nachthemd nt. ~**fall** n **at** ~**fall** bei Einbruch der Dunkelheit. ~**gown** n, (fam) ~**ie** /ˈnaɪtɪ/ n Nachthemd nt

nightingale /ˈnaɪtɪŋɡeɪl/ n Nachtigall f

night: ~**life** n Nachtleben nt.
~**ly** a nächtlich □ adv jede Nacht.
~**mare** n Alptraum m. ~**shade** n (Bot) **deadly** ~**shade** Tollkirsche f. ~**time** n **at** ~**time** bei Nacht.
~'**watchman** n Nachtwächter m

nil /nɪl/ n null

nimble /ˈnɪmbl/ a (-r, -st), -**bly** adv flink

nine /naɪn/ a neun □ n Neun f.
~'**teen** a neunzehn. ~'**teenth** a neunzehnte(r, s)

ninetieth /ˈnaɪntɪθ/ a neunzigste(r, s)

ninety /ˈnaɪntɪ/ a neunzig

ninth /naɪnθ/ a neunte(r, s)

nip /nɪp/ n Kniff m; (bite) Biss m □ vt kneifen; (bite) beißen; ~ **in the bud** (fig) im Keim ersticken □ vi (fam: run) laufen

nipple /ˈnɪpl/ n Brustwarze f; (Amer: on bottle) Sauger m

nippy /ˈnɪpɪ/ a (-ier, -iest) (cold) frisch; (quick) flink nitrate /'naɪtreɪt/ n Nitrat nt

nitrogen /'naɪtrədʒən/ n Stickstoff m

nitwit /'nɪtwɪt/ n (fam) Dummkopf m

no /nəʊ/ adv nein □ n (pl noes) Nein nt □ a keine(r); (pl) keine; in no time [sehr] schnell; no parking/smoking Parken/Rauchen verboten; no one = nobody

nobility /nəʊ'bɪlɪtɪ/ n Adel m

noble /'nəʊbl/ a (-r, -st) edel; (aristocratic) adlig. ~man n Adlige(r) m

nobody /'nəʊbədɪ/ pron niemand, keiner; he knows ~ er kennt niemanden od keinen □ n a ~ ein Niemand m

nocturnal /nɒk'tɜːnl/ a nächtlich; (animal, bird) Nacht-

nod /nɒd/ n Nicken nt □ v (pt/pp nodded) □ vi nicken □ vt ~ one's head mit dem Kopf nicken. ~ off vi einnicken

nodule /'nɒdjuːl/ n Knötchen nt

noise /nɔɪz/ n Geräusch nt; (loud) Lärm m. ~less a, ~ly adv geräuschlos

noisy /'nɔɪzɪ/ a (-ier, -iest), -ily adv laut; (eater) geräuschvoll

nomad /'nəʊmæd/ n Nomade m. ~ic /-'mædɪk/ a nomadisch; (life, tribe) Nomaden-

nominal /'nɒmɪnl/ a, -ly adv nominell

nominat|e /'nɒmɪneɪt/ vt nominieren, aufstellen; (appoint) ernennen. ~ion /-'neɪʃn/ n Nominierung f; Ernennung f

nominative /'nɒmɪnətɪv/ a & n (Gram) ~[case] Nominativ m

nonchalant /'nɒnʃələnt/ a, -ly adv nonchalant; (gesture) lässig

non-com'missioned /nɒn-/ a ~ officer Unteroffizier m

non-com'mittal a unverbindlich; be ~ sich nicht festlegen

nondescript /'nɒndɪskrɪpt/ a unbestimmbar; (person) unscheinbar

none /nʌn/ pron keine(r)/keins; ~ of us keiner von uns; ~ of this/this nichts davon □ adv ~ too nicht gerade; ~ too soon [um] keine Minute zu früh; ~ the wiser um nichts klüger; ~ the less dennoch

nonentity /nɒ'nentətɪ/ n Null f

non-ex'istent a nicht vorhanden; be ~ nicht vorhanden sein

non-'fiction n Sachliteratur f

non-'iron a bügelfrei

nonplussed /nɒn'plʌst/ a verblüfft

nonsense /'nɒnsəns/ n Unsinn m. ~ical /-'sensɪkl/ a unsinnig

non-'smoker n Nichtraucher m; (compartment) Nichtraucherabteil nt

non-'stop adv ununterbrochen; (fly) nonstop; ~ 'flight Nonstopflug m

non-'swimmer n Nichtschwimmer m

non-'violent a gewaltlos

noodles /'nuːdlz/ npl Bandnudeln pl

nook /nʊk/ n Eckchen nt, Winkel m

noon /nuːn/ n Mittag m; at ~ um 12 Uhr mittags

noose /nuːs/ n Schlinge f

nor /nɔː(r)/ adv noch □ conj auch nicht

Nordic /'nɔːdɪk/ a nordisch

norm /nɔːm/ n Norm f

normal /'nɔːml/ a & normal. ~ity /-'mælətɪ/ n Normalität f. ~ly adv normal; (usually) normalerweise

north /nɔːθ/ n Norden m; to the ~ of nördlich von □ a Nord-, nord- □ adv nach Norden

north: N~ America n Nordamerika m. ~-east n Nordost- □ n Nordosten m

norther|ly /'nɔːðəlɪ/ a nördlich. ~n a nördlich. N~n Ireland n Nordirland nt

north: N~ **'Pole** n Nordpol m. N~ 'Sea n Nordsee f. ~**ward[s]** /-wəd[z]/ adv nach Norden. ~**west** n Nordwest- □n Nordwesten m

Nor|way /'nɔ:wei/ n Norwegen nt. ~**wegian** /-'wi:dʒn/ a norwegisch □ n Norweger(in) m(f)

nose /nəuz/ n Nase f □ vi ~ **about** herumschnüffeln

nose: ~**bleed** n Nasenbluten nt. ~**dive** n (Aviat) Sturzflug m

nostalg|ia /nɒ'stældʒɪə/ n Nostalgie f. ~**ic** a nostalgisch

nostril /'nɒstrəl/ n Nasenloch nt; (of horse) Nüster f

nosy /'nəuzɪ/ a (-ier, -iest) (fam) neugierig

not /nɒt/ adv nicht; ~ a kein; if ~ wenn nicht; ~ at all gar nicht; ~ **a bit** kein bisschen; ~ **even** nicht mal; ~ **yet** noch nicht; **he is** ~ **a German** er ist kein Deutscher

notab|le /'nəutəbl/ a bedeutend; (remarkable) bemerkenswert. ~**ly** adv insbesondere

notary /'nəutərɪ/ n ~ **'public** ≈ Notar m

notation /nəu'teɪʃn/ n Notation f; (Mus) Notenschrift f

notch /nɒtʃ/ n Kerbe f. ~ **up** vt (score) erzielen

note /nəut/ n (written comment) Notiz f, Anmerkung f; (short letter) Briefchen nt, Zettel m; (bank ~) Banknote f, Schein m; (Mus) Note f; (sound) Ton m; (on piano) Taste f; **eighth/quarter** ~ (Amer) Achtel-/Viertelnote f; **half/whole** ~ (Amer) halbe/ganze Note f; **of** ~ von Bedeutung; **make a** ~ **of** notieren □ vt bemerken; (notice) bemerken (that dass). ~ **down** vt notieren

'notebook n Notizbuch nt

noted /'nəutɪd/ a bekannt (for für)

note: ~**paper** n Briefpapier nt. ~**worthy** a beachtenswert

nothing /'nʌθɪŋ/ n, ron & adv nichts; for ~ umsonst; ~ **but** nichts als; ~ **much** nicht viel; ~ **interesting** nichts Interessantes; **it's** ~ **to do with you** das geht dich nichts an

notice /'nəutɪs/ n (on board) Anschlag m, Bekanntmachung f; (announcement) Anzeige f; (review) Kritik f; (termination of lease, employment) Kündigung f; **[advance]** ~ Bescheid m; **give [in one's]** ~ kündigen; **give s.o.** ~ jdm kündigen; **take no** ~ **of** keine Notiz nehmen von; **take no** ~! ignoriere es! □ vt bemerken. ~**able** /-əbl/, a, -**bly** adv merklich. ~**board** n Anschlagbrett nt

noti|fication /nəutɪfɪ'keɪʃn/ n Benachrichtigung f. ~**fy** /'nəutɪfaɪ/ vt (pt/pp -**ied**) benachrichtigen

notion /'nəuʃn/ n Idee f; ~**s** pl (Amer: haberdashery) Kurzwaren pl

notorious /nəu'tɔ:rɪəs/ a berüchtigt

notwith'standing prep trotz (+ gen) □ adv trotzdem, dennoch

nought /nɔ:t/ n Null f

noun /naun/ n Substantiv nt

nourish /'nʌrɪʃ/ vt nähren. ~**ing** a nahrhaft. ~**ment** n Nahrung f

novel /'nɒvl/ a neu[artig] □ n Roman m. ~**ist** n Romanschriftsteller(in) m(f). ~**ty** n Neuheit f; ~**ties** pl kleine Geschenkartikel pl

November /nəu'vembə(r)/ n November m

novice /'nɒvɪs/ n Neuling m; (Relig) Novize m/Novizin f

now /nau/ adv & conj jetzt; ~ **[that]** jetzt, wo; **just** ~ gerade, eben; **right** ~ sofort; ~ **and again** hin und wieder; **now, now!** na, na!

'nowadays adv heutzutage

nowhere /'nəu-/ adv nirgendwo, nirgends

noxious /'nɒkʃəs/ a schädlich

nozzle /ˈnɒzl/ n Düse f

nuance /ˈnjuːɑ̃s/ n Nuance f

nuclear /ˈnjuːklɪə(r)/ a Kern-. ~ de'terrent n nukleares Abschreckungsmittel nt

nucleus /ˈnjuːklɪəs/ n (pl -lei /-lɪaɪ/) Kern m

nude /njuːd/ a nackt □ n (Art) Akt m; in the ~ nackt

nudge /nʌdʒ/ n Stups m □ vt stupsen

nud|ist /ˈnjuːdɪst/ n Nudist m. ~ity n Nacktheit f

nugget /ˈnʌgɪt/ n [Gold]klumpen m

nuisance /ˈnjuːsns/ n Ärgernis nt; (pest) Plage f; be a ~ ärgerlich sein; (person:) lästig sein; what a ~! wie ärgerlich!

null /nʌl/ a ~ and void null und nichtig. ~ify /ˈnʌlɪfaɪ/ vt (pt/pp -ied) für nichtig erklären

numb /nʌm/ a gefühllos, taub; ~ with cold taub vor Kälte □ vt betäuben

number /ˈnʌmbə(r)/ n Nummer f; (amount) Anzahl f; (Math) Zahl f □ vt nummerieren; (include) zählen (among zu). ~plate n Nummernschild nt

numeral /ˈnjuːmərl/ n Ziffer f

numerate /ˈnjuːmərət/ a be ~ rechnen können

numerical /njuːˈmerɪkl/ a, -ly adv numerisch; in ~ order zahlenmäßig geordnet

numerous /ˈnjuːmərəs/ a zahlreich

nun /nʌn/ n Nonne f

nuptial /ˈnʌpʃl/ a Hochzeits-. ~s npl (Amer) Hochzeit f

nurse /nɜːs/ n [Kranken]schwester f; (male) Krankenpfleger m; children's ~ Kindermädchen nt □ vt pflegen. ~maid n Kindermädchen nt

nursery /ˈnɜːsərɪ/ n Kinderzimmer nt; (Hort) Gärtnerei f; [day] ~ Kindertagesstätte f. ~

rhyme n Kinderreim m. ~ school n Kindergarten m

nursing /ˈnɜːsɪŋ/ n Krankenpflege f. ~ home n Pflegeheim nt

nurture /ˈnɜːtʃə(r)/ vt nähren; (fig) hegen

nut /nʌt/ n Nuss f; (Techn) [Schrauben]mutter f; (fam: head) Birne f (fam); be ~s (fam) spinnen (fam). ~crackers npl Nussknacker m. ~meg n Muskat m

nutrient /ˈnjuːtrɪənt/ n Nährstoff m

nutrit|ion /njuːˈtrɪʃn/ n Ernährung f. ~ious /-ʃəs/ a nahrhaft

'nutshell n Nussschale f; in a ~ (fig) kurz gesagt

nuzzle /ˈnʌzl/ vt beschnüffeln

nylon /ˈnaɪlɒn/ n Nylon nt; ~s pl Nylonstrümpfe pl

nymph /nɪmf/ n Nymphe f

O

O /əʊ/ n (Teleph) null

oaf /əʊf/ n (pl oafs) Trottel m

oak /əʊk/ n Eiche f □ attrib Eichen-

OAP abbr (old-age pensioner) Rentner(in) m(f)

oar /ɔː(r)/ n Ruder nt. ~sman n Ruderer m

oasis /əʊˈeɪsɪs/ n (pl oases -siːz/) Oase f

oath /əʊθ/ n Eid m; (swear-word) Fluch m

oatmeal /ˈəʊt-/ n Hafermehl nt

oats /əʊts/ npl Hafer m; (Culin) [rolled] ~ Haferflocken pl

obedien|ce /əˈbiːdɪəns/ n Gehorsam m. ~t a, -ly adv gehorsam

obese /əʊˈbiːs/ a fettleibig. ~ity n Fettleibigkeit f

obey /əˈbeɪ/ vt/i gehorchen (+ dat); befolgen (instructions, rules)

obituary /əˈbɪtjʊərɪ/ n Nachruf m; (notice) Todesanzeige f

object¹ /ˈɒbdʒɪkt/ n Gegenstand m; (aim) Zweck m; (intention) Absicht f; (Gram) Objekt nt; **money is no ~** Geld spielt keine Rolle

object² /əbˈdʒɛkt/ vi Einspruch erheben (**to** gegen); (**be against**) etwas dagegen haben

objection /əbˈdʒɛkʃn/ n Einwand m; **have no ~** nichts dagegen haben. **~able** /-əbl/ a anstößig; (person) unangenehm

objective /əbˈdʒɛktɪv/ a, **-ly** adv objektiv □ n Ziel nt. **~ity** /-ˈtɪvətɪ/ n Objektivität f

objector /əbˈdʒɛktə(r)/ n Gegner m

obligation /ɒblɪˈgeɪʃn/ n Pflicht f; **be under an ~** verpflichtet sein; **without ~** unverbindlich

obligatory /əˈblɪgətrɪ/ a obligatorisch; **be ~** Vorschrift sein

oblige /əˈblaɪdʒ/ vt verpflichten; (compel) zwingen; (do a small service) einen Gefallen tun (+ dat); **much ~d!** vielen Dank! **~ing** a entgegenkommend

oblique /əˈbliːk/ a schräg; (angle) schief; (fig) indirekt. **~ stroke** n Schrägstrich m

obliterate /əˈblɪtəreɪt/ vt auslöschen

oblivion /əˈblɪvɪən/ n Vergessenheit f

oblivious /əˈblɪvɪəs/ a **be ~** sich (dat) nicht bewusst sein (**of** or **to** gen)

oblong /ˈɒblɒŋ/ a rechteckig □ n Rechteck nt

obnoxious /əbˈnɒkʃəs/ a widerlich

oboe /ˈəʊbəʊ/ n Oboe f

obscene /əbˈsiːn/ a obszön; (atrocious) abscheulich. **~ity** /-ˈsenɪtɪ/ n Obszönität f; Abscheulichkeit f

obscur|e /əbˈskjʊə(r)/ a dunkel; (unknown) unbekannt □ vt verdecken; (confuse) verwischen. **~ity** n Dunkelheit f; Unbekanntheit f

obsequious /əbˈsiːkwɪəs/ a unterwürfig

observa|nce /əbˈzɜːvns/ n (of custom) Einhaltung f. **~nt** a aufmerksam. **~tion** /ɒbzəˈveɪʃn/ n Beobachtung f; (remark) Bemerkung f

observatory /əbˈzɜːvətrɪ/ n Sternwarte f; (weather) Wetterwarte f

observe /əbˈzɜːv/ vt beobachten; (say, obey) bemerken; (keep, celebrate) feiern; (obey) einhalten. **~r** n Beobachter m

obsess /əbˈses/ vt **be ~ed by** besessen sein von. **~ion** /-eʃn/ n Besessenheit f; (persistent idea) fixe Idee f. **~ive** /-ɪv/ a, **-ly** adv zwanghaft

obsolete /ˈɒbsəliːt/ a veraltet

obstacle /ˈɒbstəkl/ n Hindernis nt

obstetrician /ɒbstəˈtrɪʃn/ n Geburtshelfer m. **obstetrics** /-ˈstetrɪks/ n Geburtshilfe f

obstina|cy /ˈɒbstɪnəsɪ/ n Starrsinn m. **~te** /-nət/ a, **-ly** adv starrsinnig; (refusal) hartnäckig

obstreperous /əbˈstrepərəs/ a widerspenstig

obstruct /əbˈstrʌkt/ vt blockieren; (hinder) behindern. **~ion** /-ʌkʃn/ n Blockierung f; Behinderung f; (obstacle) Hindernis nt. **~ive** /-ɪv/ a **be ~ive** Schwierigkeiten bereiten

obtain /əbˈteɪn/ vt erhalten, bekommen □ vi gelten. **~able** /-əbl/ a erhältlich

obtrusive /əbˈtruːsɪv/ a aufdringlich; (thing) auffällig

obtuse /əbˈtjuːs/ a (Geom) stumpf; (stupid) begriffsstutzig

obviate /ˈɒbvɪeɪt/ vt beseitigen

obvious /ˈɒbvɪəs/ a, **-ly** adv offensichtlich, offenbar

occasion /əˈkeɪʒn/ n Gelegenheit f; (time) Mal nt; (event) Ereignis nt; (cause) Anlass m, Grund m; **on ~** gelegentlich, hin und wieder;

on the ~ of anlässlich (+ *gen*) □ *vt* veranlassen

occasional /əˈkeɪʒənl/ *a* gelegentlich; **he has the ~ glass of wine** er trinkt gelegentlich ein Glas Wein. **~ly** *adv* gelegentlich, hin und wieder

occult /ɒˈkʌlt/ *a* okkult

occupant /ˈɒkjupənt/ *n* Bewohner(in) *m(f)*; *(of vehicle)* Insasse *m*

occupation /ɒkjuˈpeɪʃn/ *n* Beschäftigung *f*; *(job)* Beruf *m*; *(Mil)* Besetzung *f*; *(period)* Besatzung *f*. **~al** *a* Berufs-. **~al therapy** *n* Beschäftigungstherapie *f*

occupier /ˈɒkjupaɪə(r)/ *n* Bewohner(in) *m(f)*

occupy /ˈɒkjupaɪ/ *vt* (*pt/pp* **occupied**) besetzen *(seat, Mil country)*; einnehmen *(space)*; in Anspruch nehmen *(time)*; *(live in)* bewohnen; *(fig)* bekleiden *(office)*; *(keep busy)* beschäftigen; **~ oneself** sich beschäftigen

occur /əˈkɜː(r)/ *vi* (*pt/pp* **occurred**) geschehen; *(exist)* vorkommen, auftreten; **it ~red to me that** es fiel mir ein, dass. **occurrence** /əˈkʌrəns/ *n* Auftreten *nt*; *(event)* Ereignis *nt*

ocean /ˈəʊʃn/ *n* Ozean *m*

o'clock /əˈklɒk/ *adv* **[at] 7 ~** [um] 7 Uhr

octagonal /ɒkˈtægənl/ *a* achteckig

octave /ˈɒktɪv/ *n* (*Mus*) Oktave *f*

October /ɒkˈtəʊbə(r)/ *n* Oktober *m*

octopus /ˈɒktəpəs/ *n* (*pl* **-puses**) Tintenfisch *m*

odd /ɒd/ *a* (**-ier, -est**) seltsam, merkwürdig; *(number)* ungerade; *(not of set)* einzeln; **forty ~** über vierzig; **~ jobs** Gelegenheitsarbeiten *pl*; **the ~ one out** die Ausnahme; **at ~ moments** zwischendurch; **have the ~ glass of wine** gelegentlich ein Glas Wein trinken

odd|ity /ˈɒdɪti/ *n* Kuriosität *f*. **~ly** *adv* merkwürdig; **~ly enough** merkwürdigerweise. **~ment** *n* *(of fabric)* Rest *m*

odds /ɒdz/ *npl* *(chances)* Chancen *pl*; **at ~** uneinig; **~ and ends** Kleinkram *m*; **it makes no ~** es spielt keine Rolle

ode /əʊd/ *n* Ode *f*

odious /ˈəʊdɪəs/ *a* widerlich, abscheulich

odour /ˈəʊdə(r)/ *n* Geruch *m*. **~less** *a* geruchlos

oesophagus /iːˈsɒfəɡəs/ *n* Speiseröhre *f*

of /ɒv, *unbetont* əv/ *prep* von (+ *dat*); *(made of)* aus (+ *dat*); **the two of us** wir zwei; **a child of three** ein dreijähriges Kind; **the fourth of January** der vierte Januar; **a pound of butter** ein Pfund Butter; **a cup of tea/ coffee** eine Tasse Tee/Kaffee; **a bottle of wine** eine Flasche Wein; **half of it** die Hälfte davon; **the whole of the room** das ganze Zimmer

off /ɒf/ *prep* von (+ *dat*); **£10 ~ the price** £10 Nachlass; **~ the coast** vor der Küste; **get ~ the ladder/bus** von der Leiter/aus dem Bus steigen; **take/leave the lid ~** den Topf abdecken/nicht zudecken □ *adv* weg; *(button, lid, handle)* ab; *(light)* aus; *(brake)* los; *(machine)* abgeschaltet; *(tap)* zu; *(on appliance)* **'off'** 'aus'; **2 kilometres ~** 2 Kilometer entfernt; **a long way ~** weit weg; *(time)* noch lange hin; **~ and on** hin und wieder; **with his hat/coat ~** ohne Hut/ Mantel; **with the light/lid ~** ohne Licht/Deckel; **20% ~** 20% Nachlass; **be ~** *(leave)* weggehen; *(Sport)* starten; *(food)* schlecht/*(all gone)* alle sein; **be better/worse ~** besser/ schlechter dran sein; **be well ~** gut dran sein; *(financially)* wohlhabend sein; **have a day ~**

einen freien Tag haben; **go/drive** ~ weggehen/-fahren; **turn/take** sth ~ etw abdrehen/-nehmen

offal /'ɒfl/ n (Culin) Innereien pl

offence /ə'fens/ n (illegal act) Vergehen nt; **give/take** ~ Anstoß erregen/nehmen (**at** an + dat)

offend /ə'fend/ vt beleidigen. ~**er** n (Jur) Straftäter m

offensive /ə'fensɪv/ a anstößig; (Mil, Sport) offensiv □ n Offensive f

offer /'ɒfə(r)/ n Angebot nt; **on special** ~ im Sonderangebot □ vt anbieten (**to** dat); leisten (resistance); ~ **s.o.** sth jdm etw anbieten; ~ **to do** sth sich anbieten, etw zu tun. ~**ing** n Gabe f

off'hand a brüsk; (casual) lässig □ adv so ohne weiteres

office /'ɒfɪs/ n Büro nt; (post) Amt nt; **in** ~ im Amt; ~ **hours** pl Dienststunden pl

officer /'ɒfɪsə(r)/ n Offizier m; (official) Beamte(r) m/ Beamtin f; (police) Polizeibeamte(r) m/ -beamtin f

official /ə'fɪʃl/ a offiziell, amtlich □ n Beamte(r) m/ Beamtin f; (Sport) Funktionär m. ~**ly** adv offiziell

officiate /ə'fɪʃɪeɪt/ vi amtieren

officious /ə'fɪʃəs/ a, -**ly** adv übereifrig

offing n **in the** ~ in Aussicht

off-licence n Wein- und Spirituosenhandlung f

off-load vt ausladen

off-putting a (fam) abstoßend

off'set vt (pt/pp -set, pres p -setting) ausgleichen

offshoot n Schössling m; (fig) Zweig m

offshore a offshore-. ~ **rig** n Bohrinsel f

off'side a (Sport) abseits

offspring n Nachwuchs m

off'stage adv hinter den Kulissen

off-'white a fast weiß

often /'ɒfn/ adv oft; **every so** ~ von Zeit zu Zeit

ogle /'əʊgl/ vt beäugeln

ogre /'əʊgə(r)/ n Menschenfresser m

oh /əʊ/ int oh! ach! **oh dear!** o weh!

oil /ɔɪl/ n Öl nt; (petroleum) Erdöl nt □ vt ölen

oil: ~**cloth** n Wachstuch nt. ~**field** n Ölfeld nt. ~**painting** n Ölgemälde nt. ~ **refinery** n [Erd]ölraffinerie f. ~**skins** npl Ölzeug nt. ~**slick** n Ölteppich m. ~**tanker** n Öltanker m. ~ **well** n Ölquelle f

oily /'ɔɪlɪ/ a (-ier, -iest) ölig

ointment /'ɔɪntmənt/ n Salbe f

OK /əʊ'keɪ/ a & int (fam) in Ordnung; okay □ adv (well) gut □ vt (auch okay) (pt/pp okayed) genehmigen

old /əʊld/ a (-er, -est) alt; (former) ehemalig

old: ~ **age** n Alter nt. ~**age** 'pensioner n Rentner(in) m(f). ~**boy** n ehemaliger Schüler. ~-**fashioned** a altmodisch. ~ **girl** ehemalige Schülerin f. ~ **maid** n alte Jungfer f

olive /'ɒlɪv/ n Olive f; (colour) Oliv nt □ a olivgrün. ~ **branch** n Ölzweig m; (fig) Friedensangebot nt. ~ **oil** n Olivenöl nt

Olympic /ə'lɪmpɪk/ a olympisch □ n **the** ~**s** die Olympischen Spiele pl

omelette /'ɒmlɪt/ n Omelett nt

omen /'əʊmən/ n Omen nt

ominous /'ɒmɪnəs/ a bedrohlich

omission /ə'mɪʃn/ n Auslassung f; (failure to do) Unterlassung f

omit /ə'mɪt/ vt (pt/pp omitted) auslassen; ~ **to do** sth es unterlassen, etw zu tun

omnipotent /ɒm'nɪpətənt/ a allmächtig

on /ɒn/ prep auf (+ dat/(on to) + acc); (on vertical surface) an (+ dat/(on to) + acc); (about) über

(+ *acc*); **on Monday** [am] Montag; **on Mondays** montags; **on the first of May** am ersten Mai; **on arriving** als ich ankam; **on one's finger** am Finger; **on the right/left** rechts/links; **on the Rhine/Thames** am Rhein/an der Themse; **on the radio/television** im Radio/Fernsehen; **on the bus/train** im Bus/Zug; **go on the bus/train** mit dem Bus/Zug fahren; **get on the bus/train** in den Bus/Zug einsteigen; **on me** (*with me*) bei mir; **it's on me** (*fam*) das spendiere ich □ *adv* (*further on*) weiter; (*switched on*) an; (*brake*) angezogen; (*machine*) angeschaltet; (*on appliance*) 'an', 'ein'; **with/without his hat/coat on** mit/ohne Hut/Mantel; **with/without the lid on** mit/ohne Deckel; **be on** (*film:*) laufen; (*event:*) stattfinden; **be on at** (*fam*) bedrängen (zu to); **it's not on** (*fam*) das geht nicht; **on and on** immer weiter; **on and off** hin und wieder; **and so on** und so weiter; **later on** später; **move/drive on** weitergehen/-fahren; **stick/sew on** ankleben/-nähen

once /wʌns/ *adv* einmal; (*formerly*) früher; **at ~** sofort; (*at the same time*) gleichzeitig; **~ and for all** ein für alle Mal □ *conj* wenn; (*with past tense*) als. **~over** *n* (*fam*) **give s.o./sth the ~over** sich (*dat*) jdn/etw kurz ansehen

'oncoming *a* **~ traffic** Gegenverkehr *m*

one /wʌn/ *a* ein(e); (*only*) einzig; **not ~** kein(e); **~ day/evening** eines Tages/Abends □ *n* Eins *f* □ *pron* eine(r)/eins; (*impersonal*) man; **which ~** welche(r,s); **~ another** einander; **~ by ~** einzeln; **~ never knows** man kann nie wissen

one: **~-eyed** *a* einäugig. **~-parent 'family** *n* Einelternfamilie *f*.

~'self *pron* selbst; (*refl*) sich; **by ~self** allein. **~-sided** *a* einseitig. **~-way** *a* (*street*) Einbahn-; (*ticket*) einfach

onion /'ʌnjən/ *n* Zwiebel *f*

'onlooker *n* Zuschauer(in) *m(f)*

only /'əʊnlɪ/ *a* einzig; **an ~ child** ein Einzelkind *nt* □ *adv* & *conj* nur; **~ just** gerade erst; (*barely*) gerade noch

'onset *n* Beginn *m*; (*of winter*) Einsetzen *nt*

onslaught /'ɒnslɔːt/ *n* heftiger Angriff *m*

onus /'əʊnəs/ *n* **the ~ is on me** es liegt an mir (**to** zu)

onward[s] /'ɒnwəd[z]/ *adv* vorwärts; **from then ~** von der Zeit an

ooze /uːz/ *vi* sickern

opal /'əʊpl/ *n* Opal *m*

opaque /əʊ'peɪk/ *a* undurchsichtig

open /'əʊpən/ *a*, **-ly** *adv* offen; **be ~** (*shop:*) geöffnet sein; **in the ~ air** im Freien □ *n* **in the ~** im Freien □ *vt* öffnen, aufmachen; (*start, set up*) eröffnen □ *vi* sich öffnen; (*flower:*) aufgehen; (*shop:*) öffnen, aufmachen; (*be started*) eröffnet werden. **~ up** *vt* öffnen, aufmachen; (*fig*) eröffnen □ *vi* sich öffnen; (*fig*) sich eröffnen

open: **~-air** **'swimming pool** *n* Freibad *nt*. **~ day** *n* Tag *m* der offenen Tür

opener /'əʊpənə(r)/ *n* Öffner *m*

opening /'əʊpənɪŋ/ *n* Öffnung *f*; (*beginning*) Eröffnung *f*; (*job*) Einstiegsmöglichkeit *f*. **~ hours** *npl* Öffnungszeiten *pl*

open: **~-minded** *a* aufgeschlossen. **~-plan** *a* **~-plan office** Großraumbüro *nt*. **~ 'sandwich** *n* belegtes Brot *nt*

opera /'ɒprə/ *n* Oper *f*

operable /'ɒprəbl/ *a* operierbar

opera: **~-glasses** *npl* Opernglas *nt*. **~-house** *n* Opernhaus *nt*. **~-singer** *n* Opernsänger(in) *m(f)*

operate /'ɒpəreɪt/ vt bedienen (machine, lift); betätigen (lever, brake); (fig: run) betreiben □ vi (Techn) funktionieren; (be in action) in Betrieb sein; (Mil & fig) operieren; ~ [on] (Med) operieren

operatic /ɒpə'rætɪk/ a Opern-

operation /ɒpə'reɪʃn/ n (see operate) Bedienung f; Betätigung f; Operation f; **in** ~ (Techn) in Betrieb; **come into** ~ (fig) in Kraft treten; **have an** ~ (Med) operiert werden. ~**al a be** ~ in Betrieb sein; (law:) in Kraft sein

operative /'ɒpərətɪv/ a wirksam

operator /'ɒpəreɪtə(r)/ n (user) Bedienungsperson f; (Teleph) Vermittlung f

operetta /ɒpə'retə/ n Operette f

opinion /ə'pɪnjən/ n Meinung f; **in my** ~ meiner Meinung nach. ~**ated** a rechthaberisch

opium /'əʊpɪəm/ n Opium nt

opponent /ə'pəʊnənt/ n Gegner(in) m(f)

opportune /'ɒpətjuːn/ a günstig. ~**ist** /-'tjuːnɪst/ a, ~**ist** n Opportunist m

opportunity /ɒpə'tjuːnətɪ/ n Gelegenheit f

oppose /ə'pəʊz/ vt Widerstand leisten (+ dat); (argue against) sprechen gegen; **be** ~**ed to** sth gegen etw sein; **as** ~**ed to** im Gegensatz zu. ~**ing** a gegnerisch; (opposite) entgegengesetzt

opposite /'ɒpəzɪt/ a entgegengesetzt; (house, side) gegenüberliegend; ~ **number** (fig) Gegenstück nt; **the** ~ **sex** das andere Geschlecht □ n Gegenteil nt □ adv gegenüber □ prep gegenüber (+ dat)

opposition /ɒpə'zɪʃn/ n Widerstand m; (pol) Opposition f

oppress /ə'pres/ vt unterdrücken. ~**ion** /-eʃn/ n Unterdrücken f. ~**ive** /-ɪv/ a tyrannisch; (heat) drückend. ~**or** n Unterdrücker m

opt /ɒpt/ vi ~ **for** sich entscheiden für; ~ **out** ausscheiden (of aus)

optical /'ɒptɪkl/ a optisch; ~ **illusion** optische Täuschung f

optician /ɒp'tɪʃn/ n Optiker m

optics /'ɒptɪks/ n Optik f

optimis|m /'ɒptɪmɪzm/ n Optimismus m. ~**t** /-mɪst/ n Optimist m. ~**tic** /-'mɪstɪk/ a, ~**ally** adv optimistisch

optimum /'ɒptɪməm/ a optimal □ n (pl -**ima**) Optimum nt

option /'ɒpʃn/ n Wahl f; (Comm) Option f. ~**al** a auf Wunsch erhältlich; (subject) wahlfrei; ~**al extras** pl Extras pl

opulen|ce /'ɒpjuləns/ n Prunk m; (wealth) Reichtum m. ~**lent** a prunkvoll; (wealthy) sehr reich

or /ɔː(r)/ conj oder; (after negative) noch; **or [else]** sonst; **in a year or two** in ein bis zwei Jahren

oracle /'ɒrəkl/ n Orakel nt

oral /'ɔːrl/ a, ~**ly** adv mündlich; (Med) oral □ n (fam) Mündliche(s) nt

orange /'ɒrɪndʒ/ n Apfelsine f, Orange f; (colour) Orange nt □ a orangefarben. ~**ade** /-'dʒeɪd/ n Orangeade f

oration /ə'reɪʃn/ n Rede f

orator /'ɒrətə(r)/ n Redner m

oratorio /ɒrə'tɔːrɪəʊ/ n Oratorium nt

oratory /'ɒrətərɪ/ n Redekunst f

orbit /'ɔːbɪt/ n Umlaufbahn f □ vt umkreisen. ~**al a** ~**al road** Ringstraße f

orchard /'ɔːtʃəd/ n Obstgarten m

orches|tra /'ɔːkɪstrə/ n Orchester nt. ~**tral** /-'kestrl/ a Orchester-. ~**trate** vt orchestrieren

orchid /'ɔːkɪd/ n Orchidee f

ordain /ɔː'deɪn/ vt bestimmen; (Relig) ordinieren

ordeal /ɔː'diːl/ n (fig) Qual f

order /'ɔːdə(r)/ n Ordnung f; (sequence) Reihenfolge f; (condition) Zustand m; (command) Befehl m;

(in *restaurant*) Bestellung f; (*Comm*) Auftrag m; (*Relig, medal*) Orden m; **out of** ~ (*machine*) außer Betrieb; **in** ~ **that** damit; **in** ~ **to help** um zu helfen; **take holy** ~s Geistlicher werden □ vt (*put in* ~) ordnen; (*command*) befehlen (+ dat); (*Comm, in restaurant*) bestellen; (*prescribe*) verordnen

orderly /'ɔ:dəlɪ/ a ordentlich; (*not unruly*) friedlich □ n (*Mil, Med*) Sanitäter m

ordinary /'ɔ:dɪnərɪ/ a gewöhnlich, normal; (*meeting*) ordentlich

ordination /ɔ:dɪ'neɪʃn/ n (*Relig*) Ordination f

ore /ɔ:(r)/ n Erz nt

organ /'ɔ:gən/ n (*Biol & fig*) Organ nt; (*Mus*) Orgel f

organic /ɔ:'gænɪk/ a, **-ally** adv organisch; (*without chemicals*) biodynamisch; (*crop*) biologisch angebaut; (*food*) Bio-; ~**ally grown** biologisch angebaut. ~ **farm** n Biohof m. ~ **farming** n biologischer Anbau m

organism /'ɔ:gənɪzm/ n Organismus m

organist /'ɔ:gənɪst/ n Organist m

organization /ɔ:gənaɪ'zeɪʃn/ n Organisation f

organize /'ɔ:gənaɪz/ vt organisieren; veranstalten (*event*). ~**r** n Organisator m; Veranstalter m

orgasm /'ɔ:gæzm/ n Orgasmus m

orgy /'ɔ:dʒɪ/ n Orgie f

Orient /'ɔ:rɪənt/ n Orient m. **o~al** /-'entl/ a orientalisch; ~**al carpet** Orientteppich m □ n Orientale m/Orientalin f

orient|ate /'ɔ:rɪənteɪt/ vt ~**ate oneself** sich orientieren. ~**ation** /-'teɪʃn/ n Orientierung f

orifice /'ɒrɪfɪs/ n Öffnung f

origin /'ɒrɪdʒɪn/ n Ursprung m; (*of person, goods*) Herkunft f

original /ə'rɪdʒənl/ a ursprünglich; (*not copied*) original; (*new*) originell □ n Original nt. ~**ity**

/-'nælətɪ/ n Originalität f. ~**ly** adv ursprünglich

originat|e /ə'rɪdʒɪneɪt/ vi entstehen □ vt hervorbringen. ~**or** n Urheber m

ornament /'ɔ:nəmənt/ n Ziergenstand m; (*decoration*) Verzierung f. ~**al** /-'mentl/ a dekorativ. ~**ation** /-'teɪʃn/ n Verzierung f

ornate /ɔ:'neɪt/ a reich verziert

ornithology /ɔ:nɪ'θɒlədʒɪ/ n Vogelkunde f

orphan /'ɔ:fn/ n Waisenkind nt, Waise f □ vt zur Waise machen; ~**ed** verwaist. ~**age** /-ɪdʒ/ n Waisenhaus nt

orthodox /'ɔ:θədɒks/ a orthodox

orthography /ɔ:'θɒgrəfɪ/ n Rechtschreibung f

orthopaedic /ɔ:θə'pi:dɪk/ a orthopädisch

oscillate /'ɒsɪleɪt/ vi schwingen

ostensible /ɒ'stensəbl/ a, **-bly** adv angeblich

ostentat|tion /ɒsten'teɪʃn/ n Protzerei f (*fam*). ~**ious** /-ʃəs/ a protzig (*fam*)

osteopath /'ɒstɪəpæθ/ n Osteopath m

ostracize /'ɒstrəsaɪz/ vt ächten

ostrich /'ɒstrɪtʃ/ n Strauß m

other /'ʌðə(r)/ a, pron & n andere(r,s); **the** ~ [**one**] der/die/das andere; **the** ~ **two** die zwei anderen; **two** ~s zwei andere; (*more*) noch zwei; **no** ~s sonst keine; **any** ~ **questions?** sonst noch Fragen? **every** ~ **day** jeden zweiten Tag; **the** ~ **day** neulich; **the** ~ **evening** neulich abends; **someone/something or** ~ irgendjemand/-etwas □ adv anders; ~ **than him** außer ihm; **somehow/somewhere or** ~ irgendwie/irgendwo

otherwise adv sonst; (*differently*) anders

otter /'ɒtə(r)/ n Otter m

ouch /aʊtʃ/ int autsch

ought /ɔːt/ v aux I/we ~ to stay ich sollte/wir sollten eigentlich bleiben; **he ~ not to have done it** er hätte es nicht machen sollen; **that ~ to be enough** das sollte eigentlich genügen

ounce /aʊns/ n Unze f (28, 35 g)

our /'aʊə(r)/ a unser

ours /'aʊəz/ poss pron unsere(r,s); **a friend of ~** ein Freund von uns; **that is ~** das gehört uns

ourselves /aʊə'selvz/ pron selbst; (refl) uns; **by ~** allein

oust /aʊst/ vt entfernen

out /aʊt/ adv (not at home) weg; (outside) draußen; (not alight) aus; (unconscious) bewusstlos; **be ~** (sun:) scheinen; (flower) blühen; (workers) streiken; (calculation:) nicht stimmen; (Sport) aus sein; (fig: not feasible) nicht infrage kommen; **~ and about** unterwegs; **have it ~ with s.o.** (fam) jdn zur Rede stellen; **get ~!** (fam) raus! **~ with it!** (fam) heraus damit! **go/send ~** hinausgehen/-schicken; **come/bring ~** herauskommen/ -bringen □ prep ~ **of** aus (+ dat); **go ~ of the door** zur Tür hinausgehen; **be ~ of bed/ the room** nicht im Bett/im Zimmer sein; **~ of breath/danger** außer Atem/Gefahr; **~ of work** arbeitslos; **nine ~ of ten** neun von zehn; **be ~ of sugar/bread** keinen Zucker/kein Brot mehr haben □ prep go ~ (+ dat); **go ~ the door** zur Tür hinausgehen

out'bid vt (pt/pp -**bid**, pres p -**bidding**) überbieten

outboard a **~ motor** Außenbordmotor m

outbreak n Ausbruch m

outbuilding n Nebengebäude nt

outburst n Ausbruch m

outcast n Ausgestoßene(r) m/f

outcome n Ergebnis nt

outcry n Aufschrei m [der Entrüstung]

out'dated a überholt

out'do vt (pt -**did**, pp -**done**) übertreffen, übertrumpfen

'outdoor a (life, sports) im Freien; **~ shoes** pl Straßenschuhe pl; **~ swimming pool** Freibad nt

out'doors adv draußen; **go ~** nach draußen gehen

outer a äußere(r,s)

'outfit n Ausstattung f; (clothes) Ensemble nt; (fam: organization) Betrieb m; (fam) Laden m. **~ter** n men's **~ter's** Herrenbekleidungsgeschäft nt

'outgoing a ausscheidend; (mail) ausgehend; (sociable) kontaktfreudig. **~s** npl Ausgaben pl

out'grow vi (pt -**grew**, pp -**grown**) herauswachsen aus

'outhouse n Nebengebäude nt

outing /'aʊtɪŋ/ n Ausflug m

outlandish /aʊt'lændɪʃ/ a ungewöhnlich

'outlaw n Geächtete(r) m/f □ vt ächten

'outlay n Auslagen pl

'outlet n Abzug m; (for water) Abfluss m; (fig) Ventil nt; (Comm) Absatzmöglichkeit f

'outline n Umriss m; (summary) kurze Darstellung f □ vt umreißen

out'live vt überleben

'outlook n Aussicht f; (future prospect) Aussichten pl; (attitude) Einstellung f

'outlying a entlegen; **~ areas** pl Außengebiete pl

out'moded a überholt

out'number vt zahlenmäßig überlegen sein (+ dat)

'out-patient n ambulanter Patient m; **~s' department** Ambulanz f

'outpost n Vorposten m

'output n Leistung f; Produktion f

'outrage n Gräueltat f; (fig) Skandal m; (indignation) Empörung f

□ vt empören. ~ous /-'reɪdʒəs/ a
empörend

'outright² adv ganz; (at once) sofort; (frankly) offen

'outset n Anfang m; from the ~
von Anfang an

'outside¹ a äußere(r,s); ~ wall
Außenwand f □ n Außenseite f;
from the ~ von außen; at the ~
höchstens

out'side² adv außen; (out of doors)
draußen; go ~ nach außen
gehen □ prep außerhalb (+ gen);
(in front of) vor (+ dat/acc)

out'sider n Außenseiter m

'outsize a übergroß

'outskirts npl Rand m

out'spoken a offen; be ~ kein
Blatt vor den Mund nehmen

out'standing a hervorragend;
(conspicuous) bemerkenswert;
(not settled) unerledigt; (Comm)
ausstehend

'outstretched a ausgestreckt

out'strip vt (pt/pp -stripped) davonlaufen (+ dat); (fig) übertreffen

'outvote vt überstimmen

'outward /-wəd/ a äußerlich; ~
journey Hinreise f □ adv nach
außen; be ~ bound ⟨ship:⟩ auslaufen. ~ly adv nach außen hin,
äußerlich. ~s adv nach außen

out'weigh vt überwiegen

out'wit vt (pt/pp -witted) überlisten

oval /'əʊvl/ a oval □ n Oval nt

ovary /'əʊvəri/ n (Anat) Eierstock m

ovation /ə'veɪʃn/ n Ovation f

oven /'ʌvn/ n Backofen m. ~-
ready a bratfertig

over /'əʊvə(r)/ prep über (+
acc/dat); ~ dinner beim Essen;
~ the weekend übers Wochenende; ~ the phone am Telefon; ~ the page auf der nächsten
Seite; all ~ Germany in ganz

Deutschland; (travel) durch ganz
Deutschland; all ~ the place
(fam) überall □ adv (remaining)
übrig; (ended) zu Ende; ~ again
noch einmal; ~ and ~ immer
wieder; ~ here/there hier/da
drüben; all ~ (everywhere) überall; it's all ~ es ist vorbei; I ache
all ~ mir tut alles weh; go/drive
~ hinübergehen/-fahren; come/
bring ~ herüberkommen/
-bringen; turn ~ herumdrehen

overall¹ /'əʊvərɔːl/ n Kittel m; ~s
pl Overall m

overall² /əʊvər'ɔːl/ a gesamt;
(general) allgemein □ adv insgesamt

over'awe vt (fig) überwältigen

over'balance vi das Gleichgewicht verlieren

over'bearing a herrisch

'overboard adv (Naut) über Bord

'overcast a bedeckt

over'charge vt ~ s.o. jdm zu viel
berechnen □ vi zu viel verlangen

'overcoat n Mantel m

over'come vt (pt -came, pp
-come) überwinden; be ~ by
überwältigt werden von

over'crowded a überfüllt

over'do vt (pt -did, pp -done)
übertreiben; (cook too long) zu
lange kochen; ~ it (fam: do too
much) sich übernehmen

'overdose n Überdosis f

'overdraft n [Konto]überziehung
f; have an ~ sein Konto überzogen haben

over'draw vt (pt -drew, pp
-drawn) (Comm) überziehen

over'due a überfällig

over'estimate vt überschätzen

'overflow¹ n Überschuss m; (outlet) Überlauf m

over'flow² vi überlaufen

over'grown a (garden) überwachsen

'overhang¹ n Überhang m

over'hang² vt/i (pt/pp -hung)
überhängen (über + acc)

'over'haul[1] n Überholung f
over'haul[2] vt überholen
over'head[1] adv oben
'overhead[2] a Ober-; (ceiling) Decken-. ~s npl allgemeine Unkosten pl
over'hear vt (pt/pp -heard) mit anhören (conversation); I over-heard him saying it ich hörte zufällig, wie er das sagte
over'heat vi zu heiß werden □ vt zu stark erhitzen
over'joyed a überglücklich
over'land a adv /-'-/ auf dem Landweg; ~ route Landroute f
over'lap v (pt/pp -lapped) □ vi sich überschneiden □ vt über-lappen
over'leaf adv umseitig
over'load vt überladen; (Electr) überlasten
'overlook[1] n (Amer) Aussichts-punkt m
over'look[2] vt überblicken; (fail to see, ignore) übersehen
overly /'əuvəli/ adv übermäßig
over'night adv über Nacht; stay ~ übernachten
'overnight[2] a Nacht-; ~ stay Übernachtung f
'overpass n Überführung f
over'pay vt (pt/pp -paid) über-bezahlen
over'populated a überbevölkert
over'power vt überwältigen. ~ing a überwältigend
over'priced a zu teuer
overpro'duce vt überproduzie-ren
over'rate vt überschätzen. ~d a überbewertet
over'reach vt ~ oneself sich übernehmen
overre'act vi überreagieren. ~ion n Überreaktion f
over'ride vt (pt -rode, pp -ridden) sich hinwegsetzen über (+ acc). ~ing a Haupt-
over'rule vt ablehnen; we were ~d wir wurden überstimmt

over'run vt (pt -ran, pp -run, pres p -running) überrennen; überschreiten (time); be ~ with überlaufen sein von
over'seas[1] adv in Übersee; go ~ nach Übersee gehen
'overseas[2] a Übersee-
over'see vt (pt -saw, pp -seen) be-aufsichtigen
'overseer /-siə(r)/ n Aufseher m
over'shadow vt überschatten
over'shoot vt (pt/pp -shot) hi-nausschießen über (+ acc)
'oversight n Versehen nt
over'sleep vi (pt/pp -slept) [sich] verschlafen
over'step vt (pt/pp -stepped) überschreiten
over'strain vt überanstrengen
overt /əu'vɜːt/ a offen
over'take v/i (pt -took, pp -taken) überholen. ~ing n Über-holen nt; no ~ing Überholverbot nt
over'tax vt zu hoch besteuern; (fig) überfordern
'overthrow[1] n (Pol) Sturz m
over'throw[2] vt (pt -threw, pp -thrown) (Pol) stürzen
'overtime n Überstunden pl □ adv work ~ Überstunden machen
over'tired a übermüdet
'overtone n (fig) Unterton m
overture /'əuvətjuə(r)/ n (Mus) Ouvertüre f; ~s pl (fig) Annä-herungsversuche pl
over'turn v umstoßen □ vi umkippen
'overweight a übergewichtig; be ~ Übergewicht haben
overwhelm /-'welm/ vt überwäl-tigen. ~ing a überwältigend
over'work n Überarbeitung f □ vt überfordern □ vi sich über-arbeiten
over'wrought a überreizt
ovulation /ɒvjʊ'leɪʃn/ n Ei-sprung m

owe /əʊ/ vt schulden; (fig) verdanken (**[to]** s.o. jdm); ~ **e** s.o. sth jdm etw schuldig sein; **be** ~**ing** (money:) ausstehen. '~**ing** to prep wegen (+ gen)

owl /aʊl/ n Eule f

own[1] /əʊn/ a & pron eigen; it's my ~ es gehört mir; **a car of my** ~ mein eigenes Auto; **on one's** ~ allein; **hold one's** ~ sich behaupten; **get one's** ~ **back** (fam) sich revanchieren

own[2] vt besitzen; (confess) zugeben; **I don't** ~ es ist nicht mein. ~ **up** vi es zugeben

owner /'əʊnə(r)/ n Eigentümer(in) m(f), Besitzer(in) m(f); (of shop) Inhaber(in) m(f). ~**ship** n Besitz m

ox /ɒks/ n (pl **oxen**) Ochse m

oxide /'ɒksaɪd/ n Oxid nt

oxygen /'ɒksɪdʒən/ n Sauerstoff m

oyster /'ɔɪstə(r)/ n Auster f

ozone /'əʊzəʊn/ n Ozon nt. ~-'**friendly** a ≈ ohne FCKW. ~ **layer** n Ozonschicht f

P

pace /peɪs/ n Schritt m; (speed) Tempo nt; **keep** ~ **with** Schritt halten mit □ vi ~ **up and down** auf und ab gehen. ~**maker** n (Sport & Med) Schrittmacher m

Pacific /pə'sɪfɪk/ a & n **the** ~ [**Ocean**] der Pazifik

pacifier /'pæsɪfaɪə(r)/ n (Amer) Schnuller m

pacifist /'pæsɪfɪst/ n Pazifist m

pacify /'pæsɪfaɪ/ vt (pt/pp -**ied**) beruhigen

pack /pæk/ n Packung f; (Mil) Tornister m; (of cards) (Kartenspiel nt; (gang) Bande f; (of hounds) Meute f; (of wolves) Rudel nt; **a** ~ **of lies** ein Haufen Lügen □ vt/i packen; einpacken

(article); **be** ~**ed** (crowded) [gedrängt] voll sein; **send** s.o. ~**ing** (fam) jdn wegschicken. ~ **up** vt einpacken □ vi (fam) (machine:) kaputtgehen; (person:) einpacken (fam)

package /'pækɪdʒ/ n Paket nt □ vt verpacken. ~ **holiday** n Pauschalreise f

packed 'lunch n Lunchpaket nt

packet /'pækɪt/ n Päckchen nt; **cost a** ~ (fam) einen Haufen Geld kosten

packing /'pækɪŋ/ n Verpackung f

pact /pækt/ n Pakt m

pad[1] /pæd/ n Polster nt; (for writing) [Schreib]block m; (fam: home) Wohnung f □ vt (pt/pp **padded**) polstern

pad[2] vi (pt/pp **padded**) tappen

padding /'pædɪŋ/ n Polsterung f; (in written work) Füllwerk nt

paddle[1] /'pædl/ n Paddel nt □ vt (row) paddeln

paddle[2] vi waten

paddock /'pædək/ n Koppel f

padlock /'pædlɒk/ n Vorhängeschloss nt □ vt mit einem Vorhängeschloss verschließen

paediatrician /piːdɪə'trɪʃn/ n Kinderarzt m /-ärztin f

pagan /'peɪgən/ a heidnisch □ n Heide m/Heidin f

page[1] /peɪdʒ/ n Seite f

page[2] n (boy) Page m □ vt ausrufen (person)

pageant /'pædʒənt/ n Festzug m. ~**ry** n Prunk m

paid /peɪd/ see **pay** □ a bezahlt; **put** ~ **to** (fam) zunichte machen

pail /peɪl/ n Eimer m

pain /peɪn/ n Schmerz m; **be in** ~ Schmerzen haben; **take** ~**s** sich (dat) Mühe geben; ~ **in the neck** (fam) Nervensäge f □ vt (fig) schmerzen

pain: ~**ful** a schmerzhaft; (fig) schmerzlich. ~**killer** n schmerzstillendes Mittel *nt*. ~**less** *a*, ~**ly** *adv* schmerzlos

painstaking /'peɪnzteɪkɪŋ/ *a* sorgfältig

paint /peɪnt/ *n* Farbe *f* □*vt/i* streichen; (*artist.*) malen. ~**brush** *n* Pinsel *m*. ~**er** *n* Maler *m*; (*decorator*) Anstreicher *m*. ~**ing** *n* Malerei *f*; (*picture*) Gemälde *nt*

pair /peə(r)/ *n* Paar *nt*; ~ **of trousers** Hose*f*; ~ **of scissors** Schere *f* □*vt* paaren □*vi* ~ **off** Paare bilden

pajamas /pə'dʒɑːməz/ *n pl* (*Amer*) Schlafanzug *m*

Pakistan /pɑːkɪ'stɑːn/ *n* Pakistan *nt*. ~**i** *a* pakistanisch □*n* Pakistaner(in) *m(f)*

pal /pæl/ *n* Freund(in) *m(f)*

palace /'pælɪs/ *n* Palast *m*

palatable /'pælətəbl/ *a* schmackhaft

palate /'pælət/ *n* Gaumen *m*

palatial /pə'leɪʃl/ *a* palastartig

palaver /pə'lɑːvə(r)/ *n* (*fam: fuss*) Theater *nt* (*fam*)

pale[1] *n* (*stake*) Pfahl *m*; **beyond the ~** (*fam*) unmöglich

pale[2] *a* (**-r, -st**) blass □*vi* blass werden. ~**ness** *n* Blässe *f*

Palestine /'pælɪstaɪn/ *n* Palästina *nt*. ~**ian** /pælə'stɪnɪən/ *a* palästinensisch □*n* Palästinenser(in) *m(f)*

palette /'pælɪt/ *n* Palette *f*

pall /pɔːl/ *n* Sargtuch *nt*; (*fig*) Decke *f* □*vi* an Reiz verlieren

pallid /'pælɪd/ *a* bleich. ~**or** *n* Blässe *f*

palm /pɑːm/ *n* Handfläche *f*; (*tree, symbol*) Palme *f* □*vt* ~ **sth off on s.o.** jdm etw andrehen. **P~-'Sunday** *n* Palmsonntag *m*

palpable /'pælpəbl/ *a* tastbar; (*perceptible*) spürbar

palpitate /'pælpɪteɪt/ *vi* klopfen. ~**ions** /-'teɪʃnz/ *npl* Herzklopfen *nt*

paltry /'pɔːltrɪ/ *a* (**-ier, -iest**) armselig

pamper /'pæmpə(r)/ *vt* verwöhnen

pamphlet /'pæmflɪt/ *n* Broschüre *f*

pan /pæn/ *n* Pfanne *f*; (*saucepan*) Topf *m*; (*of scales*) Schale *f* □*vt* (*pt/pp* **panned**) (*fam*) verreißen

panacea /pænə'siːə/ *n* Allheilmittel *nt*

panache /pə'næʃ/ *n* Schwung *m*

pancake *n* Pfannkuchen *m*

pancreas /'pæŋkrɪəs/ *n* Bauchspeicheldrüse *f*

panda /'pændə/ *n* Panda *m*. ~ **car** *n* Streifenwagen *m*

pandemonium /pændɪ'məʊnɪəm/ *n* Höllenlärm *m*

pander /'pændə(r)/ *vi* ~ **to s.o.** jdm zu sehr nachgeben

pane /peɪn/ *n* [Glas]scheibe *f*

panel /'pænl/ *n* Tafel *f*, Platte *f*; ~ **of experts** Expertenrunde *f*; ~ **of judges** Jury *f*. ~**ling** *n* Täfelung *f*

pang /pæŋ/ *n* ~**s of hunger** Hungergefühl *nt*; ~**s of conscience** Gewissensbisse *pl*

panic /'pænɪk/ *n* Panik *f* □*vi* (*pt/pp* **panicked**) in Panik geraten. ~**stricken** *a* von Panik ergriffen

panorama /pænə'rɑːmə/ *n* Panorama *nt*. ~**ic** /-'ræmɪk/ *a* Panorama-

pansy /'pænzɪ/ *n* Stiefmütterchen *nt*

pant /pænt/ *vi* keuchen; (*dog:*) hecheln

pantechnicon /pæn'teknɪkən/ *n* Möbelwagen *m*

panther /'pænθə(r)/ *n* Panther *m*

panties /'pæntɪz/ *npl* [Damen]slip *m*

pantomime /'pæntəmaɪm/ *n* [zu Weihnachten aufgeführte] Märchenvorstellung *f*

pantry /'pæntrɪ/ *n* Speisekammer *f*

pants /pænts/ *npl* Unterhose *f*; (*woman's*) Schlüpfer *m*; (*trousers*) Hose *f*

'pantyhose n (Amer) Strumpfhose f

papal /'peɪpl/ a päpstlich

paper /'peɪpə(r)/ n Papier nt; (wall~) Tapete f; (newspaper) Zeitung f; (exam~) Testbogen m; (exam) Klausur f; (treatise) Referat nt. ~s pl (documents) Unterlagen pl; (for identification) [Ausweis]papiere pl; **on ~** schriftlich □ vt tapezieren

paper: ~back n Taschenbuch nt. ~clip n Büroklammer f. ~knife n Brieföffner m. ~weight n Briefbeschwerer m. ~work n Schreibarbeit f

par /pɑː(r)/ n (Golf) Par nt; **on a ~** gleichwertig (with dat); **feel below ~** sich nicht ganz auf der Höhe fühlen

parable /'pærəbl/ n Gleichnis nt

parachut|e /'pærəʃuːt/ n Fallschirm m □ vi [mit dem Fallschirm] abspringen. ~ist n Fallschirmspringer m

parade /pə'reɪd/ n Parade f; (procession) Festzug m □ vi marschieren □ vt (show off) zur Schau stellen

paradise /'pærədaɪs/ n Paradies nt

paradox /'pærədɒks/ n Paradox nt. ~ical /-'dɒksɪkl/ paradox

paraffin /'pærəfɪn/ n Paraffin nt

paragon /'pærəgən/ n ~ **of virtue** Ausbund m der Tugend

paragraph /'pærəgrɑːf/ n Absatz m

parallel /'pærəlel/ a & adv parallel □ n (Geog) Breitenkreis m; (fig) Parallele f

paralyse /'pærəlaɪz/ vt lähmen; (fig) lahmlegen

paralysis /pə'ræləsɪs/ n (pl -ses /-siːz/) Lähmung f

paramount /'pærəmaʊnt/ a überragend; **be ~** vorgehen

paranoid /'pærənɔɪd/ a [krankhaft] misstrauisch

parapet /'pærəpɪt/ n Brüstung f

paraphernalia /pærəfə'neɪlɪə/ n Kram m

paraphrase /'pærəfreɪz/ n Umschreibung f □ vt umschreiben

paraplegic /pærə'pliːdʒɪk/ a querschnittsgelähmt □ n Querschnittsgelähmte(r) m/f

parasite /'pærəsaɪt/ n Parasit m, Schmarotzer m

parasol /'pærəsɒl/ n Sonnenschirm m

paratrooper /'pærətruːpə(r)/ n Fallschirmjäger m

parcel /'pɑːsl/ n Paket nt

parch /pɑːtʃ/ vt austrocknen; **be ~ed** (person.) einen furchtbaren Durst haben

parchment /'pɑːtʃmənt/ n Pergament nt

pardon /'pɑːdn/ n Verzeihung f; (Jur) Begnadigung f; ~? (fam) bitte? **I beg your ~** wie bitte? (sorry) Verzeihung! □ vt verzeihen; (Jur) begnadigen

pare /peə(r)/ vt (peel) schälen

parent /'peərənt/ n Elternteil m; ~s pl Eltern pl. ~al /pə'rentl/ a elterlich

parenthesis /pə'renθəsɪs/ n (pl -ses /-siːz/) Klammer f

parish /'pærɪʃ/ n Gemeinde f. ~ioner /pə'rɪʃənə(r)/ n Gemeindemitglied nt

parity /'pærətɪ/ n Gleichheit f

park /pɑːk/ n Park m □ vt/i parken

parking /'pɑːkɪŋ/ n Parken nt; **'no ~'** 'Parken verboten'. ~lot n (Amer) Parkplatz m. ~meter n Parkuhr f. ~ space n Parkplatz m

parliament /'pɑːləmənt/ n Parlament nt. ~ary /-'mentərɪ/ a parlamentarisch

parlour /'pɑːlə(r)/ n Wohnzimmer nt

parochial /pə'rəʊkɪəl/ a Gemeinde-; (fig) beschränkt

parody /'pærədɪ/ n Parodie f □ vt (pt/pp -ied) parodieren

parole /pə'rəʊl/ n on ~ auf Bewährung

paroxysm /'pærəksɪzm/ n Anfall m

parquet /'pɑːkeɪ/ n ~ **floor** Parkett nt

parrot /'pærət/ n Papagei m

parry /'pærɪ/ vt (pt/pp -ied) abwehren (blow); (Fencing) parieren

parsimonious /pɑːsɪ'məʊnɪəs/ a geizig

parsley /'pɑːslɪ/ n Petersilie f

parsnip /'pɑːsnɪp/ n Pastinake f

parson /'pɑːsn/ n Pfarrer m

part /pɑːt/ n Teil m, nt; (Techn) Teil nt; (area) Gegend f; (Theat) Rolle f; (Mus) Part m; **spare** ~ Ersatzteil nt; **for my** ~ meinerseits; **on the** ~ **of** vonseiten (+ gen); **take s.o.'s** ~ für jdn Partei ergreifen; **take** ~ **in** teilnehmen an (+ dat) □ adv teils □ vt trennen; scheiteln (hair); □ vi (people:) sich trennen; ~ **with** sich trennen von

partake /pɑː'teɪk/ vt (pt -took, pp -taken) teilnehmen; ~ **of** (eat) zu sich nehmen

part-ex'change n take in ~ in Zahlung nehmen

partial /'pɑːʃl/ a Teil-; **be** ~ **to** mögen. ~**ity** /pɑːʃɪ'ælɪtɪ/ n Voreingenommenheit f; (liking) Vorliebe f. ~**ly** adv teilweise

participant /pɑː'tɪsɪpənt/ n Teilnehmer(in) m(f). ~**ate** /-peɪt/ vi teilnehmen (**in** an + dat). ~**ation** /-'peɪʃn/ n Teilnahme f

participle /'pɑːtɪsɪpl/ n Partizip nt; **present/past** ~ erstes/zweites Partizip nt

particle /'pɑːtɪkl/ n Körnchen nt; (Phys) Partikel m; (Gram) Partikel f

particular /pə'tɪkjʊlə(r)/ a besondere(r,s); (precise) genau; (fastidious) penibel; **in** ~ besonders. ~**ly** adv besonders. ~**s** npl nähere Angaben pl

parting /'pɑːtɪŋ/ n Abschied m; (in hair) Scheitel m □ attrib Abschieds-

partition /pɑː'tɪʃn/ n Trennwand f; (Pol) Teilung f □ vt teilen. ~ **off** vt abtrennen

partly /'pɑːtlɪ/ adv teilweise

partner /'pɑːtnə(r)/ n Partner(in) m(f); (Comm) Teilhaber m. ~**ship** n Partnerschaft f; (Comm) Teilhaberschaft f

partridge /'pɑːtrɪdʒ/ n Rebhuhn nt

part-'time a & adv Teilzeit-; **be** or **work** ~ Teilzeitarbeit machen

party /'pɑːtɪ/ n Party f, Fest nt; (group) Gruppe f; (Pol, Jur) Partei f; **be** ~ **to** sich beteiligen an (+ dat)

'party line[1] n (Teleph) Gemeinschaftsanschluss m

'party line[2] n (Pol) Parteilinie f

pass /pɑːs/ n Ausweis m; (Geog, Sport) Pass m; (Sch) ~ ausreichend; **get a** ~ bestehen □ vt vorbeigehen/-fahren an (+ dat); (overtake) überholen; (hand) reichen; (Sport) abgeben, abspielen; (approve) annehmen; (exceed) übersteigen; bestehen (exam); machen (remark); fällen (judgement); (Jur) verhängen (sentence); ~ **water** Wasser lassen; ~ **the time** sich (dat) die Zeit vertreiben; ~ **sth off as sth** etw als etw ausgeben; ~ **one's hand over sth** mit der Hand über etw (acc) fahren □ vi vorbeigehen/-fahren; (get by) vorbeikommen; (overtake) überholen; (time:) vergehen; (in exam) bestehen; **let sth** ~ (fig) etw übergehen; [**I**] ~! [ich] passe! ~ **away** vi sterben. ~ **down** vt herunterreichen; (fig) weitergeben. ~ **out** vi ohnmächtig werden. ~ **round** vt herumreichen. ~ **up** vt heraufreichen; (fam: miss) vorübergehen lassen

passable /'pɑːsəbl/ a (road) befahrbar; (satisfactory) passabel

passage /'pæsɪdʒ/ n Durchgang m; (corridor) Gang m; (voyage) Überfahrt f; (in book) Passage f

passenger /'pæsɪndʒə(r)/ n Fahrgast m, (Naut, Aviat) Passagier m; (in car) Mitfahrer m. ~ **seat** n Beifahrersitz m

passer-by /pɑːsə'baɪ/ n (pl **-s-by**) Passant(in) m(f)

'passing place n Ausweichstelle f

passion /'pæʃn/ n Leidenschaft f. ~**ate** /-ət/ a, **-ly** adv leidenschaftlich

passive /'pæsɪv/ a passiv □ n Passiv nt

Passover /'pɑːsəʊvə(r)/ n Passah nt

pass: ~**port** n (Reise)pass m. ~**word** n Kennwort nt; (Mil) Losung f

past /pɑːst/ a vergangene(r,s); (former) ehemalig; **in the** ~ **few days** in den letzten paar Tagen; **that's all** ~ das ist jetzt vorbei □ n Vergangenheit f □ prep an (+ dat)... vorbei; (after)nach; **at** ~ **two** um zehn nach zwei □ adv vorbei; **go/come** ~ vorbeigehen/-kommen

pasta /'pæstə/ n Nudeln pl

paste /peɪst/ n Brei m; (dough) Teig m; (fish-, meat-) Paste f; (adhesive) Kleister m; (jewellery) Strass m □ vt kleistern

pastel /'pæstl/ n Pastellfarbe f; (crayon) Pastellstift m; (drawing) Pastell nt □ attrib Pastell-

pasteurize /'pɑːstʃəraɪz/ vt pasteurisieren

pastille /'pæstɪl/ n Pastille f

pastime /'pɑːstaɪm/ n Zeitvertreib m

pastoral /'pɑːstərl/ a ländlich; (care) seelsorgerisch

pastry /'peɪstrɪ/ n Teig m; **cakes and** ~**ies** Kuchen und Gebäck

pasture /'pɑːstʃə(r)/ n Weide f

pasty[1] /'pæstɪ/ n Pastete f

pasty[2] /'peɪstɪ/ a blass, (fam) käsig

pat /pæt/ n Klaps m; (of butter) Stückchen nt □ adv **have sth off** ~ etw aus dem Effeff können □ vt (pt/pp patted) tätscheln; ~ **s.o. on the back** jdm auf die Schulter klopfen

patch /pætʃ/ n Flicken m; (spot) Fleck m; **not a** ~ **on** (fam) gar nicht zu vergleichen mit □ vt flicken. ~ **up** vt [zusammen]-flicken; beilegen (quarrel)

patchy /'pætʃɪ/ a ungleichmäßig

pâté /'pæteɪ/ n Pastete f

patent /'peɪtnt/ a, **-ly** adv offensichtlich □ n Patent nt □ vt patentieren. ~ **leather** n Lackleder nt

patern|al /pə'tɜːnl/ a väterlich. ~**ity** n Vaterschaft f

path /pɑːθ/ n (pl ~**s** /pɑːðz/) [Fuß]weg m, Pfad m; (orbit, track) Bahn f; (fig) Weg m

pathetic /pə'θetɪk/ a mitleidernd; (attempt) erbärmlich

patholog|ical /pæθə'lɒdʒɪkl/ a pathologisch. ~**ist** /pə'θɒlə-dʒɪst/ n Pathologe m

pathos /'peɪθɒs/ n Rührseligkeit f

patience /'peɪʃns/ n Geduld f; (game) Patience f

patient /'peɪʃnt/ a, **-ly** adv geduldig □ n Patient(in) m(f)

patio /'pætɪəʊ/ n Terrasse f

patriot /'pætrɪət/ n Patriot(in) m(f). ~**ic** /-'ɒtɪk/ a patriotisch. ~**ism** n Patriotismus m

Patrol /pə'trəʊl/ n Patrouille f □ vt/i patrouillieren [in (+ dat)]; (police:) auf Streife gehen/fahren [in (+ dat)]. ~ **car** n Streifenwagen m

patron /'peɪtrən/ n Gönner m; (of charity) Schirmherr m; (of the arts) Mäzen m; (customer) Kunde m/Kundin f; (Theat) Besucher m. ~**age** /'pætrənɪdʒ/ n Schirmherrschaft f

patroniz|e /'pætrənaiz/ *vt* (fig) herablassend behandeln. **~ing** *a*, **-ly** *adv* gönnerhaft

patter¹ /'pætə(r)/ *n* Getrippel *nt*; (of rain) Plätschern *nt* □ *vi* trippeln; plätschern

patter² *n* (speech) Gerede *nt*

pattern /'pætn/ *n* Muster *nt*

paunch /pɔ:ntʃ/ *n* [Schmer]bauch *m*

pauper /'pɔ:pə(r)/ *n* Arme(r) *m/f*

pause /pɔ:z/ *n* Pause *f* □ *vi* innehalten

pave /peiv/ *vt* pflastern; **~ the way** den Weg bereiten (for dat). **~ment** *n* Bürgersteig *m*

pavilion /pə'viljən/ *n* Pavillon *m*; (Sport) Klubhaus *nt*

paw /pɔ:/ *n* Pfote *f*; (of large animal) Pranke *f*, Tatze *f*

pawn¹ /pɔ:n/ *n* (Chess) Bauer *m*; (fig) Schachfigur *f*

pawn² *vt* verpfänden □ *n* **in ~** verpfändet. **~ broker** *n* Pfandleiher *m*. **~shop** *n* Pfandhaus *nt*

pay /pei/ *n* Lohn *m*; (salary) Gehalt *nt*; **be in the ~ of** bezahlt werden von □ *v* (pt/pp **paid**) □ *vt* bezahlen; zahlen (money); **~ s.o. a visit** jdm einen Besuch abstatten; **~ s.o. a compliment** jdm ein Kompliment machen □ *vi* zahlen; (be profitable) sich bezahlt machen; (fig) sich lohnen; **~ for sth** etw bezahlen. **~ back** *vt* zurückzahlen. **~ in** *vt* einzahlen. **~ off** *vt* abzahlen (debt) □ *vi* (fig) sich auszahlen. **~ up** *vi* zahlen

payable /'peiəbl/ *a* zahlbar; **make ~ to** ausstellen auf (+ acc)

payee /pei'i:/ *n* [Zahlungs]empfänger *m*

payment /'peimənt/ *n* Bezahlung *f*; (amount) Zahlung *f*

pay: ~ packet *n* Lohntüte *f*. **~ phone** *n* Münzfernsprecher *m*

pea /pi:/ *n* Erbse *f*

peace /pi:s/ *n* Frieden *m*; **for my ~ of mind** zu meiner eigenen Beruhigung

peace|able /'pi:səbl/ *a* friedlich. **~ful** *a*, **-ly** *adv* friedlich. **~maker** *n* Friedensstifter *m*

peach /pi:tʃ/ *n* Pfirsich *m*

peacock /'pi:kɒk/ *n* Pfau *m*

peak /pi:k/ *n* Gipfel *m*; (fig) Höhepunkt *m*. **~ed 'cap** *n* Schirmmütze *f*. **~ hours** *npl* Hauptbelastungszeit *f*; (for traffic) Hauptverkehrszeit *f*

peaky /'pi:ki/ *a* kränklich

peal /pi:l/ *n* (of bells) Glockengeläut *nt*; **~s of laughter** schallendes Gelächter *nt*

'peanut *n* Erdnuss *f*; **for ~s** (fam) für einen Apfel und ein Ei

pear /peə(r)/ *n* Birne *f*

pearl /pɜ:l/ *n* Perle *f*

peasant /'peznt/ *n* Bauer *m*

peat /pi:t/ *n* Torf *m*

pebble /'pebl/ *n* Kieselstein *m*

peck /pek/ *n* Schnabelhieb *m*; (kiss) flüchtiger Kuss *m* □ *vt/i* picken/(nip) hacken (at nach). **~ing order** *n* Hackordnung *f*

peckish /'pekiʃ/ *a* **be ~** (fam) Hunger haben

peculiar /pi'kju:liə(r)/ *a* eigenartig, seltsam; **~ to** eigentümlich (+ dat). **~ity** /-'æriəti/ *n* Eigenart *f*

pedal /'pedl/ *n* Pedal *nt* □ *vt* fahren (bicycle) □ *vi* treten. **~ bin** *n* Treteimer *m*

pedantic /pi'dæntik/ *a*, **-ally** *adv* pedantisch

peddle /'pedl/ *vt* handeln mit

pedestal /'pedistl/ *n* Sockel *m*

pedestrian /pi'destriən/ *n* Fußgänger(in) *m(f)* □ *a* (fig) prosaisch. **~ 'crossing** *n* Fußgängerüberweg *m*. **~ 'precinct** *n* Fußgängerzone *f*

pedicure /'pedikjuə(r)/ *n* Pediküre *f*

pedigree /'pedigri:/ *n* Stammbaum *m* □ *attrib* (animal) Rasse-

pedlar /'pedlə(r)/ *n* Hausierer *m*

pee /piː/ *vi* (*pt/pp* **peed**) (*fam*) pinkeln

peek /piːk/ *vi* (*fam*) gucken

peel /piːl/ *n* Schale *f* □ *vt* schälen; □ *vi* (*skin:*) sich schälen; (*paint:*) abblättern. **~ings** *npl* Schalen *pl*

peep /piːp/ *n* kurzer Blick *m* □ *vi* gucken. **~-hole** *n* Guckloch *nt*. **P~ing Tom** *n* (*fam*) Spanner *m*

peer[1] /pɪə(r)/ *vi* ~ **at** forschend ansehen

peer[2] *n* Peer *m*; **his** ~s *pl* seinesgleichen

peeve|d /piːvd/ *a* (*fam*) ärgerlich. **~ish** *a* reizbar

peg /peg/ *n* (*hook*) Haken *m*; (*for tent*) Pflock *m*, Hering *m*; (*for clothes*) [Wäsche]klammer *f*; **off the** ~ (*fam*) von der Stange □ *vt* (*pt/pp* **pegged**) anpflocken; anklammern (*washing*)

pejorative /pɪˈdʒɒrətɪv/ *a*, **-ly** *adv* abwertend

pelican /ˈpelɪkən/ *n* Pelikan *m*

pellet /ˈpelɪt/ *n* Kügelchen *nt*

pelt[1] /pelt/ *n* (*skin*) Pelz *m*, Fell *nt*

pelt[2] *vt* bewerfen □ *vi* (*fam: run fast*) rasen; ~ [**down**] (*rain:*) [hernieder]prasseln

pelvis /ˈpelvɪs/ *n* (*Anat*) Becken *nt*

pen[1] /pen/ *n* (*for animals*) Hürde *f*

pen[2] *n* Federhalter *m*; (*ball-point*) Kugelschreiber *m*

penal /ˈpiːnl/ *a* Straf-. **~ize** *vt* bestrafen; (*fig*) benachteiligen

penalty /ˈpenltɪ/ *n* Strafe *f*; (*fine*) Geldstrafe *f*; (*Sport*) Strafstoß *m*; (*Football*) Elfmeter *m*

penance /ˈpenəns/ *n* Buße *f*

pence /pens/ *see* **penny**

pencil /ˈpensl/ *n* Bleistift *m* □ *vt* (*pt/pp* **pencilled**) mit Bleistift schreiben. **~-sharpener** *n* Bleistiftspitzer *m*

pendant /ˈpendənt/ *n* Anhänger *m*

pending /ˈpendɪŋ/ *a* unerledigt □ *prep* bis zu

pendulum /ˈpendjʊləm/ *n* Pendel *nt*

penetrat|e /ˈpenɪtreɪt/ *vt* durchdringen; **~e [into]** eindringen in (+ *acc*). **~ing** *a* durchdringend. **~ion** /-ˈtreɪʃn/ *n* Durchdringung *f*

'penfriend *n* Brieffreund(in) *m*(*f*)

penguin /ˈpeŋgwɪn/ *n* Pinguin *m*

penicillin /penɪˈsɪlɪn/ *n* Penizillin *nt*

peninsula /pəˈnɪnsʊlə/ *n* Halbinsel *f*

penis /ˈpiːnɪs/ *n* Penis *m*

peniten|ce /ˈpenɪtəns/ *n* Reue *f*. **~t** *a* reuig □ *n* Büßer *m*

penitentiary /penɪˈtenʃərɪ/ *n* (*Amer*) Gefängnis *nt*

pen|knife *n* Taschenmesser *nt*. **~-name** *n* Pseudonym *nt*

pennant /ˈpenənt/ *n* Wimpel *m*

penniless /ˈpenɪlɪs/ *a* mittellos

penny /ˈpenɪ/ *n* (*pl* **pence**; *single coins* **pennies**) Penny *m*; (*Amer*) Centstück *nt*; **spend a** ~ (*fam*) mal verschwinden; **the ~'s dropped** (*fam*) der Groschen ist gefallen

pension /ˈpenʃn/ *n* Rente *f*; (*of civil servant*) Pension *f*. **~er** *n* Rentner(in) *m*(*f*); Pensionär(in) *m*(*f*)

pensive /ˈpensɪv/ *a* nachdenklich

Pentecost /ˈpentɪkɒst/ *n* Pfingsten *nt*

pent-up /ˈpentʌp/ *a* angestaut

penultimate /peˈnʌltɪmət/ *a* vorletzte(r,s)

penury /ˈpenjʊrɪ/ *n* Armut *f*

peony /ˈpiːənɪ/ *n* Pfingstrose *f*

people /ˈpiːpl/ *npl* Leute *pl*, Menschen *pl*; (*citizens*) Bevölkerung *f*; **the ~** das Volk; **English ~** die Engländer; ~ **say** man sagt; **for four ~** für vier Personen □ *vt* bevölkern

pep /pep/ *n* (*fam*) Schwung *m*

pepper /ˈpepə(r)/ *n* Pfeffer *m*; (*vegetable*) Paprika *m* □ *vt* (*Culin*) pfeffern

pepper: ~**corn** n Pfefferkorn nt. ~**mint** n Pfefferminz nt; (Bot) Pfefferminze f. ~**pot** n Pfefferstreuer m

per /pɜː(r)/ prep pro; ~**cent** Prozent nt

perceive /pə'siːv/ vt wahrnehmen

percentage /pə'sentɪdʒ/ n Prozentsatz m; (part) Teil m

perceptible /pə'septəbl/ a wahrnehmbar

percept|ion /pə'sepʃn/ n Wahrnehmung f. ~**ive** /-tɪv/ a feinsinnig

perch[1] /pɜːtʃ/ n Stange f □ vi ⟨bird:⟩ sich niederlassen

perch[2] n inv ⟨fish⟩ Barsch m

percolat|e /'pɜːkəleɪt/ vi durchsickern. ~**or** n Kaffeemaschine f

percussion /pə'kʌʃn/ n Schlagzeug nt. ~ **instrument** n Schlaginstrument nt

peremptory /pə'remptərɪ/ a herrisch

perennial /pə'renɪəl/ a ⟨problem⟩ immer wiederkehrend □ n ⟨plant⟩ mehrjährige Pflanze f

perfect[1] /'pɜːfɪkt/ a perfekt, vollkommen; (fam: utter) völlig □ n (Gram) Perfekt nt

perfect[2] /pə'fekt/ vt vollkommen. ~**ion** /-ekʃn/ n Vollkommenheit f; **to** ~**ion** perfekt

perfectly /'pɜːfɪktlɪ/ adv perfekt; (completely) vollkommen, völlig

perforate /'pɜːfəreɪt/ vt perforieren; (make a hole in) durchlöchern. ~**d** a perforiert

perform /pə'fɔːm/ vt ausführen; erfüllen ⟨duty⟩; (Theat) aufführen ⟨play⟩; spielen ⟨role⟩ □ vi ⟨Theat⟩ auftreten; (Techn) laufen. ~**ance** n Durchführung f; (at theatre, cinema) Vorstellung f; (Techn) Leistung f. ~**er** n Künstler(in) m(f)

perfume /'pɜːfjuːm/ n Parfüm nt; (smell) Duft m

perfunctory /pə'fʌŋktərɪ/ a flüchtig

perhaps /pə'hæps/ adv vielleicht

peril /'perəl/ n Gefahr f. ~**ous** /-əs/ a gefährlich

perimeter /pə'rɪmɪtə(r)/ n [äußere] Grenze f; (Geom) Umfang m

period /'pɪərɪəd/ n Periode f; (Sch) Stunde f; (full stop) Punkt m □ attrib ⟨costume⟩ zeitgenössisch; ⟨furniture⟩ antik. ~**ic** /-'ɒdɪk/ a, ~**ally** adv periodisch. ~**ical** /-'ɒdɪkl/ n Zeitschrift f

peripher|al /pə'rɪfərl/ a nebensächlich. ~**y** n Peripherie f

periscope /'perɪskəʊp/ n Periskop nt

perish /'perɪʃ/ vi ⟨rubber:⟩ verrotten; ⟨food:⟩ verderben; (die) ums Leben kommen. ~**able** /-əbl/ a leicht verderblich. ~**ing** a (fam: cold) eiskalt

perjur|e /'pɜːdʒə(r)/ vt ~**e** oneself einen Meineid leisten. ~**y** n Meineid m

perk[1] /pɜːk/ n (fam) [Sonder]vergünstigung f

perk[2] vi ~ **up** munter werden

perky /'pɜːkɪ/ a munter

perm /pɜːm/ n Dauerwelle f □ vt ~ **s.o.'s** **hair** jdm eine Dauerwelle machen

permanent /'pɜːmənənt/ a ständig; ⟨job, address⟩ fest. ~**ly** adv ständig; ⟨work, live⟩ dauernd, permanent; ⟨employed⟩ fest

permeable /'pɜːmɪəbl/ a durchlässig

permeate /'pɜːmɪeɪt/ vt durchdringen

permissible /pə'mɪsəbl/ a erlaubt

permission /pə'mɪʃn/ n Erlaubnis f

permissive /pə'mɪsɪv/ a ⟨society⟩ permissiv

permit[1] /pə'mɪt/ vt (pt/pp -mitted) erlauben (s.o. jdm); ~ me! gestatten Sie!

permit[2] /'pɜːmɪt/ n Genehmigung f

pernicious /pəˈnɪʃəs/ a schädlich; (Med) perniziös

perpendicular /pɜːpənˈdɪkjʊlə(r)/ a senkrecht □n Senkrechte f

perpetrat|e /ˈpɜːpɪtreɪt/ vt begehen. **~or** n Täter m

perpetual /pəˈpetjʊəl/ a, **-ly** adv ständig, dauernd

perpetuate /pəˈpetjʊeɪt/ vt bewahren; verewigen (error)

perplex /pəˈpleks/ vt verblüffen. **~ed** a verblüfft. **~ity** n Verblüffung f

persecut|e /ˈpɜːsɪkjuːt/ vt verfolgen. **~ion** /-ˈkjuːʃn/ n Verfolgung f

perseverance /pɜːsɪˈvɪərəns/ n Ausdauer f

persever|e /pɜːsɪˈvɪə(r)/ vi beharrlich weitermachen. **~ing** a ausdauernd

Persia /ˈpɜːʃə/ n Persien nt

Persian /ˈpɜːʃn/ a persisch; (cat, carpet) Perser-

persist /pəˈsɪst/ vi beharrlich weitermachen; (continue) anhalten; (view:) weiter bestehen; **~ in doing sth** dabei bleiben, etw zu tun. **~ence** n Beharrlichkeit f. **~ent** a, **-ly** adv beharrlich; (continuous) anhaltend

person /ˈpɜːsn/ n Person f; **in ~** persönlich

personal /ˈpɜːsənl/ a, **-ly** adv persönlich. **~ 'hygiene** n Körperpflege f

personality /pɜːsəˈnælətɪ/ n Persönlichkeit f

personify /pəˈsɒnɪfaɪ/ vt (pt/pp -ied) personifizieren, verkörpern

personnel /pɜːsəˈnel/ n Personal nt

perspective /pəˈspektɪv/ n Perspektive f

perspicacious /pɜːspɪˈkeɪʃəs/ a scharfsichtig

perspir|ation /pɜːspɪˈreɪʃn/ n Schweiß m. **~e** /-ˈspaɪə(r)/ vi schwitzen

persua|de /pəˈsweɪd/ vt überreden; (convince) überzeugen. **~sion** /-eɪʒn/ n Überredung f; (powers of ~sion) Überredungskunst f; (belief) Glaubensrichtung f

persuasive /pəˈsweɪsɪv/ a, **-ly** adv beredsam; (convincing) überzeugend

pert /pɜːt/ a, **-ly** adv kess

pertain /pəˈteɪn/ vi **~ to** betreffen; (belong) gehören zu

pertinent /ˈpɜːtɪnənt/ a relevant (to für)

perturb /pəˈtɜːb/ vt beunruhigen

peruse /pəˈruːz/ vt lesen

pervade /pəˈveɪd/ vt durchdringen. **~sive** /-sɪv/ a durchdringend

pervers|e /pəˈvɜːs/ a eigensinnig. **~ion** /-ʒn/ n Perversion f

pervert[1] /pəˈvɜːt/ vt verdrehen; verführen (person)

pervert[2] /ˈpɜːvɜːt/ n Perverse(r) m

perverted /pəˈvɜːtɪd/ a abartig

pessimis|m /ˈpesɪmɪzm/ n Pessimismus m. **~t** /-mɪst/ n Pessimist m. **~tic** /-ˈmɪstɪk/ a, **-ally** adv pessimistisch

pest /pest/ n Schädling m; (fam: person) Nervensäge f

pester /ˈpestə(r)/ vt belästigen; **~ s.o. for sth** jdm wegen etw in den Ohren liegen

pesticide /ˈpestɪsaɪd/ n Schädlingsbekämpfungsmittel nt

pet /pet/ n Haustier nt; (favourite) Liebling m □ vt (pt/pp petted) liebkosen

petal /ˈpetl/ n Blütenblatt nt

peter /ˈpiːtə(r)/ vi **~ out** allmählich aufhören; (stream:) versickern

petite /pəˈtiːt/ a klein und zierlich

petition /pəˈtɪʃn/ n Bittschrift f □ vt eine Bittschrift richten an (+ acc)

pet 'name n Kosename m

petrif|y /ˈpetrɪfaɪ/ *vt/i* (*pt/pp* **-ied**) versteinern; **~ied** (*frightened*) vor Angst wie versteinert

petrol /ˈpetrl/ *n* Benzin *nt*

petroleum /pɪˈtrəʊlɪəm/ *n* Petroleum *nt*

petrol: ~pump *n* Zapfsäule *f*. **~ station** *n* Tankstelle *f*. **~ tank** *n* Benzintank *m*

'pet shop *n* Tierhandlung *f*

petticoat /ˈpetɪkəʊt/ *n* Unterrock *m*

petty /ˈpetɪ/ *a* (**-ier, -iest**) kleinlich. **~'cash** *n* Portokasse *f*

petulant /ˈpetjʊlənt/ *a* gekränkt

pew /pjuː/ *n* [Kirchen]bank *f*

pewter /ˈpjuːtə(r)/ *n* Zinn *nt*

phantom /ˈfæntəm/ *n* Gespenst *nt*

pharmaceutical /fɑːməˈsjuːtɪkl/ *a* pharmazeutisch

pharmac|ist /ˈfɑːməsɪst/ *n* Apotheker(in) *m(f)*. **~y** *n* Pharmazie *f*; (*shop*) Apotheke *f*

phase /feɪz/ *n* Phase *f* □ *vt* **~ in/ out** allmählich einführen/abbauen

Ph.D. (*abbr of* **Doctor of Philosophy**) Dr. phil.

pheasant /ˈfeznt/ *n* Fasan *m*

phenomen|al /fɪˈnɒmɪnl/ *a* phänomenal. **~on** *n* (*pl* **-na**) Phänomen *nt*

phial /ˈfaɪəl/ *n* Fläschchen *nt*

philanderer /fɪˈlændərə(r)/ *n* Verführer *m*

philanthrop|ic /fɪlənˈθrɒpɪk/ *a* menschenfreundlich. **~ist** /fɪˈlænθrəpɪst/ *n* Philanthrop *m*

philately /fɪˈlætlɪ/ *n* Philatelie *f*, Briefmarkenkunde *f*

philharmonic /fɪlɑːˈmɒnɪk/ *n* (*orchestra*) Philharmoniker *pl*

Philippines /ˈfɪlɪpiːnz/ *npl* Philippinen *pl*

philistine /ˈfɪlɪstaɪn/ *n* Banause *m*

philosoph|er /fɪˈlɒsəfə(r)/ *n* Philosoph *m*. **~ical** /fɪləˈsɒfɪkl/ *a*, **-ly**

adv philosophisch. **~y** *n* Philosophie *f*

phlegm /flem/ *n* (*Med*) Schleim *m*

phlegmatic /flegˈmætɪk/ *a* phlegmatisch

phobia /ˈfəʊbɪə/ *n* Phobie *f*

phone /fəʊn/ *n* Telefon *nt*; **be on the ~** Telefon haben; (*be phoning*) telefonieren □ *vt* anrufen □ *vi* telefonieren. **~ back** *vt/i* zurückrufen. **~ book** *n* Telefonbuch *nt*. **~ box** *n* Telefonzelle *f*. **~ card** *n* Telefonkarte *f*. **~-in** *n* (*Radio*) Hörersendung *f*. **~ number** *n* Telefonnummer *f*

phonetic /fəˈnetɪk/ *a* phonetisch. **~s** *n* Phonetik *f*

phoney /ˈfəʊnɪ/ *a* (**-ier, -iest**) falsch; (*forged*) gefälscht

phosphorus /ˈfɒsfərəs/ *n* Phosphor *m*

photo /ˈfəʊtəʊ/ *n* Foto *nt*, Aufnahme *f*. **~copier** *n* Fotokopiergerät *nt*. **~copy** *n* Fotokopie *f* □ *vt* fotokopieren

photogenic /fəʊtəʊˈdʒenɪk/ *a* fotogen

photograph /ˈfəʊtəɡrɑːf/ *n* Fotografie *f*, Aufnahme *f* □ *vt* fotografieren

photograph|er /fəˈtɒɡrəfə(r)/ *n* Fotograf(in) *m(f)*. **~ic** /fəʊtəˈɡræfɪk/ *a*, **-ally** *adv* fotografisch. **~y** *n* Fotografie *f*

phrase /freɪz/ *n* Redensart *f* □ *vt* formulieren. **~book** *n* Sprachführer *m*

physical /ˈfɪzɪkl/ *a*, **-ly** *adv* körperlich; (*geography, law*) physikalisch. **~ edu'cation** *n* Turnen *nt*

physician /fɪˈzɪʃn/ *n* Arzt *m*/Ärztin *f*

physic|ist /ˈfɪzɪsɪst/ *n* Physiker(in) *m(f)*. **~s** *n* Physik *f*

physiology /fɪzɪˈɒlədʒɪ/ *n* Physiologie *f*

physio'therap|ist /fɪzɪəʊ-/ *n* Physiotherapeut(in) *m(f)*. **~y** *n* Physiotherapie *f*

physique /fɪ'ziːk/ n Körperbau m
pianist /'pɪənɪst/ n Klavierspie-
ler(in) m(f); (professional) Pia-
nist(in) m(f)
piano /pɪ'ænəʊ/ n Klavier nt
pick¹ /pɪk/ n Spitzhacke f
pick² n Auslese f; take one's ~
sich (dat) aussuchen □ vt/i
(pluck) pflücken; (select) wählen,
sich (dat) aussuchen; ~ and
choose wählerisch sein; ~ one's
nose in der Nase bohren; ~ a
quarrel einen Streit anfangen; ~
a hole in sth ein Loch in etw (acc)
machen; ~ holes in (fam) kritisieren; ~ at one's food im Essen
herumstochern. ~ on vt wählen;
(fam: find fault with) herum-
hacken auf (+ dat). ~ up vt in
die Hand nehmen; (off the
ground) aufheben; hochnehmen
(baby); (learn) lernen; (acquire)
erwerben; (buy) kaufen; (Teleph)
abnehmen (receiver); auffangen
(signal); (collect) abholen; aufnehmen (passengers); (police:) auf-
greifen (criminal); sich holen
(illness); (fam) aufgabeln (girl); ~
oneself up aufstehen □ vi (improve) sich bessern
¹pickaxe n Spitzhacke f
picket /'pɪkɪt/ n Streikposten m
□ vt Streikposten aufstellen vor
(+ dat). ~ line n Streikposten-
kette f
pickle /'pɪkl/ n (Amer: gherkin)
Essiggurke f; ~s pl [Mixed] Pick-
les pl □ vt einlegen
pick: ~pocket n Taschendieb m.
~-up n (truck) Lieferwagen m;
(on record-player) Tonabnehmer
m
picnic /'pɪknɪk/ n Picknick nt □ vi
(pt/pp -nicked) picknicken
pictorial /pɪk'tɔːrɪəl/ a bildlich
picture /'pɪktʃə(r)/ n Bild nt;
(film) Film m; as pretty as a ~
bildhübsch; put s.o. in the ~
(fig) jdn ins Bild setzen □ vt (imagine) sich (dat) vorstellen

picturesque /pɪktʃə'resk/ a malerisch
pie /paɪ/ n Pastete f; (fruit)
Kuchen m
piece /piːs/ n Stück nt; (of set) Teil
nt; (in game) Stein m; (Journ) Artikel m; a ~ of bread/paper ein
Stück Brot/Papier; a ~ of news/
advice eine Nachricht/ein Rat;
take to ~s auseinander nehmen
□ vt ~ together zusammen-
setzen; (fig) zusammenstückeln.
~meal adv stückweise. ~work
n Akkordarbeit f
pier /pɪə(r)/ n Pier m; (pillar)
Pfeiler m
pierc|e /pɪəs/ vt durchstechen;
~e a hole in sth ein Loch in etw
(acc) stechen. ~ing a durchdringend
piety /'paɪətɪ/ n Frömmigkeit f
piffle /'pɪfl/ n (fam) Quatsch m
pig /pɪg/ n Schwein m
pigeon /'pɪdʒɪn/ n Taube f. ~-
hole n Fach nt
piggy /'pɪgɪ/ n (fam)
Schweinchen nt. ~back n give
s.o. a ~back jdn huckepack
tragen. ~ bank n Sparschwein
nt
pig|headed a (fam) starrköpfig.
~ment /'pɪgmənt/ n Pigment nt.
~ation /-men'teɪʃn/ n Pigmen-
tierung f
pig: ~skin n Schweinsleder nt.
~sty n Schweinestall m. ~tail n
(fam) Zopf m
pike /paɪk/ n inv (fish) Hecht m
pilchard /'pɪltʃəd/ n Sardine f
pile¹ /paɪl/ n (of fabric) Flor m
pile² n Haufen m □ vt ~ sth on to
sth etw auf etw (acc) häufen. ~
up vt häufen □ vi sich häufen
piles /paɪlz/ npl Hämorrhoiden pl
pile-up n Massenkarambolage f
pilfer /'pɪlfə(r)/ vt stehlen
pilgrim /'pɪlgrɪm/ n Pilger(in)
m(f). ~age /-ɪdʒ/ n Pilgerfahrt f,
Wallfahrt f
pill /pɪl/ n Pille f

pillage /'pɪlɪdʒ/ vt plündern

pillar /'pɪlə(r)/ n Säule f. **~box** n Briefkasten m

pillion /'pɪljən/ n Sozius[sitz] m

pillory /'pɪlərɪ/ n Pranger m □ vt (pt/pp **-ied**) anprangern

pillow /'pɪləʊ/ n Kopfkissen nt. **~case** n Kopfkissenbezug m

pilot /'paɪlət/ n Pilot m; (Naut) Lotse m □ vt fliegen (plane); lotsen (ship). **~-light** n Zündflamme f

pimp /pɪmp/ n Zuhälter m

pimple /'pɪmpl/ n Pickel m

pin /pɪn/ n Stecknadel f; (Techn) Bolzen m, Stift m; (Med) Nagel m; **I have ~s and needles in my leg** (fam) mein Bein ist eingeschlafen □ vt (pt/pp **pinned**) anstecken (**to/on** an + acc); (sewing) stecken; (hold down) festhalten; **~ sth on s.o.** (fam) jdm etw anhängen. **~ up** vt hochstecken; (on wall) anheften, anschlagen

pinafore /'pɪnəfɔː(r)/ n Schürze f. **~ dress** n Kleiderrock m

pincers /'pɪnsəz/ npl Kneifzange f; (Zool) Scheren pl

pinch /pɪntʃ/ n Kniff m; (of salt) Prise f; **at a ~** (fam) zur Not □ vt kneifen, zwicken; (fam; steal) klauen; **~ one's finger** sich (dat) den Finger klemmen □ vi (shoe:) drücken

'pincushion n Nadelkissen nt

pine¹ /paɪn/ n (tree) Kiefer f

pine² vi **~ for** sich sehnen nach; **~ away** sich verzehren

pineapple /'paɪn-/ n Ananas f

ping /pɪŋ/ n Klingeln nt

ping-pong n Tischtennis nt

pink /pɪŋk/ a rosa

pinnacle /'pɪnəkl/ n Gipfel m; (on roof) Turmspitze f

pin: **~point** vt genau festlegen. **~stripe** n Nadelstreifen m

pint /paɪnt/ n Pint nt (0,571, Amer: 0,47 l)

'pin-up n Pin-up-Girl nt

pioneer /paɪə'nɪə(r)/ n Pionier m □ vt bahnbrechende Arbeit leisten für

pious /'paɪəs/ a, **-ly** adv fromm

pip¹ /pɪp/ n (seed) Kern m

pip² n (sound) Tonsignal nt

pipe /paɪp/ n Pfeife f; (for water, gas) Rohr nt □ vt in Rohren leiten; (Culin) spritzen. **~ down** vi (fam) den Mund halten

pipe: **~dream** n Luftschloss nt. **~line** n Pipeline f; **in the ~line** (fam) in Vorbereitung

piper /'paɪpə(r)/ n Pfeifer m

piping /'paɪpɪŋ/ a **~ hot** kochend heiß

piquant /'piːkənt/ a pikant

pique /piːk/ n **in a fit of ~** beleidigt

pirate /'paɪərət/ n Pirat m

Pisces /'paɪsiːz/ n (Astr) Fische pl

piss /pɪs/ vi (sl) pissen

pistol /'pɪstl/ n Pistole f

piston /'pɪstən/ n (Techn) Kolben m

pit /pɪt/ n Grube f; (for orchestra) Orchestergraben m □ vt (pt/pp **pitted**) (fig) messen (**against** an + dat)

pitch¹ /pɪtʃ/ n (steepness) Schräge f; (of voice) Stimmlage f; (of sound) [Ton]höhe f; (Sport) Feld nt; (of street-trader) Standplatz m; (fig: degree) Grad m □ vt werfen; aufschlagen (tent) □ vi fallen

pitch² n (tar) Pech nt. **~'black** a pechschwarz. **~'dark** a stockdunkel

pitcher /'pɪtʃə(r)/ n Krug m

'pitchfork n Heugabel f

piteous /'pɪtɪəs/ a erbärmlich

pitfall n (fig) Falle f

pith /pɪθ/ n (Bot) Mark nt; (of orange) weiße Haut f; (fig) Wesentliche(s) nt

pithy /'pɪθɪ/ a (**-ier, -iest**) (fig) prägnant

piti|ful /'pɪtɪfʊl/ a bedauernswert. **~less** a mitleidslos

pittance /'pɪtns/ n Hungerlohn m

pity /'pɪtɪ/ n Mitleid nt, Erbarmen nt; **[what a] ~!** [wie] schade! **take ~ on** sich erbarmen über (+ acc) □ vt bemitleiden

pivot /'pɪvət/ n Drehzapfen m; (fig) Angelpunkt m □ vi sich drehen (**on** um)

pixie /'pɪksɪ/ n Kobold m

pizza /'pi:tsə/ n Pizza f

placard /'plækɑ:d/ n Plakat nt

placate /plə'keɪt/ vt beschwichtigen

place /pleɪs/ n Platz m; (spot) Stelle f; (town, village) Ort m; (fam: house) Haus nt; **out of ~** fehl am Platze; **take ~** stattfinden; **all over the ~** überall □ vt setzen; (upright) stellen; (flat) legen; (remember) unterbringen (fam); **~ an order** eine Bestellung aufgeben; **be ~d** (in race) sich platzieren. **~mat** n Set nt

placid /'plæsɪd/ a gelassen

plagiar|ism /'pleɪdʒərɪzm/ n Plagiat nt. **~ize** vt plagiieren

plague /pleɪg/ n Pest f □ vt plagen

plaice /pleɪs/ n inv Scholle f

plain /pleɪn/ a (-er, -est) klar; (simple) einfach; (not pretty) nicht hübsch; (not patterned) einfarbig; (chocolate) zartbitter; **in ~ clothes** in Zivil □ adv (simply) einfach □ n Ebene f; (Knitting) linke Masche f. **~ly** adv klar, deutlich; (simply) einfach; (obviously) offensichtlich

plaintiff /'pleɪntɪf/ n (Jur) Kläger(in) m(f)

plaintive /'pleɪntɪv/ a, **-ly** adv klagend

plait /plæt/ n Zopf m □ vt flechten

plan /plæn/ n Plan m □ vt (pt/pp planned) planen; (intend) vorhaben

plane¹ /pleɪn/ n (tree) Platane f

plane² n Flugzeug nt; (Geom & fig) Ebene f

plane³ n (Techn) Hobel m □ vt hobeln

planet /'plænɪt/ n Planet m

plank /plæŋk/ n Brett nt; (thick) Planke f

planning /'plænɪŋ/ n Planung f. **~ permission** n Baugenehmigung f

plant /plɑ:nt/ n Pflanze f; (Techn) Anlage f; (factory) Werk nt □ vt pflanzen; (place in position) setzen; **~ oneself in front of s.o.** sich vor jdn hinstellen. **~ation** /plæn'teɪʃn/ n Plantage f

plaque /plɑ:k/ n [Gedenk]tafel f; (on teeth) Zahnbelag m

plasma /'plæzmə/ n Plasma nt

plaster /'plɑ:stə(r)/ n Verputz m; (sticking ~) Pflaster nt; **~ [of Paris]** Gips m □ vt verputzen (wall); (cover) bedecken mit. **~ed** a (sl) besoffen. **~er** n Gipser m

plastic /'plæstɪk/ n Kunststoff m, Plastik nt □ a Kunststoff-, Plastik-; (malleable) formbar, plastisch

Plasticine (P) /'plæstɪsi:n/ n Knetmasse f

plastic 'surgery n plastische Chirurgie f

plate /pleɪt/ n Teller m; (flat sheet) Platte f; (with name, number) Schild nt; (gold and silverware) vergoldete/versilberte Ware f; (in book) Tafel f □ vt (with gold) vergolden; (with silver) versilbern

plateau /'plætəʊ/ n (pl ~x /-əʊz/) Hochebene f

platform /'plætfɔ:m/ n Plattform f; (stage) Podium nt; (Rail) Bahnsteig m; **~ 5** Gleis 5

platinum /'plætɪnəm/ n Platin nt

platitude /'plætɪtju:d/ n Platitüde f

platonic /plə'tɒnɪk/ a platonisch

platoon /plə'tu:n/ n (Mil) Zug m

platter /'plætə(r)/ n Platte f

plausible /'plɔ:zəbl/ a plausibel

play /pleɪ/ n Spiel nt; [Theater]stück nt; (Radio) Hörspiel nt; (TV) Fernsehspiel nt; **~ on**

words Wortspiel *nt* □*vt/i* spielen; **ausspielen** ⟨*card*⟩; ~ **safe** sichergehen. ~ **down** *vt* herunterspielen. ~ **up** *vi* (*fam*) Mätzchen machen

play: ~**boy** *n* Playboy *m*. ~**er** *n* Spieler(in) *m(f)*. ~**ful** *a*, **-ly** *adv* verspielt. ~**ground** *n* Spielplatz *m*; (*Sch*) Schulhof *m*. ~**group** *n* Kindergarten *m*

playing: ~**card** *n* Spielkarte *f*. ~**field** *n* Sportplatz *m*

play: ~**mate** *n* Spielkamerad *m*. ~**pen** *n* Laufstall *m*, Laufgitter *nt*. ~**thing** *n* Spielzeug *nt*. ~**wright** /-raɪt/ *n* Dramatiker *m*

plc *abbr* (**public limited company**) ≈ GmbH

plea /pliː/ *n* Bitte *f*; **make a** ~ **for** bitten um

plead /pliːd/ *vt* vorschützen; (*Jur*) vertreten ⟨*case*⟩ □ *vi* flehen (**for** um); ~ **guilty** sich schuldig bekennen; ~ **with s.o.** jdn anflehen

pleasant /'plezənt/ *a* angenehm; (*person*) nett. ~**ly** *adv* angenehm; (*say, smile*) freundlich

pleas|e /pliːz/ *adv* bitte □*vt* gefallen (+ *dat*); ~ **s.o.** jdm eine Freude machen; ~**e oneself** tun, was man will. ~**ed** *a* erfreut; **be** ~**ed with/about sth** sich über etw (*acc*) freuen. ~**ing** *a* erfreulich

pleasurable /'pleʒərəbl/ *a* angenehm

pleasure /'pleʒə(r)/ *n* Vergnügen *nt*; (*joy*) Freude *f*; **with** ~ gern[e]

pleat /pliːt/ *n* Falte *f* □*vt* fälteln. ~**ed 'skirt** *n* Faltenrock *m*

plebiscite /'plebɪsɪt/ *n* Volksabstimmung *f*

pledge /pledʒ/ *n* Pfand *nt*; (*promise*) Versprechen *nt* □*vt* verpfänden; versprechen

plentiful /'plentɪfl/ *a* reichlich; **be** ~ reichlich vorhanden sein

plenty /'plentɪ/ *n* eine Menge; (*enough*) reichlich; ~ **of money/people** viel Geld/viele Leute

pleurisy /'pluərəsɪ/ *n* Rippenfellentzündung *f*

pliable /'plaɪəbl/ *a* biegsam

pliers /'plaɪəz/ *npl* [Flach]zange *f*

plight /plaɪt/ *n* [Not]lage *f*

plimsolls /'plɪmsəlz/ *npl* Turnschuhe *pl*

plinth /plɪnθ/ *n* Sockel *m*

plod /plɒd/ *vi* (*pt/pp* **plodded**) trotten; (*work hard*) sich abmühen

plonk /plɒŋk/ *n* (*fam*) billiger Wein *m*

plot /plɒt/ *n* Komplott *nt*; (*of novel*) Handlung *f*; ~ **of land** Stück *n* Land □*vt* einzeichnen □ *vi* ein Komplott schmieden

plough /plaʊ/ *n* Pflug *m* □*vt/i* pflügen. ~ **back** *vt* (*Comm*) wieder investieren

ploy /plɔɪ/ *n* (*fam*) Trick *m*

pluck /plʌk/ *n* Mut *m* □*vt* zupfen; rupfen ⟨*bird*⟩; pflücken ⟨*flower*⟩. ~ **up courage** Mut fassen

plucky /'plʌkɪ/ *a* (**-ier, -iest**) tapfer, mutig

plug /plʌg/ *n* Stöpsel *m*; (*wood*) Zapfen *m*; (*cotton wool*) Bausch *m*; (*Electr*) Stecker *m*; (*Auto*) Zündkerze *f*; (*fam: advertisement*) Schleichwerbung *f* □*vt* zustopfen; (*fam: advertise*) Schleichwerbung machen für. ~ **in** *vt* (*Electr*) einstecken

plum /plʌm/ *n* Pflaume *f*

plumage /'pluːmɪdʒ/ *n* Gefieder *nt*

plumb /plʌm/ *n* Lot *nt* □ *adv* lotrecht □*vt* loten. ~ **in** *vt* installieren

plumb|er /'plʌmə(r)/ *n* Klempner *m*. ~**ing** *n* Wasserleitungen *pl*

'plumb-line *n* [Blei]lot *nt*

plume /pluːm/ *n* Feder *f*

plummet /'plʌmɪt/ *vi* herunterstürzen

plump /plʌmp/ *a* (**-er, -est**) mollig, rundlich □*vt* ~ **for** wählen

plunder /'plʌndə(r)/ n Beute f
□ vt plündern

plunge /plʌndʒ/ n Sprung m;
take the ~ (fam) den Schritt
wagen □ vt/i tauchen

plu'perfect /plu:-/ n Plusquam-
perfekt nt

plural /'plʊərl/ a pluralisch □n
Mehrzahl f, Plural m

plus /plʌs/ prep plus (+ dat) □n
Plus- □ n Pluszeichen nt; (advantage) Plus nt

plush[y] /'plʌʃ[ɪ]/ a luxuriös

ply /plaɪ/ vt (pt/pp **plied**)
(trade); **~ s.o.** with drink jdm
ein Glas nach dem anderen ein-
gießen. **~wood** n Sperrholz nt

p.m. adv (abbr of **post meridiem**)
nachmittags

pneumatic /nju:'mætɪk/ a pneu-
matisch. **~ 'drill** n Pressluft-
hammer m

pneumonia /nju:'məʊnɪə/ n Lun-
genentzündung f

poach /pəʊtʃ/ vt (Culin) pochieren; (steal) wildern. **~er** n
Wilddieb m

pocket /'pɒkɪt/ n Tasche f; **~ of
resistance** Widerstandsnest nt;
be out of ~ [an einem Geschäft]
verlieren □ vt einstecken. **~
book** n Notizbuch nt; (wallet)
Brieftasche f. **~money** n Ta-
schengeld nt

pock-marked /'pɒk-/ a pocken-
narbig

pod /pɒd/ n Hülse f

podgy /'pɒdʒɪ/ a (-ier, -iest) dick

poem /'pəʊɪm/ n Gedicht nt

poet /'pəʊɪt/ n Dichter(in) m(f).
~ic /-'etɪk/ a dichterisch

poetry /'pəʊɪtrɪ/ n Dichtung f

poignant /'pɔɪnjənt/ a ergreifend

point /pɔɪnt/ n Punkt m; (sharp
end) Spitze f; (meaning) Sinn m;
(purpose) Zweck m; (Electr) Steckdose f; **~s** pl (Rail) Weiche f; **~
of view** Standpunkt m; **good/
bad ~s** gute/schlechte Seiten;
what is the ~? wozu? **the ~ is**

es geht darum; **I don't see the ~**
das sehe ich nicht ein; **up to a ~**
bis zu einem gewissen Grade; **be
on the ~ of doing sth** im Begriff
sein, etw zu tun □ vt zeigen (**at**
auf + acc); ausfügen (brickwork)
□ vi deuten (**at/to** auf + acc);
(with finger) mit dem Finger
zeigen. **~ out** vt zeigen auf (+
acc); **~ sth out to s.o.** jdn auf etw
(acc) hinweisen

point'blank a aus nächster
Entfernung; (fig) rundweg

point|ed /'pɔɪntɪd/ a spitz; (ques-
tion) gezielt. **~er** n (hint) Hinweis
m. **~less** a zwecklos, sinnlos

poise /pɔɪz/ n Haltung f. **~d** a
(confident) selbstsicher; **~d to** bereit zu

poison /'pɔɪzn/ n Gift nt □ vt ver-
giften. **~ous** a giftig

poke /pəʊk/ n Stoß m □ vt stoßen;
schüren (fire); (put) stecken;
~ fun at sich lustig machen über
(+ acc)

poker[1] /'pəʊkə(r)/ n Schüreisen
nt

poker[2] n (Cards) Poker nt

poky /'pəʊkɪ/ a (-ier, -iest) eng

Poland /'pəʊlənd/ n Polen nt

polar /'pəʊlə(r)/ a Polar-. **~bear**
n Eisbär m. **~ize** nt polarisieren

Pole /pəʊl/ n Pole m/Polin f

pole[1] n Stange f

pole[2] n (Geog, Electr) Pol m

polecat n Iltis m

pole-star n Polarstern m

pole-vault n Stabhochsprung m

police /pə'li:s/ npl Polizei f □ vt
polizeilich kontrollieren

police: **~man** n Polizist m.
~state n Polizeistaat m. **~
station** n Polizeiwache f.
~woman n Polizistin f

policy[1] /'pɒlɪsɪ/ n Politik f

policy[2] n (insurance) Police f

polio /'pəʊlɪəʊ/ n Kinderläh-
mung f

Polish /'pəʊlɪʃ/ a polnisch

polish /'pɒlɪʃ/ n (shine) Glanz m; (for shoes) [Schuh]creme f; (for floor) Bohnerwachs m; (for furniture) Politur f; (for silver) Putzmittel nt; (for nails) Lack m; (fig) Schliff m □ vt polieren; (for shoes) cremen; (floor). ~ off vt (fam) verputzen (food); erledigen (task)

polisher /'pɒlɪʃə(r)/ n (machine) Poliermaschine f; (for floor) Bohnermaschine f

polite /pə'laɪt/ a, **-ly** adv höflich. ~ness f Höflichkeit f

politic /'pɒlɪtɪk/ a ratsam

political /pə'lɪtɪkl/ a, **-ly** adv politisch. ~**ian** /pɒlɪ'tɪʃn/ n Politiker(in) m(f)

politics /'pɒlɪtɪks/ n Politik f

polka /'pɒlkə/ n Polka f

poll /pəʊl/ n Abstimmung f; (election) Wahl f; [opinion] ~ [Meinungs]umfrage f; go to the ~s wählen □ vt erhalten (votes)

pollen /'pɒlən/ n Blütenstaub m, Pollen m

polling /'pəʊlɪŋ/: ~**booth** n Wahlkabine f. ~**station** n Wahllokal nt

'poll tax n Kopfsteuer f

pollutant /pə'luːtənt/ n Schadstoff m

pollute /pə'luːt/ vt verschmutzen. ~**ion** /-u:ʃn/ n Verschmutzung f

polo /'pəʊləʊ/ n Polo nt. ~**neck** n Rollkragen m. ~ **shirt** n Polohemd nt

polyester /pɒlɪ'estə(r)/ n Polyester m

polystyrene /pɒlɪ'staɪriːn/ n Polystyrol nt; (for packing) Styropor (P) nt

polytechnic /pɒlɪ'teknɪk/ n ≈ technische Hochschule f

polythene /'pɒlɪθiːn/ n Polyäthylen nt. ~ **bag** n Plastiktüte f

polyunsaturated a mehrfach ungesättigt

pomegranate /'pɒmɪɡrænɪt/ n Granatapfel m

pomp /pɒmp/ n Pomp m

pompon /'pɒmpɒn/ n Pompon m

pompous /'pɒmpəs/ a, **-ly** adv großspurig

pond /pɒnd/ n Teich m

ponder /'pɒndə(r)/ vi nachdenken

ponderous /'pɒndərəs/ a schwerfällig

pong /pɒŋ/ n (fam) Mief m

pony /'pəʊnɪ/ n Pony nt. ~**tail** n Pferdeschwanz m. ~**trekking** n Ponyreiten nt

poodle /'puːdl/ n Pudel m

pool¹ /puːl/ n [Schwimm]becken nt; (pond) Teich m; (of blood) Lache f

pool² n (common fund) [gemeinsame] Kasse f; ~s pl (Fußball)toto nt □ vt zusammenlegen

poor /pʊə(r)/ a (-er, -est) arm; (not good) schlecht; in ~ health nicht gesund □ npl the ~ die Armen. ~**ly** a be ~**ly** krank sein □ adv ärmlich; (badly) schlecht

pop¹ /pɒp/ n Knall m; (drink) Brause f □ v (pt/pp popped) □ vt (fam: put) stecken (in in + acc) □ vi knallen; (burst) platzen. ~ **in** vi (fam) reinschauen. ~ **out** vi (fam) kurz rausgehen

pop² n (fam) Popmusik f, Pop m □ attrib Pop-

popcorn n Puffmais m

pope /pəʊp/ n Papst m

poplar /'pɒplə(r)/ n Pappel f

poppy /'pɒpɪ/ n Mohn m

popular /'pɒpjʊlə(r)/ a beliebt, populär; (belief) volkstümlich. ~**ity** /-'lærəti/ n Beliebtheit f, Popularität f

populate /'pɒpjʊleɪt/ vt bevölkern. ~**ion** /-'leɪʃn/ n Bevölkerung f

porcelain /'pɔːsəlɪn/ n Porzellan nt

porch /pɔːtʃ/ n Vorbau m; (Amer) Veranda f

porcupine /'pɔːkjʊpaɪn/ n Stachelschwein nt

pore[1] /pɔː(r)/ n Pore f

pore[2] vi ~ over studieren

pork /pɔːk/ n Schweinefleisch nt

porn /pɔːn/ n (fam) Porno m

pornograph|ic /pɔːnə'græfɪk/ a pornographisch. ~y /-'nɒɡrəfɪ/ n Pornographie f

porous /'pɔːrəs/ a porös

porpoise /'pɔːpəs/ n Tümmler m

porridge /'pɒrɪdʒ/ n Haferbrei m

port[1] /pɔːt/ n Hafen m; (town) Hafenstadt f

port[2] n (Naut) Backbord nt

port[3] n (wine) Portwein m

portable /'pɔːtəbl/ a tragbar

porter /'pɔːtə(r)/ n Portier m; (for luggage) Gepäckträger m

portfolio /pɔːt'fəʊlɪəʊ/ n Mappe f; (Comm) Portefeuille f

porthole n Bullauge nt

portion /'pɔːʃn/ n Portion f; (part, share) Teil m

portly /'pɔːtlɪ/ a (-ier, -iest) beleibt

portrait /'pɔːtrɪt/ n Porträt nt

portray /pɔː'treɪ/ vt darstellen. ~al n Darstellung f

Portug|al /'pɔːtjʊɡl/ n Portugal nt. ~uese /-'giːz/ a portugiesisch □ n Portugiese m/-giesin f

pose /pəʊz/ n Pose f □ vt aufwerfen (problem); stellen (question) □ vi posieren; (for painter) Modell stehen; ~ as sich ausgeben als

posh /pɒʃ/ a (fam) feudal

position /pə'zɪʃn/ n Platz m; (posture) Haltung f; (job) Stelle f; (situation) Lage f, Situation f; (status) Stellung f □ vt platzieren; ~ oneself sich stellen

positive /'pɒzətɪv/ a, ~ly adv positiv; (definite) eindeutig; (real) ausgesprochen □ n Positiv nt

possess /pə'zes/ vt besitzen. ~ion /pə'zeʃn/ n Besitz m; ~ions pl Sachen pl

possess|ive /pə'zesɪv/ a Possessiv-; be ~ive zu sehr an jdm hängen. ~or n Besitzer m

possibility /pɒsə'bɪlətɪ/ n Möglichkeit f

possib|le /'pɒsəbl/ a möglich. ~ly adv möglicherweise; not ~ly unmöglich

post[1] /pəʊst/ n (pole) Pfosten m □ vt anschlagen (notice)

post[2] n (place of duty) Posten m; (job) Stelle f □ vt postieren; (transfer) versetzen

post[3] n (mail) Post f; by~ mit der Post □ vt aufgeben (letter); (send by~) mit der Post schicken; keep s.o. ~ed jdn auf dem Laufenden halten

postage /'pəʊstɪdʒ/ n Porto nt. ~ stamp n Briefmarke f

postal /'pəʊstl/ a Post-. ~ order n ≈ Geldanweisung f

post: ~box n Briefkasten m. ~card n Postkarte f; (picture) Ansichtskarte f. ~code n Postleitzahl f. ~date vt vordatieren

poster /'pəʊstə(r)/ n Plakat nt

posterior /pɒ'stɪərɪə(r)/ a hinter(e,r,s) □ n (fam) Hintern m

posterity /pɒ'sterətɪ/ n Nachwelt f

posthumous /'pɒstjʊməs/ a, ~ly adv postum

post: ~man n Briefträger m. ~mark n Poststempel m

post-mortem /-'mɔːtəm/ n Obduktion f

'post office n Post f

postpone /pəʊst'pəʊn/ vt aufschieben; ~ until verschieben auf (+ acc). ~ment n Verschiebung f

postscript /'pəʊstskrɪpt/ n Nachschrift f

posture /'pɒstʃə(r)/ n Haltung f

post-'war a Nachkriegs-

posy /'pəʊzɪ/ n Sträußchen nt

pot /pɒt/ n (for tea, coffee) Kanne f; ~s of money (fam) eine Menge Geld; go to ~ (fam) herunterkommen

potassium /pə'tæsɪəm/ n Kalium nt

potato /pəˈteɪtəʊ/ n (pl -es) Kartoffel f

poten|cy /ˈpəʊtənsɪ/ n Stärke f. **~t** a stark

potential /pəˈtenʃl/ a, -ly adv potenziell □ n Potenzial nt

pot: **~hole** n Höhle f; (in road) Schlagloch nt. **~holer** n Höhlenforscher m. **~shot** n take a **~shot at** schießen auf (+ acc)

potted /ˈpɒtɪd/ a eingemacht; (shortened) gekürzt. **~plant** n Topfpflanze f

potter¹ /ˈpɒtə(r)/ vi **~ [about]** herumwerkeln

potter² n Töpfer(in) m(f). **~y** n Töpferei f; (articles) Töpferwaren pl

potty /ˈpɒtɪ/ a (-ier, -iest) (fam) verrückt □ n Töpfchen n

pouch /paʊtʃ/ n Beutel m

pouffe /puːf/ n Sitzkissen nt

poultry /ˈpəʊltrɪ/ n Geflügel nt

pounce /paʊns/ vi zuschlagen; **~ on** sich stürzen auf (+ acc)

pound¹ /paʊnd/ n (money & 0,454 kg) Pfund nt

pound² vt hämmern □ vi (heart:) hämmern; (run heavily) stampfen

pour /pɔː(r)/ vt gießen; einschenken (drink) □ vi strömen; (with rain) gießen. **~ out** vi ausströmen □ vt ausschütten; einschenken (drink)

pout /paʊt/ vi einen Schmollmund machen

poverty /ˈpɒvətɪ/ n Armut f

powder /ˈpaʊdə(r)/ n Pulver nt; (cosmetic) Puder m □ vt pudern. **~y** a pulverig

power /ˈpaʊə(r)/ n Macht f; (strength) Kraft f; (Electr) Strom m; (nuclear) Energie f; (Math) Potenz f. **~cut** n Stromsperre f. **~ed** a betrieben (by mit); **~ed by electricity** mit Elektroantrieb. **~ful** a mächtig; (strong) stark. **~less** a machtlos. **~ station** n Kraftwerk nt

practicable /ˈpræktɪkəbl/ a durchführbar, praktikabel

practical /ˈpræktɪkl/ a, -ly adv praktisch. **~ 'joke** n Streich m

practice /ˈpræktɪs/ n Praxis f; (custom) Brauch m; (habit) Gewohnheit f; (exercise) Übung f; (Sport) Training nt; **in ~** (in reality) in der Praxis; **out of ~** außer Übung; **put into ~** ausführen

practise /ˈpræktɪs/ vt üben; (carry out) praktizieren; ausüben (profession) □ vi üben; (doctor:) praktizieren. **~d** a geübt

pragmatic /præɡˈmætɪk/ a, **~ally** adv pragmatisch

praise /preɪz/ n Lob nt □ vt loben. **~worthy** a lobenswert

pram /præm/ n Kinderwagen m

prance /prɑːns/ vi herumhüpfen; (horse:) tänzeln

prank /præŋk/ n Streich m

prattle /ˈprætl/ vi plappern

prawn /prɔːn/ n Garnele f, Krabbe f. **~ 'cocktail** n Krabbencocktail m

pray /preɪ/ vi beten. **~er** /preə(r)/ n Gebet nt; **~ers** pl (service) Andacht f

preach /priːtʃ/ vt/i predigen. **~er** n Prediger m

preamble /ˈpriːæmbl/ n Einleitung f

pre-ar'range /priː-/ vt im Voraus arrangieren

precarious /prɪˈkeərɪəs/ a, -ly adv unsicher

precaution /prɪˈkɔːʃn/ n Vorsichtsmaßnahme f; **as a ~** zur Vorsicht. **~ary** a Vorsichts-

precede /prɪˈsiːd/ vt vorangehen (+ dat)

preceden|ce /ˈpresɪdəns/ n Vorrang m. **~t** n Präzedenzfall m

preceding /prɪˈsiːdɪŋ/ a vorhergehend

precinct /ˈpriːsɪŋkt/ n Bereich m; (traffic-free) Fußgängerzone f; (Amer: district) Bezirk m

precious /'preʃəs/ a kostbar; ⟨style⟩ preziös □ adv ⟨fam⟩ ~ little recht wenig

precipice /'presɪpɪs/ n Steilabfall m

precipitate¹ /prɪ'sɪpɪtət/ a voreilig

precipitat|e² /prɪ'sɪpɪteɪt/ vt schleudern; ⟨fig: accelerate⟩ beschleunigen. ~ion /-'teɪʃn/ n ⟨Meteorol⟩ Niederschlag m

précis /'preɪsiː/ n ⟨pl précis /-siːz⟩ Zusammenfassung f

precis|e /prɪ'saɪs/ a, -ly adv genau. ~ion /-'sɪʒn/ n Genauigkeit f

preclude /prɪ'kluːd/ vt ausschließen

precocious /prɪ'kəʊʃəs/ a frühreif

pre|con'ceived /priː-/ a vorgefasst. ~con'ception n vorgefasste Meinung f

precursor /priː'kɜːsə(r)/ n Vorläufer m

predator /'predətə(r)/ n Raubtier nt

predecessor /'priːdɪsesə(r)/ n Vorgänger(in) m(f)

predicament /prɪ'dɪkəmənt/ n Zwangslage f

predicat|e /'predɪkət/ n ⟨Gram⟩ Prädikat nt. ~ive /prɪ'dɪkətɪv/ a, -ly adv prädikativ

predict /prɪ'dɪkt/ vt voraussagen. ~able /-əbl/ a voraussehbar; ⟨person⟩ berechenbar. ~ion /-'dɪkʃn/ n Voraussage f

pre'dominant /prɪ-/ a vorherrschend. ~antly adv hauptsächlich, überwiegend. ~ate vi vorherrschen

pre-'eminent /priː-/ a hervorragend

pre-empt /priː'empt/ vt zuvorkommen (+ dat)

preen /priːn/ vt putzen; ~ oneself ⟨fig⟩ selbstgefällig tun

pre|'fab /'priːfæb/ n ⟨fam⟩ [einfaches] Fertighaus nt. ~'fabricated a vorgefertigt

preface /'prefɪs/ n Vorwort nt

prefect /'priːfekt/ n Präfekt m

prefer /prɪ'fɜː(r)/ vt ⟨pt/pp preferred⟩ vorziehen; I ~ to walk ich gehe lieber zu Fuß; I ~ wine ich trinke lieber Wein

prefer|able /'prefərəbl/ a be ~able vorzuziehen sein (to dat). ~ably adv vorzugsweise

preferen|ce /'prefərəns/ n Vorzug m. ~tial /-'renʃl/ a bevorzugt

prefix /'priːfɪks/ n Vorsilbe f

pregnan|cy /'pregnənsɪ/ n Schwangerschaft f. ~t a schwanger; ⟨animal⟩ trächtig

prehi'storic /priː-/ a prähistorisch

prejudice /'predʒʊdɪs/ n Vorurteil nt; ⟨bias⟩ Voreingenommenheit f □ vt einnehmen (against gegen). ~d a voreingenommen

preliminary /prɪ'lɪmɪnərɪ/ a Vor-

prelude /'preljuːd/ n Vorspiel nt

pre-'marital /priː-/ a vorehelich

premature /'premətjʊə(r)/ a vorzeitig; ⟨birth⟩ Früh-. ~ly adv zu früh

pre'meditated /priː-/ a vorsätzlich

premier /'premɪə(r)/ a führend □ n ⟨Pol⟩ Premier[minister] m

première /'premɪeə(r)/ n Premiere f

premises /'premɪsɪz/ npl Räumlichkeiten pl; on the ~ im Haus

premiss /'premɪs/ n Prämisse f

premium /'priːmɪəm/ n Prämie f; be at a ~ hoch im Kurs stehen

premonition /premə'nɪʃn/ n Vorahnung f

preoccupied /priː'ɒkjʊpaɪd/ a [in Gedanken] beschäftigt

prep /prep/ n ⟨Sch⟩ Hausaufgaben pl

pre-'packed /priː-/ a abgepackt

preparation /prepə'reɪʃn/ n Vorbereitung f; ⟨substance⟩ Präparat nt

preparatory /prɪˈpærətrɪ/ *a* Vor-
□ *adv* ~ **to** vor (+ *dat*)

prepare /prɪˈpeə(r)/ *vt* vorbereiten; anrichten ⟨*meal*⟩ □ *vi* sich
vorbereiten (**for** auf + *acc*); ~**d**
to bereit zu

pre'pay /prɪ-/ *vt* (*pt/pp* -**paid**) im
Voraus bezahlen

preposition /prepəˈzɪʃn/ *n* Präposition *f*

prepossessing /priːpəˈzesɪŋ/ *a*
ansprechend

preposterous /prɪˈpɒstərəs/ *a* absurd

prerequisite /priːˈrekwɪzɪt/ *n* Voraussetzung *f*

prerogative /prɪˈrɒgətɪv/ *n* Vor-
recht *nt*

Presbyterian /prezbɪˈtɪərɪən/ *a*
presbyterianisch □ *n* Presbyteri-
aner(in) *m(f)*

prescribe /prɪˈskraɪb/ *vt* vor-
schreiben; (*Med*) verschreiben

prescription /prɪˈskrɪpʃn/ *n*
(*Med*) Rezept *nt*

presence /ˈprezns/ *n*
Anwesenheit *f*, Gegenwart *f*; ~
of mind Geistesgegenwart *f*

present¹ /ˈpreznt/ *a* gegenwärtig;
be ~ anwesend sein; (*occur*) vorkommen □ *n* Gegenwart *f*;
(*Gram*) Präsens *nt*; **at** ~ zurzeit;
for the ~ vorläufig

present² *n* (*gift*) Geschenk *nt*

present³ /prɪˈzent/ *vt* überreichen; (*show*) zeigen; vorlegen
⟨*cheque*⟩; (*introduce*) vorstellen;
~ **s.o. with sth** jdm etw überreichen. ~**able** /-əbl/ *a* **be** ~**able**
sich zeigen lassen können

presentation /preznˈteɪʃn/ *n*
Überreichung *f*. ~ **ceremony** *n*
Verleihungszeremonie *f*

presently /ˈprezntlɪ/ *adv*
nachher; (*Amer: now*) zurzeit

preservation /prezəˈveɪʃn/ *n* Erhaltung *f*

preservative /prɪˈzɜːvətɪv/ *n*
Konservierungsmittel *nt*

preserve /prɪˈzɜːv/ *vt* erhalten;
(*Culin*) konservieren; (*bottle*) einmachen □ *n* (*Hunting & fig*) Revier *nt*; (*jam*) Konfitüre *f*

preside /prɪˈzaɪd/ *vi* den Vorsitz
haben (**over** bei)

presidency /ˈprezɪdənsɪ/ *n* Präsi-
dentschaft *f*

president /ˈprezɪdənt/ *n* Präsident *m*; (*Amer: chairman*) Vorsit-
zende(r) *m/f*. ~**ial** /-ˈdenʃl/ *a*
Präsidenten-; (*election*) Präsi-
dentschafts-

press /pres/ *n* Presse *f* □ *vt/i* drücken; drücken auf (+ *acc*) ⟨*button*⟩; pressen ⟨*flower*⟩; (*iron*)
bügeln; (*urge*) bedrängen; ~ **for**
drängen auf (+ *acc*); **be** ~**ed for
time** in Zeitdrucke sein. ~ **on** *vi*
weitergehen/-fahren; (*fig*) weitermachen

press: ~ **cutting** *n* Zeitungs-
ausschnitt *m*. ~**ing** *a* dringend.
~**stud** *n* Druckknopf *m*. ~**up** *n*
Liegestütz *m*

pressure /ˈpreʃə(r)/ *n* Druck *m*
□ *vt* = **pressurize**. ~**cooker** *n*
Schnellkochtopf *m*. ~ **group** *n*
Interessengruppe *f*

pressurize /ˈpreʃəraɪz/ *vt* Druck
ausüben auf (+ *acc*). ~**d** *a* Druck-

prestige /preˈstiːʒ/ *n* Prestige *nt*.
~**ious** /-ˈstɪdʒəs/ *a* Prestige-

presumably /prɪˈzjuːməblɪ/ *adv*
vermutlich

presume /prɪˈzjuːm/ *vt* vermuten;
~ **to do sth** (*dare*) anmaßen,
etw zu tun □ *vi* ~ **on** ausnutzen

presumpt|ion /prɪˈzʌmpʃn/ *n*
Vermutung *f*; (*boldness*) An-
maßung *f*. ~**uous** /-ˈzʌmptjʊəs/
a, **-ly** *adv* anmaßend

presup'pose /priː-/ *vt* vorausset-
zen

pretence /prɪˈtens/ *n* Verstellung
f; (*pretext*) Vorwand *m*; **it's all** ~
das ist alles gespielt

pretend /prɪˈtend/ *vt* (*claim*) vorgeben; ~ **that** so tun, als ob; ~
to be sich ausgeben als

pretentious /prɪˈtenʃəs/ a protzig

pretext /ˈpriːtekst/ n Vorwand m

pretty /ˈprɪtɪ/ a (-ier, -iest), ~ily adv hübsch □ adv (fam: fairly) ziemlich

pretzel /ˈpretsl/ n Brezel f

prevail /prɪˈveɪl/ vi siegen; (custom:) vorherrschen; ~ on s.o. to do sth jdn dazu bringen, etw zu tun

prevalen|ce /ˈprevələns/ n Häufigkeit f. ~t a vorherrschend

prevent /prɪˈvent/ vt verhindern, verhüten; ~ s.o. [from] doing sth jdn daran hindern, etw zu tun. ~able /-əbl/ a vermeidbar. ~ion /-enʃn/ n Verhinderung f, Verhütung f. ~ive /-ɪv/ a vorbeugend

preview /ˈpriːvjuː/ n Voraufführung f

previous /ˈpriːvɪəs/ a vorhergehend; ~ to vor (+ dat). ~ly adv vorher, früher

pre-'war /priː-/ a Vorkriegs-

prey /preɪ/ n Beute f; **bird of ~** Raubvogel m □ vi ~ **on** Jagd machen auf (+ acc); ~ **on s.o.'s mind** jdm schwer auf der Seele liegen

price /praɪs/ n Preis m □ vt (Comm) auszeichnen. ~**less** a unschätzbar; (fig) unbezahlbar

prick /prɪk/ n Stich m □ vt/i stechen; ~ **up one's ears** die Ohren spitzen

prickl|e /ˈprɪkl/ n Stachel m; (thorn) Dorn m. ~**y** a stachelig; (sensation) stechend

pride /praɪd/ n Stolz m; (arrogance) Hochmut m; (of lions) Rudel nt □ vt ~ **oneself on** stolz sein auf (+ acc)

priest /priːst/ n Priester m

prig /prɪg/ n Tugendbold m

prim /prɪm/ a (**primmer, primmest**) prüde

primarily /ˈpraɪmərɪlɪ/ adv hauptsächlich, in erster Linie

primary /ˈpraɪmərɪ/ a Haupt-. ~ **school** n Grundschule f

prime[1] /praɪm/ a (first-rate) erstklassig □ n **be in one's** ~ in den besten Jahren sein

prime[2] vt scharf machen (bomb); grundieren (surface); (fig) instruieren

Prime Minister /praɪˈmɪnɪstə(r)/ n Premierminister(in) m(f)

primeval /praɪˈmiːvl/ a Ur-

primitive /ˈprɪmɪtɪv/ a primitiv

primrose /ˈprɪmrəʊz/ n gelbe Schlüsselblume f

prince /prɪns/ n Prinz m

princess /prɪnˈses/ n Prinzessin f

principal /ˈprɪnsəpl/ a Haupt- □ n (Sch) Rektor(in) m(f)

principality /prɪnsɪˈpælətɪ/ n Fürstentum nt

principally /ˈprɪnsəplɪ/ adv hauptsächlich

principle /ˈprɪnsəpl/ n Prinzip nt, Grundsatz m; **in/on** ~ im/aus Prinzip

print /prɪnt/ n Druck m; (Phot) Abzug m; **in** ~ gedruckt; (available) erhältlich; **out of** ~ vergriffen □ vt drucken; (write in capitals) in Druckschrift schreiben; (Computing) ausdrucken; (Phot) abziehen. ~**ed matter** n Drucksache f

print|er /ˈprɪntə(r)/ n Drucker m. ~**ing** n Druck m

'printout n (Computing) Ausdruck m

prior /ˈpraɪə(r)/ a frühere(r,s); ~ **to** vor (+ dat)

priority /praɪˈɒrətɪ/ n Priorität f, Vorrang m; (matter) vordringliche Sache f

prise /praɪz/ vt ~ **open/up** aufstemmen/hochstemmen

prism /ˈprɪzm/ n Prisma nt

prison /ˈprɪzn/ n Gefängnis nt. ~**er** n Gefangene(r) m/f

pristine /ˈprɪstiːn/ a tadellos

privacy /'prɪvəsɪ/ n Privatsphäre f; **have no ~** nie für sich sein

private /'praɪvət/ a, **-ly** adv privat; (confidential) vertraulich; (car, secretary, school) Privat- □ n (Mil) [einfacher] Soldat m; **in ~** privat; (confidentially) vertraulich

privation /praɪ'veɪʃn/ n Entbehrung f

privatize /'praɪvətaɪz/ vt privatisieren

privilege /'prɪvɪlɪdʒ/ n Privileg nt. **~d** a privilegiert

privy /'prɪvɪ/ a **be ~ to** wissen

prize /praɪz/ n Preis m □ vt schätzen. **~-giving** n Preisverleihung f. **~-winner** n Preisgewinner(in) m(f)

pro /prəʊ/ n (fam) Profi m; the **~s and cons** das Für und Wider

probability /prɒbə'bɪlɪtɪ/ n Wahrscheinlichkeit f

probable /'prɒbəbl/ a, **-bly** adv wahrscheinlich

probation /prə'beɪʃn/ n (Jur) Bewährung f. **~ary** a Probe-; **~ary period** Probezeit f

probe /prəʊb/ n Sonde f; (fig: investigation) Untersuchung f □ vt/i **~ [into]** untersuchen

problem /'prɒbləm/ n Problem nt; (Math) Textaufgabe f. **~atic** /-'mætɪk/ a problematisch

procedure /prə'siːdʒə(r)/ n Verfahren nt

proceed /prə'siːd/ vi gehen; (in vehicle) fahren; (continue) weitergehen/-fahren; (speaking) fortfahren; (act) verfahren □ vt **~ to do sth** anfangen, etw zu tun

proceedings /prə'siːdɪŋz/ npl Verfahren nt; (Jur) Prozess m

proceeds /'prəʊsiːdz/ npl Erlös m

process /'prəʊses/ n Prozess m; (procedure) Verfahren nt; **in the ~** dabei □ vt verarbeiten; (Admin) bearbeiten; (Phot) entwickeln

procession /prə'seʃn/ n Umzug m, Prozession f

proclaim /prə'kleɪm/ vt ausrufen

proclamation /prɒklə'meɪʃn/ n Proklamation f

procure /prə'kjʊə(r)/ vt beschaffen

prod /prɒd/ n Stoß m □ vt stoßen; (fig) einen Stoß geben (+ dat)

prodigal /'prɒdɪgl/ a verschwenderisch

prodigious /prə'dɪdʒəs/ a gewaltig

prodigy /'prɒdɪdʒɪ/ n [infant] **~** Wunderkind nt

produce¹ /'prɒdjuːs/ n landwirtschaftliche Erzeugnisse pl

produce² /prə'djuːs/ vt erzeugen, produzieren; (manufacture) herstellen; (bring out) hervorholen; (cause) hervorrufen; inszenieren (play); (Radio, TV) redigieren. **~r** n Erzeuger m, Produzent m; Hersteller m; (Theat) Regisseur m; (Radio, TV) Redakteur(in) m(f)

product /'prɒdʌkt/ n Erzeugnis nt, Produkt nt. **~ion** /prə'dʌkʃn/ n Produktion f; (Theat) Inszenierung f

productive /prə'dʌktɪv/ a produktiv; (land, talks) fruchtbar. **~ity** /-'tɪvətɪ/ n Produktivität f

profane /prə'feɪn/ a weltlich; (blasphemous) [gottes]lästerlich. **~ity** /-'fænətɪ/ n (oath) Fluch m

profess /prə'fes/ vt behaupten; bekennen (faith)

profession /prə'feʃn/ n Beruf m. **~al** a, **-ly** adv beruflich; (not amateur) Berufs-; (expert) fachmännisch; (Sport) professionell □ n Fachmann m; (Sport) Profi m

professor /prə'fesə(r)/ n Professor m

proficien|cy /prə'fɪʃnsɪ/ n Können nt. **~t** a **be ~t in** beherrschen

profile /'prəʊfaɪl/ n Profil nt; (character study) Porträt nt

profit /'prɒfɪt/ n Gewinn m, Profit m □ vi **~ from** profitieren von.

~**able** /-əbl/ *a,* -**bly** *adv* gewinnbringend; *(fig)* nutzbringend

profound /prə'faʊnd/ *a,* -**ly** *adv* tief

profus|e /prə'fjuːs/ *a,* -**ly** *adv* üppig; *(fig)* überschwenglich. ~**ion** /-juːʒn/ *n* in Beförderung *f;* in großer Fülle

progeny /'prɒdʒənɪ/ *n* Nachkommenschaft *f*

program /'prəʊgræm/ *n* Programm *nt;* □ *vt (pt/pp* **programmed)** programmieren

programme /'prəʊgræm/ *n* Programm *nt; (Radio, TV)* Sendung *f.* ~**r** *n (Computing)* Programmierer(in) *m(f)*

progress¹ /'prəʊgres/ *n* Vorankommen *nt; (fig)* Fortschritt *m;* **in** ~ im Gange; **make** ~ *(fig)* Fortschritte machen

progress² /prə'gres/ *vi* vorankommen; *(fig)* fortschreiten. ~**ion** /-eʃn/ *n* Folge *f; (development)* Entwicklung *f*

progressive /prə'gresɪv/ *a* fortschrittlich; *(disease)* fortschreitend. ~**ly** *adv* zunehmend

prohibit /prə'hɪbɪt/ *vt* verbieten *(s.o. jdm).* ~**ive** /-ɪv/ *a* unerschwinglich

project¹ /'prɒdʒekt/ *n* Projekt *nt; (Sch)* Arbeit *f*

project² /prə'dʒekt/ *vt* projizieren *(film); (plan)* planen □ *vi (jut out)* vorstehen

projectile /prə'dʒektaɪl/ *n* Geschoss *nt*

projector /prə'dʒektə(r)/ *n* Projektor *m*

proletariat /prəʊlɪ'teərɪət/ *n* Proletariat *nt*

prolific /prə'lɪfɪk/ *a* fruchtbar; *(fig)* produktiv

prologue /'prəʊlɒg/ *n* Prolog *m*

prolong /prə'lɒŋ/ *vt* verlängern

promenade /prɒmə'nɑːd/ *n* Promenade *f* □ *vi* spazieren gehen

prominent /'prɒmɪnənt/ *a* vorstehend; *(important)* prominent;

(conspicuous) auffällig; *(place)* gut sichtbar

promiscu|ity /prɒmɪ'skjuːətɪ/ *n* Promiskuität *f.* ~**ous** /prə'mɪskjʊəs/ *a* **be** ~**ous** häufig den Partner wechseln

promis|e /'prɒmɪs/ *n* Versprechen *nt* □ *vt/i* versprechen *(s.o. jdm);* **the P** ~**ed Land** das Gelobte Land. ~**ing** *a* viel versprechend

promot|e /prə'məʊt/ *vt* befördern; *(advance)* fördern; *(publicize)* Reklame machen für; **be** ~**ed** *(Sport)* aufsteigen. ~**ion** /-əʊʃn/ *n* Beförderung *f; (Sport)* Aufstieg *m; (Comm)* Reklame *f*

prompt /prɒmpt/ *a* prompt, unverzüglich; *(punctual)* pünktlich □ *adv* pünktlich □ *vt/i* veranlassen *(to* zu); *(Theat)* soufflieren *(+ dat).* ~**er** *n* Souffleur *m*/Souffleuse *f.* ~**ly** *adv* prompt

prone /prəʊn/ *a* **be or lie** ~ auf dem Bauch liegen; **be** ~ **to** neigen zu; **be** ~ **to do sth** dazu neigen, etw zu tun

prong /prɒŋ/ *n* Zinke *f*

pronoun /'prəʊnaʊn/ *n* Fürwort *nt,* Pronomen *nt*

pronounce /prə'naʊns/ *vt* aussprechen; *(declare)* erklären. ~**d** *a* ausgeprägt; *(noticeable)* deutlich. ~**ment** *n* Erklärung *f*

pronunciation /prənʌnsɪ'eɪʃn/ *n* Aussprache *f*

proof /pruːf/ *n* Beweis *m; (Typ)* Korrekturbogen *m* □ *a* ~ **against water/theft** wasserfest/diebessicher. ~**reader** *n* Korrektor *m*

prop¹ /prɒp/ *n* Stütze *f* □ *vt (pt/pp* **propped)** ~ **open** offen halten; ~ **against** *(lean)* lehnen an *(+ acc).* ~ **up** *vt* stützen

prop² /prɒp/ *n (Theat, fam)* Requisit *nt*

propaganda /prɒpə'gændə/ *n* Propaganda *f*

propagate /'prɒpəgeɪt/ *vt* vermehren; *(fig)* verbreiten, propagieren

propel /prə'pel/ vt (pt/pp **propelled**) [an]treiben. **~ler** n Propeller m. **~ling 'pencil** n Drehbleistift m

propensity /prə'pensətɪ/ n Neigung f (for zu)

proper /'prɒpə(r)/ a, **-ly** adv richtig; (decent) anständig. **~'name, ~ 'noun** n Eigenname m

property /'prɒpətɪ/ n Eigentum nt; (quality) Eigenschaft f; (Theat) Requisit nt; (land) [Grund]besitz m; (house) Haus nt. **~ market** n Immobilienmarkt m

prophecy /'prɒfəsɪ/ n Prophezeiung f

prophesy /'prɒfɪsaɪ/ vt (pt/pp -ied) prophezeien

prophet /'prɒfɪt/ n Prophet m. **~ic** /prə'fetɪk/ a prophetisch

proportion /prə'pɔ:ʃn/ n Verhältnis nt; (share) Teil m; **~s** pl Proportionen; (dimensions) Maße. **~al** a, **-ly** adv proportional

proposal /prə'pəʊzl/ n Vorschlag m; (of marriage) [Heirats]antrag m

propose /prə'pəʊz/ vt vorschlagen; (intend) vorhaben; einbringen (motion); ausbringen (toast) □ vi einen Heiratsantrag machen

proposition /prɒpə'zɪʃn/ n Vorschlag m

propound /prə'paʊnd/ vt darlegen

proprietor /prə'praɪətə(r)/ n Inhaber(in) m(f)

propriety /prə'praɪətɪ/ n Korrektheit f; (decorum) Anstand m

propulsion /prə'pʌlʃn/ n Antrieb m

prosaic /prə'zeɪɪk/ a prosaisch

prose /prəʊz/ n Prosa f

prosecut|e /'prɒsɪkju:t/ vt strafrechtlich verfolgen. **~ion** /-'kju:ʃn/ n strafrechtliche Verfolgung f; **the ~ion** die Anklage. **~or** n [**Public**] **P~or** Staatsanwalt m

prospect[1] /'prɒspekt/ n Aussicht f

prospect[2] /prə'spekt/ vi suchen (for nach)

prospect|ive /prə'spektɪv/ a (future) zukünftig. **~or** n Prospektor m

prospectus /prə'spektəs/ n Prospekt m

prosper /'prɒspə(r)/ vi gedeihen, florieren; (person) Erfolg haben. **~ity** /-'sperətɪ/ n Wohlstand m

prosperous /'prɒspərəs/ a wohlhabend

prostitut|e /'prɒstɪtju:t/ n Prostituierte f. **~ion** /-'tju:ʃn/ n Prostitution f

prostrate /'prɒstreɪt/ a ausgestreckt; **~ with grief** (fig) vor Kummer gebrochen

protagonist /prəʊ'tægənɪst/ n Kämpfer m; (fig) Protagonist m

protect /prə'tekt/ vt schützen (from vor + dat); beschützen (person). **~ion** /-ekʃn/ n Schutz m. **~ive** /-ɪv/ a Schutz-; (fig) beschützend. **~or** n Beschützer m

protégé /'prɒtɪʒeɪ/ n Schützling m, Protegé m

protein /'prəʊti:n/ n Eiweiß nt

protest[1] /'prəʊtest/ n Protest m

protest[2] /prə'test/ vi protestieren

Protestant /'prɒtɪstənt/ a protestantisch, evangelisch □ n Protestant(in) m(f), Evangelische(r) m/f

protester /prə'testə(r)/ n Protestierende(r) m/f

protocol /'prəʊtəkɒl/ n Protokoll nt

prototype /'prəʊtə-/ n Prototyp m

protract /prə'trækt/ vt verlängern. **~or** n Winkelmesser m

protrude /prə'tru:d/ vi [her]vorstehen

proud /praʊd/ a, **-ly** adv stolz (of auf + acc)

prove /pru:v/ vt beweisen □ vi **~to be** sich erweisen als

proverb /'prɒvɜːb/ n Sprichwort nt. ~**ial** /prə'vɜːbɪəl/ a sprichwörtlich

provide /prə'vaɪd/ vt zur Verfügung stellen; spenden ⟨shade⟩; ~ **s.o. with sth** jdn mit etw versorgen od versehen □ vi ~ **for** sorgen für

provided /prə'vaɪdɪd/ conj ~ **[that]** vorausgesetzt [dass]

providen|ce /'prɒvɪdəns/ n Vorsehung f. ~**tial** /-'denʃl/ a be ~**tial** ein Glück sein

providing /prə'vaɪdɪŋ/ conj = **provided**

provin|ce /'prɒvɪns/ n Provinz f; ⟨fig⟩ Bereich m. ~**ial** /prə'vɪnʃl/ a provinziell

provision /prə'vɪʒn/ n Versorgung f ⟨of mit⟩; ~**s** pl Lebensmittel pl. ~**al** a, **-ly** adv vorläufig

proviso /prə'vaɪzəʊ/ n Vorbehalt m

provocat|ion /prɒvə'keɪʃn/ n Provokation f. ~**ive** /prə'vɒkətɪv/ a, **-ly** adv provozierend; ⟨sexually⟩ aufreizend

provoke /prə'vəʊk/ vt provozieren; ⟨cause⟩ hervorrufen

prow /praʊ/ n Bug m

prowess /'praʊɪs/ n Kraft f

prowl /praʊl/ vi herumschleichen □ n **be on the** ~ herumschleichen

proximity /prɒk'sɪmətɪ/ n Nähe f

proxy /'prɒksɪ/ n Stellvertreter(in) m(f); ⟨power⟩ Vollmacht f

prude /pruːd/ n **be a** ~ prüde sein

pruden|ce /'pruːdns/ n Umsicht f. ~**t** a, **-ly** adv umsichtig; ⟨wise⟩ klug

prudish /'pruːdɪʃ/ a prüde

prune¹ /pruːn/ n Backpflaume f

prune² vt beschneiden

pry /praɪ/ vi ⟨pt/pp **pried**⟩ neugierig sein

psalm /sɑːm/ n Psalm m

pseudonym /'sjuːdənɪm/ n Pseudonym nt

psychiatric /saɪkɪ'ætrɪk/ a psychiatrisch

psychiatr|ist /saɪ'kaɪətrɪst/ n Psychiater(in) m(f). ~**y** n Psychiatrie f

psychic /'saɪkɪk/ a übersinnlich; **I'm not** ~ ich kann nicht hellsehen

psycho|'analyse /saɪkəʊ-/ vt psychoanalysieren. ~**a'nalysis** n Psychoanalyse f. ~**'analyst** Psychoanalytiker(in) m(f)

psychological /saɪkə'lɒdʒɪkl/ a, **-ly** adv psychologisch; ⟨illness⟩ psychisch

psycholog|ist /saɪ'kɒlədʒɪst/ n Psychologe m/ -login f. ~**y** n Psychologie f

psychopath /'saɪkəpæθ/ n Psychopath(in) m(f)

P.T.O. abbr (**please turn over**) b.w

pub /pʌb/ n ⟨fam⟩ Kneipe f

puberty /'pjuːbətɪ/ n Pubertät f

public /'pʌblɪk/ a, **-ly** adv öffentlich; **make** ~ publik machen □ n **the** ~ die Öffentlichkeit f; **in** ~ in aller Öffentlichkeit

publican /'pʌblɪkən/ n [Gast]wirt m

publication /pʌblɪ'keɪʃn/ n Veröffentlichung f

public: ~ **con'venience** n öffentliche Toilette f. ~ **'holiday** n gesetzlicher Feiertag m. ~ **'house** n [Gast]wirtschaft f

publicity /pʌb'lɪsɪtɪ/ n Reklame f; ⟨advertising⟩ Reklame f

publicize /'pʌblɪsaɪz/ vt Reklame machen für

public: ~ **'library** n öffentliche Bücherei f. ~ **'school** n Privatschule f; ⟨Amer⟩ staatliche Schule f. ~**'spirited** a **be** a ~**spirited** Gemeinsinn haben. ~**'transport** n öffentliche Verkehrsmittel pl

publish /'pʌblɪʃ/ vt veröffentlichen. ~**er** n Verleger(in) m(f); ⟨firm⟩ Verlag m. ~**ing** n Verlagswesen nt

pucker /'pʌkə(r)/ vt kräuseln

pudding /'pudɪŋ/ n Pudding m; (course) Nachtisch m

puddle /'pʌdl/ n Pfütze f

puerile /'pjuəraɪl/ a kindisch

puff /pʌf/ n (of wind) Hauch m; (of smoke) Wölkchen nt; (for powder) Quaste f □ vt blasen, pusten; ~ out ausstoßen. □ vi keuchen; ~ at paffen an (+ dat) (pipe). ~ed a (out of breath) aus der Puste. ~ pastry n Blätterteig m

puffy /'pʌfɪ/ a geschwollen

pugnacious /pʌg'neɪʃəs/ a, -ly adv aggressiv

pull /pul/ n Zug m; (jerk) Ruck m; (fam: influence) Einfluss m □ vt ziehen; zerren an (+ dat) (rope); ~ a muscle sich (dat) einen Muskel zerren; ~ oneself together sich zusammennehmen; ~ one's weight tüchtig mitarbeiten; ~ s.o.'s leg (fam) jdn auf den Arm nehmen. ~ down vt herunterziehen; (demolish) abreißen. ~ in vt hereinziehen □ vi (Auto) einscheren. ~ off vt abziehen; (fam) schaffen. ~ out vt herausziehen □ vi (Auto) ausscheren. ~ through vt durchziehen □ vi (recover) durchkommen. ~ up vt heraufziehen; ausziehen (plant); (reprimand) zurechtweisen □ vi (Auto) anhalten

pulley /'pulɪ/ n (Techn) Rolle f

pullover /'puləuvə(r)/ n Pullover m

pulp /pʌlp/ n Brei m; (of fruit) [Frucht]fleisch nt

pulpit /'pulpɪt/ n Kanzel f

pulsate /pʌl'seɪt/ vi pulsieren

pulse /pʌls/ n Puls m

pulses /'pʌlsɪz/ npl Hülsenfrüchte pl

pulverize /'pʌlvəraɪz/ vt pulverisieren

pumice /'pʌmɪs/ n Bimsstein m

pummel /'pʌml/ vt (pt/pp pummelled) mit den Fäusten bearbeiten

pump /pʌmp/ n Pumpe f □ vt pumpen; (fam) aushorchen. ~ up vt hochpumpen; (inflate) aufpumpen

pumpkin /'pʌmpkɪn/ n Kürbis m

pun /pʌn/ n Wortspiel nt

punch¹ /pʌntʃ/ n Faustschlag m; (device) Locher m □ vt boxen; lochen (ticket); stanzen (hole)

punch² /pʌntʃ/ n (drink) Bowle f

punch: ~ line n Pointe f. ~-up n Schlägerei f

punctual /'pʌŋktjuəl/ a, -ly adv pünktlich. ~ity /-'ælətɪ/ n Pünktlichkeit f

punctuat|e /'pʌŋktjueɪt/ vt mit Satzzeichen versehen. ~ion /-'eɪʃn/ n Interpunktion f. ~ion mark n Satzzeichen nt

puncture /'pʌŋktʃə(r)/ n Loch nt; (tyre) Reifenpanne f □ vt durchstechen

pundit /'pʌndɪt/ n Experte m

pungent /'pʌndʒənt/ a scharf

punish /'pʌnɪʃ/ vt bestrafen. ~able /-əbl/ a strafbar. ~ment n Strafe f

punitive /'pju:nɪtɪv/ a Straf-

punnet /'pʌnɪt/ n Körbchen nt

punt /pʌnt/ n (boat) Stechkahn m

punter /'pʌntə(r)/ n (gambler) Wetter m; (client) Kunde m

puny /'pju:nɪ/ a (-ier, -iest) mickerig

pup /pʌp/ n = puppy

pupil /'pju:pl/ n Schüler(in) m(f); (of eye) Pupille f

puppet /'pʌpɪt/ n Puppe f; (fig) Marionette f

puppy /'pʌpɪ/ n junger Hund m

purchase /'pɜ:tʃəs/ n Kauf m; (leverage) Hebelkraft f □ vt kaufen. ~r n Käufer m

pure /pjuə(r)/ a (-r, -st,) -ly adv rein

purée /'pjuəreɪ/ n Püree nt, Brei m

purgatory /'pɜ:gətrɪ/ n (Relig) Fegefeuer nt; (fig) Hölle f

purge /pɜːdʒ/ n (Pol) Säuberungsaktion f □ vt reinigen; (Pol) säubern

puri|fication /pjʊərɪfɪˈkeɪʃn/ n Reinigung f. **~fy** /ˈpjʊərɪfaɪ/ vt (pt/pp -ied) reinigen

puritanical /pjʊərɪˈtænɪkl/ a puritanisch

purity /ˈpjʊərɪtɪ/ n Reinheit f

purl /pɜːl/ n (Knitting) linke Masche f □ vt/i links stricken

purple /ˈpɜːpl/ a [dunkel]lila

purport /pəˈpɔːt/ vt vorgeben

purpose /ˈpɜːpəs/ n Zweck m; (intention) Absicht f; (determination) Entschlossenheit f; **on ~** absichtlich; **to no ~** unnützeweise. **~ful** a, **-ly** adv entschlossen. **~ly** adv absichtlich

purr /pɜː(r)/ vi schnurren

purse /pɜːs/ n Portemonnaie nt; (Amer: handbag) Handtasche f □ vt schürzen (lips)

pursue /pəˈsjuː/ vt verfolgen; (fig) nachgehen (+ dat). **~r** /-ə(r)/ n Verfolger m

pursuit /pəˈsjuːt/ n Verfolgung f; Jagd f; (pastime) Beschäftigung f; **in ~** hinterher

pus /pʌs/ n Eiter m

push /pʊʃ/ n Stoß m, (fam) Schubs m; **get the ~** (fam) hinausfliegen □ vt/i schieben; (press) drücken; (roughly) stoßen; **be ~ed for time** (fam) unter Zeitdruck stehen. **~ off** vt hinunterstoßen □ vi (fam: leave) abhauen □ vi (continue) weitertergehen/-fahren; (with activity) weitermachen. **~ up** vt hochschieben; hochtreiben (price)

push: **~-button** n Druckknopf m. **~chair** n [Kinder]sportwagen m. **~over** n (fam) Kinderspiel nt. **~-up** n (Amer) Liegestütz m

pushy /ˈpʊʃɪ/ a (fam) aufdringlich

puss /pʊs/ n, **pussy** /ˈpʊsɪ/ n Mieze f

put /pʊt/ vt (pt/pp **put**, pres p putting) tun; (place) setzen; (upright) stellen; (flat) legen; (express) ausdrücken; (say) sagen; (estimate) schätzen (at auf + acc); **~ aside** or **by** beiseite legen; **~ one's foot down** (fam) energisch werden; (Auto) Gas geben □ vi **~ to sea** auslaufen □ vt **stay ~** dableiben. **~ away** vt wegräumen. **~ back** vt wieder hinsetzen/-stellen/-legen; zurückstellen (clock). **~ down** vt hinsetzen/-stellen/-legen; (suppress) niederschlagen; (kill) töten; (write) niederschreiben; (attribute) zuschreiben (to dat). **~ forward** vt vorbringen; vorstellen (clock). **~ in** vt hineinsetzen/-stellen/-legen; (insert) einstecken; (submit) einreichen □ vi **~ in for** beantragen. **~ off** vt ausmachen (light); (postpone) verschieben; s.o. off jdn abbestellen; (disconcert) jdn aus der Fassung bringen. **~ s.o. off sth** jdm etw verleiden. **~ on** vt anziehen (clothes, brake); sich (dat) aufsetzen (hat); (Culin) aufsetzen; anmachen (light); aufführen (play); annehmen (accent); **~ on weight** zunehmen. **~ out** vt hinausstellen/-stellen/-legen; ausmachen (fire, light); ausstrecken (hand); (disconcert) aus der Fassung bringen; s.o./oneself out jdm/sich Umstände machen. **~ through** vt durchstecken; (Telephon) verbinden (to mit). **~ up** vt errichten (building); aufschlagen (tent); aufspannen (umbrella); anschlagen (notice); erhöhen (price); unterbringen (guest); **~ s.o. up to sth** jdn zu etw anstiften □ vi (at hotel) absteigen in (+ dat); **~ up with sth** sich (dat) etw bieten lassen

putrefy /ˈpjuːtrɪfaɪ/ vi (pt/pp -ied) verwesen

putrid /ˈpjuːtrɪd/ a faulig

putty /ˈpʌtɪ/ n Kitt m

put-up /ˈpʊtʌp/ a a ~ job ein abgekartetes Spiel nt

puzzl|e /ˈpʌzl/ n Rätsel nt; (jigsaw) Puzzlespiel nt □ vt it ~es me es ist mir rätselhaft □ vi ~e over sich (dat) den Kopf zerbrechen über (+ acc). ~ing a rätselhaft

pyjamas /pəˈdʒɑːməz/ npl Schlafanzug m

pylon /ˈpaɪlən/ n Mast m

pyramid /ˈpɪrəmɪd/ n Pyramide f

python /ˈpaɪθn/ n Pythonschlange f

Q

quack¹ /kwæk/ n Quaken nt □ vi quaken

quack² n (doctor) Quacksalber m

quad /kwɒd/ n (fam: court) Hof m; ~s pl = quadruplets

quadrangle /ˈkwɒdræŋgl/ n Viereck nt; (court) Hof m

quadruped /ˈkwɒdrʊped/ n Vierfüßer m

quadruple /ˈkwɒdrʊpl/ a vierfach □ vt vervierfachen □ vi sich vervierfachen. ~ts /-plɪts/ npl Vierlinge pl

quagmire /ˈkwɒgmaɪə(r)/ n Sumpf m

quaint /kweɪnt/ a (-er, -est) malerisch; (odd) putzig

quake /kweɪk/ n (fam) Erdbeben nt □ vi beben; (with fear) zittern

Quaker /ˈkweɪkə(r)/ n Quäker(in) m(f)

qualification /kwɒlɪfɪˈkeɪʃn/ n Qualifikation f; (reservation) Einschränkung f. ~ied /-faɪd/ a qualifiziert; (trained) ausgebildet; (limited) bedingt

qualify /ˈkwɒlɪfaɪ/ v (pt/pp -ied) □ vt qualifizieren; (entitle) berechtigen; (limit) einschränken □ vi sich qualifizieren

quality /ˈkwɒlətɪ/ n Qualität f; (characteristic) Eigenschaft f

qualm /kwɑːm/ n Bedenken pl

quandary /ˈkwɒndərɪ/ n Dilemma nt

quantity /ˈkwɒntɪtɪ/ n Quantität f, Menge f; in ~ in großen Mengen

quarantine /ˈkwɒrəntiːn/ n Quarantäne f

quarrel /ˈkwɒrl/ n Streit m □ vi (pt/pp quarrelled) sich streiten. ~some a streitsüchtig

quarry¹ /ˈkwɒrɪ/ n (prey) Beute f

quarry² n Steinbruch m

quart /kwɔːt/ n Quart nt

quarter /ˈkwɔːtə(r)/ n Viertel nt; (of year) Vierteljahr nt; (Amer) 25-Cent-Stück nt; ~s pl Quartier nt; at [a] ~ to six um Viertel vor sechs; from all ~s aus allen Richtungen □ vt vierteln; (Mil) einquartieren (on bei). ~-final n Viertelfinale nt

quarterly /ˈkwɔːtəlɪ/ a & adv vierteljährlich

quartet /kwɔːˈtet/ n Quartett nt

quartz /kwɔːts/ n Quarz m. ~ watch n Quarzuhr f

quash /kwɒʃ/ vt aufheben; niederschlagen (rebellion)

quaver /ˈkweɪvə(r)/ n (Mus) Achtelnote f □ vi zittern

quay /kiː/ n Kai m

queasy /ˈkwiːzɪ/ a I feel ~ mir ist übel

queen /kwiːn/ n Königin f; (Cards, Chess) Dame f

queer /kwɪə(r)/ a (-er, -est) eigenartig; (dubious) zweifelhaft; (ill) unwohl; (fam: homosexual) schwul □ n (fam) Schwule(r) m

quell /kwel/ vt unterdrücken

quench /kwentʃ/ vt löschen

query /ˈkwɪərɪ/ n Frage f; (question mark) Fragezeichen nt □ vt (pt/pp -ied) infrage stellen; reklamieren (bill)

quest /kwest/ n Suche f (for nach)

question /ˈkwestʃn/ n Frage f; (for discussion) Thema nt; out of the ~ ausgeschlossen; without ~ ohne Frage; the person in ~ die fragliche Person □ vt infrage stellen; ~ s.o. jdn ausfragen; (police:) jdn verhören. ~**able** /-əbl/ a zweifelhaft. ~ **mark** n Fragezeichen nt

questionnaire /kwestʃəˈneə(r)/ n Fragebogen m

queue /kjuː/ n Schlange f □ vi ~ [up] Schlange stehen, sich anstellen (**for** nach)

quibble /ˈkwɪbl/ vi Haarspalterei treiben

quick /kwɪk/ a (-er, -est), -ly adv schnell; **be** ~! mach schnell! **have a** ~ **meal** schnell etwas essen □ adv schnell □ n cut to the ~ (fig) bis ins Mark getroffen. ~**en** vt beschleunigen □ vi sich beschleunigen

quick: ~**sand** n Treibsand m. ~**tempered** a aufbrausend

quid /kwɪd/ n inv (fam) Pfund nt

quiet /ˈkwaɪət/ a (-er, -est), -ly adv still; (calm) ruhig; (soft) leise; **keep** ~ **about** (fam) nichts sagen von □ n Stille f; Ruhe f; **on the** ~ heimlich

quiet|en /ˈkwaɪətn/ vt beruhigen □ vi ~**en down** ruhig werden. ~**ness** n (see **quiet**) Stille f; Ruhe f

quill /kwɪl/ n Feder f; (spine) Stachel m

quilt /kwɪlt/ n Steppdecke f. ~**ed** a Stepp-

quince /kwɪns/ n Quitte f

quins /kwɪnz/ npl (fam) = **quintuplets**

quintet /kwɪnˈtet/ n Quintett nt

quintuplets /ˈkwɪntjʊplɪts/ npl Fünflinge pl

quip /kwɪp/ n Scherz m □ vi (pt/pp **quipped**) scherzen

quirk /kwɜːk/ n Eigenart f

quit /kwɪt/ v (pt/pp **quitted** or **quit**) □ vt verlassen; (give up) aufgeben; ~ **doing sth** aufhören,

etw zu tun □ vi gehen; **give s.o. notice to** ~ jdm die Wohnung kündigen

quite /kwaɪt/ adv ganz; (really) wirklich; (somewhat) ziemlich; ~ [so]! genau! ~ **a few** ziemlich viele

quits /kwɪts/ a quitt

quiver /ˈkwɪvə(r)/ vi zittern

quiz /kwɪz/ n Quiz nt □ vt (pt/pp **quizzed**) ausfragen. ~**zical** a, -ly adv fragend

quorum /ˈkwɔːrəm/ n **have a** ~ beschlussfähig sein

quota /ˈkwəʊtə/ n Anteil m; (Comm) Kontingent nt

quotation /kwəʊˈteɪʃn/ n Zitat nt; (price) Kostenvoranschlag m; (of shares) Notierung f. ~ **marks** npl Anführungszeichen pl

quote /kwəʊt/ n (fam) = **quotation**; **in** ~**s** in Anführungszeichen □ vt/i zitieren

R

rabbi /ˈræbaɪ/ n Rabbiner m; (title) Rabbi m

rabbit /ˈræbɪt/ n Kaninchen nt

rabble /ˈræbl/ n **the** ~ der Pöbel

rabid /ˈræbɪd/ a fanatisch; (animal) tollwütig

rabies /ˈreɪbiːz/ n Tollwut f

race[1] /reɪs/ n Rasse f

race[2] /reɪs/ n Rennen nt; (fig) Wettlauf m □ vi [am Rennen] teilnehmen; (athlete, horse:) laufen; (fam: rush) rasen □ vt um die Wette laufen mit; an einem Rennen teilnehmen lassen (horse)

race: ~**course** n Rennbahn f. ~**horse** n Rennpferd nt. ~**track** n Rennbahn f

racial /ˈreɪʃl/ a, -ly adv rassisch; (discrimination, minority) Rassen-

racing /ˈreɪsɪŋ/ n Rennsport m; (horse-) Pferderennen nt. ~ **car** n

Rennwagen m. **~ driver** n Rennfahrer m

racis|m /'reisizm/ n Rassismus m. **~t** /-ist/ a rassistisch □ n Rassist m

rack[1] /ræk/ n Ständer m; (for plates) Gestell n □ vt **~ one's brains** sich (dat) den Kopf zerbrechen

rack[2] n **go to ~ and ruin** verfallen; (fig) herunterkommen

racket[1] /'rækit/ n (Sport) Schläger m

racket[2] n(din) Krach m; (swindle) Schwindelgeschäft nt

racy /'reisi/ a (-ier, -iest) schwungvoll; (risqué) gewagt

radar /'reidɑ:(r)/ n Radar m

radian|ce /'reidiəns/ n Strahlen nt. **~t** a, **-ly** adv strahlend

radiat|e /'reidieit/ vt ausstrahlen □ vi ⟨heat:⟩ ausgestrahlt werden; ⟨roads:⟩ strahlenförmig ausgehen. **~ion** /-'eiʃn/ n Strahlung f

radiator /'reidieitə(r)/ n Heizkörper m; (Auto) Kühler m

radical /'rædikl/ a, **-ly** adv radikal □ n Radikale(r) m/f

radio /'reidiəʊ/ n Radio nt; **by ~** über Funk □ vt funken ⟨message⟩

radio|'active a radioaktiv. **~ac-'tivity** n Radioaktivität f

radiography /reidi'ɒgrəfi/ n Röntgenographie f

'radio ham n Hobbyfunker m

radio'therapy n Strahlenbehandlung f

radish /'rædiʃ/ n Radieschen nt

radius /'reidiəs/ n (pl **-dii** /-diai/) Radius m, Halbmesser m

raffle /'ræfl/ n Tombola f □ vt verlosen

raft /rɑ:ft/ n Floß nt

rafter /'rɑ:ftə(r)/ n Dachsparren m

rag[1] /ræg/ n Lumpen m; (pej: newspaper) Käseblatt nt; **in ~s** in Lumpen

rag[2] vt (pt/pp ragged) (fam) aufziehen

rage /reidʒ/ n Wut f; **all the ~** (fam) der letzte Schrei □ vi rasen; ⟨storm:⟩ toben

ragged /'rægid/ a zerlumpt; (edge) ausgefranst

raid /reid/ n Überfall m; (Mil) Angriff m; (police) Razzia f □ vt überfallen; (Mil) angreifen; (police) eine Razzia durchführen in (+ dat); (break in) eindringen in (+ acc). **~er** n Eindringling m; (of bank) Bankräuber m

rail /reil/ n Schiene f; (pole) Stange f; (hand~) Handlauf m; (Naut) Reling f; **by ~** mit der Bahn

railings /'reiliŋz/ npl Geländer nt

'railroad n (Amer) = **railway**

'railway n [Eisen]bahn f. **~man** n Eisenbahner m. **~ station** n Bahnhof m

rain /rein/ n Regen m □ vi regnen. **~bow** n Regenbogen m. **~check** n (Amer) **take a ~check on** aufschieben. **~coat** n Regenmantel m. **~fall** n Niederschlag m

rainy /'reini/ a (-ier, -iest) regnerisch

raise /reiz/ n (Amer) Lohnerhöhung f □ vt erheben; (upright) aufrichten; (make higher) erhöhen; (lift) [hoch]heben; lüften ⟨hat⟩; aufziehen ⟨children, animals⟩; aufwerfen ⟨question⟩; aufbringen ⟨money⟩

raisin /'reizn/ n Rosine f

rake /reik/ n Harke f, Rechen m □ vt harken, rechen. **~ up** vt zusammenharken; (fam) wieder aufführen

'rake-off n (fam) Prozente pl

rally /'ræli/ n Versammlung f; (Auto) Rallye f; (Tennis) Ballwechsel m □ vt sammeln □ vi sich sammeln; (recover strength) sich erholen

ram /ræm/ *n* Schafbock *m*; (*Astr*) Widder *m* □ *vt* (*pt/pp* **rammed**) rammen

rambl|e /'ræmbl/ *n* Wanderung *f* □ *vi* wandern; (*in speech*) irrereden. **~er** *n* Wanderer *m*; (*rose*) Kletterrose *f*. **~ing** *a* weitschweifig, (*club*) Wander-

ramp /ræmp/ *n* Rampe *f*; (*Aviat*) Gangway *f*

rampage¹ /'ræmpeɪdʒ/ *n* **be/go on the ~** randalieren

rampage² /ræm'peɪdʒ/ *vi* randalieren

rampant /'ræmpənt/ *a* weit verbreitet; (*in heraldry*) aufgerichtet

rampart /'ræmpɑːt/ *n* Wall *m*

ramshackle /'ræmʃækl/ *a* baufällig

ran /ræn/ *see* **run**

ranch /rɑːntʃ/ *n* Ranch *f*

rancid /'rænsɪd/ *a* ranzig

rancour /'ræŋkə(r)/ *n* Groll *m*

random /'rændəm/ *a* willkürlich; **a ~ sample** eine Stichprobe *f*; **at ~** aufs Geratewohl; (*choose*) willkürlich

randy /'rændɪ/ *a* (**-ier, -iest**) (*fam*) geil

rang /ræŋ/ *see* **ring²**

range /reɪndʒ/ *n* Serie *f*, Reihe *f*; (*Comm*) Auswahl *f*, Angebot *nt* (**of** an + *dat*); (*of mountains*) Kette *f*; (*Mus*) Umfang *m*; (*distance*) Reichweite *f*; (*for shooting*) Schießplatz *m*; (*stove*) Kohlenherd *m*; **at a ~ of** aus einer Entfernung von □ *vi* reichen; **~ from … to** gehen von … bis. **~r** *n* Aufseher *m*

rank¹ /ræŋk/ *n* (*row*) Reihe *f*; (*Mil*) Rang *m*; (*social position*) Stand *m*; **the ~ and file** die breite Masse; **the ~s** *pl* die gemeinen Soldaten □ *vt/i* einstufen; **~ among** zählen zu

rank² *a* (*bad*) übel; (*plants*) üppig; (*fig*) krass

ransack /'rænsæk/ *vt* durchwühlen; (*pillage*) plündern

ransom /'rænsəm/ *n* Lösegeld *nt*; **hold s.o. to ~** Lösegeld für jdn fordern

rant /rænt/ *vi* rasen

rap /ræp/ *n* Klopfen *nt*; (*blow*) Schlag *m* □ *v* (*pt/pp* **rapped**) □ *vt* klopfen auf (+ *acc*) □ *vi* **~ at/on** klopfen an/auf (+ *acc*)

rape¹ /reɪp/ *n* (*Bot*) Raps *m*

rape² *n* Vergewaltigung *f* □ *vt* vergewaltigen

rapid /'ræpɪd/ *a*, **-ly** *adv* schnell. **~ity** /rə'pɪdətɪ/ *n* Schnelligkeit *f*

rapids /'ræpɪdz/ *npl* Stromschnellen *pl*

rapist /'reɪpɪst/ *n* Vergewaltiger *m*

rapport /ræ'pɔː(r)/ *n* [innerer] Kontakt *m*

rapt /ræpt/ *a*, **-ly** *adv* gespannt; (*look*) andächtig; **~ in** versunken in (+ *acc*)

raptur|e /'ræptʃə(r)/ *n* Entzücken *nt*. **~ous** /-rəs/ *a*, **-ly** *adv* begeistert

rare¹ /reə(r)/ *a* (**-r, -st**), **-ly** *adv* selten

rare² *a* (*Culin*) englisch gebraten

rarefied /'reərɪfaɪd/ *a* dünn

rarity /'reərətɪ/ *n* Seltenheit *f*

rascal /'rɑːskl/ *n* Schlingel *m*

rash¹ /ræʃ/ *n* (*Med*) Ausschlag *m*

rash² *a* (**-er, -est**), **-ly** *adv* voreilig

rasher /'ræʃə(r)/ *n* Speckscheibe *f*

rasp /rɑːsp/ *n* Raspel *f*

raspberry /'rɑːzbərɪ/ *n* Himbeere *f*

rat /ræt/ *n* Ratte *f*; (*fam: person*) Schuft *m*; **smell a ~** (*fam*) Lunte riechen

rate /reɪt/ *n* Rate *f*; (*speed*) Tempo *nt*; (*of payment*) Satz *m*; (*exchange*) Kurs *m*; **~s** *pl* (*taxes*) ≈ Grundsteuer *f*; **at any ~** auf jeden Fall; **at this ~** auf diese Weise □ *vt* einschätzen; **~ among** zählen zu □ *vi* **~ as** gelten als

rather /'rɑːðə(r)/ adv lieber; (fairly) ziemlich; ∼! und ob!

ratification /rætɪfɪ'keɪʃn/ n Ratifizierung f. ∼**fy** /'rætɪfaɪ/ vt (pt/pp -ied) ratifizieren

rating /'reɪtɪŋ/ n Einschätzung f; (class) Klasse f; (sailor) [einfacher] Matrose m; ∼s pl (Radio, TV) ≈ Einschaltquote f

ratio /'reɪʃɪəʊ/ n Verhältnis nt

ration /'ræʃn/ n Ration f □ vt rationieren

rational /'ræʃənl/ a, **-ly** adv rational. ∼**ize** vt/i rationalisieren

'rat race n (fam) Konkurrenzkampf m

rattle /'rætl/ n Rasseln nt; (of china, glass) Klirren nt; (of windows) Klappern nt; (toy) Klapper f □ vi rasseln; klirren; klappern □ vt rasseln mit; (shake) schütteln. ∼ **off** vt herunterrasseln

'rattlesnake n Klapperschlange f

raucous /'rɔːkəs/ a rauh

ravage /'rævɪdʒ/ vt verwüsten, verheeren

rave /reɪv/ vi toben; ∼ **about** schwärmen von

raven /'reɪvn/ n Rabe m

ravenous /'rævənəs/ a heißhungrig

ravine /rə'viːn/ n Schlucht f

raving /'reɪvɪŋ/ a ∼ **mad** (fam) total verrückt

ravishing /'rævɪʃɪŋ/ a hinreißend

raw /rɔː/ a (-er, -est) roh; (not processed) Roh-; (skin) wund; (weather) nasskalt; (inexperienced) unerfahren; **get a ∼ deal** (fam) schlecht weggekommen. ∼ **ma'terials** npl Rohstoffe pl

ray /reɪ/ n Strahl m; ∼ **of hope** Hoffnungsschimmer m

raze /reɪz/ vt ∼ **to the ground** dem Erdboden gleichmachen

razor /'reɪzə(r)/ n Rasierapparat m. ∼ **blade** n Rasierklinge f

re /riː/ prep betreffs (+ gen)

reach /riːtʃ/ n Reichweite f; (of river) Strecke f; **within/out of ∼** in/außer Reichweite; **within easy ∼** leicht erreichbar □ vt erreichen; (arrive at) ankommen in (+ dat); (∼ as far as) reichen bis; kommen zu (decision, conclusion); (pass) reichen □ vi reichen (to bis zu); ∼ **for** greifen nach; I **can't ∼** ich komme nicht daran

re'act /rɪ-/ vi reagieren (to auf + acc)

re'action /rɪ-/ n Reaktion f. ∼**ary** a reaktionär

reactor /rɪ'æktə(r)/ n Reaktor m

read /riːd/ vt/i (pt/pp read /red/) lesen; (aloud) vorlesen (to dat); (Univ) studieren; ablesen (meter). ∼ **out** vt vorlesen

readable /'riːdəbl/ a lesbar

reader /'riːdə(r)/ n Leser(in) m(f); (book) Lesebuch nt

readily /'redɪlɪ/ adv bereitwillig; (easily) leicht. ∼**ness** n Bereitschaft f; in ∼**ness** bereit

reading /'riːdɪŋ/ n Lesen nt; (Pol, Relig) Lesung f

rea'djust /riː-/ vt neu einstellen □ vi sich umstellen (to auf + acc)

ready /'redɪ/ a (-ier, -iest) fertig; (willing) bereit; (quick) schnell; **get ∼** sich fertig machen; (prepare to) sich bereitmachen

ready: ∼**'made** a fertig. ∼**'money** n Bargeld m. ∼**-to-'wear** a Konfektions-

real /rɪəl/ a wirklich; (genuine) echt; (actual) eigentlich □ adv (Amer, fam) echt. ∼ **estate** n Immobilien pl

realism /'rɪəlɪzm/ n Realismus m. ∼**t** /-lɪst/ n Realist m. ∼**tic** /-'lɪstɪk/ a, **-ally** adv realistisch

reality /rɪ'ælətɪ/ n Wirklichkeit f, Realität f

realization /rɪəlaɪ'zeɪʃn/ n Erkenntnis f

realize /'rɪəlaɪz/ vt einsehen; (become aware) gewahr werden; verwirklichen (hopes, plans);

(Comm) realisieren; einbringen *(price)*; **I didn't ~** das wusste ich nicht

really /'rɪəlɪ/ *adv* wirklich; *(actually)* eigentlich

realm /relm/ *n* Reich *nt*

realtor /'rɪːəltə(r)/ *n (Amer)* Immobilienmakler *m*

reap /riːp/ *vt* ernten

reap'pear /riː-/ *vi* wiederkommen

rear¹ /rɪə(r)/ *n* Hinter-; *(Auto)* Heck-. □ **in the ~** der hintere Teil; **from the ~** von hinten

rear² *vt* aufziehen □ *vi* ~ **[up]** *(horse:)* sich aufbäumen

'rear-light *n* Rücklicht *nt*

re'arm /riː-/ *vi* wieder aufrüsten

rear'range /riː-/ *vt* umstellen

rear-view 'mirror *n (Auto)* Rückspiegel *m*

reason /'riːzn/ *n* Grund *m*; *(good sense)* Vernunft *f*; *(ability to think)* Verstand *m*; **within ~** in vernünftigen Grenzen □ *vi* argumentieren; **~ with** vernünftig reden mit. **~able** /-əbl/ *a* vernünftig; *(not expensive)* preiswert. **~ably** /-əblɪ/ *adv (fairly)* ziemlich

reas'sur|ance /riː-/ *n* Beruhigung *f*; Versicherung *f*. **~e** *vt* beruhigen; **~e s.o. of sth** jdm etw *(gen)* versichern

rebate /'riːbeɪt/ *n* Rückzahlung *f*; *(discount)* Nachlass *m*

rebel¹ /'rebl/ *n* Rebell *m*

rebel² /rɪ'bel/ *vi (pt/pp* rebelled*)* rebellieren. **~lion** /-ɪən/ *n* Rebellion *f*. **~lious** /-ɪəs/ *a* rebellisch

re'bound¹ /rɪ-/ *vi* abprallen

re'bound² /riː-/ *n* Rückprall *m*

rebuff /rɪ'bʌf/ *n* Abweisung *f* □ *vt* abweisen; eine Abfuhr erteilen *(s.o. jdm)*

re'build /riː-/ *vt (pt/pp* -built*)* wieder aufbauen

rebuke /rɪ'bjuːk/ *n* Tadel *m* □ *vt* tadeln

rebuttal /rɪ'bʌtl/ *n* Widerlegung *f*

re'call /rɪ-/ *n* Erinnerung *f*; **beyond ~** unwiderruflich □ *vt* zurückrufen; abberufen *(diplomat)*; vorzeitig einberufen *(parliament)*; *(remember)* sich erinnern an (+ *acc)*

recant /rɪ'kænt/ *vi* widerrufen

recap /'riːkæp/ *vt/i (fam)* = **recapitulate**

recapitulate /riːkə'pɪtjʊleɪt/ *vt/i* zusammenfassen; rekapitulieren

re'capture /riː-/ *vt* wieder gefangen nehmen *(person)*; wieder einfangen *(animal)*

reced|e /rɪ'siːd/ *vi* zurückgehen. **~ing** *a (forehead, chin)* fliehend; **~ing hair** Stirnglatze *f*

receipt /rɪ'siːt/ *n* Quittung *f*; *(receiving)* Empfang *m*; **~s** *pl (Comm)* Einnahmen *pl*

receive /rɪ'siːv/ *vt* erhalten, bekommen; empfangen *(guests)*. **~r** *n (Teleph)* Hörer *m*; *(Radio, TV)* Empfänger *m*; *(of stolen goods)* Hehler *m*

recent /'riːsənt/ *a* kürzlich erfolgte(r,s). **~ly** *adv* in letzter Zeit; *(the other day)* kürzlich, vor kurzem

receptacle /rɪ'septəkl/ *n* Behälter *m*

reception /rɪ'sepʃn/ *n* Empfang *m*; **~ [desk]** *(in hotel)* Rezeption *f*. **~ist** *n* Empfangsdame *f*

receptive /rɪ'septɪv/ *a* aufnahmefähig; **~ to** empfänglich für

recess /rɪ'ses/ *n* Nische *f*; *(holiday)* Ferien *pl*; *(Amer, Sch)* Pause *f*

recession /rɪ'seʃn/ *n* Rezession *f*

re'charge /riː-/ *vt* [wieder] aufladen

recipe /'resəpɪ/ *n* Rezept *nt*

recipient /rɪ'sɪpɪənt/ *n* Empfänger *m*

recipro|cal /rɪ'sɪprəkl/ *a* gegenseitig. **~cate** /-keɪt/ *vt* erwidern

recital /rɪ'saɪtl/ *n (of poetry songs)* Vortrag *m*; *(on piano)* Konzert *nt*

recite /rɪ'saɪt/ *vt* aufsagen; *(before audience)* vortragen; *(list)* aufzählen

reckless /'reklɪs/ *a*, **-ly** *adv* leichtsinnig; *(careless)* rücksichtslos. **~ness** *n* Leichtsinn *m*; Rücksichtslosigkeit *f*

reckon /'rekən/ *vt* rechnen; *(consider)* glauben □ *vi* **~ on/with** rechnen mit

re'claim /rɪ-/ *vt* zurückfordern; zurückgewinnen *(land)*

recline /rɪ'klaɪn/ *vi* liegen. **~ing seat** *n* Liegesitz *m*

recluse /rɪ'klu:s/ *n* Einsiedler(in) *m(f)*

recognition /rekəg'nɪʃn/ *n* Erkennen *nt*; *(acknowledgement)* Anerkennung *f*; **in ~** als Anerkennung *(of gen)*; **beyond ~** nicht wieder zu erkennen sein

recognize /'rekəgnaɪz/ *vt* erkennen; *(know again)* wieder erkennen; *(acknowledge)* anerkennen

re'coil /rɪ-/ *vi* zurückschnellen; *(in fear)* zurückschrecken

recollect /rekə'lekt/ *vt* sich erinnern an (+ *acc*). **~ion** /-ekʃn/ *n* Erinnerung *f*

recommend /rekə'mend/ *vt* empfehlen. **~ation** /-'deɪʃn/ *n* Empfehlung *f*

recompense /'rekəmpens/ *n* Entschädigung *f* □ *vt* entschädigen

recon|cile /'rekənsaɪl/ *vt* versöhnen; **~cile oneself to** sich abfinden mit. **~ciliation** /-sɪlɪ'eɪʃn/ *n* Versöhnung *f*

recon'dition /ri:-/ *vt* generalüberholen. **~ed engine** *n* Austauschmotor *m*

reconnaissance /rɪ'kɒnɪsns/ *n (Mil)* Aufklärung *f*

reconnoitre /rekə'nɔɪtə(r)/ *vi (pres p -tring)* auf Erkundung ausgehen

recon'sider /ri:-/ *vt* sich *(dat)* noch einmal überlegen

recon'struct /ri:-/ *vt* wieder aufbauen; rekonstruieren *(crime)*. **~ion** *n* Wiederaufbau *m*; Rekonstruktion *f*

record¹ /rɪ'kɔ:d/ *vt* aufzeichnen; *(register)* registrieren; *(on tape)* aufnehmen

record² /'rekɔ:d/ *n* Aufzeichnung *f*; *(Jur)* Protokoll *nt*; *(Mus)* [Schall]platte *f*; *(Sport)* Rekord *m*; **~s** *pl* Unterlagen *pl*; **keep a ~** of sich *(dat)* notieren; **off the ~** inoffiziell; **have a [criminal] ~** vorbestraft sein

recorder /rɪ'kɔ:də(r)/ *n (Mus)* Blockflöte *f*

recording /rɪ'kɔ:dɪŋ/ *n* Aufzeichnung *f*, Aufnahme *f*

'record-player *n* Plattenspieler *m*

re-'count¹ /ri:-/ *vt* erzählen

re-'count² /ri:-/ *vt* nachzählen

're-count² /ri:-/ *n (Pol)* Nachzählung *f*

recoup /rɪ'ku:p/ *vt* wieder einbringen; ausgleichen *(losses)*

recourse /rɪ'kɔ:s/ *n* **have ~ to** Zuflucht nehmen zu

re-'cover /ri:-/ *vt* neu beziehen

recover /rɪ'kʌvə(r)/ *vt* zurückbekommen; bergen *(wreck)* □ *vi* sich erholen. **~y** *n* Wiedererlangung *f*; Bergung *f*; *(of health)* Erholung *f*

recreation /rekrɪ'eɪʃn/ *n* Erholung *f*; *(hobby)* Hobby *nt*. **~al** *a* Freizeit-; **be ~al** erholsam sein

recrimination /rɪkrɪmɪ'neɪʃn/ *n* Gegenbeschuldigung *f*

recruit /rɪ'kru:t/ *n (Mil)* Rekrut *m*; **new ~** *(member)* neues Mitglied *nt*; *(worker)* neuer Mitarbeiter *m* □ *vt* rekrutieren; anwerben *(staff)*. **~ment** *n* Rekrutierung *f*; Anwerbung *f*

rectangle /'rektæŋgl/ *n* Rechteck *nt*. **~ular** /-'tæŋgjʊlə(r)/ *a* rechteckig

rectify /'rektɪfaɪ/ *vt (pt/pp -ied)* berichtigen

rector /'rektə(r)/ *n* Pfarrer *m*; (*Univ*) Rektor *m*. **~y** *n* Pfarrhaus *nt*

recuperat|e /rɪ'kju:pəreɪt/ *vi* sich erholen. **~ion** /-'reɪʃn/ *n* Erholung *f*

recur /rɪ'kɜ:(r)/ *vi* (*pt/pp* recurred) sich wiederholen; (*illness:*) wiederkehren

recurren|ce /rɪ'kʌrəns/ *n* Wiederkehr *f*. **~t** *a* wiederkehrend

recycle /ri:'saɪkl/ *vt* wieder verwerten. **~d paper** *n* Umweltschutzpapier *nt*

red /red/ *a* (redder, reddest) rot □*n* Rot *nt*. **~currant** *n* rote Johannisbeere *f*

redd|en /'redn/ *vt* röten □*vi* rot werden. **~ish** *a* rötlich

re'decorate /ri:-/ *vt* renovieren; (*paint*) neu streichen; (*wallpaper*) neu tapezieren

redeem /rɪ'di:m/ *vt* einlösen; (*Relig*) erlösen

redemption /rɪ'dempʃn/ *n* Erlösung *f*

rede'ploy /ri:-/ *vt* an anderer Stelle einsetzen

red: **~-haired** *a* rothaarig. **~-handed** *a* catch s.o. **~-handed** jdn auf frischer Tat ertappen. **~herring** *n* falsche Spur *f*. **~-hot** *a* glühend heiß. **R~ 'Indian** *n* Indianer(in) *m(f)*

redi'rect /ri:-/ *vt* nachsenden (*letter*); umleiten (*traffic*)

red: **~ 'light** *n* (*Auto*) rote Ampel *f*. **~ness** *n* Röte *f*

re'do /ri:-/ *vt* (*pt* -did, *pp* -done) noch einmal machen

re'double /ri:-/ *vt* verdoppeln

redress /rɪ'dres/ *n* Entschädigung *f* □*vt* wieder gutmachen; wiederherstellen (*balance*)

red 'tape *n* (*fam*) Bürokratie *f*

reduc|e /rɪ'dju:s/ *vt* verringern, vermindern; (*in size*) verkleinern; ermäßigen (*costs*); herabsetzen (*price, goods*); (*Culin*) einkochen lassen. **~tion**

/-'dʌkʃn/ *n* Verringerung *f*; (*in price*) Ermäßigung *f*; (*in size*) Verkleinerung *f*

redundan|cy /rɪ'dʌndənsɪ/ *n* Beschäftigungslosigkeit *f*; (*payment*) Abfindung *f*. **~t** *a* überflüssig; **make ~t** entlassen; **be made ~t** beschäftigungslos werden

reed /ri:d/ *n* [Schilf]rohr *nt*; **~s** *pl* Schilf *nt*

reef /ri:f/ *n* Riff *nt*

reek /ri:k/ *vi* riechen (*of* nach)

reel /ri:l/ *n* Rolle *f*, Spule *f* □*vi* (*stagger*) taumeln □*vt* **~ off** (*fig*) herunterrasseln

refectory /rɪ'fektərɪ/ *n* Refektorium *nt*; (*Univ*) Mensa *f*

refer /rɪ'fɜ:(r)/ *v* (*pt/pp* referred) □*vt* verweisen (**to an** + *acc*); übergeben, weiterleiten (*matter*) (**to an** + *acc*) □*vi* **~ to** sich beziehen auf (+ *acc*); (*mention*) erwähnen; (*concern*) betreffen; (*consult*) sich wenden an (+ *acc*); nachschlagen in (+ *dat*) (*book*); **are you ~ring to me?** meinen Sie mich?

referee /refə'ri:/ *n* Schiedsrichter *m*; (*Boxing*) Ringrichter *m*; (*for Job*) Referenz *f* □*vt/i* (*pt/pp* refereed) Schiedsrichter/Ringrichter sein (**bei**)

reference /'refərəns/ *n* Erwähnung *f*; (*in book*) Verweis *m*; (*for Job*) Referenz *f*; (*Comm*) 'your ~' 'Ihr Zeichen'; **with ~ to** in Bezug auf (+ *acc*); (*in letter*) unter Bezugnahme auf (+ *acc*); **make [a] ~ to** erwähnen. **~ book** *n* Nachschlagewerk *nt*. **~ number** *n* Aktenzeichen *nt*

referendum /refə'rendəm/ *n* Volksabstimmung *f*

re'fill[1] /ri:-/ *vt* nachfüllen

'refill[2] /ri:-/ *n* (*for pen*) Ersatzmine *f*

refine /rɪ'faɪn/ *vt* raffinieren. **~d** *a* fein, vornehm. **~ment** *n* Vornehmheit *f*; (*Techn*) Verfeinerung *f*. **~ry** /-ərɪ/ *n* Raffinerie *f*

reflect /rɪ'flekt/ vt reflektieren; ⟨mirror:⟩ [wider]spiegeln; **be ~ed in** sich spiegeln in (+ dat) □ vi nachdenken (on über + acc); ~ **badly upon s.o.** (fig) jdn in ein schlechtes Licht stellen. **~ion** /-ekʃn/ n Reflexion f; (image) Spiegelbild nt; **on ~ion** nach nochmaliger Überlegung. **~ive** /-ɪv/ a, **-ly** adv nachdenklich. **~or** n Rückstrahler m

reflex /'ri:fleks/ n Reflex m □ attrib Reflex-.

reflexive /rɪ'fleksɪv/ a reflexiv

reform /rɪ'fɔ:m/ n Reform f □ vt reformieren □ vi sich bessern. **R~ation** /refə'meɪʃn/ n (Relig) Reformation f. **~er** n Reformer m; (Relig) Reformator m

refract /rɪ'frækt/ vt (Phys) brechen

refrain¹ /rɪ'freɪn/ n Refrain m

refrain² vi **~ from doing sth** etw nicht tun

refresh /rɪ'freʃ/ vt erfrischen. **~ing** a erfrischend. **~ments** npl Erfrischungen pl

refrigerat|e /rɪ'frɪdʒəreɪt/ vt kühlen. **~or** n Kühlschrank m

re'fuel /ri:-/ vt/i (pt/pp **-fuelled**) auftanken

refuge /'refju:dʒ/ n Zuflucht f; **take ~ in** Zuflucht nehmen in (+ dat)

refugee /refjo'dʒi:/ n Flüchtling m

'refund /ri:-/ n; **get a ~** sein Geld zurückbekommen

re'fund² /rɪ-/ vt zurückerstatten

refurbish /ri:'fɜ:bɪʃ/ vt renovieren

refusal /rɪ'fju:zl/ n (see **refuse¹**) Ablehnung f; Weigerung f

refuse¹ /rɪ'fju:z/ vt ablehnen; (not grant) verweigern; **~ to do sth** sich weigern, etw zu tun □ vi ablehnen; sich weigern

refuse² /'refju:s/ n Müll m, Abfall m. **~ collection** n Müllabfuhr f

refute /rɪ'fju:t/ vt widerlegen

re'gain /rɪ-/ vt wiedergewinnen

regal /'ri:gl/ a, **-ly** adv königlich

regalia /rɪ'geɪlɪə/ npl Insignien pl

regard /rɪ'gɑ:d/ n (heed) Rücksicht f; (respect) Achtung f; **~s** pl Grüße mpl; **with ~ to** in Bezug auf (+ acc) □ vt ansehen, betrachten (as als); **as ~s** in Bezug auf (+ acc). **~ing** prep bezüglich (+ gen). **~less** adv ohne Rücksicht (of auf + acc)

regatta /rɪ'gætə/ n Regatta f

regenerate /rɪ'dʒenəreɪt/ vt regenerieren □ vi sich regenerieren

regime /reɪ'ʒi:m/ n Regime nt

regiment /'redʒɪmənt/ n Regiment nt. **~al** /-'mentl/ a Regiments-. **~ation** /-'teɪʃn/ n Reglementierung f

region /'ri:dʒən/ n Region f; **in the ~ of** (fig) ungefähr. **~al** a, **-ly** adv regional

register /'redʒɪstə(r)/ n Register nt; (Sch) Anwesenheitsliste f □ vt registrieren; (report) anmelden; einschreiben (letter); ~ aufgeben (luggage) □ vi (report) sich anmelden; **it didn't ~** (fig) ich habe es nicht registriert

registrar /redʒɪ'strɑ:(r)/ n Standesbeamte(r) m

registration /redʒɪ'streɪʃn/ n Registrierung f; Anmeldung f. **~ number** n Autonummer f

registry office /'redʒɪstrɪ-/ n Standesamt f

regret /rɪ'gret/ n Bedauern nt □ vt (pt/pp **regretted**) bedauern. **~fully** adv mit Bedauern

regrettab|le /rɪ'gretəbl/ a bedauerlich. **~ly** adv bedauerlicherweise

regular /'regjolə(r)/ a, **-ly** adv regelmäßig; (usual) üblich; (Mil) Berufs- □ n Berufssoldat m; (in pub) Stammgast m; (in shop) Stammkunde m. **~ity** /-'lærətɪ/ n Regelmäßigkeit f

regulate /'regjuleɪt/ vt regulieren. **~ion** /-'leɪʃn/ n (rule) Vorschrift f

rehabilitate /ri:hə'bɪlɪteɪt/ vt rehabilitieren. **~ion** /-'teɪʃn/ n Rehabilitation f

rehears|al /rɪ'hɜːsl/ n (Theat) Probe f. **~e** vt proben

reign /reɪn/ n Herrschaft f □ vi herrschen, regieren

reimburse /ri:ɪm'bɜːs/ vt ~ s.o. for sth jdm etw zurückerstatten

rein /reɪn/ n Zügel m

reincarnation /ri:ɪnkɑ:'neɪʃn/ f **Reinkarnation** f, Wiedergeburt f

reindeer /'reɪndɪə(r)/ n inv Rentier nt

reinforce /ri:ɪn'fɔːs/ vt verstärken. **~d 'concrete** n Stahlbeton m. **~ment** n Verstärkung f; **send ~ments** Verstärkung schicken

reinstate /ri:ɪn'steɪt/ vt wieder einstellen; (to office) wieder einsetzen

reiterate /ri:'ɪtəreɪt/ vt wiederholen

reject /rɪ'dʒekt/ vt ablehnen. **~ion** /-ekʃn/ n Ablehnung f

rejects /'ri:dʒekts/ npl (Comm) Ausschussware f

rejoic|e /rɪ'dʒɔɪs/ vi (liter) sich freuen. **~ing** n Freude f

re'join /rɪ-/ vt sich wieder anschließen (+ dat); wieder beitreten (+ dat) (club, party); (answer) erwidern

rejuvenate /rɪ'dʒu:vəneɪt/ vt verjüngen

relapse /rɪ'læps/ n Rückfall m □ vi einen Rückfall erleiden

relate /rɪ'leɪt/ vt (tell) erzählen; (connect) verbinden □ vi zusammenhängen (to mit). **~d** a verwandt (to mit)

relation /rɪ'leɪʃn/ n Beziehung f; (person) Verwandte(r) m/f. **~ship** n Beziehung f; (blood tie) Verwandtschaft f; (affair) Verhältnis nt

relative /'relətɪv/ n Verwandte(r) m/f □ a relativ; (Gram) Relativ-. **~ly** adv relativ, verhältnismäßig

relax /rɪ'læks/ vt lockern, entspannen □ vi sich lockern, sich entspannen. **~ation** /-'seɪʃn/ n Entspannung f. **~ing** a entspannend

relay¹ /ri:'leɪ/ vt (pt/pp -layed) weitergeben; (Radio, TV) übertragen

relay² /'ri:leɪ/ n (Electr) Relais nt; **work in ~s** sich bei der Arbeit ablösen. **~ [race]** n Staffel f

release /rɪ'li:s/ n Freilassung f, Entlassung f; (Techn) Auslöser m □ vt freilassen; (let go of) loslassen; (Techn) auslösen; veröffentlichen (information)

relegate /'relɪgeɪt/ vt verbannen; **be ~d** (Sport) absteigen

relent /rɪ'lent/ vi nachgeben. **~less, -ly** adv erbarmungslos; (unceasing) unaufhörlich

relevan|ce /'reləvəns/ n Relevanz f. **~t** a relevant (to für)

reliab|ility /rɪlaɪə'bɪlətɪ/ n Zuverlässigkeit f. **~le** /-'laɪəbl/ a, **-ly** adv zuverlässig

relian|ce /rɪ'laɪəns/ n Abhängigkeit f (on von). **~t** a angewiesen (on auf + acc)

relic /'relɪk/ n Überbleibsel nt; (Relig) Reliquie f

relief /rɪ'li:f/ n Erleichterung f; (assistance) Hilfe f; (replacement) Ablösung f; (Art) Relief nt; **in ~** im Relief. **~ map** n Reliefkarte f. **~ train** n Entlastungszug m

relieve /rɪ'li:v/ vt erleichtern; (take over from) ablösen; **~ of** entlasten von

religion /rɪ'lɪdʒən/ n Religion f

religious /rɪ'lɪdʒəs/ a religiös. **~ly** adv (conscientiously) gewissenhaft

relinquish /rɪ'lɪŋkwɪʃ/ vt loslassen; (give up) aufgeben

relish /'relɪʃ/ n Genuss m; (Culin) Würze f □ vt genießen

relo'cate /riː-/ vt verlegen

reluctan|ce /rɪ'lʌktəns/ n Widerstreben nt. ~t a widerstrebend; **be** ~t zögern (**to** zu). ~**tly** adv ungern, widerstrebend

rely /rɪ'laɪ/ vi (pt/pp -ied) ~ **on** sich verlassen auf (+ acc); (be dependent on) angewiesen sein auf (+ acc)

remain /rɪ'meɪn/ vi bleiben; (be left) übrig bleiben. ~**der** n Rest m. ~**ing** a restlich. ~**s** npl Reste pl; **[mortal]** ~**s** [sterbliche] Überreste pl

remand /rɪ'mɑːnd/ n **on** ~ in Untersuchungshaft □ vt ~ in **custody** in Untersuchungshaft schicken

remark /rɪ'mɑːk/ n Bemerkung f □ vt bemerken. ~**able** /-əbl/ a, -**bly** adv bemerkenswert

re|marry /riː-/ vi wieder heiraten

remedial /rɪ'miːdɪəl/ a Hilfs-; (Med) Heil-

remedy /'remədɪ/ n [Heil]mittel nt (**for** gegen); (fig) Abhilfe f □ vt (pt/pp -ied) abhelfen (+ dat); beheben (fault)

remember /rɪ'membə(r)/ vt sich erinnern an (+ acc); ~**r to do** sth daran denken, etw zu tun; ~**r me to him** grüßen Sie ihn von mir □ vi sich erinnern. ~**rance** n Erinnerung f

remind /rɪ'maɪnd/ vt erinnern (**of** an + acc). ~**er** n Andenken nt; (letter, warning) Mahnung f

reminisce /remɪ'nɪs/ vi sich seinen Erinnerungen hingeben. ~**nces** /-ənsɪz/ npl Erinnerungen pl. ~**nt** a **be** ~**nt of** erinnern an (+ acc)

remiss /rɪ'mɪs/ a nachlässig

remission /rɪ'mɪʃn/ n Nachlass m; (of sentence) [Straf]erlass m; (Med) Remission f

remit /rɪ'mɪt/ vt (pt/pp **remitted**) überweisen (money). ~**tance** n Überweisung f

remnant /'remnənt/ n Rest m

remonstrate /'remənstreɪt/ vi protestieren; ~ **with** s.o. jdm Vorhaltungen machen

remorse /rɪ'mɔːs/ n Reue f. ~**ful** a, -**ly** adv reumütig. ~**less** a, -**ly** adv unerbittlich

remote /rɪ'məʊt/ a fern; (isolated) abgelegen; (slight) gering. ~ **control** n Fernsteuerung f; (for TV) Fernbedienung f. ~-**con'trolled** a ferngesteuert; fernbedient

remotely /rɪ'məʊtlɪ/ adv entfernt; **not** ~ nicht im Entferntesten

re'movable /rɪ-/ a abnehmbar

removal /rɪ'muːvl/ n Entfernung f; (from house) Umzug m. ~ **van** n Möbelwagen m

remove /rɪ'muːv/ vt entfernen; (take off) abnehmen; (take out) herausnehmen

remunerat|e /rɪ'mjuːnəreɪt/ vt bezahlen. ~**ion** /-'reɪʃn/ n Bezahlung f. ~**ive** /-ətɪv/ a einträglich

render /'rendə(r)/ vt machen; erweisen (service); (translate) wiedergeben; (Mus) vortragen

renegade /'renɪgeɪd/ n Abtrünnige(r) m/f

renew /rɪ'njuː/ vt erneuern; verlängern (contract). ~**al** n Erneuerung f; Verlängerung f

renounce /rɪ'naʊns/ vt verzichten auf (+ acc); (Relig) abschwören (+ dat)

renovat|e /'renəveɪt/ vt renovieren. ~**ion** /-'veɪʃn/ n Renovierung f

renown /rɪ'naʊn/ n Ruf m. ~**ed** a berühmt

rent /rent/ n Miete f □ vt mieten; (hire) leihen; ~ **[out]** vermieten; verleihen. ~**al** n Mietgebühr f; Leihgebühr f

renunciation /rɪnʌnsɪ'eɪʃn/ n Verzicht m

re'open /riː-/ vt/i wieder aufmachen

re'organize /riː-/ vt reorganisieren

rep /rep/ n (fam) Vertreter m

repair /rɪ'peə(r)/ n Reparatur f;
in good/bad ~ in gutem/
schlechtem Zustand □ vt reparieren

repartee /repɑː'tiː/ n piece of ~
schlagfertige Antwort f

repatriat|e /riː'pætrɪeɪt/ vt repa-
triieren. **~ion** /-'eɪʃn/ n Repatri-
ierung f

re'pay /riː-/ vt (pt/pp **-paid**) zurückzahlen; ~ **s.o. for sth** jdm
etw zurückzahlen. **~ment** n
Rückzahlung f

repeal /rɪ'piːl/ n Aufhebung f □ vt
aufheben

repeat /rɪ'piːt/ n Wiederholung f
□ vt/i wiederholen; ~ **after me**
sprechen Sie mir nach. **~ed** a, **-ly**
adv wiederholt

repel /rɪ'pel/ vt (pt/pp **repelled**)
abwehren; (fig) abstoßen. **~lent**
a abstoßend

repent /rɪ'pent/ vi Reue zeigen.
~ance n Reue f. **~ant** a reuig

repercussions /riːpə'kʌʃnz/ npl
Auswirkungen pl

repertoire /'repətwɑː(r)/ n Repertoire nt

repertory /'repətrɪ/ n Repertoire
nt

repetit|ion /repɪ'tɪʃn/ n Wieder-
holung f. **~ive** /rɪ'petɪtɪv/ a eintönig

re'place /rɪ-/ vt zurücktun; (take
the place of) ersetzen; (exchange)
austauschen, auswechseln.
~ment n Ersatz m. **~ment part**
n Ersatzteil nt

'replay /rɪ-/ n (Sport) Wiederho-
lungsspiel nt; **[action]** ~ Wiederholung f

replenish /rɪ'plenɪʃ/ vt auffüllen
(stocks); (refill) nachfüllen

replete /rɪ'pliːt/ a gesättigt

replica /'replɪkə/ n Nachbildung
f

reply /rɪ'plaɪ/ n Antwort f (to auf
+ acc) □ vt/i (pt/pp **replied**)
antworten

report /rɪ'pɔːt/ n Bericht m; (Sch)
Zeugnis nt; (rumour) Gerücht nt;

(of gun) Knall m □ vt berichten;
(notify) melden; ~ **s.o. to the
police** jdn anzeigen □ vi berichten (on über + acc); (present
oneself) sich melden (to bei). **~er**
n Reporter(in) m(f)

repose /rɪ'pəʊz/ n Ruhe f

repos'sess /riː-/ vt wieder in Besitz nehmen

reprehensible /reprɪ'hensəbl/ a
tadelnswert

represent /reprɪ'zent/ vt darstellen; (act for) vertreten, reprä-
sentieren. **~ation** /-'teɪʃn/ n
Darstellung f; **make ~ations to**
vorstellig werden bei

representative /reprɪ'zentətɪv/ a
repräsentativ (of für) □ n Be-
vollmächtigte(r) m(f); (Comm)
Vertreter(in) m(f); (Amer, Pol)
Abgeordnete(r) m/f

repress /rɪ'pres/ vt unterdrücken. **~ion** /-eʃn/ n Unterdrückung f. **~ive** /-ɪv/ a repressiv

reprieve /rɪ'priːv/ n Begnadigung
f; (postponement) Strafaufschub
m; (fig) Gnadenfrist f □ vt begnadigen

reprimand /'reprɪmɑːnd/ n Tadel
m □ vt tadeln

'reprint /riː-/ n Nachdruck m

re'print /riː-/ vt neu auflegen

reprisal /rɪ'praɪzl/ n Vergeltungs-
maßnahme f

reproach /rɪ'prəʊtʃ/ n Vorwurf m
□ vt Vorwürfe pl machen (+ dat).
~ful a, **-ly** adv vorwurfsvoll

repro'duc|e /riː-/ vt wiedergeben;
reproduzieren □ vi sich fortpflanzen. **~tion** /-'dʌkʃn/ n
Reproduktion f; (Biol) Fort-
pflanzung f. **~tion furniture**
n Stilmöbel pl. **~tive**
/-'dʌktɪv/ a Fortpflanzungs-

reprove /rɪ'pruːv/ vt tadeln

reptile /'reptaɪl/ n Reptil nt

republic /rɪ'pʌblɪk/ n Republik f.
~an a republikanisch □ n Republi-
kaner(in) m(f)

repudiate /rɪ'pjuːdɪeɪt/ vt zurückweisen

repugnan|ce /rɪ'pʌgnəns/ n Widerwille m. **~t** a widerlich

repuls|e /rɪ'pʌls/ vt abwehren; (fig) abweisen. **~ion** /-ʌlʃn/ n Widerwille m. **~ive** /-ɪv/ a abstoßend, widerlich

reputable /'repjutəbl/ a (firm) von gutem Ruf; (respectable) anständig

reputation /repjʊ'teɪʃn/ n Ruf m

repute /rɪ'pjuːt/ n Ruf m. **~d** /-ɪd/ a, **-ly** adv angeblich

request /rɪ'kwest/ n Bitte f ⫽ vt bitten. **~ stop** n Bedarfshaltestelle f

require /rɪ'kwaɪə(r)/ vt (need) brauchen; (demand) erfordern; **be ~d to do sth** etw tun müssen. **~ment** n Bedürfnis nt; (condition) Erfordernis nt

requisite /'rekwɪzɪt/ a erforderlich ⫽ n **toilet/travel ~s** pl Toiletten-/Reiseartikel pl

requisition /rekwɪ'zɪʃn/ n **[order]** Anforderung f ⫽ vt anfordern

re'sale /riː-/ n Weiterverkauf m

rescind /rɪ'sɪnd/ vt aufheben

rescue /'reskjuː/ n Rettung f ⫽ vt retten. **~r** n Retter m

research /rɪ's3ːtʃ/ n Forschung f ⫽ vt erforschen; (Journ) recherchieren ⫽ vi **~ into** forschen. **~er** n Forscher m; (Journ) Rechercheur m

resem|blance /rɪ'zembləns/ n Ähnlichkeit f. **~ble** /-bl/ vi ähneln (+ dat)

resent /rɪ'zent/ vt übel nehmen; einen Groll hegen gegen ⟨person⟩. **~ful** a, **-ly** adv verbittert. **~ment** n Groll m

reservation /rezə'veɪʃn/ n Reservierung f; (doubt) Vorbehalt m; (enclosure) Reservat nt

reserve /rɪ'z3ːv/ n Reserve f; (for animals) Reservat nt; (Sport) Reservespieler(in) m(f) ⫽ vt reservieren; ⟨client:⟩ reservieren lassen; (keep) aufheben; sich (dat)

vorbehalten ⟨right⟩. **~d** a reserviert

reservoir /'rezəvwɑː(r)/ n Reservoir nt

re'shape /riː-/ vt umformen

re'shuffle /riː-/ n (Pol) umbildung f ⫽ vt (Pol) umbilden

reside /rɪ'zaɪd/ vi wohnen

residence /'rezɪdəns/ n Wohnsitz m; (official) Residenz f; (stay) Aufenthalt m. **~ permit** n Aufenthaltsgenehmigung f

resident /'rezɪdənt/ a ansässig (in in + dat); (housekeeper, nurse) im Haus wohnend ⫽ n Bewohner(in) m(f); (of street) Anwohner m. **~ial** /-'denʃl/ a Wohn-

residue /'rezɪdjuː/ n Rest m; (Chem) Rückstand m

resign /rɪ'zaɪn/ vt **~ oneself to** sich abfinden mit ⫽ vi kündigen; (from public office) zurücktreten. **~ation** /rezɪg'neɪʃn/ n Resignation f; (from job) Kündigung f; Rücktritt m. **~ed** a, **-ly** adv resigniert

resilient /rɪ'zɪlɪənt/ a federnd; (fig) widerstandsfähig

resin /'rezɪn/ n Harz nt

resist /rɪ'zɪst/ vt/i sich widersetzen (+ dat); (fig) widerstehen (+ dat). **~ance** n Widerstand m. **~ant** a widerstandsfähig

resolut|e /'rezəluːt/ a, **-ly** adv entschlossen. **~ion** /-'luːʃn/ n Entschlossenheit f; (intention) Vorsatz m; (Pol) Resolution f

resolve /rɪ'zɒlv/ n Entschlossenheit f; (decision) Beschluss m ⫽ vt beschließen; (solve) lösen. **~d** a entschlossen

resonan|ce /'rezənəns/ n Resonanz f. **~t** a klangvoll

resort /rɪ'zɔːt/ n (place) Urlaubsort m; **as a last ~** wenn alles andere fehlschlägt ⫽ vi **~ to** (fig) greifen zu

resound /rɪ'zaʊnd/ vi widerhallen. **~ing** a widerhallend; (loud) laut; (notable) groß

resource /rɪ'sɔːs/ n ~s pl
Ressourcen pl. ~ful a findig.
~fulness n Findigkeit f

respect /rɪ'spekt/ n Respekt m,
Achtung f (for vor + dat); (aspect) Hinsicht f; with ~ to in Bezug auf (+ acc) □ vt respektieren,
achten

respectability /rɪspektə'bɪlətɪ/ n
(see respectable) Ehrbarkeit f;
Anständigkeit f

respect|able /rɪ'spektəbl/ a, -bly
adv ehrbar; (decent) anständig;
(considerable) ansehnlich. ~ful
a, -ly adv respektvoll

respective /rɪ'spektɪv/ a jeweilig.
~ly adv beziehungsweise

respiration /respə'reɪʃn/ n Atmung f

respite /'respaɪt/ n [Ruhe]pause
f; (delay) Aufschub m

resplendent /rɪ'splendənt/ a
glänzend

respond /rɪ'spɒnd/ vi antworten;
(react) reagieren (to auf + acc);
(patient:) ansprechen (to auf +
acc)

response /rɪ'spɒns/ n Antwort f;
Reaktion f

responsibility /rɪspɒnsɪ'bɪlətɪ/ n
Verantwortung f; (duty)
Verpflichtung f

responsib|le /rɪ'spɒnsəbl/ a ver-
antwortlich; (trustworthy) ver-
antwortungsvoll. ~ly adv
verantwortungsbewusst

responsive /rɪ'spɒnsɪv/ a be ~
reagieren

rest1 /rest/ n Ruhe f; (holiday) Erholung f; (interval & Mus) Pause
f; have a ~ eine Pause machen;
(rest) sich ausruhen □ vt ausruhen; (lean) lehnen (on an/auf
+ acc) □ vi ruhen; (have a rest)
sich ausruhen

rest2 n the ~ der Rest; (people) die
Übrigen pl □ vi it ~s with you
es ist an Ihnen (to do)

restaurant /'restərɒnt/ n Restaurant nt, Gaststätte f. ~ car n
Speisewagen m

restful /'restfl/ a erholsam

restitution /restɪ'tjuːʃn/ n Entschädigung f; (return) Rückgabe
f

restive /'restɪv/ a unruhig

restless /'restlɪs/ a, -ly adv unruhig

restoration /restə'reɪʃn/ n (of
building) Restaurierung f

restore /rɪ'stɔː(r)/ vt wiederherstellen; restaurieren (building);
(give back) zurückgeben

restrain /rɪ'streɪn/ vt zurückhalten; ~ oneself sich beherrschen. ~ed a
zurückhaltend. ~t n Zurück-
haltung f

restrict /rɪ'strɪkt/ vt einschränken; ~ to beschränken auf (+
acc). ~ion /-ɪkʃn/ n Einschränkung f; Beschränkung f. ~ive
/-ɪv/ a einschränkend

rest room n (Amer) Toilette f

result /rɪ'zʌlt/ n Ergebnis nt, Resultat nt; (consequence) Folge f;
as a ~ als Folge (of gen) □ vi sich
ergeben (from aus); ~ in enden
in (+ dat); (lead to) führen zu

resume /rɪ'zjuːm/ vt wieder aufnehmen; wieder einnehmen
(seat) □ vi wieder beginnen

résumé /'rezʊmeɪ/ n Zusammenfassung f

resumption /rɪ'zʌmpʃn/ n Wieder-
aufnahme f

resurgence /rɪ'sɜːdʒəns/ n Wie-
deraufleben nt

resurrect /rezə'rekt/ vt (fig) wieder beleben. ~ion /-ekʃn/ n the
R~ion (Relig) die Auferstehung

resuscitat|e /rɪ'sʌsɪteɪt/ vt wie-
der beleben. ~ion /-'teɪʃn/ n
Wiederbelebung f

retail /'riːteɪl/ n Einzelhandel m
□ a Einzelhandels- □ adv im Einzelhandel □ vt im Einzelhandel
verkaufen □ vi ~ at im Einzelhandel kosten. ~er n Einzel-
händler m. ~ price n Ladenpreis
m

retain /rɪ'teɪn/ vt behalten

retaliat|e /rɪ'tælɪeɪt/ vi zurückschlagen. **~ion** /-'eɪʃn/ n Vergeltung f; **in ~ion** als Vergeltung

retarded /rɪ'tɑːdɪd/ a zurückgeblieben

retentive /rɪ'tentɪv/ a ⟨memory⟩ gut

reticen|ce /'retɪsns/ n Zurückhaltung f. **~t** a zurückhaltend

retina /'retɪnə/ n Netzhaut f

retinue /'retɪnjuː/ n Gefolge nt

retire /rɪ'taɪə(r)/ vi in den Ruhestand treten; ⟨withdraw⟩ sich zurückziehen. **~d** a im Ruhestand. **~ment** n Ruhestand m; **since my ~ment** seit ich nicht mehr arbeite

retiring /rɪ'taɪərɪŋ/ a zurückhaltend

retort /rɪ'tɔːt/ n scharfe Erwiderung f; ⟨Chem⟩ Retorte f □ vt scharf erwidern

re'touch /riː-/ vt ⟨Phot⟩ retuschieren

re'trace /rɪ-/ vt zurückverfolgen; **~ one's steps** denselben Weg zurückgehen

retract /rɪ'trækt/ vt einziehen; zurücknehmen ⟨remark⟩ □ vi widerrufen

re'train /riː-/ vt umschulen □ vi umgeschult werden

retreat /rɪ'triːt/ n Rückzug m; ⟨place⟩ Zufluchtsort m □ vi sich zurückziehen

re'trial /riː-/ n Wiederaufnahmeverfahren nt

retribution /retrɪ'bjuːʃn/ n Vergeltung f

retrieve /rɪ'triːv/ vt zurückholen; ⟨from wreckage⟩ bergen; ⟨Computing⟩ wieder auffinden; ⟨dog:⟩ apportieren

retrograde /'retrəgreɪd/ a rückschrittlich

retrospect /'retrəspekt/ n **in ~** rückblickend. **~ive** /-'ɪv/ a, **-ly** adv rückwirkend; ⟨looking back⟩ rückblickend

return /rɪ'tɜːn/ n Rückkehr f; ⟨giving back⟩ Rückgabe f; ⟨Comm⟩ Ertrag m; ⟨ticket⟩ Rückfahrkarte f; ⟨Aviat⟩ Rückflugschein m; **by ~ [of post]** postwendend; **in ~** dafür; **in ~ for** für; **many happy ~s!** herzlichen Glückwunsch zum Geburtstag! □ vt zurückgehen/-fahren; ⟨come back⟩ zurückkommen □ vt zurückgeben; ⟨put back⟩ zurückstellen/-legen; ⟨send back⟩ zurückschicken; ⟨elect⟩ wählen

return: **~ flight** n Rückflug m. **~ match** n Rückspiel nt. **~ ticket** n Rückfahrkarte f; ⟨Aviat⟩ Rückflugschein m

reunion /riː'juːnɪən/ n Wiedervereinigung f; ⟨social gathering⟩ Treffen nt

reunite /riːjuː'naɪt/ vt wieder vereinigen □ vi sich wieder vereinigen

re'us|able /riː-/ a wieder verwendbar. **~e** vt wieder verwenden

rev /rev/ n ⟨Auto, fam⟩ Umdrehung f □ vt/i **~ [up]** den Motor auf Touren bringen

reveal /rɪ'viːl/ vt zum Vorschein bringen; ⟨fig⟩ enthüllen. **~ing** a ⟨fig⟩ aufschlussreich

revel /'revl/ vi ⟨pt/pp revelled⟩ **~ in sth** etw genießen

revelation /revə'leɪʃn/ n Offenbarung f, Enthüllung f

revelry /'revlrɪ/ n Lustbarkeit f

revenge /rɪ'vendʒ/ n Rache f; ⟨fig & Sport⟩ Revanche f □ vt rächen

revenue /'revənjuː/ n [Staats]einnahmen pl

reverberate /rɪ'vɜːbəreɪt/ vi nachhallen

revere /rɪ'vɪə(r)/ vt verehren. **~nce** /'revərəns/ n Ehrfurcht f

Reverend /'revərənd/ a **the ~ a** B pfarrer X; ⟨Catholic⟩ Hochwürden X

reverent /'revərənt/ a, **-ly** adv ehrfürchtig

reverie /'revərı/ n Träumerei f

revers /rɪ'vɪə/ n (pl revers /-z/) Revers nt

reversal /rɪ'vɜːsl/ n Umkehrung f

reverse /rɪ'vɜːs/ a umgekehrt □ n Gegenteil nt; (back) Rückseite f; (Auto) Rückwärtsgang m □ vt umkehren; (Auto) zurücksetzen; ~ the charges (Teleph) ein R-Gespräch führen □ vi zurücksetzen

revert /rɪ'vɜːt/ vi ~ to zurückfallen an (+ acc); zurückkommen auf (+ acc) (topic)

review /rɪ'vjuː/ n Rückblick m (of auf + acc); (re-examination) Überprüfung f; (Mil) Truppenschau f; (of book, play) Kritik f, Rezension f □ vt zurückblicken auf (+ acc); überprüfen (situation); (Mil) besichtigen; kritisieren, rezensieren (book, play). ~er n Kritiker m, Rezensent m

revile /rɪ'vaɪl/ vt verunglimpfen

revis|e /rɪ'vaɪz/ vt revidieren; (for exam) wiederholen. ~ion /-'vɪʒn/ n Revision f; Wiederholung f

revival /rɪ'vaɪvl/ n Wiederbelebung f

revive /rɪ'vaɪv/ vt wieder beleben; (fig) wieder aufleben lassen □ vi wieder aufleben

revoke /rɪ'vəʊk/ vt aufheben; widerrufen (command, decision)

revolt /rɪ'vəʊlt/ n Aufstand m □ vi rebellieren □ vt anwidern. ~ing a widerlich, eklig

revolution /revə'luːʃn/ n Revolution f; (Auto) Umdrehung f. ~ary /-ərɪ/ a revolutionär. ~ize vt revolutionieren

revolve /rɪ'vɒlv/ vi sich drehen; ~ around kreisen um

revolv|er /rɪ'vɒlvə(r)/ n Revolver m. ~ing a Dreh-

revue /rɪ'vjuː/ n Revue f; (satirical) Kabarett nt

revulsion /rɪ'vʌlʃn/ n Abscheu m

reward /rɪ'wɔːd/ n Belohnung f □ vt belohnen. ~ing a lohnend

re'write /riː-/ vt (pt rewrote, pp rewritten) noch einmal [neu] schreiben; (alter) umschreiben

rhapsody /'ræpsədɪ/ n Rhapsodie f

rhetoric /'retərɪk/ n Rhetorik f. ~al /rɪ'tɒrɪkl/ a rhetorisch

rheuma|tic /ruː'mætɪk/ a rheumatisch. ~tism /'ruːmətɪzm/ n Rheumatismus m, Rheuma nt

Rhine /raɪn/ n Rhein m

rhinoceros /raɪ'nɒsərəs/ n Nashorn nt, Rhinozeros nt

rhubarb /'ruːbɑːb/ n Rhabarber m

rhyme /raɪm/ n Reim m □ vt reimen □ vi sich reimen

rhythm /'rɪðm/ n Rhythmus m. ~ic[al] a, -ally adv rhythmisch

rib /rɪb/ n Rippe f □ vt (pt/pp ribbed) (fam) aufziehen (fam)

ribald /'rɪbld/ a derb

ribbon /'rɪbən/ n Band nt; (for typewriter) Farbband nt; in ~s in Fetzen

rice /raɪs/ n Reis m

rich /rɪtʃ/ a (-er, -est), -ly adv reich; (food) gehaltvoll; (heavy) schwer □ n the ~ pl die Reichen; ~es pl Reichtum m

rickets /'rɪkɪts/ n Rachitis f

rickety /'rɪkətɪ/ a wackelig

ricochet /'rɪkəʃeɪ/ vi abprallen

rid /rɪd/ vt (pt/pp rid, pres p ridding) befreien (of von); get ~ of loswerden

riddance /'rɪdns/ n good ~! auf Nimmerwiedersehen!

ridden /'rɪdn/ see ride

riddle /'rɪdl/ n Rätsel nt

riddled /'rɪdld/ a ~ with durchlöchert mit

ride /raɪd/ n Ritt m; (in vehicle) Fahrt f; take s.o. for a ~ (fam) jdn reinlegen □ v (pt rode, pp ridden) □ vt reiten (horse); fahren mit (bicycle) □ vi reiten; (in vehicle) fahren. ~r n Reiter(in) m(f); (on bicycle) Fahrer(in) m(f); (in document) Zusatzklausel f

ridge /rɪdʒ/ n Erhebung f; (on roof) First m; (of mountain) Grat m, Kamm m; (of high pressure) Hochdruckkeil m

ridicule /'rɪdɪkjuːl/ n Spott m □ vt verspotten, spotten über (+ acc)

ridiculous /rɪ'dɪkjʊləs/ a, **-ly** adv lächerlich

riding /'raɪdɪŋ/ n Reiten nt □ attrib Reit-

rife /raɪf/ a be ∼ weit verbreitet sein

riff-raff /'rɪfræf/ n Gesindel nt

rifle /'raɪfl/ n Gewehr nt □ vt plündern; ∼ **through** durchwühlen

rift /rɪft/ n Spalt m; (fig) Riss m

rig¹ /rɪg/ n Ölbohrturm m; (at sea) Bohrinsel f □ vt (pt/pp **rigged**) ∼ **out** ausrüsten; ∼ **up** aufbauen

rig² vt (pt/pp **rigged**) manipulieren

right /raɪt/ a richtig; (not left) rechte(r,s); be ∼ 〈person:〉 Recht haben; 〈clock:〉 richtig gehen; put ∼ wieder in Ordnung bringen; (fig) richtig stellen; that's ∼! das stimmt! □ adv richtig; (directly) direkt; (completely) ganz; (not left) rechts; 〈go〉 nach rechts; ∼ **away** sofort □ n Recht nt; (not left) rechte Seite f; on the ∼ rechts; from/to the ∼ von/nach rechts; be in the ∼ Recht haben; by ∼s eigentlich; the R∼ (Pol) die Rechte. ∼ **angle** n rechter Winkel m

righteous /'raɪtʃəs/ a rechtschaffen

rightful /'raɪtfl/ a, **-ly** adv rechtmäßig

right: ∼-'**handed** a rechtshändig. ∼**-hand 'man** n (fig) rechte Hand f

rightly /'raɪtlɪ/ adv mit Recht

right: ∼ of way n Durchgangsrecht nt; (path) öffentlicher Fußweg m; (Auto) Vorfahrt f. ∼-'**wing** a (Pol) rechte(r,s)

rigid /'rɪdʒɪd/ a starr; (strict) streng. ∼**ity** /-'dʒɪdətɪ/ n Starrheit f; Strenge f

rigmarole /'rɪgmərəʊl/ n Geschwätz nt; (procedure) Prozedur f

rigorous /'rɪgərəs/ a, **-ly** adv streng

rigour /'rɪgə(r)/ n Strenge f

rile /raɪl/ vt (fam) ärgern

rim /rɪm/ n Rand m; (of wheel) Felge f

rind /raɪnd/ n (on fruit) Schale f; (on cheese) Rinde f; (on bacon) Schwarte f

ring¹ /rɪŋ/ n Ring m; (for circus) Manege f; **stand in a** ∼ im Kreis stehen □ vt umringen; ∼ **in red** rot einkreisen

ring² n Klingeln nt; **give s.o. a** ∼ (Teleph) jdn anrufen □ v (pt **rang**, pp **rung**) □ vt läuten; (Teleph) anrufen □ vi läuten, klingeln. ∼ **back** vt/i (Teleph) zurückrufen. ∼ **off** vi (Teleph) auflegen

ring: ∼**leader** n Rädelsführer m. ∼ **road** n Umgehungsstraße f

rink /rɪŋk/ n Eisbahn f

rinse /rɪns/ n Spülung f; (hair colour) Tönung f □ vt spülen; tönen 〈hair〉. ∼ **off** vt abspülen

riot /'raɪət/ n Aufruhr m; ∼**s** pl Unruhen pl; ∼ **of colours** bunte Farbenpracht f; **run** ∼ randalieren □ vi randalieren. ∼**er** n Randalierer m. ∼**ous** /-əs/ a aufrührerisch; (boisterous) wild

rip /rɪp/ n Riss m □ vt/i (pt/pp **ripped**) zerreißen; ∼ **open** aufreißen. ∼ **off** vt (fam) neppen

ripe /raɪp/ a (-r, -st) reif

ripen /'raɪpn/ vi reifen □ vt reifen lassen

ripeness /'raɪpnɪs/ n Reife f

'**rip-off** n (fam) Nepp m

ripple /'rɪpl/ n kleine Welle f □ vt kräuseln □ vi sich kräuseln

rise /raɪz/ n Anstieg m; (fig) Aufstieg m; (increase) Zunahme f; (in wages) Lohnerhöhung f; (in salary) Gehaltserhöhung f; **give** ∼ **to** Anlass geben zu □ vi (pt **rose**, pp risen) steigen; ⟨ground:⟩ ansteigen; ⟨sun, dough:⟩ aufgehen; ⟨river:⟩ entspringen; ⟨get up⟩ aufstehen; ⟨fig⟩ aufsteigen (to zu); ⟨rebel⟩ sich erheben; ⟨court:⟩ sich vertagen. **~r** n early ~r Frühaufsteher m

rising /'raɪzɪŋ/ a steigend; ⟨sun⟩ aufgehend; the **~ generation** die heranwachsende Generation □ n ⟨revolt⟩ Aufstand m

risk /rɪsk/ n Risiko nt; **at one's own ~** auf eigene Gefahr □ vt riskieren

risky /'rɪskɪ/ a (-ier, -iest) riskant

risqué /'rɪskeɪ/ a gewagt

rissole /'rɪsəʊl/ n Frikadelle f

rite /raɪt/ n Ritus m; **last ~s** Letzte Ölung f

ritual /'rɪtjʊəl/ a rituell □ n Ritual nt

rival /'raɪvl/ a rivalisierend □ n Rivale m/Rivalin f; **~s** pl ⟨Comm⟩ Konkurrenten pl □ vt ⟨pt/pp rivalled⟩ gleichkommen (+ dat); ⟨compete with⟩ rivalisieren mit. **~ry** n Rivalität f; ⟨Comm⟩ Konkurrenzkampf m

river /'rɪvə(r)/ n Fluss m. **~-bed** n Flussbett nt

rivet /'rɪvɪt/ n Niete f □ vt [ver]nieten; ⟨fig⟩ fesseln. **~ed by** ⟨fig⟩ gefesselt von

road /rəʊd/ n Straße f; ⟨fig⟩ Weg m

road: **~-block** n Straßensperre f. **~-hog** n ⟨fam⟩ Straßenschreck m. **~-map** n Straßenkarte f. **~ safety** n Verkehrssicherheit f. **~ sense** n Verkehrssinn m. **~side** n Straßenrand m. **~way** n Fahrbahn f. **~works** npl Straßenarbeiten pl. **~worthy** a verkehrssicher

roam /rəʊm/ vi wandern

roar /rɔː(r)/ n Gebrüll nt; **~s of laughter** schallendes Gelächter nt □ vi brüllen; ⟨with laughter⟩ schallend lachen. **~ing** a ⟨fire⟩ prasselnd; **do a ~ing trade** ⟨fam⟩ ein Bombengeschäft machen

roast /rəʊst/ a gebraten, Brat-; **~ beef/pork** Rinder-/Schweinebraten m □ n Braten m □ vt/i braten; rösten ⟨coffee, chestnuts⟩

rob /rɒb/ vt ⟨pt/pp **robbed**⟩ berauben (**of** gen); ausrauben ⟨bank⟩. **~ber** n Räuber m. **~bery** n Raub m

robe /rəʊb/ n Robe f; ⟨Amer: bathrobe⟩ Bademantel m

robin /'rɒbɪn/ n Rotkehlchen nt

robot /'rəʊbɒt/ n Roboter m

robust /rəʊ'bʌst/ a robust

rock[1] /rɒk/ n Fels m; **stick of ~** Zuckerstange f; **on the ~s** ⟨ship⟩ aufgelaufen; ⟨marriage⟩ kaputt; ⟨drink⟩ mit Eis

rock[2] /rɒk/ vt/i schaukeln

rock[3] n ⟨Mus⟩ Rock m

rock-'bottom n Tiefpunkt m

rockery /'rɒkərɪ/ n Steingarten m

rocket /'rɒkɪt/ n Rakete f □ vi in die Höhe schießen

rocking: **~-chair** n Schaukelstuhl m. **~-horse** n Schaukelpferd nt

rocky /'rɒkɪ/ a (-ier, -iest) felsig; ⟨unsteady⟩ wackelig

rod /rɒd/ n Stab m; ⟨stick⟩ Rute f; ⟨for fishing⟩ Angel[rute] f

rode /rəʊd/ see ride

rodent /'rəʊdnt/ n Nagetier nt

roe[1] /rəʊ/ n Rogen m; ⟨soft⟩ Milch f

roe[2] n (pl roe or roes) **~[-deer]** Reh nt

rogue /rəʊg/ n Gauner m

role /rəʊl/ n Rolle f

roll /rəʊl/ n Rolle f; ⟨bread⟩ Brötchen nt; ⟨list⟩ Liste f; ⟨of drum⟩ Wirbel m □ vt/i rollen; be **~ing in money** ⟨fam⟩ Geld wie Heu haben □ vt rollen; walzen ⟨lawn⟩; ausrollen ⟨pastry⟩. **~ over** vi sich auf die andere Seite rollen. **~ up** vt aufrollen; hochkrempeln ⟨sleeves⟩ □ vi ⟨fam⟩ auftauchen

'roll-call n Namensaufruf m; (Mil) Appell m

roller /'rəʊlə(r)/ n Rolle f; (lawn, road) Walze f; (hair) Lockenwickler m. ~ blind n Rollo nt. ~coaster n Berg-und-Talbahn f. ~skate n Rollschuh m

'rolling-pin n Teigrolle f

Roman /'rəʊmən/ a römisch □ n Römer(in) m(f)

romance /rə'mæns/ n Romantik f; (love-affair) Romanze f; (book) Liebesgeschichte f

Romania /rʊ'meɪnɪə/ n Rumänien nt. ~n a rumänisch □ n Rumäne m/-nin f

romantic /rəʊ'mæntɪk/ a, -ally adv romantisch. ~ism /-tɪsɪzm/ n Romantik f

Rome /rəʊm/ n Rom nt

romp /rɒmp/ n Tollen nt □ vi [herum]tollen. ~ers npl Strampelhöschen nt

roof /ruːf/ n Dach nt; (of mouth) Gaumen m □ vt ~ over überdachen. ~rack n Dachgepäckträger m. ~-top n Dach nt

rook /rʊk/ n Saatkrähe f; (Chess) Turm m □ vt (fam: swindle) schröpfen

room /ruːm/ n Zimmer nt; (for functions) Saal m; (space) Platz m. ~y a geräumig

roost /ruːst/ n Hühnerstange f □ vi schlafen

root¹ /ruːt/ n Wurzel f; take ~ anwachsen □ vi Wurzel schlagen. ~ out vt (fig) ausrotten

root² /ruːt/ vi ~ about wühlen; ~ for s.o. (Amer, fam) für jdn sein

rope /rəʊp/ n Seil nt; know the ~s (fam) sich auskennen. ~ in vt (fam) einspannen

rope-ladder n Strickleiter f

rosary /'rəʊzərɪ/ n Rosenkranz m

rose¹ /rəʊz/ n Rose f; (of watering-can) Brause f

rose² see rise

rosemary /'rəʊzmərɪ/ n Rosmarin m

rosette /rəʊ'zet/ n Rosette f

roster /'rɒstə(r)/ n Dienstplan m

rostrum /'rɒstrəm/ n Podest nt, Podium nt

rosy /'rəʊzɪ/ a (-ier, -iest) rosig

rot /rɒt/ n Fäulnis f; (fam: nonsense) Quatsch m □ vi (pt/pp rotted) [ver]faulen

rota /'rəʊtə/ n Dienstplan m

rotary /'rəʊtərɪ/ a Dreh-; (Techn) Rotations-

rotat|e /rəʊ'teɪt/ vt drehen; im Wechsel anbauen (crops) □ vi sich drehen; (Techn) rotieren. ~ion /-eɪʃn/ n Drehung f; (of crops) Fruchtfolge f; in ~ion im Wechsel

rote /rəʊt/ n by ~ auswendig

rotten /'rɒtn/ a faul; (fam) mies; (person) fies

rotund /rəʊ'tʌnd/ a rundlich

rough /rʌf/ a (-er, -est) rau; (uneven) uneben; (coarse, not gentle) grob; (brutal) roh; (turbulent) stürmisch; (approximate) ungefähr □ adv sleep ~ im Freien übernachten; play ~ holzen □ n do sth in ~ etw ins Unreine schreiben □ vt ~ it primitiv leben; ~ out vt im Groben entwerfen

roughage /'rʌfɪdʒ/ n Ballaststoffe pl

rough 'draft n grober Entwurf m

rough|ly /'rʌflɪ/ adv (see rough) rau; grob; roh; ungefähr. ~ness n Rauheit f

'rough paper n Konzeptpapier nt

round /raʊnd/ a (-er, -est) rund □ n Runde f; (slice) Scheibe f; do one's ~s seine Runde machen □ prep um (+ acc); ~ the clock rund um die Uhr □ adv all ~ ringsherum; ~ and ~ im Kreis; ask s.o. ~ jdn einladen; turn/look ~ sich umdrehen/umsehen □ vt biegen um (corner) □ vi ~ on s.o. jdn anfahren. ~ off vt abrunden. ~ up vt aufrunden; zusammentreiben (animals); festnehmen (criminals)

roundabout /'raʊndəbaʊt/ a ~
route Umweg m ≈ Karussell nt;
(for traffic) Kreisverkehr m

round: ~:'shouldered a mit einem runden Rücken. ~ 'trip n
Rundreise f

rous|e /raʊz/ vt wecken; (fig) erregen. ~ing a mitreißend

route /ruːt/ n Route f; (of bus) Linie f

routine /ruː'tiːn/ a, **-ly** adv routinemäßig □ n Routine f; (Theat)
Nummer f

roux /ruː/ n Mehlschwitze f

rove /rəʊv/ vi wandern

row¹ /rəʊ/ n (line) Reihe f; in a ~
(one after the other) nacheinander

row² vt/i rudern

row³ /raʊ/ n (fam) Krach m □ vi
(fam) sich streiten

rowan /'rəʊən/ n Eberesche f

rowdy /'raʊdɪ/ a (-ier, -iest) laut

rowing boat /'rəʊɪŋ-/ n Ruderboot nt

royal /'rɔɪəl/ a, **-ly** adv königlich

royal|ty /'rɔɪəltɪ/ n Königtum nt;
(persons) Mitglieder pl der königlichen Familie; **-ies** pl (payments)
Tantiemen pl

rub /rʌb/ n give sth a ~ etw reiben/(polish) polieren □ vt (pt/pp
rubbed) reiben; (polish) polieren; don't ~ it in (fam) reib
es mir nicht unter die Nase. ~
off vt abreiben □ vi abgehen; ~
off on abfärben auf (+ acc). ~
out vt ausradieren

rubber /'rʌbə(r)/ n Gummi m;
(eraser) Radiergummi m. **~band**
n Gummiband nt. **~y** a gummiartig

rubbish /'rʌbɪʃ/ n Abfall m, Müll
m; (fam: nonsense) Quatsch m;
(fam: junk) Plunder m, Kram m
□ vt (fam) schlecht machen. ~
bin n Mülleimer m, Abfalleimer
m. **~ dump** n Abfallhaufen m;
(official) Müllhalde f

rubble /'rʌbl/ n Trümmer pl,
Schutt m

ruby /'ruːbɪ/ n Rubin m

rucksack /'rʌksæk/ n Rucksack
m

rudder /'rʌdə(r)/ n [Steuer]ruder
nt

ruddy /'rʌdɪ/ a (-ier, -iest) rötlich; (sl) verdammt

rude /ruːd/ a (-r, -st), **-ly** adv unhöflich; (improper) unanständig.
~ness n Unhöflichkeit f

rudiment /'ruːdɪmənt/ n **~s** pl
Anfangsgründe pl. **~ary** /-'mentərɪ/ a elementar; (Biol) rudimentär

rueful /'ruːfl/ a, **-ly** adv reumütig

ruffian /'rʌfɪən/ n Rüpel m

ruffle /'rʌfl/ n Rüsche f □ vt zerzausen

rug /rʌg/ n Vorleger m, [kleiner]
Teppich m; (blanket) Decke f

rugged /'rʌgɪd/ a (coastline) zerklüftet

ruin /'ruːɪn/ n Ruine f; (fig) Ruin
m □ vt ruinieren. **~ous** /-əs/ a
ruinös

rule /ruːl/ n Regel f; (control)
Herrschaft f; (government) Regierung f; (for measuring) Lineal
nt; as a ~ in der Regel □ vt regieren, herrschen über (+ acc);
(fig) beherrschen; (decide) entscheiden; ziehen (line) □ vi regieren, herrschen. ~ **out** vt
ausschließen

ruled /ruːld/ a (paper) liniert

ruler /'ruːlə(r)/ n Herrscher(in)
m/f; (measure) Lineal nt

ruling /'ruːlɪŋ/ a herrschend;
(factor) entscheidend; (Pol) regierend □ n Entscheidung f

rum /rʌm/ n Rum m

rumble /'rʌmbl/ n Grollen nt □ vi
grollen; (stomach:) knurren

ruminant /'ruːmɪnənt/ n Wiederkäuer m

rummage /'rʌmɪdʒ/ vi wühlen;
~ **through** durchwühlen

rummy /'rʌmɪ/ n Rommé nt

rumour /'ruːmə(r)/ n Gerücht nt
□ vt it is ~ed that es geht das
Gerücht, dass

rump /rʌmp/ n Hinterteil nt. ~
steak n Rumpsteak nt

rumpus /'rʌmpəs/ n (fam) Spektakel m

run /rʌn/ n Lauf m; (journey)
Fahrt f; (series) Serie f, Reihe f;
(Theat) Laufzeit f; (Skiing)
Abfahrt f; (enclosure) Auslauf m;
(Amer: ladder) Laufmasche f; **at
a** ~ im Laufschritt; ~ **of bad
luck** Pechsträhne f; **be on the** ~
flüchtig sein; **have the** ~ **of sth**
etw zu seiner freien Verfügung
haben; **in the long** ~ auf lange
Sicht □ vi (pt **ran**, pp **run**, pres p
running) □ vi laufen; (flow)
fließen; (eyes:) tränen; (bus:) verkehren, fahren; (butter, ink:) zer-
fließen; (colours:) [ab]färben; (in
election) kandidieren; ~ **across**
s.o./sth auf jdn/ etw stoßen □ vt
laufen lassen; einlaufen lassen
(bath); (manage) führen, leiten;
(drive) fahren; eingehen (risk);
(Journ) bringen (article); ~ **one's
hand over sth** mit der Hand über
etw (acc) fahren. ~ **away** vi weglaufen. ~ **down** vi hinunter-/
herunterlaufen; (clockwork:) ablaufen; (stocks:) sich verringern
□ vt (run over) überfahren; (reduce) verringern; (fam: criticize)
heruntermachen. ~ **in** vi hinein-/
hereinlaufen. ~ **off** vi weglaufen
□ vt abziehen (copies). ~ **out** vi
hinaus-/herauslaufen; (supplies,
money:) ausgehen; **I've** ~ **out of
sugar** Ich habe keinen Zucker
mehr. ~ **over** vi hinüber-/
herüberlaufen; (overflow) überlaufen □ vt überfahren. ~
through vi durchlaufen. ~ **up** vi
hinauf-/herauflaufen; (towards)
hinlaufen □ vt machen (debts);
auflaufen lassen (bill); (sew)
schnell nähen

'runaway n Ausreißer m

run-'down a (area) verkommen

rung¹ /rʌŋ/ n (of ladder) Sprosse
f

rung² see **ring²**

runner /'rʌnə(r)/ n Läufer m;
(Bot) Ausläufer m; (on sledge)
Kufe f. ~ **bean** n Stangenbohne
f. ~**up** n Zweite(r) m/f

running /'rʌnɪŋ/ a laufend;
(water) fließend; **four times** ~
viermal nacheinander □ n
Laufen nt; (management)
Führung f, Leitung f; **be/not be
in the** ~ eine/keine Chance
haben. ~ **'commentary** n
fortlaufender Kommentar m

runny /'rʌnɪ/ a flüssig

run: ~**-of-the-'mill** a gewöhnlich. ~**up** n (Sport) Anlauf m; (to
election) Zeit f vor der Wahl.
~**way** n Start- und Landebahn f,
Piste f

rupture /'rʌptʃə(r)/ n Bruch m
□ vt/i brechen; ~ **oneself** sich
(dat) einen Bruch heben

rural /'rʊərəl/ a ländlich

ruse /ruːz/ n List f

rush¹ /rʌʃ/ n (Bot) Binse f

rush² n Hetze f; **in a** ~ in Eile □ vi
sich hetzen; (run) rasen; (water:)
rauschen □ vt hetzen, drängen; ~
s.o. to hospital jdn schnellstens
ins Krankenhaus bringen. ~
hour n Hauptverkehrszeit f,
Stoßzeit f

rusk /rʌsk/ n Zwieback m

Russia /'rʌʃə/ n Russland nt. ~**n**
a russisch □ n Russe m/Russin f;
(Lang) Russisch nt

rust /rʌst/ n Rost m □ vi rosten

rustic /'rʌstɪk/ a bäuerlich;
(furniture) rustikal

rustle /'rʌsl/ vi rascheln □ vt rascheln mit; (Amer) stehlen (cattle).
~ **up** vt (fam) improvisieren

'rustproof a rostfrei

rusty /'rʌstɪ/ a (-ier, -iest) rostig

rut /rʌt/ n Furche f; **be in a** ~
(fam) aus dem alten Trott nicht
herauskommen

ruthless /'ruːθlɪs/ a, **-ly** adv rück-

rye

sichtlos. **~ness** n Rücksichtslosigkeit f
rye /raɪ/ n Roggen m

S

sabbath /'sæbəθ/ n Sabbat m
sabbatical /sə'bætɪkl/ n (Univ) Forschungsurlaub m
sabot|age /'sæbɑtɑːʒ/ n Sabotage f □ vt sabotieren. **~eur** /-'tɜː(r)/ n Saboteur m
sachet /'sæʃeɪ/ n Beutel m; (scented) Kissen nt
sack¹ /sæk/ vt (plunder) plündern
sack² n Sack m; **get the ~** (fam) rausgeschmissen werden □ vt (fam) rausschmeißen. **~ing** n Sackleinen nt; (fam: dismissal) Rausschmiss m
sacrament /'sækrəmənt/ n Sakrament nt
sacred /'seɪkrɪd/ a heilig
sacrifice /'sækrɪfaɪs/ n Opfer nt □ vt opfern
sacrilege /'sækrɪlɪdʒ/ n Sakrileg nt
sad /sæd/ a (**sadder, saddest**) traurig; (loss, death) schmerzlich. **~den** vt traurig machen
saddle /'sædl/ n Sattel m □ vt satteln; **~ s.o. with sth** (fam) jdm etw aufhalsen
sadis|m /'seɪdɪzm/ n Sadismus m. **~t** /-dɪst/ n Sadist m. **~tic** /sə-'dɪstɪk/ a, **~ally** adv sadistisch
sad|ly /'sædlɪ/ adv traurig; (unfortunately) leider. **~ness** n Traurigkeit f
safe /seɪf/ a (**-r, -st**) sicher; (journey) gut; (not dangerous) ungefährlich; **~ and sound** gesund und wohlbehalten □ n Safe m. **~guard** n Schutz m □ vt schützen. **~ly** adv sicher; (arrive) gut
safety /'seɪftɪ/ n Sicherheit f. **~-belt** n Sicherheitsgurt m. **~-pin** n Sicherheitsnadel f. **~-valve** n [Sicherheits] ventil nt

sag /sæg/ vi (pt/pp **sagged**) durchhängen
saga /'sɑːgə/ n Saga f; (fig) Geschichte f
sage¹ n (herb) Salbei m
sage² a weise □ n Weise(r) m
Sagittarius /sædʒɪ'teərɪəs/ n (Astr) Schütze m
said /sed/ see **say**
sail /seɪl/ n Segel nt; (trip) Segelfahrt f □ vi segeln; (on liner) fahren; (leave) abfahren (for nach) □ vt segeln mit
'sailboard n Surfbrett nt. **~ing** n Windsurfen nt
sailing /'seɪlɪŋ/ n Segelsport m. **~-boat** n Segelboot m. **~-ship** n Segelschiff nt
sailor /'seɪlə(r)/ n Seemann m; (in navy) Matrose m
saint /seɪnt/ n Heilige(r) m/f. **~ly** a heilig
sake /seɪk/ n **for the ~ of ...** um ... (gen) willen; **for my/your ~** um meinet-/deinetwillen
salad /'sæləd/ n Salat m. **~-cream** n ≈ Mayonnaise f. **~-dressing** n Salatsoße f
salary /'sælərɪ/ n Gehalt nt
sale /seɪl/ n Verkauf m; (event) Basar m; (at reduced prices) Schlussverkauf m; **for ~** zu verkaufen
sales|man n Verkäufer m. **~woman** n Verkäuferin f
salient /'seɪlɪənt/ a wichtigste(r,s)
saliva /sə'laɪvə/ n Speichel m
sallow /'sæləʊ/ a (-er, -est) bleich
salmon /'sæmən/ n Lachs m. **~pink** a lachsrosa
saloon /sə'luːn/ n Salon m; (Auto) Limousine f; (Amer: bar) Wirtschaft f
salt /sɔːlt/ n Salz nt □ a salzig; (water, meat) Salz- □ vt salzen; (cure) pökeln; streuen (road). **~-cellar** n Salzfass nt. **~'water** n Salzwasser nt. **~y** a salzig

salutary /'sæljotərɪ/ a heilsam

salute /sə'lu:t/ n (Mil) Gruß m
□ vt/i (Mil) grüßen

salvage /'sælvɪdʒ/ n (Naut)
Bergung f □ vt bergen

salvation /sæl'veɪʃn/ n Rettung f;
(Relig) Heil nt. S~ 'Army n
Heilsarmee f

salvo /'sælvəʊ/ n Salve f

same /seɪm/ a & pron the ~
der/die/das gleiche; (pl) die
gleichen; (identical) der-/die-/
dasselbe; (pl) dieselben □ adv the
~ gleich; all the ~ trotzdem; the
~ to you gleichfalls

sample /'sɑːmpl/ n Probe f;
(Comm) Muster nt □ vt probieren,
kosten

sanatorium /sænə'tɔːrɪəm/ n
Sanatorium nt

sanctify /'sæŋktɪfaɪ/ vt (pt/pp
-fied) heiligen

sanctimonious /sæŋktɪ'məʊ-
nɪəs/ a, -ly adv frömmlerisch

sanction /'sæŋkʃn/ n Sanktion f
□ vt sanktionieren

sanctity /'sæŋktɪtɪ/ n Heiligkeit
f

sanctuary /'sæŋktjʊərɪ/ n (Relig)
Heiligtum nt; (refuge) Zuflucht f;
(for wildlife) Tierschutzgebiet nt

sand /sænd/ n Sand m □ vt ~
[down] [ab]schmirgeln

sandal /'sændl/ n Sandale f

sand: ~bank n Sandbank f.
~paper n Sandpapier nt □ vt
[ab]schmirgeln. ~-pit n Sand-
kasten m

sandwich /'sænwɪdʒ/ n ≈ belegtes Brot nt; Sandwich m □ vt
~ed between eingeklemmt
zwischen

sandy /'sændɪ/ a (-ier, -iest) san-
dig; (beach, soil) Sand-; (hair) rotblond

sane /seɪn/ a (-r, -st) geistig normal; (sensible) vernünftig

sang /sæŋ/ see sing

sanitary /'sænɪtərɪ/ a hygie-
nisch; (system) sanitär. ~ napkin

n (Amer), ~ towel n [Damen]-
binde f

sanitation /sænɪ'teɪʃn/ n Kana-
lisation und Abfallbeseitigung pl

sanity /'sænɪtɪ/ n (gesunder) Verstand m

sank /sæŋk/ see sink

sap /sæp/ n (Bot) Saft m □ vt (pt/pp
sapped) schwächen

sapphire /'sæfaɪə(r)/ n Saphir m

sarcasm /'sɑːkæzm/ n Sarkas-
mus m. ~tic /-'kæstɪk/ a, -ally
adv sarkastisch

sardine /sɑː'diːn/ n Sardine f

Sardinia /sɑː'dɪnɪə/ n Sardinien
nt

sardonic /sɑː'dɒnɪk/ a, -ally adv
höhnisch; (smile) sardonisch

sash /sæʃ/ n Schärpe f

sat /sæt/ see sit

satanic /sə'tænɪk/ a satanisch

satchel /'sætʃl/ n Ranzen m

satellite /'sætəlaɪt/ n Satellit m.
~ dish n Satellitenschüssel f.
~ television n Satelliten-
fernsehen nt

satin /'sætɪn/ n Satin m

satire /'sætaɪə(r)/ n Satire f

satirical /sə'tɪrɪkl/ a, -ly adv satirisch

satir|ist /'sætərɪst/ n Satiri-
ker(in) m(f). ~ize vt satirisch
darstellen; (book:) eine Satire
sein auf (+ acc)

satisfaction /sætɪs'fækʃn/ n Be-
friedigung f; to my ~ zu meiner
Zufriedenheit

satisfactory /sætɪs'fæktərɪ/ a,
-ily adv zufrieden stellend

satisfy /'sætɪsfaɪ/ vt (pt/pp-fied)
befriedigen; zufrieden stellen
(customer); (convince) über-
zeugen; be ~ied zufrieden sein.
~ying a befriedigend; (meal)
sättigend

saturate /'sætʃəreɪt/ vt durch-
tränken; (Chem & fig) sättigen.
~ed a durchnässt; (fat) gesättigt

Saturday /ˈsætədeɪ/ *n* Samstag *m*, Sonnabend *m*

sauce /sɔːs/ *n* Soße *f*; ⟨cheek⟩ Frechheit *f*. **~pan** *n* Kochtopf *m*

saucer /ˈsɔːsə(r)/ *n* Untertasse *f*

saucy /ˈsɔːsɪ/ *a* (-ier, -iest) frech

Saudi Arabia /saʊdɪəˈreɪbɪə/ *n* Saudi-Arabien *nt*

sauna /ˈsɔːnə/ *n* Sauna *f*

saunter /ˈsɔːntə(r)/ *vi* schlendern

sausage /ˈsɒsɪdʒ/ *n* Wurst *f*

savage /ˈsævɪdʒ/ *a* wild; ⟨fierce⟩ scharf; ⟨brutal⟩ brutal □ *n* Wilde(r) *m/f* □ *vt* anfallen. **~ry** *n* Brutalität *f*

save /seɪv/ *n* (Sport) Abwehr *f* □ *vt* retten (from vor + dat); ⟨keep⟩ aufheben; ⟨not waste⟩ sparen; ⟨collect⟩ sammeln; ⟨avoid⟩ ersparen; (Sport) verhindern ⟨goal⟩ □ *vi* ~ [up] sparen □ *prep* außer (+ dat), mit Ausnahme (+ gen)

saver /ˈseɪvə(r)/ *n* Sparer *m*

saving /ˈseɪvɪŋ/ *n* (see save) Rettung *f*; Sparen *nt*; Ersparnis *f*; (money) Ersparnisse *pl*. **~s** *pl* ⟨money⟩ Ersparnisse *pl*. **~s account** *n* Sparkonto *nt*. **~s bank** *n* Sparkasse *f*

saviour /ˈseɪvjə(r)/ *n* Retter *m*

savour /ˈseɪvə(r)/ *n* Geschmack *m* □ *vt* auskosten. **~y** *a* herzhaft, würzig; (fig) angenehm

saw[1] /sɔː/ see **see**

saw[2] *n* Säge *f* □ *vt/i* (pt sawed, pp sawn or sawed) sägen. **~dust** *n* Sägemehl *nt*

saxophone /ˈsæksəfəʊn/ *n* Saxophon *nt*

say /seɪ/ *n* Mitspracherecht *nt*; **have one's ~** seine Meinung sagen □ *vt/i* (pt/pp **said**) sagen; sprechen ⟨prayer⟩; **that is to ~** das heißt; **that goes without ~ing** das versteht sich von selbst; **when all is said and done** letzten Endes; **I ~!** ⟨attracting attention⟩ hallo! **~ing** *n* Redensart *f*

scab /skæb/ *n* Schorf *m*; (pej) Streikbrecher *m*

scaffold /ˈskæfəld/ *n* Schafott *nt*. **~ing** *n* Gerüst *nt*

scald /skɔːld/ *vt* verbrühen

scale[1] /skeɪl/ *n* ⟨of fish⟩ Schuppe *f*

scale[2] *n* Skala *f*; (Mus) Tonleiter *f*; ⟨ratio⟩ Maßstab *m*; **on a grand ~** in großem Stil □ *vt* ⟨climb⟩ erklettern. **~ down** *vt* verkleinern

scales /skeɪlz/ *npl* ⟨for weighing⟩ Waage *f*

scalp /skælp/ *n* Kopfhaut *f* □ *vt* skalpieren

scalpel /ˈskælpl/ *n* Skalpell *nt*

scam /skæm/ *n* (fam) Schwindel *m*

scamper /ˈskæmpə(r)/ *vi* huschen

scan /skæn/ *n* (Med) Szintigramm *nt* □ *v* (pt/pp **scanned**) □ *vt* absuchen; ⟨quickly⟩ flüchtig ansehen; (Med) szintigraphisch untersuchen □ *vi* ⟨poetry:⟩ das richtige Versmaß haben

scandal /ˈskændl/ *n* Skandal *m*; ⟨gossip⟩ Skandalgeschichten *pl*. **~ize** /-dəlaɪz/ *vt* schockieren. **~ous** /-əs/ *a* skandalös

Scandinavia /skændɪˈneɪvɪə/ *n* Skandinavien *nt*. **~n** *a* skandinavisch □ *n* Skandinavier(in) *m(f)*

scant /skænt/ *a* wenig

scanty /ˈskæntɪ/ *a* (-ier, -iest), **-ily** *adv* spärlich; ⟨clothing⟩ knapp

scapegoat /ˈskeɪp-/ *n* Sündenbock *m*

scar /skɑː(r)/ *n* Narbe *f* □ *vt* (pt/pp **scarred**) eine Narbe hinterlassen auf (+ dat)

scarce /skeəs/ *a* (-r, -st) knapp; **make oneself ~** (fam) sich aus dem Staub machen. **~ly** *adv* kaum. **~ity** *n* Knappheit *f*

scare /skeə(r)/ *n* Schreck *m*; ⟨panic⟩ [allgemeine] Panik *f*; ⟨bomb⟩ ~ Bombendrohung *f* □ *vt* Angst machen (+ dat); **be ~d** Angst haben (+ dat)

'scarecrow *n* Vogelscheuche *f*

scarf /skɑːf/ *n* (pl **scarves**) Schal *m*; ⟨square⟩ Tuch *nt*

scarlet /'skɑ:lət/ *a* scharlachrot. **~ 'fever** *n* Scharlach *m*

scary /'skeəri/ *a* unheimlich

scathing /'skeɪðɪŋ/ *a* bissig

scatter /'skætə(r)/ *vt* verstreuen; (*disperse*) zerstreuen □ *vi* sich zerstreuen. **~-brained** *a* (*fam*) schusselig. **~ed** *a* verstreut; (*showers*) vereinzelt

scatty /'skætɪ/ *a* (**-ier, -iest**) (*fam*) verrückt

scavenge /'skævɪndʒ/ *vi* [im Abfall] Nahrung suchen; (*animal*) Aas fressen. **~r** *n* Aasfresser *m*

scenario /sɪ'nɑ:rɪəʊ/ *n* Szenario *nt*

scene /si:n/ *n* Szene *f*; (*sight*) Anblick *m*; (*place of event*) Schauplatz *m*; **behind the ~s** hinter den Kulissen; **~ of the crime** Tatort *m*

scenery /'si:nərɪ/ *n* Landschaft *f*; (*Theat*) Szenerie *f*

scenic /'si:nɪk/ *a* landschaftlich schön; (*Theat*) Bühnen-

scent /sent/ *n* Duft *m*; (*trail*) Fährte *f*; (*perfume*) Parfüm *nt*. **~ed** *a* parfümiert

sceptic|al /'skeptɪkl/ *a*, **-ly** *adv* skeptisch. **~ism** /-tɪsɪzm/ *n* Skepsis *f*

schedule /'ʃedju:l/ *n* Programm *nt*; (*of work*) Zeitplan *m*; (*timetable*) Fahrplan *m*; **behind ~** im Rückstand; **according to ~** planmäßig □ *vt* planen. **~d flight** *n* Linienflug *m*

scheme /ski:m/ *n* Programm *nt*; (*plan*) Plan *m*; (*plot*) Komplott *nt* □ *vi* Ränke schmieden

schizophren|ia /skɪtsə'fri:nɪə/ *n* Schizophrenie *f*. **~ic** /-'frenɪk/ *a* schizophren

scholar /'skɒlə(r)/ *n* Gelehrte(r) *m/f*. **~ly** *a* gelehrt. **~ship** *n* Gelehrtheit *f*; (*grant*) Stipendium *nt*

school /sku:l/ *n* Schule *f*; (*Univ*) Fakultät *f* □ *vt* schulen; dressieren (*animal*)

school: **~boy** *n* Schüler *m*. **~girl** *n* Schülerin *f*. **~ing** *n* Schulbildung *f*. **~master** *n* Lehrer *m*. **~mistress** *n* Lehrerin *f*. **~teacher** *n* Lehrer(in) *m(f)*

sciatica /saɪ'ætɪkə/ *n* Ischias *m*

scien|ce /'saɪəns/ *n* Wissenschaft *f*. **~tific** /-'tɪfɪk/ *a* wissenschaftlich. **~tist** *n* Wissenschaftler *m*

scintillating /'sɪntɪleɪtɪŋ/ *a* sprühend

scissors /'sɪzəz/ *npl* Schere *f*; **a pair of ~** eine Schere

scoff[1] /skɒf/ *vi* **~ at** spotten über (+ *acc*)

scoff[2] *vt* (*fam*) verschlingen

scold /skəʊld/ *vt* ausschimpfen

scoop /sku:p/ *n* Schaufel *f*; (*Culin*) Portionierer *m*; (*Journ*) Exklusivmeldung *f* □ *vt* **~ out** aushöhlen; (*remove*) auslöffeln; **~ up** schaufeln; schöpfen (*liquid*)

scoot /sku:t/ *vi* (*fam*) rasen. **~er** *n* Roller *m*

scope /skəʊp/ *n* Bereich *m*; (*opportunity*) Möglichkeiten *pl*

scorch /skɔ:tʃ/ *vt* versengen. **~ing** *a* glühend heiß

score /skɔ:(r)/ *n* [Spiel]stand *m*; (*individual*) Punktzahl *f*; (*Mus*) Partitur *f*; (*Cinema*) Filmmusik *f*; **a ~ [of]** (*twenty*) zwanzig; **keep [the] ~** zählen; (*written*) aufschreiben; **on that ~** was das betrifft □ *vt* erzielen; schießen (*goal*); (*cut*) einritzen □ *vi* Punkte erzielen; (*Sport*) ein Tor schießen; (*keep score*) Punkte zählen. **~r** *n* Punktezähler *m*; (*of goals*) Torschütze *m*

scorn /skɔ:n/ *n* Verachtung *f* □ *vt* verachten. **~ful** *a*, **-ly** *adv* verächtlich

Scorpio /'skɔ:pɪəʊ/ *n* (*Astr*) Skorpion *m*

scorpion /'skɔ:pɪən/ *n* Skorpion *m*

Scot /skɒt/ *n* Schotte *m*/Schottin *f*

Scotch /skɒtʃ/ a Schottisch □n (whisky) Scotch m

scotch vt unterbinden

scot-'free a get off ~ straffrei ausgehen

Scot|land /'skɒtlənd/ n Schottland nt. ~s, ~tish a schottisch

scoundrel /'skaʊndrl/ n Schurke m

scour¹ /'skaʊə(r)/ vt (search) absuchen

scour² vt (clean) scheuern

scourge /skɜːdʒ/ n Geißel f

scout /skaʊt/ n (Mil) Kundschafter m □vi ~ for Ausschau halten nach

Scout n [Boy] ~ Pfadfinder m

scowl /skaʊl/ n böser Gesichtsausdruck m □vi ein böses Gesicht machen

scraggy /'skrægi/ a (-ier, -iest) (pej) dürr, hager

scram /skræm/ vi (fam) abhauen

scramble /'skræmbl/ n Gerangel nt □vi klettern; ~ for sich drängen nach □vt (Teleph) verschlüsseln. ~d 'egg[s] n[pl] Rührei nt

scrap¹ /skræp/ n (fam: flight) Rauferei f □vi sich raufen

scrap² n Stückchen nt; (metal) Schrott m; ~s pl Reste; not a ~ kein bisschen □vt (pt/pp scrapped) aufgeben

'scrap-book n Sammelalbum nt

scrape /skreɪp/ n schaben; (clean) abkratzen; (damage) [ver]schrammen. ~ through vi gerade noch durchkommen. ~ together vt zusammenkriegen

scraper /'skreɪpə(r)/ n Kratzer m

'scrap iron n Alteisen nt

scrappy /'skræpɪ/ a lückenhaft

'scrap-yard n Schrottplatz m

scratch /skrætʃ/ n Kratzer m; start from ~ von vorne anfangen; not be up to ~ zu wünschen übrig lassen □vt/i kratzen; (damage) zerkratzen

scrawl /skrɔːl/ n Gekrakel nt □vt/i krakeln

scrawny /'skrɔːnɪ/ a (-ier, -iest) (pej) dürr, hager

scream /skriːm/ n Schrei m □vt/i schreien

screech /skriːtʃ/ n Kreischen nt □vt/i kreischen

screen /skriːn/ n Schirm m; (Cinema) Leinwand f; (TV) Bildschirm m □vt schützen; (conceal) verdecken; vorführen (film); (examine) überprüfen; (Med) untersuchen. ~ing n (Med) Reihenuntersuchung f. ~play n Drehbuch nt

screw /skruː/ n Schraube f □vt schrauben. ~ up vt festschrauben; (crumple) zusammenknüllen; zusammenkneifen (eyes); (sl: bungle) vermasseln; ~ up one's courage seinen Mut zusammennehmen

'screwdriver n Schraubenzieher m

screwy /'skruːɪ/ a (-ier, -iest) (fam) verrückt

scribble /'skrɪbl/ n Gekritzel nt □vt/i kritzeln

script /skrɪpt/ n Schrift f; (of speech, play) Text m; (Radio, TV) Skript m; (of film) Drehbuch nt

Scripture /'skrɪptʃə(r)/ n (Sch) Religion f; the ~s pl die Heilige Schrift f

scroll /skrəʊl/ n Schriftrolle f; (decoration) Volute f

scrounge /skraʊndʒ/ vt/i schnorren. ~r n Schnorrer m

scrub¹ /skrʌb/ n (land) Buschland nt, Gestrüpp nt

scrub² vt/i (pt/pp scrubbed) schrubben; (fam: cancel) absagen; fallen lassen (plan)

scruff /skrʌf/ n by the ~ of the neck beim Genick

scruffy /'skrʌfɪ/ a (-ier, -iest) vergammelt

scrum /skrʌm/ n Gedränge nt

scruple /'skruːpl/ n Skrupel m

scrupulous /'skru:pjʊləs/ a, **-ly** adv gewissenhaft

scrutin|ize /'skru:tɪnaɪz/ vt [genau] ansehen. **~y** n (look) prüfender Blick m

scuff /skʌf/ vt abstoßen

scuffle /'skʌfl/ n Handgemenge nt

scullery /'skʌlərɪ/ n Spülküche f

sculpt|or /'skʌlptə(r)/ n Bildhauer(in) m(f). **~ure** /-tʃə(r)/ n Bildhauerei f; (piece of work) Skulptur f, Plastik f

scum /skʌm/ n Schmutzschicht f; (people) Abschaum m

scurrilous /'skʌrɪləs/ a niederträchtig

scurry /'skʌrɪ/ vi (pt/pp **-ied**) huschen

scuttle[1] /'skʌtl/ n Kohleneimer m

scuttle[2] vt versenken (ship)

scuttle[3] vi schnell krabbeln

scythe /saɪð/ n Sense f

sea /si:/ n Meer nt, See f; **at ~** auf See; **by ~** mit dem Schiff. **~board** n Küste f. **~food** n Meeresfrüchte pl. **~gull** n Möwe f

seal[1] /si:l/ n (Zool) Seehund m

seal[2] n Siegel nt; (Techn) Dichtung f □ vt versiegeln; (Techn) abdichten; (fig) besiegeln. **~ off** vt abriegeln

'sea-level n Meeresspiegel m

seam /si:m/ n Naht f; (of coal) Flöz nt

seaman n Seemann m; (sailor) Matrose m

seamless /'si:mlɪs/ a nahtlos

seance /'seɪɑ:ns/ n spiritistische Sitzung f

sea: ~plane n Wasserflugzeug nt. **~port** n Seehafen m

search /sɜ:tʃ/ n Suche f; (official) Durchsuchung f □ vt durchsuchen; absuchen (area) □ vi suchen (**for** nach). **~ing** a prüfend, forschend

search: ~light n [Such]scheinwerfer m. **~party** n Suchmannschaft f

sea: ~sick a seekrank. **~side** n **at/to the ~side** am/ans Meer

season /'si:zn/ n Jahreszeit f; (social, tourist, sporting) Saison f □ vt (flavour) würzen. **~able** /-əbl/ a der Jahreszeit gemäß. **~al** a Saison-. **~ing** n Gewürze pl

'season ticket n Dauerkarte f

seat /si:t/ n Sitz m; (place) Sitzplatz m; (bottom) Hintern m; **take a ~** Platz nehmen □ vt setzen; (have seats for) Sitzplätze bieten (+ dat); **remain ~ed** sitzen bleiben. **~-belt** n Sicherheitsgurt m; **fasten one's ~-belt** sich anschnallen

sea: ~weed n [See]tang m. **~worthy** a seetüchtig

secateurs /sekə'tɜ:z/ npl Gartenschere f

seclu|de /sɪ'klu:d/ vt absondern. **~ded** a abgelegen. **~sion** /-ʒn/ n Zurückgezogenheit f

second[1] /'sekənd/ vt (transfer) [vorübergehend] versetzen

second[2] /'sekənd/ a zweite(r,s); **on ~ thoughts** nach weiterer Überlegung □ n Sekunde f; (Sport) Sekundant m; **~s** pl (goods) Waren zweiter Wahl; **the ~** der/die/das Zweite □ adv (in race) an zweiter Stelle □ vt unterstützen (proposal)

secondary /'sekəndrɪ/ a zweitrangig; (Phys) Sekundär-. **~ school** n höhere Schule f

second: ~-best a zweitbeste(r,s). **~'class** adv (travel, send) zweiter Klasse. **~-class** a zweitklassig

'second hand n (on clock) Sekundenzeiger m

second-'hand a gebraucht □ adv aus zweiter Hand

secondly /'sekəndlɪ/ adv zweitens

second-'rate a zweitklassig

secrecy /'si:krəsɪ/ n Heimlichkeit f

secret /'si:krɪt/ a geheim; (agent, police) Geheim-; (drinker, lover) heimlich □ n Geheimnis nt

secretarial /sekrə'teəriəl/ a Sekretärinnen-; (work, staff) Sekretariats-

secretary /'sekrətəri/ n Sekretär(in) m(f)

secrete /sɪ'kriːt/ vt absondern. **~ion** /-ɪʃn/ n Absonderung f

secretive /'siːkrətɪv/ a geheimtuerisch. **~ness** n Heimlichtuerei f

secretly /'siːkrɪtlɪ/ adv heimlich

sect /sekt/ n Sekte f

section /'sekʃn/ n Teil m; (of text) Abschnitt m; (of firm) Abteilung f; (of organization) Sektion f

sector /'sektə(r)/ n Sektor m

secular /'sekjʊlə(r)/ a weltlich

secure /sɪ'kjʊə(r)/ a, **-ly** adv sicher; (firm) fest; (emotionally) geborgen □ vt sichern; (fasten) festmachen; (obtain) sich (dat) sichern

security /sɪ'kjʊərətɪ/ n Sicherheit f; (emotional) Geborgenheit f; **~ies** pl Wertpapiere pl; (Fin) Effekten pl

sedan /sɪ'dæn/ n (Amer) Limousine f

sedate¹ /sɪ'deɪt/ a, **-ly** adv gesetzt

sedate² vt sedieren

sedation /sɪ'deɪʃn/ n Sedierung f; **be under ~** sediert sein

sedative /'sedətɪv/ a beruhigend □ n Beruhigungsmittel nt

sedentary /'sedəntərɪ/ a sitzend

sediment /'sedɪmənt/ n [Boden]satz m

seduce /sɪ'djuːs/ vt verführen

seduct|ion /sɪ'dʌkʃn/ n Verführung f. **~ive** /-tɪv/ a, **-ly** adv verführerisch

see¹ /siː/ v (pt saw, pp seen) □ vt sehen; (understand) einsehen; (imagine) sich (dat) vorstellen; (escort) begleiten; **go and ~** nachsehen; (visit) besuchen; **~ you later!** bis nachher! **~ing that** da □ vi sehen; (check) nachsehen; **~ about** sich kümmern um. **~ off** vt verabschieden; (chase away)

vertreiben. **~ through** vi durchsehen □ vt (fig) **~ through** s.o. jdn durchschauen

see² n (Relig) Bistum nt

seed /siːd/ n Samen m; (of grape) Kern m; (fig) Saat f; (Tennis) gesetzter Spieler m; **go to ~** Samen bilden; (fig) herunterkommen. **~ed** a (Tennis) gesetzt. **~ling** n Sämling m

seedy /'siːdɪ/ a (**-ier, -iest**) schäbig; (area) heruntergekommen

seek /siːk/ vt (pt/pp **sought**) suchen

seem /siːm/ vi scheinen. **~ingly** adv scheinbar

seemly /'siːmlɪ/ a schicklich

seen /siːn/ see **see¹**

seep /siːp/ vi sickern

see-saw /'siːsɔː/ n Wippe f

seethe /siːð/ vi **~ with anger** vor Wut schäumen

'see-through a durchsichtig

segment /'segmənt/ n Teil m; (of worm) Segment nt; (of orange) Spalte f

segregat|e /'segrɪgeɪt/ vt trennen. **~ion** /-'geɪʃn/ n Trennung f

seize /siːz/ vt ergreifen; (Jur) beschlagnahmen; **~ s.o. by the arm** jdn am Arm packen. **~ up** vi (Techn) sich festfressen

seizure /'siːʒə(r)/ n (Jur) Beschlagnahme f; (Med) Anfall m

seldom /'seldəm/ adv selten

select /sɪ'lekt/ a ausgewählt; (exclusive) exklusiv □ vt auswählen; aufstellen (team). **~ion** /-ekʃn/ n Auswahl f. **~ive** /-ɪv/ a, **-ly** adv selektiv; (choosy) wählerisch

self /self/ n (pl **selves**) Ich nt

self: **~-ad'dressed** a adressiert. **~-ad'hesive** a selbstklebend. **~as'surance** n Selbstsicherheit f. **~as'sured** a selbstsicher. **~'catering** n Selbstversorgung f. **~-'centred** a egozentrisch. **~-'confidence** n Selbstbewusstsein *nt*, Selbstvertrauen *nt*. ~·'**con-fident** *a* selbstbewusst. ~·'**conscious** *a* befangen. ~·**con'tained** *a* ⟨*flat*⟩ abgeschlossen. ~·**con'trol** *n* Selbstbeherrschung *f*. ~·**de'fence** *n* Selbstverteidigung *f*; ⟨*Jur*⟩ ~·**de'nial** *n* Selbstverleugnung *f*. ~·**deter-mi'nation** *n* Selbstbestimmung *f*. ~·**em'ployed** selbstständig. ~·**e'steem** *n* Selbstachtung *f*. ~·'**evident** *a* offensichtlich. ~·'**governing** *a* selbst verwaltet. ~·'**help** *n* Selbsthilfe *f*. ~·**in'dulgent** *a* maßlos. ~·'**interest** *n* Eigennutz *m*

selfish /'selfɪʃ/ *a*, **-ly** *adv* egoistisch, selbstsüchtig. ~**less** *a*, **-ly** *adv* selbstlos

self: ~·'**pity** *n* Selbstmitleid *nt*. ~·'**portrait** *n* Selbstporträt *nt*. ~·**pos'sessed** *a* selbstbeherrscht. ~·**preser'vation** *n* Selbsterhaltung *f*. ~·**re'spect** *n* Selbstachtung *f*. ~·'**righteous** *a* selbstgerecht. ~·'**sacrifice** *n* Selbstaufopferung *f*. ~·'**satisfied** *a* selbstgefällig. ~·'**service** *n* Selbstbedienung *f* □*attrib* Selbstbedienungs-. ~·**suf'ficient** *a* selbstständig. ~·'**willed** *a* eigenwillig

sell /sel/ *v* ⟨*pt/pp* **sold**⟩ □*vt* verkaufen; *be sold out* ausverkauft sein □ *vi* sich verkaufen. ~ **off** *vt* verkaufen

seller /'selə(r)/ *n* Verkäufer *m*

Sellotape (P) /'seləʊ-/ *n* ≈ Tesafilm (P) *m*

sell-out *n* **be a** ~ ausverkauft sein; ⟨*fam: betrayal*⟩ Verrat sein

selves /selvz/ *see* **self**

semblance /'semblans/ *n* Anschein *m*

semen /'siːmən/ *n* ⟨*Anat*⟩ Samen *m*

semester /sɪ'mestə(r)/ *n* ⟨*Amer*⟩ Semester *m*

semi|breve /'semibriːv/ *n* ⟨*Mus*⟩ ganze Note *f*. ~**circle** *n* Halbkreis *m*. ~**circular** *a*

halbkreisförmig. ~**colon** *n* Semikolon *nt*. ~**de'tached** *a* & *n* ~**detached** [**house**] Doppelhaushälfte *f*. ~**'final** *n* Halbfinale *nt*

seminar /'seminɑː(r)/ *n* Seminar *nt*. **-y** /-nəri/ *n* Priesterseminar *nt*

'**semitone** *n* ⟨*Mus*⟩ Halbton *m*

semolina /semə'liːnə/ *n* Grieß *m*

senat|e /'senət/ *n* Senat *m*. ~**or** *n* Senator *m*

send /send/ *vt/i* ⟨*pt/pp* **sent**⟩ schicken; ~ *one's regards* grüßen lassen; ~ *for* kommen lassen ⟨*person*⟩; *sich* ⟨*dat*⟩ schicken lassen ⟨*thing*⟩. ~·**er** *n* Absender *m*. ~·**off** *n* Verabschiedung *f*

senile /'siːnaɪl/ *a* senil. ~**ity** /sɪ'nɪlɪti/ *n* Senilität *f*

senior /'siːnɪə(r)/ *a* älter; ⟨*in rank*⟩ höher □ *n* Ältere(r) *m/f*; ⟨*in rank*⟩ Vorgesetzte(r) *m/f*. ~ '**citizen** *n* Senior(in) *m(f)*

seniority /siːnɪ'ɒrəti/ *n* höheres Alter *nt*; ⟨*in rank*⟩ höherer Rang *m*

sensation /sen'seɪʃn/ *n* Sensation *f*; ⟨*feeling*⟩ Gefühl *nt*. ~**al** *a*, **-ly** *adv* sensationell

sense /sens/ *n* Sinn *m*; ⟨*feeling*⟩ Gefühl *nt*; ⟨*common* ~⟩ Verstand *m*; **in a** ~ in gewisser Hinsicht; **make** ~ Sinn ergeben □*vt* spüren. ~**less** *a*, **-ly** *adv* sinnlos; ⟨*unconscious*⟩ bewusstlos

sensible /'sensəbl/ *a*, **-bly** *adv* vernünftig; ⟨*suitable*⟩ zweckmäßig

sensitiv|e /'sensətɪv/ *a*, **-ly** *adv* empfindlich; ⟨*understanding*⟩ einfühlsam. ~**ity** /-'tɪvəti/ *n* Empfindlichkeit *f*

sensory /'sensəri/ *a* Sinnes-

sensual /'sensjʊəl/ *a* sinnlich. **-ity** /-'ælətɪ/ *n* Sinnlichkeit *f*

sensuous /'sensjʊəs/ *a* sinnlich

sent /sent/ *see* **send**

sentence /'sentəns/ *n* Satz *m*; ⟨*Jur*⟩ Urteil *nt*; ⟨*punishment*⟩ Strafe *f* □ *vt* verurteilen

sentiment

sentiment /'sentimənt/ n Gefühl nt; (opinion) Meinung f; (sentimentality) Sentimentalität f. **~al** /-'mentl/ a sentimental. **~ality** /-'tælətɪ/ n Sentimentalität f

sentry /'sentrɪ/ n Wache f

separable /'sepərəbl/ a trennbar

separate¹ /'sepərət/ a, **-ly** adv getrennt, separat

separat|e² /'sepəreɪt/ vt trennen □ vi sich trennen. **~ion** /-'reɪʃn/ n Trennung f

September /sep'tembə(r)/ n September m

septic /'septɪk/ a vereitert; **go ~** vereitern

sequel /'siːkwl/ n Folge f; (fig) Nachspiel nt

sequence /'siːkwəns/ n Reihenfolge f

sequin /'siːkwɪn/ n Paillette f

serenade /serə'neɪd/ n Ständchen nt □ vt ~ s.o. jdm ein Ständchen bringen

seren|e /sɪ'riːn/ a, **-ly** adv gelassen. **~ity** /-'renətɪ/ n Gelassenheit f

sergeant /'sɑːdʒənt/ n (Mil) Feldwebel m; (in police) Polizeimeister m

serial /'sɪərɪəl/ n Fortsetzungsgeschichte f; (Radio, TV) Serie f. **~ize** vt in Fortsetzungen veröffentlichen/(Radio, TV) senden

series /'sɪəriːz/ n inv Serie f

serious /'sɪərɪəs/ a, **-ly** adv ernst; (illness, error) schwer. **~ness** n Ernst m

sermon /'sɜːmən/ n Predigt f

serpent /'sɜːpənt/ n Schlange f

serrated /se'reɪtɪd/ a gezackt

serum /'sɪərəm/ n Serum nt

servant /'sɜːvənt/ n Diener(in) m(f)

serve /sɜːv/ n (Tennis) Aufschlag m □ vt dienen (+ dat); bedienen (customer, guest); servieren (food); (Jur) zustellen (on s.o. jdm); verbüßen (sentence); **~ its**

purpose seinen Zweck erfüllen; **it ~s you right!** das geschieht dir recht! **~s two** für zwei Personen □ vi dienen; (Tennis) aufschlagen

service /'sɜːvɪs/ n Dienst m; (Relig) Gottesdienst m; (in shop, restaurant) Bedienung f; (transport) Verbindung f; (maintenance) Wartung f; (set of crockery) Service nt; (Tennis) Aufschlag m; **~s** pl Dienstleistungen pl; (on motorway) Tankstelle und Raststätte f; **in the ~s** beim Militär; **be of ~** nützlich sein; **out of/in ~** (machine:) außer/in Betrieb □ vt (Techn) warten. **~able** /-əbl/ a nützlich; (durable) haltbar

service: **~ area** n Tankstelle und Raststätte f. **~ charge** n Bedienungszuschlag m. **~man** n Soldat m. **~ station** n Tankstelle

serviette /sɜːvɪ'et/ n Serviette f

servile /'sɜːvaɪl/ a unterwürfig

session /'seʃn/ n Sitzung f; (Univ) Studienjahr nt

set /set/ n Satz m; (of crockery) Service nt; (of cutlery) Garnitur f; (TV, Radio) Apparat m; (Math) Menge f; (Theat) Bühnenbild nt; (Cinema) Szenenaufbau m; (of people) Kreis m; **shampoo and ~** (ready) Waschen und Legen m; (ready) fertig, bereit; (rigid) fest; (book) vorgeschrieben; **be ~ on doing sth** entschlossen sein, etw zu tun; **be ~ in one's ways** in seinen Gewohnheiten festgefahren sein □ v (pt/pp set, pres p setting) □ vt setzen; (adjust) einstellen; stellen (task, alarm clock); festsetzen, festlegen (date, limit); aufgeben (homework); zusammenstellen (questions); [ein]fassen (gem); einrichten (bone); legen (hair); decken (table) □ vi (sun:) untergehen; (become hard) fest werden; **~ about sth** sich an etw (acc) machen; **~ about doing sth** sich daranmachen, etw zu tun. **~ back** vt zurücksetzen; (hold up)

aufhalten; ⟨*fam: cost*⟩ kosten. ~
off *vi* losgehen; ⟨*in vehicle*⟩ losfahren □ *vt* auslösen ⟨*alarm*⟩; explodieren lassen ⟨*bomb*⟩. ~ **out**
vi losgehen; ⟨*in vehicle*⟩ losfahren;
~ **out to do sth** sich vornehmen,
etw zu tun □ *vt* auslegen; ⟨*state*⟩
darlegen. ~ **up** *vt* aufbauen; ⟨*fig*⟩
gründen

set meal *n* Menü *nt*

settee /se'ti:/ *n* Sofa *nt*, Couch *f*

setting /'setıŋ/ *n* Rahmen *m*; ⟨*surroundings*⟩ Umgebung *f*; ⟨*of*⟩
Untergang *m*; ⟨*of jewel*⟩ Fassung
f

settle /'setl/ *vt* ⟨*decide*⟩ entscheiden; ⟨*agree*⟩ regeln; ⟨*fix*⟩
festsetzen; ⟨*calm*⟩ beruhigen;
⟨*pay*⟩ bezahlen □ *vi* sich niederlassen; ⟨*snow, dust.*⟩ liegen
bleiben; ⟨*subside*⟩ sich senken;
⟨*sediment:*⟩ sich absetzen. ~
down *vi* sich beruhigen; ⟨*permanently*⟩ seßhaft werden. ~ **up**
vi abrechnen

settlement /'setlmənt/ *n* ⟨*see*
settle⟩ Entscheidung *f*; Regelung
f; Bezahlung *f*; ⟨*Jur*⟩ Vergleich *m*;
⟨*colony*⟩ Siedlung *f*

settler /'setlə(r)/ *n* Siedler *m*

'set-to *n* ⟨*fam*⟩ Streit *m*

'set-up *n* System *nt*

seven /'sevn/ *a* sieben. ~**teen** *a*
siebzehn. ~**teenth** *a* siebzehnte(r,s)

seventh /'sevnθ/ *a* siebte(r,s)

seventieth /'sevntııθ/ *a* siebzigste(r,s)

seventy /'sevntı/ *a* siebzig

sever /'sevə(r)/ *vt* durchtrennen;
abbrechen ⟨*relations*⟩

several /'sevrl/ *a* & *pron* mehrere,
einige

sever|e /sı'vıə(r)/ *a* (-**r**, -**st**,) -**ly**
adv streng; ⟨*pain*⟩ stark; ⟨*illness*⟩
schwer. ~**ity** /-'verətı/ *n* Strenge
f; Schwere *f*

sew /səʊ/ *vt/i* (*pt* **sewed**, *pp* **sewn**
or **sewed**) nähen. ~ **up** *vt* zunähen

sewage /'su:ıdʒ/ *n* Abwasser *nt*

sewer /'su:ə(r)/ *n* Abwasserkanal
m

sewing /'səʊıŋ/ *n* Nähen *nt*;
⟨*work*⟩ Näharbeit *f*. ~ **machine**
n Nähmaschine *f*

sewn /səʊn/ *see* **sew**

sex /seks/ *n* Geschlecht *nt*;
⟨*sexuality, intercourse*⟩ Sex *m*.
~**ist** *a* sexistisch. ~ **offender** *n*
Triebverbrecher *m*

sexual /'seksjʊəl/ *a*, -**ly** *adv* sexuell. ~ **'intercourse** *n* Geschlechtsverkehr *m*

sexuality /seksjʊ'ælətı/ *n*
Sexualität *f*

sexy /'seksı/ *a* (-**ier**, -**iest**) sexy

shabby /'ʃæbı/ *a* (-**ier**, -**iest**), -**ily**
adv schäbig

shack /ʃæk/ *n* Hütte *f*

shackles /'ʃæklz/ *npl* Fesseln *pl*

shade /ʃeɪd/ *n* Schatten *m*; ⟨*of colour*⟩ [Farb]ton *m*; ⟨*for lamp*⟩
[Lampen]schirm *m*; ⟨*Amer: window-blind*⟩ Jalousie *f* □ *vt* beschatten; ⟨*draw lines on*⟩
schattieren

shadow /'ʃædəʊ/ *n* Schatten *m*
□ *vt* ⟨*follow*⟩ beschatten. ~**y** *a*
schattenhaft

shady /'ʃeɪdı/ *a* (-**ier**, -**iest**) schattig; ⟨*fam: disreputable*⟩ zwielichtig

shaft /ʃɑ:ft/ *n* Schaft *m*; ⟨*Techn*⟩
Welle *f*; ⟨*of light*⟩ Strahl *m*; ⟨*of lift*⟩
Schacht *m*; ~**s** *pl* ⟨*of cart*⟩ Gabeldeichsel *f*

shaggy /'ʃægı/ *a* (-**ier**, -**iest**) zottig

shake /ʃeɪk/ *n* Schütteln *nt* □ *v* (*pt*
shook, *pp* **shaken**) □ *vt* schütteln; ⟨*cause to tremble, shock*⟩ erschüttern; ~ **hands with s.o.**
jdm die Hand geben □ *vi* wackeln;
⟨*tremble*⟩ zittern. ~ **off** *vt* abschütteln

shaky /'ʃeɪkı/ *a* (-**ier**, -**iest**) wackelig; ⟨*hand, voice*⟩ zittrig

shall /ʃæl/ *v aux* **I** ~ **go** ich werde
gehen; **we** ~ **see** wir werden
sehen; **what** ~ **I do?** was soll ich
machen? **I'll come too,** ~ **I?** ich

komme mit, ja? **thou shalt not kill** (*liter*) du sollst nicht töten

shallow /'ʃæləʊ/ a (-er, -est) seicht; ⟨dish⟩ flach; (*fig*) oberflächlich

sham /ʃæm/ a unecht □n Heuchelei *f*; (*person*) Heuchler(in) m(*f*) □ vt (*pt/pp* **shammed**) vortäuschen

shambles /'ʃæmblz/ n Durcheinander *nt*

shame /ʃeɪm/ n Scham *f*; (*disgrace*) Schande *f*; **be a ∼** schade sein; **what a ∼!** wie schade! **∼-faced** a betreten

shame|ful /'ʃeɪmfl/ a, **-ly** adv schändlich. **∼less** a, **-ly** adv schamlos

shampoo /ʃæm'pu:/ n Shampoo *nt* □ vt schamponieren

shandy /'ʃændɪ/ n Radler m

shan't /ʃɑ:nt/ = **shall not**

shape /ʃeɪp/ n Form *f*; (*figure*) Gestalt *f*; **take ∼** Gestalt annehmen □ vt formen (**into** zu) □ vi **∼ up** sich entwickeln. **∼less** a formlos; ⟨clothing⟩ unförmig

shapely /'ʃeɪplɪ/ a (-ier, -iest) wohlgeformt

share /ʃeə(r)/ n An|teil *m*; (*Comm*) Aktie *f* □ vt/i teilen. **∼holder** n Aktionär(in) m(*f*)

shark /ʃɑ:k/ n Hai[fisch] m

sharp /ʃɑ:p/ a (-er, -est), -ly adv scharf; ⟨pointed⟩ spitz; (*severe*) heftig; (*sudden*) steil; (*alert*) clever; (*unscrupulous*) gerissen □ adv scharf; (*Mus*) zu hoch; **at six o'clock** ∼ Punkt sechs Uhr; **look ∼!** beeil dich! □ n (*Mus*) Kreuz *nt*. **∼en** vt schärfen; [an]spitzen ⟨pencil⟩

shatter /'ʃætə(r)/ vt zertrümmern; (*fig*) zerstören; **be ∼ed** (*person*) erschüttert sein; (*fam: exhausted*) kaputt □ vi zersplittern

shave /ʃeɪv/ n Rasur *f*; **have a ∼** sich rasieren □ vt rasieren □ vi sich rasieren. **∼r** n Rasierapparat m

shaving /'ʃeɪvɪŋ/ n Rasieren *nt*. **∼-brush** n Rasierpinsel m

shawl /ʃɔ:l/ n Schultertuch *nt*

she /ʃi:/ pron sie

sheaf /ʃi:f/ n (*pl* **sheaves**) Garbe *f*; (*of papers*) Bündel *nt*

shear /ʃɪə(r)/ vt (*pt* **sheared**, *pp* **shorn** or **sheared**) scheren

shears /ʃɪəz/ npl [große] Schere *f*

sheath /ʃi:θ/ n (*pl* ∼s /ʃi:ðz/) Scheide *f*

sheaves /ʃi:vz/ see **sheaf**

shed1 /ʃed/ n Schuppen m; (*for cattle*) Stall m

shed2 vt (*pt/pp* **shed**, *pres p* **shedding**) verlieren; vergießen ⟨blood, tears⟩; **∼ light on** Licht bringen in (+ *acc*)

sheen /ʃi:n/ n Glanz m

sheep /ʃi:p/ n *inv* Schaf *nt*. **∼-dog** n Hütehund m

sheepish /'ʃi:pɪʃ/ a, -ly adv verlegen

'sheepskin n Schaffell *nt*

sheer /ʃɪə(r)/ a rein; (*steep*) steil; (*transparent*) hauchdünn □ adv steil

sheet /ʃi:t/ n Laken *nt*, Betttuch *nt*; (*of paper*) Blatt *nt*; (*of glass, metal*) Platte *f*

sheikh /ʃeɪk/ n Scheich m

shelf /ʃelf/ n (*pl* **shelves**) Brett *nt*, Bord *nt*; (*set of shelves*) Regal *nt*

shell /ʃel/ n Schale *f*; (*of snail*) Haus *nt*; (*of tortoise*) Panzer *m*; (*on beach*) Muschel *f*; (*of unfinished building*) Rohbau *m*; (*Mil*) Granate *f* □ vt pellen; enthülsen ⟨peas⟩; (*Mil*) [mit Granaten] beschießen. **∼ out** vi (*fam*) blechen

'shellfish n *inv* Schalentiere *pl*; (*Culin*) Meeresfrüchte *pl*

shelter /'ʃeltə(r)/ n Schutz *m*; (*air-raid* ∼) Luftschutzraum *m* □ vt schützen (**from** vor + *dat*) □ vi sich unterstellen. **∼ed** a geschützt; (*life*) behütet

shelve /ʃelv/ vt auf Eis legen; (*abandon*) aufgeben □ vi ⟨slope:⟩ abfallen shelves /ʃelvz/ *see* shelf

shelving /'ʃelvɪŋ/ *n* (*shelves*) Regale *pl*

shepherd /'ʃepəd/ *n* Schäfer *m*; (*Relig*) Hirte *m* □ *vt* führen. **~ess** *n* Schäferin *f*. **~'s pie** *n* Auflauf *m* aus mit Kartoffelbrei bedecktem Hackfleisch

sherry /'ʃerɪ/ *n* Sherry *m*

shield /ʃiːld/ *n* Schild *m*; (*for eyes*) Schirm *m*; (*Techn* & *fig*) Schutz *m* □ *vt* schützen (**from** vor + *dat*)

shift /ʃɪft/ *n* Verschiebung *f*; (*at work*) Schicht *f*; **make** ~ sich (*dat*) behelfen (**with** mit) □ *vt* rücken; (*take away*) wegnehmen; (*rearrange*) umstellen; schieben (*blame*) (**on to** auf + *acc*) □ *vi* sich verschieben; (*fam: move quickly*) rasen

'**shift work** *n* Schichtarbeit *f*

shifty /'ʃɪftɪ/ *a* (**-ier**, **-iest**) (*pej*) verschlagen

shilly-shally /'ʃɪlɪʃælɪ/ *vi* fackeln (*fam*)

shimmer /'ʃɪmə(r)/ *n* Schimmer *m* □ *vi* schimmern

shin /ʃɪn/ *n* Schienbein *nt*

shine /ʃaɪn/ *n* Glanz *m* □ *v* (*pt/pp* shone) □ *vi* leuchten; (*reflect light*) glänzen; (*sun:*) scheinen □ *vt* **a light on** beleuchten

shingle /'ʃɪŋgl/ *n* (*pebbles*) Kiesel *pl*

shingles /'ʃɪŋglz/ *n* (*Med*) Gürtelrose *f*

shiny /'ʃaɪnɪ/ *a* (**-ier**, **-iest**) glänzend

ship /ʃɪp/ *n* Schiff *nt* □ *vt* (*pt/pp* shipped) verschiffen

ship: **~building** *n* Schiffbau *m*. **~ment** *n* Sendung *f*. **~per** *n* Spediteur *m*. **~ping** *n* Versand *m*; (*traffic*) Schiffahrt *f*. **~shape** *a* & *adv* in Ordnung. **~wreck** *n* Schiffbruch *m*. **~wrecked** *a* schiffbrüchig. **~yard** *n* Werft *f*

shirk /ʃɜːk/ *vt* sich drücken vor (+ *dat*). **~er** *n* Drückeberger *m*

shirt /ʃɜːt/ *n* [Ober]hemd *nt*; (*for woman*) Hemdbluse *f*

shit /ʃɪt/ *n* (*vulg*) Scheiße *f* □ *vi* (*pt/pp* shit) (*vulg*) scheißen

shiver /'ʃɪvə(r)/ *n* Schauder *m* □ *vi* zittern

shoal /ʃəʊl/ *n* (*of fish*) Schwarm *m*

shock /ʃɒk/ *n* Schock *m*; (*Electr*) Schlag *m*; (*impact*) Erschütterung *f* □ *vt* einen Schock versetzen (+ *dat*); (*scandalize*) schockieren. **~ing** *a* schockierend; (*fam: dreadful*) fürchterlich

shod /ʃɒd/ *see* shoe

shoddy /'ʃɒdɪ/ *a* (**-ier**, **-iest**) minderwertig

shoe /ʃuː/ *n* Schuh *m*; (*of horse*) Hufeisen *nt* □ *vt* (*pt/pp* shod, *pres p* shoeing) beschlagen (*horse*)

shoe: **~horn** *n* Schuhanzieher *m*. **~lace** *n* Schnürsenkel *m*. **~maker** *n* Schuhmacher *m*. **~-string** *n* **on a ~-string** (*fam*) mit ganz wenig Geld

shone /ʃɒn/ *see* shine

shoo /ʃuː/ *vt* scheuchen □ *int* sch!

shook /ʃʊk/ *see* shake

shoot /ʃuːt/ *n* (*Bot*) Trieb *m*; (*hunt*) Jagd *f* □ *v* (*pt/pp* shot) □ *vt* schießen; (*kill*) erschießen; drehen (*film*) □ *vi* schießen. **~ down** *vt* abschießen. **~ out** *vi* (*rush*) herausschießen. **~ up** *vi* (*grow*) in die Höhe schießen; (*prices:*) schnellen

'**shooting-range** *n* Schießstand *m*

shop /ʃɒp/ *n* Laden *m*, Geschäft *nt*; (*workshop*) Werkstatt *f*; **talk** ~ (*fam*) fachsimpeln □ *vi* (*pt/pp* shopped, *pres p* shopping) einkaufen; **go** **~ping** einkaufen gehen

shop: ~ **assistant** *n* Verkäufer(in) *m(f)*. **~keeper** *n* Ladenbesitzer(in) *m(f)*. **~lifter** *n* Ladendieb *m*. **~lifting** *n* Ladendiebstahl *m*

shopping /'ʃɒpɪŋ/ *n* Einkaufen *nt*; (*articles*) Einkäufe *pl*; **do the**

~ einkaufen. ~ **bag** n Einkaufstasche f ~ **centre** n Einkaufszentrum nt. ~ **trolley** n Einkaufswagen m

shop: ~ **'steward** n [gewerkschaftlicher] Vertrauensmann m. ~-'**window** n Schaufenster nt

shore /ʃɔː(r)/ n Strand m; (of lake) Ufer nt

shorn /ʃɔːn/ see **shear**

short /ʃɔːt/ (er, -est) kurz; (person) klein; (curt) schroff; a ~ **time ago** vor kurzem; **be** ~ zu wenig ... haben; **be in** ~ **supply** knapp sein □ adv kurz; (abruptly) plötzlich; ~ **of** angebunden; in ~ kurzum; ~ **of** (except) außer; **go** ~ Mangel leiden; **stop** ~ **of doing sth** davor zurückschrecken, etw zu tun

shortage /'ʃɔːtɪdʒ/ n Mangel m (of an + dat); (scarcity) Knappheit f

short: ~**bread** n ≈ Mürbekekse pl. ~ **circuit** n Kurzschluss m. ~**coming** n Fehler m. ~ '**cut** n Abkürzung f

shorten /'ʃɔːtn/ vt [ab]kürzen; kürzer machen (garment)

short: ~**hand** n Kurzschrift f, Stenographie f. ~**handed** a be ~**handed** zu wenig Personal haben. ~**hand 'typist** n Stenotypistin f. ~ **list** n engere Auswahl f. ~-'**lived** /-lɪvd/ a kurzlebig

short|ly /'ʃɔːtlɪ/ adv in Kürze; ~**ly before/after** kurz vorher/ danach. ~**ness** n Kürze f; (of person) Kleinheit f

shorts /ʃɔːts/ npl kurze Hose f, Shorts pl

short: ~'**sighted** a kurzsichtig. ~**sleeved** a kurzärmelig. ~'**staffed** a be ~**staffed** zu wenig Personal haben. ~ '**story** n Kurzgeschichte f. ~-'**tempered** a aufbrausend. ~**term** a kurzfristig. ~ **wave** n Kurzwelle f

shot /ʃɒt/ see **shoot** n Schuss m; (pellets) Schrot m; (person)

Schütze m; (Phot) Aufnahme f; (injection) Spritze f; (fam: attempt) Versuch m; **like a** ~ (fam) sofort. ~**gun** n Schrotflinte f. ~-**putting** n (Sport) Kugelstoßen nt

should /ʃʊd/ v aux **you** ~ **go** du solltest gehen; **I** ~ **have seen him** ich hätte ihn sehen sollen; **I** ~ **like** ich möchte; **this** ~ **be enough** das müsste eigentlich reichen; **if he** ~ **be there** falls er da sein sollte

shoulder /'ʃəʊldə(r)/ n Schulter f □ vt schultern; (fig) auf sich (acc) nehmen. ~**blade** n Schulterblatt nt. ~**strap** n Tragriemen m; (on garment) Träger m

shout /ʃaʊt/ n Schrei m □ vt/i schreien. ~ **down** vt niederschreien

shouting /'ʃaʊtɪŋ/ n Geschrei nt

shove /ʃʌv/ n Stoß m; (fam) Schubs m □ vt stoßen; (fam) schubsen; (fam: put) tun □ vi drängeln. ~ **off** vi (fam) abhauen

shovel /'ʃʌvl/ n Schaufel f (pt/pp **shovelled**) schaufeln

show /ʃəʊ/ n (display) Pracht f; (exhibition) Ausstellung f, Schau f; (performance) Vorstellung f; (Theat, TV) Show f; **on** ~ ausgestellt □ vt (pt **showed**, pp **shown**) zeigen; (put on display) ausstellen; vorführen (film) □ vi sichtbar sein; (film:) gezeigt werden. ~ **in** vt hereinführen. ~ **off** vi (fam) angeben □ vt vorführen; (flaunt) angeben mit. ~ **up** vi [deutlich] zu sehen sein; (fam: arrive) auftauchen □ vt deutlich zeigen; (fam: embarrass) blamieren

'show-down n Entscheidungskampf m

shower /'ʃaʊə(r)/ n Dusche f; (of rain) Schauer m; **have a** ~ duschen □ vt ~ **with** überschütten mit □ vi duschen. ~**proof** a regendicht. ~**y** a regnerisch

'show-jumping n Springreiten nt

shown /ʃəʊn/ *see* **show**

show: ∼**off** *n* Angeber(in) *m(f)*. ∼**piece** *n* Paradestück *nt*. ∼**room** *n* Ausstellungsraum *m*

showy /'ʃəʊɪ/ *a* protzig

shrank /ʃræŋk/ *see* **shrink**

shred /ʃred/ *n* Fetzen *m*; (*fig*) Spur *f* □ *vt* (*pt/pp* **shredded**) zerkleinern; (*Culin*) schnitzeln. ∼**der** *n* Reißwolf *m*; (*Culin*) Schnitzelwerk *nt*

shrewd /ʃruːd/ *a* (**-er, -est**), **-ly** *adv* klug. ∼**ness** *n* Klugheit *f*

shriek /ʃriːk/ *n* Schrei *m* □ *vt/i* schreien

shrift /ʃrɪft/ *n* **give s.o. short** ∼ jdn kurz abfertigen

shrill /ʃrɪl/ *a*, **-y** *adv* schrill

shrimp /ʃrɪmp/ *n* Garnele *f*, Krabbe *f*

shrine /ʃraɪn/ *n* Heiligtum *nt*

shrink /ʃrɪŋk/ *vi* (*pt* **shrank**, *pp* **shrunk**) schrumpfen; (*garment:*) einlaufen; (*draw back*) zurückschrecken (**from** *vor* + *dat*)

shrivel /'ʃrɪvl/ *vi* (*pt/pp* **shrivelled**) verschrumpeln

shroud /ʃraʊd/ *n* Leichentuch *nt*; (*fig*) Schleier *m*

Shrove /ʃrəʊv/ *n* ∼ '**Tuesday** Fastnachtsdienstag *m*

shrub /ʃrʌb/ *n* Strauch *m*

shrug /ʃrʌg/ *n* Achselzucken *nt* □ *vt/i* (*pt/pp* **shrugged**) ∼ [**one's shoulders**] die Achseln zucken

shrunk /ʃrʌŋk/ *see* **shrink**. ∼**en** *a* geschrumpft

shudder /'ʃʌdə(r)/ *n* Schauder *m* □ *vi* schaudern; (*tremble*) zittern

shuffle /'ʃʌfl/ *vi* schlurfen □ *vt* mischen (*cards*)

shun /ʃʌn/ *vt* (*pt/pp* **shunned**) meiden

shunt /ʃʌnt/ *vt* rangieren

shush /ʃʊʃ/ *int* sch!

shut /ʃʌt/ *v* (*pt/pp* **shut**, *pres p* **shutting**) □ *vt* zumachen, schließen; ∼ **one's finger in the door** sich (*dat*) den Finger in der Tür einklemmen □ *vi* sich

schließen; (*shop:*) schließen, zumachen. ∼ **down** *vt* schließen; stillegen (*factory*) □ *vi* schließen; (*factory:*) stillgelegt werden. ∼ **up** *vt* abschließen; (*lock in*) einsperren □ *vi* (*fam*) den Mund halten

shut-down *n* Stillegung *f*

shutter /'ʃʌtə(r)/ *n* [Fenster]laden *m*; (*Phot*) Verschluss *m*

shuttle /'ʃʌtl/ *n* (*Tex*) Schiffchen *nt* □ *vi* pendeln

shuttle: ∼**cock** *n* Federball *m*. ∼ **service** *n* Pendelverkehr *m*

shy /ʃaɪ/ *a* (**-er, -est**), **-ly** *adv* schüchtern; (*timid*) scheu □ *vi* (*pt/pp* **shied**) (*horse:*) scheuen. ∼**ness** *n* Schüchternheit *f*

Siamese /saɪə'miːz/ *a* siamesisch

siblings /'sɪblɪŋz/ *npl* Geschwister *pl*

Sicily /'sɪsɪlɪ/ *n* Sizilien *nt*

sick /sɪk/ *a* krank; (*humour*) makaber; **be** ∼ (*vomit*) sich übergeben; **be** ∼ **of sth** (*fam*) etw satt haben; **I feel** ∼ mir ist schlecht

sicken /'sɪkn/ *vt* anwidern □ *vi* **be** ∼**ing for something** krank werden

sickle /'sɪkl/ *n* Sichel *f*

sick|ly /'sɪklɪ/ *a* (**-ier, -iest**) kränklich. ∼**ness** *n* Krankheit *f*; (*vomiting*) Erbrechen *nt*

sick-room *n* Krankenzimmer *nt*

side /saɪd/ *n* Seite *f*; **on the** ∼ (*as sideline*) nebenbei; ∼ **by** ∼ nebeneinander; (*fig*) Seite an Seite; **take** ∼**s** Partei ergreifen (**with** für); **to be on the safe** ∼ vorsichtshalber □ *attrib* Seiten- □ *vi* ∼ **with** Partei ergreifen für

side: ∼**board** *n* Anrichte *f*. ∼**burns** *npl* Koteletten *pl*. ∼**effect** *n* Nebenwirkung *f*. ∼**lights** *npl* Standlicht *nt*. ∼**line** *n* Nebenbeschäftigung *f*. ∼**show** *n* Nebenattraktion *f*. ∼**step** *vt* ausweichen (+ *dat*). ∼**track** *vt* ablenken. ∼**walk** *n* (*Amer*) Bürgersteig *m*. ∼**ways** *adv* seitwärts

siding /'saɪdɪŋ/ n Abstellgleis nt

sidle /'saɪdl/ vi sich heranschleichen (**up to** an + acc)

siege /si:dʒ/ n Belagerung f; (by police) Umstellung f

sieve /sɪv/ n Sieb nt □ vt sieben

sift /sɪft/ vt sieben; (fig) durchsehen

sigh /saɪ/ n Seufzer m □ vi seufzen

sight /saɪt/ n Sicht f; (faculty) Sehvermögen nt; (spectacle) Anblick m; (on gun) Visier nt; ~s pl Sehenswürdigkeiten pl; **at first** ~ auf den ersten Blick; **within/out of** ~ in/außer Sicht; **lose** ~ **of** aus dem Auge verlieren; **know by** ~ vom Sehen kennen; **have bad** ~ schlechte Augen haben □ vt sichten

'sightseeing n **go** ~ die Sehenswürdigkeiten besichtigen

sign /saɪn/ n Zeichen nt; (notice) Schild nt □ vt/i unterschreiben; (author, artist:) signieren. ~ **on** vi (as unemployed) sich arbeitslos melden; (Mil) sich verpflichten

signal /'sɪgnl/ n Signal nt □ vt/i (pt/pp **signalled**) signalisieren; ~ **to s.o.** jdm ein Signal geben (**to** zu). ~**box** n Stellwerk nt

signature /'sɪgnətʃə(r)/ n Unterschrift f; (of artist) Signatur f. ~ **tune** n Kennmelodie f

signet-ring /'sɪgnɪt-/ n Siegelring m

significan|ce /sɪg'nɪfɪkəns/ n Bedeutung f. ~**t** a, **-ly** adv bedeutungsvoll; (important) bedeutend

signify /'sɪgnɪfaɪ/ vt (pt/pp **-ied**) bedeuten

signpost /'saɪn-/ n Wegweiser m

silence /'saɪləns/ n Stille f; (of person) Schweigen nt □ vt zum Schweigen bringen. ~**r** n (on gun) Schalldämpfer m; (Auto) Auspufftopf m

silent /'saɪlənt/ a, **-ly** adv still; (without speaking) schweigend; **remain** ~ schweigen. ~ **film** n Stummfilm m

silhouette /sɪlu:'et/ n Silhouette f; (picture) Schattenriss m □ vt **be** ~**d** sich als Silhouette abheben

silicon /'sɪlɪkən/ n Silizium nt

silk /sɪlk/ n Seide f □ attrib Seiden-. ~**worm** n Seidenraupe f

silky /'sɪlkɪ/ a (**-ier**, **-iest**) seidig

sill /sɪl/ n Sims m & nt

silly /'sɪlɪ/ a (**-ier**, **-iest**) dumm, albern

silo /'saɪləʊ/ n Silo m

silt /sɪlt/ n Schlick m

silver /'sɪlvə(r)/ a silbern; (coin, paper) Silber- □ n Silber nt

silver: ~**-plated** a versilbert. ~**ware** n Silber nt. ~ **wedding** n Silberhochzeit f

similar /'sɪmɪlə(r)/ a, **-ly** adv ähnlich. ~**ity** /-'lærətɪ/ n Ähnlichkeit f

simile /'sɪmɪlɪ/ n Vergleich m

simmer /'sɪmə(r)/ vi leise kochen, ziehen □ vt ziehen lassen

simple /'sɪmpl/ a (**-r**, **-st**) einfach; (person) einfältig. ~**-minded** a einfältig. ~**ton** /'sɪmpltən/ n Einfaltspinsel m

simplicity /sɪm'plɪsətɪ/ n Einfachheit f

simpli|fication /sɪmplɪfɪ'keɪʃn/ n Vereinfachung f. ~**fy** /'sɪmplɪfaɪ/ vt (pt/pp **-ied**) vereinfachen

simply /'sɪmplɪ/ adv einfach

simulat|e /'sɪmjʊleɪt/ vt vortäuschen; (Techn) simulieren. ~**ion** /-'leɪʃn/ n Vortäuschung f; Simulation f

simultaneous /sɪml'teɪnɪəs/ a, **-ly** adv gleichzeitig; (interpreting) Simultan-

sin /sɪn/ n Sünde f □ vi (pt/pp **sinned**) sündigen

since /sɪns/ prep seit (+ dat) □ adv seitdem □ conj seit; (because) da

sincere /sɪn'sɪə(r)/ a aufrichtig; (heartfelt) herzlich. ~**ly** adv aufrichtig; **Yours** ~**ly** Mit freundlichen Grüßen sincerity /sɪn'serətɪ/ n Aufrichtigkeit f

sinew /'sɪnjuː/ n Sehne f

sinful /'sɪnfl/ a sündhaft

sing /sɪŋ/ vt/i (pt sang, pp sung) singen

singe /sɪndʒ/ vt (pres p singeing) versengen

singer /'sɪŋə(r)/ n Sänger(in) m(f)

single /'sɪŋgl/ a einzeln; (one only) einzig; (unmarried) ledig; (ticket) einfach; (room, bed) Einzel- □ n (ticket) einfache Fahrkarte f; (record) Single f; ~s pl (Tennis) Einzel nt □ vt ~ out auswählen

single: ~-breasted a einreihig. ~-handed a & adv allein. ~-minded a zielstrebig. ~ 'parent n Alleinerziehende(r) m/f

singlet /'sɪŋglɪt/ n Unterhemd nt

singly /'sɪŋglɪ/ adv einzeln

singular /'sɪŋgjʊlə(r)/ a eigenartig; (Gram) im Singular □ n Singular m. ~ly adv außerordentlich

sinister /'sɪnɪstə(r)/ a finster

sink /sɪŋk/ n Spülbecken nt □ v (pt sank, pp sunk) □ vi sinken (ship); senken (shaft). ~ in vi einsinken; (fam: be understood) kapiert werden

'sink unit n Spüle f

sinner /'sɪnə(r)/ n Sünder(in) m(f)

sinus /'saɪnəs/ n Nebenhöhle f

sip /sɪp/ n Schlückchen nt □ vt (pt/pp sipped) in kleinen Schlucken trinken

siphon /'saɪfn/ n (bottle) Siphon m. ~ off vt mit einem Saugheber ablassen

sir /sɜː(r)/ n mein Herr; S~ (title) Sir; Dear S~s Sehr geehrte Herren

siren /'saɪrən/ n Sirene f

sissy /'sɪsɪ/ n Waschlappen m

sister /'sɪstə(r)/ n Schwester f. ~ (nurse) Oberschwester f. ~-in-law n (pl ~s-in-law) Schwägerin f. ~ly a schwesterlich

sit /sɪt/ v (pt/pp sat, pres p sitting) □ vi sitzen; (sit down) sich setzen; (committee:) tagen □ vt setzen; machen (exam). ~ back vi sich zurücklehnen. ~ down vi sich setzen. ~ up vi (aufrecht) sitzen; (rise) sich aufsetzen; (not slouch) gerade sitzen; (stay up) aufbleiben

site /saɪt/ n Gelände nt; (for camping) Platz m; (Archaeol) Stätte f □ vt legen

sitting /'sɪtɪŋ/ n Sitzung f; (for meals) Schub m

situate /'sɪtjʊeɪt/ vt legen; be ~ed liegen. ~ion /-'eɪʃn/ n Lage f; (circumstances) Situation f; (job) Stelle f

six /sɪks/ a sechs. ~teen a sechzehn. ~teenth a sechzehnte(r,s)

sixth /sɪksθ/ a sechste(r,s)

sixtieth /'sɪkstɪɪθ/ a sechzigste(r,s)

sixty /'sɪkstɪ/ a sechzig

size /saɪz/ n Größe f □ vt ~ up (fam) taxieren

sizeable /'saɪzəbl/ a ziemlich groß

sizzle /'sɪzl/ vi brutzeln

skate[1] /skeɪt/ n inv (fish) Rochen m

skate[2] n Schlittschuh m; (roller-) Rollschuh m □ vi Schlittschuh/Rollschuh laufen. ~r n Eisläufer(in) m(f); Rollschuhläufer(in) m(f)

skating /'skeɪtɪŋ/ n Eislaufen nt. ~-rink n Eisbahn f

skeleton /'skelɪtn/ n Skelett nt. ~ 'key n Dietrich m. ~ 'staff n Minimalbesetzung f

sketch /sketʃ/ n Skizze f; (Theat) Sketch m □ vt skizzieren

sketchy /'sketʃɪ/ a (-ier, -iest). -ily adv skizzenhaft

skew /skjuː/ n on the ~ schräg

skewer /'skjʊə(r)/ n [Brat]spieß m

ski /skiː/ n Ski m □ vi (pt/pp skied, pres p skiing) Ski fahren or laufen

skid /skɪd/ n Schleudern nt □ vi (pt/pp **skidded**) schleudern

skier /'skiːə(r)/ n Skiläufer(in) m(f)

skiing /'skiːɪŋ/ n Skilaufen nt

skilful /'skɪlfl/ a, **-ly** adv geschickt

skill /skɪl/ n Geschick nt. **~ed** a geschickt; (trained) ausgebildet

skim /skɪm/ vt (pt/pp **skimmed**) entrahmen ⟨milk⟩. **~ off** vt abschöpfen. **~ through** vt überfliegen

skimp /skɪmp/ vt sparen an (+ dat)

skimpy /'skɪmpɪ/ a (**-ier, -iest**) knapp

skin /skɪn/ n Haut f; (on fruit) Schale f □ vt (pt/pp **skinned**) häuten; schälen ⟨fruit⟩

skin: **~-deep** a oberflächlich. **~-diving** n Sporttauchen nt

skinflint /'skɪnflɪnt/ n Geizhals m

skinny /'skɪnɪ/ a (**-ier, -iest**) dünn

skip¹ /skɪp/ n Container m

skip² n Hüpfer m □ v (pt/pp **skipped**) vi hüpfen; (with rope) seilspringen □ vt überspringen

skipper /'skɪpə(r)/ n Kapitän m

'skipping-rope n Sprungseil nt

skirmish /'skɜːmɪʃ/ n Gefecht nt

skirt /skɜːt/ n Rock m □ vt herumgehen um

skit /skɪt/ n parodistischer Sketch m

skittle /'skɪtl/ n Kegel m

skive /skaɪv/ vi (fam) blaumachen

skulk /skʌlk/ vi lauern

skull /skʌl/ n Schädel m

skunk /skʌŋk/ n Stinktier nt

sky /skaɪ/ n Himmel m. **~light** n Dachluke f. **~scraper** n Wolkenkratzer m

slab /slæb/ n Platte f; (slice) Scheibe f; (of chocolate) Tafel f

slack /slæk/ a (**-er, -est**) schlaff, locker; (person) nachlässig; (Comm) flau □ vi bummeln

slacken /'slækn/ vi sich lockern; (diminish) nachlassen; (speed:)

sich verringern □ vt lockern; (diminish) verringern

slacks /slæks/ npl Hose f

slag /slæg/ n Schlacke f

slain /sleɪn/ see **slay**

slake /sleɪk/ vt löschen

slam /slæm/ v (pt/pp **slammed**) □ vt zuschlagen; (put) knallen (fam); (fam: criticize) verreißen □ vi zuschlagen

slander /'slɑːndə(r)/ n Verleumdung f □ vt verleumden. **~ous** /-rəs/ a verleumderisch

slang /slæŋ/ n Slang m. **~y** a salopp

slant /slɑːnt/ n Schräge f; **on the ~** schräg □ vt abschrägen; (fig) färben ⟨report⟩ □ vi sich neigen

slap /slæp/ n Schlag m □ vt (pt/pp **slapped**) schlagen; (put) knallen (fam) □ adv direkt

slap: **~-dash** a (fam) schludrig. **~-up** a (fam) toll

slash /slæʃ/ n Schlitz m □ vt aufschlitzen; [drastisch] reduzieren ⟨prices⟩

slat /slæt/ n Latte f

slate /sleɪt/ n Schiefer m; (fam) heruntermachen; verreißen ⟨performance⟩

slaughter /'slɔːtə(r)/ n Schlachten nt; (massacre) Gemetzel nt □ vt schlachten; abschlachten. **~house** n Schlachthaus nt

Slav /slɑːv/ a slawisch □ n Slawe m/ Slawin f

slave /sleɪv/ n Sklave m/ Sklavin f □ vi **~ [away]** schuften. **~-driver** n Leuteschinder m

slav|ery /'sleɪvərɪ/ n Sklaverei f. **~ish** a, **-ly** adv sklavisch

Slavonic /slə'vɒnɪk/ a slawisch

slay /sleɪ/ vt (pt **slew**, pp **slain**) ermorden

sleazy /'sliːzɪ/ a (**-ier, -iest**) schäbig

sledge /sledʒ/ n Schlitten m. **~-hammer** n Vorschlaghammer m

sleek /sliːk/ a (-er, -est) seidig; (well-fed) wohlgenährt

sleep /sliːp/ n Schlaf m; go to ~ einschlafen; put to ~ einschläfern □v (pt/pp slept) □vi schlafen □vt (accommodate) Unterkunft bieten für. ~er n Schläfer(in) m(f); (Rail) Schlafwagen m; (on track) Schwelle f

sleeping: ~-bag n Schlafsack m. ~-car n Schlafwagen m. ~-pill n Schlaftablette f

sleep: ~less a schlaflos. ~-walking n Schlafwandeln n

sleepy /ˈsliːpɪ/ a (-ier, -iest), -ily adv schläfrig

sleet /sliːt/ n Schneeregen m □vi it is ~ing es gibt Schneeregen

sleeve /sliːv/ n Ärmel m; (for record) Hülle f. ~less a ärmellos

sleigh /sleɪ/ n [Pferde]schlitten m

sleight /slaɪt/ n ~ of hand Taschenspielerei f

slender /ˈslendə(r)/ a schlank; (fig) gering

slept /slept/ see sleep

sleuth /sluːθ/ n Detektiv m

slew[1] /sluː/ vi schwenken

slew[2] see slay

slice /slaɪs/ n Scheibe f □vt in Scheiben schneiden; ~d bread Schnittbrot nt

slick /slɪk/ a clever □n (of oil) Ölteppich m

slid|e /slaɪd/ n Rutschbahn f; (for hair) Spange f; (Phot) Dia nt □v (pt/pp slid) □vi rutschen □vt schieben. ~ing a gleitend; (door, seat) Schiebe-

slight /slaɪt/ a (-er, -est), -ly adv leicht; (importance) gering; (acquaintance) flüchtig; (slender) schlank; not in the ~est nicht im Geringsten; ~ly better ein bisschen besser □vt kränken, beleidigen □n Beleidigung f

slim /slɪm/ a (slimmer, slimmest) schlank; (volume) schmal; (fig) gering □vi eine Schlankheitskur machen

slim|e /slaɪm/ n Schleim m. ~y a schleimig

sling /slɪŋ/ n (Med) Schlinge f □vt (pt/pp slung) (fam) schmeißen

slip /slɪp/ n (mistake) Fehler m, (fam) Patzer m; (petticoat) Unterrock m; (for pillow) Bezug m; (paper) Zettel m; give s.o. the ~ (fam) jdm entwischen; ~ of the tongue Versprecher m □v (pt/pp slipped) □vi rutschen; (fall) ausrutschen; (go quickly) schlüpfen; (decline) nachlassen □vt schieben; ~ s.o.'s mind jdm entfallen. ~ away vi sich fortschleichen; (time:) verfliegen. ~ up vi (fam) einen Schnitzer machen

slipped 'disc n (Med) Bandscheibenvorfall m

slipper /ˈslɪpə(r)/ n Hausschuh m

slippery /ˈslɪpərɪ/ a glitschig; (surface) glatt

slipshod /ˈslɪpʃɒd/ a schludrig

'slip-up n (fam) Schnitzer m

slit /slɪt/ n Schlitz m □vt (pt/pp slit) aufschlitzen

slither /ˈslɪðə(r)/ vi rutschen

sliver /ˈslɪvə(r)/ n Splitter m

slobber /ˈslɒbə(r)/ vi sabbern

slog /slɒg/ n [hard] ~ Schinderei f □v (pt/pp slogged) □vi schuften □vt schlagen

slogan /ˈsləʊgən/ n Schlagwort nt; (advertising) Werbespruch m

slop /slɒp/ v (pt/pp slopped) □vt verschütten □vi ~ over überschwappen. ~s npl Schmutzwasser nt

slop|e /sləʊp/ n Hang m; (inclination) Neigung f □vi sich neigen. ~ing a schräg

sloppy /ˈslɒpɪ/ a (-ier, -iest) schludrig; (sentimental) sentimental

slosh /slɒʃ/ vi (fam) platschen; (water:) schwappen □vt (fam: hit) schlagen

slot

slot /slɒt/ n Schlitz m; (TV) Sendezeit f □ v (pt/pp **slotted**) □ vt einfügen □ vi sich einfügen (**in** in + acc)

sloth /sləʊθ/ n Trägheit f

slot-machine n Münzautomat m; (for gambling) Spielautomat m

slouch /slaʊtʃ/ vi sich schlecht halten

slovenly /'slʌvnlɪ/ a schlampig

slow /sləʊ/ a (-er, -est), -ly adv langsam; **be** ~ (clock:) nachgehen; **in** ~ **motion** in Zeitlupe □ adv langsam □ vt verlangsamen □ vi ~ **down**, ~ **up** langsamer werden

slow: ~**coach** n (fam) Trödler m. ~**ness** n Langsamkeit f

sludge /slʌdʒ/ n Schlamm m

slug /slʌg/ n Nacktschnecke f

sluggish /'slʌgɪʃ/ a, -ly adv träge

sluice /sluːs/ n Schleuse f

slum /slʌm/ n (house) Elendsquartier nt; ~**s** pl Elendsviertel nt

slumber /'slʌmbə(r)/ n Schlummer m □ vi schlummern

slump /slʌmp/ n Sturz m □ vi fallen; (crumple) zusammensacken; (prices:) stürzen; (sales:) zurückgehen

slung /slʌŋ/ see **sling**

slur /slɜː(r)/ n (discredit) Schande f □ vt (pt/pp **slurred**) undeutlich sprechen

slurp /slɜːp/ vt/i schlürfen

slush /slʌʃ/ n [Schnee]matsch m; (fig) Kitsch m. ~ **fund** n Fonds m für Bestechungsgelder

slushy /'slʌʃɪ/ a matschig; (sentimental) kitschig

slut /slʌt/ n Schlampe f (fam)

sly /slaɪ/ a (-er, -est), -ly adv verschlagen □ n **on the** ~ heimlich

smack¹ /smæk/ n Schlag m, Klaps m □ vt schlagen; ~ **one's lips** mit den Lippen schmatzen □ adv (fam) direkt

smithereens

smack² vi ~ **of** (fig) riechen nach

small /smɔːl/ a (-er, -est) klein; **in the** ~ **hours** in den frühen Morgenstunden □ adv chop up ~ klein hacken □ n ~ **of the back** Kreuz nt

small: ~ **ads** npl Kleinanzeigen pl. ~ '**change** n Kleingeld nt. ~ **holding** n landwirtschaftlicher Kleinbetrieb m. ~**pox** n Pocken pl. ~ **talk** n leichte Konversation f

smarmy /'smɑːmɪ/ a (-ier, -iest) (fam) ölig

smart /smɑːt/ a (-er, -est), -ly adv schick; (clever) schlau, clever; (brisk) flott; (Amer fam: cheeky) frech □ vi brennen

smarten /'smɑːtn/ vt ~ **oneself up** mehr auf sein Äußeres achten

smash /smæʃ/ n Krach m; (collision) Zusammenstoß m; (Tennis) Schmetterball m □ vt zerschlagen; (strike) schlagen; (Tennis) schmettern □ vi zerschmettern; (crash) krachen (**into** gegen). ~**ing** a (fam) toll

smattering /'smætərɪŋ/ n a ~ **of German** ein paar Brocken Deutsch

smear /smɪə(r)/ n verschmierter Fleck m; (Med) Abstrich m; (fig) Verleumdung f □ vt schmieren; (coat) beschmieren (with mit); (fig) verleumden □ vi schmieren

smell /smel/ n Geruch m; (sense) Geruchssinn m □ vt (pt/pp **smelt** or **smelled**) □ vt riechen; (sniff) riechen an (+ dat) □ vi riechen (**of** nach)

smelly /'smelɪ/ a (-ier, -iest) übel riechend

smelt¹ /smelt/ see **smell**

smelt² vt schmelzen

smile /smaɪl/ n Lächeln nt □ vi lächeln; ~ **at** anlächeln

smirk /smɜːk/ vi feixen

smith /smɪθ/ n Schmied m

smithereens /smɪðə'riːnz/ npl **smash to** ~ in tausend Stücke schlagen

smitten /'smɪtn/ a ~ **with** sehr
angetan von

smock /smɒk/ n Kittel m

smog /smɒg/ n Smog m

smoke /sməʊk/ n Rauch m □vt/i
rauchen; (Culin) räuchern.
~less a rauchfrei; (fuel) rauchlos

smoker /'sməʊkə(r)/ n Raucher
m; (Rail) Raucherabteil nt

'**smoke-screen** n [künstliche] Ne-
belwand f

smoking /'sməʊkɪŋ/ n Rauchen
nt; 'no ~' 'Rauchen verboten'

smoky /'sməʊkɪ/ a (-ier, -iest)
verraucht; (taste) rauchig

smooth /smu:ð/ a (-er, -est), -ly
adv glatt □vt glätten. ~ **out** vt
glatt streichen

smother /'smʌðə(r)/ vt ersticken;
(cover) bedecken; (suppress)
unterdrücken

smoulder /'sməʊldə(r)/ vi schwelen

smudge /smʌdʒ/ n Fleck m □vt
verwischen □vi schmieren

smug /smʌg/ a (smugger, smug-
gest), **-ly** adv selbstgefällig

smuggl|e /'smʌgl/ vt schmug-
geln. ~**er** n Schmuggler m. ~**ing**
n Schmuggel m

smut /smʌt/ n Rußflocke f;
(mark) Rußfleck m; (fig) Schmutz
m

smutty /'smʌtɪ/ a (-ier, -iest)
schmutzig

snack /snæk/ n Imbiss m. ~**bar**
n Imbissstube f

snag /snæg/ n Schwierigkeit f,
(fam) Haken m

snail /sneɪl/ n Schnecke f; **at a**
~'**s pace** im Schneckentempo

snake /sneɪk/ n Schlange f

snap /snæp/ n Knacken nt; (photo)
Schnappschuss m □attrib (decision) plötzlich □v (pt/pp
snapped) □vi [entzwei]brechen;
~ **at** (bite) schnappen nach;
(speak sharply) [scharf] anfahren
□vt zerbrechen; (say) fauchen;

(Phot) knipsen. ~ **up** vt weg
schnappen

snappy /'snæpɪ/ a (-ier, -iest)
bissig; (smart) flott; **make it** ~
ein bisschen schnell!

'**snapshot** n Schnappschuss m

snare /sneə(r)/ n Schlinge f

snarl /snɑ:l/ vi [mit gefletschter
Zähnen] knurren

snatch /snætʃ/ n (fragment
Fetzen pl; (theft) Raub m; **make**
a ~ **at** greifen nach □v
schnappen; (steal) klauen
entführen (child); ~ **sth fron**
s.o. jdm etw entreißen

sneak /sni:k/ n (fam) Petze f □v
schleichen; (fam: tell tales
petzen □vt (take) mitgeher
lassen □vi ~ **in/out** sich hi
nein-/hinausschleichen

sneakers /'sni:kəz/ npl (Amer
Turnschuhe pl

sneaking /'sni:kɪŋ/ a heimlich
(suspicion) leise

sneaky /'sni:kɪ/ a hinterhältig

sneer /snɪə(r)/ vi höhnisch lä
cheln; (mock) spotten

sneeze /sni:z/ n Niesen nt □v
niesen

snide /snaɪd/ a (fam) abfällig

sniff /snɪf/ vi schnüffeln □v
schnüffeln an (+ dat); schnüffel
(glue)

snigger /'snɪgə(r)/ vi (boshaf
kichern

snip /snɪp/ n Schnitt m; (fam: bar
gain) günstiger Kauf m □vt/i ~
[at] schnippeln an (+ dat)

snipe /snaɪp/ vi ~ **at** aus dem Hir
terhalt schießen auf (+ acc); (fig
anschießen. ~**r** n Heckenschütz
m

snippet /'snɪpɪt/ n Schnipsel m
(of information) Bruchstück nt

snivel /'snɪvl/ vi (pt/pp **sniv**
elled) flennen

snob /snɒb/ n Snob m. ~**bery**
Snobismus m. ~**bish** a snobis
tisch

snoop /snu:p/ vi (fam) schnüffel

snooty /'snu:tɪ/ a (fam) hochnäsig

snooze /snu:z/ n Nickerchen nt □ vi dösen

snore /snɔː(r)/ vi schnarchen

snorkel /'snɔːkl/ n Schnorchel m

snort /snɔːt/ vi schnauben

snout /snaʊt/ n Schnauze f

snow /snəʊ/ n Schnee m □ vi schneien; **~ed under with** (fig) überhäuft mit

snow: **~ball** n Schneeball m □ vi lawinenartig anwachsen. **~drift** n Schneewehe f. **~drop** n Schneeglöckchen nt. **~fall** n Schneefall m. **~flake** n Schneeflocke f. **~flurry** n Schneegestöber nt. **~man** n Schneemann m. **~plough** n Schneepflug m. **~storm** n Schneesturm m

snub /snʌb/ n Abfuhr f □ vt (pt/pp snubbed) brüskieren

'snub-nosed a stupsnasig

snuff¹ /snʌf/ n Schnupftabak m

snuff² vt **~[out]** löschen

snuffle /'snʌfl/ vi schnüffeln

snug /snʌg/ a (snugger, snuggest) behaglich, gemütlich

snuggle /'snʌgl/ vi sich kuscheln (**up to** an + acc)

so /səʊ/ adv so; **not so fast** nicht so schnell; **so am I** ich auch; **so does he** er auch; **so I see** ach, sehe ich; **that is so** das stimmt; **so much the better** umso besser; **so it is** tatsächlich; **if so** wenn ja; **so as to** um zu; **so long!** (fam) tschüs! □ pron **I hope so** hoffentlich; **I think so** ich glaube schon; **I told you so** ich hab's dir gleich gesagt; **because I say so** weil ich es sage; **I'm afraid so** leider ja; **so saying/doing, he/she ...** indem er/sie das sagte/tat, ...; **an hour or so** eine Stunde oder so; **very much so** durchaus □ conj (therefore) also; **so that** damit; **so there!** fertig! **so what!** na und! **so you see** wie du

siehst; **so where have you been?** wo warst du denn?

soak /səʊk/ vt nass machen; (steep) einweichen; (fam: fleece) schröpfen □ vi weichen; (liquid:) sickern. **~ up** vt aufsaugen

soaking /'səʊkɪŋ/ a & adv **~ [wet]** patschnass (fam)

soap /səʊp/ n Seife f. **~ opera** n Seifenoper f. **~ powder** n Seifenpulver nt

soapy /'səʊpɪ/ a (-ier, -iest) seifig

soar /sɔː(r)/ vi aufsteigen; (prices:) in die Höhe schnellen

sob /sɒb/ n Schluchzer m □ vi (pt/pp sobbed) schluchzen

sober /'səʊbə(r)/ a, **-ly** adv nüchtern; (serious) ernst; (colour) gedeckt. **~ up** vi nüchtern werden

'so-called a sogenannt

soccer /'sɒkə(r)/ n (fam) Fußball m

sociable /'səʊʃəbl/ a gesellig

social /'səʊʃl/ a gesellschaftlich; (Admin, Pol, Zool) sozial

socialis|m /'səʊʃəlɪzm/ n Sozialismus m. **~t** -ist/ a sozialistisch □ n Sozialist m

socialize /'səʊʃəlaɪz/ vi [gesellschaftlich] verkehren

socially /'səʊʃəlɪ/ adv gesellschaftlich; **know ~** privat kennen

social: **~ se'curity** n Sozialhilfe f. **~ work** n Sozialarbeit f. **~ worker** n Sozialarbeiter(in) m(f)

society /sə'saɪətɪ/ n Gesellschaft f; (club) Verein m

sociolog|ist /səʊsɪ'ɒlədʒɪst/ n Soziologe m. **~y** n Soziologie f

sock¹ /sɒk/ n Socke f; (kneelength) Kniestrumpf m

sock² n (fam) Schlag m □ vt (fam) hauen

socket /'sɒkɪt/ n (of eye) Augenhöhle f; (of joint) Gelenkpfanne f; (wall plug) Steckdose f; (for bulb) Fassung f

soda /'səʊdə/ n Soda nt; (Amer) Limonade f. **~ water** n Sodawasser nt

sodden /'sɒdn/ a durchnässt

sodium /'səʊdɪəm/ n Natrium nt

sofa /'səʊfə/ n Sofa nt. ~ **bed** n Schlafcouch f

soft /sɒft/ a (-er, -est), -ly adv weich; (quiet) leise; (gentle) sanft; (fam: silly) dumm; **have a ~ spot for s.o.** jdn mögen. ~ **drink** n alkoholfreies Getränk nt

soften /'sɒfn/ vt weich machen; (fig) mildern □ vi weich werden

soft: ~ **toy** n Stofftier nt. ~**ware** n Software f

soggy /'sɒgɪ/ a (-ier, -iest) aufgeweicht

soil[1] /sɔɪl/ n Erde f, Boden m

soil[2] vt verschmutzen

solace /'sɒləs/ n Trost m

solar /'səʊlə(r)/ a Sonnen-

sold /səʊld/ see **sell**

solder /'səʊldə(r)/ n Lötmetall nt □ vt löten

soldier /'səʊldʒə(r)/ n Soldat m □ vi ~ **on** [unbeirrbar] weitermachen

sole[1] /səʊl/ n Sohle f

sole[2] n (fish) Seezunge f

sole[3] a einzig. ~**ly** adv einzig und allein

solemn /'sɒləm/ a, -ly adv feierlich; (serious) ernst. ~**ity** /sə'lemnətɪ/ n Feierlichkeit f; Ernst m

solicit /sə'lɪsɪt/ vt bitten um □ vi (prostitute:) sich an Männer heranmachen

solicitor /sə'lɪsɪtə(r)/ n Rechtsanwalt m/-anwältin f

solicitous /sə'lɪsɪtəs/ a besorgt

solid /'sɒlɪd/ a fest; (sturdy) stabil; (not hollow, of same substance) massiv; (unanimous) einstimmig; (complete) ganz □ n (Geom) Körper m; ~s pl (food) feste Nahrung f

solidarity /sɒlɪ'dærətɪ/ n Solidarität f

solidify /sə'lɪdɪfaɪ/ vi (pt/pp -ied) fest werden

soliloquy /sə'lɪləkwɪ/ n Selbstgespräch nt

solitary /'sɒlɪtərɪ/ a einsam; (sole) einzig. ~ **con'finement** n Einzelhaft f

solitude /'sɒlɪtjuːd/ n Einsamkeit f

solo /'səʊləʊ/ n Solo nt □ a Solo-; (flight) Allein- □ adv solo. ~**ist** n Solist(in) m(f)

solstice /'sɒlstɪs/ n Sonnenwende f

soluble /'sɒljʊbl/ a löslich; (solvable) lösbar

solution /sə'luːʃn/ n Lösung f

solvable /'sɒlvəbl/ a lösbar

solve /sɒlv/ vt lösen

solvent /'sɒlvənt/ a zahlungsfähig; (Chem) lösend □ n Lösungsmittel nt

sombre /'sɒmbə(r)/ a dunkel; (mood) düster

some /sʌm/ a & pron etwas; (a little) ein bisschen; (with pl noun) einige; (a few) ein paar; (certain) manche(r,s); (one or the other) [irgend]ein; ~ **day** eines Tages; I **want** ~ ich möchte etwas; (pl) welche; **will you have** ~ **wine?** möchten Sie Wein? I **need** ~ **money/books** ich brauche Geld/Bücher; **do** ~ **shopping** einkaufen

some: ~**body** /-bədɪ/ pron & n jemand; (emphatic) irgendjemand. ~**how** adv irgendwie. ~**one** pron & n = **somebody**

somersault /'sʌməsɔːlt/ n Purzelbaum m (fam); (Sport) Salto m; **turn a** ~ einen Purzelbaum schlagen/einen Salto springen

'something pron & adv etwas; (emphatic) irgendetwas; ~ **different** etwas anderes; ~ **like** so etwas wie; **see** ~ **of s.o.** jdn mal sehen

some: ~**time** adv irgendwann □ a ehemalig. ~**times** adv manchmal. ~**what** adv ziemlich. ~**where** adv irgendwo; (go) irgendwohin

son /sʌn/ n Sohn m

sonata /sə'nɑːtə/ n Sonate f

song /sɒŋ/ n Lied nt. **~bird** n Singvogel m

sonic /'sɒnɪk/ a Schall-. **~ 'boom** n Überschallknall m

'son-in-law n (pl **~s-in-law**) Schwiegersohn m

soon /suːn/ adv (-er, -est) bald; (quickly) schnell; **too ~** zu früh; **as ~ as** sobald; **as ~ as possible** so bald wie möglich; **~er or later** früher oder später; **no ~er had I arrived than ...** kaum war ich angekommen, da ...; **I would ~er stay** ich würde lieber bleiben

soot /sʊt/ n Ruß m

soothe /suːð/ vt beruhigen; lindern (pain). **~ing** a, **-ly** adv beruhigend; lindernd

sooty /'sʊtɪ/ a rußig

sop /sɒp/ n Beschwichtigungsmittel nt

sophisticated /sə'fɪstɪkeɪtɪd/ a weltgewandt; (complex) hoch entwickelt

soporific /sɒpə'rɪfɪk/ a einschläfernd

sopping /'sɒpɪŋ/ a & adv **~ [wet]** durchnässt

soppy /'sɒpɪ/ a (-ier, -iest) (fam) rührselig

soprano /sə'prɑːnəʊ/ n Sopran m; (woman) Sopranistin f

sordid /'sɔːdɪd/ a schmutzig

sore /sɔː(r)/ a (-r, -st) wund; (painful) schmerzhaft; **have a ~ throat** Halsschmerzen haben □ n wunde Stelle f. **~ly** adv sehr

sorrow /'sɒrəʊ/ n Kummer m, Leid nt. **~ful** a traurig

sorry /'sɒrɪ/ a (-ier, -iest) (sad) traurig; (wretched) erbärmlich; **I am ~** es tut mir Leid; **she is** or **feels ~ for him** er tut ihr Leid; **I am ~ to say** leider; **~!** Entschuldigung!

sort /sɔːt/ n Art f; (brand) Sorte f; **he's a good ~** (fam) er ist in

Ordnung; **be out of ~s** (fam) nicht auf der Höhe sein □ vt sortieren. **~ out** vt sortieren; (fig) klären

sought /sɔːt/ see **seek**

soul /səʊl/ n Seele f. **~ful** a gefühlvoll

sound¹ /saʊnd/ a (-er, -est) gesund; (sensible) vernünftig; (secure) solide; (thorough) gehörig □ adv **be ~ asleep** fest schlafen

sound² vt (Naut) loten. **~ out** vt (fig) aushorchen

sound³ n (strait) Meerenge f

sound⁴ n Laut m; (noise) Geräusch nt; (Phys) Schall m; (Radio, TV) Ton m; (of bells, music) Klang m; **I don't like the ~ of it** (fam) das hört sich nicht gut an □ vi [er]tönen; (seem) sich anhören □ vt (pronounce) aussprechen; schlagen (alarm); (Med) abhorchen (chest). **~ barrier** n Schallmauer f. **~less** a, **-ly** adv lautlos

soundly /'saʊndlɪ/ adv solide; (sleep) fest; (defeat) vernichtend

'soundproof a schalldicht

soup /suːp/ n Suppe f. **~ed-up** a (fam) (engine) frisiert

soup: ~plate n Suppenteller m. **~spoon** n Suppenlöffel m

sour /'saʊə(r)/ a (-er, -est) sauer; (bad-tempered) griesgrämig, verdrießlich

source /sɔːs/ n Quelle f

south /saʊθ/ n Süden m; **to the ~ of** südlich von □ a Süd-, süd- □ adv nach Süden

south: S~ 'Africa n Südafrika nt. **S~ A'merica** n Südamerika nt. **~'east** n Südosten m

southerly /'sʌðəlɪ/ a südlich

southern /'sʌðən/ a südlich

South 'Pole n Südpol m

'southward[s] /-wəd[z]/ adv nach Süden

souvenir /suːvə'nɪə(r)/ n Andenken nt, Souvenir nt

sovereign /'sɒvrɪn/ *a* souverän □ *n* Souverän *m*. **~ty** *n* Souveränität *f*

Soviet /'səʊvɪət/ *a* sowjetisch; **~ Union** Sowjetunion *f*

sow¹ /saʊ/ *n* Sau *f*

sow² /səʊ/ *vt* (*pt* sowed, *pp* sown *or* sowed) säen

soya /'sɔɪə/ *n* **~ bean** Sojabohne *f*

spa /spɑ:/ *n* Heilbad *nt*

space /speɪs/ *n* Raum *m*; (*gap*) Platz *m*; (*Astr*) Weltraum *m*; **leave/clear a ~** Platz lassen; **schaffen** □ *vt* **~ [out]** [in Abständen] verteilen

space: ~craft *n* Raumfahrzeug *nt*. **~ship** *n* Raumschiff *nt*

spacious /'speɪʃəs/ *a* geräumig

spade /speɪd/ *n* Spaten *m*; (*for child*) Schaufel *f*; **~s** *pl* (*Cards*) Pik *nt*; **call a ~ a ~** das Kind beim rechten Namen nennen. **~work** *n* Vorarbeit *f*

Spain /speɪn/ *n* Spanien *nt*

span¹ /spæn/ *n* Spanne *f*; (*of arch*) Spannweite *f* □ *vt* (*pt/pp* spanned) überspannen; umspannen (*time*)

span² *see* **spick**

Spaniard /'spænjəd/ *n* Spanier(in) *m(f)*. **~ish** *a* spanisch □ *n* (*Lang*) Spanisch *nt*; **the ~ish** *pl* die Spanier

spank /spæŋk/ *vt* verhauen

spanner /'spænə(r)/ *n* Schraubenschlüssel *m*

spar /spɑ:(r)/ *vi* (*pt/pp* sparred) (*Sport*) sparren; (*argue*) sich zanken

spare /speə(r)/ *a* (*surplus*) übrig; (*additional*) zusätzlich; (*seat, time*) frei; (*room*) Gäste-; (*bed, cup*) Extra- □ *n* (*part*) Ersatzteil *nt* □ *vt* ersparen; (*not hurt*) verschonen; (*do without*) entbehren; (*afford to give*) erübrigen; **to ~** (*surplus*) übrig. **~ 'wheel** *n* Reserverad *nt*

sparing /'speərɪŋ/ *a*, **-ly** *adv* sparsam

spark /spɑ:k/ *n* Funke *m* □ *vt* **~ off** zünden; (*fig*) auslösen. **~ing-plug** *n* (*Auto*) Zündkerze *f*

sparkle /'spɑ:kl/ *n* Funkeln *nt* □ *vi* funkeln. **~ing** *a* funkelnd (*wine*) Schaum-

sparrow /'spærəʊ/ *n* Spatz *m*

sparse /spɑ:s/ *a* spärlich. **~ly** *adv* spärlich; (*populated*) dünn

Spartan /'spɑ:tn/ *a* spartanisch

spasm /'spæzm/ *n* Anfall *m*; (*cramp*) Krampf *m*. **~odic** /-'mɒdɪk/ *a*, **-ally** *adv* sporadisch; (*Med*) krampfartig

spastic /'spæstɪk/ *a* spastisch (gelähmt) □ *n* Spastiker(in) *m(f)*

spat /spæt/ *see* **spit**²

spate /speɪt/ *n* Flut *f*; (*series*) Serie *f*; **be in full ~** Hochwasser führen

spatial /'speɪʃl/ *a* räumlich

spatter /'spætə(r)/ *vt* spritzen; **~ with** bespritzen mit

spatula /'spætjʊlə/ *n* Spachtel *m*; (*Med*) Spatel *m*

spawn /spɔ:n/ *n* Laich *m* □ *vi* laichen □ *vt* (*fig*) hervorbringen

spay /speɪ/ *vt* sterilisieren

speak /spi:k/ *v* (*pt* spoke, *pp* spoken) □ *vi* sprechen (**to mit**) **~ing!** (*Teleph*) am Apparat! □ *vt* sprechen; sagen (*truth*). **~ up** *vi* lauter sprechen; **~ up for one self** seine Meinung äußern

speaker /'spi:kə(r)/ *n* Sprecher(in) *m(f)*; (*in public*) Redner(in) *m(f)*; (*loudspeaker*) Lautsprecher *m*

spear /spɪə(r)/ *n* Speer *m* □ *vt* aufspießen. **~head** *vt* (*fig*) anführen

spec /spek/ *n* **on ~** (*fam*) auf gut Glück

special /'speʃl/ *a* besondere(r,s); speziell. **~ist** *n* Spezialist *m*; (*Med*) Facharzt *m*/-ärztin *f*. **~ity** /-ʃɪ'ælətɪ/ *n* Spezialität *f*

specialize /'speʃəlaɪz/ *vi* sich spezialisieren (**in** auf + *acc*). **~d** *adv* speziell; (*particularly*) besonders

species /'spiːʃiːz/ n Art f

specific /spə'sɪfɪk/ a bestimmt; (precise) genau; (Phys) spezifisch. **~ally** adv ausdrücklich

specification /spesɪfɪ'keɪʃn/ n & **~s** pl genaue Angaben pl

specify /'spesɪfaɪ/ vt (pt/pp -ied) [genau] angeben

specimen /'spesɪmən/ n Exemplar nt; (sample) Probe f; (of urine) Urinprobe f

speck /spek/ n Fleck m; (particle) Teilchen nt

speckled /'spekld/ a gesprenkelt

specs /speks/ npl (fam) Brille f

spectacle /'spektəkl/ n (show) Schauspiel nt; (sight) Anblick m. **~s** npl Brille f

spectacular /spek'tækjʊlə(r)/ a spektakulär

spectator /spek'teɪtə(r)/ n Zuschauer(in) m(f)

spectre /'spektə(r)/ n Gespenst nt; (fig) Schreckgespenst nt

spectrum /'spektrəm/ n (pl -tra) Spektrum nt

speculat|e /'spekjʊleɪt/ vi spekulieren. **~ion** /-'leɪʃn/ n Spekulation f. **~or** n Spekulant m

sped /sped/ see **speed**

speech /spiːtʃ/ n Sprache f; (address) Rede f. **~less** a sprachlos

speed /spiːd/ n Geschwindigkeit f; (rapidity) Schnelligkeit f; (gear) Gang m; at **~** mit hoher Geschwindigkeit □ vi (pt/pp sped) schnell fahren □ (pt/pp speeded) (go too fast) zu schnell fahren. **~ up** (pt/pp speeded up) □ vt beschleunigen □ vi schneller werden; (vehicle:) schneller fahren

speed: ~boat n Rennboot nt. **~ing** n Geschwindigkeitsüberschreitung f. **~ limit** n Geschwindigkeitsbeschränkung f

speedometer /spiː'dɒmɪtə(r)/ n Tachometer m

speedy /'spiːdɪ/ a (-ier, -iest), -ily adv schnell

spell¹ /spel/ n Weile f; (of weather) Periode f

spell² v (pt/pp spelled or spelt) □ vt schreiben; (aloud) buchstabieren; (fig: mean) bedeuten □ vi richtig schreiben; (aloud) buchstabieren. **~ out** vt buchstabieren; (fig) genau erklären

spell³ n Zauber m; (words) Zauberspruch m. **~bound** a wie verzaubert

spelling /'spelɪŋ/ n Schreibweise f; (orthography) Rechtschreibung f

spelt /spelt/ see **spell²**

spend /spend/ vt/i (pt/pp spent) ausgeben; verbringen (time)

spent /spent/ see **spend**

sperm /spɜːm/ n Samen m

spew /spjuː/ vt/i speien

spher|e /sfɪə(r)/ n Kugel f; (fig) Sphäre f. **~ical** /'sferɪkl/ a kugelförmig

spice /spaɪs/ n Gewürz nt; (fig) Würze f

spick /spɪk/ a **~ and span** blitzsauber

spicy /'spaɪsɪ/ a würzig, pikant

spider /'spaɪdə(r)/ n Spinne f

spik|e /spaɪk/ n Spitze f; (Bot, Zool) Stachel m; (on shoe) Spike m. **~y** a stachelig

spill /spɪl/ v (pt/pp spilt or spilled) □ vt verschütten; vergießen (blood) □ vi überlaufen

spin /spɪn/ v (pt/pp spun, pres p spinning) □ vt drehen; spinnen (wool); schleudern (washing) □ vi sich drehen. **~ out** vt in die Länge ziehen

spinach /'spɪnɪdʒ/ n Spinat m

spinal /'spaɪnl/ a Rückgrat-. **~ cord** n Rückenmark nt

spindl|e /'spɪndl/ n Spindel f. **~y** a spindeldürr

spin-'drier n Wäscheschleuder f

spine /spaɪn/ n Rückgrat nt; (of book) [Buch]rücken m; (Bot, Zool) Stachel m. **~less** a (fig) rückgratlos

spinning /'spɪnɪŋ/ *n* Spinnen *nt*. **~-wheel** *n* Spinnrad *nt*

'spin-off *n* Nebenprodukt *nt*

spinster /'spɪnstə(r)/ *n* ledige Frau *f*

spiral /'spaɪərəl/ *a* spiralig □ *n* Spirale *f* □ *vi* (*pt/pp* **spiralled**) sich hochwinden; (*smoke:*) in einer Spirale aufsteigen. **~ 'staircase** *n* Wendeltreppe *f*

spire /'spaɪə(r)/ *n* Turmspitze *f*

spirit /'spɪrɪt/ *n* Geist *m*; (*courage*) Mut *m*; **~s** *pl* (*alcohol*) Spirituosen *pl*; **in high ~s** in gehobener Stimmung; **in low ~s** niedergedrückt. **~ away** *vt* verschwinden lassen

spirited /'spɪrɪtɪd/ *a* lebhaft; (*courageous*) beherzt

spirit: **~-level** *n* Wasserwaage *f*. **~ stove** *n* Spirituskocher *m*

spiritual /'spɪrɪtjʊəl/ *a* geistig; (*Relig*) geistlich. **~ism** /-ɪzm/ *n* Spiritismus *m*. **~ist** /-ɪst/ *a* spiritistisch □ *n* Spiritist *m*

spit¹ /spɪt/ *n* (*for roasting*) [Brat]spieß *m*

spit² *n* Spucke *f* □ *vt/i* (*pt/pp* **spat**, *pres p* **spitting**) spucken; (*cat:*) fauchen; (*fat:*) spritzen; **it's ~ting with rain** es tröpfelt; **be the ~ting image of s.o.** jdm wie aus dem Gesicht geschnitten sein

spite /spaɪt/ *n* Bosheit *f*; **in ~ of** trotz (+ *gen*) □ *vt* ärgern. **~ful** *a*, **-ly** *adv* gehässig

spittle /'spɪtl/ *n* Spucke *f*

splash /splæʃ/ *n* Platschen *nt*; (*fam: drop*) Schuss *m*; **~ of colour** Farbfleck *m* □ *vt* spritzen; **~ s.o. with sth** jdn mit etw bespritzen □ *vi* spritzen □ *vi* planschen

spleen /spli:n/ *n* Milz *f*

splendid /'splendɪd/ *a* herrlich, großartig

splendour /'splendə(r)/ *n* Pracht *f*

splint /splɪnt/ *n* (*Med*) Schiene *f*

splinter /'splɪntə(r)/ *n* Splitter *m* □ *vi* zersplittern

split /splɪt/ *n* Spaltung *f*; (*Pol*) Bruch *m*; (*tear*) Riss *m* □ *v* (*pt/pp* **split**, *pres p* **splitting**) □ *vt* spalten; (*share*) teilen; (*tear*) zerreißen; **~ one's sides** sich kaputtlachen □ *vi* sich spalten; (*tear*) zerreißen. **~ on s.o.** jdn verpfeifen. **~ up** *vt* aufteilen □ *vi* (*couple:*) sich trennen

splutter /'splʌtə(r)/ *vi* prusten

spoil /spɔɪl/ *n* **~s** *pl* Beute *f* □ *v* (*pt/pp* **spoilt** *or* **spoiled**) □ *vt* verderben; verwöhnen (*person*) □ *vi* verderben. **~sport** *n* Spielverderber *m*

spoke¹ /spəʊk/ *n* Speiche *f*

spoke², spoken /'spəʊkn/ *see* **speak**

spokesman *n* Sprecher *m*

sponge /spʌndʒ/ *n* Schwamm *m* □ *vt* abwaschen □ *vi* **~ on s.o.** schmarotzen bei jdm. **~-bag** *n* Waschbeutel *m*. **~-cake** *n* Biskuitkuchen *m*

sponger /'spʌndʒə(r)/ *n* Schmarotzer *m*. **~y** *a* schwammig

sponsor /'spɒnsə(r)/ *n* Sponsor *m*; (*god-parent*) Pate *m*/Patin *f*; (*for membership*) Bürge *m* □ *vt* sponsern; bürgen für

spontaneous /spɒn'teɪnɪəs/ *a*, **-ly** *adv* spontan

spoof /spu:f/ *n* (*fam*) Parodie *f*

spooky /'spu:kɪ/ *a* (**-ier, -iest**) (*fam*) gespenstisch

spool /spu:l/ *n* Spule *f*

spoon /spu:n/ *n* Löffel *m* □ *vt* löffeln. **~-feed** *vt* (*pt/pp* **-fed**) (*fig*) alles vorkauen (+ *dat*). **~ful** *n* Löffel *m*

sporadic /spə'rædɪk/ *a*, **-ally** *adv* sporadisch

sport /spɔːt/ *n* Sport *m*; (*amusement*) Spaß *m* □ *vt* [stolz] tragen. **~ing** *a* sportlich; **a ~ing chance** eine faire Chance

sports: **~-car** *n* Sportwagen *m*. **~-coat** *n*, **~-jacket** *n* Sakko *m*. **~-man** *n* Sportler *m*. **~-woman** *n* Sportlerin *f*

sporty /'spɔːtɪ/ *a* (**-ier, -iest**) sportlich

spot /spɒt/ n Fleck m; (place) Stelle f; (dot) Punkt m; (drop) Tropfen m; (pimple) Pickel m; ~s pl (rash) Ausschlag m; **a ~ of** (fam) ein bisschen; **on the ~** auf der Stelle; **be in a tight ~** (fam) in der Klemme sitzen □ vt (pt/pp **spotted**) entdecken

spot: ~ **'check** n Stichprobe f. ~**less** a makellos; (fam: very clean) blitzsauber. ~**light** n Scheinwerfer m; (fig) Rampenlicht nt

spotted /'spɒtɪd/ a gepunktet

spotty /'spɒtɪ/ a (-ier, -iest) fleckig; (pimply) pickelig

spouse /spaʊz/ n Gatte m/Gattin f

spout /spaʊt/ n Schnabel m, Tülle f □ vi schießen (**from** aus)

sprain /spreɪn/ n Verstauchung f □ vt verstauchen

sprang /spræŋ/ see **spring²**

sprat /spræt/ n Sprotte f

sprawl /sprɔːl/ vi sich ausstrecken; (fall) der Länge nach hinfallen

spray¹ /spreɪ/ n (of flowers) Strauß m

spray² n (from sea) Sprühnebel m; (from sea) Gischt m; (device) Spritze f; (container) Sprühdose f; (preparation) Spray nt □ vt spritzen; (with aerosol) sprühen

spread /spred/ n Verbreitung f; (paste) Aufstrich m; (fam: feast) Festessen nt □ v (pt/pp **spread**) □ vt ausbreiten; streichen (butter, jam); bestreichen (bread, surface); streuen (sand, manure); verbreiten (news, disease); verteilen (payments) □ vi sich ausbreiten. ~ **out** vt ausbreiten; (space out) verteilen □ vi sich verteilen

spree /spriː/ n (fam) **go on a shopping** ~ groß einkaufen gehen

sprig /sprɪg/ n Zweig m

sprightly /'spraɪtlɪ/ a (-ier, -iest) rüstig

spring¹ /sprɪŋ/ n Frühling m □ attrib Frühlings-

spring² n (jump) Sprung m; (water) Quelle f; (device) Feder f; (elasticity) Elastizität f □ v (pt sprang, pp sprung) □ vi springen; (arise) entspringen (**from** dat) □ vt ~ **sth on s.o.** jdn mit etw überfallen

spring: ~**board** n Sprungbrett nt. ~'**cleaning** n Frühjahrsputz m. ~**time** n Frühling m

sprinkle /'sprɪŋkl/ vt sprengen; (scatter) streuen; bestreuen (surface). ~**er** n Sprinkler m; (Hort) Sprenger m. ~**ing** n dünne Schicht f

sprint /sprɪnt/ n Sprint m □ vi rennen; (Sport) sprinten. ~**er** n Kurzstreckenläufer(in) m(f)

sprout /spraʊt/ n Trieb m; [Brussels] ~**s** pl Rosenkohl m □ vi sprießen

spruce /spruːs/ a gepflegt □ n Fichte f

sprung /sprʌŋ/ see **spring²** □ a gefedert

spry /spraɪ/ a (-er, -est) rüstig

spud /spʌd/ n (fam) Kartoffel f

spun /spʌn/ see **spin**

spur /spɜː(r)/ n Sporn m; (stimulus) Ansporn m; (road) Nebenstraße f; **on the ~ of the moment** ganz spontan □ vt (pt/pp **spurred**) ~ [**on**] (fig) anspornen

spurious /'spjʊərɪəs/ a, ~**ly** adv falsch

spurn /spɜːn/ vt verschmähen

spurt /spɜːt/ n Strahl m; (Sport) Spurt m; **put on a ~** spurten □ vi spritzen

spy /spaɪ/ n Spion(in) m(f) □ vi spionieren; ~ **on s.o.** jdm nachspionieren □ vt (fam: see) sehen. ~ **out** vt auskundschaften

spying /'spaɪɪŋ/ n Spionage f

squabble /'skwɒbl/ n Zank m □ vi sich zanken

squad /skwɒd/ n Gruppe f; (Sport) Mannschaft f

squadron /'skwɒdrən/ n (Mil) Geschwader nt

squalid /'skwɒlɪd/ a, **-ly** adv schmutzig

squall /skwɔ:l/ n Bö f □ vi brüllen

squalor /'skwɒlə(r)/ n Schmutz m

squander /'skwɒndə(r)/ vt vergeuden

square /skweə(r)/ a quadratisch; ⟨metre, mile⟩ Quadrat-; ⟨meal⟩ anständig; **all ~** (fam) quitt □ n Quadrat nt; ⟨area⟩ Platz m; ⟨on chessboard⟩ Feld nt □ vt ⟨settle⟩ klären; (Math) quadrieren □ vi ⟨agree⟩ übereinstimmen

squash /skwɒʃ/ n Gedränge nt; ⟨drink⟩ Fruchtsaftgetränk nt; (Sport) Squash nt □ vt zerquetschen; ⟨suppress⟩ niederschlagen. **~y** a weich

squat /skwɒt/ a gedrungen □ n (fam) besetztes Haus nt □ vi (pt/pp **squatted**) hocken; **~ in a house** ein Haus besetzen. **~ter** n Hausbesetzer m

squawk /skwɔ:k/ vi krächzen

squeak /skwi:k/ n Quieken nt; ⟨of hinge, brakes⟩ Quietschen nt □ vi quieken; quietschen

squeal /skwi:l/ n Schrei m; ⟨screech⟩ Kreischen nt □ vi schreien; kreischen

squeamish /'skwi:mɪʃ/ a empfindlich

squeeze /skwi:z/ n Druck m; ⟨crush⟩ Gedränge nt □ vt drücken; ⟨to get juice⟩ ausdrücken; ⟨force⟩ zwängen; ⟨extort⟩ herauspressen (**from** aus) □ vi **~ in/out** sich hinein-/hinauszwängen

squelch /skweltʃ/ vi quatschen

squid /skwɪd/ n Tintenfisch m

squiggle /'skwɪgl/ n Schnörkel m

squint /skwɪnt/ n Schielen nt □ vi schielen

squire /'skwaɪə(r)/ n Gutsherr m

squirm /skwɜ:m/ vi sich winden

squirrel /'skwɪrl/ n Eichhörnchen nt

squirt /skwɜ:t/ n Spritzer m □ vt/i spritzen

St abbr ⟨Saint⟩ St.; ⟨Street⟩ Str.

stab /stæb/ n Stich m; ⟨fam: attempt⟩ Versuch m □ vt (pt/pp **stabbed**) stechen; ⟨to death⟩ erstechen

stability /stə'bɪlətɪ/ n Stabilität f

stabilize /'steɪbɪlaɪz/ vt stabilisieren □ vi sich stabilisieren

stable¹ /'steɪbl/ a (**-r, -st**) stabil

stable² n Stall m; ⟨establishment⟩ Reitstall m

stack /stæk/ n Stapel m; ⟨of chimney⟩ Schornstein m; ⟨fam: large quantity⟩ Haufen m □ vt stapeln

stadium /'steɪdɪəm/ n Stadion nt

staff /stɑ:f/ n ⟨stick & Mil⟩ Stab m □(& pl) ⟨employees⟩ Personal nt; (Sch) Lehrkräfte pl □ vt mit Personal besetzen. **~room** n (Sch) Lehrerzimmer nt

stag /stæg/ n Hirsch m

stage /steɪdʒ/ n Bühne f; ⟨in journey⟩ Etappe f; ⟨in process⟩ Stadium nt; **by** or **in ~s** in Etappen □ vt aufführen; ⟨arrange⟩ veranstalten

stage:- ~door n Bühneneingang m. **~ fright** n Lampenfieber nt

stagger /'stægə(r)/ vi taumeln □ vt staffeln ⟨holidays⟩; versetzt anordnen ⟨seats⟩; **I was ~ed** es hat mir die Sprache verschlagen. **~ing** a unglaublich

stagnant /'stægnənt/ a stehend; (fig) stagnierend

stagnat|e /stæg'neɪt/ vi (fig) stagnieren. **~ion** /-'neɪʃn/ n Stagnation f

staid /steɪd/ a gesetzt

stain /steɪn/ n Fleck m; ⟨for wood⟩ Beize f □ vt färben; beizen ⟨wood⟩; (fig) beflecken; **~ed glass** farbiges Glas nt. **~less** a fleckenlos; ⟨steel⟩ rostfrei. **~ remover** n Fleckentferner m

stair /steə(r)/ n Stufe f; **~s** pl Treppe f. **~case** n Treppe f

stake /steɪk/ n Pfahl m; ⟨wager⟩ Einsatz m; ⟨Comm⟩ Anteil m; **be at ~** auf dem Spiel stehen □ vt [an einem Pfahl] anbinden; ⟨wager⟩

stale

setzen; **~ a claim to sth** Anspruch auf etw *(acc)* erheben

stale /steɪl/ *a* (-r, -st) alt; *(air)* verbraucht. **~mate** *n* Patt *nt*

stalk¹ /stɔːk/ *n* Stiel *m*, Stängel *m*

stalk² *vt* pirschen auf (+ *acc*) □ *vi* stolzieren

stall /stɔːl/ *n* Stand *m*; **~s** *pl* *(Theat)* Parkett *nt* □ *vi* *(engine:)* stehen bleiben; *(fig)* ausweichen □ *vt* abwürgen *(engine)*

stallion /ˈstæljən/ *n* Hengst *m*

stalwart /ˈstɔːlwət/ *a* treu □ *n* treuer Anhänger *m*

stamina /ˈstæmɪnə/ *n* Ausdauer *f*

stammer /ˈstæmə(r)/ *n* Stottern *nt* □ *vt/i* stottern

stamp /stæmp/ *n* Stempel *m*; *(postage ~)* [Brief]marke *f* □ *vt* stempeln; *(impress)* prägen; *(put postage on)* frankieren; **~ one's feet** mit den Füßen stampfen □ *vi* stampfen. **~ out** *vt* [aus]stanzen; *(fig)* ausmerzen

stampede /stæmˈpiːd/ *n* wilde Flucht *f*; *(fam)* Ansturm *m* □ *vi* in Panik fliehen

stance /stɑːns/ *n* Haltung *f*

stand /stænd/ *n* Stand *m*; *(rack)* Ständer *m*; *(pedestal)* Sockel *m*; *(Sport)* Tribüne *f*; *(fig)* Einstellung *f* □ *v* *(pt/pp* **stood)** □ *vi* stehen; *(rise)* aufstehen; *(be candidate)* kandidieren; *(stay valid)* gültig bleiben; **~ still** stillstehen. **~ firm** *(fig)* festbleiben; **~ together** zusammenhalten; **~ to lose / gain** gewinnen / verlieren können; **~ to reason** logisch sein; **~ in for** vertreten; *(mean)* bedeuten; **I won't ~ for that** das lasse ich mir nicht bieten □ *vt* stellen; *(withstand)* standhalten (+ *dat*); *(endure)* ertragen; vertragen *(climate)*; *(put up with)* aushalten; haben *(chance)*; **~ one's ground** nicht nachgeben; **~ the test of time** sich bewähren; **~ s.o. a beer** jdm ein Bier spendieren; **I can't ~**

her *(fam)* ich kann sie nicht ausstehen. **~ by** *vi* daneben stehen; *(be ready)* sich bereithalten □ *vt* **by s.o.** *(fig)* zu jdm stehen. **~ down** *vi* *(retire)* zurücktreten. **~ out** *vi* hervorstehen; *(fig)* herausragen. **~ up** *vi* aufstehen; **~ up for** eintreten für; **~ up to** sich wehren gegen

standard /ˈstændəd/ *a* Normal-; **be ~ practice** allgemein üblich sein □ *n* Maßstab *m*; *(Techn)* Norm *f*; *(level)* Niveau *nt*; *(flag)* Standarte *f*; **~s** *pl* *(morals)* Prinzipien *pl*; **~ of living** Lebensstandard *m*. **~ize** *vt* standardisieren; *(Techn)* normen

'standard lamp *n* Stehlampe *f*

'stand-in *n* Ersatz *m*

standing /ˈstændɪŋ/ *a* *(erect)* stehend; *(permanent)* ständig □ *n* Rang *m*; *(duration)* Dauer *f*. **~ 'order** *n* Dauerauftrag *m*. **~room** *n* Stehplätze *pl*

stand: **~offish** /stændˈɒfɪʃ/ *a* distanziert. **~point** *n* Standpunkt *m*. **~still** *n* Stillstand *m*; **come to a ~still** zum Stillstand kommen

stank /stæŋk/ *see* **stink**

staple¹ /ˈsteɪpl/ *a* Grund- □ *n* *(product)* Haupterzeugnis *nt*

staple² *n* Heftklammer *f* □ *vt* heften. **~r** *n* Heftmaschine *f*

star /stɑː(r)/ *n* Stern *m*; *(asterisk)* Sternchen *nt*; *(Theat, Sport)* Star *m* □ *vi* *(pt/pp* **starred)** die Hauptrolle spielen

starboard /ˈstɑːbəd/ *n* Steuerbord *nt*

starch /stɑːtʃ/ *n* Stärke *f* □ *vt* stärken. **~y** *a* stärkehaltig; *(fig)* steif

stare /steə(r)/ *n* Starren *nt* □ *vi* starren; **~ at** anstarren

'starfish *n* Seestern *m*

stark /stɑːk/ *a* (-r, -est) scharf; *(contrast)* krass □ *adv* **~ naked** splitternackt

starling /ˈstɑːlɪŋ/ *n* Star *m*

starlit *a* sternhell

starry /ˈstɑːrɪ/ *a* sternklar

start /stɑːt/ n Anfang m, Beginn m; (departure) Aufbruch m; (Sport) Start m; from the ~ von Anfang an; for a ~ erstens □ vi anfangen, beginnen; (set out) aufbrechen; (engine:) anspringen; (Auto, Sport) starten; (jump) aufschrecken; to ~ with zuerst □ vt anfangen, beginnen; (cause) verursachen; (found) gründen; starten (car, race); in Umlauf setzen (rumour). ~er n (Culin) Vorspeise f; (Auto, Sport) Starter m. ~ing-point n Ausgangspunkt m

startle /'stɑːtl/ vt erschrecken

starvation /stɑː'veɪʃn/ n Verhungern nt

starve /stɑːv/ vi hungern; (to death) verhungern □ vt verhungern lassen

stash /stæʃ/ vt (fam) ~ [away] beiseite schaffen

state /steɪt/ n Zustand m; (grand style) Prunk m; (Pol) Staat m; ~ of play Spielstand m; be in a ~ (person:) aufgeregt sein; lie in ~ feierlich aufgebahrt sein □ attrib Staats-, staatlich □ vt erklären; (specify) angeben. ~-aided a staatlich gefördert. ~less a staatenlos

stately /'steɪtlɪ/ a (-ier, -iest) stattlich. ~ 'home n Schloss nt

statement /'steɪtmənt/ n Erklärung f; (Jur) Aussage f; (Banking) Auszug m

statesman n Staatsmann m

static /'stætɪk/ a statisch; remain ~ unverändert bleiben

station /'steɪʃn/ n Bahnhof m; (police) Wache f; (radio) Sender m; (space, weather) Station f; (Mil) Posten m; (status) Rang m □ vt stationieren; (post) postieren. ~ary /-ərɪ/ a stehend; be ~ary stehen

stationer /'steɪʃənə(r)/ n ~'s [shop] Schreibwarengeschäft nt. ~y n Briefpapier nt; (writing-materials) Schreibwaren pl

'station-wagon n (Amer) Kombi[wagen] n

statistic /stə'tɪstɪk/ n statistische Tatsache f. ~al a, -ly adv statistisch. ~s n & pl Statistik f

statue /'stætjuː/ n Statue f

stature /'stætʃə(r)/ n Statur f; (fig) Format nt

status /'steɪtəs/ n Status m, Rang m. ~ symbol n Statussymbol nt

statut|e /'stætjuːt/ n Statut nt. ~ory a gesetzlich

staunch /stɔːntʃ/ a, -ly adv treu

stave /steɪv/ vt ~ off abwenden

stay /steɪ/ n Aufenthalt m □ vi bleiben; (reside) wohnen; ~ the night übernachten; ~ put dableiben □ vt ~ the course durchhalten. ~ away vi wegbleiben. ~ behind vi zurückbleiben. ~ in vi zu Hause bleiben; (Sch) nachsitzen. ~ up vi oben bleiben; (upright) stehen bleiben; (on wall) hängen bleiben; (person:) aufbleiben

stead /sted/ n in his ~ an seiner Stelle; stand s.o. in good ~ jdm zustatten kommen. ~fast a, -ly adv standhaft

steadily /'stedɪlɪ/ adv fest; (continually) stetig

steady /'stedɪ/ a (-ier, -iest) fest; (not wobbly) stabil; (hand) ruhig; (regular) regelmäßig; (dependable) zuverlässig

steak /steɪk/ n Steak nt

steal /stiːl/ vt/i (pt stole, pp stolen) stehlen (from dat). ~ in/out vi sich hinein-/hinausstehlen

stealth /stelθ/ n Heimlichkeit f; by ~ heimlich. ~y a heimlich

steam /stiːm/ n Dampf m; under one's own ~ (fam) aus eigener Kraft □ vt (Culin) dämpfen, dünsten □ vi dampfen. ~ up vi beschlagen

'steam-engine n Dampfmaschine f; (Rail) Dampflokomotive f

steamer /'stiːmə(r)/ n Dampfer m

steamroller n Dampfwalze f

steamy /'sti:mɪ/ a dampfig

steel /sti:l/ n Stahl m ○ vt ~ oneself allen Mut zusammennehmen

steep¹ /sti:p/ vt (soak) einweichen

steep² a, **-ly** adv steil; (fam: exorbitant) gesalzen

steeple /'sti:pl/ n Kirchturm m. ~chase n Hindernisrennen nt

steer /stɪə(r)/ vt/i steuern; ~ clear of s.o./sth jdm/ etw aus dem Weg gehen. ~ing n (Auto) Steuerung f. ~ing-wheel n Lenkrad nt

stem¹ /stem/ n Stiel m; (of word) Stamm m ○ vi (pt/pp stemmed) ~ from zurückzuführen sein auf (+ acc)

stem² vt (pt/pp stemmed) eindämmen; stillen (bleeding)

stench /stentʃ/ n Gestank m

stencil /'stensl/ n Schablone f; (for typing) Matrize f

step /step/ n Schritt m; (stair) Stufe f; ~s pl (ladder) Trittleiter f; **in** ~ im Schritt; ~ **by** ~ Schritt für Schritt; **take** ~s (fig) Schritte unternehmen ○ vi (pt/pp stepped) treten; ~ **in** (fig) eingreifen; ~ **into s.o.'s shoes** in jds Stelle treten; ~ **out of line** aus der Reihe tanzen. ~ **up** vi hinaufsteigen ○ vt (increase) erhöhen, steigern; verstärken (efforts)

step: ~**brother** n Stiefbruder m. ~**child** n Stiefkind nt. ~**daughter** n Stieftochter f. ~**father** n Stiefvater m. ~**ladder** n Trittleiter f. ~**mother** n Stiefmutter f

stepping-stone n Trittstein m; (fig) Sprungbrett nt

step: ~**sister** n Stiefschwester f. ~**son** n Stiefsohn m

stereo /'sterɪəʊ/ n Stereo nt; (equipment) Stereoanlage f; **in** ~ stereo. ~**phonic** /-'fɒnɪk/ a stereophon

stereotype /'sterɪətaɪp/ n stereotype Figur f. ~**d** a stereotyp

sterile /'steraɪl/ a steril. ~**ity** /stə'rɪlɪtɪ/ n Sterilität f

steriliza|tion /sterəlaɪ'zeɪʃn/ n Sterilisation f. ~**e** vt sterilisieren

sterling /'stɜːlɪŋ/ a Sterling-; (fig) gediegen ○ n Sterling m

stern¹ /stɜːn/ a (-er, -est), **-ly** adv streng

stern² n (of boat) Heck nt

stew /stju:/ n Eintopf m; **in a** ~ (fam) aufgeregt ○ vt/i schmoren; ~**ed fruit** Kompott nt

steward /'stju:əd/ n Ordner m; (on ship, aircraft) Steward m. ~**ess** n Stewardess f

stick¹ /stɪk/ n Stock m; (of chalk) Stück nt; (of rhubarb) Stange f; (Sport) Schläger m

stick² v (pt/pp stuck) ○ vt stecken; (stab) stechen; (glue) kleben; (fam: put) tun; (fam: endure) aushalten ○ vi stecken; (adhere) kleben, haften (**to** an + dat); (jam) klemmen; ~ **to sth** (fig) bei etw bleiben; ~ **at it** (fam) dranbleiben; ~ **at nothing** (fam) vor nichts zurückschrecken; ~ **up for** (fam) eintreten für; **be stuck** nicht weiterkönnen; (vehicle:) festsitzen, festgefahren sein; (drawer:) klemmen; **be stuck with sth** (fam) etw am Hals haben. ~ **out** vi abstehen; (project) vorstehen ○ vt (fam) hinausstrecken; herausstrecken (tongue)

sticker /'stɪkə(r)/ n Aufkleber m

sticking plaster n Heftpflaster nt

stickler /'stɪklə(r)/ n **be a** ~ **for** es sehr genau nehmen mit

sticky /'stɪkɪ/ a (-ier, -iest) klebrig; (adhesive) Klebe-

stiff /stɪf/ a (-er, -est), **-ly** adv steif; (brush) hart; (dough) fest; (difficult) schwierig; (penalty) schwer; **be bored** ~ (fam) sich zu Tode langweilen. ~**en** vt steif machen ○ vi steif werden. ~**ness** n Steifheit f

stifl|e /'staɪfl/ vt ersticken; (fig)
unterdrücken. **~ing** a be **~ing**
zum Ersticken sein

stigma /'stɪgmə/ n Stigma nt

stile /staɪl/ n Zauntritt m

stiletto /stɪ'letəʊ/ n Stilett nt; (heel) Bleistiftabsatz m

still¹ /stɪl/ n Destillierapparat m

still² a (of) (drink) ohne Kohlensäure; **keep ~** stillhalten; **stand ~** stillstehen □ n Stille f □ adv noch; (emphatic) immer noch; (nevertheless) trotzdem; **~ not** immer noch nicht

'stillborn a tot geboren

still 'life n Stilleben nt

stilted /'stɪltɪd/ a gestelzt, geschraubt

stilts /stɪlts/ npl Stelzen pl

stimulant /'stɪmjʊlənt/ n Anregungsmittel nt

stimulat|e /'stɪmjʊleɪt/ vt anregen. **~ion** /-'leɪʃn/ n Anregung f

stimulus /'stɪmjʊləs/ n (pl -li /-laɪ/) Reiz m

sting /stɪŋ/ n Stich m; (from nettle, jellyfish) Brennen nt; (organ) Stachel m □ v (pt/pp stung) □ vt stechen □ vi brennen; (insect:) stechen. **~ing nettle** n Brennnessel f

stingy /'stɪndʒi/ a (-ier, -iest) geizig, (fam) knauserig

stink /stɪŋk/ n Gestank m □ vi (pt stank, pp stunk) stinken (of nach)

stint /stɪnt/ n Pensum nt □ vi **~ on** sparen an (+ dat)

stipulat|e /'stɪpjʊleɪt/ vt vorschreiben. **~ion** /-'leɪʃn/ n Bedingung f

stir /stɜː(r)/ n (commotion) Aufregung f □ v (pt/pp stirred) vt rühren □ vi sich rühren

stirrup /'stɪrəp/ n Steigbügel m

stitch /stɪtʃ/ n Stich m; (Knitting) Masche f; (pain) Seitenstechen nt; **be in ~es** (fam) sich kaputtlachen □ vt nähen

stoat /stəʊt/ n Hermelin nt

stock /stɒk/ n Vorrat m (of an + dat); (in shop) [Waren]bestand m; (livestock) Vieh nt; (lineage) Abstammung f; (Finance) Wertpapiere pl; (Culin) Brühe f; (plant) Levkoje f; **in/out of ~** vorrätig/nicht vorrätig; **take ~** (fig) Bilanz ziehen □ a Standard- □ vt (shop:) führen; auffüllen (shelves). **~ up** vi sich eindecken (with mit)

stock: ~broker n Börsenmakler m. **~ cube** n Brühwürfel m. **S~ Exchange** n Börse f

stocking /'stɒkɪŋ/ n Strumpf m

stockist /'stɒkɪst/ n Händler m

stock: ~market n Börse f. **~pile** vt horten; anhäufen (weapons). **~'still** a bewegungslos. **~taking** n (Comm) Inventur f

stocky /'stɒki/ a (-ier, -iest) untersetzt

stodgy /'stɒdʒi/ a pappig [und schwer verdaulich]

stoical /'stəʊɪkl/ a, **-ly** adv stoisch

stoke /stəʊk/ vt heizen

stole¹ /stəʊl/ n Stola f

stole², **stolen** /'stəʊlən/ see **steal**

stolid /'stɒlɪd/ a, **-ly** adv stur

stomach /'stʌmək/ n Magen m □ vt vertragen. **~ache** n Magenschmerzen pl

stone /stəʊn/ n Stein m; (weight) 6,35kg □ a steinern; (wall, Age) Stein- □ vt mit Steinen bewerfen; entsteinen (fruit). **~-cold** a eiskalt. **~'deaf** n (fam) stocktaub

stony /'stəʊni/ a steinig

stood /stʊd/ see **stand**

stool /stuːl/ n Hocker m

stoop /stuːp/ n **walk with a ~** gebeugt gehen □ vi sich bücken; (fig) sich erniedrigen

stop /stɒp/ n Halt m; (break) Pause f; (for bus) Haltestelle f; (for train) Station f; (Gram) Punkt m; (on organ) Register nt; **come to a ~** stehen bleiben; **put a ~ to sth** etw unterbinden □ v

stop (*pt/pp* **stopped**) □ *vt* anhalten, stoppen; (*switch off*) abstellen; (*plug, block*) zustopfen; (*prevent*) verhindern; ~ **s.o. doing sth** jdn daran hindern, etw zu tun; ~ **doing sth** aufhören, etw zu tun; ~ **that!** hör auf damit! lass das sein! □ *vi* anhalten; (*cease*) aufhören; (*clock:*) stehen bleiben; (*fam: stay*) bleiben (**with bei**) □ *int* halt! stopp!

stop: ~**gap** *n* Notlösung *f.* ~**over** *n* Zwischenaufenthalt *m*; (*Aviat*) Zwischenlandung *f*

stoppage /ˈstɒpɪdʒ/ *n* Unterbrechung *f*; (*strike*) Streik *m*; (*deduction*) Abzug *m*

stopper /ˈstɒpə(r)/ *n* Stöpsel *m*

stop: ~**press** *n* letzte Meldungen *pl.* ~**watch** *n* Stoppuhr *f*

storage /ˈstɔːrɪdʒ/ *n* Aufbewahrung *f*; (*in warehouse*) Lagerung *f*; (*Computing*) Speicherung *f*

store /stɔː(r)/ *n* (*stock*) Vorrat *m*; (*shop*) Laden *m*; (*department* ~) Kaufhaus *nt*; (*depot*) Lager *nt*; **in** ~ auf Lager; **put in** ~ lagern; **set great** ~ **by** großen Wert legen auf (+ *acc*); **be in** ~ **for s.o.** (*fig*) jdm bevorstehen □ *vt* aufbewahren; (*in warehouse*) lagern; (*Computing*) speichern. ~**room** *n* Lagerraum *m*

storey /ˈstɔːrɪ/ *n* Stockwerk *nt*

stork /stɔːk/ *n* Storch *m*

storm /stɔːm/ *n* Sturm *m*; (*with thunder*) Gewitter *nt* □ *vt/i* stürmen. ~**y** *a* stürmisch

story /ˈstɔːrɪ/ *n* Geschichte *f*; (*in newspaper*) Artikel *m*; (*fam: lie*) Märchen *nt*

stout /staʊt/ *a* (**-er, -est**) beleibt; (*strong*) fest

stove /stəʊv/ *n* Ofen *m*; (*for cooking*) Herd *m*

stow /stəʊ/ *vt* verstauen. ~**away** *n* blinder Passagier *m*

straddle /ˈstrædl/ *vt* rittlings sitzen auf (+ *dat*); (*standing*) mit gespreizten Beinen stehen über (*dat*)

straggl|e /ˈstrægl/ *vi* hinterherhinken. ~**er** *n* Nachzügler *m.* ~**y** *a* strähnig

straight /streɪt/ *a* (**-er, -est**) gerade; (*direct*) direkt; (*clear*) klar; (*hair*) glatt; (*drink*) pur; **be** ~ (*tidy*) in Ordnung sein □ *adv* gerade; (*directly*) direkt, geradewegs; (*clearly*) klar; ~ **away** sofort; ~ **on** or **ahead** geradeaus; ~ **out** (*fig*) geradeheraus; **go** ~ (*fam*) ein ehrliches Leben führen; **put sth** ~ etw in Ordnung bringen; **sit/stand up** ~ gerade sitzen/stehen

straighten /ˈstreɪtn/ *vt* gerade machen; (*put straight*) gerade richten □ *vi* gerade werden; ~ **[up]** (*person:*) sich aufrichten. ~ **out** *vt* gerade biegen

straightforward *a* offen; (*simple*) einfach

strain[1] /streɪn/ *n* Rasse *f*; (*Bot*) Sorte *f*; (*of virus*) Art *f*

strain[2] *n* Belastung *f*; ~**s** *pl* (*of music*) Klänge *pl* □ *vt* belasten; (*overexert*) überanstrengen; (*injure*) zerren (*muscle*); (*Culin*) durchseihen; abgießen (*vegetables*) □ *vi* sich anstrengen. ~**ed** *a* (*relations*) gespannt. ~**er** *n* Sieb *nt*

strait /streɪt/ *n* Meerenge *f*; **in dire** ~**s** in großen Nöten. ~**jacket** *n* Zwangsjacke *f.* ~**laced** *a* puritanisch

strand[1] /strænd/ *n* (*of thread*) Faden *m*; (*of beads*) Kette *f*; (*of hair*) Strähne *f*

strand[2] *vt* **be** ~**ed** festsitzen

strange /streɪndʒ/ *a* (**-r, -st**) fremd; (*odd*) seltsam, merkwürdig. ~**r** *n* Fremde(r) *m/f*

strangely /ˈstreɪndʒlɪ/ *adv* seltsam, merkwürdig; ~ **enough** seltsamerweise

strangle /ˈstræŋgl/ *vt* erwürgen; (*fig*) unterdrücken

strangulation /stræŋgjʊˈleɪʃn/ *n* Erwürgen *nt*

strap /stræp/ *n* Riemen *m*; (*for safety*) Gurt *m*; (*to grasp in vehicle*) Halteriemen *m*; (*of watch*) Armband *nt*; (*shoulder-*) Träger *m* □ *vt* (*pt/pp* **strapped**) schnallen; **~ in** or **down** festschnallen

strapping /'stræpɪŋ/ *a* stramm

strata /'strɑːtə/ *npl see* **stratum**

stratagem /'strætədʒəm/ *n* Kriegslist *f*

strategic /strə'tiːdʒɪk/ *a*, **-ally** *adv* strategisch

strategy /'strætədʒɪ/ *n* Strategie *f*

stratum /'strɑːtəm/ *n* (*pl* **strata**) Schicht *f*

straw /strɔː/ *n* Stroh *nt*; (*single piece, drinking*) Strohhalm *m*; **that's the last ~** jetzt reicht's aber

strawberry /'strɔːbərɪ/ *n* Erdbeere *f*

stray /streɪ/ *a* streunend □ *n* streunendes Tier *nt* □ *vi* sich verirren; (*deviate*) abweichen

streak /striːk/ *n* Streifen *m*; (*in hair*) Strähne *f*; (*fig: trait*) Zug *m* □ *vi* flitzen. **~y** *a* streifig; (*bacon*) durchwachsen

stream /striːm/ *n* Bach *m*; (*flow*) Strom *m*; (*current*) Strömung *f*; (*Sch*) Parallelzug *m* □ *vi* strömen; **~ in/out** hinaus-/herausströmen

streamer /'striːmə(r)/ *n* Luftschlange *f*; (*flag*) Wimpel *m*

'streamline *vt* (*fig*) rationalisieren. **~d** *a* stromlinienförmig

street /striːt/ *n* Straße *f*. **~car** *n* (*Amer*) Straßenbahn *f*. **~lamp** *n* Straßenlaterne *f*

strength /streŋθ/ *n* Stärke *f*; (*power*) Kraft *f*; **on the ~ of** auf Grund (+ *gen*). **~en** *vt* stärken; (*reinforce*) verstärken

strenuous /'strenjʊəs/ *a* anstrengend

stress /stres/ *n* (*emphasis*) Betonung *f*; (*strain*) Belastung *f*; (*mental*) Stress *m* □ *vt* betonen;

(*put a strain on*) belasten. **~ful** *a* stressig (*fam*)

stretch /stretʃ/ *n* (*of road*) Strecke *f*; (*elasticity*) Elastizität *f*; **at a ~** ohne Unterbrechung; **a long ~** eine lange Zeit; **have a ~** sich strecken □ *vt* strecken; (*widen*) dehnen; (*spread*) ausbreiten; □ *vi* (*person*); **~ one's legs** sich (*dat*) die Beine vertreten □ *vt* sich erstrecken; (*become wider*) sich dehnen; (*person:*) sich strecken. **~er** *n* Tragbahre *f*

strew /struː/ *vt* (*pp* **strewn** or **strewed**) streuen

stricken /'strɪkn/ *a* betroffen; **~ with** heimgesucht von

strict /strɪkt/ *a* (**-er**, **-est**), **-ly** *adv* streng; **~ly speaking** streng genommen

stride /straɪd/ *n* [großer] Schritt *m*; **make great ~s** (*fig*) große Fortschritte machen; **take sth in one's ~** mit etw gut fertig werden □ *vi* (*pt* **strode**, *pp* **stridden**) [mit großen Schritten] gehen

strident /'straɪdnt/ *a*, **-ly** *adv* schrill; (*colour*) grell

strife /straɪf/ *n* Streit *m*

strike /straɪk/ *n* Streik *m*; (*Mil*) Angriff *m*; **be on ~** streiken □ *vt* (*pt/pp* **struck**) □ *vt* schlagen; (*knock against, collide with*) treffen; prägen (*coin*); anzünden (*match*); stoßen auf (+ *acc*) (*oil, gold*); abbrechen (*camp*); (*delete*) streichen; (*impress*) beeindrucken; (*occur to*) einfallen (+ *dat*); (*Mil*) angreifen; **~ s.o. a blow** jdm einen Schlag versetzen □ *vi* treffen; (*lightning:*) einschlagen; (*clock:*) schlagen; (*attack*) zuschlagen; (*workers:*) streiken; **~ lucky** Glück haben. **~breaker** *n* Streikbrecher *m*

striker /'straɪkə(r)/ *n* Streikende(r) *m/f*

striking /'straɪkɪŋ/ *a* auffallend

string /strɪŋ/ n Schnur f; (thin) Bindfaden m; (of musical instrument, racket) Saite f; (of bow) Sehne f; (of pearls) Kette f; the ~s (Mus) die Streicher pl; **pull** ~s (fam) seine Beziehungen spielen lassen, Fäden ziehen □ vt (pt/pp **strung**) (thread) aufziehen (beads). ~**ed** a (Mus) Saiten-; (played with bow) Streich-

stringent /'strɪndʒənt/ a streng

strip /strɪp/ n Streifen m □ v (pt/pp **stripped**) □ vt ablösen; ausziehen (clothes); abziehen (bed); abbeizen (wood, furniture); auseinander nehmen (machine); (deprive) berauben (of gen); ~ **sth off** etw von etw entfernen □ vi (undress) sich ausziehen. ~ **club** n Stripteaselokal nt

stripe /straɪp/ n Streifen m. ~**d** a gestreift

'striplight n Neonröhre f

stripper /'strɪpə(r)/ n Stripperin f; (male) Stripper m

strip-'tease n Striptease m

strive /straɪv/ vi (pt **strove**, pp **striven**) sich bemühen (to zu); ~ **for** streben nach

strode /strəʊd/ see stride

stroke[1] /strəʊk/ n Schlag m; (of pen) Strich m; (Swimming) Zug m; (style) Stil m; (Med) Schlaganfall m; ~ **of luck** Glücksfall m; **put s.o. off his** ~ jdn aus dem Konzept bringen

stroke[2] □ vt streicheln

stroll /strəʊl/ n Spaziergang m, (fam) Bummel m □ vi spazieren, (fam) bummeln. ~**er** n (Amer: push-chair) [Kinder]sportwagen m

strong /strɒŋ/ a (-er -gə(r), -est -gɪst), **-ly** adv stark; (powerful, healthy) kräftig; (severe) streng; (sturdy) stabil; (convincing) gut

strong: ~**-box** n Geldkassette f. ~**hold** n Festung f; (fig) Hochburg f. ~**-'minded** a willensstark. ~**-room** n Tresorraum m

stroppy /'strɒpɪ/ a widerspenstig

strove /strəʊv/ see strive

struck /strʌk/ see strike

structural /'strʌktʃərl/ a, **-ly** adv baulich

structure /'strʌktʃə(r)/ n Struktur f; (building) Bau m

struggle /'strʌgl/ n Kampf m; **with a** ~ mit Mühe □ vt kämpfen; ~ **for breath** nach Atem ringen; ~ **to do sth** sich abmühen, etw zutun; ~ **to one's feet** mühsam aufstehen

strum /strʌm/ v (pt/pp **strummed**) □ vt klimpern auf (+ dat) □ vi klimpern

strung /strʌŋ/ see string

strut[1] /strʌt/ n Strebe f

strut[2] vi (pt/pp **strutted**) stolzieren

stub /stʌb/ n Stummel m; (counterfoil) Abschnitt m □ vt (pt/pp **stubbed**) ~ **one's toe** sich (dat) den Zeh stoßen (on an + dat). ~ **out** vt ausdrücken (cigarette)

stubble /'stʌbl/ n Stoppeln pl. ~**ly** a stoppelig

stubborn /'stʌbən/ a, **-ly** adv starrsinnig; (refusal) hartnäckig

stubby /'stʌbɪ/ a, (-ier, -iest) kurz und dick

stucco /'stʌkəʊ/ n Stuck m

stuck /stʌk/ see stick[2]. ~**-'up** a (fam) hochnäsig

stud[1] /stʌd/ n Nagel m (on clothes) Niete f; (for collar) Kragenknopf m; (for ear) Ohrstecker m

stud[2] n (of horses) Gestüt nt

student /'stjuːdnt/ n Student(in) m(f); (Sch) Schüler(in) m(f). ~ **nurse** n Lernschwester f

studied /'stʌdɪd/ a gewollt

studio /'stjuːdɪəʊ/ n Studio nt; (for artist) Atelier nt

studious /'stjuːdɪəs/ a lerneifrig; (earnest) ernsthaft

study /'stʌdɪ/ n Studie f; (room) Studierzimmer nt; (investigation)

Untersuchung f; ∼ies pl Studium nt □ v (pt/pp studied) □ vt studieren; (examine) untersuchen □ vi lernen; (at university) studieren

stuff /stʌf/ n Stoff m; (fam: things) Zeug nt □ vt vollstopfen; (with padding, Culin) füllen; ausstopfen (animal); ∼ sth into sth etw in etw (acc) hineinstopfen. ∼ing n Füllung f

stuffy /'stʌfɪ/ a (-ier, -iest) stickig; (old-fashioned) spießig

stumble /'stʌmbl/ vi stolpern; ∼e across zufällig stoßen auf (+ acc). ∼ing-block n Hindernis nt

stump /stʌmp/ n Stumpf m □ ∼ up vt/i (fam) blechen. ∼ed a (fam) überfragt

stun /stʌn/ vt (pt/pp stunned) betäuben; ∼ned by (fig) wie betäubt von

stung /stʌŋ/ see sting

stunk /stʌŋk/ see stink

stunning /'stʌnɪŋ/ a (fam) toll

stunt[1] /stʌnt/ n (fam) Kunststück nt

stunt[2] vt hemmen. ∼ed a verkümmert

stupendous /stju:'pendəs/ a, -ly adv enorm

stupid /'stju:pɪd/ a dumm. ∼ity /-'pɪdətɪ/ n Dummheit f. ∼ly adv dumm; ∼ly [enough] dummerweise

stupour /'stju:pə(r)/ n Benommenheit f

sturdy /'stɜ:dɪ/ a (-ier, -iest) stämmig; (furniture) stabil; ⟨shoes⟩ fest

stutter /'stʌtə(r)/ n Stottern nt □ vt/i stottern

sty[1] /staɪ/ n (pl sties) Schweinestall m

sty[2], **stye** n (pl styes) (Med) Gerstenkorn nt

style /staɪl/ n Stil m; (fashion) Mode f; (sort) Art f; (hair∼) Frisur f; **in** ∼ in großem Stil

stylish /'staɪlɪʃ/ a, -ly adv stilvoll

stylist /'staɪlɪst/ n Friseur m/ Friseuse f. ∼ic /-'lɪstɪk/ a, -ally adv stilistisch

stylized /'staɪlaɪzd/ a stilisiert

stylus /'staɪləs/ n (on record-player) Nadel f

suave /swɑ:v/ a (pej) gewandt

sub·conscious /sʌb-/ a, -ly adv unterbewusst □ n Unterbewusstsein nt

subcon'tract vt [vertraglich] weitervergeben (**to an** + acc)

sub·di'vide vt unterteilen. ∼sion n Unterteilung f

subdue /səb'dju:/ vt unterwerfen; (make quieter) beruhigen. ∼d a gedämpft; ⟨person⟩ still

subject[1] /'sʌbdʒɪkt/ a be ∼ to sth etw (dat) unterworfen sein □ n Staatsbürger(in) m(f); (of ruler) Untertan m; (theme) Thema nt; (of investigation) Gegenstand m; (Sch) Fach nt; (Gram) Subjekt nt

subject[2] /səb'dʒekt/ vt unterwerfen (**to** dat); (expose) aussetzen (**to** dat)

subjective /səb'dʒektɪv/ a, -ly adv subjektiv

subjugate /'sʌbdʒugeɪt/ vt unterjochen

subjunctive /səb'dʒʌŋktɪv/ n Konjunktiv m

sub'let vt (pt/pp -let) untervermieten

sublime /sə'blaɪm/ a, -ly adv erhaben

subliminal /sʌ'blɪmɪnl/ a unterschwellig

sub-ma'chine-gun n Maschinenpistole f

subma'rine n Unterseeboot nt

submerge /səb'mɜ:dʒ/ vt untertauchen; **be** ∼**d** unter Wasser stehen □ vi tauchen

submis·sion /səb'mɪʃn/ n Unterwerfung f. ∼**ive** /-sɪv/ a gehorsam; (pej) unterwürfig

submit /səb'mɪt/ v (pt/pp -mitted, pres p -mitting) □ vt vorlegen (**to** dat); (hand in) einreichen □ vi sich unterwerfen (**to** dat)

subordinate¹ /sə'bɔ:dɪnət/ a untergeordnet □ n Untergebene(r) m/f

subordinate² /sə'bɔ:dɪneɪt/ vt unterordnen (to dat)

subscribe /səb'skraɪb/ vi spenden; ~ **to** abonnieren (newspaper); (fig) n spenden. **~r** n Spender m; Abonnent m

subscription /səb'skrɪpʃn/ n (to club) [Mitglieds]beitrag m; (to newspaper) Abonnement nt; **by** ~ mit Spenden; (buy) im Abonnement

subsequent /'sʌbsɪkwənt/ a, **-ly** adv folgend; (later) später

subservient /səb'sɜ:vɪənt/ a, **-ly** adv untergeordnet; (servile) unterwürfig

subside /səb'saɪd/ vi sinken; (ground:) sich senken; (storm:) nachlassen

subsidiary /səb'sɪdɪərɪ/ a untergeordnet □ n Tochtergesellschaft f

subsid|ize /'sʌbsɪdaɪz/ vt subventionieren. **~y** n Subvention f

subsist /səb'sɪst/ vi leben (on von). **~ence** n Existenz f

substance /'sʌbstəns/ n Substanz f

sub'standard a unzulänglich; (goods) minderwertig

substantial /səb'stænʃl/ a solide; (meal) reichhaltig; (considerable) beträchtlich. **~ly** adv solide; (essentially) im Wesentlichen

substantiate /səb'stænʃɪeɪt/ vt erhärten

substitut|e /'sʌbstɪtjuːt/ n Ersatz m; (Sport) Ersatzspieler(in) m(f) □ vt ~ **A for B** B durch A ersetzen □ vi ~ **for s.o.** jdn vertreten. **~ion** /-'tjuːʃn/ n Ersetzung f

subterfuge /'sʌbtəfjuːdʒ/ n List f

subterranean /sʌbtə'reɪnɪən/ a unterirdisch

'subtitle n Untertitel m

subtle /'sʌtl/ a (-r, -st), **-tly** adv fein; (fig) subtil

subtract /səb'trækt/ vt abziehen, subtrahieren. **~ion** /-ækʃn/ n Subtraktion f

suburb /'sʌbɜːb/ n Vorort m; **in the** ~**s** am Stadtrand. **~an** /sə'bɜːbən/ a Vorort-; (pej) spießig. **~ia** /sə'bɜːbɪə/ n die Vororte pl

subversive /səb'vɜːsɪv/ a subversiv

'subway n Unterführung f; (Amer: railway) U-Bahn f

succeed /sək'siːd/ vi Erfolg haben; (plan:) gelingen; (follow) nachfolgen (+ dat); **I** ~**ed** es ist mir gelungen; **he** ~**ed in escaping** es gelang ihm zu entkommen □ vt folgen (+ dat). **~ing** a folgend

success /sək'ses/ n Erfolg m. **~ful** a, **-ly** adv erfolgreich

succession /sək'seʃn/ n Folge f; (series) Serie f; (to title, office) Nachfolge f; (to throne) Thronfolge f; **in** ~ hintereinander

successive /sək'sesɪv/ a aufeinander folgend. **~ly** adv hintereinander

successor /sək'sesə(r)/ n Nachfolger(in) m(f)

succinct /sək'sɪŋkt/ a, **-ly** adv prägnant

succulent /'sʌkjʊlənt/ a saftig

succumb /sə'kʌm/ vi erliegen (to dat)

such /sʌtʃ/ a solche(r,s); ~ **a book** ein solches od solch ein Buch; ~ **a thing** so etwas; ~ **a long time** so lange; **there is no** ~ **thing** das gibt es gar nicht; **there is no** ~ **person** eine solche Person gibt es nicht □ pron **as** ~ als solche(r,s); (strictly speaking) an sich; ~ **as** wie [zum Beispiel]; **and** ~ und dergleichen. **~like** pron (fam) dergleichen

suck /sʌk/ vt/i saugen; lutschen (sweet). ~ **up** vt aufsaugen □ vi ~ **up to s.o.** (fam) sich bei jdm einschmeicheln

sucker /'ʃʌkə(r)/ n (Bot) Ausläufer m; (fam: person) Dumme(r) m/f

suckle /'sʌkl/ vt säugen

suction /'sʌkʃn/ n Saugwirkung f

sudden /'sʌdn/ a, -ly adv plötzlich; (abrupt) jäh □ n all of a ~ auf einmal

sue /su:/ vt (pres p suing) verklagen (for auf + acc) □ vi klagen

suede /sweid/ n Wildleder nt

suet /'su:it/ n [Nieren]talg m

suffer /'sʌfə(r)/ vi leiden (from an + dat) □ vt erleiden; (tolerate) dulden. ~ance /-əns/ n on ~ance bloß geduldet. ~ing n Leiden nt

suffice /sə'faɪs/ vi genügen

sufficient /sə'fɪʃnt/ a, -ly adv genug, genügend; be ~ genügen

suffix /'sʌfɪks/ n Nachsilbe f

suffocat|e /'sʌfəkeit/ vt/i ersticken. ~ion /-'keiʃn/ n Ersticken nt

sugar /'ʃugə(r)/ n Zucker m □ vt zuckern; (fig) versüßen. ~ basin, ~bowl n Zuckerschale f. ~y a süß; (fig) süßlich

suggest /sə'dʒest/ vt vorschlagen; (indicate, insinuate) andeuten. ~ion /-estʃn/ n Vorschlag m; Andeutung f; (trace) Spur f. ~ive /-ɪv/ a, -ly adv anzüglich; be ~ive of schließen lassen auf (+ acc)

suicidal /su:ɪ'saɪdl/ a selbstmörderisch

suicide /'su:ɪsaɪd/ n Selbstmord m

suit /su:t/ n Anzug m; (woman's) Kostüm nt; (Cards) Farbe f; (Jur) Prozess m; follow ~ (fig) das Gleiche tun □ vt (adapt) anpassen (to dat); (be convenient for) passen (+ dat); (go with) passen zu; (clothing:) stehen (s.o. jdm); be ~ed for geeignet sein für; ~ yourself! wie du willst!

suit|able /'su:təbl/ a geeignet; (convenient) passend; (appropriate) angemessen; (for weather,

activity) zweckmäßig. ~ably adv angemessen; zweckmäßig

'suitcase n Koffer m

suite /swi:t/ n Suite f; (of furniture) Garnitur f

sulk /sʌlk/ vi schmollen. ~y a schmollend

sullen /'sʌlən/ a, -ly adv mürrisch

sulphur /'sʌlfə(r)/ n Schwefel f. ~ic /-'fjuərik/ a ~ic acid Schwefelsäure f

sultana /sʌl'tɑːnə/ n Sultanine f

sultry /'sʌltrɪ/ a (-ier, -iest) (weather) schwül

sum /sʌm/ n Summe f; (Sch) Rechenaufgabe f □ vt/i (pt/pp summed) ~ up zusammenfassen; (assess) einschätzen

summar|ize /'sʌmərɑɪz/ vt zusammenfassen. ~y n Zusammenfassung f □ a, -ily adv summarisch; (dismissal) fristlos

summer /'sʌmə(r)/ n Sommer m. ~house n [Garten]laube f. ~time n Sommer m

summery /'sʌmərɪ/ a sommerlich

summit /'sʌmɪt/ n Gipfel m. ~ conference n Gipfelkonferenz f

summon /'sʌmən/ vt rufen; bitten (help); (Jur) vorladen. ~ up vt aufbringen

summons /'sʌmənz/ n (Jur) Vorladung f □ vt vorladen

sump /sʌmp/ n (Auto) Ölwanne f

sumptuous /'sʌmptjʊəs/ a, -ly adv prunkvoll; (meal) üppig

sun /sʌn/ n Sonne f □ vt (pt/pp sunned) ~ oneself sich sonnen

sun: ~bathe vi sich sonnen. ~bed n Sonnenbank f. ~burn n Sonnenbrand m

sundae /'sʌndeɪ/ n Eisbecher m

Sunday /'sʌndeɪ/ n Sonntag m

'sundial n Sonnenuhr f

sundry /'sʌndrɪ/ a verschiedene pl; all and ~ alle pl

'sunflower n Sonnenblume f

sung /sʌŋ/ see sing

'sun-glasses *npl* Sonnenbrille *f*

sunk /sʌŋk/ *see* **sink**

sunken /'sʌŋkn/ *a* gesunken; ⟨eyes⟩ eingefallen

sunny /'sʌnɪ/ *a* (**-ier, -iest**) sonnig

sun: **∼rise** *n* Sonnenaufgang *m*. **∼-roof** *n* (*Auto*) Schiebedach *nt*. **∼set** *n* Sonnenuntergang *m*. **∼shade** *n* Sonnenschirm *m*. **∼shine** *n* Sonnenschein *m*. **∼stroke** *n* Sonnenstich *m*. **∼-tan** *n* [Sonnen]bräune *f*. **∼-tanned** *a* braun [gebrannt]. **∼-tan oil** *n* Sonnenöl *nt*

super /'su:pə(r)/ *a* (*fam*) prima, toll

superb /su:'pɜ:b/ *a* erstklassig

supercilious /su:pə'sɪlɪəs/ *a* überlegen

superficial /su:pə'fɪʃl/ *a*, **-ly** *adv* oberflächlich

superfluous /su'pɜ:fluəs/ *a* überflüssig

super human *a* übermenschlich

superintendent /su:pərɪn-'tendənt/ *n* (*of police*) Kommissar *m*

superior /su:'pɪərɪə(r)/ *a* überlegen; (*in rank*) höher □ *n* Vorgesetzte(r) *m/f*. **∼ity** /-'ɒrətɪ/ *n* Überlegenheit *f*

superlative /su:'pɜ:lətɪv/ *a* unübertrefflich □ *n* Superlativ *m*

superman *n* Übermensch *m*

'supermarket *n* Supermarkt *m*

super'natural *a* übernatürlich

'superpower *n* Supermacht *f*

supersede /su:pə'si:d/ *vt* ersetzen

super'sonic *a* Überschall-

superstiti|on /su:pə'stɪʃn/ *n* Aberglaube *m*. **∼ous** /-'stɪʃəs/ *a*, **-ly** *adv* abergläubisch

supervis|e /'su:pəvaɪz/ *vt* beaufsichtigen; überwachen ⟨work⟩. **∼ion** /-'vɪʒn/ *n* Aufsicht *f*; Überwachung *f*. **∼or** *n* Aufseher(in) *m(f)*

supper /'sʌpə(r)/ *n* Abendessen *nt*

supple /'sʌpl/ *a* geschmeidig

supplement /'sʌplɪmənt/ *n* Ergänzung *f*; (*addition*) Zusatz *m*; (*to fare*) Zuschlag *m*; (*book*) Ergänzungsband *m*; (*to newspaper*) Beilage *f* □ *vt* ergänzen. **∼ary** /-'mentərɪ/ *a* zusätzlich

supplier /sə'plaɪə(r)/ *n* Lieferant *m*

supply /sə'plaɪ/ *n* Vorrat *m*; **supplies** *pl* (*Mil*) Nachschub *m* □ *vt* (*pt/pp* **-ied**) liefern; **∼ s.o. with sth** jdn mit etw versorgen

support /sə'pɔ:t/ *n* Stütze *f*; (*fig*) Unterstützung *f* □ *vt* stützen; (*bear weight of*) tragen; (*keep*) ernähren; (*give money to*) unterstützen; (*speak in favour of*) befürworten; (*Sport*) Fan sein von. **∼er** *n* Anhänger(in) *m(f)*; (*Sport*) Fan *m*. **∼ive** /-ɪv/ *a* be **∼ive** [**to s.o.**] [jdm] eine große Stütze sein

suppose /sə'pəʊz/ *vt* annehmen; (*presume*) vermuten; (*imagine*) sich *(dat)* vorstellen; **be ∼d to do sth** etw tun sollen; **not be ∼d to** (*fam*) nicht dürfen; **I ∼ so** vermutlich. **∼dly** /-ɪdlɪ/ *adv* angeblich

supposition /sʌpə'zɪʃn/ *n* Vermutung *f*

suppository /sʌ'pɒzɪtrɪ/ *n* Zäpfchen *nt*

suppress /sə'pres/ *vt* unterdrücken. **∼ion** /-eʃn/ *n* Unterdrückung *f*

supremacy /su:'preməsɪ/ *n* Vorherrschaft *f*

supreme /su:'pri:m/ *a* höchste(r,s); (*court*) oberste(r,s)

surcharge /'sɜ:tʃɑ:dʒ/ *n* Zuschlag *m*

sure /ʃʊə/ *a* (**-r, -st**) sicher; **make ∼** sich vergewissern (**of** gen); (*check*) nachprüfen; **be ∼ to do it** sieh zu, dass du es tust □ *adv* (*Amer, fam*) sicher; (*really*) tatsächlich. **∼ly** *adv* sicher; (*for emphasis*) doch; (*Amer: gladly*) gern

surety /'ʃʊərətɪ/ *n* Bürgschaft *f*; **stand ∼ for** bürgen für

surf /'sɜːf/ n Brandung f

surface /'sɜːfɪs/ n Oberfläche f □ vi (emerge) auftauchen. **~ mail** n by ~ mail auf dem Land-/Seeweg

'**surfboard** n Surfbrett nt

surfeit /'sɜːfɪt/ n Übermaß nt

surfing /'sɜːfɪŋ/ n Surfen nt

surge /sɜːdʒ/ n (of sea) Branden nt; (fig) Welle f □ vi branden; ~ **forward** nach vorn drängen

surgeon /'sɜːdʒən/ n Chirurg(in) m(f)

surgery /'sɜːdʒərɪ/ n Chirurgie f; (place) Praxis f; (room) Sprechzimmer nt; (hours) Sprechstunde f; **have ~** operiert werden

surgical /'sɜːdʒɪkl/ a, **-ly** adv chirurgisch

surly /'sɜːlɪ/ a (-ier, -iest) mürrisch

surmise /sə'maɪz/ vt mutmaßen

surmount /sə'maʊnt/ vt überwinden

surname /'sɜːneɪm/ n Nachname m

surpass /sə'pɑːs/ vt übertreffen

surplus /'sɜːpləs/ a überschüssig; **be ~ to requirements** nicht benötigt werden □ n Überschuss m (**of** an + dat)

surprise /sə'praɪz/ n Überraschung f □ vt überraschen; **be ~ed** sich wundern (**at** über + acc). **~ing** a, **-ly** adv überraschend

surrender /sə'rendə(r)/ n Kapitulation f □ vi sich ergeben; (Mil) kapitulieren □ vt aufgeben

surreptitious /sʌrəp'tɪʃəs/ a, **-ly** adv heimlich, verstohlen

surrogate /'sʌrəgət/ n Ersatz m. **~ 'mother** n Leihmutter f

surround /sə'raʊnd/ vt umgeben; (encircle) umzingeln; **~ed by** umgeben von. **~ing** a umliegend. **~ings** npl Umgebung f.

surveillance /sə'veɪləns/ n Überwachung f; **be under ~** überwacht werden

survey[1] /'sɜːveɪ/ n Überblick m; (poll) Umfrage f; (investigation) Untersuchung f; (of land) Vermessung f; (of house) Gutachten nt

survey[2] /sə'veɪ/ vt betrachten; vermessen ⟨land⟩; begutachten ⟨building⟩. **~or** n Landvermesser m; Gutachter m

survival /sə'vaɪvl/ n Überleben nt; (of tradition) Fortbestand m

survive /sə'vaɪv/ vt überleben; ⟨tradition:⟩ erhalten bleiben. **~ or** n Überlebende(r) m/f; **be a ~or** (fam) nicht unterzukriegen sein

susceptible /sə'septəbl/ a empfänglich/ (Med) anfällig (**to** für)

suspect[1] /sə'spekt/ vt verdächtigen; (assume) vermuten; **he ~s nothing** er ahnt nichts

suspect[2] /'sʌspekt/ a verdächtig □ n Verdächtige(r) m/f

suspend /sə'spend/ vt aufhängen; (stop) [vorläufig] einstellen; (from duty) vorläufig beurlauben. **~er belt** n Strumpfbandgürtel m. **~ders** npl Strumpfbänder pl; (Amer: braces) Hosenträger pl

suspense /sə'spens/ n Spannung f

suspension /sə'spenʃn/ n (Auto) Federung f. **~ bridge** n Hängebrücke f

suspicion /sə'spɪʃn/ n Verdacht m; (mistrust) Misstrauen nt; (trace) Spur f. **~ous** /-ɪʃəs/ a, **-ly** adv misstrauisch; (arousing suspicion) verdächtig

sustain /sə'steɪn/ vt tragen; (fig) aufrechterhalten; erhalten ⟨life⟩; erleiden ⟨injury⟩

sustenance /'sʌstɪnəns/ n Nahrung f

swab /swɒb/ n (Med) Tupfer m; (specimen) Abstrich m

swagger /'swægə(r)/ vi stolzieren

swallow¹ /'swɒləʊ/ vt/i schlucken. **~ up** vt verschlucken; verschlingen ⟨resources⟩

swallow² n (bird) Schwalbe f

swam /swæm/ see **swim**

swamp /swɒmp/ n Sumpf m □ vt überschwemmen. **~y** a sumpfig

swan /swɒn/ n Schwan m

swank /swæŋk/ vi (fam) angeben

swap /swɒp/ n (fam) Tausch m □ vt/i (pt/pp swapped) (fam) tauschen (for gegen)

swarm /swɔːm/ n Schwarm m □ vi schwärmen; **be ~ing with** wimmeln von

swarthy /'swɔːðɪ/ a (-ier, -iest) dunkel

swastika /'swɒstɪkə/ n Hakenkreuz nt

swat /swɒt/ vt (pt/pp swatted) totschlagen

sway /sweɪ/ n (fig) Herrschaft f □ vi schwanken; (gently) sich wiegen □ vt wiegen; (influence) beeinflussen

swear /sweə(r)/ v (pt swore, pp sworn) □ vt schwören □ vi schwören (by auf + acc); (curse) fluchen. **~-word** n Kraftausdruck m

sweat /swet/ n Schweiß m □ vi schwitzen

sweater /'swetə(r)/ n Pullover m

sweaty /'swetɪ/ a verschwitzt

swede /swiːd/ n Kohlrübe f

Swede n Schwede m /-din f. **~en** n Schweden nt. **~ish** a schwedisch

sweep /swiːp/ n Schornsteinfeger m; (curve) Bogen m; (movement) ausholende Bewegung f; **make a clean ~** (fig) gründlich aufräumen □ v (pt/pp swept) □ vt fegen, kehren □ vi (go swiftly) rauschen; ⟨wind:⟩ fegen. **~ up** vt zusammenfegen/-kehren

sweeping /'swiːpɪŋ/ a ausholend; (statement) pauschal; (changes) weit reichend

sweet /swiːt/ n a (-er, -est) süß; **have a ~ tooth** gern Süßes mögen □ n Bonbon m & nt; (dessert) Nachtisch m. **~ corn** n [Zucker]mais m

sweeten /'swiːtn/ vt süßen. **~er** n Süßstoff m; (fam: bribe) Schmiergeld nt

sweet: ~heart n Schatz m. **~shop** n Süßwarenladen m. **~ness** n Süße f. **~ pea** n Wicke f

swell /swel/ n Dünung f □ v (pt swelled, pp swollen or swelled) □ vi [an]schwellen; ⟨sails:⟩ sich blähen; ⟨wood:⟩ aufquellen □ vt anschwellen lassen; (increase) vergrößern. **~ing** n Schwellung f

swelter /'sweltə(r)/ vi schwitzen

swept /swept/ see **sweep**

swerve /swɜːv/ vi einen Bogen machen

swift /swɪft/ a (-er, -est), **-ly** adv schnell

swig /swɪg/ n (fam) Schluck m, Zug m □ vt (pt/pp swigged) (fam) [herunter]kippen

swill /swɪl/ n (for pigs) Schweinefutter nt □ vt **~ [out]** [aus]spülen

swim /swɪm/ n **have a ~** schwimmen □ vi (pt swam, pp swum) schwimmen; **my head is ~ming** mir dreht sich der Kopf. **~mer** n Schwimmer(in) m(f)

swimming /'swɪmɪŋ/ n Schwimmen nt. **~-baths** npl Schwimmbad nt. **~-pool** n Schwimmbecken nt; (private) Swimmingpool m

'swim-suit n Badeanzug m

swindle /'swɪndl/ n Schwindel m, Betrug m □ vt betrügen. **~r** n Schwindler m

swine /swaɪn/ n Schwein nt

swing /swɪŋ/ n Schwung m; (shift) Schwenk m; (seat) Schaukel f; **in full ~** in vollem Gange □ v (pt/pp swung) □ vi schwingen; (on swing) schaukeln; (sway) schwanken; (dangle) baumeln; (turn) schwenken □ vt

schwingen; (*influence*) beeinflussen. ~'door n Schwingtür f
swingeing /'swɪndʒɪŋ/ a hart;
(*fig*) drastisch
swipe /swaɪp/ n (*fam*) Schlag m
□ vt (*fam*) knallen; (*steal*) klauen
swirl /swɜ:l/ n Wirbel m □ vt/i
wirbeln
swish /swɪʃ/ a (*fam*) schick □ vi
zischen
Swiss /swɪs/ a Schweizer, schwei-
zerisch □ n Schweizer(in) m(f);
the ~ pl die Schweizer. **~ 'roll** n
Biskuitrolle f
switch /swɪtʃ/ n Schalter m;
(*change*) Wechsel m; (*Amer, Rail*)
Weiche f □ vt wechseln; (*exchange*) tauschen □ vi wechseln;
~ to umstellen auf (+ *acc*). **~ off**
vt ausschalten; abschalten (*engine*). **~ on** vt einschalten, anschalten
switch: ~**back** n Achterbahn f.
~**board** n [Telefon]zentrale f
Switzerland /'swɪtsələnd/ n die
Schweiz
swivel /'swɪvl/ v (*pt/pp* **swiv-
elled**) □ vt drehen □ vi sich drehen
swollen /'swəʊlən/ *see* **swell** □ a
geschwollen. ~-'**headed** a eingebildet
swoop /swu:p/ n Sturzflug m; (*by
police*) Razzia f □ vi **~ down** he-
rabstoßen
sword /sɔ:d/ n Schwert nt
swore /swɔ:(r)/ *see* **swear**
sworn /swɔ:n/ *see* **swear**
swot /swɒt/ n (*fam*) Streber m
□ vt (*pt/pp* **swotted**) (*fam*) büf-
feln
swum /swʌm/ *see* **swim**
swung /swʌŋ/ *see* **swing**
syllable /'sɪləbl/ n Silbe f
syllabus /'sɪləbəs/ n Lehrplan m;
(*for exam*) Studienplan m

symbol /'sɪmbl/ n Symbol nt (of
für). **~ic** /-'bɒlɪk/ a, **-ally** adv
symbolisch **~ism** /-ɪzm/ n Sym-
bolik f. **~ize** vt symbolisieren

symmetr|ical /sɪ'metrɪkl/ a, **-ly**
adv symmetrisch. **~y** /'sɪmətrɪ/
n Symmetrie f
sympathetic /sɪmpə'θetɪk/ a,
-ally adv mitfühlend; (*likeable*)
sympathisch
sympathize /'sɪmpəθaɪz/ vi mitfühlen. **~r** n (*Pol*) Sympathisant
m
sympathy /'sɪmpəθɪ/ n Mitgefühl
nt; (*condolences*) Beileid nt
symphony /'sɪmfənɪ/ n Sinfonie
f
symptom /'sɪmptəm/ n Symptom
nt. **~atic** /-'mætɪk/ a symptoma-
tisch (of für)
synagogue /'sɪnəgɒg/ n
Synagoge f
synchronize /'sɪŋkrənaɪz/ vt
synchronisieren
syndicate /'sɪndɪkət/ n Syndikat
nt
syndrome /'sɪndrəʊm/ n Syndrom nt
synonym /'sɪnənɪm/ n Synonym
nt. **~ous** /-'nɒnɪməs/ a, **-ly** adv
synonym
synopsis /sɪ'nɒpsɪs/ n (pl **-opses**
/-si:z/) Zusammenfassung f; (of
opera, ballet) Inhaltsangabe f
syntax /'sɪntæks/ n Syntax f
synthesis /'sɪnθəsɪs/ n (pl **-ses**
/-si:z/) Synthese f
synthetic /sɪn'θetɪk/ a synthe-
tisch □ n Kunststoff m
Syria /'sɪrɪə/ n Syrien nt
syringe /sɪ'rɪndʒ/ n Spritze f □ vt
spritzen; ausspritzen (ears)
syrup /'sɪrəp/ n Sirup m
system /'sɪstəm/ n System nt.
~atic /-'mætɪk/ a, **-ally** adv systematisch

T

tab /tæb/ n (*projecting*) Zunge f;
(*with name*) Namensschild nt;
(*loop*) Aufhänger m; **keep ~s on**

tabby *(fam)* [genau] beobachten; **pick up the ~** ihn bezahlen

tabby /'tæbɪ/ *n* getigerte Katze *f*

table /'teɪbl/ *n* Tisch *m*; *(list)* Tabelle *f*; **at [the]** ~ bei Tisch □ *vt* einbringen. ~**cloth** *n* Tischdecke *f*, Tischtuch *nt*. ~**spoon** *n* Servierlöffel *m*

tablet /'tæblɪt/ *n* Tablette *f*; *(of soap)* Stück *nt*; *(slab)* Tafel *f*

'table tennis *n* Tischtennis *nt*

tabloid /'tæblɔɪd/ *n* kleinformatige Zeitung *f*; *(pej)* Boulevardzeitung *f*

taboo /tə'buː/ *a* tabu □ *n* Tabu *nt*

tacit /'tæsɪt/ *a*, **-ly** *adv* stillschweigend

taciturn /'tæsɪtɜːn/ *a* wortkarg

tack /tæk/ *n* *(nail)* Stift *m*; *(stitch)* Heftstich *m*; *(Naut & fig)* Kurs *m* □ *vt* festnageln; *(sew)* heften □ *vi* *(Naut)* kreuzen

tackle /'tækl/ *n* Ausrüstung *f* □ *vt* angehen

tacky /'tækɪ/ *a* klebrig

tact /tækt/ *n* Takt *m*, Taktgefühl *nt*. ~**ful** *a*, **-ly** *adv* taktvoll

tactic|al /'tæktɪkl/ *a*, **-ly** *adv* taktisch. ~**s** *npl* Taktik *f*

tactless /'tæktlɪs/ *a*, **-ly** *adv* taktlos. ~**ness** *n* Taktlosigkeit *f*

tadpole /'tædpəʊl/ *n* Kaulquappe *f*

tag¹ /tæg/ *n* *(label)* Schild *nt* □ *vi* *(pt/pp* **tagged**) ~ **along** mitkommen

tag² /tæg/ *n* *(game)* Fangen *nt*

tail /teɪl/ *n* Schwanz *m*; ~**s** *pl* *(tailcoat)* Frack *m*; **heads or ~s?** Kopf oder Zahl? □ *vt* *(fam: follow)* beschatten □ *vi* ~ **off** zurückgehen

tail: ~**back** *n* Rückstau *m*. ~**coat** *n* Frack *m*. ~**-end** *n* Ende *nt*. ~**light** *n* Rücklicht *nt*

tailor /'teɪlə(r)/ *n* Schneider *m*. ~**-made** *a* maßgeschneidert

'tail wind *n* Rückenwind *m*

taint /teɪnt/ *vt* verderben

take /teɪk/ *v* *(pt* **took**, *pp* **taken**) □ *vt* nehmen; *(with one)* mitnehmen; *(take to a place)* bringen;

(steal) stehlen; *(win)* gewinnen; *(capture)* einnehmen; *(require)* brauchen; *(last)* dauern; *(teach)* geben; machen *(exam, subject holiday, photograph)*; messen *(pulse, temperature)*; ~ **s.o. home** jdn nach Hause bringen; ~ **sth to the cleaner's** etw in die Reinigung bringen; ~ **s.o. prisoner** jdn gefangen nehmen; **be ~ ill** krank werden; ~ **sth calmly** etw gelassen aufnehmen □ *vi* *(plant:)* angehen; ~ **after s.o.** jdm nachschlagen; *(in looks)* jdm ähnlich sehen; ~ **to** *(like)* mögen; *(as a habit)* sich *(dat)* angewöhnen. ~ **away** *vt* wegbringen; *(remove)* wegnehmen; *(subtract)* abziehen; **'to ~ away'** 'zum Mitnehmen'. ~ **back** *vt* zurücknehmen; *(return)* zurückbringen. ~ **down** *vt* herunternehmen; *(remove)* abnehmen; *(write down)* aufschreiben. ~ **in** *vt* hineinbringen; *(bring indoors)* hereinholen; *(to one's home)* aufnehmen; *(understand)* begreifen; *(deceive)* hereinlegen; *(make smaller)* enger machen. ~ **off** *vt* abnehmen; ablegen *(coat)*; sich *(dat)* ausziehen *(clothes)*; *(deduct)* abziehen; *(mimic)* nachmachen; ~ **time off** sich *(dat)* freinehmen; ~ **oneself off** [fort]gehen □ *vi* *(Aviat)* starten. ~ **on** *vt* annehmen; *(undertake)* übernehmen; *(engage)* einstellen; *(as opponent)* antreten gegen. ~ **out** *vt* hinausbringen; *(for pleasure)* ausgehen mit; ausführen *(dog)*; *(remove)* herausnehmen; *(withdraw)* abheben *(money)*; *(from library)* ausleihen; ~ **out a subscription to sth** etw abonnieren; ~ **it out on s.o.** *(fam)* seinen Ärger an jdm auslassen. ~ **over** *vt* hinüberbringen; übernehmen *(firm, control)* □ *vi* ~ **over from s.o.** jdn ablösen. ~ **up** *vt* hinaufbringen; annehmen *(offer)*; ergreifen *(profession)*; sich

(*dat*) zulegen ⟨*hobby*⟩; in Anspruch nehmen ⟨*time*⟩; einnehmen ⟨*space*⟩; aufreißen ⟨*floorboards*⟩; ~ sth up with s.o. mit jdm über etw (*acc*) sprechen □ *vi* ~ up with s.o. sich mit jdm einlassen

take: ~**away** *n* Essen *nt* zum Mitnehmen; ⟨*restaurant*⟩ Restaurant *nt* mit Straßenverkauf. ~**off** *n* (*Aviat*) Start *m*, Abflug *m*. ~**over** *n* Übernahme *f*

takings /'teɪkɪŋz/ *npl* Einnahmen *pl*

talcum /'tælkəm/ *n* ~ [**powder**] Körperpuder *m*

tale /teɪl/ *n* Geschichte *f*

talent /'tælənt/ *n* Talent *nt*. ~**ed** *a* talentiert

talk /tɔːk/ *n* Gespräch *nt*; ⟨*lecture*⟩ Vortrag *m*; **make small** ~ Konversation machen □ *vi* reden, sprechen (**to/with** mit) □ *vt* reden; ~ **s.o. into sth** jdn zu etw überreden. ~ **over** *vt* besprechen

talkative /'tɔːkətɪv/ *a* gesprächig

'**talking-to** *n* Standpauke *f*

tall /tɔːl/ *a* (**-er, -est**) groß; ⟨*building, tree*⟩ hoch; **that's a** ~ **order** das ist ziemlich viel verlangt. ~**boy** *n* hohe Kommode *f*. ~'**story** *n* übertriebene Geschichte *f*

tally /'tælɪ/ *n* keep a ~ of Buch führen über (+ *acc*) □ *vi* übereinstimmen

talon /'tælən/ *n* Klaue *f*

tambourine /tæmbə'riːn/ *n* Tamburin *nt*

tame /teɪm/ *a* (**-r, -st**), -**ly** *adv* zahm; ⟨*dull*⟩ lahm (*fam*) □ *vt* zähmen. ~**r** *n* Dompteur *m*

tamper /'tæmpə(r)/ *vi* ~ **with** sich (*dat*) zu schaffen machen an (+ *dat*)

tampon /'tæmpɒn/ *n* Tampon *m*

tan /tæn/ *a* gelbbraun □ *n* Gelbbraun *nt*; ⟨*from sun*⟩ Bräune *f* □ *v* (*pt/pp* **tanned**) □ *vt* gerben ⟨*hide*⟩ □ *vi* braun werden

tang /tæŋ/ *n* herber Geschmack *m*; ⟨*smell*⟩ herber Geruch *m*

tangent /'tændʒənt/ *n* Tangente *f*; **go off at a** ~ (*fam*) vom Thema abschweifen

tangible /'tændʒɪbl/ *a* greifbar

tangle /'tæŋgl/ *n* Gewirr *nt*; ⟨*in hair*⟩ Verfilzung *f* □ *vt* ~ [**up**] verheddern □ *vi* sich verheddern

tango /'tæŋgəʊ/ *n* Tango *m*

tank /tæŋk/ *n* Tank *m*; (*Mil*) Panzer *m*

tankard /'tæŋkəd/ *n* Krug *m*

tanker /'tæŋkə(r)/ *n* Tanker *m*; ⟨*lorry*⟩ Tank[last]wagen *m*

tantalize /'tæntəlaɪz/ *vt* quälen. ~**ing** *a* verlockend

tantamount /'tæntəmaʊnt/ *a* **be** ~ **to** gleichbedeutend sein mit

tantrum /'tæntrəm/ *n* Wutanfall *m*

tap /tæp/ *n* Hahn *m*; ⟨*knock*⟩ Klopfen *nt*; **on** ~ zur Verfügung □ *v* (*pt/pp* **tapped**) □ *vt* klopfen an (+ *acc*); anzapfen ⟨*barrel, tree*⟩; erschließen ⟨*resources*⟩; abhören ⟨*telephone*⟩ □ *vi* klopfen. ~**dance** *n* Stepp[tanz] *m* □ *vi* Stepp tanzen, steppen

tape /teɪp/ *n* Band *nt*; ⟨*adhesive*⟩ Klebstreifen *m*; ⟨*for recording*⟩ Tonband *nt* □ *vt* mit Klebstreifen zukleben; ⟨*record*⟩ auf Band aufnehmen

'**tape-measure** *n* Bandmaß *nt*

taper /'teɪpə(r)/ *n* dünne Wachskerze *f* □ *vt* sich verjüngen

'**tape recorder** *n* Tonbandgerät *nt*

tapestry /'tæpɪstrɪ/ *n* Gobelinstickerei *f*

'**tapeworm** *n* Bandwurm *m*

'**tap water** *n* Leitungswasser *nt*

tar /tɑː/ *n* Teer *m* □ *vt* (*pt/pp* **tarred**) teeren

tardy /'tɑːdɪ/ *a* (**-ier, -iest**) langsam; ⟨*late*⟩ spät

target /'tɑːgɪt/ *n* Ziel *nt*; ⟨*board*⟩ [Ziel]scheibe *f*

tariff /'tærɪf/ *n* Tarif *m*; ⟨*duty*⟩ Zoll *m*

tarnish /'tɑːnɪʃ/ vi anlaufen

tarpaulin /tɑː'pɔːlɪn/ n Plane f

tarragon /'tærəgən/ n Estragon m

tart¹ /tɑːt/ a (-er, -est) sauer; (fig) scharf

tart² n ≈ Obstkuchen m; (individual) Törtchen nt; (sl: prostitute) Nutte f □ vt ~ oneself up (fam) sich auftakeln

tartan /'tɑːtn/ n Schottenmuster nt; (cloth) Schottenstoff m □ attrib schottisch kariert

tartar /'tɑːtə(r)/ n (on teeth) Zahnstein m

tartar 'sauce /tɑːtə-/ n ≈ Remouladensoße f

task /tɑːsk/ n Aufgabe f; take s.o. to ~ jdm Vorhaltungen machen. ~ force n Sonderkommando nt

tassel /'tæsl/ n Quaste f

taste /teɪst/ n Geschmack m; (sample) Kostprobe f □ vt kosten, probieren; schmecken (flavour) □ vi schmecken (of nach). ~ful a, -ly adv (fig) geschmackvoll. ~less a, -ly adv geschmacklos

tasty /'teɪstɪ/ a (-ier, -iest) lecker, schmackhaft

tat /tæt/ see tit²

tatter|ed /'tætəd/ a zerlumpt; (pages) zerfleddert. ~s npl in ~s in Fetzen

tattoo¹ /tə'tuː/ n Tätowierung f □ vt tätowieren

tattoo² n (Mil) Zapfenstreich m

tatty /'tætɪ/ a (-ier, -iest) schäbig; (book) zerfleddert

taught /tɔːt/ see teach

taunt /tɔːnt/ n höhnische Bemerkung f □ vt verhöhnen

Taurus /'tɔːrəs/ n (Astr) Stier m

taut /tɔːt/ a straff

tavern /'tævən/ n (liter) Schenke f

tawdry /'tɔːdrɪ/ a (-ier, -iest) billig und geschmacklos

tawny /'tɔːnɪ/ a gelbbraun

tax /tæks/ n Steuer f □ vt besteuern; (fig) strapazieren; ~ with beschuldigen (+ gen). ~able /-əbl/ a steuerpflichtig. ~ation /-'seɪʃn/ n Besteuerung f. ~-free a steuerfrei

taxi /'tæksɪ/ n Taxi nt □ vi (pt/pp taxied, pres p taxiing) (aircraft:) rollen. ~ driver n Taxifahrer m. ~ rank n Taxistand m

taxpayer n Steuerzahler m

tea /tiː/ n Tee m. ~-bag n Teebeutel m. ~-break n Teepause f

teach /tiːtʃ/ vt/i (pt/pp taught) unterrichten; ~ s.o. sth jdm etw beibringen. ~er n Lehrer(in) m(f)

tea: ~-cloth n (for drying) Geschirrtuch nt. ~cup n Teetasse f

teak /tiːk/ n Teakholz nt

team /tiːm/ n Mannschaft f; (fig) Team nt; (of animals) Gespann nt □ vi ~ up sich zusammentun

team-work n Teamarbeit f

teapot n Teekanne f

tear¹ /teə(r)/ n Riss m □ vi (pt tore, pp torn) □ vt reißen; (damage) zerreißen; ~ open aufreißen; ~ oneself away sich losreißen □ vi [zer]reißen; (run) rasen. ~ up vt zerreißen

tear² /tɪə(r)/ n Träne f. ~ful a weinend. ~fully adv unter Tränen. ~gas n Tränengas nt

tease /tiːz/ vt necken

tea: ~-set n Teeservice nt. ~shop n Café nt. ~spoon n Teelöffel m. ~strainer n Teesieb nt

teat /tiːt/ n Zitze f; (on bottle) Sauger m

tea-towel n Geschirrtuch nt

technical /'teknɪkl/ a technisch; (specialized) fachlich. ~ity /-'kælɪtɪ/ n technisches Detail nt; (Jur) Formfehler m. ~ly adv technisch; (strictly) streng genommen. ~ term n Fachausdruck m

technician /tek'nɪʃn/ n Techniker m

technique /tek'niːk/ n Technik f

technological /teknə'lɒdʒɪkl/ a,
-ly adv technologisch

technology /tek'nɒlədʒɪ/ n Technologie f

teddy /'tedɪ/ n ∼ **[bear]** Teddybär m

tedious /'tiːdɪəs/ a langweilig

tedium /'tiːdɪəm/ n Langeweile f

teem /tiːm/ vi (rain) in Strömen gießen; **be ∼ing with** (full of) wimmeln von

teenage /'tiːneɪdʒ/ a Teenager-; ∼
boy/girl Junge m/Mädchen nt
im Teenageralter. ∼**r** n Teenager m

teens /tiːnz/ npl **die** ∼ **die** Teenagerjahre pl

teeny /'tiːnɪ/ a (-ier, -iest) winzig

teeter /'tiːtə(r)/ vi schwanken

teeth /tiːθ/ see **tooth**

teethe /tiːð/ vi zahnen. ∼**ing
troubles** npl (fig) Anfangsschwierigkeiten pl

teetotal /tiː'təʊtl/ a abstinent.
∼**ler** n Abstinenzler m

telecommunications /telɪkəmjuːnɪ'keɪʃnz/ npl Fernmeldewesen nt

telegram /'telɪgræm/ n Telegramm nt

telegraph /'telɪgrɑːf/ n Telegraf m. ∼**ic** /-'græfɪk/ a telegrafisch.
∼ **pole** n Telegrafenmast m

telepathy /tɪ'lepəθɪ/ n Telepathie f; **by** ∼ telepathisch

telephone /'telɪfəʊn/ n Telefon nt; **be on the** ∼ Telefon haben;
(be telephoning) telefonieren □ vt
anrufen □ vi telefonieren

telephone: ∼ **book** n Telefonbuch nt. ∼ **booth** n, ∼ **box** n Telefonzelle f. ∼ **directory** n
Telefonbuch nt. ∼ **number** n
Telefonnummer f

telephonist /tɪ'lefənɪst/ n Telefonist(in) m(f)

tele'photo /telɪ-/ a ∼ **lens** Teleobjektiv nt

teleprinter /'telɪ-/ n Fernschreiber m

telescop|e /'telɪskəʊp/ n Teleskop nt, Fernrohr nt. ∼**ic** /-'skɒpɪk/ a
teleskopisch; (collapsible) ausziehbar

televise /'telɪvaɪz/ vt im Fernsehen übertragen

television /'telɪvɪʒn/ n Fernsehen nt; **watch** ∼ fernsehen. ∼
set n Fernsehapparat m, Fernseher m

telex /'teleks/ n Telex nt □ vt telexen

tell /tel/ vt/i (pt/pp **told**) sagen
(s.o. jdm); (relate) erzählen;
(know) wissen; (distinguish) erkennen; ∼ **the time** die Uhr lesen; **time will** ∼ das wird man
erst sehen; **his age is beginning
to** ∼ sein Alter macht sich bemerkbar; **don't** ∼ **me** sag es mir
nicht; **you mustn't** ∼ du darfst
nichts sagen. ∼ **off** vt ausschimpfen

teller /'telə(r)/ n (cashier) Kassierer(in) m(f)

telly /'telɪ/ n (fam) = **television**

temerity /tɪ'merətɪ/ n Kühnheit f

temp /temp/ n (fam) Aushilfssekretärin f

temper /'tempə(r)/ n (disposition)
Naturell nt; (mood) Laune f;
(anger) Wut f; **lose one's** ∼ wütend werden □ vt (fig) mäßigen

temperament /'tempərəmənt/ n
Temperament nt. ∼**al** /-'mentl/ a
temperamentvoll; (moody) launisch

temperance /'tempərəns/ n
Mäßigung f; (abstinence) Abstinenz f

temperate /'tempərət/ a gemäßigt

temperature /'temprətʃə(r)/ n
Temperatur f; **have** or **run a** ∼
Fieber haben

tempest /'tempɪst/ n Sturm m.
∼**uous** /-'pestjʊəs/ a stürmisch

template /'templɪt/ n Schablone f

temple[1] /'templ/ n Tempel m

temple² n (Anat) Schläfe f

tempo /'tempəʊ/ n Tempo nt

temporary /'tempərərɪ/ a, **-ily** adv vorübergehend; (measure, building) provisorisch

tempt /tempt/ vt verleiten; (Relig) versuchen; herausfordern ⟨fate⟩; (entice) ⟨person⟩ locken; be **~ed** versucht sein (to zu); I am **~ed** by it es lockt mich. **~ation** /-'teɪʃn/ n Versuchung f. **~ing** a verlockend

ten /ten/ a zehn

tenable /'tenəbl/ a (fig) haltbar

tenaci|ous /tɪ'neɪʃəs/ a, **-ly** adv hartnäckig. **~ty** /-'næsɪtɪ/ n Hartnäckigkeit f

tenant /'tenənt/ n Mieter(in) m(f); (Comm) Pächter(in) m(f)

tend¹ /tend/ vt ⟨look after⟩ sich kümmern um

tend² vi **~ to do sth** dazu neigen, etw zu tun

tendency /'tendənsɪ/ n Tendenz f; (inclination) Neigung f

tender¹ /'tendə(r)/ n (Comm) Angebot nt; **legal ~** gesetzliches Zahlungsmittel nt □ vt anbieten; einreichen ⟨resignation⟩

tender² a zart; (loving) zärtlich; (painful) empfindlich. **~ly** adv zärtlich. **~ness** n Zartheit f; Zärtlichkeit f

tendon /'tendən/ n Sehne f

tenement /'tenəmənt/ n Mietshaus nt

tenet /'tenɪt/ n Grundsatz m

tenner /'tenə(r)/ n (fam) Zehnpfundschein m

tennis /'tenɪs/ n Tennis nt. **~-court** n Tennisplatz m

tenor /'tenə(r)/ n Tenor m

tense¹ /tens/ n (Gram) Zeit f

tense² a (-r, -st) gespannt □ vt anspannen ⟨muscle⟩

tension /'tenʃn/ n Spannung f

tent /tent/ n Zelt nt

tentacle /'tentəkl/ n Fangarm m

tentative /'tentətɪv/ a, **-ly** adv vorläufig; (hesitant) zaghaft

tenterhooks /'tentəhʊks/ npl be on **~** wie auf glühenden Kohlen sitzen

tenth /tenθ/ a zehnte(r,s) □ n Zehntel nt

tenuous /'tenjʊəs/ a (fig) schwach

tepid /'tepɪd/ a lauwarm

term /tɜ:m/ n Zeitraum m; (Sch) ≈ Halbjahr nt; (Univ) ≈ Semester nt; (expression) Ausdruck m; **~s** pl ⟨conditions⟩ Bedingungen f; **~ of office** Amtszeit f; **in the short/long ~** kurz-/langfristig; **be on good/bad ~s** gut miteinander auskommen; **come to ~s with** sich abfinden mit

terminal /'tɜ:mɪnl/ a End-; (Med) unheilbar □ n (Aviat) Terminal m; (of bus) Endstation f; (on battery) Pol m; (Computing) Terminal nt

terminat|e /'tɜ:mɪneɪt/ vt beenden; lösen ⟨contract⟩; unterbrechen ⟨pregnancy⟩ □ vi enden. **~ion** /-'neɪʃn/ n Beendigung f; (Med) Schwangerschaftsabbruch m

terminology /tɜ:mɪ'nɒlədʒɪ/ n Terminologie f

terminus /'tɜ:mɪnəs/ n (pl **-ni** /-naɪ/) Endstation f

terrace /'terəs/ n Terrasse f; (houses) Häuserreihe f; the **~s** (Sport) die [Steh]ränge pl. **~d house** n Reihenhaus nt

terrain /te'reɪn/ n Gelände nt

terrible /'terəbl/ a, **-bly** adv schrecklich

terrier /'terɪə(r)/ n Terrier m

terrific /tə'rɪfɪk/ a (fam) (excellent) sagenhaft; (huge) riesig

terri|fy /'terɪfaɪ/ vt (pt/pp **-ied**) Angst machen (+ dat); be **~fied** Angst haben. **~fying** a Furcht erregend

territorial /terɪ'tɔ:rɪəl/ a Territorial-

territory /'terɪtərɪ/ n Gebiet nt

terror /'terə(r)/ n [panische]
Angst f; (Pol) Terror m. **~ism**
/-ɪzm/ n Terrorismus m. **~ist**
/-ɪst/ n Terrorist m. **~ize** vt terrorisieren

terse /tɜːs/ a, **-ly** adv kurz, knapp

test /test/ n Test m; (Sch) Klassenarbeit f; **put to the ~** auf die Probe stellen □ vt prüfen; (examine) untersuchen (for auf + acc)

testament /'testəmənt/ n Testament nt; **Old/New T~** Altes/Neues Testament nt

testicle /'testɪkl/ n Hoden m

testify /'testɪfaɪ/ v (pt/pp -ied)
□ vt beweisen; **~ that** bezeugen,
dass □ vi aussagen; **~ to** bezeugen

testimonial /testɪ'məʊnɪəl/ n
Zeugnis nt

testimony /'testɪmənɪ/ n Aussage f

'test-tube n Reagenzglas nt. **~
'baby** n (fam) Retortenbaby nt

testy /'testɪ/ a gereizt

tetanus /'tetənəs/ n Tetanus m

tetchy /'tetʃɪ/ a gereizt

tether /'teðə(r)/ n **be at the end
of one's ~** am Ende seiner Kraft
sein □ vt anbinden

text /tekst/ n Text m. **~book** n
Lehrbuch nt

textile /'tekstaɪl/ a Textil- □ n **~s**
pl Textilien pl

texture /'tekstʃə(r)/ n Beschaffenheit f; (Tex) Struktur f

Thai /taɪ/ a thailändisch. **~land**
n Thailand nt

Thames /temz/ n Themse f

than /ðən, betont ðæn/ conj als;
older ~ me älter als ich

thank /θæŋk/ vt danken (+ dat);
~ you [very much] danke
[schön]. **~ful** a, **-ly** adv dankbar.
~less a undankbar

thanks /θæŋks/ npl Dank m; **~!**
(fam) danke! **~ to** dank (+ dat or
gen)

that /ðæt/ a & pron (pl **those**)
der/die/das; (pl) die; **~ one**
der/die/das da; **I'll take ~** ich
nehme den/die/das; **I don't like
those** die mag ich nicht; **~ is** das
heißt; **is ~ you?** bist du es? **who
is ~?** wer ist da? **with/after ~**
damit/danach; **like ~** so; **a man
like ~** so ein Mann; **~ is why**
deshalb; **~'s it!** genau! **all ~ I
know** alles was ich weiß; **the day
~ I saw him** an dem Tag, als ich
ihn sah □ adv so; **~ good/hot** so
gut/heiß □ conj dass

thatch /θætʃ/ n Strohdach nt.
~ed a strohgedeckt

thaw /θɔː/ n Tauwetter nt □ vt/i
auftauen; **it's ~ing** es taut

the /ðə, vor einem Vokal ðiː/ def
art der/die/das; (pl) die; **play ~
piano/violin** Klavier/Geige
spielen □ adv **~ more ~ better** je
mehr, desto besser; **all ~ better**
umso besser

theatre /'θɪətə(r)/ n Theater nt;
(Med) Operationssaal m

theatrical /θɪ'ætrɪkl/ a Theater-;
(showy) theatralisch

theft /θeft/ n Diebstahl m

their /ðeə(r)/ a ihr

theirs /ðeəz/ poss pron ihre(r);
ihrs; **a friend of ~** ein Freund
von ihnen; **those are ~** die gehören ihnen

them /ðem/ pron (acc) sie; (dat)
ihnen; **I know ~** ich kenne sie;
give ~ the money gib ihnen das
Geld

theme /θiːm/ n Thema nt

them'selves pron selbst; (refl)
sich; **by ~** allein

then /ðen/ adv damals; (at that time
in past) damals; **by ~** bis dahin;
since ~ seitdem; **before ~**
vorher; **from ~ on** von da an;
now and ~ dann und wann;
there and ~ auf der Stelle □ a
damalig

theolog|ian /θɪə'ləʊdʒɪən/ n
Theologe m. **~y** /-'ɒlədʒɪ/ n
Theologie f

theorem /'θɪərəm/ n Lehrsatz m

theoretical /θɪə'retɪkl/ a, **-ly** adv theoretisch

theory /'θɪərɪ/ n Theorie f; **in ~** theoretisch

therapeutic /θerə'pju:tɪk/ a therapeutisch

therap|ist /'θerəpɪst/ n Therapeut(in) m(f). **~y** n Therapie f

there /ðeə(r)/ adv da; (with movement) dahin, dorthin; **down/up ~** da unten/oben; **~ is/are** da ist/sind; (in existence) es gibt; **~ he/she is** da ist er/sie; **send/ take ~** hinschicken/-bringen ☐ int there, there! nun, nun!

there: **~abouts** adv da [in der Nähe]; **~abouts** (roughly) ungefähr. **~after** adv danach. **~by** adv dadurch. **~fore** /-fɔ:(r)/ adv deshalb, also

thermal /'θɜ:ml/ a Thermal-; **~ 'underwear** n Thermowäsche f

thermometer /θə'mɒmɪtə(r)/ n Thermometer m

Thermos (P) /'θɜ:məs/ n **~ [flask]** Thermosflasche (P) f

thermostat /'θɜ:məstæt/ n Thermostat m

these /ði:z/ see **this**

thesis /'θi:sɪs/ n (pl **-ses** /-si:z/) Dissertation f; (proposition) These f

they /ðeɪ/ pron sie; **~ say** (generalizing) man sagt

thick /θɪk/ a (-er, -est), **-ly** adv dick; (dense) dicht; (liquid) dickflüssig; (fam: stupid) dumm ☐ adv dick n **in the ~ of** mitten in (+ dat). **~en** vt dicker machen; eindicken (sauce) ☐ vi dicker werden; (fog:) dichter werden; (plot:) komplizierter werden. **~ness** n Dicke f; Dichte f; Dickflüssigkeit f

thick: **~set** a untersetzt. **~-'skinned** a (fam) dickfellig

thief /θi:f/ n (pl **thieves**) Dieb(in) m(f)

thieving /'θi:vɪŋ/ a diebisch ☐ n Stehlen nt

thigh /θaɪ/ n Oberschenkel m

thimble /'θɪmbl/ n Fingerhut m

thin /θɪn/ a (thinner, thinnest), **-ly** adv dünn ☐ adv dünn ☐ v (pt/pp thinned) ☐ vt verdünnen (liquid) ☐ vi sich lichten. **~ out** vt ausdünnen

thing /θɪŋ/ n Ding nt; (subject, affair) Sache f; **~s** pl (belongings) Sachen pl; **for one ~** erstens; **the right ~** das Richtige; **just the ~** genau das Richtige; **how are ~s?** wie geht's? **the latest ~** (fam) der letzte Schrei; **the best ~ would be** am besten wäre es

think /θɪŋk/ vt/i (pt/pp thought) denken (about/of an + acc); (believe) meinen; (consider) nachdenken; (regard as) halten für; **I ~ so** ich glaube schon; **what do you ~?** was meinen Sie? **what do you ~ of it?** was halten Sie davon? **~ better of it** es sich (dat) anders überlegen. **~ over** vt sich (dat) überlegen. **~ up** vt sich (dat) ausdenken

third /θɜ:d/ a dritte(r,s) ☐ n Drittel m. **~ly** adv drittens. **~-rate** a drittrangig

thirst /θɜ:st/ n Durst m. **~y** a, **-ily** adv durstig; **be ~y** Durst haben

thirteen /θɜ:'ti:n/ a dreizehn. **~th** a dreizehnte(r,s)

thirtieth /'θɜ:tɪɪθ/ a dreißigste(r,s)

thirty /'θɜ:tɪ/ a dreißig

this /ðɪs/ a (pl **these**) diese(r,s); (pl) diese; **~ one** diese(r,s) da; **I'll take ~** ich nehme diesen/diese/dieses; **~ evening/morning** heute Abend/Morgen; **~ days** heutzutage ☐ pron (pl these) dies, dies[es]; (pl) die, diese; **~ and that** dies und das; **~ or that** dieses oder das dies; **like ~ so**; **~ is Peter** das ist Peter; (Teleph) hier [spricht] Peter; **who is ~?** wer ist das? (Teleph, Amer) wer ist am Apparat?

thistle /'θɪsl/ n Distel f

thorn /θɔːn/ n Dorn m. **~y** a dornig

thorough /'θʌrə/ a gründlich

thorough: **~bred** n reinrassiges Tier nt; (horse) Rassepferd nt. **~fare** n Durchfahrtsstraße f; 'no **~fare'** 'keine Durchfahrt'

thorough|ly /'θʌrəlɪ/ adv gründlich; (completely) völlig; (extremely) äußerst. **~ness** n Gründlichkeit f

those /ðəuz/ see that

though /ðəu/ conj obgleich, obwohl; **as ~** als ob □ adv (fam) doch

thought /θɔːt/ see think □ n Gedanke m; (thinking) Denken nt. **~ful** a, **-ly** adv nachdenklich; (considerate) rücksichtsvoll. **~less** a, **-ly** adv gedankenlos

thousand /'θauznd/ a one/a **~** [ein]tausend □ n Tausend nt; **~s** of Tausende von. **~th** a tausendste(r,s) □ n Tausendstel nt

thrash /θræʃ/ vt verprügeln; (defeat) [vernichtend] schlagen. **~ about** vi sich herumwerfen; (fish:) zappeln. **~ out** vt ausdiskutieren

thread /θred/ n Faden m; (of screw) Gewinde nt □ vt einfädeln; auffädeln (beads); **~ one's way through** sich schlängeln durch. **~bare** a fadenscheinig

threat /θret/ n Drohung f; (danger) Bedrohung f

threaten /'θretn/ vt drohen (+ dat); (with weapon) bedrohen; **~ to do sth** drohen, etw zu tun; **~ s.o. with sth** jdm etw androhen □ vi drohen. **~ing** a, **-ly** adv drohend; (ominous) bedrohlich

three /θriː/ a drei. **~fold** a & adv dreifach. **~some** /-səm/ n Trio nt

thresh /θreʃ/ vt dreschen

threshold /'θreʃəuld/ n Schwelle f

threw /θruː/ see throw

thrift /θrɪft/ n Sparsamkeit f. **~y** a sparsam

thrill /θrɪl/ n Erregung f; (fam) Nervenkitzel m □ vt (excite) erregen; **be ~ed with** sich sehr freuen über (+ acc). **~er** n Thriller m. **~ing** a erregend

thrive /θraɪv/ vi (pt thrived or throve, pp thrived or thriven) /'θrɪvn/) gedeihen (on bei); (business:) florieren

throat /θrəut/ n Hals m; **sore ~** Halsschmerzen pl; **cut s.o.'s ~** jdm die Kehle durchschneiden

throb /θrɒb/ n Pochen nt □ vi (pt/pp throbbed) pochen; (vibrate) vibrieren

throes /θrəuz/ npl **in the ~ of** (fig) mitten in (+ dat)

thrombosis /θrɒm'bəusɪs/ n Thrombose f

throne /θrəun/ n Thron m

throng /θrɒŋ/ n Menge f

throttle /'θrɒtl/ vt erdrosseln

through /θruː/ prep durch (+ acc); (during) während (+ gen); (Amer: up to & including) bis einschließlich □ adv durch; **all ~** die ganze Zeit; **~ and ~** durch und durch; **wet ~** durch und durch nass; **read sth ~** etw durchlesen; **let/walk ~** durchlassen/-gehen □ a (train) durchgehend; **be ~** (finished) fertig sein; (Teleph) durch sein

throughout /θruː'aut/ prep **~ the country** im ganzen Land; **~ the night** die ganze Nacht durch □ adv ganz; (time) die ganze Zeit

throve /θrəuv/ see thrive

throw /θrəu/ n Wurf m □ vt (pt threw, pp thrown) werfen; schütten (liquid); betätigen (switch); abwerfen (rider); (fam: disconcert) aus der Fassung bringen; (fam) geben (party); **~ sth to s.o.** jdm etw zuwerfen; **~ sth at s.o.** etw nach jdm werfen; (pelt with) jdn mit etw bewerfen. **~ away** vt wegwerfen. **~ out** vt hinauswerfen; (~ away) wegwerfen; verwerfen (plan). **~ up**

vt hochwerfen □ *vi* (*fam*) sich übergeben

'throw-away *n* Wegwerf-

thrush /θrʌʃ/ *n* Drossel *f*

thrust /θrʌst/ *n* Stoß *m*; (*Phys*) Schub *m* □ *vt* (*pt/pp* **thrust**) stoßen; (*insert*) stecken; ~ [**up**]**on** aufbürden (s.o. jdm)

thud /θʌd/ *n* dumpfer Schlag *m*

thug /θʌg/ *n* Schläger *m*

thumb /θʌm/ *n* Daumen *m*; **rule of** ~ Faustregel *f*; **under s.o.'s** ~ unter jds Fuchtel □ *vt* ~ **a lift** (*fam*) per Anhalter fahren. ~**index** *n* Daumenregister *nt*. ~**tack** *n* (*Amer*) Reißzwecke *f*

thump /θʌmp/ *n* Schlag *m*; (*noise*) dumpfer Schlag *m* □ *vt* schlagen □ *vi* hämmern (**on** an/auf + *acc*); ⟨*heart*:⟩ pochen

thunder /ˈθʌndə(r)/ *n* Donner *m* □ *vi* donnern. ~**clap** *n* Donnerschlag *m*. ~**storm** *n* Gewitter *nt*. ~**y** *a* gewittrig

Thursday /ˈθɜːzdeɪ/ *n* Donnerstag *m*

thus /ðʌs/ *adv* so

thwart /θwɔːt/ *vt* vereiteln; ~ **s.o.** jdm einen Strich durch die Rechnung machen

thyme /taɪm/ *n* Thymian *m*

thyroid /ˈθaɪrɔɪd/ *n* Schilddrüse *f*

tiara /tɪˈɑːrə/ *n* Diadem *nt*

tick[1] /tɪk/ *n* on ~ (*fam*) auf Pump

tick[2] *n* (*sound*) Ticken *nt*; (*mark*) Häkchen *nt*; (*fam: instant*) Sekunde *f* □ *vi* ticken □ *vt* abhaken. ~ **off** *vt* abhaken; (*fam*) rüffeln. ~ **over** *vt* ⟨*engine*:⟩ im Leerlauf laufen

ticket /ˈtɪkɪt/ *n* Karte *f*; (*for bus, train*) Fahrschein *m*; (*Aviat*) Flugschein *m*; (*for lottery*) Los *nt*; (*for article deposited*) Schein *m*; (*label*) Schild *nt*; (*for library*) Lesekarte *f*; (*fine*) Strafzettel *m*. ~**collector** *n* Fahrkartenkontrolleur *m*. ~**office** *n* Fahrkartenschalter *m*; (*for entry*) Kasse *f*

tickle /ˈtɪkl/ *n* Kitzeln *nt* □ *vt/i* kitzeln. ~**lish** /ˈtɪklɪʃ/ *a* kitzlig

tidal /ˈtaɪdl/ *a* ⟨*river, harbour*⟩ Tide-. ~ **wave** *n* Flutwelle *f*

tiddly-winks /ˈtɪdlɪwɪŋks/ *n* Flohspiel *nt*

tide /taɪd/ *n* Gezeiten *pl*; (*of events*) Strom *m*; **the** ~ **is in/out** es ist Flut/Ebbe □ *vt* ~ **s.o. over** jdm über die Runden helfen

tidiness /ˈtaɪdɪnɪs/ *n* Ordentlichkeit *f*

tidy /ˈtaɪdɪ/ *a* (-**ier**, -**iest**), -**ily** *adv* ordentlich □ *vt* ~ [**up**] aufräumen; ~ **oneself up** sich zurechtmachen

tie /taɪ/ *n* Krawatte *f*; Schlips *m*; (*cord*) Schnur *f*; (*fig: bond*) Band *nt*; (*restriction*) Bindung *f*; (*Sport*) Unentschieden *nt*; (*in competition*) Punktgleichheit *f* □ *v* (*pres p* **tying**) □ *vt* binden; machen (*knot*) □ *vi* (*Sport*) unentschieden spielen; ⟨*have equal scores, votes*⟩ punktgleich sein; ~ **in with** passen zu. ~ **up** *vt* festbinden; verschnüren (*parcel*); fesseln (*person*); **be** ~**d up** (*busy*) beschäftigt sein

tier /tɪə(r)/ *n* Stufe *f*; (*of cake*) Etage *f*; (*in stadium*) Rang *m*

tiff /tɪf/ *n* Streit *m*, (*fam*) Krach *m*

tiger /ˈtaɪgə(r)/ *n* Tiger *m*

tight /taɪt/ *a* (-**er**, -**est**), -**ly** *adv* fest; (*taut*) straff; (*clothes*) eng; (*control*) streng; (*fam: drunk*) blau; **in a** ~ **corner** (*fam*) in der Klemme □ *adv* fest

tighten /ˈtaɪtn/ *vt* fester ziehen; straffen (*rope*); anziehen (*screw*); verschärfen (*control*) □ *vi* sich spannen

tight: ~**fisted** *a* knauserig. ~**rope** *n* Hochseil *nt*

tights /taɪts/ *npl* Strumpfhose *f*

tile /taɪl/ *n* Fliese *f*; (*on wall*) Kachel *f*; (*on roof*) [Dach]ziegel *m* □ *vt* mit Fliesen auslegen; kacheln (*wall*); decken (*roof*)

till[1] /tɪl/ *prep & conj* = **until**

till² n Kasse f

tiller /'tɪlə(r)/ n Ruderpinne f

tilt /tɪlt/ n Neigung f; **at full ~** mit voller Wucht □ vt kippen; [zur Seite] neigen ⟨head⟩ □ vi sich neigen

timber /'tɪmbə(r)/ n [Nutz]holz nt

time /taɪm/ n Zeit f; (occasion) Mal nt; (rhythm) Takt m; **~s** (Math) mal; **at any ~** jederzeit; **this ~** dieses Mal, diesmal; **at ~s** manchmal; **~ and again** immer wieder; **two at a ~** zwei auf einmal; **on ~** pünktlich; **in ~** rechtzeitig; (eventually) mit der Zeit; **in no ~** im Handumdrehen; **in a year's ~** in einem Jahr; **behind ~** verspätet; **behind the ~s** rückständig; **for the ~ being** vorläufig; **what is the ~?** wie spät ist es? wie viel Uhr ist es? **by the ~ we arrive** bis wir ankommen; **did you have a nice ~?** hat es dir gut gefallen? **have a good ~!** viel Vergnügen! □ vt stoppen ⟨race⟩; **be well ~d** gut abgepaßt sein

time: **~ bomb** n Zeitbombe f. **~ lag** n Zeitdifferenz f. **~less** a zeitlos. **~ly** a rechtzeitig. **~ switch** n Zeitschalter m. **~ table** n Fahrplan m; (Sch) Stundenplan m

timid /'tɪmɪd/ a, **-ly** adv scheu; (hesitant) zaghaft

timing /'taɪmɪŋ/ n Wahl f des richtigen Zeitpunkts; (Sport, Techn) Timing nt

tin /tɪn/ n Zinn nt; (container) Dose f □ vt (pt/pp **tinned**) in Dosen od Büchsen konservieren. **~ foil** n Stanniol nt; (Culin) Alufolie f

tinge /tɪndʒ/ n Hauch m □ vt **~d with** mit einer Spur von

tingle /'tɪŋgl/ n kribbeln

tinker /'tɪŋkə(r)/ vi herumbasteln (**with** an + dat)

tinkle /'tɪŋkl/ n Klingeln nt □ vi klingeln

tinned /tɪnd/ a Dosen-, Büchsen-

'tin opener n Dosen-/Büchsenöffner m

'tinpot a (pej) ⟨firm⟩ schäbig

tinsel /'tɪnsl/ n Lametta nt

tint /tɪnt/ n Farbton m □ vt tönen

tiny /'taɪnɪ/ a (**-ier, -iest**) winzig

tip¹ /tɪp/ n Spitze f

tip² n (money) Trinkgeld nt; (advice) Rat m, (fam) Tipp m; (for rubbish) Müllhalde f □ v (pt/pp **tipped**) □ vt (tilt) kippen; (reward) Trinkgeld geben (**s.o.** jdm) □ vi kippen. **~ off** vt **s.o. off** jdm einen Hinweis geben. **~ out** vt auskippen. **~ over** vt/i umkippen

'tip-off n Hinweis m

tipped /tɪpt/ a Filter-

tipsy /'tɪpsɪ/ a (fam) beschwipst

tiptoe /'tɪptəʊ/ n **on ~** auf Zehenspitzen

tiptop /tɪp'tɒp/ a (fam) erstklassig

tire /'taɪə(r)/ vt/i ermüden. **~d** a müde; **be ~d of sth** etw satt haben; **~d out** [völlig] erschöpft. **~less** a, **-ly** adv unermüdlich. **~some** /-səm/ a lästig

tiring /'taɪrɪŋ/ a ermüdend

tissue /'tɪʃu:/ n Gewebe nt; (handkerchief) Papiertaschentuch nt. **~-paper** n Seidenpapier nt

tit¹ /tɪt/ n (bird) Meise f

tit² n **~ for tat** wie du mir, so ich dir

'titbit n Leckerbissen m

titilate /'tɪtɪleɪt/ vt erregen

title /'taɪtl/ n Titel m. **~-role** n Titelrolle f

tittle-tattle /'tɪtltætl/ n Klatsch m

titular /'tɪtjʊlə(r)/ a nominell

to /tu:, unbetont tə/ prep zu (+ dat); (with place, direction) nach; (to cinema, theatre) in (+ acc); (to wedding, party) auf (+ acc); (address, send, fasten) an (+ acc); (per) pro; (up to, until) bis; **to the**

station zum Bahnhof; **to Germany/Switzerland** nach Deutschland/ in die Schweiz; **to the toilet/one's room** auf die Toilette/sein Zimmer; **to the office/an exhibition** ins Büro/ in eine Ausstellung; **to university** auf die Universität; **twenty/quarter to eight** zwanzig/Viertel vor acht; **5 to 6 pounds** 5 bis 6 Pfund; **to the end** bis zum Schluss; **to this day** bis heute; **to the best of my knowledge** nach meinem besten Wissen; **give/say sth to s.o.** jdm etw geben/sagen; **go/come to s.o.** zu jdm gehen/kommen; **I've never been to Berlin** ich war noch nie in Berlin; **there's nothing to it** es ist nichts dabei □ *verbal construction* to go gehen; **to stay** bleiben; **want to/have to** go gehen wollen/ müssen; **be easy/difficult to forget** leicht/schwer zu vergessen sein; **too ill/tired to go** zu krank/müde, um zu gehen; **he did it to annoy me** er tat es, um mich zu ärgern; **you have to** du musst; **I don't want to** ich will nicht; **I'd love to** gern; **I forgot to** ich habe es vergessen; **he wants to be a teacher** er will Lehrer werden; **live to be 90** 90 werden; **he was the last to arrive** er kam als Letzter; **to be honest** ehrlich gesagt □ *adv* **pull to** anlehnen; **to and fro** hin und her

toad /təʊd/ *n* Kröte *f*. **~stool** *n* Giftpilz *m*

toast /təʊst/ *n* Toast *m* □ *vt* toasten (*bread*); (*drink* ~ *a* ~ *to*) trinken auf (+ *acc*). **~er** *n* Toaster *m*

tobacco /tə'bækəʊ/ *n* Tabak *m*. **~nist's [shop]** *n* Tabakladen *m*

toboggan /tə'bɒgən/ *n* Schlitten *m* □ *vi* Schlitten fahren

today /tə'deɪ/ *n* & *adv* heute; **~ week** heute in einer Woche; **~'s paper** die heutige Zeitung

toddler /'tɒdlə(r)/ *n* Kleinkind *nt*

to-do /tə'du:/ *n* (*fam*) Getue *nt*, Theater *nt*

toe /təʊ/ *n* Zeh *m*; (*of footwear*) Spitze *f* □ *vt* **~ the line** spuren. **~nail** *n* Zehennagel *m*

toffee /'tɒfɪ/ *n* Karamell *m* & *nt*

together /tə'geðə(r)/ *adv* zusammen; (*at the same time*) gleichzeitig

toil /tɔɪl/ *n* [harte] Arbeit *f* □ *vi* schwer arbeiten

toilet /'tɔɪlɪt/ *n* Toilette *f*. **~ bag** *n* Kulturbeutel *m*. **~ paper** *n* Toilettenpapier *nt*

toiletries /'tɔɪlɪtrɪz/ *npl* Toilettenartikel *pl*

toilet: **~ roll** *n* Rolle *f* Toilettenpapier. **~ water** *n* Toilettenwasser *nt*

token /'təʊkən/ *n* Zeichen *nt*; (*counter*) Marke *f*; (*voucher*) Gutschein *m* □ *attrib* symbolisch

told /təʊld/ *see* **tell** □ *a* **all ~** insgesamt

tolerable /'tɒlərəbl/ *a*, **-bly** *adv* erträglich; (*not bad*) leidlich

toleran|ce /'tɒlərəns/ *n* Toleranz *f*. **~t** *a*, **-ly** *adv* tolerant

tolerate /'tɒləreɪt/ *vt* dulden, tolerieren; (*bear*) ertragen

toll /təʊl/ *n* Gebühr *f*; (*for road*) Maut *f* (*Aust*); **death ~** Zahl *f* der Todesopfer; **take a heavy ~** einen hohen Tribut fordern

toll[2] *vi* läuten

tom /tɒm/ *n* (*cat*) Kater *m*

tomato /tə'mɑ:təʊ/ *n* (*pl* **-es**) Tomate *f*. **~ purée** *n* Tomatenmark *nt*

tomb /tu:m/ *n* Grabmal *nt*

tomboy /'tɒm-/ *n* Wildfang *m*

'tombstone *n* Grabstein *m*

'tom-cat *n* Kater *m*

tome /təʊm/ *n* dicker Band *m*

tomfoolery /tɒm'fu:lərɪ/ *n* Blödsinn *m*

tomorrow /tə'mɒrəʊ/ n & adv morgen; ~ **morning** morgen früh; **the day after** ~ übermorgen; **see you** ~! bis morgen!

ton /tʌn/ n Tonne f; ~**s of** (fam) jede Menge

tone /təʊn/ n Ton m; (colour) Farbton m □ vt ~ **down** dämpfen; (fig) mäßigen. ~ **up** vt kräftigen; straffen ⟨muscles⟩

tongs /tɒŋz/ npl Zange f

tongue /tʌŋ/ n Zunge f; ~ **in cheek** (fam) nicht ernst. ~**twister** m Zungenbrecher m

tonic /'tɒnɪk/ n Tonikum nt; (for hair) Haarwasser nt; (fig) Wohltat f; ~ [**water**] Tonic nt

tonight /tə'naɪt/ n & adv heute Nacht; (evening) heute Abend

tonne /tʌn/ n Tonne f

tonsil /'tɒnsl/ n (Anat) Mandel f. ~**litis** /-sə'laɪtɪs/ n Mandelentzündung f

too /tu:/ adv zu; (also) auch; ~ **much/little** zu viel/zu wenig

took /tʊk/ see **take**

tool /tu:l/ n Werkzeug nt; (for gardening) Gerät nt

toot /tu:t/ n Hupsignal nt □ vi tuten; (Auto) hupen

tooth /tu:θ/ n (pl **teeth**) Zahn m

tooth: ~**ache** n Zahnschmerzen pl. ~**brush** n Zahnbürste f. ~**less** a zahnlos. ~**paste** n Zahnpasta f. ~**pick** n Zahnstocher m

top¹ /tɒp/ n (toy) Kreisel m

top² n oberer Teil m; (apex) Spitze f; (summit) Gipfel m; (Sch) Erste(r) m/f; (top part or half) Oberteil nt; (head) Kopfende nt; (of road) oberes Ende nt; (upper surface) Oberfläche f; (lid) Deckel m; (of bottle) Verschluss m; (garment) Top nt; **at the/on** ~ oben; **on** ~ **of** oben auf (+ dat/acc); oben ~ **of that** (besides) obendrein; **from** ~ **to bottom** von oben bis unten □ a oberste(r,s); (best) höchste(r,s); (best) beste(r,s) □ vt (pt/pp **topped**) an erster Stelle stehen auf (+ dat) ⟨list⟩; (exceed)

übersteigen; (remove the ~ of) die Spitze abschneiden von. ~ **up** vt auffüllen, auffüllen

top: ~ **hat** n Zylinder[hut] m. ~**heavy** a kopflastig

topic /'tɒpɪk/ n Thema nt. ~**al** a aktuell

top: ~**less** a & adv oben ohne. ~**most** a oberste(r,s)

topple /'tɒpl/ vt/i umstürzen. ~ **off** vi stürzen

top-secret a streng geheim

topsy-turvy /tɒpsɪ'tɜːvɪ/ adv völlig durcheinander

torch /tɔːtʃ/ n Taschenlampe f; (flaming) Fackel f

tore /tɔː(r)/ see **tear¹**

torment¹ /'tɔːment/ n Qual f

torment² /tɔː'ment/ vt quälen

torn /tɔːn/ see **tear¹** □ a zerrissen

tornado /tɔː'neɪdəʊ/ n (pl -es) Wirbelsturm m

torpedo /tɔː'piːdəʊ/ n (pl -es) Torpedo m □ vt torpedieren

torrent /'tɒrənt/ n reißender Strom m. ~**ial** /tə'renʃl/ a ⟨rain⟩ wolkenbruchartig

torso /'tɔːsəʊ/ n Rumpf m; (Art) Torso m

tortoise /'tɔːtəs/ n Schildkröte f. ~**shell** n Schildpatt nt

tortuous /'tɔːtjʊəs/ a verschlungen; (fig) umständlich

torture /'tɔːtʃə(r)/ n Folter f; (fig) Qual f □ vt foltern; (fig) quälen

toss /tɒs/ vt werfen; (into the air) hochwerfen; (shake) schütteln; (unseat) abwerfen; mischen ⟨salad⟩; wenden ⟨pancake⟩; ~ **a coin** mit einer Münze losen □ vi ~ **and turn** (in bed) sich [schlaflos] im Bett wälzen. ~ **up** vi [mit einer Münze] losen

tot¹ /tɒt/ n kleines Kind nt; (fam: of liquor) Gläschen nt

tot² vt (pt/pp **totted**) ~ **up** (fam) zusammenzählen

total /'təʊtl/ a gesamt; (complete) völlig, total □ n Gesamtzahl f; (sum) Gesamtsumme f □ vt *(pt/pp* **totalled)** zusammenzählen; *(amount to)* sich belaufen auf (+ *dat)*

totalitarian /təʊtælɪˈteərɪən/ *a* totalitär

totally /ˈtəʊtəlɪ/ *adv* völlig, total

totter /ˈtɒtə(r)/ *vi* taumeln; *(rock)* schwanken. **∼y** *a* wackelig

touch /tʌtʃ/ *n* Berührung *f*; *(sense)* Tastsinn *m*; *(Mus)* Anschlag *m*; *(contact)* Kontakt *m*; *(trace)* Spur *f*; *(fig)* Anflug *m*; **get/be in ∼** sich in Verbindung setzen/in Verbindung stehen **(with** mit) □ *vt* berühren; *(get hold of)* anfassen; *(lightly)* tippen auf/an (+ *acc)*; *(brush against)* streifen [gegen]; *(reach)* erreichen; *(equal)* herankommen an (+ *acc; fig: move)* rühren; anrühren *(food, subject)*; **don't ∼ that!** fass das nicht an! **∼ on** *vt* sich berühren. **∼ on** *(fig)* berühren. **∼ down** *vi (Aviat)* landen. **∼ up** *vt* ausbessern

touch|ing /ˈtʌtʃɪŋ/ *a* rührend. **∼y** *a* empfindlich; *(subject)* heikel

tough /tʌf/ *a* (-er, -est) zäh; *(severe, harsh)* hart; *(difficult)* schwierig; *(durable)* strapazierfähig

toughen /ˈtʌfn/ *vt* härten; **∼ up** abhärten

tour /tʊə(r)/ *n* Reise *f*, Tour *f*; *(of building, town)* Besichtigung *f*; *(Theat, Sport)* Tournee *f*; *(of duty)* Dienstzeit *f* □ *vt* fahren durch; besichtigen *(building)* □ *vi* herumreisen

touris|m /ˈtʊərɪzm/ *n* Tourismus *m*, Fremdenverkehr *m*. **∼t** /-rɪst/ *n* Tourist(in) *m(f)* □ *attrib* Touristen-. **∼t office** *n* Fremdenverkehrsbüro *nt*

tournament /ˈtʊənəmənt/ *n* Turnier *nt*

'tour operator *n* Reiseveranstalter *m*

tousle /ˈtaʊzl/ *vt* zerzausen

tout /taʊt/ *n* Anreißer *m*; *(ticket* **∼)** Kartenschwarzhändler *m* □ *vi* **∼ for customers** Kunden werben

tow /təʊ/ *n* **give s.o./a car a ∼** jdn/ein Auto abschleppen; **'on ∼'** 'wird geschleppt'; **in ∼** *(fam)* im Schlepptau □ *vt* schleppen; ziehen *(trailer)*. **∼ away** *vt* abschleppen

toward[s] /təˈwɔːd(z)/ *prep* zu (+ *dat)*; *(with time)* gegen (+ *acc)*; *(with respect to)* gegenüber (+ *dat)*

towel /ˈtaʊəl/ *n* Handtuch *nt*. **∼ling** *n (Tex)* Frottee *nt*

tower /ˈtaʊə(r)/ *n* Turm *m* □ *vi* **∼ above** überragen. **∼ block** *n* Hochhaus *nt*. **∼ing** *a* hoch aufragend

town /taʊn/ *n* Stadt *f*. **∼ 'hall** *n* Rathaus *nt*

tow: **∼path** *n* Treidelpfad *m*. **∼ rope** *n* Abschleppseil *nt*

toxic /ˈtɒksɪk/ *a* giftig. **∼ 'waste** *n* Giftmüll *m*

toxin /ˈtɒksɪn/ *n* Gift *nt*

toy /tɔɪ/ *n* Spielzeug *nt* □ *vi* **∼ with** spielen mit; stochern in (+ *dat) (food)*. **∼shop** *n* Spielwarengeschäft *nt*

trac|e /treɪs/ *n* Spur *f* □ *vt* folgen (+ *dat); (find)* finden; *(draw)* zeichnen; *(with tracing-paper)* durchpausen. **∼ing-paper** *n* Pauspapier *nt*

track /træk/ *n* Spur *f*; *(path)* [unbefestigter] Weg *m*; *(Sport)* Bahn *f*; *(Rail)* Gleis *nt*; **keep ∼ of** im Auge behalten □ *vt* verfolgen. **∼ down** *vt* aufspüren; *(find)* finden

'tracksuit *n* Trainingsanzug *m*

tract¹ /trækt/ *n (land)* Gebiet *nt*

tract² *n (pamphlet)* [Flug]schrift *f*

tractor /ˈtræktə(r)/ *n* Traktor *m*

trade /treɪd/ *n* Handel *m*; *(line of business)* Gewerbe *nt*; *(business)* Geschäft *nt*; *(craft)* Handwerk *nt*; **by ∼** von Beruf □ *vt* tauschen; **∼**

in ⟨give in part exchange⟩ in Zahlung geben □ vi handeln (**in** mit)

'**trade mark** n Warenzeichen nt

trader /'treɪdə(r)/ n Händler m

trade: ~ **union** n Gewerkschaft f. ~ '**unionist** n Gewerkschaftler(in) m(f)

trading /'treɪdɪŋ/ n Handel m. ~ **estate** n Gewerbegebiet nt. ~ **stamp** n Rabattmarke f

tradition /trə'dɪʃn/ n Tradition f. ~**al** a, **-ly** adv traditionell

traffic /'træfɪk/ n Verkehr m; ⟨trading⟩ Handel m □ vi handeln (**in** mit)

traffic: ~ **circle** n (Amer) Kreisverkehr m. ~ **jam** n [Verkehrs]stau m. ~ **lights** npl [Verkehrs]ampel f. ~ **warden** n ≈ Hilfspolizist m; ⟨woman⟩ Politesse f

tragedy /'trædʒədɪ/ n Tragödie f

tragic /'trædʒɪk/ a, **-ally** adv tragisch

trail /treɪl/ n Spur f; ⟨path⟩ Weg m, Pfad m □ vi schleifen; ⟨plant:⟩ sich ranken; ~ [**behind**] zurückbleiben; (Sport) zurückliegen □ vt verfolgen, folgen (+ dat); ⟨drag⟩ schleifen

trailer /'treɪlə(r)/ n (Auto) Anhänger m; (Amer: caravan) Wohnwagen m; ⟨film⟩ Vorschau f

train /treɪn/ n Zug m; ⟨of dress⟩ Schleppe f; ~ **of thought** Gedankengang m □ vt ausbilden; (Sport) trainieren; ⟨aim⟩ richten auf (+ acc); erziehen ⟨child⟩; abrichten/⟨to do tricks⟩ dressieren ⟨animal⟩; ziehen ⟨plant⟩ □ vi eine Ausbildung machen; (Sport) trainieren. ~**ed** a ausgebildet

trainee /treɪ'niː/ n Auszubildende(r) m/f; (Techn) Praktikant(in) m(f)

train|er /'treɪnə(r)/ n (Sport) Trainer m; ⟨in circus⟩ Dompteur m; ~**ers** pl Trainingsschuhe pl. ~**ing** n Ausbildung f; (Sport) Training nt; ⟨of animals⟩ Dressur f

traipse /treɪps/ vi (fam) latschen

trait /treɪt/ n Eigenschaft f

traitor /'treɪtə(r)/ n Verräter m

tram /træm/ n Straßenbahn f. ~**lines** npl Straßenbahnschienen pl

tramp /træmp/ n Landstreicher m; ⟨hike⟩ Wanderung f □ vi stapfen; ⟨walk⟩ marschieren

trample /'træmpl/ vt/i trampeln (**on** auf + acc)

trampoline /'træmpəliːn/ n Trampolin nt

trance /trɑːns/ n Trance f

tranquil /'træŋkwɪl/ a ruhig. ~**lity** /-'kwɪlətɪ/ n Ruhe f

tranquillizer /'træŋkwɪlaɪzə(r)/ n Beruhigungsmittel nt

transact /træn'zækt/ vt abwickeln. ~**ion** /-ækʃn/ n Transaktion f

transcend /træn'send/ vt übersteigen

transcript /'trænskrɪpt/ n Abschrift f; ⟨of official proceedings⟩ Protokoll nt. ~**ion** /-'skrɪpʃn/ n Abschrift f

transept /'trænsept/ n Querschiff nt

transfer[1] /'trænsfɜː(r)/ n (see **transfer**[2]) Übertragung f; Verlegung f; Versetzung f; Überweisung f; (Sport) Transfer m; ⟨design⟩ Abziehbild nt

transfer[2] /træns'fɜː(r)/ v ⟨pt/pp **transferred**⟩ □ vt übertragen; verlegen ⟨firm, prisoners⟩; versetzen ⟨employee⟩; überweisen ⟨money⟩; (Sport) transferieren □ vi [über]wechseln; ⟨when travelling⟩ umsteigen. ~**able** /-əbl/ a übertragbar

transform /træns'fɔːm/ vt verwandeln. ~**ation** /-fə'meɪʃn/ n Verwandlung f. ~**er** n Transformator m

transfusion /træns'fjuːʒn/ n Transfusion f

transient /'trænzɪənt/ a kurzlebig; ⟨life⟩ kurz

transistor /træn'zɪstə(r)/ n Transistor m

transit /'trænsɪt/ n Transit m; (of goods) Transport m; **in ~** (goods) auf dem Transport

transition /træn'sɪʒn/ n Übergang m. **~al** a Übergangs-

transitive /'trænsɪtɪv/ a, **-ly** adv transitiv

transitory /'trænsɪtərɪ/ a vergänglich; (life) kurz

translat|e /træns'leɪt/ vt übersetzen. **~ion** n Übersetzung f. **~or** n Übersetzer(in) m(f)

translucent /trænz'luːsnt/ a durchscheinend

transmission /trænz'mɪʃn/ n Übertragung f

transmit /trænz'mɪt/ vt (pt/pp transmitted) übertragen. **~ter** n Sender m

transparen|cy /træns'pærənsɪ/ n (Phot) Dia nt. **~t** a durchsichtig

transpire /træn'spaɪə(r)/ vi sich herausstellen; (fam: happen) passieren

transplant¹ /'trænsplɑːnt/ n Verpflanzung f, Transplantation f

transplant² /træns'plɑːnt/ vt umpflanzen; (Med) verpflanzen

transport¹ /'trænspɔːt/ n Transport m

transport² /træn'spɔːt/ vt transportieren. **~ation** /-'teɪʃn/ n Transport m

transpose /træns'pəʊz/ vt umstellen

transvestite /træns'vestaɪt/ n Transvestit m

trap /træp/ n Falle f; (fam: mouth) Klappe f; **pony and ~** Einspänner m ● vt (pt/pp trapped) [mit einer Falle] fangen; (jam) einklemmen; **be ~ped** festsitzen; (shut in) eingeschlossen sein; (cut off) abgeschnitten sein. **~door** n Falltür f

trapeze /trə'piːz/ n Trapez nt

trash /træʃ/ n Schund m; (rubbish) Abfall m; (nonsense) Quatsch m. **~can** n (Amer) Mülleimer m. **~y** a Schund-

trauma /'trɔːmə/ n Trauma nt. **~tic** /-'mætɪk/ a traumatisch

travel /'trævl/ n Reisen nt ● v (pt/pp travelled) ● vi reisen; (go in vehicle) fahren; (light, sound:) sich fortpflanzen; (Techn) sich bewegen ● vt bereisen; fahren (distance). **~ agency** n Reisebüro nt. **~ agent** n Reisebürokaufmann m

traveller /'trævələ(r)/ n Reisende(r) m/f; (Comm) Vertreter m; **~s** pl (gypsies) Zigeuner pl. **~'s cheque** n Reisescheck m

trawler /'trɔːlə(r)/ n Fischdampfer m

tray /treɪ/ n Tablett nt; (for baking) [Back]blech nt; (for documents) Ablagekorb m

treacher|ous /'tretʃərəs/ a treulos; (dangerous, deceptive) tückisch. **~y** n Verrat m

treacle /'triːkl/ n Sirup m

tread /tred/ n Schritt m; (step) Stufe f; (of tyre) Profil n ● v (pt trod, pp trodden) ● vi (walk) gehen; **~ on/in** treten auf/ in (+ acc) ● vt treten

treason /'triːzn/ n Verrat m

treasure /'treʒə(r)/ n Schatz m ● vt in Ehren halten. **~r** n Kassenwart m

treasury /'treʒərɪ/ n Schatzkammer f; **the T~** das Finanzministerium

treat /triːt/ n [besonderes] Vergnügen n; **give s.o. a ~** jdm etwas Besonderes bieten ● vt behandeln; **~ s.o. to sth** jdm etw spendieren

treatise /'triːtɪz/ n Abhandlung f

treatment /'triːtmənt/ n Behandlung f

treaty /'triːtɪ/ n Vertrag m

treble /'trebl/ a dreifach; **~ the amount** dreimal so viel ● n (Mus) Diskant m; (voice) Sopran m ● vt

verdreifachen □ *vi* sich verdreifachen. ~ **clef** *n* Violinschlüssel
m

tree /triː/ *n* Baum *m*

trek /trek/ *n* Marsch *m* □ *vi (pt/pp*
trekked) latschen

trellis /ˈtrelɪs/ *n* Gitter *nt*

tremble /ˈtrembl/ *vi* zittern

tremendous /trɪˈmendəs/ *a*, **-ly**
adv gewaltig; *(fam: excellent)*
großartig

tremor /ˈtremə(r)/ *n* Zittern *nt*;
[earth] ~ Beben *nt*

trench /trentʃ/ *n* Graben *m*; *(Mil)*
Schützengraben *m*

trend /trend/ *n* Tendenz *f*;
(fashion) Trend *m*. ~**y** *a* (**-ier**,
-iest) *(fam)* modisch

trepidation /trepɪˈdeɪʃn/ *n* Be-
klommenheit *f*

trespass /ˈtrespəs/ *vi* ~ **on** unerlaubt betreten. ~**er** *n* Unbe-
fugte(r) *m/f*

trial /ˈtraɪəl/ *n (Jur)* [Gerichts]-
verfahren *nt*, Prozess *m*; *(test)*
Probe *f*; *(ordeal)* Prüfung *f*; **be on**
~ auf Probe sein; *(Jur)* angeklagt
sein (**for** wegen); **by** ~ **and error**
durch Probieren

triangle /ˈtraɪæŋgl/ *n* Dreieck *nt*;
(Mus) Triangel *m*. ~**ular**
/-ˈæŋgjʊlə(r)/ *a* dreieckig

tribe /traɪb/ *n* Stamm *m*

tribulation /trɪbjʊˈleɪʃn/ *n*
Kummer *m*

tribunal /traɪˈbjuːnl/ *n*
Schiedsgericht *nt*

tributary /ˈtrɪbjʊtərɪ/ *n* Neben-
fluss *m*

tribute /ˈtrɪbjuːt/ *n* Tribut *m*; **pay**
~ Tribut zollen (**to** *dat*)

trice /traɪs/ *n* **in a** ~ im Nu

trick /trɪk/ *n* Trick *m*; *(joke)*
Streich *m*; *(Cards)* Stich *m*;
(feat of skill) Kunststück *nt*; **that
should do the** ~ *(fam)* damit
dürfte es klappen □ *vt* täuschen;
(fam) hereinlegen

trickle /ˈtrɪkl/ *vi* rinnen

trick|ster /ˈtrɪkstə(r)/ *n*
Schwindler *m*. ~**y** *a* (**-ier**, **-iest**)
a schwierig

tricycle /ˈtraɪsɪkl/ *n* Dreirad *nt*

tried /traɪd/ *see* **try**

trifle /ˈtraɪfl/ *n* Kleinigkeit *f*;
(Culin) Trifle *nt*. ~**ing** *a* unbedeutend

trigger /ˈtrɪgə(r)/ *n* Abzug *m*; *(fig)*
Auslöser *m* □ *vt* ~ **[off]** auslösen

trigonometry /trɪgəˈnɒmɪtrɪ/ *n*
Trigonometrie *f*

trim /trɪm/ *a* (**trimmer**, **trim-
mest**) gepflegt □ *n (cut)* Nach-
schneiden *nt*; *(decoration)*
Verzierung *f*; *(condition)* Zustand
m □ *vt* schneiden; *(decorate)* besetzen; *(Naut)* trimmen. ~**ming**
n Besatz *m*; ~**mings** *pl (accessories)* Zubehör *nt*; *(decorations)* Ver-
zierungen *pl*; **with all the**
~**mings** mit allem Drum und
Dran

Trinity /ˈtrɪnətɪ/ *n* **the [Holy]** ~
die [Heilige] Dreieinigkeit *f*

trinket /ˈtrɪŋkɪt/ *n* Schmuck-
gegenstand *m*

trio /ˈtriːəʊ/ *n* Trio *nt*

trip /trɪp/ *n* Reise *f*; *(excursion)*
Ausflug *m* □ *v (pt/pp* **tripped***)*
□ *vt* ~ s.o. **up** jdm ein Bein
stellen □ *vi* stolpern (**on/over**
über + *acc*)

tripe /traɪp/ *n* Kaldaunen *pl*; *(nonsense)* Quatsch *m*

triple /ˈtrɪpl/ *a* dreifach □ *vt*
verdreifachen □ *vi* sich verdreifachen

triplets /ˈtrɪplɪts/ *npl* Drillinge *pl*

triplicate /ˈtrɪplɪkət/ *n* **in** ~ in
dreifacher Ausfertigung

tripod /ˈtraɪpɒd/ *n* Stativ *nt*

tripper /ˈtrɪpə(r)/ *n* Ausflügler *m*

trite /traɪt/ *a* banal

triumph /ˈtraɪʌmf/ *n* Triumph *m*
□ *vi* triumphieren (**over** über +
acc). ~**ant** /-ˈʌmfnt/ *a*, **-ly** *adv*
triumphierend

trivial /ˈtrɪvɪəl/ *a* belanglos. ~**ity**
/-ˈælətɪ/ *n* Belanglosigkeit *f*

trod, trodden /trɒd, 'trɒdn/ *see* **tread**

trolley /'trɒlɪ/ *n* (*for serving food*) Servierwagen *m*; (*for shopping*) Einkaufswagen *m*; (*for luggage*) Kofferkuli *m*; (*Amer: tram*) Straßenbahn *f*. **~ bus** *n* O-Bus *m*

trombone /trɒm'bəʊn/ *n* Posaune *f*

troop /truːp/ *n* Schar *f*; **~s** *pl* Truppen *pl* □ *vi* **~ in/out** hinein-/hinausströmen

trophy /'trəʊfɪ/ *n* Trophäe *f*; (*in competition*) Pokal *m*

tropic /'trɒpɪk/ *n* Wendekreis *m*; **~s** *pl* Tropen *pl*. **~al** *a* tropisch; ⟨*fruit*⟩ Süd-

trot /trɒt/ *n* Trab *m* □ *vi* (*pt/pp* **trotted**) traben

trouble /'trʌbl/ *n* Ärger *m*; (*difficulties*) Schwierigkeiten *pl*; (*inconvenience*) Mühe *f*; (*conflict*) Unruhe *f*; (*Med*) Beschwerden *pl*; (*Techn*) Probleme *pl*; **get into ~** Ärger bekommen; **take ~** sich (*dat*) Mühe geben □ *vt* (*disturb*) stören; (*worry*) beunruhigen □ *vi* sich bemühen. **~-maker** *n* Unruhestifter *m*. **~some** /-səm/ *a* schwierig; ⟨*flies, cough*⟩ lästig

trough /trɒf/ *n* Trog *m*

trounce /traʊns/ *vt* vernichtend schlagen; (*thrash*) verprügeln

troupe /truːp/ *n* Truppe *f*

trousers /'traʊzəz/ *npl* Hose *f*

trousseau /'truːsəʊ/ *n* Aussteuer *f*

trout /traʊt/ *n inv* Forelle *f*

trowel /'traʊəl/ *n* Kelle *f*; (*for gardening*) Pflanzkelle *f*

truant /'truːənt/ *n* **play ~** die Schule schwänzen

truce /truːs/ *n* Waffenstillstand *m*

truck /trʌk/ *n* Last[kraft]wagen *m*; (*Rail*) Güterwagen *m*

truculent /'trʌkjʊlənt/ *a* aufsässig

trudge /trʌdʒ/ *n* [mühseliger] Marsch *m* □ *vi* latschen

true /truː/ *a* (*-r, -st*) wahr; (*loyal*) treu; (*genuine*) echt; **come ~** in Erfüllung gehen; **is that ~?** stimmt das?

truism /'truːɪzm/ *n* Binsenwahrheit *f*

truly /'truːlɪ/ *adv* wirklich; (*faithfully*) treu; **Yours ~** Hochachtungsvoll

trump /trʌmp/ *n* (*Cards*) Trumpf *m* □ *vt* übertrumpfen. **~ up** *vt* (*fam*) erfinden

trumpet /'trʌmpɪt/ *n* Trompete *f*. **~er** *n* Trompeter *m*

truncheon /'trʌntʃn/ *n* Schlagstock *m*

trundle /'trʌndl/ *vt/i* rollen

trunk /trʌŋk/ *n* [Baum]stamm *m*; (*body*) Rumpf *m*; (*of elephant*) Rüssel *m*; (*for travelling*) [Überseekoffer *m*; (*for storage*) Truhe *f*; (*Amer: of car*) Kofferraum *m*. **~s** *pl* Badehose *f*

truss /trʌs/ *n* (*Med*) Bruchband *nt*

trust /trʌst/ *n* Vertrauen *nt*; (*group of companies*) Trust *m*; (*organization*) Treuhandgesellschaft *f*; (*charitable*) Stiftung *f* □ *vt* trauen (+ *dat*), vertrauen (+ *dat*); (*hope*) hoffen □ *vi* vertrauen (*in/to* auf + *acc*)

trustee /trʌs'tiː/ *n* Treuhänder *m*

'trust|ful /'trʌstfl/ *a*, **-ly** *adv* vertrauensvoll. **~ing** *a* vertrauensvoll. **~worthy** *a* vertrauenswürdig

truth /truːθ/ *n* (*pl* **-s** /truːðz/) Wahrheit *f*. **~ful** *a*, **-ly** *adv* ehrlich

try /traɪ/ *n* Versuch *m* □ *v* (*pt/pp* **tried**) □ *vt* versuchen; (*sample, taste*) probieren; (*be a strain on*) anstrengen; (*Jur*) vor Gericht stellen; verhandeln (*case*) □ *vi* versuchen; (*make an effort*) sich bemühen. **~ on** *vt* anprobieren; aufprobieren ⟨*hat*⟩. **~ out** *vt* ausprobieren

trying /'traɪɪŋ/ *a* schwierig

T-shirt /'tiː-/ *n* T-Shirt *nt*

tub /tʌb/ n Kübel m; (carton) Becher m; (bath) Wanne f

tuba /'tjuːbə/ n (Mus) Tuba f

tubby /'tʌbɪ/ a (-ier, -iest) rundlich

tube /tjuːb/ n Röhre f; (pipe) Rohr nt; (flexible) Schlauch m; (of toothpaste) Tube f; (Rail, fam) U-Bahn f

tuber /'tjuːbə(r)/ n Knolle f

tuberculosis /tjuːbɜːkjʊ'ləʊsɪs/ n Tuberkulose f

tubing /'tjuːbɪŋ/ n Schlauch m

tubular /'tjuːbjʊlə(r)/ a röhrenförmig

tuck /tʌk/ n Saum m; (decorative) Biese f □ vt (put) stecken. ~ **in** vt hineinstecken; ~ **s.o. in** jdn zudecken □ vi (fam: eat) zulangen. ~ **up** vt hochkrempeln ⟨sleeves⟩; (in bed) zudecken

Tuesday /'tjuːzdeɪ/ n Dienstag m

tuft /tʌft/ n Büschel m

tug /tʌg/ n Ruck m; (Naut) Schleppdampfer m □ v (pt/pp **tugged**) □ vt ziehen □ vi zerren (**at** an + dat). ~ **of war** n Tauziehen nt

tuition /tjuː'ɪʃn/ n Unterricht m

tulip /'tjuːlɪp/ n Tulpe f

tumble /'tʌmbl/ n Sturz m □ vi fallen; ~ **to sth** (fam) etw kapieren. ~**down** a verfallen. ~**drier** n Wäschetrockner m

tumbler /'tʌmblə(r)/ n Glas nt

tummy /'tʌmɪ/ n (fam) Magen m; (abdomen) Bauch m

tumour /'tjuːmə(r)/ n Geschwulst f, Tumor m

tumult /'tjuːmʌlt/ n Tumult m. ~**uous** /-'mʌltjʊəs/ a stürmisch

tuna /'tjuːnə/ n Thunfisch m

tune /tjuːn/ n Melodie f; (of ⟨instrument⟩ verstimmt; **to the ~ of** (fam) in Höhe von □ vt stimmen; (Techn) einstellen. ~ **in** vt einstellen □ vi ~ **in to a station** einen Sender einstellen. ~ **up** vi (Mus) stimmen

tuneful /'tjuːnfl/ a melodisch

tunic /'tjuːnɪk/ n (Mil) Uniformjacke f; (Sch) Trägerkleid nt

Tunisia /tjuː'nɪzɪə/ n Tunesien nt

tunnel /'tʌnl/ n Tunnel m □ vi (pt/pp **tunnelled**) einen Tunnel graben

turban /'tɜːbən/ n Turban m

turbine /'tɜːbaɪn/ n Turbine f

turbot /'tɜːbət/ n Steinbutt m

turbulen|ce /'tɜːbjʊləns/ n Turbulenz f. ~**t** a stürmisch

tureen /tjʊə'riːn/ n Terrine f

turf /tɜːf/ n Rasen m; (segment) Rasenstück nt. ~ **out** vt (fam) rausschmeißen

'**turf accountant** n Buchmacher m

Turk /tɜːk/ n Türke m/Türkin f

turkey /'tɜːkɪ/ n Pute f, Truthahn m

Turk|ey n die Türkei. ~**ish** a türkisch

turmoil /'tɜːmɔɪl/ n Aufruhr m; (confusion) Durcheinander m

turn /tɜːn/ n (rotation) Drehung f; (in road) Kurve f; (change of direction) Wende f; (short walk) Runde f; (Theat) Nummer f; (fam: attack) Anfall m; **do s.o. a good ~** jdm einen guten Dienst erweisen; **take ~s** sich abwechseln; **in ~** der Reihe nach; **out of ~** außer der Reihe; **it's your ~** du bist an der Reihe □ vt drehen; (~ over) wenden; (reverse) umdrehen; (Techn) drechseln ⟨wood⟩; **~ the page** umblättern; **~ the corner** um die Ecke biegen □ vi sich drehen; (~ round) sich umdrehen; ⟨car:⟩ wenden; ⟨leaves:⟩ sich färben; ⟨weather:⟩ umschlagen; (become) werden; **~ right/left** nach rechts/links abbiegen; **~ to s.o.** sich an jdn wenden; **have ~ed against s.o.** gegen jdn sein. **~ away** vt abweisen □ vi sich abwenden. **~ down** vt herunterschlagen ⟨collar⟩; heruntendrehen ⟨heat, gas⟩; leiser stellen ⟨sound⟩; (reject) ablehnen; abweisen ⟨person⟩. **~ in**

vt einschlagen *(edges)* □ *vi (car.)* einbiegen; *(fam: go to bed)* ins Bett gehen. **~ off** *vt* zudrehen *(tap)*; ausschalten *(light, radio)*; abstellen *(water, gas, engine, machine)* □ *vi* abbiegen. **~ on** *vt* aufdrehen *(tap)*; einschalten *(light, radio)*; anstellen *(water, gas, engine, machine)*. **~ out** *vt (expel)* vertreiben, *(fam)* hinauswerfen; ausschalten *(light)*; abdrehen *(gas)*; *(produce)* produzieren; *(empty)* ausleeren; [gründlich] aufräumen *(room, cupboard)* □ *vi (go out)* hinausgehen; *(transpire)* sich herausstellen; **~ out well/badly** gut/schlecht gehen. **~ over** *vt* umdrehen. **~ up** *vt* hochschlagen *(collar)*; aufdrehen *(heat, gas)*; lauter stellen *(sound, radio)* □ *vi* auftauchen

turning /'tɜːnɪŋ/ *n* Abzweigung *f*. **~-point** *n* Wendepunkt *m*

turnip /'tɜːnɪp/ *n* weiße Rübe *f*

turn: **~-out** *n (of people)* Teilnahme *f*, Beteiligung *f*; *(of goods)* Produktion *f*. **~-over** *n (Comm)* Umsatz *m*; *(of staff)* Personalwechsel *m*. **~pike** *n (Amer)* gebührenpflichtige Autobahn *f*. **~stile** *n* Drehkreuz *nt*. **~table** *n* Drehscheibe *f*; *(on record-player)* Plattenteller *m*. **~-up** *n* [Hosen]aufschlag *m*

turpentine /'tɜːpəntaɪn/ *n* Terpentin *nt*

turquoise /'tɜːkwɔɪz/ *a* türkis[farben] *f* □ *n (gem)* Türkis *m*

turret /'tʌrɪt/ *n* Türmchen *nt*

turtle /'tɜːtl/ *n* Seeschildkröte *f*

tusk /tʌsk/ *n* Stoßzahn *m*

tussle /'tʌsl/ *n* Balgerei *f*; *(fig)* Streit *m* □ *vi* sich balgen

tutor /'tjuːtə(r)/ *n* [Privat]lehrer *m*

tuxedo /tʌk'siːdəʊ/ *n (Amer)* Smoking *m*

TV /tiː'viː/ *abbr of* **television**

twaddle /'twɒdl/ *n* Geschwätz *nt*

twang /twæŋ/ *n (in voice)* Näseln *nt* □ *vt* zupfen

tweed /twiːd/ *n* Tweed *m*

tweezers /'twiːzəz/ *npl* Pinzette *f*

twelfth /twelfθ/ *a* zwölfter(r,s)

twelve /twelv/ *a* zwölf

twentieth /'twentɪθ/ *a* zwanzigste(r,s)

twenty /'twentɪ/ *a* zwanzig

twerp /twɜːp/ *n (fam)* Trottel *m*

twice /twaɪs/ *adv* zweimal

twiddle /'twɪdl/ *vt* drehen an (+ *dat*)

twig¹ /twɪg/ *n* Zweig *m*

twig² /twɪg/ *vt/i (pt/pp* **twigged)** *(fam)* kapieren

twilight /'twaɪ-/ *n* Dämmerlicht *nt*

twin /twɪn/ *n* Zwilling *m* □ *attrib* Zwillings-. **~ beds** *npl* zwei Einzelbetten *pl*

twine /twaɪn/ *n* Bindfaden *m* □ *vi* sich winden; *(plant:)* sich ranken

twinge /twɪndʒ/ *n* Stechen *nt*; **~ of conscience** Gewissensbisse *pl*

twinkle /'twɪŋkl/ *n* Funkeln *nt* □ *vi* funkeln

twin 'town *n* Partnerstadt *f*

twirl /twɜːl/ *vt/i* herumwirbeln

twist /twɪst/ *n* Drehung *f*; *(curve)* Kurve *f*; *(unexpected occurrence)* überraschende Wendung *f* □ *vt* drehen; *(distort)* verdrehen; *(fam: swindle)* beschummeln; **~ one's ankle** sich *(dat)* den Knöchel verrenken □ *vi* sich drehen; *(road:)* sich winden. **~er** *n (fam)* Schwindler *m*

twit /twɪt/ *n (fam)* Trottel *m*

twitch /twɪtʃ/ *n* Zucken *nt* □ *vi* zucken

twitter /'twɪtə(r)/ *n* Zwitschern *nt* □ *vi* zwitschern

two /tuː/ *a* zwei

two: **~-faced** *a* falsch. **~-piece** *a* zweiteilig. **~some** /-səm/ *n* Paar *nt*. **~-way** *a* **~-way traffic** Gegenverkehr *m*

tycoon /taɪ'kuːn/ *n* Magnat *m*

tying /'taɪɪŋ/ *see* **tie**

type /taɪp/ n Art f, Sorte f; (person) Typ m; (printing) Type f □ vt mit der Maschine schreiben, (fam) tippen; **~d letter** maschinegeschriebener Brief □ vi Maschine schreiben, (fam) tippen. **~writer** n Schreibmaschine f. **~written** a maschinegeschrieben

typhoid /'taɪfɔɪd/ n Typhus m

typical /'tɪpɪkl/ a, **-ly** adv typisch (of für)

typify /'tɪpɪfaɪ/ vt (pt/pp -ied) typisch sein für

typing /'taɪpɪŋ/ n Maschineschreiben nt. **~ paper** n Schreibmaschinenpapier nt

typist /'taɪpɪst/ n Schreibkraft f

typography /taɪ'pɒgrəfɪ/ n Typographie f

tyrannical /tɪ'rænɪkl/ a tyrannisch

tyranny /'tɪrənɪ/ n Tyrannei f

tyrant /'taɪrənt/ n Tyrann m

tyre /'taɪə(r)/ n Reifen m

U

ubiquitous /juː'bɪkwɪtəs/ a allgegenwärtig; **be ~** überall zu finden sein

udder /'ʌdə(r)/ n Euter nt

ugl|iness /'ʌglɪnɪs/ n Hässlichkeit f. **~y** a (-ier, -iest) hässlich; (nasty) übel

UK abbr see **United Kingdom**

ulcer /'ʌlsə(r)/ n Geschwür nt

ulterior /ʌl'tɪərɪə(r)/ a **~ motive** Hintergedanke m

ultimate /'ʌltɪmət/ a letzte(r,s); (final) endgültig; (fundamental) grundlegend, eigentlich. **~ly** adv schließlich

ultimatum /ʌltɪ'meɪtəm/ n Ultimatum nt

ultrasound /'ʌltrə-/ n (Med) Ultraschall m

ultra'violet a ultraviolett

umbilical /ʌm'bɪlɪkl/ a **~ cord** Nabelschnur f

umbrella /ʌm'brelə/ n (Regen)schirm m

umpire /'ʌmpaɪə(r)/ n Schiedsrichter m □ vt/i Schiedsrichter sein (bei)

umpteen /ʌmp'tiːn/ a (fam) zig. **~th** a (zig(s)te(r,s); **for the ~th time** zum zigsten Mal

un'able /ʌn-/ a **be ~ to do sth** etw nicht tun können

una'bridged a ungekürzt

unac'companied a ohne Begleitung; (luggage) unbegleitet

unac'countab|e a unerklärlich. **~y** adv unerklärlicherweise

unac'customed a ungewohnt; **be ~ to sth** etw nicht gewohnt sein

una'dulterated a unverfälscht, (utter) völlig

un'aided a ohne fremde Hilfe

unal'loyed /ʌnə'lɔɪd/ a (fig) ungetrübt

unanimity /juːnə'nɪmətɪ/ n Einstimmigkeit f

unanimous /juː'nænɪməs/ a, **-ly** adv einmütig; (vote, decision) einstimmig

un'armed a unbewaffnet; **~ combat** Kampf m ohne Waffen

unas'suming a bescheiden

unat'tached a nicht befestigt; (person) ungebunden

unat'tended a unbeaufsichtigt

un'authorized a unbefugt

una'voidable a unvermeidlich

una'ware a **be ~ of sth** sich (dat) etw (gen) nicht bewusst sein. **~s** /-eəz/ adv **catch s.o. ~s** jdn überraschen

un'balanced a unausgewogen; (mentally) unausgeglichen

un'bearable a, **-bly** adv unerträglich

unbeat|able /ʌn'biːtəbl/ a unschlagbar. **~en** a ungeschlagen; (record) ungebrochen

unbeknown /ʌnbɪ'nəʊn/ a (fam) **~ to me** ohne mein Wissen

unbe'lievable *a* unglaublich

un'bend *vi* (*pt*/*pp* -**bent**) (*relax*) aus sich herausgehen

un'biased *a* unvoreingenommen

un'block *vt* frei machen

un'bolt *vt* aufriegeln

un'breakable *a* unzerbrechlich

un'bridled /ʌn'braɪdld/ *a* ungezügelt

un'burden *vt* ~ **oneself** (*fig*) sich aussprechen

un'button *vt* aufknöpfen

uncalled-for /ʌn'kɔ:ldfɔ:(r)/ *a* unangebracht

un'canny *a* unheimlich

un'ceasing *a* unaufhörlich

uncere'monious *a*, **-ly** *adv* formlos; (*abrupt*) brüsk

un'certain *a* (*doubtful*) ungewiss; ⟨*origins*⟩ unbestimmt; **be** ~ nicht sicher sein; **in no** ~ **terms** ganz eindeutig. ~**ty** *n* Ungewissheit *f*

un'changed *a* unverändert

un'charitable *a* lieblos

uncle /'ʌŋkl/ *n* Onkel *m*

un'comfortable *a*, **-bly** *adv* unbequem; **feel** ~ (*fig*) sich nicht wohl fühlen

un'common *a* ungewöhnlich

un'compromising *a* kompromisslos

uncon'ditional *a*, **~ly** *adv* bedingungslos

un'conscious *a* bewusstlos; (*unintended*) unbewusst; **be** ~ **of sth** sich (*dat*) etw (*gen*) nicht bewusst sein. ~**ly** *adv* unbewusst

uncon'ventional *a* unkonventionell

unco'operative *a* nicht hilfsbereit

un'cork *vt* entkorken

uncouth /ʌn'ku:θ/ *a* ungehobelt

un'cover *vt* aufdecken

unctuous /'ʌŋktjʊəs/ *a*, **-ly** *adv* salbungsvoll

unde'cided *a* unentschlossen; (*not settled*) nicht entschieden

undeniable /ʌndɪ'naɪəbl/ *a*, **-bly** *adv* unbestreitbar

under /'ʌndə(r)/ *prep* unter (+ *dat*/*acc*); ~ **it** darunter; ~ **there** da drunter; ~ **repair** in Reparatur; ~ **construction** im Bau; ~ **age** minderjährig; ~ **way** unterwegs; (*fig*) im Gange □ *adv* darunter

'undercarriage *n* (*Aviat*) Fahrwerk *nt*, Fahrgestell *nt*

'underclothes *npl* Unterwäsche *f*

under'cover *a* geheim

'undercurrent *n* Unterströmung *f*; (*fig*) Unterton *m*

under'cut *vt* (*pt*/*pp* -**cut**) (*Comm*) unterbieten

'underdog *n* Unterlegene(r) *m*

under'done *a* nicht gar; (*rare*) nicht durchgebraten

under'estimate *vt* unterschätzen

under'fed *a* unterernährt

under'foot *adv* am Boden; **trample** ~ zertrampeln

under'go *vt* (*pt* -**went**, *pp* -**gone**) durchmachen; sich unterziehen (+ *dat*) ⟨*operation*, *treatment*⟩; ~ **repairs** repariert werden

under'graduate *n* Student(in) *m*(*f*)

under'ground¹ *adv* unter der Erde; ⟨*mining*⟩ unter Tage

'underground² *a* unterirdisch; (*secret*) Untergrund- □ *n* (*railway*) U-Bahn *f*. ~ **car park** *n* Tiefgarage *f*

'undergrowth *n* Unterholz *nt*

'underhand *a* hinterhältig

'underlay *n* Unterlage *f*

under'lie *vt* (*pt* -**lay**, *pp* -**lain**, *pres p* -**lying**) (*fig*) zugrunde liegen (+ *dat*)

under'line *vt* unterstreichen

underling /'ʌndəlɪŋ/ *n* (*pej*) Untergebene(r) *m*/*f*

under'lying *a* (*fig*) eigentlich

under'mine *vt* (*fig*) unterminieren, untergraben

underneath /ʌndə'ni:θ/ *prep* unter (+ *dat*/*acc*); ~ **it** darunter □ *adv* darunter

'under|pants npl Unterhose f
'under|pass n Unterführung f
under'privileged a unterprivile-
giert

under'rate vt unterschätzen
'under|seal n (Auto) Unterboden-
schutz m
'under|shirt n (Amer) Unterhemd
nt
under|staffed /-'stɑːft/ a unter-
besetzt

under'stand vt/i (pt/pp -stood)
verstehen; I ~ that ... (have
heard) ich habe gehört, dass ...
~able /-əbl/ a verständlich.
~ably /-əblɪ/ adv verständli-
cherweise

under'standing a verständnis-
voll □n Verständnis int; (agreement) Vereinbarung f; reach an
~ sich verständigen; on the ~
that unter der Voraussetzung,
dass

'understatement n Untertrei-
bung f
'understudy n (Theat) Ersatz-
spieler(in) m(f)

under'take vt (pt -took, pp
-taken) unternehmen; ~ to do
sth sich verpflichten, etw zu tun
~r n Leichenbestatter
m; [firm of] ~s Bestattungsinstitut n

under'taking n Unternehmen nt;
(promise) Versprechen nt
'undertone n (fig) Unterton m; in
an ~ mit gedämpfter Stimme
under'value vt unterbewerten
'under|water¹ a Unterwasser-
under'water² adv unter Wasser
'underwear n Unterwäsche f
'underweight a untergewichtig;
be ~ Untergewicht haben
'underworld n Unterwelt f
'underwriter n Versicherer m
unde'sirable a unerwünscht
undies /'ʌndɪz/ npl (fam) [Da-
men]unterwäsche f
un'dignified a würdelos

un'do vt (pt -did, pp -done) aufmachen; (fig) ungeschehen
machen; (ruin) zunichte machen
un'done a offen; (not accomplished) unerledigt
un'doubted a unzweifelhaft. ~ly
adv zweifellos
un'dress vt ausziehen; get ~ed
sich ausziehen □ vi sich ausziehen
un'due a übermäßig
undulating /'ʌndjʊleɪtɪŋ/ a Wel-
len-; (country) wellig
und'uly adv übermäßig
un'dying a ewig
un'earth vt ausgraben; (fig) zutage bringen. ~ly a unheimlich;
at an ~ly hour (fam) in aller
Herrgottsfrühe
un'ease n Unbehagen nt. ~y a
unbehaglich; I feel ~y mir ist unbehaglich zumute
un'eatable a ungenießbar
uneco'nomic a, -ally adv unwirtschaftlich
uneco'nomical a verschwenderisch
unem'ployed a arbeitslos □npl
the ~ die Arbeitslosen
unem'ployment n Arbeitslosig-
keit f. ~ benefit n Arbeitslo-
senunterstützung f
un'ending a endlos
un'equal a unterschiedlich;
(struggle) ungleich; be ~ to a
task einer Aufgabe nicht gewachsen sein. ~ly adv ungleichmäßig
unequivocal /ʌnɪ'kwɪvəkl/ a, -ly
adv eindeutig
unerring /ʌn'ɜːrɪŋ/ a unfehlbar
un'ethical a unmoralisch; be ~
gegen das Berufsethos verstoßen
un'even a uneben; (unequal) ungleich; (not regular) ungleichmäßig; (number) ungerade. ~ly
adv ungleichmäßig
unex'pected a, -ly adv unerwartet
un'failing a nie versagend

un'fair a, **-ly** adv ungerecht, unfair. **~ness** n Ungerechtigkeit f

un'faithful a untreu

unfa'miliar a ungewohnt; (*unknown*) unbekannt

un'fasten vt aufmachen; (*detach*) losmachen

un'favourable a ungünstig

un'feeling a gefühllos

un'finished a unvollendet; ⟨*business*⟩ unerledigt

un'fit a ungeeignet; (*incompetent*) unfähig; (*Sport*) nicht fit; **~ for work** arbeitsunfähig

un'flinching /ʌn'flɪntʃɪŋ/ a unerschrocken

un'fold vt auseinander falten, entfalten; (*spread out*) ausbreiten □ vi sich entfalten

unfore'seen a unvorhergesehen

unfor'gettable /ʌnfə'getəbl/ a unvergesslich

unfor'givable /ʌnfə'gɪvəbl/ a unverzeihlich

unfortunate /ʌn'fɔːtʃənət/ a unglücklich; (*unfavourable*) ungünstig; (*regrettable*) bedauerlich; **be ~** ⟨*person:*⟩ Pech haben. **~ly** adv leider

un'founded a unbegründet

unfurl /ʌn'fɜːl/ vt entrollen □ vi sich entrollen

un'furnished a unmöbliert

ungainly /ʌn'geɪnlɪ/ a unbeholfen

un'godly /ʌn'gɒdlɪ/ a gottlos; **at an ~ hour** (*fam*) in aller Herrgottsfrühe

un'grateful a, **-ly** adv undankbar

un'happi|ly adv unglücklich; (*unfortunately*) leider. **~ness** n Kummer m

un'happy a unglücklich; (*not content*) unzufrieden

un'harmed a unverletzt

un'healthy a ungesund

un'hook vt vom Haken nehmen; aufhaken (*dress*)

un'hurt a unverletzt

unhy'gienic a unhygienisch

unicorn /'juːnɪkɔːn/ n Einhorn nt

unification /juːnɪfɪ'keɪʃn/ n Einigung f

uniform /'juːnɪfɔːm/ a, **-ly** adv einheitlich □ n Uniform f

unify /'juːnɪfaɪ/ vt (pt/pp **-ied**) einigen

uni'lateral /juːnɪ-/ a, **-ly** adv einseitig

uni'maginable a unvorstellbar

unim'portant a unwichtig

unin'habited a unbewohnt

unin'tentional a, **-ly** adv unabsichtlich

union /'juːnɪən/ n Vereinigung f; (*Pol*) Union f; (*trade ~*) Gewerkschaft f. **~ist** n (*Pol*) Unionist m

unique /juː'niːk/ a einzigartig. **~ly** adv einmalig

unison /'juːnɪsn/ n **in ~** einstimmig

unit /'juːnɪt/ n Einheit f; (*Math*) Einer m; (*of furniture*) Teil nt, Element nt

unite /juː'naɪt/ vt vereinigen □ vi sich vereinigen

united /juː'naɪtɪd/ a einig. **U~ 'Kingdom** n Vereinigtes Königreich nt. **U~ 'Nations** n Vereinte Nationen pl. **U~ States [of America]** n Vereinigte Staaten pl [von Amerika]

unity /'juːnətɪ/ n Einheit f; (*harmony*) Einigkeit f

universal /juːnɪ'vɜːsl/ a, **-ly** adv allgemein

universe /'juːnɪvɜːs/ n [Welt]all nt, Universum nt

university /juːnɪ'vɜːsətɪ/ n Universität f □ attrib Universitäts-

un'just a, **-ly** adv ungerecht

unkempt /ʌn'kempt/ a ungepflegt

un'kind a, **-ly** adv unfreundlich; (*harsh*) hässlich. **~ness** n Unfreundlichkeit f; Hässlichkeit f

un'known a unbekannt

un'lawful a, **-ly** adv gesetzwidrig

unleaded /ʌn'ledɪd/ a bleifrei

un'leash vt (*fig*) entfesseln

unless /ən'les/ *conj* wenn ... nicht; ~ **I am mistaken** wenn ich mich nicht irre

un'like *a* nicht ähnlich, unähnlich; *(not the same)* ungleich □ *prep* im Gegensatz zu (+ *dat*)

un'likely *a* unwahrscheinlich

un'limited *a* unbegrenzt

un'load *vt* entladen; ausladen ⟨*luggage*⟩

un'lock *vt* aufschließen

un'lucky *a* unglücklich; ⟨*day, number*⟩ Unglücks-; **be ~** Pech haben; ⟨*thing:*⟩ Unglück bringen

un'manned *a* unbemannt

un'married *a* unverheiratet. ~ '**mother** *n* ledige Mutter *f*

un'mask *vt* ⟨*fig*⟩ entlarven

unmistakable /ʌnmɪ'steɪkəbl/ *a*, **-bly** *adv* unverkennbar

un'mitigated *a* vollkommen

un'natural *a*, **-ly** *adv* unnatürlich; *(not normal)* nicht normal

un'necessary *a*, **-ily** *adv* unnötig

un'noticed *a* unbemerkt

unob'tainable *a* nicht erhältlich

unob'trusive *a*, **-ly** *adv* unaufdringlich; ⟨*thing*⟩ unauffällig

unof'ficial *a*, **-ly** *adv* inoffiziell

un'pack *vt/i* auspacken

un'paid *a* unbezahlt

un'palatable *a* ungenießbar

un'paralleled *a* beispiellos

un'pick *vt* auftrennen

un'pleasant *a*, **-ly** *adv* unangenehm. ~**ness** *n* (*bad feeling*) Ärger *m*

un'plug *vt* (*pt/pp* **-plugged**) den Stecker herausziehen von

un'popular *a* unbeliebt

un'precedented *a* beispiellos

unpre'dictable *a* unberechenbar

unpre'meditated *a* nicht vorsätzlich

unpre'pared *a* nicht vorbereitet

unprepos'sessing *a* wenig attraktiv

unpre'tentious *a* bescheiden

un'principled *a* skrupellos

unpro'fessional *a* **be ~** gegen das Berufsethos verstoßen *(Sport)* unsportlich sein

un'profitable *a* unrentabel

un'qualified *a* unqualifiziert *(fig: absolute)* uneingeschränkt

un'questionable *a* unbezweifelbar; ⟨*right*⟩ unbestreitbar

unravel /ʌn'rævl/ *vt* (*pt/pp* **-ravelled**) entwirren; *(Knitting)* aufziehen

un'real *a* unwirklich

un'reasonable *a* unvernünftig **be ~** zu viel verlangen

unre'lated *a* unzusammenhängend; **be ~** nicht verwandt sein ⟨*events:*⟩ nicht miteinander zusammenhängen

unre'liable *a* unzuverlässig

unrequited /ʌnrɪ'kwaɪtɪd/ *a* unerwidert

unre'servedly /ʌnrɪ'zɜ:vɪdlɪ/ *adv* uneingeschränkt; *(frankly)* offen

un'rest *n* Unruhen *pl*

un'rivalled *a* unübertroffen

un'roll *vt* aufrollen □ *vi* sich aufrollen

unruly /ʌn'ru:lɪ/ *a* ungebärdig

un'safe *a* nicht sicher

un'said *a* ungesagt

un'salted *a* ungesalzen

unsatis'factory *a* unbefriedigend

un'savoury *a* unangenehm; *(fig)* unerfreulich

unscathed /ʌn'skeɪðd/ *a* unversehrt

un'screw *vt* abschrauben

un'scrupulous *a* skrupellos

un'seemly *a* unschicklich

un'selfish *a* selbstlos

un'settled *a* ungeklärt; ⟨*weather*⟩ unbeständig; *(bill)* unbezahlt

unshakeable /ʌn'ʃeɪkəbl/ *a* unerschütterlich

unshaven /ʌn'ʃeɪvn/ *a* unrasiert

unsightly /ʌn'saɪtlɪ/ *a* unansehnlich

un'skilled a ungelernt; ⟨work⟩ unqualifiziert

un'sociable a ungesellig

unso'phisticated a einfach

un'sound a krank, nicht gesund; ⟨building⟩ nicht sicher; ⟨advice⟩ unzuverlässig; ⟨reasoning⟩ nicht stichhaltig; **of ~ mind** unzurechnungsfähig

unspeakable /ʌn'spiːkəbl/ a unbeschreiblich

un'stable a nicht stabil; ⟨mentally⟩ labil

un'steady a, **-ily** adv unsicher; ⟨wobbly⟩ wackelig

un'stuck a **come ~** sich lösen; ⟨fam: fail⟩ scheitern

unsuc'cessful a, **-ly** adv erfolglos; **be ~** keinen Erfolg haben

un'suitable a ungeeignet; ⟨inappropriate⟩ unpassend; ⟨for weather, activity⟩ unzweckmäßig

unsu'specting a ahnungslos

un'sweetened a ungesüßt

unthinkable /ʌn'θɪŋkəbl/ a unvorstellbar

un'tidiness n Unordentlichkeit f

un'tidy a, **-ily** adv unordentlich

un'tie vt aufbinden; losbinden ⟨person, boat, horse⟩

until /ən'tɪl/ prep bis (+ acc); **not ~ erst**; ⟨the evening⟩ bis zum Abend; **~ his arrival** bis zu seiner Ankunft □ conj bis; **not ~ erst wenn**; ⟨in past⟩ erst als

untimely /ʌn'taɪmlɪ/ a ungelegen; ⟨premature⟩ vorzeitig

un'tiring a unermüdlich

un'told a unermesslich

unto'ward a ungünstig; ⟨unseemly⟩ ungehörig; **if nothing ~ happens** wenn nichts dazwischenkommt

un'true a unwahr; **that's ~** das ist nicht wahr

unused[1] /ʌn'juːzd/ a unbenutzt; ⟨not utilized⟩ ungenutzt

unused[2] /ʌn'juːst/ a **be ~ to sth** etw nicht gewohnt sein

un'usual a, **-ly** adv ungewöhnlich

un'veil vt enthüllen

un'versed a nicht bewandert (**in** in + dat)

un'wanted a unerwünscht

un'warranted a ungerechtfertigt

un'welcome a unwillkommen

un'well a **be** or **feel ~** sich nicht wohl fühlen

unwieldy /ʌn'wiːldɪ/ a sperrig

un'willing a, **-ly** adv widerwillig; **be ~ to do sth** etw nicht tun wollen

un'wind v ⟨pt/pp **unwound**⟩ □ vt abwickeln □ vi sich abwickeln; ⟨fam: relax⟩ sich entspannen

un'wise a, **-ly** adv unklug

un'witting /ʌn'wɪtɪŋ/ a, **-ly** adv unwissentlich

un'worthy a unwürdig

un'wrap vt ⟨pt/pp **-wrapped**⟩ auswickeln; auspacken ⟨present⟩

un'written a ungeschrieben

up /ʌp/ adv oben; ⟨with movement⟩ nach oben; ⟨not in bed⟩ auf; ⟨collar⟩ hochgeklappt; ⟨road⟩ aufgerissen; ⟨price⟩ gestiegen; ⟨curtains⟩ aufgehängt; ⟨shelves⟩ angebracht; ⟨notice⟩ angeschlagen; ⟨tent⟩ aufgebaut; ⟨building⟩ gebaut; **be up for sale** zu verkaufen sein; **up there** da oben; **up to** ⟨as far as⟩ bis; **time's up** die Zeit ist um; **what's up?** ⟨fam⟩ was ist los? **what's he up to?** ⟨fam⟩ was hat er vor? **I don't feel up to it** ich fühle mich dem nicht gewachsen; **be one up on s.o.** ⟨fam⟩ jdm etwas voraushaben; **go up** hinaufgehen; **come up** heraufkommen □ prep **be up on sth** [oben] auf etw ⟨dat⟩ sein; **up the mountain** oben am Berg; ⟨movement⟩ den Berg hinauf; **be up the tree** oben im Baum sein; **up the road** die Straße entlang; **up the river** stromaufwärts; **go up the stairs** die Treppe hinaufgehen; **be up the pub** ⟨fam⟩ in der Kneipe sein

'upbringing n Erziehung f

up'date *vt* auf den neuesten Stand bringen

up'grade *vt* aufstufen

upheaval /ʌpˈhiːvl/ *n* Unruhe *f*; (*Pol*) Umbruch *m*

up'hill *a* (*fig*) mühsam □ *adv* bergauf

up'hold *vt* (*pt/pp* upheld) unterstützen; bestätigen (*verdict*)

upholster /ʌpˈhəʊlstə(r)/ *vt* polstern. **~er** *n* Polsterer *m*. **~y** *n* Polsterung *f*

'upkeep *n* Unterhalt *m*

up-'market *a* anspruchsvoll

upon /əˈpɒn/ *prep* auf (+ *dat/acc*)

upper /ˈʌpə(r)/ *a* obere(r,s); (*deck, jaw, lip*) Ober-; **have the ~ hand** die Oberhand haben □ *n* (*of shoe*) Obermaterial *nt*

upper: ~ circle *n* zweiter Rang *m*. **~ class** *n* Oberschicht *f*. **~most** *a* oberste(r,s)

'upright *a* aufrecht □ *n* Pfosten *m*

'uprising *n* Aufstand *m*

'uproar *n* Aufruhr *m*

up'root *vt* entwurzeln

up'set¹ *vt* (*pt/pp* upset, *pres p* upsetting) umstoßen; (*spill*) verschütten; (*distress*) erschüttern; (*food:*) nicht bekommen (+ *dat*); **get ~ about sth** sich über etw (*acc*) aufregen; **be very ~** sehr bestürzt sein

'upset² *n* Aufregung *f*; **have a stomach ~** einen verdorbenen Magen haben

'upshot *n* Ergebnis *nt*

upside 'down *adv* verkehrt herum; **turn ~** umdrehen

up'stairs¹ *adv* oben; (*go*) nach oben

'upstairs² *a* im Obergeschoss

'upstart *n* Emporkömmling *m*

up'stream *adv* stromaufwärts

'upsurge *n* Zunahme *f*

'uptake *n* **slow on the ~** schwer von Begriff; **be quick on the ~** schnell begreifen

up'tight *a* nervös

'upturn *n* Aufschwung *m*

upward /ˈʌpwəd/ *a* nach oben; (*movement*) Aufwärts-; **~ slope** Steigung *f* □ *adv* **~[s]** aufwärts, nach oben

uranium /jʊˈreɪnɪəm/ *n* Uran *nt*

urban /ˈɜːbən/ *a* städtisch

urbane /ɜːˈbeɪn/ *a* weltmännisch

urge /ɜːdʒ/ *n* Trieb *m*, Drang *m* □ *vt* drängen; **~ on** antreiben

urgen|cy /ˈɜːdʒənsɪ/ *n* Dringlichkeit *f*. **~t a**. **-ly** *adv* dringend

urinate /ˈjʊərɪneɪt/ *vi* urinieren

urine /ˈjʊərɪn/ *n* Urin *m*, Harn *m*

urn /ɜːn/ *n* Urne *f*; (*for tea*) Teemaschine *f*

us /ʌs/ *pron* uns; **it's us** wir sind es

US[A] *abbr* USA *pl*

usable /ˈjuːzəbl/ *a* brauchbar

usage /ˈjuːzɪdʒ/ *n* Brauch *m*; (*of word*) [Sprach]gebrauch *m*

use¹ /juːs/ *n* (*see* use²) Benutzung *f*; Verwendung *f*; Gebrauch *m*; **be of no ~** nichts nützen; **make ~ of** Gebrauch machen von; (*exploit*) ausnutzen; **it is no ~** es hat keinen Zweck; **what's the ~?** wozu

use² /juːz/ *vt* benutzen (*implement, room, lift*); verwenden (*ingredient, method, book, money*); gebrauchen (*words, force, brains*); **~ [up]** aufbrauchen

used¹ /juːzd/ *a* benutzt; (*car*) gebraucht

used² /juːst/ *pt* **be ~ to sth** an etw (*acc*) gewöhnt sein; **get ~ to sth** sich gewöhnen an (+ *acc*); **he ~ to say** er hat immer gesagt; **he ~ to live here** er hat früher hier gewohnt

useful /ˈjuːsfl/ *a* nützlich. **~ness** *n* Nützlichkeit *f*

useless /ˈjuːslɪs/ *a* nutzlos; (*not usable*) unbrauchbar; (*pointless*) zwecklos

user /ˈjuːzə(r)/ *n* Benutzer(in) *m(f)*. **~-'friendly** *a* benutzerfreundlich

usher /'ʌʃə(r)/ n Platzanweiser m; (in court) Gerichtsdiener m □ vt ~ in hineinführen

usherette /ʌʃə'ret/ n Platzanweiserin f

USSR abbr UdSSR f

usual /'juːʒʊəl/ a üblich. **~ly** adv gewöhnlich

usurp /juː'zɜːp/ vt sich (dat) widerrechtlich aneignen

utensil /juː'tensl/ n Gerät nt

uterus /'juːtərəs/ n Gebärmutter f

utilitarian /juːtɪlɪ'teərɪən/ a zweckmäßig

utility /juː'tɪlətɪ/ a Gebrauchs- □ n Nutzen m. **~ room** n ≈ Waschküche f

utiliz|ation /juːtɪlaɪ'zeɪʃn/ n Nutzung f. **~e** /'juːtɪlaɪz/ vt nutzen

utmost /'ʌtməʊst/ a äußerste(r,s), größte(r,s) □ n one's ~ sein Möglichstes tun

utter¹ /'ʌtə(r)/ a, **-ly** adv völlig

utter² vt von sich geben ⟨sigh, sound⟩; sagen ⟨word⟩. **~ance** /-əns/ n Äußerung f

U-turn /'juː-/ n (fig) Kehrtwendung f; 'no ~s' (Auto) 'Wenden verboten'

V

vacan|cy /'veɪkənsɪ/ n (job) freie Stelle f; (room) freies Zimmer nt; 'no ~cies' 'belegt'. **~t** a frei; ⟨look⟩ [gedanken]leer

vacate /və'keɪt/ vt räumen

vacation /və'keɪʃn/ n (Univ & Amer) Ferien pl

vaccinate /'væksɪneɪt/ vt impfen. **~ion** /-'neɪʃn/ n Impfung f

vaccine /'væksiːn/ n Impfstoff m

vacuum /'vækjʊəm/ n Vakuum nt, luftleerer Raum m □ vt saugen. **~ cleaner** n Staubsauger m. **~ flask** n Thermosflasche (P) f. **~-packed** a vakuumverpackt

vagaries /'veɪɡərɪz/ npl Launen pl

vagina /və'dʒaɪnə/ n (Anat) Scheide f

vagrant /'veɪɡrənt/ n Landstreicher m

vague /veɪɡ/ a (-r,-st), **-ly** adv vage; ⟨outline⟩ verschwommen

vain /veɪn/ a (-er,-est) eitel; ⟨hope, attempt⟩ vergeblich; **in ~** vergeblich. **~ly** adv vergeblich

vale /veɪl/ n (liter) Tal nt

valet /'væleɪ/ n Kammerdiener m

valiant /'vælɪənt/ a, **-ly** adv tapfer

valid /'vælɪd/ a gültig; ⟨claim⟩ berechtigt; ⟨argument⟩ stichhaltig; ⟨reason⟩ triftig. **~ate** vt ⟨confirm⟩ bestätigen. **~ity** /və'lɪdətɪ/ n Gültigkeit f

valley /'vælɪ/ n Tal nt

valour /'vælə(r)/ n Tapferkeit f

valuable /'væljʊəbl/ a wertvoll. **~s** npl Wertsachen pl

valuation /vælju'eɪʃn/ n Schätzung f

value /'væljuː/ n Wert m; ⟨usefulness⟩ Nutzen m □ vt schätzen. **~ added 'tax** n Mehrwertsteuer f

valve /vælv/ n Ventil nt; (Anat) Klappe f; (Electr) Röhre f

vampire /'væmpaɪə(r)/ n Vampir m

van /væn/ n Lieferwagen m

vandal /'vændl/ n Rowdy m. **~ism** /-ɪzm/ n mutwillige Zerstörung f. **~ize** vt demolieren

vanilla /və'nɪlə/ n Vanille f

vanish /'vænɪʃ/ vi verschwinden

vanity /'vænətɪ/ n Eitelkeit f. **~ bag** n Kosmetiktäschchen nt

vantage-point /'vɑːntɪdʒ-/ n Aussichtspunkt m

vapour /'veɪpə(r)/ n Dampf m

variable /'veərɪəbl/ a unbeständig; (Math) variabel; ⟨adjustable⟩ regulierbar

variance /'veərɪəns/ n be at ~ nicht übereinstimmen

variant /'veərɪənt/ n Variante f

variation /ˌveərɪˈeɪʃn/ n Variation f; (difference) Unterschied m

varicose /ˈværɪkəʊs/ a ~ veins Krampfadern pl

varied /ˈveərɪd/ a vielseitig; (diet:) abwechslungsreich

variety /vəˈraɪətɪ/ n Abwechslung f; (quantity) Vielfalt f; (Comm) Auswahl f; (type) Art f; (Bot) Abart f; (Theat) Varieté nt

various /ˈveərɪəs/ a verschieden. ~ly adv unterschiedlich

varnish /ˈvɑːnɪʃ/ n Lack m □ vt lackieren

vary /ˈveərɪ/ v (pt/pp -ied) □ vi sich ändern; (be different) verschieden sein □ vt (ver)ändern; (add variety to) abwechslungsreicher gestalten. ~ing a wechselnd; (different) unterschiedlich

vase /vɑːz/ n Vase f

vast /vɑːst/ a riesig; (expanse) weit. ~ly adv gewaltig

vat /væt/ n Bottich m

VAT /viːeɪˈtiː, væt/ abbr (value added tax) Mehrwertsteuer f, MwSt.

vault[1] /vɔːlt/ n (roof) Gewölbe nt; (in bank) Tresor m; (tomb) Gruft f

vault[2] n Sprung m □ vt/i ~ [over] springen über (+ acc)

VDU abbr (visual display unit) Bildschirmgerät nt

veal /viːl/ n Kalbfleisch nt □ attrib Kalbs-

veer /vɪə(r)/ vi sich drehen; (Naut) abdrehen; (Auto) ausscheren

vegetable /ˈvedʒtəbl/ n Gemüse nt. ~s pl Gemüse nt □ attrib Gemüse-; (oil, fat) Pflanzen-

vegetarian /vedʒɪˈteərɪən/ a vegetarisch □ n Vegetarier(in) m(f)

vegetate /ˈvedʒɪteɪt/ vi dahinvegetieren. ~ion /-ˈteɪʃn/ n Vegetation f

vehemen|ce /ˈviːəməns/ n Heftigkeit f. ~t a, -ly adv heftig

vehicle /ˈviːɪkl/ n Fahrzeug nt; (fig: medium) Mittel nt

veil /veɪl/ n Schleier m □ vt verschleiern

vein /veɪn/ n Ader f; (mood) Stimmung f; (manner) Art f; ~s and arteries Venen und Arterien. ~ed a geädert

Velcro (P) /ˈvelkrəʊ/ n ~ fastening Klettverschluss m

velocity /vɪˈlɒsətɪ/ n Geschwindigkeit f

velvet /ˈvelvɪt/ n Samt m. ~y a samtig

vending-machine /ˈvendɪŋ-/ n [Verkaufs]automat m

vendor /ˈvendə(r)/ n Verkäufer(in) m(f)

veneer /vəˈnɪə(r)/ n Furnier nt; (fig) Tünche f. ~ed a furniert

venerable /ˈvenərəbl/ a ehrwürdig

venereal /vɪˈnɪərɪəl/ a ~ disease Geschlechtskrankheit f

Venetian /vəˈniːʃn/ a venezianisch. v~ blind n Jalousie f

vengeance /ˈvendʒəns/ n Rache f; with a ~ (fam) gewaltig

Venice /ˈvenɪs/ n Venedig nt

venison /ˈvenɪsn/ n (Culin) Wild nt

venom /ˈvenəm/ n Gift nt; (fig) Hass m. ~ous /-əs/ a giftig

vent[1] /vent/ n Öffnung f; (fig) Ventil n; give ~ to Luft machen (+ dat) □ vt Luft machen (+ dat)

vent[2] n (in jacket) Schlitz m

ventilat|e /ˈventɪleɪt/ vt belüften. ~ion /-ˈleɪʃn/ n Belüftung f; (in stallation) Lüftung f. ~or n (Med) Beatmungsgerät nt

ventriloquist /venˈtrɪləkwɪst/ n Bauchredner m

venture /ˈventʃə(r)/ n Unternehmung f □ vt wagen □ vi wagen

venue /ˈvenjuː/ n Treffpunkt m; (for event) Veranstaltungsort m

veranda /vəˈrændə/ n Veranda f

verb /vɜːb/ n Verb nt. **~al a, -ly** adv mündlich; (Gram) verbal

verbatim /vɜːˈbeɪtɪm/ a & adv [wort]wörtlich

verbose /vɜːˈbəʊs/ a weitschweifig

verdict /ˈvɜːdɪkt/ n Urteil nt

verge /vɜːdʒ/ n Rand m; **be on the ~ of doing sth** im Begriff sein, etw zu tun □ vi **~ on** (fig) grenzen an (+ acc)

verger /ˈvɜːdʒə(r)/ n Küster m

verify /ˈverɪfaɪ/ vt (pt/pp -ied) überprüfen; (confirm) bestätigen

vermin /ˈvɜːmɪn/ n Ungeziefer nt

vermouth /ˈvɜːməθ/ n Wermut m

vernacular /vəˈnækjʊlə(r)/ n Landessprache f

versatil|e /ˈvɜːsətaɪl/ a vielseitig. **~ity** /-ˈtɪlətɪ/ n Vielseitigkeit f

verse /vɜːs/ n Strophe f; (of Bible) Vers m; (poetry) Lyrik f

version /ˈvɜːʃn/ n Version f; (translation) Übersetzung f; (model) Modell nt

versus /ˈvɜːsəs/ prep gegen (+ acc)

vertebra /ˈvɜːtɪbrə/ n (pl -brae /-briː/) (Anat) Wirbel m

vertical /ˈvɜːtɪkl/ a, -ly adv senkrecht □ n Senkrechte f

vertigo /ˈvɜːtɪgəʊ/ n (Med) Schwindel m

verve /vɜːv/ n Schwung m

very /ˈverɪ/ adv sehr; **~ much** sehr; (quantity) sehr viel; **~ little** sehr wenig; **~ probably** höchstwahrscheinlich; **at the ~ most** allerhöchstens □ a (mere) bloß; **the ~ first** der/die/das allererste; **the ~ thing** genau das Richtige; **at the ~ end/beginning** ganz am Ende/Anfang; **only a ~ little** nur ein ganz kleines bisschen

vessel /ˈvesl/ n Schiff nt; (receptacle & Anat) Gefäß nt

vest /vest/ n [Unter]hemd nt; (Amer: waistcoat) Weste f □ vt **~ sth in s.o.** jdm etw verleihen;

have a ~ed interest in sth ein persönliches Interesse an etw (dat) haben

vestige /ˈvestɪdʒ/ n Spur f

vestment /ˈvestmənt/ n (Relig) Gewand nt

vestry /ˈvestrɪ/ n Sakristei f

vet /vet/ n Tierarzt m /-ärztin f □ vt (pt/pp vetted) überprüfen

veteran /ˈvetərən/ n Veteran m. **~ car** n Oldtimer m

veterinary /ˈvetərɪnərɪ/ a tierärztlich. **~ surgeon** n Tierarzt m /-ärztin f

veto /ˈviːtəʊ/ n (pl -es) Veto nt □ vt sein Veto einlegen gegen

vex /veks/ vt ärgern. **~ation** /-ˈseɪʃn/ n Ärger m. **~ed** a verärgert; **~ed question** viel diskutierte Frage f

VHF abbr (very high frequency) UKW

via /ˈvaɪə/ prep über (+ acc)

viable /ˈvaɪəbl/ a lebensfähig; (fig) realisierbar; (firm) rentabel

viaduct /ˈvaɪədʌkt/ n Viadukt m

vibrant /ˈvaɪbrənt/ a (fig) lebhaft

vibrat|e /vaɪˈbreɪt/ vi vibrieren. **~ion** /-ˈbreɪʃn/ n Vibrieren nt

vicar /ˈvɪkə(r)/ n Pfarrer m. **~age** /-rɪdʒ/ n Pfarrhaus nt

vicarious /vɪˈkeərɪəs/ a nachempfunden

vice¹ /vaɪs/ n Laster nt

vice² n (Techn) Schraubstock m

vice 'chairman n stellvertretender Vorsitzender m

vice 'president n Vizepräsident m

vice versa /vaɪsɪˈvɜːsə/ adv umgekehrt

vicinity /vɪˈsɪnətɪ/ n Umgebung f; **in the ~ of** in der Nähe von

vicious /ˈvɪʃəs/ a, -ly adv boshaft; (animal) bösartig. **~ 'circle** n Teufelskreis m

victim /ˈvɪktɪm/ n Opfer nt. **~ize** vt schikanieren

victor /ˈvɪktə(r)/ n Sieger m

victor|ious /vɪkˈtɔːrɪəs/ *a* sieg-reich. **~y** /ˈvɪktərɪ/ *n* Sieg *m*

video /ˈvɪdɪəʊ/ *n* Video *nt*; (*re-corder*) Videorecorder *m* □ *attrib* Video- □ *vt* [auf Videoband] auf-nehmen

video: **~ cas'sette** *n* Videokas-sette *f*. **~ game** *n* Videospiel *nt*. **~ 'nasty** *n* Horrorvideo *nt*. **~ re-corder** *n* Videorecorder *m*

vie /vaɪ/ *vi* (*pres p* **vying**) wettei-fern

Vienn|a /vɪˈenə/ *n* Wien *nt*. **~ese** /vɪəˈniːz/ *a* Wiener

view /vjuː/ *n* (*sight*), (*scene*) An-sicht *f*, Blick *m*; (*picture, opinion*) Ansicht *f*; **in my ~** meiner An-sicht nach; **in ~ of** angesichts (+ *gen*); **keep/have sth in ~** etw im Auge behalten/haben; **be on ~** besichtigt werden können □ *vt* sich (*dat*) ansehen; besichtigen (*house*); (*consider*) betrachten □ *vi* (*TV*) fernsehen. **~er** *n* (*TV*) Zu-schauer(in) *m(f)*; (*Phot*) Dia-betrachter *m*

view: **~finder** *n* (*Phot*) Sucher *m*. **~point** *n* Standpunkt *m*

vigil /ˈvɪdʒɪl/ *n* Wache *f*

vigilan|ce /ˈvɪdʒɪləns/ *n* Wach-samkeit *f*. **~t a**, **-ly** *adv* wachsam

vigorous /ˈvɪgərəs/ *a*, **-ly** *adv* kräftig; (*fig*) heftig

vigour /ˈvɪgə(r)/ *n* Kraft *f*; (*fig*) Heftigkeit *f*

vile /vaɪl/ *a* abscheulich

villa /ˈvɪlə/ *n* (*for holidays*) Fe-rienhaus *nt*

village /ˈvɪlɪdʒ/ *n* Dorf *nt*. **~r** *n* Dorfbewohner(in) *m(f)*

villain /ˈvɪlən/ *n* Schurke *m*; (*in story*) Bösewicht *m*

vim /vɪm/ *n* (*fam*) Schwung *m*

vindicate /ˈvɪndɪkeɪt/ *vt* rechtfertigen. **~ion** /-ˈkeɪʃn/ *n* Rechtfertigung *f*

vindictive /vɪnˈdɪktɪv/ *a* nachtra-gend

vine /vaɪn/ *n* Weinrebe *f*

vinegar /ˈvɪnɪgə(r)/ *n* Essig *m*

vineyard /ˈvɪnjɑːd/ *n* Weinberg *m*

vintage /ˈvɪntɪdʒ/ *a* erlesen □ *n* (*year*) Jahrgang *m*. **~ 'car** *n* Old-timer *m*

viola /vɪˈəʊlə/ *n* (*Mus*) Bratsche *f*

violat|e /ˈvaɪəleɪt/ *vt* verletzen; (*break*) brechen; (*disturb*) stören; (*defile*) schänden. **~ion** /-ˈleɪʃn/ *n* Verletzung *f*; Schändung *f*

violen|ce /ˈvaɪələns/ *n* Gewalt *f*; (*fig*) Heftigkeit *f*. **~t a** gewalttä-tig; (*fig*) heftig. **~tly** *adv* bruta[l]; (*fig*) heftig

violet /ˈvaɪələt/ *a* violett □ *n* (*flower*) Veilchen *nt*

violin /vaɪəˈlɪn/ *n* Geige *f*, Violine *f*. **~ist** *n* Geiger(in) *m(f)*

VIP *abbr* (**very important per-son**) Prominente(r) *m/f*

viper /ˈvaɪpə(r)/ *n* Kreuzotter *f*; (*fig*) Schlange *f*

virgin /ˈvɜːdʒɪn/ *a* unberührt □ *n* Jungfrau *f*. **~ity** /-ˈdʒɪnətɪ/ *n* Unschuld *f*

Virgo /ˈvɜːgəʊ/ *n* (*Astr*) Jungfrau *f*

viril|e /ˈvɪraɪl/ *a* männlich. **~ity** /-ˈrɪlətɪ/ *n* Männlichkeit *f*

virtual /ˈvɜːtjʊəl/ *a* **a ~ ...** prak-tisch ein ... **-ly** *adv* praktisch

virtue /ˈvɜːtjuː/ *n* Tugend *f*; (*ad-vantage*) Vorteil *m*; **by or in ~ of** auf Grund (+ *gen*)

virtuoso /vɜːtjʊˈəʊzəʊ/ *n* (*pl* **-si** /-ziː/) Virtuose *m*

virtuous /ˈvɜːtjʊəs/ *a* tugendhaft

virulent /ˈvɪrʊlənt/ *a* bösartig; (*poison*) stark; (*fig*) scharf

virus /ˈvaɪrəs/ *n* Virus *nt*

visa /ˈviːzə/ *n* Visum *nt*

vis-à-vis /viːzɑːˈviː/ *adv* & *prep* ge-genüber (+ *dat*)

viscous /ˈvɪskəs/ *a* dickflüssig

visibility /vɪzəˈbɪlɪtɪ/ *n* Sichtbar-keit *f*; (*Meteorol*) Sichtweite *f*

visible /ˈvɪzəbl/ *a*, **-bly** *adv* sicht-bar

vision /ˈvɪʒn/ *n* Vision *f*; (*sight*) Sehkraft *f*; (*foresight*) Weitblick *m*

visit /'vɪzɪt/ n Besuch m □ vt besuchen; besichtigen ⟨town, building⟩. **~ing hours** npl Besuchszeiten pl. **~or** n Besucher(in) m(f); (in hotel) Gast m; **have ~ors** Besuch haben

visor /'vaɪzə(r)/ n Schirm m; (on helmet) Visier nt; (Auto) [Sonnen]blende f

vista /'vɪstə/ n Aussicht f

visual /'vɪzjuəl/ a, **-ly** adv visuell; **~ly handicapped** sehbehindert. **~ aids** npl Anschauungsmaterial nt. **~ dis'play unit** n Bildschirmgerät nt

visualize /'vɪzjuəlaɪz/ vt sich ⟨dat⟩ vorstellen

vital /'vaɪtl/ a unbedingt notwendig; (essential to life) lebenswichtig. **~ity** /vaɪ'tælətɪ/ n Vitalität f. **~ly** /'vaɪtlɪ/ adv äußerst

vitamin /'vɪtəmɪn/ n Vitamin nt

vitreous /'vɪtrɪəs/ a glasartig; (enamel) Glas-

vivacious /vɪ'veɪʃəs/ a, **-ly** adv lebhaft. **~ty** /-'væsətɪ/ n Lebhaftigkeit f

vivid /'vɪvɪd/ a, **-ly** adv lebhaft; (description) lebendig

vixen /'vɪksn/ n Füchsin f

vocabulary /və'kæbjʊlərɪ/ n Wortschatz m; (list) Vokabelverzeichnis nt; **learn ~** Vokabeln lernen

vocal /'vəʊkl/ a, **-ly** adv stimmlich; (vociferous) lautstark. **~ cords** npl Stimmbänder pl

vocalist /'vəʊkəlɪst/ n Sänger(in) m(f)

vocation /və'keɪʃn/ n Berufung f. **~al** a Berufs-

vociferous /və'sɪfərəs/ a lautstark

vodka /'vɒdkə/ n Wodka m

vogue /vəʊg/ n Mode f; **in ~** in Mode

voice /vɔɪs/ n Stimme f □ vt zum Ausdruck bringen

void /vɔɪd/ a leer; (not valid) ungültig. **~ of** ohne □ n Leere f

volatile /'vɒlətaɪl/ a flüchtig; (person) sprunghaft

volcanic /vɒl'kænɪk/ a vulkanisch

volcano /vɒl'keɪnəʊ/ n Vulkan m

volition /və'lɪʃn/ n of one's own **~** aus eigenem Willen

volley /'vɒlɪ/ n (of gunfire) Salve f; (Tennis) Volley m

volt /vəʊlt/ n Volt nt. **~age** /-ɪdʒ/ n (Electr) Spannung f

voluble /'vɒljʊbl/ a, **-bly** adv redselig; (protest) wortreich

volume /'vɒljuːm/ n (book) Band m; (Geom) Rauminhalt m; (amount) Ausmaß nt; (Radio, TV) Lautstärke f. **~ control** n Lautstärkeregler m

voluntary /'vɒləntərɪ/ a, **-ily** adv freiwillig

volunteer /vɒlən'tɪə(r)/ n Freiwillige(r) m/f □ vt anbieten; geben (information) □ vi sich freiwillig melden

voluptuous /və'lʌptjʊəs/ a sinnlich

vomit /'vɒmɪt/ n Erbrochene(s) nt □ vt erbrechen □ vi sich übergeben

voracious /və'reɪʃəs/ a gefräßig; (appetite) unbändig

vot|e /vəʊt/ n Stimme f; (ballot) Abstimmung f; (right) Wahlrecht nt; **take a ~ on** abstimmen über (+ acc) □ vi abstimmen; (in election) wählen □ vt **~e s.o. president** jdn zum Präsidenten wählen. **~er** n Wähler(in) m(f)

vouch /vaʊtʃ/ vi **~ for** sich verbürgen für. **~er** n Gutschein m

vow /vaʊ/ n Gelöbnis nt; (Relig) Gelübde nt □ vt geloben

vowel /'vaʊəl/ n Vokal m

voyage /'vɔɪɪdʒ/ n Seereise f; (in space) Reise f, Flug m

vulgar /'vʌlgə(r)/ a vulgär, ordinär. **~ity** /-'gærɪtɪ/ n Vulgarität f

vulnerable /'vʌlnərəbl/ a verwundbar

vulture /'vʌltʃə(r)/ n Geier m

vying /'vaɪɪŋ/ see vie

W

wad /wɒd/ n Bausch m; (bundle) Bündel nt. **~ding** n Wattierung f

waddle /'wɒdl/ vi watscheln

wade /weɪd/ vi waten; **~ through** (fam) sich durchackern durch ⟨book⟩

wafer /'weɪfə(r)/ n Waffel f; (Relig) Hostie f

waffle¹ /'wɒfl/ vi (fam) schwafeln

waffle² n (Culin) Waffel f

waft /wɒft/ vt/i wehen

wag /wæg/ v (pt/pp wagged) □ vt wedeln mit; **~ one's finger at s.o.** jdm mit dem Finger drohen □ vi wedeln

wage¹ /weɪdʒ/ vt führen

wage² n, & **~s** pl Lohn m. **~ packet** n Lohntüte f

wager /'weɪdʒə(r)/ n Wette f

waggle /'wægl/ vt wackeln mit □ vi wackeln

wagon /'wægən/ n Wagen m; (Rail) Waggon m

wail /weɪl/ n [klagender] Schrei m □ vi heulen; (lament) klagen

waist /weɪst/ n Taille f. **~coat** /'weɪskəʊt/ n Weste f. **~line** n Taille f

wait /weɪt/ n Wartezeit f; **lie in ~ for** auflauern (+ dat) □ vi warten (for auf + acc); (at table) servieren; **~ on** bedienen □ vt **~ one's turn** warten, bis man an der Reihe ist

waiter /'weɪtə(r)/ n Kellner m; **~!** Herr Ober!

waiting: **~-list** n Warteliste f. **~room** n Warteraum m; (doctor's) Wartezimmer n

waitress /'weɪtrɪs/ n Kellnerin f

waive /weɪv/ vt verzichten auf (+ acc)

wake¹ /weɪk/ n Totenwache f □ v (pt woke, pp woken) **~ [up]** □ vt [auf]wecken □ vi aufwachen

wake² n (Naut) Kielwasser nt; **in the ~ of** im Gefolge (+ gen)

waken /'weɪkn/ vt [auf]wecken □ vi aufwachen

Wales /weɪlz/ n Wales nt

walk /wɔːk/ n Spaziergang m; (gait) Gang m; (path) Weg m; **go for a ~** spazieren gehen □ vi gehen; (not ride) laufen, zu Fuß gehen; (ramble) wandern; **learn to ~** laufen lernen □ vt ausführen ⟨dog⟩. **~ out** vi hinausgehen; ⟨workers:⟩ in den Streik treten; **~ out on s.o.** jdn verlassen

walker /'wɔːkə(r)/ n Spaziergänger(in) m(f); (rambler) Wanderer m/Wanderin f

walking /'wɔːkɪŋ/ n Gehen nt; (rambling) Wandern nt. **~-stick** n Spazierstock m

walk: **~-out** n Streik m. **~-over** n (fig) leichter Sieg m

wall /wɔːl/ n Wand f; (external) Mauer f; **go to the ~** (fam) eingehen; **drive s.o. up the ~** (fam) jdn auf die Palme bringen □ vt **~ up** zumauern

wallet /'wɒlɪt/ n Brieftasche f

'wallflower n Goldlack m

wallop /'wɒləp/ n (fam) Schlag m □ vt (pt/pp walloped) (fam) schlagen

wallow /'wɒləʊ/ vi sich wälzen; (fig) schwelgen

'wallpaper n Tapete f □ vt tapezieren

walnut /'wɔːlnʌt/ n Walnuss f

waltz /wɔːls/ n Walzer m □ vi Walzer tanzen; **come ~ing up** (fam) angetanzt kommen

wan /wɒn/ a bleich

wand /wɒnd/ n Zauberstab m

wander /'wɒndə(r)/ vi umherwandern, (fam) bummeln; (fig. digress) abschweifen. **~ about** vi umherwandern. **~lust** n Fernweh nt

wane /weɪn/ n be on the ~
schwinden; ⟨moon:⟩ abnehmen
□ vi schwinden; abnehmen

wangle /'wæŋgl/ vt (fam) organisieren

want /wɒnt/ n Mangel m (of an
+ dat); ⟨hardship⟩ Not f; ⟨desire⟩
Bedürfnis nt □ vt wollen; ⟨need⟩
brauchen; ~ **[to have] sth** etw
haben wollen; ~ **to do sth** etw
tun wollen; **we** ~ **you to go** wir
wollen bleiben; **I** ~ **you to go** ich
will, dass du gehst; **it** ~s **painting** es müsste gestrichen werden;
you ~ **to learn to swim** du solltest schwimmen lernen □ vi **he**
doesn't ~ **for anything** ihm
fehlt es an nichts. ~**ed** a gesucht.
~**ing** a be ~**ing** fehlen; **he is**
~**ing** in ihm fehlt es an (+ dat)

wanton /'wɒntən/ a, **-ly** adv mutwillig

war /wɔː(r)/ n Krieg m; **be at** ~
sich im Krieg befinden

ward /wɔːd/ n [Kranken]saal m;
⟨unit⟩ Station f; ⟨of town⟩
Wahlbezirk m; ⟨child⟩ Mündel nt
□ vt ~ **off** abwehren

warden /'wɔːdn/ n Heimleiter(in)
m(f); ⟨of youth hostel⟩ Herbergs-
vater m; ⟨supervisor⟩ Auf-
seher(in) m(f)

warder /'wɔːdə(r)/ n Wärter(in)
m(f)

wardrobe /'wɔːdrəʊb/ n Klei-
derschrank m; ⟨clothes⟩ Garderobe f

warehouse /'weəhaʊs/ n Lager
nt; ⟨building⟩ Lagerhaus nt

wares /weəz/ npl Waren pl

war: ~**fare** n Krieg m. ~**head** n
Sprengkopf m. ~**like** a kriegerisch

warm /wɔːm/ a (-er, -est), **-ly** adv
warm; ⟨welcome⟩ herzlich; **I am**
~ mir ist warm □ vt wärmen. ~
up vt aufwärmen □ vi warm
werden; ⟨Sport⟩ sich aufwärmen.
~**-hearted** a warmherzig

warmth /wɔːmθ/ n Wärme f

warn /wɔːn/ vt warnen ⟨of vor +
dat⟩. ~**ing** n Warnung f; ⟨advance
notice⟩ Vorwarnung f; ⟨caution⟩
Verwarnung f

warp /wɔːp/ vt verbiegen □ vi sich
verziehen

war-path n on the ~ auf dem
Kriegspfad

warrant /'wɒrənt/ n ⟨for arrest⟩
Haftbefehl m; ⟨for search⟩ Durch-
suchungsbefehl m □ vt ⟨justify⟩
rechtfertigen; ⟨guarantee⟩ garantieren

warranty /'wɒrənti/ n Garantie
f

warrior /'wɒrɪə(r)/ n Krieger m

warship n Kriegsschiff nt

wart /wɔːt/ n Warze f

wartime n Kriegszeit f

wary /'weərɪ/ a (-ier, -iest), **-ily**
adv vorsichtig; ⟨suspicious⟩
misstrauisch

was /wɒz/ see **be**

wash /wɒʃ/ n Wäsche f; ⟨Naut⟩
Wellen pl; **have a** ~ sich waschen
□ vt waschen; spülen ⟨dishes⟩;
aufwischen ⟨floor⟩; ⟨flow over⟩ be-
spülen; ~ **one's hands** sich ⟨dat⟩
die Hände waschen □ vi sich
waschen; ⟨fabric:⟩ sich waschen
lassen. ~ **out** vt auswaschen; ausspülen ⟨mouth⟩. ~ **up** vt abwaschen, spülen □ vi ab-
waschen, spülen

washable /'wɒʃəbl/ a waschbar

wash: ~**basin** n Waschbecken
nt. ~**cloth** n (Amer) Waschlappen m

washed 'out a ⟨faded⟩ verwaschen; ⟨tired⟩ abgespannt

washer /'wɒʃə(r)/ n ⟨Techn⟩
Dichtungsring m; ⟨machine⟩
Waschmaschine f

washing /'wɒʃɪŋ/ n Wäsche f. ~
machine n Waschmaschine f. ~
powder n Waschpulver nt. ~**'up**
n Abwasch m; **do the** ~**'up** abwaschen, spülen. ~**'up liquid** n
Spülmittel nt

wash: ~**out** n Pleite f; ⟨person⟩
Niete f. ~**room** n Waschraum m

wasp /wɒsp/ n Wespe f
wastage /ˈweɪstɪdʒ/ n Schwund m
waste /weɪst/ n Verschwendung
f; ⟨rubbish⟩ Abfall m; **~s** pl Öde
f; **~ of time** Zeitverschwendung
f □ a ⟨product⟩ Abfall-; **lay ~** verwüsten □ vt verschwenden □ vi **~
away** immer mehr abmagern
waste: ~diˈsposal unit n Müllzerkleinerer m. **~ful** a
verschwenderisch. **~land** n Ödland nt. **~ˈpaper** n Altpapier nt.
~ˈpaper basket n Papierkorb m
watch /wɒtʃ/ n Wache f; ⟨timepiece⟩ [Armband]uhr f; **be on the
~** aufpassen □ vt beobachten;
sich ⟨dat⟩ ansehen ⟨film, match⟩;
⟨be careful of, look after⟩ achten
auf (+ acc); **~ television**
fernsehen □ vi zusehen. **~ out** vi
Ausschau halten (for nach); ⟨be
careful⟩ aufpassen
watch: ~dog n Wachhund m.
~ful a, **-ly** adv wachsam.
~maker n Uhrmacher m. **~man**
n Wachmann m. **~strap** n
Uhrarmband nt. **~tower** n
Wachturm m. **~word** n Parole f
water /ˈwɔːtə(r)/ n Wasser nt; **~s**
pl Gewässer pl □ vt gießen ⟨garden, plant⟩; ⟨dilute⟩ verdünnen;
⟨give drink to⟩ tränken □ vi ⟨eyes:⟩
tränen; **my mouth was ~ing**
mir lief das Wasser im Munde
zusammen. **~ down** vt verwässern
water: ~colour n Wasserfarbe f;
⟨painting⟩ Aquarell nt. **~cress** n
Brunnenkresse f. **~fall** n Wasserfall m
ˈwatering-can n Gießkanne f
water: ~lily n Seerose f. **~
logged** a **~logged** ⟨ground:⟩
unter Wasser stehen. **~main** n
Hauptwasserleitung f. **~mark** n
Wasserzeichen n. **~ polo** n Wasserball m. **~power** n Wasserkraft f. **~proof** a wasserdicht.
~shed n Wasserscheide f; ⟨fig⟩

Wendepunkt m. **~skiing** n Wasserskilaufen nt. **~tight** a wasserdicht. **~way** n Wasserstraße f
watery /ˈwɔːtərɪ/ a wässrig
watt /wɒt/ n Watt nt
wave /weɪv/ n Welle f; ⟨gesture⟩
Handbewegung f; ⟨as greeting⟩
Winken nt □ vt winken mit;
⟨brandish⟩ schwingen; ⟨threateningly⟩ drohen mit; wellen ⟨hair⟩;
~ one's hand winken □ vi
winken ⟨to dat⟩; ⟨flag:⟩ wehen.
~length n Wellenlänge f
waver /ˈweɪvə(r)/ vi schwanken
wavy /ˈweɪvɪ/ a wellig
wax¹ /wæks/ vi ⟨moon:⟩ zunehmen; ⟨fig: become⟩ werden
wax² n Wachs nt; ⟨in ear⟩ Schmalz
nt □ vt wachsen. **~works** n
Wachsfigurenkabinett nt
way /weɪ/ n Weg m; ⟨direction⟩
Richtung f; ⟨respect⟩ Hinsicht f;
⟨manner⟩ Art f; ⟨method⟩ Art und
Weise f; **~s** pl Gewohnheiten pl;
in the ~ im Weg; **on the ~** auf
dem Weg ⟨to nach/zu⟩; ⟨under
way⟩ unterwegs; **a little/long
~ off** weit weg; **this ~** hierher;
⟨like this⟩ so; **which ~** in welche
Richtung; ⟨how⟩ wie; **by the ~**
übrigens; **in some ~s** in gewisser Hinsicht; **either ~** so oder
so; **in this ~** auf diese Weise; **in
a ~** in gewisser Weise; **in a bad
~** ⟨person⟩ in schlechter Verfassung; **lead the ~** vorausgehen;
make ~ Platz machen ⟨for dat⟩;
'give ~' ⟨Auto⟩ 'Vorfahrt beachten'; **go out of one's ~** ⟨fig⟩
sich ⟨dat⟩ besondere Mühe geben
⟨to zu⟩; **get one's [own] ~** seinen
Willen durchsetzen □ adv weit; **~
behind** weit zurück. **~in** n Eingang m
wayˈlay vt ⟨pt/pp **-laid**⟩ überfallen; ⟨fam: intercept⟩ abfangen
way 'out n Ausgang m; ⟨fig⟩
Ausweg m
way-'out a ⟨fam⟩ verrückt

wayward /ˈweɪwəd/ a eigenwillig

WC abbr WC nt

we /wiː/ pron wir

weak /wiːk/ a (-er, -est), **-ly** adv schwach; ⟨liquid⟩ dünn. **~en** vt schwächen □ vi schwächer werden. **~ling** n Schwächling m. **~ness** n Schwäche f

wealth /welθ/ n Reichtum m; (fig) Fülle f (of an + dat). **~y** a (-ier, -iest) reich

wean /wiːn/ vt entwöhnen

weapon /ˈwepən/ n Waffe f

wear /weə(r)/ n (clothing) Kleidung f; **~ and tear** Abnutzung f, Verschleiß m □ v (pt **wore**, pp **worn**) □ vt tragen; (damage) abnutzen; **~ a hole in sth** etw durchwetzen; **what shall I ~?** was soll ich anziehen? □ vi sich abnutzen; (last) halten. **~ off** vi abgehen; (effect:) nachlassen. **~ out** vt abnutzen; (exhaust) erschöpfen □ vi sich abnutzen

wearable /ˈweərəbl/ a tragbar

weary /ˈwɪərɪ/ a (-ier, -iest), **-ily** adv müde □ v (pt/pp **wearied**) □ vt ermüden □ vi **~ of sth** etw (gen) überdrüssig werden

weasel /ˈwiːzl/ n Wiesel nt

weather /ˈweðə(r)/ n Wetter nt; **in this ~** bei diesem Wetter; **under the ~** (fam) nicht ganz auf dem Posten □ vt abwettern (storm); (fig) überstehen

weather: **~-beaten** a verwittert; wettergegerbt (face). **~-cock** n Wetterhahn m. **~-forecast** n Wettervorhersage f. **~-vane** n Wetterfahne f

weave¹ /wiːv/ vi (pt/pp **weaved**) sich schlängeln (through durch)

weave² n (Tex) Bindung f □ vt (pt **wove**, pp **woven**) weben; (plait) flechten; (fig) einflechten (in in + acc). **~r** n Weber m

web /web/ n Netz nt. **~bed feet** npl Schwimmfüße pl

wed /wed/ vt/i (pt/pp **wedded**) heiraten. **~ding** n Hochzeit f; (ceremony) Trauung f

wedding: **~ day** n Hochzeitstag m. **~ dress** n Hochzeitskleid nt. **~-ring** n Ehering m, Trauring m

wedge /wedʒ/ n Keil m; (of cheese) [keilförmiges] Stück nt □ vt festklemmen

wedlock /ˈwedlɒk/ n (liter) Ehe f; **in/out of ~** ehelich/unehelich

Wednesday /ˈwenzdeɪ/ n Mittwoch m

wee /wiː/ a (fam) klein □ vi Pipi machen

weed /wiːd/ n & **~s** pl Unkraut nt □ vt/i jäten. **~ out** vt (fig) aussieben

'weed-killer n Unkrautvertilgungsmittel nt

weedy /ˈwiːdɪ/ a (fam) spillerig

week /wiːk/ n Woche f. **~day** n Wochentag m. **~end** n Wochenende nt

weekly /ˈwiːklɪ/ a & adv wöchentlich □ n Wochenzeitschrift f

weep /wiːp/ vi (pt/pp **wept**) weinen. **~ing 'willow** n Trauerweide f

weigh /weɪ/ vt/i wiegen; **~ anchor** den Anker lichten. **~ down** vt (fig) niederdrücken. **~ up** vt (fig) abwägen

weight /weɪt/ n Gewicht nt; **put on/lose ~** zunehmen/abnehmen. **~ing** n (allowance) Zulage f

weight: **~lessness** n Schwerelosigkeit f. **~-lifting** n Gewichtheben nt

weighty /ˈweɪtɪ/ a (-ier, -iest) schwer; (important) gewichtig

weir /wɪə(r)/ n Wehr nt.

weird /wɪəd/ a (-er, -est) unheimlich; (bizarre) bizarr

welcome /ˈwelkəm/ a willkommen; **you're ~!** nichts zu danken! **you're ~ to have it** das können Sie gerne haben □ n Willkommen nt □ vt begrüßen

weld /weld/ vt schweißen. **~er** n
Schweißer m

welfare /'welfeə(r)/ n Wohl nt;
(Admin) Fürsorge f. **W~** State n
Wohlfahrtsstaat m

well[1] /wel/ n Brunnen m; (oil ~)
Quelle f; (of staircase) Treppen-
haus nt

well[2] adv (better, best) gut; as ~
auch; **as ~ as** (in addition)
sowohl ... als auch; **~ done!** gut
gemacht! □ a gesund; **he is not ~**
es geht ihm nicht gut; **get ~
soon!** gute Besserung! □ int nun,
na

well: **~-behaved** a artig. **~-
being** n Wohl nt. **~-bred** a
wohlerzogen. **~-heeled** a (fam)
gut betucht

wellingtons /'welɪŋtənz/ npl
Gummistiefel pl

well: **~-known** a bekannt. **~-
meaning** a wohlmeinend. **~-
meant** a gut gemeint. **~-off** a
wohlhabend; **be ~-off** gut dran
sein. **~-read** a belesen. **~-to-do**
a wohlhabend

Welsh /welʃ/ a walisisch □ n
(Lang) Walisisch nt; **the ~** pl die
Waliser. **~ man** n Waliser m. **~
rabbit** n überbackenes Käsebrot
nt

went /went/ see **go**

wept /wept/ see **weep**

were /wɜ:(r)/ see **be**

west /west/ n Westen m; **to the ~
of** westlich von □ a West-, west-
□ adv nach Westen; **go ~** (fam)
flöten gehen. **~erly** a westlich.
~ern a westlich □ n Western m

West: **~ 'Germany** n
Westdeutschland nt. **~ 'Indian** a
westindisch □ n Westinder(in)
m(f). **~ 'Indies** /-'ɪndɪz/ npl
Westindische Inseln pl

'westward[s] /-wəd[z]/ adv nach
Westen

wet /wet/ a (wetter, wettest)
nass; (fam: person) weichlich;

lasch; '~ **paint** 'frisch gestrichen' □ vt (pt/pp wet or wet-
ted) nass machen. **~ 'blanket** n
Spaßverderber m

whack /wæk/ n (fam) Schlag m
□ vt (fam) schlagen. **~ed** a (fam)
kaputt

whale /weɪl/ n Wal m; **have a ~ of
a time** (fam) sich toll amüsieren

wharf /wɔ:f/ n Kai m

what /wɒt/ pron & int was; **~ for?**
wozu? **~ is it like?** wie ist es? **~
is your name?** wie ist Ihr Name?
~ is the weather like? wie ist
das Wetter? **~'s he talking
about?** wovon redet er? □ a
welche(r,s); **~ kind of a** was für
ein(e); **at ~ time?** um wie viel
Uhr?

what'ever /wɒt'evə(r)/ a [egal] welche(r,s)
□ pron was ... auch; **~ is it?** was
ist das bloß? **~ he does** was er
auch tut; **~ happens** was auch
geschieht; **nothing ~** überhaupt
nichts

whatso'ever pron & a ≈ **whatever**

wheat /wi:t/ n Weizen m

wheedle /'wi:dl/ vt gut zureden
(+ dat); **~ sth out of s.o.** jdm
etw ablocken

wheel /wi:l/ n Rad nt; (pottery)
Töpferscheibe f; (steering ~)
Lenkrad nt; **at the ~** am Steuer
□ vt (push) schieben □ vi kehrt-
machen; (circle) kreisen

wheel: **~barrow** n Schubkarre f.
~chair n Rollstuhl m. **~clamp**
n Parkkralle f

wheeze /wi:z/ vi keuchen

when /wen/ adv wann; **the day ~**
der Tag, an dem □ conj wenn; (in
the past) als; (although) wo ...
doch; **~ swimming/reading**
beim Schwimmen/Lesen

whence /wens/ adv (liter) woher

when'ever conj & adv [immer]
wenn; (at whatever time) wann
immer; **~ did it happen?** wann
ist das bloß passiert?

where /weə(r)/ adv & conj wo; ~ [to] wohin; ~ [from] woher

whereabouts¹ /weərə'baʊts/ adv wo

whereabouts² n Verbleib m; (of person) Aufenthaltsort m

where'as conj während; (in contrast) wohingegen

where'by adv wodurch

whereu'pon adv worauf[hin]

wher'ever conj & adv wo immer; (to whatever place) wohin immer; (from whatever place) woher immer; (everywhere) überall wo; ~ **is he?** wo ist er bloß? ~ **possible** wenn irgend möglich

whet /wet/ vt (pt/pp whetted) wetzen; anregen (appetite)

whether /'weðə(r)/ conj ob

which /wɪtʃ/ a & pron welche(r,s); ~ **one** welche(r,s) □ rel pron der/die/das, (pl) die; (after clause) was; **after** ~ wonach; **on** ~ worauf

which'ever a & pron [egal] welche(r,s); ~ **it is** was es auch ist

whiff /wɪf/ n Hauch m

while /waɪl/ n Weile f; **a long** ~ lange; **be worth** ~ lohnen; **its worth my** ~ es lohnt sich für mich □ conj während; (as long as) solange; (although) obgleich □ vt ~ **away** sich (dat) vertreiben

whilst /waɪlst/ conj während

whim /wɪm/ n Laune f

whimper /'wɪmpə(r)/ vi wimmern; (dog:) winseln

whimsical /'wɪmzɪkl/ a skurril

whine /waɪn/ n Winseln nt □ vi winseln

whip /wɪp/ n Peitsche f; (Pol) Einpeitscher m □ vt (pt/pp whipped) peitschen; (Culin) schlagen; (snatch) reißen; (fam: steal) klauen. ~ **up** vt (incite) anheizen; (fam) schnell hinzaubern (meal). ~**ped 'cream** n Schlagsahne f

whirl /wɜːl/ n Wirbel m; **I am in a** ~ mir schwirrt der Kopf □ vt/i

wirbeln. ~**pool** n Strudel m. ~**wind** n Wirbelwind m

whirr /wɜː(r)/ vi surren

whisk /wɪsk/ n (Culin) Schneebesen m □ vt (Culin) schlagen. ~ **away** vt wegreißen

whisker /'wɪskə(r)/ n Schnurrhaar nt; ~**s** pl (on man's cheek) Backenbart m

whisky /'wɪskɪ/ n Whisky m

whisper /'wɪspə(r)/ n Flüstern nt; (rumour) Gerücht nt; **in a** ~ im Flüsterton □ vt/i flüstern

whistle /'wɪsl/ n Pfiff m; (instrument) Pfeife f □ vt/i pfeifen

white /waɪt/ a (-r, -st) weiß □ n Weiß nt; (of egg) Eiweiß nt; (person) Weiße(r) m/f

white: ~**'coffee** n Kaffee m mit Milch. ~**'collar worker** n Angestellte(r) m. ~**'lie** n Notlüge f

whiten /'waɪtn/ vt weiß machen □ vi weiß werden

whiteness /'waɪtnɪs/ n Weiß nt

'whitewash n Tünche f; (fig) Schönfärberei f □ vt tünchen

Whitsun /'wɪtsn/ n Pfingsten (pl)

whittle /'wɪtl/ vt ~ **down** reduzieren; kürzen (list)

whiz[z] /wɪz/ vi (pt/pp whizzed) zischen. ~**kid** n (fam) Senkrechtstarter m

who /huː/ pron wer; (acc) wen; (dat) wem □ rel pron der/die/das, (pl) die

who'ever pron wer [immer]; ~ **he is** wer er auch ist; ~ **is it?** wer ist das bloß?

whole /həʊl/ a ganz; (truth) voll □ n Ganze(s) nt; **as a** ~ als Ganzes; **on the** ~ im Großen und Ganzen; **the** ~ **lot** alle; (everything) alles; **the** ~ **of Germany** ganz Deutschland; **the** ~ **time** die ganze Zeit

whole: ~**food** n Vollwertkost f. ~**'hearted** a rüc[ ]. ~**meal** a Vollkorn-

'wholesale a Großha[ ]en gros; (fig) in [ ] Bogen. ~**r** n Groß[ ]

wholesome /ˈhəʊlsəm/ *a* gesund

wholly /ˈhəʊlɪ/ *adv* völlig

whom /huːm/ *pron* wen; **to ~** wem □ *rel pron* den/die/das, *(pl)* die; *(dat)* dem/der/dem, *(pl)* denen

whooping cough /ˈhuːpɪŋ-/ *n* Keuchhusten *m*

whopping /ˈwɒpɪŋ/ *a (fam)* Riesen-

whore /hɔː(r)/ *n* Hure *f*

whose /huːz/ *pron* wessen; **~ is that?** wem gehört das? □ *rel pron* dessen/deren/dessen, *(pl)* deren

why /waɪ/ *adv* warum; *(for what purpose)* wozu; **that's ~** darum □ *int* na

wick /wɪk/ *n* Docht *m*

wicked /ˈwɪkɪd/ *a* böse; *(mischievous)* frech, boshaft

wicker /ˈwɪkə(r)/ *n* Korbgeflecht *nt* □ *attrib* Korb-

wide /waɪd/ *a* (-**r**,-**st**) weit; *(broad)* breit; *(fig)* groß; **be ~** *(far from target)* danebengehen □ *adv* weit; *(off target)* daneben; **~ awake** hellwach; **far and ~** weit und breit. **~ly** *adv* weit; *(known, accepted)* weithin; *(differ)* stark

widen /ˈwaɪdn/ *vt* verbreitern; *(fig)* erweitern □ *vi* sich verbreitern

widespread *a* weit verbreitet

widow /ˈwɪdəʊ/ *n* Witwe *f*. **~ed** *a* verwitwet. **~er** *n* Witwer *m*

width /wɪdθ/ *n* Weite *f*; *(breadth)* Breite *f*

wield /wiːld/ *vt* schwingen; ausüben *(power)*

wife /waɪf/ *n (pl* **wives**) [Ehe]frau *f*

wig /wɪg/ *n* Perücke *f*

wiggle /ˈwɪgl/ *vi* wackeln □ *vt* wackeln mit

wild /waɪld/ *a* (-**er**, -**est**), -**ly** *adv* wild; *(animal)* wild lebend; *(flower)* wild wachsend; *(furious)* wütend; **be ~ about** *(keen on)* wild sein auf (+ *acc*) □ *adv* wild; **n ~** frei herumlaufen □ *n* in

the **~** wild; **the ~s** *pl* die Wildnis *f*

wildcat strike *n* wilder Streik *m*

wilderness /ˈwɪldənɪs/ *n* Wildnis *f*; *(desert)* Wüste *f*

wild: **~ goose chase** *n* aussichtslose Suche *f*. **~life** *n* Tierwelt *f*

wilful /ˈwɪlfl/ *a*, -**ly** *adv* mutwillig; *(self-willed)* eigenwillig

will[1] /wɪl/ *v aux* wollen; *(forming future tense)* werden; **he ~ arrive tomorrow** er wird morgen kommen; **~ you go?** gehst du? **you ~ be back soon, won't you?** du kommst doch bald wieder, nicht? **he ~ be there, won't he?** er wird doch da sein? **she ~ be there by now** sie wird jetzt schon da sein; **~ you be quiet!** willst du wohl ruhig sein! **~ you have some wine?** möchten Sie Wein? **the engine won't start** der Motor will nicht anspringen

will[2] *n* Wille *m*; *(document)* Testament *nt*

willing /ˈwɪlɪŋ/ *a* willig; *(eager)* bereitwillig; **be ~** bereit sein. **~ly** *adv* bereitwillig; *(gladly)* gern. **~ness** *n* Bereitwilligkeit *f*

willow /ˈwɪləʊ/ *n* Weide *f*

will-power *n* Willenskraft *f*

willy-nilly *adv* wohl oder übel

wilt /wɪlt/ *vi* welk werden, welken

wily /ˈwaɪlɪ/ *a* (-**ier**, -**iest**) listig

wimp /wɪmp/ *n* Schwächling *m*

win /wɪn/ *n* Sieg *m*; **have a ~** gewinnen □ *v (pt/pp* **won**; *pres p* **winning**) □ *vi* gewinnen; bekommen *(scholarship)* □ *vi* gewinnen; *(in battle)* siegen. **~ over** *vt* auf seine Seite bringen

wince /wɪns/ *vi* zusammenzucken

winch /wɪntʃ/ *n* Winde *f* □ *vt* **~ up** hochwinden

wind[1] /wɪnd/ *n* Wind *m*; *(breath)* Atem *m*; *(fam: flatulence)* Blähungen *pl*; **have the ~ up** *(fam)* Angst haben □ *vt* **~ s.o.** jdm den Atem nehmen

wind² /waɪnd/ v (pt/pp **wound**) □ vt (wrap) wickeln; (move by turning) kurbeln; (clock) ~ vi (road): sich winden. ~ **up** vt aufziehen (clock); schließen (proceedings)

wind /wɪnd/: ~**fall** n unerwarteter Glücksfall m. ~**falls** pl (fruit) Fallobst nt. ~**instrument** n Blasinstrument nt. ~**mill** n Windmühle f

window /ˈwɪndəʊ/ n Fenster nt; (of shop) Schaufenster nt

window: ~-**box** n Blumenkasten m. ~-**cleaner** n Fensterputzer m. ~-**dresser** n Schaufensterdekorateur(in) m(f). ~-**dressing** n Schaufensterdekoration f; (fig) Schönfärberei f. ~-**pane** n Fensterscheibe f. ~-**shopping** n Schaufensterbummel m. ~-**sill** n Fensterbrett nt

windpipe n Luftröhre f

windscreen n, (Amer) **'windshield** n Windschutzscheibe f. ~ **washer** n Scheibenwaschanlage f. ~**wiper** n Scheibenwischer m

wind: ~ **surfing** n Windsurfen nt. ~**swept** a windgepeitscht; (person) zersaust

windy /ˈwɪndɪ/ a (-ier, -iest) windig; **be** ~ (fam) Angst haben

wine /waɪn/ n Wein m

wine: ~-**bar** n Weinstube f. ~**glass** n Weinglas nt. ~-**list** n Weinkarte f

winery /ˈwaɪnərɪ/ n (Amer) Weingut nt

'wine-tasting n Weinprobe f

wing /wɪŋ/ n Flügel m; (Auto) Kotflügel m. ~**s** pl (Theat) Kulissen pl

wink /wɪŋk/ n Zwinkern nt; **not sleep a** ~ kein Auge zutun □ vi zwinkern; (light:) blinken

winner /ˈwɪnə(r)/ n Gewinner(in) m(f); (Sport) Sieger(in) m(f)

winning /ˈwɪnɪŋ/ a siegreich; (smile) gewinnend. ~-**post** n Zielpfosten m. ~**s** npl Gewinn m

wint|er /ˈwɪntə(r)/ n Winter m. ~**ry** a winterlich

wipe /waɪp/ n give sth a ~ etw abwischen □ vt abwischen; aufwischen (floor); (dry) abtrocknen. ~ **off** vt abwischen; (erase) auslöschen. ~ **out** vt (cancel) löschen; (destroy) ausrotten. ~ **up** vt aufwischen; abtrocknen (dishes)

wire /ˈwaɪə(r)/ n Draht m. ~-**haired** a rauhaarig

wireless /ˈwaɪəlɪs/ n Radio nt

wire 'netting n Maschendraht m

wiring /ˈwaɪərɪŋ/ n [elektrische] Leitungen pl

wiry /ˈwaɪərɪ/ a (-ier, -iest) drahtig

wisdom /ˈwɪzdəm/ n Weisheit f; (prudence) Klugheit f. ~ **tooth** n Weisheitszahn m

wise /waɪz/ a (-r, -st), **-ly** adv weise; (prudent) klug

wish /wɪʃ/ n Wunsch m □ vt wünschen; ~ **s.o. well** jdm alles Gute wünschen; **I** ~ **you could stay** ich wünschte, du könntest hier bleiben □ vi sich (dat) etwas wünschen. ~**ful** a ~**ful thinking** Wunschdenken nt

wishy-washy /ˈwɪʃɪwɒʃɪ/ a labberig; (colour) verwaschen; (person) lasch

wisp /wɪsp/ n Büschel nt; (of hair) Strähne f; (of smoke) Fahne f

wisteria /wɪsˈtɪərɪə/ n Glyzinie f

wistful /ˈwɪstfl/ a, **-ly** adv wehmütig

wit /wɪt/ n Geist m, Witz m; (intelligence) Verstand m; (person) geistreicher Mensch m; **be at one's ~s' end** sich (dat) keinen Rat mehr wissen; **scared out of one's ~s** zu Tode erschrocken

witch /wɪtʃ/ n Hexe f. ~**craft** n Hexerei f. ~-**hunt** n Hexenjagd f

with /wɪð/ prep mit (+ dat); ~ **fear/cold** vor Angst/Kälte; ~ **it** damit; **I'm going** ~ **you** ich gehe mit; **take it** ~ **you** nimm es mit;

I haven't got it ~ me ich habe
es nicht bei mir; **I'm not ~ you**
(fam) ich komme nicht mit

with'draw v (pt -**drew**, pp
-**drawn**) □ vt zurückziehen; abheben (money) □ vi sich zurückziehen. **~al** n Zurückziehen nt;
(of money) Abhebung f; (from
drugs) Entzug m. **~al symptoms**
npl Entzugserscheinungen pl

with'drawn see **withdraw** □ a
(person) verschlossen

wither /'wɪðə(r)/ vi [ver]welken

with'hold vt (pt/pp -**held**) vorenthalten (from s.o. jdm)

with'in prep innerhalb (+ gen); ~
the law im Rahmen des Gesetzes
□ adv innen

with'out prep ohne (+ acc); ~ **my
noticing** it ohne dass ich es
merkte

with'stand vt (pt/pp -**stood**)
standhalten (+ dat)

witness /'wɪtnɪs/ n Zeuge m/ Zeugin f; (evidence) Zeugnis nt □ vt
Zeuge/Zeugin sein (+ gen); bestätigen (signature). **~-box** n,
(Amer) **~-stand** n Zeugenstand
m

witticism /'wɪtɪsɪzm/ n geistreicher Ausspruch m

wittingly /'wɪtɪŋlɪ/ adv wissentlich

witty /'wɪtɪ/ a (-**ier, -iest**) witzig,
geistreich

wives /waɪvz/ see **wife**

wizard /'wɪzəd/ n Zauberer m.
~ry n Zauberei f

wizened /'wɪznd/ a verhutzelt

wobble /'wɒbl/ vi wackeln. **~ly**
a wackelig

woe /wəʊ/ n (liter) Jammer m; ~
is me! wehe mir!

woke, woken /wəʊk, 'wəʊkn/ see
wake¹

wolf /wʊlf/ n (pl **wolves** /wʊlvz/)
Wolf m □ vt ~ [**down**] hinunterschlingen

woman /'wʊmən/ n (pl **women**)
Frau f. **~izer** n Schürzenjäger m.
~ly a fraulich

womb /wuːm/ n Gebärmutter f

women /'wɪmɪn/ npl see **woman**;
W~'s Libber /'lɪbə(r)/ n Frauen-
rechtlerin f. **W~'s Liberation** n
Frauenbewegung f

won /wʌn/ see **win**

wonder /'wʌndə(r)/ n Wunder nt;
(surprise) Staunen nt □ vt/i wundern; (be surprised) sich wundern; **I ~ da** frage ich mich; **I ~
whether she is ill** ob sie wohl
krank ist? **~ful a, -ly** adv wunderbar

won't /wəʊnt/ = **will not**

woo /wuː/ vt (liter) werben um;
(fig) umwerben

wood /wʊd/ n Holz nt; (forest)
Wald m; **touch ~!** unberufen!

wood: **~cut** n Holzschnitt m. **~ed**
/-ɪd/ a bewaldet. **~en** a Holz-,
(fig) hölzern. **~pecker** n Specht
m. **~wind** n Holzbläser pl.
~work n (wooden parts) Holz-
teile pl; (craft) Tischlerei f.
~worm n Holzwurm m. **~y** a
holzig

wool /wʊl/ n Wolle f □ attrib
Woll-. **~len** a wollen. **~lens** npl
Wollsachen pl

woolly /'wʊlɪ/ a (-**ier, -iest**) wol-
lig; (fig) unklar

word /wɜːd/ n Wort nt; (news)
Nachricht f; **by ~ of mouth**
mündlich; **have a ~ with**
sprechen mit; **have ~s** einen
Wortwechsel haben. **~ing** n
Wortlaut m. **~ processor** n
Textverarbeitungssystem nt

wore /wɔː(r)/ see **wear**

work /wɜːk/ n Arbeit f; (Art,
Literature) Werk nt; **~s** pl
(factory, mechanism) Werk nt; **at
~** bei der Arbeit; **out of ~** arbeitslos □ vi arbeiten; (machine,
system:) funktionieren; (have
effect) wirken; (study) lernen; **it
won't ~** (fig) es klappt nicht □ vt
arbeiten lassen; bedienen
(machine); betätigen (lever); **~
one's way through sth** sich
durch etw hindurcharbeiten.

off *vt* abarbeiten. ~ **out** *vt* ausrechnen; (*solve*) lösen □ *vi* gut gehen, (*fam*) klappen. ~ **up** *vt* aufbauen; sich (*dat*) holen (*appetite*); **get** ~**ed up** sich aufregen

workable /'wɜːkəbl/ *a* (*feasible*) durchführbar

workaholic /wɜːkə'hɒlɪk/ *n* arbeitswütiger Mensch *m*

worker /'wɜːkə(r)/ *n* Arbeiter(in) *m(f)*

working /'wɜːkɪŋ/ *a* berufstätig; (*day, clothes*) Arbeits-; **be in ~ order** funktionieren. ~ **class** *n* Arbeiterklasse *f*. ~**class** *a* Arbeiter-. ~**class** zur Arbeiterklasse gehören

work: ~**man** *n* Arbeiter *m*; (*craftsman*) Handwerker *m*. ~**manship** *n* Arbeit *f*. ~**out** *n* [Fitness]training *nt*. ~**shop** *n* Werkstatt *f*

world /wɜːld/ *n* Welt *f*; **in the** ~ auf der Welt; **a** ~ **of difference** ein himmelweiter Unterschied; **think the** ~ **of s.o.** große Stücke auf jdn halten. ~**ly** *a* weltlich; (*person*) weltlich gesinnt. ~**wide** *a & adv* /-'-/ weltweit

worm /wɜːm/ *n* Wurm *m* □ *vi* ~ **one's way into s.o.'s confidence** sich in jds Vertrauen einschleichen. ~**eaten** *a* wurmstichig

worn /wɔːn/ *see* **wear** □ *a* abgetragen. ~**out** *a* abgetragen; (*carpet*) abgenutzt; (*person*) erschöpft

worried /'wʌrɪd/ *a* besorgt

worry /'wʌrɪ/ *n* Sorge *f* □ *v* (*pt/pp* **worried**) □ *vt* beunruhigen, Sorgen machen (+ *dat*); (*bother*) stören □ *vi* sich beunruhigen, sich (*dat*) Sorgen machen. ~**ing** *a* beunruhigend

worse /wɜːs/ *a & adv* schlechter; (*more serious*) schlimmer □ *n* Schlechtere(s) *nt*; Schlimmere(s) *nt*

worsen /'wɜːsn/ *vt* verschlechtern □ *vi* sich verschlechtern

worship /'wɜːʃɪp/ *n* Anbetung *f*; (*service*) Gottesdienst *m*;

Your/His W ~ Euer/Seine Ehren □ *v* (*pt/pp* **-shipped**) □ *vt* anbeten □ *vi* am Gottesdienst teilnehmen

worst /wɜːst/ *a* schlechteste(r,s); (*most serious*) schlimmste(r,s) □ *adv* am schlechtesten; **am schlimmsten** □ *n* **the** ~ das Schlimmste; **get the** ~ **of it** den Kürzeren ziehen

worsted /'wʊstɪd/ *n* Kammgarn *m*

worth /wɜːθ/ *a* Wert *m*; **£10's ~ of petrol** Benzin für £10 □ *a* **be ~ £5** £5 wert sein; **be ~ it** (*fig*) sich lohnen. ~**less** *a* wertlos. ~**while** *a* lohnend

worthy /'wɜːðɪ/ *a* würdig

would /wʊd/ *v aux* **I ~ do it** ich würde es tun, ich täte es; ~ **you go?** würdest du gehen? **he said he ~n't** er sagte, er würde es nicht tun; **what ~ you like?** was möchten Sie?

wound[1] /wuːnd/ *n* Wunde *f* □ *vt* verwunden

wound[2] /waʊnd/ *see* **wind**[2]

wove, woven /wəʊv, 'wəʊvn/ *see* **weave**[1]

wrangle /'ræŋgl/ *n* Streit *m* □ *vi* sich streiten

wrap /ræp/ *n* Umhang *m* □ *vt* (*pt/pp* **wrapped**) ~ **[up]** wickeln; einpacken (*present*) □ *vi* ~ **up** warmly sich warm einpacken; **be ~ped up in** (*fig*) aufgehen in (+ *dat*). ~**per** *n* Hülle *f*. ~**ping** *n* Verpackung *f*. ~**ping paper** *n* Einwickelpapier *nt*

wrath /rɒθ/ *n* Zorn *m*

wreak /riːk/ *vt* ~ **havoc** Verwüstungen anrichten

wreath /riːθ/ *n* (*pl* ~**s** /-ðz/) Kranz *m*

wreck /rek/ *n* Wrack *nt* □ *vt* zerstören; zunichte machen (*plans*); zerrütten (*marriage*). ~**age** /-ɪdʒ/ *n* Wrackteile *pl*; (*fig*) Trümmer *pl*

wren /ren/ *n* Zaunkönig *m*

wrench /rentʃ/ n Ruck m; (tool) Schraubenschlüssel m; **be a ~** (fig) weh tun □ vt reißen; **~sth from s.o.** jdm etw entreißen

wrest /rest/ vt entwinden (**from s.o.** jdm)

wrestl|e /'resl/ vi ringen. **~er** n Ringer m. **~ing** n Ringen nt

wretch /retʃ/ n Kreatur f. **~ed** /-ɪd/ a elend; (very bad) erbärmlich

wriggle /'rɪgl/ n Zappeln nt □ vi zappeln; (move forward) sich schlängeln; **~ out of sth** (fam) sich vor etw (dat) drücken

wring /rɪŋ/ vt (pt/pp **wrung**) wringen; (**~ out**) auswringen; umdrehen (neck); ringen (hands); **be ~ing wet** tropfnass sein

wrinkle /'rɪŋkl/ n Falte f; (on skin) Runzel f □ vt kräuseln □ vi sich kräuseln, sich falten. **~d** a runzlig

wrist /rɪst/ n Handgelenk nt. **~watch** n Armbanduhr f

writ /rɪt/ n (Jur) Verfügung f

write /raɪt/ vt/i (pt **wrote**, pp **written**, pres.p **writing**) schreiben. **~ down** vt aufschreiben. **~ off** vt abschreiben; zu Schrott fahren (car)

'write-off n ≈ Totalschaden m

writer /'raɪtə(r)/ n Schreiber(in) m(f); (author) Schriftsteller(in) m(f)

'write-up n Bericht m; (review) Kritik f

writhe /raɪð/ vi sich winden

writing /'raɪtɪŋ/ n Schreiben nt; (handwriting) Schrift f; **in ~** schriftlich. **~-paper** n Schreibpapier nt

written /'rɪtn/ see **write**

wrong /rɒŋ/ a, **-ly** adv falsch; (morally) unrecht; (not just) ungerecht; **be ~** nicht stimmen; (person:) Unrecht haben; **what's ~?** was ist los? □ adv falsch; **go ~** (person:) etwas falsch machen; (machine:) kaputtgehen; (plan:) schief gehen □ n Unrecht nt □ vt

Unrecht tun (+ dat). **~ful** a ungerechtfertigt. **~fully** adv (accuse) zu Unrecht

wrote /rəʊt/ see **write**

wrought 'iron /rɔːt-/ n Schmiedeeisen nt □ attrib schmiedeeisern

wrung /rʌŋ/ see **wring**

wry /raɪ/ a (-er, -est) ironisch; (humour) trocken

X

xerox (P) /'zɪərɒks/ vt fotokopieren

Xmas /'krɪsməs, 'eksməs/ n (fam) Weihnachten nt

X-ray /'eks-/ n (picture) Röntgenaufnahme f; **~s** pl Röntgenstrahlen pl; **have an ~** geröntgt werden □ vt röntgen; durchleuchten (luggage)

Y

yacht /jɒt/ n Jacht f; (for racing) Segelboot nt. **~ing** n Segeln nt

yank /jæŋk/ vt (fam) reißen

Yank n (fam) Amerikaner(in) m(f), (fam) Ami m

yap /jæp/ vi (pt/pp **yapped**) (dog:) kläffen

yard¹ /jɑːd/ n Hof m; (for storage) Lager nt

yard² n Yard nt (= 0,91 m). **~stick** n (fig) Maßstab m

yarn /jɑːn/ n Garn nt; (fam: tale) Geschichte f

yawn /jɔːn/ n Gähnen nt □ vi gähnen. **~ing** a gähnend

year /jɪə(r)/ n Jahr nt; (of wine) Jahrgang m; **for ~s** jahrelang. **~book** n Jahrbuch nt. **~ly** a & adv jährlich

yearn /jɜːn/ vi sich sehnen (**for** nach). **~ing** n Sehnsucht f

yeast /jiːst/ n Hefe f

yell /jel/ n Schrei m □ vi schreien

yellow /'jeləʊ/ a gelb □ n Gelb nt. ~**ish** a gelblich

yelp /jelp/ vi jaulen

yen /jen/ n Wunsch m (**for** nach)

yes /jes/ adv ja; (contradicting) doch □ n Ja nt

yesterday /'jestədeɪ/ n & adv gestern; ~'**s paper** die gestrige Zeitung; **the day before** ~ vorgestern

yet /jet/ adv noch; (in question) schon; (nevertheless) doch; **as** ~ bisher; **not** ~ noch nicht; **the best** ~ das bisher beste □ conj doch

yew /juː/ n Eibe f

Yiddish /'jɪdɪʃ/ n Jiddisch nt

yield /jiːld/ n Ertrag m □ vt bringen; abwerfen (profit) □ vi nachgeben; (Amer, Auto) die Vorfahrt beachten

yodel /'jəʊdl/ vi (pt/pp yodelled) jodeln

yoga /'jəʊgə/ n Yoga m

yoghurt /'jɒgət/ n Joghurt m

yoke /jəʊk/ n Joch nt; (of garment) Passe f

yokel /'jəʊkl/ n Bauerntölpel m

yolk /jəʊk/ n Dotter m, Eigelb nt

yonder /'jɒndə(r)/ adv (liter) dort drüben

you /juː/ pron du; (acc) dich; (dat) dir; (pl) ihr; (acc, dat) euch; (formal) (nom & acc, dat) Sie; (dat, sg & pl) Ihnen; (one) man; (acc) einen; (dat) einem; **all of** ~ ihr/Sie alle; **I know** ~ ich kenne dich/euch/Sie; **I'll give** ~ **the money** ich gebe dir/euch/Ihnen das Geld; **it does** ~ **good** es tut einem gut; **it's bad for** ~ es ist ungesund

young /jʌŋ/ a (-er /-gə(r)/, -est /-gɪst/) jung □ npl (animals) Junge pl; **the** ~ die Jugend f. ~**ster** n Jugendliche(r) m/f; (child) Kleine(r) m/f

your /jɔː(r)/ a dein; (pl) euer; (formal) Ihr

yours /jɔːz/ poss pron deine(r), deins; (pl) eure(r), euers; (formal, sg & pl) Ihre(r), Ihr[e]s; **a friend of** ~ ein Freund von dir/Ihnen/euch; **that is** ~ das gehört dir/Ihnen/euch

your'self pron (pl -selves) selbst; (refl) dich; (dat) dir; euch; (formal) sich; **by** ~ allein

youth /juːθ/ n (pl youths /-ðːz/) Jugend f; (boy) Jugendliche(r) m. ~**ful** a jugendlich. ~ **hostel** n Jugendherberge f

Yugoslav /'juːgəslɑːv/ a jugoslawisch. ~**ia** /-'slɑːvɪə/ n Jugoslawien nt

Z

zany /'zeɪnɪ/ a (-ier, -iest) närrisch, verrückt

zeal /ziːl/ n Eifer m

zealous /'zeləs/ a, -ly adv eifrig

zebra /'zebrə/ n Zebra nt. ~ '**crossing** n Zebrastreifen m

zenith /'zenɪθ/ n Zenit m; (fig) Gipfel m

zero /'zɪərəʊ/ n Null f

zest /zest/ n Begeisterung f

zigzag /'zɪgzæg/ n Zickzack m □ vi (pt/pp -zagged) im Zickzack laufen; (in vehicle) fahren

zinc /zɪŋk/ n Zink nt

zip /zɪp/ n ~ [**fastener**] Reißverschluss m □ vt ~ [**up**] den Reißverschluss zuziehen an (+ acc)

'Zip code n (Amer) Postleitzahl f

zipper /'zɪpə(r)/ n Reißverschluss m

zither /'zɪðə(r)/ n Zither f

zodiac /'zəʊdɪæk/ n Tierkreis m

zombie /'zɒmbɪ/ n (fam) **like a** ~ ganz benommen

zone /zəʊn/ n Zone f
zoo /zu:/ n Zoo m
zoological /zəʊə'lɒdʒɪkl/ a zoological

zoolog|ist /zəʊ'ɒlədʒɪst/ n Zoo-
loge m /-gin f. ~y – Zoologie f
zoom /zu:m/ vi sausen. ~ **lens** n
Zoomobjektiv nt

Phonetic symbols used for German words

a	Hand	hant	ŋ	lang	laŋ
a:	Bahn	ba:n	o	Moral	mo'ra:l
ɐ	Ober	'o:bɐ	o:	Boot	bo:t
ɐ̯	Uhr	u:ɐ̯	ǫ	Foyer	fǫa'je:
ã	Conférencier	kõferã'sje:	õ	Konkurs	kõ'kurs
ã:	Abonnement	abɔnə'mã:	õ:	Ballon	ba'lõ:
aɪ	weit	vaɪt	ɔ	Post	pɔst
aʊ	Haut	haʊt	ø	Ökonom	øko'no:m
b	Ball	bal	ø:	Öl	ø:l
ç	ich	ıç	œ	göttlich	'gœtlıç
d	dann	dan	ɔʏ	heute	'hɔʏtə
dʒ	Gin	dʒın	p	Pakt	pakt
e	Metall	me'tal	r	Rast	rast
e:	Beet	be:t	s	Hast	hast
ɛ	mästen	'mɛstən	ʃ	Schal	ʃa:l
ɛ:	wählen	'vɛ:lən	t	Tal	ta:l
ẽ:	Cousin	ku'zẽ:	ts	Zahl	tsa:l
ə	Nase	'na:zə	tʃ	Couch	kaʊtʃ
f	Faß	fas	u	kulant	ku'lant
g	Gast	gast	u:	Hut	hu:t
h	haben	'ha:bən	ʊ	aktuell	ak'tʊɛl
i	Rivale	ri'va:lə	ʊ	Pult	pʊlt
i:	viel	fi:l	v	was	vas
j	Aktion	ak'tsjo:n	x	Bach	bax
ɪ	Birke	'bɪrkə	y	Physik	fy'zi:k
j	ja	ja:	'y:	Rübe	'ry:bə
k	kalt	kalt	ỹ	Nuance	'nỹã:sə
l	Last	last	ʏ	Fülle	'fʏlə
m	Mast	mast	z	Nase	'na:zə
n	Naht	na:t	ʒ	Regime	re'ʒi:m

ʔ Glottal stop, e.g. Koordination /koʔɔrdina'tsjo:n/.
: Length sign after a vowel, e.g. Chrom /kro:m/.
' Stress mark before stressed syllable, e.g. Balkon /bal'kõ:/.

Die für das Englische verwendeten Zeichen der Lautschrift

ɑː	barn	bɑːn	l	lot	lɒt
ã	nuance	ˈnjuːãs	m	mat	mæt
æ	fat	fæt	n	not	nɒt
æ̃	lingerie	ˈlæ̃ʒərɪ	ŋ	sing	sɪŋ
aɪ	fine	faɪn	ɒ	got	gɒt
aʊ	now	naʊ	ɔː	paw	pɔː
b	bat	bæt	ɔɪ	boil	bɔɪl
d	dog	dɒg	p	pet	pet
dʒ	jam	dʒæm	r	rat	ræt
e	met	met	s	sip	sɪp
eɪ	fate	feɪt	ʃ	ship	ʃɪp
eə	fairy	ˈfeərɪ	t	tip	tɪp
əʊ	goat	gəʊt	tʃ	chin	tʃɪn
ə	ago	əˈgəʊ	θ	thin	θɪn
ɜː	fur	fɜː(r)	ð	the	ðə
f	fat	fæt	uː	boot	buːt
g	good	gʊd	ʊ	book	bʊk
h	hat	hæt	ʊə	tourism	ˈtʊərɪzm
ɪ	bit, happy	bɪt, ˈhæpɪ	ʌ	dug	dʌg
ɪə	near	nɪə(r)	v	van	væn
iː	meet	miːt	w	win	wɪn
j	yet	jet	z	zip	zɪp
k	kit	kɪt	ʒ	vision	ˈvɪʒn

ː bezeichnet Länge des vorhergehenden Vokals, z. B. boot [buːt].

ˈ Betonung, steht unmittelbar vor einer betonten Silbe, z. B. ago [əˈgəʊ].

(r) Ein „r" in runden Klammern wird nur gesprochen, wenn im Textzusammenhang ein Vokal unmittelbar folgt, z. B. fire /ˈfaɪə(r); fire at /ˈfaɪər æt/.

Guide to German pronunciation

Consonants are pronounced as in English with the following exceptions:

b	as	p	
d	as	t	*at the end of a word or syllable*
g	as	k	

ch   as in Scottish lo**ch** *after a, o, u, au*

        like an exaggerated h as in **h**uge
                     after i, e, ä, ö, ü, eu, ei

-chs	as	x	(as in bo**x**)
-ig	as	-ich /ıç/	*when a suffix*
j	as	y	(as in **y**es)

ps
pn   the p is pronounced

qu	as	k + v	
s	as	z	(as in **z**ero) *at the beginning of a word*
	as	s	(as in bu**s**) *at the end of a word or syllable, before a consonant, or when doubled*
sch	as	sh	
sp	as	shp	*at the beginning of a word*
st	as	sht	
v	as	f	(as in **f**or)
	as	v	(as in **v**ery) *within a word*
w	as	v	(as in **v**ery)
z	as	ts	

Vowels are approximately as follows:

a	short	as	u	(as in b<u>u</u>t)
	long	as	a	(as in c<u>a</u>r)
e	short	as	e	(as in p<u>e</u>n)
	long	as	a	(as in p<u>a</u>per)
i	short	as	i	(as in b<u>i</u>t)
	long	as	ee	(as in qu<u>ee</u>n)
o	short	as	o	(as in h<u>o</u>t)
	long	as	o	(as in p<u>o</u>pe)
u	short	as	oo	(as in f<u>oo</u>t)
	long	as	oo	(as in b<u>oo</u>t)

Vowels are always short before a double consonant, and long when followed by an h or when double

ie	is pronounced ee			(as in k<u>ee</u>p)

Diphthongs

au	as	ow	(as in h<u>ow</u>)
ei ai	as	y	(as in m<u>y</u>)
eu äu	as	oy	(as in b<u>oy</u>)

German irregular verbs

1st, 2nd and 3rd person present are given after the infinitive, and past subjunctive after the past indicative, where there is a change of vowel or any other irregularity.

Compound verbs are only given if they do not take the same forms as the corresponding simple verb, e.g. *befehlen*, or if there is no corresponding simple verb, e.g. *bewegen*.

An asterisk (*) indicates a verb which is also conjugated regularly.

....

Infinitive Infinitiv	Past Tense Präteritum	Past Participle 2. Partizip
abwägen	wog (wöge) ab	abgewogen
ausbedingen	bedang (bedänge) aus	ausbedungen
*backen (du bäckst, er bäckt)	buk (büke)	gebacken
befehlen (du befiehlst, er befiehlt)	befahl (beföhle, befähle)	befohlen
beginnen	begann (begänne)	begonnen
beißen (du/er beißt)	biss (bisse)	gebissen
bergen (du birgst, er birgt)	barg (bärge)	geborgen
bersten (du/er birst)	barst (bärste)	geborsten
bewegen²	bewog (bewöge)	bewogen
biegen	bog (böge)	gebogen
bieten	bot (böte)	geboten
binden	band (bände)	gebunden
bitten	bat (bäte)	gebeten
blasen (du/er bläst)	blies	geblasen
bleiben	blieb	geblieben
*bleichen	blich	geblichen
braten (du brätst, er brät)	briet	gebraten
brechen (du brichst, er bricht)	brach (bräche)	gebrochen
brennen	brannte (brennte)	gebrannt
bringen	brachte (brächte)	gebracht
denken	dachte (dächte)	gedacht
dreschen (du drischst, er drischt)	drosch (drösche)	gedroschen

Infinitive	Past Tense	Past Participle
Infinitiv	Präteritum	2. Partizip

dringen	drang (dränge)	gedrungen
dürfen (ich/er darf, du darfst)	durfte (dürfte)	gedurft
empfehlen (du empfiehlst, er empfiehlt)	empfahl (empföhle)	empfohlen
erlöschen (du erlischst, er erlischt)	erlosch (erlösche)	erloschen
*erschallen	erscholl (erschölle)	erschollen
*erschrecken (du erschrickst, er erschrickt)	erschrak (erschräke)	erschrocken
erwägen	erwog (erwöge)	erwogen
essen (du/er isst)	aß (äße)	gegessen
fahren (du fährst, er fährt)	fuhr (führe)	gefahren
fallen (du fällst, er fällt)	fiel	gefallen
fangen (du fängst, er fängt)	fing	gefangen
fechten (du fichtst, er ficht)	focht (föchte)	gefochten
finden	fand (fände)	gefunden
flechten (du flichtst, er flicht)	flocht (flöchte)	geflochten
fliegen	flog (flöge)	geflogen
fliehen	floh (flöhe)	geflohen
fließen (du/er fließt)	floss (flösse)	geflossen
fressen (du/er frisst)	fraß (fräße)	gefressen
frieren	fror (fröre)	gefroren
*gären	gor (göre)	gegoren
gebären (du gebierst, sie gebiert)	gebar (gebäre)	geboren
geben (du gibst, er gibt)	gab (gäbe)	gegeben
gedeihen	gedieh	gediehen
gehen	ging	gegangen
gelingen	gelang (gelänge)	gelungen
gelten (du giltst, er gilt)	galt (gölte, gälte)	gegolten
genesen (du/er genest)	genas (genäse)	genesen
genießen (du/er genießt)	genoss (genösse)	genossen
geschehen (es geschieht)	geschah (geschähe)	geschehen
gewinnen	gewann (gewönne, gewänne)	gewonnen
gießen (du/er gießt)	goss (gösse)	gegossen
gleichen	glich	geglichen

Infinitive	Past Tense	Past Participle
Infinitiv	Präteritum	2. Partizip
gleiten	glitt	geglitten
glimmen	glomm (glömme)	geglommen
graben (du gräbst, er gräbt)	grub (grübe)	gegraben
greifen	griff	gegriffen
haben (du hast, er hat)	hatte (hätte)	gehabt
halten (du hältst, er hält)	hielt	gehalten
hängen²	hing	gehangen
hauen	haute	gehauen
heben	hob (höbe)	gehoben
heißen (du/er heißt)	hieß	geheißen
helfen (du hilfst, er hilft)	half (hülfe)	geholfen
kennen	kannte (kennte)	gekannt
klingen	klang (klänge)	geklungen
kneifen	kniff	gekniffen
kommen	kam (käme)	gekommen
können (ich/er kann, du kannst)	konnte (könnte)	gekonnt
kriechen	kroch (kröche)	gekrochen
laden (du lädst, er lädt)	lud (lüde)	geladen
lassen (du/er lässt)	ließ	gelassen
laufen (du läufst, er läuft)	lief	gelaufen
leiden	litt	gelitten
leihen	lieh	geliehen
lesen (du/er liest)	las (läse)	gelesen
liegen	lag (läge)	gelegen
lügen	log (löge)	gelogen
mahlen	mahlte	gemahlen
meiden	mied	gemieden
melken	molk (mölke)	gemolken
messen (du/er misst)	maß (mäße)	gemessen
misslingen	misslang (misslänge)	misslungen
mögen (ich/er mag, du magst)	mochte (möchte)	gemocht
müssen (ich/er muss, du musst)	musste (müsste)	gemusst
nehmen (du nimmst, er nimmt)	nahm (nähme)	genommen
nennen	nannte (nennte)	genannt
pfeifen	pfiff	gepfiffen
preisen (du/er preist)	pries	gepriesen
quellen (du quillst, er quillt)	quoll (quölle)	gequollen

Infinitive Infinitiv	Past Tense Präteritum	Past Participle 2. Partizip
raten (du rätst, er rät)	riet	geraten
reiben	rieb	gerieben
reißen (du/er reißt)	riss	gerissen
reiten	ritt	geritten
rennen	rannte (rennte)	gerannt
riechen	roch (röche)	gerochen
ringen	rang (ränge)	gerungen
rinnen	rann (ränne)	geronnen
rufen	rief	gerufen
*salzen (du/er salzt)	salzte	gesalzen
saufen (du säufst, er säuft)	soff (söffe)	gesoffen
*saugen	sog (söge)	gesogen
schaffen[1]	schuf (schüfe)	geschaffen
scheiden	schied	geschieden
scheinen	schien	geschienen
scheißen (du/er scheißt)	schiss	geschissen
schelten (du schiltst, er schilt)	schalt (schölte)	gescholten
scheren[1]	schor (schöre)	geschoren
schieben	schob (schöbe)	geschoben
schießen (du/er schießt)	schoss (schösse)	geschossen
schinden	schindete	geschunden
schlafen (du schläfst, er schläft)	schlief	geschlafen
schlagen (du schlägst, er schlägt)	schlug (schlüge)	geschlagen
schleichen	schlich	geschlichen
schleifen[2]	schliff	geschliffen
schließen (du/er schließt)	schloss (schlösse)	geschlossen
schlingen	schlang (schlänge)	geschlungen
schmeißen (du/er schmeißt)	schmiss (schmisse)	geschmissen
schmelzen (du/er schmilzt)	schmolz (schmölze)	geschmolzen
schneiden	schnitt	geschnitten
*schrecken (du schrickst, er schrickt)	schrak (schräke)	geschreckt
…ben	schrieb	geschrieben
	schrie	geschrie[e]n
	schritt	geschritten
	schwieg	geschwiegen
…schwillst,	schwoll (schwölle)	geschwollen

Infinitive Infinitiv	Past Tense Präteritum	Past Participle 2. Partizip
schwimmen	schwamm (schwömme)	geschwommen
schwinden	schwand (schwände)	geschwunden
schwingen	schwang (schwänge)	geschwungen
schwören	schwor (schwüre)	geschworen
sehen (du siehst, er sieht)	sah (sähe)	gesehen
sein (ich bin, du bist, er ist, wir sind, ihr seid, sie sind)	war (wäre)	gewesen
senden[1]	sandte (sendete)	gesandt
sieden	sott (sötte)	gesotten
singen	sang (sänge)	gesungen
sinken	sank (sänke)	gesunken
sinnen	sann (sänne)	gesonnen
sitzen (du/er sitzt)	saß (säße)	gesessen
sollen (ich/er soll, du sollst)	sollte	gesollt
*spalten	spaltete	gespalten
speien	spie	gespie[e]n
spinnen	spann (spönne, spänne)	gesponnen
sprechen (du sprichst, er spricht)	sprach (spräche)	gesprochen
sprießen (du/er sprießt)	spross (sprösse)	gesprossen
springen	sprang (spränge)	gesprungen
stechen (du stichst, er sticht)	stach (stäche)	gestochen
stehen	stand (stünde, stände)	gestanden
stehlen (du stiehlst, er stiehlt)	stahl (stähle)	gestohlen
steigen	stieg	gestiegen
sterben (du stirbst, er stirbt)	starb (stürbe)	gestorben
stinken	stank (stänke)	gestunken
stoßen (du/er stößt)	stieß	gestoßen
streichen	strich	gestrichen
streiten	stritt	gestritten
tragen (du trägst, er trägt)	trug (trüge)	getragen
treffen (du triffst, er trifft)	traf (träfe)	getroffen
treiben	trieb	getrieben
treten (du trittst, er tritt)	trat (träte)	getreten
*triefen	troff (tröffe)	getroffen
trinken	trank (tränke)	getrunken

Infinitive Infinitiv	Past Tense Präteritum	Past Participle 2. Partizip
trügen	trog (tröge)	getrogen
tun (du tust, er tut)	tat (täte)	getan
verderben (du verdirbst, er verdirbt)	verdarb (verdürbe)	verdorben
vergessen (du/er vergisst)	vergaß (vergäße)	vergessen
verlieren	verlor (verlöre)	verloren
verschleißen (du/er verschleißt)	verschliss	verschlissen
verzeihen	verzieh	verziehen
wachsen¹ (du/er wächst)	wuchs (wüchse)	gewachsen
waschen (du wäschst, er wäscht)	wusch (wüsche)	gewaschen
weichen²	wich	gewichen
weisen (du/er weist)	wies	gewiesen
*wenden²	wandte (wendete)	gewandt
werben (du wirbst, er wirbt)	warb (würbe)	geworben
werden (du wirst, er wird)	wurde (würde)	geworden
werfen (du wirfst, er wirft)	warf (würfe)	geworfen
wiegen¹	wog (wöge)	gewogen
winden	wand (wände)	gewunden
wissen (ich/er weiß, du weißt)	wusste (wüsste)	gewusst
wollen (ich/er will, du willst)	wollte	gewollt
wringen	wrang (wränge)	gewrungen
ziehen	zog (zöge)	gezogen
zwingen	zwang (zwänge)	gezwungen